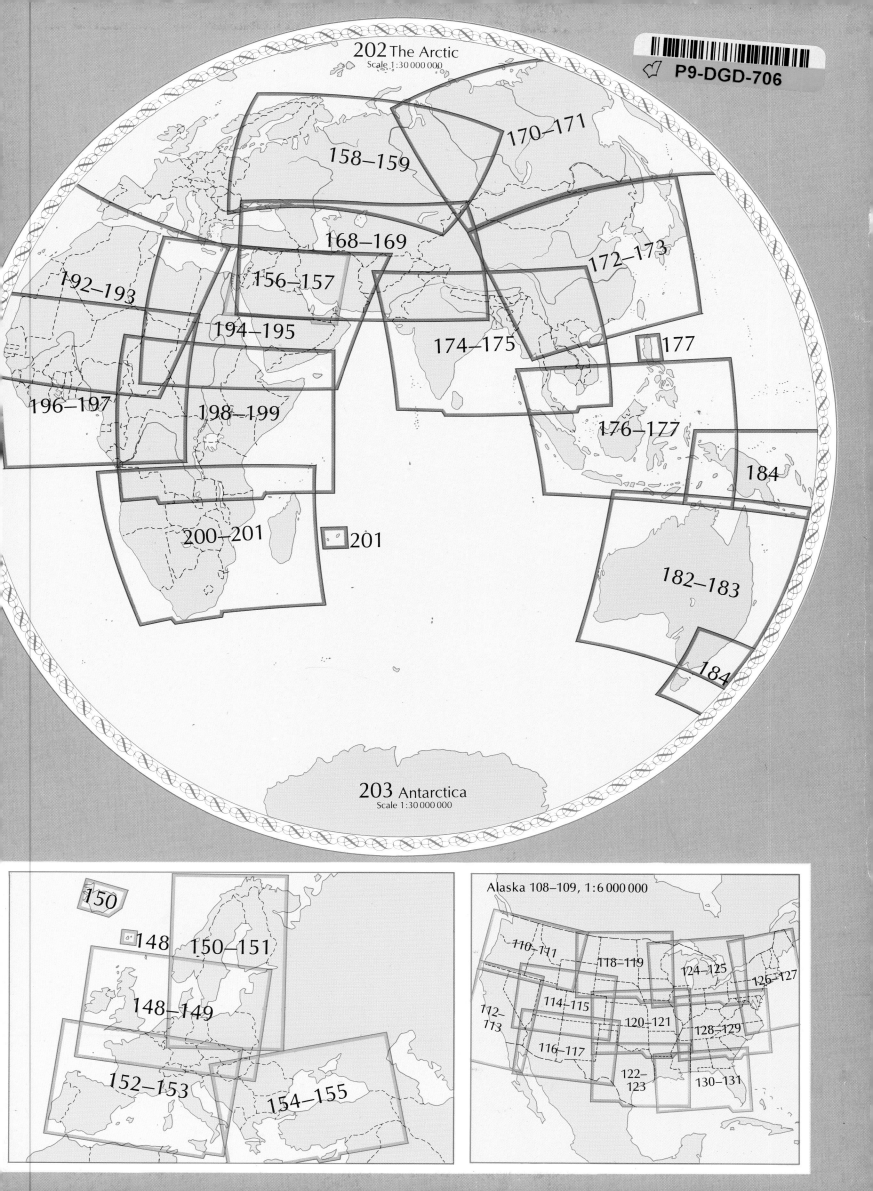

202 The Arctic
Scale 1:30 000 000

P9-DGD-706

170–171

158–159

168–169

192–193

156–157

172–173

194–195

174–175

177

196–197

198–199

176–177

184

200–201

201

182–183

184

203 Antarctica
Scale 1:30 000 000

150

148   150–151

148–149

152–153   154–155

Alaska 108–109, 1:6 000 000

110–111   118–119   124–125   126–127

112–113   114–115

120–121   128–129

116–117   122–123   130–131

Ruthie,

Though we don't live in the same house
this world is our home.
Isn't it beautiful?

Love
Dad
12/3/89

GRAPHIC LEARNING

EARTH BOOK

WORLD ATLAS

ENCYCLOPEDIA OF THE EARTH

Produced in cooperation between Esselte Map Service and Lidman Production AB.

Visualisation	Lidman Production AB	Photographs	AAA photo
			Air France
Direction	Sven Lidman		Ragnar Andersson/TIOFOTO
Text	Lars Bergquist		AP/Pressens bild
			Bildarkiver/Ellbergs bilder
Art Director	Sten Pettersson		Camera Press/IBL
			Bo Dahlin/Bildhuset
Translator	Alan Tapsell		J. Arthur Dixon
			DPA/Pressens bild
Consultants	Bertil Hedenstierna		ESA
	Ralph Mårtenson		Börje Försäter/Hallandsbild
Illustrators	Bob Chapman		J. Gaumy/Magnum
	David Cook		Claes Grundsten/Naturfotograferna
	John Flynn		Gunnar Gustafson
	Tony Gibbon		Mats Halling
	Rob Hillier		Bengt Hedberg/Naturbild
	John Potter		IBL
	Les Smith		Páll Imsland
	David West		Kjell Johansson/Bildhuset
	Maurice Wilson		Sture Karlsson/TIOFOTO
			Kungliga biblioteket
Photo research	Per Axel Nordfeldt		Frank W. Lane
			Örnulf Lautitzen
			J. Berry/Magnum
			Mount Wilson and Las Campanas observatories
			Norman Myers/TIOFOTO
			Ralph Mårtensson
			NASA
			Pål-Nils Nilsson/TIOFOTO
			Lars Olsson/Pressens bild
			G. Rodger/Magnum
			Ann Ronan
			SAS
			Per-Olle Stackman/TIOFOTO
			UPI/Pressens bild
			ZEFA
			Östasiatiska museet

THE WORLD IN MAPS

Designed, edited, drawn and reproduced by cartographers, geographers, artists and technicians at ESSELTE MAP SERVICE.

Published in The United States of America by Graphic Learning International Publishing Corporation, Boulder, Colorado.

M.L. (Mert) Yockstick, Publisher

Consultants for United States Edition   Sharryl Davis Hawke
James E. Davis

Design Counsel   Turnbull & Company,
Cambridge, Massachusetts USA

Base material for the U.S. maps in scale 1:3 Million supplied by National Cartographic Center, U.S. Geological Survey.

Copyright 1987 ESSELTE MAP SERVICE AB STOCKHOLM

Library of Congress 86-072452

Esselte Map Service AB (Sweden)
   [Title] EARTH BOOK

Includes glossary and index
   1. Atlases.   I. Title
[Card No.]
ISBN 0-87746-100-7

Printed in Sweden

The Age of Information brought a new perspective to the planet Earth. Immediate access to information fostered a broader understanding of the world and precipitated a planetary mind change. As a result, communities and countries are slowly losing their prominence as our place of residence. The entire Earth is becoming our home. People on the other side of the oceans or continents no longer seem so foreign. We are beginning to realize our dependency on each other as human beings sharing the Earth and its environments.

With this understanding, we created Earthbook to bring this world and a geographic consciousness home to you.

As the Age of Information continues to acclerate and prepare us for the year 2000 and beyond, our capacity to view and understand the Earth will continue to expand. But so will our capacity to create damage to the already delicate condition of Earth's environments. The waste of resources, depletion of natural life forms and erosion of human conditions are issues and phenomena that affect us all. When an error in human judgment affects the lives, well being, happiness and health of millions of people across many nations, we are no longer dealing with cultural, spiritual or political ideologies. The very survival of humanity now depends upon the mutual respect for the Earth and its people.

Through the use of satellite photography, EarthBook introduces a new style of environmental mapping which offers you greater insight into the land use and life conditions of humans, animals and plants throughout the world. This new age atlas presents the Earth with relief, color and clarity that more accurately represent the environments of the natural world. Combining the comprehensive Encyclopedia of the Earth with innovative mapping, EarthBook offers you a level of detail, information and understanding never before achieved in a volume of this kind.

Our survival and the survival of other species on Earth ultimately depend upon understanding our planet and the interrelationships that exist between the human and physical environments. To these ends, and to the strengthening of our geographic literacy at home, office and in our classrooms or boardrooms, we proudly present EarthBook — an atlas of our world.

M.L. (Mert) Yockstick
Publisher

ENCYCLOPEDIA OF THE EARTH

Air 2–3

Air – the Earth's shield 4–5
The atmosphere, its different layers, chemical and physical properties, and its power to protect us from dangerous radiation from outer space.

A matter of life and death 6–7
The air we breathe – the oxygen and carbon cycles. Interplay of atmosphere with animals and green plants.

Air conditioning the Earth 8–9
Large scale air circulation. Earth's heat balance. Local and regional winds. Energy from winds.

Among the clouds 10–11
Vertical circulation of the atmosphere. Fronts, clouds and precipitation. Thunderstorms and lightning.

Seasons and climates 12–13
Climatic differences and seasonal variations. Climates of the world.

Signs in the sky 14–15
Pre-scientific weather forecasting. Weather data from meteorological balloons and satellites. Computerized forecasting.

Life in the air 16–17
Adaptations to aerial existence – from the flying saurians of the Mesozoic to today's birds, bats and insects.

People take to the air 18–19
People's dream of conquering the air, from Icarus and Leonardo da Vinci to the Wright brothers and Concorde.

Air routes 20–21
The modest beginnings of commercial air traffic and its expansion. Air lanes, traffic control, airports.

The leap into space 22–23
Early concepts of space and space travel. From naked-eye astronomy to radio telescopes and space flights.

People's impact on the atmosphere 24–25
Polluted air around the whole globe. Acid rain over European forests. The danger of burning of fossil fuels.

Water 26–27

Water, the prerequisite of life 28–29
The necessity of water for living organisms, including people, and its unique physical and chemical properties.

The water cycle 30–31
The circulation of water, from the seas through the atmosphere to the ground and back to the sea. Salt and fresh water. Irrigation.

The realm of ice 32–33
Ice Ages in the history of Earth. The polar ice caps. Glaciers and glaciated landscapes. Winter – the annual Ice Age.

The oceans 34–35
The seas, their physical geography in three dimensions. Oceans and marginal seas. Salinity.

The powerful sea 36–37
The energy of the sea. Waves, currents and tides. Beach processes. Utilizing power from the sea.

Aquatic life 38–39
Vertical distribution of life in the sea. Adaptations for life in water. The ecological chain of the sea.

Food from the deep 40–41
Sea and freshwater fisheries. Overfishing and international management of fisheries.

The conquest of the seas 42–43
The age of discovery. Navigation. Exploration of the ocean depths.

Sea routes 44–45
Seafaring and navigation. Sea transport, different kinds of cargo.

People's imact on the hydrosphere 46–47
People's pollution of the oceans, and mismanagement of water resources. Mining the sea floor. Marine economic zones.

Earth 48–49

The crust 50–51
Alfred Wegener and the modern theory of plate tectonics. Kinds of bedrock and their genesis. Vertical displacements in the crust.

The restless Earth 52–53
Plate tectonics – the crust in constant motion, creating mid-ocean ridges, mountain ranges, island arcs – and earthquakes.

Weathering 54–55
Weathering in cold, warm and humid climates and limestone areas.

Erosion 56–57
Exogenic processes – erosion, slope processes and transportation. Denudation and sculpturing the Earth.

Life on land 58–59
Plants' and animals' conquest of dry land and their adaptations to terrestrial life. Evolution of species into new ecological niches.

Tropical forests 60–61
Rain forests and deciduous monsoon forests, their flora and fauna and their climatic prerequisites.

The grasslands 62–63
Savanna and steppe. The annual cycle of grasslands. Climatic control of vegetation and animal life. Effects of people's activities.

Deserts 64–65
Classification of deserts. Life in the deserts and the adaptation of animals and plants to heat and to lack of water. Desert spreading.

Temperate forests 66–67
Deciduous, coniferous and mixed forests. Flora, fauna, silviculture and forestry.

The tundras 68–69
The barren environment and its conditions. How frost modifies the soil. Flora and fauna.

Mountain environments 70–71
Formation of mountains. Mountains in different parts of the world, their physical setting and land use. Animal life and vegetation.

Living off the land 72–73
People's livelihood from the soil. Types of agriculture. Historical agriculture and distribution of agricultural systems.

Urbanization 74–75
Historical development of urbanized areas, from the small farming village through medieval towns to the modern conurbation.

Treasures underground 76–77
Mineral resources in the crust of the Earth. Mining and refining of metals.

The ravaged Earth 78–79
People's destruction of their own environment and the battle for survival.

People's impact on the Earth's crust 80–81
People as a geological force, remodeling the face of the planet.

Fire 82–83

The primordial fire 84–85
The creation of the Cosmos in the "big bang". The birth of galaxies and stars.

The sun and its offspring 86–87
The Sun as a star. The source of the Sun's energy. The planetary system and the exploration of nearest space.

Mountains of fire 88–89
Volcanoes – an open contact with the hot interior. Ancient and recent vulcanism. Hot spots. Vulcanism on other planets.

Energy from the Earth's interior 90–91
Resources beneath the ground—coal, oil, and geothermal energy. The creation and capture of preserved energy.

Fire—the servant of people 92–93
The use of fire from Homo Erectus to the age of industrialism. Steam power.

Using energy 94–95
People's use of increasing knowledge to improve their daily life. The energy staircase.

THE WORLD IN MAPS

UNITED STATES

Alabama	128, 130–131	Indiana	124, 128	Nebraska	118–119, 120–121	South Carolina	128–129
Alaska	108–109	Iowa	119	Nevada	112–113	South Dakota	118–119
Arizona	116	Kansas	120–121	New Hampshire	126	Tennessee	128–129
Arkansas	121	Kentucky	128–129	New Jersey	127	Texas	117, 122
California	112–113	Louisiana	123	New Mexico	116–117	Utah	114
Colorado	114–115	Maine	126	New York	125, 126–127	Vermont	126
Connecticut	126–127	Maryland	129	North Carolina	128–129	Virginia	128–129
Delaware	127	Massachusetts	126	North Dakota	118–119	Washington	110
Florida	130–131	Michigan	124–125	Ohio	125, 128–129	West Virginia	129
Georgia	128–129, 131	Minnesota	119	Oklahoma	120–121	Wisconsin	124
Hawaii	113	Mississippi	121, 130	Oregon	110	Wyoming	111, 118
Idaho	110–111	Missouri	121	Pennsylvania	125, 126–127	District of Columbia	127
Illinois	121, 124	Montana	111, 118	Rhode Island	126–127		

NORTH AMERICA

North America   98–99
Population, political divisions environment

North America   100–101
Organic and inorganic production, climate, soils

Alaska and Western Canada   102–103
incl. the Aleutian Islands

Eastern Canada   104–105

The United States   106–107
incl. Mexico

Central America and the West Indies   132–133
Belize, The Caribbean Archipelago, Costa Rica, Cuba, El Salvador, Guatemala, Honduras, Mexico, Nicaragua

SOUTH AMERICA

South America   134–135
Population, political divisions, environment

South America   136–137
Organic and inorganic production, climate, soils

South America, north   138–139
Brazil, Colombia, Ecuador, Guyana, Panama, Peru, Surinam, Venezuela

South America, central   140–141
Bolivia, Brazil, Chile, Peru

South America, south   142–143
Argentina, Bolivia, Brazil, Chile, Paraguay, Uruguay

EUROPE

Europe   144–145
Population, political divisions, environment

Europe   146–147
Organic and inorganic production, climate, soils

The British Isles and Central Europe   148–149
Belgium, Czechoslovakia, Federal Republic of Germany, German Democratic Republic, Luxembourg, The Netherlands, Poland

Northern Europe   150–151
Denmark, Finland, Iceland, Norway, Sweden

South-West Europe   152–153
Austria, France, Italy, Liechtenstein, Portugal, Spain, Switzerland, Yugoslavia

The Balkans   154–155
Bulgaria, Cyprus, Greece, Hungary, Romania, Turkey

Near East   156–157

Western Soviet Union   158–159
European USSR, Western Siberia

ASIA

Northern Asia   160–161
environment

Southern Asia   162–163
environment

Asia   164–165
organic and inorganic production, climate, soils

Asia   166–167
physical, precipitation, temperature, population, political divisions

The Middle East   168–169
Afghanistan, Iran, Pakistan

Eastern Soviet Union   170–171
Eastern Siberia, Mongolia

China and Japan   172–173
incl. Mongolia, North Korea, South Korea, Taiwan

India and South-East Asia   174–175
incl. Bangladesh, Bhutan, Burma, Kampuchea, Laos, Nepal, Sri Lanka, Thailand, Vietnam

The East Indies   176–177
Brunei, Indonesia, Malaysia, Philippines

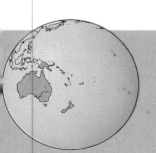

AUSTRALIA

Australasia   178–179
Population, political divisions, environment

Australasia   180–181
Organic and inorganic production, climate, soils

Australia   182–183

New Guinea and New Zealand   184–185

Oceania   186–187
Melanesia, Micronesia, Polynesia

AFRICA

Africa   188–189
Population, political divisions, environment

Africa   190–191
Organic and inorganic production, climate, soils

North-West Africa   192–193
Algeria, Libya, Morocco, Mauretania, Niger, Tunisia

The Nile Valley and Arabia   194–195
Bahrain, Egypt, Iraq, Israel, Jordan, Kuwait, Lebanon, Oman, Qatar, Saudi-Arabia, Southern Yemen, Sudan, Syria, United Arab Emirates, Yemen

West Africa   196–197
Benin, Burkina, Cameroon, Chad, Congo, Equatorial Guinea, Gabon, The Gambia, Ghana, Guinea, Guinea-Bissau, Ivory Coast, Liberia, Mali, Niger, Nigeria, Sao Tomé and Principe, Senegal, Sierra Leone, Togo

East Africa   198–199
Central Africa, Ethiopia, Kenya, Sudan, Tanzania, Uganda, Zaire

Central and Southern Africa   200–201
Angola, Botswana, Comoros, Madagascar, Malawi, Mauritius, Mozambique, Namibia, Lesotho, South Africa, Swaziland, Zambia, Zimbabwe

THE ARCTIC AND ANTARCTIC

The Arctic   202
Environment

Antarctica   203
Environment

THE WORLD

The World   204–205
Environment

The World   206–207
Climate

The World   208–209
Oceans and the ocean floor

The World   210–211
Population

The World   212–213
Political divisions

The World   214–215
Energy

The World   216
Languages, religions, time zones

Glossary, Index   217–327

ENCYCLOPEDIA of the Earth

Research undertaken during the past few decades has resulted in a dramatic increase in scientific knowledge. In the fields of biology and the earth sciences, discoveries have led to a growing awareness of the interrelationships between areas of knowledge which were previously regarded as totally separate disciplines. From mineralogy to microbiology and from botany to bathymetry the pieces are fitting together like an immense jigsaw puzzle in which gaps remain but are fewer with each passing decade.

As knowledge expands, it becomes increasingly difficult to present a brief scientific account of the Earth as a whole since a systemized treatment with subjects grouped in distinct categories is no longer the ideal choice. The Encyclopedia of the Earth in this volume has turned to the pattern of the philosophical elements—air, water, fire and earth—to provide a basic framework within which a more free-ranging presentation can be achieved. It is said that a picture is worth a thousand words. Too often in books the pictures add nothing to the information in the text. In the following pages the coordination of words and pictures encompasses infinitely more in 96 pages than would have been possible with words alone.

Air

Of all the elements air is the most elusive and the most mystical. Among Greek thinkers of the 6th century BC Anaximenes of Miletus was the greatest philosopher on the subject of air. He elaborated upon the ancient concept that breath is the spirit of life in believing that air is the fundamental element of the earth: "Just as our soul, which is air, holds the body together so wind and air encompass our whole world." All the other elements, claimed Anaximenes, originated from densified or rarified air.

It was not until the 17th century, however, that scientists like the Frenchman Pascal and the Italian Torricelli discovered how to measure air pressure and so transformed the Greek philosopher's mystical, fundamental element into a tangible physical substance. A century later chemists discovered that air is a mixture of gases and identified its primary elements as nitrogen and oxygen.

The science of meteorology was developed in the 19th century and gradually replaced the old rules of thumb of peasant and seaman with more dependable weather forecasts. The meteorologists of the present century have studied the outer strata of the atmosphere in detail. This is a part of geophysics, the science of the Earth as a planet.

The Earth's atmosphere, in the depths of which we dwell, protects us against deadly radiation from outer space and provides us with the oxygen that our life processes depend upon. It evens out what would otherwise be unendurable extremes of heat and cold and transports moisture from the oceans across the continents in a never ending global circulation system.

Oxygen is a product of living green plants and hence was absent from the primeval atmosphere. A precondition for the development of life on Earth was that no free oxygen existed to oxidize and so break down the first unprotected living molecules. It took billions of years to build up the present oxygen content of our atmosphere.

The type of atmosphere that will surround our world in the future is a vital consideration and one that is dependent largely upon people. Only if we halt the destruction of the continents' forests and the poisoning of the oceans' plankton and cease using the air as a sort of universal sewer, can higher organisms hope to survive on our planet.

Air – the Earth's shield

At sea level the atmospheric pressure is about 1,000 millibars (mb). The measurement for this pressure was formerly expressed as 30.5 in. mercury.

At ground level the atmosphere contains not only nitrogen but also oxygen and carbon dioxide, vital substances for plants and animals alike. It protects us from violent alternations between hot and cold and against being bombarded by charged particles—cosmic radiation—and meteorites.

The atmosphere also functions as an immense energy transport system between the hot tropical and cold polar regions. The efficiency of the atmosphere as a heat carrier depends on its humidity. Part of this moisture content is discernible as cloud, mist or haze. It is the capacity of water to retain heat when vaporized and then release it during condensation which evens out the climate on Earth and makes both tropics and polar regions habitable.

It is only the lower 49 mi. of our atmosphere, however, which is of the same chemical composition as the air at ground level and even within this zone conditions vary so greatly that we usually divide it into three distinct strata. The lowest is the *troposphere* extending 6–11 mi. upward from the ground. Practically all our weather is contained within this stratum and only the very highest tropical storm clouds reach up to the lower limit of the *stratosphere*. Here ultraviolet light from the sun forms a layer of ozone, triatomic oxygen, which absorbs the deadly radiation from outer space. The *mesosphere* is a transitional stratum where the air pressure falls to a mere 10,000th part of what it is at sea level.

The uppermost region of the mesosphere is the threshold to outer space. Because of the intense solar radiation the upper atmosphere is ionized and electrically conductive. This stratum is known as the *ionosphere*. Charged particles from the sun—electrons, protons and heavier atomic nuclei—moving within the rarefied gas produce the aurora, a discharge phenomenon similar to that in a fluorescent tube. The outermost stratum from about 248 mi. outward might best be described as condensed outer space. Here there exists practically nothing but hydrogen and helium, the thin gas between the stars.

The lower atmosphere

Balloons
filled with helium carried people to an altitude of 12.5 mi. as early as the 1930's.

The air pressure
in the lower stratosphere is one tenth of what it is at sea level.

Jet aircraft
with pressurized cabins operate routinely at altitudes of 6 mi. and more. The absence of weather changes up here makes flying safer.

Tropical thunder clouds
rise to the limit between troposphere and stratosphere: the tropopause.

The highest mountains
rise more than 5 mi. above sea level. But even at 2.5 mi. most people have difficulty in breathing because of the rarefied air.

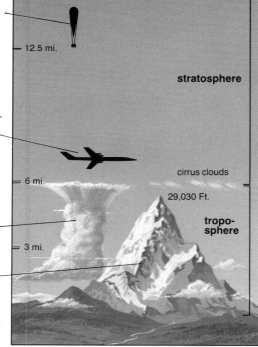

- 12.5 mi.

stratosphere

- 6 mi.

cirrus clouds

29,030 Ft.

tropo-
sphere

- 3 mi.

Satellites
launched by people orbit the Earth at altitudes ranging from 186–248 mi. up to c. 22,369 mi. in the case of the geostationary communication satellites.

The aurora
often appears at altitudes of up to 621.5 mi. where the blast of electrically charged particles from the sun encounters the Earth's atmosphere.

X-rays
and short wave ultraviolet radiation from the sun is largely absorbed by the atmosphere. Certain wavelengths of electromagnetic radiation reach the ground however. Our eyes have evolved to utilize this radiation alone, which is why we call it "visible light".

Cosmic radiation
consists of high energy particles from both the sun and from radiation sources far away in the universe. When such a particle encounters one of our atmosphere's atoms it gives rise to a shower of secondary particles.

Military satellites
for reconnaissance often fly relatively low so as to be able to detect objects as small as possible on the ground. Air resistance at such low altitudes reduces the lifespan of these satellites.

Probe rockets
are used for the scientific study of the upper regions of the atmosphere.

Meteors
become extremely hot and gasify through friction on entering the atmosphere. These "falling stars" are caused by particles no larger than sand grains. Only the largest meteors reach the ground.

Charged layers
in the ionosphere reflect radio short waves which can rebound several times around the Earth.

The lowest aurora
can occur as far down as the ionosphere.

Noctilucent clouds
are the only clouds above the troposphere. These are the subject of intensive study.

The ozone layer
in the atmosphere halts most of the ultraviolet radiation.

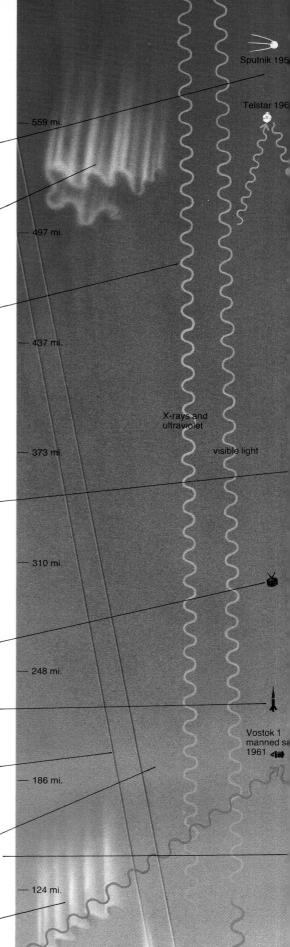

Sputnik 195

Telstar 196

- 559 mi.

- 497 mi.

- 437 mi.

X-rays and ultraviolet

visible light

- 373 mi.

- 310 mi.

- 248 mi.

- 186 mi.

Vostok 1 manned s 1961

- 124 mi.

- 62 mi.

rocket aircraft 1961

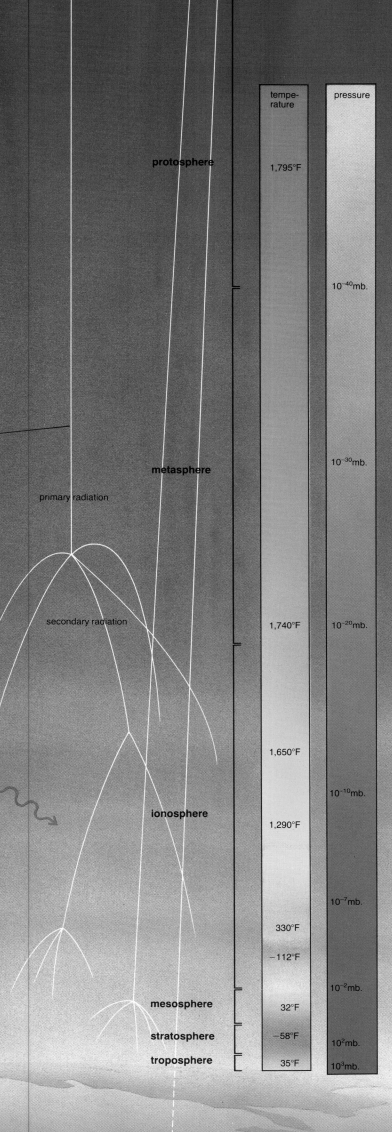

protosphere

temperature

pressure

1,795°F

10⁻⁴⁰mb.

metasphere

10⁻³⁰mb.

primary radiation

secondary radiation

1,740°F · 10⁻²⁰mb.

ionosphere

1,650°F

10⁻¹⁰mb.

1,290°F

10⁻⁷mb.

330°F

−112°F

10⁻²mb.

mesosphere

32°F

stratosphere

−58°F

10²mb.

troposphere

35°F

10³mb.

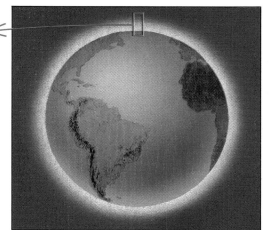

The atmosphere from outside
The 621.5 mi. of the large diagram is shown (left) in correct proportion to the Earth. It is only the innermost 6–11 mi., the troposphere, that has sufficient water vapor and dust for it to be visible to the naked eye. Beyond that is the blackness of space (photo below). Clouds seem to hang immediately above the ground.

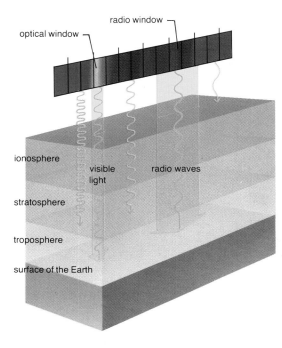

radio window

optical window

ionosphere

visible light

radio waves

stratosphere

troposphere

surface of the Earth

Two "windows"
The atmosphere is impenetrable for most types of electromagnetic radiation. Only two "windows" admit radiation with distinctly limited wavelengths. The "optical window" is open for visible light and the adjoining parts of the ultraviolet and infrared areas; the "radio window" admits certain radio wavelengths. Short radio waves which normally pass through the atmosphere without hindrance can, however, sometimes bounce off charged layers in the ionosphere (see large diagram).

A matter of life and death

The Earth's atmosphere is associated with the life processes by two vital cycles: oxygen and carbon.

Oxygen is a decisive factor in the energy systems of nearly all plants and animals. These living organisms liberate energy by oxidizing large organic molecules, obtaining the oxygen through respiration. This oxygen consumption is compensated for by a corresponding process: photosynthesis or assimilation, whereby green plants build up their energy-abundant substance as they grow. This fundamental process, without which life on Earth would be impossible, is driven by solar energy and takes, as raw materials, hydrogen from water and carbon from carbon dioxide. Oxygen is the most important by-product of photosynthesis. Most living creatures have evolved complex defences against what is, to the delicate organic substances within their cells, a corrosive poisonous gas. Only in hot springs in the depths of the oceans, in seabed mud and in a few other extremely oxygen–deficient environments do there exist anaerobic bacteria, i.e. bacteria which are not dependent upon oxygen and which can survive without protection.

Carbon is the fundamental component in all organic compounds. It is the primary element of life. There is only a limited supply of carbon, however, and consequently it must be constantly recycled. The carbon in the biosphere—the Earth's thin film of life circulates continuously through death, living matter and death again. Carbon in the atmosphere is fixed by green plants, the autotrophs. It thus becomes part of the biomass of both these and the heterotrophs—all of us from fungi to humans who are not endowed with chlorophyll but must sustain ourselves by consuming organic matter that the autotrophs have synthesized.

Our respiration process and likewise the decomposers, which dispose of our waste products and ultimately of our bodies, restore the carbon to the atmosphere in the form of carbon dioxide. The very fact that the carbon in the air is in the form of carbon dioxide means that the oxygen and carbon cycles are closely interwoven with each other.

These two cycles are connected in turn with cycles on a larger geological scale. Ultraviolet radiation dissociates water into hydrogen and oxygen in the outer atmosphere and some oxygen is fixed by the oxidizing of certain minerals. The carbon cycle is more closed, but carbon is fixed as calcium carbonate, in the form of limestone and chalk. In this part of the carbon cycle the duration is reckoned in millions of years.

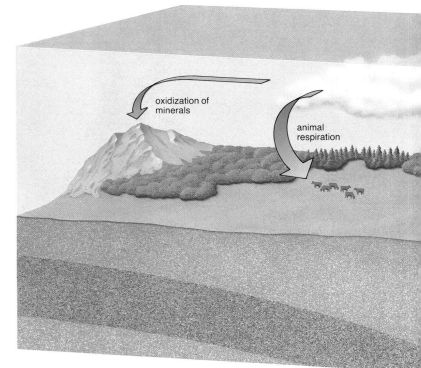

The oxygen cycle

The air contains about 21 % oxygen and this concentration is the result of millions of years of green plant photosynthesis. Such oxygen as may have existed in the primeval atmosphere has long since leaked away into outer space. Forests and plankton produce the greater part of the oxygen content in the atmosphere. Deforestation and oceanic pollution can thus have dangerous consequences by reducing the production of the oxygen that we breathe. In their turn the respiratory processes of animals and plants fix the oxygen, which is subsequently released as a component of carbon dioxide—a cycle analyzed in the panorama below.

The carbon cycle

Carbon dioxide is a common component in the atmosphere of the planets and is present, for example, around both Venus and Mars. The average CO_2 content of the Earth's atmosphere is only 0.033%. The free oxygen content of the air is over 600 times greater. The total quantity of carbon in the atmosphere is in fact no more than about one and a half times that which is fixed in the living organisms. In other words carbon is in short supply and must be recycled much more rapidly than oxygen. Enormous quantities of carbon dioxide are dissolved in the oceans, but this carbon is not directly available to the 90 % (reckoned as per biomass) of all living organisms which are on land. The carbon cycle is complex but amounts mainly to carbon being fixed in green plant photosynthesis and liberated through breathing.

Leaves absorb solar energy through a photo-chemical process conducted by the green substance chlorophyll.

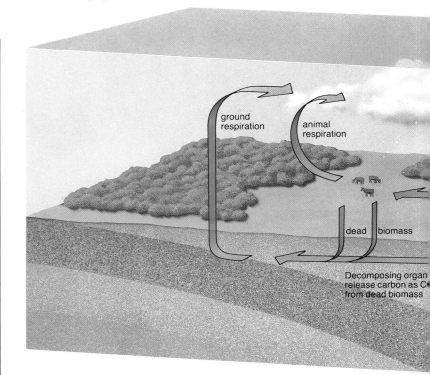

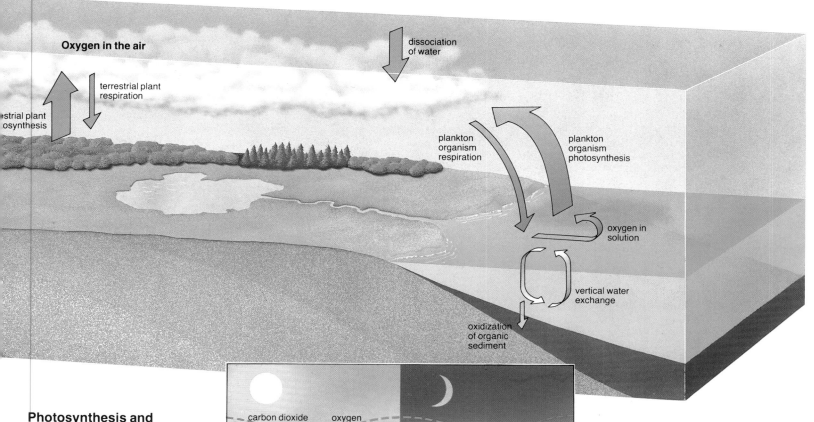

Oxygen in the air

terrestrial plant
respiration

strial plant
osynthesis

dissociation
of water

plankton
organism
respiration

plankton
organism
photosynthesis

oxygen in
solution

vertical water
exchange

oxidization
of organic
sediment

Photosynthesis and respiration

Photosynthesis extracts carbon from the atmosphere and the respiration of the green plants liberates carbon. The carbon dioxide content of the atmosphere is thus determined by a tug of war between these two processes. The life processes of animals have not affected the outcome to any great extent, since more than 90 % of all the living biomass is in plant life. Only now with their combustion of coal and oil are people threatening to disrupt this equilibrium.

carbon dioxide   oxygen

The forest respires around the clock
Photosynthesis takes place in daylight, increasing the oxygen level of the atmosphere and decreasing the CO_2 content. After dark photosynthesis ceases but respiration continues. The CO_2 level rises, reaching a peak around dawn when it can be more than 20 % higher than average.

Where is the carbon?

There may be some 40,000 billion tons of carbon available in the biosphere for the life processes. This is distributed approximately as follows (all figures are in billions of tons):

Atmosphere		700
Dissolved in the oceans		35,000
Living biomass:	on land	450
	in the sea	<5
Dead biomass		3,700

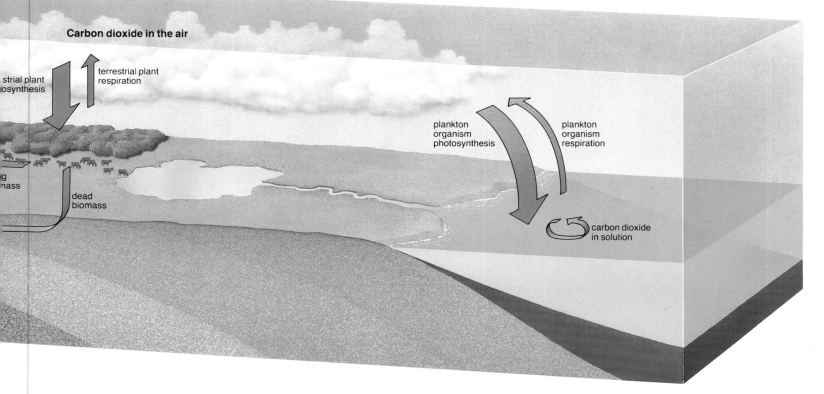

Carbon dioxide in the air

terrestrial plant
respiration

strial plant
osynthesis

plankton
organism
photosynthesis

plankton
organism
respiration

g
ass

dead
biomass

carbon dioxide
in solution

Airconditioning the Earth

The circulation of air in the atmosphere is activated by convection, the transference of heat resulting from the fact that warm gases or fluids rise while cold gases or fluids sink. For example: if one wall of a room is heated while the opposite wall is cooled, air will rise against the warm wall and flow across the ceiling to the cold wall before descending to flow back across the floor to the warm wall again.

The real atmosphere, however, is like a very long room with a very low ceiling. The distance from equator to pole is 6,214 mi. while the "ceiling height" to the tropopause is only about 6 mi. The air therefore splits up into a number of smaller loops or "convection cells". Between the equator and each pole there are three such cells and within these the circulation is mainly north-south.

Large-scale air conditioning

The result of this circulation is a flow of heat energy towards the poles and a leveling out of the climate so that both equatorial and polar regions are habitable. The atmosphere generally retains its state of equilibrium as every north-going air current is counter-balanced by a south-going one. In the same way depressions at lower levels in the troposphere are counter-balanced by areas of high pressure in the upper levels, and vice versa. The atmospheric transference of heat is closely associated with the movement of moisture between sea and continent and between different latitudes. Moist air can transport much greater quantities of energy than dry air.

Because the belts of convection cells run east to west, both climate and weather vary according to latitude. In the equatorial convergence zone (the doldrums), and around the Tropic of Cancer and Tropic of Capricorn known as "horse latitudes", sailing ships could drift for weeks unable to steer, while the "roaring forties" of the South Atlantic (40°–50°S) were notorious among mariners for their terrible winds. Climatic zones are particularly distinguishable at sea where there are no land masses to disturb the pattern.

People and the winds

For thousands of years people have been dependent upon the winds: they brought rain to the land and carried ships across the seas. Thus the westerly wind belts, the trade winds and the monsoon winds of the global circulation system, have been known to us for many centuries. As recently as the present century Arab ships sailed on the south-west monsoon winds from East Africa to India and back again on the north-east monsoon winds, without need of a compass. The winds alone were sufficient.

It was not until the development of the balloon at the end of the 18th century, however, that it became possible to study meteorological conditions at high altitudes. The balloon is still a significant research device although today it carries a radar reflector or a set of instruments and a radio transmitter, rather than the scientists themselves. Nowadays high-flying aircraft and satellites are also important aids to meteorology. Through them we have discovered the west to east jet stream. This blows at speeds of up to 310 mi/h at altitudes of 29,529–32,810 ft. along the border between the Arctic and temperate zone convection belts.

Weather fronts

The circulation within the different convection cells is greater than the exchange of air between them and therefore the temperature in two cells that are close to each other can differ greatly. Consequently the borders between the different convection cells are areas in which warm and cold air masses oppose each other, advancing and withdrawing. In the northern hemisphere the dividing line between the Arctic and temperate convection zones is the polar front, and it is this which determines the weather in northern Europe and North America. This front is unstable, weaving sometimes northward, sometimes southward, of an average latitude of 60°N. Depressions become trapped within the deep concavities of this front and these subsequently move eastward along it with areas of rain and snowfall. In this way global air circulation determines not only the long-term climate but also the immediate weather.

North Pole

Global circulation

The large-scale circulation of air takes place through convection. Warm air rises at the equator and then flows north or south, while corresponding flows of cold air move from the poles towards the equator. Each hemisphere has three belts of convection cells and the circulation within each belt is greater than it is between them.

If the Earth did not rotate, the winds would blow largely in a north/south direction. The earth's rotation causes them to veer off course (oblique arrows). The model above is schematic and presupposes a planet totally covered by sea. The continents create local wind systems.

At ground level, air streams towards the equator from both hemispheres. An equatorial convergence zone runs along the equator and seafarers of the past sought to avoid this because of its feeble and undependable winds. The exchange of air between the northern and southern hemispheres is a fairly slow process.

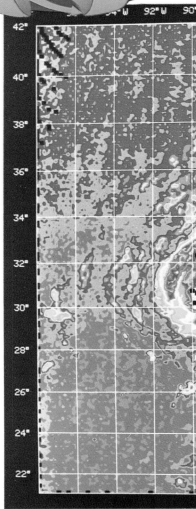

A tropical cyclone

A hurricane in the Gulf of Mexico heading towards the US coast is kept under surveillance by temperature sensing instruments in a weather satellite. At the ground station, numeric data is converted into a chart (right). The nucleus of the hurricane is a small but very intense depression and the spiral of air on its way into this "eye" is clearly visible.

The colors are produced by the computer which constructs the picture and these indicate the temperatures in the upper troposphere at about 32,810 ft. The color scale, far right, is graduated in Kelvins. One Kelvin (K) equates to 34°F., but the scale's zero is absolute zero, −459.7°F.

Utilizing the wind

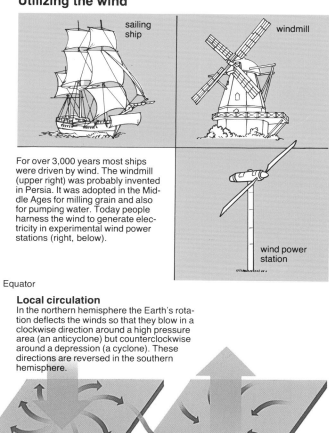

For over 3,000 years most ships were driven by wind. The windmill (upper right) was probably invented in Persia. It was adopted in the Middle Ages for milling grain and also for pumping water. Today people harness the wind to generate electricity in experimental wind power stations (right, below).

Local circulation

In the northern hemisphere the Earth's rotation deflects the winds so that they blow in a clockwise direction around a high pressure area (an anticyclone) but counterclockwise around a depression (a cyclone). These directions are reversed in the southern hemisphere.

high pressure   low pressure

Mountains, winds and rain

When a mountain range lies right across the direction of the prevailing wind the upward moving air on the windward side of the range is cooled down and the moisture precipitates as rain. It is for this reason that the hills in Assam get as much as 97.5 in. rain in one month during the south-west monsoon. The terrain on the leeward side is in the "rain-shadow" and has a dry climate.

Diurnal winds

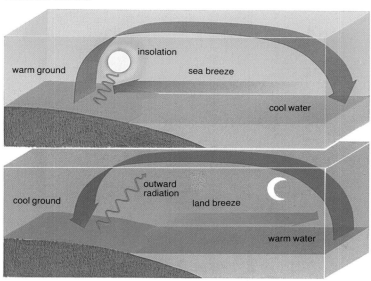

During the day the land is warmed more rapidly than the sea and the air over the land rises. Its place is taken by cooler air from over the water, creating a sea breeze. At night the grounds cools off quickly while the water retains its warmth. The air then rises over the sea instead, causing a land breeze. At higher altitudes these directions are reversed, unless larger scale wind systems upset the pattern.

Seasonal winds

The monsoons are large scale sea and land breezes, activated by annual rather than daily temperature changes. They give rise to rainy and dry periods in south and east Asia.

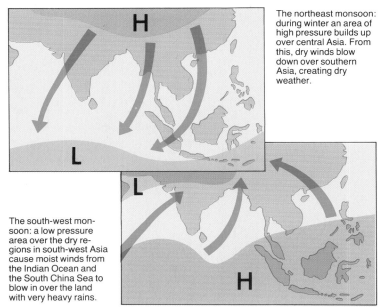

The northeast monsoon: during winter an area of high pressure builds up over central Asia. From this, dry winds blow down over southern Asia, creating dry weather.

The south-west monsoon: a low pressure area over the dry regions in south-west Asia cause moist winds from the Indian Ocean and the South China Sea to blow in over the land with very heavy rains.

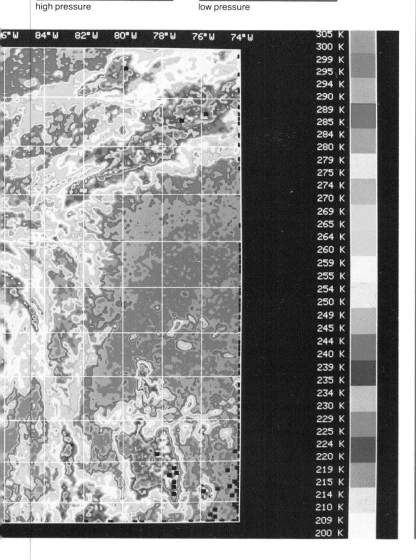

Among the clouds

The solar energy which heats the Earth's atmosphere is not only responsible for the global circulation system, it also causes local air circulation. The global circulation takes place mainly in a horizontal direction, moving warm air from the tropics to the polar regions and cold air in the opposite direction. Local circulation on the other hand functions mainly vertically, giving rise to upwinds and fall winds. We cannot see these vertical winds and neither do we feel them—except in an aircraft when turbulence can produce uncomfortably "bumpy" intervals. Every day we see a by-product of the vertical winds: the clouds above our heads. Some well-known local winds, such as the mistral and the sirocco, are mainly "horizontal" winds.

Air and water
The air in the troposphere always contains a certain amount of water vapor. The actual quantity depends upon evaporation: over the sea the humidity is high, over the desert it is very low. There is also a maximum quantity and that is related to the temperature. At 68°F a cubic foot of air can contain as much as .6 oz. of water. If the temperature is reduced to zero the same air volume can only retain .17 oz. of water, the rest precipitating in the form of microscopically small droplets. These droplets form around condensation nuclei which can either be dust particles or small salt crystals from the surface of the sea. When this takes place at ground level it is called mist, while at higher altitudes it produces clouds. These droplets are so tiny that they can remain suspended almost indefinitely on even the slightest upwinds. If they merge into larger drops then they fall as rain.

Mountains, fronts and thermals
How can a warm air mass be cooled down rapidly? In certain instances this heat loss can occur through thermal conduction when it passes over cold ground or an icy sea, or through radiation at night. But a swifter means is to force the air mass upward so that it expands because of the reduced pressure around it. This sort of adiabatic expansion (expansion without more heat being added) is always followed by a fall in temperature.

A mountain range right across the direction of the wind can, naturally, compel the air to rise. In this way rain clouds are often formed on the windward side of mountains or hills while the lee side is in a "rain shadow". For example, the Himalayas cause the moist monsoon winds to release most of the rain over northern India while the Tibetan plateau remains dry. Fronts function like moving mountain ranges: along a cold front air wedges its way in beneath a warm air mass, forcing the latter upward, often with violent rain and thunderstorms. A warm front occurs when warm air moves upward over a cold air mass and displaces it.

Thermal upwinds, known simply as "thermals" by glider pilots, derive from local heating of the ground and the air above it by the sun. The warm air rises because of its temperature and humidity in relation to the surrounding air mass. When the air reaches a certain altitude, the "cloud base", the water vapor condenses. Billowy cumulus is thus formed over this level.

The thunderstorm
Strong upwinds, either of a thermal nature or deriving from the passage of a cold front, are often followed by thunderstorms. The circulating water droplets in the cloud develop different electrical charges and enormous voltage differences build up in various parts of the cloud until these are finally discharged as lightning. The interior of a thundercloud is a complex environment, however, and we are still not entirely sure how the positive and negative charges are separated and conveyed to different parts of the cloud. The total energy of an electrical storm can be of the same magnitude as in a nuclear explosion. However, only a small proportion of this energy is released in the lightning flashes.

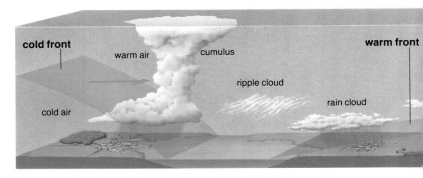

Cold and warm fronts
determine the changes in the weather in the temperate latitudes. When cold air (left) pushes its way in beneath warm air it often results in a severe storm. A warm front (right) occurs when warm, usually moist air moves in over the cold air. The result is then steady rain rather than heavy showers. The cold front is always steeper than the warm front; the slope angles are approx. 5° and 2.5°, respectively. The different fronts are heralded by typical cloud forms.

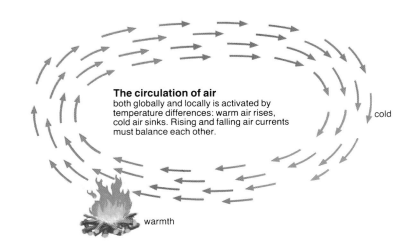

The circulation of air
both globally and locally is activated by temperature differences: warm air rises, cold air sinks. Rising and falling air currents must balance each other.

Precipitation

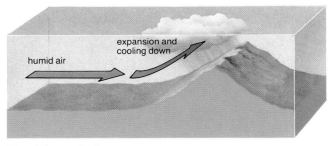

Mountains and rain
When moist winds are forced upward by mountains in their path, the resultant reduction in pressure at higher altitudes causes a fall in temperature and the formation of cloud. In this way places south of the Himalayas can get 97.5 in. of rain in a month.

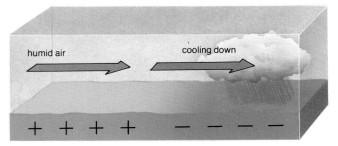

Cold and rain
A cooling process can also occur as a result of thermal conduction to the cold ground or cold water, or through radiation. This process also produces mist, i.e. cloud at ground level.

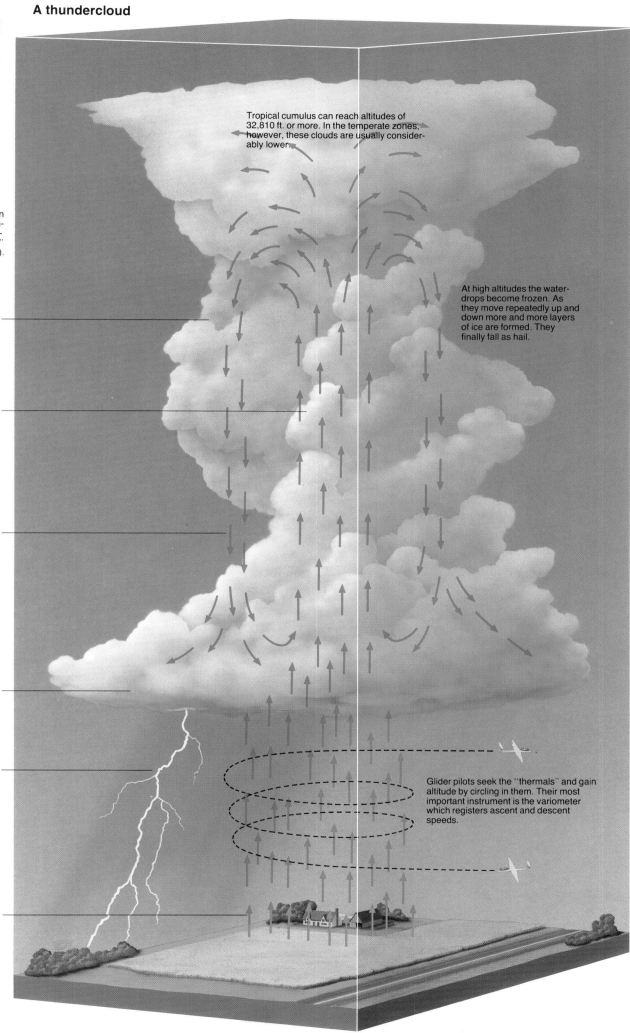

A thundercloud

cirrus

...tus

warm air

cold air

Tropical cumulus can reach altitudes of 32,810 ft. or more. In the temperate zones, however, these clouds are usually considerably lower.

At high altitudes the waterdrops become frozen. As they move repeatedly up and down more and more layers of ice are formed. They finally fall as hail.

Glider pilots seek the "thermals" and gain altitude by circling in them. Their most important instrument is the variometer which registers ascent and descent speeds.

Cumulus
is not only fine weather cloud. It can turn into thundercloud (Cumulonimbus or Cumulus tonans) and sometimes the cloud assumes an "anvil" shape (Cumulonimbus incus, right).

The upper part
of the cloud often consists of ice crystals. The level at which the waterdrops freeze depends on the temperature.

Upwinds
sometimes attaining gale force blow inside the cloud. They are strongest immediately above the cloud base, as condensation releases heat, increasing the "buoyancy" of the air.

Fall winds
are not as strong as the upwinds but can be quite violent. Fall and upwinds give rise to turbulence which has been known to break the wings of light aircraft.

The cloud base
is that level at which the temperature allows condensation to commence.

Thunderstorms
occur in clouds with violent circulation. Air currents form a gigantic electrostatic generator.

Warm air
gathers over warm ground until it loses contact with the surface and ascends like a hot-air balloon. It is then replaced by cool air which in its turn becomes warmer.

11

Seasons and climates

The Earth orbits the sun along an elliptical path and the sun, the central body in our planetary system, is at one of the focal points of this ellipse. In astronomical terms the distance between Earth and the sun does not vary greatly. The average distance is a little less than 93 million mi. The Earth orbits the sun in just over 365 days 6 hours, the odd hours making up a leap day once every four years.

It is easy enough to comprehend that the seasonal variations are not a result of the Earth's varying distance from the sun—if that were the case then both northern and southern hemispheres would have summer at the same time. Seasonal variations in temperature and in hours of day and night derive from the Earth's oblique axis which leans one hemisphere and then the other towards the sun. If the Earth lacked an atmosphere and a hydrosphere then this oblique axis would be of no particular consequence. Our sister planet, the moon, has nothing in the way of seasons. On Earth, however, the movements of both air and sea are activated in a daily or annual cycle by differences in the distribution of incoming solar energy over the Earth's surface. Winds, waves and currents, the humid warmth of the rain forests and the bitter cold of the tundra; all these arise from local and periodic variations. The consequences extend even further: Climate determines vegetation type and the fauna that derives its nourishment from the plants. Every type of climate has its own particular ecological system.

Climate is the mean value of weather. Climatologists calculate this average over a 30-year period so as to produce representative figures upon which to base their classifications. In the 1910's the Austrian Köppen drew up a classification of the world's climates founded on only two variables: temperature and precipitation. This is still generally used and is the basis for the climate chart shown here. Other variables can be used: the balance between precipitation and evaporation, the number of hours of sunshine, elevation above sea level, the balance between inward and outward radiation, and so on. The radiation balance, in particular, is of fundamental significance. The hot days and cold nights of the Sahara, for example, result from the fact that the dry atmosphere in no way hinders either the daytime inward radiation or the outward radiation at night.

The coldness of winter is intensified when white snow and ice reflect back a large proportion of the incoming solar heat. Distance from the sea causes the difference between a continental and a maritime climate. The continental climate tends to be dry with great differences between summer and winter temperatures, while the maritime climate is more humid and has a more even temperature. At Verkhoyansk on the Siberian tundra, the difference between the mean temperatures of the warmest and coldest months of the year is 154°F. In Godthåb on the west coast of Greenland it is only 62°F.

Scientists are attempting to learn something about the Earth's climate during past geological eras—the paleo-climate. Geology itself provides certain keys. There are rock types in England, for example, which were formed during a desert climate. Study of the annual growth rings in living and fossil trees—dendrochronology—enables us to look several thousand years into the past. Quotients between different oxygen isotopes in Greenland's inland ice and between samples of deepsea ooze give us some insight into past climatic changes. But this is a complex subject and it is by no means easy to correlate the different results.

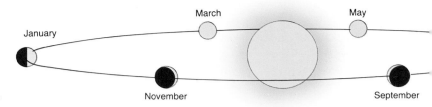

Around the sun
During the course of a year the Earth makes one complete orbit around the sun. This orbit, c. 584 million mi., is elliptical but this is of no importance in relation to the seasonal changes. In fact the Earth is closest to the sun in January. The seasons are caused instead by the angle of the Earth's axis.

The seasons

The Earth's axis from North Pole to South Pole leans at 23°27' in relation to the plane of its orbit, the ecliptic. Like the axis of the gyroscope or the spinning top, the Earth's axis always points in the same direction, despite the fact that the planet circles the sun. This is why the two hemispheres alternately face the sun, creating summer and winter respectively.

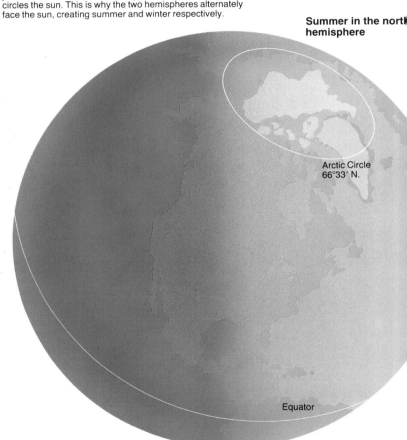

Summer in the north hemisphere

Arctic Circle 66°33' N.

Equator

Heat, humidity and vegetation

Equatorial lowland rain forest: high, steady temperature and humidity all the year round.

Savanna: high steady temperature but rainfall is unevenly distributed with often two rain periods a year.

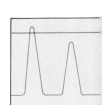

Climates and the biosphere
Water is the universal solvent and it is of vital significance to all organisms. Sunlight is the energy source of plants and hence in the final analysis of animals too. The temperature also determines whether water shall be available as liquid or ice. Precipitation (the blue graph lines in the small diagrams) and the temperature (red lines) determine between them the vegetation (large illustrations). Apart from these principal types there are many other variants as a result of local conditions, for example a mountain massif or irregularities in wind direction, etc.

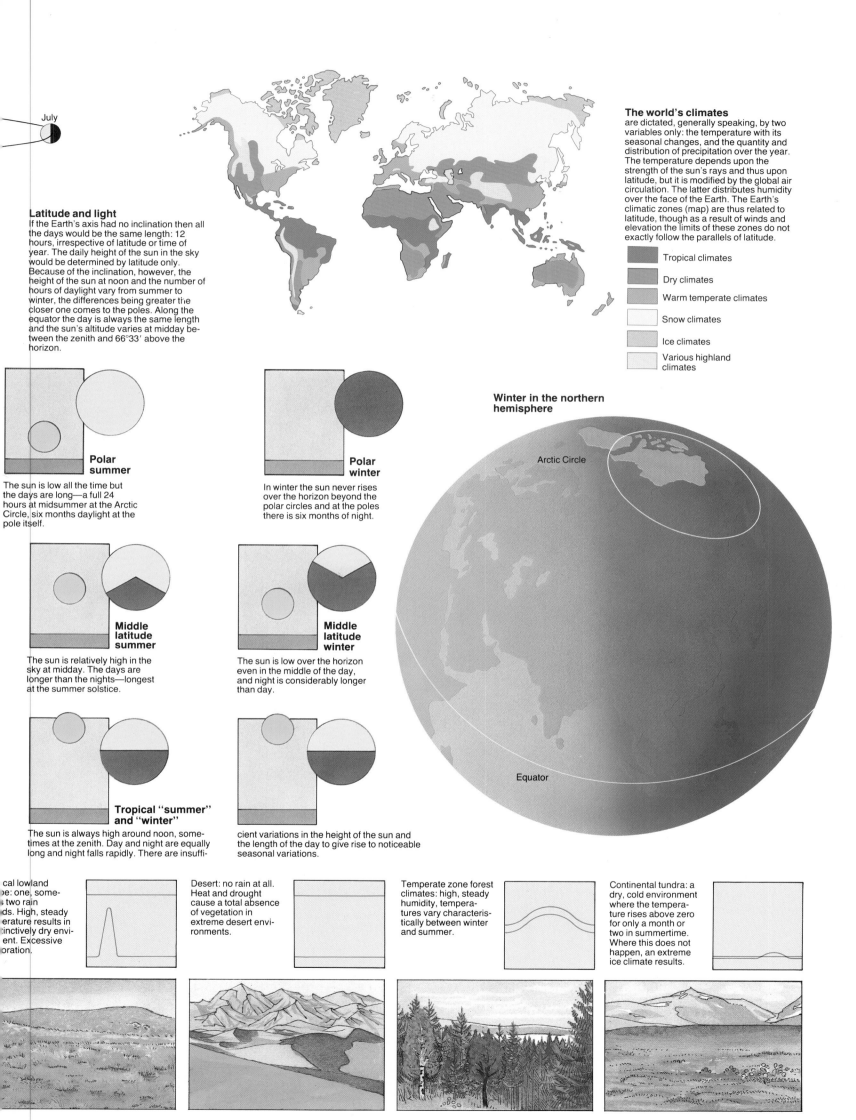

July

Latitude and light

If the Earth's axis had no inclination then all the days would be the same length: 12 hours, irrespective of latitude or time of year. The daily height of the sun in the sky would be determined by latitude only. Because of the inclination, however, the height of the sun at noon and the number of hours of daylight vary from summer to winter, the differences being greater the closer one comes to the poles. Along the equator the day is always the same length and the sun's altitude varies at midday between the zenith and 66°33' above the horizon.

The world's climates

are dictated, generally speaking, by two variables only: the temperature with its seasonal changes, and the quantity and distribution of precipitation over the year. The temperature depends upon the strength of the sun's rays and thus upon latitude, but it is modified by the global air circulation. The latter distributes humidity over the face of the Earth. The Earth's climatic zones (map) are thus related to latitude, though as a result of winds and elevation the limits of these zones do not exactly follow the parallels of latitude.

- Tropical climates
- Dry climates
- Warm temperate climates
- Snow climates
- Ice climates
- Various highland climates

Polar summer

The sun is low all the time but the days are long—a full 24 hours at midsummer at the Arctic Circle, six months daylight at the pole itself.

Polar winter

In winter the sun never rises over the horizon beyond the polar circles and at the poles there is six months of night.

Middle latitude summer

The sun is relatively high in the sky at midday. The days are longer than the nights—longest at the summer solstice.

Middle latitude winter

The sun is low over the horizon even in the middle of the day, and night is considerably longer than day.

Winter in the northern hemisphere

Arctic Circle

Equator

Tropical "summer" and "winter"

The sun is always high around noon, sometimes at the zenith. Day and night are equally long and night falls rapidly. There are insuffi- cient variations in the height of the sun and the length of the day to give rise to noticeable seasonal variations.

cal lowland pe: one, some- s two rain ds. High, steady erature results in inctively dry envi- ent. Excessive oration.

Desert: no rain at all. Heat and drought cause a total absence of vegetation in extreme desert environments.

Temperate zone forest climates: high, steady humidity, temperatures vary characteristically between winter and summer.

Continental tundra: a dry, cold environment where the temperature rises above zero for only a month or two in summertime. Where this does not happen, an extreme ice climate results.

13

Signs in the sky

Meteorological folklore

Mariners' meteorology
"Rain before wind, bring your mainsail in. Wind before rain, set your mainsail again." In the past, seamen and farmers were always dependent upon being able to foresee changes in the weather. In time their experience produced a wealth of lore expressed in rhyme and doggerel. A lot of this made sense, but there was no real understanding of the causal relationship between "signs in the sky" and the next few hours' weather before the development of modern meteorological science (three examples, right).

Old signs—new science

Cirrus clouds form high up on the forward edge of a warm front. At ground level, the front is still a long way off though it will eventually bring a change in the weather, probably rain.

Haloes occur when a front forces a mass of air to rise to an altitude where ice crystals form. This also is a sign of a change in the weather—a warm front is on the way.

"Red sky at night, shepherd's delight. Red sky in the morning, shepherd's warning." A red sky is caused by light refraction in moist air, normal after a warm day. A red sunrise on the other hand indicates that the atmosphere is exceptionally humid, which can result in rain and gusty winds.

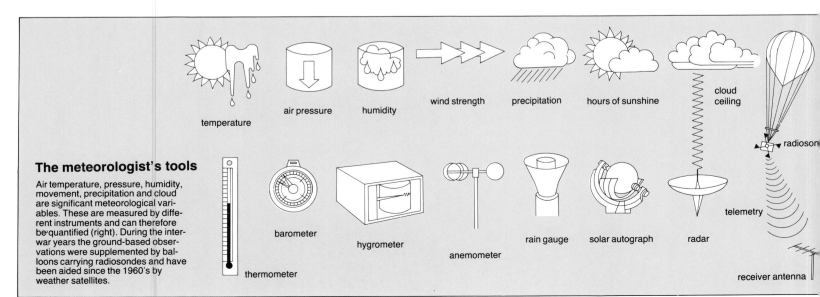

The meteorologist's tools

Air temperature, pressure, humidity, movement, precipitation and cloud are significant meteorological variables. These are measured by different instruments and can therefore be quantified (right). During the inter-war years the ground-based observations were supplemented by balloons carrying radiosondes and have been aided since the 1960's by weather satellites.

temperature · air pressure · humidity · wind strength · precipitation · hours of sunshine · cloud ceiling · radioson

thermometer · barometer · hygrometer · anemometer · rain gauge · solar autograph · radar · telemetry · receiver antenna

The science of meteorology owes much to the development of telegraphic communication. Previously meteorologists could work only with what they actually saw. Other information beyond their field of vision was no longer of any significance by the time it reached them. The telegraph, however, made it possible to assemble simultaneous observations from a wide area, thereby enabling the scientists to produce a synoptic picture of current weather conditions and to begin the analysis of atmospheric phenomena.

This capacity for swiftly collecting and processing data is of fundamental importance to the work of the meteorologist. Temperature, air pressure, wind, precipitation and cloud reports are continuously being received from weather stations, unmanned instruments and satellites.

Meteorologists could be overwhelmed by this never-ending flow of information, but the data is necessary. The recording of precise values allows scientists to subject different phenomena to mathematical analysis and thereby make meteorology an exact science. Since the beginning of this century simple equations have been known which can be applied to predict the behavior of air masses. If these are to be used to produce practical forecasts, then the atmosphere has to be divided up into a large number of relatively small "air cubes" with sides of perhaps only 1.2 mi. When each such cube has been analyzed individually the results are adjusted in relation to what has happened in the adjoining spaces. This process has to be repeated several times over. This, of course, requires an enormous calculating capability. Before this capability existed the meteorologist, engrossed in synoptic charts, had to predict the course of the weather on the strength of rules of thumb and personal experience. The duration of the forecast was never greater than 24 hours and, furthermore, it was often inaccurate.

Now for the first time modern high speed computers enable meteorologists to work out these complex equations within a reasonable time. The forecasts drawn up by the computers are no longer qualitative but quantitative, expressed in degrees, feet per second, millibars and inches of precipitation. Predictions have become more reliable. The forecast durations have increased during the 1970's from 24 hours to five days. Forecasts extending over much longer periods, weeks and even months, are also being made on an experimental basis, and although these are not yet adequately accurate they are likely to become so in the not too distant future. New super-computers of even greater capacity will most likely make possible dependable long-range forecasts before the close of the 1980's. In addition, meteorologists are receiving more and more information upon which to base their forecasts. Modern satellites register not only cloud conditions but also temperatures in the upper atmosphere and at ground and sea level. They record snow cover and sea ice. All this data is of the utmost importance to long-range meteorological predictions.

Many of our economically important activities are dependent upon the weather and this makes meteorology a science of great practical value. Farming, shipping and aviation rely heavily on correct forecasts as do many different industries. Thus, despite the high costs, weather satellites and super-computers are well worth the expense.

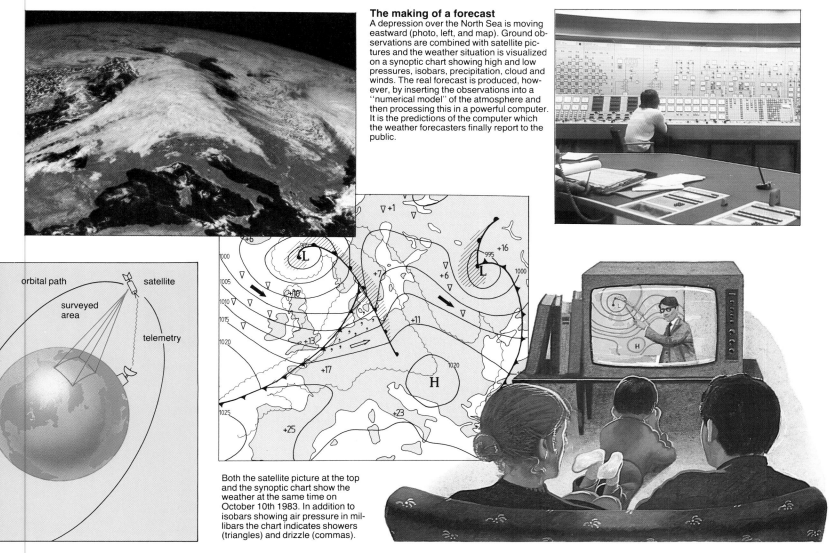

The making of a forecast
A depression over the North Sea is moving eastward (photo, left, and map). Ground observations are combined with satellite pictures and the weather situation is visualized on a synoptic chart showing high and low pressures, isobars, precipitation, cloud and winds. The real forecast is produced, however, by inserting the observations into a "numerical model" of the atmosphere and then processing this in a powerful computer. It is the predictions of the computer which the weather forecasters finally report to the public.

orbital path
satellite
surveyed area
telemetry

Both the satellite picture at the top and the synoptic chart show the weather at the same time on October 10th 1983. In addition to isobars showing air pressure in millibars the chart indicates showers (triangles) and drizzle (commas).

Life in the air

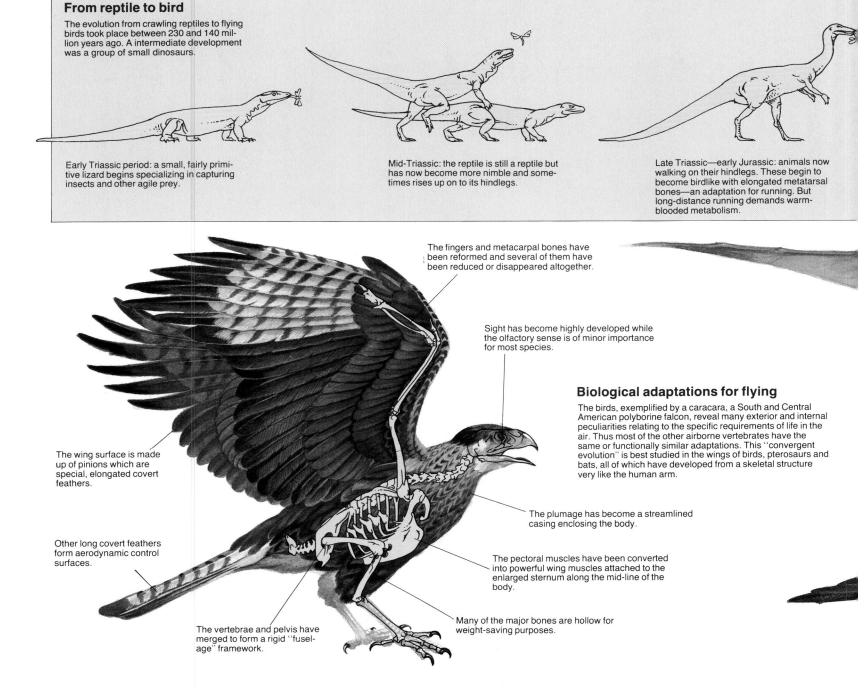

From reptile to bird

The evolution from crawling reptiles to flying birds took place between 230 and 140 million years ago. A intermediate development was a group of small dinosaurs.

Early Triassic period: a small, fairly primitive lizard begins specializing in capturing insects and other agile prey.

Mid-Triassic: the reptile is still a reptile but has now become more nimble and sometimes rises up on to its hindlegs.

Late Triassic—early Jurassic: animals now walking on their hindlegs. These begin to become birdlike with elongated metatarsal bones—an adaptation for running. But long-distance running demands warmblooded metabolism.

The fingers and metacarpal bones have been reformed and several of them have been reduced or disappeared altogether.

Sight has become highly developed while the olfactory sense is of minor importance for most species.

Biological adaptations for flying

The birds, exemplified by a caracara, a South and Central American polyborine falcon, reveal many exterior and internal peculiarities relating to the specific requirements of life in the air. Thus most of the other airborne vertebrates have the same or functionally similar adaptations. This "convergent evolution" is best studied in the wings of birds, pterosaurs and bats, all of which have developed from a skeletal structure very like the human arm.

The wing surface is made up of pinions which are special, elongated covert feathers.

Other long covert feathers form aerodynamic control surfaces.

The plumage has become a streamlined casing enclosing the body.

The pectoral muscles have been converted into powerful wing muscles attached to the enlarged sternum along the mid-line of the body.

The vertebrae and pelvis have merged to form a rigid "fuselage" framework.

Many of the major bones are hollow for weight-saving purposes.

The ability to fly is one of the most curious of all the biological adaptations. It is also very difficult to attain. Among other things it necessitates a restructuring of the body and once this has taken place it is irreversible. But in the struggle for survival flying is so advantageous that this adaptation has occurred not merely once but four times in the history of evolution: among insects, pterosaurs, birds and mammals.

The insects are a special case. The enormous success of the flying insects is attributable to their small size. An animal's weight varies according to volume but muscle power depends upon the cross-sectional area of the muscle. If an animal is scaled down to half its size then its weight diminishes to one eighth, but the muscle power is only reduced to one quarter. Thus at one stroke the power-to-weight ratio becomes twice as favorable. Moreover in minute quantities air behaves more like a fluid than a thin gas. Insects can thus generate lift by entirely different processes than birds.

Insects took to the air during the Carboniferous period about 300 million years ago. The pterosaurs evolved in the Triassic period some 200 million years ago. These were not really "flying reptiles". Reptiles are unable to fly; no cold-blooded animal is capable of prolonged muscular effort. The inner structure of the bones reveal that the pterosaurs were warm-blooded like birds and mammals and we know now from fossil finds that at least the smaller species grew an insulating fur. Some pterosaurs were no larger than sparrows while others had a wingspan of more than 33 ft.

Birds first appeared during the Jurassic period about 150 million years ago. They inherited their warm blood and insulating plumage from their ancestors, the small predatory dinosaurs. The birds displaced the pterosaurs, probably because they were more robust. A bird which loses some of its pinions can manage until new ones grow, but those incredible living sails, the pterosaurs, were doomed if their wing membrane was torn. They were helpless on the ground.

Today birds dominate our airspace so effectively that bats, the only flying mammals, are compelled to live a largely nocturnal life. People fly, too, of course, but their flight technology is mechanical rather than biological.

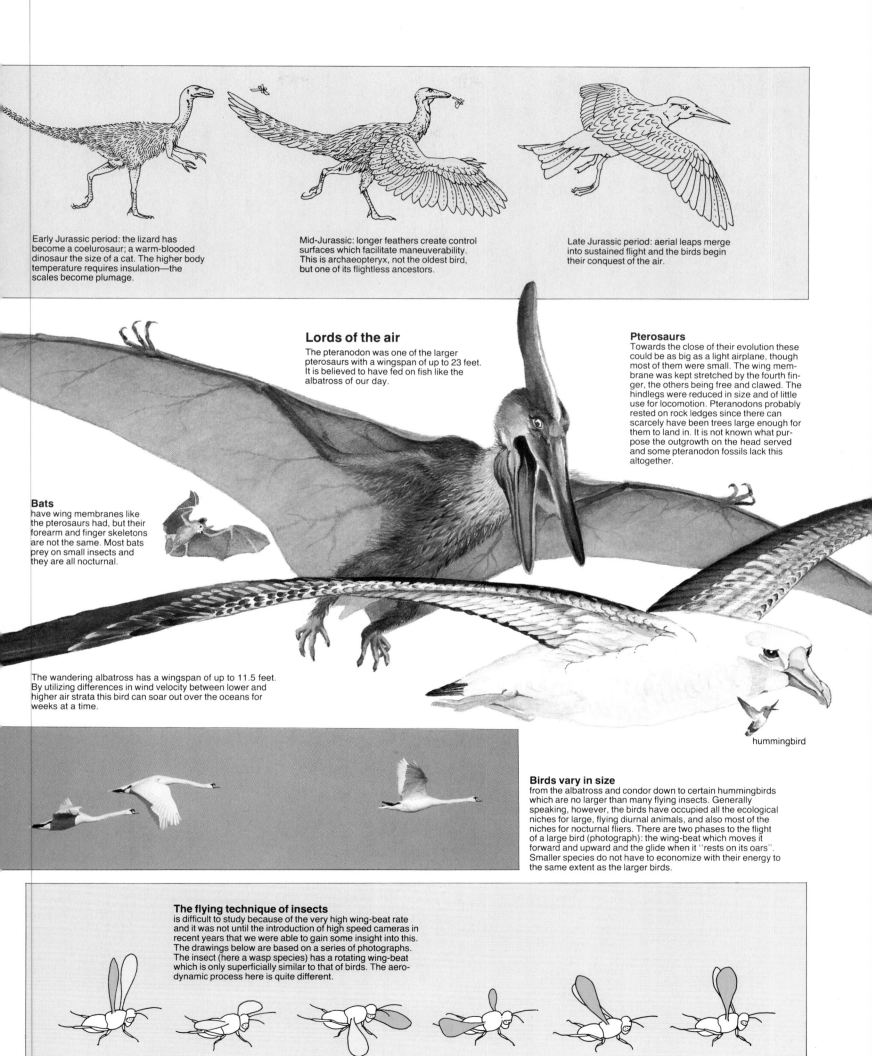

Early Jurassic period: the lizard has become a coelurosaur; a warm-blooded dinosaur the size of a cat. The higher body temperature requires insulation—the scales become plumage.

Mid-Jurassic: longer feathers create control surfaces which facilitate maneuverability. This is archaeopteryx, not the oldest bird, but one of its flightless ancestors.

Late Jurassic period: aerial leaps merge into sustained flight and the birds begin their conquest of the air.

Lords of the air
The pteranodon was one of the larger pterosaurs with a wingspan of up to 23 feet. It is believed to have fed on fish like the albatross of our day.

Pterosaurs
Towards the close of their evolution these could be as big as a light airplane, though most of them were small. The wing membrane was kept stretched by the fourth finger, the others being free and clawed. The hindlegs were reduced in size and of little use for locomotion. Pteranodons probably rested on rock ledges since there can scarcely have been trees large enough for them to land in. It is not known what purpose the outgrowth on the head served and some pteranodon fossils lack this altogether.

Bats
have wing membranes like the pterosaurs had, but their forearm and finger skeletons are not the same. Most bats prey on small insects and they are all nocturnal.

The wandering albatross has a wingspan of up to 11.5 feet. By utilizing differences in wind velocity between lower and higher air strata this bird can soar out over the oceans for weeks at a time.

hummingbird

Birds vary in size
from the albatross and condor down to certain hummingbirds which are no larger than many flying insects. Generally speaking, however, the birds have occupied all the ecological niches for large, flying diurnal animals, and also most of the niches for nocturnal fliers. There are two phases to the flight of a large bird (photograph): the wing-beat which moves it forward and upward and the glide when it "rests on its oars". Smaller species do not have to economize with their energy to the same extent as the larger birds.

The flying technique of insects
is difficult to study because of the very high wing-beat rate and it was not until the introduction of high speed cameras in recent years that we were able to gain some insight into this. The drawings below are based on a series of photographs. The insect (here a wasp species) has a rotating wing-beat which is only superficially similar to that of birds. The aerodynamic process here is quite different.

17

People take to the air

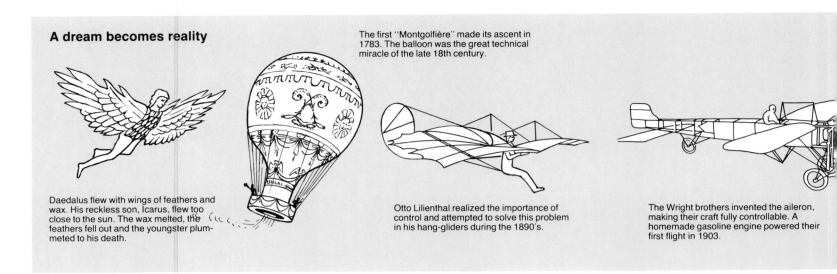
As long as we have been capable of contemplating the birds circling above our heads, we have yearned to be liberated from our bondage under the force of gravity. In myths and legends human beings had no difficulty in flying. The Greeks described how Daedalus and Icarus took to the air to escape King Minos of Crete, and Völund too, the accomplished blacksmith of the Germanic sagas, had mastered the art of flying. In reality, however, it was not until the present century that we realized our dreams.

It would have been quite possible in Leonardo da Vinci's day to have built an operable hang glider of the type in use today, but no one did so. The apparent simplicity of the hang glider is in fact deceptive. Three problems must be overcome in order to fly properly: lift, motive power and steering.

The first of these was solved after a fashion in 1783 when the Montgolfier brothers sent their first hot-air ballon up over Paris and this was followed soon afterwards by a hydrogen balloon. The balloon was widely used in the 19th century as a research device, as a moored observation platform and for sport. It was never a real flying machine however for the winds took it wherever they blew. Even when it was equipped with engines it nevertheless proved too frail to cope with wind squalls, not to mention the danger of conflagration.

It was realized early that aerodynamic lift could be attained by means of cambered wing profiles. The principle is simple enough. Air flows more swiftly over the curved, longer upper wing surface than along the straight, shorter under wing surface. In other words there is less pressure on the wing's upper side, and this difference in pressure produces lift. This requires that the aircraft move forward through the air. Not until the close of the last century could an engine be built that was light and powerful enough to propel an aircraft. Many valiant attempts were made to get airborne but the short hops invariably ended in a crash. It was not sufficient simply to hurl a flying machine up into the air: once up there it had to be steered.

The German pioneer Lilienthal realized this. He was unable to control his hang glider properly, however, and was killed in 1896. The Wright brothers experimented extensively with gliders before they made their first powered flight in 1903. This was the advent of aviation.

Since then the technique of flying has developed rapidly. Aircraft built of light metals, radio, jet engines and new navigational methods have increased the safety, speed, range and transport capabilities. The decisive step forward however was made by men like Otto Lilienthal and Orville and Wilbur Wright who first recognized the three problems—lift, motive power and control—and who prepared the way for dealing with these barriers.

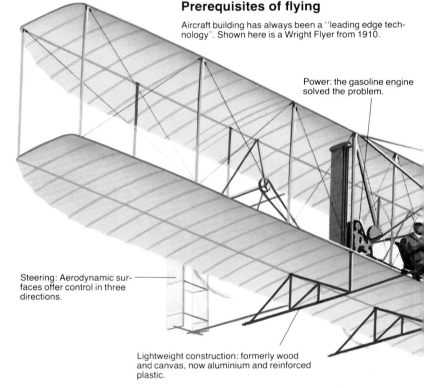

Prerequisites of flying

Aircraft building has always been a "leading edge technology". Shown here is a Wright Flyer from 1910.

Power: the gasoline engine solved the problem.

Steering: Aerodynamic surfaces offer control in three directions.

Lightweight construction: formerly wood and canvas, now aluminium and reinforced plastic.

Highly technological flying

For the uninitiated the cockpit of the Concorde is a bewildering array af dials and buttons. But in the days of piston engines there were even more instruments and gauges to keep check on. The jet engine has produced considerable technical simplification, while on the other hand communication and navigation equipment now plays a more prominent part than during the era of propeller planes.

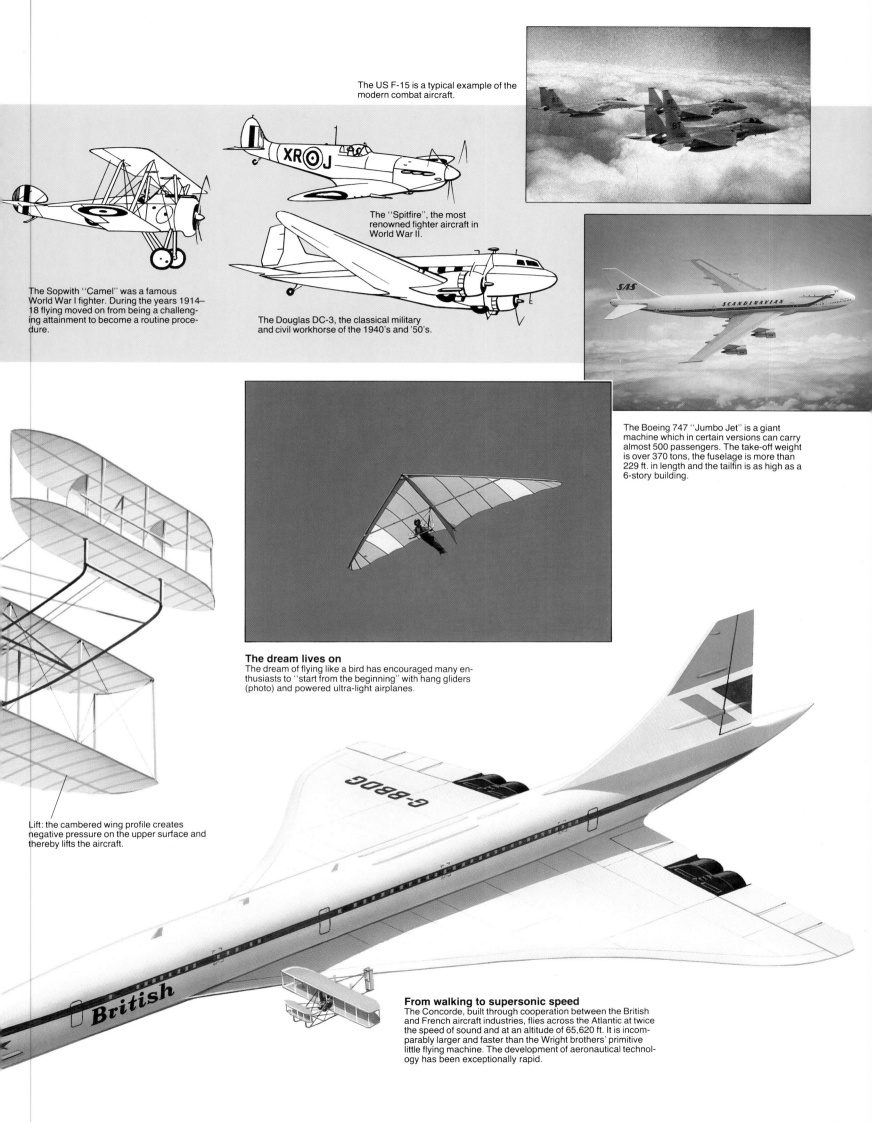

The US F-15 is a typical example of the modern combat aircraft.

The "Spitfire", the most renowned fighter aircraft in World War II.

The Sopwith "Camel" was a famous World War I fighter. During the years 1914–18 flying moved on from being a challenging attainment to become a routine procedure.

The Douglas DC-3, the classical military and civil workhorse of the 1940's and '50's.

The Boeing 747 "Jumbo Jet" is a giant machine which in certain versions can carry almost 500 passengers. The take-off weight is over 370 tons, the fuselage is more than 229 ft. in length and the tailfin is as high as a 6-story building.

Lift: the cambered wing profile creates negative pressure on the upper surface and thereby lifts the aircraft.

The dream lives on
The dream of flying like a bird has encouraged many enthusiasts to "start from the beginning" with hang gliders (photo) and powered ultra-light airplanes.

From walking to supersonic speed
The Concorde, built through cooperation between the British and French aircraft industries, flies across the Atlantic at twice the speed of sound and at an altitude of 65,620 ft. It is incomparably larger and faster than the Wright brothers' primitive little flying machine. The development of aeronautical technology has been exceptionally rapid.

19

Air routes

The history of commercial aviation begins in the 1920's and this "air taxi" from 1928 gives some indication of how primitive things were at that time. Fares were nevertheless high. Flying was a mode of travel—or rather an adventure—for the privileged few.

In less than sixty years, aviation has developed into one of the most important means of communication, recruiting its passengers from every walk of life. Below, vacationers board a DC-9 at a small airport in central Sweden.

Commercial aviation did not really appear until the period immediately after World War I. It was then that bold fliers in open machines first began flying sacks of mail between the larger European and North American cities. Sometimes they would take a passenger as well, thoroughly wrapped up against the cold air. It was not long, however, before the aircraft designers, utilizing their wartime experience, began building proper passenger planes. A network of air routes developed in Europe, extending to the British Empire's outposts in the east, and likewise connecting the east and west coasts of the United States.

Before World War II flying remained, nevertheless, a secondary form of travel. The services were irregular and the planes flew contact; in other words, they kept in sight of the ground and were thus dependent upon good weather conditions. World War II produced improved meteorological services, extended radio communications, radar, more airfields and, particularly, the jet engine. Thus the 1950's and '60's were the real turning point for commercial airlines.

The great advantage of flying is its speed. All types of goods which have to be delivered in a hurry and are valuable are potential air freight, everything from electronic chips to circus elephants. Many people have had contact, of course, with passenger aircraft (regular or charter) but for the airline the passenger is little more than an exceptionally demanding consignment of goods.

There are two types of air routes, one connecting big cities and crossing the oceans and the other consisting of feeder lines. Different types of aircraft are used on each and on the shortest feeder lines propeller aircraft are still a competitive alternative. Commercial aviation has not really kept abreast of the military trend towards increasingly high speeds. Cruising speeds of 510–559 mi/h. are most economical and the Anglo-French Concorde is the only supersonic passenger aircraft operating today. Modern navigation systems are electronic, incorporating radio beacons and similar equipment. Transoceanic airliners employ inertial navigation with a complex system of gyroscopes, accelerometers and computers.

Airfields have also developed, from idyllic green pastures into vast industrial concerns. At the beginning of the 1980's the busiest airport in the world was Chicago's O'Hare, with a daily average of nearly 2,000 arrivals and departures and more than 120,000 passengers. London's Heathrow was the largest in Europe with over 1,000 arrivals and departures a day.

Ground service
Once on the ground the aircraft becomes surrounded by service vehicles—towing tractors, tank trucks, fire engines and various vehicles for technical maintenance and catering. All this servicing has to be done quickly; it costs a lot to let an aircraft stand idle.

Airways and airports

Traffic in the air is carefully regulated. Each airport (right) is surrounded by a meticulously supervised terminal area within which incoming aircraft are "stacked" at different altitudes while awaiting their turn to land. These terminal areas are connected by airways through which aircraft fly at different altitudes in different directions. All traffic is watched over by radar and controlled by radio from traffic control towers. An airport (below) has several miles of runways with lights and instrument landing systems. There are taxi strips so that aircraft moving on the ground do not interfere with take-off and landings. The aircraft are assembled at the ramp; grouped around this are buildings for flight control, passengers and freight, technical services and administration.

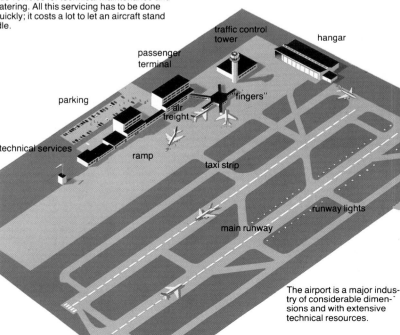

The airport is a major industry of considerable dimensions and with extensive technical resources.

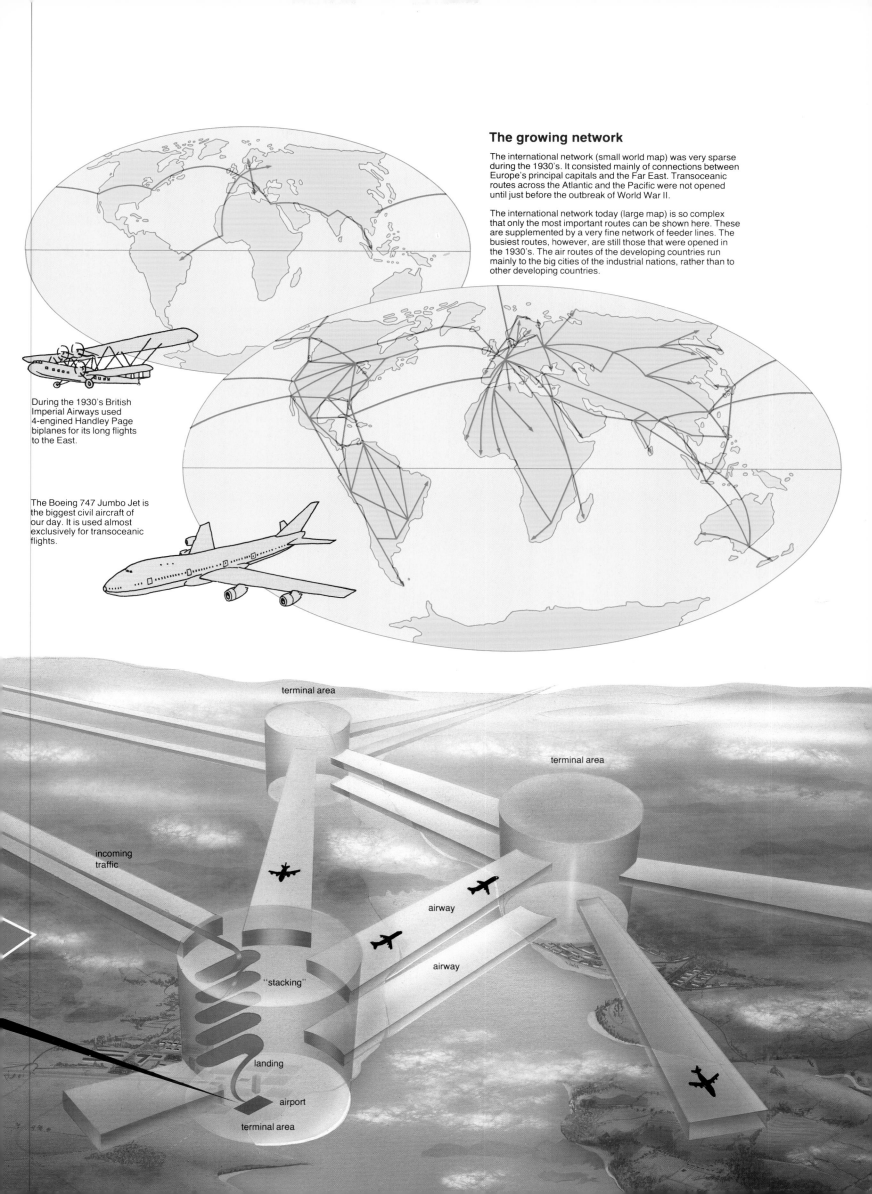

The growing network

The international network (small world map) was very sparse during the 1930's. It consisted mainly of connections between Europe's principal capitals and the Far East. Transoceanic routes across the Atlantic and the Pacific were not opened until just before the outbreak of World War II.

The international network today (large map) is so complex that only the most important routes can be shown here. These are supplemented by a very fine network of feeder lines. The busiest routes, however, are still those that were opened in the 1930's. The air routes of the developing countries run mainly to the big cities of the industrial nations, rather than to other developing countries.

During the 1930's British Imperial Airways used 4-engined Handley Page biplanes for its long flights to the East.

The Boeing 747 Jumbo Jet is the biggest civil aircraft of our day. It is used almost exclusively for transoceanic flights.

terminal area

terminal area

incoming traffic

airway

"stacking"

airway

landing

airport

terminal area

The leap into space

Looking out into space

Since time immemorial the stars have served people as both clock and signpost. Most "primitive" peoples have a better practical knowledge of astronomical time and celestial navigation than the average modern urban citizen.

Before the invention of the telescope astronomical instruments had to be made very large in order to attain sufficient accuracy. Sometimes such instruments grew into entire buildings (right).

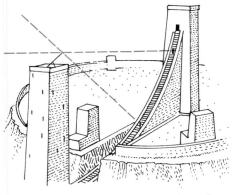

A quadrant for determining the positions of the stars, in Ulugh Begh's observatory in Samarkand, built in the 1440's.

Galileo constructed the first telescope (the idea as such was Dutch, however) and immediately directed this instrument at the stars. This brought about a scientific revolution, for now people could see farther out into space and distinguish the planets as celestial bodies instead of mere points of light. Galileo discovered the moons of Jupiter and the rings around Saturn.

Galileo's first telescope, made in 1609.

All radiation carries information about its source. Modern astronomers use radio telescopes (below) and register images by means of ultra-violet and infrared light and X-rays.

A dream becomes reality

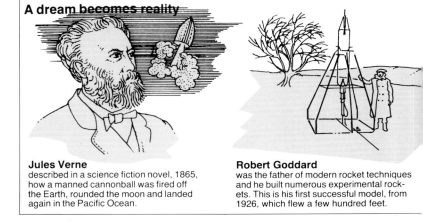

Jules Verne
described in a science fiction novel, 1865, how a manned cannonball was fired off the Earth, rounded the moon and landed again in the Pacific Ocean.

Robert Goddard
was the father of modern rocket techniques and he built numerous experimental rockets. This is his first successful model, from 1926, which flew a few hundred feet.

The departure of people into space began one April day in 1961 when the Soviet test pilot Yuri Gagarin orbited the Earth in one hour and forty-eight minutes in a space capsule. People were now on their way out into an entirely new environment which makes new demands on them but also opens entirely new prospects.

We have only been aware of the existence of outer space for about 300 years. Though Copernicus in the 1500's made deductions about our planetary system it was the new physics of Galileo and Newton which replaced the medieval concepts of the universe. Newton would have been well able to understand how a rocket could continue to function in the vacuum of space. Ejecting combustion gases backward at high velocity increases the forward impulse in accordance with the laws of motion which Newton himself formulated. He would also have understood the artificial satellites of our day. Like the moon—whose orbit Newton was the first to calculate—these satellites fall constantly towards the Earth. Their orbital velocity is so high (2–5 mi/sec) that their trajectory remains parallel with the Earth's surface. Consequently the satellites do not crash to the ground but continue orbiting for years.

Traveling and surviving in space requires advanced technical aids. Human beings need oxygen to breathe and protection against radiation and extreme temperatures. Prolonged weightlessness sometimes leads to mental confusion, deteriorating blood counts and skeletal decalcification. Keeping people alive in space calls for fundamental research and new, life-sustaining technology. If people are not merely to survive but also to work there then the technological requirements will become even greater.

Today some 300 active satellites are orbiting the Earth and permanent space stations are already on the drawing board. Space exploration and research will give our civilization new dimensions. New knowledge awaits us, knowledge relating to the origins, history and ultimate fate of the planetary system and the universe. It is to be hoped that such knowledge will also lead to a clearer understanding of our place in the infinity of the cosmos.

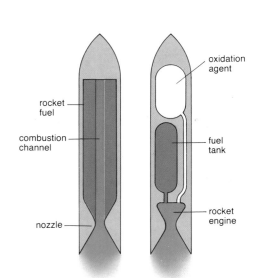

rocket fuel

combustion channel

nozzle

oxidation agent

fuel tank

rocket engine

Solid and liquid fuel
The solid propellant rocket (left) is a sophisticated version of the popular firework rocket. The fuel—usually synthetic rubber mixed with an oxidation agent—has a combustion channel through the middle and the gases are emitted through a nozzle. The liquid fuel rocket (right) has separate tanks for fuel and oxidation agent. A vehicle with such an engine can thus be refuelled and used again, while the solid propellant rocket can normally only be used once.

nher von Braun
...oped the V2 rocket at the German
...emünde base during World War II. He
...equently worked on ballistic missiles
...atellite projects in the USA.

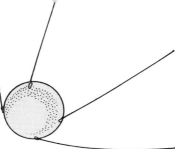

Sputnik 1
was the first human-made satellite. The
Soviet Union put this into orbit in 1957,
thereby beginning the space race with
the USA which is still going on.

The lunar voyages
in the late 1960's and early 70's rounded off
an epoch in the history of space travel.
Since then the emphasis has been more on
practical applications and scientific results
than on prestigious feats.

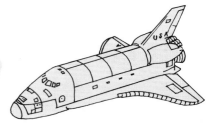

The space shuttle
was developed by the USA and made its
first flight in 1982. This recoverable space
vehicle has greatly reduced the cost of
placing small satellites in orbit and of con-
ducting scientific experiments in a weight-
less state or in the vacuum of space.

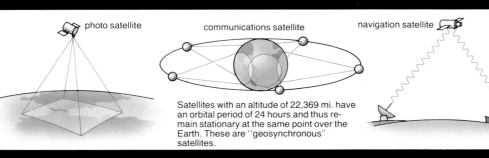

photo satellite

communications satellite

navigation satellite

Satellites with an altitude of 22,369 mi. have
an orbital period of 24 hours and thus remain stationary at the same point over the
Earth. These are "geosynchronous"
satellites.

Uses of space

Today there is intensive activity in our "immediate
space". Meteorological, resource and reconnaissanc...
satellites are constantly photographing our planet an...
studying its surface with different instruments.
Satellites have revolutionized international tele-
communications and navigation satellites are alread...
in use. But people will not really be established in
space until they have installed proper space stations
as envisaged for the next century.(panorama below)
Such stations will probably rotate so as to create an
artificial sense of weight for the people manning the...

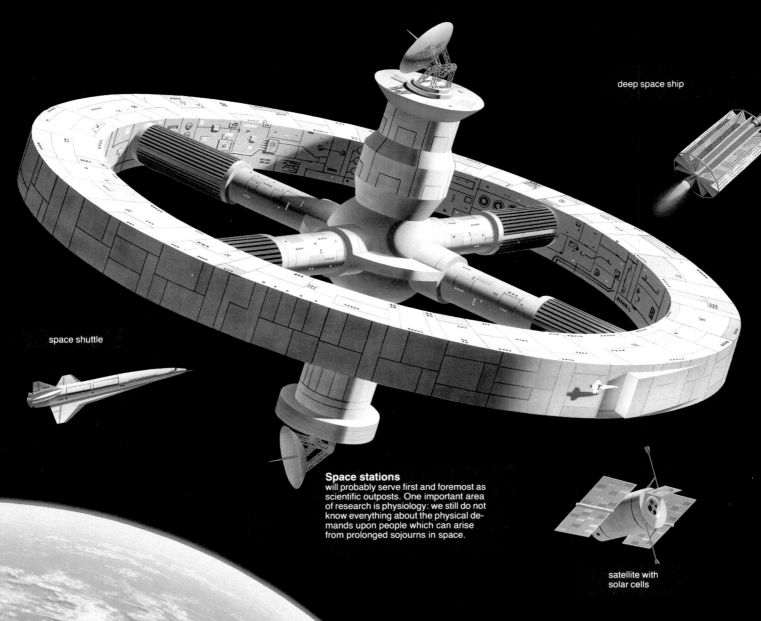

deep space ship

space shuttle

Space stations
will probably serve first and foremost as
scientific outposts. One important area
of research is physiology: we still do not
know everything about the physical demands upon people which can arise
from prolonged sojourns in space.

satellite with
solar cells

Long-distance pollution

Pollution from a region of heavy industry follows the same distribution pattern as fallout from a nuclear detonation. The heavier particles (soot, ash) descend near the chimneys. Over an elliptical area to leeward of the source pollution is acute. At greater distances some of the material rises and becomes diluted, but nevertheless this can be returned to the ground by rain.

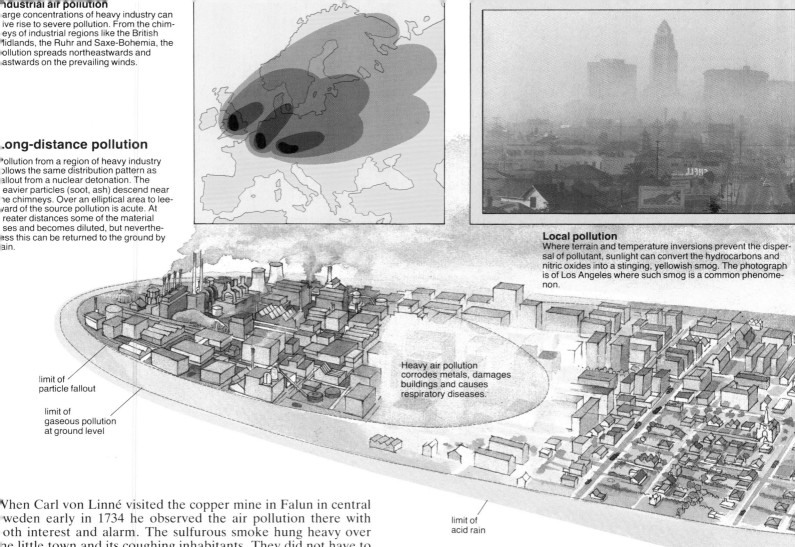

Local pollution
Where terrain and temperature inversions prevent the dispersal of pollutant, sunlight can convert the hydrocarbons and nitric oxides into a stinging, yellowish smog. The photograph is of Los Angeles where such smog is a common phenomenon.

Heavy air pollution corrodes metals, damages buildings and causes respiratory diseases.

limit of particle fallout

limit of gaseous pollution at ground level

limit of acid rain

When Carl von Linné visited the copper mine in Falun in central Sweden early in 1734 he observed the air pollution there with both interest and alarm. The sulfurous smoke hung heavy over the little town and its coughing inhabitants. They did not have to go far to find fresh air, however, for the pollution was localized.

Modern industry is not located in remote mining communities but within large cities. Consequently more and more people are being afflicted by air pollution. The growing discharge of fumes and airborne poisons is becoming more than the atmosphere's circulation system can cope with, and the capacity of vegetation to purify the air also diminishes as the plants themselves become poisoned.

Air pollution is caused mainly by the combustion of oil and coal. The burning of these substances releases heavy metals which have been fixed in the Earth's crust for millions of years. The most serious problem of all is created by sulfur. This is discharged into the atmosphere as sulfur dioxide (SO_2) but in contact with water it is converted into sulfurous acid (H_2SO_3) and ultimately into sulfuric acid (H_2SO_4). This acid corrodes machinery and metal components and damages stone buildings, the Acropolis in Athens being a good example. Even more seriously it engenders respiratory and lung diseases in millions of people.

For many years people refused to accept that this problem extended beyond the industrial centers themselves. But acids can be carried great distances on the wind, from the Ruhr to Scandinavia and from USA to Canada, before falling as acid rain. In both Scandinavia and Canada the bedrock has a low lime content and the ground thus lacks a protective alkaline reserve to neutralize the acid. The damage quickly becomes visible. Forest growth is disrupted and the debilitated trees become prone to disease and parasitic attack. Today, the forests of central Europe are beginning to die as the alkaline reserves in the bedrock become exhausted. In lakes and waterways all life ceases when the pH value falls below about 4. Many lakes in Scandinavia are already devoid of all organic life.

Scientists are worried about two long-term problems. One concerns the atmosphere's stratum of ozone, triatomic oxygen, which absorbs most of the sun's ultraviolet radiation. If this stratum disappears or deteriorates the Earth's vegetation will be severely damaged. One of the results of a nuclear war would be the destruction of the ozone stratum. The release of freon gas from spray containers and air conditioners and the exhaust of jet aircraft in the stratosphere can also damage the protective stratum.

The second problem is created by carbon dioxide. If the combustion of coal and oil further increases the carbon dioxide content in the atmosphere, then the presence of this gas could diminish the radiation of heat from Earth into space. Such an upset in the planet's radiation balance would have major effects on our climate which are only partly understood. The carbon dioxide content in the air has certainly increased during this century, but it has not been established that the Earth's mean temperature has also risen. The destruction of the forests also discharges large quantities of carbon dioxide into the atmosphere from burned and decomposed biomass creating a threat to our oxygen supplies.

These problems are not insurmountable. Industry can adopt cleaner processes. The problem of car exhaust can be overcome by better purification devices and/or other types of engines and fuels. Ruthless deforestation can be halted. Swift measures and cooperation between nations can secure clean air for future generations to breathe.

Temperature inversion

In some instances the atmosphere can be stratified in such a way that the temperature at a certain altitude can begin to rise again instead of falling. Such a temperature inversion keeps the pollution in place as though under a lid and in a short time it can reach a dangerous level of concentration.

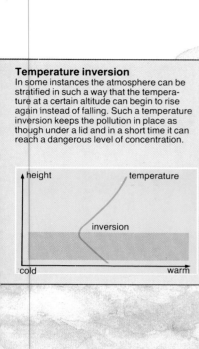

Air pollution in the past

Air pollution existed in the 16th century before industrialization. It occured mainly in the mining districts where sulfide ores were processed (map). This was on such a small scale, however, that the air pollution was limited to very small areas.

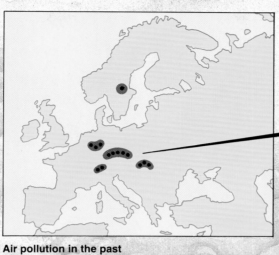

16th century metallurgy

was primitive. The furnaces were inefficient and the sulfide ores were often processed on open hearths giving off an enormous volume of smoke. The release of sulfur dioxide in this way frequently destroyed the vegetation in the surrounding area.

Toxic substances in the air can enter food plants, reaching dangerous levels. The plants' own growth can also be seriously disturbed.

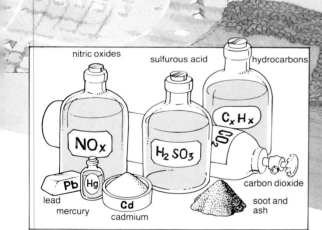

nitric oxides — sulfurous acid — hydrocarbons — C_xH_x — NO_x — H_2SO_3 — CO_2 — carbon dioxide — Pb lead — Hg mercury — Cd cadmium — soot and ash

The air we breathe

often contains foreign substances (above, some examples). These are derived from different sources such as industry, vehicle exhaust, heating and refuse burning.

Long-term threats

Nuclear detonations and high flying jet aircraft can destroy the ozone stratum which protects us from the sun's dangerous ultraviolet radiation.

Carbon dioxide from coal and oil combustion could be a hindrance to the outward radiation of heat (greenhouse effect) and thereby change the world's climate.

Forests fix carbon dioxide through photosynthesis and emit it through respiration. Cleared areas can only emit carbon dioxide, never fix it.

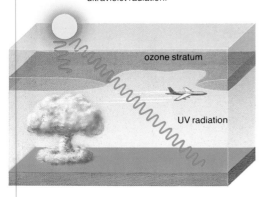

ozone stratum — UV radiation

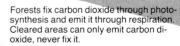

incoming shortwave radiation — carbon dioxide — longwave radiation

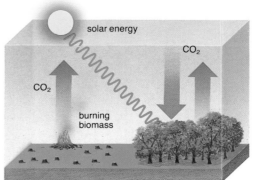

solar energy — CO_2 — CO_2 — burning biomass

Water

The seafarers of ancient Greece thought of the Earth as a flat disk encircled by a great outer sea, – Oceanus. The first of all the Greek philosophers, Thales, who lived c. 600 BC, believed that water was the origin of the world.

When 18th century chemists demonstrated that water was a compound of hydrogen and oxygen it was deprived of its status as a primary element. But hardly had water suffered this setback when the dawning science of physiology discovered its fundamental importance to the processes of life, in that it is an excellent solvent for carbon compounds which are themselves the chemical building blocks of life. Scientists now believe that life first evolved in water, probably in a sheltered tidal water basin along the shore of the primeval sea.

Throughout our cultural development water has always been an influence. Early people avoided arid deserts and impenetrable rain forests. The first advanced civilizations emerged where the great rivers—the Euphrates and Tigris, the Nile, the Indus and the Huang He—permitted people to irrigate their fields. Finally people also put sails on their still-primitive ships and sailed forth across the oceans.

Today access to water is still a vital factor in our lives. It is not only in the parched regions of the Near East and south-western USA that diminishing water supplies have become a threat to the future. In central Europe, too, shortage of water is becoming an increasing obstacle to the expansion of towns and industries.

Our constant interest in water has resulted in the emergence of a whole group of "water sciences". Meteorology is one of these since it is closely concerned with the water cycle. Hydrology embraces studies of the surface- and sub-surface water, while limnology is the science of fresh water biology. Probably the most fascinating of all to the general public, however, are oceanography and marine biology. It was not until the last century that the ocean depths were sounded and their organisms studied and classified. In our day we have descended to the uttermost depths of the seas and found life there. All this has made us more conscious of the significance of water and of the folly of polluting it. The threatened extinction of some of its species is also constraining us to take worldwide measures to save them.

Water, the prerequisite of life

Reproduction in and out of water

   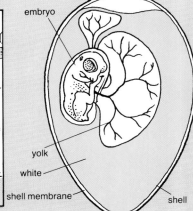

Fishes
have external fertilization: the male and female empty their milt and roe simultaneously into the water. They mingle and sperm-cell and ovum merge. The ovum hatches very swiftly and the fry emerge at an early stage of development.

Amphibians
have taken their first step onto land but the reproductive system is still the same as that of the fish. However the mating position in which the male attaches itself to the female is a step towards copulation and internal fertilization.

Reptiles
present two innovations. Copulation makes fertilization possible out of the water. The protective eggshell means that the egg can be laid on land and the embryo can develop at higher temperatures than would be possible in water.

The bird's egg
has a rigid shell with a sealing membrane inside. The mammal's fetus (right) develops in a similar fashion to that of the bird embryo, though this development takes place in the mammal's uterus.

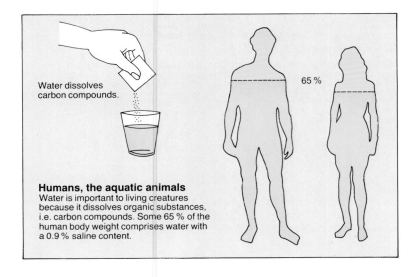

Water dissolves carbon compounds.

Humans, the aquatic animals
Water is important to living creatures because it dissolves organic substances, i.e. carbon compounds. Some 65 % of the human body weight comprises water with a 0.9 % saline content.

Water is a simple compound of hydrogen and oxygen. A chemist encountering this substance for the first time would refer to it as dihydrogen oxide. Such a term, however, would lack the pleasant associations which the word "water" affords us: the clear, pure liquid that quenches our thirst, cools us, cleanses us, sustains the woodland verdure and the golden cornfields. Water has engendered all these associations because it truly is a vital substance; the prerequisite of life.

What are the unique qualities which make water so important to all living things?

Physical properties
The mean temperature of the Earth's surface is about 35°F and the air temperature normally keeps within 104°F above and below this. The freezing point of water is therefore just below the Earth's mean temperature, while its boiling point is 208° higher. This means that water can exist in liquid form for at least part of the year over most of the face of the Earth. Nowhere, however, does it get so hot that the water becomes gasified—a state which would be incompatible with life as we know it.

On our planet water exists in all three of its physical states: ice, water and vapor. Water can be present simultaneously in the atmosphere, in the hydrosphere, in the Earth's crust and in the living organisms—fulfilling vital functions.

Water has a high specific heat: a great deal of energy is needed to vaporize one quart of water. This heat can then be transported long distances as latent heat in atmospheric humidity and released again as heat in the air when moisture condenses into cloud, rain or snow. In this way water performs an important role in the leveling out of temperature differences.

Water and life
Water is important to living organisms because it is an effective and generally available solvent for carbon compounds. Most biochemical reactions can take place only in water solutions. This means that water can transport dissolved substances between different parts of the body, for example in the blood, the serum of which is water-based. The functions of water in the organism have their equivalents outside it. The water we drink and wash ourselves with is a solvent but water is also used to carry away our waste.

Life originated in water. For aquatic organisms the fluid environment is much the same outside and inside the cell and embryo. On land however fertilization and fetal development demand different mechanisms. The eggs of reptiles and birds are like miniature pools of water inside a protective shell which retains the liquid but admits oxygen. The mammalian fetus is suspended in an inner sea of fluid which supports and protects it. Water is important at all stages of development. An adult requires between 2.5 and 3 quarts a day for his or her physiological processes. We get some of this water through our food, the rest we simply drink.

Water and people
Because of their dependence upon water people have always sought to live close to it, even if this were merely a waterhole in the desert. They would usually invent mystical protective rituals for their water source and would react fiercely and even irrationally to any threat to their supply. In the Middle Ages massacres of the Jews were justified on the grounds that they were supposed to have generated the Black Death by poisoning the wells. In the industrial countries, the village pump has been replaced by pipes which bring in domestic water and carry away waste, often over considerable distances.

Practically all our water problems arise simply because the two prime functions of water are not properly separated: dirty water becomes mixed with pure. Diseases transmitted by water spread mainly where there are dense populations combined with poor standards of technology. Today most of the peoples of the world lack a sufficient supply of pure water, even though it is our most fundamental need.

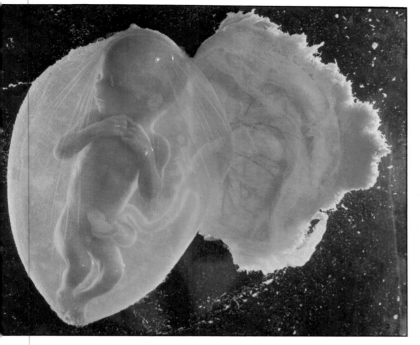

Our daily water
An adult human being needs about 3 quarts of water a day to survive, excluding household water. Women in the rural districts of poor nations spend a large part of their working day hauling water from wells and rivers—water which is often unsanitary.

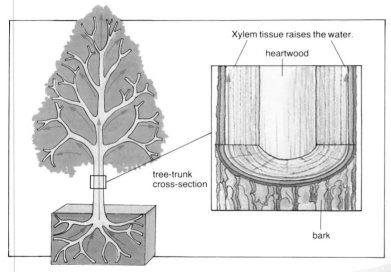

Xylem tissue raises the water.

heartwood

tree-trunk
cross-section

bark

The vital fluid

Vascular plants (exemplified by the tree, above) were the first organisms to adapt themselves completely to life on land. A complex fluid transport system raises the water from the roots of the tree up to its crown which may be 65–98 ft. above the ground. In this manner the cells in the trunk and leaves acquire the moisture they need. This is a one-way system, however: the tree transpires through its foliage as much moisture as it absorbs through its roots.

swimming pool

bathroom

irrigation

kitchen

laundry

garage

water piping

boiler-room

main drain

surface water pipe

People's water consumption

Apart from the body's internal requirements water is essential to people in many other ways. It is used for cleaning and bathing, in cooking and for drinking, in central heating systems and, ultimately, for washing away our waste products. A modern building has separate systems for the different functions. In the illustration hot and cold running water is shown in red and blue respectively, the water in the central heating system in orange and the drainage in green.

People's water consumption has increased enormously during the last hundred years. The UN recommends 16 gallons per 24 hours per person as the minimum limit for an acceptable water standard, but the industrial countries use 66–110 gallons a day per capita. The greater part of this is not domestic but industrial water consumption.

The water cycle

To the best of our knowledge the Earth is the only place in the solar system where water exists in all three of its forms: gaseous (water vapor), liquid, and solid (ice). Closer to the sun or farther away from it, temperatures are either too hot or too cold for water to exist in liquid form. It is now believed that the Earth's waters were not part of the primeval atmosphere, but were expelled from the planet's interior when radioactive decay heated the cold minerals.

Water is essential to all forms of life and access to water is a limiting factor for many types of vegetation. During the course of one summer day a birch tree consumes 44–66 gallons of water and many tropical trees require even more than this. The moisture is returned to the atmosphere through transpiration from the leaf surfaces. At the same time, however, vegetation is important to the hydrological cycle. Vegetation reduces evaporation from the ground and also protects the ground against run-off erosion. Surface roots and dense ground vegetation form innumerable barriers that slow down running water. Dead vegetation absorbs moisture like blotting paper. An unbroken covering of plantlife, especially forest, evens out the flow of surface water and hence the amount of water in the rivers and lakes. It also helps to increase the infiltration of water into the subsoil.

Most of the water on Earth is salt. The salt is believed to derive from the weathering of continental rocks. Fresh water can be equally unfit for plants and animals because of excessive mud

Water, air and soil
In the hydrological cycle water evaporates from the sea and is carried over land in air masses. It then falls as rain or snow and returns to the sea as surface or sub-surface water.

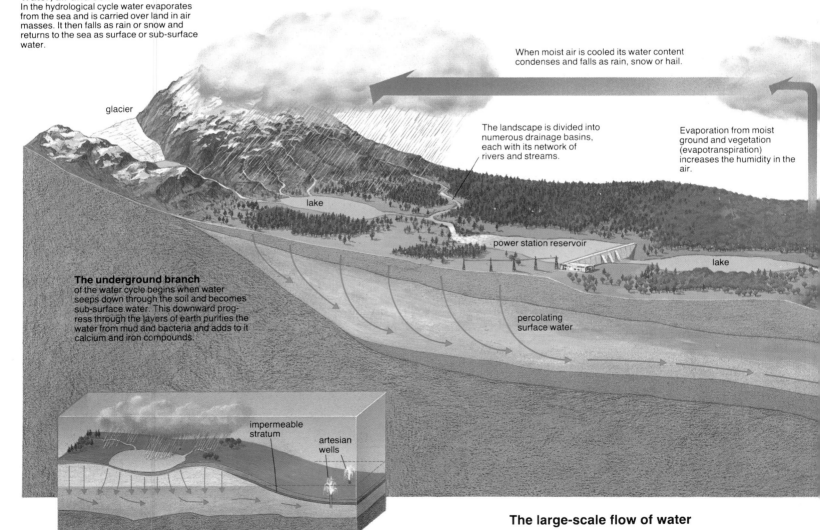

When moist air is cooled its water content condenses and falls as rain, snow or hail.

glacier

The landscape is divided into numerous drainage basins, each with its network of rivers and streams.

Evaporation from moist ground and vegetation (evapotranspiration) increases the humidity in the air.

lake

power station reservoir

lake

The underground branch
of the water cycle begins when water seeps down through the soil and becomes sub-surface water. This downward progress through the layers of earth purifies the water from mud and bacteria and adds to it calcium and iron compounds.

percolating surface water

impermeable stratum

artesian wells

Sub-surface water
(arrows) saturates the ground up to the level of the water table. Impermeable rocks or soils above the water-bearing strata create pressure when the ground surface is

below the natural water table (dotted line). If a hole is drilled through the impermeable strata the water spouts up, forming an artesian well.

The large-scale flow of water
The hydrological cycle unites the atmosphere, the hydrosphere and the Earth's crust. In the atmospheric sector of this cycle the water is present mainly in the form of water vapor. In the terrestrial sector there are two important branches: the surface water's course along streams, rivers and lakes, and the slow progress of sub-surface water through the aquifers, the water-bearing strata. Both of these normally terminate in the sea.

content and other impurities. Consequently, pure water can be a very valuable commodity. For the greater part of the year not a drop of water from the Colorado River reaches the Pacific Ocean. It is all used for irrigation and industrial purposes—distributed according to a water rights system that keeps teams of lawyers constantly employed.

The rivers' alluvial deposits created fertile river plains where the earliest civilizations emerged: in Mesopotamia and Egypt, along the Indus and in China. The Huang He, which in its upper reaches runs through loess country, moves about 10 % of all the alluvial silt in the world and its flow looks more like liquid mud than water. In the lower reaches this silt is deposited in the river bed, thereby raising it. This has many times caused the Huang He to burst its embankments, resulting in devastating floods. The silt which is not deposited but reaches the coast has given the Yellow Sea its name.

Nearly all fresh water is sub-surface water and the greater part of the total fresh water flow from rain pools to the sea probably also takes place underground. The normal cycle of sub-surface water can be reckoned in years or at the most in a few centuries. Beneath the Sahara, however, there is a layer of "fossil" water, which has been there since the rains of the last glaciation and which has been on its way towards the sea for tens of thousands of years. It was not until recently that people first discovered the presence of this vast reservoir and began to utilize it.

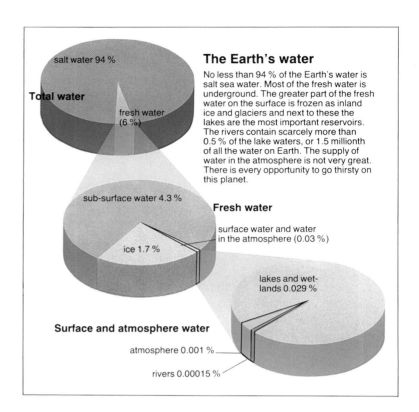

The Earth's water

No less than 94 % of the Earth's water is salt sea water. Most of the fresh water is underground. The greater part of the fresh water on the surface is frozen as inland ice and glaciers and next to these the lakes are the most important reservoirs. The rivers contain scarcely more than 0.5 % of the lake waters, or 1.5 millionth of all the water on Earth. The supply of water in the atmosphere is not very great. There is every opportunity to go thirsty on this planet.

Total water — salt water 94 % — fresh water (6 %)

Fresh water — sub-surface water 4.3 % — ice 1.7 % — surface water and water in the atmosphere (0.03 %)

Surface and atmosphere water — lakes and wetlands 0.029 % — atmosphere 0.001 % — rivers 0.00015 %

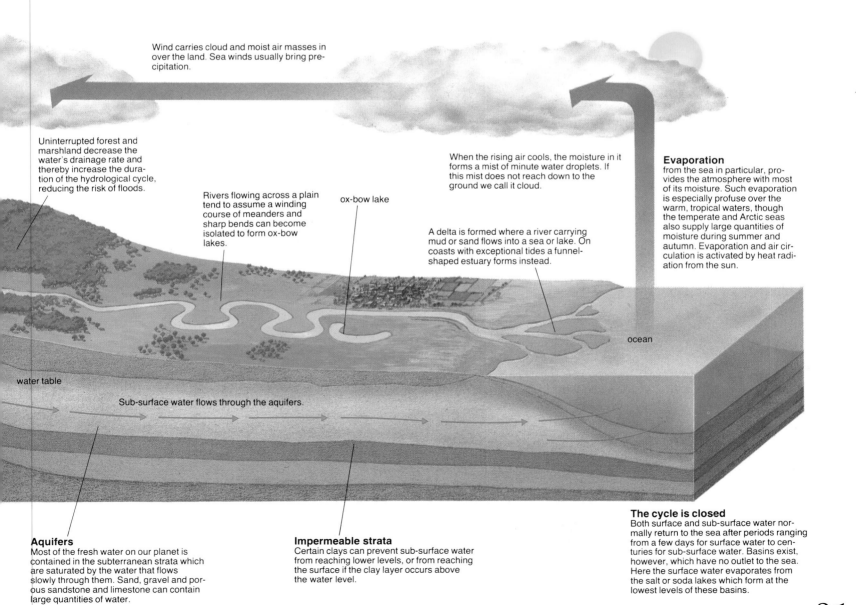

Wind carries cloud and moist air masses in over the land. Sea winds usually bring precipitation.

Uninterrupted forest and marshland decrease the water's drainage rate and thereby increase the duration of the hydrological cycle, reducing the risk of floods.

Rivers flowing across a plain tend to assume a winding course of meanders and sharp bends can become isolated to form ox-bow lakes.

ox-bow lake

When the rising air cools, the moisture in it forms a mist of minute water droplets. If this mist does not reach down to the ground we call it cloud.

A delta is formed where a river carrying mud or sand flows into a sea or lake. On coasts with exceptional tides a funnel-shaped estuary forms instead.

Evaporation
from the sea in particular, provides the atmosphere with most of its moisture. Such evaporation is especially profuse over the warm, tropical waters, though the temperate and Arctic seas also supply large quantities of moisture during summer and autumn. Evaporation and air circulation is activated by heat radiation from the sun.

ocean

water table

Sub-surface water flows through the aquifers.

The cycle is closed
Both surface and sub-surface water normally return to the sea after periods ranging from a few days for surface water to centuries for sub-surface water. Basins exist, however, which have no outlet to the sea. Here the surface water evaporates from the salt or soda lakes which form at the lowest levels of these basins.

Aquifers
Most of the fresh water on our planet is contained in the subterranean strata which are saturated by the water that flows slowly through them. Sand, gravel and porous sandstone and limestone can contain large quantities of water.

Impermeable strata
Certain clays can prevent sub-surface water from reaching lower levels, or from reaching the surface if the clay layer occurs above the water level.

31

The realm of ice

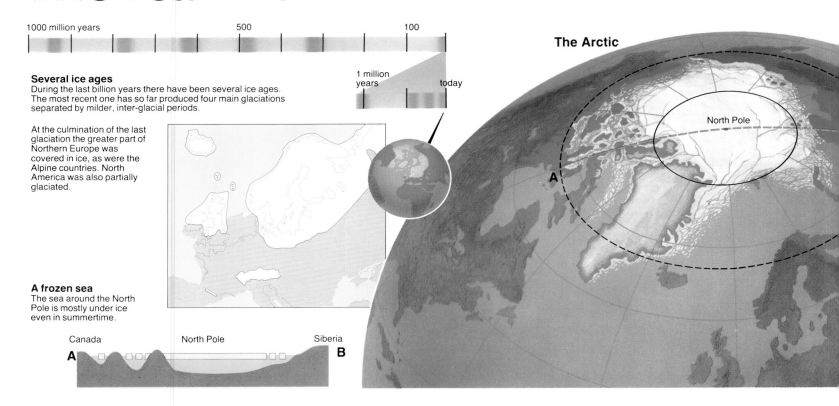

1000 million years · 500 · 100

1 million years · today

The Arctic

North Pole

A

Several ice ages
During the last billion years there have been several ice ages. The most recent one has so far produced four main glaciations separated by milder, inter-glacial periods.

At the culmination of the last glaciation the greater part of Northern Europe was covered in ice, as were the Alpine countries. North America was also partially glaciated.

A frozen sea
The sea around the North Pole is mostly under ice even in summertime.

Canada · North Pole · Siberia

A · B

The Earth has two extensive ice covers: the arctic region around the North Pole and the antarctic region of the South Pole. At these extreme latitudes the sun never climbs very high in the heavens and it thus provides little heat. The ice regions also have their outposts all the way down to the equator; wherever there is enough precipitation and sufficient elevation above sea level to keep temperatures below freezing glaciers can form.

The Earth has not always had these ice covers however. When snow falls on to open sea the flakes immediately melt. On a planet where over 70 % of the surface is covered in water, the poles are within sea areas most of the time and thus no ice forms around them. Polar ice can form in two conditions only: either the pole must be on a continent or else in a closed sea basin, so that the exchange of water with warm seas is counteracted and pack ice can form. Our present geological epoch is unusual in that both these requirements are fulfilled, at the South Pole and the North Pole respectively. The result is an ice age in both hemispheres, though we have the good fortune to exist in one of

its milder inter-glacial periods. Most of the Earth's earlier ice ages have apparently affected only one hemisphere. The current ice age will continue until the continental drift opens up the Arctic Ocean to warm currents from the south and pushes the antarctic continent away from the South Pole.

Between them the very warm tropics and the cold polar tracts create a gigantic heat engine where the equatorial belts are the boiler and the polar regions serve as the cooling system. This engine drives the global air circulation which transports enormous quantities of air around the world. In other words the climate and weather is determined to a large extent by the polar regions. Oceanic currents also transport ice from the polar regions and thereby influence local climate.

People reached the Arctic as long ago as the close of the last ice age, but not until this century have they succeeded in penetrating the Antarctic. In both places in our time the pursuit of natural resources has become a grave threat to the delicately balanced polar environments.

A · B

Antarctica

A frozen continent
The South Pole continent is a vast land mass beneath an icecap up to 2.5 mi. thick and surrounded by pack ice and shelf ice.

Extreme cold, gales, winter darkness and treacherous fissures in the ice make traveling here both physically demanding and hazardous. It is somewhat easier than it was, however, thanks to modern tracked vehicles and airborne supplies.

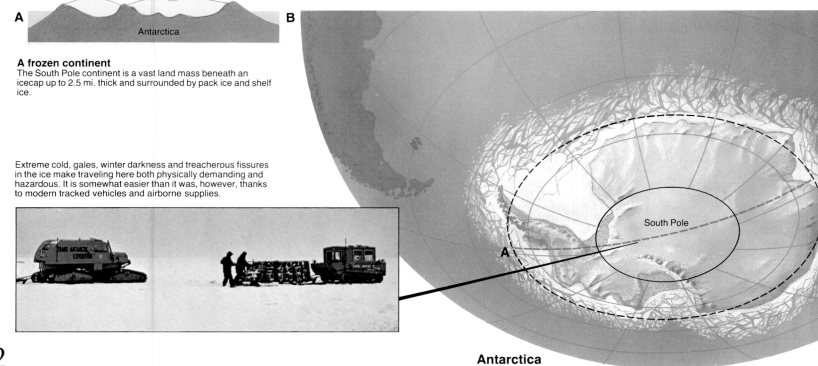

South Pole

A

Antarctica

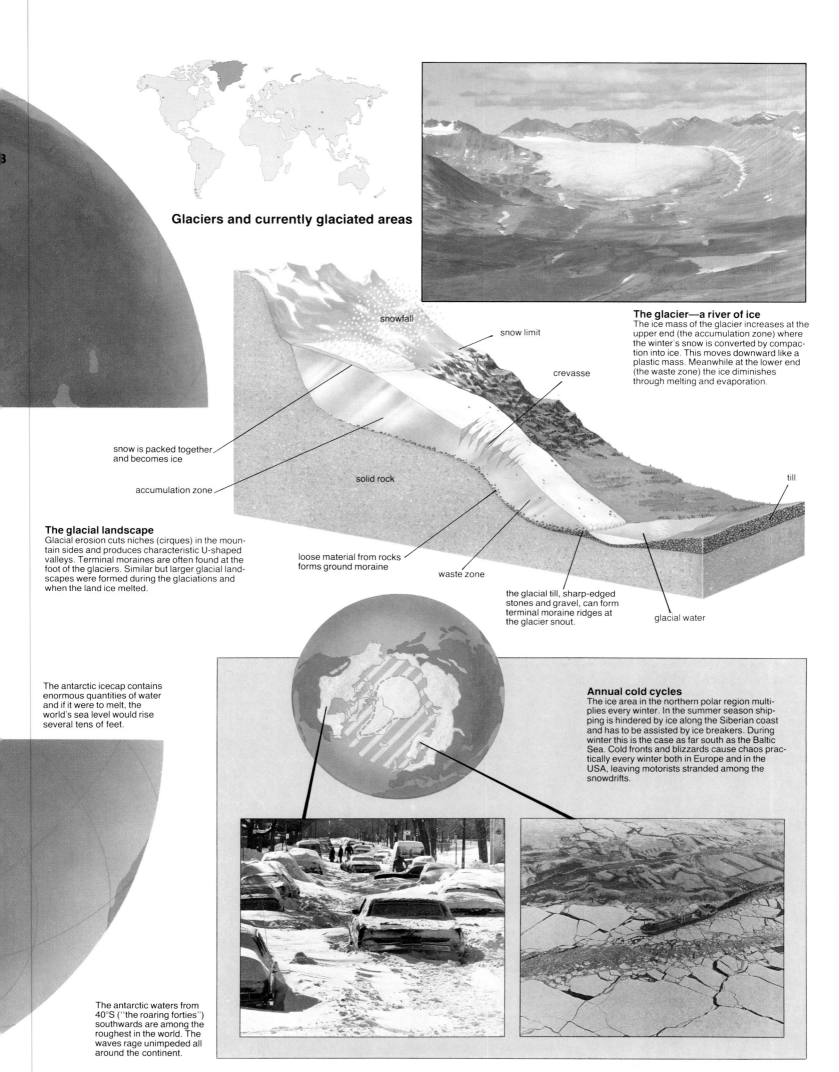

Glaciers and currently glaciated areas

snowfall

snow limit

crevasse

The glacier—a river of ice
The ice mass of the glacier increases at the upper end (the accumulation zone) where the winter's snow is converted by compaction into ice. This moves downward like a plastic mass. Meanwhile at the lower end (the waste zone) the ice diminishes through melting and evaporation.

snow is packed together and becomes ice

solid rock

till

accumulation zone

The glacial landscape
Glacial erosion cuts niches (cirques) in the mountain sides and produces characteristic U-shaped valleys. Terminal moraines are often found at the foot of the glaciers. Similar but larger glacial landscapes were formed during the glaciations and when the land ice melted.

loose material from rocks forms ground moraine

waste zone

the glacial till, sharp-edged stones and gravel, can form terminal moraine ridges at the glacier snout.

glacial water

The antarctic icecap contains enormous quantities of water and if it were to melt, the world's sea level would rise several tens of feet.

Annual cold cycles
The ice area in the northern polar region multiplies every winter. In the summer season shipping is hindered by ice along the Siberian coast and has to be assisted by ice breakers. During winter this is the case as far south as the Baltic Sea. Cold fronts and blizzards cause chaos practically every winter both in Europe and in the USA, leaving motorists stranded among the snowdrifts.

The antarctic waters from 40°S ("the roaring forties") southwards are among the roughest in the world. The waves rage unimpeded all around the continent.

The oceans

Viewed from space the Earth is an oceanic planet which might have more aptly been named Water, since 71 % of its area is covered by seas. The deep seas comprise about 55 % of the Earth's surface.

The beds of the deep seas and their unique geology were far beyond our reach until well into the present century. After World War II when studies were finally begun, the findings created a scientific revolution. The oceanic crust is not, as was formerly believed, one of Earth's oldest geological formations, instead it is among the most recent. Nowhere is it more than 200 million years old, while the earliest known continental rocks are almost four *billion* years old. The reason why the oceanic crust is not particularly ancient is because it is constantly being melted down and renewed.

The scientific study of the Earth's oceans is known as oceanography. As early as the 17th century mariners and geographers attempted to chart the oceanic currents, a task made more difficult due to their lack of instruments for precise navigation. Oceanic research in the modern sense of the term did not emerge until the 19th century. Since the seabed was still inaccessible this research was then directed mainly at marine bio-

logy, although important geophysical and geological discoveries were also made. One of the first of these was Darwin's theory on the origin of atolls: islands sink beneath the sea but the coral polyps, which can only live near the surface, tend constantly to build their reefs upwards towards the surface. It was Darwin's observations on the origins of new species on isolated oceanic islands which provided him with the material for his theory on evolution through natural selection. Thus our studies of the sea have given rise to not one but two scientific revolutions: biological and geophysical.

We now have a good knowledge of the basic features of ocean bed topography and are learning more about the sedimentation and rock types. Oceanic research is still by no means a complete science. New technology, especially in space, constantly provides us with fresh knowledge. From satellites it is now possible not only to chart the seabeds by gravimetry (the measurement of gravitational forces exerted by the bedrock and sediments on the ocean floor) but we can also measure the phytoplankton content of the water. There is little doubt that many more surprises await us in the depths of the oceans.

Ocean topography

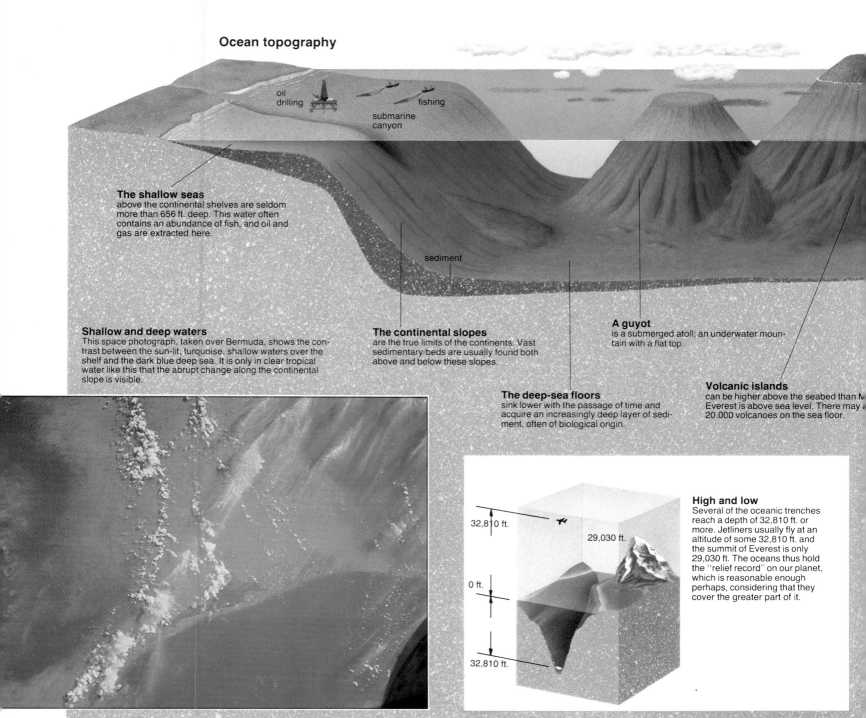

oil drilling

fishing

submarine canyon

sediment

The shallow seas
above the continental shelves are seldom more than 656 ft. deep. This water often contains an abundance of fish, and oil and gas are extracted here.

Shallow and deep waters
This space photograph, taken over Bermuda, shows the contrast between the sun-lit, turquoise, shallow waters over the shelf and the dark blue deep sea. It is only in clear tropical water like this that the abrupt change along the continental slope is visible.

The continental slopes
are the true limits of the continents. Vast sedimentary beds are usually found both above and below these slopes.

A guyot
is a submerged atoll; an underwater mountain with a flat top.

The deep-sea floors
sink lower with the passage of time and acquire an increasingly deep layer of sediment, often of biological origin.

Volcanic islands
can be higher above the seabed than M Everest is above sea level. There may 20.000 volcanoes on the sea floor.

32,810 ft.

29,030 ft.

0 ft.

32,810 ft.

High and low
Several of the oceanic trenches reach a depth of 32,810 ft. or more. Jetliners usually fly at an altitude of some 32,810 ft. and the summit of Everest is only 29,030 ft. The oceans thus hold the "relief record" on our planet, which is reasonable enough perhaps, considering that they cover the greater part of it.

The four oceans

The oceans and their percentage shares of the planet's total sea area.

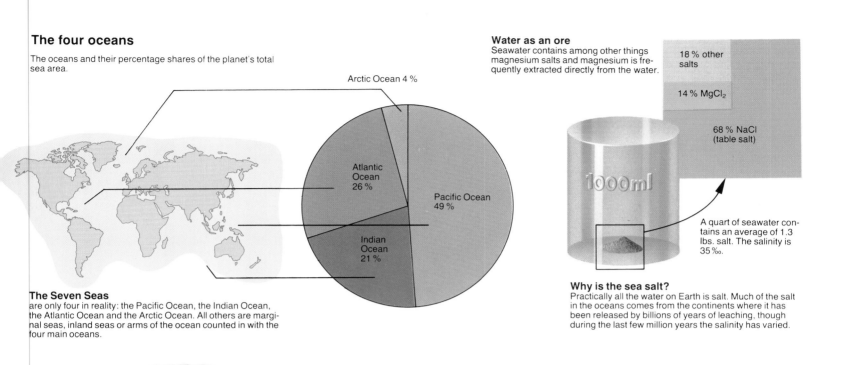

Arctic Ocean 4 %

Atlantic Ocean 26 %

Pacific Ocean 49 %

Indian Ocean 21 %

The Seven Seas

are only four in reality: the Pacific Ocean, the Indian Ocean, the Atlantic Ocean and the Arctic Ocean. All others are marginal seas, inland seas or arms of the ocean counted in with the four main oceans.

Water as an ore

Seawater contains among other things magnesium salts and magnesium is frequently extracted directly from the water.

18 % other salts

14 % $MgCl_2$

68 % NaCl (table salt)

1000ml

A quart of seawater contains an average of 1.3 lbs. salt. The salinity is 35 ‰.

Why is the sea salt?

Practically all the water on Earth is salt. Much of the salt in the oceans comes from the continents where it has been released by billions of years of leaching, though during the last few million years the salinity has varied.

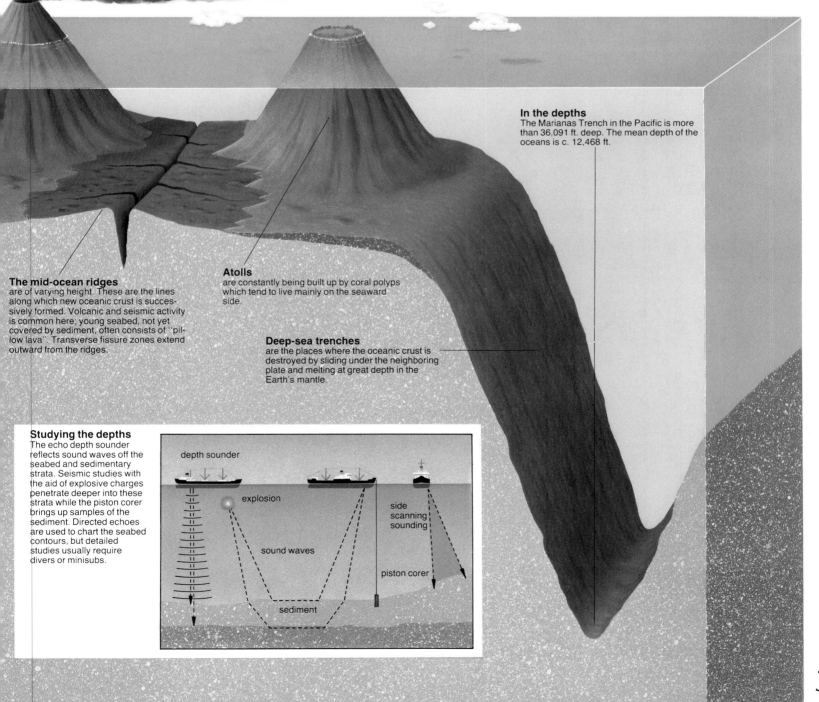

In the depths

The Marianas Trench in the Pacific is more than 36,091 ft. deep. The mean depth of the oceans is c. 12,468 ft.

The mid-ocean ridges

are of varying height. These are the lines along which new oceanic crust is successively formed. Volcanic and seismic activity is common here; young seabed, not yet covered by sediment, often consists of "pillow lava". Transverse fissure zones extend outward from the ridges.

Atolls

are constantly being built up by coral polyps which tend to live mainly on the seaward side.

Deep-sea trenches

are the places where the oceanic crust is destroyed by sliding under the neighboring plate and melting at great depth in the Earth's mantle.

Studying the depths

The echo depth sounder reflects sound waves off the seabed and sedimentary strata. Seismic studies with the aid of explosive charges penetrate deeper into these strata while the piston corer brings up samples of the sediment. Directed echoes are used to chart the seabed contours, but detailed studies usually require divers or minisubs.

depth sounder

explosion

sound waves

side scanning sounding

piston corer

sediment

The powerful sea

Standing on a rocky coast during a gale makes one dramatically aware of the enormous energy contained in the sea. The movements of the sea, the waves and currents, represent solar energy converted mainly by winds in the atmosphere.

Atmosphere and sea
The interplay between air and water is complex. One example is the apparently simple oceanic current, driven by the wind. On the surface there is a flow of water along the direction of the wind, as would be expected. With increasing depth, however, this flow is deflected by the rotation of the Earth—so much so that at a depth of about 328 ft. it is running in the opposite direction to the wind. The net or mean current runs at right-angles to the wind direction—to the right in the northern hemisphere and to the left in the southern hemisphere. Normal surface currents move at an average of a few miles every 24 hours.

There is also a chemical exchange, between the atmosphere and the sea, principally of carbon dioxide and oxygen, thereby stabilizing the content of these gases in both air and sea alike. This gas exchange takes place mainly through diffusion, i.e. the direct exchange of atoms. The wind also whips up aerosols consisting of almost invisible droplets of water which contain dissolved salts. When the water has evaporated the salt crystals are carried by the wind and then serve as condensation nuclei around which form larger water drops, producing mist, cloud and rain.

The wind creates small ripples on the water surface and these quickly grow into waves. The waves catch much of the wind, thereby absorbing even more of the wind's energy. This energy does not penetrate very far, however, diminishing to a mere 4–5% at a depth corresponding to one third the distance between the wave crests. As the wave rolls forward a small part of this energy is lost through friction, though the ocean swell can carry energy across great distances. Finally the energy is lost altogether when the waves break on the shore—the shore being eroded and re-formed by this process.

Oceanic currents
Currents can be activated by density and temperature variations in different masses of water, but the big surface current systems of the oceans are driven by the winds. The trade winds determine the patterns of the equatorial currents and counter-currents. The Gulf Stream is created by water which is carried by the Northern Equatorial Current towards the Antilles and on

Wind and waves
Seventy-one percent of the surface of our planet is covered by water and over this area a complex physical interplay takes place between atmosphere and hydrosphere. The waves are an easily observed and dramatic example of this.

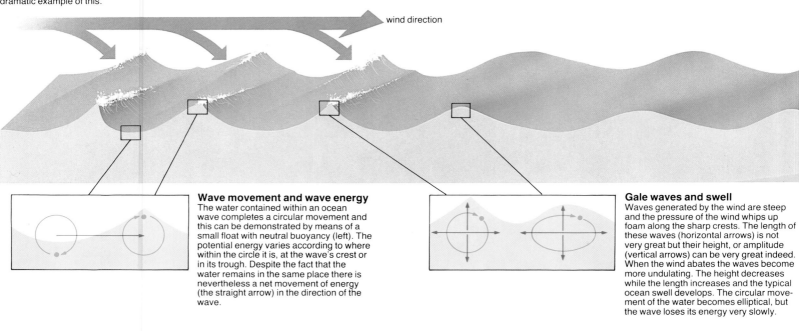

Wave movement and wave energy
The water contained within an ocean wave completes a circular movement and this can be demonstrated by means of a small float with neutral buoyancy (left). The potential energy varies according to where within the circle it is, at the wave's crest or in its trough. Despite the fact that the water remains in the same place there is nevertheless a net movement of energy (the straight arrow) in the direction of the wave.

Gale waves and swell
Waves generated by the wind are steep and the pressure of the wind whips up foam along the sharp crests. The length of these waves (horizontal arrows) is not very great but their height, or amplitude (vertical arrows) can be very great indeed. When the wind abates the waves become more undulating. The height decreases while the length increases and the typical ocean swell develops. The circular movement of the water becomes elliptical, but the wave loses its energy very slowly.

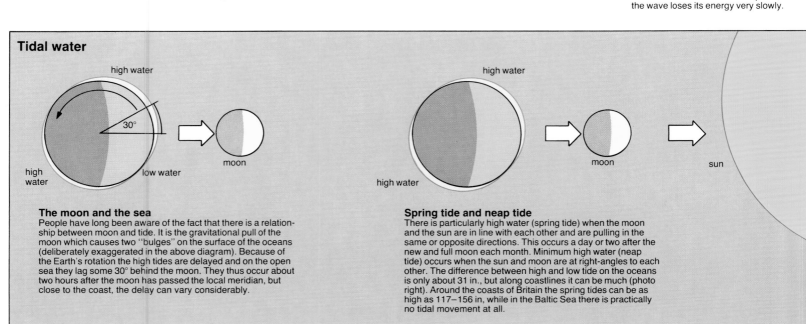

Tidal water

The moon and the sea
People have long been aware of the fact that there is a relationship between moon and tide. It is the gravitational pull of the moon which causes two "bulges" on the surface of the oceans (deliberately exaggerated in the above diagram). Because of the Earth's rotation the high tides are delayed and on the open sea they lag some 30° behind the moon. They thus occur about two hours after the moon has passed the local meridian, but close to the coast, the delay can vary considerably.

Spring tide and neap tide
There is particularly high water (spring tide) when the moon and the sun are in line with each other and are pulling in the same or opposite directions. This occurs a day or two after the new and full moon each month. Minimum high water (neap tide) occurs when the sun and moon are at right-angles to each other. The difference between high and low tide on the oceans is only about 31 in., but along coastlines it can be much (photo right). Around the coasts of Britain the spring tides can be as high as 117–156 in, while in the Baltic Sea there is practically no tidal movement at all.

into the Caribbean Sea and which then "spills over" in a north-easterly direction. A steady westerly drift flows around the Antarctic where there are no continents to hinder it.

Where winds and currents drive the surface water out from the coast this is replaced by other water rising from deeper levels. The latter is often rich in nutrients, yielding an abundance of fish. Currents of nutritious water from the polar seas create other productive fisheries, to the east of Japan for example.

Dangerous aspects

The energy of sea can sometimes become a hazard even on land. A combination of spring tides and strong on-shore winds can cause devastating floods, as have occurred along the coast of Holland. Seabed earthquakes or volcanic explosions can produce sea waves, called tsunamis. Out at sea these may be no more than half a foot or so high and perhaps 12.5 mi. from one crest to the next. But they can travel at several hundred mi/h, striking land with tremendous force. The wave which was created when the island of Krakatau between Java and Sumatra exploded in 1883 rose to a height of 115 ft. when it hit the coast of Java. Small ships were thrown far up onto the land and 35,000 people are believed to have perished.

Energy from the sea

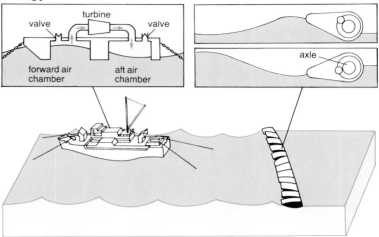

Wave energy

One way of deriving energy from waves is to anchor barges in the sea, each barge having two air chambers, separated by half a wavelength. When waves pass under the barges air is pumped in through the intake wave in the force chamber, from there through the turbine to the aft chamber and then out again.

In a sea inlet duckbill-shaped floats mounted on flexible axles can be used. The movements of the floats are transmitted via gears to the axles which in their turn drive electric generators set up ashore.

Solar energy from the sea

Ocean Thermal Energy Conversion (OTEC) is a technique regarded as being particularly applicable in tropical waters. Here the sun-warmed surface water is used to gasify a suitable agent, for example freon or ammonia, whereupon the gas is harnessed to drive a turbine generator. The agent is subsequently condensed by means of deeper, cold water brought up by a syphon system. The agent, now in liquid form, is passed on again to the heat exchanger and the circuit is complete. Plans exist to build floating power stations and bring the electricity ashore through flexible cables.

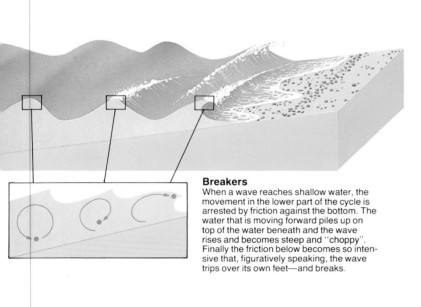

Breakers

When a wave reaches shallow water, the movement in the lower part of the cycle is arrested by friction against the bottom. The water that is moving forward piles up on top of the water beneath and the wave rises and becomes steep and "choppy". Finally the friction below becomes so intensive that, figuratively speaking, the wave trips over its own feet—and breaks.

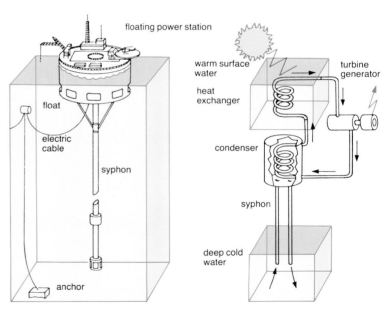

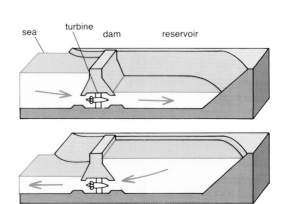

Tidal energy

In places where tides run high a narrow bay can be transformed into a power station reservoir by building a dam across the entrance, so that both inflowing and outflowing water can be used to drive reversible propeller turbines. There are not many places, however, with the right combination of a deep, narrow bay and sufficient ebb and flow.

Aquatic life

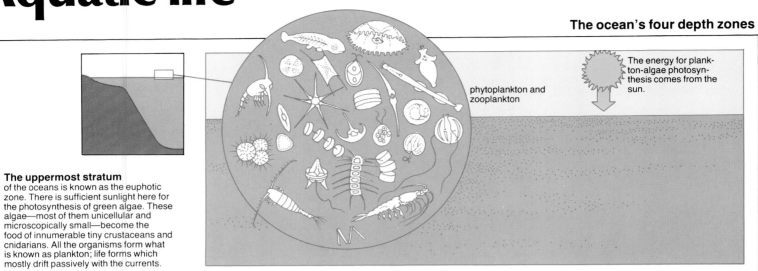

phytoplankton and zooplankton

The energy for plankton-algae photosynthesis comes from the sun.

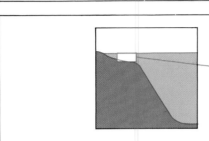

The uppermost stratum
of the oceans is known as the euphotic zone. There is sufficient sunlight here for the photosynthesis of green algae. These algae—most of them unicellular and microscopically small—become the food of innumerable tiny crustaceans and cnidarians. All the organisms form what is known as plankton; life forms which mostly drift passively with the currents.

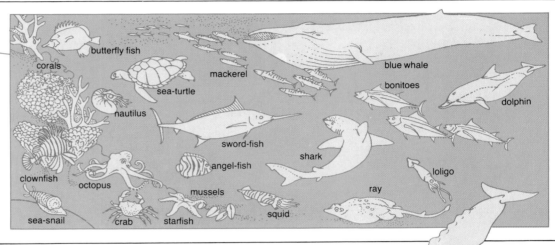

butterfly fish, corals, mackerel, blue whale, sea-turtle, bonitoes, nautilus, dolphin, sword-fish, shark, clownfish, angel-fish, loligo, octopus, mussels, ray, squid, sea-snail, crab, starfish

The coastal zones
and productive areas of the open seas contain fish which feed on plankton or prey upon each other. These accomplished swimmers are known collectively as nekton. Coral reefs are built of the calcareous shells of billions of cnidarians. Evertebrates such as mussels, starfish, crabs and squids are common on the seabed in shallow waters.

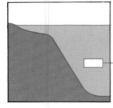

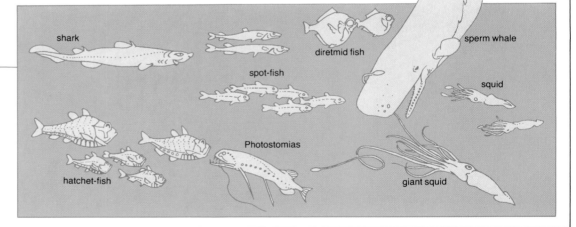

shark, diretmid fish, sperm whale, spot-fish, squid, Photostomias, hatchet-fish, giant squid

The twilight zone
and its organisms derive their nutrition from upper levels, either in the form of detritus (the steady rain of dead biomass) or through predation. The sperm whale dives to immense depths in search of its most important food, the giant squid Architeuthis. We still know very little about the habits of the fish in this zone. There are no plants here; bacteria play a vital role as decomposers.

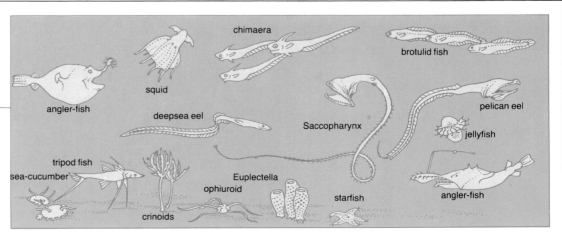

chimaera, squid, brotulid fish, angler-fish, deepsea eel, pelican eel, Saccopharynx, jellyfish, tripod fish, sea-cucumber, ophiuroid, Euplectella, starfish, angler-fish, crinoids

The deepest waters
make up the abyssal zone. In the eternal darkness practically all organisms live either on detritus or on other detritus-eaters. Many of the predators have luminous organs and grotesquely over-developed jaws for trapping their prey. Most of these deepsea fish are only a few inches in length.

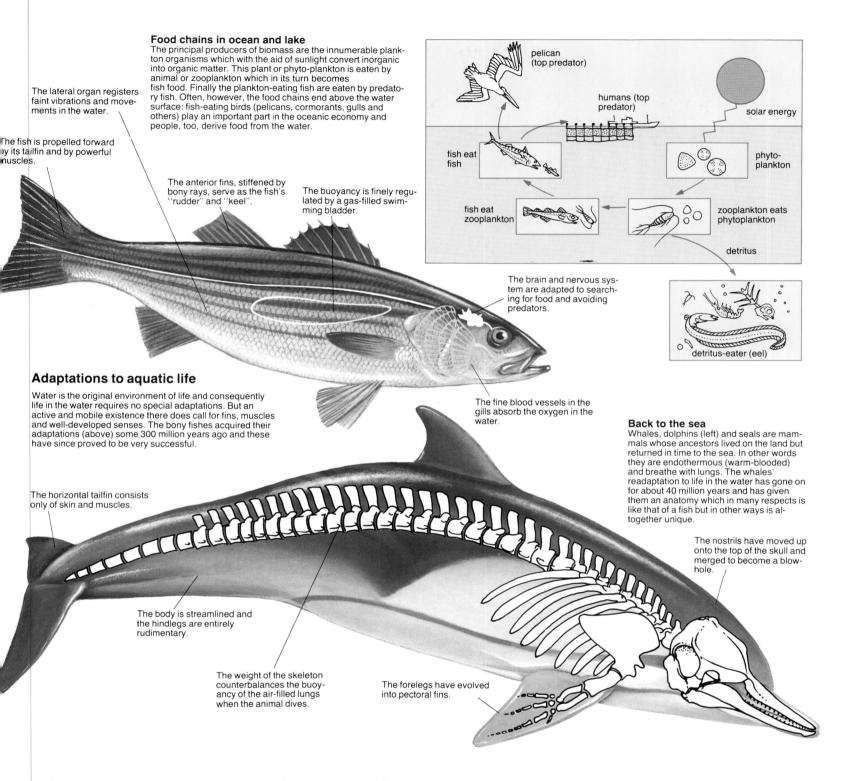

Food chains in ocean and lake

The principal producers of biomass are the innumerable plankton organisms which with the aid of sunlight convert inorganic into organic matter. This plant or phyto-plankton is eaten by animal or zooplankton which in its turn becomes fish food. Finally the plankton-eating fish are eaten by predatory fish. Often, however, the food chains end above the water surface: fish-eating birds (pelicans, cormorants, gulls and others) play an important part in the oceanic economy and people, too, derive food from the water.

The lateral organ registers faint vibrations and movements in the water.

The fish is propelled forward by its tailfin and by powerful muscles.

The anterior fins, stiffened by bony rays, serve as the fish's "rudder" and "keel".

The buoyancy is finely regulated by a gas-filled swimming bladder.

The brain and nervous system are adapted to searching for food and avoiding predators.

The fine blood vessels in the gills absorb the oxygen in the water.

pelican (top predator)

humans (top predator)

solar energy

fish eat fish

phyto-plankton

fish eat zooplankton

zooplankton eats phytoplankton

detritus

detritus-eater (eel)

Adaptations to aquatic life

Water is the original environment of life and consequently life in the water requires no special adaptations. But an active and mobile existence there does call for fins, muscles and well-developed senses. The bony fishes acquired their adaptations (above) some 300 million years ago and these have since proved to be very successful.

The horizontal tailfin consists only of skin and muscles.

The body is streamlined and the hindlegs are entirely rudimentary.

The weight of the skeleton counterbalances the buoyancy of the air-filled lungs when the animal dives.

The forelegs have evolved into pectoral fins.

Back to the sea

Whales, dolphins (left) and seals are mammals whose ancestors lived on the land but returned in time to the sea. In other words they are endothermous (warm-blooded) and breathe with lungs. The whales' readaptation to life in the water has gone on for about 40 million years and has given them an anatomy which in many respects is like that of a fish but in other ways is altogether unique.

The nostrils have moved up onto the top of the skull and merged to become a blow-hole.

Fluid is the natural environment of the living cell. Ingenious molecular mechanisms pump vital substances from the surrounding fluid in through the cell membrane and pump the waste out in the opposite direction. Thus unicellular organisms do not need any particular adaptation to life in the water. An organism which moves requires a means of locomotion—in the case of fish, muscles and fins. Muscles in their turn have to be supplied with large quantities of oxygen, hence the gills. Finally, senses and a nervous system are essential to ensure that movement is both purposeful and effective.

The demands made by water of its inhabitants are the same in principle for practically all of them. Animals which readapt to life in the water have therefore many anatomical features in common with fishes. This applies to whales and seals, and, to the same extent, to the Mesozoic ichthyosaurs of 200 million years ago. All these share or shared the same handicap in that their ancestors' fundamental adaptation to life on land, the breathing of air, has been impossible to reverse.

The principal agents of organic production of ocean and lake are the green plankton plants. In order to grow, they need not only sunlight but also oxygen, carbon dioxide and salts. It is often the availability of phosphates which determines how much biomass, i.e. living matter, can exist in a cubic foot of water. Too little phosphate means sterile water, while too much can lead to an algal bloom which consumes the oxygen in the water. The phosphates then move on through the food chain from phytoplankton via zooplankton and predators to top predators such as pelicans and humans. At the same time phosphates, in the form of organic waste, descend constantly into the depths.

In the open seas this detritus sinks beyond the reach of the organic producers and is incorporated with sediment and sedimentary rocks. The shallow seas, on the other hand, are supplied with nutrients (nitrates and phosphates) from two sources: from water draining off the land and from the decomposition of organic matter in the sea. The organic production is high because almost all available nutrients are incorporated in biomass. The shallow seas are therefore very important fishing areas and one shoal can run into hundreds of thousands.

Food from the deep

People have not always fished. It was not until the close of the Ice Age that ecological changes and the demands of an increasing population compelled the former big game hunters to turn to small game and ultimately to seafood in the form of mussels and oysters. This development can be studied archaeologically at certain sites through statistical analysis of household refuse. Fishing in the general sense of the term emerged during the Mesolithic period (c. 8,000 years ago) when the basic implements were devised: hook, spear, net and creel.

Fishing remained a largely local trade until first the steam engine and then the diesel engine brought about its industrialization during the last hundred years. Canning and refrigeration have further increased the scope of fishing. Fishing fleets are now accompanied by factory ships and mechanical equipment makes the hard work somewhat easier.

During the 1950's and '60's it was generally thought that food from the seas would be sufficient to provide for a limitless world population. But overfishing resulted in greatly diminished catches at the beginning of the '70's. Today the total annual haul, including fish farming and algae, is around 68 million tons. Nearly 40% consists of different herring and cod species. Aquaculture (mussel and oyster beds, fish breeding in coastal and inland waters, etc.) contributes about nine per cent, a proportion which is increasing rapidly. In south-east Asia in particular the breeding of carp in pools is an important source of protein.

The most important fishing grounds are the shallow waters above the continental shelves, and those areas where water rising from the deep, or currents from the polar regions provide nutritive salts, primarily phosphates. Here biological productivity is at its greatest and the food chains are usually shorter than in the more complex ecological systems of the open oceanic waters. However these highly productive areas are more vulnerable to interference. At the beginning of the 1970's the Peruvian anchovy catches – then the world's largest fishing industry – suddenly failed when a cold, very nutritious oceanic current changed course. When this nutrition disappeared the anchovies did likewise, and the entire industry collapsed.

Traditional fishing is biologically ineffective. One ton of plankton can never become more than 22–44 lbs. of mackerel since mackerel are high up in the food chain, top predators like ourselves. It is a tempting idea to resort to the lowest possible trophic level and utilize the sea's primary producers, algae, and the secondary, pelagic crustaceans such as krill. This might become possible in the near future. Meanwhile one thing remains quite clear: if we are to use the Earth's waters for the production of food then we must cease polluting them. The oceans are no longer inexhaustible.

Inland water fishing

This is an important source of protein in many parts of the world. The equipment used here is mainly simple and light.

Sea fishing

Sea fishing is very diversified. There is a big difference between coastal and deep-sea fishing and the methods vary greatly, according to the fish species. Deep-sea fishing in particular has developed into a major industry, supported by floating factories, canneries ashore and extensive distribution networks.

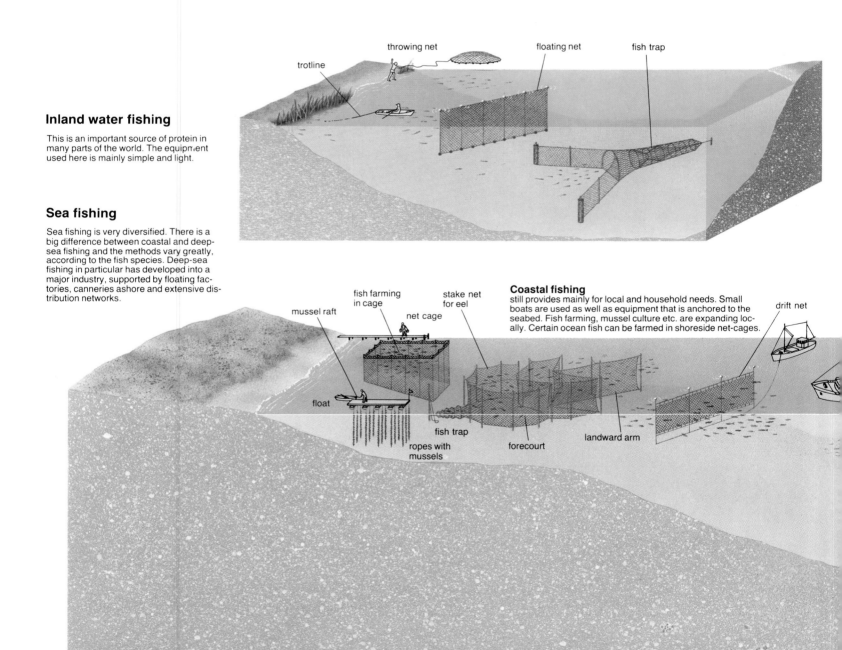

trotline · throwing net · floating net · fish trap

mussel raft · fish farming in cage · net cage · stake net for eel · float · ropes with mussels · fish trap · forecourt · landward arm · drift net

Coastal fishing
still provides mainly for local and household needs. Small boats are used as well as equipment that is anchored to the seabed. Fish farming, mussel culture etc. are expanding locally. Certain ocean fish can be farmed in shoreside net-cages.

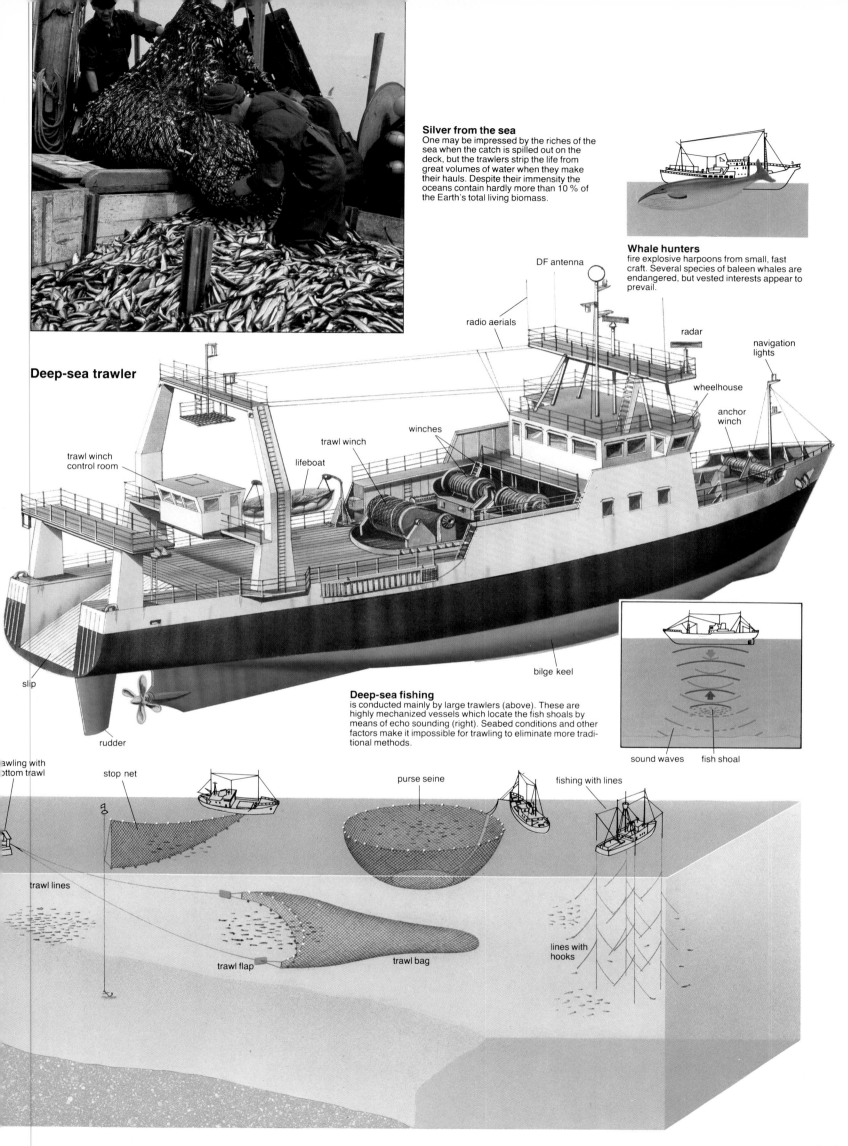

Silver from the sea
One may be impressed by the riches of the sea when the catch is spilled out on the deck, but the trawlers strip the life from great volumes of water when they make their hauls. Despite their immensity the oceans contain hardly more than 10 % of the Earth's total living biomass.

Whale hunters
fire explosive harpoons from small, fast craft. Several species of baleen whales are endangered, but vested interests appear to prevail.

Deep-sea trawler

DF antenna

radio aerials

radar

navigation lights

wheelhouse

anchor winch

winches

trawl winch

trawl winch control room

lifeboat

slip

rudder

bilge keel

Deep-sea fishing
is conducted mainly by large trawlers (above). These are highly mechanized vessels which locate the fish shoals by means of echo sounding (right). Seabed conditions and other factors make it impossible for trawling to eliminate more traditional methods.

sound waves   fish shoal

awling with ottom trawl

stop net

purse seine

fishing with lines

trawl lines

trawl flap

trawl bag

lines with hooks

The conquest of the seas

The Vikings
reached the Caspian Sea in the east and "Vinland" (presumably Newfoundland) in the west. In the 10th century they settled in Iceland and Greenland, although their voyages along the rivers of Russia were economically and historically more significant.

Early explorers
There were bold mariners on the seas long before the era of the great voyages of discovery. Chinese, Arabs, Polynesians and Vikings voyaged far beyond their own coastlines, but their fields of activity (map) were limited nevertheless. It was not until the 16th century that Europeans began voyaging all over the world.

The Chinese
were probably the best shipbuilders of the Middle Ages. Their junks carried several masts, they were fitted with a sternpost rudder and had watertight bulkheads. In the early 15th century Chinese explorers found their way as far west as India and East Africa.

The Polynesians
sailed vast distances during their voyages of colonization in the Pacific about 2,000 years ago. Their craft were outrigger canoes with a triangular sail. They used simple charts made of sticks and shells.

The Arabs
were accomplished sailors. In their lateen-rigged ships and aided by the steady monsoon winds they traded by sea during the Middle Ages from East Africa ("Azania") in the west to the Indonesian spice islands in the east.

Great seafarers
In 1492 Columbus sailed westward in search of a new sea route from Europe to India. Instead he discovered a new continent: America. The voyages of Columbus were followed by intensive colonization by the Spanish and Portuguese.

In 1496 Vasco da Gama sailed the eastward route to India, around Africa, using an Arab pilot on the last leg of the voyage. This was the culmination of eighty years of Portuguese maritime explorations.

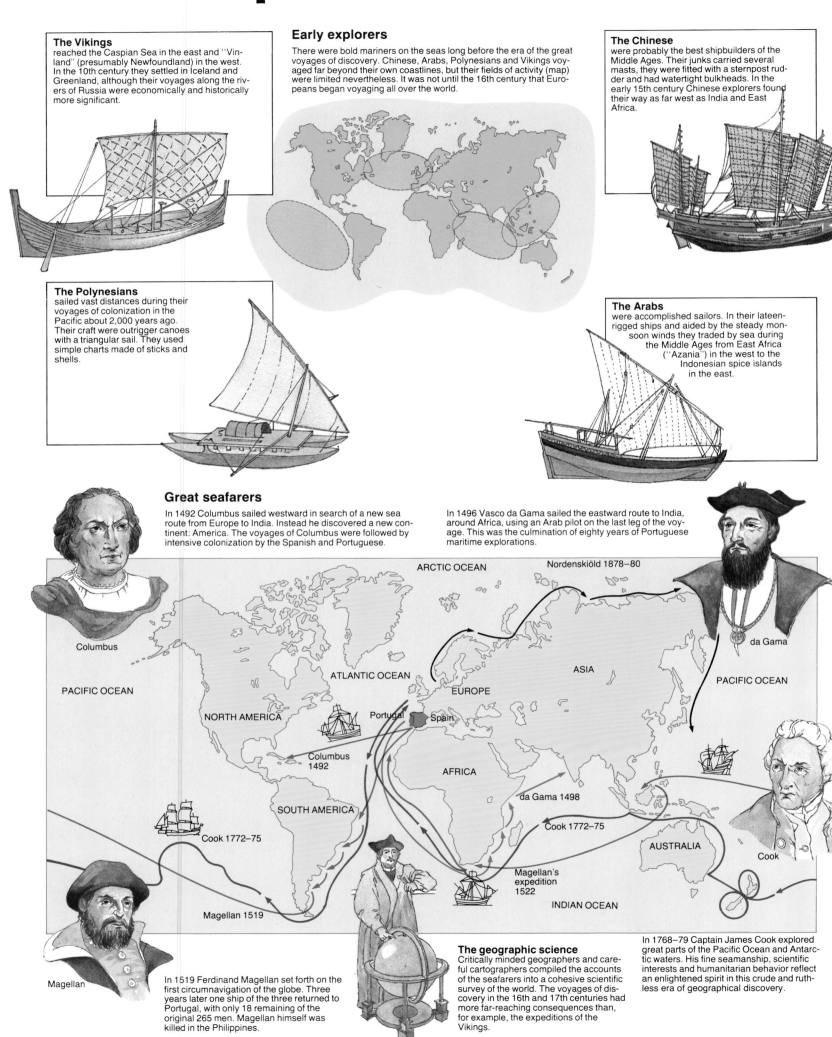

ARCTIC OCEAN
Nordenskiöld 1878–80
Columbus
PACIFIC OCEAN
ATLANTIC OCEAN
NORTH AMERICA
Portugal
Spain
EUROPE
ASIA
da Gama
PACIFIC OCEAN
Columbus 1492
AFRICA
da Gama 1498
Cook 1772–75
SOUTH AMERICA
Cook 1772–75
AUSTRALIA
Cook
Magellan's expedition 1522
INDIAN OCEAN
Magellan 1519
Magellan

The geographic science
Critically minded geographers and careful cartographers compiled the accounts of the seafarers into a cohesive scientific survey of the world. The voyages of discovery in the 16th and 17th centuries had more far-reaching consequences than, for example, the expeditions of the Vikings.

In 1519 Ferdinand Magellan set forth on the first circumnavigation of the globe. Three years later one ship of the three returned to Portugal, with only 18 remaining of the original 265 men. Magellan himself was killed in the Philippines.

In 1768–79 Captain James Cook explored great parts of the Pacific Ocean and Antarctic waters. His fine seamanship, scientific interests and humanitarian behavior reflect an enlightened spirit in this crude and ruthless era of geographical discovery.

With increasing competence in shipbuilding came the development of the high seas as important travel routes. Busy shipping traffic developed early in the Mediterranean and the Baltic, for example, where the waters were fairly protected and landfall distances relatively short. In the Mediterranean, Cretans, Phoenicians, Greeks, Romans, Arabs and Italians succeeded each other as the leading seafarers—until world trade moved out to the great oceans and the Mediterranean declined into an economic backwater.

The new trade routes were the result of the great discoveries of the 15th and 16th centuries. Hundreds of years of voyaging along stormy coastlines had compelled western Europeans to develop good ships but the real impetus behind their maritime expansion was the idea of by-passing the Arab-Italian monopoly to trade with the Far East. Though it was not scientific fervor which sent Columbus and da Gama to sea, nevertheless, their voyages had important scientific consequences.

It is often asserted that it was the Indians and not Columbus who first discovered America. It is true that the original inhabitants of the New World knew their own hunting grounds well, but they had no idea that this land was an isolated continent separated by sea from other continents, such as Europe, Asia and Africa. They possessed no geographical science. The Europeans, however, developed one and this gave them a practical grasp of world geography unparalleled in earlier history. The epoch of the great voyages of discovery can be said to have terminated with Cook's travels in the 1770's. These represented the transition to the golden age of scientific expeditions in the 19th century: the Challenger expedition, Darwin, Nordenskiöld and many more.

Mariners and people who fish have always had some knowledge of sea depths, but the skindivers' capacity is limited to a few dozen feet and a duration of a couple of minutes. In the 17th century the diving bell was invented for salvaging operations and in the 1830's Siebe designed the modern diving suit for the same purpose. Breathing sets for "scuba divers" were introduced in World War II. Today divers work as a matter of routine at depths of down to several hundred feet.

It was the invention of the torpedo around the close of the 19th century which turned the submarine into a practical military weapon. It remained a military craft until the 1960's when marine researchers developed specially built diving craft for scientific use. Since then the quest for oil under the sea has brought rapid advances in diving techniques.

People are now beginning to probe the mysteries of the ocean depths. The "inner space" of the sea, is, like outer space, a new and promising frontier.

Exploring the depths

Divers breathing oxygen are limited to depths of 33–49 feet. Under pressure oxygen has a poisonous effect.

Using the simplest possible equipment pearl and sponge divers ("skindivers") reach depths of 98–164 ft. for brief periods.

Scuba divers using scuba equipment can go down to about 197 ft. Beyond that depth special gas mixtures are needed.

Helmet divers can work at depths of 492–820 ft. breathing heliox, a mixture of helium and oxygen.

Commercial submarines can be used for repairs and maintenance work at a depth of 1,312–1,640 ft. in the offshore oilfields for ex-

In 1934, using a bathysphere, a steel ball suspended on a cable from a ship, the American zoologist William Beebe descended to a depth of more than 2,953 ft. This hazardous device made it possible for people to observe for the first time the eternally dark world of the ocean depths.

Research submarines built of new materials such as titanium, aluminium and plexiglass are being used to carry out scientific observations at depths of several thousand feet. With the aid of this type of craft important biological and geological discoveries have been made along the mid-ocean ridges.

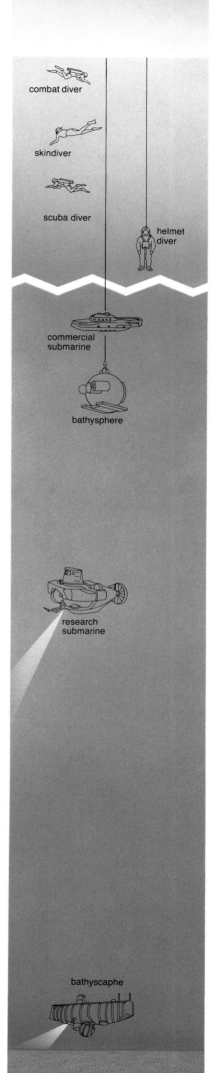

combat diver

skindiver

scuba diver

helmet diver

commercial submarine

bathysphere

research submarine

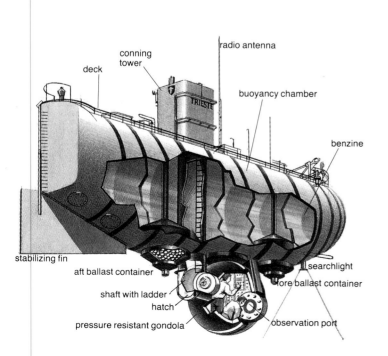

deck

conning tower

radio antenna

buoyancy chamber

benzine

stabilizing fin

aft ballast container

shaft with ladder

hatch

pressure resistant gondola

searchlight

fore ballast container

observation port

The greatest depths

The greatest known depth in the world's oceans is the MARINA TRENCH in the Pacific: 36,202 ft. Here, in 1960, a bathyscaphe (right and in greater detail, left) descended to 35,815 ft. In principle a bathyscaphe is a sort of underwater zeppelin. The hull is filled with benzine which is lighter than water, just as the gas in an airship is lighter than air. Beneath this hull or buoyancy chamber there is a steel, pressure resistant gondola with observation ports. The buoyancy is trimmed by means of steel balls released from two containers. The crew numbers two or three. The vehicle can remain on the seabed for a few hours at depths of 32,810 ft. or more.

bathyscaphe

Sea routes

The Egyptians are believed to have built the first sailing ships. They collected luxury goods such as hard woods, gold, ivory and slaves from Lebanon and Punt (probably Somalia). For a long time shipping remained something which hardly affected or concerned ordinary people. The Greeks and after them the Romans, were the first to be dependent upon transport of staple goods across the seas: grain, olive oil, wine and metals. With the collapse of the Roman Empire around 500 AD this traffic ceased and it was not until the late Middle Ages that everyday commodities once again began to become an important factor in shipping. During all this time most ships sailed more or less inshore, passing from point to point along the coasts. The Arabs and Chinese conducted some oceanic traffic, aided by the monsoon winds, in the Middle Ages. But the Europeans did not embark on such ventures until around 1500.

Nowadays the major part of shipping freight consists of bulk goods like oil, ore, minerals, industrial chemicals and grain. Manufactured goods for shipment comprise mainly of heavy industrial products such as machinery, vehicles and various semi-finished goods. Passenger traffic is largely restricted to cruises and ferry lines, aircraft having taken over the trans-oceanic passenger trade. During the course of the last hundred years there have been immense advances in shipbuilding. The modern

Ships from two centuries
Greyhounds of the seas
Centuries of development in square-rigged sailing vessels culminated in the British and American clippers of the mid-19th century. These swift ships were created to fulfill a particular requirement: costly and perishable cargoes from the Far East, especially tea, had to be carried to Europe and North America. The season's first deliveries could fetch very high prices and this led to the famous races across the high seas. The golden era of the clippers was brief for within a few decades they were replaced by steamships.

A modern cargo vessel
Because of industrial demands for fast, regular, sea transport services the tramp steamers of yesterday, the "casual workers" of the sea, have been almost eclipsed by regular-service cargo liners. These ships are swift and specially built for different cargoes. They usually have two crews who alternate, since it costs too much to have a ship lying idle while the entire crew is on leave.

The container revolution
Non-bulk cargo is no longer loaded and unloaded bit by bit, it is handled instead in unit loads, i.e. large standard-sized containers. This has reduced the alongside time of ships in port from days to hours. Special roll on-roll off ships carry cars and trucks on short routes between ports. The illustration below portrays both types of cargo in one vessel.

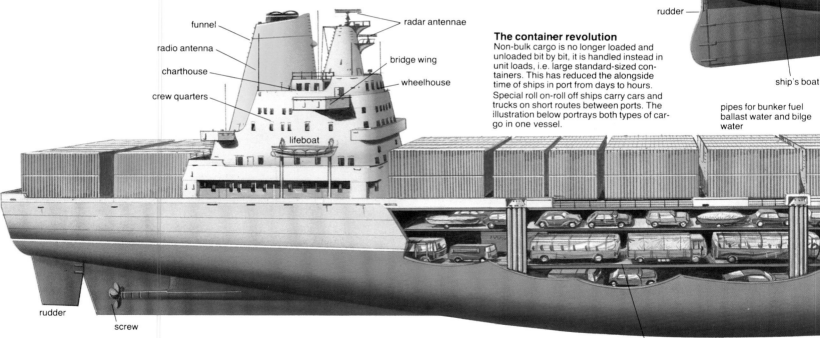

funnel / radar antennae / radio antenna / bridge wing / charthouse / wheelhouse / crew quarters / lifeboat / rudder / screw / through deck for vehicles

mizzenmast / mizzen topgallant staysail / mizzenmast staysail / mizzen / rudder / ship's boat / pipes for bunker fuel ballast water and bilge water

cargo liner has the same size crew as a clipper ship, 20 to 30 people, while the freight capacity can be as much as one hundred times greater; 30,000 tons or more. Noise, vibration and stress are the principal complaints of the modern crew, just as accidents, cramped conditions, cold, heat and damp plagued their predecessors.

Ports, like ships, have changed as well. Increasingly large ships and the growing demands for freight-handling space have resulted in the ports being moved out of the towns to new deep water sites. Another significant change is the container. The idea is not new; the Middle Ages had their own unit load system in the barrel or cask. The French word for cask, "tonne", gave its name to the unit of measurement. The modern standard containers (24 and 48 ft. in length) have already greatly altered designs and routines of ports and ships alike. Ships now have a very short turnaround time and shipping tends to be concentrated on fewer and larger centers. The world's busiest port today is considered to be Rotterdam with a turnover of some 270 million tons of freight in 1978.

Finding the way at sea
On the high seas and in dangerous coastal waters alike, it is of vital importance to know a vessel's exact location. Modern navigators make use of many different methods:

Astronavigation
The height over the horizon of the sun or a suitable star when in a position due south, gives the latitude. Longitude can be established by recording the exact moment when the reading takes place. The altitude of the sun is measured with a sextant.

Bearings
The bearings (horizontal angles) of two land marks of known position can be read off on a bearing plate, then determining one's position.

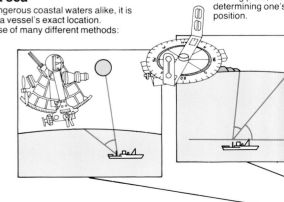

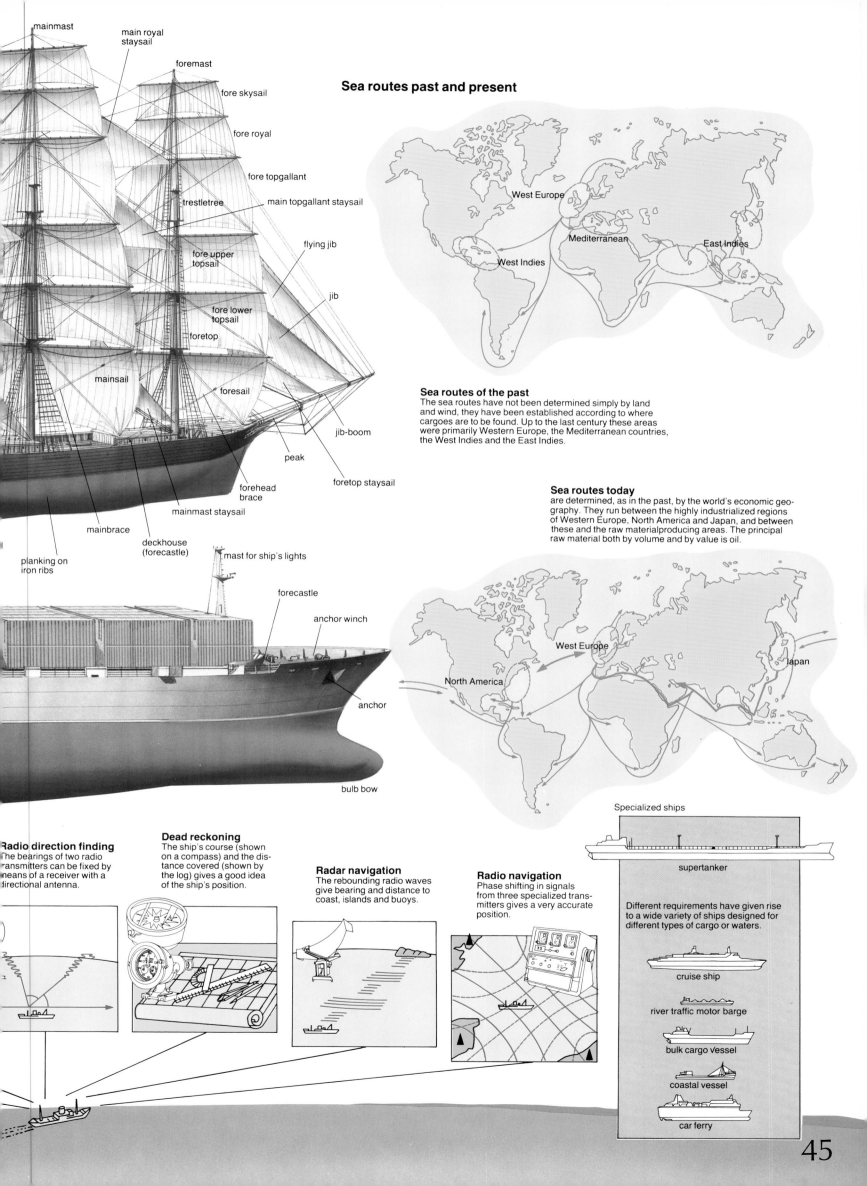

mainmast

main royal
staysail

foremast

fore skysail

fore royal

fore topgallant

trestletree

main topgallant staysail

fore upper
topsail

flying jib

fore lower
topsail

foretop

jib

mainsail

foresail

jib-boom

peak

forehead
brace

foretop staysail

mainmast staysail

mainbrace

deckhouse
(forecastle)

planking on
iron ribs

mast for ship's lights

forecastle

anchor winch

anchor

bulb bow

Sea routes past and present

Sea routes of the past

The sea routes have not been determined simply by land and wind, they have been established according to where cargoes are to be found. Up to the last century these areas were primarily Western Europe, the Mediterranean countries, the West Indies and the East Indies.

West Europe

Mediterranean

East Indies

West Indies

Sea routes today

are determined, as in the past, by the world's economic geography. They run between the highly industrialized regions of Western Europe, North America and Japan, and between these and the raw material-producing areas. The principal raw material both by volume and by value is oil.

West Europe

Japan

North America

Radio direction finding

The bearings of two radio transmitters can be fixed by means of a receiver with a directional antenna.

Dead reckoning

The ship's course (shown on a compass) and the distance covered (shown by the log) gives a good idea of the ship's position.

Radar navigation

The rebounding radio waves give bearing and distance to coast, islands and buoys.

Radio navigation

Phase shifting in signals from three specialized transmitters gives a very accurate position.

Specialized ships

supertanker

Different requirements have given rise to a wide variety of ships designed for different types of cargo or waters.

cruise ship

river traffic motor barge

bulk cargo vessel

coastal vessel

car ferry

People's impact on the hydrosphere

Surface and sub-surface water

In dry regions and industrialized areas alike clean water is a scarce and valuable substance.

Surface and sub-surface water

The ancient Persians living in steppe and desert tracts regarded all running water as sacred. In rain-abundant Europe this healthy reverence for water has been lacking. The water in rivers flowing through the big cities was recognized as being dangerous to drink more than five hundred years ago and industrialization, growing population and new, toxic chemicals have steadily worsened the problem.

The laying of drainage systems and the increased use of cleaning agents have added growing quantities of phosphates to our waterways and lakes. This excessive nourishment, or eutrophication, results in an explosive growth of algae which in turn consumes the oxygen in the water and leads to the death of fish and the impoverishment of the ecological system. Serious water contamination has also resulted from the careless disposal of mercury compounds and other heavy metals from industry. During its progress through the food chains, mercury becomes increasingly concentrated until it causes acute nerve damage to fish-eating birds or human beings.

Waste water can be cleansed. Formerly this was a mechanical process involving sedimentation and filtering. Nowadays chemical methods are being used to precipitate the nutritive salts and biological methods to add oxygen to the waste water, thus accelerating the decomposition of organic matter. Thanks to a successful sewage treatment program the River Thames now boasts 105 species of fish and in August 1983 a salmon was caught with rod and line for the first time in 150 years.

Sub-surface water is threatened as well, partly because too much of it is being drawn off and used. Oil and phenols from refuse dumps and nitrogen fertilizers can poison ground water. Once in the ground the nitrates in nitrogen fertilizers are converted into nitrite which in the human body can be transformed into substances that breed cancer.

Inland seas and oceans

Inland seas with their limited water turnover have much in common with lakes. Eutrophication leads to a shortage of oxygen in deep water. Hydrogen sulfide is generated in the water when the normal decomposition of organic matter no longer functions. Poisons like mercury and chlorinated hydrocarbons can reach high concentrations and in the Baltic these have affected fish and, indirectly, seals and eagles.

In the oceans with their much greater water masses these problems are not as manifest, but in the long term they are equally serious. There is a danger that the production of vegetable plankton will be reduced by chlorinated hydrocarbons such as DDT insecticide, which has even been traced in penguins in the Antarctic. The dumping of chemical and radioactive waste in deepsea areas has aroused equal anxiety in recent years. We do not know enough about the circulation of seawater between deep and surface strata and these poisons may well invade the food chains and become concentrated within them.

Land and sea water rights

The right to use the waters of rivers which cross national frontiers has frequently caused local conflict. Sea rights, by comparison, create dissent on a global scale. The "freedom of the seas" doctrine of the 18th and 19th centuries is now a thing of the past. In the 1970's nations began to claim vast areas of sea, and land-enclosed waters like the North Sea are now entirely divided up into economic zones. Disputes over the right to utilize the resources of the remaining free oceans have created international disagreement. The industrial nations with the necessary technology assert their right to exploit the high seas. Poorer countries and those without coastline demand that these resources should be administered supranationally as the common inheritance of all mankind. The tension has diminished to some extent now that the exaggerated expectations of high-profit seabed mining have abated.

The prospects are not entirely negative. International agreements on the release of oil in especially vulnerable waters have been introduced and implemented, even though these are all too often violated. This shows that agreements can be reached on individual issues, and it is in this spirit that we should continue.

Human mismanagement

Destruction of ground vegetation and the draining of wetlands diminishes the infiltration of surface water and thereby lowers the water table. The latter can be lowered further by excessive demand for municipal and industrial purposes: fresh water is pumped up, used in households and industries and then released again as polluted surface water. Intensive irrigation, on the other hand, can increase infiltration until the water table reaches the surface. Then in dry regions, exceptional evaporation from the water-logged ground causes the precipitation of salts from this sub-surface water and in time the salty soil becomes useless for farming.

clearcut watershed

sub-surface water

bedrock

Death by oil

The dumping of ballast water mixed with oil is illegal in many waters, but it still occurs. The real oil disasters take place, however, when big tankers founder (below). The subsequent cleaning up is a costly and time-consuming undertaking. The death of many seafowl (right) arouses widespread public indignation, but the oil pollution is even more dangerous to organisms beneath the surface: fish and fish fry, crustaceans and algae. This is why we now try to remove the oil from the water instead of sinking it by the application of chemicals.

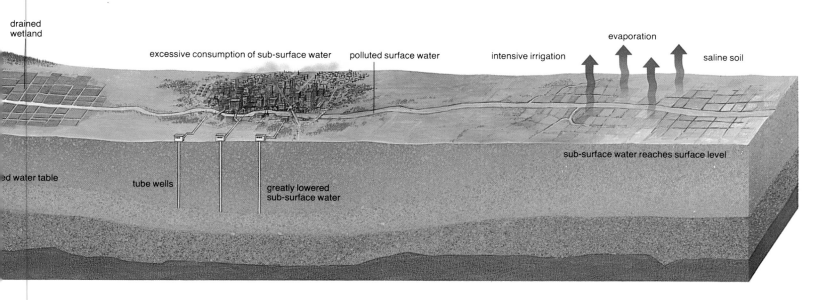

drained wetland

excessive consumption of sub-surface water

polluted surface water

intensive irrigation

evaporation

saline soil

ed water table

tube wells

greatly lowered sub-surface water

sub-surface water reaches surface level

Poisoning the world's water

Dumping at sea

The practice of dumping chemical and radioactive waste in the sea's depths has been going on for years. In time, however, containers can erode away and the poisonous contents can be released into the sea water. We do not know a great deal about the circulation of deep and surface water (arrows) and this process may take place faster than we formerly realized, so that the poisons spread to the biologically active water strata. Oceanographers have discovered currents even in the very deepest parts of the oceans.

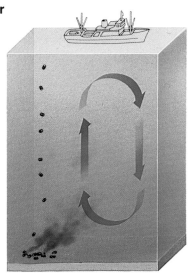

Eutrophication

the over-nourishing of water results in algal blooms and lack of oxygen in the water. This can be caused by phosphorus of nitrogen in sewage or, as here, by nitrogen fertilizer draining off agricultural land.

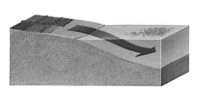

Environmental poisons

are spread mainly by industry and agriculture. Poisonous substances such as DDT and PCB cause serious damage to inland seas like the Baltic where the water exchange rate is not very great.

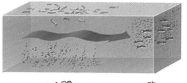

Excessive fishing

does not necessarily lead to extermination but it does upset the balance between the different fish species. When catches diminish drastically serious problems arise for both people and industries who depend on fish.

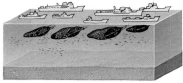

---

copper

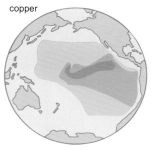

☐ less than 0.5 %

☐ 0.5–1 %

■ more than 1 %

nickel

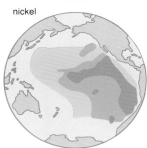

Mining on the seabed

Large areas of the ocean floors are scattered with fist-sized mineral nodules. These contain principally manganese plus a certain amount of copper, nickel and cobalt, varying in proportion according to where they are found (map, left). There are advanced plans to exploit these mineral resources. One such project is to dredge them up from the bed of the Pacific by means of a vast bucket dredger system (below).

cobalt

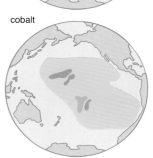

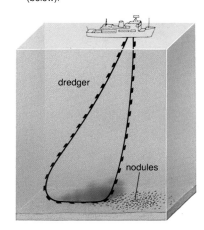

dredger

nodules

Fences in the sea

have become a reality in recent years, not physically but legally. The continental shelves have been divided among the nations bordering the seas, giving each of these the right to exploit the natural resources (below, the North Sea). Countries with a short coastline or no coast at all have been the losers.

Faroe Islands

Danish zone

Norwegian zone

Shetland Islands

Orkney Islands

British zone

Aberdeen

Stavanger

Oslo

Danish zone

West German zone

Dutch zone

Copenhagen

Hamburg

London

Amsterdam

Earth

Earth is a tangible substance. There is nothing immediately remarkable about it so perhaps its elevation to one of the four primary elements occurred reluctantly and only because matter in the solid state also demanded a place among the primary substances, alongside gaseous air and fluid water. It is not surprising that none of the early philosophers recognized earth's fundamental importance.

This is not to say, however, that the Earth's crust and the matter contained in it were not subjected to philosophical speculation. Metals were extracted from the ground, and their transformation from grey ore through incandescent fire to gleaming metal fired people's imagination: if stone could become metal then could not lead and other base metals be transmuted into gold?

Thus alchemy was born in ancient Alexandria and was passed via the Arabs to medieval Europe. Alchemists' theories consisted almost entirely of occult speculation. But their practical experiments produced new techniques: for example, distillation led to the discovery of new elements such as phosphorus and, in time, sowed the seeds of scientific chemistry.

Geology, the science of the Earth's crust, originated as late as 1830, when the English scientist Lyell had the courage to assert in print that our Earth was not created in the year 4004 BC as claimed by the learned theologians, but was in fact millions of years old. Geophysics, geology and mineralogy form the basis for a group of special sciences which are collectively known as earth science. In our generation a revolution has occurred in the way we view the Earth. The crust is now seen as a mosaic of plates with the continents moving across the face of the globe. This new theory of "plate tectonics" has enabled insight into the formation of minerals and ores, but it has also forced scientists to re-evaluate seemingly unrelated disciplines such as paleontology, the science of extinct animals and plants.

People have become a geological force, excavating and blasting, draining and filling in, to such an extent that in many places their ruthless activities have exposed the ground to the ravages of erosion. The shallow stratum of life that covers the Earth's crust – the biosphere – is essentially dependent upon the fragile layer of soil that exists beneath the green surface. We are ourselves part of that vulnerable stratum even though we usually overlook this in our pursuit of short-term gains.

The crust

The structure of the Earth

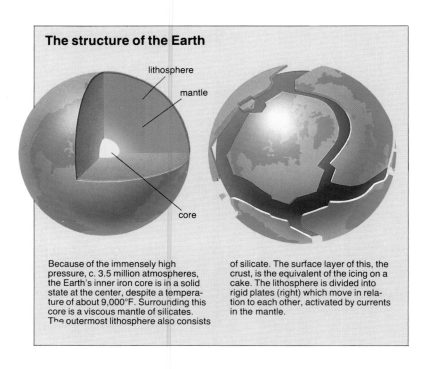

lithosphere
mantle
core

Because of the immensely high pressure, c. 3.5 million atmospheres, the Earth's inner iron core is in a solid state at the center, despite a temperature of about 9,000°F. Surrounding this core is a viscous mantle of silicates. The outermost lithosphere also consists of silicate. The surface layer of this, the crust, is the equivalent of the icing on a cake. The lithosphere is divided into rigid plates (right) which move in relation to each other, activated by currents in the mantle.

Alfred Wegener

published his theory on "continental drift" in 1912. He had evolved this idea because Africa and South America fit together along their continental shelf limits and also because the same fossils have been found on both sides of the South Atlantic. But this theory was not generally accepted until the mid-1960's. Wegener himself died during an expedition to Greenland in 1930.

AFRICA

SOUTH AMERICA

Drifting continents

With the aid of paleomagnetic data scientists are seeking to reconstruct the appearance of the Earth during earlier geological periods. Paleomagnetic data relates to how magnetic particles in minerals were aligned by the Earth's magnetic field at the time when the mineral was formed. This is a complicated task, however, and the various reconstructions can often differ in detail.

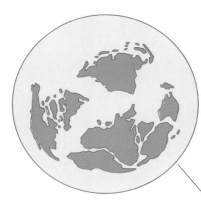

The Earth 300 million years ago

During the Carboniferous period the continents moved towards each other. Then in the Mesozoic era they formed a super-continent, Wegener's "Pangaea".

180 million years ago

By the time of the Jurassic period the super-continent had begun to split up. This was the heyday of the dinosaurs.

60 million years ago

At the beginning of the Cainozoic era, after the dinosaurs had become extinct, the South Atlantic had already opened up. India was moving towards Asia, but Australia was still attached to the Antarctic.

The Earth today

The contours of the continents have not altered much in 300 million years. But their present positions represent merely the latest phase in a constantly shifting pattern. Studies of mid-ocean ridges (below) and fracture zones have enabled scientists to decipher the movements of the crustal plates.

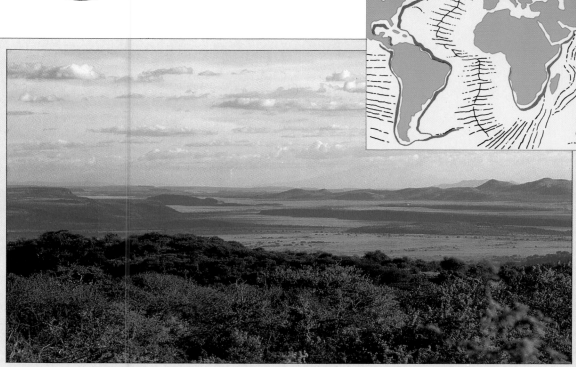

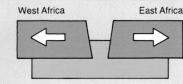

West Africa   East Africa

A continent splits

Continents can become welded together and they can split up. The latter process is taking place today along East Africa's Rift Valley (photo). West and East Africa are being pulled apart along this 2,485 mi. fault line (above). Vulcanism is common in the Rift Valley. When, in the future, East Africa from southern Ethiopia to northern Mozambique becomes a "mini-continent", the Rift Valley will be an arm of the sea.

By studying the way in which earthquake shock waves progress through the Earth, scientists have found that it is vertically stratified. The molten iron core is surrounded by a mantle of viscous silicates. The Earth's crust is 12–43 mi. thick beneath the continents but only about 3–4 mi. under the oceans, i.e. roughly one thousandth part of the Earth's radius. Combined with the upper stratum of the mantle, the crust forms a zone known as the lithosphere.

As recently as a couple of decades ago we believed that this thin crust was rigid and motionless. At the beginning of the century, the German climatologist Alfred Wegener observed that the climate had varied in an apparently erratic fashion during the past geological epochs. He attempted to explain this by postulating that the continents had "drifted". During the early Mesozoic era about 200 million years ago all the land on Earth formed a single huge continent, "Pangaea", which subsequently split up. Wegener declared that the continents had actively plowed their way through the immobile oceanic crust. With good reason, geologists refused to accept this theory.

But in the early 1960's, using new instruments, oceanographers began measuring gravitation, magnetism and heat flow along the mid-ocean ridges. They discovered that these ridges are fractures where new oceanic crust is constantly formed until, possibly 150–200 million years later, it disintegrates in the oceanic trenches, far from its origin.

We know now that the lithosphere is divided up into plates which are comparatively rigid. They move in relation to each other like ice-floes in a current of water. These plates incorporate blocks of continental crust or "cratons". While, geologically speaking, the seabeds are recent and consist of homogenous volcanic rocks, the continents are extremely ancient and are made up of many different types of rock. They have repeatedly split and collided and fragments of oceanic sediment and rock have fastened on to their flanks. These movements have resulted in folding, faulting and vulcanism around the periphery of the continents. This new plate tectonic theory has created a veritable revolution in geology.

Scientific studies into the structure of the continents have been going on for two hundred years and have produced important knowledge as to the origins of rocks and soils. Even as early as the 18th century we understood how magmatic rocks rise from the Earth's interior, how they are then weathered and how the mineral fragments form sediment far away from the original rocks. In time, chemical processes cement these fragments into sedimentary rock. High pressures and temperatures in the crustal collision zones can then convert the sedimentary rock into metamorphic rock. If this is raised to the surface and is exposed to weathering the entire rock cycle begins again: transportation, sedimentation, consolidation, metamorphosis. On land, this cycle is fragmentary and erratic when compared with the immense geological machinery of the oceans.

Vertical crustal movements

The large-scale movements in the Earth's crust are almost entirely horizontal, but the local shifts are often vertical. These derive their motive power mainly from the horizontal movements of the plates, but they can occur a long way from the plate limits. The mechanics of geological faulting (right) were being studied in detail long before the geologists themselves understood or even suspected any movement of the plates.

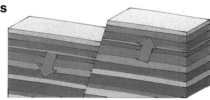

fault

Faults, horsts and grabens

A simple fault (uppermost, right) occurs through vertical movements on both sides of a fault line. Horsts (middle) arise when a long, narrow block of bedrock is pressed upward, while a graben (below) is formed when the bedrock block sinks downward. These drawings are stylized. In actual fact the contours of the blocks would be softened by slope wasting.

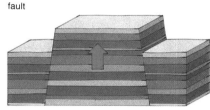

horst

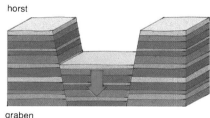

graben

Rocks of the Earth's crust

Magmatic rocks
are formed when molten magma wells up from the Earth's upper mantle. Shown here is a coarse-grained granite. Magma on the surface is called lava.

Sedimentary rocks
are usually deposited in water. This Jurassic period limestone has a clearly stratified structure.

Metamorphic rocks
(shown here: gneiss) are formed when magmatic or sedimentary rocks are transformed through high pressure and/or high temperatures.

How rock types are formed
Unlike the homogenous oceanic crust, the continental crust is a patchwork of rock types from different periods and different origins. The magmatic rocks are the most primitive, though not always the oldest. The other rock types—with the exception of organic formations such as coal—are secondary products from the weathering, erosion, transportation, deposition and transformation of older rocks. Because of movements in the crust these rocks can now be found far from the places where they were originally formed. But their structure and composition give scientists important clues in determining their origin.

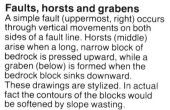

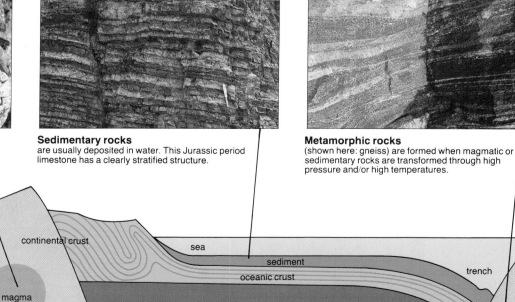

continental crust

sea

sediment

oceanic crust

trench

magma

lithosphere

The restless Earth

The interiors of the continents
are built around large granitic shields which have long been unaffected by the more dramatic geological processes. Consequently the continental rocks are the oldest in the world—as much as 3.8 billion years.

The shallow seas over the shelves
are strictly speaking flooded continents. Some of these sea areas were dry land in earlier epochs, while elsewhere the sea covered areas that form the continents of today. Small fluctuations of the sea level cause major changes in the coastline.

The mid-ocean ridges
are zones where new crust is constantly being formed. Active vulcanism sometimes raises parts of such a ridge above the surface of the sea. Typical examples of this include Iceland, Ascension Island and Tristan da Cunha.

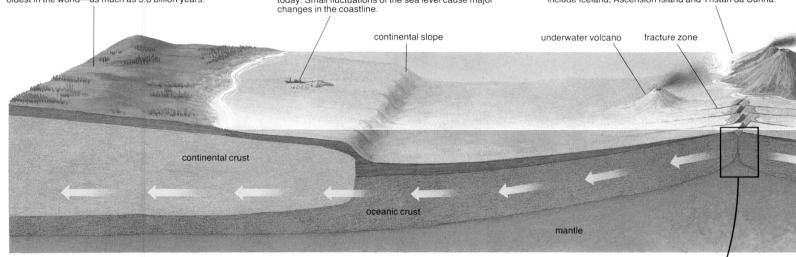

continental slope

underwater volcano   fracture zone

continental crust

oceanic crust

mantle

Continental and oceanic crust

SOUTH AMERICA   ATLANTIC OCEAN

Patagonia   Falkland Islands

Tierra del Fuego

Cape Horn

PACIFIC OCEAN

continental crust

oceanic crust

mantle

crust

mantle

core

Two types of crust
The continental crust is c 16 % lighter than the basalts of the oceanic crust. The continents can thus be said to be floating like ice floes on the oceanic beds. This isostatic effect explains why the surfaces of the continents are mainly above sea level. It also explains why the continents are not drawn down into the Earth's mantle like the seabed and, therefore, why the continents are older than the oceanic crust. Beneath the highest mountain ranges the Earth's crust is thickest.

How new crust is formed:

New crust is formed where two plates are drawn apart by movements in the underlying mantle, which consists of liquid magma. New formation takes place mainly along the mid-ocean ridges, but can also occur where continents are splitting up.

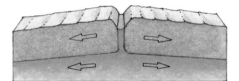

The newly formed fracture between the plates is immediately sealed by magma welling up from the mantle beneath. The oceanic crust is formed by these lava rocks, which develop a cushion-like shape when they harden rapidly beneath the water.

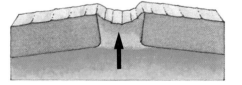

Meanwhile the movements in the mantle continue so that the process is quickly repeated: fractures form, fractures are sealed, fractures re-form . . .

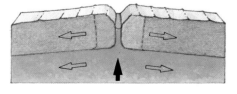

Because of this repeated process the oceanic crust is made up of long strips of simultaneously formed rock running parallel with the mid-ocean ridge. This ridge often has a central valley which is where the fissure is found. Transversal fracture zones extend outward from the ridge. Along these zones the crust is somewhat displaced, since the mantle movements are not equally great at all points along the mid-ocean ridge.

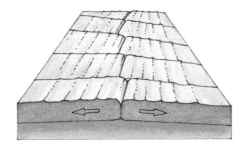

The movement of the continents across the face of the Earth is only one consequence of the phenomenon known as "seafloor spreading". This begins at the mid-ocean ridges where oceanic Earth crust is constantly being formed. The crust then moves away from the spreading zone at a rate of .5 to 4 in. a year. At first the newly formed seabed lava is fully exposed but gradually it becomes covered by sediment. Thus a recently formed seabed near the spreading zone has only a thin layer of sediment, while older parts farther away can be covered by sediment several miles deep. By its own weight this sediment becomes compressed to form sedimentary rock such as sandstone.

At the same time that the oceanic plate is being renewed in the spreading zones, it is disintegrating in the subduction or consumption zones. These are found in oceanic trenches, which

Subduction zones
are areas where the oceanic crust is disintegrating. If the subduction zone is in the open sea then the result is a volcanic island arch, but if it adjoins a continent a mountain range like the Andes is formed.

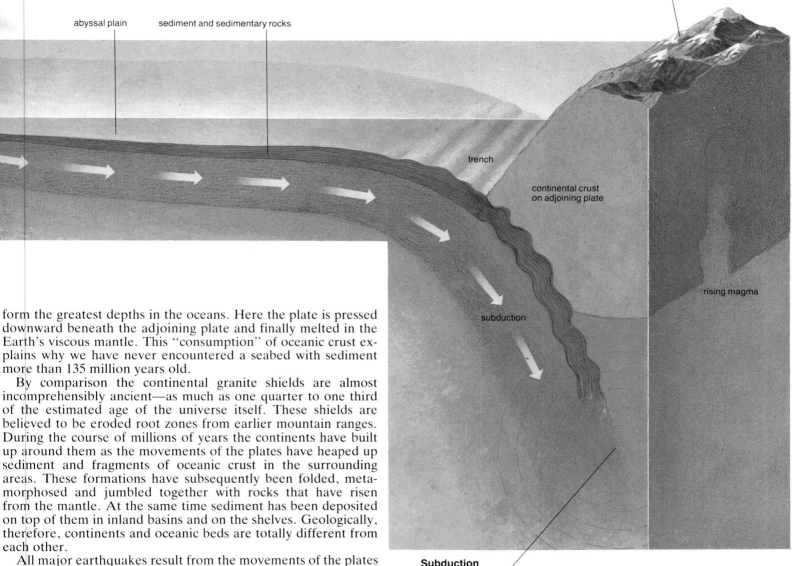

abyssal plain

sediment and sedimentary rocks

trench

continental crust on adjoining plate

rising magma

subduction

form the greatest depths in the oceans. Here the plate is pressed downward beneath the adjoining plate and finally melted in the Earth's viscous mantle. This "consumption" of oceanic crust explains why we have never encountered a seabed with sediment more than 135 million years old.

By comparison the continental granite shields are almost incomprehensibly ancient—as much as one quarter to one third of the estimated age of the universe itself. These shields are believed to be eroded root zones from earlier mountain ranges. During the course of millions of years the continents have built up around them as the movements of the plates have heaped up sediment and fragments of oceanic crust in the surrounding areas. These formations have subsequently been folded, metamorphosed and jumbled together with rocks that have risen from the mantle. At the same time sediment has been deposited on top of them in inland basins and on the shelves. Geologically, therefore, continents and oceanic beds are totally different from each other.

All major earthquakes result from the movements of the plates against each other. Surface tremors occur when two adjacent plates move in opposite directions, as along the San Andreas fault in California. Deep earthquakes take place when a plate penetrates the mantle at an angle of about 45°. Consequently the very deepest tremors occur at quite a distance beneath the upper plate, sometimes at a depth of more than 435 mi. Both surface and deep-level earthquakes have their true centers far beneath the surface. No matter how great the devastation may be at the epicenter on the surface, this is nevertheless a mere echo of what has taken place deep down in the bowels of the Earth.

Vulcanism is a common enough phenomenon throughout the solar system, but plate tectonic processes appear to be restricted to Earth. It will be for the scientists of the future to determine just what special features of the Earth's interior structure give our planet this unique status.

Subduction
The movements of the plate when it is drawn down (subducted) into the mantle cause deep earthquakes.

island arch

When the plate melts, lighter parts of the molten mass rise upward. These thicken the continental plate from beneath which results in isostatic lifting. They also cause vulcanism.

53

Weathering

Weathering is the common term for a series of mechanical and chemical processes which decompose both rock and soil. Nearly all of these processes are governed to some extent by climate. Precipitation and temperature are key factors which, along with the hardness and chemical composition of the rocks and soils, determine how the weathering process develops.

Mechanical weathering

In cold climates frost action is the most common form of weathering. Changes in temperature cause small inclusions of moisture in rock and earth to freeze and thaw alternately. Frost action will only occur where local temperatures vary above and below zero and where liquid water is present.

The pressure of growing ice crystals can shatter boulders and bedrock. There are other types of crystal, however, which can have the same shattering effect. All surface and sub-surface water contains dissolved salts which have been leached out of minerals and soils. When the moisture evaporates, salt crystals can split porous rocks.

This salt shattering action occurs particularly in sandstone and in desert regions where there is exceptional evaporation. Even in very arid conditions there is sufficient moisture present in rocks to cause this form of shattering. The process attacks not only rock formations, however, but also buildings. In modern times dam building and large scale irrigation have raised the water table in the Nile valley to such an extent that ancient monuments there are becoming damaged by the saline water that is soaking upward through the porous stone. In European cities, too, the foundations of historic buildings are being damaged by salt. This penetrates the masonry via dampness from the surrounding ground and then crystallizes.

Extreme changes of temperature between day and night can shatter stone through the constant expansion and contraction that takes place. This is a common phenomenon in the desert where, because of the dry air, there is a great difference between daytime and nighttime temperatures. This type of shattering is consequently related to the absence, rather than to the presence, of moisture. One form of mechanical weathering which is of secondary significance is the shattering effect of growing roots.

Chemical weathering

This takes place primarily when weak acids in surface and sub-surface water dissolve different minerals. When carbon dioxide dissolves in water, part of it combines with the water and produces carbonic acid, H_2CO_3. This acid in turn dissolves the calcium carbonate in limestone. Water circulation in this pervious type of bedrock can thus form caves and tunnels. When the calcareous water evaporates, the calcium carbonate is precipitated again as limestone formations. In regions with a limestone bedrock and abundant precipitation this type of weathering is associated with karst landscapes (named after the ancient province of Karst on the Yugoslavian-Italian border) with ravines, dolines, poljes and caverns.

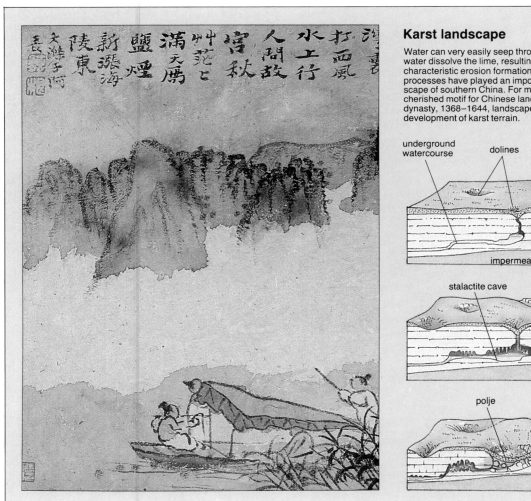

Karst landscape

Water can very easily seep through limestone. Weak acids in the water dissolve the lime, resulting in the creation of caves and the characteristic erosion formations which form a karst landscape. Karst processes have played an important part in the forming of the landscape of southern China. For many centuries this has been a cherished motif for Chinese landscape painters (left: detail of a Ming dynasty, 1368–1644, landscape painting). Below: an analysis of the development of karst terrain.

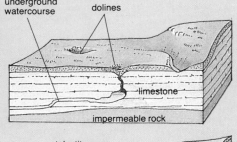

Because of the perviousness of the bedrock and rapid chemical weathering, watercourses flow largely underground. They disappear through funnel-shaped dolines and sinkholes in the ground.

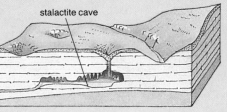

The acid in the water enlarges the limestone caves. Dripping, calcareous water forms stalactites on the cave roof and stalagmites on its floor.

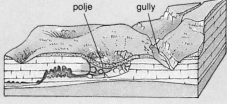

The dolines are gradually enlarged and collapsing cave systems result in kettle-shaped poljes. Precipices and ravines with exposed limestone surfaces are other characteristic features of a karst landscape.

In places where the air is polluted, limestone masonry suffers damage as airborne sulphuric acid decomposes the stone. The Acropolis, the hill citadel of Athens, is threatened with disintegration and the authorities are now considering removing these edifices altogether to a museum with purified air and erecting plastic models instead on the site—a solution which it is thought would be less expensive than attempting to clean up the notoriously polluted atmosphere of the Greek capital.

Organic acids, formed in a surface layer of humus, are an important factor in wet climates. Not only acids destroy stone, however; oxidation (attack by the oxygen in the air) and hydrolysis (minerals in the rocks combine with water), also result in weathering. Feldspar and mica in even the hardest of granites can break down and cause the stone to disintegrate. The feldspar and mica are transformed into hydrous oxides of iron and aluminium and hydrous alumino-silicates, clay minerals which form kaolin and bauxite. All that remains of the granite is loose grains of quartz. These can then sedimentate and become converted into rocks. When these rocks in their turn are weathered the geological rock cycle is completed.

In nature the process of weathering is so slow that it is often difficult to discern. But it is nevertheless highly significant for it is the first stage in denudation, the leveling out of the landscape. The products of weathering also form soils which in their turn are essential to the existence of vegetation and animal life on land. Weathering has therefore been a factor of fundamental importance in the creation of life environments on our planet.

Folding and denudation

The history of the Earth's surface constitutes a constant struggle between constructive and destructive forces. The most significant building-up processes are uplifting and folding while the principle disintegrating processes are weathering and erosion. The disintegration is part of a process known as denudation—a process which through geological time reduces even the highest mountains to mere hillocks (below). Weathering makes this process possible by breaking down even the hardest of rocks.

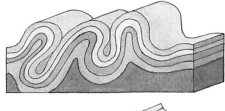

Horizontal forces in the Earth's crust fold the formerly level strata of sedimentary rocks. This diagram is schematic only—in reality no landforms such as these occur...

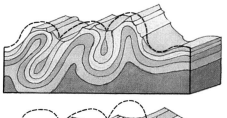

...since denudation is taking place simultaneously with folding and uplifting. Rapid uplifting and erosion together produce an "Alpine" relief with dramatic precipices, ridges and peaks.

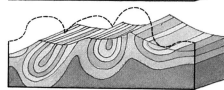

The ultimate result of denudation is a low, undulating relief, the highest points of which are much lower in many cases than the original mountain ridge (dotted line).

Frost action

The volume of water increases by 9 % when it freezes—a unique quality among naturally occurring fluids. In this way the water that always exists in cracks and pores in stone can shatter and split bedrock and boulders alike (left). In rocky regions with pronounced variations between warm and cold temperatures, frost action produces "boulder fields" or "felsenmeers", whole areas consisting of sharp-edged, split boulders and smaller stones.

Weathering in the tropics
In warm, humid climates weathering processes penetrate to 262 ft. or more beneath the surface. Deep weathering of the bedrock often creates red, ferruginous laterite soil (right). A recently exposed "inselberg" reveals the results of weathering in earlier, wetter epochs in the form of rounded blocks and rock surfaces (below).

Erosion

Abraded coast

The kinetic energy in waves makes wave erosion, or abrasion, very effective, especially along exposed, rocky coasts. The waves undermine the rock until part of it falls away. It is this process which creates the steep faces of rock known as cliffs, for example the famous white cliffs of Dover in England. Harder parts remain standing as isolated pillars or "stacks". In front of the cliff an abrasion platform is formed and this is usually exposed at low water on tidal coasts. Loose material brought down by erosion gathers here. The stones are kept in constant movement by the waves and become rounded into smooth pebbles. On softer faces the abrasion process is more rapid and of a somewhat different nature.

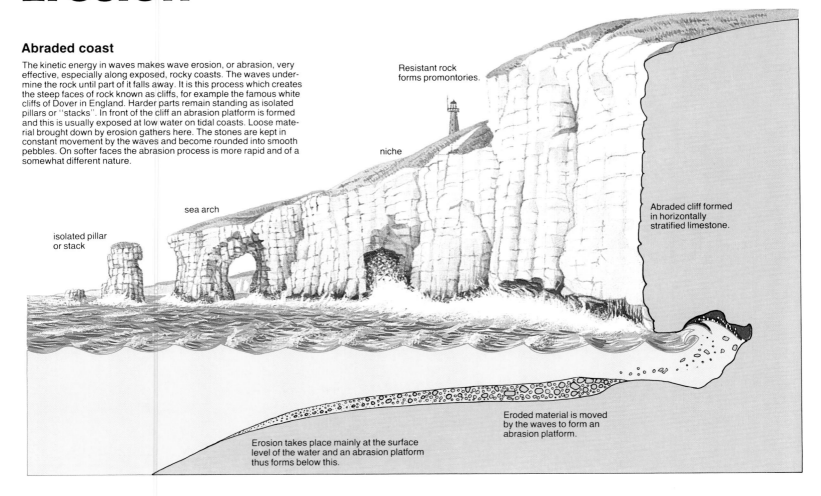

Resistant rock forms promontories.

niche

sea arch

isolated pillar or stack

Abraded cliff formed in horizontally stratified limestone.

Eroded material is moved by the waves to form an abrasion platform.

Erosion takes place mainly at the surface level of the water and an abrasion platform thus forms below this.

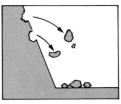

In a rockslide rocks or a whole cliff face will fall away. This usually happens on very steep slopes.

Rock, soil and gravity

When weathering or excessive moisture reduces the cohesion in a slope the force of gravity can set it in motion downward. This slope wasting may vary in manner according to the nature of the material (solid rock, boulders, moist or dry soils) and also according to the angle of the slope. When the material is dry and the slope only moderate then the process is normally slow. Creep and solifluction can take place almost indiscernibly and this occurs to some extent on all slopes. Rockslides or landslides on the other hand happen suddenly and violently and if this occurs in a built-up area the loss of life and property can be enormous. Landslides can take place on quite moderate slopes. When the moisture content in very fine-grained material, especially clays, rises beyond a specific limit the cohesion of that material diminishes dramatically.

A talus is formed when repeated small slides pile up debris at the foot of a steep face. The "angle of repose" of the talus is about 35°, depending on the material in it.

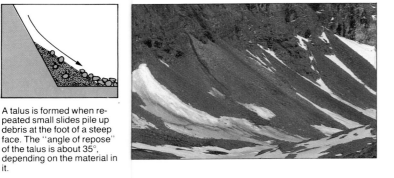

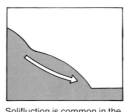

Solifluction is common in the polar regions where the soil above the permafrost becomes saturated with water in the summer.

Creep in loose ground can create steep ravines (right). Trees and posts are displaced from the vertical.

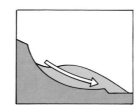

Landslides occur when the moisture content in fine-grained soils exceeds a certain limit, abruptly transforming the ground into mush.

Erosion is part of an extensive process which earth scientists call denudation—the stripping of the ground by the forces of wind, ice and running water. Denudation causes the gradual lowering of the ground level. It has been calculated that this takes place at a mean rate of 164–295 ft. per million years, at least during the present geological epoch.

Denudation embraces a whole series of processes. Climatic conditions cause disintegration by weathering when particles and larger fragments break away from the bedrock. Gravity, water, ice and strong winds set this loose material in motion and erosion as such takes place when the particles, and the medium which carries them along, wears away the surface of the ground. Denudation could be described as the sum total of weathering, slope wasting and erosion.

The ground is most effectively eroded by running water and consequently heavy rainfall often results in severe erosion. Steep slopes increase the kinetic energy of the water and thereby further intensify the erosion process, as in the Alps or the Himalayas for example. The loose material which rivers and streams carry along with them is sooner or later deposited in deltas or sedimentation basins. This occurs at the point where the flow of water has diminished to the extent that the loose material is no longer kept moving.

The process of erosion has not continued at the same rate throughout geological time. For long periods the continents were considerably flatter than at present because the formation of mountain ranges proceeded slowly or did not take place at all. During other epochs when the plates in the Earth's crust collided with each other, new mountain ranges were folded and large areas of the continents were raised relative to sea level. Erosion then increased again. In dry regions wind erosion has been predominant while in the polar regions it is the slowly advancing ice of the glaciers which is the erosive element, but the principal factor on a global scale has always been running water.

The flow of water, in miniature gullies and great rivers alike,

wears away the surface in characteristic V-shaped grooves. Glaciers carve out a broader valley, with a U-shaped profile. The valley sides are then smoothed out by slope wasting, especially in moist climates. The contours of the landscape become increasingly gentle, finally leveling out into a plain. By then denudation can have lowered the ground level so much that the slow flow of rivers is no longer sufficient to sustain erosion. This "peneplain" is the final product of denudation.

The surface of the Earth has never been reduced to one great peneplain since at many times in the past a new rising movement in the Earth's crust has increased the flow of water, transformed quiet rivers into raging torrents and thereby speeded up erosion once again. This struggle between the disintegrating forces of atmosphere and hydrosphere and the building forces of the crust will continue as long as the heat in the Earth's interior is sufficient to sustain the plate tectonic processes.

Erosion's agents

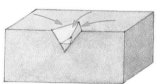

Running water dislodges and carries away bedrock fragments and soil particles, thereby forming ravines.

Waves abrade exposed coasts forming steep cliffs—anything from less than a foot to a hundred feet or more high.

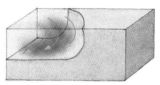

The river current erodes the shoreline, especially on the outer side of a bend. Rivers thus tend to develop an increasingly winding or meandering course.

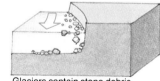

Glaciers contain stone debris, called till and this wears away and polishes the bedrock.

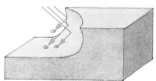

In dry areas the wind carries innumerable grains of sand which "blast" and sculpture exposed rocks.

The impact of raindrops throws up loose particles which gradually move downward over a slope.

From plain to peneplain

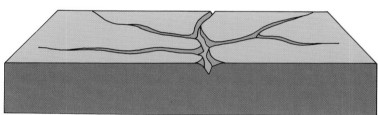

On a plain, rivers and streams run slowly and the valleys and gullies which these cut have the typical V-shaped profile of fluvial erosion. However, they are shallow—the slower the current, the less the erosion.

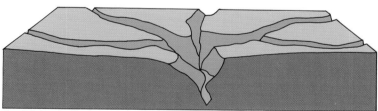

If a plain is raised by forces in the Earth's interior then the swiftness of the waterflow increases, and the rivers cut deep gorges with steep sides. In dry regions the areas between these gorges can remain intact for a long time . . .

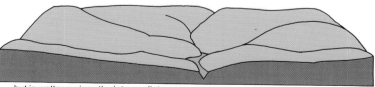

. . . but in wetter regions the intermediate areas are worn away by slope wasting. The entire plain becomes "denuded" and as its level sinks the flow of the rivers becomes slower and slower.

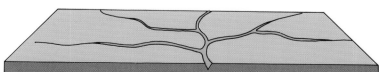

Finally denudation flattens out the entire area into a "peneplain". Erosion is now very slow because of the leisurely flow of the water. Peneplains are found in the granite regions of Canada and Scandinavia. Details of the terrain here have often been modified by glacial processes during the final stages of the last Ice Age.

Life on land

Living in water
A fish is a relatively uncomplicated creature. Its means of locomotion—muscles, fins—are simpler than those of terrestrial animals. The fish has no urgent need to regulate its body temperature.

Adaptations to life on dry land

The elephant, the largest and heaviest of all living terrestrial animals, can be used here as a fairly drastic example of the biological adaptations necessary for survival ashore. Mammals, with their complex temperature control mechanism, are the animals which have most efficiently adapted themselves to living on land.

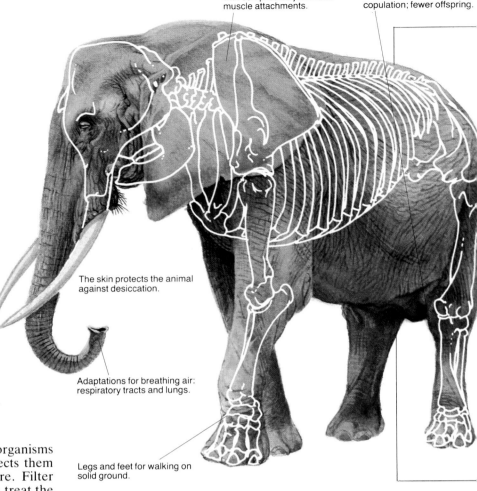

Rigid supporting skeleton with complicated joints and muscle attachments.

Internal fertilization through copulation; fewer offspring.

The skin protects the animal against desiccation.

Adaptations for breathing air: respiratory tracts and lungs.

Legs and feet for walking on solid ground.

Life began in the sea and the life environment of those organisms which still live there is not particularly harsh. It protects them against desiccation and sudden changes in temperature. Filter feeders from the sea cucumber to the baleen whale can treat the water quite simply as a nutrient solution. On the other hand the move on to land—a step which the multicellular plants took about 400 million years ago—required drastic biological adaptations.

Two of these adaptations are especially manifest. The first of them relates to locomotion. In order to be able to move on land the terrestrial animal had to evolve a complex motive apparatus with legs and feet, an apparatus which had, and continues to have, a low degree of energy efficiency. A small, running quadruped, a dog for example, has to use five times more energy than a swimming salmon to move one-half mile.

The second of these adaptations concerns reproduction. In the water fertilization is an external process: the female cod ejects her spawn whereupon the male secretes his milt over it. Fertilization occurs freely in the water and tens of thousands of offspring are left to their own resources.

Reproduction on land demands internal fertilization by means of copulation, incubation and usually care of the offspring. The mammal has gone a stage further; an "internal incubation" of the fertilized ovum is followed by delivery, i.e. birth. The tendency, in other words, has been towards greater attention to each individual offspring.

Yet despite these severe demands the colonization of the continents has been extraordinarily successful. The first amphibian to make a brief but arduous land crossing—probably from one pool of water to another—has through an incredible process of adaptation given rise to some 13,000 vertebrate species now dwelling on, in and above the ground, and also in the seas (seals and whales). The adaptation program of the insects has been even more successful; there are now about one million insect species. The number of terrestrial plant species is probably in the region of 300,000. One reason for this vast variation may be that land, in contrast to water, is divided into numerous environments with different attributes.

In response to varying environmental characteristics organisms have been compelled to develop more differentiated forms and more complex behavior patterns than would ever have been necessary in water. This is a course of development which has led to our own species.

Life has colonized the land
The invasion of life on dry land has totally transformed the environment. This photograph shows lifeforms of different levels of sophistication, from grassplants to elephants.

Adaptive radiation

In evolution biology the term "adaptive radiation" is applied to a parent species which produces later species that in their turn occupy specialized ecological niches.

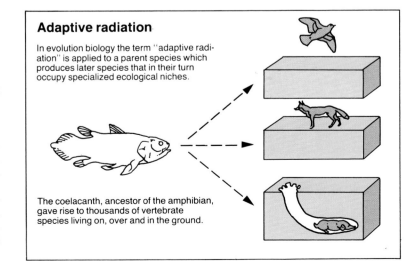

The coelacanth, ancestor of the amphibian, gave rise to thousands of vertebrate species living on, over and in the ground.

Plants on dry land

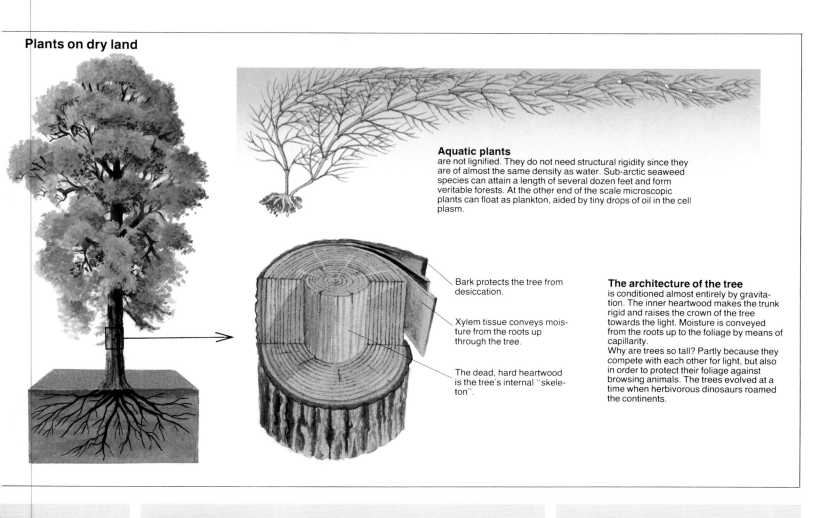

Aquatic plants

are not lignified. They do not need structural rigidity since they are of almost the same density as water. Sub-arctic seaweed species can attain a length of several dozen feet and form veritable forests. At the other end of the scale microscopic plants can float as plankton, aided by tiny drops of oil in the cell plasm.

Bark protects the tree from desiccation.

Xylem tissue conveys moisture from the roots up through the tree.

The dead, hard heartwood is the tree's internal "skeleton".

The architecture of the tree

is conditioned almost entirely by gravitation. The inner heartwood makes the trunk rigid and raises the crown of the tree towards the light. Moisture is conveyed from the roots up to the foliage by means of capillarity.

Why are trees so tall? Partly because they compete with each other for light, but also in order to protect their foliage against browsing animals. The trees evolved at a time when herbivorous dinosaurs roamed the continents.

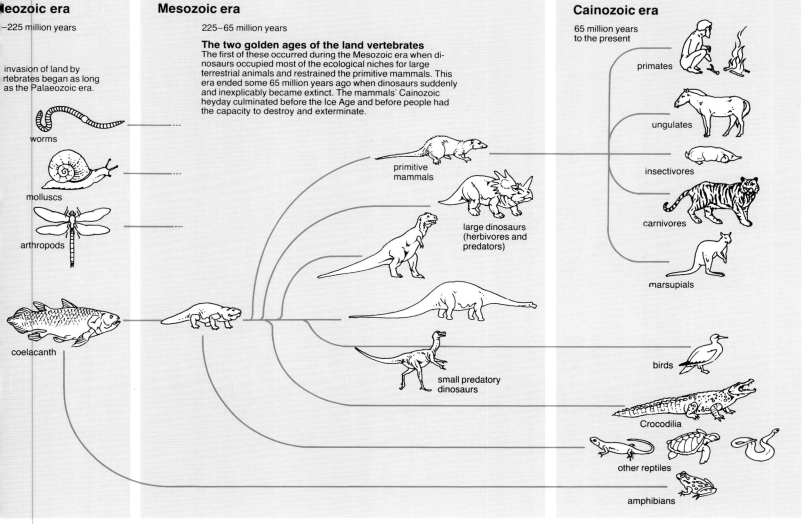

Meozoic era

–225 million years

invasion of land by rtebrates began as long as the Palaeozoic era.

worms

molluscs

arthropods

coelacanth

Mesozoic era

225–65 million years

The two golden ages of the land vertebrates

The first of these occurred during the Mesozoic era when dinosaurs occupied most of the ecological niches for large terrestrial animals and restrained the primitive mammals. This era ended some 65 million years ago when dinosaurs suddenly and inexplicably became extinct. The mammals' Cainozoic heyday culminated before the Ice Age and before people had the capacity to destroy and exterminate.

primitive mammals

large dinosaurs (herbivores and predators)

small predatory dinosaurs

Cainozoic era

65 million years to the present

primates

ungulates

insectivores

carnivores

marsupials

birds

Crocodilia

other reptiles

amphibians

59

Tropical forests

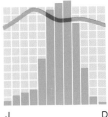

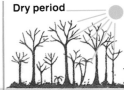

Rain period   Dry period

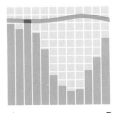

Monsoon and rain forests
form distinct ecological systems, because of climatic differences. Monsoon forest (above) has an annual dry period; the columns in the climate diagram show the rainfall distribution over the year. During the dry period most of the trees shed their leaves. The rain forest (below) remains green all the year around, because the rainfall is more evenly distributed. The temperature (graph curves) remains high and steady in all tropical lowland areas.

Monsoon forests (above) are found in south and south-west Asia. Lowland rain forests grow in an equatorial belt and are most extensive in the Amazon and Congo river basins (below).

Rain all the year around

Forest requires moisture. In tropical regions where there is abundant rain, monsoon or rain forests flourish according to how the rainfall is distributed over the year. Lowland rain forests and the more unusual mountain rain forests are also distinctly different to each other. In regions where there is less rain, savanna and other types of vegetation emerge.

It is the competition for the sun's energy which gives the rain forest its particular character. The plants cling to and scramble over each other to reach upward to the light. The forest floor, on the other hand, is dark and humid. The tropical forests lack the abundant ground vegetation of the temperate zones.

There is a greater variety of plant and animal species in the rain forests than in any other ecosystem; probably half of all the known species on Earth exist here. The reason for this enormous wealth of species is that the equatorial ecosystems have remained stable for several million years. No Ice Age has moved through these regions.

The rain forests give the impression of superabundant vitality, and yet this is to some extent misleading. There is a great difference between the high-productive conditions of the treetops and the inhospitable forest floor. Moreover the rain forest environment is exceptionally delicate. In the temperate zone forest, only a small proportion of the organic carbon present occurs in the living plants; most of it is stored in a thick layer of humus on the ground. In a rain forest, however, the carbon is converted almost immediately into new vegetation. In other words, the humus stratum is very thin and is destroyed rapidly when the forest cover disappears. Beneath the humus are infertile soils which easily become fused into laterite, a brick-like mass.

People's endeavors to exploit the rain forests can therefore have disastrous results. Traditional land clearance is not particularly hazardous but poverty and desperation can lead to reckless stripping that can be totally destructive. When international timber and food producing concerns move into the forests with their heavy machinery and demands for quick returns, the consequences can be equally grave. After a few good harvests the ground becomes exhausted and can sustain little more than scrub. The process of devastation is now moving so swiftly that the rain forests and their life forms could face total extinction within a few decades.

The rain forests of the Old and New Worlds differ in their flora and fauna. Shown here is a South American forest, but the threat to existence is the same for all tropical forests and that threat is people.

The canopy
Because of the abundance of sunlight, the biomass production is highest among the treetops. Consequently large numbers of birds, insects and monkeys have their habitat on this level.

The lower trees
Lower down there are other treetop strata. These intermediate levels consist of tree species which are better adapted to shade than the trees that form the canopy. These lower levels, too, harbor their particular fauna.

Epiphytes
Many plants, for example lianas and some orchids, grow up among the trees. Certain of these epiphytes are parasites which feed on their host plants, while others merely make use of the trees to climb upwards towards the light. Other epiphytes are saprophytes, living on decaying organic matter.

Palms
do not normally grow as tall as deciduous trees. They are thus not common in the shadowy interior of the rain forests though they do occur where the sun can reach them, along the watercourses, for example.

Constant shade
prevails over the forest floor so that this environment is not very productive. Fallen leaves are decomposed by various organisms which have their habitat here.

Stranglers
Many of the epiphytes are stranglers which gradually choke and destroy the host plant.

The soil
beneath the thin layer of humus is often infertile, latosolic earth, reddish in color from iron oxides.

The highest trees

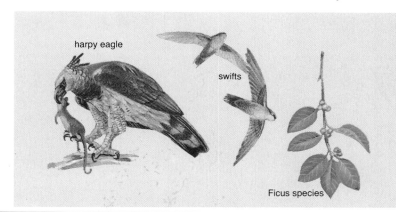

harpy eagle

swifts

Ficus species

protruding above the canopy and known as "emergents" harbor a number of bird species, including swifts that are closely related to the species of the Old World. The harpy eagle preys chiefly on the monkeys of the canopy.

The treetops

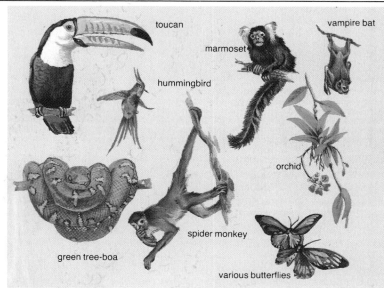

toucan

marmoset

vampire bat

hummingbird

orchid

green tree-boa

spider monkey

various butterflies

are the habitat of a great variety of fauna. There are many bird species here, from grotesque toucans to graceful humming-birds that are often no bigger than a large butterfly. The green tree-boa slithers through the foliage in pursuit of monkeys and birds. Nocturnal vampire bats sleep away the hours of daylight while orchids bloom in branch-forks and bark fissures. Brilliant butter-flies swarm among and over the tree crowns.

In the lower trees

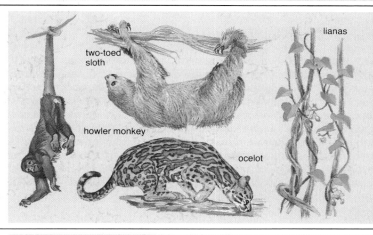

two-toed sloth

lianas

howler monkey

ocelot

great troops of howler monkeys greet the sunrise in clamorous chorus. Their screams can be heard several miles away. The two-toed sloth ambles leisurely through the branches; this crea-ture has no natural enemies and thus no need for speed or agility. Unlike the heavier jaguar, the agile ocelot hunts up among the branches with ease.

On the ground

giant armadillo

agouti

jaguar

anaconda

low bush vegetation

the giant armadillo roots among fallen leaves while the agouti, a rodent, scuttles about in search of fallen fruit. The jaguar fre-quents the tracts around the watercourses in which swim anacondas, the largest snakes in the world, up to 33 feet in length.

Underground

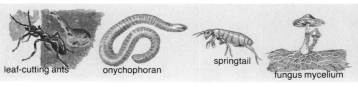

leaf-cutting ants

onychophoran

springtail

fungus mycelium

a multitude of invertebrates, fungi and bacteria decompose dead organic matter to recycle the nutrients for further biological production.

61

The grasslands

Tropical or temperate zone forest thins out and becomes grassland because the rainfall there is inadequate in relation to evaporation, or because it is not sufficiently evenly distributed over the year to sustain an overall woodland coverage. The great grasslands of the world are located in places where the global air circulation system produces a predominance of dry, descending air masses.

The grasslands of the world
The grass plains constitute not one but several environments. The tropical savannas, the temperate zone prairies and the continental steppes differ in many ways. First and foremost the savannas have no winter; located as they are between the tropics of Cancer and Capricorn the savannas merely have two dry periods each year. Where the savanna gives way to steppe the vegetation becomes lower and sparser, more thorny and with smaller leaves, as the climate becomes drier. Lowland steppe forms the transitional zone between savanna and desert. Another type of steppe is the continental plateau as in Anatolia and central Asia.

The East African savannas are the best studied of all the world's grasslands. Compared with the monotonous and impoverished steppes the savannas are varied and highly productive. The prairie is a sort of intermediate environment between savanna and steppe, though it scarcely exists any longer in its natural state; most of it has been modifed by cultivation. The savanna can have the appearance of sparse woodland, have a park landscape, or be almost treeless, depending upon the humidity. The watercourses are lined by a narrow strip of forest often little more than a few dozen feet in breadth.

The food chain
Grasses represent the basic element in the food chain although they emerged only during the last 50–60 million years, i.e. in the Cainozoic era. The same also applies to the grazing animals. The teeth and the digestive systems of the ungulates have become adapted to the cellulose-abundant grass diet, especially in the case of the ruminants, while the grass in its turn has also adapted to the grazers. Unlike most other vascular plants, grass does not grow at the top but out from the bottom so that the stems can survive being constantly nibbled off.

Herbivores have specialized eating habits. Giraffes eat leaves and twigs from high up on the trees, elephants leaves and branches farther down, and zebras, antelopes and gazelles graze on grasses of different height and coarseness. In this way the herbivores make maximum use of the flora. The huge herds of animals represent an adaptation to the threat from predators. Large animals are unable to conceal themselves on the plains, but they can hide among their own kind. Thus the strong animals of high status are found in the herd's center while the weaker individuals have to stay on the periphery.

The predators of the plains are interesting subjects of study, though their total living weight is at most one tenth that of the herbivores. There is not always a clear difference between the so-called predators and carrion-eaters. Nocturnal studies using image intensifiers have revealed that the hyena is an accomplished hunter and when one sees lions and hyenas around the same carcass it is by no means certain that it was the lions which brought down the prey.

People on the grasslands
The human race evolved on the grass plains of Africa and people have continued to live on the savannas and steppes as hunters/gatherers, livestock nomads, and farmers. Hunters and nomads alike follow the animals which in their turn follow the rain seasons and vegetation cycles. The farmer departs from this pattern. In many places increasing population results in imprudent methods of cultivation, over-grazing and the laying waste of delicately balanced environments. In this way the productive savanna can become impoverished and reduced to steppe which in its turn can deteriorate into desert. Finally the soil itself can be blown away leaving only a sterile layer of small stones—a desert pavement.

Grassland regions
All the continents, except the Antarctic, have their grasslands: North America's prairies, South America's llanos and pampas, Africa's savanna and steppe belts north and south of the equatorial forests, Eastern Europe and Central Asia's steppes. The "grass continent" of them all, however, is Australia, the vast "outback" consisting of grassland enclosing an inner core of desert.

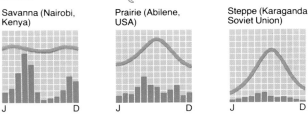

Savanna (Nairobi, Kenya)   Prairie (Abilene, USA)   Steppe (Karaganda, Soviet Union)

J   D   J   D   J   D

Savanna, prairie, steppe
These diagrams show the climates of savanna, prairie and steppe. Precipitation (columns) often has two annual peak periods but is greater on the savanna than on the steppe. The temperatures (graph curves) are constantly high on the savanna while on the steppe the winter is cold. For both precipitation and temperature the prairie is intermediate. It is found between humid and arid climates.

Savanna flora
is not as well adapted to drought as that of the desert; the dry periods on the savanna are shorter than in the desert. Grasses are the principal producers of biomass and thereby also the main sustenance for the animals, but trees like umbrella thorn and baobab are also characteristic plants.

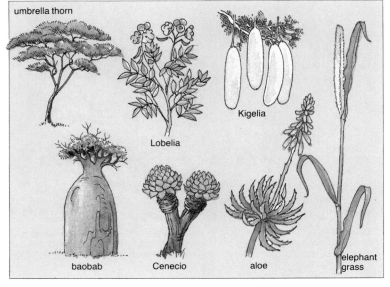

umbrella thorn

Kigelia

Lobelia

baobab   Cenecio   aloe   elephant grass

Savanna animals

Hunters and scavengers
The puff-adder hunts stealthily on its own, the lions hunt in prides. Hunting dogs chase their prey until it collapses. Hyenas are not only carrion-eaters but also skilled nocturnal hunters. Vultures are specialized carrion-eaters – and outstanding gliders.

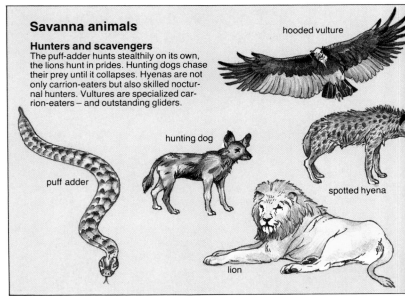

hooded vulture

hunting dog

puff adder

spotted hyena

lion

The great herds
do not wander at random over the East African savannas. They undertake regular seasonal migrations governed ultimately by the periodic variations in rainfall and vegetation. Herd behavior is an adaptation to the threat of predators, reducing the danger for the individual animal. Shown here is a mixed herd of wildebeest and zebra in East Africa.

A grazing succession

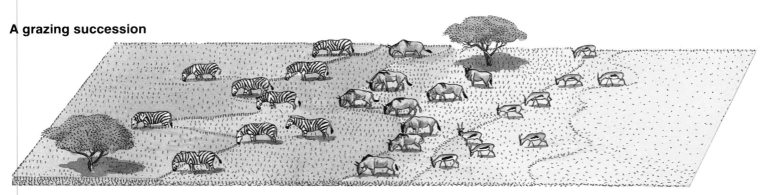

After the rain the new grass grows very rapidly and this is grazed by an ordered succession of animals: zebras move in first, eating the tallest and coarsest grass followed by the wildebeest that eat the medium-length stalks. Finally the Thomson gazelles nibble off the tenderest leaves. This grazing succession makes maximum use of the grass.

Savanna year

| January | February | March | April | May | June | July | August | September | October | November | December |

The two annual rain periods are most pronounced on the African savannas. The "long rains" continue for a couple of months, the "short rains" for about one month. The rain causes the ground to change its hue abruptly from yellow-brown to green. Between these rain periods the ground gradually resumes the color of the dry period.

Grazers and browsers
Herbivores are also specialized. The elephant seeks its food in the trees, the wart-hog mainly in the ground. The zebra, wildebeest and gazelle form between them a distinct grazing succession, shown in the upper panorama on this page.

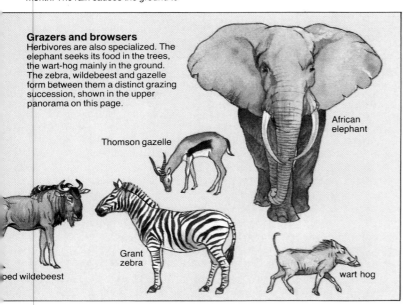

African elephant

Thomson gazelle

Grant zebra

wart hog

ped wildebeest

People and the grasslands

On the dry savanna, agricultural productivity is low. But commercial monoculture is more dangerous to the environment than varied subsistence farming. Intensive livestock rearing often causes the total destruction of the ground vegetation. One introduced species—cattle—makes less efficient use of the pasture than animals in a natural grazing succession. Rational game protection and game ranching would give the highest yield but this is difficult to organize and tends also to conflict with customs and traditions. A nomad's wealth is reckoned in terms of how many head of livestock he or she owns and without such affluence dowry payments and many other social transactions become impossible.

Deserts

From bushland to desert
The dry bushland (above, far left) has a continuous cover of drought-resistant grasses and thorn bushes. The semi-desert has patches of vegetation, surrounded by bare ground, while the desert itself (far right) is barren with only isolated plantlife here and there.

Deserts of the world
These cover some 15 % of the Earth's land area and are located mainly between the tropics and the subtropical regions where dry air masses descend towards the ground. A vast belt of desert extends from the Atlantic to central Asia.

Sand, stone and rock

Desert types:
Local geology, elevation and winds create different types of desert. The principal ones are sand desert ("erg" in Arabic), stony desert ("sarir") and rock desert ("hammamet"). All of these types are represented in many desert regions.

Wind and sand
Barchan dunes are formed when the wind moves the sand up on the windward side. Eddies behind the crest cause the sand to be deposited and the dune to move forward. These dunes arise in areas where the wind blows in one direction only and they form at right angles to the wind direction.

A sea of sand
is what we generally envisage when we think of a desert. In fact, however, the sand desert is not very common – it is only nine percent of the Sahara, for example. The wind moves the sand into the area from adjacent rock and stone deserts and deposits it as dunes (above, right).

Sand desert
is characterized by dunes which do not always cover the entire area. Shifting dunes can bury cultivated land and sometimes entire communities.

Stony desert
is littered with stones of varying size, from boulders to coarse gravel. These stones are often so densely packed that they create a "desert pavement".

sand dunes

oasis

butte

playa

The deserts are the outcome of the large-scale air circulation system which distributes precipitation unevenly over the surface of the Earth. The large deserts are located along the border regions between the tropic and sub-tropic zones. Here, tropical air, which has risen in the equatorial convergence zone and thereby disposed of its moisture, descends again on the other side of the convection cell. Local conditions can also contribute. Mountain ranges can function as gigantic dehumidifiers whereupon areas sheltered by them can easily become desert or semi-desert. The main cause of coastal deserts is cold oceanic currents which compel the sea winds to deposit their rain out over the water.

It rains only seldom in the desert – but when it does rain the effect is dramatic. Roaring flash floods surge down the dry river beds, salt-pans become short-lived lakes and millions of seeds which have lain dormant in the ground are transformed into dazzling vegetation. Soon afterwards the desert becomes its customary, arid self again, but the rain has replenished the aquifers which often lie beneath the surface.

Deserts vary greatly in appearance. Most common are different types of stone and rock desert. Sand desert is created when over a long period steady winds bring in mineral particles from adjacent desert areas. A common feature of all dry deserts, however, is the extreme range in temperature; a result of the dry, clear air which produces very strong insolation in the daytime and equally strong loss of heat through outward radiation at night.

Survival in this extreme environment demands far-reaching biological adaptation. Desert plants often have a leathery or wax-like skin which protects them against desiccation. Certain animals, for example the desert rats, can manage without access to water. Through their behavior, too, animals have contrived to adjust to desert conditions. Burying themselves by day and moving about by night, aided by very keen hearing, is a tactic used by both predators and their prey.

The deserts have varied in magnitude during different geological epochs. In our day, however, a new influence has entered the scene—people. Attempts to farm land and raise livestock in places where the precipitation is inadequate have resulted in large areas becoming desert which should otherwise have been bushland, savanna or even forest. As a rule the inhabitants are well aware of what is happening, yet poverty is forcing them to ruin their environment by overgrazing, overfarming and fuel collecting simply for the sake of day-to-day survival.

Wind and dust

Light dust particles are often carried away from desert areas by winds and deposited elsewhere as aeolian soils, e.g. the northern Chinese loess. Such soils are usually extremely fertile, if there is sufficient water present. Dust carried out over the sea produces red deep-sea clays.

How a salt-pan is formed

The infrequent but very heavy rains and intensive evaporation – the potential evaporation can be tens of times greater than the actual annual precipitation – produce salt pans ("chott" in Arabic), shallow saline lakes which often dry out altogether.

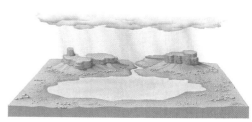

Wadis lead the rainwater out into the desert where it can form an extensive, though shallow and temporary lake. The water contains salts which have been leached out of the soil strata higher up in the drainage area.

Evaporation is rapid and the lake shrinks. Pure water disappears into the atmosphere while the salts remain. The salinity of the water increases and salts – chlorides and sulphates – are precipitated.

The open water is transformed into a corrosive salt slush, or disappears altogether. A smooth, firm "playa" is left if the water has had a high clay and sand content. Salt from salt–pans has been an important commodity in the north-south caravan trade through the Sahara for thousands of years.

Sandstorm over the Atlantic
Strong winds can carry desert dust very great distances. This satellite photograph shows how an easterly gale has blown a vast cloud of dust out over the Atlantic and all the way to the Cape Verde Islands, a distance of some 600 mi. The smallest particles can remain airborne long enough to cross the Atlantic.

photo

AFRICA

Rock desert
is bedrock where the wind has stripped off all loose soil. Like the stony desert, it is criss-crossed by wadis, riverbeds that are usually dry.

wind eroded rocks

talus slopes

wadi

Wind and rock
The desert winds carry sand with which they carve out many characteristically rounded shapes in the hard desert rocks. This process is known as abrasion.

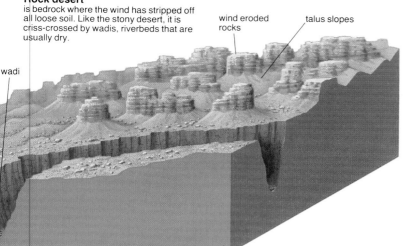

Cereus (giant saguaro)

yucca

Opuntia

Cereus

Desert adaptations

Desert flora and fauna are very characteristic. This cross-section is from western North America, but parallel adaptations are found in many deserts. Both the fox and the mouse below, for example, have almost exact counterparts in the Sahara.

rattlesnake

agave

road runner

kangaroo mouse

Mamillaria

scorpion

kit fox

The desert mammals are often nocturnal and bury themselves in the daytime, both as a protection against the heat and to avoid predators. The fox has enormous ears, an adaptation to enable it to locate its prey almost solely by hearing. The kangaroo mouse is built so as to have minimum possible contact with the hot sand. Insects, arachnids and reptiles which have difficulty in regulating their body temperatures, survive by shifting between sun and shade. Snakes are common in sand desert where they can move more easily than quadrupeds. Most of the desert plants have a tough, leather-like skin as protection against dehydration, and thorns or prickles to save them from the animals that seek their stored water. Flowering occurs at infrequent intervals and is greatly dependent upon moisture and temperature. But certain plants can survive many years of drought, by lying dormant as seeds. When the rain does come, leaves, flowers and seeds are produced with a suddenness which seems little short of miraculous. The cacti in this panorama are typical of the New World's deserts and semi-deserts.

Temperate forests

Northern forests

The most extensive temperate forest regions are in the northern hemisphere. Between the tundra limit and roughly 50°N a belt of coniferous forest extends through northern North America, Europe and Asia. South of this there is another belt, of varying width, comprising mixed and deciduous woodland. Areas with a Mediterranean climate have permanently green deciduous trees.

The diagrams show two temperate climate types: right, a dry continental climate with greatly varying temperatures (graph lines) and maximum precipitation in summertime (columns); far right, a Mediterranean-type climate where the annual temperature is more even and precipitation greatest in wintertime.

Kuopio, Finland   Algiers, Algeria

Coniferous forest

The coniferous forest regions are an important raw material source for sawn timber, wood pulp and fuel. As a rule the same tree species grow over very big areas which facilitates large-scale, highly mechanized forestry. Towards the tree limit, both on mountain slopes and adjoining the tundra in the north, the conifers give way to birch and brush vegetation which becomes increasingly stunted as conditions grow more severe.

Mixed forest

In the mixed forestland hardy deciduous trees, such as birch and various Salix species (sallow, willow etc.), are commonest. Conifers grow mainly in meager soils. The varied environments of the mixed woodlands offer a wide selection of specialized ecological niches and thereby a very diversified fauna. Such mixed forest is rare nowadays however. Large areas of it have been cleared for cultivation and what remains is in danger of being replaced by the fast-growing and commercially more attractive coniferous monoculture.

Deciduous forest

The deciduous forest consists mainly of hardwood trees such as oak, beech, elm, lime and maple. In areas with a distinctly maritime climate the evergreen holly is a characteristic feature. Because of the dense, shadowing canopy the ground vegetation is not as profuse here as in mixed forest, though the environment is still very productive. Hardwood forest of this type is even more scarce than mixed forest because, ever since the Middle Ages, it has been subject to clearance to facilitate cultivation.

The annual cycle

The deciduous forest undergoes seasonal changes with a growing season lasting from spring to autumn, followed by a period of dormancy throughout winter.

Throughout the greater part of the Earth's temperate zones forest is the natural vegetation. The climatic requirements for temperate forest are relatively abundant precipitation, moderate temperatures and a distinct difference between summer and winter. A belt of coniferous forest runs from east to west through Asia, Europe and North America, the southernmost limit of which generally coincides with the southern limit of the snow climate according to the Austrian climatologist Köppen's definition, i.e. where the mean temperature of the coldest month is below 27°F. In the southern hemisphere these latitudes are mostly sea areas so there is practically no temperate forest at all. That which does exist, in South Africa and south-west Australia, is of the evergreen Mediterranean type.

In areas with a cold temperate or snow climate podsolic soils are the most common. Precipitation leaches out the humus substances of the uppermost layer and deposits these as a brown stratum deeper down. Farther south deciduous forest grows on soils which have not been leached but are brown with humus, from the surface layer's rotting vegetation down to the subsoil.

During the last Ice Age, temperate forest gave way to ice and tundra and in Europe, forest survived only in a few sheltered places. When the ice retreated northward the tundra withdrew in its wake and the forest advanced again. The spruce, or fir, which now flourishes in large areas throughout the northern forests, was a latecomer. Pollen analysis (the use of pollen grains collected from peat bogs and sediment to determine plant species in ancient times) has revealed that during the post-glacial warm period deciduous forest extended very far northward in Europe. Thickets of hazel were common.

For the hunters and gatherers of the early Stone Age the forest was both a source of food and a habitat. During the late Stone Age the inhabitants cleared ground in the deciduous forest regions, establishing in time the first agricultural settlements. Greeks and Romans deforested large areas around the Mediterranean, but it was not until the Middle Ages that serious inroads were made on the European forests (in North America not before the colonists began to settle in the 19th century). The fact that hunting was a jealously guarded feudal privilege was the salvation of many forests in Western Europe. "Forest" and "hunting ground" were synonymous words in many languages. When the Swedish peasants were granted the right to hunt in the late 18th century on the other hand, the large animals were driven to the brink of extinction in a few years.

In deciduous forest areas income from game rights is still a significant consideration and ecologically productive mixed forest environments are permitted to survive to some extent. In the sparsely populated coniferous regions, on the other hand, the forests are used more specifically as a source of raw materials for the timber and pulp industries.

spring   summer   autumn   wi[n]

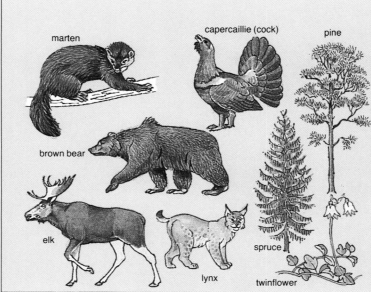

Woodland flora and fauna

The species, left, are native to Europe and Asia. North America has similar plants and animals, however, in corresponding ecological niches. In the coniferous forestlands the species are to a large extent identical on both sides of the Atlantic.

Coniferous forest regions

Pines grow mostly in meager soils while spruce, or fir, prefer richer, moister soils. The twinflower is used here to represent the relatively abundant ground vegetation of the coniferous forest. The marten is a carnivore which catches a lot of its prey in the trees. The capercaillie is encountered mainly in old, tall-trunked forest. The brown bear is Europe's only bear species. It is both herbivore and carnivore. The lynx is found from northern to southern Europe, mainly in mountainous areas. The elk is the largest of the deer family, feeding on broadleaf foliage and the young twigs and shoots of the conifers. Bear, lynx (bobcat) and elk (moose) are also native to North America.

Mixed forest

The birch is the most typical tree of northern deciduous forestlands, while the larch is a "deciduous conifer" which sheds its needles in winter. The dog-rose is common in open places where there is plenty of light, for example forest edge and pastureland. The wide variety of vegetation supports an abundance of bird species. The great tit is found throughout temperate Eurasia. The tawny owl is specifically nocturnal and thus more often heard than seen. The red deer is primarily a leaf-eater. The fox is an opportunist frequenting both the depths of the forests and farmland or suburb, while the beaver confines itself exclusively to aquatic surroundings.

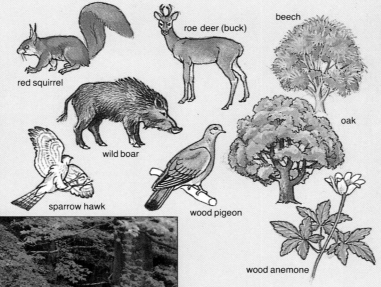

Deciduous forest

Oak and beech are typical of the European deciduous woodlands and their fruit, acorn and beechnut, are a vital source of food for wild boar and many other woodland animals. The oak lets in more light than the beech, thereby permitting a more diversified ground vegetation. Wood anemones bloom in profusion during early spring, before and while the trees are budding. The roe-deer move about mostly at twilight and dawn and can thus adapt themselves to environments which are modified by people. The wild boar likewise is mainly nocturnal. The European, red squirrel is not limited to deciduous woodland but can survive just as well on pine seeds as acorns. The sparrow hawk preys on small birds and the wood pigeon modestly conceals itself in the very depths of the woods.

The forest floor

In temperate climates the decomposition of dead biomass is a slow process and consequently the ground is covered in a deep layer of last year's leaves, pine needles, twigs, and so on, the layer beneath this being more thoroughly broken down. Consequently there is plenty of nutrition available at ground level and instead light is the limiting factor for the growth of ground vegetation. The beech forest (left) with its extremely dense canopy has very little ground flora and it is only those plants which bloom early in spring that can survive here.

The tundras

The world's tundra

Tundra is the vegetation zone between the coniferous forest and the arctic wasteland. The line of demarcation between forest and tundra is determined by the climate; it runs farther south in the New than in the Old World. Height above sea-level is another determining factor: tundra-like vegetation is encountered far south of the normal tundra limit in mountainous areas like the Rockies and the Urals.

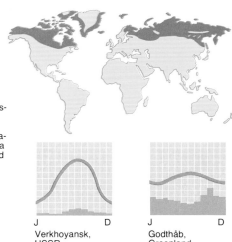

Tundra climate

can vary greatly from place to place. Both the precipitation and its yearly distribution (columns in the climate diagrams) and the temperature (graph curves) depend upon whether the location is maritime or continental. The sea evens out changes in temperature and produces precipitation. The common factor, that which prevents the forest from invading the tundra, is the long, severe winter and the brief summer. The warmest month does not exceed +50°F on average.

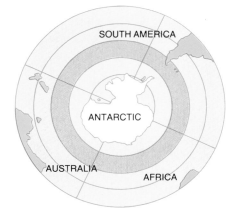

J   D   J   D
Verkhoyansk,   Godthåb,
USSR   Greenland

No tundra in the south

In the southern hemisphere the regions which could be covered with tundra (shown on map below) are nearly all sea. Consequently environments similar to maritime tundra are found only at Tierra del Fuego and in certain oceanic islands. For the same reasons there is no equivalent in the southern hemisphere to the northern coniferous forest region.

Earth, frost and water

When very wet ground freezes, cracks form and fine earth particles fall down into these cracks. Thus every winter fine material moves downwards and coarse material upwards. This process produces different types of stony terrain which on slopes often becomes terraced.

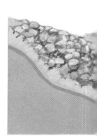

The climatologists have a simple definition for tundra: an area in which the highest monthly mean temperature is between 32°F and 50°F. For ecologists and Eskimos the tundra is the zone between the termination of the forest belt and the ice and barren ground of the arctic wasteland. The climate and natural environment of the tundra is a question not only of latitude but also of elevation. Tundra-like environments are common in mountain ranges far from the normal tundra limits. The tundra climate may be of the maritime type with relatively moderate temperature variations and abundant precipitation, or the continental type: very dry and with extremely cold winters.

The tundra is a world of dramatic seasonal changes. In summertime the landscape throngs with animals and birds which depart in the autumn. Only a few cold-adapted species remain behind and survive the winter. The nature of the ground also changes with the seasons. All year around the permafrost keeps the ground deep-frozen. In northern Siberia it is as deep as 4,921 feet. In the summer a few inches on the surface thaw out, forming an "active zone" in which biological production is possible.

During the most recent glaciation, which came to an end about 10,000 years ago, the greater part of Europe, Asia and North America became tundra. The Ice Age environment and today's tundra have much in common. They are both characterized by few species but many individuals. One single plant species can cover a very large area and birds and mammals are often present in vast flocks or herds. In this unstable environment evolution has not yet had time to create any refined ecological niches.

The hunters and nomads of the tundra employed a simple but sophisticated technology. They did not upset the balance of nature, contenting themselves instead with a "tithe" of the summer's abundant biological production. The food standard could be very high, even though meager years and hunger were by no means unusual. From the mid-18th century onwards Europeans began to move into the arctic regions. The pursuit of furred animals for profit decimated the fauna while at the same time the natives became stricken by disease and alcohol. Military operations in World War II, post-war industrial fishing and drilling for oil have all imposed further strains on the tundra environment.

Newcomers to the tundra have been made to realize, however, that this is an alien world. Those who devote a winter to removing the upper, insulating layer of the ground for the purpose of building an airfield, for example, may find that in the summer when the permafrost thaws out it sinks down into a mire of mud. Destroying the tundra environment is easy enough. To live with it, on the other hand, is difficult; this demands a properly adapted technology and adequate consideration—things with which industrial people are not always overendowed.

Permafrost

Frozen ground

During winter the tundra ground is frozen to a great depth (above) and during the brief summer season only a shallow stratum of surface ground thaws out (right). Below that the ground remains perma- nently frozen, hence the term permafrost. Because this permafrost prevents the absorption of the surface water, the sur- face layer is water-logged and marshy in summertime.

Why the tundra is treeless

Permafrost prevents tree roots from penetrating deep into the ground. Shallow roots are only poorly anchored in the marshy ground and such trees as might grow are blown down by high winds.

Tundra environment

Marshland
The permafrost hinders ground drainage since the surface water is unable to seep down into the subsoil. As a result, during the summer season, large areas turn into marshland where billions of blood-sucking midges are hatched which can drive grazing reindeer into frenzy and death.

Sea and shore
The arctic waters contain abundant nutrition and produce large quantities of crustaceans. As soon as the ice disappears in the spring, large flocks of seafowl and waders appear. Because of the plentiful food they nest in the region, though once their young have learned to fly they return southwards again.

People and the tundra
The early hunters did little harm to the environment. Industrial people do not live on the tundra but they exploit its natural resources, such as oil. Because the season of biological activity is brief, nature has only a limited capacity for decomposing wastes and repairing damage to the vegetation.

Mountain plateaus
Mountain plateaus, worn away and rounded off during past geological epochs, are a common feature of the tundra landscape. The word tundra itself, of Finnish derivation, means a low, barren mountain ridge.

Summer fauna
The few very long summer days produce a wealth of food and this attracts reindeer, for example, and many different species of birds which have spent the winter in the forest belts or even farther south. But the ecological balance is unstable and the animal populations can vary greatly from year to year.

The tundra's vegetation
consists of scrub, mosses, lichens and algae. It seldom grows above knee-height because perennials need the protection of insulating snow in order to survive the winter. Persistent winds also contribute to keeping the brush vegetation low and flattened.

Tundra flora and fauna

On the tundra the winter is the main task-master; the "bottleneck" through which all forms of life have to pass. Adaptations are many and varied: fur, small ears, feathered legs reduce loss of heat. The reindeer move southwards, the lemmings burrow into the ground. The lemmings are well known for their fluctuating population though in fact they share this characteristic with voles and other small rodents. The "rodent explosions" and subsequent population collapses lead to corresponding variations among predators such as the snowy owl and the arctic fox. The non-migratory bird species like the ptarmigan normally turn white during wintertime. The perennial plants adapt themselves to winter conditions by growing low to the ground.

snowy owl · crane · ptarmigan · snow goose · stonecrop · lemming · arctic fox · ice loon · reindeer moss · musk ox · ermine · arctic hare · reindeer (caribou) · bilberry · cup moss

Turf and ice

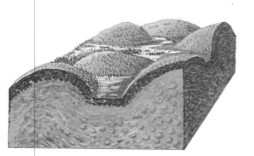

The marshlands of the tundra are made up of small rises, palsas, with swampy depressions between them. When the wet turf freezes it rises to form miniature hills. In the summer only the few top inches thaw out. The following winter more water is absorbed and this freezes, causing the palsas to grow.

Winter camouflage

The appearance of the tundra landscape changes drastically from summer to winter. The lack of protective vegetation makes it doubly necessary for predators and prey alike to assume a white winter camouflage. Because of its white coat the hare is in less danger of being spotted, while the arctic fox's winter color makes it easier for it to stalk its prey. This change in hue is not triggered directly by the snow but by the waning and increasing daylight. Therefore, during winters with little snow, white-colored animals are clearly discernible against the dark ground, while the opposite applies in springs with a lot of snow. Animals that migrate (reindeer) and those that burrow (lemmings) do not need to change color.

Mountain environments

In relation to the size of the Earth even the highest mountains are mere wrinkles on its face. Mt. Everest's height is only one seven hundredth part of the globe's radius and the Himalayas would scarcely be discernible from space, except for the varying colors in the vegetation at different levels. The really high mountain areas are equally small in relation to the lowland plains.

Seemingly minor differences in height above sea level result in major differences in climate, flora and fauna. With an increase of a few hundred feet the environment can change as much as with a shift of several hundred miles towards one of the poles. The ecology of the mountains is therefore very distinct compared with that of the adjoining lowlands. The mountains also influence the lowland climate by affecting air circulation, precipitation and river flow.

Mountains' ecological zones

The mountainside's clearly visible arrangement of "stories", each with its own vegetation, demonstrates the relationship between ecology and elevation. In many instances the highest peaks are entirely devoid of vegetation, with bare rock, permanent snow and glaciers. Glaciers are most usual on the leeward side of the peaks where air turbulence builds up deep snowdrifts.

Below the snow line is found alpine pasture and scrub-covered moorland. The species here are not usually the same as on the arctic tundra but the conditions are similar. In mountainous regions where there are steep slopes the treeline is very sharply demarcated, while on lower subarctic mountains is found a tran-

sitional zone frequently like that between coniferous forest and tundra with increasingly stunted birch forest. It is mainly temperature which determines the level of the treeline, just as it determines the boundary between woodland and tundra, although the wind and the duration of spring snows also play important parts. In tropical mountain regions one encounters specific, very distinctive transitional areas with cloud and mist forest.

In temperate areas the coniferous forest sometimes begins directly at the treeline without the transitional zone of stunted birch forest. In the Alps the silver fir is the most characteristic tree. In this zone pasture is also common. The term "Alp" in German does, in fact, mean a mountain pasture. As the woodland descends the mountainside the proportion of deciduous trees increases steadily, though further down the natural vegetation has been considerably changed through the influence of agriculture.

Because of their mobility, animals are less confined than plants to specific zones. Even above the treeline there are numerous large animal species including reindeer, golden eagles and, in Asia, snow leopards.

Mountains and people

Precipitation is abundant in mountainous regions. Streams tumble down the slopes from mountains and glaciers, forming rapids and waterfalls. Lower down these streams merge into rivers. The Alps are the source of Europe's largest rivers (Rhine, Rhone, Danube, Po) while the Indus, the Ganges, the Mekong and the

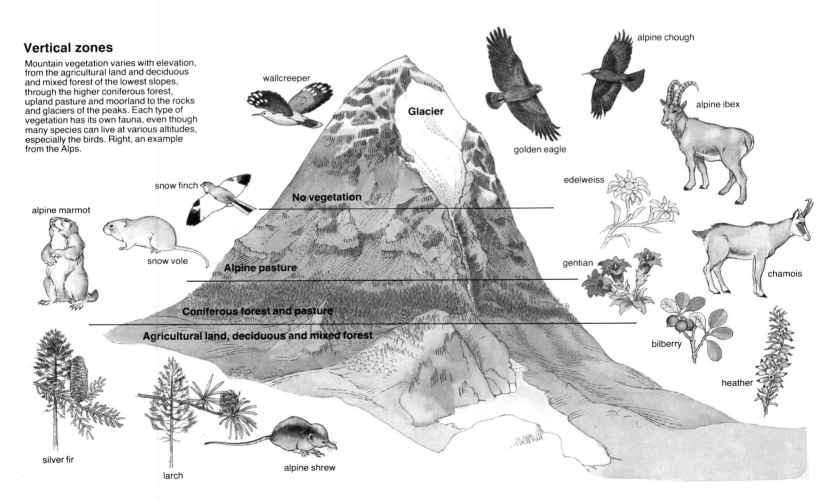

Vertical zones

Mountain vegetation varies with elevation, from the agricultural land and deciduous and mixed forest of the lowest slopes, through the higher coniferous forest, upland pasture and moorland to the rocks and glaciers of the peaks. Each type of vegetation has its own fauna, even though many species can live at various altitudes, especially the birds. Right, an example from the Alps.

alpine chough

wallcreeper

Glacier

golden eagle

alpine ibex

edelweiss

snow finch

No vegetation

alpine marmot

snow vole

Alpine pasture

gentian

chamois

Coniferous forest and pasture

Agricultural land, deciduous and mixed forest

bilberry

heather

silver fir

larch

alpine shrew

Mountains of four continents

Right, profiles across North America, South America, Africa, all in a west/east direction along one line of latitude, and north/south through Asia, i.e. along a meridian. They are all on the same longitudinal scale though the vertical scale is greatly exaggerated. The impression that the plain and mountain regions are distinctly delimited is nevertheless correct.

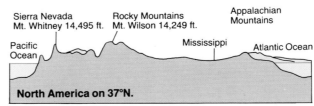

Sierra Nevada Mt. Whitney 14,495 ft. Rocky Mountains Mt. Wilson 14,249 ft. Appalachian Mountains

Pacific Ocean Mississippi Atlantic Ocean

North America on 37°N.

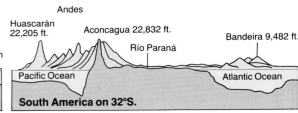

Andes

Huascarán 22,205 ft. Aconcagua 22,832 ft.

Río Paraná Bandeira 9,482 ft.

Pacific Ocean Atlantic Ocean

South America on 32°S.

70

Chang Jiang all rise in the Himalayas. The water flows more slowly through the valleys, depositing sediment. Consequently the valley floors are usually fertile and thickly populated.

In contrast the mountain environment is harsh. Many of our customary crops will not grow at high altitudes. The tribes and peoples who were able to settle in the lowlands preferred to remain there, thereby engendering the traditional antagonism between the "civilized" lowlanders and the "barbaric" mountain folk found all over the world. In the West even in quite recent times "educated" people regarded the mountain world as a horrifying wilderness. From the Renaissance onward there were exceptions—Petrarch and Rousseau among others—though the great change in attitude did not occur before the development of Romanticism in the early 19th century. By this time, roads, railways, bridges and tunnels had made it easier for people to cross and to visit the mountains. Today the mountains of Europe and North America are recreational areas where vacationers seek relaxation and peace, increasingly elusive objectives in the frenzy of modern resorts.

The world's mountain regions
are located where the plates of the Earth's crust have collided, resulting in folding. The Andes, Alps and Himalayas are still being formed through continuing plate movement. The mountains of Scandinavia and Scotland, on the other hand, were first formed some 500 million years ago.

Mountain building

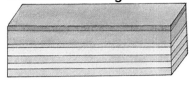

As a rule the rocks that make up the Earth's crust lie in horizontal layers over each other, because the sediments were deposited in water. Uppermost is a layer of loose soils with vegetation.

Mountain climbing
is a dramatic and dangerous hobby cherished by few. Other, less well trained people also seek recreation in the mountains, instead of avoiding such surroundings as they did in the past.

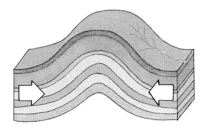

Compression forces of plate-tectonic origin cause the crust to fold, thereby forming a mountain range. The water runs very swiftly down the steep slopes, causing exceptionally rapid erosion.

Elevation zones and climate
The vegetation zones of mountains are largely the same everywhere. The snows of Kilimanjaro and Mt. Kenya are fragments of the Arctic on the equator and below these are moorland tracts and tundra-like vegetation. The snow line is much higher in Africa than it is in Canada, just as are the other zones. The equatorial mountains of Africa also have a belt of mountain rain forest which exists only in the tropics. In Canada, the chilly climate and abundant precipitation causes the west coast glaciers to extend down the mountainsides all the way to the shores of the Pacific.

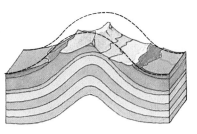

Erosion by running water and glaciers carves out the typical mountain terrain with its pinnacles and precipices, though at the same time this erosion also lowers the ground surface beneath its original level (marked with broken line).

Subarctic and tropical mountains

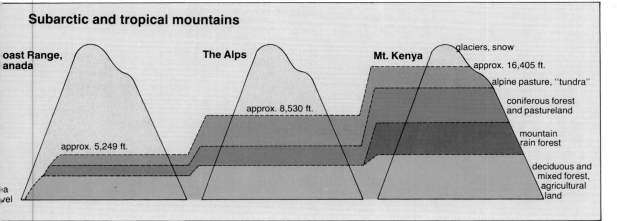

Coast Range, Canada

The Alps

Mt. Kenya

glaciers, snow

approx. 16,405 ft.

alpine pasture, "tundra"

coniferous forest and pastureland

approx. 8,530 ft.

mountain rain forest

approx. 5,249 ft.

deciduous and mixed forest, agricultural land

sea level

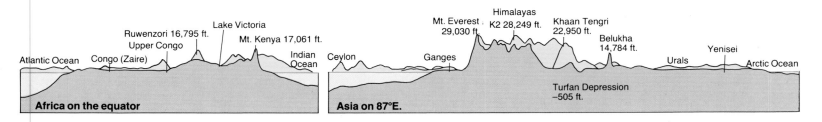

Ruwenzori 16,795 ft.
Upper Congo
Lake Victoria
Mt. Kenya 17,061 ft.
Atlantic Ocean
Congo (Zaire)
Indian Ocean

Africa on the equator

Himalayas
Mt. Everest 29,030 ft.
K2 28,249 ft.
Khaan Tengri 22,950 ft.
Belukha 14,784 ft.
Ceylon
Ganges
Urals
Yenisei
Arctic Ocean
Turfan Depression −505 ft.

Asia on 87°E.

71

Living off the land

The crop cycle

Tropical land clearance
Clearance by burning in forest and savanna regions is one of the earliest of all forms of farming. This is how it is employed (right) in the mountains of New Guinea. After 14–24 months the fields are abandoned and the forest reclaims the land, which is then left undisturbed for several decades. If the revegetation is allowed to continue uninterrupted then the effects on the environment are minimal. But where an expanding population and indigence lead to more ruthless clearing methods the outcome can be a breakdown in the entire ecological system.

clearing the ground

fencing in and planting

The ground is cleared and trees and branches burned. Minerals in the ash add to the soil's nutrition. Tree stumps and large trunks are left where they are, which prevents erosion in steep mountainous terrain.

The fields are fenced in to keep animals out. Taro, yams, beans, bananas, etc. are planted in mixed lots so that several layers of foliage protect the ground against violent rains, while the maximum benefit is derived from the sun.

Rice growing
Of all the world's cereals rice is the most widely used as a staple food, and most of this is paddy rice which requires an efficient irrigation system. The communities of S.E. Asia and S. China are greatly influenced by the needs and routines of rice growing. Depending upon the local climate a rice field can give as much as three crops a year though most farmers use a crop rotation system, growing rice during only part of the growing season. An alternative "crop" is fish, which can be bred in the flooded paddy fields.

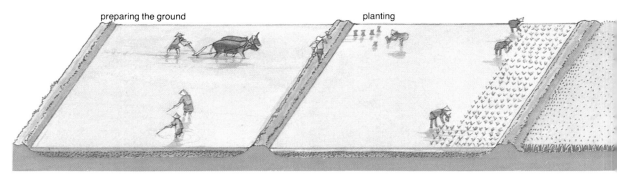

preparing the ground

planting

The field is inundated. The ground is prepared with hoes, water buffalo-hauled plows and motor-cultivators. This produces a layer of mud on the bottom. Banks between the fields retain the water and serve as pathways.

The rice plants, germinated in seed beds, are set out by hand in the mud. Rice growing requires a large workforce, but labor is abundant and so cheap that full mechanization of the system would not be worthwhile.

Autumn wheat
is an important crop in the temperate zones. All cereals are cultivated grass species and the autumn sowing of wheat imitates the normal reproductive cycle of the grasses: the mature plants spread their seed in the autumn, these lie dormant during the winter and germinate in the spring. Another variety is spring wheat: the seed is sown in the spring and harvested the same autumn. In this latter case, however, harvesting has to be later in the season. Autumn wheat is therefore more suitable in regions where the growing season is short.

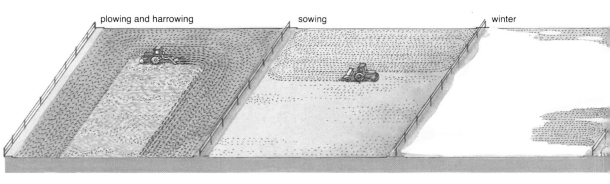

plowing and harrowing

sowing

winter

The land is first plowed and harrowed. This keeps the weeds down and gives the wheat shoots a vital head start. Sowing, formerly done by hand, is now entirely mechanized.

It is an advantage if during the winter season the ground is protected against frost by an insulating layer of snow. A cold winter with a shortage of snow often leads to a poor crop. As soon as the snow melts and the sun warms the ground the seeds begin to germinate.

In many cases a transition to farming has occurred in response to a local food crisis. People who hunt and gather have an excellent knowledge of practical biology and it is not usually ignorance that deters them from farming. But as long as they can continue the free life of the hunter they are disinclined to become involved in the arduous and monotonous toil of agriculture. Farming emerges in areas where a growing population has already initiated permanent settlement and where the traditional sources of food have begun to fail. In the Near East this took place some eight to ten thousand years ago. There the Triticum genus of cereal grasses came to play an important role as food. When the seeds were no longer collected from wild stands but were harvested from cultivated fields, then grass became domesticated wheat.

Earlier prehistorians regarded the rearing of livestock as more "primitive" and therefore of older date than arable farming. This is not the case. It was the farmers who first began rearing sheep and goats, cattle and pigs in order to add meat and milk to their cereal diet. Livestock nomadism is an ecological adaptation to arid areas where agriculture is an uncertain occupation.

The transition to permanent inhabitation and farming was a revolution: the population could increase and taxes could be extracted from the peasants to feed kings, priests, scribes and soldiers. Farming paved the way for social differentiation and specialization, though for all that it was not altogether a blessing. Unbalanced diet and contagious disease are believed to have shortened the average lifespan and many early settlements literally became buried in their own refuse.

The greater part of the world's population is still engaged in farming. Between 75–90 % of Third World inhabitants work the land, though what they produce is scarcely sufficient to meet their needs. The saleable surplus is small: the farming is aimed at self-subsistence. In the industrial countries, on the other hand, seldom more than five to ten per cent of the people are engaged in commercial farming, yet their "cash crops" feed the nation. Just how has this difference come about?

Agriculture "fixes" solar energy in energy-abundant foodstuffs. This output of comestible energy requires an input of work energy. In "primitive" farming the input consists mainly of muscle work—the energy of people and animals which in turn derives from food that has recently been produced. This agricultural energy balance yields a surplus which can be utilized for other

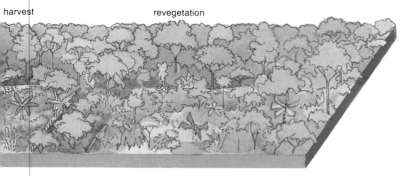

harvest   revegetation

New trees start growing even during the short cultivation period and the farmers encourage these; the fences protect them against animals. Thus when these fields are ultimately abandoned the revegetation process is very swift.

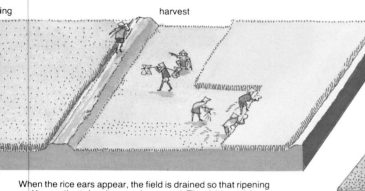

ing   harvest

When the rice ears appear, the field is drained so that ripening and harvesting take place on dry ground. The sickle and the carrying pole are still the most important implements in the Asian rice-growing areas.

growth   harvest

Weeds usually have to be combatted during the growing season. The harvest is a critical operation, dependent on fine weather since wet grain quickly deteriorates. Harvesting thus has to be a rapid process and is therefore highly mechanized.

Agricultural revolutions
The earliest advance from hunting and gathering to farming occurred independently in at least four regions: the Iran highlands, S.E. Asia, W. Africa and Central America. Many important cultivated plants have also been domesticated outside these areas.

bare ground   grasses and   perennials   young wood   climax
               annuals   and bushes   forest

The natural succession
If a piece of land is cleared, and then left untended, grasses and annuals are the first plants to grow there. After 1–2 years perennials emerge and these are followed by young trees. In climatically favorable areas the final vegetation consists of full-grown forest. In the first stage of this succession (dotted rectangle) the growth rate of the biomass is greatest. The farmer keeps the land at this peak-production stage by combatting weeds, periodic harvests and plowing-in of surplus biomass.

Using productive land
Subsistence agriculture using simple implements is still practised in most parts of the Third World. Terraced rice fields have created a unique "rice landscape" in E. Asia. Wheat and milk production are predominant in the temperate zones while extensive livestock rearing is important where there is little rainfall and irrigation is not possible. Forestry is a mechanized industry. Trees grow slowly, maturing from 20 years in the tropics to as much as 150 years in cold climates.

activities. Modern farming methods are far more productive, but this high productivity is attained through a massive contribution of energy from elsewhere—industrially generated energy invested in fuels, fertilizers, biocides, mechanized irrigation and transport. This overall contribution is so great that it cannot be derived from fixed solar energy; most of it originates in coal and oil. Thus, strictly in terms of energy, modern agriculture produces a deficit. But the overall yield is impressive, even though the labor intensive farming of South-east Asia probably gives the greatest return per unit area.

Modern agriculture is thus impossible without an industrial foundation. But the food we consume in the industrial society comes almost exclusively from farming and in that respect we all live in an agricultural society. If our agricultural system were to break down then no amount of advanced industrial technology could save us from starvation.

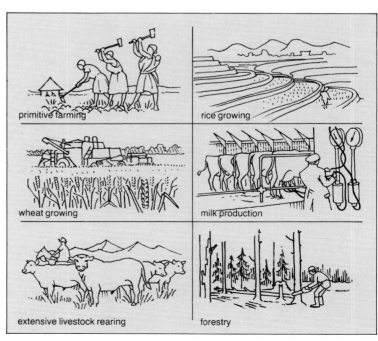

primitive farming   rice growing

wheat growing   milk production

extensive livestock rearing   forestry

Urbanization

Urbanization of the landscape

The sites upon which our great cities stand were once virgin land onto which people gradually encroached. Populations have grown steadily through the centuries. This gradual, continuous process does not in itself lead to urbanization, but at one stage in the progression the town forms. It usually becomes clearly demarcated from the surrounding countryside and an exchange and interaction develops between these two environments.

Medieval town
Villages at an intersection of two trade routes or where a temporal or church authority is established begin to turn to trade. The inhabitants protect their property and privileges by building a city wall. But for a long time to come there remain both orchards and cowsheds within the walls. It is not until an increase in prosperity and population has taken place that the towns begin to assume a really urban character.

Natural landscape
The greater part of northern Europe was once primeval forest with an occasional simple shelter for hunters or farmers engaged in primitive farming. The only forms of transport were foot and packhorse. People still lived in tribes and clans.

The pioneers
Because of the shortage of land in the farming districts, people clear new ground in the forests. Increasing populations make shifting agriculture difficult and necessitate a more settled life. This in its turn demands improved farming methods and a more established social organization.

Farming landscape
The clearings merge and form farming districts and the farms grow into villages. Woods are now permitted to remain only on land that is difficult to work. Marginal land is used for grazing and this and the woodland are common land belonging to the village.

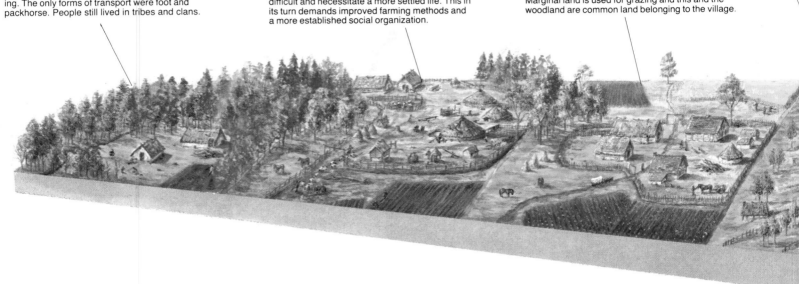

A collection of buildings or a gathering of people in one place does not necessarily create a town. There are farming areas on Java, for example, where the population density is greater than in many European cities, yet these areas are not urban. The definition of the city or town is primarily functional: the inhabitants specialize in things other than the production of foodstuffs and raw materials. They are engaged in industry, trade, service, administration, research and development.

The town-country relationship has not always been a benign one. In most early civilizations, the rural population would have managed just as well or even better without towns. It was not until the emergence of the industrial town that the urban community was able to offer its rural counterpart something worthwhile in exchange for the latter's foodstuffs and raw materials: industrial products (machines, chemicals) which could increase agricultural production.

The earliest towns
The villages where those in power resided and where they gathered in the surplus products of their subjects, grew into the first towns. Here dwelled not only the rulers but also the priests who vindicated the rulers' powers, the soldiers who slaughtered the rulers' enemies, the clerks, the artisans and the servants, and the merchants who managed the exchange of goods between the different towns. This pattern existed not only in the city-states of the Near East some 5,000 years ago (Sumerian, Egyptian) but throughout all Asia.

The oldest cities grew organically and with little planning. Successive layers of refuse gradually accumulated in Ur and Troy and beneath the foundations of modern London lie the remains of Roman Londinium. Defense and traffic sometimes gave rise to a certain degree of planning but first and foremost it was the ruling faction which determined developments according to its own particular requirements. Broad avenues and palaces contrasted harshly with the hovels of the poor.

The cities of western Asia often have a continuous history extending back to the most ancient civilizations. Jericho is probably the world's oldest inhabited city (from c. 8000 BC) and Damascus is believed to be the next oldest.

Town planning
In the West the Romans were the first to engage in large-scale town planning. Most of the European medieval towns expanded spontaneously, but newly established towns were planned with a regular network of streets. Renaissance and Baroque planning was aesthetic and symbolic in intention; to the honor of God or a worldly prince. The achievements of this planning can still be studied in papal Rome and the Paris of the absolute monarchs. Practical, social and hygienic needs were ignored. In the 18th century the traveler could recognize the stench of Hamburg long before the city came into sight. The urban population growth arising from industrialization was accompanied by appalling sanitation and social misery. A series of cholera epidemics in the mid-19th century compelled the authorities to install sewer and water pipes and to introduce elementary building by-laws at least in the western European cities. This legislation represented the advent of the highly regulated urban communities of our day.

Megalopolis—and afterwards?
The cities of the industrial world have grown very large, but more characteristic still of our century is the tendency for these large cities to merge into urban agglomerations. Typical examples of this are the Boston-Washington area in the USA, Randstad in the Netherlands and the Rhine-Ruhr district in Germany. In the Third World it is the core cities which are growing or which, rather, are being stifled by their explosively expanding peripheral slums.

The latest censuses in the USA indicate that the agglomeration growth there has come to a standstill. Is the centuries-old urbanization trend about to turn? It has occurred before in history that big cities have reverted to mere villages, or disappeared altogether as the fates of Babylon, Carthage and Troy amply testify.

Urban landscape

The once compact and centralized town has expanded into a widespread urban landscape. Rising land prices have led to taller and taller buildings while increasingly large areas are covered by motorways and complex traffic systems. The big cities of the Third World (right: Mexico City) have a superficially modern appearance, though their productive functions are relatively poorly developed and a large proportion of the inhabitants lack regular employment. The social mobility in these cities and the chances of temporary work attract a constant influx of people from the rural areas where conditions are still worse.

Industrial town

Towns now develop a more regular layout with paved streets and piped water and drainage systems. Factories grow up on the outskirts, their chimneys competing with church towers and steeples to form the skyline. A structural pattern is established with administrative and commercial activities in the center and industry and workers' accommodation around the outskirts.

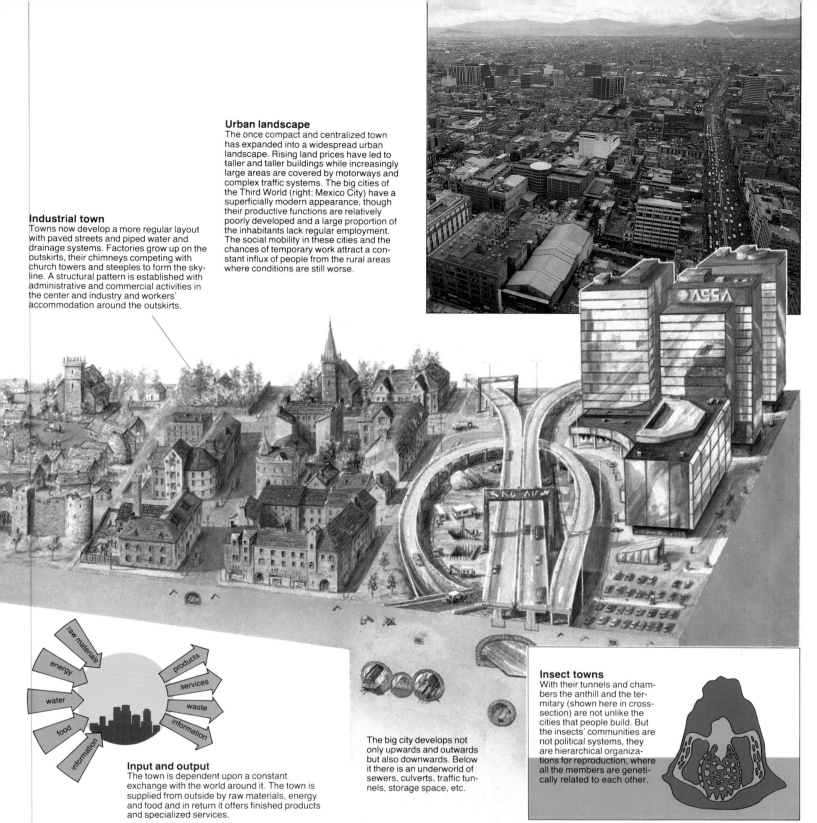

Input and output

The town is dependent upon a constant exchange with the world around it. The town is supplied from outside by raw materials, energy and food and in return it offers finished products and specialized services.

raw materials · energy · water · food · information · products · services · waste · information

The big city develops not only upwards and outwards but also downwards. Below it there is an underworld of sewers, culverts, traffic tunnels, storage space, etc.

Insect towns

With their tunnels and chambers the anthill and the termitary (shown here in cross-section) are not unlike the cities that people build. But the insects' communities are not political systems, they are hierarchical organizations for reproduction, where all the members are genetically related to each other.

The expanding towns

The largest cities

The trading and industrial centers of Europe and North America were once the biggest cities in the world. Presently, however, the growing cities of the Third World often contain larger populations. Lack of consistency between administrative and demographic limits and uncertain statistics make comparisons difficult. Consequently the following table of the ten largest cities of the world must be regarded as approximate only:

Mexico City	14.0 million inhabitants
Tokyo	11.6 million inhabitants
Shanghai	10.8 million inhabitants
Buenos Aires	10.3 million inhabitants
New York	9.2 million inhabitants
Beijing (Peking)	8.5 million inhabitants
Paris	8.4 million inhabitants
Moscow	8.0 million inhabitants
Seoul	7.8 million inhabitants
São Paulo	7.2 million inhabitants

How the city expands

The growth of a city creates a system of differentiated zones. The historical nucleus, comprising administrative and commercial functions, is surrounded by densely built older housing. Beyond this there is a belt of industry and beyond that again more recent housing areas. Pressure on the city center is relieved by satellite towns, which are smaller editions of the city itself with their own centers and industrial areas. The system of radial transport routes reveals that their independence is illusory. This city plan is based on Paris; for historical reasons other cities, especially those outside Europe, may have quite another structure.

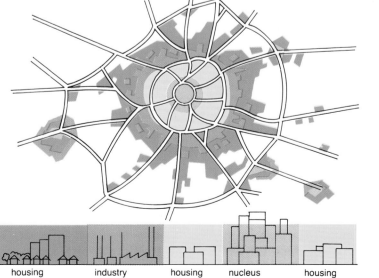

satellite town

industry · nucleus · housing · housing · industry · housing · nucleus · housing

Treasures underground

Ore is a mineral which contains a concentration of metal that is worth extracting. Consequently, the definition of "ore" is essentially an economic matter. Because of great variations in raw material prices a mineral that is not worth mining today may easily be worth mining tomorrow, and vice versa. But it is not only ores that are of economic significance; numerous industrial minerals are also mined, from quartzite and dolomite for steel mill furnaces to sand and clay for the cement and building industries.

Metal ores
Metals are rare components of the Earth's crust. Workable ores appear either when metal-abundant magma rises from deeper strata within the Earth's interior, or when metal compounds in the ground or beneath the sea become concentrated through natural processes.

We have long known how ores form in the continental crust, but we remained ignorant for a long time of how they formed under the sea. Remarkable discoveries were made at the close of the 1970's when research submarines descended to the mid-ocean ridges along the bed of the Pacific. Scientists observed how hot springs spewed up black, metalliferous water and built up cones of metal minerals. The plate tectonic theory also explains how other ores are formed; showing how, why and where magma rises upwards through the crust. This takes place mainly in areas adjoining those where an oceanic crustal plate is pressed down under a neighboring plate to become remelted within the mantle.

Mining through the ages
Mining is of earlier origin than our use of metals. A number of flint mines from the late Stone Age have been found in northwest and central Europe. Extracting metals from ores required metallurgic skills and the ability to generate and regulate heat. The mine and mining operations did not change very much, however, before the end of the Middle Ages. By then the mines of central Europe had become so deep that they required pumps and haulage equipment driven by water power. During the 19th

How ores are formed:
Most of the metals we use are heavy elements, but these are not often encountered in the Earth's crust, the principal components of which are silica and aluminium. The heavier metals, mainly iron, sank downwards into the Earth's interior when the young planet began to heat up from the inside and developed its present structure with a core, a mantle and a lithosphere, each with different chemical compositions. Ores are formed when metalliferous magmas or solutions move upwards from the Earth's mantle. We still know very little about the processes in the mantle, but we do know what happens when the molten minerals reach the crust. The more significant of these processes are analyzed on the right. Ores of magmatic origin can subsequently be weathered, swept away as grains or nuggets and then be deposited by sedimentation far from their place of origin. Finally, certain ores may have formed by precipitation from metalliferous solutions in marshland with a high content of hydrogen sulfide.

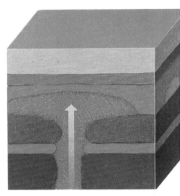

Intrusion
Metalliferous magma rises from below in the Earth's mantle and forms a distinctly defined ore-body higher up in the Earth's crust, or on the surface as lava.

century mining operations became mechanized through such innovations as steam-powered lift-cages and fans. The deepest mine in the world today is a South African gold mine which reaches 12,661 ft. in depth.

Many ores come mainly from open-cast mines, others from underground. Nowadays the ore is concentrated at the site of the mine and further refined as pulverized ore concentrate or as small pellets. Nonferrous ores, principally sulfide ores, contain various metals which have to be separated by chemical and physical processes.

Metallurgy
Until the 18th century practically all metallurgic processes used charcoal, which served both as a source of heat and as an agent for reducing the oxides in the ore. Later, however, the steel industry moved on to coke processes. The modern steel industry

The world's metals
The most important metals and annual production (in millions of tons) at the beginning of the 1980's:

Iron	530.2
Aluminium	83.9
Manganese	9.4
Copper	7.9
Zinc	5.7
Chrome	4.3
Lead	3.5

Underground mining
Main shaft, ventilation and pumping shafts are drilled down to the ore-body which is then worked in galleries, i.e. large chambers, at increasingly deep levels. The ore is transported on small railways or by trucks. At each level there are complete systems incorporating transport tunnels, workshops, stores etc.

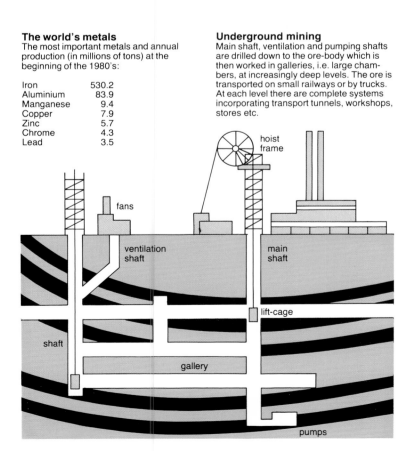

Mining—then and now
The Stone Age flint mines, the Bronze Age copper mines and the medieval iron mines all looked much the same (left). The modern mine on the other hand is a highly mechanized, large-scale industry. Below: open-cast iron mining in Liberia. Many important mining areas are now located far away from traditional industrial centers.

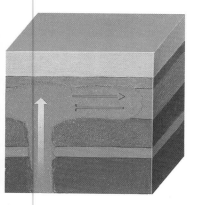

Contact metamorphosis
The magma heats up and transmutes the rock with which it comes into contact. An exchange of atoms occurs so that metal atoms from the magma move into the transmuted (metamorphic) rock.

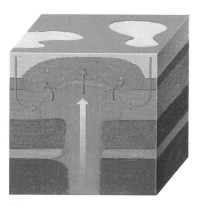

Water-carried minerals
Water from above, seeping down to a magma intrusion, can dissolve certain ion complexes which are subsequently precipitated and left behind in adjacent rock.

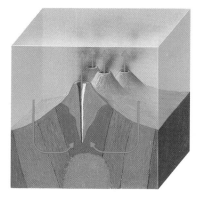

Mineral springs under the sea
Along the mid-ocean ridges, sea water can penetrate downwards to meet the rising magma. When the now hot and metalliferous water is suddenly cooled off through contact with sea water, copper, nickel and manganese minerals are precipitated on the seabed.

Sedimentation
Decomposition products from an ore-body that has reached the surface can result in metal in the sediment. An example of this process is gold sand and nuggets on the beds of river valleys and deltas.

primarily uses electricity for heat, and oxygen as a reducing agent. Electro-chemical separation processes are becoming more and more common since these conserve more energy: the metal does not have to be heated repeatedly as it did formerly.

Metallurgy has developed new products such as alloy steel and various light metals. Also, metals now have competition in the form of new, synthetic materials. Yet despite this and despite the immense recycling capacity of the scrap-metal industry, our civilization remains dependent upon ore production. A medium-sized car contains 1,763 lbs. steel and 286 lbs. of nonferrous metals. However, the treasures under the ground are not inexhaustible and if the level of car ownership in the world as a whole were as high per capita as that in western Europe and the USA, then the car industry alone would exhaust all known reserves of iron ore.

The tapping, when the molten steel is run off into transport vessels or molds, is a critical phase in the manufacturing process.

From blast furnace to scrap yard

In the modern steel mill many of the manufacturing phases are integrated in a semi-continuous process. The blast furnace is charged with ore, limestone and coke which reduce the oxides in the ore. The coal content in the molten iron is lowered by injection of oxygen or air. Alloying materials are added in an electrically heated oven. The molten steel is then cast in blocks which are afterwards reheated and rolled into sheeting or sections in a hydraulically powered rolling mill.

The scrap yard is the final resting place of the car, but not of the steel in that car. Scrap metal is one of the most important raw materials of the industrial world and forms the basis of a busy international trade.

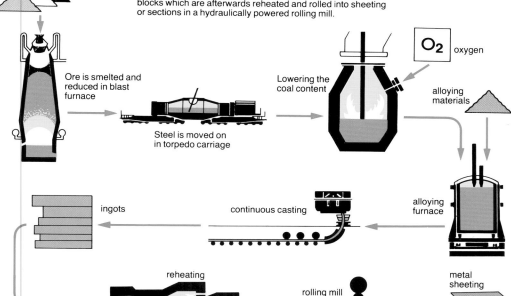

dolomite
coke
ore

Ore is smelted and reduced in blast furnace

Steel is moved on in torpedo carriage

Lowering the coal content

O_2 oxygen

alloying materials

ingots

continuous casting

alloying furnace

reheating

rolling mill

metal sheeting

The ravaged Earth

Gone forever

No species survives forever. But a large number of plant and animal species has been exterminated prematurely with the help of people.

The migration of people to America via the Bering Strait (arrow on map, left) probably had disastrous consequences for the continent's fauna.

Humans are suspected

At the close of the Ice Age there were large numbers of animal species on the North American prairies, including the giant ground sloth Mylodon (left). This "megafauna" suddenly died out at about the time people arrived on the scene. Many scientists suspect people that exterminated them. Slow moving and slow thinking creatures like the mylodon had no chance of survival against the super-predator, humans.

Humans are guilty

The dodo was a turkey-sized, flightless bird which lived on Mauritius in the Indian Ocean. When European seafarers arrived they began killing and eating the dodos and any that managed to escape became the victims of feral dogs and swine. The last specimen died around 1680 and all that remains of the dodo today is a preserved head in Copenhagen and a foot in London.

Threatened environments

Deforestation

The greatest threat to the world's flora and fauna is the destruction of living environments. No species can survive outside the environment to which it has been adapted. One of the most species-abundant habitats in the world is the rain forest, which is now being destroyed at an increasing rate. In fact all natural forests throughout the world are threatened. At best they are replaced by commercial forest monoculture, at worst by a meager scrub terrain broken up by erosion.

Cultivating the grass plains

The prairies of North America have more or less disappeared. The growing population of Africa is burning off the savannas with their wealth of animal life to make way for an agriculture of doubtful viability. Traditional farming methods are both uncertain and dangerous in dry areas. Attempts to cultivate the steppes of Central Asia have led to many disastrous setbacks.

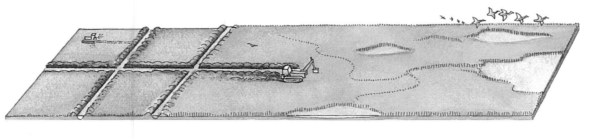

Draining the wetlands

The wetlands are not only living environments in themselves, they also play an important part in the hydrological cycle. They even out the flow rate of the rivers and improve the sub-surface water supply. But many wetlands are either drained off or filled in to make industrial or housing developments. Attempts to turn wetlands into arable land usually result in a low yield from poor soil.

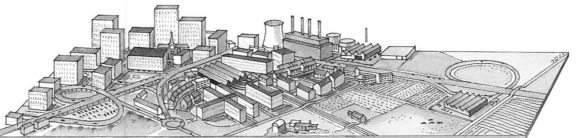

Asphalting the fields

Towns usually develop in good agricultural areas and urbanization has often meant the sacrifice of productive land for housing developments, streets and parking lots. In this way arable land is transformed into a biologically unproductive wasteland. It will be economically and probably physically impossible to restore such land to farmland again.

Endangered animal species

Many animal species are threatened with extinction; the list of endangered vertebrates alone is frightening. The nature of the threat varies: European birds of prey are menaced by egg-collectors while the tiger's jungle is being felled. Some of the species shown here are probably already beyond saving, while others may survive provided they are given protection. The numbers of threatened plants and lower animals are even higher, but despite the fact that their extinction can have grave consequences to us, little attention is paid to their fate.

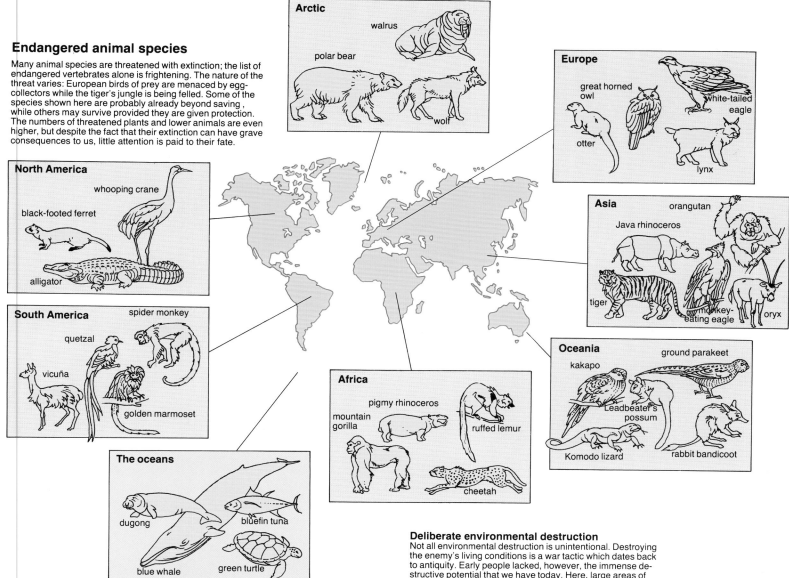

Through evolution every animal and plant species has adapted to its particular habitat; its living environment. This environment is shaped by climate and soil, but above all by the other species within it. About 300 years ago one of the species of tree on Mauritius suddenly ceased reproducing and today only a few specimens remain. Research has revealed that the seeds in the tree's fruit would only grow after having first passed through the digestive system of the dodo—and this bird became extinct towards the end of the 17th century. Indirect extermination through the destruction of a habitat is even more disastrous than direct assault with gun and axe.

People believe they have "conquered" nature and made themselves independent of it, but that is not so. People are biological creatures with biological needs. Without nature civilization is impossible. We are therefore dependent upon other animals and plants in our habitat, from whales and tigers to microscopic bacteria. No species can destroy its own living environment without perishing.

Because of this we must safeguard our own environment by protecting threatened species and vulnerable habitats—partly through the establishment of nature reserves but above all by learning how to use the world prudently and considerately. Ultimately, however, all this is both insufficient and impossible; the laws of change and evolution prescribe that no species can live forever and that no environment can be made eternally stable. We have to accept the responsibility to not only preserve but also create living environments for ourselves and for the other species we are going to share them with. Those who now destroy must become creators. Only then can the Earth be made permanently inhabitable for people, and for the species into which we will ultimately evolve.

Deliberate environmental destruction

Not all environmental destruction is unintentional. Destroying the enemy's living conditions is a war tactic which dates back to antiquity. Early people lacked, however, the immense destructive potential that we have today. Here, large areas of forest in Vietnam have been defoliated in attempts to prevent guerrilla troops from utilizing woodland cover.

People's impact on the Earth's crus

1

Humans as diggers

Ever since the late Stone Age, people have been engaged in re-arranging the surface of the Earth using the simplest of tools such as spades, mattocks, baskets, carts and wheelbarrows. These laborious but cheap methods are still useful in developing countries where large numbers of people can be mobilized for large undertakings. Such methods were an important factor in China's huge water regulating projects in the 1950's and 1960's (right). Industrialized countries use fewer people and larger machines (left).

Forest is felled excessively for timber or fuel, to make way for commercial agriculture or, in many countries, for primitive, subsistence farming.

When the protective trees are felled the humus layer is easily destroyed and running water erodes the land.

Humans, the geological force

In the long term our interference with the Earth can have unfortunate consequences (right). The destruction is usually of an indirect nature, when the protective covering of vegetation is removed and erosion commences. Drainage, irrigation projects and open-cast mining are other examples of our modification of the land. The destruction of the land is sometimes the result of a deliberate undertaking for immediate financial gain, though more often it is caused by poor people's day-to-day struggle for survival; need rather than profit being the motivation.

The draining of wetlands eliminates important ecosystems and also reduces the percolation of sub-surface water.

Open-cast mining leaves lasting scars. The water table often sinks and waste heaps can leak heavy metals.

People create their own landscape, for better or for worse. This fact is immediately evident in the agricultural regions of Western Europe, China and South-east Asia, but even in the more sparsely populated countries the landscape is scarcely "natural". Maps showing "natural vegetation" tend to show how things would have looked without intervention by people.

People do not only interfere with the vegetation however, they also alter the Earth's crust. Even the simplest of tools such as shovels and carts are sufficient to bring about large scale changes on the face of the Earth. The methods used to build the great Pyramids and the Chinese Wall are still employed today. The scope for re-forming the landscape is, of course, much greater in industrial countries where use is made of earth-moving machinery, heavy trucks and explosives. When people operate as a geological force it is usually in an indirect fashion, by modifying or removing the vegetation. The results can be destructive (soil erosion, desert spreading or waterlogging), though people also create stable, highly productive environments. In South-east Asia, for example, there are terraced fields which, according to archaeologists, have been used continuously for five or six thousand years. On the other hand, in the American prairie states a few decades of ruthless cultivation in a dry climate led in

the 1930's to the dustbowl disasters when the wind carried all the soil away. Vast, fertile areas around the Euphrates, the Tigris and the Indus which once sustained the earliest civilizations, have since become sterile or waterlogged and excessively saline because of imprudent farming methods.

Interference with vegetation also leads to changes in the hydrological cycle which in their turn can cause changes in the landscape. A high proportion of silt in river water can clog up reservoirs and irrigation ditches and even cause the river itself to change course. A high silt content often derives from deforestation around the upper reaches of the river. Silting up of this kind can be combated by reafforestation and other anti-erosion measures. A high silt content can sometimes have advantages. Silt from the Nile fertilized the Egyptian fields every year until the Aswan High Dam terminated the annual flooding. Damming has increased the need for expensive, imported artificial fertilizers, has ruined fishing in the delta and has put the delta itself, the most fertile region in Egypt, in danger of being washed away altogether by the sea. Our capacity to change the face of the Earth is great, but our willingness to recognize the consequences of our actions is often considerably less.

Changing the course of rivers

Six million years ago the Caspian Sea was a deep basin in an inland sea which stretched from the Carpathians to the Aral Sea. Today it is in danger of drying up because of the high rate of evaporation and inadequate inflow from the rivers. Large areas (dark blue on map, left) are below sea level. Already some of the Don's water is being redirected into the Volga (shorter red arrow) and there are plans to lead water from the Sea of Azov to the Caspian (long arrow). This would make it possible to stabilize the water in the latter at its existing level.

Dams and silting

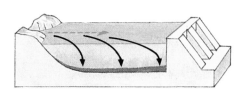

The rivers' silt transport capacity depends upon the flow of water. If a river is dammed up the speed of the current is reduced. The silt particles can no longer remain suspended in the water . . .

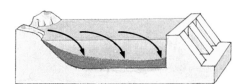

. . . but sink to the bottom. This process covers the bottom with an increasingly thick layer of sediment and the reservoir above the dam becomes progressively shallower.

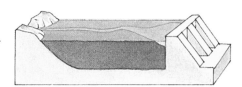

In the end the reservoir is completely silted up except for a channel down the center. This process is a long-term threat to regulated, silt-abundant rivers like the Nile and the Huang He.

Heavy machines tear up the ground, destroy the vegetation and thereby upset the microclimate and the ground level environment.

Overgrazing destroys the turf itself, the pasture is trampled out of existence and the wind blows the soil away.

In dry climates, grass burning followed by the planting of crops can also result in the ruination of the ground through soil erosion.

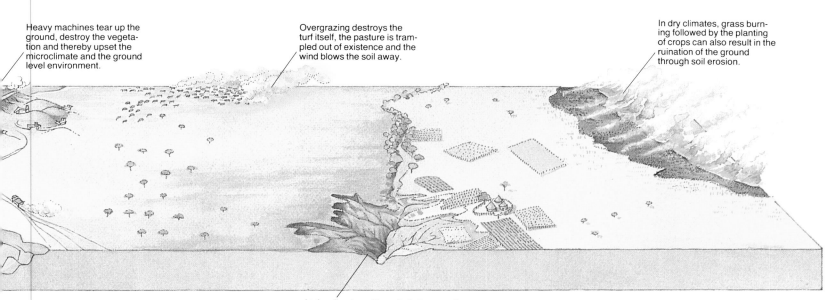

In dry climates with periodic heavy rains excessive cultivation can lead to gully erosion.

Dust storms

arise when strong winds stir up fine particles on the ground and carry them away. This can only happen where there is no ground vegetation to impede the wind and consequently dust storms are common in desert regions. As a result of extensive farming, the farmlands of the US prairie states were turned into barren dustbowls by storms in the 1930's. Measures to restore ground vegetation are now overcoming the wind-erosion problem, but local dust storms do still occur (below).

Our landscape

A landscape like the one below (north-east USA) is the product of our civilization. There is no natural vegetation at all. Prudent farming methods properly adapted to terrain and climate can make such an environment stable and productive for centuries.

The land can be protected

Careful cultivation methods, the retaining of woodland and new shelter plantations can give protection against wind erosion. Contour plowing, with the furrows parallel to the elevation contours of the terrain, prevents water from washing the soil away. These methods have been applied on the farmland, right.

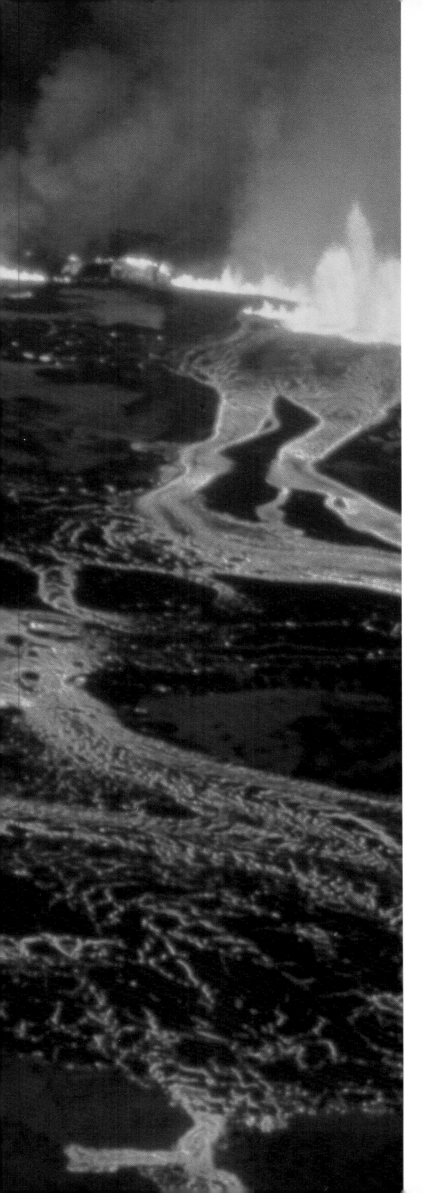

Fire

Crouched around their night fires our early ancestors gazed out into the darkness. Occasionally they saw the gleam of a pair of eyes. That blackness beyond the circle of their fire was a realm of terror, the haunt of real beasts of prey and imagined spirits and monsters.

According to Greek mythology the cultural awakening came when Prometheus stole fire from the gods and gave it to humans. As myth gave way to philosophy, fire found a new advocate in Heracleitus—a thinker who lived around 500 BC in the Greek city of Ephesus in Asia Minor.

Heracleitus was a dialectic philosopher. He regarded the world not as an object or as a state but as a continuous process, a flux. He claimed that everything flows, that one cannot step twice into the same river because the water in it is never the same. In the all-consuming and constantly changing fire he saw the primary element. Today we know that fire is not an element at all, but a transformation, a process.

As recently as the 18th century chemists regarded heat as a physical substance called phlogiston. Warm bodies contained more phlogiston than cold bodies. In combustion, it was believed, the phlogiston was released from the fuel.

With the discovery of oxygen by the English chemist Priestley and the Swede Scheele, it became evident that combustion was an oxidization process and the phlogiston theory was rendered untenable. It was finally dispelled through the study of thermodynamics, a science which was inspired by the steam engine and which describes energy conversions, such as the conversion of heat into motion. Today the term heat describes a form of electromagnetic radiation and also molecular movements.

Heracleitus has to some extent been vindicated by modern cosmology. Scientists are now inclined to believe that the universe was actually born in the fireball of the "big bang". All the energy around us, from the heat in the bowels of the Earth and the light of the sun's nuclear fires, to the cosmic background radiation only a few degrees above absolute zero, is ultimately a remnant of the "big bang": the primary fire. Sometime in the incomprehensibly far-off future fire may fail and darkness fall over the cosmos.

The primordial fire

No matter how often we gaze up at the stars we are unlikely to observe any changes from one night to the next. The idea of the universe being in a steady state with neither beginning nor end seems natural enough. Nevertheless every civilization has had its own legend about creation. The biblical account is found in the Book of Genesis: "And God said: Let there be Light; and there was Light".

The idea of the steady state was reinforced by natural science and this, despite biblical beliefs, was the predominant cosmological theory well into our century. In the 1920's the American astronomer Hubble discovered that light from distant galaxies is shifted further towards the red, longwave end of the spectrum, the farther away these galaxies are. Not until after prolonged debate did scientists accept the most simple explanation for this: the shifting results from the Doppler effect and the galaxies are moving out and away from us at tremendous speed. Finally by the 1960's it became clear that the universe is indeed expanding. It was then a simple matter for the cosmologists to determine the

The creation

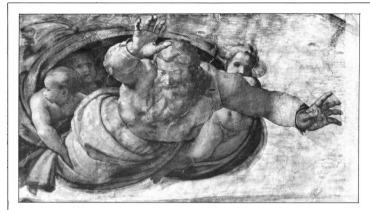

In the Bible's account of the creation (above, detail from Michelangelo's painting) God made the difference between light and darkness, thereby establishing the visible universe.

12 billion years	11	10	9	8	7	6	5

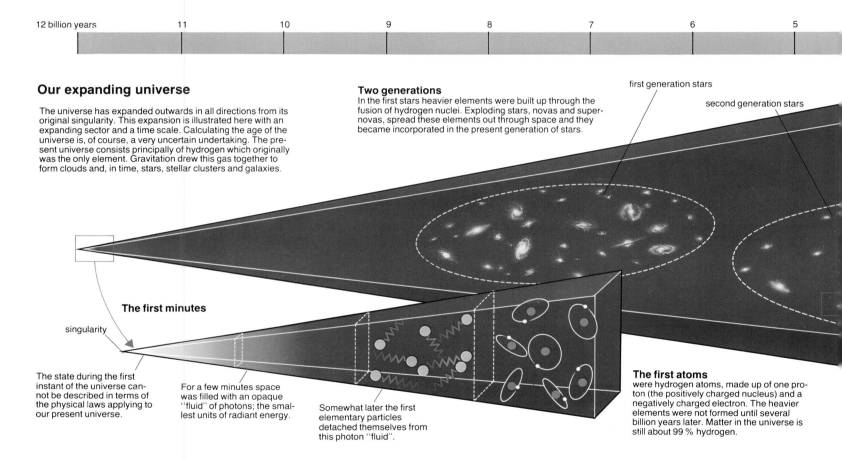

Our expanding universe

The universe has expanded outwards in all directions from its original singularity. This expansion is illustrated here with an expanding sector and a time scale. Calculating the age of the universe is, of course, a very uncertain undertaking. The present universe consists principally of hydrogen which originally was the only element. Gravitation drew this gas together to form clouds and, in time, stars, stellar clusters and galaxies.

Two generations

In the first stars heavier elements were built up through the fusion of hydrogen nuclei. Exploding stars, novas and supernovas, spread these elements out through space and they became incorporated in the present generation of stars.

first generation stars

second generation stars

The first minutes

singularity

The state during the first instant of the universe cannot be described in terms of the physical laws applying to our present universe.

For a few minutes space was filled with an opaque "fluid" of photons; the smallest units of radiant energy.

Somewhat later the first elementary particles detached themselves from this photon "fluid".

The first atoms

were hydrogen atoms, made up of one proton (the positively charged nucleus) and a negatively charged electron. The heavier elements were not formed until several billion years later. Matter in the universe is still about 99 % hydrogen.

age of the universe on the basis of its present rate of expansion. It was concluded that the universe probably originated in a single dimensionless point, a "singularity" without extent in either space or time, containing the entire mass of the cosmos. The universe and space itself exploded out of this point at least 12–15 billion years ago. This "creation" was dubbed the "big bang".

As the universe expanded so it cooled. A few minutes after the bang the temperature had fallen to around one billion degrees and the first elementary particles were then formed. Two to three billion years later the first stars appeared among the hydrogen gas clouds. In this initial generation of stars, nuclear reactions fused hydrogen nuclei into the heavier elements, from helium to carbon and uranium, which subsequently became incorporated in the present stars and planets—and in our own bodies.

What, then of the future? There are two possibilities. One is that the expansion will continue forever, the universe becoming increasingly sparse and cold, with the stars burning out and expiring, until finally matter itself decays and nothing remains but cosmic background radiation—cold radio noise a fraction of a degree above absolute zero. The other alternative is more dramatic; the expansion ceases and is replaced by contraction. Finally the universe reverts to a singularity—an implosion which the irreverent cosmologists refer to as the "big crunch".

Which of the alternatives is most likely depends upon the total mass of the universe, a value physicists are unable to calculate. If it is less than a certain critical value then the expansion will continue. If it is greater than that value then we are heading for the "big crunch". Does the neutrino, the most common of the elementary particles, have any mass? Are there large quantities of non-radiant, invisible matter in the cosmos? If the answer to either of these questions is yes then the total gravitational force is sufficient to halt the expansion and the history of the universe will become a leap from the primordial frying pan into the ultimate fire.

Steady state . . .

For centuries scientists believed that the universe had not changed essentially, but only in minor detail. This theory could no longer be maintained, however, when it was discovered that space itself was expanding.

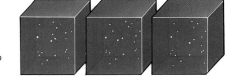

. . . or a big bang?

Cosmologists—scientists who study the structure and development of the universe—now believe that in the comparatively short space of some 12–15 billion years the universe has expanded out of a single point. The first explosive expansion is referred to as the "big bang".

The curvature of space

From Euclid to Newton

geometric space was conceived of as being rectilinear, rightangled and basically uniform everywhere. In the universe described by Einstein, (right) however, space is deformed or bent by the masses present within it (below).

Space and mass

The curvature of three-dimensional space is almost impossible to visualize. We show it below as a two-dimensional plane deformed by the mass of a star. The curvature of space is conformed to not only by masses and particles but also by light rays. It was, in fact, the bending of light rays adjacent to a star which confirmed the correctness of Einstein's theory, when this phenomenon was first observed in the 1920's.

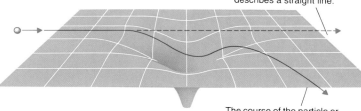

On a nondeformed plane a mass particle or a photon describes a straight line.

The mass of the star bends three-dimensional space in the same way that it bends this two-dimensional plane.

The course of the particle or photon is deflected when it passes close to the mass which is bending the space.

Our own sun

and its planetary system was formed between 4½ and 5 billion years ago. The sun thus belongs to the second generation of stars in the universe.

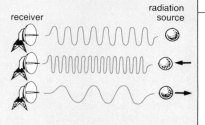

The red-shift

The red-shift (caused by the Doppler effect, right) shows that the distant galaxies are moving away from us. This does not imply, however, that the Earth or our galaxy is the center point of the universe. A simple experiment can demonstrate this. Stick a number of pieces of tape to a deflated balloon and then blow up the balloon (below, right). It can be seen that all the pieces move away from each other, i.e. in all instances the distance from one piece to all the others increases.

The Doppler effect

Light or radio waves have a specific wavelength (top). If the radiation source moves towards us we perceive the wavelength as shorter (middle). If the source moves away from us the wavelength increases—the frequency diminishes—and the light is red-shifted (bottom). Police traffic speed control radar is based on the Doppler effect.

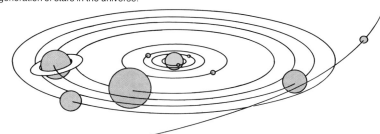

receiver

radiation source

observation point

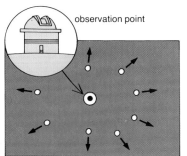

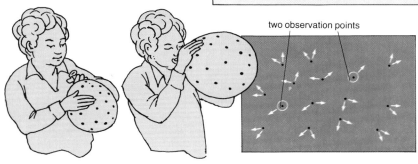

two observation points

The same everywhere

Since the universe expands uniformly it makes no difference where in the cosmos the astronomer sets up instruments. From either of the two observation points in the diagram (left) one can see how all the other points are retreating (arrows).

85

The sun and its offspring

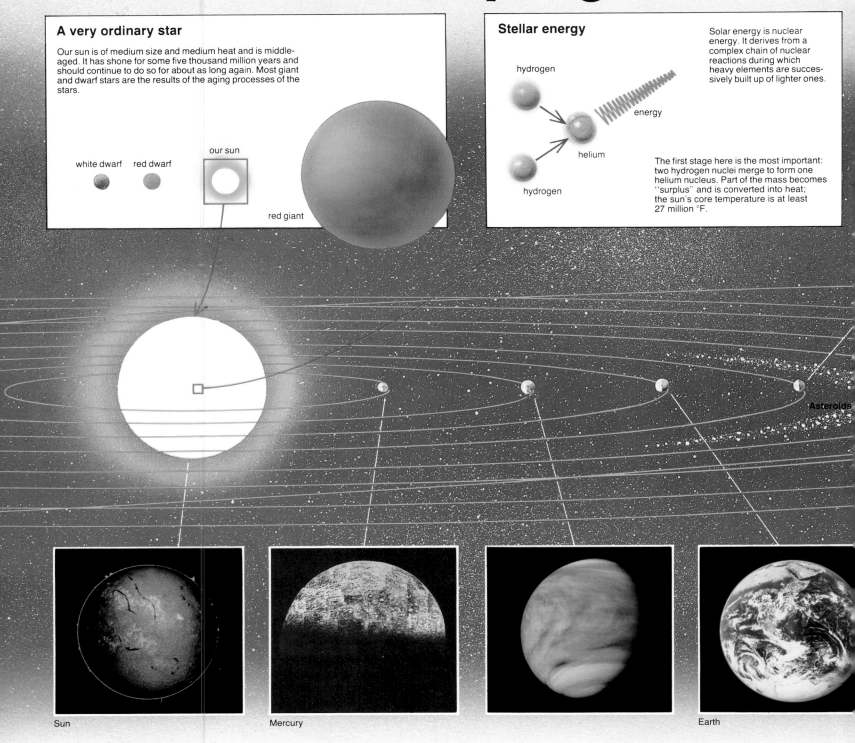

Asteroids

Sun

Mercury

Earth

Our sun is an average star, neither very large nor very small; neither hot nor cold; neither old nor recent. It is located on the edge of a very common type of spiral galaxy. If it is usual for such stars to have a planetary system – and most astronomers believe it is – then there must be many Earth-like planets in the universe, and on some of these there ought also to be life.

The planets in our solar system are of two entirely different categories. The inner planets, *Mercury*, *Venus*, *Earth* and *Mars*, are what are sometimes known as "cannonball worlds": compact mineral orbs encompassed by a shallow belt of atmosphere. The outer planets are mainly gaseous.

Mercury, in fact, lacks atmosphere altogether and is not unlike our moon, though its ground-level temperature would melt lead. Venus is a hot desert shrouded in a yellowish fog of carbon dioxide. It is only our Earth that has an oxygenous atmosphere and liquid water. So far as we know it is also the only one of the planets with life on its surface. Mars has a rarefied atmosphere consisting principally of carbon dioxide,

like that of Venus. But the surface of Mars is a frigid wasteland where only dust storms move. Contrary to earlier theories *asteroids* are not fragments of an exploded planet, instead they are the material for a planet which never actually formed, because the gravitational force of the giant planet Jupiter constantly dissipated the pieces.

The outer planets, *Jupiter*, *Saturn*, *Uranus* and *Neptune*, are gigantic balls of very cold gases, primarily hydrogen, helium, methane and ammonia. The density is low—in Neptune's case lower than water—but because of their enormous size the gravitational fields of these planets are of immense power. The rings around Saturn consist of ice particles. Uranus and Neptune, too, have faint ring systems. Each of these planets also has its imposing array of moons, many of these being as big as the planet Mercury. *Pluto*, finally, is an erratic among the planets. Its orbit is oblique and eccentric, and it is a "cannonball world" like the inner planets. Pluto could possibly be an adopted planet; a celestial body recruited from elsewhere.

Mars

Saturn

Pluto

Panorama of planets
In this diagram, for the sake of clarity, both distances and differences in magnitude have had to be diminished. The system's radius out to Pluto's orbit is 8,500 times that of the sun's radius and almost 10,000 times that of Earth. In correct scale the planets would not be visible. The small pictures are photographs, except for Uranus, Neptune and Pluto which are drawings.

Jupiter

Uranus

Neptune

The first steps in space

When in 1969 Neil Armstrong set foot on the moon (right) it was, as he put it, "a gaint leap for mankind". But because of the enormous costs of manned space travel, the further study of the planets is being conducted with remote-controlled devices. These have photographed Mercury, Jupiter and Saturn, penetrated the atmosphere of Venus and landed on Mars. In 1983 a US space-probe in the Pioneer series became the first device built by people to leave our solar system and continue on out into interstellar space.

Mountains of fire

Most geological processes are so slow that we do not have the time during our brief lifespan to observe them directly. Their cumulative effects do not emerge for thousands or millions of years. But vulcanism is an exception. A volcanic cone can be built up in only a few days, a mountain can explode and be thrown up into the stratosphere as fine dust in a matter of seconds.

Vulcanism occurs when magma rises up through the Earth's crust. Why it takes place, when and where it does, remained a mystery until the emergence of the modern plate tectonic theory. We now know that the Earth's "fire belts" generally follow the limits of the geological plates. Ninety percent of all the active volcanoes are located either along the spreading lines (e.g. in Iceland) or in the subduction zones (Andes, Japan). In the spreading areas new earth-crust is formed when magma wells upward from the mantle, while in the subduction zones it is destroyed by being forced down into the mantle and remelted. The magma which formed the Andean volcanoes, for example, consists mainly of "recycled" crust. The hot spots which give rise to whole chains of volcanoes as the earth-crust slides over the top of them are still a scientific riddle however; they appear to have remained in the same place in the mantle for millions of years.

The nature of vulcanism varies according to the composition of the magma. Certain volcanoes, in addition to nitrogen, water vapor and gasified sulfur, produce mainly stones—volcanic "bombs" and smaller "lapilli"—and ash. One example is Vesuvius which buried Pompeii in 79 AD. It is this type of volcano which builds up the characteristically steep cone profile. Other volcanoes erupt incandescent gas clouds, like Mont Pelée on Martinique which killed 30,000 people in 1902. Very liquid lava produces the more shallow contoured shield volcanoes. Volcanic domes caused by magma intrusions, hot springs and gas vents are other characteristic phenomena.

We tend to regard volcanoes as basically destructive. They have caused the death of vast numbers of people and lava flows and ash have had disastrous economic consequences. So much dust was spouted into the atmosphere during the eruption of Tambora in Indonesia in 1815 that there was practically no summer at all the following year. But there is another aspect to this. All the organic carbon and all the water on our planet is believed to be of volcanic origin—it was not part of the primeval atmosphere but came out of the Earth's mantle. Thus, vulcanism may be regarded as a prerequisite for life on our planet.

The earthquake zones
(orange color) are also where most volcanos are found (red dots). These fire belts are areas where the crustal plates move relative to each other. Other important volcanic areas include the mid-ocean ridges (lines) and the "hot spots".

Stratovolcanoes
are steep cones built up of layers of ash, lava and pumice.

crater

volcanic cone

funnel

Magma rises upward from deep down in the Earth's mantle. The consistency of the magma, and thereby the nature of the eruption, depends to a large extent upon its composition, especially the gas and silicic acid content.

Extraterrestrial vulcanism

Our solar system's biggest volcano is Olympus Mons on Mars. This is a gigantic shield volcano with a diameter of nearly 373 mi. and the summit, a caldera, some 75,463 ft. above the surrounding desertland. The gradually sloping sides terminate abruptly in a 13,124 ft. sheer fall down to the ground level. This is all clearly discernible in the mosaic, composed of a series of vertical photographs taken by a space probe in orbit. There appears also to be volcanic activity on a couple of Jupiter's satellites, though the familiar craters on our moon and Mercury have nothing to do with vulcanism. These are merely impact craters caused by falling meteorites back in the time when the celestial bodies were being formed.

Mount Saint Helens—a volcanic case study

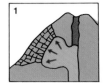 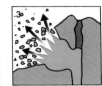

Mount Saint Helens in the northwestern USA produced a violent eruption in 1980. The funnel to the top crater had become blocked and the pressure of the magma caused the entire side of the mountain to bulge and fracture (1). A landslide then released the pressure that enclosed the magma (2) and the whole mountainside burst (3). The result was probably the most photographed volcanic eruption in history.

Boulders and small stones fall down around the crater, but the ash is spread over vast areas.

Lateral fissures can release lava or gas but also widen into lateral craters.

Shield volcanoes
are formed from fluid and gaseous lavas. They are lower and flatter but also larger than typical stratovolcanoes.

Geysers
and other hot springs arise when ground water reaches hot geological strata. These eruptions occur at intervals when the water comes to a violent boil.

How a caldera is formed:

A caldera is formed after a large magma chamber has developed underground. No normal funnel has formed here.

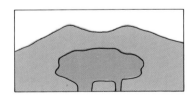

Instead the pressure is relieved through an explosion which shatters the rock above the chamber. The lighter material is then ejected into the air . . .

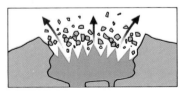

. . . but most of the heavy rock falls down into the empty chamber. The waning volcanic activity can build up a small volcanic cone out in the caldera.

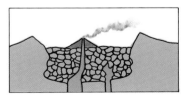

The final result is a circular depression enclosed by a ridge and often containing a lake. The diameter can be 12.5 mi. or more.

Hawaii's hot spot

Kauai
Oahu
Molokai
Maui
Hawaii
Mauna Loa

The islands northwest of Hawaii itself are extinct volcanic cones.

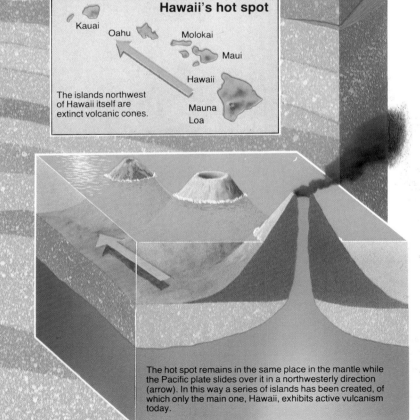

The hot spot remains in the same place in the mantle while the Pacific plate slides over it in a northwesterly direction (arrow). In this way a series of islands has been created, of which only the main one, Hawaii, exhibits active vulcanism today.

Energy from the Earth's interior

Industrial society is sustained by energy resources in the ground beneath our feet—coal and oil. Both of these are, in fact, fossilized solar energy from remote geological epochs.

Pit coal was formed during the Carboniferous Period about 300 million years ago. In conditions of immense pressure and heat, dead vegetation was gradually transformed into the mineral we now mine. Brown coal or lignite is of somewhat more recent origin. It is not as completely transformed as black or pit coal and its energy content is less. Petroleum and natural gas are also of organic origin, although in their case it was unicellular organisms which absorbed the sun's rays during the era of the dinosaurs a couple of hundred million years ago. According to another theory, however, at least some natural gas is "deep gas", hydrocarbons which have existed in the Earth's interior even since the planet was formed, seeping out during the course of billions of years. Some of this gas has been trapped beneath impenetrable rock strata in the same way as the organic gas.

Early interest in coal and oil developed through the availability of surface deposits. Fossil fuel was first used on a large scale in 16th century England where deforestation had resulted in a shortage of firewood for the expanding towns. Coal was later used to fuel the steam engines of the industrial revolution. The large-scale exploitation of petroleum began in the USA in the 1850's, the principal products at that time being axle grease and lamp paraffin. Gasoline was a useless by-product. A little of it was sold for spot-removing while the rest was simply burned as a last means of disposal.

A further sort of energy in the Earth's interior is geothermal; heat in the bowels of our planet. This is a legacy from the creation of the solar system five thousand million years ago. The heat has been generated through the decay of radioactive elements which gathered in the core of Earth when the planet was formed.

How pit coal was formed:

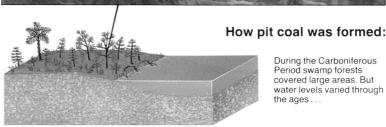

During the Carboniferous Period swamp forests covered large areas. But water levels varied through the ages . . .

. . . and when the water rose the vegetation died. If the dead vegetation was covered so that oxygen could not reach it, it did not disintegrate but formed an organic stratum in the ground instead.

dead plants

new vegetation

In time this stratum would be transformed into a coal seam. In the soil on top of the seam a new swamp forest grew—this would become the next coal seam.

vegetable matter is fossilized

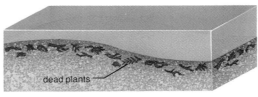

The world's coal
The USA, Western Europe, the Soviet Union, China and Australia are the principal producers.

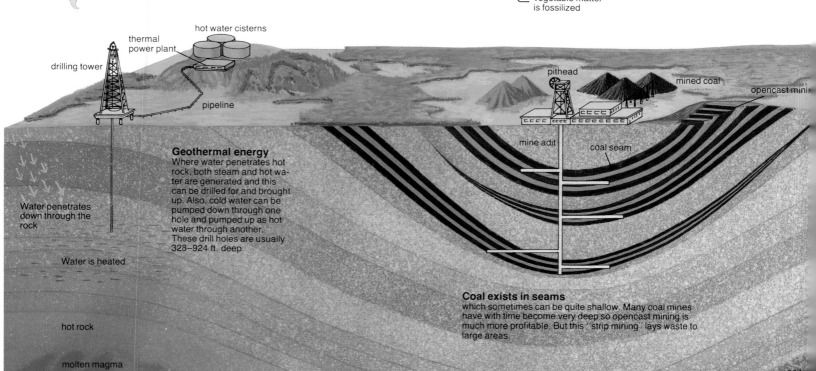

hot water cisterns

thermal power plant

drilling tower

pipeline

pithead

mined coal

opencast mini

mine adit

coal seam

Geothermal energy
Where water penetrates hot rock, both steam and hot water are generated and this can be drilled for and brought up. Also, cold water can be pumped down through one hole and pumped up as hot water through another. These drill holes are usually 328–924 ft. deep.

Water penetrates down through the rock

Water is heated

hot rock

molten magma

Coal exists in seams
which sometimes can be quite shallow. Many coal mines have with time become very deep so opencast mining is much more profitable. But this "strip mining" lays waste to large areas.

salt w

How oil was formed:

From seabed mud . . .

In shallow lakes and lagoons multitudes of tiny water organisms thrived. When they expired they sank to the bottom and formed a layer of mud rich in organic matter. A dinosaur or two probably went the same way, but these, of course, were not the main contributors to the process.

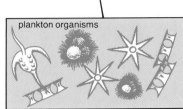

plankton organisms

. . . to petroleum

The water at the bottom, containing little oxygen, protected the hydrocarbons in the dead organisms against disintegration. Pressure and heat converted simple hydrocarbons into the large molecules of petroleum. In this way oil-yielding sandstone, oil shale and tar sand were formed.

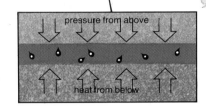

pressure from above

heat from below

Immense energy sources are concealed beneath the desolate surface of the desert.

The world's oil

is usually found far from where it is most in demand. The search for new reserves goes on constantly and rising prices have made it worthwhile to bring up oil from the continental shelves and in the Arctic.

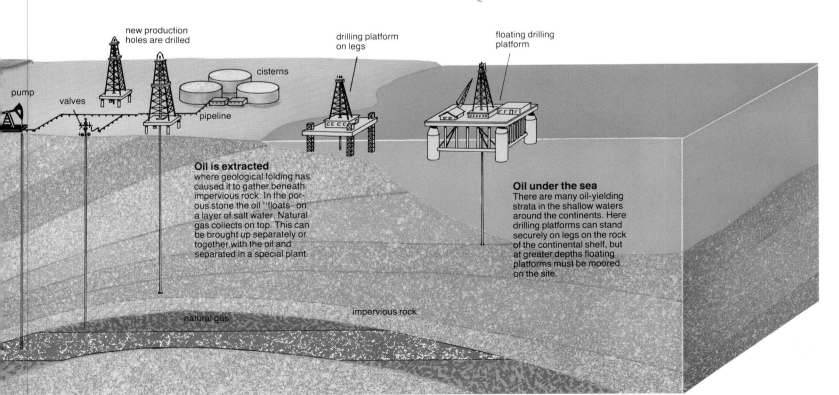

new production holes are drilled

drilling platform on legs

floating drilling platform

pump

valves

cisterns

pipeline

Oil is extracted

where geological folding has caused it to gather beneath impervious rock. In the porous stone the oil "floats" on a layer of salt water. Natural gas collects on top. This can be brought up separately or together with the oil and separated in a special plant.

Oil under the sea

There are many oil-yielding strata in the shallow waters around the continents. Here drilling platforms can stand securely on legs on the rock of the continental shelf, but at greater depths floating platforms must be moored on the site.

natural gas

impervious rock

Fire, the servant of people

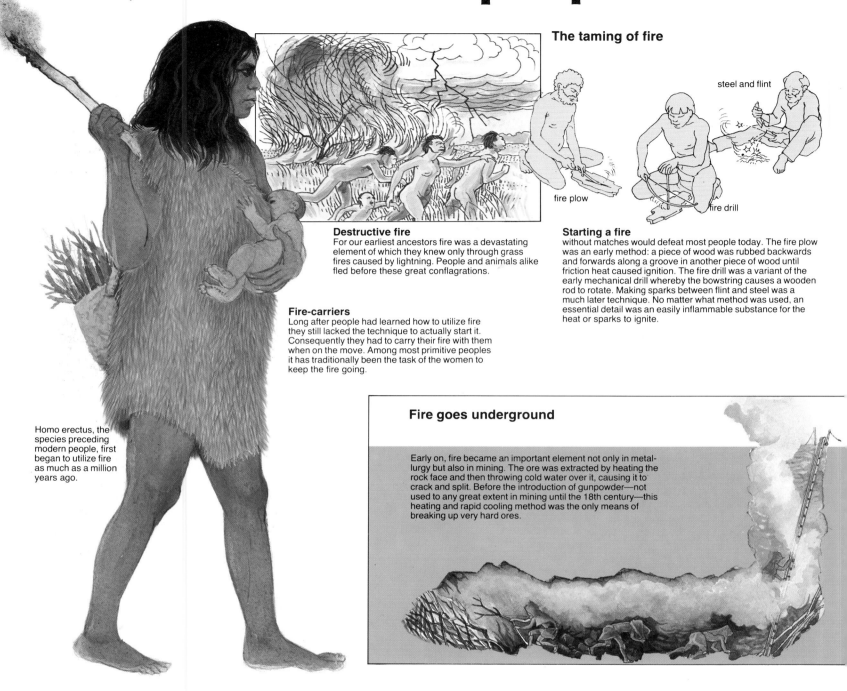

Homo erectus, the species preceding modern people, first began to utilize fire as much as a million years ago.

The taming of fire

steel and flint

fire plow

fire drill

Destructive fire
For our earliest ancestors fire was a devastating element of which they knew only through grass fires caused by lightning. People and animals alike fled before these great conflagrations.

Fire-carriers
Long after people had learned how to utilize fire they still lacked the technique to actually start it. Consequently they had to carry their fire with them when on the move. Among most primitive peoples it has traditionally been the task of the women to keep the fire going.

Starting a fire
without matches would defeat most people today. The fire plow was an early method: a piece of wood was rubbed backwards and forwards along a groove in another piece of wood until friction heat caused ignition. The fire drill was a variant of the early mechanical drill whereby the bowstring causes a wooden rod to rotate. Making sparks between flint and steel was a much later technique. No matter what method was used, an essential detail was an easily inflammable substance for the heat or sparks to ignite.

Fire goes underground

Early on, fire became an important element not only in metallurgy but also in mining. The ore was extracted by heating the rock face and then throwing cold water over it, causing it to crack and split. Before the introduction of gunpowder—not used to any great extent in mining until the 18th century—this heating and rapid cooling method was the only means of breaking up very hard ores.

Ask a chemist to define fire and he or she will probably reply that it is an exothermic oxidation reaction. If certain carbon or hydrogen compounds are heated sufficiently then the carbon or hydrogen will combine with the oxygen in the air (oxidation). This process gives off large quantities of heat (it is exothermic)—so much so that it heats up the rest of the fuel sufficiently for the oxidation to continue and spread. Fire, in other words, is a chemical chain reaction.

On the grass plains where early people developed, fire played an important role as a periodic regenerator of the vegetation. When our ancestors first began to make use of fire for their own purposes—between 1,500,000 and 500,000 years ago—they probably employed it to raise game in their organized hunts. It was not until later around 7000 BC, that Neolithic people utilized it regularly as a source of warmth and light and as a means of keeping nocturnal predators at bay. And it was much later still that they learned how to use the heat from fire to roast food. Fire probably became a necessity in the movement from the warm plains of Africa to colder, more inhospitable regions.

The initial, simple hearth, a ring of stones, was gradually built higher. The next step, to the oven, was soon achieved and in time the potter's kiln developed into the early metalworker's

primitive smelting furnace. The enclosed oven made it possible to control simple oxidation and reduction processes. Subsequently, development remained largely at a standstill until about the 15th century when the low smelting furnace was replaced by a tall blast furnace with improved fuel economy and better process regulation.

In early Alexandria, Greek inventors had examined the idea of converting heat energy into kinetic energy. The concept was revived in the latter part of the 17th century when European mines had become so deep that it was impossible to pump them out manually. The first steam engines were therefore built to power the mine pumps. These were of the atmospheric type. Steam was injected into the cylinder when the piston was in its outermost position. Water was then added and the cooling-down process created a vacuum, causing the piston to be drawn inwards. The piston rate was about one stroke a minute and the machines had to be of enormous size to attain the required power.

The man who changed all this was James Watt. In 1769 he added a condenser to the steam engine. This greatly improved the fuel economy and the stroke rate. He introduced the piston rod, which converted the piston's backwards and forwards

Large quantities of wood were used to produce char-coal for the smelting furnaces.

Process heat

Early iron manufacturing
For thousands of years iron was smelted in low beehive-shaped furnaces. These were filled with alternate layers of iron ore and charcoal. When the latter had burned out it left behind a sponge-like cake of iron at the bottom. There were many local variations of the process. Furnaces of this type were being used in Africa up until this century.

Slag inclusions were removed from the still red-hot iron by hammering.

A blower, manual or wind-driven, increased the temperature in the furnace to iron's melting point, 2,782°F.

Early heat technology
The metallurgy of ancient peoples was part of a development which had been going on for thousands of years. The potter's kiln was adopted by the bronze-founder and when the blower was added this furnace could be used for iron smelting. The simple furnace could likewise be used for making glass (above: an oriental glassblower).

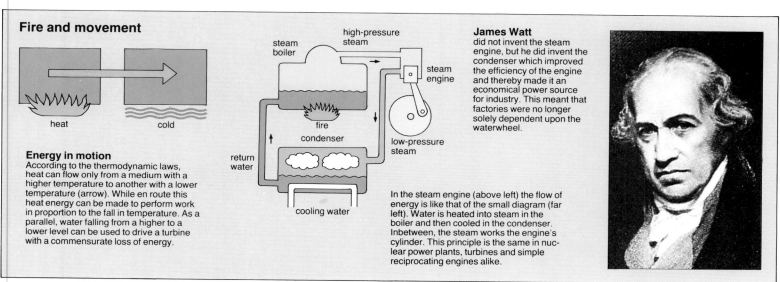

Fire and movement

heat   cold

Energy in motion
According to the thermodynamic laws, heat can flow only from a medium with a higher temperature to another with a lower temperature (arrow). While en route this heat energy can be made to perform work in proportion to the fall in temperature. As a parallel, water falling from a higher to a lower level can be used to drive a turbine with a commensurate loss of energy.

steam boiler   high-pressure steam   steam engine   fire   condenser   low-pressure steam   return water   cooling water

James Watt
did not invent the steam engine, but he did invent the condenser which improved the efficiency of the engine and thereby made it an economical power source for industry. This meant that factories were no longer solely dependent upon the waterwheel.

In the steam engine (above left) the flow of energy is like that of the small diagram (far left). Water is heated into steam in the boiler and then cooled in the condenser. Inbetween, the steam works the engine's cylinder. This principle is the same in nuclear power plants, turbines and simple reciprocating engines alike.

movement to a rotational movement, and also the governor which controlled the stroke rate. Watt was a self-taught mill-builder and instrument-maker and it was pure intuition which inspired him to invent the condenser. The scientific analysis of this invention was made by the Frenchman Sadi Carnot in 1824, who thereby founded thermodynamics, the science of energy conversion.

The role of steam in Europe's industrialization has often been misconstrued. Steam did not create industrialization—industry and machines had existed prior to Watt. As much as half a century after Watt's first patent, the waterwheel was just as important as steam as a power source in British industry—the most advanced in the world at that time. The steam engine did however liberate industry from the limitations of water power with regard to factory location and size.

It was in the realm of transport that the real revolution arose. Steamboats opened up the Mississippi valley, steam locomotives opened the way to the American West and Siberia for international trade and development. Steam helped carry the products of the industrialized nations out across the world, and brought back the raw materials to these same nations. The rise of steam signaled the advent of the modern world.

The factories of the 19th century
were run by steam engines, the power being distributed to the different machines through a maze of shafts and belts. Production increased, though it also became more centralized since the individual artisans could not afford their own steam engines. The many exposed belt drives in the early factory made working conditions there exceedingly dangerous.

93

Using energy

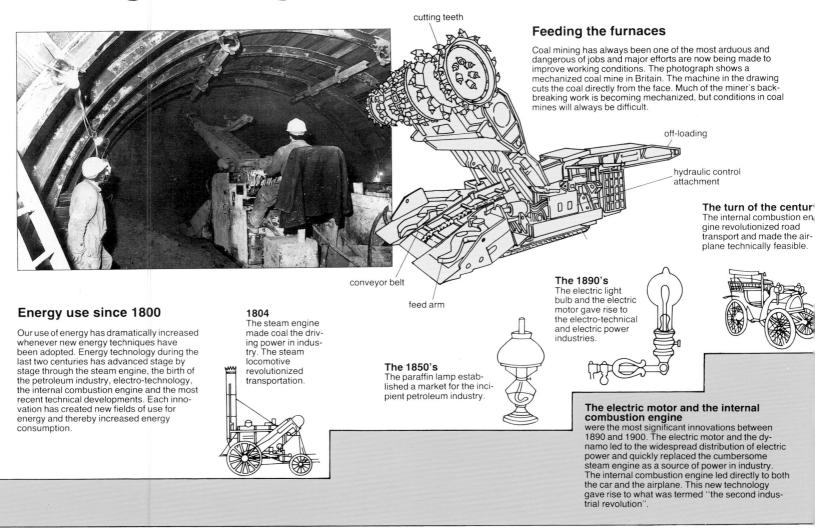

cutting teeth

Feeding the furnaces

Coal mining has always been one of the most arduous and dangerous of jobs and major efforts are now being made to improve working conditions. The photograph shows a mechanized coal mine in Britain. The machine in the drawing cuts the coal directly from the face. Much of the miner's back-breaking work is becoming mechanized, but conditions in coal mines will always be difficult.

off-loading

hydraulic control attachment

The turn of the centur
The internal combustion en gine revolutionized road transport and made the air-plane technically feasible.

conveyor belt

feed arm

The 1890's
The electric light bulb and the electric motor gave rise to the electro-technical and electric power industries.

The 1850's
The paraffin lamp estab-lished a market for the inci-pient petroleum industry.

Energy use since 1800

Our use of energy has dramatically increased whenever new energy techniques have been adopted. Energy technology during the last two centuries has advanced stage by stage through the steam engine, the birth of the petroleum industry, electro-technology, the internal combustion engine and the most recent technical developments. Each inno-vation has created new fields of use for energy and thereby increased energy consumption.

1804
The steam engine made coal the driv-ing power in indus-try. The steam locomotive revolutionized transportation.

The electric motor and the internal combustion engine
were the most significant innovations between 1890 and 1900. The electric motor and the dy-namo led to the widespread distribution of electric power and quickly replaced the cumbersome steam engine as a source of power in industry. The internal combustion engine led directly to both the car and the airplane. This new technology gave rise to what was termed "the second indus-trial revolution".

The sun is the main source of energy in our planetary system. Electromagnetic radiation of almost incomprehensible mag-nitude floods out into space from its surface. This flow can be calculated at 4×10^{23} kilowatts, i.e. a 4 followed by twenty-three zeros. Of this vast output the Earth picks up about 127,500 billion kW on its daylight side, or 1 kW/m². This energy then streams through the atmosphere and hydrosphere until it again flows out into space. All life processes are sustained by the energy which organisms divert from this flow in order to utilize it in their own metabolism and life environment.

This applies to people. Our earliest ancestors had no more energy at their disposal than their own muscular strength. Two major steps were taken when people tamed fire about a million years ago and when they learned to harness draft animals during the agricultural revolution some 8,000 years ago. But the princi-ple remained unchanged. The wood with which people fuelled their fires and the fodder that sustained their animals were recon-stituted solar energy, as was the food that they consumed.

The situation changed drastically when people began using fossil fuels; coal and oil. It then became possible to utilize large amounts of energy in transport, industry and agriculture and this prepared the way for increasingly high productivity. It seemed as though all the natural limitations had been overcome. This ener-gy optimism culminated with the advent of nuclear power when we were promised almost costless energy in unlimited quantities forever.

Now, however, we are becoming aware that our energy resour-ces are not inexhaustible, that their exploitation is costly and that such exploitation is ultimately harmful to the environment.

The laws of thermodynamics indicate that energy is indestruct-ible. We can neither produce nor consume energy, merely har-ness it by converting it from one form to another. The electric current from a wall socket may amount to only 40 % of the ener-gy in oil, uranium or running water which has been used to keep the power station generators going. The light from an electric bulb represents about one tenth of the bulb's rated power, i.e. ten watts out of a hundred. What happens to the rest and where does the light go when the lamp is switched off? All this energy, including light energy, is converted into low-grade heat which flows out into space as long-wave infrared radiation.

Radiation from a body is proportional to that body's tempera-ture. The Earth's temperature has become stabilized at a point where incoming and outgoing radiation balance each other exactly. Heat emanating from fossil fuels and nuclear reaction does not derive from the sun, however. It is additional heat, thermal pollution, which increases the temperature of the atmosphere. As a result, the mean temperature of the Earth must increase in order that a radiation balance may once more be achieved. Until now this thermic environmental upset has been apparent only at the local level when cooling towers and cooling water releases have affected the microclimate in the immediate vicinity. What has been described above shows that there are limits to energy production. The way to greater pros-perity is no longer an increased output of energy, but rather production processes and life styles that are more energy-saving and less environmentally destructive.

The 1950's:
The development of commercial nuclear power began: unlimited access to cheap energy was still regarded as the key to every form of technical and economic progress. The technology behind this "peaceful" nuclear power derived from the military nuclear weapons programs, however.

Clean energy?
The processing of fuel and distribution of energy takes place under far more tolerable conditions than are found below ground. The photograph shows the control room at a nuclear power plant. The control room of a coal-fired power plant looks much the same, although the instrument panels may be somewhat less imposing. Despite the cleanliness of the power plant control room, threats to the environment do exist. All technical energy conversion, even the domestic fire, results in environmental damage of some sort. Large energy systems are very efficient, but they can break down. A major power failure can bring an entire region practically to a standstill.

The energy-saturated community
During the 1950's and 1960's energy consumption increased rapidly in industrial countries; doubling every five years in some cases. This increase was caused less by nuclear power than by the expansion of electric power networks and gas pipeline systems on a continental scale. During the 1970's energy consumption stagnated, partly because of the need to save expensive oil and partly because of a general slowdown in economic expansion. Industrial countries now foresee their energy consumption leveling off while the needs of Third World will continue to increase.

Humans and the energy staircase
Homo sapiens and their predecessors have always been somewhere on the "energy staircase", but there were thousands or even millions of years from one step to another. Fire and the utilizing of beasts of burden such as oxen, donkeys and horses, were the most important advances until the advent of industrialism. Between these big changes the energy consumption per capita remained at a fairly steady level.

industrial age

agricultural revolution

Homo erectus tames fire

primeval human

Flowing versus capital energy
Utilizing flowing energy sources means that we divert solar energy on its way through the atmosphere, hydrosphere and biosphere, just as our ancestors did. With properly developed techniques this energy might even be sufficient for the needs of modern times. Capital energy on the other hand is energy from nonreplenishable sources, such as fossil fuels and uranium. No matter where the energy comes from, it all ends up as waste heat in the atmosphere.

constantly flowing solar energy

direct solar energy

waste heat into the atmosphere

photosynthesis

atmospheric energy

biomass

capital energy: coal, oil, natural gas, uranium

Energy-impoverished societies
Energy resources are unevenly distributed. Industrialized countries use 90 % of the available energy while for the most part people in the developing countries have to manage with whatever "subsistence energy" they can find. Their pursuit of fuel (below) takes up an immense amount of time and labor, and often causes great damage to the vegetation.

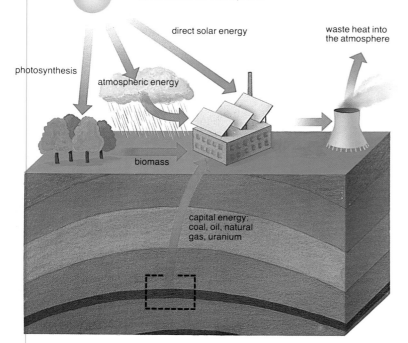

95

Tundra

Coniferous forest

Mixed forest

Arable land

Grassland, pasture

Semi-desert,
Steppe

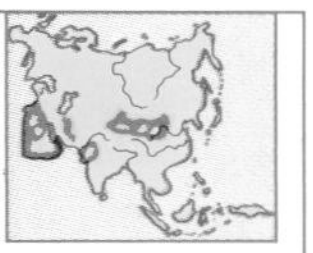

Other desert

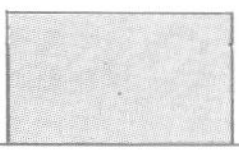

Sand desert

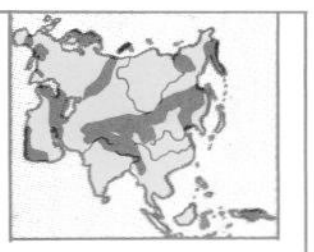

Mountain

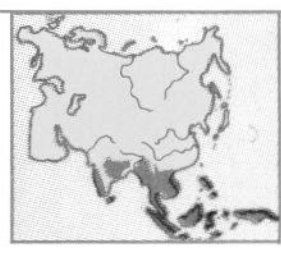

Tropical
rain forest

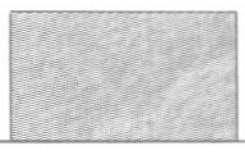

THE WORLD
in maps

A map is a representation of the face of the Earth. It lacks, however, the realism of an aerial photograph since it is abstract; mountains, rivers, seas and cities are indicated by signs and colors. The Earth's surface in all its endless variety has to be sorted out and arranged so that it may be presented in a form that is easily understood. In the past cartography has perhaps been a little too abstract; most people will recall the traditional school atlas where the lowland Sahara was shown in lush green, while upland Africa's rich vegetation was represented in parched brown; the map gave no intimation of the specific characteristics of the landscape with its forests and grasslands, its deserts and cultivated plains.

Satellite imagery and photographs of the Earth taken from space have inspired a new era in cartography. The environmental maps in this atlas bring the representation of the Earth's surface much closer to reality. The former, schematic levels of elevation have been succeeded by plastic relief effects and colors which are closer to those of the natural world. This new form of cartography represents the surface of the Earth at a level of detail never achieved before in an atlas of this kind.

The key on the left indicates the main classes into which different environments have been grouped. Certain specific environments not shown here have their own unique color classification. A complete display of all the classes can be found inside the back cover. It should be noted that the United States has a separate series of color classifications which is also displayed inside the back cover.

POLITICAL DIVISIONS

Names of the American states, with their standard abbreviations

AL.	Alabama		
AK.	Alaska		
AZ.	Arizona		
AR.	Arkansas		
CA.	California		
CO.	Colorado		
CT.	Connecticut		
DE.	Delaware		
FL.	Florida		
GA.	Georgia		
HI.	Hawaii		
ID.	Idaho		
IL.	Illinois		
IN.	Indiana		
IA.	Iowa		
KS.	Kansas		
KY.	Kentucky		
LA.	Louisiana		
ME.	Maine		
MD.	Maryland		
MA.	Massachusetts		
MI.	Michigan		
MN.	Minnesota		
MS.	Mississippi	PA.	Pennsylvania
MO.	Missouri	R.I.	Rhode Island
MT.	Montana	S.C.	South Carolina
NE.	Nebraska	S.D.	South Dakota
NV.	Nevada	TN.	Tennessee
N.H.	New Hampshire	TX.	Texas
N.J.	New Jersey	UT.	Utah
N.M.	New Mexico	VT.	Vermont
N.Y.	New York	VA.	Virginia
N.C.	North Carolina	WA.	Washington
N.D.	North Dakota	W.V.	West Virginia
OH.	Ohio	WI.	Wisconsin
OK.	Oklahoma	WY.	Wyoming
OR.	Oregon	D.C.	District of Columbia (Federal)

POPULATION

Population distribution 1982

• 500 000 inhabitants

●³ Figures show populations (cities with suburbs) in millions

uninhabited (less than 1 person per sq.km)

Population increase per country 1972–1982

50%
40
30
20 Average for North and
10 Central America 15%
0

Scale 1:60 000 000

0   1000   2000 km
0   500   1000 miles

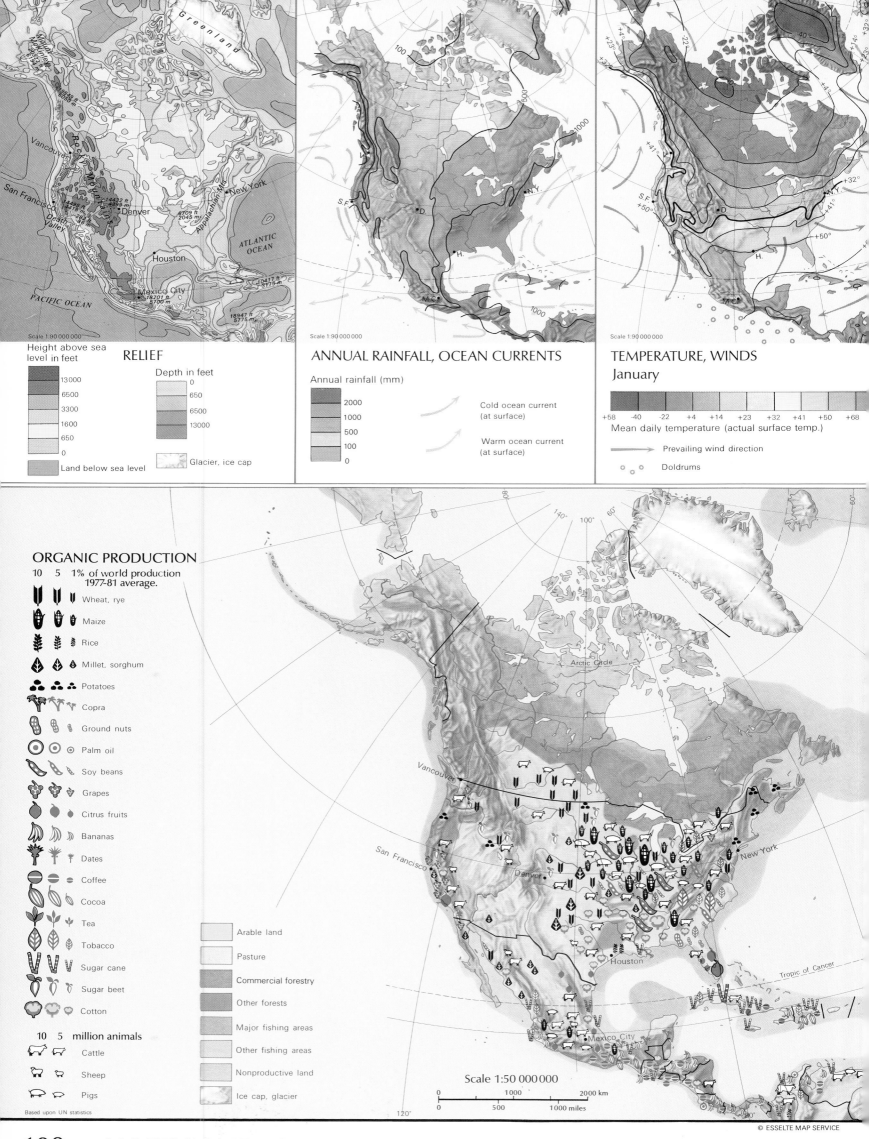

RELIEF

Scale 1:90 000 000

Height above sea level in feet

- 13000
- 6500
- 3300
- 1600
- 650
- 0
- Land below sea level

Depth in feet

- 0
- 650
- 6500
- 13000
- Glacier, ice cap

ANNUAL RAINFALL, OCEAN CURRENTS

Scale 1:90 000 000

Annual rainfall (mm)

- 2000
- 1000
- 500
- 100
- 0

→ Cold ocean current (at surface)

→ Warm ocean current (at surface)

TEMPERATURE, WINDS

January

Scale 1:90 000 000

Mean daily temperature (actual surface temp.)

+58 -40 -22 +4 +14 +23 +32 +41 +50 +68

→ Prevailing wind direction

∘ ∘ ∘ Doldrums

ORGANIC PRODUCTION

10 5 1% of world production 1977-81 average.

- Wheat, rye
- Maize
- Rice
- Millet, sorghum
- Potatoes
- Copra
- Ground nuts
- Palm oil
- Soy beans
- Grapes
- Citrus fruits
- Bananas
- Dates
- Coffee
- Cocoa
- Tea
- Tobacco
- Sugar cane
- Sugar beet
- Cotton

10 5 million animals

- Cattle
- Sheep
- Pigs

- Arable land
- Pasture
- Commercial forestry
- Other forests
- Major fishing areas
- Other fishing areas
- Nonproductive land
- Ice cap, glacier

Based upon UN statistics

Scale 1:50 000 000

0   1000   2000 km
0   500   1000 miles

© ESSELTE MAP SERVICE

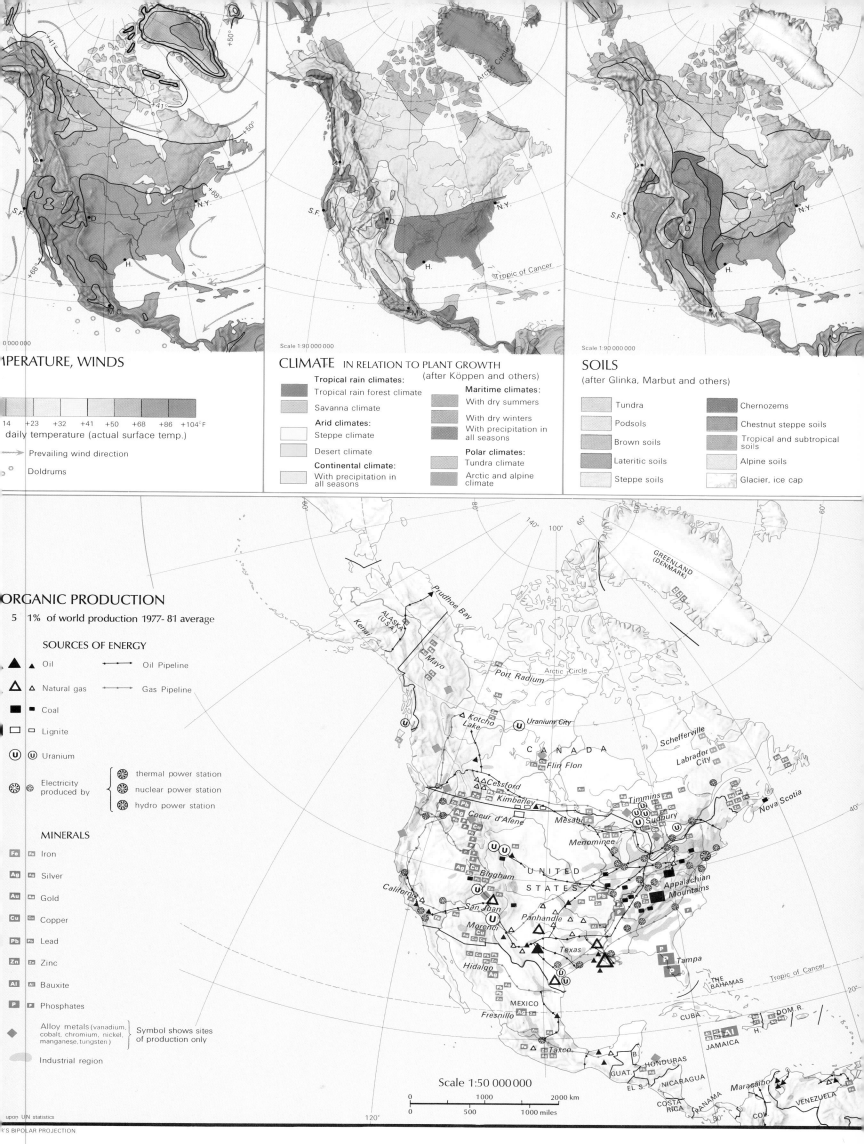

TEMPERATURE, WINDS

14	+23	+32	+41	+50	+68	+86	+104°F

daily temperature (actual surface temp.)

→ Prevailing wind direction

○ Doldrums

CLIMATE IN RELATION TO PLANT GROWTH (after Köppen and others)

Scale 1:90 000 000

Tropical rain climates:
- Tropical rain forest climate
- Savanna climate

Arid climates:
- Steppe climate
- Desert climate

Continental climate:
- With precipitation in all seasons

Maritime climates:
- With dry summers
- With dry winters
- With precipitation in all seasons

Polar climates:
- Tundra climate
- Arctic and alpine climate

SOILS

Scale 1:90 000 000

(after Glinka, Marbut and others)

- Tundra
- Podsols
- Brown soils
- Lateritic soils
- Steppe soils
- Chernozems
- Chestnut steppe soils
- Tropical and subtropical soils
- Alpine soils
- Glacier, ice cap

INORGANIC PRODUCTION

5 1% of world production 1977-81 average

SOURCES OF ENERGY

▲ ▲ Oil	●—● Oil Pipeline
△ △ Natural gas	—○— Gas Pipeline
■ ▪ Coal	
▢ ▫ Lignite	
Ⓤ Ⓤ Uranium	

⊛ ⊛ Electricity produced by
- thermal power station
- nuclear power station
- hydro power station

MINERALS

Fe	▫ Iron
Ag	▫ Silver
Au	▫ Gold
Cu	▫ Copper
Pb	▫ Lead
Zn	▫ Zinc
Al	▫ Bauxite
P	▫ Phosphates

◆ Alloy metals (vanadium, cobalt, chromium, nickel, manganese, tungsten) } Symbol shows sites of production only

⊙ Industrial region

Scale 1:50 000 000

0	1000	2000 km
0	500	1000 miles

upon UN statistics

...'S BIPOLAR PROJECTION

101

© ESSELTE MAP SERVICE

Scale 1:10 000 000

© ESSELTE MAP SERVICE

© ESSELTE MAP SERVIC

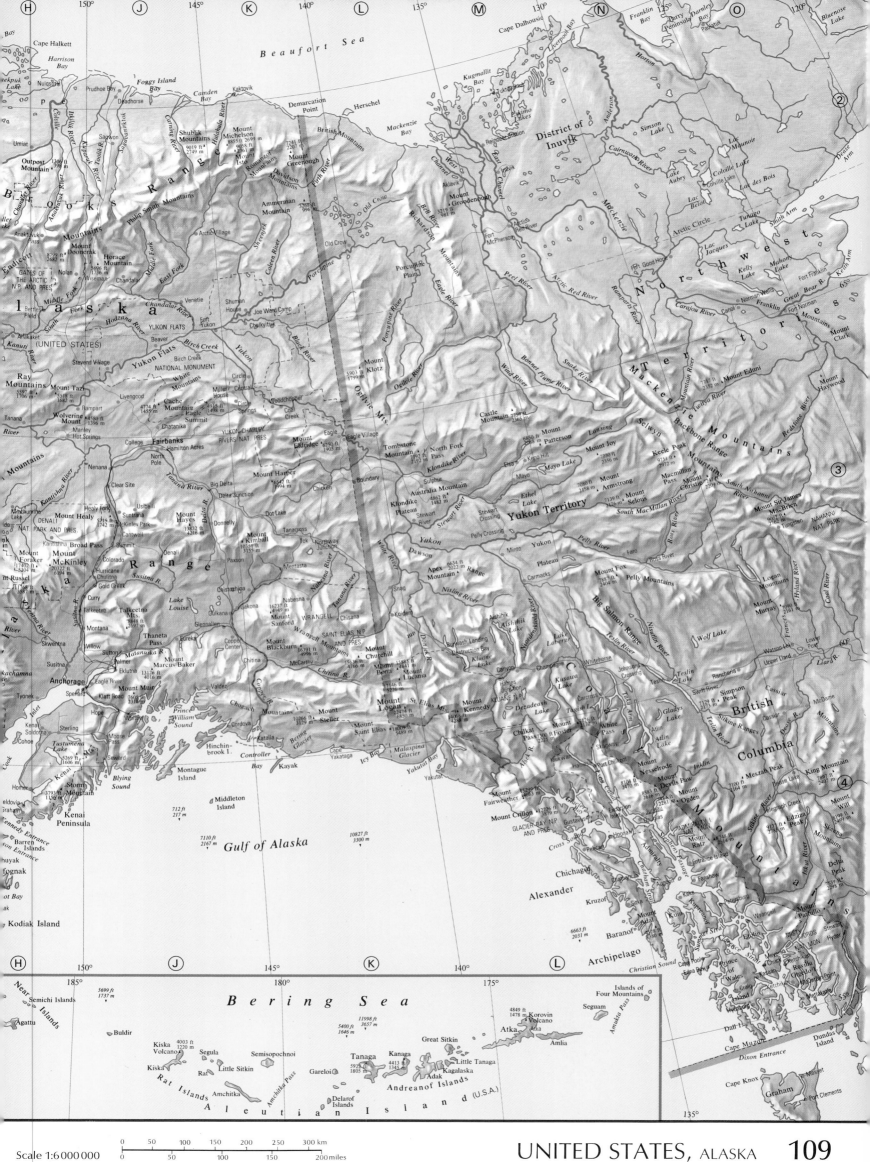

Scale 1:6 000 000

Scale 1:3 000 000

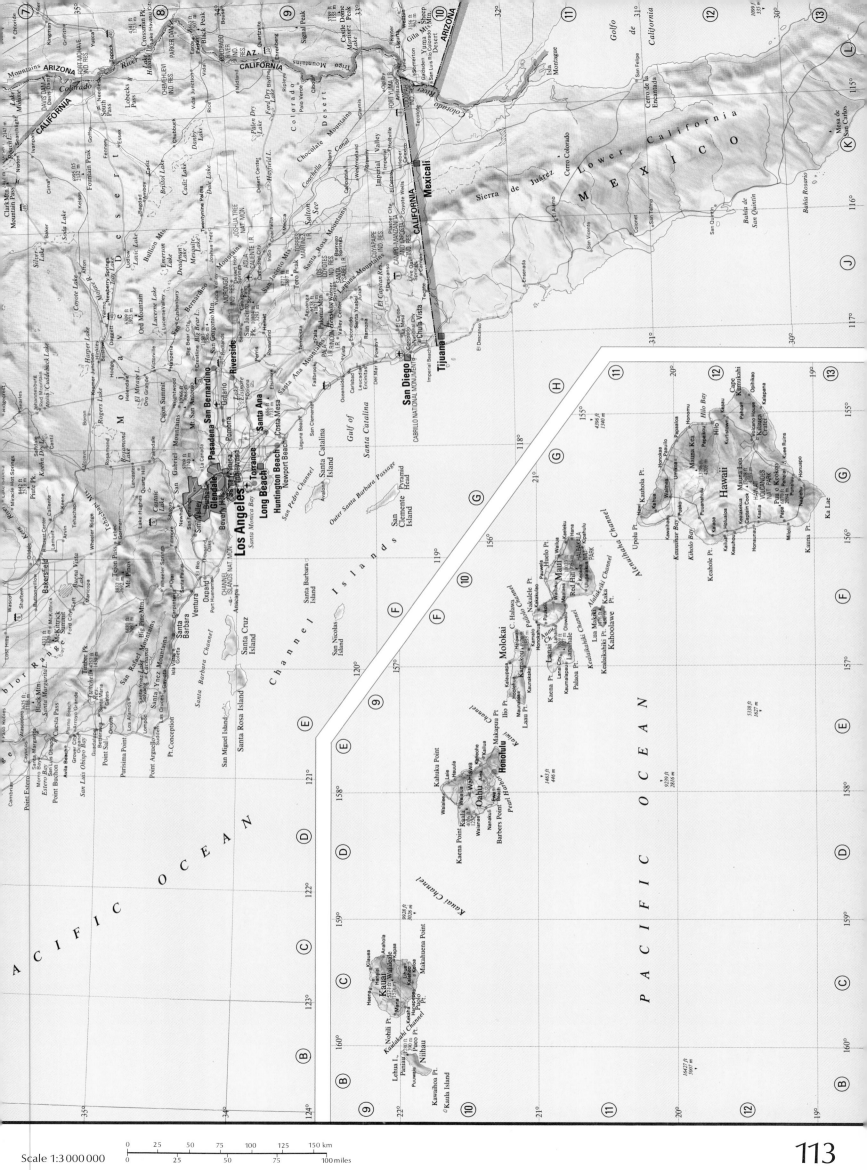

Scale 1:3 000 000

0 25 50 75 100 125 150 km
0   25   50   75   100 miles

113

© ESSELTE MAP SERVICE

Scale 1:3 000 000

0 25 50 75 100 125 150 km

0   25   50   75   100 miles

Scale 1:3 000 000

UNITED STATES, IOWA, MINNESOTA, MONTANA, NEBRASKA, N.DAKOTA, S.DAKOTA, WYOMING

© ESSELTE MAP SERVICE

Scale 1:3 000 000

GULF OF MEXICO

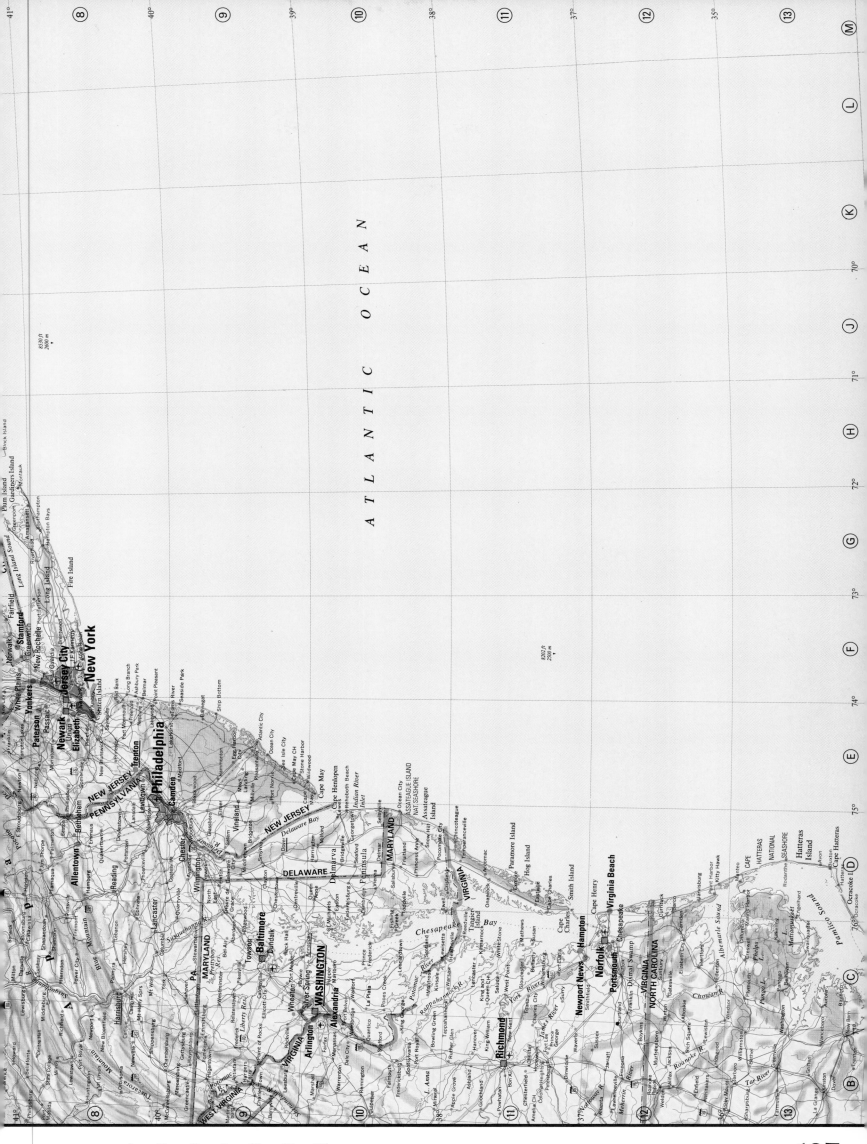

© ESSELTE MAP SERVICE

© ESSELTE MAP SERVICE

Scale 1:10 000 000

POLITICAL DIVISIONS

Scale 1:60 000 000

| 0 | 1000 | 2000 km |
| 0 | 500 | 1000 miles |

POPULATION

Population distribution 1982

- 500 000 inhabitants
- **5** Figures show populations (cities with suburbs) in millions

uninhabited (less than 1 person per sq.km)

Population increase per country 1972–1982

50 %
40
30 — Average for South America 24%
20
10
0

© ESSELTE MAP SERVICE

JAMACA © Puerto Rico D ANTIGUA AND E 60° F 50° G 40° 30°

Caribbean Sea
St. KITTS AND BARBUDA
NEVIS Guadeloupe (France) Pointe-à-Pitre
DOMINICA
Martinique (France)
Fort-de-France
ST. LUCIA
ST. VINCENT BARBADOS
GRENADA Bridgetown

ATLANTIC

OCEAN

P. Gallinas
Santa Marta
Barranquilla Aruba I. Curaçao I. (Neth.)
Cartagena Colón Maracaibo Barquisimeto Maracay CARACAS Cumaná
PANAMÁ Mt. Cristóbal Ciudad Valencia Barcelona TRINIDAD AND TOBAGO
NAMÁ Cúcuta Ojeda PORT OF SPAIN
San Cristóbal Ciudad
Medellín Bucaramanga Bolívar Ciudad Guayana
Manizales Cerro Bolívar GEORGETOWN PARAMARIBO
BOGOTÁ VENEZUELA Angel Falls Kaieteur Falls Cayenne
Ibagué Mt. Roraima French
Buenaventura Guaviare R. Guiana Highlands SURINAM Guiana
Cali COLOMBIA Orinoco R. Roraima Boa Vista

St. Peter and
St. Paul Rocks
(Braz.)
Equator

QUITO Mt. Cotopaxi R. Negro Amapá
ADOR Macapá
Guayaquil Fonte Boa Amazon R. Marajó I. Belém Fernando
Iquitos Manaus Santarém São Luís de Noronha I.
Cajamarca Amazonas Pará Parnaíba Sobral (Braz.)
Marañón R. Selvas Tapajós R. Fortaleza
Mt. Huascarán Juruá R. Madeira R. Ceará C. São Roque
himbote Pôrto Velho Maranhão Teresina Rio Grande Natal
Cerro de Pasco Acre Pôrto Velho Caatingas Piauí do Norte
PERU Rio Branco BRAZIL Paraíba Campina Grande
Huánuco Guajará Mirim Rondônia Juàzeiro do Norte Recife
LIMA La Oroya Cobija Barreiras Pernambuco Caruaru
Callao Huancayo Xingu R. Mato Grosso Bahia Aracaju Alagoas
Huancavelica Trinidad Goiás Feira Alagoinhas Maceió
Ica Cuzco BOLIVIA Cuiabá São Francisco R. Salvador
Pisco Lake Titicaca Mt. Ancohuma Distrito Jequié
Mt. Corupuna Puno LA PAZ Federal BRASÍLIA Itabuna
Arequipa Oruro Cochabamba Goiânia Montes Claros Ilhéus
Mollendo Lake SUCRE Santa Cruz Anápolis Vitória
Tacna Paopó Llallagua Mato Grosso Brazilian Teófilo Otoni
Arica Potosí do Sul Minas Gerais Governador Valadares
Iquique Tarija Campo Uberlândia Highlands Espírito
Antofagasta Grande Uberaba Belo Itabira Santo
Mt. Llullaillaco Paraguay R. São José Horizonte Mt. Bandeira Vitória
Salta PARAGUAY Campo Grande Presidente São Paulo Juiz Campos
Jujuy Chaco Prudente Ribeirão de Fora Rio
CHILE Mt. Galán ASUNCIÓN Paraná R. Bauru Prêto Volta Redonda de Janeiro
Copiapó Tucumán Formosa Londrina Sorocaba Niterói C. Frio
Mr.Ojos del Salado Resistencia Corrientes Campinas Rio de Janeiro
Catamarca Posadas Paraná Santos São Paulo
La Serena La Rioja Santiago Iguaçu Falls Ponta Grossa Curitiba
del Estero Salado R. Santa Catarina Joinville
San Juan Salinas Paraná R. Blumenau
Grandes Santa Fe Florianópolis
Mendoza Córdoba Uruguaiana Rio Grande
Mt. Aconcagua Rosario do Sul Passo Fundo
Viña del Mar San Luis Río Cuarto Santa Caxias do Sul
Valparaíso SANTIAGO Junín Zárate Paraná Paysandú Maria Pôrto Alegre
Rancagua ARGENTINA La Plata Salto L. dos Patos
Talca Santa Rosa BUENOS AIRES URUGUAY Pelotas
Azul Tandil MONTEVIDEO Río Grande
Talcahuano Río Plate Lake Mirim
Concepción Colorado R. Mar del Plata

ATLANTIC
OCEAN

Chillán
Temuco Bahía Blanca
Valdivia Neuquén
Osorno Plaza Huincul
Puerto Montt Viedma
San Carlos Gulf of
de Bariloche San Matías

Chiloé I. Rawson

OCEAN

Puerto Aisén Gulf of
Cerro San Valentín San Jorge
Comodoro Rivadavia
Puerto Deseado

Falkland Islands
(U.K.)
Río Gallegos Stanley

B 80° C 70° D Strait of Magellan E 60° F 50° G 40° 20°
Punta Arenas Tierra del Fuego South Georgia
Ushuaia (U.K.)
Cape Horn

Polar Projection
0 500 1000 km
0 200 400 600 miles
1 hour

135

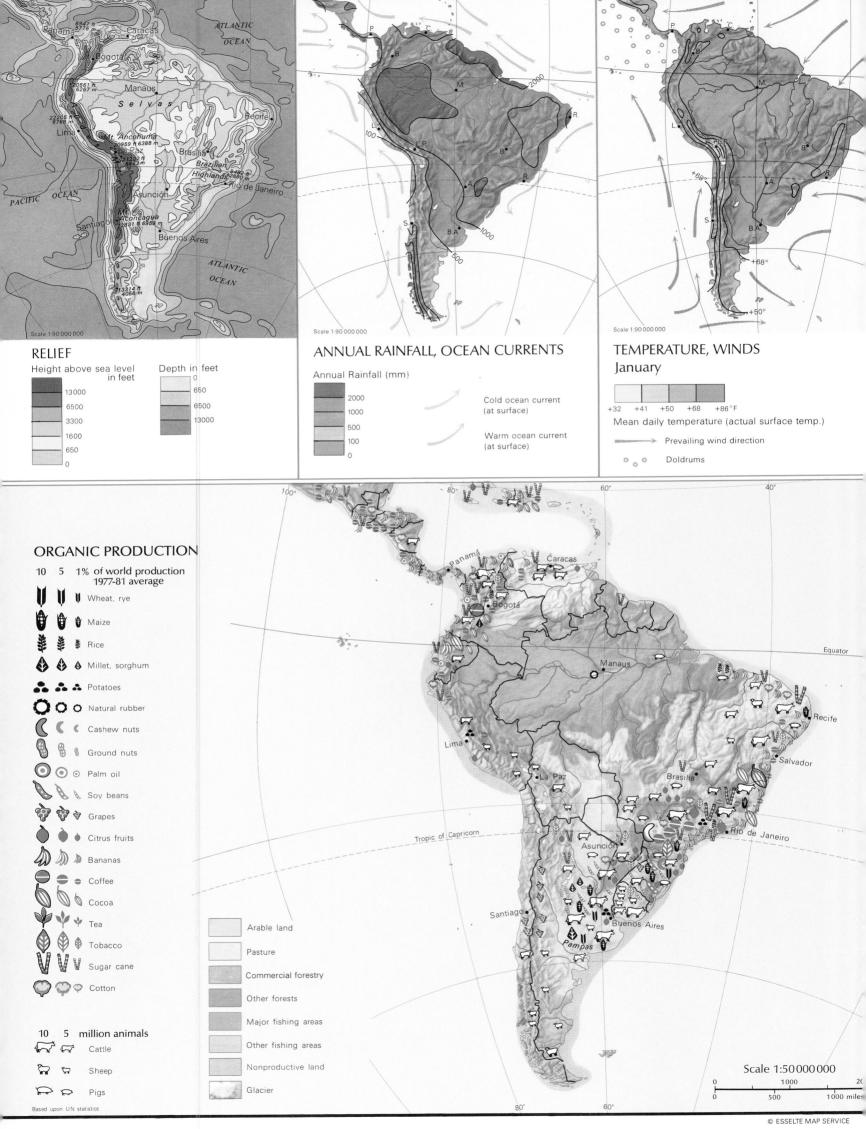

RELIEF

Height above sea level in feet

13000
6500
3300
1600
650
0

Depth in feet

0
650
6500
13000

ANNUAL RAINFALL, OCEAN CURRENTS

Annual Rainfall (mm)

2000
1000
500
100
0

Cold ocean current (at surface)

Warm ocean current (at surface)

Scale 1:90 000 000

TEMPERATURE, WINDS
January

+32 +41 +50 +68 +86 °F

Mean daily temperature (actual surface temp.)

Prevailing wind direction

Doldrums

Scale 1:90 000 000

Scale 1:90 000 000

ORGANIC PRODUCTION

10 5 1% of world production 1977-81 average

Wheat, rye
Maize
Rice
Millet, sorghum
Potatoes
Natural rubber
Cashew nuts
Ground nuts
Palm oil
Soy beans
Grapes
Citrus fruits
Bananas
Coffee
Cocoa
Tea
Tobacco
Sugar cane
Cotton

10 5 million animals

Cattle
Sheep
Pigs

Based upon UN statistics

Arable land
Pasture
Commercial forestry
Other forests
Major fishing areas
Other fishing areas
Nonproductive land
Glacier

Scale 1:50 000 000

© ESSELTE MAP SERVICE

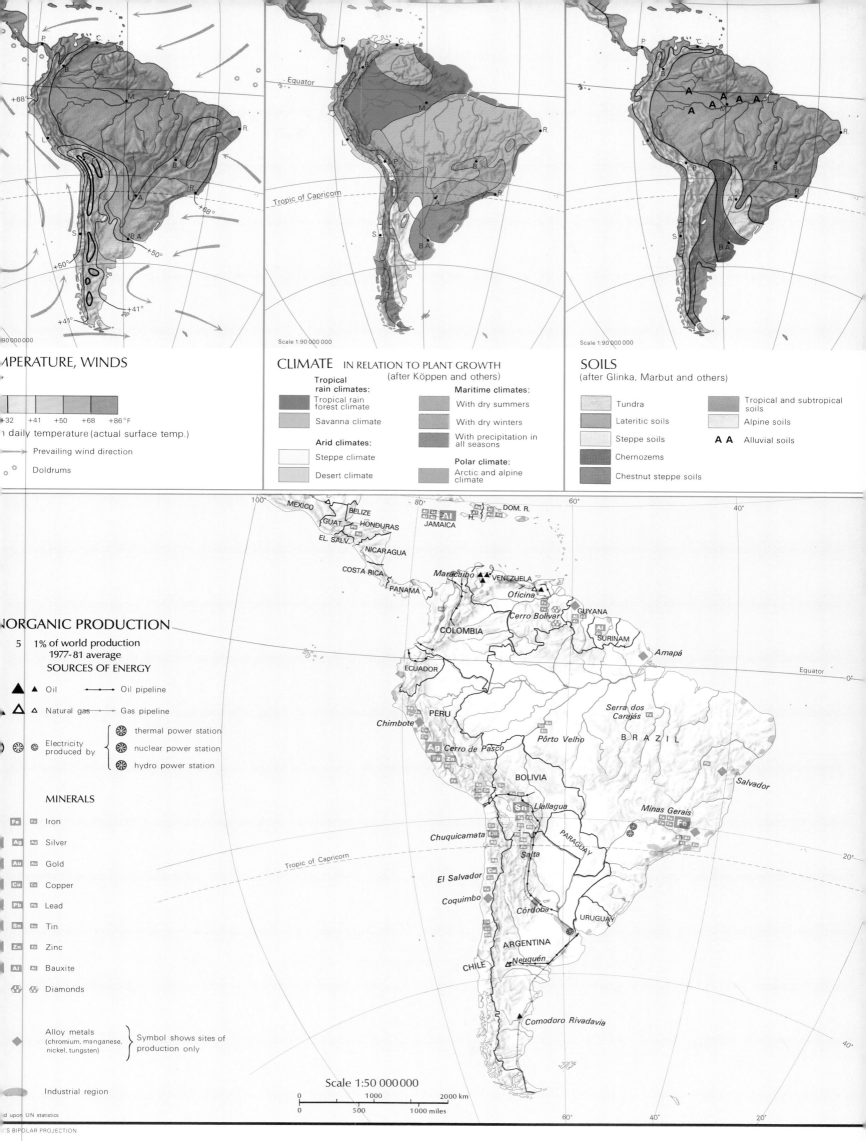

TEMPERATURE, WINDS

+32 +41 +50 +68 +86°F
daily temperature (actual surface temp.)

Prevailing wind direction

Doldrums

CLIMATE IN RELATION TO PLANT GROWTH
(after Köppen and others)

Tropical rain climates:
Tropical rain forest climate
Savanna climate

Arid climates:
Steppe climate
Desert climate

Maritime climates:
With dry summers
With dry winters
With precipitation in all seasons

Polar climate:
Arctic and alpine climate

SOILS
(after Glinka, Marbut and others)

Tundra
Lateritic soils
Steppe soils
Chernozems
Chestnut steppe soils

Tropical and subtropical soils
Alpine soils
A A Alluvial soils

Scale 1:90 000 000

INORGANIC PRODUCTION

5 1% of world production
1977-81 average

SOURCES OF ENERGY

Oil   Oil pipeline
Natural gas Gas pipeline

Electricity produced by:
thermal power station
nuclear power station
hydro power station

MINERALS

Fe Iron
Ag Silver
Au Gold
Cu Copper
Pb Lead
Sn Tin
Zn Zinc
Al Bauxite
    Diamonds

Alloy metals
(chromium, manganese, nickel, tungsten) Symbol shows sites of production only

Industrial region

Scale 1:50 000 000

0   1000   2000 km
0   500   1000 miles

based upon UN statistics

'S BIPOLAR PROJECTION

137

© ESSELTE MAP SERVICE

Scale 1:10 000 000

0 100 200 300 400 km
0   100   200 miles

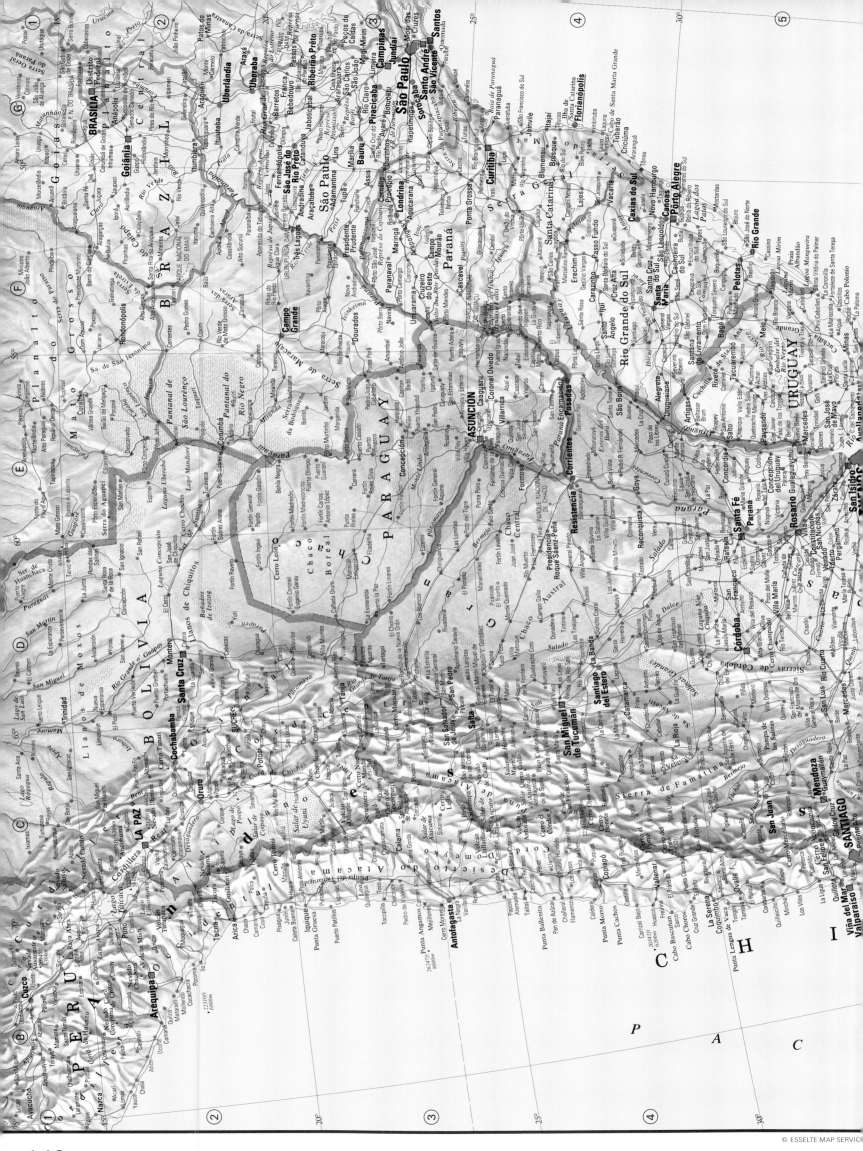

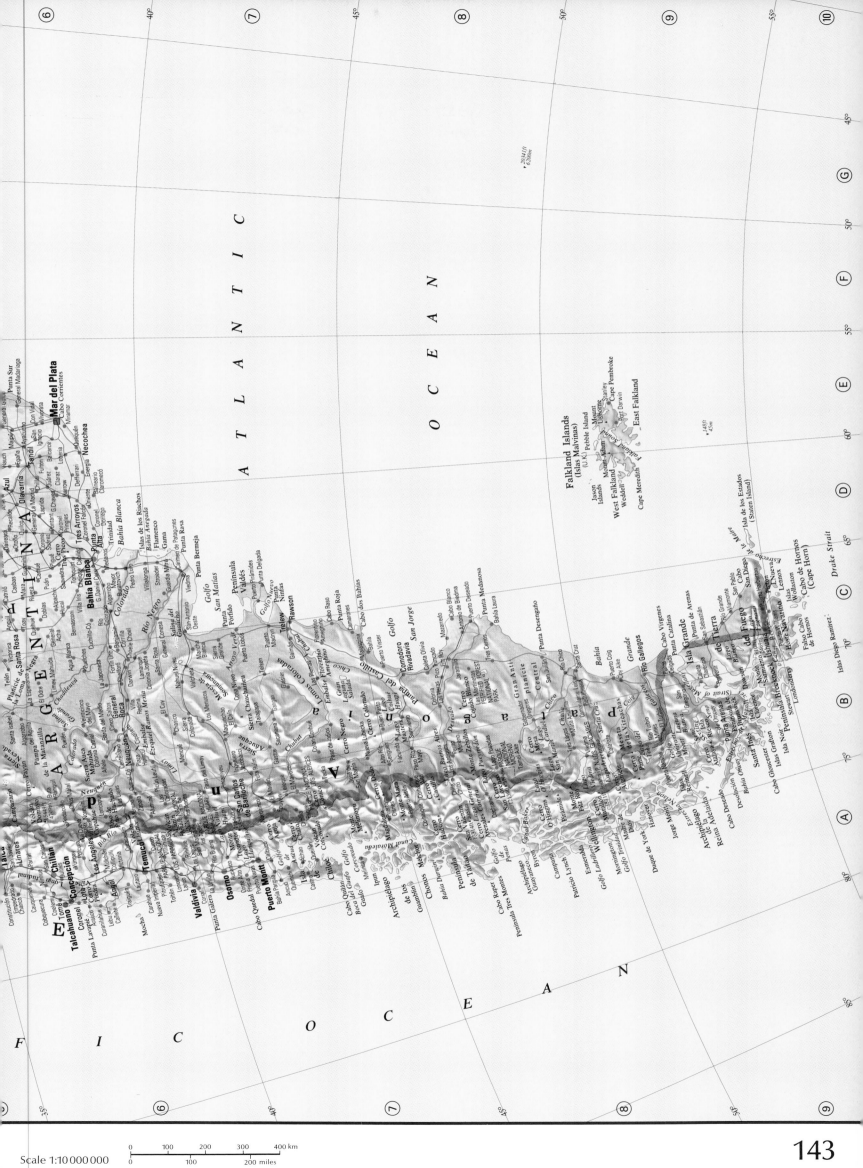

Scale 1:10 000 000

0 100 200 300 400 km
0 100 200 miles

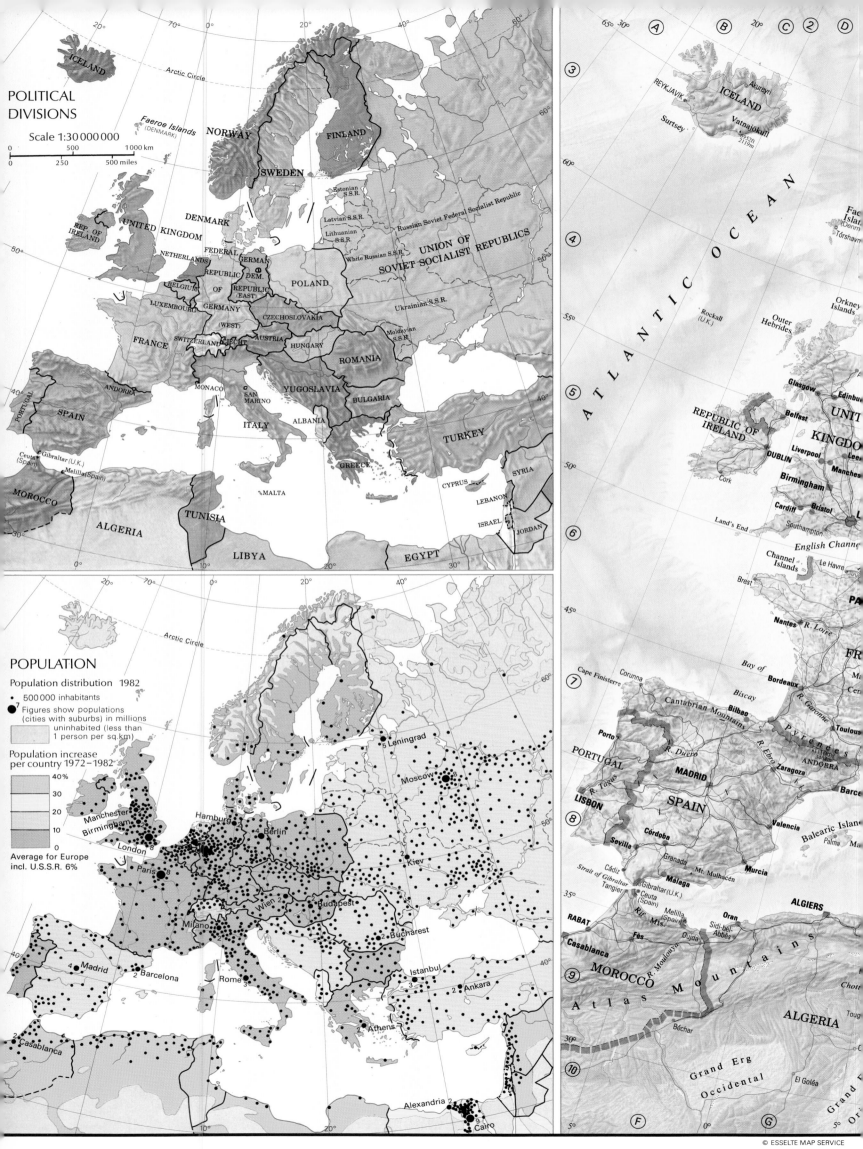

EUROPE, environment, political divisions, population

LAMBERT'S CONFORMAL CONIC PROJECTION

Scale 1:15 000 000

0   200   400   600 km

0   200   300   400 miles
      1/2 hour

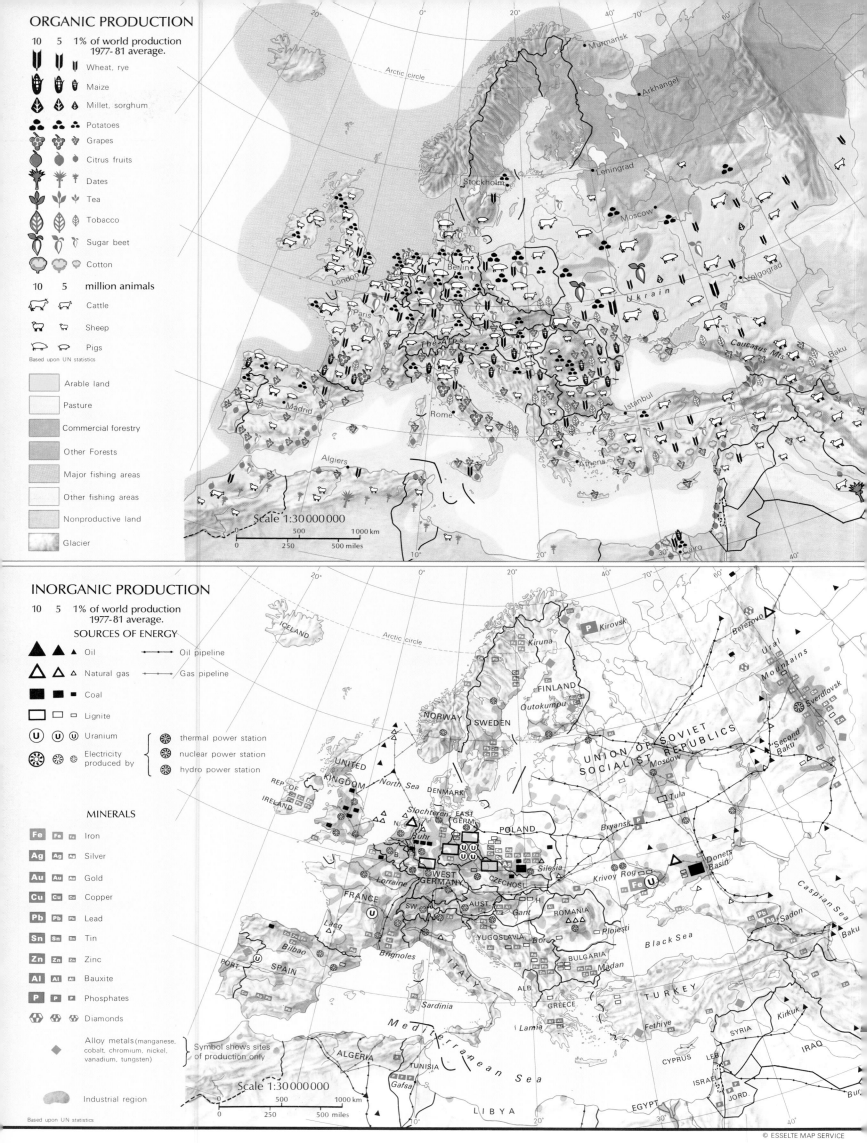

ORGANIC PRODUCTION

10   5   1% of world production
1977-81 average.

Wheat, rye
Maize
Millet, sorghum
Potatoes
Grapes
Citrus fruits
Dates
Tea
Tobacco
Sugar beet
Cotton

10   5   million animals

Cattle
Sheep
Pigs

Based upon UN statistics

Arable land
Pasture
Commercial forestry
Other Forests
Major fishing areas
Other fishing areas
Nonproductive land
Glacier

Scale 1:30 000 000

0   500   1000 km
0   250   500 miles

Arctic circle
Murmansk
Arkhangel
Leningrad
Stockholm
Moscow
Volgograd
Ukrain
The Alps
London
Paris
Madrid
Rome
Algiers
Athens
Istanbul
Caucasus Mts
Baku
Cairo

INORGANIC PRODUCTION

10   5   1% of world production
1977-81 average.

SOURCES OF ENERGY

Oil   Oil pipeline
Natural gas   Gas pipeline
Coal
Lignite
Uranium
Electricity
produced by   thermal power station
                       nuclear power station
                       hydro power station

MINERALS

Fe   Iron
Ag   Silver
Au   Gold
Cu   Copper
Pb   Lead
Sn   Tin
Zn   Zinc
Al   Bauxite
P   Phosphates
     Diamonds

Alloy metals (manganese,
cobalt, chromium, nickel,
vanadium, tungsten)

Symbol shows sites
of production only

Industrial region

Based upon UN statistics

Scale 1:30 000 000

0   500   1000 km
0   250   500 miles

ICELAND
Arctic circle
Kirovsk
Kiruna
Berezovo
Ural Mountains
NORWAY
SWEDEN
FINLAND
Outokumpu
Sverdlovsk
UNION OF SOVIET
SOCIALIST REPUBLICS
Second Baku
Moscow
REP OF
IRELAND
UNITED
KINGDOM
North Sea
DENMARK
Slochteren EAST
GERM
Tula
Caspian Sea
Ruhr
POLAND
Silesia
Bryansk
Donets Basin
Krivoy Rog
Baku
Lorraine
WEST
GERMANY
CZECHOSL
Sadon
FRANCE
AUST
Gant
ROMANIA
Lacq
SW
Bor
Ploiesti
Black Sea
Ladq
YUGOSLAVIA
Brignoles
Bilbao
ITALY
BULGARIA
Madan
PORT
SPAIN
Sardinia
ALB
TURKEY
GREECE
Lamia
Fethiye
Kirkuk
SYRIA
CYPRUS
LEB
IRAQ
Mediterranean Sea
ALGERIA
TUNISIA
ISRAEL
JORD
Gafsa
LIBYA
EGYPT

© ESSELTE MAP SERVICE

146   EUROPE, physical, economic

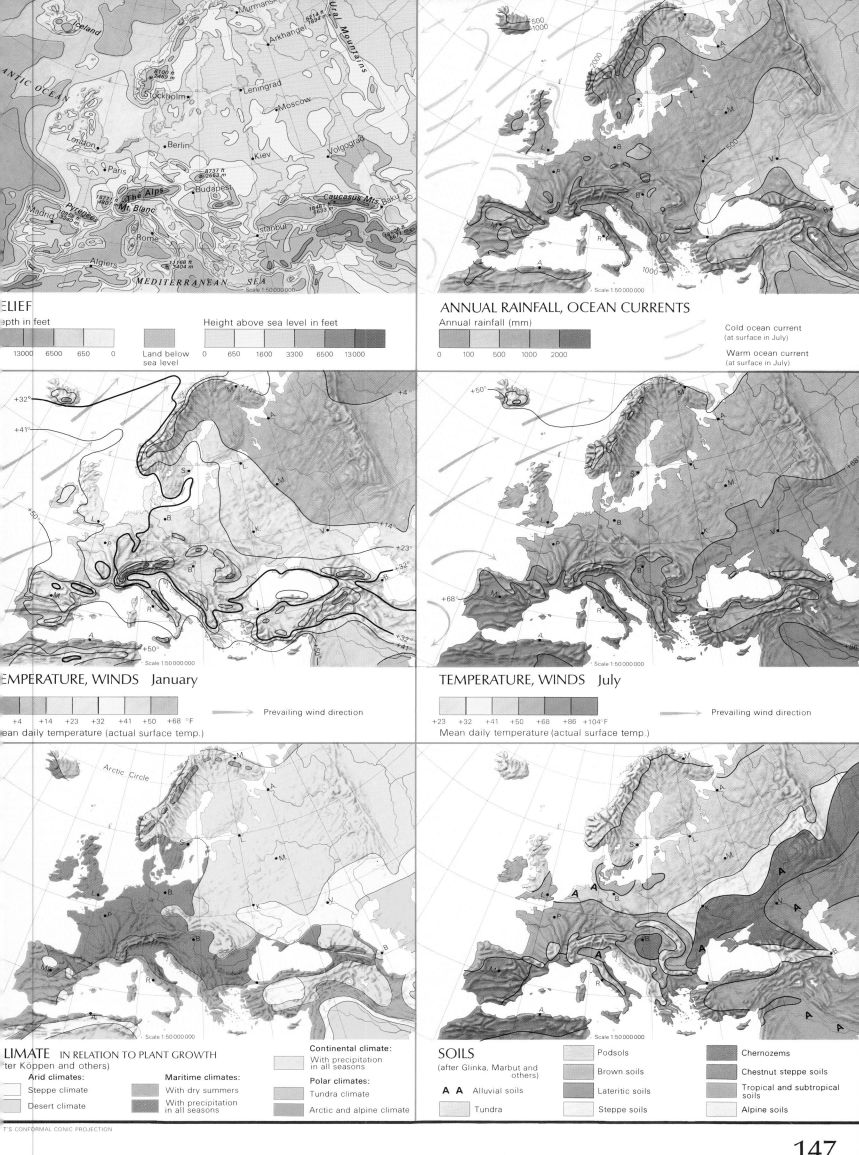

RELIEF

Depth in feet

13000   6500   650   0   Land below sea level

Height above sea level in feet

0   650   1600   3300   6500   13000

ANNUAL RAINFALL, OCEAN CURRENTS

Annual rainfall (mm)

0   100   500   1000   2000

Cold ocean current (at surface in July)

Warm ocean current (at surface in July)

TEMPERATURE, WINDS   January

+4   +14   +23   +32   +41   +50   +68 °F

Mean daily temperature (actual surface temp.)

Prevailing wind direction

TEMPERATURE, WINDS   July

+23   +32   +41   +50   +68   +86   +104°F

Mean daily temperature (actual surface temp.)

Prevailing wind direction

CLIMATE IN RELATION TO PLANT GROWTH
(after Köppen and others)

Arid climates:
- Steppe climate
- Desert climate

Maritime climates:
- With dry summers
- With precipitation in all seasons

Continental climate:
- With precipitation in all seasons

Polar climates:
- Tundra climate
- Arctic and alpine climate

SOILS
(after Glinka, Marbut and others)

A A   Alluvial soils

- Tundra
- Podsols
- Brown soils
- Lateritic soils
- Steppe soils
- Chernozems
- Chestnut steppe soils
- Tropical and subtropical soils
- Alpine soils

LAMBERT'S CONFORMAL CONIC PROJECTION

147

© ESSELTE MAP SERVICE

Scale 1:5 000 000

0 50 100 200 km
0   50   100 miles

Scale 1:5 000 000

0   100   200 km

0   50   100 miles

© ESSELTE MAP SERVICE

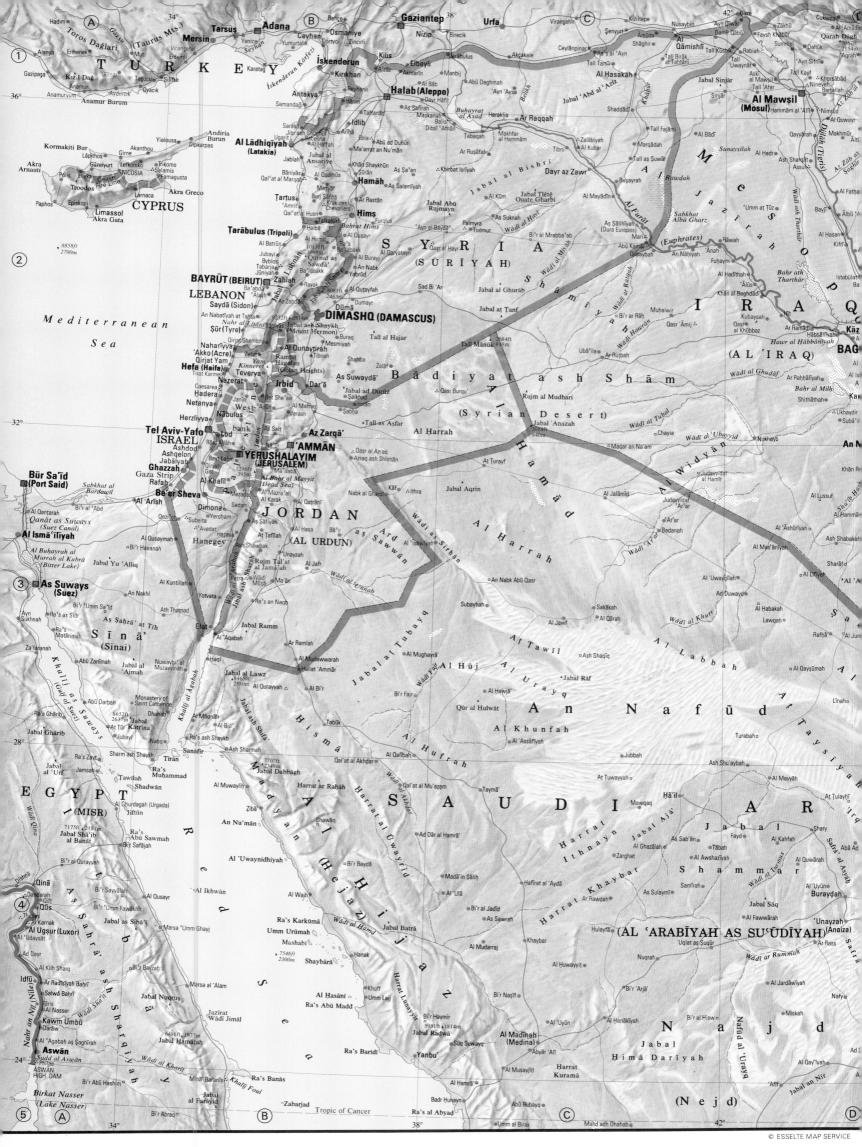

© ESSELTE MAP SERVICE

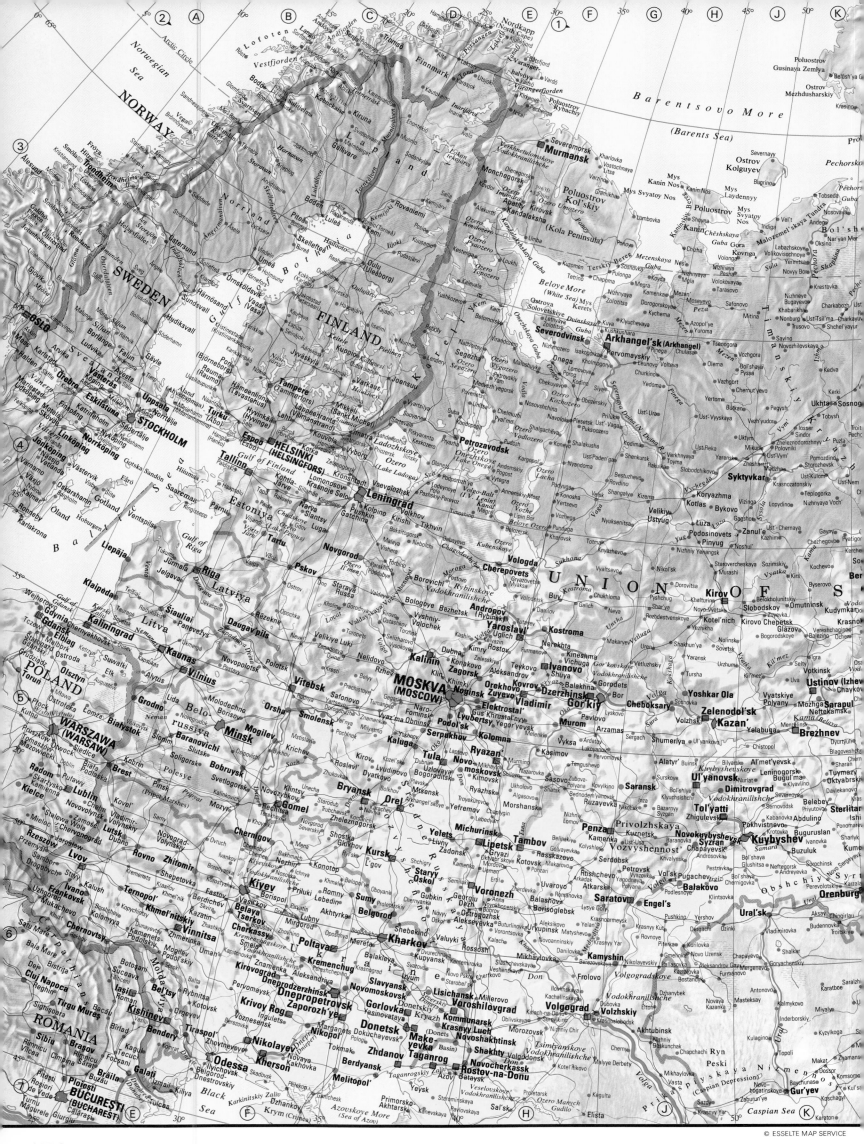

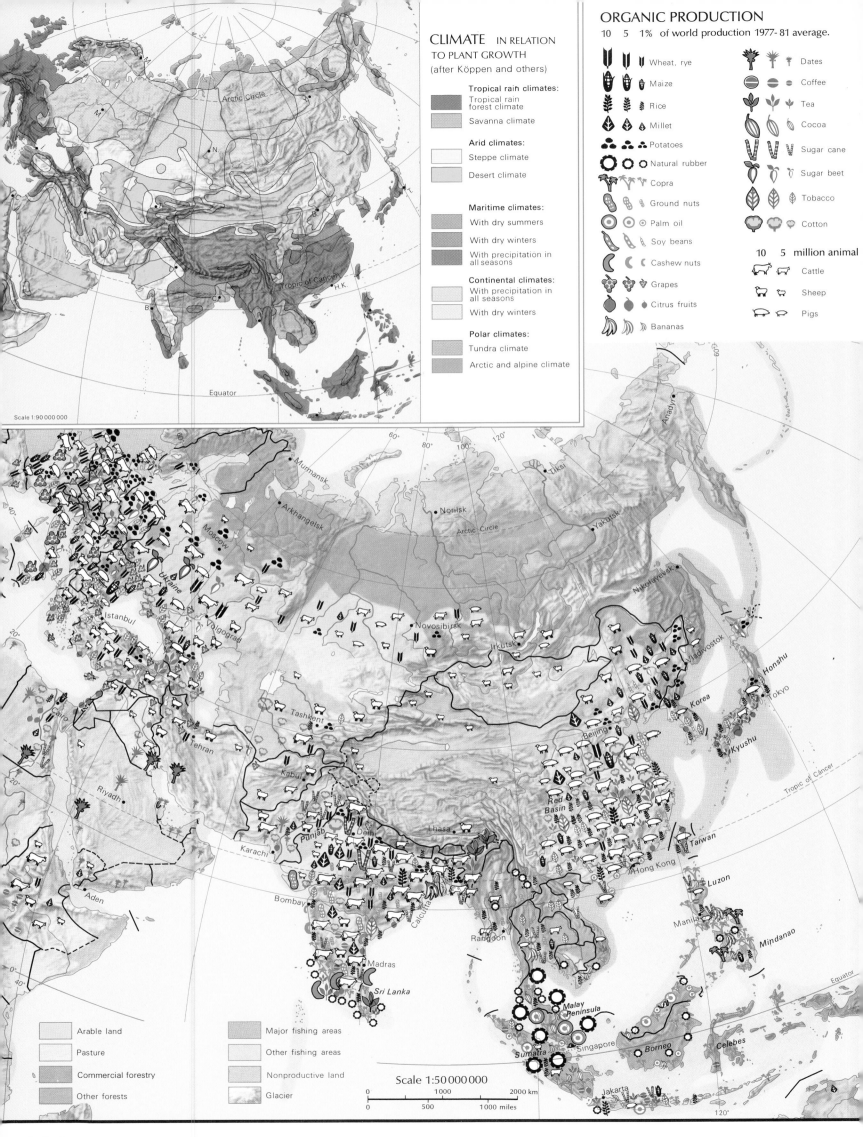

CLIMATE IN RELATION TO PLANT GROWTH
(after Köppen and others)

Tropical rain climates:
- Tropical rain forest climate
- Savanna climate

Arid climates:
- Steppe climate
- Desert climate

Maritime climates:
- With dry summers
- With dry winters
- With precipitation in all seasons

Continental climates:
- With precipitation in all seasons
- With dry winters

Polar climates:
- Tundra climate
- Arctic and alpine climate

Scale 1:90 000 000

ORGANIC PRODUCTION
10 5 1% of world production 1977- 81 average.

- Wheat, rye
- Maize
- Rice
- Millet
- Potatoes
- Natural rubber
- Copra
- Ground nuts
- Palm oil
- Soy beans
- Cashew nuts
- Grapes
- Citrus fruits
- Bananas
- Dates
- Coffee
- Tea
- Cocoa
- Sugar cane
- Sugar beet
- Tobacco
- Cotton

10 5 million animal
- Cattle
- Sheep
- Pigs

- Arable land
- Pasture
- Commercial forestry
- Other forests
- Major fishing areas
- Other fishing areas
- Nonproductive land
- Glacier

Scale 1:50 000 000

| 0 | 1000 | 2000 km |
| 0 | 500 | 1000 miles |

SOILS
(after Glinka, Marbut and others)

- Tundra
- Podsols
- Brown soils
- Lateritic soils
- Steppe soils
- Chernozems
- Chestnut steppe soils
- Tropical and subtropical soils
- Alpine soils
- Glacier, ice cap

A A Alluvial soils

INORGANIC PRODUCTION

MINERALS

10   5   1% of world production 1977-81 average.

Fe Fe Fe	Iron	**Sn** Sn Sn	Tin
Ag Ag Ag	Silver	**Zn** Zn Zn	Zinc
Au Au Au	Gold	**Al** Al Al	Bauxite
Cu Cu Cu	Copper	**P** P P	Phosphates
Pb Pb Pb	Lead		Diamonds

◆ Alloy metals (chrome, manganese, cobalt, nickel, vanadium, tungsten) — Symbol shows sites of production only

Industrial region

Based on UN statistics

SOURCES OF ENERGY

10   5   1% of world production 1977-81 average.

- ▲ ▲ ▲ Oil — ⟷ Oil Pipeline
- △ △ △ Natural gas — ⟷ Gas Pipeline
- ■ ■ ▪ Coal
- ▭ ▭ ▭ Lignite
- Ⓤ Ⓤ Ⓤ Uranium
- ✷ ✷ ✷ Electricity produced by

- ✷ thermal power station
- ✷ nuclear power station
- ✷ hydro power station

Based on UN statistics

Scale 1:50 000 000

0   1000   2000 km

0   500   1000 miles

'T'S AZIMUTHAL EQUAL-AREA PROJECTION

165

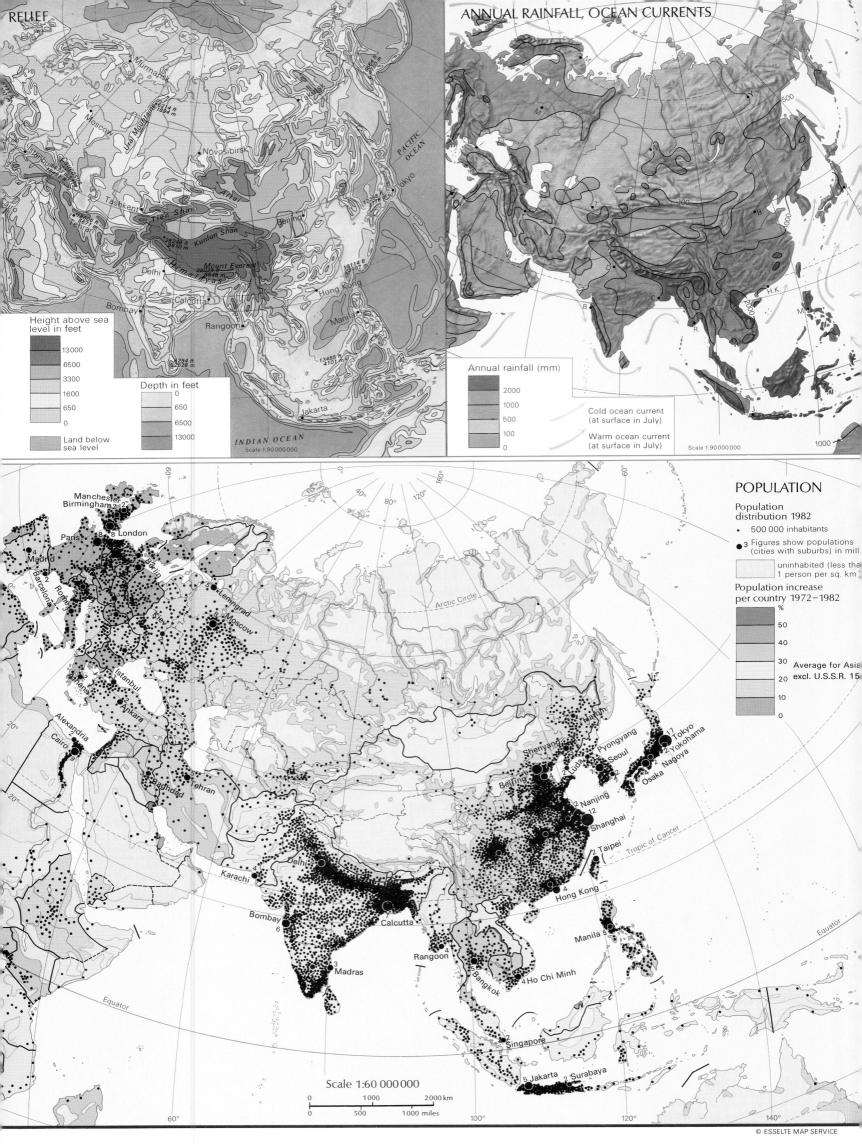

RELIEF

Murmansk
Moscow
Ural Mountains 6214 ft / 1894 m
Novosibirsk
Yakutsk
Altai
PACIFIC OCEAN
Tokyo
Tashkent
Tien Shan
Kunlun Shan 28248 ft / 8610 m
Beijing
Delhi
Mount Everest 29028 ft / 8848 m
Himalayas
Hong Kong
Bombay
Calcutta
Manila
Rangoon
3294 ft / 2528 m
13114 ft / 3997 m
13455 ft / 4101 m
INDIAN OCEAN
Jakarta

Scale 1:90 000 000

Height above sea level in feet
13000
6500
3300
1600
650
0

Depth in feet
0
650
6500
13000

Land below sea level

ANNUAL RAINFALL, OCEAN CURRENTS

500
100
1000
2000
1000

Annual rainfall (mm)
2000
1000
500
100
0

→ Cold ocean current (at surface in July)
→ Warm ocean current (at surface in July)

Scale 1:90 000 000

POPULATION

Population distribution 1982
· 500 000 inhabitants
● 3 Figures show populations (cities with suburbs) in mill

uninhabited (less tha 1 person per sq. km

Population increase per country 1972–1982
%
50
40
30
20
10
0

Average for Asia excl. U.S.S.R. 15

Manchester
Birmingham 2
Paris 8
8 London
4 Madrid
Barcelona 2
Rome 3
Berlin
Leningrad 5
Moscow
Athens
Istanbul
Ankara 2
Alexandria
Cairo
Baghdad
Tehran
Harbin
Shenyang
Pyongyang
2 Luda
Seoul 7
17 Tokyo
2 Yokohama
Osaka Nagoya
Beijing
2 Nanjing
Shanghai 12
Karachi
Delhi 4
Taipei 2
Bombay 6
Calcutta
4 Hong Kong
Rangoon 4
Madras 3
Bangkok
Manila 5
Ho Chi Minh 4
2 Singapore
5 Jakarta
2 Surabaya

Arctic Circle
Tropic of Cancer
Equator

Scale 1:60 000 000

0   1000   2000 km
0   500   1000 miles

© ESSELTE MAP SERVICE

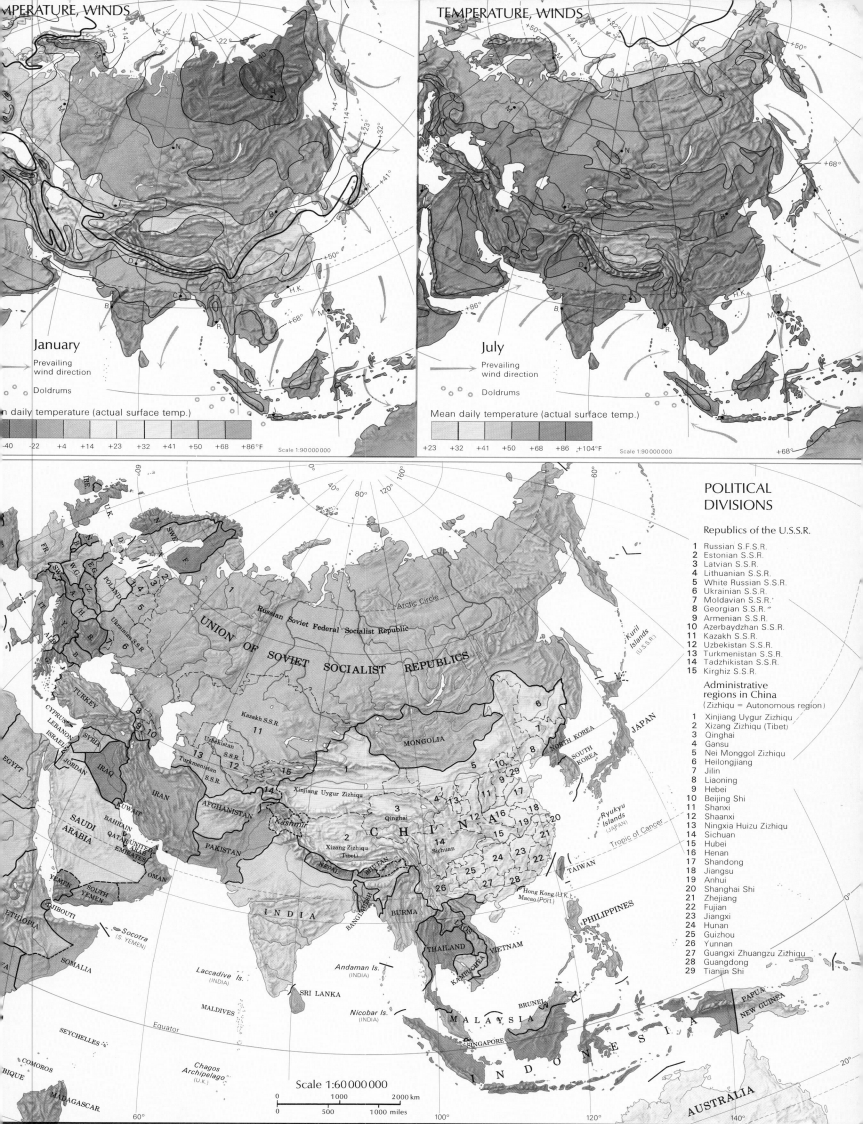

January

→ Prevailing
   wind direction

○ ○ Doldrums

n daily temperature (actual surface temp.)

| -40 | -22 | +4 | +14 | +23 | +32 | +41 | +50 | +68 | +86°F |

Scale 1:90 000 000

July

→ Prevailing
   wind direction

○ ○ Doldrums

Mean daily temperature (actual surface temp.)

| +23 | +32 | +41 | +50 | +68 | +86 | +104°F |

Scale 1:90 000 000

+68°

POLITICAL DIVISIONS

Republics of the U.S.S.R.

1 Russian S.F.S.R.
2 Estonian S.S.R.
3 Latvian S.S.R.
4 Lithuanian S.S.R.
5 White Russian S.S.R.
6 Ukrainian S.S.R.
7 Moldavian S.S.R.'
8 Georgian S.S.R.'
9 Armenian S.S.R.
10 Azerbaydzhan S.S.R.
11 Kazakh S.S.R.
12 Uzbekistan S.S.R.
13 Turkmenistan S.S.R.
14 Tadzhikistan S.S.R.
15 Kirghiz S.S.R.

Administrative regions in China
(Zizhiqu = Autonomous region)

1 Xinjiang Uygur Zizhiqu
2 Xizang Zizhiqu (Tibet)
3 Qinghai
4 Gansu
5 Nei Monggol Zizhiqu
6 Heilongjiang
7 Jilin
8 Liaoning
9 Hebei
10 Beijing Shi
11 Shanxi
12 Shaanxi
13 Ningxia Huizu Zizhiqu
14 Sichuan
15 Hubei
16 Henan
17 Shandong
18 Jiangsu
19 Anhui
20 Shanghai Shi
21 Zhejiang
22 Fujian
23 Jiangxi
24 Hunan
25 Guizhou
26 Yunnan
27 Guangxi Zhuangzu Zizhiqu
28 Guangdong
29 Tianjin Shi

Scale 1:60 000 000

0   1000   2000 km

0   500   1000 miles

'S AZIMUTHAL EQUAL-AREA PROJECTION

167

© ESSELTE MAP SERVICE

Scale 1:10 000 000

169

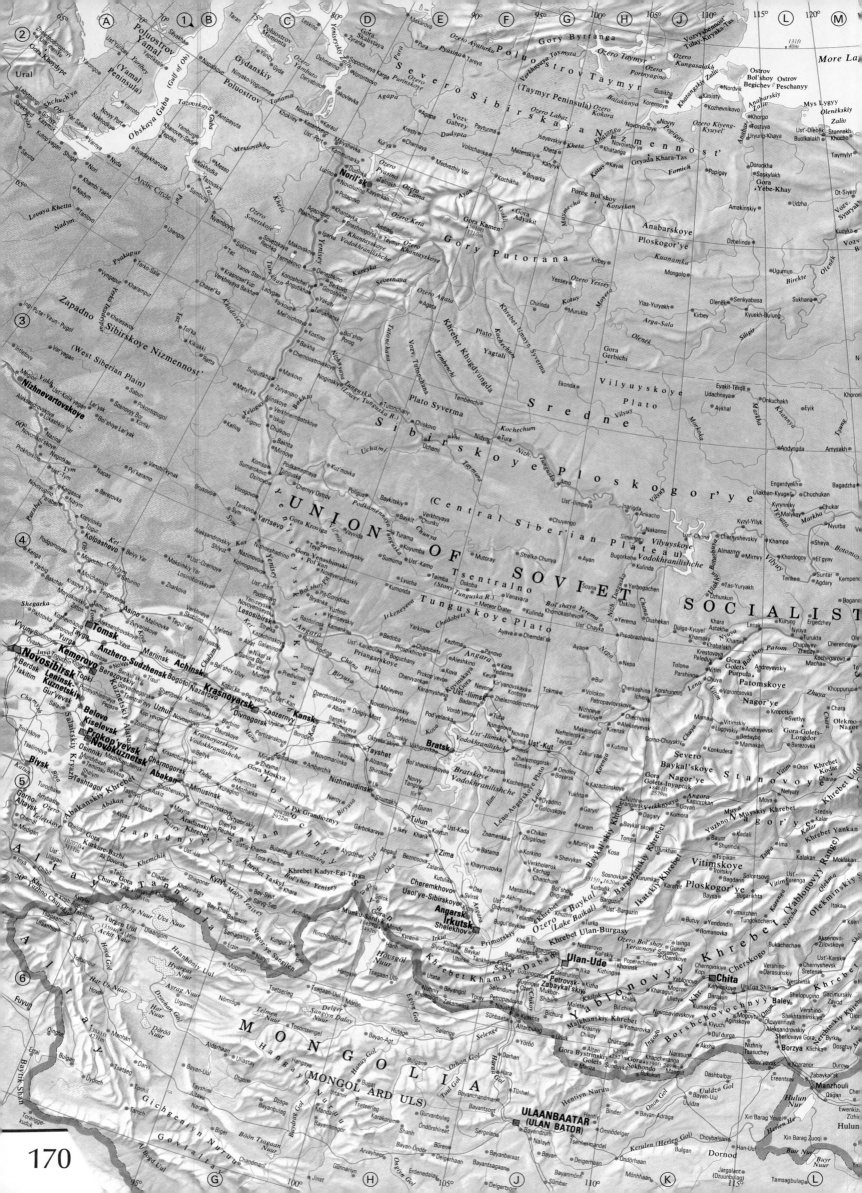

© ESSELTE MAP SERVICE

Scale 1:10 000 000

0   100   200   300   400 km
0   100   200 miles

173

175

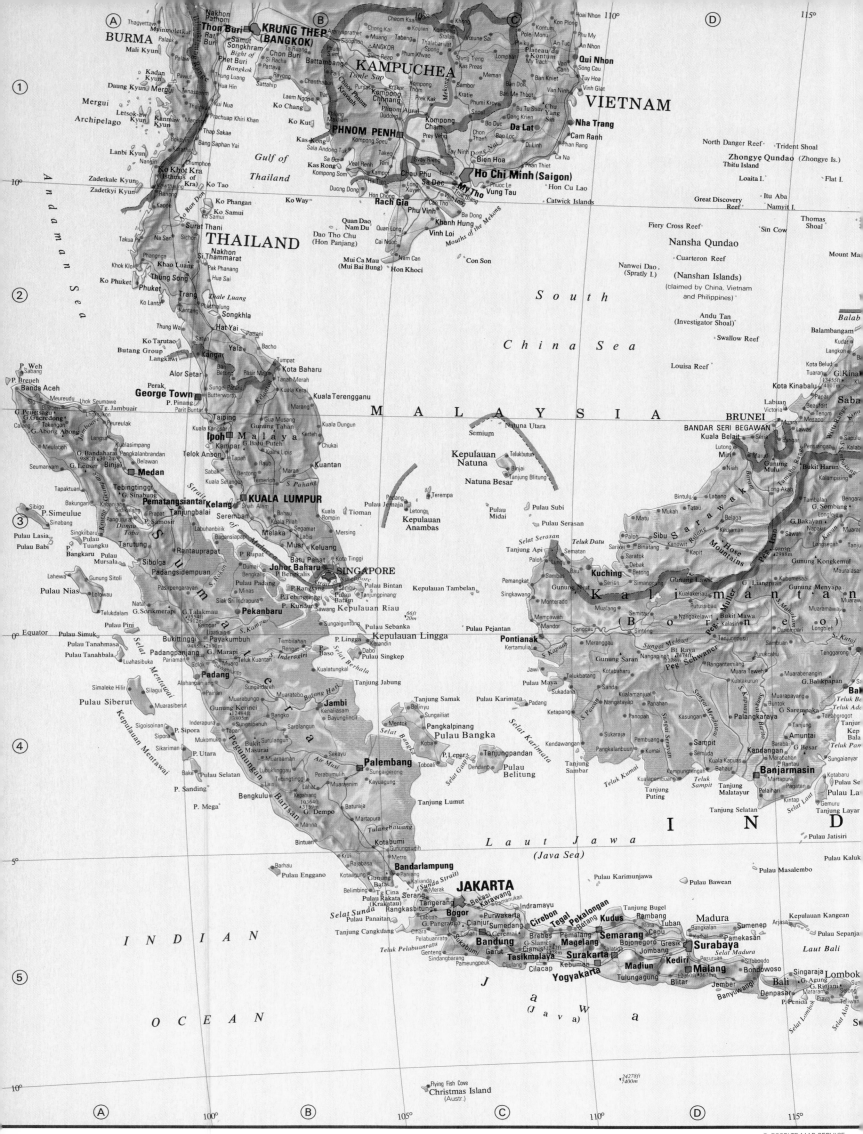

Scale 1:10 000 000

0   100   200   300   400 km
0   100   200 miles

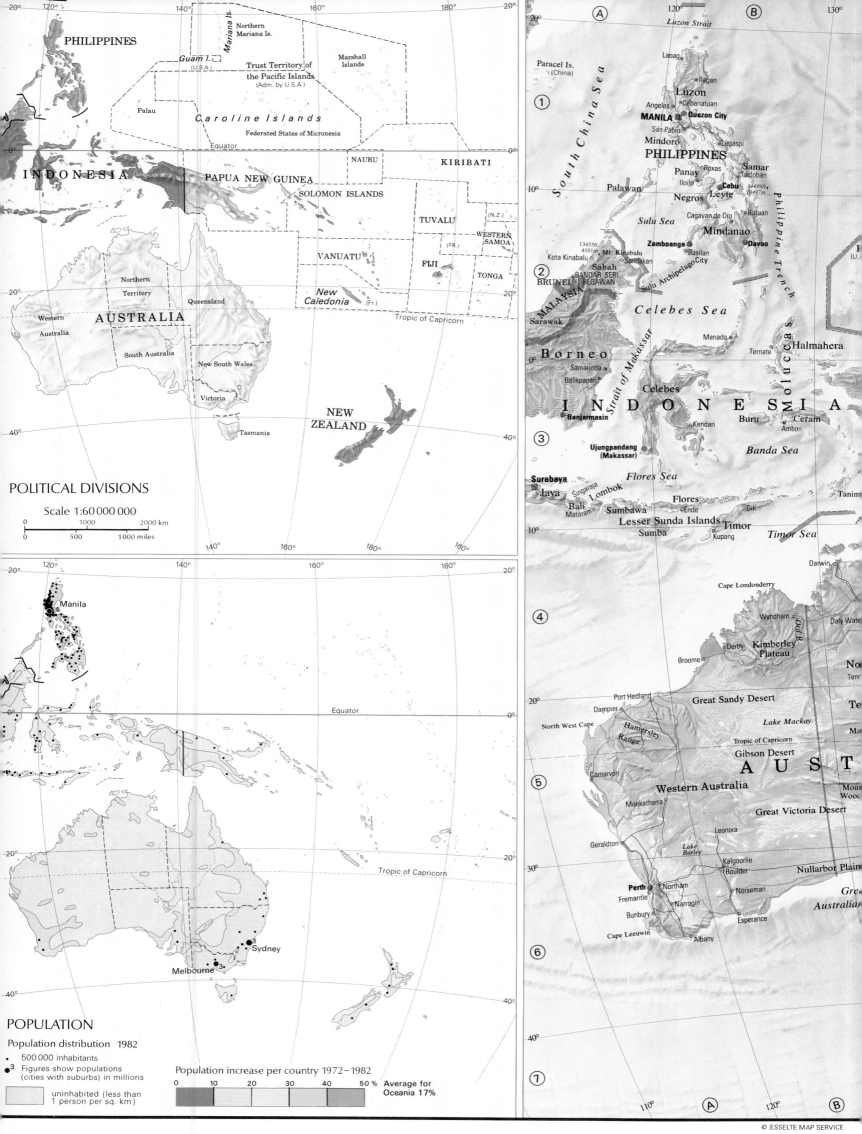

POLITICAL DIVISIONS

Scale 1:60 000 000

POPULATION

Population distribution 1982

• 500 000 inhabitants

●3 Figures show populations (cities with suburbs) in millions

uninhabited (less than 1 person per sq. km)

Population increase per country 1972–1982

0   10   20   30   40   50 %   Average for Oceania 17%

© ESSELTE MAP SERVICE

LAMBERT'S AZIMUTHAL EQUAL-AREA PROJECTION

Scale 1:25 000 000

179

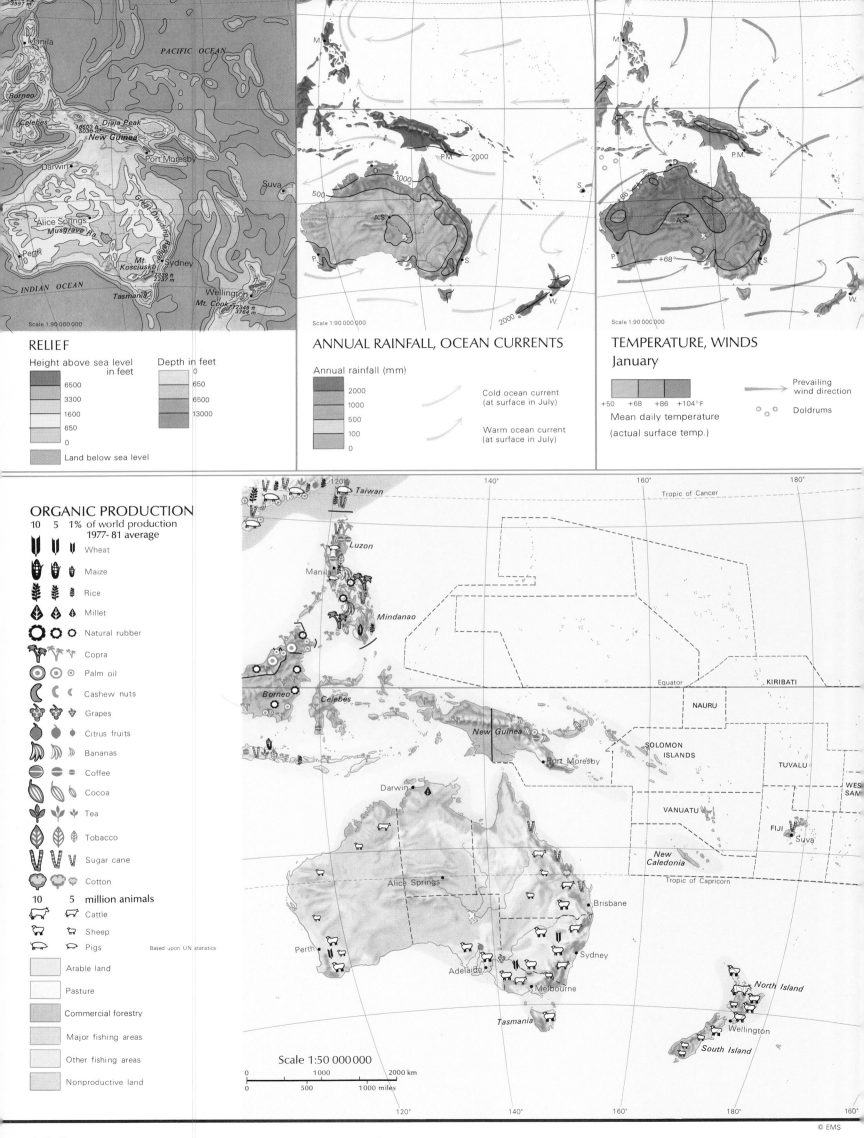

RELIEF

Height above sea level in feet

- 6500
- 3300
- 1600
- 650
- 0
- Land below sea level

Depth in feet

- 0
- 650
- 6500
- 13000

Scale 1:90 000 000

ANNUAL RAINFALL, OCEAN CURRENTS

Annual rainfall (mm)

- 2000
- 1000
- 500
- 100
- 0

→ Cold ocean current (at surface in July)

→ Warm ocean current (at surface in July)

Scale 1:90 000 000

TEMPERATURE, WINDS
January

Mean daily temperature (actual surface temp.)

+50 +68 +86 +104°F

→ Prevailing wind direction

∘ ∘ ∘ Doldrums

Scale 1:90 000 000

ORGANIC PRODUCTION

10 5 1% of world production
1977-81 average

- Wheat
- Maize
- Rice
- Millet
- Natural rubber
- Copra
- Palm oil
- Cashew nuts
- Grapes
- Citrus fruits
- Bananas
- Coffee
- Cocoa
- Tea
- Tobacco
- Sugar cane
- Cotton

10 5 million animals

- Cattle
- Sheep
- Pigs

Based upon UN statistics

- Arable land
- Pasture
- Commercial forestry
- Major fishing areas
- Other fishing areas
- Nonproductive land

Scale 1:50 000 000

0 1000 2000 km
0 500 1000 miles

© EMS

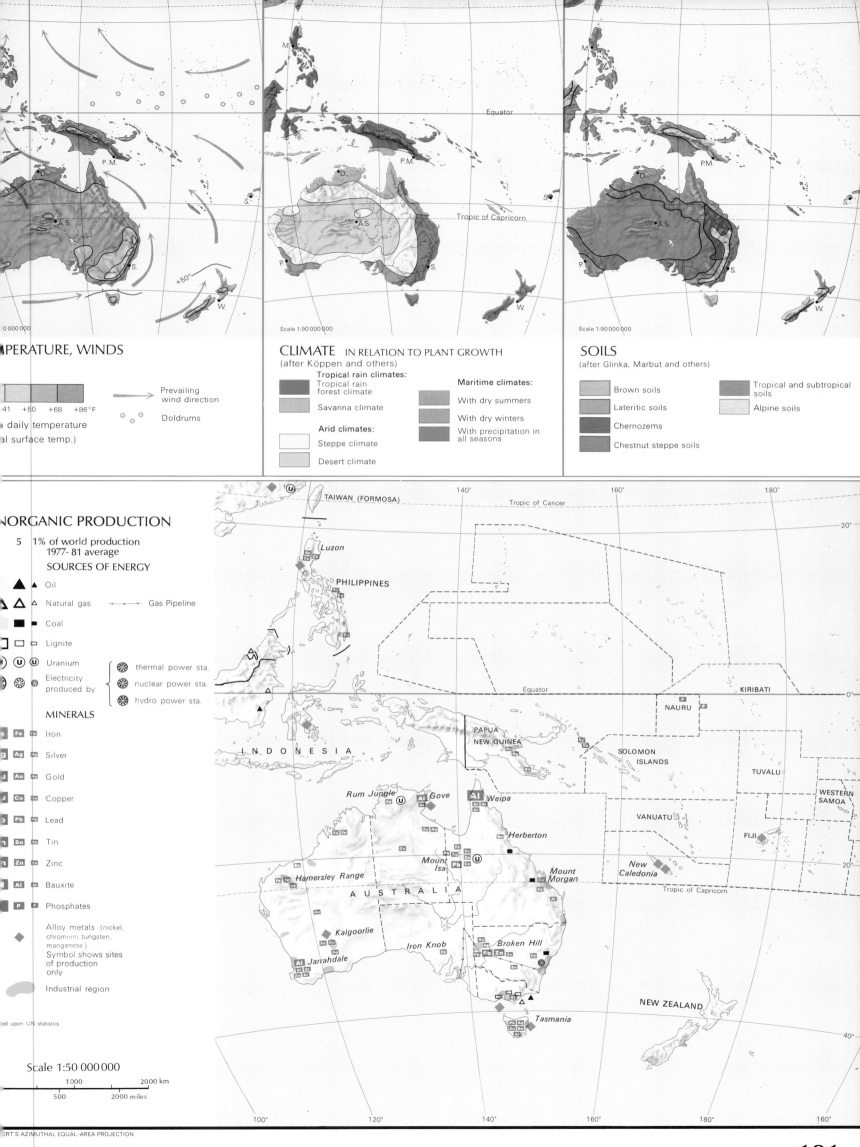

Scale 1:90 000 000

Scale 1:90 000 000

[TEM]PERATURE, WINDS

+41 +50 +68 +86°F

[Mean] daily temperature
([actual] surface temp.)

→ Prevailing wind direction

○ ○ Doldrums

CLIMATE IN RELATION TO PLANT GROWTH
(after Köppen and others)

Tropical rain climates:
- Tropical rain forest climate
- Savanna climate

Arid climates:
- Steppe climate
- Desert climate

Maritime climates:
- With dry summers
- With dry winters
- With precipitation in all seasons

SOILS
(after Glinka, Marbut and others)

- Brown soils
- Lateritic soils
- Chernozems
- Chestnut steppe soils
- Tropical and subtropical soils
- Alpine soils

[I]NORGANIC PRODUCTION

5 1% of world production
1977- 81 average

SOURCES OF ENERGY

▲ ▲ ▲ Oil
△ △ △ Natural gas   —┼— Gas Pipeline
■ ■ ■ Coal
▢ ▢ ▢ Lignite
Ⓤ Ⓤ Ⓤ Uranium

Electricity produced by:
- ⊛ thermal power sta.
- ⊛ nuclear power sta.
- ⊛ hydro power sta.

MINERALS

Fe Fe Iron
Ag Ag Silver
Au Au Gold
Cu Cu Copper
Pb Pb Lead
Sn Sn Tin
Zn Zn Zinc
Al Al Bauxite
P P Phosphates

◆ Alloy metals (nickel, chromium, tungsten, manganese)
Symbol shows sites of production only

◖ Industrial region

[Based] upon UN statistics

Scale 1:50 000 000

1000 2000 km
500 2000 miles

[Map labels:]
TAIWAN (FORMOSA)
Tropic of Cancer
Luzon
PHILIPPINES
INDONESIA
PAPUA NEW GUINEA
Equator
KIRIBATI
NAURU
SOLOMON ISLANDS
TUVALU
WESTERN SAMOA
VANUATU
FIJI
New Caledonia
Rum Jungle
Gove
Weipa
Herberton
Mount Isa
Hamersley Range
Mount Morgan
AUSTRALIA
Kalgoorlie
Iron Knob
Broken Hill
Jarrahdale
Tropic of Capricorn
NEW ZEALAND
Tasmania

[LAMB]ERT'S AZIMUTHAL EQUAL-AREA PROJECTION

181

© ESSELTE MAP SERVICE

Scale 1:10 000

183

© ESSELTE MAP SERVICE

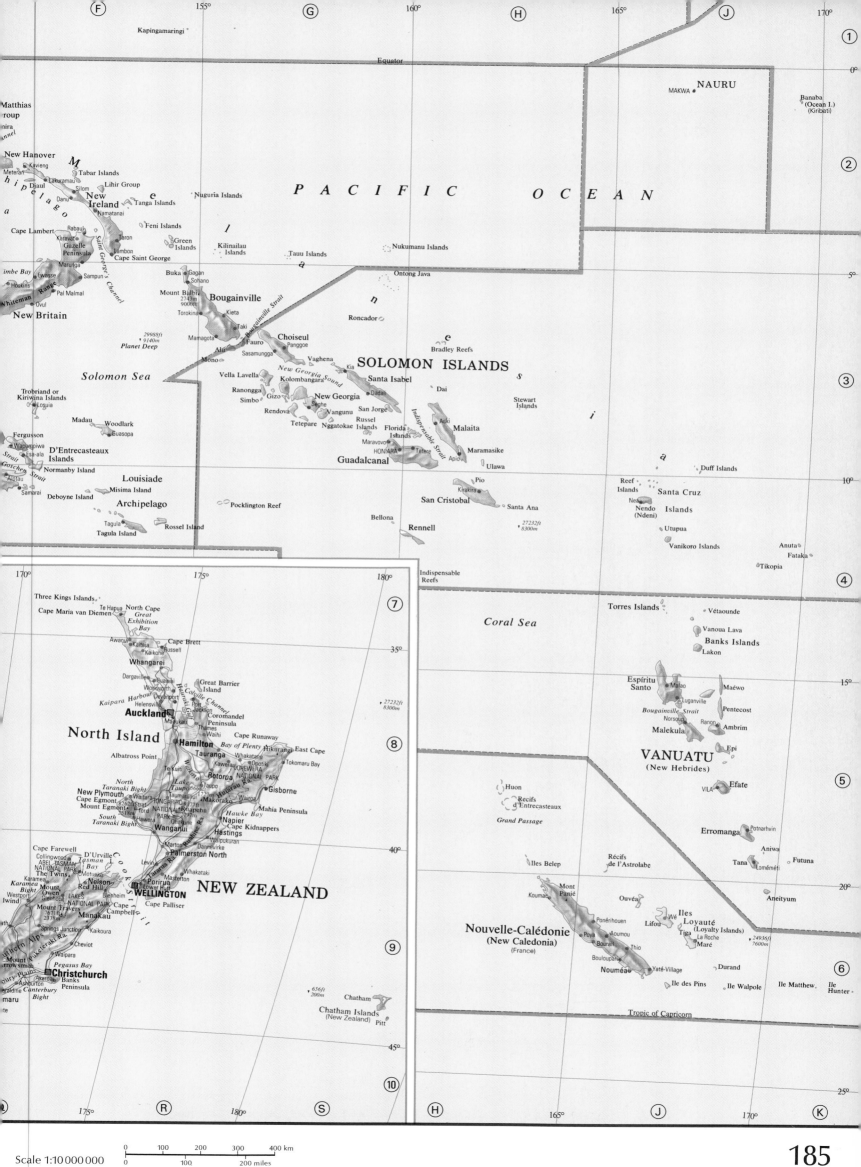

① ② ③ ④

Kapingamaringi

Equator

NAURU
MAKWA ·

Banaba
(Ocean I.)
(Kiribati)

Matthias
roup
nira
annel

New Hanover
Kavieng
Meteran
Dvaul
Danu
Silom

M

Tabar Islands
Lihir Group

New
Ireland
Namatanai
Tanga Islands

P A C I F I C   O C E A N

Nuguria Islands

e

l

a

n

e

s

i

a

Cape Lambert
Rabaul
Karavat
Gazelle
Peninsula
Marunga

Taron
Lembon
Cape Saint George

Feni Islands

Green
Islands

Kilinailau
Islands

Tauu Islands

Nukumanu Islands

imbe Bay
Ewasse
Hoskins
Whiteman
New Britain

Sampun
Pal Malmal
Ovul

Range

Buka Gagan
Sohano

Ontong Java

Mount Balbi
2743m
9008ft
Torokina

Bougainville

Bougainville Strait

Kieta
Taki

Roncador

29988ft
9140m
Planet Deep

Mamagota
Alu
Mono

Fauro
Sasamungga

Choiseul
Panggoe

Bradley Reefs

Solomon Sea

Vaghena
Kia

SOLOMON ISLANDS

Trobriand or
Kiriwina Islands
Losuia

Vella Lavella
Ranongga
Simbo

Kolombangara
Gizo
Rendova

New Georgia Sound
New Georgia
Seghe
Vangunu

Santa Isabel
Dadali
Dai

Stewart
Islands

Madau
Woodlark
Buasopa

San Jorge
Russel
Islands
Nggatokae

Auki

Fergusson
Waporomiwa
Esa-ala

D'Entrecasteaux
Islands
Normanby Island

Tetepare

Florida
Islands
Maravovo
HONIARA
Tetere

Malaita

Duff Islands

Strait
Goschen Strait
Alotau
Samarai

Louisiade

Misima Island

Deboyne Island

Guadalcanal

Indispensable Strait
Apio

Maramasike
Ulawa

Reef
Islands
Nea
Nendo
(Ndeni)

Santa Cruz
Islands

Archipelago

Pocklington Reef

Pio
Kirakira
San Cristobal

Santa Ana

Utupua

Tagula
Tagula Island

Rossel Island

Bellona

Rennell

27232ft
8300m

Vanikoro Islands

Anuta
Fataka

Tikopia

⑤ (5)

⑥ (6)

⑦ (7)

⑧ (8)

⑨ (9)

⑩ (10)

Three Kings Islands
Cape Maria van Diemen

Te Hapua North Cape
Great
Exhibition
Bay

Indispensable
Reefs

Coral Sea

Torres Islands
Vétaounde

Vanoua Lava

Banks Islands
Lakon

Awanui Kaitaia
Kaikohe
Cape Brett
Russell

Whangarei

Dargaville
Buawai
Warkworth
Great Barrier
Island

Kaipara Harbour
Devonport
Helensville
Jackson
Port

Coromandel
Peninsula
Thames

Espíritu
Santo
Malao
Luganville

Maéwo

Auckland
Manukau
Waihi

Bougainville Strait
Norsoup
Ranon

Pentecost

Ambrim

North Island

Hamilton

Bay of Plenty
Tauranga
Whakatane
Kawerau

Cape Runaway
Hikurangi East Cape
Tokomaru Bay

Malekula

Epi

VANUATU
(New Hebrides)

Albatross Point
Te Kuiti

Opotiki
UREWERA
NATIONAL PARK

Rotorua
Lake
Taupo
Taupo
Waitara

Gisborne

VILA
Efate

North
Taranaki Bight
New Plymouth
Cape Egmont
Mount Egmont
2518m 8262ft

TONGARIRO
NATIONAL
PARK
Ford
Ruapehu
2797m

Makorako
Wairoa

Huon
Recifs
d'Entrecasteaux

Grand Passage

South
Taranaki Bight
Hawera
Wanganui

Mahia Peninsula
Hawke Bay
Napier
Cape Kidnappers
Hastings
Waipukurau

Erromanga
Potnarhvin

Cape Farewell
Collingwood

D'Urville
Island
Tasman
Bay

Marton
Levin
Whakataki
Masterton

Dannevirke
Palmerston North

Aniwa

Tana
Loméméfi

Futuna

ABEL TASMAN
NATIONAL PARK
The Twins
Karamea
Bight
Westport

Motueka
Nelson
Red Hill
Blenheim

Porirua
Lower Hutt
WELLINGTON

NEW ZEALAND

Récifs
de l'Astrolabe

Iles Belep

Mont
Panié

Aneityum

LAKES
NATIONAL PARK
Mount
Owen
Glenhope
Mount Travers
7671ft
2338m

Cape
Campbell
Cape Palliser

Koumac

Poya

Ouvéa
Ponérihouen
Aoumou

Lifou
Wé

Iles
Loyauté
(Loyalty Islands)
Tiga

Springs Junction
Manakau

Kaikoura

Bourail

Thio

Maré

24936ft
7600m

Southern Alps
Mount
Arrowsmith
Pegasus Bay

Cheviot
Waipara

Nouvelle-Calédonie
(New Caledonia)
(France)

Bouloupari
Nouméa

La Roche

Akaroa

Christchurch
Banks
Peninsula

656ft
200m

Durand

maru

Ashburton
Geraldine
Canterbury
Bight

Chatham
Islands
(New Zealand)
Pitt

Ile des Pins

Yaté-Village

Ile Walpole

Tropic of Capricorn

Ile Matthew
Ile
Hunter

Scale 1:10 000 000

0   100   200   300   400 km
0   100   200 miles

185

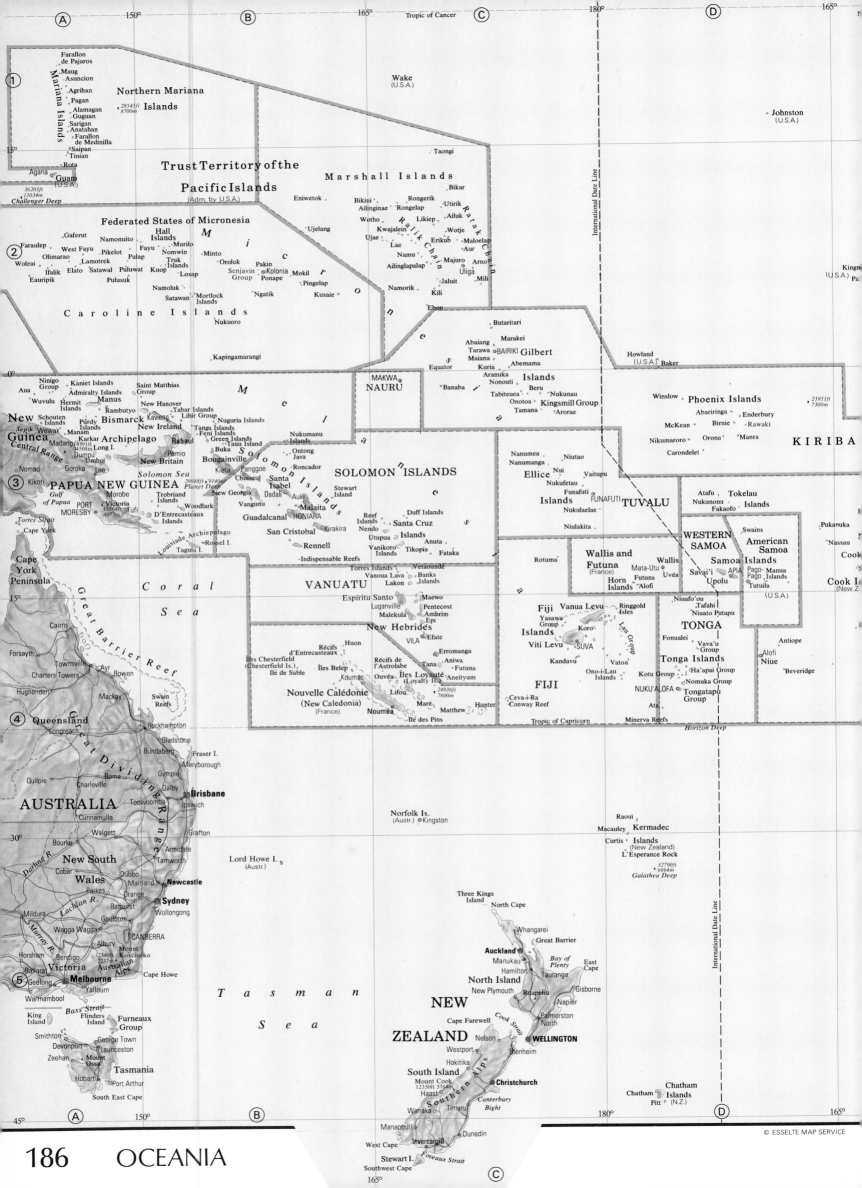

Map labels (geographic):

Coordinate grid: A 150° B 165° Tropic of Cancer C 180° D 165°

1

Farallon de Pajaros
Maug
Asuncion
Agrihan
Pagan
Alamagan
Guguan
Sarigan
Anatahan
Farallon de Medinilla
Saipan
Tinian
Rota
Agana
Guam (U.S.A.)
36203ft 11034m
Challenger Deep
Mariana Islands

Northern Mariana Islands
28545ft 8700m

Wake (U.S.A.)

Johnston (U.S.A.)

15°

Trust Territory of the Pacific Islands
(Adm. by U.S.A.)

Taongi

Marshall Islands

Federated States of Micronesia

Micronesia

2

Faraulep
Woleai
Ifalik Elato Satawal Puluwat
Eauripik
Gaferut
Namonuito
West Fayu Pikelot Fayu Nomwin
Olimarao Pulap Truk
Lamotrek Puluwat Kuop Islands
Pulusuk Losap
Namoluk
Satawan
Mortlock Islands
Ngatik
Hall Islands
Murilo
Minto
Oroluk Pakin
Senjavin Kolonia
Group Ponape
Mokil
Pingelap
Kusaie

Ujelang

Eniwetok
Bikini Rongerik
Ailinginae Rongelap Utirik Ailuk
Wotho Likiep Wotje
Kwajalein Erikub Maloelap
Ujae Lae Aur
Namu Majuro Arno
Ailinglapalap Uliga
Namorik Mili
Kili
Ebon

Butaritari
Abaiang Marakei
Tarawa BAIRIKI Gilbert
Maiana Abemama
Kuria Islands
Aranuka
Banaba Nonouti
Tabiteuea Beru Nukunau
Onotoa Kingsmill Group
Tamana Arorae

Howland (U.S.A.)
Baker (U.S.A.)

Winslow Phoenix Islands
Abariringa Enderbury
McKean Birnie Rawaki
Nikumaroro Orona Manra
Carondelet

Kingm (U.S.A.) Pa

23951ft 7300m

KIRIBA

KIRIBA

Equator

0°

Caroline Islands
Nukuoro
Kapingamarangi

MAKWA
NAURU
NAURU

Ninigo Group Kaniet Islands Saint Matthias Group
Aua Admiralty Islands New Hanover
Wuvulu Hermit Manus New Ireland
Islands Rambutyo Tabar Islands
New Schouten Purdy Kavieng Lihir Group
Guinea Islands Islands Nuguria Islands
Sepik Manam Bismarck Tanga Islands
Madang Karkar Archipelago Feni Islands
14791ft Long I. Rabaul Green Islands
4508m Dumpu Umboi New Britain Tauu Island
Central Range Goroka Lae Pomio Buka
Nomad Morobe Bougainville
Kikori PAPUA NEW GUINEA Kieta
Gulf Tufi 29988ft 9140m
of Papua 1364ft Planet Deep
PORT 4073m Choiseul
MORESBY Trobriand New Georgia
Torres Strait Islands Vanguru
Cape York D'Entrecasteaux Santa Isabel
Islands Dadali
Woodlark Auki
Rossel I. Malaita
Louisiade Archipelago HONIARA
Tagula I. Guadalcanal
San Cristobal
Rennell
Indispensable Reefs

Nukumanu Islands
Ontong Java
Roncador

Solomon Islands
SOLOMON ISLANDS

Stewart Island

Reef Islands Duff Islands
Nendo Santa Cruz
Utupua Islands
Vanikoro Anuta
Islands Tikopia Fataka

3

Nanumea Niutao
Nanumanga Nui
Nukufetau Vaitupu
Ellice Funafuti
Islands FUNAFUTI TUVALU
Nukulaelae
Niulakita

Atafu Tokelau
Nukunonu Fakaofo Islands

Swains

WESTERN SAMOA
Savai'i APIA
Upolu
Samoa Islands

American Samoa Islands
Pago- Manua
Pago Islands
Tutuila
(U.S.A.)

Pukapuka
Nassau
Cook I (New Z

Rotuma

Wallis and Futuna (France)
Horn Mata-Utu
Islands Futuna
Alofi

Wallis
Uvéa

Niuafo'ou
Tafahi
Niuato Putapu

Cook I

Fiji Vanua Levu
Yasawa Ringgold
Group Isles
Viti Levu Koro
SUVA
Kandavu Vatoa
Ono-i-Lau
Islands

Lau Group

Fonualei
Vava'u Group
TONGA

Tonga Islands
Kotu Group Ha'apai Group
NUKU'ALOFA Nomuka Group
Tongatapu Group
Ata

Antiope
Alofi Niue

Beveridge

4

Torres Islands Vetaoundé
Vanua Lava Banks
Lakon Islands

VANUATU

Espíritu Santo Maewo
Luganville Pentecost
Malekula Ambrim
Epi

New Hebrides
VILA Efate

Récifs Huon
d'Entrecasteaux
Îles Chesterfield Récifs de
(Chesterfield Is.) l'Astrolabe Tana Aniwa
Île de Sable Îles Belep Erromanga Futuna
Koumac Îles Loyauté
Ouvéa (Loyalty Is.)
Lifou Aneityum
Nouvelle Calédonie Maré
(New Caledonia) 24936ft
(France) Noumea 7600m
Île des Pins

Ceva-i-Ra
Conway Reef

FIJI

Minerva Reefs

Matthew Hunter

AUSTRALIA

Cairns
Forsayth
Townsville
Charters Towers Ayr Bowen
Hughenden Mackay
Longreach Swain
Queensland Reefs
Rockhampton
Gladstone
Great Dividing Range Bundaberg
Quilpie Roma Maryborough Fraser I.
Charleville Dalby Gympie
Cunnamulla Toowoomba Brisbane
Bourke Ipswich
Walgett Grafton
New South Armidale
Cobar Wales Tamworth
Dubbo
Parkes Maitland Newcastle
Bathurst Orange
Wagga Wagga Goulburn Sydney
Albury CANBERRA Wollongong
Bendigo Mount
Horsham Kosciusko
Victoria 7340ft 2237m
Ballarat Australian Alps Cape Howe
Geelong Melbourne
Warrnambool Yallourn

Great Barrier Reef

Coral Sea

Cape York Peninsula

15°

25°

30°

Norfolk Is. (Austr.) Kingston

Raoul
Macauley Kermadec
Curtis Islands
Islands (New Zealand)
L'Esperance Rock
32790ft 9994m
Galathea Deep

Lord Howe I. (Austr.)

Tropic of Capricorn

Horizon Deep

Tasman Sea

Three Kings Island
North Cape
Whangarei
Great Barrier
Auckland Bay of
Manukau Plenty
Hamilton Tauranga
North Island East Cape
New Plymouth
Ruapehu Gisborne
Napier
NEW Palmerston North
ZEALAND Cape Farewell WELLINGTON
Nelson Cook Strait
Westport Blenheim
Hokitika
Christchurch
South Island
Mount Cook
12350ft 3764m
Haast Timaru
Southern Alps Canterbury Bight
Wanaka
Manapouri Dunedin
West Cape Invercargill
Stewart I.
Southwest Cape Foveaux Strait

Chatham Islands
Chatham Pitt (N.Z.)

King Island Furneaux Group
Flinders Island
Smithton George Town
Devonport Launceston
Zeehan Mount Ossa
Hobart
Port Arthur
Tasmania
South East Cape

Bass Strait

Murray R. Darling R. Lachlan R.
Mildura Cobar
Wagga Wagga
Maitland
Horsham
Goulburn

5

45°

International Date Line

© ESSELTE MAP SERVICE

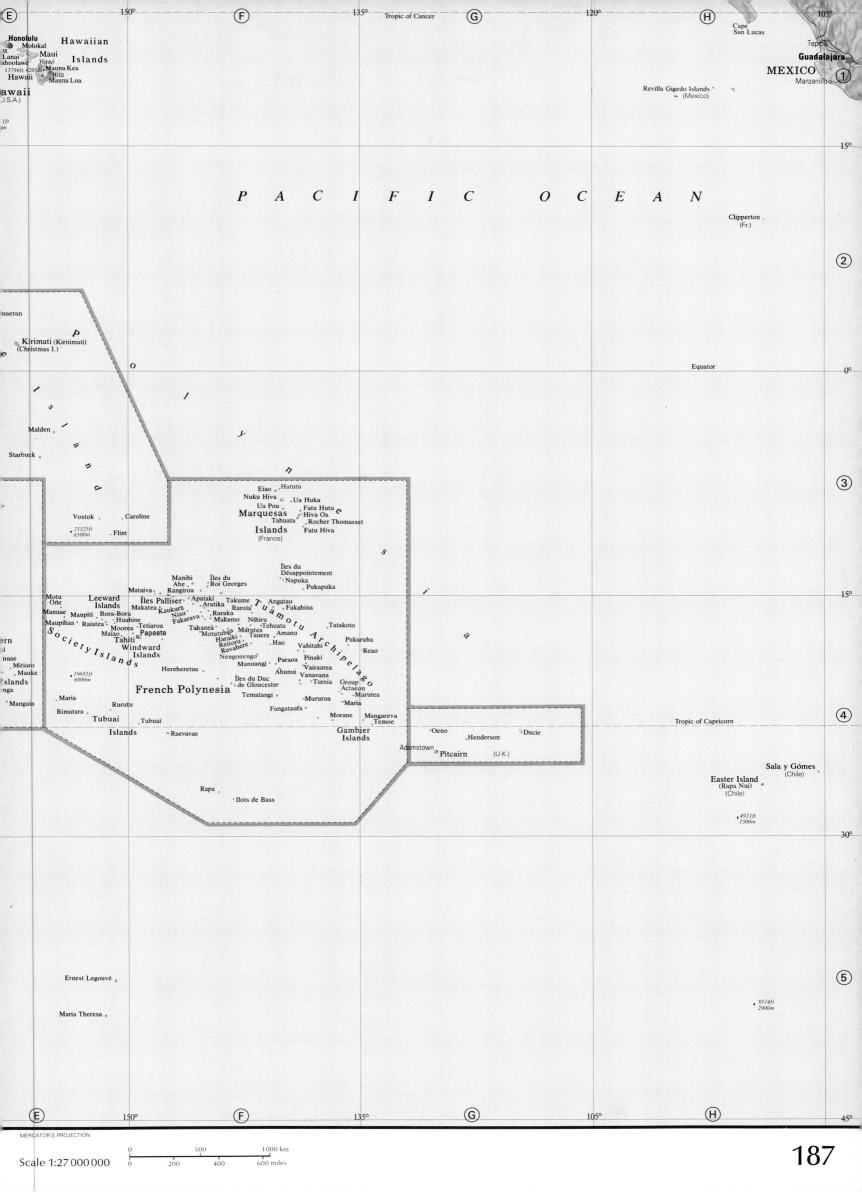

Honolulu
Hawaiian Islands
u Lanai · Molokai · Maui
Kahoolawe · Hawi · Mauna Kea
13796ft 4205m · Hilo
Hawaii · Mauna Loa
awaii
U.S.A.)

Cape
San Lucas
Tepic
Guadalajara
MEXICO
Manzanillo

Revilla Gigedo Islands
(Mexico)

①

P A C I F I C   O C E A N

Clipperton
(Fr.)

②

uaeran

Kirimati (Kiritimati)
(Christmas I.)

Equator

③

P o l y n e s i a

Malden

Starbuck

Vostok · Caroline

21325ft
6500m · Flint

Eiao · Hatutu
Nuku Hiva · Ua Huka
Ua Pou · Fatu Hutu
Marquesas · Hiva Oa
Islands · Tahuata · Rocher Thomasset
(France) · Fatu Hiva

Îles du
Désappointement
· Napuka
Pukapuka

Manihi · Îles du
Ahe · Roi Georges
Mataiva · Rangiroa
Motu · Leeward · Apataki · Takume · Angatau · Fakahina
Orie · Islands · Îles Palliser · Makatea · Aratika · Raroïa
Manuae · Maupiti · Bora-Bora · Kaukura · Niau · Raraka
Maupihaa · Raiatea · Huahine · Fakarava · Makemo · Nihiru
Moorea · Tetiaroa · Tahanea · Tehuata · Tatakoto
Society Islands · Malao · Papeete · Motutunga · Marutea · Amanu
Tahiti · Haraiki · Tauere · Hao · Pukaruha
Windward · Reitoru · Vahitahi · Reao
Islands · Ravahere
Nengonengo · Paraoa · Pinaki
Hereheretue · Manuangi · Vairaatea
19685ft · Ahunui · Vanavana
6000m · Îles du Duc · Tureia · Group
de Gloucester · Actaeon · Marutea
French Polynesia · Tematangi · Maria
Maria · Mururoa
Rurutu · Fangataufa · Morane · Mangareva
Rimatara · Temoe
Tubuai · Tubuaï · Gambier
Islands · Tubuaï · Islands
Raevavae

Tuamotu Archipelago

④ Tropic of Capricorn

Oeno · Ducie
Henderson
Adamstown
Pitcairn · (U.K.)

Sala y Gómes
(Chile)
Easter Island
(Rapa Nui)
(Chile)

Rapa
Ilots de Bass

4921ft
1500m

30°

⑤

Ernest Legouvé

9514ft
2900m

Maria Theresa

MERCATOR'S PROJECTION

Scale 1:27 000 000

0 · 500 · 1000 km
0 · 200 · 400 · 600 miles

187

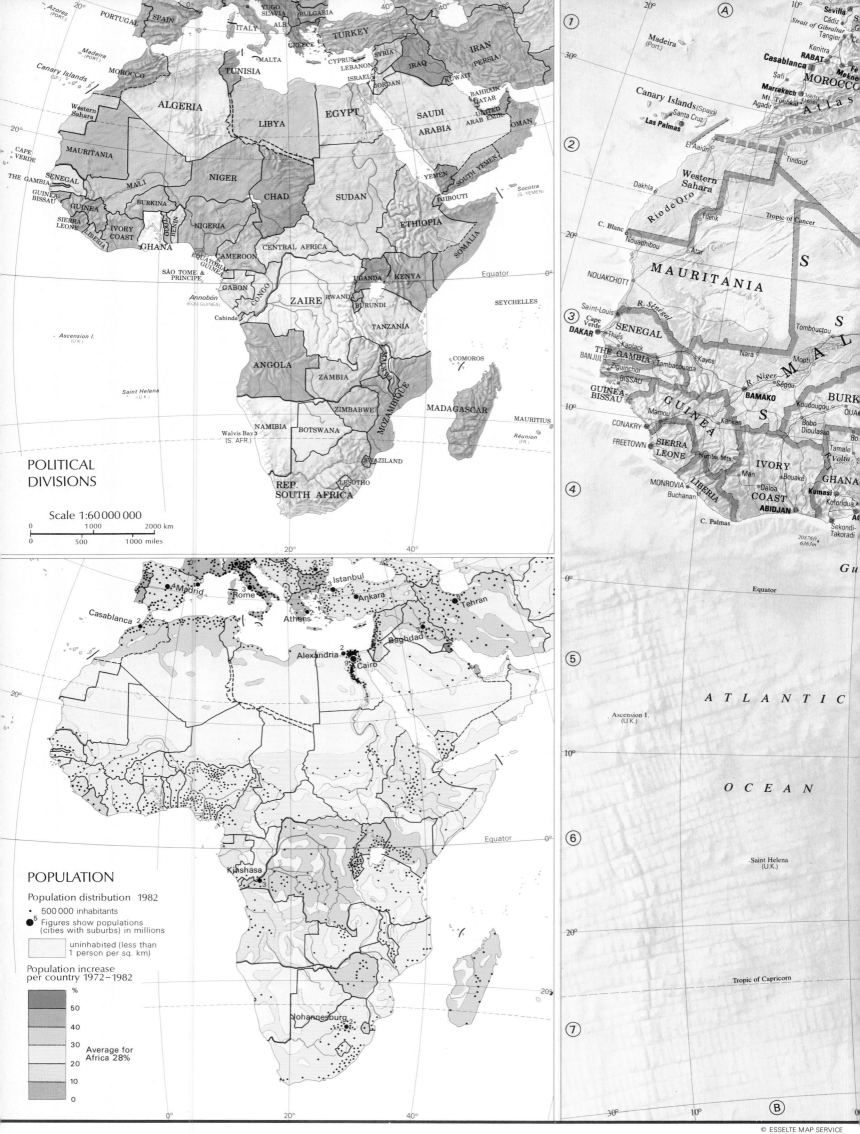

POLITICAL DIVISIONS

Scale 1:60 000 000

0 — 1000 — 2000 km
0 — 500 — 1000 miles

POPULATION

Population distribution 1982

• 500 000 inhabitants

● 5 Figures show populations (cities with suburbs) in millions

uninhabited (less than 1 person per sq. km)

Population increase per country 1972–1982

%
50
40
30
20
10
0

Average for Africa 28%

© ESSELTE MAP SERVICE

MILLER'S STEREOGRAPHIC PROJECTION

Scale 1:25 000 000

| 0 | | 500 | | 1000 km |
| 0- | 200 | 400 | | 600 miles |

1 hour

189

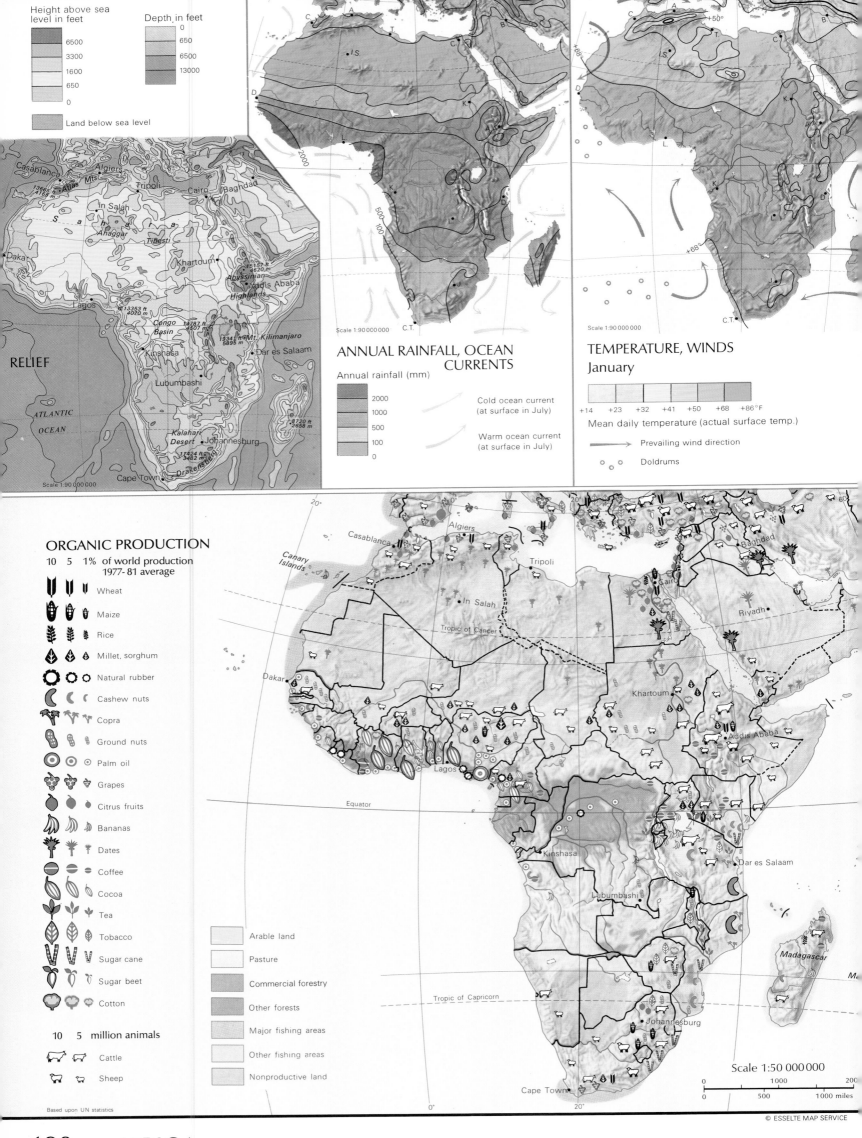

Height above sea level in feet

6500
3300
1600
650
0

Depth in feet

0
650
6500
13000

Land below sea level

RELIEF

Scale 1:90 000 000

ANNUAL RAINFALL, OCEAN CURRENTS

Annual rainfall (mm)

2000
1000
500
100
0

Cold ocean current (at surface in July)

Warm ocean current (at surface in July)

Scale 1:90 000 000

TEMPERATURE, WINDS
January

+14 +23 +32 +41 +50 +68 +86°F

Mean daily temperature (actual surface temp.)

Prevailing wind direction

Doldrums

Scale 1:90 000 000

ORGANIC PRODUCTION

10 5 1% of world production 1977-81 average

Wheat
Maize
Rice
Millet, sorghum
Natural rubber
Cashew nuts
Copra
Ground nuts
Palm oil
Grapes
Citrus fruits
Bananas
Dates
Coffee
Cocoa
Tea
Tobacco
Sugar cane
Sugar beet
Cotton

10 5 million animals

Cattle
Sheep

Arable land
Pasture
Commercial forestry
Other forests
Major fishing areas
Other fishing areas
Nonproductive land

Based upon UN statistics

Scale 1:50 000 000

0   500   1000 miles
0   1000   200

© ESSELTE MAP SERVICE

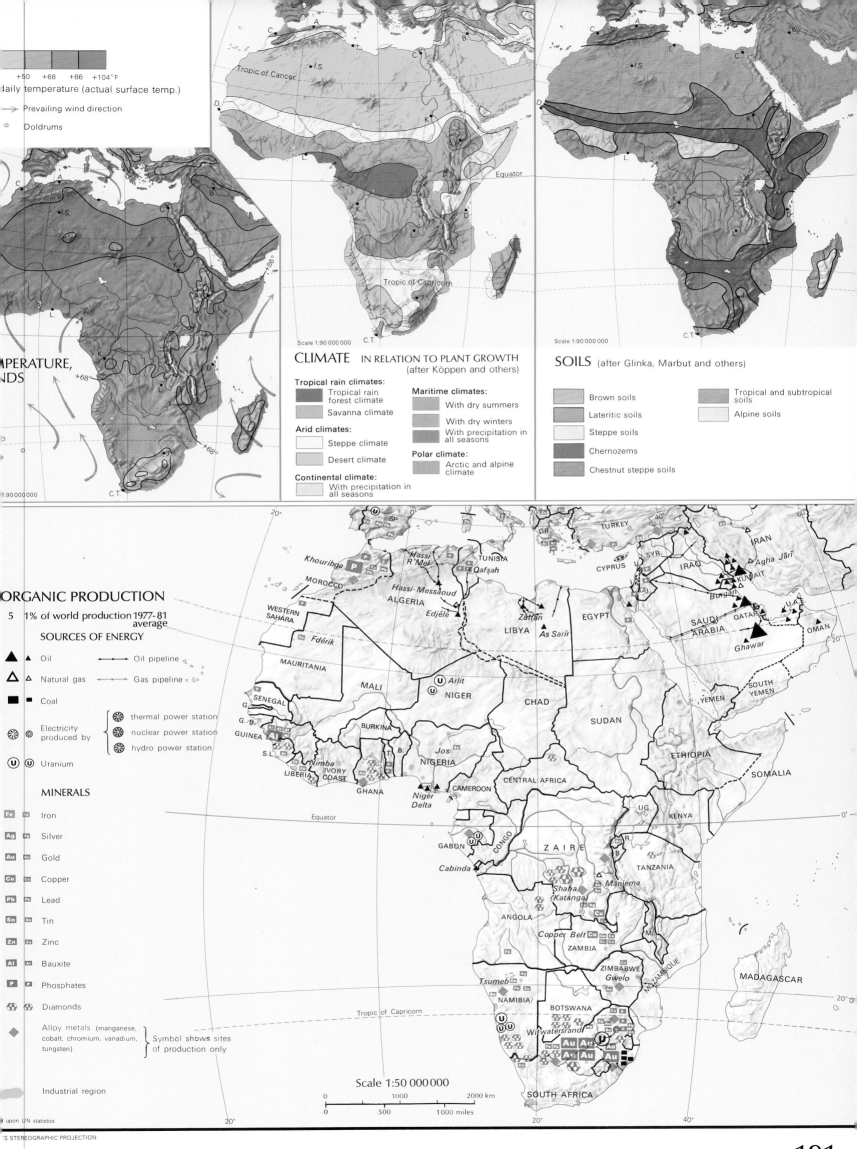

+50　+68　+86　+104°F
daily temperature (actual surface temp.)

→ Prevailing wind direction
○ Doldrums

TEMPERATURE, ...NDS

1:90 000 000

Tropic of Cancer · I.S.

Equator

Tropic of Capricorn

Scale 1:90 000 000

CLIMATE IN RELATION TO PLANT GROWTH
(after Köppen and others)

Tropical rain climates:
Tropical rain forest climate
Savanna climate

Arid climates:
Steppe climate
Desert climate

Continental climate:
With precipitation in all seasons

Maritime climates:
With dry summers
With dry winters
With precipitation in all seasons

Polar climate:
Arctic and alpine climate

Scale 1:90 000 000

Tropic of Cancer · I.S.

Equator

C.T.

SOILS (after Glinka, Marbut and others)

Brown soils
Lateritic soils
Steppe soils
Chernozems
Chestnut steppe soils

Tropical and subtropical soils
Alpine soils

...ORGANIC PRODUCTION

5　1% of world production 1977-81 average

SOURCES OF ENERGY

▲ ▲ Oil
△ △ Natural gas
■ ■ Coal

◉ ◉ Electricity produced by
　　⊛ thermal power station
　　⊛ nuclear power station
　　⊛ hydro power station

Ⓤ Ⓤ Uranium

◆—◆ Oil pipeline
○—○ Gas pipeline

MINERALS

Fe Fe Iron
Ag Ag Silver
Au Au Gold
Cu Cu Copper
Pb Pb Lead
Sn Sn Tin
Zn Zn Zinc
Al Al Bauxite
P P Phosphates
⬡⬡ Diamonds

◆ Alloy metals (manganese, cobalt, chromium, vanadium, tungsten) } Symbol shows sites of production only

Industrial region

...I upon UN statistics

...'S STEREOGRAPHIC PROJECTION

SP
Khouribga P
MOROCCO
WESTERN SAHARA
MAURITANIA
Fdérik
SENEGAL
G.
G.-B.
GUINEA Al
S.L.
LIBERIA
Nimba IVORY COAST
GHANA
Niger Delta
Hassi R'Mel
Qafşah
TUNISIA
Hassi-Messaoud
ALGERIA
Edjélé
LIBYA
Zaltan
As Sarīr
MALI
Ⓤ Arlit
NIGER
CHAD
BURKINA
Jos
NIGERIA
CAMEROON
CENTRAL AFRICA
SUDAN
EGYPT
TURKEY
GR.
CYPRUS
SYR.
IRAQ Agha Jārī
KUWAIT
Burgan
IRAN
U.A.E.
QATAR
SAUDI ARABIA
Ghawar
OMAN
YEMEN
SOUTH YEMEN
ETHIOPIA
SOMALIA
UG.
KENYA
GABON
CONGO
ZAIRE
Maniema
Shaba (Katanga)
TANZANIA
Cu
ANGOLA
Copper Belt Cu Cu Cu
ZAMBIA
ZIMBABWE Gwelo
MOZAMBIQUE
MADAGASCAR
Cabinda
Tsumeb Ag
NAMIBIA/
BOTSWANA
Witwatersrand
Au Au Au Au
Cu
SOUTH AFRICA

Equator

Tropic of Capricorn

Scale 1:50 000 000
0　1000　2000 km
0　500　1000 miles

Scale 1:10 000 000

0   100   200   300   400 km
0   100   200 miles

© ESSELTE MAP SERVIC

Scale 1:10 000 000

197

© ESSELTE MAP SERVICE

199

Scale 1:10 000 000

0   100   200   300   400 km

0   100   200 miles

© ESSELTE MAP SERVICE

Scale 1:30 000 000

0   500   1000 km
0 250 500 miles

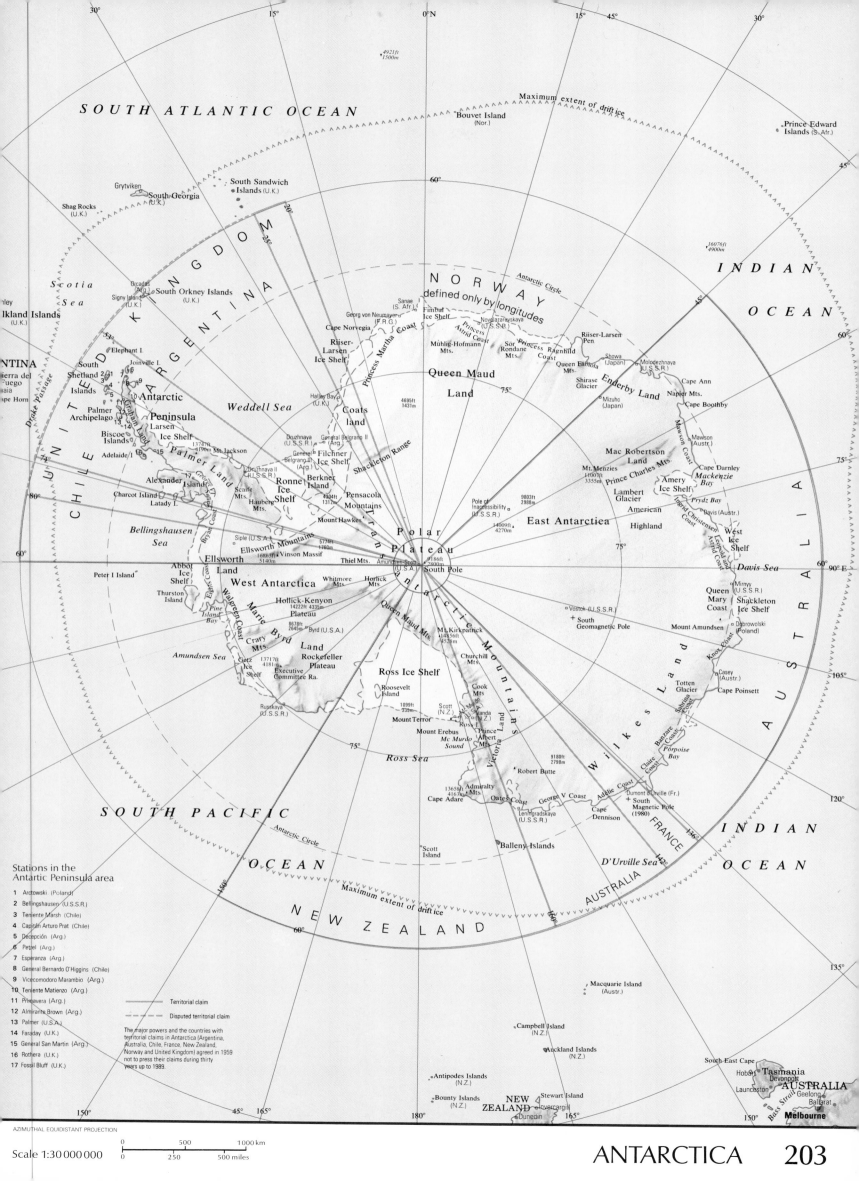

SOUTH ATLANTIC OCEAN

4921ft 1500m

Maximum extent of drift ice

Bouvet Island (Nor.)

Prince Edward Islands (S. Afr.)

30° 15° 0°N 15° 45° 30°

Grytviken

Shag Rocks (U.K.)

South Georgia (U.K.)

South Sandwich Islands (U.K.)

Scotia Sea

lkland Islands (U.K.)

60°

45°

INDIAN OCEAN

16076ft 4900m

Antarctic Circle

NTINA

ierra del uego uaia ape Horn

South Shetland Islands

Orcadas (Arg.) South Orkney Islands (U.K.)

Signy Island (U.K.)

Sanae (S. Afr.)

Georg von Neumayer (F.R.G.)

Fimbul Ice Shelf

Novolazarevskaya (U.S.S.R.)

NORWAY defined only by longitudes

Riiser-Larsen Pen.

Cape Ann

Elephant I.

Joinville I.

Cape Norvegia

Riiser-Larsen Ice Shelf

Mühlig-Hofmann Mts.

Princess Astrid Coast

Sør Rondane Mts.

Princess Ragnhild Coast

Queen Fabiola Mts.

Showa (Japan)

Molodezhnaya (U.S.S.R.)

Napier Mts.

Antarctic Peninsula

Larsen Ice Shelf

Queen Maud Land

Shirase Glacier

Mizuho (Japan)

Enderby Land

Cape Boothby

Palmer Archipelago

Biscoe Islands

Graham Land

Halley Bay (U.K.)

Coats land

4695ft 1431m

Mawson (Austr.)

Mawson Coast

Weddell Sea

13747ft 4190m Mt. Jackson

Druzhnaya (U.S.S.R.)

General Belgrano II (Arg.)

Mac Robertson Land

Cape Darnley *Mackenzie Bay*

Adelaide I.

Druzhnaya (U.S.S.R.)

General Belgrano II (Arg.)

Shackleton Range

Mt. Menzies 11007ft 3355m

Prince Charles Mts.

Amery Ice Shelf

Prydz Bay

Davis (Austr.)

Alexander Island

Scaife Mts.

Hauberg Mts.

Ronne Ice Shelf

Berkner Island

Filchner Ice Shelf

4304ft 1312m

Pensacola Mountains

Lambert Glacier

Ingrid Christensen Coast

Charcot Island

Latady I.

Mount Hawkes

9803ft 2988m

East Antarctica

American Highland

Leopold and Astrid Coast

West Ice Shelf

Bellingshausen Sea

Siple (U.S.A.)

Ellsworth Mountains

5774ft 1760m

Pole of Inaccessibility (U.S.S.R.)

14009ft 4270m

Bryan Coast

16863ft 5140m Vinson Massif

Thiel Mts.

Amundsen-Scott (U.S.A.)

Polar Plateau

9186ft 2800m

South Pole

75°

Davis Sea

90°E

Abbot Ice Shelf

Ellsworth Land

West Antarctica

Whitmore Mts.

Horlick Mts.

Vostok (U.S.S.R.)

South Geomagnetic Pole

Queen Mary Coast

Mirny (U.S.S.R.)

Shackleton Ice Shelf

Peter I Island

Thurston Island

Hollick-Kenyon Plateau 14222ft 4335m

8678ft 2645m Byrd (U.S.A.)

Queen Maud Mts.

Mt. Kirkpatrick 14856ft 4528m

Mount Amundsen

Dobrowolski (Poland)

Pine Island Bay

Walgreen Coast

Marie Byrd Land

Rockefeller Plateau

Churchill Mts.

Knox Coast

Totten Glacier

Casey (Austr.)

Amundsen Sea

Crary Mts.

Getz Ice Shelf

13717ft 4181m

Executive Committee Ra.

Ross Ice Shelf

Cook Mts.

Cape Poinsett

Sabrina Coast

Wilkes Land

Banzare Coast

Russkaya (U.S.S.R.)

1099ft 335m

Roosevelt Island

Scott (N.Z.)

Vanda (N.Z.)

Ross I.

Prince Albert Mts.

Robert Butte

9180ft 2798m

Claire Coast

Porpoise Bay

Mount Terror

Mount Erebus

Mc Murdo Sound

Victoria Land

Adélie Coast

South Magnetic Pole (1980)

AUSTRALIA

Ross Sea

13658ft 4163m

Admiralty Mts.

Cape Adare

George V Coast

Oates Coast

Leningradskaya (U.S.S.R.)

Cape Dennison

Dumont d'Urville (Fr.)

INDIAN OCEAN

Antarctic Circle

SOUTH PACIFIC OCEAN

Scott Island

Balleny Islands

D'Urville Sea

FRANCE

NEW ZEALAND

Maximum extent of drift ice

Macquarie Island (Austr.)

Campbell Island (N.Z.)

Auckland Islands (N.Z.)

South East Cape

Hobart *Tasmania* Geelong

AUSTRALIA

Launceston

Ballarat

Melbourne

Stations in the
Antarctic Peninsula area

1 Arctowski (Poland)
2 Bellingshausen (U.S.S.R.)
3 Teniente Marsh (Chile)
4 Capitán Arturo Prat (Chile)
5 Decepción (Arg.)
6 Petrel (Arg.)
7 Esperanza (Arg.)
8 General Bernardo O'Higgins (Chile)
9 Vicecomodoro Marambio (Arg.)
10 Teniente Matienzo (Arg.)
11 Primavera (Arg.)
12 Almirante Brown (Arg.)
13 Palmer (U.S.A.)
14 Faraday (U.K.)
15 General San Martin (Arg.)
16 Rothera (U.K.)
17 Fossil Bluff (U.K.)

Territorial claim

Disputed territorial claim

The major powers and the countries with territorial claims in Antarctica (Argentina, Australia, Chile, France, New Zealand, Norway and United Kingdom) agreed in 1959 not to press their claims during thirty years up to 1989.

Antipodes Islands (N.Z.)

Bounty Islands (N.Z.)

Stewart Island

NEW ZEALAND

Invercargill

Dunedin

AZIMUTHAL EQUIDISTANT PROJECTION

Scale 1:30 000 000

0 500 1000 km
0 250 500 miles

Kamchatka

Bering Strait

Alaska

Mount McKinley

Bering Sea

Aleutian Islands

Victoria Island

Baffin Island

Baffin Bay

Arctic Circle

Greenland

Iceland

NORTH AMERICA

Mackenzie River

Hudson Bay

Labrador

Labrador Current

Newfoundland

North Atlantic Drift

Missouri R.

Chicago

New York

Gulf Stream

California Current

Los Angeles

30°

Sargasso Sea

Tropic of Cancer

Canary Current

PACIFIC

Hawaiian Islands

Mexico City

West Indies

Caribbean Sea

Central America

ATLANTIC

OCEAN

P o l y n e s i a

0°

R. Amazon

Equator

OCEA

Andes

SOUTH AMERICA

Peru Current

Mount Ancohuma

Brazil Current

Tropic of Capricorn

R. Paraná

São Paulo

Rio de Janeiro

30°

New Zealand

12350ft
3764m
Mount Cook

2284m
6959ft
Mount Aconcagua

Cordillera

Buenos Aires

Cape Horn

Drake Passage

■	Million city	
→	Warm current	at surface in January
→	Cold current	
▨	Pack and drift ice	International boundary

Glacier, ice cap

Tundra

Coniferous forest

Rain

© ESSELTE MAP SERVICE

TIC OCEAN
Svalbard
North Cape
Barents Sea
Novaya Zemlya
Taymyr Peninsula
Arctic Circle
Bering Strait
Alaska
Mount McKinley
Bering Sea
Aleutian Islands

Scandinavia

EUROPE
Moscow
R. Volga
R. Ob
Ural Mountains
R. Ob
S i b e r i a
R. Yenisei
R. Lena
R. Amur
Sea of Okhotsk
Kamchatka
Sakhalin
Oya Siwo

Black Sea
Caspian Mts
Caspian Sea
Kirghiz Steppe
A S I A
Altai
Gobi
Tien Shan
Takla Makan
Kunlun Shan
Tibet
Himalayas
Mount Everest 29029ft 8848m
Manchuria
Beijing
Hwang He
Honshu
Seoul
Tokyo
Kuro Siwo
PACIFIC
OCEAN

Mediterranean Sea
Cairo
R. Euphrates
R. Nile
Red Sea
Rub al Khali
R. Indus
R. Ganges
Calcutta
Yangtze Kiang
Shanghai
Tropic of Cancer
30°

AFRICA
R. Zaire
R. Congo
Mount Kilimanjaro 19341ft 5895m
Bombay
Arabian Sea
Sri Lanka
R. Mekong
South China Sea
Philippine Islands
M i c r o n e s i a

Equator
Sumatra
Borneo
Java
Jakarta
Sunda Islands
New Guinea
M e l a n e s i a
0°

Madagascar
R. Zambezi
Kalahari Desert
I N D I A N
O C E A N
Coral Sea
Tropic of Capricorn

Cape Town of Good Hope
AUSTRALIA
Darling River
Sydney
30°

Westralian Current
Tasmania
Tasman Sea
Mount Cook 12350ft 3764m
New Zealand

West Wind Drift

R GRINTEN'S PROJECTION

Cultivated land
Savanna
Steppe
Desert

e 1:90 000 000
equator
0°0 400 800 km
30°
60°
200 600 1000 km
0°0 200 400 600 miles
30°
60°
100 300 500 miles

205

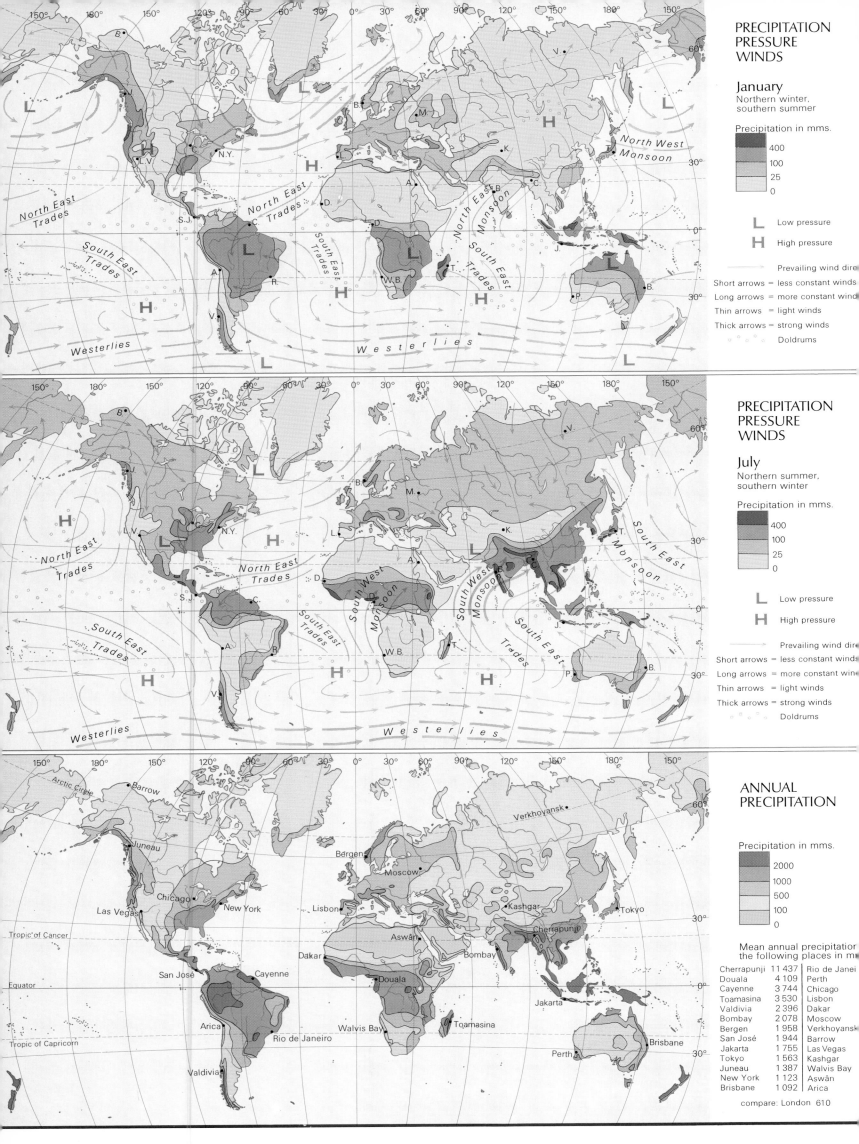

PRECIPITATION
PRESSURE
WINDS

January
Northern winter,
southern summer

Precipitation in mms.

400
100
25
0

L   Low pressure

H   High pressure

Prevailing wind dire
Short arrows = less constant winds
Long arrows = more constant wind
Thin arrows = light winds
Thick arrows = strong winds
Doldrums

PRECIPITATION
PRESSURE
WINDS

July
Northern summer,
southern winter

Precipitation in mms.

400
100
25
0

L   Low pressure

H   High pressure

Prevailing wind dir
Short arrows = less constant winds
Long arrows = more constant wine
Thin arrows = light winds
Thick arrows = strong winds
Doldrums

ANNUAL
PRECIPITATION

Precipitation in mms.

2000
1000
500
100
0

Mean annual precipitation
the following places in m

		Rio de Janei
Cherrapunji	11 437	Rio de Janei
Douala	4 109	Perth
Cayenne	3 744	Chicago
Toamasina	3 530	Lisbon
Valdivia	2 396	Dakar
Bombay	2 078	Moscow
Bergen	1 958	Verkhoyansk
San José	1 944	Barrow
Jakarta	1 755	Las Vegas
Tokyo	1 563	Kashgar
Juneau	1 387	Walvis Bay
New York	1 123	Aswân
Brisbane	1 092	Arica

compare: London 610

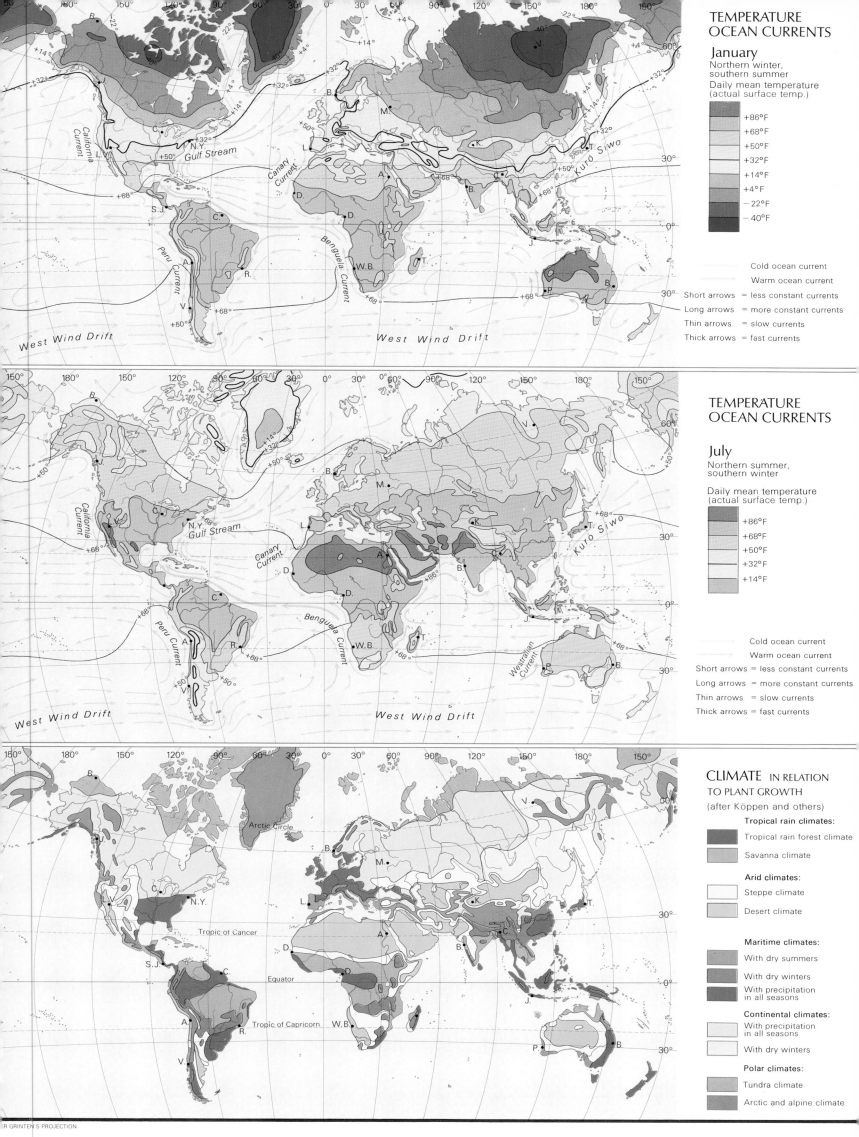

TEMPERATURE OCEAN CURRENTS

January
Northern winter,
southern summer

Daily mean temperature
(actual surface temp.)

+86°F
+68°F
+50°F
+32°F
+14°F
+4°F
−22°F
−40°F

Cold ocean current
Warm ocean current
Short arrows = less constant currents
Long arrows = more constant currents
Thin arrows = slow currents
Thick arrows = fast currents

TEMPERATURE OCEAN CURRENTS

July
Northern summer,
southern winter

Daily mean temperature
(actual surface temp.)

+86°F
+68°F
+50°F
+32°F
+14°F

Cold ocean current
Warm ocean current
Short arrows = less constant currents
Long arrows = more constant currents
Thin arrows = slow currents
Thick arrows = fast currents

CLIMATE IN RELATION TO PLANT GROWTH
(after Köppen and others)

Tropical rain climates:
Tropical rain forest climate
Savanna climate

Arid climates:
Steppe climate
Desert climate

Maritime climates:
With dry summers
With dry winters
With precipitation in all seasons

Continental climates:
With precipitation in all seasons
With dry winters

Polar climates:
Tundra climate
Arctic and alpine climate

ER GRINTEN'S PROJECTION

e 1:220 000 000
e equator

90°   Ⓐ   0°   Ⓑ   90°

① Baffin Bay   Greenland   Novaya Zemlja

Barents Sea

Mohns Ridge

Norwegian Sea

Jan Mayen Ridge   Arctic Circle

Hudson Bay   Iceland   Norwegian Basin   Scandinavia

Labrador Basin   Irminger Basin   Ural Mountains   A   S

② NORTH AMERICA   Hatton Bank   Rockall Bank   North Sea   EUROPE

Appalachians   NORTH ATLANTIC OCEAN   Celtic Shelf   Mt. Blanc 15781ft 4810m   The Alps   Tien Shan

Mid-Atlantic Ridge   Azores   Mediterranean Sea   18481ft 5633m   Caucasus   Caspian Sea   Pamir

Sohm Abyssal Plain   Atlas Mountains   Himalayas

Sargasso Sea   Canary Islands   Tropic of Cancer   Red Sea   Mt. Everest 29028ft 8848m

Kane Fracture Zone   Indus Cone

Puerto Rico Trench   AFRICA   Arabian Basin   Ganges Cone

③ Antilles   Cape Verde Islands   Cameroon Mountains   Carlsberg Ridge   Somali Basin   Seychelles Bank   Great Indian Basin

Ceara Abyssal Plain   Romanche Fracture Zone   Equator   Guinea Basin

SOUTH AMERICA   Mid-Atlantic Ridge   Mt. Kilimanjaro 19340m 5895m   Mid-Indian Ridge   INDIAN OCEAN

④ Andes Mountains   Brazil Basin   Angola Basin   Madagascar   Ninety East Ridge

Peru-Chile Trench   Mt. Aconcagua 12831ft 6959m   Grande Ridge   Rio Fracture Zone   Grande Zone   Tropic of Capricorn   Mocambique Basin

SOUTH ATLANTIC OCEAN   Walvis Ridge   Cape Abyssal Plain   Cape Agulhas   Southwest Indian Ridge

Argentine Basin   Cape Basin   Conrad Rise   Australian-Antarctic Basin

⑤ Falkland Islands   Atlantic-Indian Rise   Melville Fracture Zone   Kerguelen Gaussberg Ridge   Southeast Indian

Scotia Ridge   Meteor Depth   Enderby Abyssal Plain

Cape Horn

90°   0°   90°

FISHING

Density of animal plankton

- Over 500 milligrams per cubic metre
- 200–500 » »
- 50–200 » »
- under 50 » »

Important catch of:

- whale
- herring, cod and similar fish
- tuna
- crab, prawn and other shellfish

© EMS

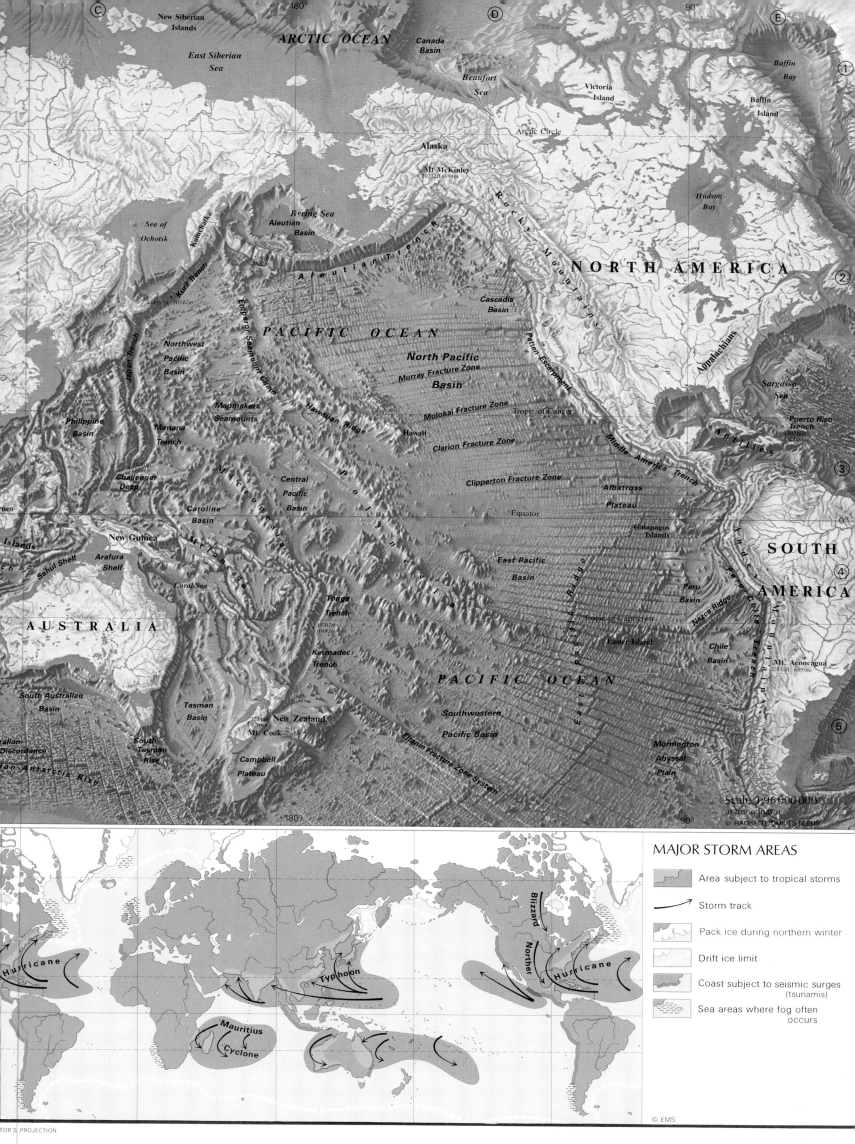

ARCTIC OCEAN

New Siberian
Islands

East Siberian
Sea

Canada
Basin

Beaufort
Sea

Baffin
Bay

Victoria
Island

Baffin
Island

Arctic Circle

Sea of
Ochotsk

Kamchatka

Bering Sea
Aleutian
Basin

Alaska

Mt McKinley
20322ft 6194m

Hudson
Bay

NORTH AMERICA

Aleutian Trench

Cascadia
Basin

Appalachians

Kuril Trench

Japan Trench

Northwest
Pacific
Basin

Emperor Seamount Chain

PACIFIC OCEAN

North Pacific
Basin

Murray Fracture Zone

Patton Escarpment

Sargasso
Sea

Mapmakers
Seamounts

Hawaiian Ridge

Molokai Fracture Zone

Tropic of Cancer

Puerto Rico
Trench
30246ft
9219m

Philippine
Basin

Mariana
Trench

Hawaii

Clarion Fracture Zone

Middle America Trench

Antilles

Challenger
Deep

Central
Pacific
Basin

Clipperton Fracture Zone

Albatross
Plateau

Micronesia

Caroline
Basin

Polynesia

Equator

Galapagos
Islands

0°

Islands

New Guinea

Melanesia

East Pacific
Basin

SOUTH
AMERICA

Sahul Shelf

Arafura
Shelf

Coral Sea

Peru
Basin

Nazca Ridge

Andes Mountains

AUSTRALIA

Tonga
Trench

Tropic of Capricorn

Easter Island

Chile
Basin

Mt. Aconcagua
22831ft 6959m

Peru-Chile Trench

Kermadec
Trench

East Pacific Ridge

South Australian
Basin

Tasman
Basin

New Zealand

Mt. Cook

PACIFIC OCEAN

Mornington
Abyssal
Plain

Australian
Discordance

South
Tasman
Rise

Southwestern
Pacific Basin

Indian Antarctic Rise

Campbell
Plateau

Eltanin Fracture Zone System

Scale 1:96 000 000
at the equator

© HACHETTE GUIDES BLEUS

MAJOR STORM AREAS

Hurricane

Blizzard

Norther

Hurricane

Typhoon

Mauritius
Cyclone

- Area subject to tropical storms
- Storm track
- Pack ice during northern winter
- Drift ice limit
- Coast subject to seismic surges (tsunamis)
- Sea areas where fog often occurs

© EMS

TOR'S PROJECTION

209

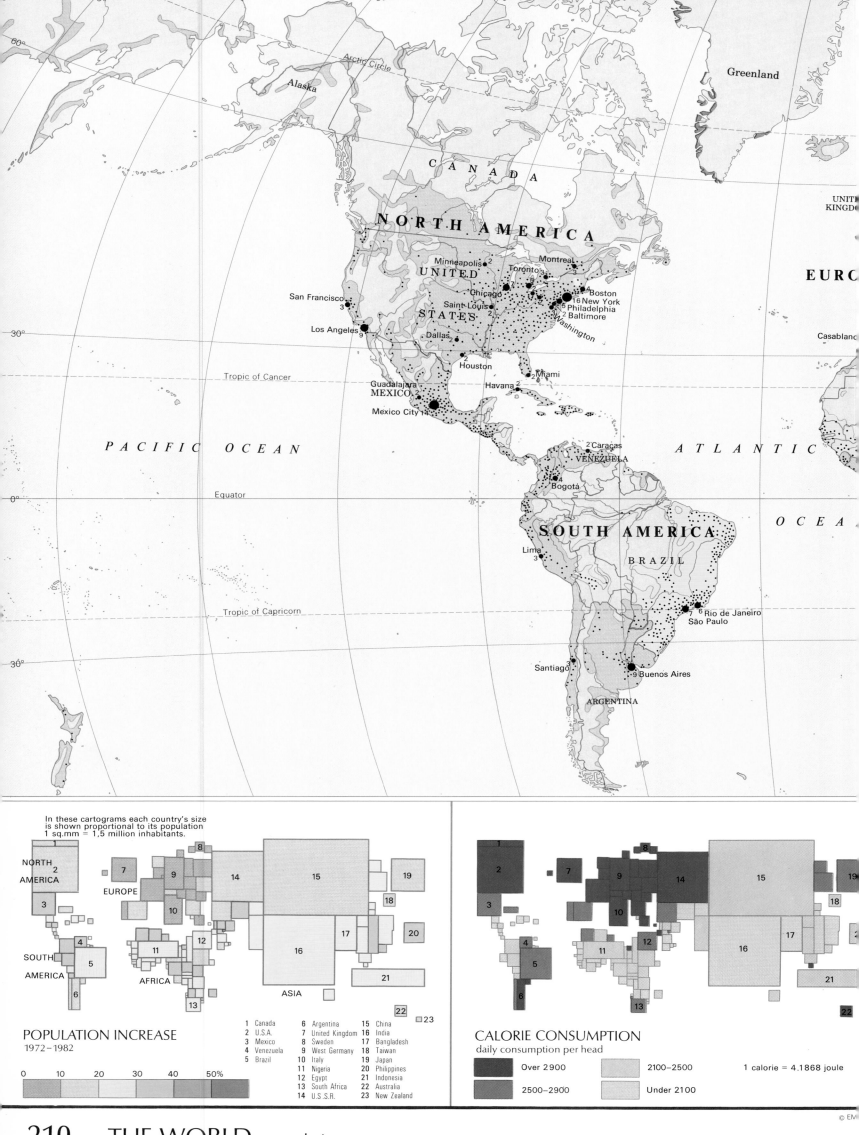

POPULATION INCREASE
1972 – 1982

| 0 | 10 | 20 | 30 | 40 | 50% |

In these cartograms each country's size is shown proportional to its population 1 sq.mm = 1,5 million inhabitants.

1	Canada	6	Argentina	15	China
2	U.S.A.	7	United Kingdom	16	India
3	Mexico	8	Sweden	17	Bangladesh
4	Venezuela	9	West Germany	18	Taiwan
5	Brazil	10	Italy	19	Japan
		11	Nigeria	20	Philippines
		12	Egypt	21	Indonesia
		13	South Africa	22	Australia
		14	U.S.S.R.	23	New Zealand

CALORIE CONSUMPTION
daily consumption per head

| Over 2900 | | 2100–2500 | | 1 calorie = 4.1868 joule |
| 2500–2900 | | Under 2100 | |

© EM

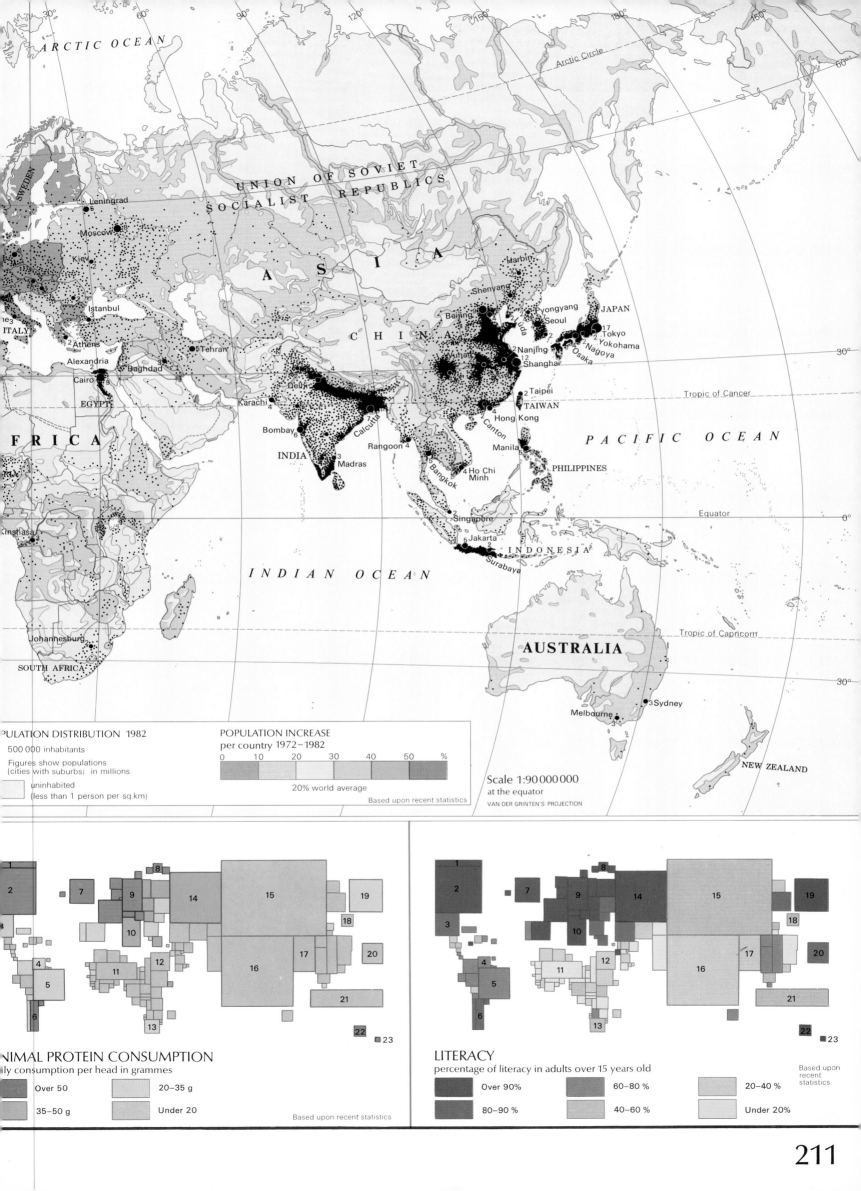

ARCTIC OCEAN

SWEDEN

Leningrad
5

Moscow
8

Kiev
2

Istanbul
3

ITALY

Athens
2

Alexandria

Baghdad
3

Cairo
9

EGYPT

AFRICA

Kinshasa

Johannesburg

SOUTH AFRICA

UNION OF SOVIET
SOCIALIST REPUBLICS

A S I A

C H I N A

Tehran
5

Karachi
4

Delhi

Bombay
6

INDIA

Madras
3

Calcutta

Rangoon
4

Bangkok
5

Singapore

Jakarta
5

Surabaya
2

INDONESIA

Harbin

Shenyang
7

Beijing
9

Juda

Wuhan

Nanjing
2

Shanghai
12

Pyongyang

Seoul
9

JAPAN

Tokyo
17

Yokohama
2

Nagoya
2

Osaka

Taipei
2

TAIWAN

Hong Kong
2

Canton
4

Manila

PHILIPPINES

Ho Chi Minh
4

PACIFIC OCEAN

Tropic of Cancer

Equator

INDIAN OCEAN

AUSTRALIA

Tropic of Capricorn

Melbourne
3

Sydney
3

NEW ZEALAND

Arctic Circle

POPULATION DISTRIBUTION 1982

500 000 inhabitants

Figures show populations
(cities with suburbs) in millions

uninhabited
(less than 1 person per sq.km)

POPULATION INCREASE
per country 1972–1982

0   10   20   30   40   50   %

20% world average

Based upon recent statistics

Scale 1:90 000 000
at the equator

VAN DER GRINTEN'S PROJECTION

ANIMAL PROTEIN CONSUMPTION

daily consumption per head in grammes

| | Over 50 | | 20–35 g |
| | 35–50 g | | Under 20 |

Based upon recent statistics

LITERACY

percentage of literacy in adults over 15 years old

| | Over 90% | | 60–80 % | | 20–40 % |
| | 80–90 % | | 40–60 % | | Under 20% |

Based upon
recent
statistics

211

MILITARY POLITICS

© ESSELTE MAP SERVICE

N.A.T.O., A.N.Z.U.S.	Warsaw Pact	Other communist states	Arab League	Other states

AMERICAN ASPECT
centre Chicago

EUROPEAN ASPECT
centre London

EAST ASIATIC ASPECT
centre Peking

W. Willia projectio

ARCTIC OCEAN

Franz Josef Land
(U.S.S.R.)

Barents
Sea

Novaya
Zemlya

SWEDEN
FINLAND
Stockholm
Helsinki
Copenhagen
Moscow
EAST
Berlin
MANY
Warsaw
POLAND
Is
Prague
Vienna
Budapest
CHOSLOVAKIA
AUSTRIA HUNGARY
Belgrade
Bucharest
ROMANIA
YUGOSLAVIA Sofia
ome
Tirana
BULGARIA
Athens
TURKEY
Valletta GREECE Nicosia
Sea
MALTA
CYPRUS
LEB.
SYRIA
Ankara
Black Sea
UNISIA
Jerusalem Amman
ISRAEL
JORDAN
Damascus
IRAQ
Baghdad
Tripoli
Cairo
KUWAIT

UNION OF SOVIET SOCIALIST REPUBLICS

R. Ob
R. Yenisey
R. Lena
R. Amur

Arctic Circle

Ulan Bator

MONGOLIA

Sea of
Okhotsk

Sakhalin

Kamchatka

Kuril Islands

Bering Sea

Alaska
(U.S.A.)

International Date Line

Aleutian Islands

CHINA

Beijing

NORTH
KOREA
Pyongyang
SOUTH
Seoul KOREA

JAPAN
Tokyo

Sunday
Monday

Midway I. (U.S.A.)

LIBYA
EGYPT

R. Nile
Red Sea

SAUDI
ARABIA

BAHRAIN
Riyadh QATAR
UNITED
ARAB EMIR.

Muscat
OMAN

Tehran

IRAN

Kabul
AFGHANISTAN

Islamabad

PAKISTAN

Delhi

Kashmir

NEPAL
Katmandu
Thimbu
BHUTAN

R. Ganges

Dacca

INDIA

BANGLADESH

Hwang Ho

Yangtze Kiang

Taipei
TAIWAN
Hong Kong (U.K.)
Macao (Port.)

Ryukyu
Islands
(JAPAN)

Bonin
Islands
(JAPAN)

Marcus I.
(JAPAN)

Tropic of Cancer

Wake I.
(U.S.A.)

PACIFIC

CHAD
N'Djamena
SUDAN
Khartoum

YEMEN
Sana
SOUTH YEMEN
Aden
DJIBOUTI

ETHIOPIA
Addis
Ababa

Arabian
Sea

BURMA
Rangoon

LAOS
Hanoi
VIETNAM
Vientiane

THAILAND
Bangkok

KAMPUCHEA
Phnom
Penh

Laccadive Is.

Bay of
Bengal

SRI LANKA
Colombo

South China Sea

PHILIPPINES
Manila

Mariana
Islands
(U.S.A.)

Guam I. (U.S.A.)
Pacific Islands
Trust Territory
(Admin. by U.S.A.)

Marshall
Islands

OCEAN

Bairiki
Equator

CENTRAL
AFRICA
Bangui

SOMALIA
Mogadishu

Male
MALDIVES

MALAYSIA
Kuala Lumpur
BRUNEI
SINGAPORE
Borneo

Palau

Federated States of Micronesia

NAURU

KIRIBATI

MMEROON
Yaoundé
Zaire
GABON
ZAIRE

UGANDA
RWANDA Kigali
KENYA
Kampala
Nairobi
BURUNDI Bujumbura

SEYCHELLES
Victoria

Chagos
Archipelago
(U.K.)

Sumatra

Jakarta

INDONESIA

Java

New Guinea

Bismarck
Archipelago

PAPUA NEW GUINEA

SOLOMON
ISLANDS

Port Moresby Honiara

TUVALU
Funafuti

Wallis &
Futuna Is.
(FR.)

WESTERN
SAMOA
Apia

azzaville
inda
uanda
Kinshasa

ANGOLA

ZAMBIA
Lusaka

TANZANIA
Dar es Salaam

MALAWI
COMOROS
Lilongwe Moroni

Cocos Islands
(AUSTR.)

VANUATU
Vila

FIJI Suva

New Caledonia
(FR.)

Harare
ZIMBABWE

MOZAMBIQUE

Tananarive
MADAGASCAR
Réunion
(FR.)
Port Louis
MAURITIUS

INDIAN

Coral Sea

Nuku'alofa TONGA

Kermadec
Islands
(N.Z.)

NAMIBIA BOTSWANA
Gaborone
Pretoria
Ivis Bay
(AFR.)
Mbabane SWAZILAND
Maputo
Maseru LESOTHO
SOUTH
AFRICA

OCEAN

Tropic of Capricorn

AUSTRALIA

Cape Town

Amsterdam I.
(FR.)

Scale 1:90 000 000

• National capital
— International boundary
--- Disputed boundary

Canberra

Tasmania

NEW ZEALAND
Wellington

Prince Edward
Islands
(S. AFR.)

Kerguelen I.
(FR.)

VAN DER GRINTEN'S PROJECTION

AMERICAN
ASPECT

Ch.

centre
Chicago

EUROPEAN
ASPECT

L

centre
London

EAST ASIATIC
ASPECT

P.

centre
Peking

ADE POLITICS

| ▧ E.E.C. | ▨ E.E.C. associated. Commonwealth | ▤ E.F.T.A. | ▥ L.A.I.A. | ▦ Comecon | ▧ Other countries | ○ O.P.E.C. |

213

OIL: production, consumption, sea transport (metric tons)

139 production (million tons/year)

83 consumption (million tons/year)

transport of crude oil (million tons/year)

less than 20
20–100
100–200
200–400
400–800
over 800

COAL: production, consumption (metric tons)

330 production (million tons/year)

394 consumption (million tons/year)

coal and lignite expresse in comparable values (coal equivalent)

© ESSELTE MAP SERVICE

ARCTIC OCEAN

Svalbard

Barents Sea

Novaya Zemlya

Vorkuta · R.Ob

S i b e r i a

Arctic Circle

Bering Strait

Alaska

Bering Sea

Aleutian Islands

R.Lena

R.Yenisei

Bratsk

Kamchatka

Sea of Okhotsk

Billingen

E U R O P E

R.Volga

Second Baku

"Third Baku"

R.Ob

R.Ural

Donets Basin

Volgograd

Ploiești

Caspian

Black Sea

Baku

Kuznetsk Basin

Lake Baikal

A S I A

Dzungaria

Fergana Basin

R.Amur

Manchuria

Sakhalin

Kuril Islands

Hokkaido

Honshu

Sakuma

Kyushu

PACIFIC

OCEAN

Mediterranean Sea

saoud

Zaltan

A F R I C A

Arlit

Bakouma

Moanda

R.Congo

Rössing U

Witwatersrand

Kirkuk

Burgān (Kuwait)

Aghā Jarī

Persian Gulf

Abu Dhabi

Ghawar

Aswān
Sadd el Aali

R.Nile

Red Sea

R.Indus

Bhakra

R.Ganges

Bihar

Assam

Hwang Ho

Szechwan (Red Basin)

Yangtze Kiang

Tropic of Cancer

30°

Gulf of Bengal

Sri Lanka

Arabian Sea

Equator

South China Sea

Brunei

Borneo

Sumatra

Sunda Islands

Philippine Islands

New Guinea

0°

Kariba

Cabora Bassa

Madagascar

I N D I A N

O C E A N

Rum Jungle

A U S T R A L I A

Coral Sea

Tropic of Capricorn

30°

Snowy Mts

Gippsland Shelf

Tasman Sea

New Zealand

LAND

deposits of:
— uranium
— crude oil
— tar sands or oil shales
— natural gas
— coal
— lignite

mentary basin (tly oil-bearing)

rock without k sediment cover

ro electric er > 500 Mw

SEA

sedimentary basin (partly oil-bearing)

shallow seabed without thick sediment cover

200 m

2000 m

shallow sea (continental shelf)

deep sea

Scale 1:90 000 000
at the equator

COMMUNIST COUNTRIES INCL. CHINA

AMERICA 2359

1533

WESTERN EUROPE 832

572

1349

3089

365

Hydro-electric & nuclear power 3,6%

21,4%

Natural gas

Coal, lignite 29,4%

Crude oil 45,6%

THE WORLD'S SOURCES OF ENERGY

CENTRAL AMERICA (INCL. VENEZUELA AND COLOMBIA)

285

428

AFRICA 500

99

408

186

REST OF ASIA

1193

MIDDLE EAST

SOUTH AMERICA 133

46

128

34

OCEANIA

RODUCTION OF ENERGY

tal annual production of primary energy
ude oil, natural gas, coal, lignite,
at, hydro-electric and nuclear power)

primary energy expressed in million tons coal

537 — 1981
99 — 1962

AFRICA

CONSUMPTION OF ENERGY

Total annual consumption of primary
energy per person by country
(expressed in kilograms of coal)

100   1000   3000   6000   kilograms per person

DER GRINTEN'S PROJECTION

215

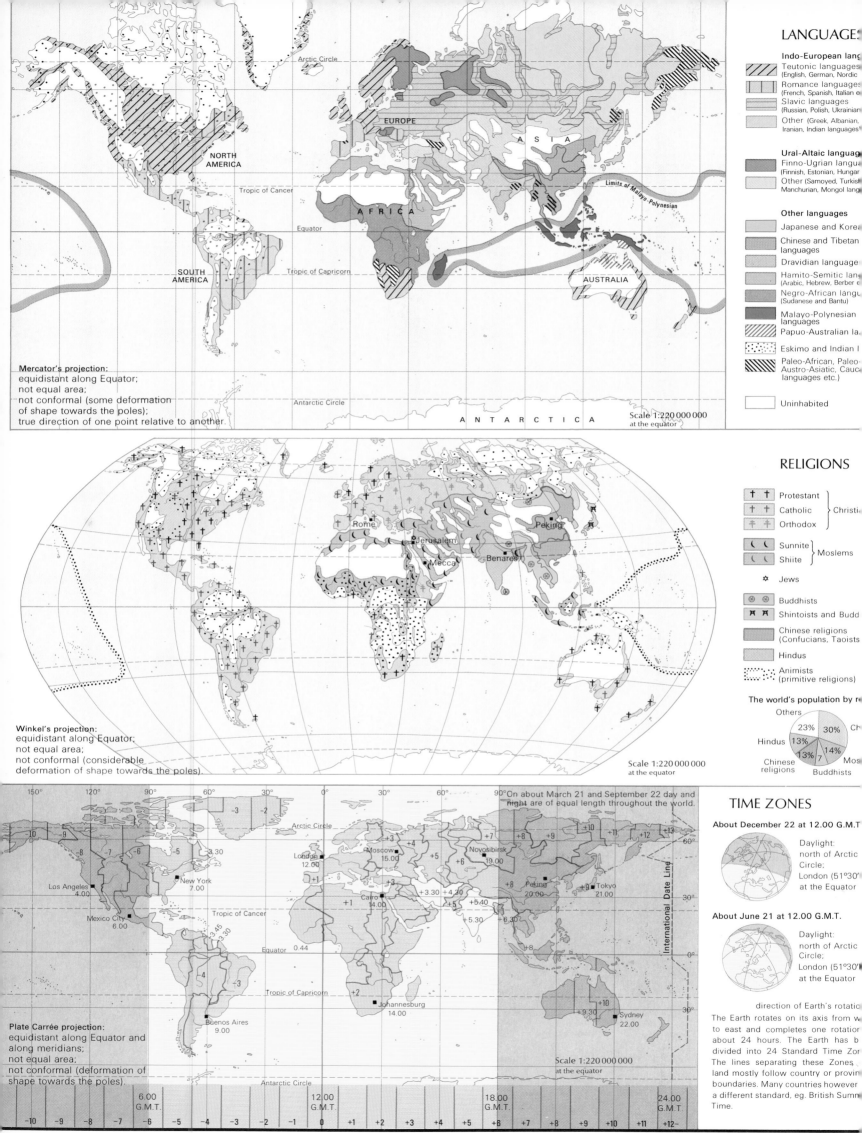

LANGUAGES

Indo-European languages
Teutonic languages
(English, German, Nordic)
Romance languages
(French, Spanish, Italian e)
Slavic languages
(Russian, Polish, Ukrainian)
Other (Greek, Albanian,
Iranian, Indian languages)

Ural-Altaic languages
Finno-Ugrian languages
(Finnish, Estonian, Hungar)
Other (Samoyed, Turkish
Manchurian, Mongol lang)

Other languages
Japanese and Korea
Chinese and Tibetan
languages
Dravidian language
Hamito-Semitic lan
(Arabic, Hebrew, Berber e)
Negro-African langu
(Sudanese and Bantu)
Malayo-Polynesian
languages
Papuo-Australian la
Eskimo and Indian l
Paleo-African, Paleo-
Austro-Asiatic, Cauca
languages etc.
Uninhabited

Mercator's projection:
equidistant along Equator;
not equal area;
not conformal (some deformation
of shape towards the poles);
true direction of one point relative to another.

Scale 1:220 000 000
at the equator

RELIGIONS

Protestant ⎫
Catholic ⎬ Christi
Orthodox ⎭

Sunnite ⎫ Moslems
Shiite ⎭

Jews

Buddhists

Shintoists and Budd

Chinese religions
(Confucians, Taoists
Hindus

Animists
(primitive religions)

The world's population by r

Others 23% | 30% Ch
Hindus 13%
Chinese 13% 7 Mos
religions | 14%
Buddhists

Winkel's projection:
equidistant along Equator;
not equal area;
not conformal (considerable
deformation of shape towards the poles).

Scale 1:220 000 000
at the equator

On about March 21 and September 22 day and
night are of equal length throughout the world.

TIME ZONES

About December 22 at 12.00 G.M.T

Daylight:
north of Arctic
Circle;
London (51°30'
at the Equator

About June 21 at 12.00 G.M.T.

Daylight:
north of Arctic
Circle;
London (51°30'
at the Equator

direction of Earth's rotatio
The Earth rotates on its axis from w
to east and completes one rotation
about 24 hours. The Earth has b
divided into 24 Standard Time Zor
The lines separating these Zones
land mostly follow country or provin
boundaries. Many countries however
a different standard, eg. British Sum
Time.

Plate Carrée projection:
equidistant along Equator and
along meridians;
not equal area;
not conformal (deformation of
shape towards the poles).

Scale 1:220 000 000
at the equator

6.00 G.M.T. | 12.00 G.M.T. | 18.00 G.M.T. | 24.00 G.M.T.

-10 -9 -8 -7 -6 -5 -4 -3 -2 -1 0 +1 +2 +3 +4 +5 +6 +7 +8 +9 +10 +11 +12 -

GLOSSARY and INDEX

The **GLOSSARY**, p. 217–219, provides an English translation of those geographical names and words which are presented on the maps in the langue of the area concerned. For languages using non-Latin alphabets, official transcriptions have been used throughout the entire atlas—in maps, glossary and index.

The words in the glossary are mostly single words, but some prefixes and suffixes are also translated into English. In some cases the name on the map is abbreviated, for instance **Khr.** for the Russian **Khrebet** (mountain chain or range). In the glossary both the full name and its abbreviation is given.

The **INDEX**, p. 220–327, contains about 57.000 names found in the map section. As a general rule each entry is referred to the map page where the place or feature is shown at the largest scale and where it is best seen in its national and environmental context. The oceans and some oceanic islands are referred to small-scale maps to show the extent of the oceans and, for the islands, their correct location.

Each name in the index is located by a map page number and an index square on that particular page. The locational reference is to the name and not, for instance, the extent of country or the position of the town. The squares are defined by letters and figures. For example the town Nyeri in Kenya is found in the index with the reference 199 F 5 which means that Nyeri is found on page 199 in index square F (marked at the top and at the bottom of the map spread) and 5 (marked at the sides of the spread).

Some names are given only a page number as reference. Some of these names appear on the maps of the Polar regions, where an index with letters and figures would be confusing. Other entries refer to names on the thematical maps of the continents which do not have index squares.

The order of names in the index is strictly alphabetical and unaffected by diacritical signs such as dots or accents.

GLOSSARY

A

å *Dan., Nor., Swe.*	river
açude *Portugese*	reservoir
adrar *Berber*	mountains
ákra, akrotition *Greek*	cape
Alb, Alp *German*	mountains, peak
alpes *French*	mountains
alpi *Italian*	mountains
-älv, -älven *Swedish*	river
ao *Thai*	bay
archipiélago *Spanish*	archipelago
arquipélago *Portugese*	archipelago
arrecife *Spanish*	reef
arroyo *Spanish*	brook
-ås, -åsen *Swedish*	hills
atol *Portugese*	atoll
aïn *Arabic*	spring

B

bab *Arabic*	strait
bælt *Danish*	strait
bahía *Spanish*	bay
bahr, baḥr *Arabic*	river, sea
baía *Portugese*	bay
baie *French*	bay
ballon *French*	mountain
balta *Romanian*	marsh
bañados *Spanish*	marsh
-bandao *Chinese*	peninsula
barrage *French*	dam
baraji *Turkish*	reservoir
batang *Indonesian*	river
batu *Malay*	mountain
Becken *German*	basin
ben *Gaelic*	mountain
Berg *German*	mountain, hill
berg *Afrikaan, Dutch*	mountains
-berg *Swedish*	mountain, hill
Berge *German*	mountains
-bergen *Swedish*	mountains
-berget *Swedish*	mountain, hill
bi'r *Arabic*	well
birkat *Arabic*	lake
boca *Spanish*	river mouth
boğazi *Turkish*	strait
bogd *Mongolian*	range
bol'shoy *Russian*	big
bong *Korean*	mountain
-breen *Norwegian*	glacier
Bucht *German*	bay
bugt *Danish*	bay
buhayrah *Arabic*	lake

buḥayrat *Arabic*	lake, lagoon
bukit *Indon., Malay*	mountain
-bukten *Swedish*	bay
burnu, burun *Turkish*	cape

C

c., cabo *Spanish*	cape
c., cabo *Port., Sp.*	cape
cachoeira *Portugese*	waterfall
canal *Fr., Port., Sp.*	canal, channel
canale *Italian*	canal, channel, strait
cao nguyen *Vietnamese*	plateau
c., cap *French*	cape
capo *Italian*	cape
causse *French*	upland
c., co., cerro *Spanish*	mountain
c., co., cerros *Spanish*	mountains
chapada *Portugese*	hills
chott *Arabic*	intermittent lake, salt marsh
chuŏr phnum *Cambod.*	mountains
ciudad *Spanish*	city
co *Chinese*	lake
col *French*	pass
colina *Spanish*	hill
colinas *Spanish*	hills
colli *Italian*	hills
collines *French*	hills
con *Vietnamese*	islands
cord., cordillera *Sp.*	mountains
corno *Italian*	mountain
costa *Spanish*	coast
côte *French*	coast, hills
crêt *French*	peak
cuevas *Spanish*	caves

D

dağ, dağı *Turkish*	mountain
dāgh *Persian*	mountains
dağlar, dağları *Turkish*	mountains
dahr *Arabic*	hill
-dal, -dalen *Nor., Swe.*	valley
danau *Indonesian*	lake
-dao *Chinese, Vietnam.*	island
daryācheh *Persian*	lake
dasht *Persian*	desert
deniz, denizi *Turkish*	sea
desierto *Spanish*	desert
détroit *French*	strait
dhar *Arabic*	escarpment
-dian *Chinese*	lake
dijk *Dutch*	dike

djebel *Arabic*	mountain, mountains
-djupet *Swedish*	deep
-do *Korean*	island
doi *Thai*	mountain
dolina *Russian*	valley
dolok *Indonesian*	mountain

E

-egga *Norwegian*	mountain
-elv, -elva *Nor.*	river
embalse *Spanish*	reservoir
erg *Arabic*	desert
espigão *Portugese*	highland
estero *Spanish*	estuary
estrecho *Spanish*	strait
étang *French*	pond
-ey *Icelandic*	island

F

falaise *French*	cliff
farsh *Arabic*	upland
-fell *Icelandic*	mountain
-feng *Chinese*	mountain
firth *Gaelic*	estuary, strait
-fjäll *Swedish*	hill, mountain
-fjällen *Swedish*	mountain, mountains
-fjället *Swedish*	mountain
-fjell, -fjellet *Norwegian*	mountain
-fjöll *Icelandic*	mountain
-fjord *Norwegian*	fjord
-fjorden *Nor., Swe.*	fjord, lake
-fjördur *Icelandic*	fjord, bay
-flói *Icelandic*	bay
foci *Italian*	river mouths
-fonni *Norwegian*	glacier
fontaine *French*	spring
-foss *Icelandic*	waterfall

G

g., gora *Russian*	mountain, hill
G., gunung *Malay*	mountain
G., gunung *Indonesian*	mountain
gebergte *Dutch*	mountains
Gebirge *German*	mountains
greçidi *Turkish*	pass
ghubbat *Arabic*	bay
Gipfel *German*	peak
gji *Albanian*	bay
gol *Mongol*	river
göl, gölü *Turkish*	lake
golfe *French*	gulf

golfo *It., Sp.*	gulf	
gora *Serbo-Croathian*	mountains	
góra *Polish*	mountain	
gorje *Serbo-Croathian*	mountains, hills	
gory *Russian*	mountains, hills	
góry *Polish*	mountains	
grotte *French*	grotto	
gryada *Russian*	mountain	
guba *Russian*	bay	
guelb *Arabic*	mountain	
-guntō *Japanese*	islands	

H

Haff *German*	lagoon
-hai *Chinese*	sea, lake
-haixia *Chinese*	strait
-halvøya *Norwegian*	peninsula
-hama *Japanese*	beach
hamada *Arabic*	desert
hammādat *Arabic*	plateau
hāmūn *Persian*	lake, marsch
harrat *Arabic*	lava flow
-hav *Swedish*	sea, bay
havre *French*	harbor
hawr *Arabic*	lake
-he *Chinese*	river
Heide *German*	heath
hka *Burmese*	river
-holm *Danish*	island
horn *German*	cape, mountain
hory *Czech., Slovenian*	mountains
-hu *Chinese*	lake

I

i., isla *Spanish*	island
idhan *Arabic*	dunes
île *French*	island
îles *French*	islands
ilha *Portugese*	islands
Insel *German*	island
Inseln *German*	islands
Insulá *Romanian*	island
'irq *Arabic*	dunes
islas *Spanish*	islands
isola *Italian*	island
isole *Italian*	islands
istmo *Spanish*	isthmus

J

jabal *Arabic*	mountain, mountains
järv *Estonian*	lake
-järvi *Finnish*	lake
-jaur *Lappish*	lake
-javre *Lappish*	lake
jazā'ir *Arabic*	islands
jazīrat *Arabic*	island
jazīreh *Persian*	island
jebel *Arabic*	mountain
jezero *Serbo-Croathian, Albanian*	lake
jezioro *Polish*	lake, lagoon
-jiang *Chinese*	river
jibāl *Arabic*	mountains
-jima *Japanese*	island
-joki *Finnish*	river
-jøkulen *Norwegian*	glacier
-jökull *Icelandic*	glacier

K

kabīr *Persian*	mountains
-kaikuō *Japanese*	strait
-kaise *Lappish*	mountain
kalns *Latvian*	mountain
Kamm *German*	ridge
kanaal *Dutch*	canal
kanal *Rus., S.C., Swe., Ger.*	canal, channel
kanava *Finnish*	canal, channel
Kap *German*	cape
-kapp *Norwegian*	cape
kas *Cambodian*	island
kavīr *Persian*	desert
kep *Albanian*	cape
k., kep., kepulauan *Indon.*	islands
khalīj *Arabic*	gulf
khashm *Arabic*	mountain
Khr., Khrebet *Russian*	mountain range
ko *Thai.*	island
-ko *Japanese*	lake, lagoon
koh *Afgan.*	mountains
kólpos *Greek*	bay
körfezi *Turkish*	gulf, bay
kórgustik *Estonian*	mountain
kosa *Russian*	spit
kotlina *Polish*	basin
-kou *Chinese*	bay, pass
krueng *Indonesian*	river

kryazh *Russian*	mountains	
kuala *Malay*	bay	
kūh *Persian*	mountain	
kūhha *Persian*	mountains	
-kulle *Swedish*	hill	
kyun *Burmese*	island	

L

l., lac *French*	lake
la *Tibethan*	pass
lacs *French*	lakes
lacul *Romanian*	lake
lago *It., Sp. Port.*	lake
lagoa *Portugese*	lake, lagoa
lagos *Port., Sp.*	lakes
lag., laguna *Spanish*	lagoon, lake
l., laut *Indonesian*	sea
les *Czechoslovakian*	forest
liman *Russian*	estuary, bay
limni *Greek*	lake
-ling *Chinese*	peak
llano *Spanish, Port.*	plain
llanos *Spanish, Port.*	plains
loch *Gaelic*	lake, inlet
lough *Gaelic*	lake

M

m., munţii *Romanian*	mountains
mae *Thai*	river
-mak *Turkish*	river
-man *Korean*	bay
mar *Spanish*	sea
marais *French*	marsch
mare *Italian*	sea
massif *French*	mountain, mountains
Meer *German*	sea, lake
meer *Afrikaans, Dutch*	sea, lake
mer *French*	sea
mesa *Spanish*	mesa
meseta *Spanish*	plateau
mierzeja *Polish*	spit
-misaki *Japanese*	cape
mont *French*	mount
montagna *Italian*	mountain
montagne *French*	mountain
montagnes *French*	mountains
montaña *Spanish*	mountain
montañas *Spanish*	mountains
monte *It., Port., Sp.*	mount
montes *Port., Sp.*	mountains
monti *Italian*	mountains
monts *French*	mountains
more *Russian*	sea
morro *Port., Sp.*	hill, mountain
motu *Polynesian*	island, rock
mui *Vietnamese*	point
munkhafad *Arabic*	depression
munţii *Romanian*	mountains
mys *Russian*	cape

N

nafūd *Arabic*	desert
najor'ye *Russian*	plateau, mountains
namakzār *Persian*	salt flat
-näs *Swedish*	peninsula
nasjonal park *Nor.*	national park
neem *Estonian*	cape
-nes *Ice., Nor.*	peninsula, point
ness *Gaelic*	promontory
nev., nevado *Spanish*	mountain
ngoc *Vietnamese*	mountain
niso *Greek*	islands
nizmennost' *Russian*	plain
nunatakk *Eskimoo*	peak
nuruu *Mongol*	mountains
nuur *Mongol*	lake

O

-ö *Swe., Dan., Nor.*	island
o., ostrov *Russian*	island
-öarna *Swedish*	islands
-ön *Swedish*	island
óri *Greek*	mountains
óros *Greek*	mountain, mountains
ostrov *Russian*	island
ostrova *Russian*	islands
ostrovul *Romanian*	island
otok *Serbo-croathian*	island
-øy, -øya *Norwegian*	island
oz., ozero *Russian*	lake
ozera *Russian*	lakes

P

pahorkatina *Czech.*	hills
palla *Italian*	peak
pampa *Spanish*	plain
pantanal *Port., Sp.*	swamp

parc nacional *French*	national park
parq. nac., parque nacional *Port., Sp.*	national park
pas *French*	strait
paso *Spanish*	pass
Pass *German*	pass
passe *French*	passage
passo *Italian*	pass
pasul *Romanian*	pass
peg., pegunungan *Indonesian*	mountains
pélagos *Greek*	sea
peña *Spanish*	peak, rock
-pendi *Chinese*	basin
península *Spanish*	peninsula
pereval *Russian*	pass
pertuis *French*	strait
peski *Russian*	desert
phnum *Cambodian*	mountain
pic *French*	peak
pico *Port., Sp.*	peak
picos *Port., Sp.*	peaks
-piggen *Norwegian*	mountains
pik *Russian*	peak
plaine *French*	plain
planalto *Portugese*	plateau
planina *Serbo-Croathian*	mountain
plato *Bulgarian, Russian*	plateau
playa *Spanish*	beach
ploskogorje *Russian*	plateau
pointe *French*	point
poluostrov *Russian*	peninsula
ponta *Portugese*	point
porog *Russian*	waterfall
presa *Spanish*	reservoir, dam
prohod *Bulgarian*	pass
proliv *Russian*	strait
promontorio *It., Sp.*	promonotyr
puerto *Spanish*	pass
puig *Catalonian*	peak
pulau *Indon., Malay*	island
puna *Spanish*	upland
punta *It., Sp.*	point, peak
puncak *Indonesian*	peak
puo *Laotian, Thai*	mountain
puy *French*	peak

Q

qanāt *Arabic*	canal
-quando *Chinese*	islands
qurnat *Arabic*	mountains

R

r. *Port., Sp.*	river
rags *Latvian*	cape
ramlat *Arabic*	dunes
ras, ra's *Arabic*	cape
rās *Persian*	cape
ravnina *Russian*	plain
récif *French*	reef
récifs *French*	reefs
représa *Portugese*	dam, reservoir
-retto *Japanese*	islands
ria *Portugese*	estuary
ría *Spanish*	estuary
rio *Portugese*	river
río *Spanish*	river
riviera *Italian*	coast
rivière *French*	river
rt *Serbo-Croathian*	cape
Ruck *German*	mountain

S

sa. *Portugese*	mountains
saar *Estonian*	island
sabkhat *Arabic*	lagoon, salt marsh
sadd *Arabic*	dam
saguia *Arabic*	wadi
şsahrā' *Arabic*	desert
salar *Spanish*	salt flat
salina, salinas *Spanish*	salt marsh, salt flat
-sälkä *Finnish*	ridge
-sanmyaku *Japanese*	range
-san *Jap., Korean*	mountain
-sanchi *Japanese*	mountains
-sanmaek *Korean*	mountains
sarīr *Arabic*	desert
Sattel *German*	pass
saurums *Latvian*	strait
sebkha *Arabic*	salt flat
sebkra *Arabic*	intermittent lake
See *German*	lake
Seen *German*	lakes
selat *Indonesian*	strait
serra *Portugese*	mountains, mountain-chain
serranía, serranías *Sp.*	mountains

serrania, serranias *Portugese*	mountains	
shamo *Chinese*	desert	
-shan *Chinese*	mountains, mountain, island	
-shankou *Chinese*	pass	
sharm *Arabic*	bay	
-shima *Japanese*	island	
-shotō *Japanese*	islands	
-shuiku *Chinese*	reservoir	
sierra *Spanish*	mountains	
silsilesi *Turkish*	mountains	
-sjö *Norwegian*	lake	
-sjön *Swedish*	lake, bay	
serrania *Spanish*	mountains	
sopka *Russian*	mountain	
Spitze *German*	peak	
sierra *Spanish*	mountains	
step' *Russian*	plain	
štit *Slovenian*	peak	
stretto *Italian*	strait	
-suidō *Japanese*	channel	
-sund *Swedish*	sound	
s., sungai *Indonesian*	river	

T

tg., tanjung *Indones.*	cape
-tangar-, tangi *Icelandic*	point
tassili *Berber*	plateau
taung *Burmese*	mountain
teluk *Indonesian*	bay
ténéré *Berber*	desert
tepe, tepesi *Turkish*	peak, hill
thiu khao *Thai.*	mountains
-tind, -tindane *Nor.*	mountain
-tō *Japanese*	island
tónlé *Cambodian*	lake
-top *Dutch*	peak
-träsk *Swedish*	lake
-tunturi *Finnish*	mountain

U–V

uul *Mongol*	mountain, mountains
-vaara *Finnish*	hill
val *French, Italian*	valley
valle *Italian, Spanish*	valley
vallée *French*	valley
-vatn *Ice., Nor.*	lake
-vesi *Finnish*	lake
-vidda *Norwegian*	plateau

-viken *Swedish*	gulf
Virful *Romanian*	mountain
vodokhranilishche *Russian*	reservoir
vol., volcán *Spanish*	volcano
vozvyshennost *Russian*	upland
vrh., vrchovina *Czech., Slo.*	mountains
-väin *Estonian*	strait
-vötn *Icelandic*	lake

W–Z

wādi *Arabic*	wadi
wāhat *Arabic*	oasis
Wald *German*	forest
-wan *Ch., Jap.*	bay
-xan *Chinese*	strait
-yama *Japanese*	mountain
y., yarimadasi *Turkish*	peninsula
yoma *Burmese*	mountains
-zaki *Japanese*	point
zalew *Polish*	lagoon
zaliv *Russian*	gulf, bay
zatoka *Polish*	gulf
zee *Dutch*	sea, lake

INDEX

A

Å 150 F 2
Aachen 148 E 4
Aalen 149 F 5
Äänekoski 150 J 3
Aansluit 200 C 5
Aare 153 E 2
Aargub 192 B 4
Aa Sumayḥ 198 D 3
Aba (China) 172 D 4
Aba (Nigeria) 197 F 4
Aba (Zaire) 198 E 4
Abā Ad Dūd (Saudi Arabia) 156 D 4
Abacaxis 139 G 5
Abadab, Jabal 194 F 5
Ābādān (Iran) 157 E 3
Ābādeh (Iran) 157 F 3
Ābādeh (Iran) 157 F 3
Abadla 192 E 2
Abaeté 141 G 4
Abaetetuba 139 J 4
Abagnar Qi 173 G 2
Abaí 142 E 4
Abaiang 186 C 2
Abaji 197 F 4
Abajo Mountains 114 H 6
Abajo Peak 114 H 6
Abakaliki 197 F 4
Abakan 159 R 5
Abakan 170 F 5
Abakanskiy Khrebet 159 S 5
Abakwasimbo 198 D 4
Abala (Congo) 197 H 6
Abala (Niger) 196 E 3
Abalak 197 F 2
Abalemma (Algeria) 193 G 4
Abalemma (Niger) 197 F 2
Abalemma (Niger) 197 F 2
Abalessa 193 F 4
Aban 170 G 4
Abancay 140 B 3
Abant Silsilesi 154 D 2
Abār al Kanā'is 194 D 2
Abariringa 186 D 3
Abarqu 168 E 4
Abarqu (Iran) 157 F 3
Abarqu, Kavir-e (Iran) 157 F 3
Abashiri 173 M 2
Abatskoye 159 O 4
Abau 184 E 4
Abava 151 H 4
Abay 159 O 6
Abaya, Lake 199 F 3
Abaza 170 F 5
Abbai 198 F 2
Abbas, Bandar (Iran) 157 G 4
Abbāsābād (Iran) 157 G 1
Abbe, Lake 199 G 2
Abbeville (AL.) 131 J 3
Abbeville (France) 152 D 1
Abbeville (GA.) 131 L 2–3
Abbeville (LA.) 123 L 6
Abbeville (MS.) 121 Q 8
Abbeville (S.C.) 129 J 7
Abborrträsk 150 GH 2
Abbot Butte 110 C 8
Abbot Ice Shelf 203
Abbotsford (WI.) 124 D 5
Abbott (N.M.) 117 M 1MO
Abbottabad 169 J 4
'Abd al Azīz, Jabal 195 F 1
'Abd al Kūrī 199 J 2
Ābdānān (Iran) 157 E 2
Abdul Ghadir 199 G 2
Abdulino 158 K 5
Abéché 197 J 3
Abel Tasman National Park 185 Q 9
Abelvær 150 F 3
Abemama 186 C 2
Abenab 200 B 3
Abengourou 196 D 4
Åbenrå 148 E 4
Abeokuta 196 E 4
Aberaeron 148 C 4
Aberdare National park 199 F 5
Aberdares → Nyanda Rua 199 F 5
Aberdeen (Andaman Is.) 175 F 5
Aberdeen (MD.) 129 P 2
Aberdeen (MS.) 121 R 9
Aberdeen (N.C.) 131 M 6
Aberdeen (S.D.) 119 K 5
Aberdeen (South Africa) 200 C 6
Aberdeen (U.K.) 148 C 3
Aberdeen (WA.) 110 B 3–4
Aberdeen Lake 103 RS 3
Aberfoyle 183 H 3

Abernant (AL.) 128 D 8
Abernathy (TX.) 117 P 4MO
Aberystwyth 148 C 4
Abez' 159 M 2
Abganerevo 155 F 1
Abhā 195 G 5
Abhar (Iran) 157 E 1
Abi Addi 199 F 2
Abidjan 196 D 4
Abilene (KS.) 120 H 4
Abilene (TX.) 122 E 4
Abingdon (VA.) 129 J 5
Abinskaya 155 E 2
Abiquiu (N.M.) 117 K 1MO
Abiquiu Reservoir 117 K 1
Abisko 150 G 2
Abitibi 105 L 5
Abja-Paluoja 151 HJ 4
Abkit 171 T 3
Abnūb 194 E 3
Åbo 151 H 3
Abo, Massif d' 197 H 1
Aboisso 196 D 4
Aboke 198 E 3
Abomey 196 E 4
Abong Abong, Gunung 176 A 3
Abong Mbang 197 G 5
Aborigen, Pik 171 R 3
Aborlan 177 E 2
Abou Deïa 197 H 3
Abou Goulem 197 J 3
Abovyan 155 F 2
Abqaiq (Saudi Arabia) 157 E 4
Abqayq → Buqayq 195 H 3
Abraham's Bay 133 H 3
Abrantes 152 B 4
Abreu e Lima 141 K 2
'Abrī 194 E 4
Abrolhos, Arquipélago dos 141 J 4
Abruka 151 H 4
Abruzzo 153 F 3
Absaroka Range 111 PQ 6
Absarokee (MT.) 111 Q 5
Abū ad Duḥūr (Syria) 156 B 2
Abū al Abyaḍ (United Arab Emirates) 157 F 4
Abū al Bukhush (United Arab Emirates) 157 F 4
Abū 'Alī (Saudi Arabia) 157 E 4
Abū 'Arīsh 195 G 5
Abū Baḥr 195 H 4
Abū Ballaṣ 194 D 4
Abū Daghmah (Syria) 156 C 1
Abū Darbah (Egypt) 156 B 3
Abu Dhabi (United Arab Emirates) 157 FG 4
Abū Dulayq 194 E 5
Abufari 139 F 5
Abū Ḥadrīyah (Saudi Arabia) 157 E 4
Abū Ḥamad 194 E 5
Abū Ḥasan, Jabal 195 G 5
Abuja 197 F 4
Abū Jābirah 194 D 6
Abū Jifān (Saudi Arabia) 157 E 4
Abū Jubayhah 194 E 6
Abū Kamāl (Syria) 156 C 2
Abū Madd, Ra's 194 F 4
Abū Maṭāriq 194 D 6
Abu Mendi 198 F 2
Abumombazi 198 C 4
Abū Njaym 193 J 2
Abūqrīn 193 J 2
Abū Qumayyis, Ra's (United Arab Emir-
ates) 157 F 4
Abu Road 174 B 3
Abū Ruayq (Saudi Arabia) 156 C 5
Abū Rubayq 195 F 4
Abū Rujmayn, Jabal 194 F 2
Abū Sa'fan (Saudi Arabia) 157 F 4
Abū Shajarah, Ra's 194 F 4
Abū Shanab 194 D 6
Abu Simbel → Abu Sunbul 194 E 4
Abū Sukhayr (Saudi Arabia) 156 D 3
Abū Sunbul 194 E 4
Abū Ṭabarī 194 D 5
Abū Ṭij 194 E 3
Abū Ṭulayh 194 E 5
Abū 'Uruq 194 E 5
Abuya Myeda 199 F 2
Abū Zabad 194 D 6
Abū Ẓaby (United Arab Emirates) 157 FG 4
Abū Zanīmah (Egypt) 156 A 3

Abwong 198 E 3
Aby, Lagune 196 D 4
Abyaḍ 194 D 6
Abyaḍ, Jabal 194 D 5
Abyaḍ, Ra's al (Saudi Arabia) 156 BC 5
Abyār 'Alī (Saudi Arabia) 156 C 4
Abydos 194 E 3
Abyei 198 D 3
Abyei 198 D 3
Âbyek (Iran) 157 F 2
Åbyn 150 H 2
Abyy 171 QR 2
Acadia, Cape 105 M 3
Acadia National Park 126 L 4
Açailândia 139 J 4
Acajutla 132 DE 5
Acalayong 197 FG 5
Acámbaro 132 B 3–4
Acandí 138 C 2
Acaponeta 132 A 3
Acapulco 132 B 4
Acará 139 J 4
Acaraú 141 HJ 1
Acaraú 141 J 1
Acari (Brazil) 141 J 2
Acarí (Peru) 140 B 4
Acarigua 138 E 2
Acatlán de Osorio 132 C 4
Acayucan 132 C 4
Accomac (VA.) 129 Q 4
Accra 196 DE 4
Acebuches 132 B 2
Acerra 153 F 3
Achaguas 138 E 2
Achalpur 174 C 3
Achao 143 B 7
Achar 142 E 5
Achegour 197 G 2
Acheloós 154 B 3
Acheng 173 J 1
Achikouya, Plateau des 197 GH 6
Achikulak 155 F 2
Achill 148 A 4
Achim 149 E 4
Achinsk 170 EF 4
Achit Nuur 170 F 6
Achuyevo 155 E 1
Acı Gölü 154 C 3
Acil Barké 196 C 3
Acipayam 154 C 3
Acireale 153 G 4
Ackerman (MS.) 121 Q 9
Ackley (IA.) 119 PQ 8
Acklins Island 133 H 3
Acme (LA.) 123 M 4
Acme (N.M.) 117 M 4MO
Acme (WA.) 110 C 2
Acme (WY.) 118 B 6
Acoma (NV.) 112 L 5
Acoma Indian Reservation 116 J 3
Acomita (N.M.) 116 J 2
Aconcagua, Cerro 142 BC 5
Acopiara 141 J 2
Acorizal 140 C 3
Acorn Hoek 201 E 4
Acquasanta Terme 153 F 3
Acqui Terme 153 E 3
Acre 138 D 5
Acre 140 C 3
Acre (Israel) 156 B 2
Acre → 'Akko 194 EF 2
Acri 153 G 4
Actaeon Group 187 F 4
Acton (MT.) 111 R 5
Actopan 132 C 3
Açu 141 J 2
Açude Araras 141 H 1
Açude Orós 141 J 2
Acuracay 138 D 5
Ada (Ghana) 196 E 4
Ada (MN.) 119 M 3
Ada (OK.) 120 J 8
Ada (WI.) 124 G 6
Adaba 199 F 3
Ada Burnu 155 D 3
'Adad 199 H 3
Adâdle 199 G 3
Adafer 192 CD 5
Adair (IA.) 119 O 9
Adair (OK.) 121 K 6
Adair, Bahia 106 D 5
Adairsville (GA.) 128 G 7
Adak (AK.) 102 B 5
Adak (Sweden) 150 G 2
Adal, Mount 109 LM 4
'Adale 199 H 4

Ådalen 150 G 3
'Ādam 195 K 4
Adam, Mount 143 DE 9
Adama Nazareth → Adama 199 F 3
Adamantina 141 F 5
Adamaoua 197 G 4
Adamello 153 F 2
Adams (MA.) 126 F 6
Adams (N.D.) 119 KL 2
Adams (N.Y.) 126 D 5
Adams (OK.) 120 DE 6
Adams (TN.) 128 DE 5
Adams (WI.) 124 E 6
Adams, Mount 110 D 4
Adams Bridge 174 C 6
Adams–McGill Reservoir 112 K 4
Adams Peak 174 D 6
Adamstown 187 G 4
Adamsville (TN.) 128 C 6
Adamsville (TX.) 122 E 4
Adamsville (UT.) 114 DE 5
Adana 155 E 3
Adana (Turkey) 156 B 1
Adang, Teluk 176 E 4
Adapazarı 154 D 2
Adarama 194 E 5
Adare, Cape 203
Adaut 177 H 5
Adavale 183 G 4
Adda 153 E 2
Aḍ Ḍab'ah 194 D 2
Ad Dabbah 194 E 5
Ad Dafinah 195 G 4
Aḍ Ḍafrah (United Arab Emirates) 157 F 5
Ad Dahnā' (Saudi Arabia) 157 DE 4
Aḍ Ḍāli' 195 GH 6
Ad Damazin 194 E 6
Ad' Dāmir 194 E 5
Ad Dammām (Saudi Arabia) 157 EF 4
Ad Darb 195 G 5
Ad Dawādimī (Saudi Arabia) 156 D 4
Ad Dawḥah (Qatar) 157 F 4
Ad Dawr (Iraq) 156 D 2
Ad Dayr (Iraq) 156 A 4
Ad Dibdibah (Saudi Arabia) 157 E 3
Aḍ Ḍiffah 193 K 2
Ad Dikākah 195 J 5
Ad Dilam (Saudi Arabia) 157 E 5
Ad Dindar 194 E 6
Ad Dirīyah (Saudi Arabia) 157 E 4
Addis (LA.) 123 M 5
Addis Ababa 199 F 3
Addis Alam 199 F 3
Addis Derra 199 F 2
Addison (N.Y.) 126 B 6
Addis Zemen 199 F 2
Ad Dīwanīyah (Iraq) 157 D 3
Ad Du'ayn 194 D 6
Ad Duwayd (Saudi Arabia) 156 CD 3
Ad Duwaym 194 E 6
Adel (GA.) 131 L 3
Adel (MT.) 111 O 3
Adel (OR.) 110 H 8
Adelaide (South Africa) 200 D 6
Adelaide (South Australia) 183 F 5
Adelaide Island 203
Adelaide Peninsula 103 S 2
Adelaide River 182 E 1
Adelaye 198 C 3
Adele Island 182 C 2
Adélie Coast 203
Aden 195 H 6
Aden, Gulf of 195 H 6
Aderbissinat 197 F 2
Adhan, Jabal (United Arab Emirates) 157 G 4
Adh Dhahībāt 193 H 2
Adh Dhayd (United Arab Emirates) 157 G 4
Adi 198 E 4
Adi, Pulau 177 H 4
Adiaké 196 D 4
Adi Arkai 199 F 2
Adige 153 F 2
Adigrat 199 F 2
Adigüzel Barajı 154 C 3
Adi Kaie 199 F 2
Adilabad 174 C 4
Adilcevaz 155 F 3
Adin (CA.) 112 E 1
Adi Quala 199 F 2
Adirondack Mountains 126 E 4–5
Adi Ugri 199 F 2

Adıyaman 155 E 3
Adjud 154 C 1
Adjuntas (P.R.) 130 C 8
Adler 155 E 2
Admer, Erg d' 193 G 4
Admiralty 102 L 4
Admiralty Gulf 182 D 1
Admiralty Island National Monument 102 L 4
Admiralty Islands 184 E 2
Admiralty Mountains 203
Ado 196 E 4
Adobe Creek Reservoir 115 O 5
Ado Ekiti 197 F 4
Adok 198 E 3
Adolphus Island 182 D 2
Adonara, Pulau 177 F 5
Adoni 174 C 4
Adour 152 C 3
Ad Ouzzeïne 196 E 2
Adra 152 C 4
Adrano 153 F 4
Adrar (Algeria) 192 E 3
Adrar (Algeria) 193 G 3–4
Adrar des Iforas 196 E 1–2
Adrar Sotuf 192 B 4
Adré 197 J 3
Adria 153 F 2
Adrian (GA.) 131 M 2
Adrian (MI.) 125 K 8
Adrian (MN.) 119 N 7
Adrian (MO.) 121 L 4
Adrian (OR.) 110 H 7
Adrian (TX.) 117 O 2MO
Adriatic Sea 153 FG 3
Adulis 199 F 1
Adusa 198 D 4
Advance (MO.) 121 Q 5
Adwa 199 F 2
Ady (TX.) 117 O 2MO
Adyakit, Gora 170 G 2
Adycha 171 P 2
Adygalakh 171 R 3
Adyk 155 G 1
Adzhar 155 F 2
Adzhima 171 P 6
Adzopáe 196 D 4
Adz'va 159 L 2
Adzva 159 M 2
Aegean Sea 154 C 3
Aeneas (WA.) 110 G 2
Ærö 151 F 5
Aesculapium 154 C 3
Aetna (KS.) 120 G 5
Afade 197 G 3
Afao, Mont 193 G 3
Affak (Iraq) 157 D 2
Affollé 192 C 4
Afghanistan 169 GH 4
Afgöye 199 H 4
Afif (Saudi Arabia) 156 D 4–5
Afikpo 197 F 4
Aflou 193 F 2
Afmadow 199 G 4
Afogados da Ingazeira 141 J 2
Afognak 102 G 4
Afore 184 E 3
Afrêra, Lake 199 G 2
African Islands 199 J 5
Afşin 155 E 3
Afton (CA.) 113 J 7
Afton (IA.) 119 O 9–10
Afton (KS.) 121 K 6
Afton (N.M.) 117 JK 5MO
Afton (NV.) 113 J 4
Aftout 192 C 5
Afuá 139 H 4
Afyonkarahisar 154 D 3
Agadem 197 G 2
Agadez 197 F 2
Agadir 192 D 2
Agadyr' 159 O 6
Agailás 192 C 4
Agalta, Sierra de 132 E 4
Agana 186 A 2
Agapa 170 E 1
Agapitovo 159 R 2
Agapovka 159 L 5
Agara 155 F 2
Agaro 199 F 3
Agartala 175 F 3
Agassiz Pool 119 N 2
Agata 170 F 2
Agata, Ozero 170 GF 2
Agate (CO.) 115 NO 4

Agate (NE.) 118 E 8
Agate Fossil Beds National Monument 118 E 8
Agats 177 J 5
Agawa Bay 104 L 6
Agawa Bay (MI.) 125 K 2
Agawam (MT.) 111 NO 3
Agbaja 197 F 4
Agboville 196 D 4
Agdam 168 D 2
Agdary 170 L 3
Agde 152 D 3
Agdz 192 D 2
Agen 152 D 3
Agency Lake 110 CD 8
Agepsta 155 F 2
Agha Jari 165
Agha Jārī (Iran) 157 EF 3
Aghireşu 154 B 1
Aghrejit 192 C 4
Agía Pelagía 154 B 3
Aginskoye 170 FG 4
Aginskoye 170 K 5
Agmar 192 C 3
Agmumuit 192 B 4
Agness (OR.) 110 AB 8
Agnew 182 C 4
Agnibilékrou 196 D 4
Agnita 154 B 1
Agön 150 G 3
Agordat 199 F 1
Agout 152 D 3
Agoza 197 J 2
Agra 174 C 2
Ágreda 152 C 3
Ağrı 155 F 3
Agrigento 153 F 4
Agrihan 186 A 1
Agrinion 154 B 3
Agrour Sfaya 192 C 4
Agto 105 R 2
Agua Blanca 143 C 6
Aguaclara 138 D 3
Água Clara 141 F 5
Aguadas 138 C 2
Aguadilla (P.R.) 130 B 8
Aguadulce 138 B 2
Agua Fria Peak 117 L 1
Agua Fria River 116 D 3–4
Aguanga (CA.) 113 J 9
Agua Nueva (TX.) 122 E 9
Aguapeí, Serra do 140 E 4
Agua Prieta 106 E 5
Aguaray 140 D 5
Aguarico 138 C 4
Águas Formosas 141 H 4
Agua Vermelha, Reprêsa 141 FG 4–5
Águeda 152 B 3
Aguelhok 196 E 2
Aguelt el Melha 192 D 4
Aguelt Némadi 192 C 5
Aguemour 193 FG 3
Aguenit 192 C 4
Aguerakertem 192 D 4
Aguezi Tigu 197 G 1
Aguila (AZ.) 116 C 4
Aguilar (CO.) 115 N 6
Aguilar de Campóo 152 DC 3
Aguilas 152 C 4
Aguililla 132 B 4
Aguja, Cerro 143 B 7
Agulhas, Cape 200 C 6
Agulhas Negras, Pico das 141 H 5
Agung, Gunung 176 E 5
Aguscalientes 132 B 3
Agustín Codazzi 138 D 1–2
Ağva 154 C 2
Agvali 155 G 2
Ahaggar 193 G 4
Aha Hills 200 C 3–4
Ahar 168 D 3
Ahe 187 F 3
Ahiri 174 D 4
Ahlat 155 F 3
Ahmadabad 174 B 3
Ahmadnagar 174 BC 4
Ahmadpur East 169 J 5
Ahmadpur West 169 J 5
Ahmar Mountains 199 G 3
Ahmeyim 192 C 4
Ahome 106 E 6
Ahoskie (N.C.) 129 P 5
Ahram (Iran) 157 F 3
Ahraura 174 D 3
Ahrensburg 149 F 4
Ähtäri 150 H 3
Ähtärinjärvi 150 H 3
Ähtäri 150 H 3
Ähtävänjoki 150 H 3
Ahunui 187 F 4
Åhus 151 F 4
Ahvāz (Iran) 157 E 3

Ahvenanmaa (Åland) 151 GH 3
Aḥwar 195 H 6
Ai-Ais 200 B 5
Aiapuá 139 F 4
Aiea (HI.) 113 E 10
Aigoual, Mont 152 D 3
Aigua 142 F 5
Aigues-Mortes 152 D 3
Aiguilete, Cerro 143 B 9
Aiguillon 152 D 3
Aihui 171 N 5
Aiken (S.C.) 129 J 8
Ailao Shan 172 D 6
Aileu 177 G 5
Ailigandí 138 C 2
Ailinginae 186 C 2
Ailinglapalap 186 C 2
Aillik 105 Q 4
Ailuk 186 C 2
Aim 171 O 4
Aimorés 141 H 4
Aimorés, Serra dos 141 H 4
Ain 153 E 2
Aïn Afalelah 193 G 4
'Ain al Khaleifa 194 D 3
'Ain al Wādī 194 D 3
Aïn Amenas 193 G 3
Aïn Amguel 193 FG 4
Ainaro 177 G 5
Aïn Athil 192 C 4
Aïn Azaoua 193 G 3
Ainaži 151 H 4
Aïn Beïda 193 G 1
Aïn Beni Mathar 192 E 2
Aïn ben Tili 192 D 3
Aïn Ebeggi 193 G 4
Aïn Ekker 193 G 4
Aïn el Barka 192 D 3
Aïn el Hadjadj 193 G 3
Aïn Ezzane 193 H 4
Aïn Galakka 197 H 2
Aïn Guezzam 193 G 5
Aínos Óros 154 B 3
Aïn Ouzzal 193 F 4
Aïn Safra 192 C 4
Aïn Sefra 192 E 2
Aïn Souf 193 F 3
Ainsworth (NE.) 118 J 8
Aïn Taya 193 D 4
Aïn Témouchent 192 E 1
Aïn Tidjoubar 193 F 3
Aïn Tiguelguemine 193 F 3
Aïn Ziza 193 F 4
Aïoun Abd el Malek 192 D 4
Aioun el Atrouss 192 D 5
Aiquile 140 C 4
Aïr 197 F 2
Airao 139 F 4
Aire-sur-l'Adour 152 CD 3
Air Force Island 105 N 2
Air Musi 176 B 4
Airolo 153 E 2
Aisaita 199 G 2
Aiscia 199 G 2
Aisega 184 E 3
Aishalton 139 G 3
Aishihik 109 L 3
Aisne 152 D 2
Aïssa, Djebel 192 E 2
Aitana, Pico 152 C 4
Aitape 184 D 2
Aitkin (MN.) 119 P 4
Aitolikón 154 B 3
Aitutaki 187 E 4
Aiud 154 B 1
Aix, Mount 110 D 4
Aix-en-Provence 153 E 3
Aix-les-Bains 153 E 2
Aiyaion Pélagos 154 C 3
Aíyina 154 B 3
Aiyion 154 B 3
Aizawl 175 F 3
Aizuwakamatsu 173 M 3
Aja, Jabal (Saudi Arabia) 156 C 4
Ajab Shīr 168 D 3
Ajaccio 153 E 3
'Ajā'iz 195 K 5
Ajajú 138 D 3
Ajanta Range 174 C 3
Aj Bogd Uul 170 FG 7
Aj Bogd Uul 172 BC 2
Ajdābiyā 193 K 2
Ajdīr, Ra's 193 H 2
Ajigasawa 173 L 2
Ajir, Mont 197 F 2
Ajka 154 A 1
'Ajlūn (Jordan) 156 B 2
'Ajmah, Jabal al (Egypt) 156 A 3
'Ajmān (United Arab Emirates) 157 G 4
Ajmer 174 B 2
Ajo (AZ.) 116 D 5
Ajo, Cabo de 152 C 3
Ajoewa 139 G 3
Aju, Kepulauan 177 H 3
Akabli 193 F 3
Akademii, Zaliv 171 P 5
Akal 154 F 5
Akalkot 174 C 4
Akanthou 155 D 3
Akanthou (Cyprus) 156 A 2

Akarnaniká Ori 154 B 3
Akaroa 185 Q 9
'Akasha 194 E 4
Akashi 173 K 4
Akbaba Tepe 155 E 3
Akbaytal, Pereval 169 J 3
Akbulak 158 L 5
Akçaabat 155 E 2
Akçadağ 155 E 3
Akçakale 155 E 3
Akcakale (Turkey) 156 C 1
Akçakara Dağı 155 F 3
Akçakışla 155 E 3
Akçakoca 154 D 2
Akcha 169 H 3
Akchar, Dunes de l' 192 C 4
Akchatau 159 O 6
Ak-Chin Indian Reservation 116 D 4
Ak Dağ 154 C 3
Ak Dağ 154 C 3
Ak Dağ (Turkey) 155 F 2
Ak Dağ (Turkey) 155 F 2
Ak Dağ (Turkey) 155 F 2
Akdağmadeni 155 E 3
Ak Dovurak 170 F 5
Akelamo 177 G 3
Akeley (MN.) 119 O 3–4
Akelo 198 E 3
Akers (LA.) 123 N 5
Akespe 168 G 2
Aketi 198 C 4
Akhalkalaki 155 F 2
Akhaltsikhe 155 F 2
Akharnai 154 B 3
Akhḍar, Jabal al 195 K 4
Akhḍar, Wādī al (Saudi Arabia) 156 B 4
Akhiny 170 J 5
Akhiok 108 M 4
Akhisar 154 C 3
Akhmīm 194 E 3
Akhsu 168 D 2
Akhtarīn (Syria) 156 B 1
Akhtubinsk 158 J 6
Akhtyrka 158 F 5
Akiachak 108 F 3
Akiak 108 F 3
Akimiski 105 L 5
Akimovka 155 E 1
Akita 173 M 3
Akjoujt 192 C 5
Akka 192 D 3
Akkabak 169 G 1
Akkajaure 150 G 2
Akkani 108 D 2
Akkavare 150 H 3
'Akko (Israel) 156 B 2
Akköy 154 C 3
Akkul' 169 J 2
Aklavik 102 K 2
Aklé Aouana 192 D 5
Akmenrags 151 H 4
Akmeqit 169 K 3
Akobo 198 E 3
Akobo 198 E 3
Akok 197 F 3
Akola 174 C 3
Akongkür 169 K 2
Akonolinga 197 G 5
Akot (India) 174 C 3
Akot (Sudan) 198 E 3
Akpatok 105 O 3
Akqi 169 K 2
Ákra Akritas 154 B 3
Ákra Ambelos 154 B 3
Ákra Áraxos 154 B 3
Akra Arnauti 155 D 3
Akra Arnauti (Cyprus) 156 A 2
Akra Gata 155 D 4
Akra Gata (Cyprus) 156 A 2
Akra Greco 155 D 4
Akra Greco (Cyprus) 156 B 2
Ákra Kafirévs 154 BC 3
Ákra Kambanós 154 BC 3
Ákra Kánestron 154 B 3
Ákra Kastéllos 154 C 3
Ákra Lithinon 154 B 4
Ákra Maleás 154 B 3
Akranes 150 A 3
Ákra Okhthonia 154 B 3
Akra Pinnes 154 B 2
Akrapkir 155 E 3
Ákra Pláka 154 C 2
Ákra Sidheros 154 C 3
Ákra Soúnion 154 B 3
Ákra Spátha 154 B 3
Ákra Taínaron 154 B 3
Akreïdil 192 B 5
Akritas, Ákra 154 B 3
Akron (CO.) 115 O 3
Akron (IA.) 119 M 8
Akron (N.Y.) 125 Q 6
Akron (OH.) 125 N 8
Aksai Chin 169 K 3
Aksaray 155 D 3
Aksay 155 F 1
Aksay 158 K 5
Aksay Kazakzu Zizhixian 172 B 3
Aksayqin Hu 169 L 3
Aksehir 154 D 3

Akşehir Gölü 154 D 3
Akseki 155 D 3
Aksenovo-Zilovskoye 170 L 5
Aksha 170 K 5
Akshiy 169 G 1
Akstafa 155 G 2
Aksu (China) 169 L 2
Aksu (Turkey) 154 D 3
Aksu (U.S.S.R.) 159 O 5
Aksu (U.S.S.R.) 159 P 6
Aksuat 159 Q 6
Aksu He 169 L 2
Aksum 199 F 2
Aksumbe 169 H 2
Aktash 169 H 3
Aktasty 159 M 5
Aktau 159 O 5
Aktau, Gora 169 G 2
Akto 169 K 3
Aktobe 168 E 2
Aktogay 159 OP 6
Aktumsyk 168 F 1
Aktyubinsk 159 L 5
Akula 198 C 4
Akun 102 D 5
Akure 197 F 4
Akureyri 150 B 2
Akutan 102 D 5
Akutan Passage 108 E 5
Akutau 108 E 5
Akwanga 197 F 4
Akyab 175 F 3
Akyazı 154 D 2
Akzhal 159 Q 6
Akzhar 169 J 2
Akzhaykyn, Ozero 169 H 1–2
Ala, Monti di 153 E 3
Alabama (North) 128 HJ 2
Alabama (South) 130–131
Alabama River 130 G 3
Alabaster (AL.) 128 E 8
Al 'Abbāsīyah 194 E 6
Al Abyaḍ, Ra's 193 G 1
Al Abyār 193 K 2
Alaca 155 DE 2
Alaçam 155 E 2
Alaçam Dağları 154 C 3
Alachakh 171 P 4
Alachevo 171 T 3
Alachua (FL.) 131 M 5
Alacrán 132 E 3
Aladağ (Turkey) 155 DE 3
Aladağ (Turkey) 155 F 3
Al 'Adam 193 K 2
Aladža manastir 154 C 2
Al 'Agabah aş Şaghīrah (Egypt) 156 A 4
Alagir 155 F 2
Alagoas 141 J 2
Alagoinhas 141 J 3
Alagón (Spain) 152 B 3–4
Alagon (Spain) 152 C 3
Alahanpanjang 176 B 4
Alahärmä 150 H 3
Al Aḥmadī (Kuwait) 157 E 3
Alaid 171 T 5
Alaita 199 G 2
Alajärvi 150 H 3
Alajuela 132 F 5
Alakanuk 108 EF 3
Al Akhḍar, Al Jabal 193 K 2
Alakol', Ozero 159 Q 6
Alakurtti 150 K 2
Al 'Alamayn 194 D 2
Alama (NV.) 112 K 5
Al Amādīyah (Iraq) 156 D 1
Alamagan 186 A 1
'Alam al Rūm, Ra's 194 D 2
Al 'Amārah (Iraq) 157 E 3
Alameda (N.M.) 117 K 2
Alamitos, Sierra de los 132 B 2
Alamo (GA.) 131 M 2
Alamo (ND.) 118 E 2
Alamo (TN.) 128 B 6
Alamo Alto (TX.) 117 KL 6
Alamogordo (N.M.) 117 L 5
Alamo Heights (TX.) 122 E 6
Alamos 106 E 6
Alamos, Sierra 132 B 2
Alamosa (CO.) 115 M 6
Åland 151 GH 3
Ålands hav 151 G 4
Alaniemi 150 J 3
Alanreed (TX.) 117 Q 2
Alanson (MI.) 125 K 4
Alanya 155 D 3
Alanya (Turkey) 156 A 1
Alaotra, Lac 201 H 3
Alapaha (GA.) 131 L 3
Alapayevsk 159 M 4
Alaplı 154 D 2
Al 'Aqabah (Jordan) 156 B 3
Al 'Aqaylah 193 J 2
Al 'Aqīq 195 G 4
Al 'Arabīyah (Saudi Arabia) 157 EF 4
Al 'Arabīyah as Su'ūdīyah (Saudi Arabia) 156 CD 4
Al Arabīyah as Su'ūdīyah → Saudi Arabia 195 GH 4

Al 'Araj 194 D 3
Alarçon, Embalse de 152 C 4
Al 'Arīsh (Egypt) 156 AB 3
Al 'Armah (Saudi Arabia) 157 DE 4
Al Arṭāwīyah (Saudi Arabia) 157 D 4
Alas, Selat 176 E 5
Al Asab (United Arab Emirates) 157 FG 5
Alaşehir 154 C 3
Al Ashkharah 195 K 4
Al 'Āshūrīyah (Iraq) 156 D 3
Alaska 102 FH 2
Alaska (SD.) 118 HJ 5
Alaska, Gulf of 102 HJ 4
Alaska Peninsula 102 E 4
Alaska Range 102 GH 3
Al 'Assāfīyah (Saudi Arabia) 156 C 3
Alassio 153 E 3
Alatau Shankou 169 L 1
Al' Athāmīn (Iraq) 156 D 3
Alatna 102 G 2
Alatri 153 F 3
Al 'Aṭrun 194 D 5
Alatyr' 158 J 5
Alava, Cape 110 A 2
Alaverdi 155 F 2
Alavíjeh (Iran) 157 F 2
Alavus 150 H 3
Al 'Awāliq 195 H 6
Al 'Awāriq 195 H 4
Al 'Awaynāt 193 H 3
Al' Awsajīyah (Saudi Arabia) 156 D 4
Al Awshazīyah (Saudi Arabia) 156 CD 4
'Alayh (Lebanon) 156 B 2
Alaykél' 169 J 2
Al Ayn (Sudan) 194 D 5
Al 'Ayn (United Arab Emirates) 157 G 4
Alayskiy Khrebet 169 J 3
Alayunt 154 D 3
Alazani 155 G 2
Alazeya 171 S 1
Alazeyskoye Ploskogor'ye 171 R 2
Al Azīzīyah 193 H 2
Alb, Crişul 154 B 1
Alba 153 E 3
Alba (TX.) 123 H 3
Alba Iulia 154 B 1
Al Balyanā 194 E 3
Albanel, Lac 105 N 5
Albania 154 AB 2
Albano Laziale 153 F 3
Albany (Australia) 182 B 5
Albany (GA.) 131 K 3
Albany (KY.) 128 F 5
Albany (MN.) 119 O 5
Albany (MO.) 121 L 2
Albany (N.Y.) 126 F 6
Albany (OH.) 129 J 2
Albany (Ontario, Can.) 104 L 5
Albany (OR.) 110 B 6
Albany (TX.) 122 D 3
Albany (WY.) 118 B 9
Albany (WY.) 118 BC 9
Albany Downs 183 H 4
Albardón 142 C 5
Al Barkāt 193 H 4
Al Barrah (Saudi Arabia) 157 D 4
Al Basrah (Iraq) 157 E 3
Al Baṭhā' (Iraq) 157 D 3
Al Baṭin (Saudi Arabia) 157 F 5
Al Bāṭinah (Saudi Arabia) 157 E 4
Al Batrīn (Iraq) 157 E 3
Albatross Bay 183 G 1
Albatross Plateau 209 D 3
Albatross Point 185 Q 8
Al Batrūn (Lebanon) 156 B 2
Al Bawīṭī 194 D 3
Al Bayāḍh 195 H 4
Al Baydā' (Libya) 193 K 2
Al Baydā' (S. Yemen) 195 H 6
Albemarle (N.C.) 129 L 6
Alberene (VA.) 129 N 4
Alberga River 182 E 4
Albert (KS.) 120 FG 4
Albert (OR.), Lake 110 E 8
Albert (TX.) 122 E 5
Albert, Lake (Uganda/Zaire) 198 E 4
Alberta (AL.) 130 D 2
Alberta (Canada) 103 OP 5
Alberta (VA.) 129 O 5
Albert City (IA.) 119 O 8
Albert Edward Bay 103 R 2
Alberti 142 DE 6
Albertkanaal 148 DE 4
Albert Lea (MN.) 119 P 7
Albert Nile 198 E 4
Alberton (MT.) 111 L 3
Albert River (Queensland, Austr.) 183 F 2
Albertville 153 E 2

Albertville (AL.) **128** E 7
Albi **152** D 3
Albia (IA.) **119** Q 9
Al Bid' (Saudi Arabia) **156** B 3
Albin (WY.) **118** DE 9
Albina **139** H 2
Albion (CA.) **112** B 3
Albion (IA.) **119** PQ 8
Albion (ID.) **111** M 8
Albion (IL.) **121** R 4
Albion (IN.) **124** J 8
Albion (MI.) **125** K 7
Albion (MT.) **118** D 5
Albion (NE.) **119** KL 9
Albion (N.Y.) **125** Q 6
Albion (OK.) **121** K 8
Albion (PA.) **125** O 8
Al Bi'r (Saudi Arabia) **156** B 3
Al Birk **195** G 5
Al Birkah **195** G 4
Alborán **152** C 4
Ålborg **151** F 4
Alborn (MN.) **119** Q 4
Albox **152** C 4
Al Brayqah **193** J 2
Albro **183** H 3
Âlbū 'Alī (Iraq) **156** D 2
Al Buhayrah al Murrah al Kubrā (Egypt) **156** A 3
Albuquerque (N.M.) **117** K 2
Albuquerque, Cayos de **133** F 5
Al Burayj (Syria) **156** B 2
Al Buraymi (Oman) **157** G 4
Al Burdī **193** L 2
Al Burmah **193** G 2
Albury **183** H 6
Al Butayn (Saudi Arabia) **157** D 4
Alcácer do Sal **152** B 4
Alcalá **152** C 3
Alcalá **152** B 4
Alcalá de Chivert **152** D 3
Alcalá la Real **152** C 4
Alcalde (N.M.) **117** KL 1
Alcamo **153** F 4
Alcañices **152** B 3
Alcañiz **152** C 3
Alcántara **139** K 4
Alcántara, Embalse de **152** B 4
Alcantarilla **152** C 4
Alcaraz **152** C 4
Alcaraz, Sierra de **152** C 4
Alcaudete **152** C 4
Alcázar de San Juan **152** C 4
Alcester (S.D.) **119** M 8
Alciéni **197** G 6
Alcira **152** C 4
Alcobaça **141** J 4
Alcobendas **152** C 3
Alcolea del Pinar **152** C 3
Alcoutim **152** B 4
Alcova (WY.) **118** B 8
Alcoy **152** C 4
Alcudia **152** D 4
Al Dab'iyyah (United Arab Emirates) **157** FG 4
Aldabra Islands **199** H 6
Aldama **106** E 6
Aldan **171** O 3
Aldan **171** N 4
Aldano-Uchurskiy Khrebet **171** N 4
Aldanskoye Nagor'ye **171** MN 4
Aldarhaan **170** G 6
Aldeburgh **148** D 4
Alden (MN.) **119** P 7
Alder (MT.) **111** N 5
Alderdale (WA.) **110** EF 5
Alder Lake **110** C 4
Alderney **148** C 5
Aldoma **171** P 4
Aledo (IL.) **124** D 8
Aleg **192** C 5
Alegrete **142** E 4
Alegros Mountain **116** H 3
Aleknagik **102** F 4
Aleksandriya (Ukraine, U.S.S.R.) **155** D 1
Aleksandrov **158** G 4
Aleksandrov Gay **158** J 5
Aleksandrovsk **159** M 4
Aleksandrovskiy **170** L 5
Aleksandrovskoye **155** F 2
Aleksandrovskoye **159** P 3
Aleksandrovskoye **159** R 4
Aleksandrovsk-Sakhalinskiy **171** Q 5
Alekseyevka (Kazakhstan, U.S.S.R.) **159** O 5
Alekseyevka (Kazakhstan, U.S.S.R.) **159** QR 6
Alekseyevka (U.S.S.R.) **158** GH 5
Alekseyevka (U.S.S.R.) **171** M 3
Alekseyev **171** R 1
Alekseyevsk **170** J 4
Aleksikovo **158** H 5
Aleksinac **154** B 2
Alemania (Argentina) **142** C 4
Alemania (Chile) **142** B 4
Além Paraíba **141** H 5
Alençon **152** D 2
Alenquer **139** H 4
Alenuihaha Channel **113** FG 11

Alépé **196** D 4
Aleppo (Syria) **156** B 1
Aléria **153** E 3
Alerta **140** B 3
Alès **152** D 3
Aleshkino **170** H 4
Alessandria **153** E 3
Ålestrup **151** E 4
Ålesund **150** E 3
Aleutian Basin **209** H 6
Aleutian Islands **102** AC 4
Aleutian Range **102** F 4
Aleutian Trench **209** D 2
Alex (OK.) **120** H 8
Alexander (ND.) **118** E 4
Alexander Archipelago **102** K 4
Alexander Bay **200** B 5
Alexander City (AL.) **131** J 2
Alexander Island **203**
Alexandra **184** P 10
Alexandra Channel **175** F 5
Alexandra Falls **103** O 3
Alexandria (Australia) **183** F 2
Alexandria (Egypt) **194** D 2
Alexandria (IN.) **124** J 9
Alexandria (KY.) **128** G 3
Alexandria (LA.) **123** L 4
Alexandria (MN.) **119** N 5
Alexandria (Romania) **154** BC 2
Alexandria (S.D.) **119** KL 7
Alexandria (South Africa) **200** D 6
Alexandria (TN.) **128** EF 5
Alexandria (VA.) **129** O 3
Alexandria Bay (N.Y.) **126** D 4
Alexandrina, Lake **183** F 6
Alexandroúpolis **154** C 2
Alexis (IL.) **124** D 8
Aleysk **159** Q 5
Alfabia, Sierra de **152** D 4
Alfalfa (OR.) **110** DE 6
Al Fallūjah (Iraq) **156** D 2
Alfambra **152** C 3
Al Farīdah (United Arab Emirates) **157** G 4
Al Fāshir **194** D 6
Al Fashn **194** E 3
Al Fatḥah (Iraq) **156** D 2
Al Faw (Iraq) **157** E 3
Al Fawwārah (Saudi Arabia) **156** D 4
Al Fayyūm **194** E 3
Al Fāzih **195** G 6
Alferovka **159** P 5
Al Fifi **194** C 6
Alfios **154** B 3
Alföld **154** AB 1
Alfred (ME.) **126** J 5
Alfred (ND.) **118** K 4
Alfred (TX.) **122** F 8
Al Fuhayhīl (Kuwait) **157** E 3
Al Fuhūd (Iraq) **157** E 3
Al Fujayrah (United Arab Emirates) **157** G 4
Al Fūlah **194** D 6
Al Fuqahā **193** J 3
Al Furāt (Iraq) **156** C 2
Al Fuwayrit (Qatar) **157** F 4
Alga **168** F 1
Al Gāga **194** E 4
Al Galhak **194** E 6
Algama **171** N 4
Alganskaya **171** W 3
Algarrobo **143** D 6
Algarrobo del Águila **143** C 6
Algarve **152** B 4
Algasovo **158** H 5
Algeciras **152** B 4
Alger → Al Jazā'ir **193** F 1
Algeria **192–193** EF 3
Al Gharbī **193** H 2
Al Ghāt (Saudi Arabia) **157** D 4
Al Ghaydah **195** J 5
Al Ghayl **195** H 4
Al Ghazālah (Saudi Arabia) **156** C 4
Alghero **153** E 3
Al Ghrayfah **193** H 3
Al Ghurdagah (Egypt) **156** AB 4
Al Ghurdaqah **194** E 3
Al Ghuwairiyah (Qatar) **157** F 4
Algibe **152** B 4
Algiers **193** F 1
Algoa Bay **200** D 6
Algodones (N.M.) **117** K 2
Algoma (WI.) **124** G 5
Algona (IA.) **119** O 7
Algood (TN.) **128** F 5
Al Habakah (Saudi Arabia) **156** D 3
Al Haḍabat al Ma'āzah **194** E 3
Al Haḍḍar **193** H 2
Al Haḍhālīl (Saudi Arabia) **156–157** D 3
Al Hadīdah **195** J 4
Al Hadīthah (Iraq) **156** CD 2
Al Haḍr (Iraq) **156** D 2
Al Hā'ir (Saudi Arabia) **157** E 4
Al Hajar al Gharbī **195** K 4
Al Hajar ash Sharqī **195** K 4
Al Ḥalfāyah (Iraq) **157** E 3
Al Hamād **156** C 2–3

Al Hamādah al Hamrā' **193** H 3
Alhama de Murcia **152** C 4
Al Hammām (Iraq) **156** D 3
Al Hamrā' (Saudi Arabia) **156** C 5
Al Hamrā', al Hamādah **193** H 3
Al Hanākīyah (Saudi Arabia) **156** C 4
Al Haniyah (Iraq) **157** DE 3
Al Hanīsh al Kabīr **195** G 6
Al Harīq (Saudi Arabia) **157** E 5
Al Harrah (Jordan) **194** F 2
Al Harrah (Saudi Arabia) **156** C 3
Al Harrah (Syria) **156** B 2
Al Harrah (Syria) **156** BC 2
Al Harūj al Aswad **193** J 3
Al Hasa (Jordan) **156** B 3
Al Hasā' (Saudi Arabia) **157** E 4
Al Hasakah (Syria) **156** C 1
Al Hasan (Iraq) **156** D 2
Al Hasānī (Saudi Arabia) **156** B 4
Al Hawātah **194** EF 6
Al Hawīyah **195** G 4
Al Hawjā' (Saudi Arabia) **156** C 3
Al Hawrah **195** H 6
Al Hawtah **195** H 6
Al Hawwārī **193** K 4
Al Hayy (Iraq) **157** DE 2
Al Hayz **194** D 3
Al Hibāk **195** J 4–5
Al Hijaz (Saudi Arabia) **156** B 4
Al Hillah (Iraq) **157** D 2
Al Hillah (Saudi Arabia) **157** E 5
Al Hillah (Sudan) **194** D 6
Al Hinnah (Saudi Arabia) **157** E 4
Al Hirmil (Lebanon) **156** B 2
Al Hoceima **192** E 1
Al Hout (Saudi Arabia) **157** E 3
Al Hudaydah **195** G 6
Al Hufrah (Libya) **193** J 3
Al Hufrah (Saudi Arabia) **156** BC 3–4
Al Hufūf (Saudi Arabia) **157** E 4
Al Hūj (Saudi Arabia) **156** C 3
Al Hunayy (Saudi Arabia) **157** E 4
Al Husayhisah **194** E 6
Al Husaymī **195** H 6
Al Huwaymi **195** H 6
Al Huwayyit (Saudi Arabia) **156** C 4
Al Huwwah **195** H 4
'Alīābād (Iran) **157** F 1
'Alīābād (Iran) **157** G 1
'Alīābād (Iran) **157** E 2
'Alīābād (Iran) **157** F 2
'Alīābād (Iran) **157** F 2
'Alīābād, Kūh-e (Iran) **157** F 2
Aliákmon **154** B 2
Alī al Gharbī (Iraq) **157** E 2
'Alī ash Sharqī (Iraq) **157** E 2
Alibag **174** B 4
Alice (TX.) **122** E 8
Alice, Punta dell' **153** G 4
Alice River **183** H 3
Alice Springs **182** E 3
Aliceville (AL.) **128** C 8
Alichur **169** J 3
Alicudi **153** F 4
Aligarh **174** C 2
Aligūdarz (Iran) **157** F 2
Alijūq, Kūh-e (Iran) **157** F 3
Alikayası **155** E 3
Al Ikhwān **199** J 2
Al Ikhwān (Egypt) **156** B 4
Alim **184** E 2
Alima **197** H 6
Alindao **198** C 3
Alingsås **151** F 4
Alipur **169** J 5
Alipur Duar **174** E 2
Aliquippa (PA.) **125** N 9
Al 'Iraq **156** D 2
Al 'Iraq al 'Arabi (Iraq) **157** DE 2–3
Alire (N.M.) **117** K 1
Al 'Irq **193** K 3
Al 'Irqah **195** H 6
Ali Sabjeh **199** G 2
Al 'Isāwīyah (Saudi Arabia) **156** B 3
'Alī Shāh 'Avaz (Iran) **157** F 2
Al Iskandarīyah (Iraq) **156** D 2
Aliskerovo **171** V 2
Al Ismā'īlīyah (Egypt) **156** A 3
Alitak, Cape **102** FG 4
Alitak Bay **108** M 4
Aliwal North **200** D 6
Al Jabal al Akhḍar **193** K 2
Al Jabalayn **194** E 6
Al Jadīdah (Saudi Arabia) **157** E 4
Al Jafr (Jordan) **156** B 3
Al Jāfūrah (Saudi Arabia) **157** F 4–5
Al Jaghbūb **193** K 3
Al Jahrah (Kuwait) **157** E 3
Al Jalāmīd (Saudi Arabia) **156** C 3
Al Jamalīyah (Qatar) **157** F 4
Al Jamm **193** H 1
Al Jardāwīyah (Saudi Arabia) **156** D 4
Al Jarid, Shaṭṭ **193** G 2
Al Jawārah **195** K 5

Al Jawb (Saudi Arabia) **157** F 5
Al Jawf (Saudi Arabia) **156** C 3
Al Jawf → Al Kufrah **193** K 4
Al Jaylī **194** E 5
Al Jazā'ir **193** F 1
Al Jazīrah **194** E 6
Al Jazīrah (Iraq) **156** CD 2
Al Jībān (Saudi Arabia) **157** F 5
Al Jifārah (Saudi Arabia) **157** D 5
Al Jiwā' (United Arab Emirates) **157** FG 5
Al Jīzah **194** E 2
Al Jubayl (Saudi Arabia) **157** E 4
Al Jubaylah (Saudi Arabia) **157** E 4
Al Jufrah, Wāhat **193** J 3
Al Jufrah Oasis → Wahat al Jufrah **193** J 3
Al Julayqah (Saudi Arabia) **157** E 4
Al Jumaymah (Iraq) **156** D 3
Al Jumaynah **194** C 6
Al Junaynah **195** G 4
Al Jurayd **157** EF 4
Al Kabā'ish (Iraq) **157** E 3
Al Kāf **193** G 1
Al Kahfah (Saudi Arabia) **156** D 4
Al Kāmilīn **194** E 5
Al Karak (Jordan) **156** B 3
Al Karnak (Egypt) **156** A 4
Al Kawah **194** E 6
Al Kāzimīyah (Iraq) **156** D 2
Al Khābūrah **195** K 4
Al Khalīl **156** B 3
Al Khāliş (Iraq) **157** D 2
Al Khalūf **195** K 4
Al Khandaq **194** E 5
Al Khārijah **194** E 3
Al Kharj (Saudi Arabia) **157** E 5
Al Khartum **194** E 5
Al Kharṭūm Baḥrī **194** E 5
Al Khasab (Oman) **157** G 4
Al Khatam (United Arab Emirates) **157** G 5
Al Khaṭṭ (United Arab Emirates) **157** G 4
Al Khazna (United Arab Emirates) **157** G 4
Al Khidr (Iraq) **157** D 3
Al Khīşah (Saudi Arabia) **157** F 4
Al Khubar (Saudi Arabia) **157** F 4
Al Khufayfīyah (Saudi Arabia) **157** D 4
Al Khums **193** H 2
Al Khunfah (Saudi Arabia) **156** C 3
Al Khunn **195** H 4
Al Khuraybah **195** H 5
Al Khurmah **195** G 4
Al Khuwayr (Qatar) **157** F 4
Al Kidn **195** J 4
Al Kifl (Iraq) **156** D 2
Al Kilh Sharq (Egypt) **156** A 4
Al Kir'āneh (Qatar) **157** F 4
Al Kirbekan **194** E 5
Alkmaar **148** D 4
Al Kubar (Syria) **156** C 2
Al Kūfah (Iraq) **156** D 2
Al Kufrah **193** K 4
Al Kufrah, Wāhat **193** K 4
Al Kūm (Syria) **156** C 2
Al Kumayt (Iraq) **157** E 2–3
Al Kuntillah (Egypt) **156** B 3
Al Kūt (Iraq) **157** D 2
Al Kuwayt (Kuwait) **157** E 3
Al Labbah (Saudi Arabia) **156** C 3
Allada **196** E 4
Al Lādhiqīyah (Syria) **156** B 2
Allagash River **126** K 2
Allahabad **174** D 2
Allahüekber Dağı **155** F 2
Allakaket **102** G 2
Allakh-Yun' **171** P 3
Allamoore (TX.) **117** LM 6
Allanmyo **175** G 4
Allanridge **200** D 5
Allardt (TN.) **128** F 5
Allatoona Lake **128** G 7
Al Layyah **194** E 6
Alldays **200** D 4
Allegan (MI.) **124** J 7
Allegany (N.Y.) **125** Q 7
Allegany Indian Reservation **125** Q 7
Allegheny Mountains **129** L 3–4
Allegheny Plateau **129** L 2–3
Allegheny Reservoir **125** Q 8
Allegheny River **125** P 8
Allen (OK.) **120** J 8
Allen (SD.) **118** G 7
Allendale (IL.) **121** S 4
Allendale (S.C.) **129** K 8
Allende **132** C 4
Allenspark (CA.) **113** F 7
Allentown (PA.) **127** D 8
Alleppey **174** C 6
Aller **149** E 4
Allevard **153** E 2

Alley (TX.) **117** P 4
Alliance (NE.) **118** EF 8
Alliance (OH.) **125** N 9
Allier **152** D 2
Al Līfīyah (Iraq) **156** D 3
Alligator River, East **182** E 1
Alligator River, South **182** E 1
Al Lişāfah (Saudi Arabia) **157** E 4
Allison (IA.) **119** Q 8
Allison (N.M.) **116** H 2
Al Līth **195** G 4
Allonnes **152** D 2
Allora **183** J 4
Allouez (WI.) **124** FG 5
Al Luḥayyah **195** G 5
Al Lussuf (Iraq) **156** D 3
Allyn (WA.) **110** C 3
Alma (AR.) **121** L 7
Alma (GA.) **131** M 3
Alma (KS.) **120** J 3
Alma (MI.) **125** K 6
Alma (NE.) **120** F 2
Alma (Quebec, Can.) **105** N 6
Alma (WI.) **124** C 5
Alma-Ata **169** K 2
Alma Center (WI.) **124** C 5
Almada **152** B 4
Almadén **152** C 4
Al Madīnah (Iraq) **157** E 3
Al Madīnah (Saudi Arabia) **156** C 4
'Al Madōw **199** H 2
Al Mafraq (Jordan) **156** B 2
Al Maghrah **194** D 2
Al Mahallah al Kubrā **194** E 2
Al Mahāwiyah **195** G 4
Al Mahdīyah **193** H 1
Al Mahmūdīyah (Iraq) **156** D 2
Al Mahrah **195** J 5
Al Majann (Saudi Arabia) **157** F 5
Al Majarr al Kabīr (Iraq) **157** E 3
Al Majma'ah (Saudi Arabia) **157** D 4
Al Makhaylī **193** K 2
Al Maks al Qiblī **194** E 4
Al Mallāhah al Baḥrīyah **193** H 2
Al Mallāhah al Gharbīyah **193** H 2
Almalyk **169** H 2
Al Manadīr (Oman) **157** G 5
Al Manadir (United Arab Emirates) **157** G 5
Al Manāmah (Qatar) **157** F 4
Al Manāqil **194** E 6
Almanor, Lake **112** D 2
Almansa **152** C 4
Al Manshāh **194** E 3
Al Manşūrah **194** E 2
Al Ma'qil (Iraq) **157** E 3
Al Māqnāh (Saudi Arabia) **156** B 3
Al Maqrūn **193** J 2
Al Maqṭa' (United Arab Emirates) **157** G 4
Al Marj **193** K 2
Al Ma'rūf **193** J 3
Al Mas'ānīyah (Saudi Arabia) **156** D 3
'Al Maskād **199** H 2
Al Matnah **194** EF 6
Al Mawdū **193** J 2
Al Mawşil (Iraq) **156** D 1
Al Mayādīn (Syria) **156** C 2
Al Mayyāh (Saudi Arabia) **156** D 4
Almazán **152** C 3
Almaznyy **170** K 3
Al Mazra'ah (Jordan) **156** B 3
Almeirim **139** H 4
Al Mellem **198** D 3
Almelo **148** E 4
Almena (KS.) **120** F 3
Almenara **141** H 4
Almenara, Sierra de la **152** C 4
Almendra, Embalse de **152** B 3
Almendralejo **152** B 4
Almería **152** C 4
Almería (NE.) **118** J 9
Almería, Golfo de **152** C 4
Al'met'yevsk **158** K 5
Älmhult **151** F 4
Al Midhnab (Saudi Arabia) **156** D 4
Al Milh, Ra's **193** L 2
Almina, Punta **192** D 1
Al Minṭirīb **195** K 4
Al Minyā **194** E 3
Al Miqdādīyah (Iraq) **157** D 2
Almira (WA.) **110** G 3
Almirante **138** B 2
Almirante Brown **203**
Almirante Montt, Golfo **143** B 9
Almirós **154** B 3
Almodóvar **152** B 4
Almogasta **142** C 4
Almond (AR.) **121** O 7
Almont (CO.) **115** L 5
Almont (MI.) **125** M 7
Almont (ND.) **118** G 4
Almonte **152** B 4
Almora **174** CD 2
Almoustarat **196** D 2
Al Mubarraz (Saudi Arabia) **157** E 4
Al Mubarraz (United Arab Emirates) **157** F 4
Al Mudarraj (Saudi Arabia) **156** C 4
Al Mudawwarah (Saudi Arabia) **156** B 3

Al Mughayrā' (Saudi Arabia) 156 B 3
Al Mughayrā' (United Arab Emirates) 157 F 5
Al Muglad 194 D 6
Al Muharraq (Qatar) 157 F 4
Al Mukallā 195 H 6
Al Mukhā 195 G 6
Al Muknīn 193 H 1
Al Munastir 193 H 1
Almuñécar 152 C 4
Al Murabbā' (Saudi Arabia) 156 D 4
Almus 155 E 2
Al Musannāh (Saudi Arabia) 157 E 3
Al Muṣawwart aş Şafra' 194 E 5
Al Musayjīd (Saudi Arabia) 156 C 4
Al Musayyib (Iraq) 156 D 2
Al Muwayh 195 G 4
Al Muwaylih (Saudi Arabia) 156 B 4
Almy (WY.) 111 P 9
Al Nasser (Egypt) 156 A 4
Alney, Gora 171 TU 4
Alnön 150 G 3
Alo 197 J 3
Alofi (Cook Is.) 186 D 4
Alofi (Wallis and Futuna) 186 D 3
Alomata 199 F 2
Along 175 F 2
Alongshan 171 M 5
Alónnisos 154 B 3
Alor, Pulau 177 F 5
Alor, Selat 177 F 5
Álora 152 C 4
Alor Setar 176 B 2
Alotau 183 J 1
Alotau 185 F 4
Alpachiri 143 D 6
Alpaugh (CA.) 113 F 7
Alpena (MI.) 125 L 4
Alpercatas, Serra das 139 JK 5
Alpes Mancelles 152 C 2
Alpha 183 H 3
Alpha (IL.) 124 D 8
Alpha (MI.) 124 F 3
Alpha River 183 H 3
Alphonse 199 J 6
Alpi Carniche 153 F 2
Alpi Dolomitiche 153 F 2
Alpi Marittime 153 E 3
Alpine (AZ.) 116 G 4
Alpine (ID.) 111 OP 7
Alpine (TX.) 117 N 7
Alpi Orobie 153 EF 2
Alps (N.M.) 117 N 1
Al Qa'āmīyāt 195 H 5
Al Qaḍārif 194 F 6
Al Qaddāhīyah 193 J 2
Al Qadīmah 195 F 4
Al Qadmūs (Syria) 156 B 2
Al Qaffay (United Arab Emirates) 157 F 4
Al Qāhirah 194 E 2
Al Qahmah 195 G 5
Al Qā'īyah (Saudi Arabia) 157 D 4
Al Qalībah (Saudi Arabia) 156 B 3
Al Qāmishlī (Syria) 156 C 1
Al Qanțarah (Egypt) 156 A 3
Al Qarābūllī 193 H 2
Al Qārah (Saudi Arabia) 156 C 3
Al Qardah 193 H 3
Al Qaryatayn (Syria) 156 B 2
Al Qaṣr 194 D 3
Al Qasrayn 193 G 1
Al Qațīf (Saudi Arabia) 157 E 4
Al Qaţn 195 H 5
Al Qatrānī (Jordan) 156 B 3
Al Qaṭrūn 193 H 3–4
Al Qay'īyah (Saudi Arabia) 156 D 4
Al Qayrawān 193 GH 1
Al Qayṣūmah (Saudi Arabia) 156 D 3
Al Qayṣūmah (Saudi Arabia) 157 E 3
Alqueva, Barragem de 152 B 4
Al Qunayṭirah (Syria) 156 B 2
Al Qunfudhah 195 G 5
Al Qurayni 195 J 4
Al Qurayyah (Saudi Arabia) 156 B 3
Al Qurayyāt 195 K 4
Al Qurnah (Iraq) 157 E 3
Al Qusaymah (Egypt) 156 AB 3
Al Quşayr (Egypt) 156 B 4
Al Quşayr (Syria) 156 B 2
Al Qūşīyah 194 E 3
Al Qūşūrīyah (Saudi Arabia) 156 D 5
Al Quţayfah (Syria) 156 B 2
Al Quţaynah 194 E 6
Al Quwārah (Saudi Arabia) 156 D 4
Al Quwayīyah (Saudi Arabia) 157 D 4
Al Quwayr (Iraq) 156 D 1–2
Al Qwārshah 193 J 2
Al Rabyānah, Wāhāt 193 K 4
Al Rayyān (Qatar) 157 F 4
Als 151 EF 5
Alsask 103 Q 5
Alsasua 152 C 3
Alsea (OR.) 110 B 6
Alsea Bay 110 A 6
Alsen (N.D.) 119 K 2
Alsfeld 149 E 4
Al Shagra (Qatar) 157 F 4
Al'skiy Khrebet 171 P 5

Alsten 150 F 2
Alta 150 H 2
Alta (IA.) 119 N 8
Altaelva 150 H 2
Altafjorden 150 H 1
Alta Gracia 142 D 5
Altagracia de Orituco 138 E 2
Altai 170 EF 6
Altair (TX.) 122 G 6
Altamachi 140 C 4
Altamaha River 131 N 3
Altamira 139 H 4
Altamont (KS.) 121 K 5
Altamont (OR.) 110 D 8
Altamont (TN.) 128 F 6
Altamont (UT.) 114 G 3
Altamont (WY.) 111 P 9
Altamura 153 G 3
Altan 170 J 6
Altanbulag 170 J 5
Altaqracia 138 D 1
Altar 106 D 5
Altas, Rías 152 B 3
Altat 170 F 4
Altata 106 E 7
Altatump 159 M 3
Altaville (CA.) 112 E 4
Alta Vista (KS.) 120 J 4
Altay (China) 169 M 1
Altay (Mongolia) 170 G 6
Altay (U.S.S.R.) 159 N 3
Altay (U.S.S.R.) 159 R 5
Altay Shan 169 M 1
Altayskiy 159 QR 5
Al Tāzirbū, Wāhāt 193 K 3
Altdorf 153 E 2
Altenburg 149 F 4
Altevatnet 150 G 2
Altheimer (AR.) 121 O 8
Altıntaş 154 D 3
Altiplanicie Mexicana 132 B 2
Altiplano 140 C 4
Altkirch 153 E 2
Altmark 149 F 4
Altmühl 149 F 5
Alto (TX.) 123 H 4
Alto-Alentejo 152 B 4
Alto Araguaia 141 F 4
Alto Chicapa 200 B 2
Alto Garças 141 F 4
Alto Molócuè 201 F 3
Alton (IA.) 119 M 8
Alton (IL.) 121 P 4
Alton (KS.) 120 FG 3
Alton (MO.) 121 O 6
Alton (N.H.) 126 H 5
Alton (UT.) 114 E 6
Alton Downs 183 F 4
Altoona (FL.) 131 N 6
Altoona (KS.) 121 K 5
Altoona (PA.) 125 Q 9
Altoona (WA.) 110 B 4
Alto Paraguai 140 E 3
Alto Parnaíba 141 G 2
Alto Purus 140 B 2–3
Alto Río Senguerr 143 B 8
Alto Sucuriú 141 F 4
Alto Turi 141 G 1
Alto Zaza 200 B 1
Altun Ha 132 E 4
Āltūn Kūprī 195 G 1
Āltūn Kūprī (Iraq) 156 D 2
Altun Shan 172 AB 3
Alturas (CA.) 112 E 1
Altus (OK.) 120 F 8
Altus, Lake 120 F 8
Altynasar 169 G 1
Alu 185 G 3
Al 'Ubaylah 195 J 4
Al Ubayyid 194 E 6
Alucra 155 E 2
Al 'Udaysāt (Egypt) 156 A 4
Al Uḍayyah 194 D 6
Al Ugsur (Egypt) 156 A 4
Aluk 198 D 3
'Alūla 199 J 2
Al 'Ulā (Saudi Arabia) 156 C 4
Alūm (Iran) 157 E 2
Aluminé 143 B 6
Alupka 155 D 2
Al 'Uqayr (Saudi Arabia) 157 E 4
Alur 174 C 4
Al Urayq (Saudi Arabia) 156 C 3
Al Urdun 156 B 3
Al 'Urūq al Mu'tariḍah 195 J 4
'Ālūs (Iraq) 156 D 2
Alushta 155 D 2
Al 'Uthmānīyah (Saudi Arabia) 157 E 4
Al 'Uwaynidhīyah (Saudi Arabia) 156 B 4
Al 'Uwayqīlah (Saudi Arabia) 156 CD 3
Al 'Uyūn (Saudi Arabia) 156 C 4
Al'Uyūn (Saudi Arabia) 156 D 4
Al 'Uzayr (Iraq) 157 E 3
Alva (OK.) 120 G 6
Alva (WY.) 118 D 6
Alvano, Kūh-e (Iran) 157 E 2
Alvarado (TX.) 122 F 3
Alvarães 139 F 4
Alvdal 150 F 3

Älvdalen 150 F 3
Älvdalen 151 F 3
Alvear 142 E 4
Alvelos, Serra de 152 B 4
Alvesta 151 F 4
Ålvik 151 E 3
Alvin (TX.) 123 H 6
Älvkarleby 151 G 3
Alvorado 141 G 3
Alvord (TX.) 122 F 2
Alvord Lake 110 G 8
Alvord Valley 110 G 8
Al Wāḥah 193 K 3
Al Waïh (Saudi Arabia) 156 B 4
Al Wajh 194 F 3
Al Wakrah (Qatar) 157 F 4
Al Wannān (Saudi Arabia) 157 E 4
Alwar 174 C 2
Al Warīah (Saudi Arabia) 157 E 4
Al Wāsiţah 194 E 3
Al Watyah 193 H 2
Al Wazz 194 D 5
Al Widyān (Iraq) 156 C 3
Al Wīgh 193 J 4
Al Wīgh, Ramlat 193 J 4
Alxa Youqi 172 D 3
Alxa Zuoqi 172 DE 3
Alyangula 183 F 1
Alyaskitovyy 171 Q 3
Alygdzher 170 G 5
Alys-Khaya 171 P 2
Alyssy-Garakh 171 Q 2
Alytus 151 H 5
Alzada (MT.) 118 D 5
Alzamay 170 G 4
Al Zukum (United Arab Emirates) 157 F 4
Amada 194 E 4
Amada Gaza 198 B 4
Amadi 198 E 3
Amadeus, Lake 182 E 3
Amadjuak Lake 105 N 2–3
Amado (AZ.) 116 E 6
Amagansett (N.Y.) 127 G 8
Amahai 177 G 4
Amain, Monts d' 152 D 2
Amakinskiy 170 K 1
Amål 151 F 4
Ämål 193 K 3
Amalfi (Colombia) 138 D 2
Amalfi (Italy) 153 F 3
Amalias 154 B 3
Amambaí 141 EF 5
Amami-ō-shima 173 J 5
Amanā, Lago 139 F 4
Amangel'dy 159 N 5
Amanino 171 T 4
Amanotkel' 169 G 1
Amanu 187 F 4
Amanzimtoti 201 E 6
Amapá 139 H 3
Amapá 139 H 3
Amar 197 FG 4
'Amara 194 E 4
Amarante 141 H 2
Amārat Abū Sinn 194 EF 5
Amargosa Range 112 J 6
Amargosa River 112 J 6–7
Amarillo (TX.) 117 P 2
Amaro Leite 141 G 3
Amarti 199 G 2
Amasa (MI.) 124 F 3
Amasra 155 D 2
Amasya 155 E 2
Amataurá 138 E 4
Amazar 170 M 5
Amazon 139 H 4
Amazonas 138–139 EF 4
Amazonas 139 H 4
Amba Farit 199 F 2
Ambala 174 C 1
Ambalavao 201 H 4
Ambam 197 G 5
Ambar 170 EF 2
Ambarchik 170 G 4
Ambarchik 171 U 2
Ambardakh 171 P 1
Ambarnyy 150 K 2
Ambato 138 C 4
Ambato Boény 201 H 3
Ambatofinandrahana 201 H 4
Ambatolampy 201 H 3
Ambatondrazaka 201 H 3
Ambatosoratra 201 H 3
Ambatry 201 G 4
Ambelos, Ákra 154 B 3
Amber (WA.) 110 H 3
Amberg 149 F 5
Amberg (WI.) 124 F 4
Ambérieu-en-Bugey 153 E 2
Ambgaon 174 D 3
Ambidédi 196 B 3
Ambikapur 174 D 3
Ambilobe 201 H 2
Ambo 140 A 3
Amboasary 201 H 4
Ambodifototra 201 HJ 3

Ambohibe 201 G 4
Ambohimahasoa 201 H 4
Ambohitralanana 201 J 3
Ambon 177 G 4
Ambon, Pulau 177 G 4
Ambositra 201 H 4
Ambovombe 201 H 5
Amboy (CA.) 113 K 8
Amboy (IL.) 124 E 8
Amboy (MN.) 119 O 7
Ambre, Cap d' 201 H 2
Ambre, Montange d' 201 H 2
Ambridge (PA.) 125 N 9
Ambrin 185 J 5
Ambriz 200 A 1
Ambrose (ND.) 118 E 2
Ambrym 186 C 4
Ambur 174 C 5
Amchitka 102 A 5
Amchitka Pass 102 AB 5
'Amd 195 H 5
Am Dam 197 J 3
Amderma 159 M 2
Amdo 172 B 4
Ameca 132 B 3
Amelia (NE.) 118 K 8
Amelia CH (VA.) 129 O 4
Amelia City (FL.) 131 N 4
Amelia Island 131 N 4
Amendolara 153 G 3–4
American Falls (ID.) 111 MN 8
American Falls Reservoir 111 N 8
American Fork (UT.) 114 C 3
American Highland 203
American Samoa 186 D 3
Americus (GA.) 131 K 2
Americus (KS.) 120 J 4
Ames (IA.) 119 P 8
Ametlla de Mar 152 D 3
Amfilokhia 154 B 3
Amfissa 154 B 3
Amga 171 O 3
Amgu 173 L 1
Amguema 102 B 2
Amguid 193 G 3
Amgun' 171 P 5
Amhara 199 F 2
Amherst (CO.) 115 PQ 3
Amherst (MA.) 126 G 6
Amherst (ME.) 126 L 4
Amherst (NE.) 120 F 2
Amherst (Nova Scotia, Can.) 105 P 6
Amherst (N.Y.) 125 Q 7
Amherst (TX.) 117 O 3
Amherst (VA.) 129 MN 4
Amherst Junction (WI.) 124 E 5
Amiak River 108 G 3
Amiata 153 F 3
Amidon (ND.) 118 E 4
Amiens 152 D 2
Amik Gölü 155 E 3
Amili 175 G 2
'Amīnābād (Iran) 157 F 3
Amindivi Islands 174 B 5
Aminuis 200 B 4
Amirante Islands 199 J 6
Amisk Lake 103 R 5
Amistad (N.M.) 117 N 2
Amistad Dam 117 PQ 8
Amistad National Recreation Area 117 P 8
Amistad Reservoir 117 P 8
Amite (LA.) 123 N 5
Amite River 123 N 5
Amity (OR.) 110 B 5
Amka 171 Q 4
Amlia 102 C 5
'Amm Adām 194 F 5
Ammān (Jordan) 156 B 3
Ammarfjället 150 G 2
Ammarnäs 150 G 2
Ammerman Mountain 109 K 2
Ammokhostos → Famagusta 155 D 3
Ammon (ID.) 111 O 7
Amo 170 H 3
Amol (Iran) 157 F 1
Amolar 140 E 4
Amoret (MO.) 121 L 4
Amorgos 154 C 3
Amory (MS.) 121 R 9
Amos 105 M 6
Åmot 151 E 4
Amour, Djebel 193 F 2
Amourj 192 D 5
Amoy 173 G 6
Ampanihy 201 G 4
Amparafaravola 201 H 3
Ampitsikana 201 H 2
Amposta 152 D 3
'Amrān 195 G 5
Amravati 174 C 3
Am Raya 197 J 3
Amri 169 H 5
'Amrit (Syria) 156 B 2
Amritsar 174 C 1

Amroha 174 C 2
Amsā'ad 193 K 2
Amsterdam (Netherlands) 148 DE 4
Amsterdam (N.Y.) 126 E 6
Amstetten 153 F 2
Am Timan 197 J 3
Amtkeli 155 F 2
Āmūda (Syria) 156 C 1
Amu-Dar'ya 169 G 2
Amudat 198 E 4
Amukta Pass 102 C 5
Amundsen Gulf 103 N 1
Amundsen-Scott 203
Amundsen Sea 203
Amungen 150 G 3
Amuntai 176 E 4
Amur 171 P 5
Amursk 171 P 5
Amvrakikos Kólpos 154 B 3
Amysakh 170 L 2
Am Zoer 197 J 3
Anabar 170 K 1
Anabarskiy Zaliv 170 KL 1
Anabarskoye Ploskogor'ye 170 J 1–2
Anaco 139 G 2
Anacoco (LA.) 123 K 4
Anaconda (MT.) 111 N 4
Anaconda Range 111 M 5
Anadarko (OK.) 120 G 7
Anadolu 154–155 CD 3
Anadyr 171 X 3
Anadyr 171 X 3
Anadyrskaja Nízmennost 171 X 2
Anadyrskiy Liman 171 X 3
Anadyrskiy Zaliv 102 B 3
Anadyrskiy Zaliv 171 Y 3
Anadyrskoye Ploskogor'ye 171 VW 2
Anáfi 154 C 3
Anáfjället 150 F 3
Anaghit 199 F 1
Anagni 153 F 3
Anah (Iraq) 156 C 2
Anahola (HI.) 113 C 9
Anahuac 132 C 2
Anahuac (TX.) 123 J 6
Anaï 193 H 4
Anaimalai Hills 174 C 5
Anajás 139 J 4
Anajatuba 141 H 1
Anakapalle 174 D 4
Anakliya 155 F 2
Anaktuvuk Pass 109 H 2
Anaktuvuk River 109 H 2
Analalava 201 H 2
Anamã 139 F 4
Ana Maria, Golfo de 133 G 3
Anambas, Kepulauan 176 C 3
Anamoose (ND.) 118 H 3
Anamosa (IA.) 119 R 8
Anamur (Turkey) 156 A 1
Anamur 155 D 3
Anamur Burnu 155 D 3
Anamur Burum (Turkey) 156 A 2
Anamuryum 155 D 3
Anangravnen, Sopka 171 U 4
Anantapur 174 C 5
Anantnag 169 K 4
Anan'yev 154 C 1
Anapa 155 E 2
Anapka 171 U 3
Anápolis 141 G 4
Anapu 139 H 4
Anār (Iran) 157 G 3
Anārak (Iran) 157 F 2
Anarisfjällen 150 F 3
Añasco (P.R.) 130 B 8
Añasco, Bahía de 130 B 8
Anatahan 186 A 1
Anatolia 154–155 D 3
Anatone (WA.) 110 H 4
Añatuya 142 D 4
Anauá 139 F 3
Anavarza 155 E 3
Anavelona 201 G 4
Anavilhanas, Arquipélago das 139 F 4
'Anazah, Jabal (Iraq) 156 C 2
Anbyŏn 173 J 3
Ancares, Sierra de 152 B 3
Ancasti, Sierra de 142 C 4
Anceney (MT.) 111 O 5
Ancenis 152 C 2
Ancha 171 P 3
Ancho (N.M.) 117 L 4
Anchorage 102 H 3
Anci 173 G 3
Anclote Keys 131 M 6
Ancohuma 140 C 4
Ancon (Ecuador) 138 B 4
Ancón (Peru) 140 A 3
Ancona 153 F 3
Ancuabe 201 F 2
Ancud 143 B 7
Ancud, Golfo de 143 B 7
Anda 173 J 1
Andacollo (Argentina) 143 B 6
Andacollo (Chile) 142 B 5
Andahuaylas 140 B 3
Andale (KS.) 120 H 5
Andalgala 142 C 4

Åndalsnes 150 E 3
Andalucía 152 BC 4
Andalusia (AL.) 131 H 3
Andaman Islands 175 F 5
Andaman Sea 175 G 5–6
Andamooka 183 F 5
Andapa 201 H 2
Andara 200 C 3
Andarab 169 H 3
Andaraí 141 H 3
Andeg 158 K 2
Andenes 150 G 2
Andéranboukane 196 E 2
Anderson (CA.) 112 C 2
Anderson (IN.) 124 J 9
Anderson (N.W.T., Can.) 102 M 2
Anderson (S.C.) 128 J 7
Anderson (TX.) 122 GH 5
Anderson Ranch Reservoir 111 K 7
Anderstorp 151 F 4
Andes (Colombia) 138 C 2
Andes, Lake 119 K 7
Andes Mountains 135 C 2–6
Andevoranto 201 H 3
Andfjorden 150 G 2
Andhra Pradesh 174 C 4
Andikira 154 B 3
Andikíthira 154 B 3
Andilamena 201 H 3
Andilanatoby 201 H 3
Andīmeshk (Iran) 157 E 2
Andípaxoi 154 AB 3
Andiria Burun 155 D 3
Andiria burun (Cyprus) 156 B 2
Andırın 155 E 3
Andirlangar 169 L 3
Andizhan 169 J 2
Andkhui 169 H 3
Andoas 138 C 4
Andomskiy Pogost 158 G 3
Andong 173 J 3
Andorra 152 D 3
Andorra la Vella 152 D 3
Andover (N.Y.) 126 B 6
Andover (OH.) 125 O 3
Andover (S.D.) 119 L 5
Andøya 150 G 2
Andrade (CA.) 113 K 10
Andradina 141 F 5
Andraitx 152 D 4
Andreafsky River 108 F 3
Andreanof Islands 102 BC 5
André Félix National Park 198 C 3
Andrepatsy 201 H 3
Andrews (S.C.) 129 M 8
Andrews (TX.) 117 O 5
Andreyevka 155 E 1
Andreyevka 158 K 5
Andreyevka 159 Q 6
Andreyevo-Ivanovka 154 D 1
Andreyevsk 170 KL 4
Andreyevskiy 170 KL 4
Andria 153 G 3
Andriamena 201 H 3
Andriba 201 H 3
Andringitra 201 H 4
Andrix (CO.) 115 O 6
Androka 201 G 5
Androna, Plateau de l' 201 H 3
Andropov 158 G 4
Ándros 154 B 3
Ándros 154 C 3
Androscoggin River 126 HJ 4
Andros Island 133 G 3
Androsovka 158 J 5
Androth 174 B 5
Andrushevka 151 J 5
Andryushka 171 S 2
Andselv 150 G 2
Andudu 198 D 4
Andújar 152 C 4
Andulo 200 B 2
Andu Tan 176 D 2
Andyngda 170 L 2
Aneby 151 FG 4
Anécho 196 E 4
Anéfis 196 E 2
Anegada 130 E 8
Anegada, Bahía 143 D 7
Anegada Passage 133 K 4
Anegam (AZ.) 116 DE 5
Añelo 143 C 6
Aneta (N.D.) 119 L 3
Aneth (UT.) 114 H 6
Aneto, Pico de 152 D 3
Aney 197 G 2
Angamos, Punta 140 B 5
Ang'angxi 173 H 1
Angar 177 H 4
Angara 170 F 4
Angarsk 170 H 5
Angas Downs 182 E 4
Angatau 187 F 4
Angaul 170 H 5
Angaur 177 H 2
Ånge 150 G 3

Angela (MT.) 118 B 4
Ángel de la Guarda, Isla 106 D 6
Angeles 177 J 1
Angeles (TX.) 117 MN 6
Angel Falls 139 F 2
Ängelholm 151 F 4
Angelina River 123 J 4
Angels Camp (CA.) 112 E 4
Angelus (KS.) 120 E 3
Angemuk, Gunung 177 J 4
Ångermanälven 150 G 3
Angers 152 C 2
Angerville (France) 152 D 2
Angical 141 H 3
Angijak Island 105 P 2
Angikuni Lake 103 S 3
Angiola (CA.) 112 F 6
Angkor 175 H 5
Angle (UT.) 114 F 5
Angle Inlet (MN.) 119 NO 1
Anglem, Mount 184 P 10
Anglesey 148 C 4
Angleton (TX.) 123 H 6
Angmagssalik 202
Ango 198 D 4
Angoche 201 G 3
Angol 143 B 6
Angola 200 B 2
Angola (IN.) 125 K 8
Angola Basin 208 B 4
Angónia, Planalto de 201 E 2
Angora (NE.) 118 E 9
Angoram 184 D 2
Angostura 106 E 6
Angostura, Salto 138 D 3
Angostura Reservoir 118 E 7
Angoulême 152 D 2
Angouma 197 G 5
Angren 169 J 2
Ang Thong 175 H 5
Angu 198 C 4
Anguil 143 D 6
Anguilla 133 K 4
Anguilla (MS.) 130 D 2
Anguille, Cape 105 PQ 6
Angul 174 E 3
Angumu 198 D 5
Anguo 172 G 3
Angutikha 159 R 2
Angwin (CA.) 112 C 4
Anholt 151 F 4
Anh Son 175 J 4
Anhua 172 F 5
Anhui 173 G 4
Aniak 102 F 3
Aniakchak National Monument
  and Preserve 102 F 4
Anié 196 E 4
Animas (N.M.) 116 H 6
Animas Peak 116 H 6
Animas River 115 K 6
Animas Valley 116 H 5–6
Anina 154 B 1
Anita (AZ.) 116 D 2
Aniuk River 108 G 2
Aniva 171 Q 6
Aniva, Mys 171 Q 6
Aniva, Zaliv 171 Q 6
Aniwa 185 J 5
Aniwa 186 C 4
Aniwa (WI.) 124 E 4
Anjala 151 J 3
Anjou 152 C 2
Anjouan 201 G 2
Anjozorobe 201 H 3
Anju 173 J 3
Anjuman 169 J 3
Anka 197 F 3
Ankacho 170 J 3
Ankang 172 E 4
Ankara 155 D 2–3
Ankaramena 201 H 4
Ankavandra 201 H 3
Ankazoabo 201 G 4
Ankazobe 201 H 3
Ankeny (IA.) 119 P 9
Ankerika 201 H 2
'Ankhor (Somalia) 199 H 2
Anklam 149 F 4
Anklesvar 174 B 3
Ankium Mountains 108 F 4
Ankober 199 F 3
Ankofa 201 H 3
Ankoro 198 D 6
Ankpa 197 F 4
Anlong 172 E 5
Anlu 172 F 4
Ånn 150 F 3
Ann, Cape 203
Anna (IL.) 121 Q 5
Anna (TX.) 122 G 4
Anna (U.S.S.R.) 158 H 5
Anna, Lake 129 O 3
Annaba 193 G 1
An Nabatīyah at Tahta (Lebanon)
  156 B 2
An Nabk (Syria) 156 B 2

An Nabk Abū Qasr (Saudi Arabia)
  156 C 3
An Nafīdah 153 F 4
An Nafūd (Saudi Arabia) 156 C 3
An Nāfūrah 193 K 3
An Nāhiyah (Iraq) 156 C 2
Annai 139 G 3
An Najaf (Iraq) 156 D 2–3
An' Nakhi (Egypt) 156 AB 3
An Nāmūs, Jabal 193 J 3–4
Annam 175 J 4
Annandale 183 H 3
Annandale (MN.) 119 O 5
Anna Plains 182 C 2
Annapolis (MD.) 129 P 3
Annapurna 174 D 2
Ann Arbor (MI.) 125 L 7
An Nashshāsh (United Arab Emirates)
  157 FG 5
An Nashwah (Iraq) 157 E 3
An Nāsirīyah (Iraq) 157 E 3
Annean, Lake 182 B 4
Annecy 153 E 2
Annemasse 153 E 2
Annenskiy-Most 158 G 3
An Nhon 175 J 5
Anning 172 D 6
Anniston (AL.) 128 F 8
Annobón 197 F 6
Annonay 153 D 2
An Nu'ayrīyah (Saudi Arabia) 157 E 4
An Nuhūd 194 D 6
An Nu'mān (Saudi Arabia) 156 B 4
An Nu'māniyah (Iraq) 157 D 2
An Nuqayr (Saudi Arabia) 157 E 4
An Nūwfalīyah 193 J 2
Anoka (MN.) 119 P 5
Anoka (NE.) 118 K 7
Anori 139 F 4
Anoshkinsk 171 N 1
Anou 196 E 2
Anoumaba 196 D 4
Anou-n Bidek 193 F 5
Ansāb (Saudi Arabia) 157 D 3
Ansariye, Jabal al (Syria) 156 B 2
Ansas 177 J 4
Ansbach 149 F 5
Anselmo (NE.) 118 J 9
Anserma 138 C 2
Anshan 173 H 2
Anshun 172 E 5
Ansina 142 E 5
Ansley (LA.) 123 L 3
Ansley (NE.) 120 F 1
Anson (TX.) 122 D 3
Anson Bay 182 D 1
Ansongo 196 E 2
Ansudu 177 J 4
Anta 140 B 3
Anta, Cachoeira de 139 F 5
Antakya 155 E 3
Antakya (Turkey) 156 B 1
Antalaha 201 J 2
Antalya 154 D 3
Antalya Körfezi 154 D 3
Antananarivo 201 H 3
Antanimora 201 H 4
Antarctic Peninsula 203
Antas 142 C 4
Antela, Laguna de 152 B 3
Antelope (MT.) 118 D 2
Antelope (OR.) 110 E 6
Antelope Peak 112 L 1
Antelope Reservoir 110 H 8
Antequera 140 E 5
Antequera 152 C 4
Antero, Mount 115 L 5
Antero Reservoir 115 M 5
Anthon (IA.) 119 N 8
Anthony (KS.) 120 GH 5
Anthony (N.M.) 117 K 5–6
Anthony Lagoon 182 F 2
Antibes 153 E 3
Anticosti, Île d 105 P 6
Antietam (MD.) 129 O 2
Antifer, Cap d' 152 CD 2
Antigo (WI.) 124 E 4
Antigonish 105 P 6
Antigua 133 K 4
Antigua Guatemala 132 D 5
Antillas Mayores 133 HJ 4
Antillas Menores 133 K 5
Antimony (UT.) 114 F 5
Antioch (CA.) 112 D 4
Antioch (NE.) 118 F 8
Antioche, Pertuis d' 152 C 2
Antiope 186 D 4
Antioquia 138 C 2
Antipayuta 159 P 2
Antipinskiy 171 N 1
Antipodes Islands 203
Antlât 193 K 2
Antler (ND.) 118 G 2
Antlers (OK.) 121 K 8
Antnäs 150 H 2
Antofagasta 140 B 5
Antofagasta de la Sierra 142 C 4
Antofalla, Salar de 142 C 4

Antofalla, Volcán 142 C 4
Anton (CO.) 115 O 4
Anton (TX.) 117 O 4
Anton Chico (N.M.) 117 L 2
Antone (OR.) 110 F 6
Antongil, Baie d' 201 HJ 3
Antonina 142 G 4
Antônio Bezerra 141 J 1
Antonio de Biedma 143 C 8
Antonito (CO.) 115 M 6
Antonovo 168 E 1
Antonto 142 D 4
Antrim Mountains 148 B 3–4
Antrodoco 153 F 3
Antsakabary 201 H 2
Antsalova 201 G 3
Antsirabe 201 H 3
Antsiranana 201 H 2
Antsohihy 201 H 2
Antu 173 J 2
An Tuc 175 J 5
Antufash 195 G 5
Anupgarh 174 B 2
Anuradhapura 174 D 6
Anuta 185 J 4
Anuta 186 C 3
Anvik 102 E 3
An Nu'ayrīyah (Saudi Arabia) 157 E 4
An Nuhūd 194 D 6
A'nyemaqen Shan 172 CD 3–4
Anyuan 172 G 5
An'yudin 159 L 3
Anyue 172 E 4
Anyuysk 171 U 2
Anyuyskiy Khrebet, Severnyy
  171 UW 2
Anyuyskiy Khrebet, Yuzhnyy 171 UV 2
Anzhero-Sudzhensk 159 R 4
Ao Ban Don 175 G 6
Aoga-shima 173 L 4
Aomori 173 M 2
Aosta 153 E 2
Aoudaghost 192 C 5
Aoudéras 197 F 2
Aouinat Legraa 192 D 3
Aouker (Mali) 192 E 4
Aouker (Mauritania) 192 CD 5
Aoulef el Arab 192–193 F 3
Aoumou 185 J 6
Apache 171 T 5
Apache (OK.) 120 G 8
Apache Junction (AZ.) 116 E 4
Apache Lake 116 E 4
Apache Mountains 117 M 6
Apache Peak 116 F 6
Apahida 154 B 1
Apalachee (GA.) 128 H 8
Apalachee Bay 131 KL 5
Apalachicola (FL.) 131 JK 5
Apalachicola Bay 131 JK 5
Apalachicola River 131 J 4
Apan 132 C 4
Apaporis 138 D 4
Aparecida do Tabuado 141 F 4
Aparri 177 J 1
Apataki 187 F 4
Apatin 154 A 1
Apatity 150 K 2
Apatzingán 132 B 4
Ape 151 J 4
Apeldoorn 148 E 4
Apere 140 C 3
Apia 186 D 3
Apiacás, Serra dos 140 E 2–3
Apiaí 141 G 5
Apiaú, Serra do 139 F 3
Apinajé 141 G 3
Apio 185 H 3
Apishapa River 115 N 6
Apizaco 132 C 4
Aplin (AR.) 121 MN 8
Apo, Mount 177 J 8
Apollo (FL.) 131 N 6
Apollo Bay 183 G 6
Apollonia 193 K 2
Apolo 140 C 3
Apopka (FL.) 131 N 6
Apopka, Lake 131 N 6
Aporé 141 F 4
Aporé 141 F 4
Aporema 139 H 3
Apostle Islands 124 D 2
Apostle Islands National Lakeshore
  124 D 3
Apóstoles 142 E 4

Apostolovo 155 D 1
Apoteri 139 G 3
Appalachia (VA.) 128 J 5
Appenino Calabro 153 G 4
Appennino Ligure 153 E 3
Appennino Lucano 153 G 3–4
Appennino Tosco-Emiliano 153 F 3
Appenzell 153 E 2
Apple Creek (OH.) 125 N 9
Apple Grove (VA.) 129 O 4
Appleton (MN.) 119 M 5
Appleton (WI.) 124 F 5
Appleton City (MO.) 121 LM 4
Appling (GA.) 129 J 8
Apollonia → Sūsah 193 K 2
Appomattox (VA.) 129 N 4
Appomattox River 129 N 4
Approuague 139 H 3
Aprilia 153 F 3
Apsheronsk 155 E 2
Apt 153 E 3
Aptos (CA.) 112 D 5
Apucarana 141 F 5
Apuka 171 W 3
Apuka Chukotskaya 171 W 3
Apure 138 D 2
Apurimac 140 B 3
Āqā Bābā (Iran) 157 E 1
Aqar 'Atabah 193 H 3
Aqdā (Iran) 157 F 2
'Aqīq 194 F 5
Āqotāq (Iran) 157 E 1
Aqrah (Iraq) 156 D 1
Aqrin, Jabal (Saudi Arabia) 156 C 3
Aquarius Plateau 4114 F 5–6
Aquibi, Cachoeira 141 E 3
Aquidauana 140 E 4
Aquilares (TX.) 122 D 8
Aquilla (TX.) 122 F 4
Ara 152 C 3
Arab (AL.) 128 E 7
'Arabah, Wādi al (Jordan) 156 B 3
Arabatskaya Strelka 155 E 1
Arabestān (Iran) 157 E 3
Arabia (NE.) 118 H 8
Arabian Basin 208 B 3
Arabian Desert → Aş Şahrā' ash-
  Sharqīyah 194 E 2–3
Arabian Sea 205
Araç 155 D 2
Aracá 139 F 3
Aracaju 141 J 3
Aracati 141 J 1
Araçatuba 141 F 5
Aracena, Sierra de 152 B 4
Árachthos 154 B 3
Araçuai 141 H 4
Arad 154 B 1
Arada 197 J 2
'Arādah (United Arab Emirates) 157 F 5
Aradanskiy Khrebet 170 F 5
Arafali 199 F 1
Arafura, Laut 177 HJ 5
Arafura Sea 177 HJ 5
Arafura Shelf 209 C 4
Aragarças 141 F 4
Aragats 155 F 2
Arago, Cape 110 A 7
Aragon 152 C 3
Araguacema 139 HJ 5
Aragua 141 G 3
Aragua de Barcelona 139 F 2
Aragua de Maturín 139 F 2
Araguaia 139 J 5
Araguaia, Parque Nacional do 141 FG 3
Araguaiana 141 F 4
Araguaína 139 J 5
Araguari (Amapá, Brazil) 139 H 3
Araguari (Minas Gerais, Brazil) 141 G 4
Araguatins 139 J 5
Arak (Algeria) 193 F 3
Arāk (Iran) 157 E 2
Araka 197 J 2
Arakaka 139 G 2
Arakamchechen, Ostrov 108 D 3
Arakan Yoma 175 FG 4
Araks 168 D 3
Aral 169 L 2
Aral'sk 169 G 1
Aral'skoye More 168–169 FG 2
Aralsul'fat 169 G 1
Aramac 183 H 3
Arambaza 138 D 4
Ārān (Iran) 157 F 2
Aran (Rep. of Irland) 148 B 3
Aranda de Duero 152 C 3
Arandai 177 H 4
Arandelovac 154 B 2
Aran Islands 148 AB 4
Aranjuez 152 C 3
Aranos 200 B 4
Aransas Pass (TX.) 122 F 8
Aranuka 186 C 3
Aranyaprathet 175 H 5
Araouane 196 D 2
Arapa, Lago 140 B 4
Arapaho (OK.) 120 FG 7
Arapaho (CO.) 115 PQ 5
Arapahoe (N.C.) 129 P 6–7
Arapahoe (NE.) 120 F 2

Araparí 139 J 5
Arapey 142 E 5
Arapongas 141 F 5
Arapiraca 141 J 2
'Ar'ar (Saudi Arabia) 156 C 3
'Ar'ar, Wādī (Saudi Arabia) 156 C 3
Araracuara, Cerros de 138 D 3–4
Araranguá 142 G 4
Araras 139 H 5
Araras, Serra das 141 F 4
Ararat (Armeniya, U.S.S.R.) 155 FG 3
Ararat (Victoria, Austr.) 183 G 6
Ararat, Mount (Turkey) 155 F 3
Ararí 141 H 1
Araro 199 F 4
Aras 155 F 2
Aras 168 D 3
Araticu 139 J 4
Aratika 187 F 4
Arauá 141 J 3
Arauca 138 D 2
Arauquita 138 D 2
Araura 138 E 2
Aravalli Range 174 B 2
Arawale Game Reserve 199 G 5
Araxá 141 G 4
Áraxos, Ákra 154 B 3
Araya 139 F 1
Arba Minch 199 F 3
'Arbat (Iraq) 157 D 2
Arbatax 153 E 4
Arboga 151 G 4
Arbon 153 E 2
Arbon (ID.) 111 N 8
Arbrå 150 G 3
Arbre du Ténéré 197 G 2
Arbroath 148 C 3
Arbuckle (CA.) 112 C 4
Arbuckle, Lake 131 N 7
Arbuckle Mountains 120 HJ 8
Arbuckle National Recreation Area 120 J 8
Arcachon 152 C 3
Arcade (CA.) 112 D 4
Arcade (N.Y.) 125 Q 7
Arcadia (FL.) 131 N 7
Arcadia (KS.) 121 L 5
Arcadia (LA.) 123 L 3
Arcadia (MI.) 124 H 5
Arcadia (NE.) 120 FG 1
Arcata (CA.) 112 A 2
Arcata Bay 112 A 2
Arc Dome 112 H 4
Arcelia 132 B 4
Archer (FL.) 131 M 5
Archer City (TX.) 122 E 2
Archer River 183 G 1
Archer River National Park 183 G 1
Archer's Post 199 F 4
Arches National Park 114 H 5
Archibald (LA.) 123 M 3
Archidona 152 C 4
Archipelago Kerimbas 201 G 2
Archipelago of the Recherche 182 C 5
Archipiélago de Camagüey 133 G 3
Archipiélago de Colón 138 B 6
Archipiélago de la Reina Adelaida 143 A 9
Archipiélago de los Canarreos 133 F 3
Archipiélago de los Chonos 143 AB 7–8
Archipiélago de los Jardines-de la Reina 133 FG 3
Archipiélago Guayaneco 143 A 8
Arckaringa River 182 E 4
Arco (ID.) 111 M 7
Arco (Italy) 153 F 2
Arcola (IL.) 121 R 3
Arcola (TX.) 123 H 6
Arcos 152 B 4
Arcos de Jalón 152 C 3
Arcos de Valdevez 152 B 3
Arcoverde 141 J 2
Arctic Ocean 202
Arctic Red River (N.W.T., Can.) 102 L 2
Arctic Red River (N.W.T., Can.) 102 L 2
Arctic Village 102 H 2
Arctowski 203
Arda 154 C 2
Ardabīl 168 D 3
Ardahan 155 F 2
Ardakān (Iran) 157 FG 2
Ardakān (Iran) 157 F 3
Ardal (Iran) 157 F 2
Årdalstangen 150 E 3
Ard as Sawwān (Jordan) 156 B 3
Ardatov 158 H 4
Ardee 148 B 4
Arden (CA.) 112 D 4
Arden (NV.) 112 K 6
Ardennes 148 E 4
Ardennes, Canal des 153 D 2
Ardenvoir (WA.) 110 E 3
Ardeşen 155 F 2
Ardestan (Iran) 157 F 2
Ardila 152 B 4
Ardmore (OK.) 120 H 8

Ardmore (SD.) 118 E 7
Ardmore (TN.) 128 E 6–7
Ardrossan 148 C 3
Ards Peninsula 148 B 4
Åre 150 F 3
Arebi 198 D 4
Arecibo 133 J 4
Arecibo (P.R.) 130 C 8
Areia Branca 141 J 1
Arena 177 F 2
Arena, Point 112 B 4
Arena, Punta 130 D 8
Arenales, Cerro 143 B 8
Arenápolis 140 E 3
Arenas 130 D 8
Arenas, Punta de 143 C 9
Arendal 151 E 4
Aréopolis 154 B 3
Arequipa 140 B 4
Arere 139 H 4
Arés 141 J 2
Åreskutan 150 F 3
Arévalo 152 C 3
Arezzaf 196 D 2
Arezzo 153 F 3
Arga 171 R 2
Argadargada 183 F 3
Arga-Emneke, Gora 171 Q 2
Argan 172 A 2
Arganda 152 C 3
Arga-Sala 170 J 2
Argens 153 E 3
Argent, Côte d' 152 C 3
Argenta 153 F 3
Argentan 152 D 2
Argentina 143 CD 6
Argentine Basin 208 A 5
Argentino, Lago 143 B 9
Argenton-sur-Creuse 152 D 2
Arges 154 C 2
Arghandab 169 H 4
Argio 199 F 3
Argo 194 E 5
Argolíkós Kólpos 154 B 3
Argonia (KS.) 120 H 5
Argonne 153 DE 2
Árgos 154 B 3
Argos (IN.) 124 H 8
Argostólion 154 B 3
Arguello, Point 113 E 8
Arguin, Cap d' 192 B 4
Argun' 170 L 5
Argungu 197 E 3
Argusville (N.D.) 119 L 3
Argyle (MN.) 119 M 2
Argyle, Lake 182 D 2
Arholma 151 G 4
Ar Horqin Qi 173 H 2
Århus 151 F 4
Ariari 138 D 3
Arias 142 D 5
Ariaú 139 G 4
Aribinda 196 D 3
Arica (Chile) 140 B 4
Arica (Colombia) 138 D 4
Arid, Cape 182 C 5
Aridal 192 C 3
Ariège 152 D 3
Ariel 143 D 6
Ariguaní 138 D 1
Arīḥā (Syria) 156 B 2
Arikaree River 115 P 4
Arima 139 F 5
Arima (Trinidad and Tobago) 139 F 1
Arinos (Mato Grosso, Brazil) 140 E 3
Arinos (Minas Gerais, Brazil) 141 G 4
Arinosa (UT.) 114 D 3
Aripuanã 139 F 5
Aripuanã 139 F 5
Ariquemes 139 F 5
Ariripina 141 H 2
Arismendi 138 E 2
Arissa 199 G 2
Ariton (AL.) 131 J 3
Aritzo 153 E 4
Arivaca (AZ.) 116 E 6
Arivonimamo 201 H 3
Ariza 152 C 3
Arizaro, Salar de 140 C 5
Arizona 116
Arizona (Argentina) 143 C 6
Ärjäng 151 F 4
Arjasa 176 DE 5
Arjeplog 150 G 2
Arjona 138 C 1
Arka 171 Q 3
Arkabutla Lake 121 P 8
Arkadak 158 H 5
Arkadelphia (AR.) 121 MN 8
Arkalyk 159 N 5
Arkansas 121
Arkansas City (AR.) 121 O 9
Arkansas City (KS.) 120 HJ 5
Arkansas Post (AR.) 121 O 8
Arkansas River 121 NO 8
Arkanū, Jabal 193 K 4
Arkatag Shan 172 AB 3
Arkhángel 158 H 3
Arkhangel'sk 158 H 3
Arkhangel'skaya 155 F 1

Arkhangel'skoye 155 F 2
Arkhangel'skoye 158 G 5
Arkhara 171 O 6
Arkhyz 155 F 2
Arklow 148 B 4
Arkonam 174 C 5
Arlberg 153 F 2
Arlee (MT.) 111 L 3
Arles 153 D 3
Arlington (CO.) 115 O 5
Arlington (GA.) 131 K 3
Arlington (KS.) 120 G 5
Arlington (MN.) 119 O 6
Arlington (NE.) 119 M 9
Arlington (OR.) 110 E 5
Arlington (S.D.) 119 LM 6
Arlington (TN.) 128 B 6
Arlington (TX.) 122 F 3
Arlington (VA.) 129 O 3
Arlington Hights (IL.) 124 FG 7
Arlit 197 F 2
Arlon 148 E 5
Arly 196 E 3
Armagnac, Collines de l' 152 D 3
Arman 171 S 4
Armant 194 E 3
Armenia 138 C 4
Armeniya 155 F 2
Armentieres 152 D 1
Armeria 132 B 4
Armero 138 D 2
Armidale 183 J 5
Armijo (N.M.) 117 K 2
Arminto (WY.) 111 S 7
Armori 174 D 3
Armour (S.D.) 119 K 7
Armstrong (MO.) 121 N 3
Armstrong (TX.) 122 F 9
Armstrong Mount 109 M 3
Armur 174 C 4
Armyansk 155 D 1
Arnaudville (LA.) 123 M 5
Arnauti, Akra (Cyprus) 156 A 2
Arnawai 169 J 3
Arnett (OK.) 120 F 6
Arney (TX.) 117 O 3
Arnhem 148 E 4
Arnhem, Cape 183 F 1
Arnhem Bay 183 F 1
Arnhem Land 182 EF 1
Arnhem Land Reserve 182 EF 1
Arni 174 C 5
Arno (Italy) 153 F 3
Arno (Marshall Is.) 186 C 2
Arno (TX.) 117 N 6
Arno Bay 183 F 5
Arnold (NE.) 120 E 1
Arnøy 150 H 1
Aroab 200 B 5
Aroche, Pico de 152 B 4
Arock (OR.) 110 H 8
Aroma 194 F 5
Arona 184 E 3
Aropuk Lake 108 F 3
Arorae 186 C 3
Arosa 153 E 2
Årösund 151 E 4
Aroya (CO.) 115 O 5
Arp (TX.) 123 H 3
Arpaçay 155 F 2
Arpajon 152 D 2
Arpavla 159 M 3
Arquipélago das Anavilhanas 139 F 4
Arquipélago dos Abrolhos 141 J 4
Arquipélago dos Bijagós 196 A 3
Ar Rachidiya 192 E 2
Ar Radīsīyah Baḥrī (Egypt) 156 A 4
Arrah 174 D 2
Ar Rahad 194 E 6
Ar Rahad 194 F 6
Ar Raḥḥāliyah (Iraq) 156 D 2
Arraias 141 G 3
Ar Ramādī (Iraq) 156 D 2
Ar Ramlah (Jordan) 156 B 3
Arran 148 B 3
Ar Rank 194 E 6
Ar Raqqah (Syria) 156 C 2
Ar Rāqūbah 193 J 3
Arras 152 D 1
Ar Rass (Saudi Arabia) 156 D 4
Ar Rastān (Syria) 156 B 2
Ar Rawḍah 195 G 3
Ar Rawḍah 195 G 4
Ar Rawḍah 195 H 6
Ar Rawḍah (Saudi Arabia) 156 C 4
Ar Rawḍatayn (Kuwait) 157 E 3
Ar Rayḥānī (Oman) 157 G 5
Ar Rayyān 195 H 5
Arrecifal 138 E 3
Arrecife 192 C 3
Arrecifes 142 D 5
Arrecifes Triángulos 132 D 3
Arrey (N.M.) 117 J 5
Arriaga 132 D 4
Arriba (CO.) 115 O 4
Ar Rifā' (Qatar) 157 F 4

Ar Rifā'ī (Iraq) 157 E 3
Ar Riḥāb (Iraq) 157 D 3
Ar Rimāh (Saudi Arabia) 157 E 4
Ar Rimāl 195 J 4
Ar Riyāḍ (Saudi Arabia) 157 E 4
Arroio Grande 142 F 5
Arrow Creek (MT.) 111 P 3
Arrowhead, Lake 122 E 2
Arrowrock Reservoir 111 K 7
Arrowsmith, Mount 185 Q 9
Arroyito 142 D 5
Arroyo de las Flores 143 DE 6
Arroyo Grande (CA.) 113 E 7
Arroyo Hondo (N.M.) 117 L 1
Arroyos y Esteros 140 E 5
Arroyo Verde 143 C 7
Ar Rubaḍ 195 F 4
Ar Rumaythah (Iraq) 157 D 3
Ar Rumaythah (Qatar) 157 F 4
Ar Ruqi (Saudi Arabia) 157 E 3
Ar Rusāfah (Syria) 156 C 2
Ar Ruṣayriṣ 194 E 6
Ar Ruṭbah (Iraq) 156 C 2
Ar Ruwaydah (Saudi Arabia) 156 D 4
Ar Ruways (Qatar) 157 F 4
Ar Ruways (United Arab Emirates) 157 F 4
Års 151 E 4
Arsenjān (Iran) 157 F 3
Arsen'yev 173 K 2
Årskogen 150 G 3
Arsuk 105 S 3
Árta 154 B 3
Artá, Cuevas de 152 D 4
Artašat 155 F 3
Arteaga 132 B 4
Artem 173 K 2
Artemisa 132 F 3
Artémou 192 C 5
Artemovsk 155 E 1
Artemovsk 170 F 5
Artemovskiy 155 F 1
Artesia (AZ.) 116 G 5
Artesia (MS.) 121 R 9
Artesia (N.M.) 117 M 5
Artesia Lake 112 F 4
Artesian (S.D.) 119 L 6
Artesia Wells (TX.) 122 D 7
Arthur (N.D.) 119 L 3
Arthur (NE.) 118 G 9
Arthur (NV.) 112 K 2
Arthur (TN.) 128 H 5
Arthur City (TX.) 123 H 2
Arthur's Town 133 G 3
Artigas 142 E 5
Artik 155 F 2
Artillery Lake 103 Q 3
Artois (CA.) 112 C 3
Artoli 194 E 5
Artsyz 154 C 1
Artux 169 K 3
Artvin 155 F 2
Artybash 159 R 5
Artyk 171 R 3
Aru 198 E 4
Aru, Kepulauan 177 HJ 5
Aru, Tanjung 176 E 4
Arua 198 E 4
Aruajá 138 E 5
Aruanã 141 F 3
Aruba, Isla 138 E 1
Aru Islands 184 C 3
Aruma 139 F 4
Arunachal 175 F 2
Arun Qi 171 M 6
Aruppukkottai 174 C 6
Arus, Tanjung 177 F 3
Arusha 199 F 5
Arusha Chini 199 F 5
Aruwimi 198 D 4
Arvada (CO.) 115 M 4
Arvada (WY.) 118 B 6
Arvana (TX.) 117 P 5
Arvayheer 172 D 1
Arvidsjaur 150 G 2
Arvika 151 F 4
Årviksand 150 GH 1
Arvin (CA.) 113 G 7
Arxan 170 L 6
Ary 170 M 1
Arys' 169 H 2
Arys, Ozero 169 H 1
Aryta 171 N 3
Arzamas 158 H 4
Arzanah (United Arab Emirates) 157 F 4
Aržano 153 G 3
Arzgir 155 F 1
Arzhan 170 G 5
Asab 200 B 5
Asaba 197 F 4
Asadabad (Afghanistan) 169 J 4
Asadābād (Iran) 157 EF 2
Asahikawa 173 M 2
'Asalūyeh (Iran) 157 F 4
Asamakka 197 F 2
Asansol 174 E 3
Åsarna 150 F 3
Asba Tafari 199 G 3
Asbest 159 M 4

Ascensión (Bolivia) 140 D 4
Ascension Island 188 A 5
Ascension Island 188 A 5
Aschaffenburg 149 E 5
Ascoli Piceno 153 F 3
Ascotán 140 C 5
Ascutney, Mount 126 G 5
Åseda 151 G 4
Asedjrad 193 F 4
Asekseme 193 F 3
Åsele 150 G 3
Aselle 199 F 3
Åsen 150 F 3
Asendabo 199 F 3
Åseral 151 E 4
Asfar, Tall as (Jordan) 156 B 2
Asha 159 L 4
Ashanti 196 D 4
As Ḥasāwinah, Jabal 193 H 3
Ashburn (GA.) 131 L 3
Ashburton 185 Q 9
Ashburton River 182 B 3
Ashbury Park (N.J.) 127 F 8
Ashby (NE.) 118 G 8
Aschikol', Ozero 169 H 1
Ashdod (Israel) 156 B 3
Ashdown (AR.) 121 L 9
Asheboro (N.C.) 129 M 6
Asher (OK.) 120 J 7–8
Asherton (TX.) 122 D 7
Asherville (KS.) 120 H 3
Asheville (N.C.) 128 J 4
Ash Flat (AR.) 121 O 6
Ashford (WA.) 110 CD 4
Ash Fork (AZ.) 116 D 2
Ashgelon (Israel) 156 B 3
Ash Grove (KS.) 120 G 3
Ash Grove (MO.) 121 M 5
Ashkhabad 168 F 3
Ashkidah 193 H 3
Ashkun 169 J 3
Ashland (AL.) 128 F 8
Ashland (IL.) 121 Q 3
Ashland (KS.) 120 F 5
Ashland (KY.) 128 J 3
Ashland (ME.) 126 L 2
Ashland (MO.) 121 N 4
Ashland (MS.) 121 Q 8
Ashland (MT.) 118 B 5
Ashland (NE.) 120 J 1
Ashland (OH.) 125 M 9
Ashland (OK.) 120 J 8
Ashland (OR.) 110 C 8
Ashland (VA.) 129 O 4
Ashland (WI.) 124 D 3
Ashland City (TN.) 128 DE 5
Ashley (IL.) 121 Q 4
Ashley (MI.) 125 K 6
Ashley (N.D.) 118 J 4
Ashmore Reef 182 C 1
Ashokan 126 E 7
Ashtabula, Lake 119 L 3
Ashtabula, Lake 119 L 3
Ashtarak 155 F 2
Ashtīyān (Iran) 157 EF 2
Ashtola (TX.) 117 PQ 2
Ashton (ID.) 111 O 6
Ashton (NE.) 120 G 1
Ashton (S.D.) 119 K 6
Ashuanipi 105 O 5
Ashuanipi Lake 105 O 5
Ashur → Assur 195 G 1
Ashville (AL.) 128 E 8
Ashwood (OR.) 110 E 6
Asia, Kepulauan 177 H 3

Asilah 192 D 1
Asimiro 177 G 3
Asinara 153 E 3
Asinara, Golfo dell' 153 E 3
Asino 159 R 4
Asir, Ra's 199 J 2
Aska 174 D 4
Aşkale 155 F 3
Askaniya Nova 155 D 1
Asker 151 F 4
Askersund 151 G 4
Askī al Mawşil (Iraq) 156 D 1
Askim 151 F 4
Askiz 170 F 5
Askja 150 B 3
Askvoll 150 E 3
Asmara 199 F 1
Åsnen 151 FG 4
Asni 192 D 2
Asop 174 B 2
Asosa 198 E 2
Asoteriba, Jabal 194 F 4
Asotin (WA.) 110 HJ 4
Asouf Mellene 193 F 3
Aspās (Iran) 157 F 3
Aspen (CO.) 115 L 4
Aspen (WY.) 111 P 9
Aspendos 154 D 3
Aspen Lake 110 C 8
Aspermont (TX.) 117 Q 4
Aspiring, Mount 184 P 9
Aspurito 138 E 2
Asqueimat 192 B 4
Assa 192 D 3
Aş Şa'an (Syria) 156 B 2
Assab 199 G 2
Assâba 192 C 5
As Sab'ān (Saudi Arabia) 156 C 4
Aş Şadr (United Arab Emirates) 157 G 4
Aş Şafīrah (Syria) 156 B 1
Aş Şāfīyah (Jordan) 156 B 3
Aş Şahm 195 K 4
Aş Şahrā' al Gharbīyah 194 D 3
Aş Şahrā' al Janūbīyah 194 D 4
Aş Şahrā' an Nūbiyah 194 E 4
Aş Şahrā' ash Sharqīyah (Egypt) 156 AB 4
Aş Şahrā' Tīh (Egypt) 156 AB 3
As Salamīyah (Saudi Arabia) 157 E 4
As Salamīyah (Syria) 156 B 2
Assale, Lake 199 G 2
As Salīf 195 G 5
Aş Şālihīyah (Syria) 156 C 2
As Sālimīyah (Kuwait) 157 E 3
As Sallūm 194 D 2
As Salmān (Iraq) 157 D 3
As Salt (Jordan) 156 B 2
Assam 175 F 2
As Samāwah (Iraq) 157 D 3
Aş Şanām 195 J 4
Assaouas 197 F 2
As Sarīr 193 K 3
As Sarir 193 K 3
Assateague Island 129 Q 3
Assateague Island National Seashore 129 Q 3
As Sawdā, Jabal 193 HJ 3
As Sawrah (Saudi Arabia) 156 C 4
Assaye 174 C 3
As Sayl al Kabīr 195 G 4
Assekaifaf 193 G 3
Assekrème 193 G 4
Assen 148 E 4
Assens 151 EF 4
as Sibā'ī, Jabal (Egypt) 156 AB 4
As Sidrah 193 J 2
As Sidrah 193 J 2
As Silā (United Arab Emirates) 157 F 4
Assini 196 D 5
Assiniboia 103 Q 6
Assiniboine 103 S 6
Assiniboine, Mount 103 O 5
Assiou 193 G 4
Assis 141 F 5
Assisi 153 F 3
Assodé 197 F 2
As Subū' 194 E 4
As Sufāl 195 H 6
Aş Şufayyah 194 E 5
Aş Şufug (United Arab Emirates) 157 F 5
Aş Şukhayrah 193 H 2
As Suknah (Jordan) 156 C 2
As Sulaymī (Saudi Arabia) 156 C 4
As Sulayyil 195 H 4
Aş Şulb (Saudi Arabia) 157 E 4
Aş Şummān (Saudi Arabia) 157 DE 4
Assumption 199 H 6
Assur (Iraq) 156 D 2
As Suwaydā' (Syria) 156 B 2
As Suwayḩ 195 K 4
Aş Şuwayrah (Iraq) 157 D 2
As Suways 156 A 3
Astakh 171 P 2
Āstāneh (Iran) 157 E 2
Astārā (Iran) 168 D 3
Asti 153 E 3
Astillero 140 C 3
Astipálaia 154 C 3
Astola 169 G 6
Astor 169 J 3
Astorga 152 B 3
Astoria (IL.) 124 D 9
Astoria (OR.) 110 B 4
Astove 199 H 6
Astrakhan 168 D 1
Astrolabe, Récifs de l' 186 C 4
Asturias 152 B 3
Asuncion (Mariana Is.) 186 A 1
Asunción (Paraguay) 142 E 4
Aswa 198 E 4
Aswān (Egypt) 156 A 4
Aswan High Dam (Egypt) 156 A 5
Asyūţ 194 E 3
Ata 186 D 4
Atacama, Desierto do 140 C 5
Atacama, Salar de 140 C 5
Atafu 186 D 3
Ataki 154 C 1
Atakora, Chaîne de l' 196 E 3
Atakpamé 196 E 4
Atalándi 154 B 3
Atalaya 140 B 3
Atalaya, Cerro (Chile) 143 B 9
Atalaya, Cerro (Peru) 140 B 3
Atalaya, Pico 130 B 8
Atalayasa 152 D 4
Atamanon Óri 154 B 3
Atambua 177 F 5
Atangmik 105 R 3
Atar 192 C 4
Atas Bogd Uul 172 C 2
Atascadero (CA.) 113 E 7
Atasu 159 O 6
Atauba 139 F 4
Atauro, Pulau 177 G 5
Ataviros 154 C 3
Atbalmin 184 D 2
'Aţbarah 194 E 5
Aţbarah 194 F 5
Atbasar 159 N 5
At-Bash 169 K 2
Atchafalaya Bay 123 M 6
Atchison (KS.) 121 K 3
Atebubu 196 D 4
Ateca 152 C 3
Atemble 184 D 2–3
Āteshān (Iran) 157 F 2
Athabasca (Alb., Can.) 103 P 4
Athabasca (Alb., Can.) 103 P 5
Athena (OR.) 110 G 5
Athens (AL.) 128 E 7
Athens (GA.) 128 H 8
Athens (OH.) 129 J 2
Athens (PA.) 126 C 7
Athens (TN.) 128 G 6
Athens (WI.) 124 DE 4
Athens → Athínai 154 B 3
Athéras 154 C 3
Atherton (Queensland, Austr.) 183 GH 2
Athi 199 F 5
Athínai 154 B 3
Athi River 199 F 5
Athlone 148 B 4
Athni 174 C 4
Athol (ID.) 110 J 3
Athol (MA.) 126 G 6
Athol (S.D.) 119 K 6
Áthos 154 B 2
Ath Thamad (Egypt) 156 B 3
Ath Thumāmī 195 G 3
Ath Thumāmī (Saudi Arabia) 157 D 4
Ati 197 H 3
Atiak 198 E 4
Atico 140 B 4
Atikokan 104 J 6
Atikonak Lake 105 P 5
Atiu 187 E 4
Atka 102 C 5
Atka (AK, U.S.A.) 102 C 5
Atka (U.S.S.R.) 171 S 3
Atkarsk 158 H 5
Atkasuk 102 F 1
Atkins (AR.) 121 N 7
Atkinson (GA.) 131 N 3
Atkinson (N.C.) 129 N 7
Atkinson (NE.) 118 J 8
Atlanta (GA.) 128 G 8
Atlanta (ID.) 111 K 7
Atlanta (MI.) 125 K 4
Atlanta (TX.) 123 J 2
Atlantic (IA.) 119 NO 9
Atlantic (N.C.) 129 P 7
Atlantic Beach (FL.) 131 N 4
Atlantic City (N.J.) 127 E 9
Atlantic City (WY.) 111 R 8
Atlantic-Indian Rise 208 B 5
Atlantic Ocean 204
Atlantic Peak 111 R 8
Atlas el Kebir 192 DE 2
Atlas el Moutaouassit 192 DE 2
Atlas es Sahir 192 D 2–3
Atlas Mountains 192 DF 2
Atlasova, Ostrov 171 ST 5
Atlin 102 L 4
Atlin Lake 102 L 4
Atna Peak 103 M 5
Atocha 140 C 5
Atoka (OK.) 120 J 8
Atoka Reservoir 120 J 8
Atolia (CA.) 113 H 7
Atomic City (ID.) 111 N 7
Atouat 175 J 4
Atoyac de Alvarez 132 B 4
Ātran 151 F 4
Atrato 138 C 2
Atrek 168 E 3
Atsy 177 J 5
Aţ Ţaff (United Arab Emirates) 157 G 4
At Tafīlah (Jordan) 156 B 3
Aţ Ţā'if 195 G 4
Attalla (AL.) 128 E 7
At Tamīmī 193 K 2
At Tarhūnī, Jabal 193 K 4
Aţ Ţarmīyah (Iraq) 156 D 2
Attawapiskat 104 KL 5
Attawapiskat 104 L 5
Attawapiskat Lake 104 K 5
At Tawīl (Saudi Arabia) 156 C 3
Aţ Ţaysīyah (Saudi Arabia) 156 D 3–4
Aţ Ţayyārah 194 E 6
Attersee 153 F 2
Aţ Ţīb, Ra's 193 H 1
Attica (KS.) 120 G 5
Attica (OH.) 125 M 8
Attikamagen Lake 105 O 5
At Tin, Ra's 193 K 2
Attleboro (MA.) 126 H 7
Attopeu 175 J 5
Attu 102 A 5
Attu 102 A 5
Aţ Ţulayḩī (Saudi Arabia) 156 D 4
Aţ Ţullāb 193 K 4
Attur 174 C 5
Aţ Ţūr (Egypt) 156 A 3
At Turayf (Saudi Arabia) 156 C 3
At Turbah 195 G 6
Aţ Ţuwayshah 194 D 6
Aţ Ţuwayyah (Saudi Arabia) 156 C 4
Atuel 143 C 6
Atura 198 E 4
Åtvidaberg 151 G 4
Atwater (CA.) 112 E 5
Atwood (CO.) 115 O 3
Atwood (KS.) 120 DE 3
Atwood Lake 125 N 9
Atyr-Meyite 171 O 2
Aua 184 D 2
Aua 186 A 3
Auadi 192 C 4
Auas Mountains 200 B 4
Auati Paraná 138 E 4
Auatu 199 G 3
Auau Channel 113 F 11
Aubagne 153 E 3
Aube 153 D 2
Aubry, Lake 103 M 2
Auburn (AL.) 131 J 2
Auburn (CA.) 112 D 4
Auburn (IL.) 121 Q 3
Auburn (IN.) 124 J 8
Auburn (KY.) 128 E 5
Auburn (MA.) 126 H 6
Auburn (ME.) 126 J 4
Auburn (NE.) 120 K 2
Auburn (N.Y.) 126 C 6
Auburn (WA.) 110 C 3
Auburn River 183 J 4
Aubusson 152 D 2
Auca Mahuida, Sierra 143 C 6
Auch 152 D 3
Auchi 197 F 4
Aucilla River 131 L 4
Auckland 185 Q 8
Auckland 186 C 5
Auckland Islands 203
Aude 152 D 3
Audo Range 199 G 3
Audubon (IA.) 119 O 9
Aue 149 F 4
Augathella 183 H 4
Aughrabies Falls 200 C 5
Augoon 109 M 4
Au Gres (MI.) 125 L 5
Augsburg 149 F 5
Augusta (AR.) 121 O 7
Augusta (Australia) 182 A 5
Augusta (GA.) 129 K 8
Augusta (Italy) 153 G 4
Augusta (KS.) 120 HJ 5
Augusta (KY.) 128 G 3
Augusta (ME.) 126 K 4
Augusta (MT.) 111 N 3
Augusta (WI.) 124 C 5
Augustów 149 H 4
Augustus, Mount 182 B 3
Auki 185 H 3
Auki 186 B 3
Auld, Lake 182 C 3
Ault (CO.) 115 N 3
Auna 197 E 3
Auning 151 F 4
Aur 186 C 2
Auraiya 174 C 2
Aurangabad 174 D 3
Aurangaband 174 C 4
Auray 152 C 2
Aure 150 E 3
Aurès, Massif de l' 193 G 1
Aurich 149 E 4
Aurilândia 141 F 4
Aurillac 152 D 3
Aurlandsfjorden 150 E 3
Aurlandsvangen 150 E 3
Aurora (CO.) 115 N 4
Aurora (IL.) 124 F 8
Aurora (IN.) 128 FG 2
Aurora (KS.) 120 H 3
Aurora (KY.) 128 C 5
Aurora (MN.) 119 Q 3
Aurora (MO.) 121 M 6
Aurora (N.C.) 129 P 6
Aurora (NE.) 120 G 2
Aurora (Philippines) 177 F 2
Aurora (W.V.) 129 M 2
Aursunden 150 F 3
Aurukun 183 G 1
Aurunci, Monti 153 F 3
Aus 200 B 5
Au Sable Forks (N.Y.) 126 F 4
Au Sable Point 125 L 5
Ausangate, Nevado 140 B 3
Ausert 192 C 4
Aust-Agder 151 E 4
Austin (Australia) 182 B 4
Austin (IN.) 128 F 3
Austin (KY.) 128 F 5
Austin (MN.) 119 Q 7
Austin (PA.) 125 Q 8
Austin (TX.) 122 F 5
Austin, Lake 182 B 4
Austintown (OH.) 125 O 8
Austinville (VA.) 129 L 5
Austonio (TX.) 123 H 4
Austral Downs 183 F 3
Australia 182–183 CG 3
Australia Mountain 109 L 3
Australian Alps 183 H 6
Australian-Antarctic Basin 208 B 5
Australian-Antarctic Discordance 209 C 5
Australian-Antarctic Rise 209 C 5
Australian Capital Territory 183 H 6
Austria 153 F 2
Austurhorn 150 C 3
Austvågöy 150 F 2
Autazes 139 G 4
Autlán 132 B 4
Autun 152 D 2
Auxerre 152 D 2 Auxonne 153 E 2
Auyuittuq National Park 105 OP 2
Ava (MO.) 121 N 6
Avakubi 198 D 4
Avallon 152 D 2
Avalon (CA.) 113 G 9
Avalon, Lake 117 M 5
Avalon Peninsula 105 R 6
Avan 168 G 1
Avanavero 139 G 3
Avanos 155 D 3
Avant (OK.) 120 J 6
Avaré 141 G 5
Avarua 187 E 4
Avaz 168 G 4
Avdhira 154 B 2
Avedat (Israel) 156 B 3
Āveh (Iran) 157 F 2
Aveiro 139 H 4
Aveiro (Portugal) 152 B 3
Āvej (Iran) 157 E 2
Āvej, Gardaneh-ye (Iran) 157 E 2
Avekova 171 U 3
Avellaneda 142 E 5
Avellino 153 FG 3
Avenal (CA.) 112 E 6
Averöya 150 E 3
Aversa 153 F 3
Avery (ID.) 111 K 3
Avery Island (LA.) 123 LM 6
Aves, Isla de 133 K 4
Aves, Islas las 138 E 1
Avesta 151 G 3
Aveyron 152 D 3
Avezzano 153 F 3
Aviá Terai 142 D 4
Avigait 105 R 3
Avignon 153 D 3
Ávila 152 C 3
Avila Beach (CA.) 113 E 7
Avilés 152 B 3
Avilla (MO.) 121 L 5
Avington 183 GH 3
Avis (PA.) 127 B 7
Avoca (IA.) 119 N 9
Avola 153 G 4
Avon 148 C 4
Avon (MT.) 111 N 4
Avon (N.C.) 129 Q 6
Avon (S.D.) 119 K 8
Avondale (CO.) 115 N 5
Avondale (PA.) 127 D 9
Avon Downs 183 F 2
Avon Park (FL.) 131 N 7
Avon River (Australia) 182 B 5
Avranches 152 C 2
Avrora 155 D 1
Awai 197 F 4
'Awālī (Qatar) 157 F 4
Awanui 185 Q 8
Awara Plain 199 G 4
Awareh 199 G 3
Awasa 199 F 3
Awash 199 G 2
Awash 199 G 3
Awash Fish River (Namibia) 200 B 5
Awasib Mountains 200 B 5
Awaso 196 D 4
Awat 169 L 2
'Awaynat Wanīn 193 H 3
Awbārī 193 H 3
Awbārī, Idhān 193 H 3
Awdēgle 199 G 4
Awjilah 193 K 3
Awka 197 F 4
Awuna River 108 G 2
Axel Heiberg Island 202
Axial (CO.) 115 K 3
Axi-les-Thermes 152 D 3
Axim 196 D 5
Axinim 139 G 4
Axioma 139 F 5
Axios 154 B 2
Axtell (NE.) 120 F 2
Axtell (NE.) 120 J 3
Ayabaca 138 BC 4
Ayachi, Jbel 192 E 2
Ayacucho (Argentina) 143 E 6
Ayacucho (Peru) 140 B 3
'Ayādh 195 H 6
Ayaguz 159 P 6
Ayaguz 159 Q 6
Ayakkum Hu 172 A 3
Ayakli 170 G 2
Ayamé 196 D 4
Ayamé Dam 196 D 4
Ayamonte 152 B 4
Ayan 170 F 2
Ayan 170 J 3
Ayan 170 J 4
Ayan 171 P 4
Ayanaka 171 V 3
Ayancık 155 D 2
Ayangba 197 F 4
Ayanka 171 U 3
Ayaş 155 D 2
Ayaturku, Ozero 170 EF 1
Ayava 170 H 4
Ayaviri 140 B 3
Ayaya 171 O 3
Aydın 154 C 3
Aydıncık 155 D 3
Aydingkol Hu 172 AB 2
Aydyrlinskiy 159 L 5
Ayelu 199 G 2
Ayerbe 152 C 3
Ayers Rock – Mount Olga National park 182 E 4
Áyion Óros 154 B 2
Áyios Evstrátios 154 C 3
Áyios Kirikos 154 C 3
Áyios Nikólaos 154 C 3
Aykhal 170 K 2
Aylmer Lake 103 Q 3
'Ayn, Ra's al (Syria) 156 C 1
Ayna 152 C 4
'Aynabo 199 H 3
'Ayn al 'Ajalīyah 195 H 4
'Ayn al Baydā' (Syria) 156 BC 2
'Ayn al Ghazāl 193 K 4
'Ayn 'Aysa (Syria) 156 C 1
'Ayn Dāllah 194 D 3
Ayn Dār (Saudi Arabia) 157 E 4
'Ayn Dīwār 195 G 1
Ayni 169 H 3
'Aynīn 195 G 4
Aynor (S.C.) 129 M 7–8
'Ayn Sifnī (Iraq) 156 D 1
'Ayn Sukhnah (Egypt) 156 A 3
'Ayn Zuwayyah 193 K 4
Ayod 198 E 3
Ayon 171 V 2
Ayorou 196 E 3
Ayr (Australia) 183 H 2
Ayr (NE.) 120 G 2
Ayr (U.K.) 148 C 3
Ayrag Nuur 170 F 6
Ayrancı 155 D 3
Ayrshire Downs 183 G 3
Aysary 159 O 5
Ayshirak 159 O 6
Aytos 154 C 2
Aytré 152 C 2
Ayuán-Tepuí 139 F 2
Ayutla 132 C 4
Ayutthaya 175 H 5
Ayvacık 154 C 3
Ayvacık 155 E 2
Ayvalık 154 C 3
Āzādshahr (Iran) 157 G 1
Azaila 152 C 3
Azambuja 152 B 4
Azamgarh 174 D 2
Azanka 159 M 4
Azaouad 196 D 2
Azaouak, Vallée de l' 196 E 2
Āzarān 168 D 3
Azare 197 G 3
A'zāz 156 B 1
Azbine 197 F 2
Az Daro 199 F 2

Azdavay 155 D 2
Azéffal, Dunes de l' 192 BC 4
Azeffoun 153 D 4
Azelik 197 F 2
Azemmour 192 D 2
Azennezal 192 F 4
Azerbaydzhan 168 D 2
Azilal 192 D 2
Aziscohos Lake 126 J 3
Aznā (Iran) 157 E 2
Azogues 138 C 4
Azopol'ye 158 J 2
Azores 192 A 1
Azoum 197 J 3
Azov 155 E 1
Azovskiy Kanal 155 EF 1
Azovskoye More 155 E 1
Azovy 159 N 3
Azozo 199 F 2
Azraq ash Shīshān (Jordan) 156 B 3
Azrou 192 D 2
Azrow 169 H 4
Az Silfī (Saudi Arabia) 157 D 4
Aztec (N.M.) 116 HJ 1
Aztec Peak 116 F 4
Aztec Ruins National Monument 116 J 1
Az Tibaghbagh 194 D 3
Azua 133 H 4
Azuaga 152 B 4
Azuero, Península de 138 B 2
Azul 143 E 6
Azul, Cordillera 138 C 5
Azur, Côte d' 153 E 3
Azzaba 193 G 1
Az Zāb al Kabīr (Iraq) 156 D 1
Az Zāb aş Şaghīr (Iraq) 156 D 2
Az Zabdānī (Syria) 156 B 2
Aẕ Ẕafīr 195 G 5
Aẕ Ẕahrah 193 J 3
Aẕ Ẕahrān (Saudi Arabia) 157 EF 4
Az Zallāq (Qatar) 157 F 4
Az Zaqāzīq 194 E 2
Az Zarqā' (United Arab Emirates) 157 F 4
Az Zarqā' (Jordan) 156 B 2
Az Zāwiyah 193 H 2
Az Zaydab 194 E 5
Az Zaydīyah 195 G 5
Az Zaytūn 194 D 3
Azzel Matti, Sebkha 192 F 3
Az Zilfī 195 G 4
Az Zubayr (Iraq) 157 E 3
Az Zugar 195 G 6
Azzuwaytīnah 193 JK 2

B

Baa 177 F 6
Bää 182 C 1
Ba'abdā (Lebanon) 156 B 2
Ba'ādwēyn 199 H 3
Baan Baa 183 H 5
Bāb (United Arab Emirates) 157 F 5
Baba Burnu 154 D 2
Baba Burun 154 C 3
Babaculândia 139 J 5
Babadag 154 C 2
Babaeski 154 C 2
Bābā Heydar (Iran) 157 F 2
Babahoyo 138 C 4
Babai Gaxun 172 D 2
Babanūsah 194 D 6
Babar, Kepulauan 177 G 5
Babati 199 F 5
Babayevo 158 G 4
Babb (MT.) 111 M 2
Babbitt (NV.) 112 G 4
Babenna (Syria) 156 B 2
Babi, Pulau 176 A 3
Babinda 197 F 3
Babine 103 M 4
Babine Lake 103 M 5
Babino Polje 153 G 3
Babo 177 H 4
Bābol (Iran) 157 F 1
Babol Sar (Iran) 157 F 1
Baboquivari Peak 116 E 6
Baborigame 106 E 6
Baboua 198 AB 3
Babushkin 170 J 5
Babuyan 177 E 1–2
Babuyan 177 J 1
Babuyan Channel 177 J 1
Babylon (Iraq) 156 D 2
Bacabal (Maranhão, Brazil) 141 GH 1
Bacabal (Pará, Brazil) 139 G 5
Bacajá 139 H 4
Bacan, Pulau 177 G 4
Bacău 154 C 1
Bac Can 175 J 3
Bachaquero 138 D 2
Bacho 175 H 6
Bachu 169 K 3
Back 103 S 2
Bačka Palanka 154 A 1

Bačka Topola 154 AB 1
Backbone Mountain 129 M 2
Backbone Range 109 N 3
Bačkovski Manastir 154 BC 2
Backus (MN.) 119 O 4
Bac Ninh 175 J 3
Bacolod 177 F 1
Bac Quang 175 H 3
Bād (Iran) 157 F 2
Badagara 174 BC 5
Badagri 196 E 4
Badain Jaran Shamo 172 D 2
Badajós 139 J 4
Badajós, Lago 139 F 4
Badajoz 152 B 4
Badakhshan 169 J 3
Badalona 152 D 3
Badami 174 C 4
Badanah (Saudi Arabia) 156 C 3
Badarma 170 H 4
Bad Aussee 153 F 2
Badda 199 F 3
Baden (Austria) 153 G 2
Baden (Ethiopia) 199 F 1
Baden (Switzerland) 153 E 2
Baden-Baden 149 E 5
Baden-Württemberg 149 E 5
Badgastein 153 F 2
Badger (CA.) 112 G 6
Badger (MN.) 119 M 2
Badger Peak 118 B 5
Bad Godesberg 149 E 4
Bad Hersfeld 149 E 4
Bad Homburg 149 E 4
Badin 169 H 6
Badin (N.C.) 129 L 6
Badin Lake 129 L 6
Badiraguato 106 E 6
Bad Ischl 153 F 2
Badiyat ash Shām 156 BC 2
Badjawa 177 F 5
Bad Kissingen 149 F 4
Bad Kreuznach 149 E 5
Badlands 117 MN 2
Badlands 118 EF 7
Badlands National Monument 118 F 7
Bado 177 J 5
Ba Dong 175 J 6
Badoumbé 196 B 3
Bad Reichenhall 149 F 5
Badr Ḥunayn (Saudi Arabia) 156 C 5
Bad River 118 GH 6
Bad River Indian Reservation 124 D 3
Bad Schwartau 149 F 4
Bad Tölz 149 F 5
Badulla 174 D 6
Badyarikha 171 R 2
Badzhal 171 O 5
Badzhal'skiy Khrebet 171 O 5
Baena 152 C 4
Baeza (Ecuador) 138 C 4
Baeza (Spain) 152 C 4
Bafa Gölü 154 C 3
Bafang 197 FG 4
Bafatá 196 B 3
Baffin Bay 202
Baffin Bay (TX.) 122 F 8
Baffin Island 105 NO 2
Bafia 197 G 5
Bafing 196 B 3
Bafing Makana 196 BC 3
Bafoulabé 196 B 3
Bafoussam 197 G 4
Baf → Paphos 155 D 4
Bāfq (Iran) 157 G 2
Bāfq, Kūh-e (Iran) 157 G 3
Bafra 155 E 2
Bafra Burnu 155 E 2
Bāft (Iran) 157 G 3
Bafwaboli 198 D 4
Bafwasende 198 D 4
Baga 197 G 3
Bagadzha 170 L 3
Bagalkot 174 C 4
Bagam 197 F 2
Baganalakh 170 L 3
Bagansiapapi 176 B 3
Baga Sola 197 G 3
Bagata 198 B 4
Bagdad (AZ.) 116 C 3
Bagdad (CA.) 113 K 8
Bagdarin 170 K 5
Bagé 142 F 5
Baghdād (Iraq) 156 D 2
Bagh-e Malek (Iran) 157 E 3
Bagheria 153 F 4
Bāghin (Iran) 157 G 3
Baghlan 169 H 3
Bagley (MN.) 119 N 3
Bağlum 155 D 2
Bagn 151 E 3
Bagnell (MO.) 121 N 4
Bagnell Dam 121 N 4
Bagnères-de-Bigorre 152 D 3
Bagoé 196 C 3

Bagrawia → Meroe 194 E 5
Bagrax → Bohu 169 M 2
Bagre 139 H 4
Bagua 138 C 5
Baguia 177 G 5
Baguio 177 J 1
Baguirmi 197 H 3
Bagusi 177 J 4
Bagzane, Monts 197 F 2
Bahama Islands 133 H 3
Ba-Illi 197 H 3
Bāhār (Iran) 157 E 2
Bahar Dar 199 F 2
Bahariya Oasis → Wāḥat al Ba-ḥarīyah 194 D 3
Bahau 176 B 3
Bahaur 176 D 4
Bahawalnagar 169 J 5
Bahawalpur 169 J 5
Bahçe 155 E 3
Bahçe (Turkey) 156 B 1
Bahi 198 F 6
Bahía (Argentina) 143 C 8
Bahía (Brazil) 141 H 3
Bahía, Islas de la 132 E 4
Bahia Adair 106 D 5
Bahía Anegada 143 D 7
Bahía Ballenas 106 D 6
Bahía Blanca 143 D 6
Bahía Blanca 143 D 6
Bahía Coatzacoalcos 132 D 4
Bahía Concepción 106 D 6
Bahía Darwin 143 AB 8
Bahía de Amatique 132 E 4
Bahía de Añasco 130 B 8
Bahía de Campeche 132 D 4
Bahía de Caráquez 138 B 4
Bahía de Chetumal 132 E 4
Bahía de Coronado 132 B 4
Bahia de La Paz 106 D 7
Bahia de Petacalco 132 B 4
Bahía de Punta Gorda 132 F 5
Bahia de San Jorge 106 D 5
Bahia de San Quintin 106 C 5
Bahía de Santa Elena 132 E 5
Bahía de Santa María 106 E 6
Bahía de Sechura 138 B 5
Bahía de Tepoca 106 D 5
Bahía de Topolobampo 106 E 6
Bahia Dulce 132 C 4
Bahia Grande 143 C 9
Bahía Kino 106 D 6
Bahia Laura 143 C 8
Bahia Magdalena 106 D 7
Bahía Negra 140 E 5
Bahía Otway 143 B 9
Bahía Pargua 143 B 7
Bahía Rosario 106 C 6
Bahías, Cabo dos 143 CD 8
Bahía → Salvador (Brazil) 141 J 3
Bahía Samborombón 143 E 6
Bahía San Luis Gonzaga 106 D 6
Bahía Santa Ines 106 D 6
Bahía Sebastián Vizcaíno 106 D 6
Bahindi 197 E 3
Baḥrah 195 F 4
Bahraich 174 D 2
Bahrain 157 F 4
Baḥr al Abyaḍ 194 E 6
Baḥr al 'Arab 194 D 6
Baḥr al Azraq 194 E 6
Baḥr al Ghazāl 198 DE 3
Baḥr al Jabal 198 E 3
Baḥr al Milk (Iraq) 156 D 2
Baḥr ar Rimāl al 'Aẕīm 194 D 3
Baḥrat Ḥimṣ (Syria) 156 B 2
Baḥr ath Tharthār (Iraq) 156 D 2
Bahrayn, Khalījal (Saudi Arabia) 157 F 4
Bahr el Ghazal 197 H 2–3
Bāhu Kālāt 169 G 5
Baía de Maputo 201 E 5
Baia de Paranaguá 142 G 4
Baía de Setúbal 152 B 4
Baía de Sofala 201 EF 4
Baia de Todos os Santos 141 J 3
Baía do Bengo 200 A 1
Baía dos Tigres 200 A 3
Baía Farta 200 A 2
Baião 139 J 4
Baïbokoum 197 H 4
Baicang 175 F 1
Baicheng 169 L 2
Baicheng 173 H 1
Baie aux Feuilles 105 O 4
Baie Comeau 105 O 6
Baie d'Antongil 201 HJ 3
Baie d'Audierne 152 C 2
Baie de Corisco 197 F 5
Baie de Lannion 152 C 2
Baie de la Seine 152 C 2
Baie de Rupert 105 LM 5
Baie-des-Moutons 105 Q 5
Baie Diana 105 O 3
Baie du Poste 105 N 5
Baie Mosquito 105 M 3
Baie Payne 105 O 4
Baie Trinité 105 O 6
Baie Verte 105 Q 6

Baihe 172 F 4
Baikal, Lake 170 J 4–5
Baikha 159 R 3
Bailang 170 M 6
Baile Átha Cliath 148 B 4
Bailén 152 C 4
Bãileşti 154 B 2
Bailey (CO.) 115 M 4
Baileys Harbor (WI.) 124 G 4
Bailique, Ilha 139 J 3
Bailundo 200 B 2
Baima 172 D 4
Baimuru 184 D 3
Bainang 174 E 2
Bainbridge (GA.) 131 K 4
Bainbridge (OH.) 128 H 2
Bain-de-Bretagne 152 C 2
Baing 177 F 6
Baingoin 174 E 1
Bainville (MT.) 118 D 2
Baiquan 171 N 6
Bā'ir (Jordan) 156 B 3
Baird (TX.) 122 D 3
Baird Inlet 102 E 3
Baird Mountains 102 E 2
Baird Peninsula 105 M 2
Bairiki 186 C 2
Bairin Youqi 173 G 2
Bairin Zuoqi 173 GH 2
Bairkum 169 H 2
Bairnsdale 183 H 6
Bairoil (WY.) 111 S 8
Bais 177 F 2
Baisha 172 E 7
Bai Thuong 175 J 4
Baixo-Alentejo 152 B 4
Baixo-Longa 200 B 3
Baiyanghe 169 M 2
Baiyer River 184 D 3
Baiyü 172 C 4
Baiyuda 194 E 5
Baiyuda Desert → Şaḥrā' Bayyū-ḍah 194 E 5
Baja 154 A 1
Baja California Norte 106 C 5
Baja California Sur 106 D 6
Baja de Marajó 139 J 4
Bājah 193 G 1
Bajas, Rías 152 B 3
Bājgīrān 168 F 3
Bajitpur 175 F 3
Bajun Islands 199 G 5
Baka 198 E 4
Bakadžicite 154 C 2
Bakala 198 C 3
Bakanas 169 K 2
Bakar 153 F 2
Bakayan, Gunung 176 E 3
Bakchar 159 Q 4
Bake 176 B 4
Bakel 196 B 3
Baker (CA.) 113 J 7
Baker (FL.) 130 H 4
Baker (LA.) 123 M 5
Baker (MT.) 111 M 5
Baker (MT.) 118 D 4
Baker (OK.) 120 DE 6
Baker (OR.) 110 H 6
Baker (Pacific Ocean, U.S.A.) 186 D 2
Baker, Canal 143 B 8
Baker, Mount 110 C 2
Baker Butte 116 E 3
Baker Lake (Australia) 182 D 4
Baker Lake (N.W.T., Can.) 103 S 3
Bakersfield (CA.) 113 F 7
Bakersfield (TX.) 117 O 7
Bakersville (N.C.) 129 J 5
Bakharden 168 F 3
Bakhardok 168 F 3
Bākharz 168 G 4
Bakhchisaray 155 D 2
Bakhma (Iraq) 156 D 1
Bakhmach 158 F 5
Bakhta 159 R 3
Bakhta 159 R 3
Bakhtegān, Daryācheh-ye (Iran) 157 FG 3
Baki 197 F 2
Bakinskikh Komissarov, Imeni 26 168 DE 3
Bakir 197 C 2
Bakırdağı 155 E 3
Bakkaflói 150 C 2
Bako (Ethiopia) 199 F 3
Bako (Ivory Coast) 196 C 4
Bakony 154 A 1
Bakouma 198 C 3
Bakoye 196 C 3
Baksanges 155 F 2
Baku 168 DE 2
Bakungan 176 A 3
Bakuriani 155 F 2
Bakwa M'Bule 198 C 5

Balabac 176 E 2
Balabac 176 E 2
Balabac Strait 176 E 2
Balabak Dağları 155 E 2
Ba'labakk (Lebanon) 156 B 2
Ba'labakk, Ra's (Syria) 156 B 2
Balabalangan, Kepulauan 176 E 4
Bālā Bolūk 169 G 4
Bal'ad 199 H 4
Balad (Iraq) 156 D 2
Bālādeh (Iran) 157 F 3
Baladek 171 O 5
Baladīyat 'Adan 195 H 6
Balad Rūz (Iraq) 157 D 2
Balagannakh 171 O 2
Balagannoye 171 R 4
Balaghat 174 D 3
Balaghat Range 174 C 4
Balaguer 152 D 3
Balakhna 158 H 4
Balakhnya 170 H 1
Balakhta 170 F 4
Balaklava 155 D 2
Balakleya 158 G 6
Balakovo 158 J 5
Balama 201 F 2
Balambangam 176 E 2
Bala Murghab 169 G 3
Balance Rock (CA.) 113 G 7
Balas 198 F 2
Balashov 158 H 5
Balasore 174 E 3
Balassagyarmat 154 A 1
Balāt 194 D 3
Balaton 154 A 1
Balaurin 177 F 5
Balavino 155 E 1
Balazhal 159 Q 6
Balazote 154 C 4
Balbi, Mount 185 F 3
Balboa 138 C 2
Balcarce 143 E 6
Balclutha 184 P 10
Balcones Escarpment 122 C–E 6
Balde 142 C 5
Bald Head 182 B 6
Bald Knob (AR.) 121 O 7
Bald Mountain 110 H 6
Bald Mountain 110 D 7
Bald Mountain 115 M 3
Bald Point 131 K 5
Baldridge (TX.) 117 O 6
Baldwin (FL.) 131 N 4
Baldwin (LA.) 123 M 6
Baldwin (MI.) 124 H 6
Baldwin (ND.) 118 H 3
Baldwin (WI.) 124 B 5
Baldwin City (KS.) 121 K 4
Baldwinsville (N.Y.) 126 C 5
Baldwyn (MS.) 121 R 8
Baldy Mountain 111 Q 2
Baldy Peak 116 G 4
Bale 199 G 3
Baleares, Islas 152 D 3–4
Balearic Islands 152 D 3
Baleia, Ponta da 141 J 4
Baleine, Grande Rivière de la 105 M 4–5
Baleine, Rivière à la 105 O 4
Baler 177 J 1
Baley 170 L 5
Balezino 158 K 4
Balgazin 170 G 5
Balguntay 169 M 2
Bal Ḥāf 195 H 6
Balho 199 G 2
Bali 176 DE 5
Bali, Laut 176 E 5
Balia 196 B 4
Balıkesir 154 C 3
Balıkpapan, Gunung 176 E 4
Balikpapan, Teluk 176 E 4
Balimbing 176 EF 2
Balimo 184 D 3
Balintang Channel 177 J 1
Balis (Syria) 156 BC 2
Baliza 141 F 4
Balkan Mountains 154 C 2
Balkashino 159 N 5
Balkh 169 H 3
Balkhab 169 H 3
Balkhash 159 O 6
Balkhash, Ozero 159 OP 6
Balladonia 182 C 5
Ballangen 150 G 2
Ballantine (MT.) 111 R 5
Ballantrae 148 C 3
Ballarat 183 G 6
Ballard, Lake 182 C 4
Ballé 196 C 3
Ballenas, Bahía 106 D 6
Ballenita, Punta 142 B 4
Balleny Islands 203
Ballia 174 D 2
Ballina (Australia) 183 J 4
Ballina (Rep. of Ireland) 148 B 4
Ballinger (TX.) 122 D 4
Ballinrobe 148 B 4

Balls Pyramid 183 K 5
Ballston Spa (N.Y.) 126 F 6
Balltown (IA.) 119 S 8
Ballyhaunis 148 B 4
Balmoral Castle 148 C 3
Balmorhea (TX.) 117 N 6-7
Balneario Claromecó 143 DE 6
Balombo 200 AB 2
Balonne River 183 H 4
Balotra 174 B 2
Balovale 200 C 2
Bal Qaf 193 J 3
Balrampur 174 D 2
Balranald 183 G 5
Bals 154 B 2
Balsas 139 J 5
Balsas (Maranhão, Brazil) 141 G 2
Balsas (Maranhão, Brazil) 141 G 2
Balsas (Mexico) 132 C 4
Balsas, Rio 132 B 4
Bålsta 151 C 4
Balta 154 C 1
Balta Brăilei 154 C 1–2
Balta Ialomiţei 154 C 2
Baltasar Brum 142 E 5
Baltaţi 154 C 1
Baltic (S.D.) 119 M 7
Baltic Sea 151 GH 4
Baltim 194 E 2
Baltimore (MD.) 129 P 2
Baltimore (OH.) 128 J 2
Baltimore (South Africa) 200 D 4
Baltiskaja Grjada 151 HJ 4–5
Baltistan 169 K 3
Baltiysk 151 H 5
Baluchistan 168–169 FG 5
Balurghat 174 E 2
Balvard (Iran) 157 G 3
Balvi 151 J 4
Balya 154 C 3
Balygychan 171 S 3
Balyksa 159 R 5
Bam 168 F 5
Bama 197 G 3
Bamaga 183 G 1
Bamako 196 C 3
Bāmbā (Libya) 193 K 2
Bamba (Mali) 196 D 2
Bamba (Zaire) 198 B 6
Bambafouga 196 B 3
Bambama 197 G 6
Bambamarca 138 C 5
Bambangando 200 C 3
Bambari 198 C 3
Bambaroo 183 H 2
Bamberg 149 F 5
Bamberg (SC.) 129 K 8
Bambesa 198 D 4
Bambesi 198 E 3
Bambey 196 A 3
Bambio 198 B 4
Bamboi 196 D 4
Bambouti 198 D 3
Bambouto, Monts 197 G 4
Bamenda 197 G 4
Bami 168 F 2
Bamingui 198 B 3
Bamingui 198 C 3
Bamingui-Bangoran, Parc National du 198 BC 3
Bamiyan 169 H 4
Bam Posht 169 G 5
Bampūr 169 G 5
Banaadir 199 GH 4
Banaba 185 J 2
Banaba 186 C 3
Bañados de Izozog 140 D 4
Banagi 198 EF 5
Banalia 198 D 4
Banamba 196 C 3
Banana 183 J 3
Banana Islands 196 B 4
Bananal, Ilha do 141 F 3
Bananga 175 F 6
Banas 174 C 2
Banās, Ra's (Egypt) 156 B 5
Banat 154 B 1
Banaz 154 C 3
Ban Ban 175 H 4
Banbar 172 B 4
Banc du Geyser 201 H 2
Banco Chinchorro 132 E 4
Banco de Serrana 133 G 5
Banco Quitasueño 133 F 5
Bancoran 177 E 2
Banco Serranilla 133 G 4
Bancroft 105 M 6
Bancroft (ID.) 111 O 8
Bancroft (NE.) 119 M 8
Banda 174 D 2
Banda 174 C 3
Banda, Kepulauan 177 G 4
Banda, Laut 177 G 5
Banda Aceh 176 A 2
Banda del Río Sali 142 D 4
Banda Elat 177 H 5
Bandahara, Gunung 176 A 3
Bandama 196 C 3
Bandama Blanc 196 C 4
Bandan Kūh 169 G 4

Bandar Abbas (Iran) 157 G 4
Bandarban 175 F 3
Bandar-e-Anzalī 168 DE 3
Bandar-e Chārak (Iran) 157 G 4
Bandar-e Chāru (Iran) 157 FG 4
Bandar-e Deylam (Iran) 157 F 3
Bandar-e Gaz (Iran) 157 F 1
Bandar-e Khomeynī (Iran) 157 E 3
Bandar-e Lengeh (Iran) 157 G 4
Bandar-e Māh Shahr (Iran) 157 E 3
Bandar-e Māqām (Iran) 157 F 4
Bandar-e Moghūyeh (Iran) 157 FG 4
Bandar-e Rig (Iran) 157 F 3
Bandar-e Shahpur → Bandar-e Khomeyni 168 D 4
Bandar-e Torkeman (Iran) 157 G 1
Bandarlampung 176 C 5
Bandar Ma'shur (Iran) 157 E 3
Bandarpunch 174 C 1
Bandar Seri Begawan 176 D 3
Bandar Shāh (Iran) 157 E 1
Banda Sea 177 G 5
Bandau 176 E 2
Band Boni 168 F 5
Bandeira 141 H 5
Bandeirante 141 F 3
Bandera 142 D 4
Bandera (TX.) 122 D 6
Bandiagara 196 D 3
Band-i-Amir 169 H 3
Band-i-Baba 169 G 4
Band-i-Baian 169 H 4
Bandırma 154 C 2
Band-i-Turkestan 169 GH 3
Ban Don 175 J 5
Bandon (OR.) 110 A 7
Band Qīr (Iran) 157 E 3
Bandundu 198 B 5
Bandundu 198 B 5
Bandung 176 C 5
Baneh (Iran) 157 D 2
Banemo 177 G 3
Banes 133 G 3
Banff 103 O 5
Banff (U.K.) 148 C 3
Banff National Park 103 O 5
Banfora 196 CD 3
Banga 198 C 6
Bangadi 198 D 4
Banganté 197 G 4
Bangar 176 E 3
Bangassou 198 C 4
Bangeta, Mount 184 E 3
Banggai 177 F 4
Banggai, Kepulauan 177 F 4
Banggi 176 E 2
Banggong Co 174 CD 1
Bang Hieng 175 J 4
Bangka, Pulau 176 C 4
Bangka, Selat 176 C 4
Bangkalan 176 D 5
Bangkaru, Pulau 176 A 3
Bangko 176 B 4
Bangkok 175 H 5
Bangkok, Bight of 175 H 5
Bangladesh 175 F 3
Bang Mun Nak 175 H 4
Bangor (ME.) 126 L 4
Bangor (MI.) 124 H 7
Bangor (N. Ireland, U.K.) 148 B 4
Bangor (Wales, U.K.) 148 C 4
Bangs (TX.) 122 D 4
Bangs, Mount 116 C 1
Bang Saphan Yai 175 GH 5
Bangsund 150 F 3
Bangui 198 B 4
Bangui (Philippines) 177 J 1
Banguru 198 D 4
Bangweulu Swamps 200 D 2
Banhã 194 E 2
Banhine National Park 201 E 4
Banī 133 H 4
Bani 196 C 3
Baniara 185 E 3
Bani Bangou 196 E 2–3
Banī Forūr (Iran) 157 G 4
Banihal Pass 169 K 4
Banī Ma'ārid 195 H 5
Banī Mazār 194 E 3
Banī Suwayf 194 E 3
Banī Tonb (Iran) 157 G 4
Banī Walīd 193 H 2
Bāniyās (Golan Heights) 156 B 2
Bāniyās (Lebanon) 156 B 2
Bāniyās (Syria) 156 B 2
Banja Koviljača 153 G 3
Banja Luka 153 G 3
Banjul 196 A 3
Banka 174 E 3
Bankas 196 D 3
Bankeryd 151 F 4
Banket 201 E 3
Ban Kniet 175 J 5
Banks (ID.) 110 J 6
Banks (ID.) 110 J 6
Banks Island (Br. Col., Can.) 102 L 5

Banks Island (Canada) 103 N 1
Banks Island (Queensland, Austr.) 183 G 1
Banks Islands (Vanuatu) 185 J 4
Banks Islands (Vanuatu) 186 C 3
Banks Lake 110 F 3
Banks Lake 131 L 3
Banks Peninsula 185 Q 9
Banks Strait 184 L 9
Bankura 174 E 3
Banmauk 175 G 3
Ban Me Thuot 175 J 5
Bann 148 B 3–4
Ban Nabo 175 J 4
Ban Ngon 175 H 4
Banning (CA.) 113 J 9
Bannock Range 111 N 8
Bannu 169 J 4
Bāno 150 G 2
Ban Sao 175 H 4
Bansi 174 D 2
Banská Bystrica 149 G 5
Ban Sop Huai Hai 175 G 4
Banswara 174 B 3
Bantaeng 177 E 5
Ban Taup 175 J 4
Bantry 148 B 4
Bantry (ND.) 118 H 2
Bantry Bay 148 AB 4
Banu 169 H 3
Banyo 197 G 4
Banyuls-sur-Mer 152 D 3
Banyuwangi 176 D 5
Banzare Coast 203
Bao Bilia 197 J 2
Baode 172 F 3
Baodi 173 G 3
Baoding 172 G 3
Baofeng 172 F 4
Bao Ha 175 H 3
Baoji 172 E 4
Bao Loc 175 J 5
Baoqing 173 K 1
Baoro 198 B 3
Baoshan 172 C 5
Baotou 172 E 2
Baoulé 192 D 6
Baoulé 196 C 3
Baoxing 172 D 4
Baoying 173 G 4
Bap 174 B 2
Bapatla 174 D 4
Baqam (Iran) 157 F 2
Baqen 172 B 4
Bāqerābād (Iran) 157 F 2
Ba' qūbah (Iraq) 157 D 2
Baquedano 140 C 5
Bar 154 A 2
Bara 197 G 3
Barabai 176 E 4
Bara Banki 174 D 2
Barabinsk 159 P 4
Barabinskaya Step' 159 P 5
Baraboo (WI.) 124 E 6
Baracaldo 152 C 3
Baragoi 199 F 4
Bārah 194 E 6
Barahona 133 H 4
Barail Range 175 F 2
Baraka 199 F 1
Barakāt 194 E 6
Barakkul' 159 N 5
Baram 176 D 3
Baramanni 139 G 2
Baramula 169 J 4
Baran 174 C 2
Baran (U.S.S.R.) 151 K 5
Barangbarang 177 F 5
Barani 196 D 3
Baranikha, Malaya 171 V 2
Baranoa 138 C 1
Baranof 102 K 4
Baranovichi 151 J 5
Baranovka 158 J 3
Barão de Capanema 140 E 3
Barão de Melgaco 140 D 3
Barão de Melgaço 140 E 4
Barapasi 177 J 4
Baratang 175 F 5
Barataria (LA.) 123 N 6
Barati 177 F 5
Baraunda 174 D 2
Barāwe 199 G 4
Barbacena 141 H 5
Barbacoas 138 C 3
Barbados 133 K 5
Barbar 194 E 5
Bárbara 138 D 4
Barbas, Cabo 192 B 4
Barbastro 152 D 3
Barbate de Franco 152 B 4
Barber (MT.) 111 Q 4
Barbers Point 113 D 10
Barberton (OH.) 125 N 8
Barberton (South Africa) 201 E 5
Barberville (FL.) 131 N 5
Barbezieux 152 C 2

Barbosa 138 D 2
Barboursville (W.V.) 129 J 3
Barbourville (KY.) 128 H 5
Barbuda 133 K 4
Barcaldine 183 H 3
Barce → Al Marj 193 K 2
Barcellona 153 FG 4
Barcelona 139 F 2
Barcelona (Spain) 152 D 3
Barcelonette 153 E 3
Barcelos 139 F 4
Barco (N.C.) 129 Q 5
Barcoo or Cooper Creek 183 F 4
Barcoo River 183 G 3
Barcoo River 183 H 3
Barda del Medio 143 C 6
Bardaï 197 H 1
Bardejov 149 H 5
Bārdēre 199 G 4
Bardeskan 168 F 3
Bardonecchia 153 E 2
Bardsey 148 BC 4
Bardwell (KY.) 128 C 5
Bardwell Lake 122 G 3
Barēda 199 J 2
Bareilly 174 CD 2
Bare Mountain 110 C 5
Barentsovo More 158 GJ 1
Barents Sea 158 GH 2
Barents Sea 202
Barentu 199 F 1
Barfleur, Pointe de 152 C 2
Bārga 150 G 2
Barga 193 D 1
Bārgāl 199 J 2
Barganshahr (Iran) 157 E 3
Bargarh 174 D 3
Barguzin 170 J 5
Barguzinskiy Khrebet 170 JK 4–5
Barhaj 174 D 2
Barhau 176 B 5
Bari 153 G 3
Bari, Mola di 153 G 3
Bari, Terra di 153 G 3
Baria 138 E 3
Barīdī, Ra's (Saudi Arabia) 156 B 4
Barikiwa 199 F 6
Barīm 195 G 6
Barinas 138 DE 2
Baring, Cape 103 O 2
Baringo, Lake 199 F 4
Baripada 174 E 3
Bariri 141 G 5
Bariri, Reprêsa 141 G 5
Bārīs 194 E 4
Bari Sadri 174 B 3
Barisal 175 F 3
Barisan, Pegunungan 176 B 4
Barito, Sungai 176 D 4
Barkā' 195 K 4
Barkam 172 D 4
Barkan, Ra's-e (Iran) 157 E 3
Barker Heights (N.C.) 128 J 6
Barkhamsted Reservoir 126 G 7
Barkley, Lake 128 D 5
Barkly East 200 D 6
Barkly Tableland 183 F 2
Barkly West 200 C 5
Barkol Kazak Zizhixian 172 B 2
Bark Point 124 C 3
Barksdale (TX.) 122 CD 6
Barladağı 154 D 3
Bar-le-Duc 153 DE 2
Barlee, Lake 182 B 3
Barlee Range 182 B 3
Barletta 153 G 3
Barlow Pass 110 D 5
Barma 177 H 4
Barmer 174 B 2
Barmera 183 G 5
Barnard (KS.) 120 GH 3
Barnaul 159 Q 5
Barnegat (N.J.) 127 E 9
Barnes Ice Cap 105 N 1–2
Barnesville (GA.) 128 G 8
Barnesville (MN.) 119 M 4
Barnesville (OH.) 129 K 2
Barnhart (TX.) 117 P 6
Barnsdall (OK.) 120 J 6
Barnstaple 148 C 4
Barnwell (S.C.) 129 K 8
Baro (Ethiopia) 198 E 3
Baro (Nigeria) 197 F 4
Baroda → Vadodara 174 B 3
Barong 172 C 4
Barotseland 200 C 3
Barouéli 196 C 3
Barq al Bishārīyīn 194 E 5
Barquisimeto 138 DE 1
Barra 148 B 3
Barra (Bahía, Brazil) 141 H 3
Barraba 183 J 4
Barracão do Barreto 139 G 5
Barra da Estiva 141 H 3
Barra do Corda 141 G 2
Barra do Dande 200 A 1
Barra do Garças 141 F 4
Barra do Ribeiro 142 F 5
Barra do São Manuel 139 G 5

Barra dos Coqueiros 141 J 3
Barragem da Rocha de Galé 152 B 4
Barragem de Alqueva 152 B 4
Barragem de Sobradinho 141 H 3
Barra Head 148 B 3
Barranca (Peru) 138 C 4
Barranca (Peru) 138 C 6
Barrancabermeja 138 D 2
Barrancas 139 F 2
Barranqueras 142 E 4
Barranquilla 138 C 1
Barranquitas (P.R.) 130 C 8
Barra Patuca 132 F 4
Barraute 105 M 6
Barre (VT.) 126 G 4
Barreiras 141 H 3
Barreirinha 139 G 4
Barreirinhas 141 H 1
Barreiro 152 B 4
Barreiros 141 JK 2
Barren 175 F 5
Barren Island, Cape 185 L 9
Barren Islands 102 G 4
Barrenitos 132 B 2
Barren Lands 103 QS 2
Barren River Lake 128 E 5
Barretos 141 G 5
Barrhead 103 P 5
Barrie 105 LM 7
Barr Lake 115 N 4
Barrocão 141 H 4
Barrow (AK., U.S.A.) 102 F 1
Barrow (Argentina) 143 DE 6
Barrow (Rep. of Ireland) 148 B 4
Barrow, Point 102 F 1
Barrow Creek 182 E 3
Barrow-in-Furness 148 C 4
Barrow Island 182 A 3
Barrow Range 182 D 4
Barry 148 C 4
Barry (IL.) 121 P 3
Barryton (MI.) 124 J 6
Barsa-Kel'mes, Ostrov 168 F 1
Barsi 174 C 4
Barstow (CA.) 113 HJ 8
Barstow (TX.) 117 N 6
Bar-sur-Aube 153 D 2
Bartallah (Iraq) 156 D 1
Bartazuga, Jabal 194 E 4
Bartibougou 196 E 3
Bartica 139 G 2
Bartın 155 D 2
Bartlesville (OK.) 120 JK 6
Bartlett (CA.) 112 G 6
Bartlett (NE.) 119 K 9
Bartlett (TX.) 122 F 5
Bartow (FL.) 131 N 7 131 N 7
Bartow (GA.) 131 M 2
Barú, Volcán 138 B 2
Bāruni 174 E 2
Baruun Urt 172 F 1
Barwa 174 D 3
Barwani 174 B 3
Barwon River 183 H 4
Barycz 149 G 4
Barzas 159 R 4
Barylas 171 O 2
Barzūk (Iran) 157 F 2
Bāsa'īdū (Iran) 157 G 4
Basalt (CO.) 115 L 4
Basankusu 198 BC 4
Basauri 152 C 3
Basekpio 198 CD 4
Basel 153 E 2
Bashi Haixia 173 H 6
Bashkend 155 G 2
Basian 177 F 4
Basilan 177 F 2
Basilan City 177 F 2
Basile (LA.) 123 L 5
Basílio 142 F 5
Basin (MT.) 111 N 4
Basin (WY.) 111 R 6
Basingstoke 148 CD 4
Baskahegan Lake 126 M 3
Başkale 155 F 3
Baskatong, Réservoir 105 MN 6
Baskil 155 E 3
Basmat 174 C 4
Baso, Pulau 176 B 4
Basoko 198 D 4
Basongo 198 C 5
Basra (Iraq) 157 E 3
Bassano del Grappa 153 F 2
Bassari 196 E 4
Bassas da India 201 F 4
Bassein 175 F 2
Bassein → Vasai 174 B 4
Basse Santa Su 196 B 3
Basse-Terre (Guadeloupe) 107 K 4
Basse Terre (Saint Kitts-Nevis) 133 K 4
Bassett (NE.) 118 J 8
Bassett (VA.) 129 M 5
Bassfield (MS.) 130 E 3
Bassikounou 192 D 5
Bassila 196 E 4
Bassinde Rennes 152 CD 2
Bassin de Thau 152 D 3
Bass Lake (CA.) 112 F 5

Basso, Plateau de 197 J 2
Bass Strait 184 L 8
Basswood Lake 119 R 2
Båstad 151 F 4
Bastak (Iran) 157 G 4
Bastam (Iran) 157 G 1
B. A. Steinhagen Reservoir 123 J 5
Bastevarri 150 H 2
Basti 174 D 2
Bastia 153 E 3
Basto, Terra de 152 B 3
Bastrop (LA.) 123 M 3
Bastrop (TX.) 122 F 5
Bastuträsk 150 G 3
Basuto 200 D 3
Baswa 174 C 2
Bata 197 F 5
Batabano, Golfo del 132–133 F 3
Batagay 171 OP 2
Batagay-Alyta 171 O 2
Batai, Gunung 176 BC 5
Bataklık Gölü 155 D 3
Batala 174 BC 1
Batam, Pulau 176 B 3
Batama (U.S.S.R.) 170 H 5
Batama (Zaire) 198 D 4
Batamay 171 N 3
Batamshinskiy 159 L 5
Batang 172 C 4
Batang (Indonesia) 176 C 5
Batang Hari 176 B 4
Batan Islands 173 H 6
Batanta, Pulau 177 H 4
Batara 198 B 3
Batangafo 198 B 3
Batangas 177 F 1
Batanga 197 F 6
Bataysk 155 EF 1
Batchawana Mountain 104 L 6
Batchelor 182 E 1
Batemans Bay 183 J 6
Bateria, Cachoeira da 139 G 3
Bates (OR.) 110 G 6
Batesburg (S.C.) 129 K 8
Batesland (SD.) 118 FG 7
Batesville (AR.) 121 O 7
Batesville (MS.) 121 Q 8
Batesville (TX.) 122 D 6—7
Bath (ME.) 126 K 5
Bath (N.Y.) 126 B 6
Bath (U.K.) 148 C D 4
Batha 197 H 3
Batha 197 H 3
Bathalha 152 B 4
Bathgate (N.D.) 119 L 2
Bathurst (Canada) 105 O 6
Bathurst (N.S.W., Austr.) 183 H 5
Bathurst, Cape 102 LM 1
Bathurst → Banjul 196 A 3
Bathurst Inlet 103 Q 2
Bathurst Island (N.T., Austr.)
    182 D 1
Bathurst Island (The Arctic) 202
Batié 196 D 4
Batie 199 G 2
Bātin, Wādi al (Iraq) 157 E 3
Batkanu 196 B 4
Bātlāq-e Gavkhūnī (Iran) 157 F 2
Batman 155 F 3
Batman 155 F 3
Batna 193 G 1
Batn al Hajar 194 E 4
Batoka 200 D 3
Batomga 171 P 4
Baton Rouge (LA.) 123 M 5
Batopilas 106 E 6
Batouri 197 G 5
Batrā, Jabal (Saudi Arabia) 156 B 4
Båtsfjord 150 J 1
Battambang 175 H 5
Batticaloa 174 D 6
Batti Malv 175 F 6
Battinga 198 C 3
Battle 103 P 5
Battle Creek (MI.) 124 J 7
Battle Creek (NE.) 119 L 9
Battle Ground (WA.) 110 C 5
Battle Lake (MN.) 119 N 4
Battlement Mesa 115 JK 4
Battle Mountain (NV.) 112 H 2
Batu 199 F 3
Batui 177 F 4
Batulantee, Gunung 176 E 5
Batumi 155 F 2
Batu Pahat 176 B 3
Batu Puteh, Gunung 176 B 3
Batuputih 177 E 3
Baturaja 176 B 4
Baturino 159 R 4
Baturinskaya 155 E 1
Baturité 141 J 1
Bau 176 D 3
Baucau 177 G 5
Bauchi 197 F 3
Bauchi Plateau 197 FG 3–4

Baud 152 C 2
Baudette (MN.) 119 O 2
Baudo 138 C 2
Baudó, Serranía de 138 C 2
Bauhinia Downs 183 H 3
Baula 177 F 4
Bauld, Cape 105 Q 5
Baunei 153 E 3
Baunt 170 K 4
Bauple 183 J 4
Baures 140 D 3
Bauru 141 G 5
Baús 141 F 4
Bauska 151 H 4
Bautzen 149 F 4
Bavaria 149 F 5
Bāw 194 E 6
Bawdwin 175 G 3
Bawean, Pulau 176 D 5
Bawku 196 D 3
Bawmi 175 F 4
Bawn 199 G 2
Ba Xian 172 E 5
Ba Xian 173 G 3
Baxley (GA.) 131 M 3
Baxoi 172 C 4
Baxter (IA.) 119 P 9
Baxter (ND.) 118 E 4
Baxter Springs (KS.) 121 L 5—6
Bay (AR.) 121 P 7
Bayamo 133 G 3
Bayamón (P.R.) 130 C 8
Bayan 170 J 6
Bayana 174 C 2
Bayan-Adraga 170 K 6
Bayan-Agt 170 H 6
Bayan-Aul 159 P 5
Bayanbaraat 172 E 1
Bayanbulag 170 G 6
Bayanbulak 169 L 2
Bayanchandman 170 J 6
Bayandalay 172 D 2
Bayanday 170 J 5
Bayandzurh 170 J 6
Bayanga 198 B 4
Bayangol 170 H J 5
Bayan Har Shan 172 CD 4
Bayan Har Shankou 172 C 4
Bayanhongor 170 H 6
Bayan Mod 172 D 2
Bayanmönh 172 E 1
Bayan Obo 172 E 2
Bayan-Öndör 172 D 1
Bayan-Öndör 172 C 2
Bayantsagaan 172 E 1
Bayantsogt 170 J 6
Bayan-Uul 170 G 6
Bayan-Uul 170 K 6
Bayard (IA.) 119 O 9
Bayard (NE.) 118 E 9
Bayat 155 D 2
Bayāz (Iran) 157 G 3
Bayāzeh (Iran) 157 G 2
Bayboro (N.C.) 129 P 6
Bayburt 155 F 2
Bay Center (WA.) 110 B 4
Baychunas 168 E 1
Bay City (MI.) 125 L 6
Bay City (OR.) 110 B 5
Bay City (TX.) 122 GH 7
Baydaratskaya Guba 159 N 2
Bay de Verde 105 R 6
Baydrag Gol 170 G 6
Bayerischer Wald 149 F 5
Bayern 149 F 5
Bayeux 152 C 2
Bayfield (CO.) 115 K 6
Bayfield (WI.) 124 D 3
Bayhān al Qisāb 195 H 6
Bayındır 154 C 3
Bayjī (Iraq) 156 D 2
Baykal 170 H 5
Baykal, Ozero 170 J 5
Baykalovo 159 N 4
Baykal'skiy Khrebet 170 J 4–5
Baykal'skoye 170 JK 4
Baykal'skoye Nagor'ye, Severo 170 K 4
Baykan 155 F 3
Bay-Khak 170 F 5
Baykit 170 G 3
Baykitskiy 170 G 3
Baykonur 169 H 1
Bay Lorne 183 G 6
Baymak 159 L 5
Bay Minette (AL.) 130 G 4
Baynūnah (United Arab Emirates)
    157 F 5
Bay of Bengal 174–175 EF 4
Bay of Biscay 152 C 2–3
Bay of Fundy 105 O 6–7
Bay of Gods Mercy 103 U 3
Bay of Islands 105 Q 6
Bay of Plenty 185 R 8
Bay of Plenty 186 C 5
Bayombong 177 J 1
Bayonne 152 C 3
Bayo Nuevo 133 G 4
Bayou D'Arbonne Lake 123 L 3

Bayou La Batre (AL.) 130 F 4
Bayovar 138 B 5
Bayport (FL.) 131 M 6
Bay Port (MI.) 125 L 6
Bayram-Ali 169 G 3
Bayramiç 154 C 3
Bayreuth 149 E 4
Bayrūt (Lebanon) 156 B 2
Baysa 170 K 5
Bay Saint Louis (MS.) 130 E 4
Bay Springs (MS.) 130 E 3
Bay-Syut 170 G 5
Bayt al Faqīh 195 G 6
Baytik Shan 169 N 1
Bayt Lahm (Israel) 156 B 3
Baytown (TX.) 123 HJ 6
Bayunglincir 176 B 4
Bayview (ID.) 110 J 3
Bayy al Kabīr, Wādī 193 H 2
Bayyūdah, Sahrā' 194 E 5
Baza 152 C 4
Bazar Dyuzi, Gora 168 D 2
Bazarnyy Syzgan 158 J 5
Bazaruto National Park 201 F 4
Bazhong 172 E 4
Bazine (KS.) 120 F 4
Baztán 152 C 3
B Bua Chum 175 H 4
Beach (ND.) 118 E 4
Beach 182 B 5
Beacon (N.Y.) 126 F 7
Beafort (NC.) 129 P 7
Beagle (KS.) 121 L 4
Beagle, Canal 143 C 9
Beagle Bay 182 C 2
Beagle Gulf 182 DE 1
Bealanana 201 H 2
Beal Range 183 G 4
Beampingaratra 201 H 4
Bear Cape 105 P 6
Bearden (AR.) 121 N 9
Bear Island 202
Bear Lake 111 O 8–9
Bear Lodge Mountains 118 CD 6
Bear Mountain 116 H 4
Bearpaw Mountains 111 Q 2
Bear Peak 111 Q 7
Bear River 111 O 8
Bears Ears 114 H 6
Bearskin Lake 104 J 5
Beartooth Mountains 111 PQ 5
Beartooth Pass 111 Q 6
Bearwallow Mountain 116 H 4
Beas 174 C 1
Beas de Segura 152 C 4
Beata, Cabo 133 H 4
Beatrice (AL.) 130 G 3
Beatrice (NE.) 120 J 2
Beatrice, Cape 183 F 1
Beattie (NE.) 120 J 3
Beatton 103 N 4
Beatton River 103 N 4
Beatty (NV.) 112 J 5
Beatty (OR.) 110 D 8
Beattyville 105 M 6
Beattyville (KY.) 128 H 4
Beau-Bassin 201 K 6
Beaucaire 153 D 3
Beaucanton 105 M 6
Beaufort 176 E 2
Beaufort (S.C.) 129 L 9
Beaufort (S.C.) 131 M 3
Beaufort Sea 102 JL 1
Beaufort West 200 C 6
Beaujolais, Monts du 153 D 2
Beaulieu (MN.) 119 N 3
Beaumont (France) 152 C 2
Beaumont (KS.) 120 J 5
Beaumont (MS.) 130 F 3
Beaumont (TX.) 123 J 5
Beaune 153 DE 2
Beaupré 105 N 6
Beausejour 103 S 5
Beauvais 152 D 2
Beaver (AK, U.S.A.) 102 H 2
Beaver (KS.) 120 G 4
Beaver (OK.) 120 E 6
Beaver (PA.) 125 O 9
Beaver (Sask., Can.)103 Q 5
Beaver (UT.) 114 E 5
Beaver City (NE.) 120 F 2
Beaver Creek 120 EF 2
Beaver Dam (WI.) 124 F 6
Beaverdam Lake 124 F 6
Beaver Falls (PA.) 125 N 9
Beaverhead Mountains 111 M 5–6
Beaver Island 124 J 4
Beaver Lake (AR.) 121 M 6
Beaver Mountains 108 G 3
Beaverton (MI.) 125 K 6
Beaverton (OR.) 110 C 5
Beawar 174 B 2
Beazley 142 C 5
Bebedouro 141 G 5
Beberibe 141 J 1
Becan 132 E 4
Bečej 154 B 1
Becerreá 152 B 3
Béchar 192 E 2
Becharof Lake 102 F 4

Becharof National Monument 102 F 4
Bechevin Bay 102 E 4
Becker (MN.) 119 P 5
Beckley (W.V.) 129 K 4
Beckum 149 E 4
Beckwourth Pass 112 E 3
Becky Peak 112 L 3
Bedeli 199 F 3
Bedford (IA.) 119 O 10
Bedford (IN.) 128 E 3
Bedford (KY.) 128 F 3
Bedford (OH.) 125 N 8
Bedford (PA.) 125 Q 10
Bedford (U.K.) 148 C 4
Bedford (VA.) 129 M 4
Bedford (WY.) 111 P 8
Bedias (TX.) 122 H 5
Bedirli 155 E 3
Bednodem'yanovsk 158 H 5
Bedoba 170 G 4
Bedourie 183 F 3
Bedrock (CO.) 114 J 5
Beebe (AR.) 121 O 7
Beecher (MI.) 125 L 6
Beecher Falls (N.H.) 126 H 4
Beech Grove (IN.) 128 E 2
Beecroft Head 183 J 5–6
Beef Island 130 E 8
Beeler (KS.) 120 E 4
Beemer (NE.) 119 M 9
Beenleigh 183 J 4
Beetaloo 182 E 2
Beeville (TX.) 122 F 7
Befale 201 H 2
Befandriana 201 H 4
Befandriana 201 G 4
Bega 183 H 6
Begambanj 175 F 3
Begejski Kanal 154 B 1
Beggs (OK.) 120 J 7
Bègle 152 C 3
Begna 151 E 3
Begoml'(U.S.S.R.) 151 J 5
Behābād (Iran) 157 G 3
Behbehān (Iran) 157 EF 3
Behleg 172 B 3
Behshar (Iran) 157 F 1
Bei'an 171 N 6
Beibu Wan 175 J 3
Beichuan 172 D 4
Beida 193 K 2
Beihai 172 E 6
Bei Hulsan Hu 172 C 3
Beijing 173 G 3
Beiliu 172 F 6
Beilu Heyan 172 B 4
Beilul 199 G 2
Beïnamar 197 H 4
Beipiao 173 H 2
Beira 201 EF 3
Beirut (Lebanon) 156 B 2
Bei Shan 172 C 2
Beishan 172 E 4
Beizhen 173 H 2
Beizhen 173 G 3
Beja 139 J 4
Beja 152 B 4
Bejaïa 193 F 1
Beji 169 H 5
Béjar 152 B 3
Bekabad 169 H 2
Bekasi 176 C 5
Bekdash 168 E 2
Békéscsaba 154 B 1
Bekily 201 H 4
Bekodoka 201 H 3
Bekopaka 201 G 3
Bekwai 196 D 4
Bela 169 H 5
Bela 174 D 2
Béla Bérim 197 G 2
Bélabo 197 G 5
Bela Crkva 154 B 2
Bela Dila 174 D 4
Belaga 170 D 3
Bel'Agach 159 Q 5
Belaia Sancai 198 F 2
Bel Air (MD.) 129 P 2
Belaka 198 C 5
Belang 177 FG 3
Bela Polanka 154 B 2
Belau 177 H 2
Belawan 176 A 3
Belaya 158 K 4
Belaya 170 J 5
Belaya (U.S.S.R.) 155 F 2
Belaya, Gora 108 A 2
Belaya Glina 155 F 1
Belaya Kalitva 155 F 1
Belaya Tserkov 158 F 6

Belcher Islands 105 L 4
Belcik 155 E 3
Belczyna 149 G 4
Belden (ND.) 118 F 2
Belding (MI.) 124 J 6
Belding (TX.) 117 NO 7
Belebey 158 K 5
Beled Wēyne 199 H 4
Belem (Amazonas, Brazil) 138 E 4
Belem (Mexico) 106 D 6
Belem (Mozambique) 201 F 2
Belém (Pará, Brazil) 139 J 4
Belém de São Francisco 141 J 2
Belén (Argentina) 142 C 4
Belén (Colombia) 138 C 3
Belen (N.M.) 117 K 3
Belén (Paraguay) 140 E 5
Belep, Îles 186 B 4
Beleuli 168 F 2
Belfast 148 B 4
Belfield (ND.) 118 E 4
Belfort 153 E 2
Belfry (MT.) 111 R 5
Belgaum 174 B 4
Belgium 148 DE 4
Belgorod 158 G 5
Belgorod-Dnestrovskiy 154 CD 1
Belgrade 154 B 2
Belgrade (MN.) 119 O 5
Belgrade (MT.) 111 O 5
Belgrade (NE.) 120 GH 1
Bel Guerdane 192 C 3
Bel Haïrane 193 G 2
Belhaven (N.C.) 129 P 6
Beli 197 G 3
Beli Drim 154 B 2
Belikh (Syria) 156 C 1
Beli Manastir 153 G 2
Belimbing 176 B 5
Belin 152 C 3
Belinga 197 G 5
Belingwe → Mberengwa 200 D 4
Belinskiy 158 H 5
Belinyu 176 C 4
Beliot (WI.) 124 F 7
Belitung, Pulau 176 C 4
Belize 132 E 4
Belize City 132 E 4
Belize River 132 E 4
Bélizon 139 H 3
Beljanica 154 B 2
Bel'kachi 171 O 4
Belknap (MT.) 111 K 3
Belkofski 108 F 4
Bell 105 M 6
Bell (FL.) 131 M 5
Bell (N.M.) 117 M 1
Bella Bella 103 M 5
Bellac 152 D 2
Bellaco 142 E 5
Bella Coola 103 M 5
Bellaire (MI.) 124 J 5
Bellaire (OH.) 125 O 9
Bellaire (TX.) 123 H 6
Bellamy (AL.) 130 F 2
Bellamy (VA.) 129 P 4
Bellary 174 C 4
Bella Vista (Argentina) 142 E 4
Bella Vista (CA.) 112 C 2
Bellavista (Peru) 138 C 4
Bellavista (Peru) 138 C 5
Bell Bay 104 L 1
Bellbrook 183 J 5
Bell City (LA.) 123 KL 5
Belle (MO.) 121 O 4
Bellefontaine (MS.) 121 Q 9
Bellefontaine (OH.) 125 L 9
Bellefonte (PA.) 127 B 8
Belle Fourche (SD.) 118 E 6
Belle Fourche Reservoir 118 E 6
Belle Fourche River 118 EF 6
Bellegarde 153 E 2
Belle Glade (FL.) 131 O 8
Belle Ile 152 C 2
Belle Isle (FL.) 131 N 6
Belle Isle 105 QR 5
Belle Isle, Strait of 105 Q 5
Belle Plain (KS.) 120 H 5
Belle Plaine (IA.) 119 Q 9
Belle Plaine (MN.) 119 P 6
Belleview (FL.) 131 MN 5
Belleville (France) 153 DE 2
Belleville (IL.) 121 Q 4
Belleville (KS.) 120 H 3
Belleville (Ontario, Can.) 105 M 7
Bellevue (IA.) 119 S 8
Bellevue (ID.) 111 L 7
Bellevue (MI.) 124 J 7
Bellevue (OH.) 125 M 8
Bellevue (TX.) 122 EF 2
Bellevue (WA.) 110 C 3
Belley 153 E 2
Belle Yella 196 B 4
Bellin 105 N 3
Bellingen 183 J 5
Bellingham (WA.) 110 C 2
Bellingshausen 203
Bellingshausen Sea 203
Bellinzona 153 E 2

Bellmead (TX.) 122 F 4
Bello 138 C 2
Bellona 185 G 4
Bellot Strait 103 T 1
Bellows Falls (VT.) 126 G 5
Bell Peninsula 103 V 3
Bell Ranch (N.M.) 117 M 2
Bell River 109 L 2
Bells (TN.) 128 B 6
Bells (TX.) 122 G 2
Belluno 153 F 2
Bell Ville 142 D 5
Bellville (OH.) 125 M 9
Bellville (TX.) 122 G 6
Bellvue (CO.) 115 M 3
Bellwood (NE.) 120 H 1
Bellyk 170 F 5
Belmond (IA.) 119 P 8
Belmont (MS.) 121 R 8
Belmont (MT.) 111 R 4
Belmont (N.Y.) 126 B 6
Belmont (WI.) 124 D 7
Belmonte 141 J 4
Belmonte (Portugal) 152 B 3
Belmonte (Spain) 152 C 4
Belmopan 132 E 4
Belmonte 152 C 4
Belogolovoye 171 T 4
Belogorsk 155 D 2
Belogorsk (U.S.S.R.) 171 N 5
Belogor'ye 159 N 3
Belogradčik 154 B 2
Belo Horizonte (Minas Gerais, Brazil)
  141 H 4
Belo Horizonte (Pará, Brazil) 139 H 5
Beloit (KS.) 120 GH 3
Belo Jardim 141 J 2
Belokholunitskiy 158 K 4
Belo Monta 139 H 4
Belomorsk 150 K 3
Belopol'ye 158 F 5
Belorechensk 155 F 2
Beloretsk 159 L 5
Belorussiya 151 J 5
Belorusskaya Gryada 151 J 5
Belo-sur-Mer 201 G 4
Belo-sur-Tsiribihina 201 G 3
Belot, Lac 103 M 2
Belousovka 154 D 1
Belovo 159 R 5
Beloyarovo 171 N 5
Beloye More 158 G 2
Beloye Ozero 155 G 1
Beloye Ozero 158 G 3
Belozerka 155 D 1
Belozersk 158 G 4
Belt (MT.) 111 P 3
Beltana 183 F 5
Belted Range 112 J 5
Belterra 139 G 4
Belton (MO.) 121 L 4
Belton (S.C.) 128 J 7
Belton (TX.) 122 F 4
Belton Reservoir 122 F 4
Bel'tsy 154 C 1
Belukha, Gora 159 R 5–6
Belush'ya Guba 158 K 1
Belush'ya Guba 202
Belvidere (IL.) 124 F 7
Belyando River 183 H 4
Belyayevka 154 D 1
Belyy 158 F 4
Belyy Yar 159 R 4
Belzoni (MS.) 130 D 1
Bełżyce 149 H 4
Bemaraha, Plateau du 201 GH 3
Bembe 200 A 1
Bemidji (MN.) 119 O 3
Bemis (TN.) 128 C 6
Bemis (W.V.) 129 M 3
Ben (Iran) 157 F 2
Benãb (Iran) 157 E 1
Bena Dibile 198 C 5
Ben Ahmadu 192 C 3
Benalla 183 H 6
Benares 174 D 2
Benavente 152 B 3
Benavides (TX.) 122 E 8
Ben Bolt (TX.) 122 E 8
Benbrook Lake 122 F 3
Bencubbin 182 B 5
Bend (OR.) 110 D 6
Bendaja 196 B 4
Bendavis (MO.) 121 N 5
Bende 197 F 4
Bendela 198 B 5
Bendeleben, Mount 108 F 2
Bendemeer 183 J 5
Bender Bãyla 199 J 3
Bender Cassim → Bõsãso 199 H 2
Bender Mur'anyo 199 HJ 2
Bender Siyada 199 H 2
Bendery 154 C 1
Bendigo 183 G 6
Benedict (MN.) 119 O 3
Benešov 149 F 5
Benevento 153 FG 3
Bengal 174 E 3
Bengal, Bay of 174–175 EF 4
Bengal, West 174 E 3
Bengara 176 E 3

Bengbis 197 G 5
Bengbu 173 G 4
Benghazi 193 J 2
Benghisa Point 153 F 4
Bengkalis 176 B 3
Bengkalis, Pulau 176 B 3
Bengkulu 176 B 4
Bengo, Baía do 200 A 1
Bengtsfors 151 F 4
Benguela 200 A 2
Benguerir 192 D 2
Ben Hope 148 C 3
Beni (Bolivia) 140 C 4
Beni (Zaire) 198 D 4
Beni Abbès 192 E 2
Benicarló 152 D 3
Benicasim 152 D 3
Benidorm 152 CD 4
Beni Mellal 192 D 2
Benin 196 E 3–4
Benin, Bight of 196 E 4
Benin City 197 F 4
Beni Ounif 192 E 2
Beni Saf 192 E 1
Beni Suef → Banī Suwayf 194 E 3
Benito Juárez 132 D 4
Benjamin (TX.) 122 D 2
Benjamin Constant 138 D 4
Benjamin Corrilla 143 CD 6
Benkelman (NE.) 120 D 2
Benkelman (NE.) 120 D 2
Ben Klibreck 148 C 3
Benkovac 153 G 3
Ben Lomond (CA.) 112 CD 5
Ben Macdhui 148 C 3
Ben Mehidi 153 E 4
Benndale (MS.) 130 F 4
Bennett (CO.) 115 N 4
Bennett (N.M.) 117 N 5
Bennettsville (S.C.) 129 M 7
Ben Nevis 148 BC 3
Bennichab 192 B 5
Bennington (ID.) 111 O 8
Bennington (KS.) 120 H 3
Bennington (TX.) 122 G 2
Benoud 192 F 2
Bénoué 197 G 4
Bénoué National Park 197 G 4
Benoy 197 H 4
Bensané 196 B 3
Bensheim 149 E 5
Benson (AZ.) 116 F 6
Benson (MN.) 119 N 5
Benson (N.C.) 129 N 6
Bent 168 F 5
Benteng 177 F 5
Bentiaba 200 A 2
Bentinck 175 G 5
Bentinck Island (Queensland, Austr.)
  183 F 2
Bentiu 198 E 3
Bento Gonçalves 142 F 4
Benton (AR.) 121 N 8
Benton (CA.) 112 G 5
Benton (IL.) 121 R 5
Benton (KY.) 128 C 5
Benton (LA.) 123 K 3
Benton (MS.) 130 D 2
Benton (TN.) 128 G 6
Benton (WI.) 124 D 7
Benton City (WA.) 110 F 4
Benton Harbor (MI.) 124 H 7
Bentonia (MS.) 130 D 2
Bentonite Spur (WY.) 118 D 6
Benton Lake 111 O 3
Bentonville (AR.) 121 L 6
Benue 197 F 4
Ben Wyvis 148 C 3
Benxi 173 H 2
Beo 177 G 3
Beograd 154 B 2
Beoumi 196 C 4
Beowawe (NV.) 112 J 2
Beppu 173 K 4
Bera 174 E 3
Berakata 201 H 4
Berati 154 A 2
Berau, Teluk 177 H 4
Berbera 199 H 2
Berbérati 198 B 4
Berca 154 C 1
Berchogur 168 F 1
Berchtesgaden 149 F 5
Berck 152 D 1
Berclair (TX.) 122 F 7
Berdâle 199 H 3
Berdale 199 G 4
Berdichev 151 J 6
Berdigestyakh 171 N 3
Berdoba 197 J 2
Berdsk 159 Q 5
Berdyansk 155 E 1
Berdyuzh'ye 159 N 4
Berea (KY.) 128 G 4
Berea (NE.) 118 E 8
Berea (TX.) 123 J 4
Beregovo 154 B 1
Bereina 184 E 3
Bereko 199 F 5

Berekum 196 D 4
Berenda (CA.) 112 E 5
Berenice → Mīnā' Baranīs 194 EF 4
Berens 103 S 5
Berens River 103 S 5
Beresford (S.D.) 119 M 7
Bereza 151 J 5
Bereznegovatoye 155 D 1
Berezniki 158 L 4
Berezovka (Russia, U.S.S.R.) 159 Q 4
Berezovka (Russia, U.S.S.R.) 170 L 4
Berezovka (Russia, U.S.S.R.) 171 T 2
Berezovka (Ukraine, U.S.S.R.) 154 D 1
Berezovo 159 N 3
Berezovo 171 W 3
Berezovskaya 158 H 5
Berezovskiy 159 R 4
Berezovskiy 159 L 5
Berg 150 F 3
Berga 152 D 3
Bergamo 153 EF 2
Bergamo 154 C 3
Bergby 151 G 3
Bergen (F.R.G.) 149 F 4
Bergen (Norway) 151 DE 3
Bergen (N.Y.) 125 Q 6
Bergerac 152 D 3
Bergkvara 151 G 4
Bergland 200 B 4
Bergland (MI.) 124 E 3
Bergö 150 H 3
Bergslagen 151 F 3
Bergviken 151 G 3
Berhala, Selat 176 B 4
Berhampore 174 E 3
Berhampur 174 D 4
Berīkān (Iran) 157 F 3
Berikul'skiy 159 R 4
Beringarra 182 B 4
Bering Glacier 102 J 3
Bering Land Bridge National
  Preserve 102 E 2
Beringovskiy 171 X 3
Bering Sea 102 CD 3–4
Bering Strait 102 CD 2–3
Berino (N.M.) 117 K 5
Berislav 155 D 1
Berkakit 171 M 4
Berkane 192 E 2
Berkeley (CA.) 112 C 5
Berkner Island 203
Berkovisa 154 B 2
Berkshire Hills 126 FG 6
Berlevåg 150 J 1
Berlin 149 F 4
Berlin (N.H.) 126 H 4
Berlin (WI.) 124 E 6
Berlin Lake 125 N 8–9
Bermeja, Punta 143 D 7
Bermeja, Sierra 152 B 4
Bermejo 142 C 5
Bermejo 142 C 5
Bermejo (Argentina) 142 D 4
Bermen, Lac 105 O 5
Bermeo 152 C 3
Bermuda Islands 133 K 1
Bern 153 E 2
Bernalillo (N.M.) 117 K 2
Bernardo (N.M.) 117 K 3
Bernardo de Irigoyen 142 F 4
Bernasconi 143 D 6
Bernay 152 D 2
Bernburg 149 F 4
Berne 153 E 2
Berne (IN.) 125 K 9
Berner Alpen 153 E 2
Bernice (LA.) 123 L 3
Bernier Island 182 A 3
Bernina 153 E 2
Bernkastel-Kues 149 E 5
Bernstein (TX.) 117 P 1
Bernstorffs Isfjord 105 T 3
Bóroroha 201 H 4
Berouanouaye 196 E 3
Beroun 149 F 5
Berovo 154 B 2
Berre, Étang de 153 E 3
Berrechid 192 D 2
Berri (Saudi Arabia) 157 E 4
Berriane 193 F 2
Berry 152 D 2
Berry (AZ.) 116 C 2
Berrydale (FL.) 130 G 4
Berryessa, Lake 112 C 4
Berry Islands 133 G 2
Berseba 200 B 5
Bershad 154 C 1
Berthold (ND.) 118 G 2
Berthoud (CO.) 115 MN 3
Berthoud Pass 115 M 4
Bertolínia 141 J 2
Bertoua 197 G 5
Bertram (IA.) 119 R 9
Bertram (TX.) 122 EF 5
Bertrand (NE.) 120 F 2
Beru 186 C 3
Beruri 139 F 4
Beruwala 174 CD 6
Berwick (LA.) 123 M 6

Berwick (ME.) 126 J 5
Berwick (PA.) 127 C 7
Berwick-upon-Tweed 148 C 3
Beryl (UT.) 114 D 6
Besalampy 201 G 3
Besançon 153 E 2
Besar, Gunung 176 E 4
Besar, Pulau 177 F 5
Beskidy Zachodny 149 GH 5
Beslan 155 F 2
Besni 155 E 3
Bessarabiya 154 C 1
Bessemer (AL.) 128 DE 8
Bessines-sur-Gartempe 152 D 2
Besskorbnaya 155 F 2
Bestamak 159 P 6
Bestepeler Geçidi 155 E 3
Bestobe 159 O 5
Bestyakh 171 MN 2
Bestyakh 171 O 3
Beswick 182 E 1
Betafo 201 H 3
Betamba 198 C 5
Betanzos 152 B 3
Bétaré Oya 197 G 4
Bethal 200 D 5
Bethanie 200 B 5
Bethany (MO.) 121 LM 2
Bethany (OK.) 120 H 7
Bethel 102 E 3
Bethel 108 F 3
Bethel (ME.) 126 J 4
Bethel (N.C.) 129 O 6
Bethel (OK.) 120 H 7
Bethel (VT.) 126 G 5
Bethlehem (PA.) 127 D 8
Bethlehem (South Africa) 200 D 5
Bethlehem → Bayt Laḥm 194 EF 2
Bethor 199 F 2
Bethulie 200 D 6
Béthune 152 D 1
Bet She'an (Israel) 156 B 2
Betsiboka 201 H 3
Bettendorf (IA.) 119 S 9
Betteravia (CA.) 113 E 8
Bettiah 174 D 2
Bettles 102 G 2
Bettola 153 E 3
Betul 174 C 3
Betwa 174 C 2
Beulah (CO.) 115 N 5
Beulah (MI.) 124 H 5
Beulah (ND.) 118 G 3
Beulah (OR.) 110 G 7
Beulah (WY.) 118 D 6
Beulah Reservoir 110 G 7
Beveridge 186 D 4
Beverley (Western Australia) 182 B 5
Beverly (KS.) 120 H 3
Beverly (WA.) 110 F 4
Beverly Hills (CA.) 113 G 8
Bexar (AL.) 128 C 7
Bexar (AR.) 121 NO 6
Beyänlū (Iran) 157 E 1
Bey Dağları 154 CD 3
Beykoz 154 C 2
Beyla 196 C 4
Beyoneisu-retsugan 173 L 4
Beypore 174 C 5
Beypazari 155 D 2
Beyra 199 H 3
Beyram (Iran) 157 F 4
Beyşehir 154 D 3
Beyşehir Gölü 154 D 3
Beysug 155 E 1
Bezaha 201 G 4
Bezdez 149 G 4
Bezhanitskaya Vozvyshennost' 151 J 4
Bezhanitsy 151 K 4
Bezhetsk 158 G 4
Béziers 152 D 3
Bezmein 168 F 3
Beznosova 170 H 5
Bhadarwah 169 K 4
Bhadgaon 174 E 2
Bhadohi 174 D 2
Bhadrachalam 174 D 4
Bhadrajan 174 B 2
Bhadrakh 174 E 3
Bhadravati 174 C 5
Bhagalpur 174 E 2
Bhakkar 169 J 4
Bhalki 174 C 4
Bhamo 175 G 3
Bhandara 174 C 3
Bhanrer Range 174 C 3
Bharatpur 174 C 2
Bharatpur 174 D 3
Bharuch 174 B 3

Bhatinda 174 BC 1
Bhatpara 174 E 3
Bhavnagar 174 B 3
Bhawanipatna 174 D 4
Bhilwara 174 BC 2
Bhima 174 C 4
Bhind 174 C 2
Bhiwani 174 C 2
Bhongir 174 C 4
Bhopal 174 C 3
Bhopalpatnam 174 D 4
Bhor 174 B 4
Bhuban 174 E 3
Bhubaneswar 174 E 3
Bhuban Hills 175 F 3
Bhuj 174 A 3
Bhumiphol Dam 175 G 4
Bhusawal 174 C 3
Bhutan 175 F 2
Biak (Indonesia) 177 F 4
Biak (New Guinea) 177 J 4
Biak, Pulau 177 J 4
Biała Podlaska 149 H 4
Białogard 149 G 4
Białowieża 149 H 4
Białystok 149 H 4
Bianco 153 G 4
Biankouma 196 C 4
Biaora 174 C 3
Biarritz 152 C 3
Biasca 153 E 2
Bibã 194 E 3
Bibai 173 M 2
Bibala 200 A 2
Bibémi 197 G 4
Biberach 149 EF 5
Bibiani 196 D 4
Bibi Hakimeh (Iran) 157 F 3
Bib Island (VA.) 129 M 4
Bichura 170 J 5
Bickerton Island 183 F 1
Bicknell (UT.) 114 F 5
Bicuari National Park 200 AB 3
Bida 197 F 4
Bidar 174 C 4
Bida Zayed (United Arab Emirates)
  157 FG 5
Bid Cypress Swamp 131 N 8
Biddeford (ME.) 126 J 5
Biddle (MT.) 118 C 5
Bidon 5 (Algeria) 193 F 4
Bidzhan 171 O 6
Bié 200 B 2
Bieber (CA.) 112 D 1
Biebrza 149 H 4
Biel 153 E 2
Bielefeld 149 E 4
Biella 153 E 2
Bielsko-Biała 149 G 5
Bielsk Podlaski 149 H 4
Bien Hoa 175 J 5
Bienville, Lac 105 N 4
Biferno 153 F 3
Bifoum 197 G 6
Biga 154 C 2
Big Bald Mountain 105 O 6
Big Baldy 111 K 6
Big Bar (CA.) 112 B 2
Big Bay (MI.) 124 G 3
Big Bay De Noc 124 H 4
Big Bear City (CA.) 113 J 8
Big Bear Lake 113 J 8
Big Bell 182 B 4
Big Belt Mountains 111 O 4
Big Bend Dam 118 J 6–7
Big Bend National Park 117 N 8
Big Black River 130 D 2
Big Blue River 120 J 2
Big Cabin (KS.) 121 K 6
Big Clifty (KY.) 128 E 4
Big Creek (ID.) 111 K 5
Big Creek Lake 130 F 4
Big Creek Peak 111 M 6
Big Cypress Indian Reservation
  131 NO 8
Big Delta 102 H 3
Big Eau Pleine Reservoir 124 E 5
Biger 170 G 6
Big Falls (MN.) 119 P 2
Big Flat (AR.) 121 N 6
Bigfork (MN.) 119 P 3
Bigfork (MT.) 111 LM 2
Biggar 103 Q 5
Biggers (AR.) 121 P 6
Biggs (CA.) 112 D 3
Big Hatchet Peak 116 H 6
Bighorn (MT.) 111 S 4
Big Horn (WY.) 118 AB 6
Bighorn Basin 111 R 6–S 7
Bighorn Canyon National Recreation-
  Area 111 RS 5
Bighorn Mountains 118 A 6–B 7
Bighorn River 111 S 5
Bight of Bangkok 175 H 5
Bight of Benin 196 E 4
Bigi 198 C 3
Big Island 105 N 3
Big Lake 126 M 3
Big Lake (CA.) 112 D 1
Big Lake (MN.) 119 P 5

Big Lake (MT.) **111** P 3
Big Lake (TX.) **117** P 6
Big Lookout Mountain **110** H 6
Bignona **196** A 3
Bigobo **198** D 6
Big Pine (CA.) **112** G 5
Big Pine (FL.) **131** N 10
Big Pine Mountain **113** F 8
Big Piney (WY.) **111** PQ 8
Big Point (MS.) **130** F 4
Big Quill Lake **103** R 5
Big Rapids (MI.) **124** J 6
Big River **103** Q 5
Big Sable Point **124** H 5
Big Sage Reservoir **112** E 1
Big Salmon Range **109** M 3
Big Sand Lake **103** S 4
Big Sandy (MT.) **111** P 2
Big Sandy (TN.) **128** CD 5
Big Sandy (TX.) **123** H 3
Big Sandy (WY.) **111** Q 8
Big Sandy Creek **115** O 4–5
Big Sandy Lake **119** P 4
Big Sandy Reservoir **111** Q 8
Big Sheep Mountains **118** C 3–4
Big Sioux River **119** M 6
Big Smoky Valley **112** H 4–J 3
Big Snowy Mountains **111** Q 4
Big Southern Butte **111** M 7
Big Spring (TX.) **117** P 5
Big Springs (NE.) **118** FG 9
Big Stone City (S.D.) **119** M 5
Big Stone Gap (VA.) **128** J 5
Big Stone Lake **119** M 5
Big Sur (CA.) **112** D 6
Big Timber (MT.) **111** Q 5
Big Trails (WY.) **111** S 7
Big Trout Lake **104** K 5
Big Trout Lake (Ontario, Can.) **104** J 5
Big Wells (TX.) **122** D 7
Bihać **153** G 3
Bihar **174** E 2
Bihar **174** E 3
Biharamulo **198** E 5
Bijapur **174** C 4
Bījār (Iran) **157** E 2
Bijawar **174** C 3
Bijeljina **153** G 3
Bijelo Polje **154** AB 2
Bijiang **172** C 5
Bijie **172** E 5
Bijnor **174** C 2
Bijou Hills (SD.) **118** JK 7
Bijoutier **199** J 6
Bikaner **174** B 2
Bikar **186** C 2
Bikin **171** O 6
Bikin **171** P 6
Bikini **186** C 2
Bikoro **198** B 5
Bilād Banī Bū 'Alī **195** K 4
Bilād Ghāmid **195** G 5
Bilād Zahrān **195** G 4
Bilala **197** G 6
Bilanga **196** E 3
Bilaspur **174** D 3
Bilauktaung Range **175** G 5
Bilbao **152** C 3
Bil'chir **170** K 5
Bileća **153** G 3
Bilecik **154** C 2
Bilesha Plain **199** G 4
Bili **198** C 4
Bili **198** D 4
Bilibino **171** V 2
Biling La **174** D 1
Bilir **171** O 2
Bill (WY.) **118** C 7
Billabalong **182** B 4
Billiluna **182** D 2
Billings (MT.) **111** R 5
Billings (OK.) **120** H 6
Billingsfors **151** F 4
Bill Williams Mountain **116** D 2
Bill Williams River **116** BC 3
Billy Chinook, Lake **110** D 6
Billy Clapp Lake **110** F 3
Bilma **197** G 2
Bilma, Grand Erg de **197** G 2
Biloela **183** J 3
Bilogora **153** G 2
Biloku **139** G 3
Biloxi (MS.) **130** F 4
Biltine **197** J 3
Bilugyun **175** G 4
Bilyarsk **158** JK 5
Bima **177** E 5
Bimbéréke **196** E 3
Bimberi, Mount **183** H 6
Bimbila (WV.) **196** E 3
Bimbo **198** B 4
Bimini Islands **133** G 2
Bimlipatam **174** D 4
Bīnab (Iran) **157** E 1
Binaiya, Gunung **177** G 4
Binatang **176** D 3
Binchuan **172** D 5
Binder **170** K 6
Bindura **201** E 3
Binga (Zaire) **198** C 4

Binga (Zaire) **200** D 3
Binga, Monte **201** E 3
Bingara **183** J 4
Bingen **149** E 5
Binger (OK.) **120** G 7
Bingham (ME.) **126** K 3
Bingham (N.M.) **117** K 4
Binghamton (N.Y.) **126** D 6
Bin Ghanīmah, Jabal **193** J 3–4
Bin Ghashir **193** H 2
Bingöl **155** F 3
Binhai **173** GH 4
Binh Son **175** J 4
Bini Erdi **197** H 1
Binjai **176** A 3
Binjai **176** C 3
Binnaway **183** H 5
Binongko, Pulau **177** F 5
Bin Qirdān **193** H 2
Bintan, Pulau **176** B 3
Bint Bayyah **193** H 3
Bintuan **176** B 4
Bintulu **176** D 3
Bintuni, Teluk **177** H 4
Bin Xian **172** E 3
Bin Xian **173** J 1
Bin Xian **173** G 3
Binyang **172** E 6
Bin Yauri **197** EF 3
Bío Bío **143** B 6
Biograd na Moru **153** G 3
Bioko **197** F 5
Biola (CA.) **112** F 6
Biorka Island **108** E 5
Bir **174** C 4
Bira **171** O 6
Bira **171** P 6
Birab **177** J 5
Bi'r Abraq (Egypt) **156** B 5
Bi'r Abū Algharab **193** H 2
Bi'r Abū al Ḥusayn **194** E 4
Bi'r Abū Gharādiq **194** D 2
Bi'r Abū Hashim (Egypt) **156** AB 5
Bi'r Abū Mingat **194** D 3
Bi'r Adh Dhikār **193** K 3
Birāk at Tahtāni, Tall (Syria) **156** C 1
Bi'r al 'Abd (Egypt) **156** A 3
Bi'r al Ḥakīm **193** K 2
Bi'r al Ḥamrā' **193** H 2
Bi'r al Ḥisw (Saudi Arabia) **156** C 4
Bi'r al Jadīd (Saudi Arabia) **156** C 4
Bi'r al Khamsah **194** D 2
Bi'r 'Allāq **193** H 2
Bi'r al Mrabba'ab (Syria) **156** C 2
Bi'r al Mushayqīq **193** H 2
Bi'r al Mushayqiq (Tunisia) **193** GH 2
Bi'r al Qurayyah (Egypt) **156** A 4
Birao **198** C 2
Bi'r Arjā' (Saudi Arabia) **156** C 4
Bi'r ar Rāh (Iraq) **156** C 2
Bi'r ar Rūmān **193** G 2
Biratnagar **174** E 2
Bi'r Bayah (Egypt) **156** B 4
Bi'r Baydā (Saudi Arabia) **156** B 4
Bi'r Baylī **194** D 2
Bi'r Bin Ghunaymah **193** K 2
Bi'r Bū Hawsh **193** K 3
Bi'r Bū Zurayyq **193** K 3
Bir Chali **192** D 4
Birch Creek **102** H 2
Birch Creek **109** J 2
Birch Lake **104** J 5
Birch Mountains **103** P 4
Birch Run (MI.) **125** L 6
Birchwood (WI.) **124** C 4
Bird **103** T 4
Bird City (KS.) **120** D 3
Bi'r Dibis **194** D 4
Bir Djedid **193** G 2
Birdsville **183** F 4
Bi'r Dūfān **193** H 2
Birdum River **182** E 2
Birecik **155** E 3
Birecik (Turkey) **156** C 1
Bir ed Deheb **192** E 3
Birekte **172** E 4
Bir el Ater **193** G 2
Bir el Hadjaj **192** E 3
Bir el Khzaim **192** D 4
Bir el Ksaib **196** C 1
Bir Enzaran **192** C 4
Bireuen **176** A 2
Bi'r Fajr (Saudi Arabia) **156** B 3
Bi'r Fardān **195** H 4
Bi'r Fu'ād **194** D 2
Bir Gandus **192** B 4
Bir Gara **197** H 3
Bi'r Ghawdah **195** G 4
Bi'r Ḥabs adh Dhur'ānī **193** K 2
Bi'r Ḥasanah (Egypt) **156** AB 3
Bi'r Ḥaymir (Tunisia) **193** GH 2
Bi'r Ibn Sarrār **195** G 5
Bir Igueni **192** C 4
Birikao → Būr Gābo **199** G 5
Birilyussy **170** F 4
Birini **198** C 3
Birjand **168** F 4
Birkat Nasser (Egypt) **156** A 5
Birkat Qārūn **194** E 3

Birkenhead **148** C 4
Birket Fatmé **197** H 3
Birksgate Range **182** D 4
Bi'r Kusaybah **194** E 4
Bir Lehlú **192** D 3
Bir Lehmar **192** C 3
Bir Lehlú **192** D 3
Bir Moghreim **192** C 3
Bi'r Murr **194** E 4
Bi'r Nāhid **194** D 2
Bi'r Nasif (Saudi Arabia) **156** C 4
Birni **196** E 3–4
Birnie **186** D 3
Birni Ngaoure **196** E 3
Birnin Gwari **197** F 3
Birnin Kebbi **197** E 3
Birni Nkonni **197** EF 3
Birnin Kudu **197** F 3
Birobidzhan **171** O 6
Bir Ould Brini **192** E 3
Bir Ounane **196** D 1
Bir Rhoraffa **193** G 2
Birrindudu **182** D 2
Bi'r Safājah (Egypt) **156** AB 4
Bi'r Ṣaḥrā' **194** D 4
Bi'r Salālah **194** F 5
Bi'r Salālbah **194** D 4
Bi'r Sayyālah (Egypt) **156** A 4
Bi'r Shalatayn **194** F 4
Bi'r Sīdī Madhkūr **193** H 2
Birsilpur **174** B 2
Birsk **158** L 4
Bi'r Ṭarfāwī (Egypt) **194** D 4
Bi'r Ṭarfāwī (Sudan) **194** E 4
Bi'r Tlākshīn **193** H 2
Biru **172** B 4
Bi'r 'Umm Fawākhīr (Egypt) **156** A 4
Bi'r 'Umm Sa'id (Egypt) **156** A 3
Bi'r Ungāt **194** E 4
Bi'r Wurshah **195** G 4
Biruni **168** G 2
Biryusa **170** G 4
Biryusinsk **170** G 4
Birẑai **151** HJ 4
Birzebbuga **153** F 4
Bir Zreigat **192** D 4
Bisaccia **153** G 3
Bisalpur **174** D 2
Bisbee (AZ.) **116** G 6
Bisbee (ND.) **118** J 2
Biscarrosse, Étang de **152** C 3
Biscay, Bay of **152** C 2–3
Biscayne Bay **131** O 9
Biscayne National Monument **131** O 9
Bisceglie **153** G 3
Bischofshofen **149** E 3
Biscoe Islands **203**
Bisekera **171** X 3
Bisert' **159** L 4
Bishan **172** E 5
Bishārīyīn, Barq al **194** E 5
Bishnath **175** F 2
Bishop (CA.) **112** G 5
Bishop (TX.) **122** F 8
Bishop Creek Reservoir **112** L 1
Bishop Rock **148** B 5
Bishop's Falls **105** Q 6
Bishopville (S.C.) **129** L 7
Bishr **193** J 2
Bishrī, Jabal al (Syria) **156** C 2
Bishui **171** M 5
Biskia **199** F 1
Biskra **193** G 2
Bislig **177** G 2
Bismarck (AR.) **121** M 8
Bismarck (MO.) **121** P 5
Bismarck (N.D.) **118** H 4
Bismarck Archipelago **184–185** EF 2
Bismarck Archipelago **186** AB 3
Bismarck Range **184** D 3
Bismarck Sea **184** E 2
Bismil **155** F 3
Bison (OK.) **120** H 6
Bison (SD.) **118** F 5
Bison Peak **115** M 4
Bisotūn (Iran) **157** E 2
Bispfors **150** G 3
Bissau **196** A 3
Bissett **103** S 5
Bissikrima **196** B 3
Bistcho Lake **103** NO 4
Bistineau, Lake **123** K 3
Bistrica **154** B 2
Bistriţa **154** B 1
Bistriţa **154** C 1
Bitam **197** G 5
Bitburg **148** E 5
Bitchana **199** F 2
Bitely (MI.) **124** J 6
Bitkiné **197** H 3
Bitlis **155** F 3
Bitlis Dağları **155** F 3
Bitola **154** B 2
Bitonto **153** G 3
Bitter Creek (WY.) **111** R 9

Bitterfeld **149** F 4
Bitterfontein **200** B 6
Bitter Lake (Egypt) **156** A 3
Bitter Lake (N.M.) **117** M 4
Bitterroot Range **111** K 3–M 6
Bitterroot River **111** L 4
Bittou **196** DE 3
Biu **197** G 3
Bivolari **154** C 1
Bivolu, Virful **154** C 1
Biwa-ko **173** L 3
Bixby (MO.) **121** O 5
Biya **159** R 5
Biyang **172** F 4
Biyārjomand **168** F 3
Biyārjomand (Iran) **157** G 1
Biylikol' **169** J 2
Biyo Kaboba **199** G 2
Biysk **159** R 5
Bizerta → Banzart **193** GH 1
Bjala Slatina **154** B 2
Bjargtangar **150** A 2
Bjästa **150** G 3
Bjelašnica **154** A 2
Bjelovar **153** G 2
Bjerkvik **150** G 2
Björkö **150** J 2
Björna **150** G 3
Björnafjorden **151** E 3
Björneborg **150** H 3
Björnevatn **150** J 2
Björnöya **202**
Bjurholm **150** G 3
Bjuröklubb **150** H 3
Bjuv **151** F 4
Bla **196** C 3
Blåsjön, Stora **150** F 3
Black (MO.) **121** O 5
Blackall **183** H 3
Blackbeard Island **131** N 3
Blackburn **148** C 4
Blackburn, Mount **102** J 3
Black Butte **111** O 6
Black Butte **114** E 6
Black Butte Lake **112** C 3
Black Canyon of the Gunnison
   National Monument **115** K 5
Black Diamond (WA.) **110** D 3
Black Eagle (MT.) **111** O 3
Black Escarpment **200** B 5
Blackfeet Indian Reservation **111** MN 2
Blackfoot (MT.) **111** N 2
Blackfoot Reservoir **111** O 8
Blackfoot River **111** M 4
Blackford (ID.) **111** L 8
Black Gap (AZ.) **116** D 5
Blackhall Mountain **118** B 9
Blackhawk (SD.) **118** E 6
Black Hills **118** D 6–E 7
Black Lake **103** R 4
Black Lake (MI.) **125** K 4
Black Lake (N.Y.) **126** D 4
Blackman (FL.) **130** H 4
Black Mesa **116** F 1
Black Mesa **120** C 6
Blackmore, Mount **111** OP 5
Black Mountain **111** N 4
Black Mountain **111** S 6
Black Mountain **113** E 7
Black Mountain **116** F 5
Black Mountain **122** C 6
Black Mountain **128** J 5
Black Mountains **116** B 2
Black Peak **116** B 3
Black Pine Peak **111** M 8
Black Point **112** B 4
Black Point **116** H 6
Blackpool **148** C 4
Black Range **116** J 4
Black River **126** D 5
Black River **129** M 8
Black River (AK.) **109** K 2
Black Rock (AR.) **121** O 6
Black Rock (N.M.) **116** H 2
Black Rock (UT.) **114** E 5
Black Rock Desert **112** F 2–G 1
Blacksburg (VA.) **129** L 4
Black Sea **155** DE 2
Blackshear (GA.) **131** M 3
Blackshear, Lake **131** M 3
Blackstone (VA.) **129** N 4
Blackville (S.C.) **129** K 8
Black Volta **196** D 4
Black Warrior River **128** D 8
Blackwater (Queensland, Austr.)
   183 H 3
Blackwater (Rep. of Ireland) **148** B 4
Blackwell (OK.) **120** H 6
Blackwell (PA.) **126** B 7
Blackwell (TX.) **122** C 3
Blackwood (N.J.) **127** DE 9
Blackwood River **182** B 5
Blaenavon (Queensland, Austr.)
   183 H 3

Blagoveshchensk **158** KL 4
Blagoveshchensk **171** N 5
Blain **152** C 2
Blaine (MN.) **119** P 5
Blair (NE.) **119** M 9
Blair (OK.) **120** F 8
Blair (WI.) **124** C 5
Blairsden (CA.) **112** E 3
Blairsville (GA.) **128** GH 7
Blairsville (PA.) **125** P 9
Blaj **154** B 1
Blakely (GA.) **131** K 3
Blakely (W.V.) **129** K 3
Blakeman (KS.) **120** D 3
Blake Point **124** F 1
Blalock (OR.) **110** E 5
Blanc, Cap (Mauritania) **192** B 4
Blanca (CO.) **115** M 6
Blanca, Cordillera **138** C 5
Blanca, Laguna **143** B 9
Blanca Peak **115** M 6
Blanchard (OK.) **120** H 7
Blanche, Lake (South Australia) **183** F 4
Blanche, Lake (Western Australia)
   182 C 3
Blanco (TX.) **122** E 5
Blanco, Cape **110** A 8
Blanco, Lago **143** C 9
Bland (VA.) **129** K 4
Blanda **150** B 2
Blanes **152** D 3
Blaney Park (MI.) **124** H 3
Blangy-sur-Bresle **152** D 2
Blanket (TX.) **122** E 4
Blansko **149** G 5
Blantyre **201** E 3
Blåsjön, Stora **150** F 3
Blåskavlen **150** E 3
Blato **153** G 3
Blåvands Huk **151** E 4
Blaye **152** C 2
Bled **153** F 2
Bledsoe (TX.) **117** NO 4
Bleecker (AL.) **131** J 2
Blei, Monti **153** F 4
Blekinge **151** FG 4
Blenheim **185** Q 9
Blenheim **186** C 3
Blessing (TX.) **122** G 7
Bleus, Monts **198** E 4
Blewett (TX.) **122** CD 6
Blewett Falls Lake **129** M 6–7
Blida **193** F 1
Blind River **104** L 6
Bliss (ID.) **111** L 8
Bliss (NV.) **112** H 1
Blissfield (MI.) **125** L 8
Blitar **176** D 5
Blitchton (GA.) **131** N 2
Blitta **196** E 4
Block Island **127** H 7
Block Island (N.Y.) **127** H 8
Block Island Sound **127** GH 7
Blocksburg (CA.) **112** B 2
Bloemfontein **200** D 5
Bloemhof **200** D 5
Bloemhof Dam **200** D 5
Blois **152** D 2
Blönduós **150** AB 2
Bloom (KS.) **120** F 5
Bloomer (WI.) **124** C 4
Bloomfield (IA.) **119** Q 10
Bloomfield (IN.) **128** E 2
Bloomfield (KY.) **128** F 4
Bloomfield (MO.) **121** P 6
Bloomfield (N.M.) **116** J 1
Blooming Grove (TX.) **122** G 3
Blooming Prairie (MN.) **119** PQ 7
Bloomington (IL.) **124** E 9
Bloomington (IN.) **128** E 2
Bloomington (MN.) **119** P 6
Bloomington (TX.) **122** G 7
Bloomington (WI.) **124** D 7
Bloomsburg (PA.) **127** C 7–8
Bloomsburg (PA.) **126** B 7
Blora **176** D 5
Blossburg (MT.) **111** N 4
Blossburg (PA.) **126** B 7
Blosseville Coast **202**
Blouberg **200** D 4
Blountstown (FL.) **131** J 4
Blountville (TN.) **129** J 5
Blowing Rock (N.C.) **129** K 5
Blue Cypress Lake **131** O 7
Blue Diamond (NV.) **112** K 6
Blue Earth (MN.) **119** O 7
Bluefield (W.V.) **129** K 4
Bluefields **132** F 5
Blue Hill (ME.) **126** L 4
Blue Hill (NE.) **120** G 2
Blue Hills Upland **120** E 4–F 3
Bluejoint Lake **110** F 8
Blue Lake (CA.) **112** A 2
Blue Mesa Reservoir **115** K 5
Blue Mound (IL.) **121** Q 3
Blue Mountain (MT.) **118** D 3
Blue Mountain (PA.) **127** C 8
Blue Mountain Lake **121** M 7
Blue Mountain Pass **110** H 8
Blue Mountain Peak **133** G 4
Blue Mountains **183** J 5

Blue Mountains (OR.) 110 G 6–H 5
Blue Mountains National Park 183 J 5
Blue Mud Bay 183 F 1
Blue Nile 194 E 6
Bluenose Lake 103 O 2
Blue Rapids (NE.) 120 J 3
Blue Ridge (GA.) 128 G 7
Blue Ridge (VA.) 129 LM 4
Blue River (OR.) 110 C 6
Blue Stack 148 B 4
Bluestone Lake 129 L 4
Bluewater (N.M.) 116 J 2
Bluewater Lake 116 H 2
Bluff 184 P 10
Bluff City (TN.) 129 J 5
Bluff Dale (TX.) 122 EF 3
Bluff Knoll 182 B 5
Bluff Park (AL.) 128 E 8
Bluff Point 182 A 4
Bluffs (IL.) 121 P 3
Bluffton (IN.) 124 J 9
Blumenau 142 G 4
Blumenthal (TX.) 122 E 5
Blunt (SD.) 118 J 6
Bly (OR.) 110 D 8
Blying Sound 109 H 4
Blythe (CA.) 113 L 9
Blytheville (AR.) 121 Q 7
Bo 196 B 4
Boac 177 F 1
Boaco 132 E 5
Boa Esperança, Reprêsa 141 H 2
Boane 201 E 1
Boano, Pulau 177 G 4
Board Camp Mountain 112 B 2
Boardman (OH.) 125 O 8
Boardman (OR.) 110 F 5
Boatasyn 171 Q 5
Boatman 183 H 4
Boa Vista (Cape Verde) 196 B 6
Boa Vista (Pará, Brazil) 139 F 3
Boa Vista (Roraima, Brazil) 139 F 3
Boaz (AL.) 128 E 7
Boaz (N.M.) 117 MN 4
Bobai 172 EF 6
Bobangi 198 B 5
Bobât (Iran) 157 G 3
Bobbili 174 D 4
Bobo Dioulasso 196 D 3
Bobonazo 138 C 4
Bobonong 200 D 4
Bobrinets 155 D 1
Bobrov 158 H 5
Bobruysk 151 J 5
Boby, Pic 201 H 4
Boca, Cachoeira da 139 GH 5
Boca de la Serpiente 139 F 2
Boca del Guafo 143 AB 7
Boca del Rio 106 E 6
Bôca do Acre 138 E 5
Bôca do Curuquetê 138 E 5
Bôca do Jari 139 H 4
Bôca do Moaço 138 E 5
Bocage Vendéen 152 C 2
Boca Grande 139 FG 2
Boca Grande (FL.) 131 M 8
Bocaiúva 141 H 4
Boca Mavaca 138 E 3
Bocaranga 198 B 3
Boca Raton (FL.) 131 O 8
Bocas del Toro 138 B 2
Bochnia 149 H 5
Bochum 149 E 4
Bocoio 200 A 2
Boconó 138 DE 2
Bocşa 154 B 1
Boda 198 B 4
Bodaybo 170 K 4
Boddington 182 B 5
Bodélé 197 H 2
Boden 150 H 2
Bodensee 153 E 2
Bodmin Moor 148 BC 4
Bodö 150 F 2
Bodoquena, Serra da 140 E 5
Bodrum 154 C 3
Bo Duc 175 J 5
Boduna 198 B 3
Boën 152 D 2
Boende 198 C 5
Boerne (TX.) 122 E 6
Boffa 196 B 3
Bogachevka 171 U 5
Bogale 175 G 4
Bogalusa (LA.) 123 O 5
Bogandé 196 DE 3
Bogangolo 198 B 3
Bogan River 183 H 5
Bogata (TX.) 123 H 2
Bogbonga 198 B 4
Bogda Feng 169 M 2
Bogdan 154 B 2
Bogda Shan 169 MN 2
Bogen 150 G 2
Bogense 151 F 4
Bogetkol'skiy 159 M 5
Boggabilla 183 HJ 4

Boggeragh Mountains 148 B 4
Boghari → Ksar el Buokhari 193 F 1
Boghra Dam 169 GH 4
Bogia 184 D 2
Bogo 177 F 1
Bogodukhov 158 G 5
Bogol Manya 199 G 4
Bogor 176 C 5
Bogoroditsk 158 G 5
Bogorodskoye 158 K 4
Bogorodskoye 171 Q 5
Bogotá 138 D 3
Bogotol 159 R 4
Bogöy 150 G 2
Bogra 174 E 3
Boguchany 170 G 4
Bogué 192 C 5
Bogue (KS.) 120 F 3
Bogue Chitto River 123 N 5
Boguillas (TX.) 117 O 8
Boguslav 158 F 6
Boğzlıyan 155 E 3
Bo Hai 173 GH 3
Bohai Haixia 173 H 3
Bohemia 149 F 5
Bohemia Downs 182 D 2
Bohicon 196 E 4
Böhmerwald 149 F 5
Bohodoyou 196 C 4
Bohol 177 F 2
Bohol Sea 177 F 2
Bohu 169 M 2
Boiaçu 139 F 4
Boim 139 G 4
Boipeba, Ilha 141 J 3
Bois 141 F 4
Bois, Lac des 103 N 2
Bois Blanc Island 125 K 4
Boise (ID.) 110 J 7
Boise (TX.) 117 O 2
Boise City (OK.) 120 C 6
Boise Mountains 111 K 7
Boise River 111 K 7
Boissevain 103 S 6
Boissevain (ND.) 118 HJ 1
Boix de Sioux River 119 M 5
Boizenburg 149 F 4
Bojador, Cabo 192 C 3
Bojnūrd 168 F 3
Bojonegoro 176 D 5
Bojuro 142 F 5
Bok 184 E 3
Boka Kotorska 154 A 2
Bokani 197 F 4
Bokatola 198 B 5
Boké 196 B 3
Bokeelia (FL.) 131 M 8
Bokhapcha 171 S 3
Boki 197 G 4
Boknafjorden 151 E 4
Boko 197 G 6
Bokora Game Reserve 198 E 4
Bokoro 197 H 3
Bokote 198 C 5
Bokpyin 175 G 5
Boksitogorsk 158 F 4
Bokspits 200 C 5
Bokungu 198 C 5
Bokwankusu 198 C 5
Bol (Chad) 197 G 3
Bol (Yugoslavia) 153 G 3
Bolafa 198 C 4
Bolaiti 198 C 5
Bolama 196 A 3
Bolangir 174 D 3
Bolan Pass 169 H 5
Bole (China) 169 L 2
Bole (Ethiopia) 199 F 3
Bole (Ghana) 196 D 4
Boles (AR.) 121 LM 8
Bolesławiec 149 G 4
Boley (OK.) 120 J 7
Bolgatanga 196 D 3
Bolgrad 154 C 1
Boli 173 K 1
Bolia 198 B 5
Boliden 150 H 3
Boligee (AL.) 130 FG 2
Bolinao 177 H 1
Bolintin Vale 154 C 2
Boliohutu, Gunung 177 F 3
Bolívar (Argentina) 143 D 6
Bolívar (Colombia) 138 C 3
Bolívar (MO.) 121 M 5
Bolivar (N.Y.) 125 O 3
Bolivar (TN.) 128 BC 6
Bolívar, Cerro 139 F 2
Bolívar, Pico 138 D 2
Bolivia 140 CD 4
Bolkar Dağları 155 D 3
Bolkhov 158 G 5
Bolléne 153 D 3
Bollnäs 150 G 3
Bollon 183 H 4
Bollstabruk 150 G 3
Bolmen 151 F 4
Bolnisi 155 F 2
Bolobo 198 B 5
Bologna 153 F 3
Bolognesi 140 B 3

Bologoye 158 F 4
Bologur 171 O 3
Bolomba 198 B 4
Bolombo 198 C 5
Bolon' 171 P 5
Bolon', Ozero 171 P 6
Bolotnoye 159 Q 4
Bolsena, Lago di 153 F 3
Bol'shaya Belozerka 155 D 1
Bol'shaya Chernigovka 158 JK 5
Bol'shaya Glushitsa 158 K 5
Bol'shaya Lepetikha 155 D 1
Bol'shaya Murta 170 F 4
Bol'shaya Novoselka 155 E 1
Bol'shaya Orlovka 155 F 1
Bol'shaya Osinovaya 108 AB 2
Bol'shaya Pyssa 158 J 3
Bol'shaya Vladimirovka 159 P 5
Bol'shaya Yerema 170 J 3
Bol'shenarymskoye 159 Q 6
Bol'sheokinskoye 170 H 4
Bol'sheretsk 171 T 5
Bol'shezemel'skaya Tundra 158 KM 2
Bol'shiye Khatymy 171 M 4
Bol'shiye Klyuchsishchi 158 J 5
Bol'shiye Lar'yak 159 Q 3
Bol'shiye Shogany 159 M 3
Bol'shiye Uki 159 O 4
Bol'shoy 171 T 1
Bol'shoy Anyuy 171 U 2
Bol'shoy Balkhan, Khrebet 168 EF 3
Bol'shoy Begichev, Ostrov 170 KL 1
Bol'shoy Berezovy, Ostrov 151 J 3
Bol'shoy Kavkaz 155 F 2
Bol'shoy Kymency 108 D 2
Bol'shoy Lyakhovskiy, Ostrov 171 Q 1
Bol'shoy Nimnyr 171 MN 4
Bol'shoy Oloy 171 TU 2
Bol'shoy Onguren 170 J 5
Bol'shoy Patom 170 KL 3–4
Bol'shoy Porog 170 F 2
Bol'shoy Salym 159 O 3
Bol'shoy Shantar, Ostrov 171 P 4–5
Bol'shoy Uluy 170 F 4
Bol'shoy Yenisey 170 G 5
Bol'shoy Yeravnoye, Ozero 170 K 5
Bol'shoy Yugan 159 O 4
Bol'shoy Yugan 159 O 4
Bolsjoj Morskoye, Ozero 171 T 1
Bolsón de Mapimi 132 B 2
Bolton 148 C 4
Bolton (N.C.) 129 N 7
Bolu 154 D 2
Bolungarvík 150 A 2
Boluntay 172 B 3
Bolvadin 154 D 3
Bolvanskiy Nos, Mys 159 LM 1
Bolzano 153 F 2
Bom 184 E 3
Boma 197 G 7
Bomarton (TX.) 122 D 2
Bomassa 197 H 5
Bombala 183 H 6
Bombarral 152 B 4
Bombay 174 B 4
Bomberai 177 H 4
Bombéré 198 B 4
Bombo 198 E 4
Bomboma 198 B 4
Bom Comercio 138 E 5
Bomdila 175 F 2
Bomi 172 C 5
Bomi Hills 196 B 4
Bomili 198 D 4
Bom Jardim 138 E 5
Bom Jesus 141 H 2
Bom Jesus da Gurguéia, Serra 141 H 2
Bom Jesus da Lapa 141 H 3
Bömlo 151 DE 4
Bomokandi 198 D 4
Bomongo 198 B 4
Bom Retiro 142 G 4
Bomu 198 C 4
Bona, Mount 102 J 3
Bon Air (VA.) 129 O 4
Bonaire, Isla 138 E 1
Bonampak 132 D 4
Bonanza 132 F 5
Bonanza (CO.) 115 L 5
Bonanza (OR.) 110 D 8
Bonanza (UT.) 114 H 3
Bonanza Peak 110 E 2
Bonaparte (IA.) 119 R 10
Bonaparte, Mount 110 F 2
Bonaparte Archipelago 182 C 1
Bonasila Dome 108 F 3
Bonavista 105 R 6
Bonavista Bay 105 R 6
Bondad (CO.) 115 K 6
Bondo 198 C 5
Bondo 198 C 5
Bondowoso 176 D 5
Bondurant (WY.) 111 P 7
Bone (ID.) 111 O 7
Bone, Teluk 177 F 4
Bonelohe 177 F 5
Boneng 175 H 4

Bonete, Cerro 142 C 4
Bonga 199 F 3
Bongabong 177 F 1
Bongandanga 198 C 4
Bongka 177 F 4
Bong Mountains 196 C 4
Bongo 197 G 6
Bongor 197 H 3
Bongou 198 C 3
Bonham (TX.) 122 G 2
Bonifacio 153 E 3
Bonifacio, Strait of 153 E 3
Bonifati, Capo 153 G 4
Bonifay (FL.) 131 J 4
Boni Game Reserve 199 G 5
Bonilla (S.D.) 119 K 6
Bonin Islands 161 R 7
Bonita Springs (FL.) 131 N 8
Bonito 140 E 5
Bonkoukou 196 E 3
Bonn 149 E 4
Bonners Ferry (ID.) 110 J 2
Bonne Terre (MO.) 121 P 5
Bonnet Plume 102 L 2–3
Bonnet Plume River 109 M 2–3
Bonneville (WY.) 111 RS 7
Bonneville Dam 110 CD 5
Bonneville Peak 111 N 8
Bonneville Salt Flats 114 D 3
Bonnie Rock 182 B 5
Bonny 197 F 5
Bonny Reservoir 115 P 4
Bonobono 176 E 2
Bontang 176 E 3
Bonthe 196 B 4
Bontoc 177 J 1
Bonwapitse 200 D 4
Bonyhád 154 A 1
Boody (ID.) 121 R 3
Booker (TX.) 117 Q 1
Boola 196 C 4
Boolaloo 182 B 3
Booligal 183 GH 5
Boologooro 182 A 3
Boon 104 L 6
Boonah 183 J 4
Boone (CO.) 115 N 5
Boone (IA.) 119 P 8
Boone (N.C.) 129 K 5
Boone Reservoir 129 J 5
Booneville (AR.) 121 LM 7
Booneville (KY.) 128 H 4
Booneville (MS.) 121 R 8
Boongoondoo 183 H 3
Boonville (CA.) 112 B 3
Boonville (IN.) 128 D 3
Boonville (MO.) 121 N 4
Boonville (N.Y.) 126 D 5
Booroorban 183 G 5
Booth (AL.) 131 H 2
Boothby, Cape 203
Boothia, Gulf of 103 T 1
Boothia Peninsula 103 T 1
Booué 197 G 5–6
Bophuthatswana 200 C 5
Bopolu 196 B 4
Boqueirão 142 F 5
Boquerón (P.R.) 130 B 8
Boquete 138 B 2
Boquillagas del Carmen 132 B 2
Boquillas Canyon 117 O 8
Bor (Sudan) 198 E 3
Bor (Turkey) 155 D 3
Bor (U.S.S.R.) 158 H 4
Bor (Yugoslavia) 154 B 2
Bora-Bora 187 E 4
Borah Peak 111 M 6
Böramo 199 G 3
Borås 151 F 4
Borasambar 174 D 3
Borāzjān (Iran) 157 F 3
Borba 139 G 4
Borborema, Planalto da 141 J 2
Borçka 155 F 2
Bordeaux 152 C 3
Border (WY.) 111 OP 8
Bordertown 183 G 6
Bordj Bou Arreridj 193 F 1
Bordj Fly Sainte Marie 192 E 3
Bordj Messouda 193 G 2
Bordj Moktar 193 F 3
Bordj Omar Driss 193 G 3
Bordj Sif Fatima 193 G 2
Borgå (Porvoo) 151 J 3
Borgarnes 150 A 3
Börgefjellet 150 F 2
Borger (TX.) 117 P 2
Borgholm 151 G 4
Borgne, Lake 123 O 5
Borinquen, Punta 130 B 8
Borisoglebsk 158 H 5
Borisovka 169 H 2

Borispol 158 F 5
Bo River 198 D 3
Borja 138 C 4
Borja 155 G 3
Borjas Blancas 152 D 3
Borkou 197 H 2
Borlänge 151 FG 3
Borlu 154 C 2
Bornholm 151 F 5
Bornu 197 G 3
Bornwee Head 148 B 4
Boro 198 D 3
Borodino 170 F 4
Borodyanka 158 E 5
Borogontsy 171 O 3
Borohoro Shan 169 L 2
Boroko 177 F 3
Borolgustakh 170 M 2
Boromo 196 D 3
Boron (CA.) 113 H 7
Borong, Khrebet 171 P 2
Bororen 183 J 3
Borotou 196 C 4
Borovichi 151 J 4
Borovichi 158 FG 4
Borovlyanka 159 Q 5
Borovo 153 G 2
Borovoye 159 O 5
Borovskiy 159 N 4
Borovskoye 159 M 5
Borrän 199 J 3
Borrby 151 F 4
Borrego Springs (CA.) 113 J 9
Borroloola 183 F 2
Borşa 154 B 1
Börselv 150 J 1
Borshchev (Ukraine, U.S.S.R.) 158 E 6
Borshchovochnyy Khrebet 170 KL 5
Borshchkev (Ukraine, U.S.S.R.) 154 C 1
Borsippa (Iraq) 156 D 2
Boru 171 Q 1
Borūjen (Iran) 157 F 3
Borūjerd (Iran) 157 E 2
Borzhomi 155 F 2
Bôrzsöny 154 A 1
Borzya 170 L 5
Bosa 153 E 3
Bosaga 159 O 6
Bosanska Gradiška 153 G 2
Bosanska Krupa 153 G 3
Bosanski Novi 153 G 2
Bosanski Petrovac 153 G 3
Bosanski Samac 153 G 2
Bösäso 199 H 2
Boscobel (WI.) 124 D 6
Bose 172 E 6
Boseki 198 B 5
Boshan 173 G 3
Boshnyakovo 171 Q 6
Boshrüyeh 168 F 4
Boshuslän 151 F 4
Bosilegrad 154 B 2
Boskamp 139 G 2
Bosler (WY.) 118 C 9
Bosna 153 G 3
Bosna 154 C 2
Bosnik 177 J 4
Bosobolo 198 B 4
Bosporus 154 C 2
Bosque (AZ.) 116 D 4–5
Bosque Bonito 106 E 5
Bossangoa 198 B 3
Bossé Bangou 196 E 3
Bossembele 198 B 3
Bossemptélé II 198 B 3
Bossier City (LA.) 123 K 3
Bosso 197 G 3
Bossut, Cape 182 C 2
Bostan 169 H 4
Bostandyk 158 J 6
Bosten Hu 172 A 2
Boston (GA.) 131 L 4
Boston (MA.) 126 HJ 6
Boston (TX.) 123 J 2
Boston (U.K.) 148 C 4
Boston Mountains 121 LM 7
Boswell (IN.) 124 G 9
Boswell (PA.) 125 P 9
Boswell (TX.) 122 H 2
Botan 169 H 4
Botev 154 C 2
Botevgrad 154 B 2
Bothaville 200 D 5
Botletle 200 C 4
Botlikh 155 J 6
Botomoyu 170 L 3
Botoşani 154 C 1
Bo Trach 175 J 4
Botrange 148 E 4
Botswana 200 CD 4
Botte Donato 153 G 4
Bottineau (ND.) 118 H 2
Bottrop 148 E 4
Botucatu 141 G 5
Botuobuya, Ulakhan 170 K 3
Botwood 105 QR 6
Bouaflé 196 C 4
Bouaké 196 D 4

Bouala 198 B 3
Bouali (Centr. Afr. Rep.) 198 B 4
Bouali (Gabon) 197 G 6
Bouânane 192 E 2
Bouar 198 B 3
Bou Arfa 192 E 2
Boubandjida 197 GH 4
Boubandjida National Park 197 GH 4
Boubin 149 F 5
Boubout 192 E 3
Bouca 198 B 3
Boucle de Baoulé, Parc National dela 196 C 3
Boudenib 192 E 2
Bou Djéhiba 196 D 2
Boufarik 152 D 4
Bougainville (Papua New Guinea) 185 G 3
Bougainville (Papua New Guinea) 186 B 3
Bougainville Reef 183 H 2
Bougainville Strait (New Hebrides) 185 J 5
Bougainville Strait (Solomon Is.) 185 G 3
Bou Garfa 192 D 3
Bougaroun, Cap 193 G 1
Bougie → Bejaïa 193 F 1
Bougouni 196 C 3
Bougtob 192 EF 2
Bouïra 193 F 1
Bou Ismaïl 152 D 4
Bou Izakarn 192 D 3
Bou Kadir 152 D 4
Boulanouar 192 B 4
Boulder (Australia) 182 C 5
Boulder (CO.) 115 M 3–4
Boulder (IL.) 121 Q 4
Boulder (MT.) 111 N 4
Boulder (UT.) 114 F 6
Boulder (WY.) 111 Q 8
Boulder City (NV.) 112 L 7
Boulder Peak 112 B 1
Boulia 183 F 3
Boulogne-sur-Mer 152 D 1
Boulouli 196 C 2
Bouloupari 185 J 6
Boulsa 196 D 3
Boultoum 197 G 3
Bouly 192 C 5
Boumdeïd 192 C 5
Bouna 196 D 3
Bou Naga 192 C 5
Boundary 109 K 3
Boundary Peak 112 G 5
Boundiali 196 C 4
Boundji 197 GH 6
Boundou 196 B 3
Boundoukou 196 D 4
Boun Neua 175 H 3
Bounoum 196 A 2
Bountiful (UT.) 114 F 3
Bounty Islands 203
Bourail 185 J 6
Bourbon (MO.) 121 O 4
Bourem 196 D 2
Bouressa 196 E 1
Bourg 153 E 2
Bourganeuf 152 D 2
Bourges 152 D 2
Bourget, Lac du 153 E 2
Bourgogne 153 DE 2
Bourgogne, Canal de 152 D 2
Bourgoin-Jallieu 153 E 2
Bou Rjeima 192 C 5
Bourke 183 H 5
Bournemouth 148 C 4
Bouroum 196 D 3
Bourtoutou 197 J 3
Bou Saâda 193 F 1
Bouse (AZ.) 116 B 4
Bouse Wash 116 C 4
Boussens 152 D 3
Bousso 197 H 3
Bouvet Island 203
Bouza 197 F 3
Bovill (ID.) 110 J 4
Bovina (TX.) 117 O 3
Bovril 142 E 5
Bow 103 P 5
Bowbells (ND.) 118 F 2
Bowdle (SD.) 118 J 5
Bowdoin (MT.) 111 S 2
Bowdoin, Lake 111 S 2
Bowdon (ND.) 118 J 3
Bowen (Argentina) 142 C 5
Bowen (Australia) 183 H 2
Bowen (IL.) 124 C 9
Bowie (AZ.) 116 G 5
Bowie (MD.) 129 P 2MO
Bowie (TX.) 122 F 2
Bowkan (Iran) 157 E 1
Bowland Forest 148 C 4
Bowling Green (FL.) 131 N 7
Bowling Green (KY.) 128 E 5
Bowling Green (MO.) 121 O 3
Bowling Green (OH.) 125 L 8
Bowling Green (VA.) 129 O 3
Bowling Green, Cape 183 H 2
Bowman (ND.) 118 E 4

Bowman Bay 105 MN 2
Bowman-Haley Lake 118 E 5
Bowral 183 J 5
Box Elder (MT.) 111 P 2
Box Elder (SD.) 118 EF 6
Boxelder (WY.) 118 C 8
Boxholm 151 G 4
Bo Xian 172 G 4
Boxing 173 G 3
Boyabat 155 D 2
Boyabo 198 B 4
Boyang 173 G 5
Boyang Hu 172 G 5
Boyarka 170 G 1
Boyarsk 170 J 4
Boyce (LA.) 123 L 4
Boyd (OK.) 120 E 6
Boyd (TX.) 122 F 2
Boydton (VA.) 129 N 5
Boyero (CO.) 115 O 5
Boyer River 119 N 9
Boyes (MT.) 118 CD 5
Boykins (VA.) 129 O 5
Boyle 148 B 4
Boyne 148 B 4
Boyne City (MI.) 125 K 4
Boynton (OK.) 121 K 7
Boynton Beach (FL.) 131 OP 8
Boysen Reservoir 111 R 7
Boys Ranch (TX.) 117 O 2
Boyuibe 140 D 5
Bozcaada 154 C 3
Bozdağ 155 D 3
Boz Dağı 154 C 3
Bozdoğan 154 C 3
Bozeman (MT.) 111 O 5
Bozene 198 B 4
Bozkır 155 D 3
Bozok Platosu 155 DE 3
Bozouls 152 D 3
Bozoum 198 B 3
Bozova 155 E 3
Bozshakul 159 OP 5
Bozüyük 154 D 3
Bra 153 E 3
Brač 153 G 3
Bracciano, Lago di 153 F 3
Bräcke 150 G 3
Brackettville (TX.) 122 C 6
Brački Kanal 153 G 3
Brad 154 B 1
Brad (TX.) 122 E 3
Bradano 153 G 3
Braddock (ND.) 118 HJ 4
Bradenton (FL.) 131 M 7
Bradford (PA.) 125 Q 8
Bradford (U.K.) 148 C 4
Bradley (AL.) 130 H 3
Bradley (FL.) 131 MN 7
Bradley (IL.) 124 F 8
Bradley (S.D.) 119 L 5
Bradley Reefs 185 H 3
Bradshaw 182 E 2
Brady (MT.) 111 O 2
Brady (NE.) 120 E 1
Brady (TX.) 122 D 4
Brady Mountains 122 CD 4
Bradys Hot Springs (NV.) 112 F 3
Braga 152 B 3
Bragado 142 D 6
Bragança 139 J 4
Bragança 152 B 3
Bragina 171 X 3
Braham (MN.) 119 P 5
Brahman Baria 175 F 3
Brahmaputra 175 F 2
Brai 105 M 2
Braidwood (IL.) 124 F 8
Brainard (NE.) 120 J 1
Brainerd (MN.) 119 O 4
Braithwaite Point 182 E 1
Bräk 193 H 3
Brakna 192 C 5
Brålanda 151 F 4
Braman (OK.) 120 H 6
Bramhapuri 174 C 3
Brämön 150 G 3
Brampton 105 L 7
Brampton (N.D.) 119 L 5
Branchville (S.C.) 129 L 8
Brand (TX.) 117 PQ 5
Brandberg 200 A 4
Brandberg West Mine 200 A 4
Brande 151 E 4
Brandenberg (MT.) 118 B 5
Brandenburg 149 F 4
Brandenburg (KY.) 128 E 4
Brandon 103 S 6
Brandon (FL.) 131 M 7
Brandon (MS.) 130 E 2
Brandon (VT.) 126 F 5
Brandvlei 200 C 6
Brandy Peak 110 B 8
Branford (FL.) 131 M 4—5
Braniewo 149 GH 4
Branson (CO.) 115 O 6
Branson (MO.) 121 M 6
Brantford 105 L 7
Brant Lake (N.Y.) 126 F 5

Brantley (AL.) 131 H 3
Brás 139 G 4
Brás d'Or Lake 105 PQ 6
Brasil, Planalto do 141 H 4
Brasiléia 140 C 3
Brasília 141 G 4
Brasília, Parque Nacional do 141 G 4
Brasília Legal 139 G 4
Braslav 151 J 4
Braşov 154 C 1
Brass 197 F 5
Brassey, Mount 182 E 3
Brasstown Bald 128 H 7
Bratca 154 B 1
Bratsk 170 H 4
Bratskoye Vodokhranilishche 170 H 4
Bratslav 154 C 1
Brattleboro (VT.) 126 G 6
Brattvåg 150 E 3
Braunau am Inn 153 F 2
Braunschweig 149 F 4
Brava 196 AB 7
Brave (PA.) 125 O 10
Bravo, Cerro 138 C 5
Brawley (CA.) 113 K 10
Brawley Peaks 112 G 4
Bray (CA.) 112 D 1
Bray (South Africa) 200 C 5
Brazil 140–141 EG 3
Brazil (IN.) 128 D 2
Brazil Basin 208 A 4
Brazo Casiquiare 138 E 3
Brazos (N.M.) 117 K 1
Brazos River 122 G 5
Brazzaville 197 G 6
Brčko 153 G 3
Brda 149 G 4
Brdy 149 F 5
Brea, Cerros de la 138 B 4
Brea, Punta 130 C 9
Breaden, Lake 182 D 4
Breaux Bridge (LA.) 123 M 5
Breaza 154 C 1
Brebes 176 C 5
Breckenbridge (CO.) 115 M 4
Breckenridge (MN.) 119 M 4
Breckenridge (TX.) 122 E 3
Brecknock, Península 143 B 9
Breclav 149 G 5
Breda 148 D 4
Bredasdorp 200 C 6
Bredbyn 150 G 3
Bredy 159 M 5
Bregenz 153 E 2
Breiðafjörður 150 A 2
Breiðdalur 150 C 3
Breien (ND.) 118 H 4
Breivikbotn 150 H 1
Brejo (Maranhão, Brazil) 141 H 1
Brejo (Piauí, Brazil) 141 H 2
Brekken 150 F 3
Brekstad 150 EF 3
Bremangerlandet 150 D 3
Bremen 149 E 4
Bremen (GA.) 128 F 8
Bremen (IN.) 124 H 8
Bremer Bay 182 B 5
Bremer Bay 182 B 5
Bremerhaven 149 E 4
Bremerton (WA.) 110 C 3
Bremond (TX.) 122 G 4
Brenda (AZ.) 116 C 4
Brenham (TX.) 122 G 5
Brenner 153 F 2
Brent (AL.) 130 G 2
Brentwood (AR.) 121 L 7
Brentwood (N.Y.) 127 F 8
Brentwood (TN.) 128 E 5
Brescia 153 F 2
Bressanone 153 F 2
Brest (France) 152 C 2
Brest (U.S.S.R.) 151 H 5
Brestova 153 F 2
Bretagne 152 C 2
Breteuil 152 D 2
Breton, Pertuis 152 C 2
Breton Islands 123 O 6
Breton Sound 123 O 6
Brett, Cape 185 Q 8
Breueh, Pulau 176 A 2
Brevard (N.C.) 128 J 6
Breves 139 H 4
Brevik 151 E 4
Brevoort Island 105 P 3
Brevort (MI.) 124 J 3
Brewarrina 183 H 4—5
Brewer (ME.) 126 L 4
Brewerville 196 B 4
Brewster (KS.) 120 D 3
Brewster (MN.) 119 N 7
Brewster (NE.) 118 J 9
Brewster (WA.) 110 EF 2
Brewster, Kap 202

Brewton (AL.) 130 GH 3
Brezhnev 158 K 4
Brežice 153 G 2
Brézina 193 F 2
Bria 198 C 3
Briançon 153 E 3
Brian Head 114 E 6
Briare, Canal de 152 D 2
Brice (TX.) 117 Q 3
Briceland (CA.) 112 AB 2
Bricelyn (MN.) 119 P 7
Brichany 154 C 1
Bridge (ID.) 111 M 8
Bridge (OR.) 110 AB 7
Bridgeboro (GA.) 131 L 3
Bridgeland (UT.) 114 G 3
Bridgeport (AL.) 128 F 7
Bridgeport (CA.) 112 F 4
Bridgeport (CT.) 127 F 7
Bridgeport (NE.) 118 E 9
Bridgeport (TX.) 122 F 2
Bridgeport, Lake 122 F 2
Bridger (MT.) 111 R 5
Bridger Peak 118 A 9
Bridgeton (N.J.) 127 D 9
Bridgetown (Australia) 182 B 5
Bridgetown (Barbados) 133 KL 5
Bridgeville (CA.) 112 B 2
Bridgeville (PA.) 127 D 10
Bridgewater 105 P 7
Bridgewater (ME.) 126 L 2
Bridgewater (S.D.) 119 L 7
Bridgman (MI.) 124 H 8
Bridgton (ME.) 126 J 4
Bridgwater 148 C 4
Bridlington Bay 148 CD 4
Brig 153 E 2
Briggs (TX.) 122 F 5
Briggsdale (CO.) 115 N 3
Brigham City (UT.) 114 F 2
Bright 183 H 6
Brighton (CO.) 115 N 4
Brighton (FL.) 131 N 7
Brighton (IA.) 119 R 9
Brighton (IL.) 121 P 3
Brighton (MI.) 125 L 7
Brighton (MO.) 121 M 5
Brighton (N.Y.) 126 B 5
Brighton Indian Reservation 131 N 7
Brignoles 146
Brijuni 153 F 3
Brikama 196 A 3
Brilliant (AL.) 128 D 7
Brillon (WI.) 124 F 5
Brindisi 153 G 3
Brinford (N.D.) 119 K 3
Brinkene 192 E 3
Brinkley (AR.) 121 O 8
Brinnon (WA.) 110 BC 3
Brisbane 183 J 4
Briscoe (TX.) 117 Q 2
Bristol (CT.) 126 FG 7
Bristol (FL.) 131 K 4
Bristol (S.D.) 119 L 5
Bristol (TN.) 129 J 5
Bristol (U.K.) 148 C 4
Bristol (VA.) 129 J 5
Bristol Bay 102 EF 4
Bristol Channel 148 C D 4
Bristol Lake 113 K 8
Bristow (OK.) 120 J 7
Britânia 141 F 4
British Columbia 103 MN 4—5
British Mountains 102 JK 2
Brits 200 D 5
Britstown 200 C 6
Britter Lake (S.D.) 119 L 5
Britton (S.D.) 119 L 5
Brive 152 D 2
Briviesca 152 C 3
Brno 149 G 5
Broadalbin (N.Y.) 126 E 5
Broadback 105 M 5
Broadford 148 B 3
Broad Pass 109 J 3
Broad River 129 K 7
Broad Sound 183 H 3
Broadview (MT.) 111 R 4
Broadview (N.M.) 117 N 3
Broadwater (NE.) 118 F 9
Broadway (VA.) 129 MN 3
Broadys (MT.) 118 C 5
Brochet 103 R 4
Brocken 149 F 4
Brockman, Mount 182 B 3
Brock's Creek 182 E 1
Brockton (MA.) 126 H 6
Brockton (MT.) 118 CD 2
Brockville 105 M 7
Brockway (MT.) 118 C 3
Brockway (PA.) 125 Q 8
Brod 154 B 2
Broderick Falls 198 EF 4
Brodhead (WI.) 124 E 7
Brodick 148 B 3
Brodnica 149 G 4
Brody 151 J 5
Brogan (OR.) 110 H 6

Broken Arrow (OK.) 121 K 6
Broken Bow (NE.) 120 F 1
Broken Bow (OK.) 121 L 8
Broken Bow Lake 121 L 8
Broken Hill 183 G 5
Brokhovo 171 ST 4
Brokopondo 139 G 3
Bromölla 151 F 4
Brønderslev 151 F 4
Bronnikovo 159 N 4
Brönnöysund 150 F 2
Bronte 153 F 4
Bronte (TX.) 122 C 4
Bronx (WY.) 111 P 8
Brookeland (TX.) 123 JK 4
Brooke's Point 176 E 2
Brookfield (MO.) 121 M 3
Brookhaven (MS.) 130 D 3
Brookings (OR.) 110 A 8
Brookings (S.D.) 119 M 6
Brooklyn (IA.) 119 Q 9
Brooklyn Park (MN.) 119 P 5
Brookneal (VA.) 129 N 4
Brooks 103 P 5
Brooks Range 102 FH 2
Brookville (AL.) 128 E 7
Brooksville (FL.) 131 M 6
Brooksville (KY.) 128 H 3
Brooksville (MS.) 121 R 9
Brookton 182 B 5
Brookville 183 H 3
Brookville (IN.) 128 F 2
Brookville (PA.) 125 P 8
Broome 182 C 2
Broome, Mount 182 D 2
Brora 148 C 3
Brothers (OR.) 110 E 7
Broughton Island 105 P 2
Broutona, Ostrov 171 S 6
Brovst 151 E 4
Browerville (MN.) 119 O 4
Brown, Mount 111 O 2
Brown, Point 110 A 4
Brownbranch (MO.) 121 N 6
Brown City (MI.) 125 L 6
Brown City (MI.) 125 M 6
Brown Deer (WI.) 124 G 6
Brownell (KS.) 120 F 4
Browne Range Nature Reserve 182 CD 3
Brownfield (TX.) 117 O 4
Browning (MT.) 111 M 2
Brown Lake 103 T 2
Brownlee (NE.) 118 H 8
Brownlee (OR.) 110 HJ 6
Brownlee Dam 110 J 6
Brownlee Reservoir 110 H 6
Brown Mountain 113 HJ 7
Brown River (Queensland, Austr.) 183 G 2
Brownstown (IN.) 128 F 3
Browns Valley (S.D.) 119 LM 5
Brownsville (OR.) 110 C 6
Brownsville (PA.) 125 P 10
Brownsville (TN.) 128 B 6
Brownsville (TX.) 122 F 10
Brownton (MN.) 119 O 6
Brownville (AL.) 128 D 8
Brownville (ME.) 126 L 3
Brownville (NE.) 121 K 2
Brownwood (TX.) 122 E 4
Brownwood, Lake 122 D 4
Browse Island 182 C 1
Broxton (GA.) 131 M 3
Bruay-en-Artois 152 D 1
Bruce (MS.) 121 Q 8—9
Bruce (WI.) 124 C 4
Bruce, Mount 182 B 3
Bruce Crossing (MI.) 124 E 3
Bruce Peninsula 105 L 7
Bruchsal 149 E 5
Bruck 153 G 2
Brückenau 149 EF 4
Brugge 148 D 4
Bruhel Point 112 B 3
Bruin Point 114 G 4
Brumado 141 H 3
Bruncio 153 F 2
Brundage (TX.) 122 D 7
Bruneau (ID.) 111 K 8
Bruneau River 111 K 8
Brunei 176 D 2
Brunflo 150 FG 3
Bruni (TX.) 122 E 8
Brunsbüttel 149 E 4
Brunswick (GA.) 131 N 3
Brunswick (ME.) 126 JK 5
Brunswick (MO.) 121 M 3
Brunswick (OH.) 125 N 8
Brunswick, Península de 143 B 9
Brunswick Bay 182 C 2
Bruny 184 L 9
Brus, Laguna de 132 F 4
Brusett (MT.) 111 S 3
Brush (CO.) 115 O 3
Brusilovka 158 KL 5
Brusovo 159 R 3
Brusque 142 G 4
Brussels 148 DE 4

Brusset, Erg **197** FG 2
Bruxelles **148** DE 4
Bruzual **138** E 2
Bryan (OH.) **125** K 8
Bryan (TX.) **122** G 5
Bryan Coast **203**
Bryanka **170** F 4
Bryansk **158** F 5
Bryanskoye **155** G 2
Bryant (S.D.) **119** L 6
Bryce Canyon (UT.) **114** E 6
Bryce Canyon National Park **114** E 6
Bryne **151** E 4
Bryn'kovskaya **155** E 1
Bryson City (N.C.) **128** H 6
Bryukhovetskaya **155** E 1
Bryungyadinskiye Gory **171** PQ 3
Brza Palanka **154** B 2
Brzeg **149** G 4
Buandougou **196** C 4
Buapinang **177** F 4
Bua Yai **175** H 4
Buba **196** A 3
Bubanza **198** D 5
Bubaque **196** A 3
Būbīyān (Kuwait) **157** E 3
Bucak **154** D 3
Bucaramanga **138** D 2
Buccaneer Archipelago **182** C 2
Buchanan **196** B 4
Buchanan (GA.) **128** F 8
Buchanan (ND.) **118** JK 3
Buchanan (N.M.) **117** M 3
Buchanan (VA.) **129** M 4
Buchanan, Lake (Queensland, Austr.) **183** H 3
Buchanan, Lake (Western Australia) **182** C 4
Buchanan Dam (TX.) **122** E 5
Buchanan Lake **122** E 5
Buchardo **142** D 5
Bucharest **154** C 2
Bucharest → București **154** C 2
Buchon, Point **113** E 7
Buchs **153** C 2
Buck, Lake **182** E 2
Buckeye (AZ.) **116** D 4
Buckhannon (W.V.) **129** L 3
Buckhorn Lake **128** H 4
Buckingham (CO.) **115** O 3
Buckingham (VA.) **129** N 4
Buckingham Bay **183** F 1
Buck Island **130** E 9
Buckland **102** E 2
Buckland River **108** F 2
Buckland Tableland **183** H 3
Buckley (WA.) **110** D 3
Bucklin (KS.) **120** F 5
Buck Mountain **110** F 2
Bucks Lake **112** D 3
Bucksport (ME.) **126** L 4
Buco Zau **197** G 6
Bu Craa **192** C 3
București **154** C 2
Bucyrus (ND.) **118** F 4
Bucyrus (OH.) **125** L 9
Buda (IL.) **124** E 8
Buda (TX.) **122** F 5
Budacu, Vîrful **154** C 1
Budapest **154** A 1
Budaun **174** C 2
Bud Bud **199** H 4
Bude **148** C 4
Bude (MS.) **130** D 2
Bude Bay **148** C 4
Budennovka **158** K 5
Budennovsk **155** F 2
Búðardalur **150** A 2
Buðir **150** C 3
Budjala **198** B 4
Buea **197** F 5
Buena (WA.) **110** E 4
Buenaventura (Colombia) **138** C 3
Buenaventura (Mexico) **106** E 6
Buenavista **106** E 7
Buena Vista **138** E 2
Buena Vista (CO.) **115** LM 5
Buena Vista (GA.) **131** K 2
Buena Vista (VA.) **129** M 4
Buena Vista Lake **113** F 7
Buendía, Embalse de **152** C 3
Buengas **200** B 1
Buenópolis **141** H 4
Buenos Aires **142** DE 5
Buenos Aires, Lago **143** B 8
Buen Pasto **143** C 8
Bueryeros (N.M.) **117** N 2
Buffalo (KS.) **121** K 5
Buffalo (MO.) **121** M 5
Buffalo (MT.) **111** Q 4
Buffalo (N.W.T., Can.) **103** P 3
Buffalo (N.Y.) **125** Q 7
Buffalo (OH.) **129** K 2
Buffalo (OK.) **120** F 6
Buffalo (SD.) **118** E 5
Buffalo (TX.) **122** G 4
Buffalo (WY.) **118** B 6
Buffalo Bill Reservoir **111** Q 6
Buffalo Center (IA.) **119** P 7
Buffalo Creek (CO.) **115** M 4

Buffalo Gap (SD.) **118** E 7
Buffalo Gap (TX.) **122** D 3
Buffalo Lake **103** OP 3
Buffalo Lake **117** O 3
Buffalo Narrows **103** Q 4
Buffalo Valley (TN.) **128** F 5
Buford (GA.) **128** G 7
Buford (ND.) **118** DE 2
Buftea **154** C 2
Bug **149** H 4
Buga **138** C 3
Bugala Island **198** E 5
Bugarach, Pech de **152** D 3
Bugarikhta **170** KL 5
Bugat **170** H 6
Bugel, Tanjung **176** D 5
Bugene **198** E 5
Bugojno **153** G 3
Bugorkan **170** J 3
Bugøynes **150** J 2
Bugrino **158** J 2
Bugsuk **176** E 2
Bugt **171** M 6
Bugul'deyka **170** J 5
Bugul'ma **158** K 5
Buguruslan **158** K 5
Bū Ḥasā' (United Arab Emirates) **157** F 5
Buhayrat al Asad (Syria) **156** C 1–2
Buhayrat Sharī (Iraq) **156** D 2
Buhera **201** E 3
Buh He **172** C 3
Buhl (ID.) **111** L 8
Búhōdle **199** H 3
Bui Dam **196** D 4
Buinsk **158** J 5
Buir Nur **170** L 6
Buist (ID.) **111** N 8
Buitepos **200** D 6
Buítrago del Lozoya **152** C 3
Bujaraloz **152** CD 3
Bujaru **139** J 4
Buje **153** F 2
Bujumbura **198** D 5
Buka **185** F 3
Buka **186** B 3
Bukachacha **170** L 5
Bukadaban Feng **172** B 3
Bukakata **198** E 5
Bukama **198** D 6
Bukanskoye **159** Q 5
Bukantau, Gory **169** G 2
Bukavu **198** D 5
Bukene **198** E 5
Bu Khanum **175** H 5
Bukhara **169** G 3
Bukit Gandadiwata **177** EF 4
Bukit Kambuno **177** EF 4
Bukit Masurai **176** B 4
Bukit Mawa **176** D 3
Bukit Raya **176** D 4
Bukit Sulat **177** G 3
Bukittinggi **176** B 4
Bukoba **198** E 5
Bukukun **170** K 6
Bukuru **197** F 4
Bukwimba **198** E 5
Būl, Kūh-e (Iran) **157** F 3
Bula **177** H 4
Bulambuk **170** G 5
Bulan **177** F 1
Bulancak **155** E 2
Bulandshahr **174** C 2
Bulanik **155** F 3
Būlāq **194** E 3
Bulawayo **200** D 4
Bulayevo **159** O 5
Buldan **154** C 3
Buldana **174** C 3
Buldir **102** A 5
Bulgan **170** F 6
Bulgan **170** H 6
Bulgan **170** K 6
Bulgaria **154** C 2
Buli **177** G 3
Buli, Teluk **177** G 3
Bulki **199** F 3
Bullahār **199** G 2
Bullard (TX.) **123** H 3
Bulla Regia **153** E 4
Bullfinch **182** B 5
Bullhead (SD.) **118** G 5
Bullion Mountains **113** J 8
Bull Island **129** M 9
Bullita **182** E 2
Bull Lake **111** Q 7
Bull Mountain **111** O 4
Bull Mountains **111** RS 4
Bulloo River **183** G 4
Bullrun Rock **110** G 6
Bull Shoals Lake **121** N 6
Bully Creek Reservoir **110** H 6
Bulnes **143** B 6
Bulo Berde **199** H 4
Bulolo **184** E 3
Bulucan **155** E 3
Bulukumba **177** F 5
Bulun **171** N 1
Bulun **171** T 2
Bulun **171** Q 4

Bulungu **198** B 5
Bumba **198** C 4
Bumba **198** B 6
Bumble Bee (AZ.) **116** D 3
Bumbuli **198** C 5
Bumbulan **177** F 3
Bumbuna **196** B 4
Buna **199** F 4
Buna (TX.) **123** K 5
Bunbury **182** B 5
Buncrana **148** B 3
Bunda **198** E 5
Bundaberg **183** J 3
Bunda Bunda **183** G 3
Bundesrepublik Deutschland **149** EF 5
Bundi **174** C 2
Bundooma **182** E 3
Bundoran **148** B 4
Bungku **177** F 3
Bungo-suidō **173** K 4
Bung Sai **175** J 4
Buni **197** G 3
Bunia **198** E 4
Bunji **169** JK 3
Bunker (MO.) **121** O 5
Bunker Hill **112** H 3
Bunker Hill (IN.) **124** H 9
Bunker Hill (OR.) **110** A 7
Bunkerville (NV.) **112** L 6
Bunkeya **200** D 2
Bunkie (LA.) **123** L 5
Bunn (N.C.) **129** N 6
Bunnell (FL.) **131** N 5
Buntok **176** DE 4
Bünyan **155** E 3
Bun Yun **175** H 4
Buol **177** F 3
Buolkalakh **170** L 1
Buorkhaya, Guba **171** O 1
Buorkhaya, Mys **171** O 1
Buotama **171** N 3
Bupul **184** D 3
Buqayq (Saudi Arabia) **157** E 4
Buqda Kōsār **199** G 4
Buqūm, Ḥarrat al **195** G 4
Bur **170** J 4
Bura **199** F 5
Buram **194** D 6
Buran **159** R 6
Burang **174** D 1
Bura'o **199** H 3
Buraq (Syria) **156** B 2
Buras (LA.) **123** O 6
Burayda (Saudi Arabia) **156** D 4
Burbank (CA.) **113** G 8
Bür Dab **199** H 3
Burdekin River **183** H 2
Burden (KS.) **120** J 5
Burdère **199** H 4
Burdett (KS.) **120** F 4
Burdock (SD.) **118** E 7
Burdur **154** D 3
Burdur Gölü **154** CD 3
Burdwan **174** E 3
Bureå **150** H 3
Burei **198** F 3
Bureinskiy, Khrebet **171** O 5
Büren **170** H 6
Bureya **171** O 5
Bureya **171** N 6
Burfjord **150** H 2
Burg **149** F 4
Bür Gābo **199** G 5
Burgakhcha **171** Q 3
Burgan **165**
Burgas **154** C 2
Burgaski zaliv **154** C 2
Burgaw (N.C.) **129** O 7
Burgdorf **153** E 2
Burgdorf (ID.) **111** K 5
Burgeo **105** Q 6
Burgersdorp **200** D 6
Burgfjället **150** G 3
Burghausen **153** F 2
Burgos (Mexico) **132** C 3
Burgos (Spain) **152** C 3
Burgsvik **151** G 4
Bür Hakkaba **199** G 4
Burhan Budai Shan **172** C 3
Burhaniye **154** C 3
Burhanpur **174** C 3
Burias **177** F 1
Buribay **159** L 5
Burica, Punta **132** F 6
Burin Peninsula **105** Q 6
Buriram **175** H 5
Buriti **140** E 4
Buritizal, Cachoeira do **139** H 3
Burjasot **152** C 4
Burji **199** F 3
Burkburnett (TX.) **122** E 1
Burke (ID.) **111** K 3
Burke River **183** F 3
Burkesville (KY.) **128** F 5
Burketown (Queensland, Austr.) **183** F 2
Burkett (TX.) **122** D 3
Burkeville (TX.) **123** K 4–5
Burkeville (VA.) **129** N 4

Burkhala **171** RS 3
Burkhaybyt **171** P 2
Burkina **196** DE 3
Burla **159** P 5
Burleson (TX.) **122** F 3
Burley (ID.) **111** M 8
Burlingame (NE.) **120** K 4
Burlington (CO.) **115** P 4
Burlington (IA.) **119** R 10
Burlington (KS.) **121** K 4
Burlington (N.C.) **129** M 5
Burlington (ND.) **118** G 2
Burlington (OK.) **120** G 6
Burlington (VT.) **126** F 4
Burlington (WI.) **124** F 7
Burlington (WY.) **111** R 6
Burlington Junction (MO.) **121** KL 2
Burlyu-Tobe **159** P 6
Burma **175** FG 3
Burmantovo **159** M 3
Burmester (UT.) **114** E 3
Burnet (TX.) **122** E 5
Burnett River **183** J 3–4
Burnie **184** L 9
Burns (KS.) **120** HJ 4
Burns (OR.) **110** F 7
Burns (WY.) **118** D 9
Burns Flat (OK.) **120** F 7
Burns Lake **103** M 5
Burnside (KY.) **128** G 5
Burnside **103** PQ 2
Burnsville (N.C.) **129** J 6
Burnsville (W.V.) **129** L 3
Burntfork (WY.) **111** P 9
Burntwood **103** S 4
Burqān (Kuwait) **157** E 3
Burqin **169** M 1
Burra (Nigeria) **197** F 3
Burra (South Australia) **183** F 5
Burriana **152** C 4
Burris (WY.) **111** Q 7
Burris (WY.) **111** R 7
Burr Oak (KS.) **120** G 3
Burrton (KS.) **120** H 4
Burruyacú **142** D 4
Burrville (UT.) **114** EF 5
Bursa **154** C 2
Bür Saīd (Egypt) **156** A 3
Bür Südān **194** F 5
Burt Lake **125** K 4
Burtnieku ezers **151** J 4
Burton (TX.) **122** G 5
Burton, Lac **105** M 5
Burton, Lake **128** H 7
Burträsk **150** H 3
Buru, Pulan **177** G 4
Burum **195** H 6
Burunday **169** K 2
Burundi **198** DE 5
Bururi **198** D 5
Burutu **197** F 4
Burwash Landing **109** L 3
Burwell (NE.) **118** JK 9
Burye **199** F 2
Bury St. Edmunds **148** D 4
Busalla **153** E 3
Busanga (Zaire) **198** C 5
Busanga (Zaire) **200** D 2
Busanga Swamp (Zambia) **200** D 2
Buşayrah (Syria) **156** C 1
Busby (MT.) **118** B 5
Büshehr (Iran) **157** F 3
Büshgān (Iran) **157** F 3
Bushimaie **198** C 6
Bushland (TX.) **117** O 2
Bushman Land **200** B 5
Bushnell (FL.) **131** M 6
Bushnell (IL.) **124** D 9
Bushnell (NE.) **118** DE 9
Bushton (KS.) **120** G 4
Busia **198** E 4
Businga **198** C 4
Busira **198** B 5
Buskerud **151** E 3
Busko-Zdrój **149** H 4
Buskul' **159** M 5
Busse **171** N 5
Busselton **182** A 5
Bussey (IA.) **119** Q 9
Bussol', Proliv **171** S 6
Bustak, Ozero **171** Q 1
Bustamante (TX.) **122** D 8–9
Busu Djanoa **198** C 4
Busu Gongo **198** C 4
Busu Melo **198** C 4
Bususulu **198** C 4
Buta **198** C 4
Butajira **199** F 3
Butang Group **175** G 6
Buta Ranquil **143** C 6
Butare **198** DE 5
Butaritari **186** C 2
Butemba **198** E 4
Butembo **198** D 4
Butere **198** E 4
Butha Qi **171** M 6
Buthidaung **175** F 3
Butía **142** F 5
Butiaba **198** E 4

Butiama **198** E 5
Butkan **158** J 3
Butler (AL.) **130** F 2
Butler (GA.) **131** K 2
Butler (IN.) **125** K 8
Butler (MO.) **121** L 4
Butler (OK.) **120** F 7
Butler (PA.) **125** P 9
Butte (MT.) **111** N 4
Butte (ND.) **118** H 3
Butte de Vaudémont **153** E 2
Butte Mountains **112** K 3
Butterfield (MN.) **119** O 7
Butterfield (MO.) **121** M 6
Butternut (WI.) **124** D 3
Butterworth (Malaysia) **176** B 2
Butterworth (South Africa) **200** D 6
Butt of Lewis **148** B 3
Button Bay **103** T 4
Button Islands **105** P 3
Buttonwillow (CA.) **113** F 7
Butuan **177** G 2
Butung, Pulau **177** F 4
Buturlinovka **158** H 5
Bu Tu Suay **175** J 5
Butuy **171** R 5
Buwayrāt al Ḥasūn **193** J 2
Buxton (N.C.) **129** Q 6
Buy **158** H 4
Buyant-Ovoo **172** E 2
Buynaksk **168** D 2
Buyo **196** C 4
Buyr Nuur **170** L 6
Büyük Ağrı Dağı **155** F 3
Büyük Menderes **154** C 3
Buyunda **171** S 3
Buzachi, Poluostrov **168** E 1–2
Buzău **154** C 1
Buzău **154** C 1
Buzet **153** F 2
Būzhān (Iran) **157** E 2
Buzi **201** E 4
Buzi **201** E 4
Buzluk Dağı **155** E 2
Buzuluk **158** K 5
Buzzards Bay **126** J 7
Bwendi **198** D 4
Byars (OK.) **120** H 8
Byblos (Lebanon) **156** B 2
Byczyna **149** G 4
Bydgoszcz **149** G 4
Byers (CO.) **115** N 4
Bygdeå **150** H 3
Bygdeträsket **150** H 3
Byglandsfjord **151** E 4
Byglandsfjorden **151** E 4
Byhalia (MS.) **121** Q 8
Bykhov **158** F 5
Bykle **151** E 4
Bykov **171** Q 6
Bykovo **158** J 3
Bykovskiy **171** NO 1
Bylas (AZ.) **116** F 4
Bylkyldak **159** OP 6
Bylot Island **202**
Bynoe River (Queensland, Austr.) **183** G 2
Bynum (N.C.) **129** M 6
Bynum (TX.) **122** FG 3–4
Bynum Reservoir **111** N 3
Byram (MS.) **130** D 2
Byrd Station **203**
Byrdstown (TN.) **128** F 5
Byraya-Tas, Vozvyshennost' **170** M 1
Byrka **170** L 5
Byro **182** B 4
Byrock **183** H 5
Byron (IL.) **124** E 7
Byron (WY.) **111** R 6
Byron, Cape **183** J 4
Byron, Isla **143** A 8
Byron Bay **183** J 4
Byrranga, Gory **170** GH 1
Byserovo **158** K 4
Byske **150** H 3
Byskeälven **150** H 2
Bystraya **171** T 5
Bystrinskiy Golets, Gora **170** J 6
Bytantay **171** O 2
Bytča **149** G 5
Bytom **149** G 4
Bytów **149** G 4
Byuchennyakh **171** QR 3
Byxelkrok **151** G 4
Byzantium **183** H 4
Bzimah **193** K 4
Bzybskiy Khrebet **155** F 2

C

Caacupé **142** E 4
Caaguazu **142** E 4
Caála **200** B 2
Caatinga (Minas Gerais, Brazil) **141** G 4
Cáatingas **141** GH 2
Caazapa **142** E 4
Caballeria, Cabo de **152** D 3

Caballo (N.M.) **117** J 4-5
Caballococha **138** D 4
Caballo Reservoir **117** J 5
Cabanatuan **177** J 1
Čabar **153** F 2
Cabazon (CA.) **113** J 9
Cabeceiras **141** G 4
Cabedelo **141** K 2
Cabeza del Buey **152** BC 4
Cabezas **140** D 4
Cabezas de San Juan **130** D 8
Cabildo (Argentina) **143** D 6
Cabildo (Chile) **142** B 5
Cabimas **138** D 1
Cabinda **197** G 7
Cabinda **197** G 7
Cabinet Mountains **111** K 2–3
Cable (WI.) **124** C 3
Cabo Barbas **192** B 4
Cabo Bascuñan **142** B 4
Cabo Beata **133** H 4
Cabo Blanco **143** C 8
Cabo Bojador **192** C 3
Cabo Camarón **132** EF 4
Cabo Cassiporé **139** H 3
Cabo Catoche **132** E 3
Cabo Choros **142** B 4
Cabo Corrientes (Argentina) **143** E 6
Cabo Corrientes (Colombia) **138** C 2
Cabo Cruz **133** G 4
Cabo das Correntes **201** F 4
Cabo de Ajo **152** C 3
Cabo de Caballeria **152** D 3
Cabo de Cala Figuera **152** D 4
Cabo de Creus **152** D 3
Cabo de Finisterre **152** B 3
Cabo de Formentor **152** D 3–4
Cabo de Gata **152** C 4
Cabo de Hornos **143** C 10
Cabo de la Nao **152** D 4
Cabo Delgado **201** G 2
Cabo de Palos **152** C 4
Cabo de Peñas **152** B 3
Cabo de Salinas **152** D 4
Cabo de San Francisco **138** B 3
Cabo de Santa Maria (Mozambique)
 201 E 5
Cabo de Santa Maria (Portugal) **152** B 4
Cabo de Santa Marta **200** A 2
Cabo de Santa Marta Grande **142** G 4
Cabo de São Brás **200** A 1–2
Cabo de São Roque **141** J 2
Cabo de São Tomé **141** H 5
Cabo de São Vicente **152** B 4
Cabo Deseado **143** AB 9
Cabo de Sines **152** B 4
Cabo de Tortosa **152** D 3
Cabo dos Bahías **143** CD 8
Cabo Engaño **133** J 4
Cabo Espichel **152** B 4
Cabo Francés **132** F 3
Cabo Freu **152** D 4
Cabo Frio **141** H 5
Cabo Frio **141** H 5
Cabo Gloucester **143** B 9
Cabo Gracias a Dios **132** F 4–5
Cabo Gurupi **139** J 4
Cabo Ledo **200** A 1
Cabo Maguarinho **139** J 4
Cabo Manglares **138** C 3
Cabo Marzo **138** C 2
Cabo Mondego **152** B 3
Cabonga, Réservoir **105** M 6
Cabo Norte **139** J 3
Cabo Orange **139** H 3
Cabo Ortegal **152** B 3
Cabo Pantoja **138** CD 4
Cabo Pasado **138** B 4
Cabo Polonio **142** F 5
Cabo Quedal **143** B 7
Cabo Quilán **143** AB 7
Cabora Bassa **201** E 3
Cabora Bassa, Lago **201** E 3
Cabo Raper **143** A 8
Cabo Raso **143** C 7
Caborca **106** D 5
Cabo Rojo **130** B 9
Cabo Rojo (Mexico) **132** C 3
Cabo Rojo (Puerto Rico) **133** J 4
Cabo San Antonio (Argentina) **143** E 6
Cabo San Antonio (Cuba) **132** EF 3
Cabo San Diego **143** C 9
Cabo San Juan **197** F 5
Cabo San Lorenzo **138** B 4
Cabo San Lucas **106** E 7
Cabo San Rafael **133** J 4
Cabo Santa Elena **132** E 5
Cabot (AR.) **121** NO 8
Cabot, Mount **126** H 4
Cabo Touriñán **152** B 3
Cabo Trafalgar **152** B 4
Cabot Strait **105** Q 6
Cabourg **152** CD 2
Cabo Verde **196** AB 6
Cabo Virgenes **143** C 9
Cabras, Stagno di **153** E 4
Cabrera **152** D 4
Cabrera, Sierra de la **152** B 3

Cabriel **152** C 3–4
Cabrillo, Point **112** B 3
Cabrillo National Monument **113** H 10
Cabrobó **141** J 2
Cabruta **138** E 2
Cabuyaro **138** D 3
Caçador **142** F 4
Čačak **154** B 2
Caçapava do Sul **142** F 5
Cacequí **142** EF 4
Caceres (Brazil) **140** E 4
Cáceres (Colombia) **138** CD 2
Cáceres (Spain) **152** B 4
Cacharí **143** E 6
Cache (OK.) **120** G 8
Cache Mountain **109** J 2
Cache Peak **111** M 8
Cache River **121** O 7
Cachi, Nevado de **140** C 5
Cachimbo **139** H 5
Cachimbo, Serra do **139** G 5
Cachinal **140** C 5
Cachingues **200** B 2
Cachoeira **141** J 3
Cachoeira Alta **141** F 4
Cachoeira Aquibi **141** E 3
Cachoeira Cantagalo **139** H 5
Cachoeira Capinzal **139** G 5
Cachoeira da Bateria **139** G 5
Cachoeira da Boca **139** GH 5
Cachoeira da Conceição **139** F 5
Cachoeira das Capoeiras **139** G 5
Cachoeira das Ilhas **139** G 4
Cachoeira das Sete Quedas **139** G 5
Cachoeira de Anta **139** F 5
Cachoeira de Paulo Afonso **141** J 2
Cachoeira do Buritizal **139** H 3
Cachoeira do Chacorão **139** G 5
Cachoeira do Inferno **139** G 4
Cachoeira dois de Novembro **139** F 5
Cachoeira do Pimenta **139** F 3
Cachoeira do Rafael **140** D 3
Cachoeira do Rebojo **139** G 5
Cachoeira dos Índios **139** G 4
Cachoeira dos Patos **139** FG 5
Cachoeira do Sul **142** F 5
Cachoeira do Tereraimbu **139** H 5
Cachoeira Figueira **139** G 5
Cachoeira Grande **139** G 3
Cachoeira Maranhão **139** G 4
Cachoeira Pereira **139** G 4
Cachoeiro de Itapemirim **141** HJ 5
Cachos, Punta **142** B 4
Cachuma, Lake **113** F 8
Cacine **196** A 3
Cacolo **200** B 2
Caconda **200** B 2
Cactus Flat **112** J 5
Cactus Peak **112** J 5
Cacuaco **200** A 1
Cacula **200** A 2
Caculé **141** H 3
Caçumba, Ilha **141** J 4
Cacuso **200** B 1
Cadarga **183** J 4
Caddo (OK.) **120** J 8
Caddo (TX.) **122** E 3
Caddoa (CO.) **115** P 5
Caddo Lake **123** J 3
Cadena del Pantiacolla **140** B 3
Cadi, Sierra del **152** D 3
Cadillac (MI.) **124** J 5
Cadiz (CA.) **113** K 8
Cadiz (KY.) **128** D 5
Cadiz (Philippines) **177** F 1
Cádiz (Spain) **152** B 4
Cadiz, Golfo de **152** B 4
Cadiz Lake **113** K 8
Cadott (WI.) **124** C 5
Cadwell (GA.) **131** LM 2
Caen **152** C 2
Caesarea (Israel) **156** B 2
Caete **141** J 4
Caetite **141** H 3
Cagayan **177** J 1
Cagayan de Oro **177** F 2
Cagayan Islands **177** F 2
Cagayan Sulu **177** E 2
Cagliari **153** E 4
Cagnes **153** E 3
Cagua **138** E 1
Caguas **133** J 4
Caguas (P.R.) **130** C 8
Caguán **138** D 3
Cahaba Heights (AL.) **128** E 8
Cahama **200** A 3
Caha Mountains **148** B 4
Cahersiveen **148** B 4
Cahone (CO.) **114** J 6
Cahore Point **148** B 4
Cahors **152** D 3
Caia **201** F 3
Caiabis, Serra dos **140** E 3
Caianda **200** C 2
Caiapó, Serra do **141** F 4
Caiapônia **141** F 4
Caibarién **133** G 3
Caicara **138** E 2
Caico **141** J 2

Caicos Islands **133** H 3
Caicos Passage **133** H 3
Cailloma **140** B 4
Caillou Bay **123** MN 6
Caiman Point **177** H 1
Caineville (UT.) **114** G 5
Cai Nuoc **175** HJ 6
Cairn Hope Peak **110** EF 4
Cairn Mountain **108** G 3
Cairns **183** H 2
Cairnwath River **109** N 2
Cairo **194** E 2
Cairo (GA.) **131** K 4
Cairo (IL.) **121** Q 5
Cairo (NE.) **120** G 1
Caiundo **200** B 3
Caja de Muertos, Isla **130** C 9
Cajamarca **138** C 5
Cajazeiras **141** J 2
Cajon Summit **113** H 8
Cajuapara **139** J 4
Caka **172** C 3
Çakırgöl Dağ **155** EF 2
Çakmak **155** D 3
Čakovec **153** G 2
Cakrani **154** A 2
Çal **154** C 3
Calabar **197** F 4
Calabozo **138** E 2
Calabria **153** G 4
Calabro, Apennino **153** G 4
Calafat **154** B 2
Calafate **143** B 9
Cala Figuera, Cabo de **152** D 4
Calagua Islands **177** F 1
Calahorra **152** C 3
Calai **200** B 3
Calais **148** D 4
Calais (ME.) **126** M 3
Calakmul **132** D 4
Calama **139** F 5
Calama (Chile) **140** C 5
Calamar **140** B 4
Calamarca **140** C 4
Calamian Group **177** E 1
Calamocha **152** C 3
Calanaque **139** F 4
Calanda **152** C 3
Calandula **200** B 1
Calang **176** A 3
Calapan **177** J 1
Calapooya Mountains **110** C 7
Călăraşi **154** C 2
Cala Ratjada **152** D 4
Calatayud **152** C 3
Calatrava, Campo de **152** C 4
Calaveras Lake **122** E 6
Calayan **177** J 1
Calbayog **177** FG 1
Calbuco **143** B 7
Calcasieu Lake **123** K 6
Calchaquí **142** D 4
Calçoene **139** H 3
Calcutta **174** E 3
Caldas **138** C 2
Caldas da Rainha **152** B 4
Caldeirão, Serra de **152** B 4
Caldera **142** B 4
Calderina **152** C 4
Çaldıran **155** F 3
Caldwell (ID.) **110** J 7
Caldwell (KS.) **120** G 7
Caldwell (OH.) **129** K 2
Caldwell (TX.) **122** G 5
Caldwell (W.V.) **129** L 4
Caledonia (MN.) **119** R 7
Caledonia (N.D.) **119** LM 3
Caledonia (N.Y.) **126** B 6
Caledonia (WI.) **124** G 7
Calera (AL.) **128** E 8
Caleta Buena **140** B 4
Caleta Clarencia **143** C 9
Caleta Olivia **143** C 8
Calexico (CA.) **113** K 10
Calgary **103** P 5
Calhan (CO.) **115** N 4
Calhoun (AL.) **131** DE 9
Calhoun (GA.) **128** G 7
Calhoun (KY.) **128** D 4
Calhoun (MO.) **121** M 4
Calhoun (TN.) **128** G 6
Calhoun City (MS.) **121** Q 9
Calhoun Falls (S.C.) **128** J 7
Cali **138** C 3
Calico Rock (AR.) **121** N 6
Calicut **174** C 5
Caliente (CA.) **113** G 7
Caliente (NV.) **112** L 5
California **112–113**
California (MO.) **121** N 4
California, Golfo de **106** DE 5–7
California Aqueduct **112** E 6
Calilegua **140** CD 5
Calimanului, Muntii **154** BC 1
Calimere, Point **174** C 5
Calingasta **142** BC 3
Calipatria (CA.) **113** K 9
Calistoga (CA.) **112** C 4
Callabonna, Lake **183** F 4
Callac **152** C 2

Callafo **199** G 3
Callaghan, Mount **112** J 3
Callahan (CA.) **112** C 1
Callahan (FL.) **131** N 4
Callan **148** B 4
Callan (TX.) **122** D 4
Callao **140** A 3
Callao (UT.) **114** D 4
Callaway (NE.) **120** F 1
Calliham (TX.) **122** E 7
Callitharra Springs **182** B 4
Calmar (IA.) **119** R 7
Caloosahatchee River **131** N 8
Calpe **152** D 4
Calpella (CA.) **112** B 3
Calpet (WY.) **111** P 8
Calpine (CA.) **112** E 3
Caltagirone **153** F 4
Caltanissetta **153** F 4
Calulo **200** B 2
Calumet (MN.) **119** P 3
Calumet (OK.) **120** G 7
Caluquembe **200** A 2
Calva (AZ.) **116** F 4
Calvert (TX.) **122** G 4—5
Calvert City (KY.) **128** C 5
Calvi **153** E 3
Calvin (OK.) **120** J 8
Calvinia **200** BC 6
Calvi **153** E 3
Cama **132** F 5
Camabatela **200** B 1
Camacá **141** J 4
Camacupa **200** B 2
Camaguán **138** E 2
Camagüey **133** G 3
Camagüey, Archipiélago de **133** G 3
Camaná **140** B 4
Camano Island **110** C 2
Camapuã **141** F 4
Camaquã **142** F 5
Camaquã **142** F 5
Camara **139** F 4
Camararé **140** E 3
Camarat, Cap **153** E 3
Camargo **140** C 5
Camargo (OK.) **120** F 6
Camariñas **152** B 3
Camarón, Cabo **132** EF 4
Camarones (Argentina) **143** C 7
Camarones (Chile) **140** B 4
Camas **152** B 4
Camas (ID.) **111** N 6
Camas (WA.) **110** C 5
Camas Valley (OR.) **110** B 7
Camatindi **140** D 5
Camaxilo **200** B 1
Cambay → Khambhat **174** B 3
Cambodia **175** HJ 5
Camboon **183** J 4
Cambrai **152** D 1
Cambria (CA.) **113** D 7
Cambrian Mountains **148** C 4
Cambridge (ID.) **110** J 6
Cambridge (IL.) **124** D 8
Cambridge (Jamaica) **133** G 4
Cambridge (MA.) **126** HJ 6
Cambridge (MD.) **129** PQ 3
Cambridge (MN.) **119** P 5
Cambridge (NE.) **120** EF 2
Cambridge (OH.) **125** N 9
Cambridge (U.K.) **148** D 4
Cambridge Bay **103** QR 2
Cambridge City (IN.) **128** F 2
Cambridge Downs **183** G 3
Cambridge Gulf **182** D 1
Cambridge Sprs (PA.) **125** P 8
Cambuci **141** H 5
Cambulo **200** C 1
Cambundi-Catembo **200** B 2
Camden (AL.) **130** G 2—3
Camden (AR.) **121** N 9
Camden (ME.) **126** H 4
Camden (MS.) **130** E 2
Camden (N.C.) **129** P 5
Camden (N.J.) **127** DE 9
Camden (N.Y.) **126** D 5
Camden (S.C.) **129** L 7
Camden (TN.) **128** C 5
Camden (WA.) **110** H 2
Camden Bay **102** HJ 1
Camdenton (MO.) **121** N 4—5
Cameia **200** C 2
Cameia National Park **200** C 2
Camelo (CO.) **115** J 4
Cameo **115** P 6
Cameo (N.M.) **117** N 3
Camerino **153** F 3
Cameron (AZ.) **116** E 2
Cameron (LA.) **123** K 6
Cameron (MO.) **121** L 3
Cameron (MT.) **111** O 5
Cameron (TX.) **122** FG 5
Cameron (WI.) **124** C 5
Cameron (W.V.) **129** L 2
Cameron Hills **103** O 4
Cameroon **197** G 4
Cameroon, Mont **197** F 5
Cametá **139** J 4

Camiguin **177** J 1
Camiguin **177** F 2
Camilla (GA.) **131** K 3
Camiña **140** C 4
Camino (CA.) **112** E 4
Camiranga **139** J 4
Camiri **140** D 5
Camisea **140** B 3
Čamlıbel Geçidi **155** E 2
Camocim **141** H 1
Camoió **141** J 3
Camoola **183** G 3
Camooweal (Queensland, Austr.)
 183 F 2
Camopi **139** H 3
Camorta **175** F 6
Camotes Sea **177** F 1
Campana **142** E 5
Campana, Isla **143** A 8
Campanario **143** BC 6
Campas **141** GH 3–4
Campbell (MO.) **121** P 6
Campbell (NE.) **120** G 2
Campbell, Cape **185** Q 9
Campbell Hill **125** L 9
Campbell Island **203**
Campbell Plateau **209** C 5
Campbellpore **169** J 4
Campbell River **103** M 6
Campbellsport (WI.) **124** F 6
Campbellsville (KY.) **128** F 4
Campbellton **105** O 6
Campbellton (FL.) **131** J 4
Campbellton (TX.) **122** E 7
Campbelltown (N.S.W., Austr.) **183** J 5
Campbeltown **148** B 3
Camp Bird (CO.) **115** K 6
Camp Century **202**
Camp Creek (AZ.) **116** E 4
Camp Creek (W.V.) **129** K 4
Camp Crook (SD.) **118** E 5
Campeche **132** D 4
Campeche **132** D 4
Campeche, Bahia de **132** D 4
Camperdown **183** G 6
Camp Hill (PA.) **127** BC 8
Camp Howard Ridge **110** J 5
Campidano **153** E 4
Campiglia Marittima **153** F 3
Campina Grande **141** J 2
Campinas **141** G 5
Campina Verde **141** G 4
Campion (CO.) **115** M 3
Campo **197** F 5
Campo (CA.) **113** J 10
Campo (CO.) **115** P 6
Campobasso **153** FG 3
Campo Belo **141** G 5
Campo Corral **138** D 2
Campo de Calatrava **152** C 4
Campo de Criptana **152** C 4
Campo de Diauaruri **141** F 3
Campo de Montiel **152** C 4
Campo Formoso **141** H 3
Campo Gallo **142** D 4
Campo Grande **141** F 5
Campo Maior **141** H 1
Campo-Manzanita and Laposta Indian-
 Reservation **113** J 10
Campomarino **153** G 3
Campo Mourão **141** F 5
Campo Quijano **140** C 5
Campos **141** GH 3–4
Campos **141** H 5
Campos Novos **142** F 4
Campos Sales **141** HJ 2
Campo Troso **138** E 3
Camp Point (IL.) **124** C 9—10
Camp San Saba (TX.) **122** D 4—5
Campti (LA.) **123** K 4
Campton (KY.) **128** H 4
Camptonville (CA.) **112** D 3
Camp Verde (AZ.) **116** E 3
Camp Verde Indian Reservation
 116 DE 3
Camp Wood (TX.) **122** CD 6
Cam Ranh **175** J 5
Camrose **103** P 5
Camsell **103** O 3
Camsell Portage **103** PQ 4
Camucuio **200** A 2
Canaan (CT.) **126** F 6
Canacassala **200** A 1
Canada **102–105**
Canada Basin **209** D 1
Cañada de Gómez **142** D 5
Cañada Oruro **140** D 5
Cañada Verde → Villa Huidobro
 142 D 5
Canadian (OK.) **121** K 7
Canadian (TX.) **117** Q 2
Canadian River **120** GH 7
Canaima **139** C 2
Canaima, Parque Nacional **139** F 2
Çanakkale **154** C 2
Canakkale Boğazı **154** C 2–3

Canal Baker 143 B 8
Canal Beagle 143 C 9
Canal de Ballenas 106 D 6
Canal de Bourgogne 152–153 D 2
Canal de Briare 152 D 2
Canal de la Marne à la Saône 153 E 2
Canal de la Mona 133 J 4
Canal de Sainte-Lucie 133 K 5
Canal des Ardennes 153 D 2
Canal des Ardennes 152–153 D 2
Canal de Yucatán 132 E 3
Canal do Norte 139 H 3
Canal do Sul 139 HJ 4
Canal du Midi 152 D 3
Canale Cavour 153 E 2
Canale de Sicilia 153 F 4
Canale di Malta 153 F 4
Canalejas 143 C 6
Canal Moraleda 143 B 7
Canama 138 D 5
Canamari 140 C 3
Canandaigua Lake 126 B 6
Canandaiqua (N.Y.) 126 B 6
Cananea 106 DE 5
Cananéia 141 G 5
Cananguchal 138 C 3
Canapiari, Cerro 138 E 3
Canary Islands 192 B 3
Canaseraga (N.Y.) 126 B 6
Canastra, Serra da 141 G 4
Cañaveral 152 B 4
Canaveral, Cape 131 O 6
Canavieiras 141 J 4
Canberra 183 H 6
Canby (CA.) 112 E 1
Canby (MN.) 119 M 6
Canby (OR.) 110 C 5
Canchas 142 B 4
Canchyuaya, Cerros de 138 D 5
Cancún 132 E 3
Candamom Hills 174 C 6
Çandarlı 154 C 3
Candeias 141 J 3
Candelaria 132 D 4
Candelaria (TX.) 117 M 7
Çandili Tepe 155 E 3
Candle 108 F 2
Cando (ND.) 118 J 2
Candoí 142 F 4
Candor (N.C.) 129 M 6
Canela (Goiás, Brazil) 141 G 3
Canela (Rio Grande do Sul, Brazil) 142 F 4
Canelones 142 E 5
Cañete (Chile) 143 B 6
Cañete (Peru) 140 A 3
Caney (OK.) 120 J 8
Canfield (AR.) 121 M 9
Cangamba 200 C 2
Cangandala 200 B 1
Cangas 152 B 3
Cangas de Narcea 152 B 3
Canguçu 142 F 5
Cangumbe 200 B 2
Cangwu 172 F 6
Cangyuan 172 C 6
Cangzhou 173 G 3
Caniapiscau 105 N 5
Caniapiscau, Lac 105 O 5
Canicatti 153 F 4
Canık Dağları 155 E 2
Canindé (Amazonas, Brazil) 138 D 5
Canindé (Ceará, Brazil) 141 J 1
Canipiscau 105 O 4
Canjilon (N.M.) 117 K 1
Çankırı 155 D 2
Cannanore 174 BC 5
Cannel City (KY.) 128 H 4
Cannelton (IN.) 128 E 4
Cannes 153 E 3
Canning (SD.) 118 J 6
Canning Basin 182 C 5
Cannon Ball Mountain 110 J 5
Cannonball River 118 G 4
Cannon Beach (OR.) 110 A 5
Cannon Falls (MN.) 119 Q 6
Cannonsville Reservoir 126 D 6
Cannonville (UT.) 114 EF 6
Cann River 183 H 6
Canoas 142 F 4
Canobie 183 G 2
Canol 109 N 2
Canoncito Indian Reservation 117 JK 2
Canon City (CO.) 115 M 5
Canones (N.M.) 117 K 1
Canon Plaza (N.M.) 117 K 1
Canoochee River 131 N 2–3
Canora 103 R 5
Canosa 153 G 3
Canova (S.D.) 119 L 7
Canso 105 P 6
Canso, Strait of 105 P 6
Canta 140 A 3
Cantabrian Mountains 152 BC 3
Cantagalo, Cachoeira 139 H 5
Cantaura 139 F 2

Canterbury 148 D 4
Canterbury Bight 185 Q 9
Canterbury Bight 186 C 5
Canterbury Plains 185 Q 9
Can Tho 175 J 6
Cantil (CA.) 113 H 7
Cantilan 177 G 2
Canto do Buriti 141 H 2
Canton (China) 172 F 6
Canton (GA.) 128 G 7
Canton (IL.) 124 D 9
Canton (MO.) 121 O 2
Canton (KS.) 120 H 4
Canton (MS.) 130 DE 2
Canton (N.C.) 128 J 6
Canton (N.Y.) 126 D 4
Canton (OH.) 125 N 9
Canton (OK.) 120 G 6
Canton (PA.) 126 C 7
Canton (S.D.) 119 M 7
Canton (TX.) 122 H 4
Canton Lake 120 G 6
Cantonment (FL.) 130 G 4
Cantù 153 E 2
Cantwell 102 H 3
Cañuelas 142 E 6
Canumã 139 G 4
Canumã (Amazonas, Brazil) 139 F 5
Canumã (Amazonas, Brazil) 139 FG 5
Canutama 139 F 5
Canutillo (TX.) 117 K 6
Canyon 109 L 3
Canyon (MN.) 119 Q 3
Canyon (TX.) 117 P 2–3
Canyon City (OR.) 110 G 6
Canyon Creek (MT.) 111 N 4
Canyon de Chelly National Monument 116 G 1
Canyon Diablo (AZ.) 116 E 2
Canyon Ferry Lake 111 O 4
Canyon Lake 122 E 6
Canyonlands National Park 114 GH 5
Canyon Valley (TX.) 117 P 4
Canyonville (OR.) 110 B 8
Cao Bang 175 J 3
Caombo 200 B 1
Càorle 153 F 2
Cao Xian 172 G 4
Capa (SD.) 118 GH 6
Capaccio 153 G 3
Capaia 200 C 1
Capanaparo 138 E 2
Capanema 139 J 4
Capão Bonito 141 G 5
Capatárida 138 D 1
Cap Blanc (Mauritania) 192 B 4
Cap Blanc → Ra's al Abyaḍ 193 G 1
Cap Bon → Ra's aṭ Ṭīb 193 H 1
Cap Bougar'oûn 193 G 1
Cap Camarat 153 E 3
Cap Corse 153 E 3
Cap Croisette 153 DE 3
Cap d'Ambre 201 J 2
Cap Dame-Marie 133 H 4
Cap d'Antifer 152 CD 2
Cap d'Arguin 192 B 4
Cap de Fer 193 G 1
Cap de Gaspé 105 P 6
Cap de la Hague 152 C 2
Cap-de-la-Madeleine 105 N 6
Cap-de-Nouvelle France 105 N 3
Cap Drâa 192 C 3
Cape, Ann 126 J 6
Cape, Lookout 129 P 7
Cape Abyssal Plain 208 B 5
Cape Acadia 105 M 3
Cape Adare 203
Cape Agulhas 200 C 6
Cape Alava 110 A 2
Cape Alitak 102 FG 4
Cape Anguille 105 PQ 6
Cape Ann 126 J 6
Cape Ann 203
Cape Arago 110 A 7
Cape Arid 182 C 5
Cape Arid National Park 182 C 5
Cape Arnhem 183 F 1
Cape Baring 103 O 2
Cape Barren Island 184 L 9
Cape Basin 208 B 5
Cape Bathurst 102 LM 1
Cape Bauld 105 QR 5
Cape Bear 105 P 6
Cape Beatrice 183 F 1
Cape Blanco 110 A 8
Cape Boothby 203
Cape Bossut 182 C 2
Cape Bowling Green 183 H 2
Cape Breton Highlands National Park 105 P 6
Cape Breton Island 105 Q 6
Cape Brett 185 Q 8
Cape Byron 183 J 4
Cape Ca Mau 163 J 6
Cape Campbell 185 Q 9
Cape Canaveral 131 O 6
Cape Capricorn 183 J 3
Cape Catastrophe 183 F 6
Cape Chapman 103 U 2

Cape Charles 129 PQ 4
Cape Charles (Newfoundl., Can.) 105 QR 5
Cape Charles (VA.) 129 Q 4
Cape Chelyuskin 202
Cape Chidley 105 P 3
Cape Churchill 103 T 4
Cape Clear 148 B 4
Cape Coast 196 D 4
Cape Cod 126 K 7
Cape Cod Bay 126 J 7
Cape Columbine 200 B 6
Cape Colville 103 T 2
Cape Comorin 174 C 6
Cape Constantine 102 EF 4
Cape Coral (FL.) 131 N 8
Cape Cornwall 148 B C 4
Cape Cretin 184 E 3
Cape Croker 182 E 1
Cape Cross 200 A 4
Cape Cuvier 182 A 3
Cape Dalhousie 102 L 1
Cape Darby 108 F 3
Cape Darnley 203
Cape Dennison 203
Cape Disappointment 110 A 4
Cape Dominion 105 M 2
Cape Dorchester 105 M 2
Cape Dorset 105 MN 3
Cape du Couedic 183 F 6
Cape Dyer 105 P 2
Cape Egmont 185 Q 8
Cape Elizabeth 110 A 3
Cape Elizabeth (ME.) 126 J 5
Cape Engaño 177 J 1
Cape Falcon 110 A 5
Cape Farewell 185 Q 9
Cape Farewell 186 C 5
Cape Farquhar 182 A 3
Cape Fear 129 O 8
Cape Fear River 129 N 7
Cape Felix 103 S 2
Cape Ferrelo 110 A 8
Cape Finniss 182 E 5
Cape Flattery 110 A 2
Cape Flattery (Queensland, Austr.) 183 H 1
Cape Foulwind 185 Q 9
Cape Freels 105 R 6
Cape Fria 200 A 3
Cape Grenville (Queensland, Austr.) 183 G 1
Cape Grim 184 K 9
Cape Guardafui 199 J 2
Cape Halawa 113 F 10
Cape Halkett 102 G 1
Cape Harrison 105 Q 5
Cape Hatteras 129 Q 6
Cape Hatteras National Seashore 129 Q 6
Cape Henlopen 127 DE 10
Cape Henrietta Maria 105 L 4
Cape Henry 129 Q 5
Cape Herluf Trolle 105 T 3
Cape Hooper 105 O 2
Cape Hope 103 O 2
Cape Horn 143 C 10
Cape Howe 183 J 6
Cape Inscription 182 A 4
Cape Island 129 M 8
Cape Jaffa 183 F 6
Cape Jones 103 T 3
Cape Kattaktoc 105 O 4
Cape Keer-Weer (Queensland, Austr.) 183 G 1
Cape Kellett 103 M 1
Cape Kendall 103 U 3
Cape Kidnappers 185 R 8
Cape Knox 102 L 5
Cape Krusenstern 108 F 2
Cape Krusenstern National Monument 102 E 2
Cape Kumukahi 113 H 12
Cape Lambert 185 F 2
Cape Lambton 103 MN 1
Cape Latouche Treville 182 C 2
Cape Leeuwin 182 A 5
Cape Lévêque 182 C 2
Cape Lisburne 102 D 2
Cape Lisburne 102 DE 2
Cape Londonderry 182 D 1
Cape Lookout 110 A 5
Cape Lookout National Seashore 129 P 7
Cape Low 103 UV 3
Cape Maria van Diemen 185 Q 7
Cape Matapan 154 B 3
Cape May 127 E 10
Cape May (N.J.) 127 E 8—9
Cape May CH (N.J.) 127 E 9
Cape Melville (Queensland, Austr.) 183 G 1
Cape Mendocino 112 A 2
Cape Mercy 105 P 3
Cape Meredith 143 D 9
Cape Michelsen 103 R 1
Cape Mohican 102 D 3

Cape Monze → Ras Muari 169 H 6
Cape Morris Jesup 202
Cape Naturaliste 182 A 5
Cape Negrais 175 F 4
Cape Nelson 183 G 6
Cape Nelson (New Guinea) 185 E 3
Cape Newenham 102 E 4
Cape North (Nova Scotia, Can.) 105 P 6
Cape Norvegia 203
Cape of Good Hope 200 B 6
Cape Otway 183 G 6
Cape Palliser 185 R 9
Cape Palmas 196 C 5
Cape Parry 103 N 1
Cape Pembroke 143 E 9
Cape Pembroke (Ontario, Can.) 105 L 3
Cape Poinsett 203
Cape Pool 109 M 4
Cape Portland 184 L 9
Cape Prince Alfred 103 M 1
Cape Prince of Wales 102 D 2
Cape Providence 184 P 10
Cape Province 200 CD 6
Cape Queen 105 M 3
Cape Race 105 R 6
Cape Raper 105 O 2
Cape Ray 105 Q 6
Cape River 183 H 3
Cape Rodney (AK, U.S.A.) 102 D 3
Cape Rodney (Papua New Guinea) 184 E 4
Cape Romain 129 M 9
Cape Romano 131 N 9
Cape Romanzof 102 D 3
Cape Runaway 185 R 8
Cape Sable 105 O 7
Cape Sable 131 N 9
Cape Saint Francis 200 CD 6
Cape Saint George 105 PQ 6
Cape Saint George (Papua New Guinea) 185 F 2
Cape Saint James 102 L 5
Cape Saint Lucia 201 E 5
Cape Saint Martin 112 L 6
Cape San Agustin 177 G 2
Cape San Blas 131 J 5
Cape Scott 102 M 5
Cape Scott 182 D 1
Cape Small 126 K 5
Cape Smith 105 M 3
Cape Southampton 103 UV 3
Cape Spencer 183 F 6
Cape Swinburne 103 RS 1
Cape Tatnam 103 TU 4
Cape Three Points 196 D 5
Cape Town 200 B 6
Cape Van Diemen 182 D 1
Cape Verde 196 AB 6
Cape Verde (Senegal) 192 B 6
Cape Vincent (N.Y.) 126 C 4
Cape Vizcaino 112 B 3
Cape Walsingham 105 P 2
Cape Wessel 183 F 1
Cape Wickham 184 K 8
Cape Wilson 103 VW 2
Cape Wrath 148 C 2
Cape Wrottesley 103 N 1
Cape Yakataga 102 J 4
Cape York 183 G 1
Cape York Peninsula (Queensland, Austr.) 183 G 1
Cape Zhelaniya 202
Cap Ferret 152 C 3
Cap Fréhel 152 C 2
Cap Gris-Nez 152 D 1
Cap-Haïtien 133 H 4
Cap Hopes Advance 105 O 3
Capibara 138 E 3
Capilla 142 E 5
Capim 139 J 4
Capim 139 J 4
Capinota 140 C 4
Capinzal, Cachoeira 139 G 5
Capitan (N.M.) 117 L 4
Capitan Arturo Prat 203
Capitan Bado 140 E 5
Capitán Meza 142 E 4
Capitan Peak 117 L 4
Capitol (MT.) 118 D 5
Capitol Peak 112 H 1
Capitol Reef National Park 114 F 5
Capivara, Represa da 141 F 5
Cap Juby 192 C 3
Cap Lopez 197 F 6
Cap Masoala 201 J 3
Capo Bonifati 153 G 4
Capo Carbonara 153 E 4
Capo Circeo 153 F 3
Capo delle Colonne 153 G 4
Capo di Pula 153 E 4
Capoeiras, Cachoeira das 139 G 5
Capo Gallo 153 F 4
Capo Linaro 153 F 3
Capo Mannu 153 E 3
Capo Marargiu 153 E 3
Capo Murro di Porco 153 G 4
Capoompeta 183 J 4
Capo Palinuro 153 FG 3
Capo Passero 153 G 4

Capo Punta Granitola 153 F 4
Capo San Marco 153 E 4
Capo Santa Maria di Leuca 153 G 4
Capo Scaramia 153 F 4
Capo Sferracavallo 153 E 4
Capo Spartivento 153 E 4
Capo Testa 153 E 3
Capo Vaticano 153 G 4
Cap Prince de Galles 105 N 3
Capps (FL.) 131 L 4
Capraia 153 E 3
Capreol 105 L 6
Capri 153 F 3
Capricorn, Cape 183 J 3
Capricorn Channel 183 J 3
Capricorn Group 183 J 3
Caprivi Game Park 200 C 3
Caprivi Strip 200 C 3
Caprock (N.M.) 117 N 4
Cap Rock (TX.) 117 P 4
Capron (OK.) 120 G 6
Cap Roxo 196 A 3
Cap Saint-André 201 G 3
Cap Sainte-Marie 201 GH 5
Cap Spartel 192 D 1
Captain Cook (HI.) 113 G 12
Captains Flat 183 H 6
Captieux 152 C 3
Cap Timiris 192 B 5
Captiva (FL.) 131 M 8
Cap Tres Forcas 192 E 1
Capulin Mountain National Monument 117 M 1
Capulin Peak 117 K 1
Capunda 200 B 2
Caputa (SD.) 118 F 6
Cap Verga 196 B 3
Cap Vert 196 A 3
Cap Wolstenholme 105 M 3
Caquetá 138 D 4
Carabaya, Cordillera de 140 B 3
Carabelle (FL.) 131 K 5
Caracal 154 B 2
Caracarai 139 F 3
Caracas 138 E 1
Caracol 141 H 2
Caraga 177 G 2
Carahue 143 B 6
Carajari 139 H 4
Carajás, Serra dos 139 H 4–5
Carajou River 109 N 2
Caramulo, Serra do 152 B 3
Caranapatuba 139 F 5
Carandotta 183 F 3
Carangola 141 H 5
Caransbeş 154 B 1
Carantuohill 148 AB 4
Carapajó 139 J 3
Caraquet 105 P 6
Caratasca, Laguna de 132 F 4
Caratinga 141 H 5
Carauari 138 E 4
Caravaca 152 C 4
Caravelas 141 J 4
Caraveli 140 B 4
Caraz 138 C 5
Carazinho 142 F 4
Carballo 152 B 3
Carbon (TX.) 122 E 3
Carbonado (WA.) 110 D 3
Carbonara, Capo 153 E 4
Carbondale (CO.) 115 K 4
Carbondale (IL.) 121 Q 5
Carbondale (KS.) 121 K 4
Carbondale (PA.) 126 D 7
Carboneras 152 C 4
Carbonia 153 E 4
Carcajou 103 O 4
Carcans-Plage 152 C 2
Carcaraña 142 D 5
Carcar Mountains → Karkār 199 H 3
Carcassonne 152 D 3
Carcross 102 K 3
Cárdenas (Cuba)133 F 3
Cárdenas (Mexico) 132 C 3
Cardenas (N.M.) 117 M 3
Cardiel, Lago 143 B 8
Cardiff 148 C 4
Cardigan 148 C 4
Cardigan Bay 148 C 4
Cardona 152 D 3
Cardozo 142 E 5
Cardston 103 P 6
Cardwell (MO.) 121 P 6
Carei 154 B 1
Careiro 139 G 4
Carentan 152 C 2
Carey (ID.) 111 M 7
Carey (OH.) 125 L 9
Carey (TX.) 117 Q 3
Carey, Lake 182 C 4
Cargèse 153 E 3
Carhaix-Plouguer 152 C 2
Carhué 143 D 6
Cariati 153 G 4
Caribbean Sea 133 GJ 4
Cariboo Mountains (Br. Col., Can.) 103 N 5

Caribou (ME.) 126 L 2
Caribou Mountains (Alb., Can.) 103 O 4
Caribou Range 111 O 7
Carimbula 200 BC 1
Cariñena 152 C 3
Carinhanha 141 H 3
Cariparé 141 G 3
Caripito 139 F 1
Caritianas 139 F 5
Carius 141 J 2
Carl Blackwell, Lake 120 H 6
Carleton (NE.) 120 H 2
Carleton Place 105 M 6
Carletonville 200 D 5
Carlile (WY.) 118 D 6
Carlin (NV.) 112 J 2
Carlinville (IL.) 121 P 3
Carlisle 148 C 4
Carlisle (AR.) 121 O 8
Carlisle (IA.) 119 P 9
Carlisle (KY.) 128 H 3
Carlisle (S.C.) 129 K 7
Carlistle (PA.) 127 E 9
Carloforte 153 E 4
Carlos Casares 143 D 6
Carlos Chagas 141 H 4
Carlow 148 B 4
Carloway 148 B 3
Carlsbad (CA.) 113 H 9
Carlsbad (N.M.) 117 M 5
Carlsbad (TX.) 122 C 4
Carlsbad Caverns National Park 117 M 5
Carlsberg Ridge 208 B 3
Carlton (MN.) 119 Q 4
Carlton (OR.) 110 B 5
Carlton (TX.) 122 E 4
Carlton (WA.) 110 E 2
Carlton Hill 182 D 2
Carlyle 103 R 6
Carlyle (IL.) 121 Q 4
Carlyle (MT.) 118 D 4
Carlyle Lake 121 Q 4
Carmacks 102 K 3
Carmagnola 153 E 3
Carmaux 152 D 3
Carmel, Point 112 CD 6
Çarmeli 154 C 3
Carmelo 142 E 5
Carmen 142 E 4
Carmen (ID.) 111 LM 5
Carmen (OK.) 120 G 6
Carmen, Isla 106 D 6
Carmen Alto 140 BC 5
Carmen de Patagones 143 D 7
Carmensa 143 C 6
Carmi (IL.) 121 R 4
Carmichael (CA.) 112 D 4
Carmila 183 H 3
Carmine (TX.) 122 G 5
Carmona 152 B 4
Carnac 152 C 2
Carnamah 182 B 4
Carnarvon 182 A 3
Carnarvon 200 C 6
Carnarvon Range 182 C 4
Carnation (WA.) 110 D 3
Carne (N.M.) 116 J 5
Carnegie 182 C 4
Carnegie (OK.) 120 G 7
Carnegie, Lake 182 C 4
Carnesville (GA.) 128 H 7
Carney (OK.) 120 NU F 7
Carniche, Alpi 153 F 2
Car Nicobar 175 F 6
Carning River 109 J 2
Carnot 198 B 3
Caro (MI.) 125 L 6
Carol City (FL.) 131 O 9
Carolina 139 J 5
Carolina (Ecuador) 138 C 3
Carolina (P.R.) 130 D 8
Carolina Beach (N.C.) 129 O 7
Caroline (Kiribati) 187 EF 3
Caroline Basin 209 C 3
Caroline Islands 186 AB 2
Carondelet 186 D 3
Caroní 139 F 2
Carora 138 DE 1
Carp (NV.) 112 L 5
Carpathians 154 C 1
Carpáţii Meridionali 154 B 1–2
Carpentaria, Gulf of 183 F 1
Carpenter (S.D.) 119 KL 6
Carpenter (WY.) 118 D 9
Carpenterville (OR.) 110 A 8
Carpentras 153 E 3
Carpi 153 F 3
Carpina 141 J 2
Carpinteria (CA.) 113 F 8
Carr (CO.) 115 N 3
Carrara 153 E 3
Carrazedo 139 H 4
Carrera 140 E 5
Carreta, Punta 140 A 3
Carribou Lake, North 104 J 5
Carrick-on-Shannon 148 B 4
Carriere (MS.) 130 E 4
Carrillo 132 B 2

Carrington (ND.) 118 JK 3
Carrión de los Condes 152 C 3
Carrizal (Colombia) 138 D 1
Carrizal (Mexico) 106 E 5
Carrizal Bajo 142 B 4
Carrizo Plateau 116 GH 1
Carrizos 106 E 5
Carrizo Springs (TX.) 122 D 7
Carrizozo (N.M.) 117 L 4
Carroll (IA.) 119 O 8
Carroll (NE.) 119 L 8
Carrollton (AL.) 128 C 8
Carrollton (GA.) 128 F 8
Carrollton (IL.) 121 P 3
Carrollton (KY.) 128 F 2
Carrollton (MO.) 121 M 3
Carrollton (MS.) 121 M 6
Carrollton (TX.) 122 G 3
Carry Falls Reservoir 126 E 4
Çarşamba 155 E 2
Çarşamba 155 D 3
Carson (ND.) 118 G 4
Carson (WA.) 110 D 5
Carson City (MI.) 125 K 6
Carson City (NV.) 112 F 3
Carson City (NV.) 112 F 3
Carson Lake 112 G 3
Carson Sink 112 G 3
Cartagena (Colombia) 138 C 1
Cartagena (Spain) 152 C 4
Cartago 138 C 3
Cartago (CA.) 112 H 6
Cartago (Costa Rica) 132 F 6
Carta Valley (TX.) 122 C 6
Carter (MT.) 111 O 3
Carter (OK.) 120 F 7
Carter (SD.) 118 H 7
Carter (WI.) 124 F 4
Carter (WY.) 111 P 9
Carter, Mount (Queensland, Austr.) 183 G 1
Carter Lake (NE.) 120 K 1
Carter Mountain 111 Q 6
Carters Lake 128 G 7
Cartersville (GA.) 128 G 7
Carthage (AR.) 121 N 8
Carthage (IL.) 124 C 9
Carthage (MO.) 121 L 5
Carthage (MS.) 130 E 2
Carthage (N.C.) 129 M 6
Carthage (N.Y.) 126 D 5
Carthage (S.D.) 119 L 6
Carthage (TN.) 128 F 5
Carthage (Tunisia) 153 F 4
Carthage (Tunisia) → Karthago 193 H 1
Carthage (TX.) 123 C 4
Cartier Island 182 C 1
Cartwright 105 Q 5
Cartwright (ND.) 118 E 3
Caruaru 141 J 2
Carúpano 139 F 1
Carutapera 139 J 4
Carvoeiro 139 F 4
Cary (MS.) 130 D 2
Cary (N.C.) 129 N 6
Caryville (TN.) 128 G 5
Casablanca 192 D 2
Casablanca (Chile) 142 B 5
Casa Branca 141 G 5
Casa Grande (AZ.) 116 E 5
Casa Grande Ruins National Monument 116 E 4–5
Casalbordino 153 F 3
Casale Monferrato 153 E 2
Casalmaggiore 153 F 3
Casalvasco 140 E 4
Casal Velino 153 G 3
Casamance 196 A 3
Casanare 138 D 2
Casa Nova 141 H 2
Casa Piedra (TX.) 117 MN 8
Casaux, Étang de 152 C 3
Casbas 143 D 6
Cascade (IA.) 119 RS 8
Cascade (ID.) 110 J 6
Cascade (MT.) 111 O 3
Cascade Head 110 A 5
Cascade Range 110 D 4–6
Cascade Reservoir 110 J 6
Cascadia (OR.) 110 C 6
Cascadia Basin 209 D 2
Cascavel 141 F 5
Cascina 153 F 3
Casco Bay 126 JK 5
Caserta 153 F 3
Caseville (MI.) 125 L 6
Casey 203
Cashmere (WA.) 110 E 3
Cashmere Mountain 110 DE 3
Casiguran 177 F 1
Casiguran 177 J 1
Casilda 142 D 5
Casino 183 J 4
Cáslav 149 G 5
Casma 138 C 5
Caspar (CA.) 112 B 3
Casper (WY.) 118 B 8
Caspian Depression 168 DE 1
Caspian Sea 168 DE 2–3

Cass (W.V.) 129 M 3
Cassai 200 C 2
Cassai Sul 200 C 2
Cassamba 200 C 2
Cass City (MI.) 125 L 6
Casselton (N.D.) 119 L 4
Cassiar 102 L 4
Cassiar Mountains 102 M 4
Cassilândia 141 F 4
Cassinga 200 A 2
Cassino 142 F 5
Cassino (Italy) 153 F 3
Cassiporé, Cabo 139 H 3
Cass Lake (MN.) 119 O 3
Cassoday (KS.) 120 J 4
Cassongue 200 A 2
Cassopolis (MI.) 124 H 8
Cassville (MO.) 121 M 6
Cassville (WI.) 124 D 7
Castaic Lake 113 G 8
Castañar, Sierra del 152 C 4
Castaneda (OK.) 120 C 6
Castanhal 139 J 4
Castanho 139 F 5
Castaño 142 C 5
Castelarrasin 152 D 3
Castel di Sangro 153 F 3
Castella (CA.) 112 C 1
Castellabate 153 F 3
Castellammare, Golfo di 153 F 4
Castellane 153 E 3
Castellaneta 153 G 3
Castelli 143 E 6
Castellón 152 D 4
Castelnaudary 152 D 3
Castelo Branco 152 B 4
Castelo de Vide 152 B 4
Castelvetrano 153 F 4
Castets 152 C 3
Castiglione 153 F 3
Castilla (Chile) 142 B 4
Castilla (Peru) 138 B 5
Castilla la Nueva 152 C 3–4
Castilla la Vieja 152 C 3
Castillejo 152 D 3
Castillo, Cerro 143 B 8
Castillo, Pampa del 143 C 8
Castillo de San Marcos National Monument 131 N 5
Castillo Incasico de Ingapirca 138 C 4
Castillonnes 152 D 3
Castillos 142 F 5
Castlebar 148 B 4
Castleberry (AL.) 130 GH 3
Castle Dale (UT.) 114 F 4
Castle Dome Peak 116 B 4
Castleford (ID.) 111 KL 8
Castlegar 103 O 6
Castle Gate (UT.) 114 G 4
Castle Hayne (N.C.) 129 O 7
Castle Hills (TX.) 122 E 6
Castlemaine 183 G 6
Castle Mountain 109 L 3
Castle Peak 111 L 6
Castle Peak 115 L 4–5
Castlereagh Bay 182 F 1
Castlereagh River 183 H 5
Castle Rock 110 G 6
Castle Rock (CO.) 115 N 4
Castle Rock (SD.) 118 E 6
Castle Rock (WA.) 110 BC 4
Castle Rock Butte 118 E 5
Castle Rock Lake 124 E 6
Castlewood (S.D.) 119 M 6
Castolon (TX.) 117 M 8
Castor 103 P 5
Castres 152 D 3
Castries (Saint Lucia) 133 K 5
Castro (Chile) 143 B 7
Castro (Paraná, Brazil) 141 G 5
Castro Daire 152 B 3
Castro del Río 152 C 4
Castro-Urdiales 152 C 3
Castro Verde 152 B 4
Castrovillari 153 G 4
Castroville (CA.) 112 D 6
Castroville (TX.) 122 E 6
Castuera 152 B 4
Casuarina, Mount 182 D 1
Casula 201 E 3
Çat 155 F 3
Catabola 200 B 2
Catacaos 138 B 5
Cataguases 141 H 5
Catahoula Lake 123 LM 4
Catalão 141 G 4
Catalina, Punta 143 C 9
Catalonia 152 D 3
Çatalzeytin 155 D 2
Catamarca 142 C 4
Catamayo 138 BC 4
Catandica 201 E 3
Catanduanes 177 F 1
Catanduva 141 G 5
Catania 153 G 4
Cataño (P.R.) 130 C 8
Catanzaro 153 G 4
Cataract Lake 128 E 2

Cataratas del Iguazú 142 F 4
Catarina (TX.) 122 D 7
Catastrophe, Cape 183 F 6
Catauera 139 G 4
Catawba River 129 L 7
Catawissa (PA.) 127 C 8
Catbalogan 177 FG 1
Cat Creek (MT.) 111 R 3
Cateel 177 G 2
Catende 141 J 2
Catesbu (OK.) 120 F 6
Catharine (KS.) 120 F 4
Cathay (ND.) 118 J 3
Cathedral City (CA.) 113 J 9
Cathedral Mountain 117 N 7
Catheys Valley (CA.) 112 EF 5
Cathlamet (WA.) 110 B 4
Catinzaco 142 C 4
Catió 196 A 3
Catisimiña 139 F 3
Cat Island 133 GH 3
Cat Island (KY.) 128 J 3
Cat Island (MS.) 130 E 4
Cat Lake 104 J 5
Catlettsburg (KY.) 128 J 3
Catnip Mountain 112 F 1
Catoche, Cabo 132 E 3
Catonsville (MD.) 129 P 2
Catoosa (OK.) 121 K 6
Catora 140 D 4
Catrilo 143 D 6
Catrimani 139 F 3
Catrimani 139 F 3
Catskill (N.Y.) 126 E 6
Catskill Mountains 126 E 6
Cattaraugus Indian Reservation 125 Q 7
Catuane 201 F 2
Catuile 200 C 3
Catuna 142 C 5
Catur 201 F 2
Cauaburi 138 E 3
Cauca 138 C 2
Caucaia 138 CD 2
Caucasus Mountains 155 F 2
Caucomgomoc Lake 126 K 2
Caudry 152 D 1
Cauga (TX.) 122 H 4
Caulfield (MO.) 121 N 6
Caulonia 153 G 4
Caungula 200 B 1
Cauquenes 143 B 6
Caura 139 F 2
Causapscal 105 O 6
Causey (N.M.) 117 N 4
Caussade 152 D 3
Causse de Gramat 152 D 3
Causse de Limogne 152 D 3
Causse du Larzac 152 D 3
Cautário 140 D 3
Cauvery 174 C 5
Cavaillon 153 D 3
Cavalcante 141 G 3
Cavalier (N.D.) 119 L 2
Cavally 196 C 4
Cavan 148 B 4
Cavarzere 153 F 2
Çavdarhisar 154 C 3
Cave City (AR.) 121 O 7
Cave City (KY.) 128 F 4
Cave Creek (AZ.) 116 E 4
Cave Creek Dam 116 DE 4
Cave Junction (OR.) 110 B 8
Cavell 104 K 5
Caviana, 139 HJ 3
Cavignac 152 C 2
Cavili 177 F 2
Cavour (WI.) 124 F 4
Cavour, Canale 153 E 2
Cavtat 153 G 3
Çavuşcu Gölü 155 D 3
Cawker City (KS.) 120 G 3
Caxias (Amazonas, Brazil) 138 D 4
Caxias (Maranhão, Brazil) 141 H 1
Caxias do Sul 142 F 4
Caxito 200 A 1
Cay 155 D 3
Cayambe 138 C 3
Cayambe 138 C 3
Çaycuma 155 D 2
Çayeli 155 F 2
Cayenne 139 H 3
Cayey (P.R.) 130 C 8
Çayıralan 155 E 3
Çayırhan 154 D 2
Cayman Brac 133 G 4
Cayman Islands 133 FG 4
Cayo Arenas 132 D 3
Cayo Norte 130 D 8
Cayo Nuevo 132 D 3
Cayos Arcas 132 D 3
Cayos de Albuquerque 133 F 5
Cayos de Roncador 133 G 5
Cayos Miskitos 132 F 5
Cay Sal 133 F 3
Cayucos (CA.) 113 E 7
Cayuga (N.D.) 119 L 4
Cayuga Lake 126 C 6

Cazenovia (N.Y.) 126 D 6
Cazombo 200 C 2
Cazongo 197 G 7
Ceará 141 J 1
Ceara Abyssal Plain 208 A 3
Ceará Mirim 141 J 2
Ceballos 132 B 2
Cebolla (N.M.) 117 K 1
Cebollar 142 C 4
Cebollatí 142 F 5
Cebollita Peak 116 J 3
Cebu 177 F 1
Cebu 177 F 2
Čechy 149 F 4
Cecil (AR.) 121 LM 7
Cecil (OR.) 110 F 5
Cecilia (KY.) 128 E 4
Cecilville (CA.) 112 B 1
Cecina 153 F 3
Cedar (UT.) 114 G 4
Cedar Bluff Reservoir 120 F 4
Cedar Bluffs (KS.) 120 E 3
Cedar Breaks National Monument 114 E 6
Cedar Butte (SD.) 118 G 7
Cedar City (MO.) 121 N 4
Cedar City (UT.) 114 D 6
Cedar Creek 118 FG 4
Cedar Creek Reservoir 122 G 3
Cedar Falls (IA.) 119 Q 8
Cedar Grove (CA.) 112 G 6
Cedar Grove (W.V.) 129 K 3
Cedar Hill (N.M.) 116 J 1
Cedar Key (FL.) 131 LM 5
Cedar Keys 131 L 5
Cedar Lake 103 RS 5
Cedar Lake (TX.) 123 H 7
Cedar Mills (MN.) 119 O 6
Cedar Park (TX.) 122 F 5
Cedar Pass 112 E 1
Cedar Rapids (IA.) 119 R 9
Cedar Rapids (NE.) 119 K 9
Cedar River (IA.) 119 Q 7
Cedar River (MI.) 124 G 4
Cedartown (GA.) 128 F 7
Cedar Vale (KS.) 120 J 5
Cedarville (CA.) 112 E 1
Cedarwood (CO.) 115 N 6
Ceder Springs (MI.) 124 J 6
Cedonia (WA.) 110 G 2
Cedros, Isla 106 C 6
Ceduna 182 E 5
Cefalù 153 F 4
Cegléd 154 A 1
Çekerek 155 E 2
Çekerek 155 E 2–3
Celaya 132 B 3
Celebes 177 EF 4
Celebes Sea 177 F 3
Çelebi 155 D 3
Celeste (TX.) 122 G 2
Celestún 132 D 3
Çelikhan 155 E 3
Celina (OH.) 125 K 9
Celina (TN.) 128 F 5
Celina (TX.) 122 G 2
Celje 153 G 2
Celle 149 F 4
Celorico da Beira 152 B 3
Celtic Sea 148 B 4
Celtic Shelf 208 A 2
Çeltikçi Geçidi 154 D 3
Cement (OK.) 120 G 8
Cement City (MI.) 125 K 7
Çemişgezek 155 E 3
Cenajo, Embalse de 152 C 4
Cencia 199 F 3
Cendrawasih 177 H 4
Centenario 143 C 6
Centennial (WY.) 118 BC 9
Centennial Mountains 111 NO 6
Centennial Wash 116 C 4
Center (CO.) 115 L 6
Center (ND.) 118 G 3
Center (NE.) 119 L 8
Center (TX.) 123 J 4
Centerburg (OH.) 125 M 9
Center City (MN.) 119 Q 5
Center City (TX.) 122 E 4
Center Hill (FL.) 131 MN 6
Center Hill Reservoir 128 F 5
Center Mountain 111 K 5
Center Point (AL.) 128 E 8
Center Point (IN.) 128 DE 2
Center Point (TX.) 117 P 5
Center Point (TX.) 122 D 6
Centerville (IA.) 119 Q 10
Centerville (PA.) 125 O 9
Centerville (S.D.) 119 M 7
Centerville (TN.) 128 D 6
Centerville (TX.) 122 GH 4
Centerville (UT.) 114 F 3
Cento 153 F 3
Central (AK.) 109 K 2
Central (N.M.) 116 H 5
Central (UT.) 114 D 6
Central, Cordillera (Colombia) 138 C 2–3
Central, Cordillera (Peru) 138 C 5
Central African Republic 198 BC 3

Central Arctic District **103** QR 1
Central Brahui Range **169** H 5
Central City (CO.) **115** M 4
Central City (IA.) **119** R 8
Central City (IL.) **121** Q 4
Central City (KY.) **128** DE 4
Central City (NE.) **120** G 1
Central City (PA.) **125** Q 9
Central City (SD.) **118** E 6
Centralia (IL.) **121** Q 4
Centralia (MO.) **121** N 3
Centralia (NE.) **120** J 3
Centralia (WA.) **110** C 4
Central Kalahari Game Reserve **200** C 4
Central Lake (MI.) **124** J 4
Central Makran Range **169** GH 5
Centralno Tungusskoye Plato
  170 GH 3–4
Central Pacific Basin **209** D 3
Central Point (OR.) **110** C 8
Central Range (Papua New Guinea)
  184 D 3
Central Range (Papua New Guinea)
  186 A 3
Central Siberian Plateau **170** GK 3
Central Square (N.Y.) **126** C 5
Central Valley (CA.) **112** C 2
Centre (AL.) **128** F 7
Centre Hall (PA.) **127** B 8
Centreville (AL.) **130** G 2
Centreville (MD.) **129** PQ 2
Centreville (MI.) **124** J 8
Centreville (MO.) **121** P 5
Centreville (MS.) **130** CD 3
Čepin **153** G 2
Cepu **176** D 5
Ceram **177** G 4
Cercal **152** B 4
Cereal **103** P 5
Ceremai, Gunung **176** C 5
Ceres (Brazil) **141** G 4
Ceres (South Africa) **200** B 6
Cereté **138** C 2
Cerf **199** J 6
Cerignola **153** G 3
Çerkeş **155** D 2
Cermenika **154** B 2
Cernavoda **154** C 2
Černi vrukh **154** B 2
Cerralvo, Isla **106** E 7
Cerra Viejo **106** D 5
Cerrillos (N.M.) **117** K 2
Cerritos **138** BC 3
Cerro Aconcagua **142** BC 5
Cerro Agua Caliente **132** A 2
Cerro Aguja **143** B 7
Cerro Aiguilete **143** B 9
Cerro Ángel **132** B 3
Cerro Arenales **143** B 8
Cerro Atalaya (Chile) **143** B 9
Cerro Atalaya (Peru) **140** B 3
Cerro Azul **132** C 3
Cerro Blanco **106** E 6
Cerro Bolívar **139** F 2
Cerro Bonete **142** C 4
Cerro Bravo **138** C 5
Cerro Canapiari **138** E 3
Cerro Candelaria **138** B 3
Cerro Castillo **143** B 8
Cerro Champaquí **142** D 5
Cerro Chato **143** B 7
Cerro Chirripó **132** F 6
Cerro Chochis **140** E 4
Cerro Cibuta **106** D 5
Cerro Coan **138** C 5
Cerro Coatepetl **132** C 4
Cerro Cojudo Blanco **143** C 8
Cerro Colorado **106** C 5
Cerro Colorado **143** C 7
Cerro Cónico **143** B 7
Cerro Dedo **143** B 7
Cerro de la Asunción **132** C 3
Cerro de la Encantada **106** CD 5
Cerro de las Mesas **132** CD 4
Cerro del Tigre **132** BC 3
Cerro del Toro **142** C 4
Cerro de Punta **133** J 4
Cerro de Punto **130** C 8
Cerro de Pasco **140** A 3
Cerro de San Felipe **152** C 3
Cerro Desmoronado **132** AB 3
Cerro de Tocorpuri **140** C 5
Cerro el Cóndor **142** C 4
Cerro el Nevado **138** D 3
Cerro el Potro **142** C 4
Cerro Galán **142** C 4
Cerro Grande **132** B 3
Cerro Guaiquinima **139** F 2
Cerro Hudson **143** B 8
Cerro La Ardilla **132** B 3
Cerro Largo **142** EF 4
Cerro Las Casilas **106** E 7
Cerro Las Minas **132** E 5
Cerro Lechiguiri **132** C 4
Cerro Lejia **140** C 5
Cerro León **140** D 5
Cerro Marahuaca **138** E 3
Cerro Mariquita **132** C 3
Cerro Mato **138** E 2
Cerro Mercedario **142** BC 5

Cerro Mesa **143** B 8
Cerro Mohinora **106** E 6
Cerro Morado **140** CD 5
Cerro Morado **140** CD 5
Cerro Moreno **140** B 5
Cerro Munchique **138** C 3
Cerro Murallón **143** B 8
Cerro Negro **143** C 7
Cerro Nevado **143** C 6
Cerro Nuevo Mundo **140** C 5
Cerro O'Higgins **143** B 8
Cerro Ojos del Salado **142** C 4
Cerro Paine Medio **143** B 9
Cerro Payún **143** C 6
Cerro Peña Nevada **132** C 3
Cerro Piedra **143** B 6
Cerro Potosí **132** B 2–3
Cerro San Lorenzo **143** B 8
Cerro Santiago **133** F 6
Cerro Santiago **138** B 2
Cerro San Valentín **143** B 8
Cerros de Araracuara **138** D 3–4
Cerros de Canchyuaza **138** C 3
Cerros de la Brea **138** B 4
Cerro Tetari **138** D 2
Cerro Toroni **140** C 4
Cerro Tres Cruces **132** C 3
Cerro Tres Picos **143** D 6
Cerro Tunari **140** C 4
Cerro Veijo **138** C 4
Cerro Ventana **106** E 7
Cerro Vista Peak **117** L 1
Cerro Yavi **138** E 2
Cerro Yucuyácua **132** C 4
Cerro Yumari **138** E 3
Cervera **152** D 3
Cervia **153** F 3
Cesano **153** F 3
Cesena **153** F 3
Čēsis **151** J 4
Česká Lípa **149** F 4
Česká Třebová **149** G 5
České Budějovice **149** F 5
Českézemě **149** FG 5
Český les **149** F 5
Çeşme **154** C 3
Cess **196** C 4
Cessford **101**
Cessnock **183** J 5
Cetina **153** G 3
Cetinje **154** A 2
Çetinkaya **155** E 3
Cetraro **153** G 4
Ceuta **192** D 1
Ceva-i-Ra **186** C 4
Cévennes **152** D 3
Ceyhan **155** E 3
Ceyhan **155** E 3
Ceyhan (Turkey) **156** B 1
Ceylanpinar (Turkey) **156** C 1
Ceylon (MN.) **119** O 7
Ceylon → Sri Lanka **174** D 6
Cézallier **152** D 2
Chabas **142** D 5
Chãboksar (Iran) **157** F 1
Chaca **140** B 4
Chacabuco **142** D 5
Chacance **140** BC 5
Chachani, Nevado **140** B 4
Chachapoyas **140** B 2
Chachoengsao **175** H 5
Chachro **169** J 3
Chaco, Parque Nacional de **142** E 4
Chaco Austral **142** D 4
Chaco Boreal **140** D 6
Chaco Canyon National Monument
  116 HJ 1–2
Chaco Central **140** DE 6
Chacorão, Cachoeira do **139** G 5
Chaco River **116** H 1
Chad **197** H 3
Chad **197** HJ 3
Chad, Lake **197** G 3
Chadan **170** F 5
Chadbourn (N.C.) **129** N 7
Chādegān (Iran) **157** F 2
Chadileuvú **143** C 6
Chadiza **201** E 2
Chadobets **170** G 4
Chadobets **170** GH 4
Chaffee (MO.) **121** Q 5
Chaffee (N.D.) **119** L 4
Chaffey (WI.) **124** B 3
Chagai **169** G 5
Chagai Hills **169** G 5
Chagda **171** O 4
Chagdo Kangri **174** D 1
Chaghcharān **169** H 4
Chagny **153** D 2
Chagodoshcha **158** G 4
Chagos Archipelago **162** F 7
Chaguaramas **138** E 2
Chagyl **168** F 2
Chahah Burjak **169** G 4
Chah Bahār **169** G 5
Chai Badan **175** H 4
Chaibassa **174** E 3
Chai Buri **175** H 4
Chaillu, Massif du **197** G 6
Chainat **175** GH 4

Chaîne de l'Atakora **196** E 3
Chain of Lakes **111** P 2
Ch'aio-ko-li Feng **169** K 3
Chaiyaphum **175** H 4
Chajari **142** E 5
Chakachamna Lake **109** H 3
Chakari **200** D 3
Chak Chak **198** D 3
Chake Chake **199** FG 6
Chakhansur **169** G 4
Chakhva **155** F 2
Chakwal **169** J 4
Chala **140** B 4
Chalabesa **201** E 2
Chalbi Desert **199** F 4
Châlesban (Iran) **157** E 2
Chalhuanca **140** B 3
Chalía **143** B 8
Chaling **172** F 5
Chalisgaon **174** C 3
Chalk Mountain (TX.) **122** F 3
Chalk Mountains **117** N 8
Chalkyitsik **109** K 2
Challapata **140** C 5
Challenger Deep **209** C 3
Challis (ID.) **111** L 6
Chalmette (LA.) **123** O 6
Chalna **174** E 3
Châlons-sur-Marne **153** D 2
Chalon-sur-Saône **153** DE 2
Chalt **149** F 5
Chama **201** E 2
Chama (N.M.) **117** K 1
Chamais **200** B 5
Chaman **169** H 4
Chamaya **138** C 5
Chamba (India) **174** C 1
Chamba (Tanzania) **201** F 2
Chambal **174** C 2
Chamberlain (SD.) **118** J 7
Chamberlain Lake **126** K 2
Chamberlain River **182** D 2
Chambers (AZ.) **116** G 2
Chambers (NE.) **119** K 8
Chambersburg (PA.) **127** B 9
Chambers Island **124** G 4
Chambery **153** E 2
Chambeshi **201** E 2
Chambishi **200** D 2
Chamchamāl (Iraq) **157** D 2
Chamela **132** B 4
Chamiapatna **174** C 5
Chamical **142** C 5
Chamo, Lake **199** F 3
Chamois (MO.) **121** O 4
Chamoli **174** C 1
Chamonix **153** E 2
Chamouchouane **105** N 6
Champa **174** D 3
Champagne **153** DE 2
Champagne **155** DE 2
Champagne (Yukon, Can.) **109** L 3
Champaign (IL.) **124** F 9
Champanha **139** G 5
Champaquí, Cerro **142** D 5
Champdoré, Lac **105** O 4
Champion (MI.) **124** F 3
Champion Creek Reservoir **122** C 3
Champlain, Lake **126** F 4
Champotón **132** D 4
Chamrajnagar **174** C 5
Chamutete **200** B 3
Chañaral **142** B 4
Chanc Changmar **174** C 1
Chancellor (TX.) **117** N 7
Chan Chan **138** C 5
Chanchelulha Peak **112** C 2
Chanchur **170** J 5
Chanco **143** B 6
Chandalar (AK.) **102** H 2
Chandalar (AK.) **102** H 2
Chandarnagar **174** E 3
Chandausi **174** C 2
Chandeleur Islands **123** P 6
Chandeleur Sound **123** OP 6
Chanderi **174** C 3
Chandigarh **174** C 1
Chandler (AZ.) **116** E 4
Chandler (IN.) **128** D 3
Chandler (OK.) **120** J 7
Chandler (Quebec, Can.) **105** P 6
Chandler (TX.) **123** H 3
Chandler Heights (AZ.) **116** E 4
Chandler Lake **109** H 2
Chandler River **109** H 2
Chandmanī **172** C 1
Chandpur **175** F 3
Chandrakona **174** E 3
Chandrapur **174** C 4
Chaneliak **108** F 3
Chanf **169** G 5
Changane **201** E 4
Changara **201** E 3
Changbai Shan **173** J 2
Changcheng (Chinese Wall) **172** E 3
Changchun **173** J 2
Changdao **173** H 3

Changde **172** F 5
Changfeng **173** G 4
Changhua **173** GH 6
Changji **169** M 2
Changjiang **172** E 7
Chang Jiang **173** G 4
Changjin **173** J 2
Changli **173** G 3
Changling **173** H 2
Changlung **169** K 4
Changning **172** CD 6
Changsha **172** F 5
Changshan **173** G 5
Changshu **173** H 4
Changshun **172** E 5
Changting **172** G 5
Changtu **173** H 2
Changwu **172** E 3
Changzhou **173** G 4
Channel Islands (CA.) **113** E 9–10
Channel Islands (U.K.) **148** C 5
Channel Islands National Monument
  113 F 8–9
Channel Port aux Basques **105** Q 6
Channing (MI.) **124** F 3
Channing (TX.) **117** O 2
Chantaburi **175** H 5
Chantilly **152** D 2
Chantrey Inlet **103** S 2
Chanute (KS.) **121** K 5
Chany **159** P 4
Chany, Ozero **159** P 5
Chao, Isla **138** C 5
Chao'an **172** G 6
Chao Hu **173** G 4
Chaor He **173** H 1
Chao Xian **173** G 4
Chaoyang **172** G 6
Chaoyang **173** GH 2
Chaoyangcun **171** MN 5
Chaozhong **171** M 5
Chapa **171** N 4
Chapada das Mangabeiras **141** G 2–3
Chapada Diamantina **141** H 3
Chapada dos Veadeiros, Parque Na-
  cional do **141** G 4
Chapadão dos Gerais **141** G 4
Chapadinha **141** H 1
Chapala **132** B 3
Chapala, Lago de **132** B 3
Chapanda **171** O 4
Chaparral **138** C 3
Chapa Tong **175** F 3
Chapayevo **158** K 5
Chapayevsk **158** J 5
Chapayev-Zheday **170** L 3
Chapchachi **158** J 6
Chapel Hill (N.C.) **129** M 6
Chapel Hill (TN.) **128** E 6
Chapiquy (IA.) **119** Q 7
Chapleau **104** L 6
Chaplinka **155** D 1
Chaplino **108** D 3
Chaplygin **158** GH 5
Chapman (MT.) **111** R 2
Chapman (NE.) **120** G 1
Chapman, Cape **103** U 2
Chapman Ranch (TX.) **122** F 8
Chapmanville (W.V.) **129** J 4
Chapoma **158** GH 2
Chappell (NE.) **118** F 9
Chapra **174** DE 2
Chaqui **140** C 4
Char **192** C 4
Chara **170** L 4
Chara **170** L 4
Chara **170** L 4
Charagua **140** D 4
Charaña **140** C 4
Charcas **132** B 3
Charco (TX.) **122** F 7
Charcot Island **203**
Chard **103** P 4
Chārdagh (Iran) **157** E 1
Chardara **169** H 2
Chardon (OH.) **125** N 8
Chardzhou **169** G 3
Charente **152** C 2
Chari **197** H 3
Charikar **169** H 3
Chariton (IA.) **119** P 9
Chariton River **121** N 2
Charity **139** G 2
Charkabozh **158** K 2
Charkayuvom **158** KL 2
Charleroi **148** DE 4
Charles **105** N 3
Charles, Cape (Newfoundl., Can.)
  105 QR 5
Charles, Cape (VA.) **129** PQ 4
Charlesbourg **105** N 6
Charles City (IA.) **119** Q 7
Charles City (VA.) **129** OP 4
Charles Louis, Pegunungan **177** J 4

Charles Mill Lake **125** M 9
Charles Peak **182** C 5
Charleston (IL.) **121** R 3
Charleston (MO.) **121** Q 6
Charleston (MS.) **121** PQ 8
Charleston (NV.) **112** K 1
Charleston (OR.) **110** A 7
Charleston (S.C.) **129** LM 9
Charleston (TN.) **128** G 6
Charleston (W.V.) **129** K 3
Charleston Peak **112** K 6
Charlestown (VA.) **129** O 2
Charleville **183** H 4
Charleville-Mézières **153** DE 2
Charlevoix (MI.) **124** J 4
Charlotte (MI.) **125** K 7
Charlotte (N.C.) **129** L 6
Charlotte (TN.) **128** D 5
Charlotte (TX.) **122** E 7
Charlotte Amalie **130** E 8
Charlotte Amalie **133** K 4
Charlotte Beach (FL.) **131** M 8
Charlotte Cort House (Can.) **129** N 4
Charlotte Harbour **131** M 8
Charlottenberg **151** F 4
Charlottesville (VA.) **129** N 3
Charlottetown **105** P 6
Charlton **105** LM 5
Charlton **183** G 6
Charmes **153** E 2
Charouîne **192** E 3
Charsadda **169** J 4
Charshanga **169** H 3
Charsk **159** Q 6
Charters Towers **183** H 3
Chartres **152** D 2
Chartreuse, Grande **153** E 2
Chāru, Bandar-e (Iran) **157** FG 4
Charyn **169** K 2
Charysh **159** Q 5
Charyshskoye **159** Q 5
Chascomus **142** E 6
Chase (AL.) **128** E 7
Chase (KS.) **120** G 4
Chase (NE.) **120** D 2
Chase (NE.) **120** D 2
Chase City (VA.) **129** N 5
Chase Lake **118** J 3–4
Chaseley (ND.) **118** J 3
Chasel'ka **159** Q 2
Chashniki **151** J 5
Chasico **143** C 7
Chaska (MN.) **119** P 6
Chasnachorr, Gora **150** K 2
Chasovnya Uchurskaya **171** O 4
Chassahowitzka (FL.) **131** M 6
Chāt **168** F 3
Čhatal Balkan **154** C 2
Chatanga **170** K 5
Chatanika **109** J 2
Chateaugay (N.Y.) **126** E 4
Châteaubriant (Can.) **109** L 3
Château-Chinon **152** D 2
Châteaudun **152** D 2
Châteaulin **152** C 2
Châteauneuf-sur-Loire **152** D 2
Châteauroux **152** D 2
Chateau-Salins **153** E 2
Château-Thierry **152** D 2
Chateaux-Arnoux **153** E 3
Châtellerault **152** D 2
Chatfield (MN.) **119** Q 7
Chatham (AK.) **109** L 4
Chatham (LA.) **123** L 3
Chatham (MA.) **126** K 7
Chatham (MI.) **124** H 3
Chatham (New Brunswick, Canada)
  105 O 6
Chatham (New Zealand) **185** S 9
Chatham (New Zealand) **186** D 5
Chatham (N.Y.) **126** F 6
Chatham (VA.) **129** M 5
Chatham Islands **185** S 9
Chatham Strait **108** K 4
Châtillon-sur-Seine **153** D 2
Chatkal **169** J 2
Chato, Cerro **143** B 7
Chatom (AL.) **130** F 3
Chatra **174** D 3
Chatrapur **174** E 4
Chatsworth (GA.) **128** G 7
Chattahoochee (FL.) **131** K 4
Chattahoochee River **131** J 3
Chattanooga (OK.) **120** G 8
Chattanooga (TN.) **128** F 6
Chatyrkel', Ozero **169** JK 2
Chauchaineu, Sierra **143** C 7
Chauk **175** F 3
Chaullay **140** B 3
Chaumont **153** DE 2
Chauncey (OH.) **129** JK 2
Chaunskaya Guba **171** VW 2
Chauny **152** D 2
Chau Phu **175** J 5
Chaura **175** F 6
Chautauqua Lake **125** P 7

Chaves 139 HJ 4
Chaves (Portugal) 152 B 3
Cháviva 138 D 3
Chavuma 200 C 2
Chayatyn, Khrebet 171 P 5
Chaydakh 171 O 2
Chayek 169 J 2
Chayia (Iraq) 156 C 2
Chaykovskiy 158 KL 4
Chayvo, Zaliv 171 Q 5
Chazhegovo 158 K 3
Chazón 142 D 5
Cheaha Mountain 128 F 8
Cheb 149 F 4
Chebarkul' 159 M 4–5
Cheboksary 158 J 4
Cheboygan (MI.) 125 K 4
Chech, Erg 192 E 3–4
Chechaouen 192 D 1
Checheng 173 H 6
Chech'on 173 J 3
Chechuysk 170 J 4
Checotah (OK.) 121 K 7
Cheduba 175 F 4
Cheektowaga (N.Y.) 125 Q 7
Cheesman Lake 115 M 4
Cheffadene 197 G 2
Chefornak 108 F 3
Cheg 192 C 3
Chegdomyn 171 O 5
Chegga (Algeria) 193 G 2
Chegga (Mauritania) 192 D 3
Cheghelvandi (Iran) 157 E 2
Chegutu 200 C 2
Chegytun 102 C 2
Chehalis (WA.) 110 C 4
Chehalis Indian Reservation 110 B 4
Chehariz (Iraq) 157 E 2
Chehel Päyeh 168 F 4
Cheikria 192 D 3
Cheil, Ra's el 199 HJ 3
Cheju 173 J 4
Cheju-do 173 J 4
Cheju-haehyŏp 173 J 4
Chekhov 171 Q 6
Chekunda 171 O 5
Chekurovka 171 N 1
Chekuyevo158 G 3
Chela, Serra da 200 A 3
Chelan (WA.) 110 F 3
Chelan, Lake 110 E 2
Cheleken 168 E 3
Chelforó 143 C 6
Chélia, Djebel 193 G 1
Cheliff 193 F 1
Chelkar 168 F 1
Chelleh Khāneh, Kūh-e (Iran) 157 E 1
Chełm 149 H 4
Chełmno 149 G 4
Chelmsford 148 D 4
Chełmża 149 G 4
Chelosh 159 R 5
Chelsea (MI.) 125 K 7
Chelsea (VT.) 126 G 5
Chelsea (WI.) 124 D 4
Cheltenham 148 C 4
Chelyabinsk 159 M 4
Chelyan (W.V.) 129 K 3
Chelyuskin, Cape 202
Chemal 159 R 5
Chemba 201 E 3
Chembe 200 D 2
Chemdal'sk 170 H 4
Chemehuevi Indian Reservation 113 L 8
Chemer 158 F 5
Chemillé 152 C 2
Chemult (OR.) 110 D 7
Chenab 169 J 3
Chenachane 192 E 3
Chenango Bridge (N.Y.) 126 D 6
Chenārbāshi (Iran) 157 E 2
Chen Barag Qi 170 L 6
Chencoyi 132 D 4
Cheney (WA.) 110 H 3
Cheney Reservoir 120 H 5
Cheng'an 172 F 3
Chengcheng 172 E 3
Chengde 173 G 2
Chengdu 172 D 4
Chenggong 172 D 5
Chengjiang 172 D 6
Chengkou 172 E 4
Chengmai 172 F 7
Cheng Xian 172 E 4
Chengzitan 173 H 3
Chenoa (IL.) 124 F 9
Chenxi 172 F 5
Chenzhou 172 F 5
Cheom Ksan 175 H 5
Chepen 138 C 5
Chepes 142 C 5
Cher 152 D 2
Cheraw (CO.) 115 O 5
Cheraw (S.C.) 129 M 7
Cherbaniani Reef 174 B 5
Cherbourg 152 C 2
Cherchell 193 F 1

Cherdyn' 158 L 3
Cherek 155 F 2
Cheremkhovo 170 H 5
Cherendey 170 L 3
Cherepanovo 159 Q 5
Chereponi 196 DE 3
Cherepovets 158 G 4
Chergui, Chott Ech 192 EF 2
Chéri 197 G 3
Cherkashina 170 J 4
Cherkassy 158 F 6
Cherkessk 155 F 2
Cherlak 159 O 5
Cherlakskiy 159 O 5
Chernaya 173 M 3
Chernaya 170 EF 1
Chernigov 158 F 5
Chernigovka 155 E 1
Chernigovka 173 K 2
Chernikovsk 158 L 5
Chernobyl 158 F 5
Chernofski 108 E 5
Chernogorsk 170 F 5
Chernolesskaya 171 P 3
Chernomorskoye 155 D 1
Chernoostrovskoye 159 R 3
Chernovskiye Kopi 170 K 5
Chernovtsy 154 C 1
Chernushka 158 L 4
Chernut'yevo 158 J 3
Cherny 168 D 1
Chernyakhovsk 151 H 5
Chernyanka 158 G 5
Chernyshevsk 170 L 5
Chernyshevskiy 170 K 4
Chernyye Brat'ya, Ostrova 171 S 6
Chernyye Zemli 155 G 1
Chernyy Ostrov 170 F 3
Chernyy Rynok 155 G 2
Cherokee (IA.) 119 N 8
Cherokee (N.C.) 128 H 6
Cherokee (OK.) 120 G 6
Cherokee (TX.) 122 E 4–5
Cherokee Indian Reservation 128 H 6
Cherokee Lake 128 H 5
Cherry Creek (NV.) 112 KL 3
Cherry Creek (SD.) 118 G 6
Cherry Creek Lake 115 N 4
Cherry Spring (TX.) 122 DE 5
Cherry Tree (PA.) 125 Q 9
Cherry Valley (AR.) 121 P 7
Cherryville (MO.) 121 O 5
Cherskiy Range 171 Q 2
Cherskogo, Khrebet 170 KL 5
Chertkovo 158 H 6
Cherven 151 J 5
Chervlennaya 155 G 2
Chervonograd 151 HJ 5
Chervonoye, Ozero 151 J 5
Chervonoznamenka 154 D 1
Chervyanka 170 J 4
Cherwell 148 C 4
Chesapeake (VA.) 129 P 5
Chesapeake Bay 129 P 3–4
Chesaw (WA.) 110 FG 2
Chëshskaya Guba 158 J 2
Chesnee (S.C.) 129 K 6
Chester 148 C 4
Chester (CA.) 112 D 2
Chester (IL.) 121 Q 5
Chester (MT.) 111 P 2
Chester (OK.) 120 G 6
Chester (PA.) 127 D 9
Chester (S.C.) 129 K 7
Chester (TX.) 123 J 5
Chester (VA.) 129 O 4
Chesterfield (ID.) 111 O 8
Chesterfield (S.C.) 129 L 7
Chesterfield (U.K.) 148 C 4
Chesterfield (VA.) 129 O 4
Chesterfield, Iles 186 B 4
Chesterfield, Récifs et Iles 183 K 2
Chesterfield Inlet (N.W.T., Can.) 103 T 3
Chesterfield Inlet (N.W.T., Can.) 103 TU 3
Chesterfield Islands 186 B 4
Chestertown (MD.) 129 PQ 2
Chestnut Mountain (GA.) 128 H 7
Chesuncook (ME.) 126 K 2
Chesuncook Lake 126 K 2–3
Chetek (WI.) 124 C 4
Chetlat 174 B 5
Chetopa (KS.) 121 K 5
Chetumal 132 E 4
Chetumal, Bahia de 132 E 4
Chetvertyy Kuril'skiy Proliv 171 ST 5–6
Cheugda 171 O 5
Cheulik 171 P 2
Chevak 108 EF 3
Cheviot (New Zealand) 185 Q 9
Chewelah (WA.) 110 H 2
Cheyenne (OK.) 120 F 7
Cheyenne (WY.) 118 D 9
Cheyenne River 118 G 6
Cheyenne River Indian Reservation 118 GH 5
Cheyenne Wells (CO.) 115 P 5
Cheyne Bay 182 B 5
Chhatarpur 174 C 3

Chhindwara 174 C 3
Chiai 173 H 6
Chiamboni, Ra's 199 G 5
Chiang Dao 175 G 4
Chiange 200 A 3
Chiang Kham 175 H 4
Chiang Khan 175 H 4
Chiang Mai 175 G 4
Chiang Rai 175 G 4
Chiang Saen 175 H 3
Chiapas 132 D 4
Chiatura 155 F 2
Chiavari 153 E 3
Chiawuli (AZ.) 116 E 6
Chiba 173 M 3
Chibabava 201 E 4
Chibagalakh 171 PQ 2
Chibemba 200 A 3
Chibia 200 A 3
Chibit 159 R 5
Chibougamau 105 N 6
Chibougamau, Lac 105 N 6
Chibuto 201 E 4
Chibwe 200 D 2
Chicago (IL.) 124 G 8
Chicago Heights (IL.) 124 G 8
Chicamba 197 G 6–7
Chicapa 200 C 1
Chic-Chocs, Mounts 105 O 6
Chicha 197 H 2
Chichagof 102 K 4
Chichaoua 192 D 2
Chichas, Cordillera de 140 C 4–5
Chicheng 173 G 2
Chichén-Itzá 132 E 3
Chichester Range National Park 182 B 3
Chickamauga Lake 128 FG 6
Chickasaw (AL.) 130 FG 4
Chickasawhay River 130 F 3
Chickasha (OK.) 120 H 7
Chicken 102 J 3
Chiclana de la Frontera 152 B 4
Chiclayo 138 C 5
Chico (CA.) 112 D 3
Chico (Chile) 143 C 7
Chico (Chile) 143 C 8
Chico (TX.) 122 F 2
Chicoana 142 C 4
Chico Hot Springs (MT.) 111 P 5
Chicomba 200 A 2
Chicomo 201 E 4
Chiconono 201 F 2
Chicopee (MA.) 126 G 6
Chicoutimi 105 N 6
Chicualacuala 201 E 4
Chicuma 200 A 2
Chidambaram 174 CD 5
Chidenguele 201 E 4
Chidester (AR.) 121 MN 9
Chidley, Cape 105 P 3
Chiefland (FL.) 131 M 5
Chiemsee 149 F 5
Chiengi 200 D 1
Chieti 153 F 3
Chifeng 173 G 2
Chifre, Serra do 141 H 4
Chifunde 201 E 2
Chigamane 201 E 4
Chiganak 159 O 6
Chiginagak, Mount 108 G 4
Chignik 102 F 4
Chignik Lagoon 108 G 4
Chigorodó 138 C 2
Chigubo 201 E 4
Chihli, Gulf of 173 GH 3
Chihuahua 106 E 6
Chiili 169 H 2
Chikan 170 J 5
Chikayevo 171 W 3
Chik Ballapur 174 C 5
Chikhacheva 171 R 1
Chikmagalur 174 C 5
Chikoy 170 J 5
Chikwawa 201 E 3
Chi-kyaw 175 F 3
Chilabombwe 200 D 2
Chilas 169 J 3
Chilaw 174 C 6
Chilca, Cordillera de 140 B 4
Chilca, Punta de 140 A 3
Chilchinbito (AZ.) 116 F 1
Childers 183 J 4
Childersburg (AL.) 128 E 8
Childress (TX.) 117 Q 3
Childs (AZ.) 116 D 5
Chile 142–143 B 4–6
Chile Basin 209 L 5
Chile Chico 143 B 8
Chilecito 142 C 4
Chilete 138 C 5
Chilgir 155 G 1
Chilicotal Mountain 117 N 8
Chilik 169 K 2
Chilili (N.M.) 117 K 3
Chilimanzi 201 E 3
Chilipa de Alvarez 132 C 4
Chilka Lake 174 E 4
Chillagoe 183 G 2

Chillán 143 B 6
Chillar 143 E 6
Chillicothe (IL.) 124 E 9
Chillicothe (MO.) 121 M 3
Chillicothe (OH.) 128 J 2
Chillicothe (TX.) 122 D 1
Chilly (ID.) 111 M 6
Chiloé, Isla de 143 B 7
Chiloquin (OR.) 110 D 8
Chilpancingo 132 BC 4
Chiltern Hills 148 C 4
Chiluage 200 C 1
Chilumba 201 E 2
Chilwa, Lago 201 F 3
Chimala 198 E 5
Chimalavera 200 A 2
Chimaltenango 132 D 5
Chimán 138 C 2
Chimanimani 201 E 3
Chimay 159 N 4
Chimbay 168 F 2
Chimborazo 138 C 4
Chimbote 138 C 5
Chimbwingombi 201 E 2
Chimeyevo 159 N 4
Chimishliya 154 C 1
Chimkent 169 H 2
Chimney Rock (CO.) 115 K 6
Chimoio 201 E 3
Chimoio, Planalto de 201 E 3
Chimtarga 169 H 3
Chin 175 F 3
China 172 DE 4
China Lake 113 H 7
Chinandega 132 E 5
Chinati Mountains 117 M 8
Chinati Peak 117 M 8
Chincha Alta 140 A 3
Chinchilla 183 J 4
Chinchilla de Monte-Aragon 152 C 4
Chinchorro, Banco 132 E 4
Chincoteague (VA.) 129 Q 4
Chindagatuy 159 R 6
Chinde 201 F 3
Chin-do 173 J 4
Chindu 172 C 4
Chindwin 175 F 3
Chinese Wall 172 E 3
Chingirlau 158 K 5
Chingiz-Tau, Khrebet 159 P 6
Chingola 200 D 2
Chinguetti 192 C 4
Chinguil 197 H 3
Chinhae 173 J 3
Chinhoyi 201 E 3
Chinipas 106 E 6
Chinju 173 J 3
Chinko 198 C 3
Chinle (AZ.) 116 G 1
Chinnur 174 C 4
Chino (AZ.) 116 CD 2
Chino (CA.) 113 H 9
Chino Valley (AZ.) 116 D 3
Chinon 152 D 2
Chinook (MT.) 111 Q 2
Chinook Pass 110 D 4
Chino Valley (AZ.) 116 D 3
Chinsali 201 E 2
Chintalnar 174 D 4
Chioco 201 E 3
Chioggia 153 F 3
Chipata 201 E 2
Chipepo 200 D 3
Chiperone 201 F 3
Chipili 200 D 2
Chipindo 200 B 2
Chipinge 201 E 4
Chipley (FL.) 131 J 4
Chipogolo 199 F 6
Chipoia 200 B 2
Chippewa, Lake 124 C 4
Chippewa Falls (WI.) 124 C 4
Chippewa River 124 C 5
Chipurupalle 174 D 4
Chiputneticook Lakes 126 M 3
Chiquián 140 A 2–3
Chiquitos, Llanos de 140 D 4
Chirala 174 D 4
Chirchik 169 HJ 2
Chiredzi 201 E 4
Chireno (TX.) 123 J 4
Chirfa 197 G 1
Chiricahua Mountains 116 G 5–6
Chiricahua National Monument 116 G 5–6
Chiricahua Peak 116 G 6
Chiriguaná 138 D 2
Chiriguanos 140 D 5
Chirikof 102 F 4
Chirinda 170 H 2
Chirinkotan, Ostrov 171 S 6
Chiriquí 138 B 2
Chiriquí, Golfo de 138 B 2
Chiromo 201 F 3
Chirpan 154 C 2
Chirundu 200 D 3
Chisamba 200 D 2
Chisana 109 K 3
Chishmy 158 L 5
Chisholm (MN.) 119 Q 3
Chisholm (TX.) 122 G 3
Chishui 172 E 5
Chishui He 172 E 5

Chisimaio → Kismāyu 199 G 5
Chiskovo 170 G 3
Chisos Mountains 117 N 8
Chistochina 109 J 3
Chistoozernoye 159 P 5
Chistopol 158 K 4
Chita 170 K 5
Chitado 200 A 3
Chitambo 201 E 2
Chitato 200 C 1
Chitembo 200 B 2
Chitina (AK.) 102 J 3
Chitina (AK.) 102 J 3
Chitipa 201 E 1
Chitokoloki 200 C 2
Chitradurga 174 C 5
Chitral 169 J 3
Chitré 138 B 2
Chittagong 175 F 3
Chittaurgarh 174 C 3
Chittoor 174 C 5
Chiumbe 200 C 1
Chiume 200 C 3
Chiure 201 G 2
Chiure Novo 201 F 2
Chiuta, Lago 201 F 2
Chivasso 153 E 2
Chivay 140 B 4
Chivilcoy 142 D 5
Chivington (CO.) 115 P 5
Chizha 158 H 2
Chkalovo 159 O 5
Chloe (N.M.) 117 K 3
Chloride (AZ.) 116 B 2
Choba 199 F 4
Chobe National Park 200 C 3
Chochis, Cerro 140 E 4
Chocolate Mountains 113 K 9
Chocontá 138 D 2
Chocope 138 C 5
Choctawhatchee Bay 131 H 4
Choctaw Indian Reservation 130 E 2
Chodzież 149 G 4
Choele Choel 143 CD 6
Choggia 153 F 2
Choique 143 D 6
Choiseul 185 G 3
Choiseul 186 B 3
Choix 106 E 6
Chojna 149 F 4
Chojnice 149 G 4
Choke Mountains 199 F 2
Choknar 169 JK 2
Chokoloskee (FL.) 131 N 9
Chokurdakh 171 R 1
Chókwè 201 E 4
Chola Shan 172 C 4
Cholet 152 C 2
Cholila 143 B 7
Choluteca 132 E 5
Choma 200 D 3
Chomo Yummo 174 E 2
Chomutov 149 F 4
Chona 170 J 3
Ch'ŏnan 173 J 3
Chon Buri 175 H 5
Chondon 171 P 1
Chone 138 B 4
Ch'ŏngjin 173 JK 2
Ch'ŏngju 173 J 3
Chŏngju 173 J 3
Chong Kal 175 H 5
Chongkü 172 C 4
Chongming Dao 173 H 4
Chongoroi 200 A 2
Chongqing 172 E 5
Chongup 173 J 3
Chongxin 172 E 3
Chongzuo 172 E 6
Chŏnju 173 J 3
Chonos, Archipiélago de los 143 AB 7–8
Chon Thanh 175 J 5
Chop 154 B 1
Cho Ra 175 J 3
Chorito, Sierra del 152 C 4
Cholorque 140 C 5
Choros, Cabo 142 B 4
Chorregon 183 G 3
Chorrillos 140 A 3
Chorrochó 141 J 2
Ch'ŏrwŏn 173 J 3
Chŏrzów 149 G 4
Chŏshi 173 M 3
Chosica 140 A 3
Chos Malal 143 BC 6
Choszczno 149 G 4
Chota 138 C 5
Chotanagpur 174 DE 3
Chota Udaipur 174 B 3
Choteau (MT.) 111 N 3
Chott Ech Chergui 192 EF 2
Chott el Hodna 193 F 1
Chott el Rharsa 193 G 2
Chott Melrhir 193 G 2
Chott Merouane 193 G 2
Choum 192 C 4
Chouteau (OK.) 121 K 6
Chowan River 129 P 5
Chowchilla (CA.) 112 E 5
Choybalsan 170 K 6

Chrisman (IL.) **121** S 3
Christchurch **185** Q 9
Christchurch (New Zealand) **186** C 5
Christiana **200** D 5
Christiansburg (VA.) **129** L 4
Christian Sound **102** KL 4
Christiansted **130** E 9
Christie, Mount **109** M 3
Christie Bay **103** PQ 3
Christina **200** D 5
Christina (MT.) **111** Q 3
Christmas (AZ.) **116** F 4
Christmas Island **176** C 6
Christmas Mountain **108** F 3
Christopher (IL.) **121** Q 5
Christoval (TX.) **122** C 4
Chromo (CO.) **115** L 6
Chrysler (AL.) **130** G 3
Chrystal Falls (MI.) **124** F 3
Chtakal'skiy Khrebet **169** J 2
Chu **169** J 2
Chu **169** J 2
Chubbuck (CA.) **113** K 8
Chubbuck (ID.) **111** N 8
Chubut **143** C 7
Chuchukan **170** L 3
Chucuito **140** BC 4
Chucul **142** D 5
Chudinovo **159** M 5
Chudleigh Park **183** G 2
Chudovo **151** K 4
Chudskoye Ozero **151** J 4
Chugach Mountains **102** H 3
Chuginadak **102** C 5
Chugwater (WY.) **118** D 9
Chuhuichupa **106** E 6
Chuichu (AZ.) **116** E 5
Chu-Iliyskiye Gory **169** JK 2
Chukai **176** B 3
Chukar **170** L 3
Chukchagirskoye, Ozero **171** P 5
Chukchi Sea **102** CD 2
Chukchi Sea **202**
Chuken **171** P 6
Chukhloma **158** H 4
Chukoch'ye **171** T 2
Chukotskiy, Mys **102** C 3
Chukotskiy Poluostrov **102** BC 2
Chukotsk Peninsula **202**
Chukotsk Range **202**
Chukuchany **171** R 2
Chulak-Kurgan **169** HJ 2
Chulakovka **155** D 1
Chulasa **158** J 3
Chula Vista (CA.) **113** H 10
Chulitna **102** H 3
Chulkovo **159** R 3
Chul'man **171** M 4
Chulucanas **138** BC 3
Chuluota (FL.) **131** N 6
Chulym **159** Q 4
Chulym **159** QR 4
Chulym **170** F 4
Chum **159** M 2
Chumakovo **159** P 4
Chumbicha **142** C 4
Chumek **159** R 6
Chumerna **154** C 2
Chumikan **171** OP 5
Chum Phae **175** H 4
Chumphon **175** G 5
Chumysh **159** Q 5
Chuña **142** D 5
Chuna **170** G 4
Ch'unch'ŏn **173** J 3
Chunchula (AL.) **130** F 4
Chundzha **169** K 2
Chunga **200** D 2
Ch'ungju **173** J 3
Chungking → Chongqing **172** E 5
Ch'ungmu **173** J 3
Chunhua **173** K 2
Chunskiy **170** G 4
Chunya (Tanzania) **198** D 6
Chunya (U.S.S.R.) **170** G 3
Chuor Phnum Kravanh **175** H 5
Chupa **150** K 2
Chüplü (Iran) **157** E 1
Chuquibama **140** B 4
Chuquibamba **138** D 2
Chuquicamata **140** C 5
Chuquillanqui **138** C 5
Chur **153** E 2
Churapcha **171** O 3
Church Ferry (ND.) **118** J 2
Churchill **103** ST 4
Churchill **105** P 5
Churchill (Man., Can.) **103** T 4
Churchill (Newfoundl., Can.) **103** R 4
Churchill, Cape **103** T 4
Churchill, Mount **109** K 3
Churchill Falls **105** P 5
Churchill Lake **103** Q 4
Churchill Mountains **203**
Churchill Peak **103** N 4
Churchville (VA.) **129** M 3
Chureg-Tag, Gora **170** F 5
Churia Range **174** E 2
Churkino **158** H 3
Churu **174** C 2
Churuguara **138** DE 1

Churún Merú **139** F 2
Chushal **169** K 4
Chushkakyl' **168** F 1
Chuska Mountains **116** H 1–2
Chuska Peak **116** H 2
Chusovaya **159** L 4
Chusovoy **159** L 4
Chusovskoy **158** L 3
Chute-des-Passes **105** N 6
Chutes de Katende **198** C 6
Chutes de Katende (Katende Falls) **198** C 6
Chutes de la Lufira **198** D 6
Chutes de Livingstone **197** G 7
Chutes Ngaliema **198** D 4
Chutes Ngaliema (Stanley Falls) **198** D 4
Chutes Tembo **198** B 6
Chuval **159** L 3
Chuvanskiye Gory **171** V 3
Chuvanskoye Petushkova **171** W 2
Chu Xian **173** G 4
Chuxiong **172** D 5
Chuya **170** K 4
Chuya **170** K 4
Chu Yang Sin **175** J 5
Chuy Cevolleti **142** F 5
Chuyengo **170** H 3
Chybydat **170** M 3
Chyul'be **171** O 4
Chyulu Range **199** F 5
Ciales (P.R.) **130** C 8
Ciamis **176** C 5
Cianjur **176** C 5
Cianorte **141** F 5
Cibola (AZ.) **116** B 4
Cícero Dantas **141** J 3
Ćićevac **154** C 2
Cide **155** D 2
Ciechanów **149** H 4
Ciego de Ávila **133** G 3
Ciénaga **138** D 1
Cienfuegos **133** F 3
Cieza **152** C 4
Çifteler **154** C 3
Cifuentes **152** C 3
Cihanbeyli **155** D 3
Cihanbeyli Platosu **155** D 3
Cihara **176** C 5
Cihuatlán **132** B 4
Cijara, Embalse de **152** BC 4
Cijulang **176** C 5
Cilacap **176** C 5
Çıldır **155** F 2
Çıldır Gölü **155** F 2
Cilo Dağı **155** F 3
Cima (CA.) **113** K 7
Cimahi **176** C 5
Cimarron (CO.) **115** K 5
Cimarron (KS.) **120** E 5
Cimarron (N.M.) **117** M 1
Cimarron River **120** G 6
Çimen Dağı **155** E 3
Cimone **153** F 3
Cîmpia Bărăganului **154** C 1–2
Cîmpia Burnazului **154** C 2
Cîmpia Turzii **154** B 1
Cîmpina **154** C 1
Cîmpulung **154** C 1
Cîmpulung Moldovenesc **154** C 1
Cina, Tanjung **176** BC 5
Çinar **155** F 3
Cinca **152** D 3
Cincinnati (OH.) **128** G 2
Cinco Saltos **143** C 6
Çine **154** C 3
Cintalapa de Figueroa **132** D 4
Cinto, Monte **153** E 3
Cintra, Golfo de **192** B 4
Cipolletti **143** C 6
Circeo, Capo **153** F 3
Circle (AK, U.S.A.) **102** J 2
Circle Cliffs **114** F 6
Circle Springs **109** K 2
Circleville (OH.) **128** J 2
Circleville (UT.) **114** E 5
Circleville Mountain **114** E 5
Cirebon **176** C 5
Cirencester **148** C 4
Cirié **153** E 2
Cirk, Gora **108** B 3
Ciro Marina **153** G 4
Cirque Mountain **105** P 4
Cisco (TX.) **122** DE 3
Cisco (UT.) **114** H 5
Ciskei **200** D 6
Cisnădie **154** B 1
Cisne (IL.) **121** R 4
Cisne, Islas del **132** F 4
Cisnéros (Colombia) **138** D 2
Citac, Nevado **140** AB 3
Citlaltépetl, Volcán **132** C 4
Citra (FL.) **131** M 5
Citronelle (AL.) **130** F 3
Citrus Heights (CA.) **112** D 4
Citrusdal **200** B 6
Citta del Vaticano **153** F 3
Città di Castello **153** F 3
City Point (FL.) **131** O 6
Ciucasu, Virful **154** C 1
Ciudad Acuña **132** B 2

Ciudad Altamirano **132** B 4
Ciudad Bolívar **139** F 2
Ciudad Bolivia **138** DE 2
Ciudad Camargo **106** E 6
Ciudad Cuauhtémoc **132** D 4
Ciudad de Dolores Hidalgo **132** BC 3
Ciudad del Carmen **132** D 4
Ciudad del Maíz **132** C 3
Ciudad de Nutrias **138** DE 2
Ciudad de Rio Grande **132** B 3
Ciudadela **152** D 3
Ciudad Guayana **139** F 2
Ciudad Guzmán **132** B 4
Ciudad Hidalgo (Mexico) **132** BC 4
Ciudad Hidalgo (Mexico) **132** D 5
Ciudad Lerdo **132** B 2
Ciudad Madero **132** C 3
Ciudad Mante **132** C 3
Ciudad Mendoza **132** C 4
Ciudad Obregón **106** E 6
Ciudad Ojeda **138** D 1
Ciudad Piar **139** F 2
Ciudad Real **152** C 4
Ciudad Río Bravo **132** C 2
Ciudad-Rodrigo **152** B 3
Ciudad Valles **132** C 3
Ciudad Victoria **132** C 3
Civa Burnu **155** E 2
Civita Castellana **153** F 3
Civitanova Marche **153** F 3
Civitavecchia **153** F 3
Çivril **154** C 3
Cizre (Turkey) **156** D 1
C. J. Strike Reservoir **111** K 8
Clacton-on-Sea **148** D 4
Claflin (KS.) **120** G 4
Claiborne (AL.) **130** G 3
Claire, Lake **103** P 4
Claire Coast **203**
Clairemont (TX.) **117** Q 4
Clair Engle Lake **112** C 2
Clairette (TX.) **122** E 3
Clairton (PA.) **125** P 9
Clallam Bay (WA.) **110** A 2
Clamecy **152** D 2
Clam Lake (WI.) **124** CD 3
Clan Alpine Mountains **112** H 3
Clanton (AL.) **130** H 2
Clanwilliam **200** B 6
Clara (MS.) **130** F 3
Clara City (MN.) **119** N 6
Claraz **143** E 6
Clare **183** F 5
Clare (MI.) **125** K 6
Claremont (CA.) **112** E 3
Claremont (N.H.) **126** G 5
Claremont (S.D.) **119** L 5
Claremore (OK.) **121** K 6
Clarence (IA.) **119** RS 9
Clarence (LA.) **123** KL 4
Clarence (PA.) **127** B 7
Clarence, Isla **143** B 9
Clarence Strait **102** L 4
Clarence Strait (N.T., Austr.) **182** E 1
Clarence Town **133** H 3
Clarendon (AR.) **121** O 8
Clarendon (TX.) **117** Q 3
Clarenville **105** R 6
Claresholm **103** P 5
Clareton (WY.) **118** D 7
Clarinda (IA.) **119** NO 10
Clarion (IA.) **119** P 8
Clarion (PA.) **125** P 8
Clarion Fracture Zone **209** D 3
Clarita (OK.) **120** J 8
Clark (S.D.) **119** L 6
Clark (WY.) **111** Q 6
Clark, Lake **108** H 3
Clark Canyon Reservoir **111** N 6
Clarkdale (AZ.) **116** D 3
Clarke **184** L 9
Clarke Range **183** H 3
Clarkesville (GA.) **128** H 7
Clarkfield (MN.) **119** N 6
Clark Fork **111** K 3
Clark Fork (ID.) **110** J 2
Clark Hill Lake **129** J 8
Clarkia (ID.) **110** J 3
Clark Mountain **113** K 7
Clark River **183** H 2
Clarks (LA.) **123** L 3
Clarks (NE.) **120** H 1
Clarksburg (W.V.) **129** L 2
Clarksdale (MS.) **121** P 8
Clarkston (WA.) **110** H 4
Clarksville (AR.) **121** M 7
Clarksville (TN.) **128** D 5
Clarksville (TX.) **123** HJ 2
Clarksville (VA.) **129** N 5
Claro **141** F 4
Clatskanie (OR.) **110** B 4
Claude (TX.) **117** P 2
Clauene (TX.) **117** O 4
Claunch (N.M.) **117** KL 3
Claveria **177** J 1
Claxton (GA.) **131** N 2
Clay (W.V.) **129** K 3

Clay Belt **104** LM 5
Clay Center (KS.) **120** H 3
Clay Center (NE.) **120** GH 2
Clay City (IN.) **128** DE 2
Clay Springs (AZ.) **116** F 3
Clayton (AL.) **131** J 3
Clayton (GA.) **128** H 7
Clayton (ID.) **111** L 6
Clayton (LA.) **123** M 4
Clayton (MO.) **121** P 4
Clayton (N.M.) **117** N 1
Clayton (N.Y.) **126** CD 4
Clayton (OK.) **121** K 8
Clayton (PA.) **127** D 9
Clayton Lake (ME.) **126** K 2
Claytor Lake **129** L 4
Clearbrook (MN.) **119** N 3
Clear Creek (CA.) **112** B 1
Clearcreek (UT.) **114** FG 4
Clearfield (IA.) **119** O 10
Clearfield (PA.) **125** Q 8
Clearfield (UT.) **114** E 2
Clear Lake (CA.) **112** C 3
Clear Lake (IA.) **119** P 7
Clear Lake (LA.) **123** K 4
Clear Lake (S.D.) **119** M 6
Clear Lake (UT.) **114** E 4
Clear Lake (UT.) **114** E 4
Clear Lake (WI.) **124** B 4
Clearlake Highlands (CA.) **112** C 4
Clearlake Oaks (CA.) **112** C 3
Clear Lake Reservoir **112** D 1
Clearmont (WY.) **118** B 6
Clear Site **109** J 3
Clearwater (FL.) **131** M 7
Clearwater (KS.) **120** H 5
Clearwater (NE.) **119** K 8
Clearwater Lake (MO.) **121** P 5
Clearwater Mountains **111** KL 4
Clearwater River **110** J 4
Cleator (AZ.) **116** D 3
Clebit (N.M.) **121** KL 8
Cleburne (TX.) **122** F 3
Cle Elum (WA.) **110** E 3
Clemson (S.C.) **128** J 7
Clendening Reservoir **125** N 9
Cleo (TX.) **122** D 5
Clere, Mount **182** B 4
Clermont **183** H 3
Clermont-Ferrand **152** D 2
Cleveland (AL.) **128** E 7–8
Cleveland (KS.) **120** G 5
Cleveland (MS.) **121** P 9
Cleveland (OH.) **125** N 8
Cleveland (OK.) **121** J 6
Cleveland (TN.) **128** G 6
Cleveland (TX.) **123** J 4
Cleveland, Mount **111** M 2
Clew Bay **148** AB 4
Clewiston (FL.) **131** NO 8
Clifford (N.D.) **119** L 3
Clifton (AZ.) **116** G 4
Clifton (KS.) **120** H 3
Clifton (LA.) **123** N 5
Clifton (TX.) **122** F 4
Clifton Forge (VA.) **129** LM 4
Clifton Hills **183** F 4
Clinch River **128** H 5
Cline (TX.) **122** C 6
Clines Corners (N.M.) **117** L 2
Clingmans Dome **128** H 6
Clinton (AL.) **130** FG 2
Clinton (AR.) **121** N 7
Clinton (Br. Col., Can.) **103** N 5
Clinton (CT.) **127** G 7
Clinton (IA.) **119** S 9
Clinton (IL.) **124** F 9
Clinton (KY.) **128** C 5
Clinton (LA.) **123** MN 5
Clinton (MA.) **126** H 5
Clinton (ME.) **126** K 4
Clinton (MI.) **125** L 7
Clinton (MO.) **121** M 4
Clinton (MS.) **130** D 2
Clinton (MT.) **111** M 4
Clinton (N.C.) **129** N 6–7
Clinton (OK.) **120** FG 7
Clinton (TN.) **128** G 5
Clinton (WI.) **124** F 5
Clinton-Colden Lake **103** Q 3
Clintonville (WI.) **124** F 5
Clintwood (KY.) **128** J 4
Clio (AL.) **131** J 3
Clio (S.C.) **129** M 7
Clipperton Fracture Zone **209** D 3
Clive (UT.) **114** C 3
Cloates, Point **182** A 3
Clodomira **142** D 4
Cloncurry **183** FG 3
Cloncurry River **183** G 2–3
Clonmel **148** B 4
Cloppenburg **149** E 4
Cloquet (MN.) **119** Q 4
Clorinda **142** E 4
Cloudcroft (N.M.) **117** L 4–5
Cloud Peak **111** S 6
Cloverdale (AL.) **128** D 7
Cloverdale (CA.) **112** B 4
Cloverdale (IN.) **128** E 2

Clovis (CA.) **112** F 6
Clovis (N.M.) **117** N 3
Cluj-Napoca **154** B 1
Cluny **153** D 2
Cluses **153** E 2
Clute (TX.) **123** H 6
Clutha River **184** P 10
Clyattville (GA.) **131** L 4
Clyde (KS.) **120** H 3
Clyde (ND.) **118** JK 2
Clyde (N.W.T., Can.) **105** O 1
Clyde (N.Y.) **126** CD 4
Clyde (TX.) **122** F 3
Clyde, Firth of **148** BC 3
Clyde Park (MT.) **111** P 5
Clymer (PA.) **125** P 9
Cnossus **154** C 3
Côa **152** B 3
Coachella (CA.) **113** J 9
Coachella Canal **113** K 9
Coahoma (TX.) **117** P 5
Coahuila **132** B 2
Coal City (IL.) **124** F 8
Coal City (IN.) **128** DE 2
Coalcoman, Sierra de **132** B 4
Coal Creek **109** K 2
Coaldale (CO.) **115** M 5
Coalgate (OK.) **120** J 8
Coal Hill (AR.) **121** M 7
Coalinga (CA.) **112** E 6
Coalmont (CO.) **115** L 3
Coal River **109** N 3
Coal River (Br. Col., Can.) **103** M 4
Coal Valley **112** K 5
Coalville (UT.) **114** F 3
Coalwood (MT.) **118** C 5
Coamo (P.R.) **130** C 8
Coan, Cerro **138** C 5
Coaraci **141** J 3
Coari **139** F 4
Coari **139** F 4
Coarsegold (CA.) **112** F 5
Coast Mountains **102–103** LM 4–5
Coast of Labrador **105** QP 4–5
Coast Range (Queensland, Austr.) **183** J 4
Coast Ranges **110** B 4–6
Coatepec **132** C 4
Coatesville (PA.) **127** D 9
Coats Island **103** V 3
Coats land **203**
Coatzacoalcos **132** D 4
Coatzacoalcos, Bahia **132** D 4
Coba **132** E 3
Cobalt (ID.) **111** L 5
Cobán **132** D 4
Cobar **183** H 5
Cobh **148** B 4
Cobija **140** C 4
Cobleskill (N.Y.) **126** E 6
Cobourg Peninsula **182** E 1
Cobquecura **143** B 6
Cobre (NV.) **112** L 1
Cobue **201** EF 2
Coburg **149** F 4
Cocachacra **140** B 4
Cocamá **140** B 3
Cochabamba **140** C 4
Cochin **174** C 6
Cochinoca **140** C 5
Cochise (AZ.) **116** FG 5
Cochiti Pueblo (N.M.) **117** K 2
Cochran (GA.) **131** L 2
Cochrane (Chile) **143** B 8
Cochrane (Man., Can.) **103** R 4
Cochrane (Ontario, Can.) **105** L 6
Cochrane (WI.) **124** C 5
Cockburn **183** G 5
Cocklebiddy **182** D 5
Cocoa (FL.) **131** O 6
Cocoa Beach (FL.) **131** O 6
Cocobeach **197** FG 5
Coco Channel **175** F 5
Cocodrie (LA.) **123** N 6
Coco Island (Costa Rica) **134** B 2
Coco Islands **175** F 5
Cocolalla (ID.) **110** J 2
Coconino (AZ.) **116** D 1
Coconino Plateau **116** D 2
Coco o Segovia, Rio **132** EF 5
Côcos **141** H 3
Cocula **132** B 3
Cocuy, Sierra Nevada de **138** D 2
Cod, Cape **126** K 7
Codajás **139** F 4
Codigoro **153** F 3
Codlea **154** C 1
Codman (TX.) **117** Q 2
Codó **141** H 1
Cody (NE.) **118** G 8
Cody (WY.) **111** Q 6
Coelemu **143** B 6
Coen (Queensland, Austr.) **183** G 1
Coeroenie **139** G 3
Coesfeld **149** E 4
Coetivy **199** K 6
Coeur d'Alene (ID.) **110** J 3
Coeur d'Alene Indian Reservation **110** J 3
Coeur d'Alene Lake **110** J 3
Coffee Creek (MT.) **111** PQ 3

Coffeen Lake **121** Q 3
Coffeeville (MS.) **121** Q 9
Coffeyville (KS.) **121** K 5
Coffin Bay **183** F 5
Coff's Harbour **183** J 5
Cofrentes **152** C 4
Coggon (IA.) **119** R 8
Cognac **152** C 2
Cogne **153** E 2
Cohagen (MT.) **118** B 3
Cohoe **109** H 3
Coiba, Isla de **138** B 2
Coig **143** B 9
Coihaique **143** B 8
Coihaique Alto **143** B 8
Coimbatore **174** C 5
Coimbra **152** B 3
Coin **152** C 4
Coipasa, Salar de **140** C 4
Cojimies **138** B 3
Cojudo Blanco, Cerro **143** C 8
Cojutepeque **132** E 5
Cokeville (WY.) **111** P 8
Colac **183** G 6
Colalao del Valle **142** C 4
Colan-Conhué **143** C 7
Colatina **141** H 4
Colbert (OK.) **120** J 9
Colbert (WA.) **110** H 3
Colby (KS.) **120** D 3
Colchester **148** D 4
Colcord (W.V.) **129** K 4
Cold Bay **102** E 4
Col de Larche **153** E 3
Col de Perthus **152** D 3
Col de Tende **153** E 3
Cold Lake **103** P 5
Cold Mountain **128** J 6
Coldspring (TX.) **123** H 5
Coldwater (KS.) **120** F 5
Coldwater (MI.) **125** K 8
Coldwater (MO.) **121** P 5
Coldwater (MS.) **121** Q 8
Coldwater (OH.) **125** K 9
Colebrook (N.H.) **126** H 4
Cole Camp (MO.) **121** M 4
Coleen River **109** K 2
Coleman (FL.) **131** MN 6
Coleman (MI.) **125** K 6
Coleman (TX.) **122** D 4
Coleman River **183** G 2
Coleraine **148** B 3
Coles Bay **184** L 9
Colesberg **200** D 6
Coleville (CA.) **112** F 4
Colfax (CA.) **112** E 3
Colfax (IL.) **124** F 9
Colfax (LA.) **123** L 4
Colfax (N.D.) **119** LM 4
Colfax (N.M.) **117** M 1
Colfax (WI.) **124** C 4
Colhué Huapí, Lago **143** C 8
Colima **132** B 4
Colinas (Goiás, Brazil) **141** G 3
Colinas (Maranhão, Brazil) **141** H 2
Coll **148** B 3
Collahuasi **140** C 5
Collbran (CO.) **115** K 4
College **102** H 3
College Grove (TN.) **128** E 6
College Heights (AR.) **121** O 9
College Station (TX.) **122** G 5
Collie **182** B 5
Collier Bay **182** C 2
Collier Ranges National Park **182** B 3
Collierville (TN.) **128** B 6
Colli Euganei **153** F 2
Collines de la Puisaye **152** D 2
Collines de l'Armagnac **152** D 3
Collines de l'Artois **152** D 1
Collines du Perche **152** D 2
Collines du Sancerrois **152** D 2
Collingwood (New Zealand) **185** Q 9
Collingwood (Ontario, Can.) **105** M 7
Collins (MS.) **130** E 3
Collinson Peninsula **103** R 1–2
Collinston (LA.) **123** M 3
Collinsville **183** H 3
Collinsville (MS.) **130** F 2
Collinwood (TN.) **128** D 6
Collipulli **143** B 6
Collison (IL.) **124** G 9
Collo **153** E 4
Collyer (KS.) **120** EF 3
Colmar **153** E 2
Colmena **142** D 4
Colmenar Viejo **152** C 3
Colmor (N.M.) **117** M 1
Cologne → Köln **149** E 4
Cololo, Nevado **140** C 4
Coloma (WI.) **124** E 5
Colombia **138** DE 3
Colombia (São Paulo, Brazil) **141** G 5
Colombo **174** C 6
Colome (SD.) **118** J 7
Colon (Argentina) **142** D 5
Colón (Argentina) **142** E 5
Colón (Cuba) **133** F 3
Colón (Panamá) **138** C 2
Colón, Archipiélago de **138** B 6
Colona **182** E 5
Colona (CO.) **115** K 5
Colonet **106** C 5
Colonia Catriel **143** C 6
Colonia Dalmacia **142** E 4
Colonia del Sacramento **142** E 5
Colonia Josefa **143** C 6
Colonia Las Heras **143** C 8
Colonial Heights (VA.) **129** O 4
Colonia Morelos **106** E 5
Colonias (N.M.) **117** M 2
Colonne, Capo delle **153** G 4
Colonsay **148** B 3
Colony (KS.) **121** K 4
Colorado **115**
Colorado (AK.) **109** J 3
Colorado (Argentina) **143** D 6
Colorado, Cerro (Argentina) **143** C 7
Colorado, Cerro (Mexico) **106** C 5
Colorado, Pico **142** C 4
Colorado City (AZ.) **116** CD 1
Colorado City (TX.) **122** C 3
Colorado Desert **113** KL 9
Colorado National Monument **114** J 4
Colorado River **113** L 7–8
Colorado River (TX.) **122** G 6
Colorado River Indian Reservation **116** B 4
Colorado Springs (CO.) **115** N 5
Colotlán **132** B 3
Colquechaca **140** C 4
Colquitt (GA.) **131** K 3
Colstrip (MT.) **118** B 5
Colt (AR.) **121** P 7
Coltax (WA.) **110** H 4
Colter Peak **111** P 6
Colton (N.Y.) **126** E 4
Colton (UT.) **114** G 4
Columbia (AL.) **131** J 3
Columbia (Br. Col., Can.) **103** O 5
Columbia (IL.) **121** P 4
Columbia (KY.) **128** F 4
Columbia (LA.) **123** L 3
Columbia (MO.) **121** N 4
Columbia (MS.) **130** E 3
Columbia (N.C.) **129** P 6
Columbia (PA.) **127** C 8
Columbia (S.C.) **129** K 7–8
Columbia (S.D.) **119** K 5
Columbia (TN.) **128** DE 6
Columbia (TN.) **128** E 6
Columbia (UT.) **114** G 4
Columbia, Mount **103** O 5
Columbia City (IN.) **124** J 8
Columbia Falls (MT.) **111** L 2
Columbia Mountains **103** NO 5
Columbiana (AL.) **128** E 8
Columbia Plateau **110** G 6–8
Columbia River **110** B 3
Columbia Road Reservoir **119** K 5
Columbine (CO.) **115** KL 3
Columbine, Cape **200** B 6
Columbria **183** H 3
Columbus (GA.) **131** K 2
Columbus (IN.) **128** F 2
Columbus (KS.) **121** L 5
Columbus (MS.) **121** R 9
Columbus (MT.) **111** Q 5
Columbus (N.C.) **129** J 6
Columbus (ND.) **118** F 2
Columbus (NE.) **120** H 1
Columbus (N.M.) **116** J 6
Columbus (OH.) **128** HJ 2
Columbus (TX.) **122** G 6
Columbus (WI.) **124** E 6
Columbus Junction (IA.) **119** R 9
Columbus Salt Marsh **112** GH 4
Colusa (CA.) **112** C 3
Colville (AK.) **102** G 2
Colville (WA.) **110** GH 2
Colville, Cape **103** T 2
Colville Channel **185** R 8
Colville Indian Reservation **110** FG 2
Colville Lake **103** MN 2
Colville Lake **103** MN 2
Colwyn Bay **148** C 4
Comacchio **153** F 3
Comai **175** F 2
Comal (TX.) **122** E 6
Comalcalco **132** D 4
Comanche (MT.) **111** R 4
Comanche (OK.) **120** GH 8
Comanche (TX.) **122** E 4
Comanche Reservoir **112** DE 4
Comandante Luis Piedrabuena **143** BC 8–9
Comandante Salas **142** C 5
Comănești **154** C 1
Comayagua **132** E 5
Combarbala **142** B 5
Combermere Bay **175** F 4
Combes (TX.) **122** F 9
Comeragh Mountains **148** B 4
Comerío (P.R.) **130** C 8
Comet **183** H 3
Comet River **183** H 3
Comfort (TX.) **122** E 5–6
Comfrey (MN.) **119** O 6
Comilla **175** F 3
Comitán de Dominguez **132** D 4
Commentry **152** D 2
Commerce (GA.) **128** H 7
Commerceo (MO.) **121** Q 5
Commercy **153** E 2
Committee Bay **103** U 2
Como **153** E 2
Como (MS.) **121** Q 8
Como, Lago di **153** E 2
Comodoro Rivadavia **143** C 8
Comondú **106** D 6
Comorin, Cape **174** C 6
Comoros **201** G 2
Compiègne **152** D 2
Comptche (CA.) **112** B 3
Comstock (NE.) **118** J 9
Comstock (TX.) **122** B 6
Cona **175** F 2
Conakry **196** B 4
Cona Niyeo **143** C 7
Concan (TX.) **122** D 6
Concarneau **152** C 2
Conceição, Cachoeira da **139** F 5
Conceição da Barra **141** J 4
Conceição do Araguaia **139** J 5
Concepción (Argentina) **142** C 4
Concepción (Bolivia) **140** C 3
Concepción (Bolivia) **140** D 4
Concepción (Chile) **143** B 6
Concepción (Paraguay) **140** E 5
Concepción, Bahía **106** D 6
Concepción del Oro **132** B 3
Concepción del Uruguay **142** E 5
Conception, Point **113** E 8
Conception Bay **105** R 6
Conception Bay (Namibia) **200** A 4
Conchas Dam (N.M.) **117** MN 2
Conchas Lake **117** M 2
Conchi **140** C 5
Concho (AZ.) **116** G 3
Concho River **122** CD 4
Conchos, Rio **106** EF 6
Conconully (WA.) **110** EF 2
Concord (CA.) **112** CD 5
Concord (MO.) **121** P 4
Concord (N.C.) **129** L 6
Concord (N.H.) **126** H 5
Concord (TN.) **128** G 6
Concórdia (Amazonas, Brazil) **138** E 4
Concordia (Argentina) **142** E 5
Concordia (KS.) **120** H 3
Concordia (Mexico) **132** A 3
Concordia (Peru) **138** C 4
Concrete (WA.) **110** D 2
Conda **200** A 2
Conda (ID.) **111** O 8
Condamine **183** J 4
Conde **141** J 3
Conde (S.D.) **119** KL 5
Condobolin **183** H 5
Condom **152** D 3
Condon (MT.) **111** M 3
Condon (OR.) **110** E 5
Condor, Cordillera del **138** C 4
Condoto **138** CD 4
Cone (TX.) **117** P 4
Conecuh River **131** H 3
Conegliano **153** F 2
Conejera **152** D 4
Conejo **106** D 7
Conejos (CO.) **115** L 6
Cone Mountain **108** G 2
Conero **153** F 3
Confluence (PA.) **125** P 10
Congaree River **129** L 8
Conghua **172** F 6
Congo **197** H 6
Congress (AZ.) **116** D 3
Cónico, Cerro **143** B 7
Conifer (CO.) **115** M 4
Conlen (TX.) **117** O 1
Conn, Lough **148** B 4
Connaught **148** B 4
Conneaut (OH.) **125** O 8
Conneauville (PA.) **125** O 8
Connecticut **126–127**
Connecticut River **126** G 5
Connell (WA.) **110** G 4
Connellsville (PA.) **125** P 9
Connemara, Mountains of **148** AB 4
Conner (MT.) **111** L 5
Connersville (IN.) **128** F 2
Conn Lake **105** N 1
Connor, Mount **182** D 1
Conover (WI.) **124** E 3
Conrad (IA.) **119** Q 8
Conrad (MT.) **111** O 2
Conrad Rise **208** B 5
Conroe (TX.) **123** H 5
Conselheiro Lafaiete **141** H 5
Con Son **175** J 6
Constance, Mount **110** B 3
Constância dos Baetas **139** F 5
Constanța **154** C 2
Constantina **152** B 4
Constantine **193** G 1
Constantine, Cape **102** F 4
Constellation (AZ.) **116** D 3
Constitución **143** B 6
Contact (NV.) **112** L 1
Contai **174** E 3
Contamana **138** CD 5
Contão **139** F 3
Cóntas **141** H 3
Continental (OH.) **125** K 8
Continental Divide (N.M.) **116** H 2
Continental Lake **112** G 1
Continental Peak **111** R 8
Contreras, Embalse de **152** C 4
Contreras, Puerto de **152** C 4
Controller Bay **109** K 3
Contwoyto Lake **103** PQ 2
Convención **138** D 2
Convent (LA.) **123** N 5
Con Vidal **143** E 6
Conway (AR.) **121** N 7
Conway (MO.) **121** N 5
Conway (N.H.) **126** H 5
Conway (S.C.) **129** MN 8
Conway (TX.) **117** P 2MO
Conway Reef → Ceva-i-Ra **186** C 4
Conway Springs (KS.) **120** H 5
Conyers (GA.) **128** GH 8
Conza, Sella di **153** G 3
Coober Pedy **182** E 4
Cooch Bihar **174** E 2
Cook **182** E 5
Cook (MN.) **119** Q 3
Cook (NE.) **120** J 2
Cook, Mount **185** Q 9
Cook, Mount **186** C 5
Cook, Strait **186** C 5
Cooke City (MT.) **111** PQ 5
Cookes Peak **116** J 5
Cookeville (TN.) **128** F 5
Cook Inlet **102** G 3
Cook Islands **186** E 3
Cook Mountains **203**
Cook Strait **185** Q 9
Cooktown **183** H 2
Coolgardie **182** C 5
Coolibah **182** E 2
Coolidge (AZ.) **116** E 4–5
Coolidge (GA.) **131** L 3–4
Coolidge (KS.) **120** D 4
Coolidge Dam **116** F 4
Cooma **183** H 6
Coonabarabran **183** H 5
Coonamble **183** H 5
Coondapoor **174** B 5
Coongoola **183** H 4
Coonoor **174** C 5
Coon Rapids (MN.) **119** P 5
Cooper (AL.) **131** H 2
Cooper (TX.) **123** H 2
Co-Operative (KY.) **128** G 5
Cooper Creek **183** G 4
Cooperstown (N.D.) **119** K 3
Cooperstown(N.Y.) **126** E 6
Coopersville (MI.) **124** J 6
Coorow **182** B 4
Cooroy **183** J 4
Coosa River **128** E 8
Coos Bay (OR.) **110** A 7
Coos Bay (OR.) **110** A 7
Cootamundra **183** H 5
Copahue **143** B 6
Copan **132** E 5
Copan (OK.) **120** JK 6
Copana **138** E 4
Copano Bay **122** F 7
Cope (CO.) **115** P 4
Copeland (FL.) **131** N 9
Copeland (ID.) **110** J 2
Copeland (KS.) **120** E 5
Copenhagen **151** F 4
Copeville (TX.) **122** G 2
Copiapó **142** BC 4
Čöpköy **154** C 2
Copper **102** J 3
Copperas Cove (TX.) **122** EF 4
Copperbelt **200** D 2
Copper Butte **110** G 2
Copper Center **102** H 3
Copper Cliff **105** L 6
Copperfield (NV.) **112** F 3
Copper Harbor (MI.) **124** G 2
Coppermine (N.W.T., Can.) **103** OP 2
Coppermine (N.W.T., Can.) **103** P 2
Copper Queen **200** D 3
Coqên **174** E 1
Coquille (OR.) **110** A 7
Coquimbo **142** B 4
Cora (WY.) **111** Q 8
Corabia **154** B 2
Coral Harbour **103** UV 3
Coral Sea **185** H 4
Coral Sea **186** B 3–4
Coral Sea Islands Territory **183** HJ 1–2
Coralville (IA.) **119** R 9
Coralville Lake **119** R 9
Coram (MT.) **111** LM 2
Corantijn **139** G 3
Corato **153** G 3
Corazon (N.M.) **117** M 2
Corbin (KY.) **128** G 5
Corbin (MT.) **111** N 4
Corcaigh **148** B 4
Corcoran (CA.) **112** F 6
Corcovado, Golfo **143** B 7
Corcovado, Volcán **143** B 7
Cordele (GA.) **131** L 3
Cordell (OK.) **120** FG 7
Cordell (WA.) **110** F 2
Cordilheiras, Serra das **139** J 5
Cordillera, Costa de la **138** E 2
Cordillera Azul **138** C 5
Cordillera Blanca **138** C 5
Cordillera Cantábrica **152** BC 3
Cordillera Central (Colombia) **138** C 2–3
Cordillera Central (Dominican Rep.) **133** H 4
Cordillera Central (Peru) **138** C 5
Cordillera Central (Philippines) **177** J 1
Cordillera de Carabaya **140** B 3
Cordillera de Chichas **140** C 4–5
Cordillera de Chilca **140** B 4
Cordillera de Huanzo **140** B 3
Cordillera de la Costa **138** E 2
Cordillera del Condor **138** C 4
Cordillera de Lípez **140** C 5
Cordillera de Mérida **138** D 2
Cordillera Domeyko **140** C 5
Cordillera Isabella **132** EF 5
Cordillera Negra **138** C 5
Cordillera Occidental **140** BC 3–4
Cordillera Occidental (Colombia) **138** C 2–3
Cordillera Oriental **140** BC 3–5
Cordillera Oriental (Colombia) **138** CD 2–3
Cordillera Real (Bolivia) **140** C 4
Cordillera Real (Ecuador) **138** C 4
Cordillera Vilcabamba **140** B 3
Córdoba (Argentina) **142** D 5
Córdoba (Mexico) **132** C 4
Córdoba (Spain) **152** BC 4
Córdoba, Sierra de **142** D 5
Cordova (AK.) **102** H 3
Cordova (AL.) **128** D 8
Cordova (IL.) **124** D 8
Córdova (Peru) **140** A 3
Core Banks **129** P 7
Corfu **154** A 3
Corguinno **141** E 4
Coria **152** B 4
Corigliano Calabro **153** G 4
Corinda (Queensland, Austr.) **183** F 2
Coringa Islands **183** J 2
Corinne (UT.) **114** E 2
Corinth (Greece) **154** B 3
Corinth (MS.) **121** R 8
Corinto **141** H 4
Corisco, Baie de **197** F 5
Corisco Island **197** F 5
Cork (Queensland, Austr.) **183** G 3
Cork (Rep. of Ireland) **148** B 4
Corleone **153** F 4
Çorlu **154** C 2
Cornelia (GA.) **128** H 7
Cornelio **106** D 6
Cornélio Procópio **141** F 5
Cornelius Grinnel Bay **105** P 3
Cornell (WI.) **124** CD 4
Corner Brook **105** Q 6
Corning (AR.) **121** P 6
Corning (CA.) **112** C 3
Corning (IA.) **119** O 10
Corning (NE.) **120** J 3
Corning (N.Y.) **126** B 6
Cornish (CO.) **115** N 3
Corno Grande **153** F 3
Cornudas (TX.) **117** L 6
Cornville (AZ.) **116** E 3
Cornwall (Ontario, Can.) **105** N 6
Cornwell (FL.) **131** N 7
Coro **138** E 1
Coroatá **141** H 1
Corocoro **140** C 4
Coroico **140** C 4
Coromandel Coast **174** D 5
Coromandel Peninsula **185** R 8
Corona (CA.) **113** H 9
Corona (N.M.) **117** KL 3
Coronado (CA.) **113** H 10
Coronado, Bahía de **132** F 6
Coronation **103** P 5
Coronation Gulf **103** P 2
Corondo **142** D 5
Coronel **143** B 6
Coronel Dorrego **143** D 6
Coronel Fabriciano **141** H 4
Coronel Falcón **143** D 6
Coronel Oviedo **142** E 4
Coronel Pringles **143** D 6
Coronel Suárez **143** D 6
Corongo **138** C 5
Coropuna, Nevado **140** B 4
Corozal **132** E 4
Corozal **138** CD 2
Çorpus **142** E 4
Corpus Christi (TX.) **122** F 8
Corpus Christi, Lake **122** F 7
Corpus Christi Bay **122** F 8
Corque **140** C 4
Corquin **132** E 5
Corral **143** B 6
Corral (ID.) **111** L 7
Corrales **142** E 5
Corrente (Bahía, Brazil) **141** H 3
Corrente (Piauí, Brazil) **141** G 3

Correntes 141 F 4
Correntes, Cabo das 201 F 4
Correntina 141 GH 3
Correo (N.M.) 117 J 3
Corrib, Lough 148 B 4
Corrientes 138 C 4
Corrientes (Argentina) 142 E 4
Corrientes (Argentina) 142 E 4
Corrientes (Peru) 138 C 4
Corrientes, Cabo (Argentina) 143 E 6
Corrientes, Cabo (Colombia) 138 C 2
Corrigan (TX.) 123 J 4–5
Corrigin 182 B 5
Corry (PA.) 125 P 8
Corryong 183 H 6
Corse 153 E 3
Corse, Cap 153 E 3
Corsica 153 E 3
Corsica (S.D.) 119 K 7
Corsicana (TX.) 122 G 3
Corte 153 E 3
Corte Alto 143 B 7
Cortegana 152 B 4
Cortez (CO.) 114 J 6
Cortez (Spain) 152 C 3
Cortez Mountains 112 J 2
Cortland (NE.) 120 J 2
Cortland (N.Y.) 126 C 6
Cortland (OH.) 125 O 8
Cortona 153 F 3
Corubal 196 B 3
Coruche 152 B 4
Çoruh 155 F 2
Çoruh Dağları 155 F 2
Çorum 155 D 2
Corumba (Goiás, Brazil) 141 G 4
Corumbá (Mato Grosso do Sul, Brazil) 140 E 4
Corumbá de Goiás 141 G 4
Corunna 152 B 3
Coruripe 141 J 3
Corvallis (MT.) 111 L 4
Corvallis (OR.) 110 B 6
Corvo 192 A 1
Corwin Springs (MT.) 111 P 5
Corydon (IA.) 119 P 10
Corydon (IN.) 128 E 3
Cosamaloapan 132 C 4
Cosenza 153 G 4
Coshocton (OH.) 125 N 9
Cosmoledo Group 199 H 6
Cosne-sur-Loire 152 D 2
Costa Blanca 152 C 4
Costa Blanca 152 C 4
Costa Brava 152 D 3
Costa de la Luz 152 B 4
Costa del Azahar 152 D 3–4
Costa del Sol 152 C 4
Costa de Mosquitos 132 F 5
Costa Dorada 152 D 3
Costa Mesa (CA.) 113 J 9
Costa Rica 132 EF 6
Costa Verde 152 B 3
Costilla (N.M.) 117 L 1
Cotabato 177 F 2
Cotagaita 140 C 5
Cotahuasi 140 B 4
Cotati (CA.) 112 C 4
Coteau (N.D.) 118 F 2
Coteau des Prairies 119 KM 5–6
Coteau du Missouri 118 H 3–5
Côte d'Argent 152 C 3
Côte d'Azur 153 E 3
Côte de l'Ile de France 152 D 2
Côte d'Ivoire → Ivory Coast 196 CD 4
Côte d'Or 153 E 2
Cotentin 152 C 2
Cotherstone 183 H 3
Cotonou 196 E 4
Cotopaxi 138 C 4
Cottage Grove (OR.) 110 B 7
Cottage Grove Lake 110 B 7
Cottbus 149 F 4
Cottica 139 H 3
Cotton (MN.) 119 Q 3
Cottondale (AL.) 128 D 8
Cottondale (FL.) 131 J 4
Cotton Plant (AR.) 121 O 7–8
Cottonwood (AZ.) 116 D 3
Cottonwood (CA.) 112 C 2
Cottonwood (ID.) 110 J 4
Cottonwood (MN.) 119 N 6
Cottonwood (SD.) 118 D 4
Cottonwood Falls (KS.) 120 J 4
Cottonwood Pass 113 E 7
Cottonwood River 119 N 6
Cotulla (TX.) 122 D 7
Coubre, Pointe de la 152 C 2
Coudersport (PA.) 125 Q 8
Cougar (WA.) 110 C 4
Cougar Reservoir 110 C 6
Couhé 152 CD 2
Čoukkarašša 150 H 2
Coulee (N.D.) 118 F 2
Coulee City (WA.) 110 F 3
Coulee Dam (WA.) 110 G 3
Coulee Dam National Recreation Area 110 G 2
Coulommiers 152 D 2
Coulterville (CA.) 112 EF 5

Coulterville (IL.) 121 Q 4
Council (AK.) 102 E 3
Council (ID.) 110 J 6
Council Bluffs (IA.) 119 N 9
Council Grove (KS.) 120 J 4
Council Grove Lake 120 J 4
Country Homes (WA.) 110 H 3
Coupeville (WA.) 110 C 2
Courantyne 139 G 3
Courland 151 H 4
Courmayeur 153 E 2
Courtenay (FL.) 131 O 6
Courtennai 103 M 6
Courtland (AL.) 128 D 7
Courtland (VA.) 129 OP 4
Coushatta (LA.) 123 K 3
Coutances 152 C 2
Coutney (TX.) 122 F 6
Coutras 152 CD 2
Couvin 148 D 4
Cove (OR.) 110 H 5
Covelo (CA.) 112 B 3
Coventry 148 C 4
Covert (KS.) 120 G 3
Covilhã 152 B 3
Covington (GA.) 128 H 8
Covington (IN.) 124 G 9
Covington (KY.) 128 G 2
Covington (LA.) 123 N 5
Covington (MI.) 124 F 3
Covington (OK.) 120 H 6
Covington (TN.) 128 B 6
Cowal, Lake 183 H 5
Cowan (TN.) 128 EF 6
Cowan, Lake 182 C 5
Cowargarze 172 C 4
Cowdrey (CO.) 115 L 3
Cowell 183 F 5
Cowen (W.V.) 129 L 3
Cowen, Mount 111 P 5
Coweta (OK.) 121 K 7
Cow Head Lake 112 EF 1
Cowles (N.M.) 117 L 2
Cowley (WY.) 111 R 6
Cowra 183 H 5
Cox's Bazar 175 F 3
Coy Aike 143 C 9
Coyame 106 E 6
Coyle → Coig 143 B 9
Coyote (N.M.) 117 L 4
Coyote Lake 113 J 7
Coyote Wells (CA.) 113 K 10
Coyotitan 106 E 7
Cozad (NE.) 120 F 2
Crab Orchard (TN.) 128 G 6
Crab Orchard Lake 121 Q 5
Crabtree (OR.) 110 C 6
Cracow 183 J 4
Cradock 200 D 6
Craig (AK.) 102 L 4
Craig (CO.) 115 K 3
Craig (MO.) 121 K 2
Craig (MT.) 111 O 3
Craigmont (ID.) 110 J 4
Craig Pass 111 P 6
Craigs Range 183 J 4
Craiova 154 B 2
Crakow 149 H 4
Crampel 192 E 2
Crampel → Kaga Bandoro 198 B 3
Cranberry Lake 126 E 4
Cranbrook 103 O 6
Cranbrook (Western Australia) 182 B 5
Crandon (WI.) 124 G 4
Crane (MO.) 121 M 6
Crane (MT.) 118 D 3
Crane (OR.) 110 G 7
Crane (TX.) 117 O 6
Crane Mountain 110 E 8
Crane Prairie Reservoir 110 D 7
Cranston (R.I.) 126 H 7
Craolândia 139 J 5
Crasna 154 B 1
Cratère du Nouveau-Québec 105 N 3
Crater Lake (OR.) 110 C 8
Crater Lake (OR.) 110 C 8
Crater Lake National Park 110 C 8
Craters of the Moon National Monument 111 M 7
Cratéus 141 H 2
Crato (Amazonas, Brazil) 139 F 5
Crato (Ceará, Brazil) 141 J 2
Cravo Norte 138 E 2
Crawford (CO.) 115 K 5
Crawford (NE.) 118 E 8
Crawford (TX.) 122 F 4
Crawfordsville (IN.) 124 H 9
Crawfordville (FL.) 131 K 4
Crawfordville (GA.) 128 H 8
Crawley (U.K.) 148 C 4
Crazy Mountains 111 P 4–5
Cree 103 Q 4
Creede (CO.) 115 KL 6
Creedmoor (N.C.) 129 N 5
Creel 106 E 6
Cree Lake 103 Q 4
Creighton (NE.) 119 L 8

Creighton (SD.) 118 F 6
Creil 152 D 2
Cremona 153 F 2
Creole (LA.) 123 K 6
Crepori 139 G 5
Cres 153 F 3
Crescent (OK.) 120 H 6–7
Crescent (OR.) 110 D 7
Crescent City (CA.) 112 A 1
Crescent City (FL.) 131 N 5
Crescent Junction (UT.) 114 H 5
Crescent Lake 131 N 5
Crescent Lake (OR.) 110 D 7
Cresco (IA.) 119 Q 7
Cresson (TX.) 122 F 3
Crest 153 DE 3
Crested Butte (CO.) 115 L 5
Crestline (CA.) 113 H 8
Crestline (NV.) 112 LM 5
Crestline (OH.) 125 M 9
Creston (IA.) 119 O 9
Creston (LA.) 123 KL 4
Creston (WA.) 110 G 3
Creston (WY.) 111 S 9
Crestview (FL.) 131 H 4
Creswell (N.C.) 129 P 6
Creswell (OR.) 110 B 7
Crête de la Neige 153 E 2
Crete 154 BC 3
Crete (NE.) 120 J 2
Cretin, Cape 184 E 3
Creus, Cabo de 152 D 3
Creuse 152 D 2
Crevillente 152 C 4
Crewe 148 C 4
Criciúma 142 G 4
Crillon, Mount 109 L 4
Crimea 155 D 1
Cripple Creek (CO.) 115 M 5
Crisfield (MD.) 129 Q 4
Crisp Point 124 J 3
Cristal, Monts de 197 G 5
Cristalândia 141 G 3
Cristino Castro 141 H 2
Cristmas Island 187 E 2
Cristóbal, Colón Pico 138 D 1
Crişul Alb 154 B 1
Crişul Repede 154 B 1
Crivitz (WI.) 124 G 4
Crkvena Planina 154 B 2
Crna Gora 154 A 2
Crna Gora 154 B 2
Crna Reka 154 B 2
Crni Drim 154 B 2
Črni Vrh (Yugoslavia) 153 G 2
Crni Vrh (Yugoslavia) 153 G 3
Croatia 153 G 2
Crocker (N.M.) 121 N 5
Crocker (N.M.) 117 J 4
Crockett (TX.) 123 H 4
Crockston (MN.) 119 M 3
Crofton (KY.) 128 D 4
Crofton (NE.) 119 L 8
Croghan (N.Y.) 126 D 5
Croissette, Cap 153 DE 3
Croix, Lac la 119 R 2
Croker, Cape 182 E 1
Croker Island 182 E 1
Cromarty 148 C 3
Cromer 148 D 4
Cromwell (AL.) 130 F 2
Cromwell (MN.) 119 Q 4
Crook (CO.) 115 P 3
Crooked Creek 102 F 3
Crooked Island 131 J 4
Crooked Island 133 H 3
Crooked Island Passage 133 GH 3
Crooked River 110 E 6
Crooksville (OH.) 129 JK 2
Crosby (MN.) 119 OP 4
Crosby (MS.) 130 C 3
Crosby (ND.) 118 E 2
Crosby, Mount 111 Q 7
Crosbyton (TX.) 117 P 4
Cross (Nigeria) 197 F 4
Cross, Cape 200 A 4
Cross City (FL.) 131 L 5
Crossett (AR.) 121 O 9
Cross Fell 148 C 4
Cross Hill (S.C.) 129 K 7
Cross Lake (Manitoba, can.) 103 S 5
Cross Lake (ME.) 126 L 1
Crossman Peak 116 B 3
Cross Plains (TX.) 122 D 3
Crossroads (N.M.) 117 N 4
Cross Sound 102 K 4
Crossville (IL.) 121 R 4
Crossville (TN.) 128 F 6
Croswell (MI.) 125 M 6
Crotone 153 G 4
Crow Agency (MT.) 111 S 5
Crow Creek Indian Reservation 118 J 6
Crowell (TX.) 122 D 1–2
Crowe Peak 111 O 4
Crowheart (WY.) 111 Q 7
Crowheart (WY.) 111 R 7
Crow Indian Reservation 111 RS 5
Crow Lake 104 J 6
Crowley (LA.) 123 L 5
Crowley, Lake 112 G 5

Crowley Ridge 121 OP 7
Crown City (OH.) 129 J 3
Crown Point (IN.) 124 G 8
Crown Point (LA.) 123 N 6
Crownpoint (N.M.) 116 H 2
Crown Prince Frederik Island 103 U 2
Crows Nest 183 J 4
Crowsnest Pass 103 OP 6
Crows Nest Peak 118 E 6
Croydon 183 G 2
Crozon 152 C 2
Cruger (MS.) 121 P 9
Crump Lake 110 F 8
Cruz, Cabo 133 G 4
Cruz Alta 142 F 4
Cruz Alta (Argentina) 142 D 5
Cruz del Eje 142 CD 5
Cruzeiro 141 G 5
Cruzeiro do Oeste 141 F 5
Cruzeiro do Sul 138 D 5
Cruz Grande (Chile) 142 B 4
Cruz Grande (Mexico) 132 C 4
Crystal (MN.) 119 P 5
Crystal (N.D.) 119 L 2
Crystal Bay (FL.) 131 M 6
Crystal Bay (NV.) 112 F 3
Crystal City (MO.) 121 P 4
Crystal City (TX.) 122 D 7
Crystal Lake (IL.) 124 F 7
Crystal River (FL.) 131 M 6
Crystal Springs (MS.) 130 D 2–3
Ctesiphon (Iraq) 157 D 2
Cuale 200 B 1
Cuamba 201 F 2
Cuando Cubango 200 BC 3
Cuangar 200 B 3
Cuango 200 B 1
Cuango 200 B 1
Cuanza 200 B 1
Cuanza Norte 200 AB 1
Cuanza Sul 200 AB 2
Cua Rao 175 H 4
Cuareim 142 E 4
Cuarterón Reef 176 D 2
Cuarto 142 D 5
Cuauhtémoc 106 E 6
Cuba 133 F 3
Cuba (AL.) 130 F 2
Cuba (IL.) 124 D 9
Cuba (KS.) 120 H 3
Cuba (MO.) 121 O 4
Cuba (N.Y.) 125 Q 7
Cubal 200 A 2
Cubango 200 B 3
Cubati 200 B 3
Cubuk 155 D 2
Cuchara (CO.) 115 M 6
Cuchilla de Santa Ana 142 EF 5
Cuchilla Grande 142 EF 5
Cuchillo-Có 143 D 6
Cuchumatanes, Sierra de los 132 D 4
Cucuí 138 E 3
Cucumbi 200 B 2
Cucurpe 106 D 5
Cúcuta 138 D 2
Cuddalore 174 CD 5
Cuddapah 174 C 5
Cuddeback Lake 113 H 7
Cuddy Mountain 110 J 6
Cudi Daği 155 F 3
Cue 182 B 4
Cuéllar 152 C 3
Cuemba 200 B 2
Cuenca (Ecuador) 138 C 4
Cuenca (Spain) 152 C 3
Cuencamé de Ceniceros 132 B 3
Cuerda del Pozo, Embalse de la 152 C 3
Cuernavaca 132 BC 4
Cuero (TX.) 122 F 6
Cuervo (N.M.) 117 M 2
Cuesta Pass 113 E 7
Cuevas del Ará 152 D 4
Cuevo 140 D 5
Cufra Oasis → Wāhāt al Kufrah 193 H 2
Cuiabá 140 E 4
Cuiabá 140 E 4
Cuiari 138 E 3
Cuilapa 132 D 5
Cuilo 200 B 1
Cuilo 200 B 1
Cuima 200 B 2
Cuito Cuanavale 200 B 3
Cuiuni 139 F 4
Cujmir 154 B 2
Çukurca 155 F 3
Çukurca (Turkey) 156 D 1
Culan 152 D 2
Cu Lao Cham 175 J 4
Cu Lao Hon 175 J 5
Cu Lao Re 175 J 4
Culbertson (MT.) 118 D 2
Culbertson (NE.) 120 E 2
Culcairn 183 H 6
Culebra, Isla 130 D 8
Culgoa River 183 H 4

Culiacán 106 E 7
Culion 177 F 1
Cullera 152 C 4
Cullison (KS.) 120 FG 5
Cullman (AL.) 128 E 7
Culloden (GA.) 131 K 2
Culp Creek (OR.) 110 C 7
Culpeper (VA.) 129 O 3
Cultowa 183 G 5
Culuene 141 F 3
Culver (OR.) 110 D 6
Culver, Point 182 C 5
Cumaná 139 F 1
Cumaria 138 D 5
Cumbal 138 C 3
Cumberland (IA.) 119 O 9
Cumberland (KY.) 128 H 5
Cumberland (MD.) 129 N 2
Cumberland (OH.) 129 K 2
Cumberland (VA.) 129 N 4
Cumberland (WI.) 124 B 4
Cumberland, Lake 128 G 5
Cumberland City (TN.) 128 D 5
Cumberland Island 131 N 4
Cumberland Island National Seashore 131 N 4
Cumberland Islands 183 H 3
Cumberland Lake (Sask., Can.) 103 R 5
Cumberland Peninsula 105 OP 2
Cumberland Plateau 128 F 5–6
Cumberland Point 124 E 2
Cumberland River 128 D 5
Cumberland Sound 105 O 2
Cûmina 139 G 4
Cuminapanema 139 GH 4
Cumming (GA.) 128 G 7
Cummins 183 F 5
Çumra 155 D 3
Cunani 139 H 3
Cunco 143 B 6
Cundiff (TX.) 122 EF 2
Cunene 200 A 3
Cunene 200 B 3
Cuneo 153 E 3
Cungena 182 E 5
Cunnamulla 183 H 4
Cupica 138 C 2
Ćuprija 154 B 2
Cuprum (ID.) 110 J 5
Curaçao, Isla 138 E 1
Curacautin 143 B 6
Curanilahue 143 B 6
Curaray 138 CD 4
Curare 138 E 3
Curcubata, Virful 154 B 1
Curdimurka 183 F 4
Curecanti National Recreation Area 115 K 5
Curepipe 201 K 6
Curepto 143 B 6
Curicó 143 B 5–6
Curicuriari 138 E 4
Curimatá 141 H 2–3
Curious, Mount 182 A 4
Curiplaya 138 C 3
Curitiba 142 FG 4
Curnamona 183 F 5
Curoca 200 A 3
Currais Novos 141 J 2
Curralinho 139 J 4
Currant Creek Peak 114 F 3
Currant Mountain 112 JK 4
Currie 183 G 6
Currie (MN.) 119 N 6
Currie (NV.) 112 L 2
Currituck (N.C.) 129 PQ 5
Curry 183 J 3
Curtea de Argeş 154 BC 1
Curtici 154 B 1
Curtin (OR.) 110 B 7
Curtina 142 E 5
Curtis 183 H 5
Curtis (NE.) 120 E 2
Curtis Channel 183 J 3
Curtis Island 183 J 3
Curuá 139 J 4
Curuá (Pará, Brazil) 139 H 4
Curuá, Ilha 139 J 3
Curuaí 139 G 4
Curuá Una 139 H 4
Curuça 139 J 4
Curuçambaba 139 J 4
Curuguaty 140 E 5
Curumu 139 H 4
Curupá 139 J 5
Curupira, Sierra de 138–139 EF 3
Curuzú Cuatiá 142 E 4
Curvelo 141 H 4
Curwood, Mount 124 F 3
Cushenbury (CA.) 113 J 8
Cushing (OK.) 120 J 6–7
Cushing, Mount 103 M 4
Cushman (OR.) 110 B 6
Cusick (WA.) 110 H 2
Cusset 152 D 2
Cusseta (GA.) 131 K 2

Custer (MT.) **111** S 4
Custer (SD.) **118** E 7
Custer Battefiled National Monument **111** S 5
Custer City (OK.) **120** G 7
Cut Bank (MT.) **111** N 2
Cutervo **138** C 5
Cuthbert (GA.) **131** K 3
Cutler (CA.) **112** F 6
Cutral-Có **143** C 6
Cuttack **174** E 3
Cutter (AZ.) **116** F 4
Cutter (N.M.) **117** J 4
Cuvelai **200** B 3
Cuvette **197** H 6
Cuvier, Cape **182** A 3
Cuxhaven **149** E 4
Cuya **140** B 4
Cuyahoga Falls (OH.) **125** N 8
Cuyapaipe Indian Reservation **113** J 10
Cuyo Islands **177** F 1
Cuzco **140** B 3
Cuzna **152** C 4
Cyangugu **198** D 5
Cyclades **154** C 3
Cygnes River **121** LM 4
Cynthiana (KY.) **128** G 3
Cypress (LA.) **123** KL 4
Cypress Hills **103** PQ 6
Cyprus **155** D 3
Cyprus **156** AB 2
Cyrenaica **193** K 2
Cyrene **193** K 2
Cyrene → Shaḥḥāt **193** K 2
Cyrus (Iran) **157** E 3
Cyrus Field Bay **105** P 3
Czechoslovakia **149** G 5
Czeremcha **149** H 4
Czersk **149** G 4
Częstochowa **149** G 4

D

Da'an **173** H 1
Dabaga **199** F 6
Dabajuro **138** D 1
Dabakala **196** D 4
Daba Shan **172** E 4
Dabat **199** F 2
Dabbāgh, Jabal (Saudi Arabia) **156** B 4
Dabeiba **138** C 2
Dabhoi **174** B 3
Dabie Shan **172** G 4
Dabney (TX.) **122** C 6
Dabnou **197** F 3
Dabo **176** B 4
Dabola **196** B 3
Daborów **199** H 3
Dabou **196** D 4
Daboya **196** D 4
Dabrash **154** B 2
Dabu **172** G 6
Dăbuleni **154** B 2
Dacca **174** E 3
Dachau **149** F 5
Dadali **185** G 3
Dadali **186** B 3
Dadanawa **139** G 3
Dade City (FL.) **131** M 6
Dadu **169** H 5
Dadu He **172** D 5
Dadynskoye, Ozero **155** FG 1
Daet **177** F 1
Dafang **172** E 5
Dafeng **173** H 4
Daflas **175** F 2
Dagabur **199** G 3
Dagadzhik **168** E 3
Daga Medo **199** G 3
Dagana (Chad) **197** H 3
Dagana (Senegal) **196** A 2
Daga Post **198** E 3
Dagary **170** K 4
Dağbası **155** E 3
Dagett (CA.) **113** J 8
Dagger Mountain **117** N 8
Dagi **171** Q 5
Daguan **172** D 5
Dagupan **177** J 1
Dagur **172** C 3
Dagworth **183** G 2
Dagzê **175** F 2
Dagzê Co **174** E 1
Dagzhuka **174** E 2
Dahabān **195** F 4
Dahanu **174** B 4
Daheiding Shan **171** NO 6
Dahei He **172** F 2
Da Hinggan Ling **173** GH 1–2
Dahlak Archipelago **199** G 1
Dahlak Kebir **199** G 1
Dahl al Furayy (Saudi Arabia) **157** E 4
Dahlgren (IL.) **121** R 4
Dahlia (N.M.) **117** L 2
Dahlonega (GA.) **128** GH 7

Dahongliutan **169** K 3
Dahra (Algeria) **152** D 4
Dahra (Senegal) **196** A 2
Dahūk (Iraq) **156** D 1
Dahy, Nafūd ad **195** GH 4
Dai **185** H 3
Daïa **193** F 2
Daicheng **173** G 3
Daik-u **175** G 4
Dailey (W.V.) **129** M 3
Daimier **152** C 4
Daingerfield (TX.) **123** J 2
Dainkog **172** C 4
Daintree River National Park **183** G 2
Daireaux **143** D 6
Dairen **173** H 3
Daitō-shotō **173** K 5
Dai Xian **172** F 3
Daiyun Shan **173** G 5–6
Dajarra **183** F 3
Dakala **196** E 3
Dakar **196** A 3
Dakha **174** E 3
Dakhla **192** B 4
Dakhla Oasis → Wāḥāt ad Dākhilah **194** E 3
Dakhlet Nouadhibou **192** B 4
Dak Kon **175** J 5
Dako **196** D 2
Dakoro **197** F 3
Dakota City (IA.) **119** O 8
Dakota City (NE.) **119** M 8
Dakovica **154** B 2
Dakovo **153** G 2
Daktuy **171** N 5
Dākura **132** F 5
Dala **200** C 2
Dalaba **196** B 3
Dalad Qi **172** E 2
Dalai Nur **173** G 2
Dalälven **151** G 3
Dalaman **154** C 3
Dalāmi **194** E 6
Dalandzadgad **172** DE 2
Dalanjargalan **172** E 1
Dalarna **151** F 3
Da Lat **175** J 5
Dalbandin **169** G 5
Dalby **183** J 4
Dalbyrdakh **171** P 2
Dale **151** E 3
Dale (OR.) **110** G 6
Dale City (VA.) **129** O 3
Dale Hollow Lake **128** F 5
Dale Lake **113** K 8
Dalen **151** E 4
Daletme **175** F 3
Dalgonally **183** G 3
Dalhart (TX.) **117** O 1
Dalhousie **105** O 6
Dalhousie, Cape **102** L 1
Dali **172** EF 4
Dali **172** D 5
Dalian → Lüda **173** H 3
Dalias **152** C 4
Dalj **153** G 2
Daljä' **194** E 3
Dall **102** L 5
Dallas (GA.) **128** G 8
Dallas (OR.) **110** B 6
Dallas (TX.) **122** G 3
Dallas Center (IA.) **119** OP 9
Dalli **174** D 3
Dall Lake **102** E 3
Dallol Bosso **196** E 3
Dalmā' (United Arab Emirates) **157** F 4
Dalmaj, Hawr (Iraq) **157** D 2
Dalnegorsk **173** L 2
Dal'nerechensk **173** K 1
Dal'nyaya **171** Q 6
Daloa **196** C 4
Dalou Shan **172** E 5
Dalqān (Saudi Arabia) **157** D 4
Dalqū **194** E 4
Dalrymple, Mount **183** H 3
Dalsfjorden **150** D 3
Dalsland **151** F 4
Dals Långed **151** F 4
Dalstroy **171** P 3
Dal'stroya **108** C 2
Daltonganj **174** D 3
Daluo **172** D 6
Dalupiri **177** J 1
Dalvík **150** B 2
Dalwallinu **182** B 5
Daly Bay **103** U 3
Daly City (CA.) **112** C 5
Daly River **182** E 1
Daly Waters **182** E 2
Daman **174** B 3
Dāmaneh (Iran) **157** F 2
Damanhūr **194** DE 2
Damar, Pulau **177** G 4
Damar, Pulau **172** G 5
Damara **198** B 3
Damaraland **200** B 4
Damascus (AR.) **121** N 7

Damascus (Syria) **156** B 2
Dāmāsh (Iran) **157** E 1
Damaturu **197** G 3
Damāvand (Iran) **157** F 2
Damāvand, Qolleh-ye **168** E 3
Damba **200** B 1
Dambarta **197** F 3
Dame Marie, Cap **133** H 4
Dāmghan (Iran) **157** FG 1
Damietta → Dumyāt **194** E 2
Damīr Qābū (Syria) **156** CD 1
Damlataş **155** D 3
Damoh **174** C 3
Damongo **196** D 4
Damot **199** H 3
Dampier **182** B 3
Dampier, Selat **177** H 4
Dampier Archipelago **182** B 3
Dampier Land **182** C 2
Dampier Strait **184** E 3
Damqawt **195** J 5
Dana **171** U 3
Danakil Depression → Kobar Sink **199** G 2
Danakil Plain **199** G 2
Danan **199** G 3
Danané **196** C 4
Da Nang **175** J 4
Danau Toba **176** A 3
Danau Towuti **177** F 4
Danba **172** D 4
Danbury (N.C.) **129** L 5
Danbury (NE.) **120** E 2
Danbury (VT.) **127** F 7
Danbury (WI.) **124** B 4
Danby Lake **113** K 8
Dandarah (Egypt) **156** A 4
Dande **200** A 1
Dandeldhura **174** D 2
Dandeli **174** B 4
Dandong **173** H 2
Dandridge (TN.) **128** H 5
Danells Fjord **105** T 3
Danfa **196** C 3
Danfeng **172** F 4
Danforth (ME.) **126** L 3
Danforth Hills **115** JK 3
Dangara **169** H 3
Dangchang **172** D 4
Dange **200** B 1
Danghe Nanshan **172** C 3
Dangila **199** F 2
Dangjin Shankou **172** B 3
Dang Krien **175** J 5
Dangriga **132** E 4
Dangshan **173** G 4
Dan Gulbi **197** F 3
Dangyang **172** F 4
Daniel (WY.) **111** P 8
Daniell **182** C 5
Daniel's Harbour **105** Q 5
Danielskuil **200** C 5
Danielsville (GA.) **128** H 7
Danilov **158** H 4
Danilovka **158** H 5
Daning **172** F 3
Danjiangkou Shuiku **172** F 4
Danjo-guntō **173** J 4
Dank (Oman) **157** G 5
Dankhar **174** C 1
Danlí **132** E 5
Danmark **151** E 4
Danmarks Havn **202**
Dannebrog (NE.) **120** G 1
Dannemora (N.Y.) **126** F 4
Dannevirke **185** R 9
Danompari **176** E 3
Dan Sai **175** H 4
Dansville (N.Y.) **126** B 6
Dante **199** J 2
Dantewara **174** D 4
Danu **185** F 2
Danube **154** C 1
Danville (AR.) **121** M 7
Danville (IL.) **124** G 9
Danville (IN.) **128** E 2
Danville (KY.) **128** G 4
Danville (PA.) **127** C 8
Danville (VA.) **129** M 5
Danville (VT.) **126** G 4
Danville (WA.) **110** G 2
Dan Xian **172** E 7
Danzhai **172** E 5
Dao **177** F 1
Daocheng **172** D 5
Daora **192** C 3
Dao Tho Chy **175** G 5
Dao Timni **197** G 1
Daoukro **196** D 4
Daoura **192** E 2
Dao Xian **172** F 3
Dapango **196** E 3
Dapchi **197** G 3
Daphabum **175** G 2
Dapoli **174** B 4
Da Qaidam **172** C 3
Daqing **173** J 1
Dar'ā (Syria) **156** B 2
Dārāb (Iran) **157** G 3

Darabani **154** C 1
Daraçya Yarımadası **154** C 3
Darāfisah **194** E 6
Daraj **193** H 2
Dar al Ḥomr **194** D 6
Dāran (Iran) **157** F 2
Darapap **184** D 2
Darasun **170** K 5
Darāw (Egypt) **156** A 4
Darazo **197** G 3
Darband **168** F 4
Darbhanga **174** E 2
Darboruk **199** G 3
Darby (MT.) **111** L 4
Darby, Cape **108** F 3
Darda **153** G 2
Dardanele (AR.) **121** M 7
Dardanelle (CA.) **112** F 4
Dardanelle Lake **121** M 7
Dardanelles **154** C 3
Dardanelles **154** C 3
Dar el Beida **192** CD 2
Dar el Kouti **198** C 3
Darende **155** E 3
Dar es Salaam **199** F 6
Darfo Boario Terme **153** EF 2
Dārfūr **194** C 6
Darganata **169** G 2
Dargaville **185** Q 8
Dargo **183** H 6
Dargol **196** E 3
Dar Ḥamar **194** D 6
Darhan **170** J 6
Darhan Muminggan Lianheqi **172** F 2
Darién **138** C 2
Darién, Golfo del **138** C 2
Darién, Serranía del **138** C 2
Darius (Iran) **157** EF 3
Darjeeling **174** E 2
Darkan **182** B 5
Darkhovin (Iran) **157** E 3
Darlag **172** C 4
Darling, Lake **118** G 2
Darling Downs **183** H 4
Darling Range **182** B 5
Darling River **183** G 5
Darlington (FL.) **131** HJ 4
Darlington (ID.) **111** M 7
Darlington (S.C.) **129** M 7
Darlington (U.K.) **148** C 4
Darlington (WI.) **124** D 7
Darlot, Lake **182** C 4
Darłowo **149** G 4
Darmstadt **149** E 5
Darnah **193** K 2
Darnley, Cape **203**
Darnley Bay **103** N 2
Dar Nūbah **194** DE 6
Daroca **152** C 3
Darreh Gaz **168** F 3
Darreh-shahr (Iran) **157** E 2
Darrington (WA.) **110** D 2
Dar Rounga **198** C 2–3
Darrouzett (TX.) **117** Q 1
Darsi **174** C 4
Dar Sila **197** J 3
Dartmoor **148** C 4
Dartmouth **105** P 7
Daru **184** D 2
Daruba **177** G 3
Darūneh (Iran) **157** G 2
Daruvar **153** G 2
Darvaza **168** F 2
Darvel, Teluk **177** E 3
Darvi **170** F 6
Darweshan **169** G 4
Darwin (Argentina) **143** C 6
Darwin (Australia) **182** E 1
Darwin (IL.) **121** S 3
Darwin, Bahía **143** AB 8
Darwin, Isla **138** B 6
Darwin, Port **182** E 1
Dāryācheh-ye **169** G 4
Dāryācheh-ye Bakhtegān (Iran) **157** FG 3
Dāryācheh-ye Hāmūn-e Hirmand **169** G 4
Dāryācheh-ye Mahārlū (Iran) **157** F 3
Dāryācheh-ye Namak (Iran) **157** F 2
Dāryācheh-ye Orūmīyeh (Iran) **157** D 1
Dāryācheh-ye Tashk (Iran) **157** FG 3
Daryā-ye Māzandarān **168** E 3
Daryā-ye Panj **169** J 3
Dās (United Arab Emirates) **157** F 4
Dashbalbar **170** K 6
Dasht (Iran) **168** F 3
Dasht (Pakistan) **169** G 5
Dashtak (Iran) **157** F 3
Dasht Āb (Iran) **157** G 3
Dasht-e Kavīr (Iran) **157** FG 2
Dasht-e Lūt (Iran) **157** G 2
Dasht-e Naomid **168–169** G 4
Dasht-i Arbu Lut **169** G 5
Dashtiari **157** G 4
Dasht-i-Margo **169** G 4
Dasht-i-Nawar **169** H 4
Dasht-i Tahlab **169** G 4
Daspalla **174** D 3
Dassel (MN.) **119** O 5

Dastgardān (Iran) **157** G 2
Dasuya **174** C 1
Datça **154** C 3
Date **173** M 2
Dateland (AZ.) **116** C 5
Datha **174** B 3
Datia **174** C 2
Datian **173** G 5
Datil (N.M.) **116** J 3
Datong **165**
Datong **172** F 2
Datong **172** D 3
Datong **173** H 1
Datong Shan **172** CD 3
Datta **171** Q 6
Datumakuta **176** E 3
Datu Piang **177** F 2
Dāuarzan **168** F 3
Daugava **151** H 4
Daulatabad **169** GH 3
Daulat Yar **169** H 4
Daule **138** B 4
Daule **138** C 4
Daung Kyun **175** G 5
Dauphin (ND.) **103** R 5
Dauphin Island **130** F 4
Dauphin Lake **103** S 5
Dauphiné **153** E 3
Daura **197** F 3
Daurskoye **170** F 4
Davangere **174** C 5
Davant (LA.) **123** O 6
Davao **177** G 2
Davao Gulf **177** G 2
Dāvarān, Kūh-e (Iran) **157** G 3
Dāvar Panāh **169** G 5
Dāvarzan (Iran) **157** G 1
Davenport (CA.) **112** C 5
Davenport (IA.) **119** S 9
Davenport (N.D.) **119** LM 4
Davenport (OK.) **120** J 7
Davenport (WA.) **110** G 3
Davenport Downs **183** G 3
David **138** B 2
David (KY.) **128** HJ 4
David City (NE.) **120** H 1
Davidson (OK.) **120** F 8
Davidson Mountains **102** J 2
Davies, Mount **182** D 4
Davis (Antarctica) **203**
Davis (CA.) **112** D 4
Davis (OK.) **120** H 8
Davis, Lake **112** E 3
Davis, Mount **125** P 10
Davis City (IA.) **119** P 10
Davis Dam **116** B 2
Davis Inlet **105** P 4
Davis Lake **110** D 7
Davis Mountains **117** MN 7
Davis River **182** C 3
Davis Sea **203**
Davisson Lake **110** C 4
Davis Strait **105** Q 2
Davlekanovo **158** K 5
Davos **153** E 2
Davydov Brod **155** D 1
Dawa **199** G 3
Dawāsir, Wādī ad **195** G 4
Dawes Range **183** J 3
Dawḥat as Salwā **195** J 3
Dawḥat as Salwā (Qatar) **157** F 4
Dawna Range **175** G 4
Dawqah (Oman) **195** J 5
Dawqah (Saudi Arabia) **195** G 5
Dawson (GA.) **131** K 3
Dawson (MN.) **119** M 6
Dawson (ND.) **118** J 4
Dawson (OR.) **110** B 6
Dawson (Yukon, Can.) **102** K 3
Dawson, Isla **143** B 9
Dawson Creek **103** N 4
Dawson Inlet **103** T 3
Dawson Range **102** K 3
Dawson River **183** HJ 3
Dawson Springs (KY.) **128** D 4
Dawsonville (GA.) **128** G 7
Dawu **172** D 4
Dawu **172** F 4
Dax **152** C 3
Daxian **172** E 4
Daxin **172** E 6
Daxing **173** G 3
Daxue Shan **172** D 4–5
Day (FL.) **131** L 4
Daya Abeidi **196** C 1
Daya Hamami **192** C 4
Dayangshu **171** M 6
Dayao **172** D 5
Dayet en Naharat **196** D 2
Daym Zubayr **198** D 3
Dayong **172** F 5
Dayr, Jabal ad **194** E 6
Dayr az Zawr (Syria) **156** C 2
Dayr Ḥāfir (Syria) **156** B 1
Dayrūt **194** E 3
Dayton (MT.) **111** L 3
Dayton (N.M.) **117** M 5
Dayton (OH.) **128** G 2
Dayton (TN.) **128** F 6

Dayton (TX.) **123** J 5
Dayton (WA.) **110** H 4
Dayton (WY.) **111** S 6
Daytona Beach (FL.) **131** NO 5
Dayu **172** F 5
Da Yunhe **173** G 4
Dayville (OR.) **110** F 6
Dayyīnah (United Arab Emirates) **157** F 4
Dazhu **172** E 4
Dazjā (Iran) **157** G 2
Dazkırı **154** C 3
Dazu **172** E 5
De Aar **200** C 6
Deadhorse **102** GH 1
Dead Knoll **111** P 8
Dead Lake **131** J 4
Deadman Bay **131** L 5
Deadman Lake **113** J 8
Deadmans Basin Reservoir **111** Q 4
Dead Sea **156** B 3
Deadwood (SD.) **118** E 6
Deadwood Reservoir **111** K 6
Deal Island (Victoria, Austr.) **183** H 6
De'an **172** G 5
Dean (Br. Col., Can.) **103** M 5
Dean (MT.) **111** Q 5
Deán Funes **142** D 5
Dearborn (MI.) **125** L 7
Deary (ID.) **110** J 4
Dease **102** M 4
Dease Arm **103** N 2
Dease Lake **102** L 4
Dease Strait **103** Q 2
Death Valley (CA.) **112** J 5
Death Valley (CA.) **112** HJ 6
Death Valley National Monument **112** HJ 6
Deatsville (AL.) **131** H 2
Deaver (WY.) **111** R 6
Debak **176** D 3
Debaltsevo **155** E 1
Debao **172** E 6
Debar **154** B 2
Debark **199** F 2
Debauch Mountain **108** G 3
De Behagle → Lai **197** H 4
De Beque (CO.) **115** J 4
Dębica **149** H 4
Dęblin **149** H 4
Dębno **149** F 4
Débo, Lac **196** D 2
Deborah, Lake **182** B 5
Deboyne Island **185** F 4
Debra Birhan **199** F 3
Debra Libanos **199** F 3
Debra Markos **199** F 2
Debra Sina **199** F 3
Debra Tabor **199** F 2
Debrecen **154** B 1
De Brie **201** H 3
Decamere **199** F 1
Decatur (AL.) **128** DE 7
Decatur (GA.) **128** G 8
Decatur (IL.) **121** R 3
Decatur (MS.) **130** E 2
Decatur (NE.) **119** M 9
Decatur (TX.) **122** F 2
Decaturville (TN.) **128** C 6
Decazeville **152** D 3
Deccan **174** CD 3–5
Decelles, Réservoir **105** M 6
Decepción **203**
Dechang **172** D 5
Děčín **149** F 4
Decker (MT.) **118** B 5
Deckerville (MI.) **125** M 6
Decorah (IA.) **119** R 7
Deda **154** B 1
Dedegöl Dağı **154** D 3
Dedo, Cerro **143** B 7
Dédougou **196** D 3
Dedovichi **151** J 4
Dedu **171** N 6
Dedza **201** E 2
Dee (Scotland, U.K.) **148** C 3
Dee (Wales, U.K.) **148** C 4
Deep Creek Lake **129** M 2
Deep Springs (CA.) **112** H 5
Deep Springs Lake **112** GH 5
Deepwater (MO.) **121** M 4
Deep Well **182** E 3
Deer Creek (MN.) **119** N 4
Deer Creek Indian Reservation **119** P 3
Deer Creek Reservoir **114** F 3
Deerfield (KS.) **120** D 5
Deering **102** E 2
Deering (ND.) **118** GH 2
Deering, Mount **182** D 3
Deer Isle **126** L 4
Deer Lake (Newfoundl., Can.) **105** Q 6
Deer Lake (Ontario, Can.) **104** J 5
Deer Lodge (MT.) **111** N 4
Deer Park (AL.) **130** F 3
Deer Park (WA.) **110** H 3
Deer River (MN.) **119** P 3
Deer Trail (CO.) **115** N 4
Deerwood (MN.) **119** P 4

Deesa **174** B 3
Deeth (NV.) **112** K 1
Defah **193** K 3
Defferrari **143** E 6
Defiance (IA.) **119** N 9
Defiance (OH.) **125** K 8
Defiance Plateau **116** G 1–2
Defirou **197** H 1
De Funiak Springs (FL.) **131** H 4
Dêgê **172** C 4
Degema **197** F 5
Dêgên **175** F 1
Degerfors **151** F 4
Deggendorf **149** F 5
de Gras, Lac **103** P 3
De Gray Lake **121** M 8
De Grey River **182** C 3
Dehaj (Iran) **157** G 3
Dehaq (Iran) **157** F 2
Deh Bārez **168** F 5
Deh Bīd (Iran) **157** F 3
Deh Dasht (Iran) **157** EF 3
Dehdez (Iran) **157** F 3
Deh-e Namak (Iran) **157** F 2
Deh-e Shīr (Iran) **157** F 3
Dehgolān (Iran) **157** E 2
Dehlorān (Iran) **157** E 2
Deh Mollā (Iran) **157** EF 3
Dehra Dun **174** C 1
Deh Shū **169** G 4
Dehua **173** G 5
Dehui **173** J 2
Deinguri, Mont **198** D 3
Dej **154** B 1
Dejiang **172** E 5
De Jong, Tanjung **177** J 5
De Kalb (IL.) **124** F 8
De Kalk **200** B 4
Dekar **200** C 4
Dekese **198** C 5
Dekina **197** F 4
Dekle Beach (FL.) **131** L 5
Dékoa **198** B 3
Delacroix (LA.) **123** O 6
De Land (FL.) **131** N 5
Delano (CA.) **113** F 7
Delano Peak **114** E 5
Delaplaine (AR.) **121** P 6
Delarof Islands **102** B 5
Delavan (IL.) **124** E 9
Delaware **127** D 9–10
Delaware (KS.) **121** K 6
Delaware (OH.) **125** L 9
Delaware Bay **127** D 9
Delaware City (PA.) **127** D 9
Delaware Mountains **117** M 6
Del Campillo **142** D 5
Del City (OK.) **120** H 7
Delco (ID.) **111** M 8
Delco (N.C.) **129** N 7
Delcommune, Lac **200** D 2
Delegate **183** H 6
Delémont **153** E 2
De Leon (TX.) **122** E 3
De Leon Springs (FL.) **131** N 5
Delevan (CA.) **112** C 3
Delft (Netherlands) **148** D 4
Delft (Sri Lanka) **174** C 6
Delgada, Point **112** A 2
Delgado, Cabo **201** G 2
Delger **170** G 6
Delgereh **172** F 1
Delgerhaan (Mongolia) **172** F 1
Delgerhaan **172** DE 1
Delgerhangay **172** D 1
Delgerhet **172** F 1
Delgertsogt **172** E 1
Delhi **174** C 2
Delhi (CO.) **115** O 6
Delhi (LA.) **123** M 3
Delhi (N.Y.) **126** D 7
Delhi (TX.) **122** F 6
Deliblatska Peščara **154** B 1–2
Deličal Dağı **154** C 2–3
Delice **155** D 3
Delicias **106** C 4
Delicirmak **155** D 2–3
Delijān (Iran) **157** F 2
Delingha **172** C 3
Dell (MT.) **111** N 6
Dellen **150** G 3
Dellenbaugh, Mount **116** C 1
Delle River **109** J 3
Dell Rapids (SD.) **119** M 7
Dellys **193** F 1
Del Mar (CA.) **113** H 10
Delmar (PA.) **127** D 10
Delmarva Peninsula **129** Q 3
Delmenhorst **149** E 4
Delmont (S.D.) **119** K 7
Delnice **153** F 2
Del Norte (CO.) **115** L 6
De Long Mountains **102** E 2
Delorme, Lac **105** O 5
Delos → Dhílos **154** C 3
Delphi **154** B 3
Delphi (IN.) **124** H 9
Delphia (MT.) **111** R 4
Delphi → Dhelfoi **154** B 3

Delphos (KS.) **120** H 3
Delphos (N.M.) **117** N 3
Delphos (OH.) **125** K 9
Delray Beach (FL.) **131** O 8
Del Rio (TX.) **122** C 6
Delsbo **150** G 3
Delta (CO.) **115** JK 5
Delta (LA.) **123** MN 3
Delta (UT.) **114** E 4
Delta del Ebro **152** D 3
Delta Downs **183** G 2
Delta Dunării **154** CD 1
Delta Dunării **154** D 1
Delta Junction **102** H 3
Delta Peak **109** MN 4
Del Valle (TX.) **122** F 5
Delvina **154** AB 3
Delyankir **171** R 3
Delyatin **154** B 1
Demanda, Sierra de la **152** C 3
Demarcation Point **109** K 2
Demavend, Mount (Iran) **157** F 2
Demba **198** C 6
Dembi **199** F 3
Dembia **198** C 3
Dembidollo **198** E 3
Deming (N.M.) **116** J 5
Deming (WA.) **110** C 2
Demini **139** F 3
Demirci **154** C 3
Demir Kapija **154** B 2
Demirköprü Barajı **154** C 3
Demmin **149** F 4
Demnate **192** D 2
Democracia **139** F 5
Demopolis (AL.) **130** G 2
Demotte (IN.) **124** G 8
Dempo, Gunung **176** B 4
Dêmqog **174** C 1
Demre **154** C 3
Dem'yanka **159** O 4
Dem'yanovka **159** N 5
Dem'yanskoye **159** N 4
Denain **152** D 1
Denale **109** J 3
Denali **102** H 3
Denali National Park and Preserve **102** GH 3
Denau **169** H 3
Dendang **176** C 4
Dendi **199** F 3
Deng Deng **197** G 4
Deng Xian **172** F 4
Denham **182** A 4
Denham Sound **182** A 4
Den Helder **148** D 4
Denhoff (ND.) **118** H 3
Denia **152** D 4
Deniliquin **183** G 6
Denio (NV.) **112** G 1
Denison (IA.) **119** N 8–9
Denison (TX.) **122** G 2
Denison, Mount **102** G 4
Denizli **154** C 3
Denkou **172** E 2
Denmark **151** E 4
Denmark (Australia) **182** B 5
Denmark (S.C.) **129** K 8
Denmark (WI.) **124** G 5
Denmark Strait **202**
Dennehotso (AZ.) **116** G 1
Dennison, Cape **203**
Denpasar **176** E 5
Denton (TX.) **122** F 2
D'Entrecasteaux, Point **182** B 5
D'Entrecasteaux Islands **185** F 3
D'Entrecasteaux Islands **186** C 3
Denver (CO.) **115** N 4
Denver City (TX.) **117** O 4–5
Deo **197** G 4
Deoatur (IN.) **125** K 9
Deogarh **174** D 3
Deoghar **174** E 3
Deolali **174** B 4
Deora (CO.) **115** P 6
Deori **174** C 3
De Pere (WI.) **124** F 5
Depew (OK.) **120** J 7
Depoe Bay (OR.) **110** A 6
Deposit (N.Y.) **126** D 6
Depósita **139** F 3
Depresión del Balsas **132** BC 4
Dépression du Mourdi **197** J 2
Deputatskiy **171** P 2
Deqên **172** C 5
Deqing **172** F 6
Der, Lac du **153** D 2
Dera Bugti **169** H 5
Dera Ghazi Khan **169** HJ 4
Deraheib **194** F 4
Dera Ismail Khan **169** J 4
Derajat **169** J 4
Derbeke **171** P 2
Derbent **168** D 2
Derbent **169** H 3

Derbino **170** F 4
Derbisaka **198** C 3
Derby (Australia) **182** C 2
Derby (KS.) **120** H 5
Derby (N.Y.) **125** P 7
Derby (TX.) **122** D 7
Derby (U.K.) **148** C 4
Derdap **154** B 2
Dereköy **154** C 2
Dergachi **158** J 5
Derik **155** T 3
Derm **200** B 4
Dermott (AR.) **121** O 9
Derna → Darnah **193** K 2
Dernieres, Isles **123** N 6
Dêrong **172** C 5
Derry (N.H.) **126** H 6
Derudeb **194** F 5
Derventa **153** G 3
Derwent River (Tasmania, Austr.) **184** L 9
Deryabino **159** Q 1
Derzhavinsk **159** N 5
Desaguadero (Argentina) **142** C 5
Desaguadero (Bolivia) **140** C 4
Des Allemands (LA.) **123** N 6
des Allemands, Lac **123** N 6
Désappointement, Îles du **187** F 3
Des Arc (AR.) **121** O 8
De Sart (ND.) **118** F 4
Descalvado **140** E 4
Descanso (CA.) **113** J 10
Deschambault Lake **103** R 5
Deschutes River **110** E 5
Deschutes-Umatilla Plateau **110** F 5
Deseado **143** C 8
Deseado, Cabo **143** AB 9
Desecheo, Isla **130** B 8
Desengaño, Punta **143** C 8
Deseret (UT.) **114** E 4
Desert (CA.) **113** K 7
Desert (N.M.) **117** K 5
Desert Center (CA.) **113** K 9
Desert Hot Springs (CA.) **113** J 9
Desert Peak (UT.) **114** D 2
Desert Peak (UT.) **114** E 3
Desert Ranch Reservoir **112** J 1
Desert Valley **112** G 1
Desierto de Sechura **138** B 5
Desierto de Vizcaíno **106** D 6
Desierto do Atacama **140** C 5
Desloge (MO.) **121** P 5
De Smet (MT.) **111** LM 4
De Smet (S.D.) **119** L 6
De Smet, Lake **118** B 6
Des Moines (IA.) **119** P 9
Des Moines (N.M.) **117** N 1
Des Moines River **119** Q 9–10
Des Plaines (IL.) **124** FG 7–8
Desrouches, Île **199** J 6
Dessau **149** F 4
Dessye **199** F 2
Deta **154** B 1
Detmold **149** E 4
De Tour Village (MI.) **125** K 3
Detroit (MI.) **125** LM 7
Detroit (OR.) **110** C 6
Détroit de Jaques-Cartier **105** P 6
Détroit d'Honguedo **105** P 6
Detroit Lake (OR.) **110** C 6
Detroit Lakes (MN.) **119** N 4
Dett **200** D 3
Deutsche Bucht **149** E 4
Deutsche Demokratische Republik **149** F 4
Deva **154** B 1
Devakottai **174** C 6
De Valls Bluff (AR.) **121** O 8
Devarkonda **174** C 4
Deveci Dağı **155** E 2–3
Develi **155** E 3
Devikot **174** B 2
Devils Den (CA.) **113** F 7
Devils Elbow **148** C 3
Devil's Island **139** H 2
Devils Lake (N.D.) **118** J 2
Devils Lake (ND.) **118** JK 2
Devils Lake (TX.) **122** C 6
Devils Paw **109** M 4
Devils Postpile National Monument **112** F 5
Devils Tower National Monument **118** D 6
Devine (TX.) **122** E 6
Devli **174** C 2
Devnya **154** C 2
Devolli **154** B 2
Devon Island **202**
Devonport (New Zealand) **185** Q 8
Devonport (Tasmania, Austr.) **184** L 9

Derbino **170** F 4
Devrek **155** D 2
Devrez **155** D 2
Dewangiri **175** F 2
Dewey (OK.) **120** JK 6
Dewey (SD.) **118** DE 7
Dewey Lake **128** J 4
Deweyville (TX.) **123** K 5
De Witt (AR.) **121** O 8
De Witt (IA.) **119** S 9
De Witt (MI.) **125** K 7
De Witt (NE.) **120** J 2
Dexing **173** G 5
Dexter (KS.) **120** J 5
Dexter (ME.) **126** K 3
Dexter (MO.) **121** Q 6
Dexter (N.M.) **117** M 4
Dexter (OR.) **110** C 7
Deyang **172** D 4
Dey Dey, Lake **182** E 4
Deyhuk **168** F 4
Deylam, Bandar-e (Iran) **157** F 3
Deynau **169** G 3
Deyyer (Iran) **157** F 4
Dez (Iran) **157** E 2
Dezadeash Lake **109** L 3
Dezfūl (Iran) **157** E 2
Dez Gerd (Iran) **157** F 3
Dezhou **173** G 3
Dháfni **154** B 3
Dhahab (Egypt) **156** B 3
Dhahran (Saudi Arabia) **157** EF 3
Dhamār **195** G 6
Dhamra **174** E 3
Dhamtari **174** D 3
Dhanbad **174** E 3
Dhangain **174** D 2
Dhang Range **174** D 2
D'Hanis (TX.) **122** D 6
Dhankuta **174** E 2
Dhar **174** C 3
Dhar Adrar **192** C 4
Dharinavaram **174** C 5
Dharmapuri **174** C 5
Dharmjaygarh **174** D 3
Dhar Oualata **192** D 5
Dhar Tagant **192** C 5
Dhar Tichit **192** D 5
Dharwar **174** C 4
Dhaulagiri **174** D 2
Dhelfoí **154** B 3
Dhenkanal **174** E 3
Dhiavlos Thásou **154** BC 2
Dhíavlos Zakínthou **154** B 3
Dhílos **154** C 3
Dhirfís Óros **154** B 3
Dhisoron Óros **154** B 2
Dhofar → Zufār **195** J 5
Dholpur **174** C 2
Dhomokós **154** B 3
Dhone **174** C 4
Dhoraji **174** B 3
Dhubāb **195** G 6
Dhule **174** B 3
Dhulian **174** E 3
Día **154** C 3
Diabakagna **196** B 3
Diable, Île du **139** H 2
Diablo (WA.) **110** D 2
Diablo Plateau **117** L 6
Diablo Range **112** D 5–6
Diaca **201** F 2
Diafarabe **196** C 3
Dialafara **196** B 3
Dialakoto **196** B 3
Diamante (Argentina) **142** D 5
Diamante (Italy) **153** G 4
Diamante, Punta del **132** C 4
Diamantina (Minas Gerais, Brazil) **141** H 4
Diamantina (Queensland, Austr.) **183** G 3
Diamantina Lakes **183** G 3
Diamentina Fracture Zone **208** C 5
Diamond Dam **117** M 4
Diamond Harbour **174** E 3
Diamond Jenness Peninsula **103** OP 1
Diamond Lake (OR.) **110** C 7
Diamond Lake (OR.) **110** C 7
Diamond Peak (ID.) **111** M 6
Diamond Peak (NV.) **112** K 3
Diamond Peak (OR.) **110** C 7
Diamond Peak (WA.) **110** H 4
Diamond Springs (CA.) **112** E 4
Diamondville (WY.) **111** P 9
Diamou **196** B 2
Diamounguel **196** B 2
Diana, Baie **105** O 3
Dianbai **172** F 6
Dian Chi **172** D 6
Diane Bank **183** H 2
Dianjiang **172** E 4
Dianópolis **141** G 3
Diapaga **196** E 3
Dibā (United Arab Emirates) **157** G 4
Dībagah (Iraq) **156** D 2
Dibang **175** G 2
Dibaya **198** C 6
Dibaya-Lubue **198** B 5

Dibella 197 G 2
Dibete 200 D 4
Dibo 199 G 3
Diboll (TX.) 123 J 4
Dibrugarh 175 FG 2
Dibsī ʿAfnān (Syria) 156 BC 2
Dickens (TX.) 117 Q 4
Dickinson (ND.) 118 F 4
Dickinson (TX.) 123 H 6
Dickson (TN.) 128 D 5
Dicle 155 F 3
Didiéni 196 C 3
Didwana 174 B 2
Didyma 154 C 3
Die 153 E 3
Diébougou 196 D 3
Diego Ramírez, Islas 143 BC 10
Diéké 196 C 4
Diéma 196 C 3
Dien Bien Phu 175 H 3
Diepholz 149 E 4
Dieppe 152 D 2
Di'er Songhua Jiang 173 J 2
Dietrich (ID.) 111 L 8
Dif 199 G 4
Diffa 197 G 3
Digba 198 D 4
Digby 105 O 7
Dighir 174 C 4
Dighton (KS.) 120 E 4
Digne 153 E 3
Digoin 152 D 2
Digos 177 G 2
Digranes 150 C 2
Digul, Sungai 177 J 5
Dihang 175 G 2
Dijlāh (Iraq) 156 F 2
Dijlāh (Iraq) 157 D 2
Dijon 153 E 2
Dik 197 H 4
Dikanäs 150 G 2
Dikchu 174 E 2
Dikebeye 200 D 4
Dikhil 199 G 2
Dikili 154 C 3
Dikmen 155 E 2
Dikmen Dağı 155 D 2
Dikodougou 196 C 4
Dikson 202
Dikwa 197 G 3
Dilaram 169 G 4
Dili 177 G 5
Dilia (N.M.) 117 LM 2
Di Linh 175 J 5
Dilizhan 155 FG 2
Dilj 153 G 2
Dilla 199 F 3
Dilley (TX.) 122 D 7
Dillia 197 G 2
Dillia Téfidinga 197 G 2
Dilling 194 D 6
Dillingham 102 F 4
Dillon (CO.) 115 L 4
Dillon (MT.) 111 N 5
Dillon (S.C.) 129 M 7
Dillon Beach (CA.) 112 C 4
Dillon Lake 125 L 9
Dillon Reservoir 115 LM 4
Dilly 196 C 2
Dilolo 200 C 2
Dimashq (Syria) 156 B 2
Dimbelenge 198 C 6
Dimbokro 196 D 4
Dimboola 183 G 6
Dimitrovgrad 154 B 2
Dimitrovgrad 154 C 2
Dimitrovgrad 158 JK 5
Dimitrya Lapteva, Proliv 171 Q 1
Dimmitt (TX.) 117 O 3
Dimock (S.D.) 119 K 7
Dimona (Israel) 156 B 3
Dimovo 154 B 2
Dīn (Iran) 157 G 4
Dinagat 177 G 1
Dinajpur 174 E 2
Dinangourou 196 D 3
Dinant 148 DE 4
Dınar 154 D 3
Dīnār, Kūh-e (Iran) 157 F 3
Dinara Planina 153 G 3
Dinard 152 C 2
Dinder National Park 194 F 6 Dindigul
174 C 5
Dindiza 201 E 4
Dindori 174 D 3
Dinero (TX.) 122 F 7
Dinga 198 B 6
Dingbian 172 E 3
Dinggyê 174 E 2
Dinghai 173 H 4
Dingle 148 A 4
Dingle Bay 148 A B 4
Dingtao 172 G 3–4
Dinguiraye 196 B 3
Dingwall 148 C 3
Dingxi 172 D 3
Dingxian 172 F 3
Ding Xian 172 FG 3
Dingxing 172 G 3
Dinh Lap 175 J 3

Diniapur 175 F 2
Dinokwe 200 D 4
Dinosaur (CO.) 114 J 3
Dinosaur National Monument 114 HJ 3
Dinskaya 155 E 1
Dīnsör 199 G 4
Dinwiddie (VA.) 129 O 4
Diois, Massif du 153 E 3
Dioka 196 B 3
Diomida, Ostrova 102 D 2
Diona 197 J 2
Dionísio Cerqueira 142 F 4
Diouloulou 196 A 3
Dioundiou 196 E 3
Dioura 196 C 3
Diourbel 196 A 3
Dipkarpas 155 D 3
Dipkarpas (Cyprus) 156 B 2
Dipolog 177 F 2
Dir 169 J 3
Diré 196 D 2
Diredawa 199 G 3
Dirico 200 C 3
Dirk Hartog Island 182 A 4
Dirkou 197 G 2
Dirranbandi 183 H 4
Dîrs 195 G 5
Dirty Devil River 114 G 5
Disappointment, Cape 110 A 4
Disappointment, Lake 182 C 3
Dishman (WA.) 110 H 3
Dishnā (Egypt) 156 A 4
Disko 202
Disko Bugt 202
Dismal Swamp 129 P 5
Disna 151 J 4
Dispur 174 F 2
District of Columbia 129 OP 3
District of Fort Smith 103 P 3
District of Inuvik 102 LM 2
District of Keewatin 103 TU 2–3
Distrito Federal 141 G 4
Ditdak 175 F 6
Diu 174 B 3
Dīvāndareeh (Iran) 157 E 1
Divénié 197 G 6
Divenskaya 151 JK 4
Diversion Lake 122 DE 2
Divide (CO.) 115 M 5
Divide (MT.) 111 N 5
Divinopolis 141 GH 5
Divisor, Serra do 138 D 5
Divnogorsk 170 F 4
Divnoye 155 F 1
Divo 196 C 4
Divriği 155 E 3
Dīvrūd (Iran) 157 F 1
Dix (NE.) 118 E 9
Dixie (AL.) 130 H 3
Dixie (ID.) 111 K 5
Dixie (WA.) 110 G 4
Dixon (CA.) 112 D 4
Dixon (IL.) 124 E 8
Dixon (KY.) 128 D 4
Dixon (MO.) 121 N 4–5
Dixon (MT.) 111 L 3
Dixon (N.M.) 117 L 1
Dixon (WY.) 111 S 9
Dixon Entrance 102 L 5
Dixons Mills (AL.) 130 G 2
Diyālā (Iraq) 157 D 2
Diyarbakır 155 F 3
Diyarbakır Havzası 155 F 3
Diza 155 G 3
Dja 197 G 5
Djado 197 G 1
Djado, Plateau du 197 G 1
Djafou 193 F 3
Djaja Peak 177 J 4
Djaja Peak 184 C 2
Djako 198 C 3
Djamaa 193 G 2
Djambala 197 G 6
Djanet 193 G 4
Djaret 193 F 3
Djaul 185 F 2
Djebel Aïssa 192 E 2
Djebel Amour 193 F 2
Djebel Chélia 193 G 1
Djebel Edough 153 E 4
Djebel Onk 193 G 2
Djebel Ounane 193 G 3
Djebel Telerhteba 193 G 3
Djebobo 196 E 4
Djédaa 197 H 3
Djedi 193 F 2
Djelfa 193 F 2
Djéma 198 D 3
Djemila 193 G 1
Djenienbou Rezg 192 E 2
Djénné 196 D 3
Djerba → Jarbah 193 H 2
Djerem 197 G 4
Djéroual 197 H 3
Djibo 196 D 3
Djibouti 199 G 2
Djibouti 199 G 2
Djiguéni 192 D 2
Djikdjik 197 J 2
Djilbabo Plain 199 F 4

Djokupunda 198 C 6
Djolu 198 C 4
Djombo 198 C 4
Djougou 196 E 4
Djoum 197 G 5
Djourab, Erg du 197 H 2
Djugu 198 E 4
Djúpivogur 150 C 3
Dmanisi 155 F 2
Dnepr 158 F 6
Dneprodzerzhinsk 155 D 1
Dnepropetrovsk 155 E 1
Dneprovskiy Liman 154 D 1
Dneprovsko-Bugskiy Kanal 151 HJ 5
Dnestr 154 C 1
Dnestrovskiy Liman 154 D 1
Dno 151 K 4
Dô, Lac 196 D 2
Doa 201 E 3
Doany 201 H 2
Doba (Chad) 197 H 4
Doba (China) 174 E 1
Dobbiaco 153 F 2
Dobel 199 F 4
Dobele 151 H 4
Döbeln 149 F 4
Doblas 143 D 6
Dobo 177 H 5
Doboj 153 G 3
Dobreta Turnu Severin 154 B 2
Dobrogea 154 C 2
Dobrowolski 203
Dobroye 171 R 7
Dobruja 154 C 2
Dobryanka 158 L 4
Dobson (N.C.) 129 L 5
Doce 141 H 4
Docksta 150 G 3
Dockton (WA.) 110 C 3
Doctor Arroyo 132 B 3
Doda Betta 174 C 5
Dod Ballapur 174 C 5
Dodecanese 154 C 3
Dodge (NE.) 119 M 9
Dodge Center (MN.) 119 Q 6–7
Dodge City (KS.) 120 E 5
Dodgeville (WI.) 124 D 7
Dodoma 199 F 6
Dodson (LA.) 123 L 3
Dodson (MT.) 111 R 2
Dofa 177 G 4
Dogai Coring 174 E 1
Doğankent 155 E 3
Dog Creek 103 N 5
Dogger Bank 148 D 4
Doghārūn 169 G 4
Dog Island 131 K 5
Dôgo 173 K 3
Dogonbadān (Iran) 157 F 3
Dogondoutchi 197 E 3
Doğubayazıt 155 F 3
Doguéraoua 197 F 3
Doğu Karadeniz Dağları 155 EF 2
Dogwaya 194 EF 5
Do'gyaling 174 E 1
Dohad 174 B 3
Dohazan 175 F 3
Döhö Nugālēd 199 H 3
Doi Inthanon 175 G 4
Doilungdêqen 175 F 2
Dois de Novembro, Cachoeira 139 F 5
Dois Irmãos 139 J 5
Dois Irmãos, Serra 141 H 2
Doka (Indonesia) 177 H 5
Doka (Sudan) 194 F 6
Dokka 151 F 3
Doko 198 D 4
Dokshitsy 151 J 5
Dokuchayevsk 155 E 1
Dolak Island 184 C 3
Doland (S.D.) 119 KL 6
Dolbeau 105 N 6
Dôle 153 E 2
Doleib Hill 198 E 3
Dolgellau 148 C 4
Dolgeville (N.Y.) 126 E 5
Dolgiy, Ostrov 159 LM 2
Dolgiy-Most 170 G 4
Dolinsk 171 Q 6
Dolinskaya 155 D 1
Dollar Bay (MI.) 124 F 2
Dolni Dŭbnik 154 B 2
Dolo 199 G 4
Dolo, Pereval 169 K 2
Dolores (Argentina) 143 E 6
Dolores (CO.) 115 J 6
Dolores (Uruguay) 142 E 5
Dolores River 114 J 5
Dolphin and Union Strait 103 OP 2
Dolzhanskaya 155 E 1
Dom, Kūh-e (Iran) 157 F 2
Domadare 199 G 4
Domaniç 154 C 3
Doma Peaks 184 D 3
Dom Aquino 141 F 4
Domažlice 149 F 5
Domba 172 C 4
Dombarovskiy 159 L 5
Dombås 150 E 3

Djokupunda 198 C 6
Dombovár 154 A 1
Dom Cavati 141 H 4
Domeyko 140 C 5
Domeyko, Cordillera 140 C 5
Domingo (N.M.) 117 K 2
Dominica 133 K 4
Dominican Republic 133 J 3–4
Dominica Passage 133 K 4
Dominion, Cape 105 M 2
Domino 105 Q 5
Domiongo 198 C 5
Domo → Damot 199 H 3
Domodossola 153 E 2
Domokos 154 B 3
Dompierre 152 D 2
Dompu 177 E 5
Domuyo, Volcán 143 BC 6
Don (Mexico) 106 E 6
Don (U.S.S.R.) 158 H 6
Dona (N.M.) 117 J 5
Dona Ana (N.M.) 117 K 5
Donadeu 142 D 4
Donald 183 G 6
Donaldson (AR.) 121 N 8
Donaldson (MN.) 119 M 2
Donaldsonville (LA.) 123 MN 5
Donalsonville (GA.) 131 K 3
Donau 149 F 5
Donauwörth 149 F 5
Don Benito 152 B 4
Dondo (Angola) 200 A 1
Dondo (Indonesia) 177 F 4
Dondo (Mozambique) 201 E 3
Dondra Head 174 D 6
Donegal 148 B 4
Donegal Bay 148 B 4
Donegal Mountains 148 B 4
Donets, Severskiy 155 F 1
Donets Basin 146
Donets Basin 155 E 1
Donetskiy Kryazh 155 E 1
Donetskiy Kryazh 155 EF 1
Donetsk 155 E 1
Donfeng 173 J 2
Donga 197 G 4
Dong'an 172 F 5
Dongara 182 AB 4
Dongargarh 174 D 3
Dongchuan 172 D 5
Dongfang 172 E 7
Donges 152 C 2
Donggala 177 E 4
Donggi Cona 172 C 3
Donggou 173 H 3
Dong Ha 175 J 4
Donghai 173 G 4
Dong Hai 173 HJ 5
Donghai Dao 172 F 6
Dong He 172 D 2
Dong Hoi 175 J 4
Dong Jiang 172 FG 6
Dongkalang 177 F 3
Dong Khe 175 J 3
Donglan 172 E 6
Donglük 172 A 3
Dongnai 175 J 5
Dongning 173 K 2
Dongo (Angola) 200 B 2
Dongo (Zaire) 198 B 4
Dongo (Zaire) 198 B 6
Dongou 197 H 5
Dongoura 196 C 3
Dongping 173 G 3
Dongshan 173 G 6
Dongshan Dao 173 G 6
Dongsheng 172 EF 3
Dongtai 173 H 4
Dong Taijnar Hu 172 B 3
Dongting Hu 172 F 5
Dongtou 173 H 5
Dong Ujimqin Qi 173 G 1
Dongwe 200 C 2
Dongxiang 172 G 5
Dongying 173 G 3
Dongzhen 172 D 3
Dongzhi 173 G 4
Donie (TX.) 122 G 4
Doniphan (MO.) 121 OP 6
Doniphan (NE.) 120 G 2
Donja Brela 153 G 3
Donjek 162 K 3
Don Khi 175 H 4
Donji Miholjac 153 G 2
Donji Vakuf 153 G 3
Don Pedro Reservoir 112 E 5
Donskoye 155 F 1
Donuzlav, Ozero 155 D 1
Doole (TX.) 122 D 4
Doon (IA.) 119 M 7
Doonerak, Mount 102 H 2
Door Peninsula 124 G 4–5
Dora (AL.) 128 D 8
Dora, Lake 182 C 3
Dora Baltea 153 E 2
Doramarkog 172 C 4
Dorbod 173 H 1

Dorchester 148 C 4
Dorchester (S.C.) 129 L 8
Dorchester (WI.) 124 D 4
Dorchester, Cape 105 M 2
Dordogne 152 D 3
Dordrecht 148 D 4
Dore (ND.) 118 E 3
Dore, Monts 152 D 2
Dore Lake 103 Q 5
Dorena Lake 110 C 7
Dores do Indaiá 141 G 4
Dori 196 D 3
Doring 200 B 6
Dormidontovka 171 P 6
Dornbin 153 E 2
Dornoch 148 C 3
Dornod 170 K 6
Dornogovĭ 172 EF 2
Doro (Indonesia) 177 G 3
Doro (Mali) 196 D 2
Dorogobuzh 158 F 5
Dorogorskoye 158 H 2
Dorohoi 154 C 1
Döröö Nuur 170 F 6
Dorotea 150 G 3
Dorovitsa 158 J 4
Dorra (Saudi Arabia) 157 E 3
Dorrance (KS.) 120 G 4
Dorre Island 182 A 4
Dorrigo 183 J 5
Dorris (CA.) 112 D 1
Dortmund 149 E 4
Dörtyol 155 E 3
Dörtyol (Turkey) 156 B 1
Doruma 198 D 4
Doruokha 170 K 1
Dosatuy 170 L 5
Dos Cabezas (AZ.) 116 G 5
Dos de Mayo 138 D 5
Doshi 169 H 3
Dos Palos (CA.) 112 E 6
Dos Rios (CA.) 112 B 3
Dosso 196 E 3
Dossor 168 E 1
Dothan (AL.) 131 J 3
Dot Lake 109 K 3
Douai 152 D 1
Douala 197 FG 5
Douandago 198 B 3
Double Mountain Fork 117 PQ 4
Double Springs (AL.) 128 D 7
Doubs 153 E 2
Doubtful Sound 184 P 10
Douentza 196 D 3
Dougga 193 G 1
Douglas (AK.) 102 L 4
Douglas (AZ.) 116 G 6
Douglas (GA.) 131 M 3
Douglas (ND.) 118 G 3
Douglas (South Africa) 200 C 5
Douglas (U.K.) 148 C 4
Douglas (WA.) 110 F 3
Douglas (WY.) 118 C 7
Douglas City (CA.) 112 C 2
Douglas Lake 128 H 4
Douglass (KS.) 120 J 5
Douglass (TX.) 123 J 4
Doumbouene 197 J 3
Doumé 197 G 5
Douna 196 D 3
Dourada, Serra 141 G 3
Dourado, Monte 139 H 4
Dourados 141 F 5
Dourbali 197 H 3
Douro 152 B 3
Douro (TX.) 117 O 6
Dove Creek (CO.) 114 J 6
Dover (AR.) 121 M 7
Dover (DE.) 127 D 9
Dover (ID.) 110 J 2
Dover (N.C.) 129 O 6
Dover (N.H.) 126 J 5
Dover (OH.) 125 N 9
Dover (OK.) 120 H 6–7
Dover (TN.) 128 D 5
Dover (U.K.) 148 D 4
Dover, Strait of 148 D 4
Dover-Foxcroft (ME.) 126 K 3
Dovre 150 E 3
Dovrefjell 150 E 3
Dowa 201 E 2
Dowagiac (MI.) 124 H 8
Dow Dehak (Iran) 157 F 2
Dowlatābād 168 F 5
Dowlatābād (Iran) 157 G 3
Downey (ID.) 111 N 8
Downieville (CA.) 112 E 3
Downpatrick 148 B 4
Downs (KS.) 120 G 3
Downs Mountain 111 Q 7
Downsville (N.Y.) 126 D 6
Dow Rūd (Iran) 157 E 2
Dows (IA.) 119 P 8
Dow Sar (Iran) 157 E 2
Doyle (CA.) 112 E 2
Doylestown (PA.) 127 D 8
Doyleville (CO.) 115 L 5
Dozois, Réservoir 105 M 6
Drâa, Cap 192 C 3

Drâa, Hamada du 192 D 3
Drâa, Wadi 192 D 3
Drabat 'Ali, Ra's 195 J 5
Drac 153 E 3
Dragan 150 FG 3
Drăgăşani 154 B 2
Dragonera 152 D 4
Dragoon (AZ.) 116 FG 5
Dragör 151 F 4
Draguignan 153 E 3
Drain (OR.) 110 B 7
Drake 183 J 4
Drake (AZ.) 116 D 2–3
Drake (MO.) 121 O 4
Drake (ND.) 118 H 3
Drakensberg 200 DE 4
Drakensberg 200 D 5
Drakensberg (Lesotho) 200 D 5–6
Drake Passage 203
Drake Peak 110 E 8
Drake Strait 143 CD 10
Dráma 154 B 2
Drammen 151 F 4
Drangajökull 150 A 2
Drangedal 151 E 4
Drangsnes 150 A 2
Dranka 171 U 4
Draper (UT.) 114 F 3
Dras 169 K 4
Drau 153 F 2
Drava 153 G 2
Dráva 154 A 1
Dravograd 153 G 2
Drawa 149 G 4
Drawsko, Jezioro 149 G 4
Drayton 183 J 4
Drayton (N.D.) 119 L 2
Drayton Plains (MI.) 125 L 7
Drayton Valley 103 O 5
Drean 153 E 4
Dresden 149 F 4
Dresden (KS.) 120 E 3
Dresden (TN.) 128 C 5
Dreux 152 D 2
Drevsjö 150 F 3
Drews Reservoir 110 E 8
Drifton (FL.) 131 N 4
Driftwood (PA.) 125 Q 8
Driggs (ID.) 111 OP 7
Drina 153 G 3
Drini 154 B 2
Driscoli (TX.) 122 F 8
Driskill Mountain 123 L 3
Driva 150 E 3
Drniš 153 G 3
Dröbak 151 F 4
Drogheda 148 B 4
Droichead Átha 148 B 4
Drokiya 154 C 1
Drôme 153 DE 3
Drosh 169 J 3
Drumheller 103 P 5
Drummond (ID.) 111 O 6
Drummond (WI.) 124 C 3
Drummond Island 125 L 4
Drummond Range 183 H 3
Drummondville 105 N 6
Drumright (OK.) 120 J 6–7
Druskininkai 151 H 5
Druzhba 154 C 2
Druzhbovka 155 D 1
Druzhina 171 R 2
Druzhkovka 155 E 1
Druzhnaya 203
Druzhnaya II 203
Drvar 153 G 3
Drvenik 153 G 3
Dryanovo 154 C 2
Dry Creek Mountain 112 J 1
Dryden (N.Y.) 126 C 6
Dryden (Ontario, Can.) 104 J 6
Dryden (TX.) 117 O 7
Dry Falls Dam 110 F 3
Dry Lake (N.D.) 118 JK 2
Dry Lake (NV.) 112 F 2
Dry Lake (NV.) 112 L 6
Dry River 182 E 2
Drysdale River 182 D 1–2
Drysdale River National Park 182 D 2
Dry Tortugas 131 M 10
Dschang 197 F 4
Duaringa 183 H 3
Dubach (LA.) 123 L 3
Dubawnt 103 R 3
Dubawnt Lake 103 R 3
Dubayy 153 JK 3
Dubayy (United Arab Emirates) 157 G 4
Dubbo 183 H 5
Dubenskiy 158 L 5
Dubica 153 G 2
Dublin (GA.) 131 M 2
Dublin (Rep. of Ireland) 148 B 4
Dublin (TX.) 122 E 3
Dublin (VA.) 129 L 4
Dubna 158 G 4
Dubna 158 G 5
Dubno 151 J 5
Dubois (ID.) 111 N 6 Du Bois (NE.)
  120 J 2

Du Bois (PA.) 125 Q 8
Dubois (WY.) 111 Q 7
Dubossary 154 C 1
Dubovka 158 J 6
Dubovskoye 155 F 1
Dubreka 196 B 4
Dubrovitsa 151 J 5
Dubrovnik 153 G 3
Dubrovnoye 159 NO 4
Dubuque (IA.) 119 S 8
Dubuque Hills 124 DE 7
Duc de Gloucester, Îles du 187 F 4
Duchesne (UT.) 114 G 3
Duchess 183 F 3
Ducie 187 G 4
Duck River 128 D 6
Ducktown (TN.) 128 G 6
Duck Valley Indian Reservation
  110 J 8–9
Duckwater (NV.) 112 K 4
Duckwater Indian Reservation 112 JK 4
Ducor (CA.) 113 FG 7
du Couedic, Cape 183 F 6
Dudhi 174 D 3
Dudinka 159 R 2
Dudley 148 C 4
Ḍudo 199 J 3
Dudub 199 H 3
Dudypta 170 F 1
Duékoué 196 C 4
Dueré 141 G 3
Duero 152 C 3
Duette (FL.) 131 M 6
Duffer Peak 112 G 1
Duff Islands 185 J 3
Duff Islands 186 C 3
Dufur (OR.) 110 D 5
Duga-Zapadnaya, Mys 171 R 4
Dugi Otok 153 F 3
Dugo Selo 153 G 2
Duḩūn Tarsū 193 J 4
Duifken Point 183 G 1
Duisburg 148 E 4
Duitama 138 D 2
Dujūma 199 G 4
Dukagjini 154 A 2
Dukān (Iraq) 157 D 2
Dukana 199 F 4
Duke (OK.) 120 F 8
Duke of York Bay 103 UV 2
Dukes (FL.) 131 M 5
Duk Fadiat 198 E 3
Duk Faiwil 198 E 3
Dukhān (Qatar) 157 F 4
Duki (Pakistan) 169 H 4
Duki (U.S.S.R.) 171 P 5
Dukou 172 D 5
Duku 197 G 3
Dukwe 200 D 4
Dulan 172 CD 3
Dulce 142 D 4
Dulce (N.M.) 117 JK 1
Dulce, Bahia 132 C 4
Dulce, Golfo 132 F 6
Dul'durga 170 K 5
Dulga-Kyuyel' 170 K 3
Dulgalakh 171 O 2
Dulla 199 F 3
Duluth (MN.) 119 Q 4
Dūmā 194 F 2
Dumaguete 177 F 2
Dumai 176 B 3
Dumanlı Dağı 155 F 3
Dumaran 177 EF 1
Dumaring 176 E 3
Dumas (AR.) 121 O 9
Dumas (TX.) 117 OP 2
Dumayr (Syria) 156 B 2
Dumboa 197 G 3
Dumfries 148 C 3
Dumont d'Urville 203
Dumpu 184 E 3
Dumpu 186 A 3
Dumraon 174 D 2
Dumyāt 194 E 2
Duna 154 A 1
Dunaföldvár 154 A 1
Dunajec 149 GH 5
Dunántúl 154 A 1
Dunărea 154 C 1
Dunaujváros 154 A 1
Dunav 154 B 2
Dunay 170 M 1
Dunay 173 K 2
Dunayevtsy 158 E 6
Dunbar (Australia) 183 G 2
Dunbar (U.K.) 148 C 3
Duncan (AZ.) 116 G 5
Duncan (MS.) 121 P 8
Duncan (OK.) 120 H 8
Duncan Passage 175 F 5
Duncansby Head 148 C 3
Dundalk 148 B 4
Dundalk (M.D.) 129 P 2
Dundalk Bay 148 B 4
Dundas, Lake 182 C 5
Dundas Island 109 N 4
Dundas Strait 182 E 1
Dún Dealgan 148 B 4
Dundee (MI.) 125 L 8

Dundee (N.Y.) 126 B 6
Dundee (South Africa) 200 E 5
Dundee (U.K.) 148 C 3
Dundgovĭ 172 E 1
Dundwa Range 174 D 2
Dunedin 185 Q 10
Dunedin 186 C 6
Dunedin (FL.) 131 M 6
Dunfanaghy 148 B 3
Dunfermline 148 C 3
Dungarpur 174 B 3
Dungas 197 F 3
Dungog 183 J 5
Dungu 198 D 4
Dungul 194 E 4
Dunhua 173 J 2
Dunhuang 172 B 2
Dunken (N.M.) 117 L 5
Dunkerque 148 D 4
Dunkirk (N.Y.) 125 P 7
Dunkirk (OH.) 125 L 9
Dunkur 198 F 2
Dunkwa 196 D 4
Dún Laoghaire 148 B 4
Dunlap (IA.) 119 N 9
Dunlap (TN.) 128 F 6
Dunlay (TX.) 122 DE 6
Dunlop (TX.) 117 Q 3
Dunmanway 148 B 4
Dunmarra 182 E 2
Dunmor (KY.) 128 E 4
Dunmore (PA.) 126 D 7
Dunn (N.C.) 129 N 6
Dunn (TX.) 122 C 3
Dunn Center (ND.) 118 F 3
Dunnellon (FL.) 131 M 5
Dunnigan (CA.) 112 C 4
Dunning (NE.) 118 H 9
Dunphy (NV.) 112 J 2
Dunqulah (al 'Ordi 194 E 5
Dunqulah al Qadīmah 194 DE 5
Dunqunāb 194 F 4
Dunrankin 104 L 6
Dunseith (ND.) 118 H 2
Dunsmuir (CA.) 112 C 1
Duolun 173 G 2
Duong Dong 175 H 5
Dupree (SD.) 118 G 5
Dupuyer (MT.) 111 N 2
Duque de York 143 A 9
Du Quoin (IL.) 121 Q 4
Durack Range 182 D 2
Dura Europos (Syria) 156 C 2
Durağan 155 DE 2
Duran (N.M.) 117 KL 3
Durance 153 E 3
Durand (IA.) 119 RS 9
Durand (MI.) 125 L 7
Durand (WI.) 124 C 5
Durango (CO.) 115 K 6
Durango (Mexico) 132 AB 3
Durango (Spain) 152 C 3
Durant (IA.) 119 RS 9
Durant (MS.) 130 E 1
Durant (OK.) 120 J 8–9
Duratón 152 C 3
Durazno 142 E 5
Durban 201 E 5
Durbin (W.V.) 129 M 3
Durdevac 153 G 2
Düren 148 E 4
Durg 174 D 3
Durgapur (Bangla Desh) 175 F 2
Durgapur (India) 174 E 3
Durham (CA.) 112 D 3
Durham (KS.) 120 H 4
Durham (N.C.) 129 N 6
Durham (OK.) 120 F 7
Durham (WY.) 118 D 9
Durham Downs 183 G 4
Durkee (OR.) 110 H 6
Durmā (Saudi Arabia) 157 E 4
Durmitor 154 A 2
Duro Europos → Aş Şālihīyah 195 G 2
Duroy 170 L 5
Durresi 154 A 2
Dursunbey 154 C 3
Duruksi 199 H 3
Durusu Gölü 154 C 2
Durūz, Jabal ad (Syria) 156 B 2
D'Urville Island 185 Q 9
D'Urville Sea 203
Dusa Mareb 199 H 3
Dushak 168 G 3
Dushan 172 E 5
Dushanbe 169 H 3
Dushekan 170 J 3
Dusheti 155 F 2
Dushore (PA.) 126 C 7
Düsseldorf 148 E 4
Dustin (OK.) 120 J 7
Dusty (WA.) 110 H 4
Dutch Harbor 102 D 5
Dutch John (UT.) 114 H 3
Dutlwe 200 C 4
Dutton (MT.) 111 O 3
Duvall (WA.) 110 D 3
Duved 150 F 3

Duvno 153 G 3
Duvogero 150 K 3
Duwayhin (United Arab Emirates)
  157 F 4
Duwisib 200 B 5
Duwwāh 195 K 4
Duye 198 D 4
Düz 193 G 2
Düzce 154 D 2
Dvina, Severnaya 158 H 3
Dvinskaya Guba 158 G 2–3
Dvorechnaya 158 G 6
Dwarka 174 A 3
Dwight (IL.) 124 F 8
Dwight (N.D.) 119 M 4
Dworshak Reservoir 110 J 4
Dwyer (WY.) 118 D 8
Dyadmo 170 J 4
Dyatkovo 158 F 5
Dyatlovo 151 J 5
Dyer (NV.) 112 G 5
Dyer, Lake 112 A 1
Dyersburg (TN.) 128 B 5
Dyersville (IA.) 119 R 8
Dygdy-Sise, Khrebet 171 O 4
Dyje 149 G 5
Dykh Tau 155 F 2
Dylewska Góra 149 GH 4
Dyrhólaey 150 B 3
Dysnų Ežeras 151 J 4
Dytike Rodhopi 154 B 2
Dyurmen'tobe 169 G 1
Dyurtyuli 158 K 4
Dzag 170 G 6
Dzamïn Uüd 172 F 2
Dzaoudzi 201 H 2
Dzavhan Gol 170 F 6
Dzenzik, Mys 155 E 1
Dzerzhinsk (Balorussiya, U.S.S.R.)
  151 J 5
Dzerzhinsk (Russiya, U.S.S.R.) 158 H 4
Dzerzhinskaya, Gora 151 J 5
Dzerzhinskoye 159 Q 6
Dzerzhinskoye 170 G 4
Dzhagdy, Khrebet 171 O 5
Dzhagry 155 G 3
Dzhaki-Unakhta Yakbyyana,
  Khrebet 171 OP 5–6
Dzhaksy 159 N 5
Dzhalagash 169 G 1
Dzhalal-Abad 169 J 2
Dzhalampyr 169 H 3
Dzhalilabad 168 D 3
Dzhalinda 171 N 5
Dzhaltyr 159 N 5
Dzhambul 159 M 5
Dzhambul 159 O 6
Dzhambul 169 J 2
Dzhamm 171 O 1
Dzhanga 168 E 2
Dzhankoy 155 D 1
Dzhanybek 158 J 6
Dzhardzhan 171 MN 2
Dzharkurgan 169 H 3
Dzhava 155 F 2
Dzhebariki 171 P 3
Dzhebel 168 E 3
Dzhelinde 170 K 1
Dzhetygara 159 M 5
Dzhezkazgan 169 H 1
Dzhigirbent 169 G 2
Dzhigudzhak 171 T 3
Dzhirgatal' 169 J 3
Dzhizak 169 H 2
Dzhubga 155 E 2
Dzhugdzhur, Khrebet 171 OP 4
Dzhugdzhur Range 171 Q 4
Dzhunkun 170 K 3
Dzhurin 154 C 1
Dzhurun 168 F 1
Dzhusaly 169 G 1
Dzibalchén 132 E 4
Dzierźoniów 149 G 4
Dzioua 193 G 2
Dziuche 132 E 4
Dzungaria 169 M 1
Dzüünbayan 172 E 2
Dzuunbulag 172 FG 1

Eads (CO.) 115 P 5
Eagar (AZ.) 116 G 3
Eagle (AK.) 102 J 3
Eagle (AK., U.S.A.) 199 J 6
Eagle (CO.) 115 L 4
Eagle (ID.) 110 J 7
Eagle, Mount 130 E 9
Eagle Bend (MN.) 119 NO 4
Eagle Butte (SD.) 118 G 6
Eagle City (OK.) 120 G 7
Eagle Flat (TX.) 117 L 6
Eagle Grove (IA.) 119 P 8
Eagle Lake (CA.) 112 E 2
Eagle Lake (ME.) 126 L 1
Eagle Lake (ME.) 126 L 1

Eagle Lake (ME.) 126 K 2
Eagle Lake (Ontario, Can.) 104 J 6
Eagle Lake (TX.) 122 G 6
Eagle Mountain 119 S 3
Eagle Mountain Lake 122 F 3
Eagle Nest (N.M.) 117 L 1
Eagle Nest Butte 118 G 7
Eagle Nest Lake 117 L 1
Eagle Pass (TX.) 122 C 7
Eagle Peak (CA.) 112 E 1
Eagle Peak (CA.) 112 F 5
Eagle River (WI.) 124 E 3
Eagle River (WI.) 124 E 4
Eagle River(Yukon, Can.) 109 L 2
Eagle Rock (VA.) 129 LM 4
Eagle Summit 102 H 2
Eagleton (MT.) 111 Q 3
Eagle Village 109 K 3
Eagleville (CA.) 112 EF 1
Eakly (OK.) 120 G 7
Ear Falls 104 J 5
Earl, Lake 112 A 1
Earlimart (CA.) 113 F 7
Earlville (IN.) 126 D 6
Earp (CA.) 113 L 8
Earth (TX.) 117 O 3
Easley (S.C.) 128 J 7
East Alligator River 182 E 1
East Amana (IA.) 119 R 9
East Antarctica 203
East Bay (FL.) 131 J 4
East Bay (LA.) 123 O 6–7
East Bay (N.W.T., Can.) 103 V 3
East Bay (TX.) 123 J 6
East Bernad (TX.) 122 G 6
Eastbourne 148 CD 4
East Brady (PA.) 125 P 9
East Brewton (AL.) 130 G 3
East Cape 185 R 8
East Cape 186 C 5
East Channel 109 M 2
East Chicago (IN.) 124 G 8
East China Sea 173 HJ 5
East Ely (NV.) 112 L 3
Eastend 103 Q 6
Easter Island 187 H 4
Eastern Ghats 174 D 4
Eastern Nara River 169 H 5
East Falkland 143 E 9
East Fork 109 J 2
Eastgate (NV.) 112 H 3
East Glacier Park (MT.) 111 M 2
East Grand Forks (MN.) 119 M 3
East Grand Rapids (MI.) 124 J 7
Easthampton (MA.) 126 G 6
East Helena (MT.) 111 O 4
East Kilbride 148 C 3
East Lake (MI.) 124 H 5
East Lake (OR.) 110 D 7
Eastland (TX.) 122 E 3
East Lansing (MI.) 125 K 7
East Las Vegas (NV.) 112 L 6
East Liverpool (OH.) 125 N 9
East London (Sout Africa) 200 D 6
East Lynn (W.V.) 129 J 3
Eastmain 105 M 5
Eastman (GA.) 131 L 2
East Nishnabotna River 119 N 9–10
East Olympia (WA.) 110 C 4
Easton (MD.) 129 Q 3
Easton (PA.) 127 D 8
Eastover (S.C.) 129 L 8
East Pacific Basin 209 D 4
East Pacific Ridge 209 D 5
East Pack Reservoir 112 C 3
East Palatka (FL.) 131 N 5
East Point (P.R.) 130 E 8
East Point(P.R.) 130 E 9
Eastport (ME.) 126 M 4
East Prairie (MO.) 121 Q 6
East Pryor Mountain 111 R 5
East Ridge (TN.) 128 F 6
East Siberian Sea 171 S 1
East Siberian Sea 202
East Stroudsburg (PA.) 127 D 7
East Troy (WI.) 124 F 7
East Turkistan 162 FG 2–3
Eastville (VA.) 129 Q 4
East Wenatchee (WA.) 110 E 3
Eaton (CO.) 115 N 3
Eaton (OH.) 128 G 2
Eaton Rapids (MI.) 125 K 7
Eatonton (GA.) 128 H 8
Eatonville (WA.) 110 C 4
Eau Claire (WI.) 124 C 5
Eau-Claire, Lac à l' 105 N 4
Eauripik 186 A 3
Ebano 132 C 3
Ebe 171 Q 3
Ebe-Basa 171 NO 3
Ebebiyin 197 G 5
Ebeltoft 151 F 4
Ebensburg (PA.) 125 Q 9
Eber Gölü 154 D 3
Eberswalde 149 F 4
Ebinur Hu 169 L 1
Ebla (Syria) 156 B 2
Ebo 200 A 2
Ebola 198 C 4

Eboli 153 G 3
Ebolowa 197 G 5
Ebombo 198 D 6
Ebon 186 C 2
Ebony 200 AB 4
Ebro 152 C 3
Ebro, Delta del 152 D 3
Ebro, Embalse del 152 C 3
Ebyakh 171 S 2
Ecbatana (Iran) 157 E 2
Ech Cheliff 193 F 1
Echdeiria 192 C 3
Echeng 172 FG 4
Echeta (WY.) 118 C 6
Echmiadzin 155 F 2
Echo (MN.) 119 N 6
Echo (UT.) 114 F 3
Echo Bay 103 O 2
Echuca 183 G 6
Écija 152 B 4
Eckerman (MI.) 124 J 3
Eckernförde 149 EF 4
Eckerö 151 G 3
Eckley (CO.) 115 P 3
Ecuador 138 D 4
E'cueils, Pointe aux 105 M 4
Ed 151 F 4
Edchera 192 C 3
Edd 199 G 2
Ed Damer → Ad' Dāmir
194 E 5
Eddaré 192 D 4
Eddéki 197 H 2
Eddyville (KY.) 128 C 4
Eddyville (NE.) 120 F 1
Ede 197 E 4
Edéa 197 FG 5
Edefors 150 H 2
Edel Land 182 A 4
Eden (MS.) 130 D 2
Eden (N.C.) 129 M 5
Eden (N.S.W., Austr.) 183 H 6
Eden (TX.) 122 D 4
Eden (U.K.) 148 C 4
Eden (WY.) 111 Q 8
Edenburg 200 D 5
Edenton (N.C.) 129 P 5
Eden Valley (MN.) 119 O 5
Eder 149 E 4
Edgar (NE.) 120 H 2
Edgard (LA.) 123 N 5–6
Edgar Range 182 C 2
Edgartown (N.Y.) 127 J 8
Edgefield (S.C.) 129 K 8
Edgeley (N.D.) 119 K 4
Edgell 105 P 3
Edgemont (SD.) 118 E 7
Edgeöya 202
Edgerton (KS.) 121 KL 4
Edgerton (MN.) 119 M 7
Edgerton (WI.) 124 E 7
Edgerton (WY.) 118 B 7
Edgewater (FL.) 131 O 6
Edgewood (IA.) 119 R 8
Edgewood (IL.) 121 R 4
Edgewood (MD.) 129 P 2
Edhessa 154 B 2
Edina (MN.) 119 P 6
Edina (MO.) 121 N 2
Edinburg (IN.) 128 E 2
Edinburg (N.D.) 119 KL 2
Edinburg (TX.) 122 E 9
Edinburgh 148 C 3
Edinga 197 H 2
Edirne 154 C 2
Edisto Island 129 L 9
Edisto River 129 L 8
Edith, Mount 111 O 4
Edjeleh 193 GH 3
Edler (CO.) 115 P 6
Edmond (KS.) 120 F 3
Edmond (OK.) 120 H 7
Edmonds (ID.) 111 NO 7
Edmonds (WA.) 110 C 3
Edmonton (Alberta, Can.) 103 P 5
Edmonton (KY.) 128 F 5
Edmore (MI.) 124 J 6
Edmore (N.D.) 119 K 2
Edmundston 105 O 6
Edna (TX.) 122 G 6–7
Edna Bay 109 M 4
Edough, Djebel 153 E 4
Edounga 197 G 6
Edremit 154 C 3
Edremit Körfezi 154 C 3
Edrengiyn Nuruu 172 C 2
Edsbyn 150 G 3
Edson 103 O 5
Edson Butte 110 A 8
E. Dubuque (WI.) 124 D 7
Eduni, Mount 102 LM 3
Eduni, Mount 109 N 3
Edwall (WA.) 110 H 3
Edward, Lake 198 D 5
Edward River 183 G 1
Edwards (MS.) 130 D 2
Edwards (N.Y.) 126 D 4
Edwards Creek 183 F 4
Edwards Plateau 117 P 6–7

Edwardsville (IL.) 121 Q 4
Edzhen 171 P 3
Edziza Peak 109 M 4
Edzo 103 O 3
Eek 102 E 3
Eel River 112 B 2
Eenhana 200 B 3
Efate 185 J 5
Efaté 186 C 4
Eferding 153 F 2
Efes 154 C 3
Effingham (IL.) 121 R 3
Effingham (S.C.) 129 M 7
Eflâni 155 D 2
Eforie 154 C 2
Egan (S.D.) 119 M 7
Egaña 143 E 6
Egbe 197 F 4
Egbert (WY.) 118 D 9
Egegik 102 F 4
Egeland (ND.) 118 JK 2
Eger 154 B 1
Egersund 151 E 4
Egerton, Mount 182 B 3
Eggan 197 F 4
Egg Harbor City (N.J.) 127 E 9
Eg Glab Tiguesmat 192 D 3–4
Eggum 150 F 2
Egilsstaðir 150 C 2
Egiyn Gol 170 H 5–6
Eglab Dersa 192 E 3
Égletons 152 D 2
Egmont, Cape 185 Q 8
Egmont, Mount 185 Q 8
Egnar (CO.) 114 J 6
Eğridir 154 D 3
Eğridir Gölü 154 D 3
Eguata 197 F 6
Egvekinot 102 B 2
Egypt 194 DE 4
Eha Amufu 197 F 4
Ehcel 196 E 2
Ehrenberg (AZ.) 116 B 4
Ehrhardt (S.C.) 129 KL 8
Ehtridge (TN.) 128 D 6
Eiao 187 F 3
Eibar 152 C 3
Eidet 150 F 3
Eidfjord 151 E 3
Eidslandet 150 E 3
Eidsvåg 150 E 3
Eidsvoll 151 F 3
Eifel 148 E 4
Eigat, Jabal 194 EF 4
Eigeröy 151 E 4
Eigg 148 B 3
Eight Degree Channel 174 B 6
Eights Coast 203
Eighty Mile Beach 182 C 2
Eigrim, Jabal 194 F 5
'Eilai 194 E 5
Eildon 183 H 6
Einasleigh 183 G 2
Einasleigh River 183 G 2
Eindhoven 148 DE 4
Eindpaal 200 B 5
Eire 148 B 4
Eiríksjökull 150 A 3
Eirunepé 138 D 5
Eisenach 149 EF 4
Eisenerz 153 F 2
Eisenhüttenstadt 149 F 4
Eisenstadt 153 G 2
Ejeda 201 G 4
Ejin Horo Qi 172 E 3
Ejin Qi 172 D 2
Ejura 196 D 4
Ekalaka (MT.) 118 D 5
Ekarma, Ostrov 171 S 6
Ekecik Dağı 155 D 3
Ekenäs (Tammisaari) 151 H 4
Eket 197 F 5
Ekiatap 108 C 2
Ekiatapskiy Khrebet 108 BC 2
Ekibastuz 159 P 5
Ekimchan 171 O 5
Ekitykiy Khrebet 108 B 2
Eklutna 109 J 3
Ekoli 198 C 5
Ekonda 170 H 2
Eksjö 151 G 4
Ekuk 108 G 4
Ekwan 104 L 5
Ekwok 108 G 4
El Aaiún 192 C 3
El Aatf 192 B 4
El Abiodh Sidi Cheikh 192 F 2
El Adeb Larache 193 G 3
El Affroun 152 D 4
El Agreb 193 G 2
Elaine (AR.) 121 P 8
El Alamein → Al 'Alamayn 194 D 2
El Alamo 106 C 4
El Alia 193 G 2
El Arahal 152 B 4
El Aráich → Larache 192 D 1
El Aricha 192 E 2
El Arrouch 153 E 4

Elassón 154 B 3
Elat (Israel) 156 B 3
Eláti 154 B 3
Elato 186 A 2
El Attar 193 F 2
Elâzığ 155 E 3
Elba 153 F 3
Elba (AL.) 131 HG 3
Elba (ID.) 111 M 8
Elba (NE.) 120 G 1
El'ban 171 P 5
El Banco 138 D 2
El Barco 152 B 3
El Barco de Ávila 152 BC 3
Elbasani 154 A 2
El Baul 138 E 2
El Bayadh 193 F 2
Elbe 149 F 4
El Bema 193 F 4
Elbert (CO.) 115 N 4
Elbert (TX.) 122 DE 2
Elbert, Mount 115 L 4
Elberta (UT.) 114 F 4
Elberton (GA.) 128 J 8
Elbeyli 156 B 1
El Bir → Teouit 193 G 3
Elbistan 155 E 3
Elbląg 149 G 4
Elbow 103 Q 5
Elbow Lake (MN.) 119 N 5
Elbrus 155 F 2
'El Bûr 199 H 4
El Burgo de Osma 152 C 3
El Buro 132 B 2
Elburz Mountains (Iran) 157 F 1
El Caín 143 C 7
El Cajon (CA.) 113 J 10
El Callao 139 F 2
El Campo (TX.) 122 G 6
El Canelo 132 BC 3
El Capitan Reservoir 113 J 10
El Carmen (Bolivia) 140 D 3
El Carmen (Colombia) 138 C 2
El Carre 199 G 3
El Casco 132 B 2
El Centro (CA.) 113 K 10
El Cerito 138 C 3
El Cerro 140 D 4
Elche 152 C 4
Elcho Island 182 F 1
El Chorro 140 D 5
El Cocuy 138 D 2
El Cóndor, Cerro 142 C 4
El Cuy 143 C 6
Elda 152 C 4
El Dab 199 H 3
El Daoud 192 D 4
El Der 199 G 3
'El Dère 199 H 4
Elderwood (CA.) 112 FG 6
El Descanso 106 C 5
El Difícil 138 D 2
El'dikan 171 P 3
El Diviso 138 C 3
El Djouf 192 D 4
Eldon (IA.) 119 Q 10
Eldon (MO.) 121 N 4
Eldon (WA.) 110 B 3
Eldora (IA.) 119 P 8
Eldora (CO.) 115 L 4
El Dorado 139 F 2
El Dorado (AR.) 121 N 9
Eldorado (Argentina) 142 EF 4
Eldorado (IL.) 121 R 5
El Dorado (KS.) 120 J 5
El Dorado (Mexico) 106 E 7
Eldorado (OH.) 128 G 2
Eldorado (OK.) 120 F 8
Eldorado (TX.) 122 C 5
Eldorado Springs (MO.) 121 LM 5
Eldoret 198 F 4
Eldridge (AL.) 128 D 8
Eldridge (ND.) 118 K 4
Eldridge, Mount 109 K 3
Electra (TX.) 122 E 1
Electra Lake 115 K 6
El Eglab 192 DE 3
Elêja 151 H 4
Elekton (VA.) 129 N 3
Elektrostal' 158 G 4
Elele 197 F 4
Elemi Triangle 198 EF 4
El Encanto 138 D 4
Elephant Butte (N.M.) 117 J 4
Elephant Butte Reservoir 117 J 4
Elephant Island 203
Elesbão Veloso 141 H 2
El Eulma 193 G 1
Eleuthera Island 133 G 2
Elevenmile Canyon Reservoir 115 M 5
Elevtheroúpolis 154 B 2
Ellaville (FL.) 131 L 4
El Farsia 192 D 3
El Fasher 194 D 6
El Ferrol del Candillo 152 B 3
Elfrida (AZ.) 116 G 6
El Fud 199 G 3
El Fuerte 132 B 3
Elgåhogna 150 F 3
El'gakan 171 M 4
'El Gâl 199 J 2
El Gassi 193 G 2

Elghena 199 F 1
El'gi 171 Q 3
Elgin (IL.) 124 F 7
Elgin (ND.) 118 G 4
Elgin (NE.) 119 K 9
Elgin (NV.) 112 L 5
Elgin (OR.) 110 H 5
Elgin (TX.) 122 F 5
Elgin (U.K.) 148 C 3
El'ginskoye Ploskogor'ye 171 PQ 2
El Goléa 193 F 2
Elgon, Mount 198 E 4
El Goran 199 G 3
El Guamo 138 C 3
El Guettara 196 D 1
El'gyay 170 L 3
El'gygytgyn, Ozero 171 W 2
El Hachchana 193 F 3
El Hajeb 192 D 2
'El Hamurre 199 H 3
El Hank 192 D 4
El Homr 193 F 3
Eliase 177 H 5
Eliasville (TX.) 122 E 3
Elida (N.M.) 117 N 4
Elikón Óros 154 B 3
Elila 198 D 5
Elila 198 D 5
Elim 102 E 3
El Indio (TX.) 122 C 7
Elingampangu 198 C 5
Elisenvaara 150 J 3
Eliseu Martins 141 H 2
Eliseyna 154 B 2
Elista 155 F 1
Elizabeth 183 F 5
Elizabeth (CO.) 115 N 4
Elizabeth (N.J.) 127 E 8
Elizabeth (W.I.) 124 D 7
Elizabeth (W.V.) 129 K 2
Elizabeth, Cape 110 A 3
Elizabeth, Mount 182 D 2
Elizabeth City (N.C.) 129 P 5
Elizabeth Falls 103 Q 4
Elizabethton (TN.) 129 J 5
Elizabethtown (IL.) 121 R 5
Elizabethtown (KY.) 128 F 4
Elizabethtown (N.C.) 129 N 7
Elizabethtown (N.Y.) 126 F 4
El Jadida 192 D 2
El Jicaral 132 E 5
Ełk 149 H 4
Elk (CA.) 112 B 3
Elk (N.M.) 117 L 5
Elk (WY.) 111 P 7
Elkader (IA.) 119 R 8
El Kala 193 G 1
El Kantara 193 G 1
El Kharga → Al Khārijah 194 E 3
Elkhart (IN.) 124 J 8
Elkhart (KS.) 120 D 5
Elkhart (TX.) 123 H 4
Elk Head Mountains 115 K 3
Elk Hill 126 D 7
El Khnâchîch 192 E 4
Elk Horn (KY.) 128 F 4
Elkhorn (OR.) 110 C 6
Elkhorn (WI.) 124 F 7
Elkhorn City (KY.) 129 J 4
Elkhorn River 119 L 8
Elkhovo 154 C 2
Elkin (N.C.) 129 L 5
Elkins (N.M.) 117 M 4
Elkins (W.V.) 129 M 3
Elk Lake 124 J 5
Elk Mountain (WY.) 118 B 9
Elk Mountain (WY.) 118 B 9
Elko (NV.) 112 K 2
Elk Peak 111 P 4
Elk Point (S.D.) 119 M 8
Elk River (ID.) 110 J 4
Elk River (MN.) 119 P 5
Elk River (TN.) 128 E 6
El Kseïbat 192 E 3
Elk Springs (CO.) 115 J 3
Elkton (KY.) 128 D 5
Elkton (OR.) 110 B 7
Elkton (S.D.) 119 M 6
Elku Kalns 151 J 4
Ell, Lake 182 D 4
Ellaval (FL.) 131 L 4
Ellaville (GA.) 131 K 2
Ellef Ringnes Island 202
Ellenabad 174 B 2
Ellenboro (W.V.) 129 K 2
Ellendale (MN.) 119 P 7
Ellendale (N.D.) 119 K 5
Ellensburg (WA.) 110 E 3–4
Ellenville (N.Y.) 126 E 7
Ellesmere Island 202
Ellice Islands 186 C 3

Ellicott (CO.) 115 N 5
Ellicott City (MD.) 129 OP 2
Ellijay (GA.) 128 G 7
Ellila 197 J 2
Ellington (MO.) 121 P 5
Elliot (Australia) 182 E 2
Elliot (South Africa) 200 D 6
Elliot, Mount 183 H 2
Elliott (IA.) 119 N 9
Elliott Key 131 O 9
Elliott Knob 129 M 3
Elliotts Bluff (GA.) 131 N 4
Ellis (ID.) 111 LM 6
Ellis (KS.) 120 F 4
Elliston 183 E 5
Ellisville (MS.) 130 E 3
Ellsinore (MO.) 121 P 6
Ellsworth (KS.) 120 G 4
Ellsworth (ME.) 126 L 4
Ellsworth (MI.) 124 J 4
Ellsworth (MN.) 119 M 7
Ellsworth (NE.) 118 F 8
Ellsworth (WI.) 124 B 5
Ellsworth Land 203
Ellsworth Mountains 203
Ellwood City (PA.) 125 N 9
Elma (IA.) 119 Q 7
Elmadağ 155 D 3
El Maestrazgo 152 CD 3
El Mahia 196 D 1
El Maitén 143 B 7
Elmali 154 C 3
Elmalı Dağı 155 DE 3
El Mamoun 196 D 2
El Mansour 192 E 3
El Mayoco 143 B 7
Elm Creek (NE.) 120 F 2
El Medo 199 G 3
El Meghaïer 193 G 2
Elmendorf (N.M.) 117 K 4
Elmer (PA.) 127 D 9
Elmer City (WA.) 110 G 2
El Mereïé 192 D 5
El Messir 197 H 2
Elmhurst (IL.) 124 FG 8
El Milhéas 192 D 3
El Milia 153 E 4
Elmira (ID.) 110 J 2
Elmira (MI.) 125 K 4
Elmira (N.Y.) 126 C 6
El Mirador 132 E 4
El Mirage (AZ.) 116 D 4
El Mirage Lake 113 H 8
Elm Lake 119 K 5
Elmo (MT.) 111 L 3
Elmo (UT.) 114 G 4
El Moïnane 192 C 5
Elmore (MN.) 119 O 7
El Morro National Monument 116 H 2
El Mreiti 192 D 4
El Mreyer 192 D 4
Elmshorn 149 EF 4
Elm Springs (SD.) 118 F 6
Elmwood (NE.) 120 J 2
Elmwood (OK.) 120 E 6
El Mzereb 192 D 4
El Mzerif 196 D 1
Elne 152 D 3
El Niabo 199 F 4
El Nido 177 E 1
El Nido (CA.) 112 E 5
El Nihuil 143 C 5
Elnora (IN.) 128 DE 3
Elnora (IN.) 128 DE 3
El Novillo 106 DE 6
El Obeid 194 E 6
El Odre 143 C 6
Elora (TN.) 128 E 6
Elorza 138 E 2
El Oso 138 E 3
El Oued 193 G 2
El Ousseukh 193 F 2
Eloy (AZ.) 116 E 5
El Palmito 132 A 2
El Palqui 142 B 5
El Paso (IL.) 124 F 9
El Paso (TX.) 117 K 6
Elphinstone 183 H 3
El Pico 140 D 4
El Pilar 139 F 1
El Pintado 140 D 5
El Portal (CA.) 112 F 5
El Portugues 138 C 5
El Porvenir (N.M.) 117 L 2
El Porvenir (Panamá) 138 C 2
El Porvenir (Venezuela) 138 E 2
El Potosi (Mexico) 132 B 3
El Potro, Cerro 142 C 4
El Progreso 132 E 4
El Puerto 106 D 6
El Puerto de Santa María 152 B 4
El Real 138 C 2
El Reno (OK.) 120 H 7
El Rio (CA.) 113 F 8
El Rito (N.M.) 117 K 1
Elsa (TX.) 122 EF 9
Elsa (Yukon, Can.) 109 L 3
El Safiya 194 E 5
El Salto 132 A 3
El Salvador 132 DE 5
El Sauca 106 D 7

El Sáuz 106 E 6
El Sáuz (TX.) 122 E 9
Elsberry (MO.) 121 P 3
El Seibo 133 J 4
Elsen Nur 172 B 3
Elsey 182 E 1
El Sharana 182 E 1
Elsie (MI.) 125 K 6
Elsie (OR.) 110 B 5
Elsinore (CA.) 113 H 9
Elsinore (UT.) 114 E 5
Elsinore, Lake 113 H 9
Elsmere (NE.) 118 H 8
El Soberbio 142 F 4
El Sueco 106 E 6
Elsworth, Lake 120 G 8
El Tajin 132 C 3
Eltanin Fracture Zone System 209 D 5
El Tigre (Colombia) 138 E 3
El Tigre (Venezuela) 139 F 2
El Tocuyo 138 E 2
El Tofo 142 B 4
Elton 158 J 6
Elton (LA.) 123 L 5
Eltopia (WA.) 110 G 4
El Toro 130 D 8
El Tránsito 142 B 4
El Trapiche 138 C 3
El Triumfo 106 D 7
El Tuito 132 A 3
El Tunal 142 E 4
El Tuparro, Parque Nacional 138 E 2
El Turbio 143 B 9
Eluru 174 D 4
Elva 151 J 4
El Vado (N.M.) 117 K 1
El Vado Reservoir 117 K 1
El Valle 138 C 2
Elvas 152 B 4
Elverum 151 F 3
El Vigía 138 D 2
Elvira 138 D 5
Elvire River 182 D 2
El Wak 199 G 4
Elwood (IN.) 124 J 9
Elwood (KS.) 121 L 3
Elwood (NE.) 120 EF 2
Ely (NV.) 112 L 3
Elyria (OH.) 125 M 8
Ema Jõgi 151 J 4
Emali 199 F 5
Emämrūd (Iran) 157 G 1
Emämzadeh ʿAbbás (Iran) 157 E 2
Emämzadeh Nasrod Dīn (Iran) 157 E 2
Eman 151 G 4
Emas, Parque Nacional do 141 F 4
Emba 168 F 1
Emba 168 F 1
Embalse de Alarcón 152 C 4
Embalse de Alcántara 152 B 4
Embalse de Almendra 152 B 3
Embalse de Buendia 152 C 3
Embalse de Cenajo 152 C 4
Embalse de Cijara 152 BC 4
Embalse de Contreras 152 C 4
Embalse de Entrepeñas 152 C 3
Embalse de Gabriel y Galan 152 B 3
Embalse de la Cuerda del Pozo 152 C 3
Embalse de la Sotonera 152 C 3
Embalse del Ebro 152 C 3
Embalse del Guárico 152 C 3
Embalse del Río Negro 142 EF 5
Embalse de Mequinenza 152 CD 3
Embalse de Ricobayo 152 B 3
Embalse de Valdecañas 152 BC 4
Embalse de Yesa 152 C 3
Embalse Ezequiel Ramos Mexia 143 C 6
Embalse Florentino Ameghino 143 C 7
Embarcación 140 D 5
Embarras Portage 103 P 4
Embarras River 121 R 3
Embira 138 D 5
Emblem (WY.) 111 R 6
Embu 199 F 5
Embudo (N.M.) 117 L 1
Emden 149 E 4
Emei Shan 172 D 5
Emelʼdzak 171 N 4
Emelle (AL.) 130 F 2
Emerado (N.D.) 119 L 3
Emerald 183 H 3
Emerson (AR.) 121 M 9
Emerson (Manitoba, Can.) 103 S 6
Emerson (MN.) 119 LM 1
Emerson (NE.) 119 M 8
Emerson Lake 113 J 8
Emery (UT.) 114 F 5
Emet 154 C 2
Emgayet 193 H 3
Emi 170 G 5
Emida (ID.) 110 J 3
Emi Fezzane 197 G 1
Emigrant (MT.) 111 P 5
Emigrant Gap (CA.) 112 E 3
Emiliano Zapata 132 D 4
Emi Lulu 197 G 1
Emily (MN.) 119 P 4
Emin 169 L 1

Eminence (KY.) 128 F 3
Emira 185 F 2
Emirdağ 154 D 3
Emlenton (PA.) 125 P 8
Emmaboda 151 G 4
Emmaste 151 H 4
Emmaus (PA.) 127 D 8
Emmelen 108 C 2–3
Emmen 148 E 4
Emmet 183 G 3
Emmet (NE.) 118 K 8
Emmetsburg (IA.) 119 O 7
Emmett (ID.) 110 J 7
Emmett (KS.) 120 J 3
Emmett (MS.) 130 F 2
Emmitsburg (MD.) 129 O 2
Emmonak 102 E 3
Emory (TX.) 123 H 3
Emory (UT.) 114 F 2
Emory Peak 117 N 8
Empalme 106 D 6
Empangeni 201 E 5
Empedrado (Argentina) 142 E 4
Empedrado (Chile) 143 B 6
Emperor Seamount Chain 209 C 2
Empire (NV.) 112 F 2
Empire Reservoir 115 N 3
Empoli 153 F 3
Emporia (KS.) 120 J 4
Emporig (VA.) 129 O 5
Emporium (PA.) 125 Q 8
Ems 149 E 4
Emumägi 151 J 4
Emundston (ME.) 126 L 1
Enånger 150 G 3
Enarotali 177 J 4
Encampment (WY.) 118 B 9
Encarnación 142 E 4
Enchi 196 D 4
Encinal (TX.) 122 D 7
Encinitas (CA.) 113 H 9
Encino (N.M.) 117 KL 3
Encino (TX.) 122 E 9
Encón 142 C 5
Encontrados 138 D 2
Encounter Bay 183 F 6
Encruzilhada do Sul 142 F 5
Enda Salassie 199 F 2
Ende 177 F 5
Endeavor (WI.) 124 E 6
Endeavour 183 H 2
Endeavour Strait 183 G 1
Endee (N.M.) 117 N 2
Enderbury 186 D 3
Enderby Abyssal Plain 208 B 5
Enderby Land 203
Enderlin (N.D.) 119 L 4
Enders (NE.) 120 D 2
Enders (NE.) 120 D 2
Enders Reservoir 120 D 2
Endicott (N.Y.) 126 C 6
Endicott (WA.) 110 H 4
Endicott Mountains (AK.) 102 G 2
Endwell, N.Y. 126 CD 6
Endybal 171 O 2
Energia 143 E 6
Enez 154 C 2
Enfer, Portes dʼ 198 D 6
Enfield (N.C.) 129 O 5
Engaño, Cabo 133 J 4
Engaño, Cape 177 J 1
Engelhard (N.C.) 129 PQ 6
Engelʼs 158 J 5
Engerdyakh 170 L 3
Engershatu 199 F 1
Engiabaia 199 F 2
England 148 CD 4
England (AR.) 121 O 8
Engle (N.M.) 117 JK 4
Englewood (CO.) 115 N 4
Englewood (KS.) 120 E 5
Englewood (TN.) 128 G 6
English (IN.) 128 E 3
English Bazar 174 E 3
English Channel 148 C 4–5
Engozero 150 K 2
Engozero, Ozero 150 K 2
Engure 151 H 4
Enibé 197 J 2
Enid (MT.) 118 D 3
Enid (OK.) 120 H 6
Enid Lake 121 Q 8
Eniwetok 186 B 2
Enji 192 D 5
Enkan 171 Q 4
Enkan, Mys 171 Q 4
Enkeldoorn 201 E 3
Enköping 151 G 4
Enmore 139 G 2
Enna 153 F 4
Ennadai 103 R 3
Ennadai Lake 103 R 3
Enned 197 J 2
Enning (S.D.) 118 F 6
Ennis 148 B 4
Ennis (MT.) 111 O 5
Ennis (TX.) 123 H 4
Enniscorthy 148 B 4
Enniskillen 148 B 4
Ennis Lake 111 O 5

Ennistymon 148 B 4
Ennore 174 D 5
Enns 153 F 2
Enns 153 F 2
Enns 153 F 2
Eno 150 K 3
Enoch (UT.) 114 D 6
Enochs (TX.) 117 O 4
Enonkoski 150 K 3
Enontekiö 150 H 2
Enosburg Falls (VT.) 126 G 4
Enosville (IN.) 128 D 3
Enrekang 177 EF 4
Enriquillo 133 J 4
Enschede 148 E 4
Ensenada 106 C 5
Enshi 172 E 4
Ensign (KS.) 120 E 5
Entebbe 198 E 4
Enterprise (AL.) 131 J 3
Enterprise (CA.) 112 C 2
Enterprise (KS.) 120 HJ 4
Enterprise (MS.) 130 F 2
Enterprise (N.W.T., Can.) 103 O 3
Enterprise (OR.) 110 H 5
Enterprise (UT.) 114 D 6
Entiat (WA.) 110 E 3
Entrance Island 109 M 4
Entrecasteaux, Récifs dʼ 186 B 4
Entrepreñas, Embalse de 152 C 3
Entre Rios (Amazonas, Brazil) 139 G 4
Entre Ríos (Bolivia) 140 D 5
Entre Rios (Pará, Brazil) 139 H 5
Entrevaux 153 E 3
Entroncamento 152 B 4
Enugu 197 F 4
Enugu Ezike 197 F 4
Enumclaw (WA.) 110 D 3
Enurmino 102 C 2
Envigado 138 CD 2
Envira 138 D 5
Enyamba 198 D 5
Enyellé 197 H 5
Eolia (MO.) 121 O 3
Eolie o Lipari, Isole 153 F 4
Epanomi 154 B 2
Epembe 200 A 3
Epéna 197 H 5
Épernay 152 D 2
Epes (AL.) 130 F 2
Ephesus 154 C 3
Ephraim (UT.) 114 F 4
Ephrata (PA.) 127 C 8
Ephrata (WA.) 110 F 3
Epi 185 J 5
Epi 186 C 4
Epidhavros 154 B 3
Épinal 153 E 2
Epira 139 G 2
Episkopi 155 D 4
Episkopi (Cyprus) 156 A 2
Epping (ND.) 118 E 2
Epping (N.H.) 126 H 5
Epps (LA.) 123 M 3
Epsie (MT.) 118 C 5
Epukiro 200 B 4
Epukiro 200 C 4
Epuyén 143 B 7
Eqlīd (Iran) 157 F 3
Équateur 198 BC 4
Equatoria 198 DE 3–4
Equatorial Guinea 197 F 5
Eraclea 153 G 3
Erap 184 E 3
Erba, Jabal 194 F 4
Erbaa 195 F 2
Erbeskopf 149 E 5
Erbīl (Iraq) 156 D 1
Erçek 155 F 3
Erçek Gölü 155 F 3
Ercis 155 F 3
Erciyas Dağı 155 E 3
Érd 154 A 1
Erdaogou 172 B 4
Erdek 154 C 2
Erdemli 155 D 3
Erdemli (Turkey) 156 B 1
Erdene 172 F 2
Erdenedalay 172 DE 1
Erech (Iraq) 157 D 3
Erechim 142 F 4
Ereentsav 170 L 6
Ereğli (Turkey) 154 D 2
Ereğli (Turkey) 155 D 3
Erenhaberga Shan 169 LM 2
Erenhot 172 F 2
Erentepe 155 F 3
Erepecu, Lago de 139 G 4
Eresma 152 C 3
Erfoud 192 E 2
Erfurt 149 F 4
Erg Afarag 193 F 4
Erg Atouila 196 D 1
Ergani 155 E 3
Erg Brusset 197 FG 2
Erg Chech 192 E 3–4
Erg dʼAdmer 193 G 4
Erg de Ténéré 197 G 2
Erg du Djourab 197 H 2
Ergedzhey 170 L 3
Erg el Ahmar 192 E 4
Ergene 154 C 2

Erg er Raoui 192 E 3
Erg Iabès 192 E 3
Erg Iguidi 192 DE 3
Erg in Sakkane 196 D 1
Ergli 151 J 4
Erg N-Ataram 193 F 4
Ergun Youqi 170 M 5
Ergun Zuoqi 171 M 5
Er Hai 172 D 5
Eriba 194 F 5
Eric 105 O 5
Erice 153 F 4
Ericeira 152 B 4
Erichsen Lake 105 L 1
Erick (OK.) 120 F 7
Ericson (NE.) 119 K 9
Eridu (Iraq) 157 D 3
Erie (CO.) 115 MN 3
Erie (KS.) 121 K 5
Erie (PA.) 125 OP 7
Erie Canal 125 Q 6
Erie, Lake 125 Q 6–7
Erigābo 199 H 3
Erikub 186 C 2
Erimbet 169 G 2
Erimo-misaki 173 M 2
Erinpura 174 B 2
Erin (TN.) 128 D 5
Erkowit 194 F 5
Erlangen 149 F 5
Erldunda 182 E 4
Ermelo 200 DE 5
Ermenek 155 D 3
Ermenek (Turkey) 156 A 1
Ermera 177 FG 5
Ermil 194 D 6
Ermióni 154 B 3
Ermoupolis 154 B 3
Ernakulam 174 C 6
Erne, Lower Lough 148 B 4
Ernest Legouvé 187 E 5
Erode 174 C 5
Erongo 200 B 4
Erongo Mountains 200 B 4
Erota 199 F 1
Erozionnyy 171 R 2
Errego 201 F 3
Er Rif 192 E 2
Errol (N.H.) 126 H 4
Erromanga 185 J 5
Erromango 186 C 4
Er Roseires → Ar Ruşayriş 194 E 6
Er rout Sanihida 197 G 1
Erskine (MN.) 119 M 3
Ertai 169 N 1
Ertil 158 H 5
Ertix He 169 M 1
Eruh (Turkey) 156 C 1
Erundu 200 B 4
Erwin (TN.) 129 J 5
Eryuan 172 C 5
Erzgebirge 149 F 4
Erzin 170 G 5
Erzincan 155 E 3
Erzurum 155 F 3
Erzurum-Kars Yaylâsı 155 F 2
Esa-ala 185 F 3
Esbjerg 151 E 4
Esbo 151 H 3
Escada 141 J 2
Escalante Desert 114 D 6
Escalante River 114 F 6
Escalón 132 B 2
Escalon (CA.) 112 D 5
Escalona 152 C 3
Escanaba (MI.) 124 GH 4
Escanaba River 124 G 3–4
Escatrón 152 C 3
Esch (sur-Alzette) 153 E 2
Eschan 171 R 3
Eschwege 149 F 4
Escobas (TX.) 122 D 8
Escondido (CA.) 113 H 9
Escorial, Serra do 141 H 3
Escudo, Puerto de 152 C 3
Escuintla 132 D 5
Eséka 197 G 5
Eşenler Dağı 155 D 3
Esfahan (Iran) 157 F 2
Esfandārān (Iran) 157 F 3
Esfandiar (Iran) 157 EF 3
Eshowe 201 E 5
Eshtehārd (Iran) 157 F 2
Eskifjörður 150 C 2
Eskilstuna 151 G 4
Eskimo Lakes 102 L 2
Eskimo Point 103 T 3
Eskipazar 155 D 2
Eskişehir 154 D 3
Eskota (TX.) 122 C 3
Eskridge (KS.) 120 J 4
Esk River 184 L 9
Esla 152 B 3
Eslamabad (Iran) 157 E 2
Eslöv 151 F 4
Eşme 154 C 3
Esmeralda 138 E 3

Esmeralda, Isla 143 A 8
Esmeraldas 138 BC 3
Esmeraldas 138 C 3
Esmond (ND.) 118 J 2
España 152 C 4
Espanola (N.M.) 117 KL 1–2
Espanola (CA.) 112 CD 4
Esparto (CA.) 112 CD 4
Esperance 182 C 5
Esperance Bay 182 C 5
Esperanza (Antarctica) 203
Esperanza (Argentina) 142 D 5
Esperanza (Mexico) 106 E 6
Esperanza (Peru) 138 D 5
Esperanza (P.R.) 130 D 8
Espichel, Cabo 152 B 4
Espigão Mestre 141 G 3
Espinal 138 D 3
Espinal 140 E 4
Espinar 140 B 3
Espinazo del Diablo, Sierra 132 A 3
Espinhaço, Serra do 141 H 4
Espinho 152 B 3
Espírito Santo (Brazil) 141 HJ 4
Espiritu Santo (Vanuatu) 185 J 5
Espiritu Santo (Vanuatu) 186 BC 4
Esplanada 141 J 3
Espoo (Esbo) 151 H 3
Espungabera 201 E 4
Esquel 143 B 7
Esquina 142 E 4
Esquinapa de Hidalgo 132 A 3
Essaouira 192 CD 2
Essen 149 E 4
Essendon, Mount 182 C 3
Essequibo 139 G 3
Essendon, Mount 182 C 3
Essex (CA.) 113 K 8
Essex (MT.) 111 M 2
Essex Junction (VT.) 126 F 4
Essexville (MI.) 125 L 6
Esslingen 149 E 5
Esso 171 T 4
Essouk 196 E 2
Est, Cap 201 J 3
Estacada (OR.) 110 C 5
Estados, Isla de los 143 D 9
Eştahbanāt (Iran) 157 G 3
Estância 141 J 3
Estancia (N.M.) 117 KL 3
Estancias, Sierra de la 152 C 4
Estarreja 152 B 3
Estats, Pic dʼ 152 D 3
Estcourt 200 D 5
Este 153 F 2
Este, Punta 130 D 8
Estelí 132 E 5
Estella 152 C 3
Estelline (S.D.) 119 M 6
Estelline (TX.) 117 Q 3
Estepona 152 BC 4
Estero, Point 113 D 7
Estero Bay 113 DE 7
Estero de Agiabampo 106 E 6
Esteros 140 D 5
Esteros del Iberá 142 E 4
Estes Park (CO.) 115 M 3
Estevan (ND.) 118 F 1
Estevan (Sask., Can.) 103 R 6
Estherville (IA.) 119 O 7
Estill (S.C.) 129 K 9
Estoniya 151 J 4
Estrecho de Gibraltar 152 B 4
Estrecho de le Maire 143 CD 9–10
Estrecho de Magallanes 143 B 9
Estrecho Nelson 143 AB 9
Estreito, Rêprêsa do 141 G 4–5
Estrela, Serra da (Mato Grosso, Brazil) 141 F 4
Estrêla, Serra de (Portugal) 152 B 3
Estrella 152 C 4
Estremadura 152 B 4
Estremoz 152 B 4
Estrondo, Serra do 139 J 5
Esztergom 154 A 1
Etadunna 183 F 4
Etah 174 C 2
Étain 153 E 2
Étampes 152 D 2
Étang de Berre 153 DE 3
Étang de Biscarrosse 152 C 3
Étang de Cazaux 152 C 3
Étang de Leucate 152 D 3
Étang de Sigean 152 D 3
Étang dʼHourtin 152 C 2
Etawah 174 C 2
Etengua 200 A 3
Ethan (S.D.) 119 K 7
Ethel (MS.) 130 E 1
Ethel Creek 182 C 3
Ethel Lake 109 L 3
Ethete (WY.) 111 R 7
Ethiopia 199 FG 3
Ethiopian Plateau 199 FG 3
Ethridge (MT.) 111 N 2
Etna 153 F 4
Etna (CA.) 112 C 1
Etna (UT.) 112 LM 1
Etna (WY.) 111 P 7
Etolin 102 L 4
Etolin Strait 102 DE 3–4

Etosha National Park **200** B 3
Etosha Pan **200** B 3
Etoumbi **197** GH 6
Etowah (TN.) **128** G 6
Etter (TX.) **117** OP 1
Etykan **171** R 2
Etzná Tixmucuy **132** D 4
Eubank (KY.) **128** G 4
Euca **139** H 3
Eucla **182** D 5
Euclid (OH.) **125** N 8
Eudora (AR.) **121** O 9
Eufaula (AL.) **131** J 3
Eufaula (OK.) **121** K 7
Eufaula Dam **121** K 7
Eufaula Lake **121** K 7
Eugene (OR.) **110** B 6
Eugenia, Punta **106** C 6
Eugmo **150** H 3
Eungella National Park **183** H 3
Eunice (LA.) **123** L 5
Eunice (N.M.) **117** N 5
Euphrates **195** G 2
Euphrates (Iraq) **156** C 2
Eupora (MS.) **121** Q 9
Eura **150** H 3
Eure **152** D 2
Eureka (AK.) **109** J 3
Eureka (CA.) **112** A 2
Eureka (IL.) **124** E 9
Eureka (KS.) **120** J 5
Eureka (MT.) **111** KL 2
Eureka (NV.) **112** JK 3
Eureka (SD.) **118** J 3
Eureka (UT.) **114** E 4
Eureka (WA.) **110** G 4
Eureka Springs (AR.) **121** M 6
Europa (Réunion) **201** G 4
Europa, Picos de **152** C 3
Europa, Picos de **152** C 3
Europa, Punta de **152** B 4
Euskirchen **148** E 4
Eustis (MT.) **111** O 4–5
Eustis (NE.) **120** E 2
Euston **183** G 5
Eutaw (AL.) **130** G 2
Eutin **149** F 4
Eva **139** G 4
Eva (LA.) **123** M 4
Eva (OK.) **120** D 6
Evadale (TX.) **123** JK 5
Evans (CO.) **115** N 3
Evans, Lac **105** M 5
Evans, Mount **115** M 4
Evans Strait **103** V 3
Evanston (IL.) **124** G 7
Evanston (WY.) **111** OP 9
Evansville (IL.) **121** Q 4
Evansville (IN.) **128** D 3–4
Evansville (WI.) **124** E 7
Evansville (WY.) **118** B 8
Evant (TX.) **122** E 4
Evart (MI.) **124** J 6
Evaz (Iran) **157** F 4
Eveleth (MN.) **119** Q 3
Evenequén **139** F 3
Evening Shade (AR.) **121** O 6
Evensk **171** T 3
Everard, Lake **183** F 5
Everard Range **182** E 4
Everest (KS.) **121** K 3
Everest, Mount **174** E 2
Everett (GA.) **131** N 3
Everett (WA.) **110** C 3
Everett Mountains **105** O 3
Everglades City (FL.) **131** N 9
Everglades National Park **131** NO 9
Evergreen (AL.) **130** H 3
Evijärvi **150** H 3
Evinayong **197** FG 5
Evje **151** E 4
Évora **152** B 4
Evreux **152** D 2
Evros **154** C 2
Evstratios, Ayios **154** C 3
Evvoia **154** B 3
Evzono **154** B 2
Ewa Beach (HI.) **113** DE 10
Ewan (WA.) **110** H 3
Ewaso Ngiri **199** F 4
Ewasse **185** F 3
Ewell (MD.) **129** Q 3
Ewenkizu Zizhqi **170** L 6
Ewing (NE.) **119** K 8
Ewirgol **169** M 2
Ewo **197** GH 6
Exaltacion **140** C 3
Excelsior Mountain (CA.) **112** F 4
Excelsior Mountains (NV.) **112** G 4
Excelsior Springs (MO.) **121** L 3
Excursion Inlet **109** L 4
Exe **148** C 4
Executive Committee Range **203**
Exeland (WI.) **124** C 4
Exeter **148** C 4
Exeter (CA.) **112** FG 6
Exeter (NE.) **120** H 2
Exeter (N.H.) **126** J 5
Exeter Sound **105** P 2
Exira (IA.) **119** O 9

Exmoor **148** C 4
Exmore (VA.) **129** Q 4
Exmouth (Australia) **182** A 3
Exmouth Gulf **182** A 3
Expedition Range **183** H 3
Extremadura **152** B 4
Extremo **140** BC 3
Exum (TX.) **117** O 1
Exuma Cays **133** G 3
Exuma Sound **133** G 3
Eyakit-Tërdë **170** K 2
Eyasi, Lake **198** E 5
Eye Peninsula **148** B 3
Eygurande **152** D 2
Eyik **170** L 2
Eyjafjallajökull **150** A 3
Eyjafjörður **150** B 2
Êyl **199** H 3
Eyrarbakki **150** A 3
Eyre **182** D 5
Eyre, Lake **183** F 4
Eyre Peninsula **183** F 5
Eyre River **183** F 3
Eysturoy **148** A 1
Eyvānaki (Iran) **157** F 2
Ezequiel Ramos Mexia, Embalse **143** C 6
Ezine **154** C 3
Ezinepazari **155** E 2
Ezop, Gora **171** S 3
Ezzell (TX.) **122** G 6

F

Fabala **196** C 4
Fabens (TX.) **117** K 6
Faber Lake **103** O 3
Fåborg **151** F 4
Fabriano **153** F 3
Facatativa **138** D 3
Faceville (GA.) **131** K 4
Fachi **197** G 2
Facundo **143** B 8
Fada **197** J 2
Fada Niamtougou **196** E 3
Fāḍilī (Saudi Arabia) **157** E 4
Faenza **153** F 3
Færingehavn **105** R 3
Faeroe Islands **148** A 1
Fafa (Centr. Afr. Rep.) **198** B 3
Fafa (Mali) **196** E 2
Fafan **199** G 3
Fagita **177** H 4
Fagnano, Lago **143** C 9
Faguibine, Lac **196** D 2
Fahūd **195** K 4
Faial **192** A 1
Fairbank (AZ.) **116** F 6
Fairbanks (AK.) **102** H 3
Fairborn (OH.) **128** H 2
Fairburn (SD.) **118** E 7
Fairbury (NE.) **120** H 2
Fairchild (WI.) **124** D 5
Fairfax (AL.) **131** J 2
Fairfax (MN.) **119** O 6
Fairfax (S.C.) **129** K 9
Fairfax (SD.) **118** JK 8
Fairfax (VA.) **129** O 3
Fairfield (AL.) **128** E 8
Fairfield (CA.) **112** C 4
Fairfield (CT.) **127** F 7
Fairfield (IA.) **119** R 9
Fairfield (ID.) **111** L 7
Fairfield (IL.) **121** R 4
Fairfield (MT.) **111** N 3
Fairfield (ND.) **118** E 3
Fairfield (NE.) **120** G 2
Fairfield (TX.) **122** G 4
Fairfield (UT.) **114** E 3
Fairfield (WA.) **110** H 3
Fair Haven (VT.) **126** F 5
Fairhope (AL.) **130** G 4
Fair Isle **148** C 3
Fairland (TX.) **122** E 5
Fairmont (MN.) **119** O 7
Fairmont (W.V.) **129** L 2
Fairmount (GA.) **128** G 7
Fairmount (N.D.) **119** M 4
Fairmount (N.Y.) **126** C 5
Fair Ness **105** N 3
Fair Oaks (AR.) **121** OP 7
Fair Plain (MI.) **124** H 7
Fairplay (CO.) **115** M 4
Fairpoint (SD.) **118** F 6
Fairport (KS.) **120** F 3
Fairport (MI.) **124** H 4
Fairvalley (OK.) **120** F 6
Fairview **183** G 2
Fairview (IL.) **124** D 9
Fairview (KS.) **121** K 3
Fairview (MI.) **125** L 5
Fairview (MT.) **118** D 3
Fairview (OK.) **120** G 6
Fairview (TX.) **117** P 5

Fairview (UT.) **114** F 4
Fairview Peak **110** C 7
Fairweather, Mount **102** K 4
Faisalabad **169** J 4
Faison (N.C.) **129** N 6
Faith (SD.) **118** F 5
Faizabad (Afghanistan) **169** J 3
Faizabad (India) **174** D 2
Fajardo (P.R.) **130** D 8
Fajr, Wādī (Saudi Arabia) **156** BC 3
Fakaina **187** F 4
Fakaofo **186** D 3
Fakarava **187** F 4
Fakfak **177** H 4
Fakhr (Iran) **157** F 3
Fakse Bugt **151** F 4
Fakse Ladeplats **151** F 4
Faku **173** H 2
Falaba **196** B 4
Falagh **198** E 3
Falaise **152** CD 2
Falaise de Tiguidit **197** F 2
Falakrón Óros **154** B 2
Falam **175** F 3
Fălciu **154** C 1
Falcon (CO.) **115** N 5
Falcon (TX.) **122** D 9
Falcon, Cape **110** A 5
Falconara Marittima **153** F 3
Falcone, Punta **153** E 3
Falcon Reservoir **122** D 9
Faléa **196** B 3
Falémé **196** B 3
Faleshty **154** C 1
Falfurrias (TX.) **122** E 8
Falkenberg **151** F 4
Falkirk (ND.) **118** G 3
Falkland Islands **143** DE 9
Falkland Sound **143** DE 9
Falköping **151** F 4
Falkville (AL.) **128** E 7
Fallbrook (CA.) **113** H 9
Fall Creek (IL.) **121** O 3
Fallon (MT.) **118** C 4
Fallon (NV.) **112** G 3
Fallon Indian Reservation **112** G 3
Fall River (KS.) **120** J 5
Fall River (MA.) **126** H 7
Fall River Lake **120** J 5
Fall River Mills (CA.) **112** D 1
Falls City (NE.) **121** K 2
Falls City (OR.) **110** B 6
Falls City (TX.) **122** E 6–7
Falls Creek (PA.) **125** Q 8
Falmouth **148** B 4
Falmouth (KY.) **128** G 3
Falmouth (MA.) **126** J 7
Falmouth (ME.) **126** J 5
Falmouth (MI.) **124** J 5
Falmouth (VA.) **129** O 3
Falmouth Bay **148** BC 4
False Bay **200** B 6
False Pass **102** E 5
Falso Cabo de Hornos **143** C 10
Falster **151** F 5
Falsterbo **151** F 4
Falterona **153** F 3
Fălticeni **154** C 1
Falun **151** G 3
Famagusta **155** D 3
Famagusta (Cyprus) **156** AB 2
Famatina **142** C 4
Famatina, Sierra de **142** C 4–5
Fana **196** C 3
Fanchang **173** G 4
Fandriana **201** H 4
Fangak **198** E 3
Fangataufa **187** F 4
Fangcheng **172** F 4
Fangcheng **172** E 6
Fangliao **173** H 6
Fangshan **173** H 2
Fang Xian **172** F 4
Fangzheng **173** J 1
Fanø **151** E 4
Fano **153** F 3
Fanø Bugt **151** E 4
Fanshaw **109** M 4
Fan si Pan **175** H 3
Faraba **196** B 3
Faradje **198** D 3
Farafangana **201** H 4
Farāfirah, Wāhāt al **194** D 3
Farafra Oasis → Wāhāt al Farā- firah **194** D 3
Farah **169** G 4
Farahābad (Iran) **157** F 1
Farah Rud **169** G 4
Faranah **196** B 3
Farasān, Jazā'ir **195** G 5
Faraulep **186** A 2
Farāyid, Jabal al (Egypt) **156** B 5
Farcău, Virful **154** B 1
Fardes **152** C 4
Farewell **102** G 3
Farewell, Cape **185** Q 9

Farewell, Cape **186** C 5
Fargo (GA.) **131** M 4
Fargo (N.D.) **119** M 4
Fargo (OK.) **120** F 6
Faribault (MN.) **119** P 6
Faribault, Lac **105** N 4
Faridabad **174** C 2
Faridpur **174** E 3
Färigh, Wādī **193** K 2
Farim **196** A 3
Fāris (Egypt) **156** A 4
Farkhato **169** HJ 3
Farkwa **199** F 6
Faro **139** G 4
Fårö **151** G 4
Faro (Cameroon) **197** G 4
Faro (N.W.T., Can.) **102** L 3
Faro (Portugal) **152** B 4
Faro, Sierra del **152** B 3
Faro National Park **197** G 4
Fårösund **151** G 4
Farquhar, Cape **182** A 3
Farquhar Group **199** J 6
Farrar **148** BC 3
Farrars Creek **183** G 3
Farrāshband (Iran) **157** F 3
Färs (Iran) **157** F 3
Fārsī (Iran) **157** F 4
Farsö **151** E 4
Farson (WY.) **111** Q 8
Farsund **151** E 4
Fartak, Ra's **195** J 5
Farthing (WY.) **118** C 9
Farwell (MI.) **125** K 6
Farwell (TX.) **117** O 3
Fasā (Iran) **157** F 3
Fasad **195** J 5
Fasano **153** G 3
Fastov **158** E 5
Fataka **185** J 4
Fataka **186** C 3
Fatehabad **174** C 2
Fatehgarh **174** CD 2
Fatehpur **174** D 2
Fath (United Arab Emirates) **157** G 4
Father Lake **105** MN 6
Fatick **196** A 3
Fatsa **155** E 2
Fatu Hiva **187** F 3
Fatu Hutu **187** F 3
Fatunda **198** B 5
Faulkton (SD.) **118** JK 5
Făurei **154** C 1
Fauro **185** G 3
Fauske **150** G 2
Faust (UT.) **114** E 3
Faux Cap **201** H 5
Faya-Largeau **197** H 2
Fayd (Saudi Arabia) **156** D 4
Fayette (AL.) **128** D 8
Fayette (IA.) **119** R 8
Fayette (MO.) **121** N 3
Fayette (MS.) **130** C 3
Fayette (OH.) **125** K 8
Fayetteville (AR.) **121** L 6
Fayetteville (GA.) **128** G 8
Fayetteville (N.C.) **129** N 6
Fayetteville (N.Y.) **126** D 5
Fayetteville (TN.) **128** E 6
Fayetteville (TX.) **122** G 6
Fayetteville (W.V.) **129** K 3
Faylakah (Kuwait) **157** E 3
Faysh Khābur (Iraq) **156** D 1
Faysville (TX.) **122** E 9
Fayu **186** B 2
Faywood (N.M.) **116** HJ 5
Fazeï **197** G 2
Fazilka **174** B 1
Fazrān (Saudi Arabia) **157** E 4
Fdérik **192** C 4
Fear, Cape **129** O 8

Feather Falls (CA.) **112** D 3
Feathertop, Mount **183** H 6
Featherville (ID.) **111** K 7
Fécamp **152** D 2
Federación **142** E 5
Federal (WY.) **118** CD 9
Federal Republic of Germany **149** E 4
Federalsburg (MD.) **129** PQ 3
Federated States of Micronesia **186** AB 2
Fedorovka **159** M 5
Fehmarn **149** F 4
Feicheng **173** G 3
Feijó **138** D 5
Feira **201** E 3
Feira de Santana **141** J 3
Feixiang **172** FG 3
Feke **155** E 3
Feklistova, Ostrov **171** P 4–5
Felanitx **152** D 4
Felch (MI.) **124** G 4
Felda (FL.) **131** N 8
Feldbach **153** G 2
Feldberg **149** E 5
Feldkirch **153** E 2
Felipe Carrillo Puerto **132** E 4
Felix, Cape **103** S 2
Felixlândia **141** H 4
Felixstowe **148** D 4
Fellsburg (KS.) **120** F 5
Fellsmere (FL.) **131** O 7
Felt (ID.) **111** O 7
Felt (OK.) **120** C 6
Feltre **153** F 2
Femer Bælt **151** F 5
Femund **150** FG 3
Fenaroa **199** F 2
Fence Lake (N.M.) **116** H 3
Fener Burnu **155** E 2
Fengcheng **173** H 2
Fengcheng **172** FG 3
Fengdu **172** E 5
Fenghuang **172** E 5
Fengjie **172** E 4
Fengning **173** G 2
Fengqing **172** CD 6
Fengqiu **172** F 3
Fengrun **173** G 2
Fengshuba Shuiku **172** G 6
Fengshui Shan **171** M 5
Fengtai **173** G 4
Feng Xian **172** E 4
Feng Xian **173** G 4
Fengxiang **172** E 4
Fengxin **172** G 5
Fengzhen **172** F 2
Fen He **172** F 3
Feni Islands **185** F 2
Feni Islands **186** B 3
Fenner (CA.) **113** K 8
Fennimore (WI.) **124** D 7
Fennville (MI.) **124** H 7
Fenoarivo Atsinanana **201** HJ 3
Fensfjorden **150** DE 2
Fentani, Monti dei **153** FG 3
Fenton (MI.) **125** L 7
Fentress (TX.) **122** F 6
Fenxi **172** F 3
Fenyang **172** F 3
Fenyi **172** F 5
Feodora (TX.) **117** O 7
Feodosiya **155** E 1
Fer, Cap de **193** G 1
Ferdows **168** F 4
Fereidoon (Iran) **157** EF 3
Feren **150** F 3
Ferfer **199** H 3
Fergana **169** J 2
Ferganskiy Khrebet **169** J 2
Fergus (MT.) **111** Q 3
Fergus Falls (MN.) **119** MN 5
Ferguson Lake **103** Q 2
Fergusson **185** F 3
Fergusson River **182** E 1
Ferjukot **150** A 3
Ferkéssédougou **196** C 4
Ferlo **199** F 3
Fermo **153** F 3
Fermoselle **152** B 3
Fernandina, **138** B 3
Fernandina Beach (FL.) **131** N 4
Fernando de la Mora **142** E 4
Fernando de Noronha Island **135** G 3
Fernandópolis **141** FG 5
Fernando Póo → Bioko **197** F 5
Ferndale (CA.) **112** A 2
Ferney (S.D.) **119** K 5
Fernley (NV.) **112** F 3
Fern Ridge Lake **110** B 6
Fernwood (ID.) **110** J 3
Ferrara **153** F 3
Ferreira Gomes **139** H 3
Ferrelo, Cape **110** A 8
Ferrenafe **138** C 5
Ferret, Cap **152** C 3
Ferriday (LA.) **123** M 4
Ferris (TX.) **122** G 3
Ferron (UT.) **114** FG 4
Ferrysburg (MI.) **124** H 6
Fertile (MN.) **119** M 3

Fertilia 153 E 3
Fès 192 E 2
Feshi 198 B 6
Fessenden (ND.) 118 J 3
Festus (MO.) 121 P 4
Feteşti 154 C 2
Fethiye 154 C 3
Fethıye Körfezi 154 C 3
Fetisovo 168 E 2
Fetlar 148 C 2
Feuilles, Baie aux 105 O 4
Feuilles, Rivière aux 105 N 4
Fezzan 193 HJ 3
Fiambalá 142 C 4
Fianarantsoa 201 H 4
Fianga 197 H 4
Fich 199 G 3
Fiche 199 F 3
Fichtelgebirge 149 F 4
Ficksburg 200 D 5
Fidenza 153 E 3
Field (KY.) 128 H 5
Fields Landing (CA.) 112 A 2
Fier 154 A 2
Fierras 150 G 2
Fiery Cross Reef 176 D 2
Fife Lake (MI.) 124 J 5
Fife Ness 148 C 3
Fifield (WI.) 124 D 4
Fifth Cataract → Ash Shallāl al Khamis 194 E 5
Figeac 152 D 3
Figtree 200 D 4
Figueira, Cachoeira 139 G 5
Figueira da Foz 152 B 3
Figueras 152 D 3
Figuig 192 E 2
Fiji 186 C 4
Fiji Islands 186 C 4
Filadélfia 139 J 5
Filadélfia (Paraguay) 140 D 5
Filchner Ice Shelf 203
Filer (ID.) 111 L 8
Filiaşi 154 B 2
Filicudi 153 F 4
Filingué 196 E 3
Filipstad 151 F 4
Fillmore (CA.) 113 G 8
Fillmore (ND.) 118 J 2
Fillmore (UT.) 114 E 5
Filtu 199 G 3
Fimbul Ice Shelf 203
Fimi 198 B 5
Fin (Iran) 157 F 2
Fındık 155 F 3
Findlay (IL.) 121 R 3
Findlay (OH.) 125 L 8
Fine (N.Y.) 126 D 4
Fingal (N.D.) 119 L 4
Fingoè 201 E 3
Finike 154 D 3
Finisterre, Cabo de 152 B 3
Finke 182 E 3
Finke, Mount 182 E 5
Finke Flood Flats River 183 F 4
Finke Gorge National Park 182 E 3
Finke River 182 E 4
Finland 150 J 3
Finland, Gulf of 151 HJ 4
Finlay 103 MN 4
Finlay Forks 103 N 4
Finley 183 H 6
Finley (OK.) 121 K 8
Finnie Bay 105 M 2
Finniss, Cape 182 E 5
Finnmark 150 H 2
Finnmarksvidda 150 H 2
Finn Mountain 108 G 3
Finnskogen 151 F 3
Finnsnes 150 G 2
Finnveden 151 F 4
Fins 195 K 4
Finspång 151 G 4
Finsterwalde 149 F 4
Fiordland National Park 184 P 9–10
Fırat 155 E 3
Firebaugh (CA.) 112 E 6
Fire Island 127 G 8
Firenze 153 F 3
Firesteel (SD.) 118 G 5
Firghia 196 B 3
Firmat 142 D 4
Firminy 152 D 2
Firovo 158 F 4
Firozabad 174 C 2
Firozpur 174 BC 1
First Cataract → Sadd al Aswān 194 E 4
Firth of Clyde 148 BC 3
Firth of Forth 148 C 3
Firth of Lorn 148 B 3
Firth River 109 K 2
Firūzābād (Iran) 157 E 2
Firūzābād (Iran) 157 G 2
Firūzābād (Iran) 157 F 2
Firūz Kūh (Iran) 157 F 2
Fischersbrunn 200 A 4
Fishers Island 127 H 7

Fishers Peak 115 N 6
Fisher Strait 103 V 3
Fishguard 148 BC 4
Fishing Creek (MD.) 129 P 3
Fish Lake 114 F 5
Fish Lake Reservoir 119 Q 4
Fish River 183 F 2
Fish River (South Africa) 200 C 6
Fisht, Gora 155 E 2
Fiskåfjället 150 F 3
Fiskárdhon 154 B 3
Fiskenæsset 105 R 3
Fitchburg (MA.) 126 H 6
Fith (ID.) 111 N 7
Fitri, Lac 197 H 3
Fitzcarrald 140 B 3
Fitzgerald (Alberta, Can.) 103 P 4
Fitzgerald (GA.) 131 L 3
Fitzgerald River National Park 182 B 5
Fitz Roy 143 C 8
Fitz Roy, Monte 143 B 8
Fitzroy Crossing 182 D 2
Fitzroy River (Queensland, Austr.) 183 J 3
Fitzroy River (Western Australia) 182 C 2
Fiumicino 153 F 3
Fivizzano 153 EF 3
Fizi 198 D 5
Fiziuli 168 D 3
Fjällbacka 151 F 4
Fjällfjällen 150 F 2
Fkih Ben Salah 192 D 2
Flacq 201 K 6
Flagler (CO.) 115 OP 4
Flagler Beach (FL.) 131 N 5
Flagstaff (AZ.) 116 E 2
Flagstaff Lake 126 J 3
Flambeau River 124 D 4
Flamenco (Argentina) 143 D 7
Flamenco (Chile) 142 B 4
Flamenco, Isla 143 D 7
Flaming Gorge Dam 114 H 3
Flaming Gorge Reservoir 111 Q 9
Flamingo (FL.) 131 O 9
Flanders 148 D 4
Flandreau (S.D.) 119 M 6
Flanigan (NV.) 112 F 2
Flannan Isles 148 B 3
Flasher (N.D.) 118 G 4
Flåsjön 150 G 3
Flat 102 F 3
Flatey 150 A 2
Flateyri 150 A 2
Flathead Indian Reservation 111 L 3
Flathead Lake 111 M 3
Flathead River 111 L 2
Flat Island 176 E 1
Flatonia (TX.) 122 F 6
Flat River (MO.) 121 P 5
Flat Rock (MI.) 125 L 7
Flats (NE.) 118 G 9
Flattery, Cape 110 A 2
Flattery, Cape (Queensland, Austr.) 183 H 1
Flat Top Mountain 114 E 3
Flat Tops 115 K 3–4
Flatwillow (MT.) 111 R 4
Flat Woods (TN.) 128 D 6
Flaxton (N.D.) 118 F 2
Flaxville (MT.) 118 D 2
Fleetwood (Queensland, Austr.) 183 H 3
Fleetwood (U.K.) 148 C 4
Flekkefjord 151 E 4
Fleming (CO.) 115 P 3
Flemingsburg (KY.) 128 H 3
Flen 151 G 4
Flensburg 149 E 4
Flers 152 C 2
Flesberg 151 E 4
Fletcher (N.C.) 128 J 6
Fletcher (OK.) 120 G 8
Fleurance 152 D 3
Flevoland 148 E 4
Flinders 184 L 8
Flinders Bay 182 B 5
Flinders Chase National Park 183 F 6
Flinders Island 183 H 6
Flinders Passage 183 H 2
Flinders Range 183 F 5
Flinders Ranges National Park 183 F 5
Flinders Reefs 183 H 2
Flinders River 183 G 2
Flin Flon 103 R 5
Flint (Kiribati) 187 E 3
Flint (MI.) 125 L 6
Flint Creek Range 111 M 4
Flint Hills 120 J 4–5
Flinton 183 H 4
Flint River 131 K 3
Flippin (AR.) 121 N 6
Flisa 151 F 3
Flisegga 151 E 4
Flomaton (AL.) 130 E 4
Flomot (TX.) 117 PQ 3
Floodwood (MN.) 119 PQ 4
Flora 150 E 3
Flora (IL.) 121 R 4
Flora (OR.) 110 H 5
Florac 152 D 3

Florala (AL.) 131 H 3–4
Floral City (FL.) 131 M 6
Floraville (Queensland, Austr.) 183 F 2
Flora Vista (N.M.) 116 H 1
Florence (AL.) 128 D 7
Florence (AZ.) 116 E 4
Florence (CO.) 115 MN 5
Florence (Italy) 153 F 3
Florence (KS.) 120 HJ 4
Florence (KY.) 128 G 2–3
Florence (MS.) 130 D 2
Florence (MT.) 111 LM 4
Florence (OR.) 110 A 7
Florence (S.C.) 129 M 7
Florence (S.D.) 119 L 5
Florence (TX.) 122 F 5
Florence (WI.) 124 F 4
Florence Junction (AZ.) 116 E 4
Florencia 138 C 3
Florentino Ameghino 143 C 7
Florentino Ameghino, Embalse 143 C 7
Flores (AZ.) 116 D 3
Flores (Azores) 192 A 1
Flores (Guatemala) 132 E 4
Flores (Indonesia) 177 F 5
Flores, Laut 177 E 5
Flores Sea 177 E 5
Floresta (AL.) 130 Q 4
Floresville (TX.) 122 E 6
Florey (TX.) 117 O 5
Floriano 141 H 2
Floriano Pleixoto 138 E 5
Florianópolis 142 G 4
Florida 131
Florida (Cuba) 133 G 3
Florida (N.M.) 116 J 5
Florida (Uruguay) 142 E 5
Floridablanca 138 D 2
Florida City (FL.) 131 O 9
Florida Islands 185 GH 3
Florida Keys 131 NO 10
Florien (LA.) 123 K 4
Flórina 154 B 2
Flórissant (MO.) 121 P 4
Florissant National Monument 115 M 5
Flowell (UT.) 114 E 5
Floyd (N.M.) 117 N 3
Floyd (VA.) 129 L 5
Floydada (TX.) 117 P 3–4
Floyd River 119 M 8
Fluk 177 G 4
Flumendosa 153 E 4
Flying Fish Cove 176 C 6
Flying H (N.M.) 117 L 4
Fly River 184 D 3
Foard City (TX.) 122 D 2
Foča 153 G 3
Fochi 197 H 2
Fochimi 197 H 2
Foci del Po 153 F 2–3
Focşani 154 C 1
Foggara ez Zoua 193 F 3
Foggia 153 G 3
Foggo 197 G 3
Foggy Island Bay 109 J 1
Fogo 185 R 6
Fogo (N.Y.) 121 M 6
Fogo (Cape Verde) 196 B 7
Fohnsdorf 153 F 2
Foix 152 D 3
Fokku 197 E 3
Folakara 201 H 3
Folda 150 F 2
Folégandros 154 B 3
Foley (AL.) 130 G 4
Foley (Botswana) 200 D 4
Foley (MN.) 119 P 5
Foley (N.W.T., Can.) 105 M 2
Foleyet 104 L 6
Folgefonni 151 E 3–4
Foligno 153 F 3
Folkestone 148 D 4
Folkston (GA.) 131 M 4
Folldal 150 EF 3
Follett (TX.) 117 Q 1
Folly Beach (S.C.) 129 M 9
Folsom (LA.) 123 N 5
Folsom (N.M.) 117 N 1
Folsom Lake 112 D 4
Fomboni 201 G 2
Fomich 170 J 1
Fomin 155 F 1
Fonda (IA.) 119 O 8
Fonda (N.Y.) 126 F 6
Fond du-Lac (Sask., Can.) 103 Q 4
Fond du Lac (Sask., Can.) 103 QR 4
Fond du Lac (WI.) 124 F 6
Fongen 150 F 3
Fonseca, Golfo de 132 E 5
Fontainebleau 152 D 2
Fontana Lake 128 H 6
Fontana Village (NC.) 128 H 6
Fontas 103 N 4
Fonte Boa 138 E 4
Fonte do Pau-d'Agua 140 E 3
Fontenay-le-Comte 152 C 2
Fontenelle (WY.) 111 Q 9
Fontenelle Reservoir 111 P 8
Fontur 150 C 2
Fonualei 186 D 4

Foraker (OK.) 120 J 6
Foraker, Mount 102 G 3
Forbes 183 H 5
Forbes (ND.) 118 K 5
Forbestown (CA.) 112 D 3
Forcados 197 F 4
Ford (KS.) 120 F 5
Ford (WA.) 110 H 3
Ford City (CA.) 113 F 7
Ford City (PA.) 125 P 9
Ford Dry Lake 113 L 9
Förde 150 E 3
Fördefjorden 150 DE 3
Fords Prairie (WA.) 110 B 4
Fordville (N.D.) 119 KL 2
Fordyce (AR.) 121 N 9
Forecariah 196 B 4
Forest (MS.) 130 E 2
Forest City (IA.) 119 P 7
Forest City (N.C.) 129 K 6
Forest City (PA.) 126 D 7
Forest Grove (OR.) 110 B 5
Foresthill (CA.) 112 E 3
Forest Hill (LA.) 123 L 4
Forest Lake (MN.) 119 PQ 5
Forest Park (GA.) 128 G 8
Forest Ranch (CA.) 112 D 3
Forest River (N.D.) 119 L 2
Forestville (Quebec, Can.) 105 O 6
Forestville (WI.) 124 G 5
Forêt d'Ecouves (CA.) 152 C 2
Forez, Plaine du 152 D 2
Forgan (OK.) 120 E 6
Forín Linares 140 D 5
Forkas 196 E 3
Fork Mountain (TN.) 128 G 5
Forks (WA.) 110 A 3
Forli 153 F 3
Forman (N.D.) 119 L 4
Formentera 152 D 4
Formentor, Cabo de 152 D 3–4
Formia 153 F 3
Formigas 192 A 1
Formosa (Goiás, Brazil) 141 G 4
Formosa (Taiwan) 173 H 6
Formosa, Serra 141 E 3
Formosa do Rio Prêto 141 G 3
Formosa Strait 173 GH 5–6
Formosa Strait → Taiwan Haixia 173 GH 5–6
Formoso 141 G 3
Formoso (Argentina) 142 E 4
Fornæs 151 F 4
Foroyar 148 A 1
Forrest 182 D 5
Forrest (IL.) 124 F 9
Forrest City (AR.) 121 P 7–8
Forsayth 183 G 2
Forshaga 151 F 4
Forsmark 151 G 3
Forsnäs 150 G 2
Forssa 151 H 3
Forst 149 F 4
Forsyth (GA.) 128 H 8
Forsyth (MO.) 121 M 6
Forsyth (MT.) 118 B 4
Fort Adams (MS.) 130 C 3
Fort Albany 105 L 5
Fortaleza (Ceará, Brazil) 141 J 1
Fortaleza (Pará, Brazil) 139 G 5
Fortaleza de Ituxi 138 E 5
Fortaleza de Santa Teresa 142 F 5
Fort Apache Indian Reservation 116 FG 4
Fort Archambault → Sarh 197 H 4
Fort Assiniboine 103 OP 5
Fort Atkinson (WI.) 124 F 7
Fort Augustus 148 C 3
Fort Basinger (FL.) 131 NO 7
Fort Beaufort 200 D 6
Fort Belknap Agency (MT.) 111 QR 2
Fort Belknap Indian Reservation 111 R 2
Fort Belvoir (VA.) 129 O 3
Fort Benjamin Harrison (IN.) 128 E 2
Fort Benning (GA.) 128 F 8
Fort Benton (MT.) 111 P 3
Fort Berthold Indian eservation 118 F 3
Fort Bidwell Indian Reservation 112 E 1
Fort Black 103 Q 4
Fort Bliss (TX.) 117 K 6
Fort Bragg (CA.) 112 B 3
Fort Bragg (N.C.) 129 MN 6
Fort Branch (IN.) 128 D 3
Fort Bridger (WY.) 111 P 9
Fort Brussaux → Markounda 198 B 3
Fort-Carnot 201 H 4
Fort Chadnourne (TX.) 122 E 4
Fort Charlet → Djanet 193 G 4
Fort Chimo 105 O 4
Fort Chipewyan 103 P 4
Fort Clark (N.D.) 118 G 3
Fort Cobb (OK.) 120 G 7
Fort Cobb Reservoir 120 G 7
Fort Collins (CO.) 115 M 3
Fort Collinson 103 O 1
Fort Covington (N.Y.) 126 E 4
Fort Davis (TX.) 117 N 7
Fort-de-France 133 K 5

Fort de Polignac → Illizi 193 G 3
Fort Dodge (IA.) 119 O 8
Fort Douglas (AR.) 121 M 7
Fort Drum (FL.) 131 O 7
Fort Duchesne (UT.) 114 H 3
Fortescue River 182 B 3
Fort Eustis (VA.) 129 P 4
Fort Flatters → Bordj Omar Driss 193 G 3
Fort Foureau → Kousseri 197 G 3
Fort Frances 104 J 6
Fort Franklin 103 N 2
Fort Fredericia National Monument 131 N 3
Fort Gaines (GA.) 131 JK 3
Fort Gardel → Zaouatallaz 193 G 4
Fort Garland (CO.) 115 M 6
Fort Gay (W.V.) 128 J 3
Fort George 105 M 5
Fort Gibson (OK.) 121 K 7
Fort Gibson Dam 121 K 7
Fort Gibson Lake 121 K 7
Fort Good Hope 102 M 2
Fort Gordon (GA.) 129 J 8
Fort Gouraud → Fdérik 192 C 4
Fort Griffin (TX.) 122 D 3
Forth, Firth of 148 C 3
Fort Hall (ID.) 111 N 7
Fort Hall Indian Reservation 111 N 7–8
Fort Hancock (TX.) 117 L 6
Fort Hood (TX.) 122 F 4
Fort Hope 104 K 5
Fortification Hill 116 B 1
Fortín Carlos Antonio López 140 E 5
Fortín Coronel Eugenio Garay 140 D 5
Fortine (MT.) 111 L 2
Fortín Falcon 140 E 5
Fortín Galpón 140 E 4
Fortín General Aquino 140 E 5
Fortín General Pando 140 E 4
Fortín Ingavi 140 E 4
Fortín Lavalle 142 D 4
Fortín Madrejón 140 E 5
Fortín Madrejoncito 140 E 5
Fortín Ravelo 140 D 4
Fortín Rojas Silva 140 E 5
Fortín Suárez Arana 140 DE 4
Fortín Uno 143 C 6
Fort Jackson (S.C.) 129 L 7
Fort Jefferson National Monument 131 M 10
Fort Jones (CA.) 112 C 1
Fort Kent (ME.) 126 L 1
Fort Kent (Quebec, Can.) 105 O 6
Fort Klamath (OR.) 110 C 8
Fort Knox (KY.) 128 F 4
Fort Lamy → N'Djamena 197 H 3
Fort Laperrine → Tamanrasset 193 G 4
Fort Laramie (WY.) 118 D 8
Fort Lauderdale (FL.) 131 OP 8
Fort Leavenworth (KS.) 121 L 3
Fort Lee (VA.) 129 O 4
Fort Leonard Wood (MO.) 121 N 5
Fort Liard 103 N 3
Fort Loudon Lake 128 G 6
Fort Lupton (CO.) 115 N 3
Fort Mackay 103 P 4
Fort Macleod 103 P 6
Fort Madison (IA.) 119 R 10
Fort Matanzas National Monument 131 N 5
Fort McClellan (AL.) 128 F 8
Fort McDermitt Indian Reservation 112 G 1
Fort McDowell Indian Reservation 116 E 4
Fort McMahon → El Homr 193 F 3
Fort McMurray 103 P 4
Fort McPherson (GA.) 128 G 8
Fort McPherson (N.W.T., Can.) 102 L 2
Fort Meade (FL.) 131 N 7
Fort Meade (MD.) 129 P 2
Fort Miribel 193 F 3
Fort Mohave Indian Reservation 116 B 1
Fort Monmouth (N.J.) 127 EF 8
Fort Morgan (AL.) 130 FG 4
Fort Morgan (CO.) 115 O 3
Fort Motylinski → Tarahouahout 193 G 4
Fort Myers (FL.) 131 N 8
Fort Myers Beach (FL.) 131 N 8
Fort Nelson (Br. Col., Can.) 103 N 3
Fort Nelson (Br. Col., Can.) 103 N 4
Fort Norman 109 NO 3
Fort Ogden (FL.) 131 N 7
Fort Ord (CA.) 112 D 6
Fort Payne (AL.) 128 F 7
Fort Peck Dam 118 B 3
Fort Peck Indian Reservation 118 C 2
Fort Peck Lake 118 B 3
Fort Phantom Hill, Lake 112 D 3
Fort Pierce (FL.) 131 O 7
Fort Pierre (SD.) 118 H 6
Fort Plain (N.Y.) 126 E 6
Fort Polk (LA.) 123 K 4
Fort Portal 198 DE 4
Fort Providence 103 O 3
Fort Pulaski National Monument 131 O 2–3

Fort Qu'Appelle 103 R 5
Fort Randall Dam 119 K 7
Fort Ransom (N.D.) 119 L 4
Fort Resolution 103 OP 3
Fortress Mountain 111 Q 6
Fort Ripley (MN.) 119 O 4
Fort Ritchie (MD.) 129 O 2
Fort Robinson (NE.) 118 E 8
Fort Rucker (AL.) 131 J 3
Fort Rupert 105 M 5
Fort Saint James 103 N 5
Fort Saint John 103 N 4
Fort Saskatchewan 103 P 5
Fort Scott (KS.) 121 L 5
Fort Severn 104 K 4
Fort Sheridan (IL.) 124 G 7
Fort Shevchenko 168 E 2
Fort Simpson 103 N 3
Fort Smith (Alb., Can.) 103 P 4
Fort Smith (AR.) 121 L 7
Fort Stewart (GA.) 131 N 3
Fort Still (OK.) 120 G 8
Fort Stockton (TX.) 117 O 7
Fort Sumner (N.M.) 117 M 3
Fort Supply (OK.) 120 F 6
Fort Supply Lake 120 F 6
Fort Thompson (SD.) 118 J 6
Fort Totten (ND.) 118 J 3
Fort Totten Indian Reservation
  118 JK 3
Fortuna (ND.) 118 E 2
Fortune Bay 105 Q 6
Fort Union National Monument 117 L 2
Fort Valley (GA.) 131 L 2
Fort Vermilion 103 O 4
Fort Victoria → Masvingo 201 E 4
Fort Walton Beach (FL.) 131 H 4
Fort Washakie (WY.) 111 QR 7
Fort Wayne (IN.) 124 J 8
Fort Wellington 139 G 2
Fort White(FL.) 131 M 5
Fort William 148 C 3
Fort Wolters (TX.) 122 E 3
Fort Worth (TX.) 122 F 3
Fort Yates (ND.) 118 H 4
Fort Yukon 102 J 2
Fort Yuma Indian Reservation 113 L 10
Forūr (Iran) 157 G 4
Forveaux Strait 186 C 6
Foshan 172 F 6
Fosna 150 F 3
Foso 196 D 4
Fossano 153 E 3
Fossil (OR.) 110 E 5
Fossil Bluff 203
Fossil Butte National Monument
  111 P 9
Fossil Lake 110 E 7
Foss Reservoir 120 F 7
Fosston (MN.) 119 N 3
Foster 183 H 6
Foster (MT.) 111 S 5
Foster, Mount 102 K 4
Foster Lake 110 F 8
Fosters (AL.) 128 D 8
Fostoria (OH.) 125 L 8
Fougamou 197 G 6
Fougères 152 C 2
Foula 148 C 2
Fouladou 196 AB 3
Foulalaba 196 C 3
Foula Morie 196 B 3
Foul Bay → Khalīj Foul 194 F 4
Foulwind, Cape 185 Q 9
Foumban 197 G 4
Foum el Hassan 192 D 3
Foum Zguid 192 D 2
Found du Lac Indian Reservation
  119 Q 4
Foundiougne 196 A 3
Fountain (CO.) 115 N 5
Fountain (FL.) 131 J 4
Fountain (MI.) 124 H 5
Fountain City (WI.) 124 C 5
Fountain Green (UT.) 114 F 4
Fountain Peak 113 K 8
Four Buttes (MT.) 118 BC 2
Four Corners (WY.) 118 D 6
Fourmies 152 D 1
Four Mountains, Islands of 102 CD 5
Four Peaks 116 E 4
Fourteen Mile Point 124 E 2–3
Fourth Cataract → Ash Shallāl ar Rābi'
  194 E 5
Four Town (MN.) 119 N 2
Fourway (TX.) 117 OP 2
Fouta Djallon 196 B 3
Fouta Ferlo 196 B 2
Foveaux Strait 184 P 10
Fowler (CA.) 112 F 6
Fowler (CO.) 115 N 5
Fowler (IN.) 124 G 9
Fowler (KS.) 120 E 5
Fowlers Bay 182 E 5
Fowlers Bay 182 E 5
Fowlerton (TX.) 122 E 7
Fowlerville (MI.) 125 L 7
Fowlkes (TN.) 128 B 6
Fowlstown (GA.) 131 K 4

Fowman 168 D 3
Fox (OR.) 110 F 6
Foxe Basin 103 VW 2
Foxe Channel 105 M 3
Foxe Peninsula 105 M 3
Fox Islands 102 D 5
Fox Lake (IL.) 124 F 7
Fox Mountain 109 M 3
Foxpark (WY.) 118 B 9
Fox River 124 F 8
Foxworth (MS.) 130 E 3
Foz do Breu 138 D 5
Foz do Copeá 139 F 4
Foz do Cunene 200 A 3
Foz do Gregório 138 D 5
Foz do Iguaçu 142 F 4
Foz do Jordão 138 D 5
Foz do Jutaí 138 E 4
Foz Tarauacá 138 E 5
Fraga 152 D 3
Franca 141 G 5
France 152 CD 2
Frances 102 M 3
Francés, Cabo 132 F 3
Frances, Lake 111 N 2
Franceville 197 G 6
Francis (UT.) 114 F 3
Francis Case, Lake 118 J 7
Francisco de Orellana (Ecuador)
  138 C 4
Francisco Escárcega 132 D 4
Francistown 200 D 4
Francofonte 153 FG 4
Francs Peak 111 Q 7
Frankenberg 149 E 4
Frankewing (TN.) 128 E 6
Frankfort (IN.) 124 H 9
Frankfort (KY.) 128 G 3
Frankfort (MI.) 124 H 5
Frankfort (NE.) 120 J 3
Frankfort (S.D.) 119 K 6
Frankfurt am Main 149 E 4
Frankfurt an der Oder 149 F 4
Franklin (AZ.) 116 G 5
Franklin (GA.) 128 F 8
Franklin (ID.) 111 O 8
Franklin (IN.) 128 E 2
Franklin (KY.) 128 E 5
Franklin (LA.) 123 M 6
Franklin (MT.) 111 Q 4
Franklin (NE.) 120 G 2
Franklin (N.H.) 126 H 5
Franklin (N.J.) 127 E 7
Franklin (OH.) 128 G 2
Franklin (PA.) 125 P 8
Franklin (TX.) 122 G 4
Franklin (VA.) 129 P 5
Franklin (WI.) 124 F 7
Franklin (W.V.) 129 M 3
Franklin Bay 103 M 1–2
Franklin Delano Roosevelt Lake
  110 G 2
Franklin Lake (NV.) 112 K 2
Franklin Lake (N.W.T., Can.) 103 S 2
Franklin Mountains 103 MN 2–3
Franklin Strait 103 S 1
Franklinton (LA.) 123 N 5
Franklinville (N.Y.) 125 Q 7
Franks Peak 111 Q 7
Frankston (TX.) 123 H 3
Frannie (WY.) 111 R 6
Fransfontein 200 A 4
Fransfontein Mountains 200 B 4
Fransisco de Orellana (Peru) 138 D 4
Franz 104 L 6
Franz Josef Land 202
Fraser 103 N 5
Fraser, Mount 182 B 4
Fraserburg (South Africa) 200 C 6
Fraserburgh (U.K.) 148 C 3
Fraserdale 105 L 6
Fraser or Great Sandy Island 183 J 4
Fraser Plateau 103 N 5
Fraser Range 182 C 5
Frauenfeld 153 E 2
Fray Bentos 142 E 5
Frazee (MN.) 119 N 4
Frazer (MT.) 118 B 2
Frederic (MI.) 125 K 5
Frederic (WI.) 124 B 4
Fredericia 151 EF 4
Frederick (MD.) 129 O 2
Frederick (OK.) 120 FG 8
Frederick (S.D.) 119 K 5
Frederick Hills 182 F 1
Frederick Reef 183 J 3
Fredericksburg (TX.) 122 E 5
Fredericksburg (VA.) 129 O 3
Fredericktown (MO.) 121 P 5
Fredericktown (OH.) 125 M 9
Fredericton 105 O 6
Frederik IX-Land 105 R 2
Frederiksdal 105 S 3
Frederikshåb 105 R 3
Frederikshavn 151 F 4
Frederikssund 151 F 4
Frederiksted 130 E 9
Frederiksted 133 J 4
Frederik VI-Coast 202
Fredônia 138 C 2

Fredonia (AZ.) 116 D 1
Fredonia (KY.) 128 C 4
Fredonia (ND.) 118 J 4
Fredonia (N.Y.) 125 P 7
Fredrika 150 G 3
Fredrikshamn 151 J 3
Fredrikstad 151 F 4
Fredvang 150 F 2
Freeburg (IL.) 121 Q 4
Freeburg (MO.) 121 O 4
Freedom (WY.) 111 P 8
Freehold (N.J.) 127 E 8
Freeland (MI.) 125 K 6
Freeling Heights 183 F 5
Freel Peak 112 F 4
Freels, Cape 105 R 6
Freeman (S.D.) 119 L 7
Freeman (WA.) 110 H 3
Freemont (MI.) 124 H 6
Freeport (FL.) 131 H 4
Freeport (IL.) 124 E 7
Freeport (TX.) 123 H 7
Freeport City 133 G 2
Freer (TX.) 122 E 8
Freetown 196 B 4
Freezeout Lake 111 N 3
Fréhel, Cap 152 C 2
Freiberg 149 F 4
Freiburg 149 E 5
Freilassing 149 F 5
Freirina 142 B 4
Freising 149 F 5
Freistadt 153 F 2
Freital 149 F 4
Fréjus 153 E 3
Fremantle 182 B 5
Fremont (CA.) 112 D 5
Fremont (IA.) 119 Q 9
Fremont (N.C.) 129 O 6
Fremont (NE.) 120 J 1
Fremont (OH.) 125 L 8
Fremont (WI.) 124 E 5
Fremount Island 114 E 2
French Broad River 128 H 6
Frenchburg (KY.) 128 H 4
French Camp (MS.) 121 Q 9
Frenchglen (OR.) 110 FG 8
French Guiana 139 H 3
French Lick (IN.) 128 E 3
Frenchman (NV.) 112 G 3
Frenchman (Sask., Can.) 103 Q 6
Frenchman Creek (MT.) 111 S 2
Frenchman Creek (NE.) 120 D 2
Frenchman Flat 112 JK 6
Frenchman Lake (CA.) 112 E 3
Frenchman Lake (NV.) 112 K 6
French Polynesia 187 F 4
Frenchtown (MT.) 111 L 3
Frenda 193 F 1
Frenier (LA.) 123 N 5
Fresco 139 H 5
Fresco (Ivory Coast) 196 C 5
Fresia 143 B 7
Fresnillo 132 B 3
Fresno (CA.) 112 F 6
Fresno (MT.) 111 Q 2
Fresno Reservoir 111 Q 2
Freu, Cabo 152 D 4
Frewen (WY.) 111 R 9
Frewsburg (N.Y.) 125 P 7
Freycinet Peninsula 184 L 9
Fria 196 B 3
Fria, Cape 200 A 3
Friant (CA.) 112 F 6
Frías 142 C 4
Fribourg 153 E 2
Friday Harbor (WA.) 110 BC 2
Friedberg 149 E 4
Friedland 153 G 2
Friend (KS.) 120 DE 4
Friend (NE.) 120 J 2
Friendship (WI.) 124 E 6
Fries (VA.) 129 M 5
Friesach 153 F 2
Friesland 148–149 E 4
Frio, Cabo 141 H 5
Friona (TX.) 117 O 3
Frio River 122 D 6–7
Frisco (CO.) 115 L 4
Frisco City (AL.) 130 G 3
Frisco Peak 114 D 5
Frisian Islands 148 E 4
Fritch (TX.) 117 P 2
Frobisher Bay 105 O 3
Frobisher Lake 103 Q 4
Froid (MT.) 118 D 2
Frolovo 158 H 6
Fromberg (MT.) 111 R 5
Frome, Lake 183 F 5
Fronteiras 141 H 2
Frontera 132 D 4
Fronteras 106 E 5
Frontier (WY.) 111 P 9
Front Range 115 M 3–4
Front Royal (VA.) 129 N 3
Frosinone 153 F 3
Frösö 150 F 3
Frostburg (MD.) 129 M 2
Frotín Cañada Oruro 140 D 5
Fröya 150 E 3
Fröysjöen 150 D 3
Frozen Strait 103 V 2

Fruita (CO.) 114 J 4
Fruita (UT.) 114 F 5
Fruitdale (AL.) 130 F 3
Fruitdale (OR.) 110 B 8
Fruitland (ID.) 110 J 6
Fruitland (MD.) 129 Q 3
Fruitland (UT.) 114 G 3
Fruitland (WA.) 110 G 2
Fruitvale (ID.) 110 J 6
Frunze 169 J 2
Frunzovka 154 C 1
Fruška Gora 154 A 1
Frutal 141 G 4
Frýdek Mistek 149 G 5
Fryeburg (LA.) 123 K 3
Fryeburg (ME.) 126 J 4
Fryken, Övre 151 F 3
Ftéri 154 B 3
Fu'an 173 G 5
Fubo 197 G 7
Fuchuan 172 F 6
Fuding 173 H 5
Fuengirola 152 C 4
Fuente de Cantos 152 B 4
Fuentes 152 B 4
Fuentesaúco 152 B 3
Fuerte Olimpo 140 E 5
Fuerteventura 192 C 3
Fuga 177 J 1
Fuglafjörður 148 A 1
Fugong 172 C 5
Fugou 172 F 4
Fugu 172 F 3
Fuguay-Varina (N.C.) 129 N 6
Fuhai 169 M 1
Fuhaymi (Iraq) 156 CD 2
Fuji 173 L 3
Fujian 173 G 5
Fujin 171 O 6
Fuji-san 173 L 3–4
Fujiyama 173 LM 4
Fūka 194 D 2
Fukang 169 M 2
Fukue 173 J 4
Fukue-jima 173 J 4
Fukui 173 L 3
Fukuoka 173 JK 4
Fukushima 173 LM 2
Fukushima 173 M 3
Fukuyama 173 K 4
Fülād Mahalleh (Iran) 157 FG 1
Fulda 149 E 4
Fulda (MN.) 119 N 7
Fuling 172 E 5
Fullerton (NE.) 120 G 1
Fullerville (TX.) 117 P 5
Fulton 143 E 6
Fulton (IL.) 124 D 8
Fulton (KY.) 128 C 5
Fulton (MO.) 121 O 4
Fulton (MS.) 121 R 8
Fulton (N.Y.) 126 C 5
Fulton (TX.) 122 FG 7
Funafuti 186 C 3
Funchal 192 B 2
Fundación 138 D 1
Fundão (Iran) 141 H 4
Fundão 152 B 3
Fundy, Bay of 105 O 7
Funhaiouro 201 E 4
Funing 172 E 6
Funing 173 G 3
Funing 173 GH 4
Funiu Shan 172 F 4
Funnel River 183 H 3
Funsi 196 D 3
Funtua 197 F 3
Fuping 172 F 3
Fuping 172 E 4
Fuqing 173 G 5
Fuquay-Varina 201 E 2
Furana 193 F 4
Furancungo 201 E 2
Furano 173 M 2
Furawiyah 194 C 5
Fürg (Iran) 157 G 3
Furmanov 158 H 4
Furmanovka 169 J 2
Furmanovo 158 JK 6
Furnas, Reprêsa de 141 G 5
Furnas Dam 141 G 5
Furneaux Group 184 L 9
Furneaux Group 186 A 5
Furqlus (Syria) 156 B 2
Fürstenberg 149 E 4
Fürstenfeld 153 G 2
Fürstenfeldbrück 149 F 5
Fürstenwalde 149 F 4
Fürth 149 F 5
Furth im Wald 149 F 5
Furudal 150 F 3
Furukawa 173 M 3
Fury and Hecla Strait 104 L 1–2
Fusagasugá 138 D 3
Fushë-Lura 154 B 2
Fushun 173 H 2
Fusong 173 J 2
Fusui 172 E 6

Futuna (Vanuatu) 185 K 5
Futuna (Vanuatu) 186 C 4
Futuna (Wallis and Futuna) 186 CD 3
Fuwaris (Saudi Arabia) 157 E 3
Fu Xian 172 E 3
Fu Xian 173 H 3
Fuxian Hu 172 D 6
Fuxin 173 H 2
Fuyang 172 G 4
Fuyu 171 M 6
Fuyu 173 H 1
Fuyuan (China) 172 D 5
Fuyuan (U.S.S.R.) 171 O 6
Fuyun 169 M 1
Fuzhou 172 G 5
Fyn 151 F 4
Fyresvatn 151 E 4
Fyrsjön 150 G 3

G

Gabba' 199 J 3
Gabela 200 A 2
Gabès 193 H 2
Gabon 197 F 5
Gabon 197 G 6
Gaborone 200 D 4
Gaboto 142 D 5
Gabras 194 D 6
Gabredarre 199 G 3
Gabrey, Vozvyshennost' 170 F 1
Gabriel Strait 105 O 3
Gabriel y Galan, Embalse de 152 B 3
Gabrovo 154 C 2
Gacé 152 D 2
Gach Sārān (Iran) 157 F 3
Gackle (ND.) 118 J 4
Gacko 153 G 3
Gada 197 F 3
Gadag 174 C 4
Gadamai 194 F 5
Gadame 198 E 3
Gäddede 150 F 3
Gadê 172 C 4
Gadhap 169 H 5
Gadsden (AL.) 128 E 7–8
Gadsden (AZ.) 116 B 5
Gadūk, Gardaneh-ye (Iran) 157 F 2
Gadwal 174 C 4
Gaeta 153 F 3
Gaeta, Golfo di 153 F 3
Gaferut 186 A 2
Gafsa 191
Gafsa → Qafsah 193 G 2
Gag, Pulau 177 G 4
Gagan 185 F 3
Gagarin 158 F 4
Gage (N.M.) 116 H 5
Gage (OK.) 120 F 6
Gagere 197 F 3
Gagnoa 196 C 4
Gagnon 105 O 5
Gagra 155 F 2
Gagshor 158 JK 3
Gahkom 157 G 3
Gaibanda 174 E 2
Gail (TX.) 117 P 5
Gaillac 152 D 3
Gaillimh 148 B 4
Gaimán 143 C 7
Gainesboro (TN.) 128 F 5
Gainesville (FL.) 131 M 5
Gainesville (GA.) 128 H 7
Gainesville (MO.) 121 N 6
Gainesville (TX.) 122 F 2
Gairdner, Lake 183 F 5
Gairloch 148 B 3
Gai Xian 173 H 2
Gaizina Kalns 151 J 4
Gakankoy 171 T 4
Gakarosa 200 C 5
Gakona 102 H 3
Gala (Greece) 154 C 2
Gala (Tibet, China) 174 E 2
Galadi (Ethiopia) 199 H 3
Galadi (Nigeria) 197 F 3
Galán, Cerro 142 C 4
Galana 199 F 5
Galanino 170 F 4
Galápagos Islands 138 B 6
Galashiels 148 C 3
Galata (MT.) 111 O 2
Galatea Deep 186 D 5
Galați 154 C 1
Galatia (KS.) 120 G 4
Galatina 153 G 3
Galax (VA.) 129 L 5
Galbraith 183 G 2
Galconda (IL.) 121 R 5
Galdhöpiggen 150 E 3
Galeana 106 E 5
Galeana (Mexico) 132 C 3
Galeh Dār (Iran) 157 F 4
Galela 177 G 3
Galena (AK.) 102 F 3
Galena (KS.) 121 L 5

Galena (MO.) 121 M 6
Galena (WI.) 124 D 7
Galera, Punta 143 B 7
Galesburg (IL.) 124 D 9
Galesville (WI.) 124 C 5
Galeton (PA.) 126 B 7
Gali 155 F 2
Galich 158 H 4
Galicia (Poland) 149 H 5
Galicia (Spain) 152 B 3
Galilee, Lake 183 H 3
Galiléa 141 H 4
Galimyy 171 T 3
Galion (OH.) 125 M 9
Galiuro Mountains 116 F 5
Gälka'yo 199 H 3
Gallarate 153 E 2
Gallatin (MO.) 121 M 3
Gallatin (TN.) 128 E 5
Gallatin River 111 O 5
Gallatin Tange 111 O 5
Galle 174 D 6
Gallego 152 C 3
Gallegos 143 B 9
Gallinas (N.M.) 117 KL 3
Gallinas, Punta 138 D 1
Gallipoli 153 G 3
Gallipolis (OH.) 129 J 3
Gällivare 150 H 2
Gallo 152 C 3
Gallo, Capo 153 E 4
Gallo Mountains 116 H 3
Galloo Island 126 C 5
Gallup (N.M.) 116 H 2
Galole 199 F 5
Galt (CA.) 112 C 4
Gal Tardo 199 H 4
Galty Mountains 148 B 4
Galva (IA.) 119 N 8
Galva (IL.) 124 E 8
Galveston (IN.) 124 H 9
Galveston (TX.) 123 J 6
Galveston Bay 123 J 6
Galveston Island 123 J 6
Galvez 142 D 5
Galway 148 B 4
Galway Bay 148 B 4
Gam 200 C 4
Gama 143 D 7
Gama, Isla 143 D 7
Gamarri, Lake 199 G 2
Gamba (Gabon) 197 F 6
Gamba (Tibet, China) 174 E 2
Gambaga 196 D 3
Gambela 198 E 3
Gambell 102 C 3
Gambia 196 A 3
Gambie 196 B 3
Gambier Islands 187 FG 4
Gamboma 197 H 6
Gamboola 183 G 2
Gamboula 198 B 4
Gamkunoro, Gunung 177 G 3
Gamleby 151 G 4
Gammelstad 150 H 2
Gamo Gofa 199 F 3
Gamud 199 F 4
Gamvik 150 J 1
Ganado (AZ.) 116 G 2
Ganado (TX.) 122 G 6
Ganale 199 G 3
Ganaly 171 T 5
Ganäveh (Iran) 157 F 3
Ganda 200 A 2
Gandadiwata, Bukit 177 EF 4
Gandajika 198 C 6
Gandak 174 D 2
Gandaua 169 H 5
Gander 105 R 6
Gandesa 152 D 3
Gandhinagar 174 B 3
Gandhi Sagar Dam 174 C 3
Gandi 197 F 3
Gandía 152 C 4
Gand-i-Zirreh 169 G 5
Gandu 141 J 3
Ganeb 192 C 5
Ganetti 194 E 5
Ganga 174 E 2
Ganga, Mont de 197 G 4
Ganga, Mouths of the 174–175 EF 3
Gangakher 174 C 4
Gangan 143 C 7
Ganganagar 174 B 2
Gangapur 174 C 2
Gangara 197 F 3
Gangaw 175 F 3
Gangawati 174 C 4
Gangca 172 D 3
Gangdisê Shan 174 DE 1
Ganges 174 E 3
Ganges Cone 208 B 3
Ganghar 174 C 3
Gangmar Co 174 D 1
Gangotri 174 C 1
Gangtok 174 E 2
Gangu 172 E 4
Gani 177 G 4
Ganina Gar' 170 F 4
Gan Jiang 172 G 5

Gannan 171 M 6
Gannat 152 D 2
Gannett (ID.) 111 L 7
Gannett Peak 111 Q 7
Gannvalley (SD.) 118 JK 7
Ganquan 172 E 3
Gansu 172 DE 3
Gant 146
Ganta 196 C 4
Gantang 172 D 3
Gantt (AL.) 131 H 3
Ganyesa 200 C 5
Ganzhou 172 F 5
Ganzurino 170 J 5
Gao 196 D 2
Gao'an 172 G 5
Gaohe 172 F 6
Gaolan 172 D 3
Gaoligong Shan 172 C 5
Gaolou Ling 172 E 5–6
Gaomi 173 GH 3
Gaona 142 D 4
Gaoping 172 F 3
Gaotai 172 C 3
Gaotang 173 G 3
Gaoua 196 D 3
Gaoual 196 B 3
Gao Xian 172 D 5
Gaoyi 172 F 3
Gaoyou 173 G 4
Gaoyou Hu 173 G 4
Gaozhou 172 F 6
Gap 153 E 3
Gapan 177 J 1
Gar 174 C 1
Gara'ad 199 H 3
Garachiné 138 C 2
Garai 169 J 3
Garaina 184 E 3
Garaldine (MT.) 111 P 3
Garamba National Park 198 D 4
Garangan (Iran) 157 F 3
Garanhuns 141 J 2
Garantah 176 E 5
Garara 184 E 3
Garba Härrey 199 G 4
Garber (OK.) 120 H 6
Garberville (CA.) 112 B 2
Garbokaray 170 G 5
Garbosh, Kūh-e (Iran) 157 EF 2
Garcia (CO.) 115 M 6
Garco 174 E 1
Garda, Lago di 153 F 2
Gardaneh-ye Āvej (Iran) 157 E 2
Gardaneh-ye Gadūk (Iran) 157 F 2
Gardaneh-ye Kandovān (Iran) 157 F 1
Gardaneh-ye Khāneh Sorkh (Iran) 157 G 3
Gardaneh-ye Kowli Kosh (Iran) 157 F 3
Garden (MI.) 124 H 4
Gardena (ID.) 110 J 6–7
Garden City (GA.) 131 N 2
Garden City (KS.) 120 E 4
Garden City (MO.) 121 L 4
Garden City (S.D.) 119 L 6
Garden City (TX.) 117 P 6
Garden City (UT.) 114 F 2
Gardendale (AL.) 130 H 3
Gardendale (MI.) 125 M 6
Gardendale (TX.) 122 D 7
Garden Island Bay 123 OP 6
Garden Plain (KS.) 120 H 5
Garden Valley (ID.) 111 K 6
Gardermoen 151 F 3
Gardez 169 H 4
Gardine (ME.) 126 K 4
Gardiner (MT.) 111 P 5
Gardiner (OR.) 110 B 7
Gardiners Island 127 G 7
Gardner (CO.) 115 MN 6
Gardner (MA.) 126 GH 6
Gardnerville (NV.) 112 F 4
Gardo → Qardo 199 H 3
Gardula 199 F 3
Gareloi 102 B 5
Garet el Djenoun 193 G 3
Garfield (KS.) 120 F 4
Garfield (N.M.) 117 J 5
Garfield (WA.) 110 H 3
Garfield Mountain 111 N 6
Gargano, Promontorio del 153 G 3
Gargnäs 150 G 2
Gargouna 196 DE 2
Gari 159 M 4
Garibaldi (OR.) 110 B 5
Garies 200 B 5
Garissa 199 FG 5
Garita (N.M.) 117 M 2
Garkida 197 G 3
Garland (AL.) 130 H 3
Garland (MT.) 118 C 4
Garland (N.C.) 129 N 7
Garland (TX.) 122 G 3
Garland (UT.) 114 EF 2
Garland (WY.) 111 R 6
Garmal 199 J 3
Garmdasht (Iran) 157 E 3
Garmisch-Partenkirchen 149 F 5
Garmsar (Iran) 157 F 2

Garner (IA.) 119 P 7
Garner (N.C.) 129 N 6
Garnet Range 111 M 4
Garnett (KS.) 121 K 4
Garonne 152 D 3
Garoua (Cameroon) 197 G 4
Garoua (Niger) 197 G 3
Garoua Boulai 197 G 4
Garōwe 199 H 3
Garphyttan 151 G 4
Garrett (TX.) 122 G 3
Garrett (WY.) 118 C 8
Garri, Kūh-e (Iran) 157 E 2
Garrison (MN.) 119 P 4
Garrison (ND.) 118 G 3
Garrison (TX.) 123 J 4
Garrison (UT.) 114 D 5
Garrison Dam 118 G 3
Garry Bay 103 U 2
Garry Lake 103 R 2
Garryowen (MT.) 111 S 5
Garsen 199 F 5
Garsila 194 C 6
Garut 176 C 5
Garwa 174 D 3
Garwolin 149 H 4
Garwood (TX.) 122 G 6
Gary (IN.) 124 G 8
Gary (S.D.) 119 M 6
Garyn' 170 J 4
Garza 142 D 4
Garza-Little Elm Reservoir 122 G 2
Garze 172 C 4
Garzón 138 C 3
Gasan-Kuli 168 E 3
Gas City (IN.) 124 J 9
Gascogne 152 CD 3
Gasconade River 121 N 5
Gascoyne Junction 182 B 4
Gascoyne River 182 A 3
Gashagar 197 G 3
Gashaka 197 G 4
Gasht 169 G 5
Gas Hu 172 B 3
Gashua 197 G 3
Gashun 155 F 1
Gaspar, Selat 176 C 4
Gasparilla Island 131 M 8
Gaspé 105 P 6
Gaspé, Cap de 105 P 6
Gaspé, Péninsule de 105 O 6
Gasquet (CA.) 112 B 1
Gassaway (W.V.) 129 KL 3
Gassi Touil 193 G 2
Gassol 197 G 4
Gastello, Iméni 171 R 3
Gaston, Lake 129 N 5
Gastonia (N.C.) 129 K 6
Gastre 143 C 7
Gästrikland 151 G 3
Gata, Akra (Cyprus) 156 A 2
Gata, Cabo de 152 C 4
Gata, Sierra de 152 B 3
Gatamaran 184 L 9
Gatchina 151 K 4
Gate (OK.) 120 E 6
Gate City (VA.) 128 J 5
Gates (N.C.) 129 P 5
Gates (N.Y.) 126 B 5
Gateshead (N.W.T., Can.) 103 S 1
Gatesville (N.C.) 129 P 5
Gatesville (TX.) 122 F 4
Gateway (CO.) 114 J 5MO
Gatineau Park 105 M 6
Gatlinburg (TN.) 128 H 6
Gato (CO.) 115 K 6
Gatooma → Kadoma 200 D 3
Gatton 183 J 4
Gatvand (Iran) 157 E 2
Gauani 199 G 2
Gauhati 175 F 2
Gauja 151 H 4
Gaula 150 E 3
Gauldalen 150 F 3
Gauley Bridge (W.V.) 129 K 3
Gaurdak 169 H 3
Gaurihar 174 CD 2
Gausta 151 E 4
Gauttier, Pegunungan 177 J 4
Gavanka 171 T 4
Gäväter 169 G 5
Gāvbandi (Iran) 157 F 4
Gāvbūs, Kūh-e (Iran) 157 FG 4
Gávdhos 154 B 4
Gave de Pau 152 C 3
Gavins Point Dam 119 L 8
Gaviota (CA.) 113 E 8
Gāv Kosh (Iran) 157 E 2
Gävle 151 G 3
Gävlebukten 151 G 3
Gawler 183 F 5
Gawler Ranges 183 F 5
Gaxun Nur 172 D 2
Gaya (India) 174 E 3
Gaya (Niger) 196 E 3
Gaya (Nigeria) 197 F 3

Gaylord (KS.) 120 G 3
Gaylord (MI.) 125 K 4
Gaylord (MI.) 119 O 6
Gayndah 183 J 4
Gayny 158 K 3
Gaysin 154 C 1
Gays Mills (WI.) 124 D 6
Gaz (Iran) 157 F 2
Gaza → Ghazzah 194 E 2
Gaza Strip 156 AB 3
Gazammi 197 G 3
Gazaoua 197 F 3
Gazelle (CA.) 112 C 1
Gazelle Peninsula 185 F 2
Gaziantep 155 E 3
Gaziantep (Turkey) 156 B 1
Gaziantep Yaylasi 155 E 3
Gazimur 170 L 5
Gazimurskiy Zavod 170 L 5
Gazipaşa 155 D 3
Gazipaşa (Turkey) 156 A 1
Gazli 169 G 2
Gbarnga 196 C 4
Gboko 197 F 4
Gcoverega 200 C 3
Gdańsk 149 G 4
Gdansk, Gulf of 149 G 4
Gdov 151 J 4
Gdynia 149 G 4
Gearhart Mountain 110 E 8
Geary (OK.) 120 G 7
Gebe, Pulau 177 G 4
Gebo (WY.) 111 R 7
Gebze 154 C 2
Gechia 198 F 3
Geddes (S.D.) 119 K 7
Gedi 199 F 5
Gediz 154 C 3
Gediz 154 C 3
Gedser 151 F 5
Geelong 183 G 6
Geelvink Channel 182 A 4
Gefara Plain → Jifārah Plain 193 H 2
Gegamskiy Khrebet 155 G 2–3
Gê'gyai 174 D 1
Gehee (AR.) 121 O 9
Geidam 197 G 3
Geigar 194 E 6
Geikie 103 R 4
Geilo 151 E 3
Geita 198 E 5
Gejiu 165
Gejiu 172 D 6
Gel 198 D 3
Gela 153 F 4
Gelai 199 F 5
Gelendzhik 155 E 2
Gelibolu 154 C 2
Gelibolu Yarimadasi 154 C 2
Gellinsör 199 H 3
Gelsenkirchen 149 E 4
Gemena 198 B 4
Gemerek 155 E 3
Gemlik 154 C 2
Gemlik Körfezi 154 C 2
Gemona 153 F 2
Gemsbok National Park 200 C 4–5
Gemuru 176 E 4
Genç (New Zealand) 185 Q 9
Gencek 154 D 3
Geneina → Al Junaynah 194 C 6
General Acha 143 D 6
General Alvear (Argentina) 143 C 5–6
General Alvear (Argentina) 143 DE 6
General Belgrano 143 E 6
General Belgrano II 203
General Belgrano III 203
General Bernardo O'Higgins 203
General Bravo 132 C 2
General Carrera, Lago 143 B 8
General Chaves 143 D 6
General Conesa 143 CD 7
General Daniel Cerri 143 D 6
General Guido 143 E 6
General La Madrid 143 D 6
General Lavalle 143 E 6
General Madariaga 143 E 6
General Martín Miguel de Güemes 140 D 5
General Paz 142 E 4
General Pico 143 D 6
General Pinedo 142 D 4
General Pinto 142 D 5
General Roca 143 C 6
General San Martin 203
General Santos 177 G 2
General Treviño 132 C 2
General Trias 106 E 6
General Vargas 142 F 4
General Villegas 142 D 6
Genesee (ID.) 110 J 4
Geneseo (KS.) 120 GH 4
Geneseo (N.Y.) 126 B 6
Geneso (IL.) 124 D 8
Geneva (AL.) 131 J 3
Geneva (ID.) 111 OP 8
Geneva (NE.) 120 H 2

Geneva (N.Y.) 126 BC 6
Geneva (OH.) 125 N 8
Genève 153 E 2
Gengma 172 C 6
Genichesk 155 DE 1
Genil 152 C 4
Genkanyy, Khrebet 108 D 2
Genoa 153 E 3
Genoa (IL.) 124 F 7
Genoa (NE.) 120 H 1
Genova 153 E 3
Genova, Golfo di 153 E 3
Genovesa Isla 138 B 6
Gent 148 D 4
Genteng 176 C 5
Gentryville (MO.) 121 N 6
Genyem 184 CD 2
Geographe Bay 182 B 5
Geographe Channel 182 A 3
Geok-Tepe 168 F 3
George (Quebec, Can.) 105 O 4
George (South Africa) 200 C 6
George (WA.) 110 EF 3
George , Lake (FL.) 131 N 5
George, Lake (N.D.) 118 J 4
George, Lake (N.Y.) 126 F 5
George, Lake (Uganda) 198 E 5
George, Lake (Western Australia) 182 C 3
Georgetown (CA.) 112 E 4
Georgetown (Cayman Is.) 133 F 4
Georgetown (CO.) 115 M 4
Georgetown (GA.) 131 JK 3
Georgetown (Gambia) 196 B 3
Georgetown (Guyana) 139 G 2
Georgetown (ID.) 111 O 8
Georgetown (KY.) 128 C 3
Georgetown (LA.) 123 L 4
George Town (Malaysia) 176 AB 2
Georgetown (MS.) 130 D 3
Georgetown (OH.) 128 H 3
Georgetown (PA.) 127 D 10
Georgetown (Queensland, Austr.) 183 G 2
Georgetown (S.C.) 129 M 8
George Town (Tasmania, Austr.) 184 L 9
George Town (Tasmania, Austr.) 186 A 5
Georgetown (The Bahamas) 133 G 3
Georgetown (TX.) 122 F 5
George V Coast 203
George VI Sound 203
George Washington Carver National-Monument 121 L 5–6
George West (TX.) 122 E 7
Georgia 196 A 3
Georgia (North) 128 HJ 2
Georgia (South) 131
Georgia (U.S.S.R.) 155 F 2
Georgiana (AL.) 130 H 3
Georgian Bay 105 L 6
Georgina River 183 F 3
Georgiu-Dezh 158 G 5
Georgiyevka 159 Q 6
Georgiyevka 169 K 2
Georgiyevsk 155 F 2
Georg von Neumayer 203
Gera 149 F 4
Gerais, Chapadão dos 141 G 4
Geral, Serra 142 F 4
Geral de Goiás, Serra 141 G 3
Geraldine (New Zealand) 185 Q 9
Geraldine (Western Australia) 182 A 4
Geral do Paraná, Serra 141 G 3
Geraldton (Ontario, Can.) 104 K 6
Geraldton (Western Australia) 182 A 4
Geral ou Grande, Serra 141 G 3
Gerâs, Serra do 152 B 3
Gerasimovka 159 O 4
Gerba 171 S 3
Gerber (CA.) 112 C 2
Gerber Reservoir 110 D 8
Gerbichi, Gora 170 J 2
Gerciüş 155 F 3
Gerðar 150 A 3
Gerede 155 D 2
Geriban → 'El Ḩamurre 199 H 3
Gering (NE.) 118 E 9
Gerlach (NV.) 112 F 2
Gerlachovský Štit 149 H 5
Gerlogubi 199 GH 3
Gerlovo 154 C 2
German Democratic Republic 149 F 4
Germânia 140 BC 3
Germania 142 D 5
Germann (AZ.) 116 E 4
Germfask (MI.) 124 H 3
Germi 168 E 3
Germi 168 E 4
Germi (Iran) 157 E 2
Gerona 152 D 3
Geronimo (AZ.) 116 F 4
Geronimo (OK.) 120 G 8
Gerze 155 DE 2
Gêrzê 174 D 1
Gesoa 184 D 3
Gestro, Webbe 199 G 3
Gesunda 151 F 4
Gesunden 150 G 3
Getafe 152 C 3

Gettysburg (PA.) **127** B 9
Gettysburg (SD.) **118** J 5
Getúlio Vargas **142** F 4
Getz Ice Shelf **203**
Geumpang, Krueng **176** A 3
Gevaş **155** F 3
Gevgelija **154** B 2
Geyik Dağı **155** D 3
Geyser (MT.) **111** P 3
Geyser, Banc du **201** H 2
Geyserville (CA.) **112** BC 4
Geysir **150** A 3
Geyve **154** D 2
Ghadāmis **193** G 2
Ghadduwah **193** H 3
Ghadīr ar Razzah **193** J 3
Ghaghara **174** D 2
Ghana **196** D 4
Ghanadah, Ra's (United Arab Emirates) **157** G 4
Ghanzi **200** C 4
Gharaqābād (Iran) **157** EF 2
Ghardaïa **193** F 2
Ghârib, Jabal (Egypt) **156** A 3
Gharib, Ra's (Egypt) **156** A 3
Gharyān **193** H 2
Ghāt **193** H 4
Ghats, Eastern **174** CD 3–5
Ghats, Western **174** BC 4–5
Ghawar (Saudi Arabia) **157** E 4
Ghayl Bā Wāzīr **195** H 6
Ghayl Bin Ymayn **195** H 5
Ghazaouet **192** E 1
Ghaziabad **174** C 2
Ghazipur **174** D 2
Ghazni **169** H 4
Ghazzah **156** B 3
Ghedo **199** F 3
Ghelemso **199** G 3
Ghemi, Jabal **198** E 3
Gheorghe Gheorghiu-Dej **154** C 1
Gheorghieni **154** C 1
Gherla **154** B 1
Ghimbi **198** F 3
Ghizao **169** H 4
Ghizar **169** J 3
Ghubaysh **194** D 6
Ghubbat al Qamar **195** J 5
Ghubbat Şawqirah **195** K 5
Ghudāf, Wādī al (Iraq) **156** D 2
Ghurāb, Jabal al (Syria) **156** C 2
Ghurayrah **195** G 5
Ghurd Abū Muharrik **194** D 3
Ghurian **169** G 4
Giamame → Jamāme **199** G 4
Giannutri **153** F 3
Gibara **133** G 3
Gibbon (NE.) **120** G 2
Gibbon (OR.) **110** G 5
Gibb River **182** D 2
Gibeon **200** B 5
Gibostad **150** G 2
Gibraltar **152** B 4
Gibraltar, Estrecho de **152** B 4
Gibraltar, Strait of **152** B 4
Gibson **182** C 5
Gibson (GA.) **128** J 8
Gibson City (IL.) **124** F 9
Gibson Desert **182** C 3
Gichgeniyn Nuruu **170** FG 6
Giddings (TX.) **122** FG 5
Gideå **150** G 3
Gideån **150** G 3
Gidgi, Lake **182** D 4
Gidole → Gardula **199** F 3
Gien **152** D 2
Giessen **149** E 4
Gifford (AR.) **121** N 8
Gifford (FL.) **131** O 7
Gifthorn **149** F 4
Gift Lake **103** O 4
Gifu **173** L 3
Gigant **155** F 1
Giganta, Sierra de la **106** D 6
Giglio **153** F 3
Gijon **152** B 3
Gila (N.M.) **116** H 5
Gila Bend (AZ.) **116** D 5
Gila Bend Indian Reservation **116** D 4
Gila Bend Mountains **116** CD 4
Gila Cliff Dwellings National Monument **116** H 4
Gila Desert **116** C 4–5
Gila Mountains (AZ.) **116** G 4
Gila Mountains (AZ.) **116** B 5
Gīlān-e Gharb (Iran) **157** DE 2
Gila River **116** C 5
Gila River Indian Reservation **116** DE 4
Gilbert (LA.) **123** M 3
Gilbert Islands **186** C 2–3
Gilberton **183** G 2
Gilbertown (AL.) **130** F 3
Gilbert Peak **110** D 4
Gilbert River **183** G 2
Gilbert River **183** G 2
Gilbués **141** G 2
Gilé **201** F 3
Giles **182** D 4
Gilett (AR.) **121** O 8

Gilgandra **183** H 5
Gilgau **154** B 1
Gilgil **199** F 5
Gilgit **169** J 3
Gilgunnia **183** H 5
Gill (CO.) **115** N 3
Gillam **103** T 4
Gillespie (IL.) **121** Q 3
Gillett (WI.) **124** F 5
Gillette (WY.) **118** C 6
Gillian, Lake **105** M 2
Gills Rock (WI.) **124** H 4
Gilluly (UT.) **114** F 4
Gilman (IL.) **124** G 9
Gilman (MT.) **111** N 3
Gilman (WI.) **124** D 4
Gilmer (TX.) **123** J 3
Gilmore City (IA.) **119** O 8
Gilo **198** E 3
Gilroy (CA.) **112** D 6
Giltner (NE.) **120** GH 4
Gīlvān (Iran) **157** E 1
Gilyuy **171** N 4
Gimli **103** S 5
Gimolskoye, Ozero **150** K 3
Gingin **182** B 5
Gingoog **177** G 2
Ginir **199** G 3
Ginzo de Limia **152** B 3
Gioher → Jōwhar **199** H 4
Gioia **153** G 3
Gioia Tauro **153** G 4
Giralia **182** A 3
Girard (IL.) **121** Q 3
Girard (KS.) **121** L 5
Girard (PA.) **125** O 4
Girard (TX.) **117** Q 4
Girardot **138** D 3
Giresun **155** E 2
Gir Forest **174** B 3
Giri **198** B 4
Giridih **174** E 3
Girishk **169** G 4
Girna **174** C 3
Girne **155** D 3
Girne (Cyprus) **156** A 2
Girón **138** C 4
Gironde **152** C 2
Girvan **148** C 3
Girvas **150** K 3
Gisborne **185** R 8
Gisborne **186** C 5
Gisenye **198** D 5
Gislaved **151** F 4
Gistral **152** B 3
Gitarama **198** DE 5
Gitega **198** E 5
Gitu (Iran) **157** E 2
Giuba → Juba **199** G 4
Giulianova **153** F 3
Giurgiu **154** C 2
Givors **153** D 2
Giza **194** DE 3
Gizhduvan **169** G 2
Gizhiga **171** U 3
Gizhiginskaya Guba **171** T 3
Gizo **185** G 3
Giżycko **149** H 4
Gjiri i Drinit **154** A 2
Gjiri i Karavastase **154** A 2
Gjiri i Vlorä **154** A 2
Gjirokastra **154** B 2
Gjoa Haven **103** S 2
Gjögur **150** B 2
Gjøvik **151** F 3
Glace Bay **105** Q 6
Glaciares, Parque Nacional los **143** B 8
Glacier (WA.) **110** D 2
Glacier Bay **102** K 4
Glacier Bay National Park and Preserve **102** K 4
Glacier National Park **111** LM 2
Glacier Peak **110** D 2
Glade (KS.) **120** F 3
Gladewater (TX.) **123** J 3
Gladstone **183** J 3
Gladstone (MI.) **124** G 4
Gladstone (MO.) **121** L 3
Gladstone (N.M.) **117** MN 1
Glad Valley (SD.) **118** FG 5
Gladwin (MI.) **125** K 6
Gladys Lake **109** M 4
Gláma **150** A 2
Glåma **151** F 3
Glamis (CA.) **113** KL 9
Glarus **153** E 2
Glasco (KS.) **120** H 3
Glasgow (KY.) **128** F 4–5
Glasgow (MT.) **118** B 2
Glasgow (U.K.) **148** C 3
Glasgow (VA.) **129** M 4
Glasier **143** C 7
Glassboro (N.J.) **127** D 9
Glass Mountains **117** N 7
Glazier (TX.) **117** Q 1–2
Glazov **158** K 4
Gleib Chileh **192** C 4
Gleisdorf **153** G 2

Glen (MT.) **111** N 5
Glen (N.H.) **126** H 4
Glen Arbor (MI.) **124** J 5
Glenbar (AZ.) **116** G 5
Glenburn (ND.) **118** G 2
Glen Canyon (UT.) **114** F 6
Glen Canyon (UT.) **114** G 6
Glen Canyon Dam **116** E 1
Glen Canyon National Recreation Area **114** FG 6
Glencoe (KY.) **128** G 3
Glencoe (MN.) **119** O 6
Glencoe (N.M.) **117** L 4
Glendale (AZ.) **116** D 4
Glendale (CA.) **113** G 8
Glendale (KS.) **120** GH 4
Glendale (NV.) **112** L 6
Glendale (OR.) **110** B 8
Glendale (UT.) **114** E 6
Glendevey (CO.) **115** LM 3
Glendive (MT.) **118** D 3
Glendo (WY.) **118** C 8
Glendo Reservoir **118** D 8
Glen Elder (KS.) **120** G 3
Glenfield (N.Y.) **126** D 5
Glenham (SD.) **118** H 5
Glenhope (ID.) **182** B 9
Glen Innes **183** J 4
Glenmora (LA.) **123** L 5
Glenn (TX.) **117** Q 4
Glennallen **102** H 3
Glenns Ferry (ID.) **111** K 8
Glennville (GA.) **131** MN 3
Glenoma (WA.) **110** CD 4
Glenormiston **183** F 3
Glenrock (WY.) **118** C 8
Glen Rose (TX.) **122** F 3
Glenrothes **148** C 3
Glens Falls (N.Y.) **126** F 5
Glenshaw (PA.) **125** OP 9
Glen Ullin (ND.) **118** G 4
Glenville (MN.) **119** P 7
Glenville (W.V.) **129** L 3
Glenwood (AR.) **121** M 8
Glenwood (MN.) **119** N 5
Glenwood (N.M.) **116** H 4
Glenwood (OR.) **110** B 5
Glenwood City (WI.) **124** B 4
Glenwood Springs (CO.) **115** K 4
Glidden (IA.) **119** O 8
Glidden (WI.) **124** D 3
Glide (OR.) **110** B 7
Glina **153** G 2
Glittertind **150** E 3
Gliwice (WI.) **149** G 4
Globe (AZ.) **116** F 4
Głogów **149** G 4
Glomfjord **150** F 2
Glommersträsk **150** GH 2
Gloppet **150** H 3
Glorieta (N.M.) **117** L 2
Glorieuses, Iles **201** H 2
Glottof, Mount **102** G 4
Gloucester (Australia) **183** J 5
Gloucester (MA.) **126** J 6
Gloucester (U.K.) **148** C 4
Gloucester (VA.) **129** P 4
Gloucester, Cabo **143** B 9
Glover (MO.) **121** P 5
Gloversville (N.Y.) **126** E 5
Glubokiy **155** F 1
Glubokoye **155** F 1
Glubokoye **159** Q 5
Glücksburg **149** E 4
Glukhov **158** F 5
Glusha **151** J 5
Glusk **151** J 5
Glybokaya **154** C 1
Gmelinka **158** J 5
Gmünd **153** F 2
Gmünd **153** G 2
Gmunden **153** F 2
Gnarp **150** G 3
Gniben **151** F 4
Gniezno **149** G 4
Gniloaksayskaya **155** F 1
Gnjilane **154** B 2
Gnowangerup **182** B 5
Goa **174** B 4
Goageb **200** B 5
Goalpara **175** F 2
Goaso **196** D 4
Goba **199** G 3
Gobabeb **200** B 4
Gobabis **200** B 4
Gobernador Crespo **142** D 5
Gobernador Gregores **143** BC 8
Gobi **172** EF 2
Gochas **200** B 4
Godār-e Sorkh (Iran) **157** G 2
Godar-i-Shah **169** G 5
Godavari **174** D 4
Godavari, Mouths of the **174** CD 3–5
Godby **151** H 3
Goðafoss **150** B 2
Godhra **174** B 3
Godinlave **199** H 3
Godoy Cruz **142** C 5
Gods Lake (Manitoba, Can.) **103** T 5
Gods Lake (Manitoba, Can.) **103** T 5

Gods Mercy, Bay of **103** U 3
Gods River **103** T 4
Godthåb **105** R 3
Godthåbfjord **105** R 3
Godwar **174** B 2
Goe **184** D 3
Goéland, Lac au **105** M 5–6
Goélands, Lac aux **105** P 4
Goes **148** D 4
Goff (KS.) **120** K 3
Goffs (CA.) **113** K 8
Gofitskoye **155** F 1
Gogebic, Lake **124** E 3
Gogebic Range **124** DE 3
Gogland, Ostrov **151** J 3
Gogolevskiy **159** O 5
Gogrial **198** D 3
Gogu, Virful **154** B 1
Gogui **196** C 2
Goiandira **141** G 4
Goianesia **141** G 4
Goiânia **141** G 4
Goianorte **139** J 5
Goiás **141** G 4
Goiás (Goiás, Brazil) **141** G 4
Göinge **151** F 4
Góis **152** B 3
Gojam **199** F 2
Gojra **169** J 4
Gökırmak **155** D 2
Goksu **155** D 3
Göksu (Turkey) **155** E 3
Göksu (Turkey) **155** F 3
Goksu (Turkey) **156** A 1
Göksum **155** E 3
Göktepe **154** C 3
Gokwe **200** D 3
Golaghat **175** F 2
Golan Heights **156** B 2
Golaya Pristan **155** D 1
Golconda (NV.) **112** H 2
Gold Beach (OR.) **110** A 8
Gold Coast **196** DE 5
Gold Coast (Australia) **183** J 4
Golden (Br. Col., Can.) **103** O 5
Golden (CO.) **115** M 4
Golden City (MO.) **121** L 5
Goldendale (WA.) **110** E 5
Golden Hinde **103** M 6
Golden Meadow (LA.) **123** N 6
Golden Vale **148** B 4
Golden Valley (ND.) **118** F 3
Goldfield (IA.) **119** P 8
Goldfield (NV.) **112** H 5
Gold Greek **109** J 3
Goldsmith (TX.) **117** O 5–6
Goldston (N.C.) **129** M 6
Goldsboro (N.C.) **129** NO 6
Goldthwaite (TX.) **122** E 4
Goldwater (TX.) **122** E 4
Gole **155** F 2
Goleniów **149** FG 4
Golestan **169** G 4
Goleta (CA.) **113** F 8
Golets-Inyaptuk, Gora **170** K 4
Golets-Longdor, Gora **170** L 4
Golets-Purpula, Gora **170** K 4
Golets-Skalistyy, Gora **170** LM 4
Golets Skalistyy, Gora **171** O 4
Golfe de la Gonâve **133** H 4
Golfe de Saint-Florent **153** E 3
Golfe de Saint-Malo **152** C 2
Golfe de Tadjourah **199** G 2
Golfe du Lion **152–153** D 3
Golfito **132** F 6
Golfo Almirante Montt **143** B 9
Golfo Aranci **153** E 3
Golfo Corcovado **143** B 7
Golfo de Almeria **152** C 4
Golfo de Ana María **133** G 3
Golfo de Ancud **143** B 7
Golfo de Cadiz **152** B 4
Golfo de California **106** DE 5–7
Golfo de Chiriquí **138** B 2
Golfo de Cintra **192** B 4
Golfo de Fonseca **132** E 5
Golfo de Guacanayabo **133** G 3
Golfo de Guayaquil **138** B 4
Golfo de Honduras **132** E 4
Golfo del Batabano **132–133** F 3
Golfo del Darién **138** B 2
Golfo del Papagayo **132** E 5
Golfo de los Mosquitos **138** B 2
Golfo de Nicoya **132** F 6
Golfo de Panamá **138** C 2
Golfo de Paria **139** F 1
Golfo de Penas **143** B 8
Golfo de Rosas **152** D 3
Golfo de San Jorge **152** D 3
Golfo de Tehuantepec **132** D 4
Golfo de Valencia **152** D 3
Golfo de Venezuela **138** D 1
Golfo di Castellammare **153** F 4
Golfo di Gaeta **153** F 3
Golfo di Genova **153** E 3

Golfo di Manfredonia **153** G 3
Golfo di Palmas **153** E 4
Golfo di Policastro **153** G 4
Golfo di Salerno **153** F 3
Golfo di Squillace **153** G 4
Golfo di Taranto **153** G 3–4
Golfo Dulce **132** F 6
Golfo Ladrillero **143** A 8
Golfo Nuevo **143** D 7
Golfo San Jorge **143** C 8
Golfo San Matías **143** D 7
Golfo Trinidad **143** A 8
Gölgeli Dağları **154** C 3
Gölhisar **154** C 3
Goliad (TX.) **122** F 7
Golija **154** B 2
Goljak **153** E 3
Goljama Syutkya **154** B 2
Gölköy **155** E 2
Golmud **172** E 3
Golmud He **172** BC 3
Golo **153** E 3
Gololcha **199** G 3
Gölören **155** E 3
Golubac **154** B 2
Golubovka **159** O 5
Golva (ND.) **118** E 4
Golyama **154** B 2
Golyam Perelik **154** B 2
Golyam Persenk **154** B 2
Golyayevka **158** H 5
Golygino **171** T 5
Golyshmanovo **159** N 4
Goma **198** D 5
Gomati **174** D 2
Gombe **197** G 3
Gombi **197** G 3
Gomel **158** F 5
Gomera **192** B 3
Goméz Palacio **132** B 2
Gomo **174** E 1
Gomo Co **174** E 1
Gomo Gomo **177** HJ 5
Gonâbād **168** F 4
Gonaïves **133** H 4
Gonam **171** O 4
Gonam **171** O 4
Gonâve, Golfe de la **133** H 4
Gonâve, Ile de la **133** H 4
Gonbad-e Qābus **168** EF 3
Gonda **174** D 2
Gondal **174** B 3
Gondar **199** F 2
Gondia **174** D 3
Gondomar **152** B 3
Gönen **154** C 2
Gongan **172** F 4
Gongbo' gyamda **172** B 5
Gonggar **175** F 2
Gongga Shan **172** D 5
Gonghe **172** D 3
Gonglee **196** C 4
Gongliu **169** L 2
Gongola **197** G 3
Gongpoquan **172** C 2
Gongshan **172** C 5
Goñi **172** E 5
Gonjo **172** C 4
Gonzales **132** C 3
Gonzales (CA.) **112** D 6
Gonzales (TX.) **122** F 6
Goochland (VA.) **129** O 4
Good Hope, Cape of **200** B 6
Goodhouse **200** B 5
Gooding (ID.) **111** L 8
Goodland (KS.) **120** D 3
Goodlettsville (TN.) **128** E 5
Goodnews Bay **102** E 4
Goodnight (TX.) **117** P 2
Goodooga **183** H 4
Goodrich (CO.) **115** NO 3
Goodrich (TX.) **123** J 5
Goodsprings (NV.) **113** K 7
Goodwater (AL.) **128** EF 8
Goodyear (AZ.) **116** D 4
Goolgowi **183** H 5
Goomalling **182** B 5
Goondiwindi **183** HJ 4
Goonyella **183** H 3
Goose Bay **105** P 5
Goose Lake **112** E 1
Goose River **119** L 3
Göppingen **149** E 5
Gora Adyakit **170** G 2
Gora Aksoran **159** P 6
Gora Aktau **169** G 2
Gora Alney **171** TU 4
Gora Arga-Emneke **171** Q 2
Gora Bazar Dyuzi **168** D 2
Gora Belaya **108** A 2
Gora Belukha **159** R 5–6

Gora Bystrinskiy Golets 170 J 6
Gora Chureg-Tag 170 F 5
Gora Cirk 108 B 3
Gora Denezhkin Kamen' 159 L 3
Gora Dzerzhinskaya 151 J 5
Gora Ezop 171 S 3
Gora Fisht 155 E 2
Gora Gerbichi 170 J 2
Gora Golets-Inyaptuk 170 K 4
Gora Golets-Longdor 170 L 4
Gora Golets-Purpula 170 K 4
Gora Golets-Skalistyy 170 LM 4
Gora Golets Skalistyy 171 O 4
Goragorskiy 155 G 2
Gora Impenekuim 108 B 2
Gora Ischodnaya 108 D 3
Gora Isherim 159 L 3
Gora Ivao 171 RS 6
Gora Kamen 170 FG 2
Gora Kekurnaya 171 V 3
Gora Kelil'vun 171 V 2
Gora Khil'mi 171 S 1
Gora Khoydype 159 N 2
Gorakhpur 174 D 2
Gora Konus 108 B 2
Gora Konus 171 O 4
Gora Konzhakovskiy Kamen' 159 LM 4
Kovriga 158 J 2
Gora Kroviga 170 F 3
Gora Kurkure-Bazhi 159 R 5
Gora Kuytun 159 R 6
Gora Ledyanaya 171 W 3
Gora Lopatina 171 Q 5
Gora Medvezh'ya 171 P 6
Gora Mil'utke 108 C 2
Gora More-Iz 159 M 2
Gora Moskva 170 F 5
Gora Munku-Sardyk 170 GH 5
Gora Nachikinskaya 171 U 4
Gora Narodnaya 159 LM 2
Gora Nelkuchan 171 P 3
Goransko 154 A 2
Gora Orlinnaya 108 B 3
Gora Orvyn 108 CD 2
Gora Ostryak 171 W 3
Gora Pal-Pal 171 VW 3
Gora Pay-Yer 159 M 2
Gora Pobeda 171 R 2
Gora Pshish 155 F 2
Gora Pyat'kovende 171 T 2
Gora Shunak 159 O 6
Gora Shunak 169 J 1
Gora Skalistaya 170 D 1
Gora Sokhondo 170 K 6
Gora Sokhor 170 J 5
Gora Syuge-Khaya 171 P 2
Gora Taklaun 171 Q 3
Gora Tardoki Yani 171 P 6
Gora Tel'pos-Iz 159 L 3
Gora Terpukhoy 171 VW 2
Gora Topko 171 P 4
Gora Tumannaya 108 B 2
Gora Volna 171 T 3
Gora Yamantau 159 L 5
Gora Yebe-Khay 170 KL 1
Gora Yenashimskiy Pol'kan 170 F 3–4
Gora Zamkowa 149 H 4
Gora Zubets 171 X 3
Gorda, Punta 112 A 2
Gördes 154 C 3
Gordil 198 C 3
Gordion 155 D 3
Gordium 155 D 3
Gordon (NE.) 118 F 8
Gordon (WI.) 124 C 3
Gordon Downs 182 D 2
Gordon Lake 103 P 3
Gordon River 184 L 9
Gordonsville (VA.) 129 N 3
Gordonvale 183 H 2
Goré (Chad) 197 H 4
Gore (Ethiopia) 198 F 3
Gore (New Zealand) 184 P 10
Gore (OK.) 121 K 7
Gore (VA.) 129 N 2
Görele 155 E 2
Gorelova 171 T 2
Göreme 155 D 3
Gorg 168 F 5
Gorgān (Iran) 157 G 1
Gorgas (AL.) 128 D 8
Gorgin (Iran) 157 E 1
Gorgona (Italy) 153 E 3
Gorgona, Isla 138 C 3
Gorgora 199 F 2
Gorgoram 197 G 3
Gorham (N.Y.) 126 B 6
Gori 155 F 2
Gorizia 153 F 2
Gorjanci 153 G 2
Gorkha 174 D 2
Gorki 159 N 2
Gor'kiy 158 H 4
Gor'kovskoye Vodokhranilishche
 158 H 4
Görlitz 149 F 4
Gorlovka 155 E 1
Gorman (CA.) 113 G 8
Gorman (TX.) 122 E 3
Gormanstown 184 L 9

Gorna Oryakhovitsa 154 C 2
Gornji Vakuf 153 G 3
Gorno-Altaysk 159 QR 5
Gorno-Chuyskiy 170 K 4
Gorno-Filinskoye 159 N 3
Gorno Slinkina 159 N 4
Gornostakhskiy Khrebet 171 P 3–4
Gornozavodsk 171 Q 6
Gornyak 159 Q 5
Gornyy 171 P 5
Gornyy Kazymsk 159 N 2
Gorodenka 154 C 1
Gorodets 158 H 4
Gorodnitsa 151 J 5
Gorodnya 158 F 4
Gorodok 151 J 4
Gorodovikovsk 155 F 1
Goroka 184 E 3
Goroka 186 A 3
Goromay 171 Q 5
Gorom-Gorom 196 D 3
Gorongosa 201 E 3
Gorongosa, Serra da 201 E 3
Gorongosa National Park 201 E 3
Gorontalo 177 F 3
Goroshikha 159 R 2
Górowo Hawieckié 149 H 4
Gorrahei 199 G 3
Goru, Virful 154 C 1
Goryachegorsk 159 R 4
Goryachenskiy 158 K 5
Goryachiy Klyuch 155 E 2
Goryachiy Klyuch 171 S 3
Gory Bukantau 169 G 2
Gory Byrranga 170 GH 1
Gory Kul'dzhuktau 169 G 2
Goryn' 151 J 5
Gory Putorana 170 FH 2
Gory Świetokrzyskie 149 H 4
Gory Ulutau 169 H 1
Gory Ushkan'iy 171 X 2
Gory Ushurakchan 171 U 2
Gory Yermentau 159 O 5
Gorzów Wielkopolski 149 G 4
Goschen Strait 185 F 4
Gosford 183 J 5
Goshen (CA.) 112 F 6
Goshen (IN.) 124 J 4
Goshen (VA.) 129 M 4
Goshogawara 173 LM 2
Goshute (UT.) 114 D 4
Goshute Indian Reservation 112 L 3
Goshute Lake 112 L 2
Goslar 149 F 4
Gospic 153 G 3
Gosport (IN.) 128 E 2
Goss (MS.) 130 E 3
Gossi 196 D 2
Gossinga 198 D 3
Goste Delčhev 154 B 2
Gostivar 154 B 2
Gostynin 149 G 4
Göta älv 151 F 4
Göta kanal 151 F 4
Gotaru 174 B 2
Göteborg 151 F 4
Gotel Mountains 197 G 4
Götene 151 F 4
Gotha 149 F 4
Gothenburg (NE.) 120 EF 2
Gothenburg (Sweden) 151 F 4
Gotheye 196 E 3
Gotland 151 G 4
Gotō-rettō 173 J 4
Gotowasi 177 G 3
Gotska Sandön 151 GH 4
Götsu 173 K 3
Göttingen 149 EF 4
Gottwaldov 149 G 5
Goubéré 198 D 3
Goubon 197 H 1
Goudge 142 C 5
Goudoumaria 197 G 3
Goulburn 183 H 5
Goulburn Islands 182 E 1
Gould, Mount 182 B 4
Gould City (MI.) 124 J 3
Goulds (FL.) 131 O 9
Goulimime 192 C 3
Goumbou 196 C 3
Goundam 196 D 2
Goundi 197 H 4
Gouradi 197 H 4
Gourara 192 F 3
Gourcy 196 D 3
Gourdon 152 D 3
Gourin 152 C 2
Gourma 196 E 3
Gourma-Rarous 196 D 2
Gouro 197 H 2
Gourounsi 196 D 3
Gourrama 192 E 3
Gouverneur (N.Y.) 126 D 4
Gouzon 152 D 2
Gove (Angola) 200 B 2
Gove (Australia) 181

Gove (KS.) 120 E 4
Govena, Poluostrov 171 V 4
Gove Peninsula 183 F 1
Goverla 154 B 1
Governador Valadares 141 H 4
Government Peak 124 E 3
Governor's Harbour 133 G 2
Goviältay 172 C 1
Govorovo 171 N 1
Gowanda (N.Y.) 125 Q 7
Gowrie (IA.) 119 O 8
Goya 142 E 4
Göynük 154 D 2
Goz Beïda 197 J 3
Gozha Co 174 D 1
Gozo 153 F 4
Graaff Reinet 200 C 6
Grabo 196 C 5
Gračac 153 G 3
Grace (ID.) 111 O 8
Grace, Lake 182 B 5
Grace City (ND.) 118 JK 3
Graceville (MN.) 119 M 5
Gracias a Dios, Cabo 132 F 5
Graciosa 192 A 1
Gradaús 139 H 5
Gradaús, Serra dos 139 H 5
Grado (Italy) 153 F 2
Grado (Spain) 152 B 3
Grady (AR.) 121 P 4
Grady (N.M.) 117 N 3
Grænalón 150 B 3
Grafing 149 F 5
Graford (TX.) 122 E 3
Grafton (IL.) 121 P 4
Grafton (N.D.) 119 L 2
Grafton (WI.) 124 F 6
Grafton (W.V.) 129 M 2
Grafton, Islas 143 B 9
Graham (Br. Col., Can.) 102 L 5
Graham (N.C.) 129 M 5
Graham (TX.) 122 E 2
Graham, Mount 116 G 5
Graham Lake 126 L 4
Graham Land 203
Grahamstown 200 D 6
Grain Coast 196 B 4–C 5
Grainfield (KS.) 120 E 3
Grajaú 139 J 5
Grajaú 141 G 2
Grajewo 149 H 4
Gramat 152 D 3
Gramat, Causse de 152 D 3
Granada (CO.) 115 P 5
Granada (Nicaragua) 132 E 5
Granada (Spain) 152 C 4
Gran Antiplanicie Central 143 C 8
Granbury (TX.) 122 F 3
Granbury, Lake 122 F 3
Granby (CO.) 115 M 3
Granby (Quebec, Can.) 105 N 6
Granby, Lake 115 M 3
Gran Canaria 192 B 3
Gran Chaco 140 D 5
Grand Bahama Island 133 G 2
Grand Ballon 153 E 2
Grand Bank 105 Q 6
Grand Bassam 196 D 4–5
Grand Bay (AL.) 130 F 4
Grand Béréby 196 C 5
Grand Canal 148 B 4
Grand Canal (China) 173 G 3
Grand Canyon 116 D 1
Grand Canyon National Park 116 D 1
Grand Cayman 133 F 4
Grand Cess 196 C 5
Grand Chenier (LA.) 123 L 6
Grand Coulee (WA.) 110 G 3
Grand Coulee Dam 110 FG 3
Grande (N.M.) 117 N 1
Grande, Ilha 141 H 5
Grande, Sierra(Mexico) 132 B 2
Grande Cache 103 O 4
Grande Chartreuse 153 E 2
Grande Comore 201 G 2
Grandeeville (W.V.) 129 K 3
Grande Prairie 103 O 4
Grand Erg de Bilma 197 G 2
Grand Erg Occidental 192–193 E 2–3
Grand Erg Oriental 193 G 2–3
Grande Ridge 208 A 5
Grande Rivière de la Baleine 105 M 4–5
Grande Ronde River 110 H 5
Grand Falls 105 Q 6
Grandfalls (TX.) 117 O 6
Grandfield (OK.) 120 G 8
Grand Forks (N.D.) 119 L 3
Grand Glaise (AR.) 121 O 7
Grand Haven (MI.) 124 H 6
Grandin, Lake 103 O 3
Grandioznyy, Pik 170 G 5
Grand Island (MI.) 124 H 3
Grand Island (NE.) 120 G 2
Grand Isle 123 O 6
Grand Junction (CO.) 114 J 4
Grand Junction (IA.) 119 O 8–9
Grand Lahou 196 CD 5

Grand Lake (CO.) 115 M 3
Grand Lake (LA.) 123 L 6
Grand Lake (ME.) 126 M 3
Grand Lake (New Brunsw., Can.)
 105 O 6
Grand Lake (Newfoundl., Can.) 105 Q 6
Grand Lake (OH.) 125 K 9
Grand Ledge (MI.) 125 K 7
Grand Lieu, Lac de 152 C 2
Grand Manan 105 O 7
Grand Manan Channel 126 MN 4
Grand Marais (MI.) 124 J 3
Grand Meadow (MN.) 119 Q 7
Grand Mesa (CO.) 115 J 4–5
Grand Mesa (CO.) 115 K 4
Grāndola 152 B 4
Grāndola, Serra de 152 B 4
Grand Passage 185 H 5
Grand Popo 196 E 4
Grand Portage Indian Reservation
 119 T 3
Grand Prairie (TX.) 122 FG 3
Grand Rapids (Man., Can.) 103 S 5
Grand Rapids (MI.) 124 J 7
Grand Rapids (MN.) 119 P 3
Grand River (MO.) 121 M 3
Grand River (S.D.) 118 G 5
Grand Santi 139 H 3
Grand Teton 111 P 7
Grand Teton National Park 111 P 7
Grand Tower (IL.) 121 Q 5
Grand Traverse Bay 124 J 4
Grand Turk 133 H 3
Grand Valley (CO.) 115 J 4
Grand View (ID.) 110 J 7
Grandview (TX.) 122 F 3
Grandview (WA.) 110 F 4
Grand Wash Cliffs 116 B 1–2
Grand Wintersberg 153 E 2
Graneros 142 B 5
Granger (TX.) 122 F 5
Granger (UT.) 114 EF 3
Granger (WA.) 110 E 4
Grangesberg 151 F 3
Grangeville (ID.) 110 J 5
Granite (CO.) 115 L 4
Granite (OR.) 110 G 6
Granite City (IL.) 121 P 4
Granite Falls (MN.) 119 N 6
Granite Mountain 108 F 2
Granite Mountains 111 S 8
Granite Pass 111 S 6
Granite Peak (MT.) 111 NO 5
Granite Peak (NV.) 112 H 1
Granite Range 112 F 1–2
Granitola, Capo Punta. 153 F 4
Graniton (NE.) 120 D 2
Graniton (NE.) 120 D 2
Granja 141 H 1
Gran Laguna Salada 143 C 7
Gran Morelos 106 E 5
Gränna 151 F 4
Granön 150 G 3
Gran Paradiso 153 E 2
Gran Pilastro 153 F 2
Gran Quivira (N.M.) 117 KL 3
Gran Quivira National Monument
 117 K 3
Gran Río 139 G 3
Gran Sasso d'Italia 153 F 3
Grant (MT.) 111 M 5
Grant (NE.) 120 D 2
Grant (NE.) 120 D 2
Grant, Mount 112 G 4
Grant City (MO.) 121 L 2
Grant Range 112 JK 4
Grants (N.M.) 117 J 2
Grantham (N.H.) 126 G 5
Grantsburg (WI.) 124 B 4
Grantsdale (MT.) 111 L 4
Grants Pass (OR.) 110 B 8
Grantsville (UT.) 114 E 3
Grantsville (W.V.) 129 K 3
Granview (MO.) 121 L 4
Granville (AZ.) 116 G 4
Granville (ND.) 118 H 2
Granville Lake 103 R 4
Grapeland (TX.) 123 H 4
Grapevine Lake 122 F 3
Grapevine Peak 112 HJ 6
Graskop 201 E 5
Grasmere (ID.) 111 K 8
Grass Creek (WY.) 111 R 7
Grasse 153 E 3
Grassrange (MT.) 111 R 3–4
Grass Valley (CA.) 112 E 3
Grass Valley (OR.) 110 E 5
Grassy Butte (ND.) 118 E 3
Gråsten 151 E 5
Graulhet 152 D 3
Gravatá 141 J 2
Grave, Pointe de 152 C 2
Gravelbourg 103 Q 6
'S-Gravenhage 148 D 4
Grave Peak 111 L 4

Gravette (AR.) 121 L 6
Gravina 153 G 3
Gravois Mills (MO.) 121 N 4
Gray 153 E 2
Gray (GA.) 128 H 8
Gray (OK.) 120 E 6
Grayback, Mount 108 M 4
Gray Horse (OK.) 120 J 6
Grayland (WA.) 110 A 4
Grayling (AK.) 108 F 2
Grayling (MI.) 125 K 5
Grayling (MT.) 111 O 6
Gray Mountain (AZ.) 116 E 2
Grays Harbor 110 A 4
Grays Lake 111 O 7
Grayson (AL.) 128 D 7
Grayson (KY.) 128 J 3
Grays River (WA.) 110 B 4
Grayville (IL.) 121 R 4
Graz 153 G 2
Grdelica 154 B 2
Great Abaco Island 133 G 2
Great Artesian Basin 183 G 3–4
Great Australian Bight 182 D 5
Great Barrier 186 C 5
Great Barrier Island 185 R 8
Great Barrier Reef 183 H 1–2
Great Barrington (MA.) 126 F 6
Great Basin 112 J 2–5
Great Bear 103 N 2
Great Bear Lake 103 NO 2
Great Bear River 109 O 2
Great Bend (KS.) 120 G 4
Great Bend (N.D.) 119 M 4
Great Berg 200 B 6
Great Camanoe 130 E 8
Great Discovery Reef 176 D 1
Great Divide Basin 111 R 8–9
Great Dividing Range 183 H 3–4
Greater Antilles 133 GJ 3–4
Greater Sunda Islands 163 JK 7
Great Exhibition Bay 185 Q 7
Great Exuma Island 133 G 3
Great Falls (MT.) 111 O 3
Great Fisher Bank 148 D 3
Greathouse Peak 111 Q 4
Great Inagua Island 133 H 3
Great Indian Basin 208 B 4
Great Indian Desert 174 B 2
Great Karas Mountains 200 B 5
Great Karroo 200 C 6
Great Khingan Mountains 173 GH 1–2
Great Lake 184 L 9
Great Malvern 148 C 4
Great Miami River 128 G 2
Great Mountains 200 A 3
Great Nicobar 175 F 6
Great North East Channel 184 D 3
Great Plain of the Koukdjuak 105 N 2
Great Plains 103 OQ 4–5
Great Plains Reservoirs 115 P 5
Great Point 127 K 7
Great Ruaha 199 F 6
Great Salt Lake 114 E 2
Great Salt Lake Desert 114 D 3
Great Salt Plains Lake 120 G 6
Great Sand Dunes National Monument
 115 M 4
Great Sand Sea → Baḥr ar Rimāl al
 Aẓim 194 D 3
Great Sandy Desert 182 C 3
Great Sandy Desert (OR.) 110 E 7
Great Scarcies 196 B 4
Great Sitkin 102 B 5
Great Slave Lake 103 P 3
Great Smoky Mountains 128 GH 6
Great Smoky Mountains National Park
 128 H 6
Great Victoria Desert 182 D 4
Great Victoria Desert Nature Reserve
 182 D 4–5
Great Yarmouth 148 D 4
Grebbestad 151 F 4
Grebenka 158 F 5
Gréboun, Mont 197 F 1
Greco, Akra (Cyprus) 156 AB 2
Greece 154 B 3
Greece (N.Y.) 126 B 5
Greeleyville (S.C.) 129 LM 8
Greely (CO.) 115 N 3
Greely (NE.) 119 K 9
Green (OR.) 110 B 7
Green (WI.) 124 D 7
Greenbank (WA.) 110 C 2
Green Bay (WI.) 124 G 5
Green Bay (WI./MI.) 124 G 4–5
Greenbrier (AR.) 121 N 7
Greenbrier River 129 L 4
Greenbush (MN.) 119 M 2
Greencastle (IN.) 128 D 2
Greencastle (PA.) 127 B 9
Green City (MO.) 121 N 2
Green Cove Springs (FL.) 131 N 4–5
Greene (N.Y.) 126 D 6
Greeneville (TN.) 128 J 5
Greenfield (CA.) 112 D 6
Greenfield (IA.) 119 O 9
Greenfield (IL.) 121 P 3
Greenfield (IN.) 128 F 2
Greenfield (IN.) 128 F 2

Greenfield (MA.) 126 G 6
Greenfield (MO.) 121 M 5
Greenfield (OH.) 128 H 2
Green Forest (AR.) 121 M 6
Green Grass (SD.) 118 GH 5
Green Island (New Zealand) 185 Q 10
Green Islands (Papua New Guinea) 185 F 2
Green Islands (Papua New Guinea) 186 B 3
Green Lake (WI.) 124 E 6
Green Lake (WI.) 124 F 6
Greenland 202
Greenland (MI.) 124 E 3
Greenland (MI.) 124 F 3
Greenland Sea 202
Greenleaf (NE.) 120 J 3
Green Mountain Reservoir 115 L 4
Green Mountains 126 G 4–5
Greenock 148 BC 3
Greenough (MT.) 111 M 4
Greenough, Mount 109 K 2
Greenough River 182 B 4
Green Peter Lake 110 C 6
Green Pond (S.C.) 129 L 9
Greenport (N.Y.) 127 G 7
Green River (KY.) 128 D 4
Green River (Papua New Guinea) 184 D 2
Green River (UT.) 114 G 4
Green River (UT.) 114 GH 4
Green River (WY.) 111 Q 9
Green River Lake 128 F 4
Greensboro (AL.) 130 G 2
Greensboro (GA.) 128 H 8
Greensboro (N.C.) 129 M 5
Greensburg (IN.) 128 F 2
Greensburg (KS.) 120 F 5
Greensburg (KY.) 128 F 4
Greensburg (LA.) 123 N 5
Greensburg (PA.) 125 P 9
Greens Peak 116 G 3
Green Swamp 129 N 7
Greenup (IL.) 121 R 3
Greenup (KY.) 128 J 3
Greenvale (Queensland, Austr.) 183 GH 2
Greenville (AL.) 130 H 3
Greenville (CA.) 112 E 2
Greenville (FL.) 131 L 4
Greenville (IL.) 121 Q 4
Greenville (KY.) 128 DE 4
Greenville (Liberia) 196 C 5
Greenville (ME.) 126 K 3
Greenville (MI.) 124 J 6
Greenville (MO.) 121 P 5
Greenville (MS.) 121 OP 9
Greenville (N.C.) 129 O 6
Greenville (N.H.) 126 H 6
Greenville (OH.) 125 K 9
Greenville (PA.) 125 O 8
Greenville (S.C.) 129 J 7
Greenville (TX.) 122 G 2
Greenway (SD.) 118 J 5
Greenwich (CT.) 127 F 7
Greenwich (OH.) 125 M 8
Greenwood (AR.) 121 L 7
Greenwood (FL.) 131 J 4
Greenwood (IN.) 128 E 2
Greenwood (KY.) 128 G 5
Greenwood (MS.) 121 P 9
Greenwood (S.C.) 129 J 7
Greenwood (WI.) 124 D 5
Greenwood, Lake 129 JK 7
Greer (ID.) 110 J 4
Greer (S.C.) 129 J 7
Greers Ferry Lake 121 N 7
Gregorio (SD.) 118 J 7
Gregory (SD.) 118 J 7
Gregory (TX.) 122 F 8
Gregory, Lake (South Australia) 183 F 4
Gregory, Lake (Western Australia) 182 D 3
Gregory, Lake (Western Australia) 182 B 4
Gregory Downs (Queensland, Austr.) 183 F 2
Gregory Range 183 G 2
Gregory River (Queensland, Austr.) 183 F 2
Greifswald 149 F 4
Grein 153 F 2
Greitz 149 F 4
Gremikha 158 G 2
Grenå 151 F 4
Grenada 133 K 5
Grenada (CA.) 112 C 1
Grenada (MS.) 121 Q 9
Grenada Lake 121 Q 9
Grenadine Islands 133 K 5
Grenchen 153 E 2
Grenen 151 F 4
Grenoble 153 E 2
Grenola (KS.) 120 J 5
Grenora (ND.) 118 E 2
Grense-Jakobselv 150 K 2
Grenville, Cape 183 G 1
Gresham (OR.) 110 C 5
Gresik 176 D 5
Gretna (NE.) 120 J 1

Gretna (VA.) 129 M 5
Grevená 154 B 2
Greybull (WY.) 111 RS 6
Greybull River 111 R 6
Greyclifﬀ (MT.) 111 Q 5
Grey Eagle (MN.) 119 O 5
Grey Islands 105 QR 5
Greylock, Mount 126 F 6
Greymouth 185 Q 9
Grey Range 183 G 4
Greystone (CO.) 114 J 3
Greytown 201 E 5
Gribingui 198 B 3
Grico 138 E 2
Gridley (CA.) 112 D 3
Gridley (KS.) 120 K 4
Griﬀin (GA.) 128 G 8
Griﬀith 183 H 5
Griﬀith (AZ.) 116 B 2
Grifton (N.C.) 129 O 6
Grigoriopol' 154 C 1
Grigston (KS.) 120 E 4
Grim, Cape 184 K 9
Grimari 198 C 3
Grimsá 150 A 3
Grimsby 148 CD 4
Grímsey 150 B 2
Grimshaw 103 O 4
Grimsley (TN.) 128 FG 5
Grímsstaðir 150 B 2
Grimstad 151 E 4
Grímsvötn 150 B 3
Grindavik 150 A 3
Grindsted 151 E 4
Grinnell (IA.) 119 Q 9
Grintavec 153 F 2
Griquatown 200 C 5
Gris-Nez, Cap 152 D 1
Grisslehamn 151 G 3
Grit (TX.) 122 D 5
Grizim 192 E 3
Grizzly (OR.) 110 E 6
Grizzly Mountain 110 G 2
Grmeč 153 G 3
Groblersdal 200 D 5
Grodekovo 173 K 2
Grodno 151 H 5
Groesbeck (TX.) 122 G 4
Groix, Ile de 152 C 2
Grójec 149 H 4
Gronau 148 E 4
Gröndalen 150 F 3
Grong 150 F 3
Groningen (Netherlands) 148 E 4
Groningen (Surinam) 139 G 2
Grønnedal 105 S 3
Groodenough, Mount 109 L 2
Groom (TX.) 117 P 2
Groote Eylandt 183 F 1
Grootfontein 200 B 3
Groot River 200 C 6
Groot Vloer 200 C 5
Groot Winter Berg 200 D 6
Gros Morne 105 Q 6
Grosser Arber 149 F 5
Grosseto 153 F 3
Grossglockner 153 F 2
Gros Ventre Range 111 P 7
Groswater Bay 105 Q 5
Grötavær 150 G 2
Grotli 150 E 3
Groton (S.D.) 119 K 5
Grottaglie 153 G 3
Grotte de Lascaux 152 D 2
Grotto (WA.) 110 D 3
Grottoes (VA.) 129 N 3
Groumania 196 D 4
Group, Actaeon 187 F 4
Grouse (ID.) 111 M 7
Grouse Creek (UT.) 114 D 2
Grouse Creek Mountain 111 M 6
Grove (KS.) 121 L 6
Grove City (MN.) 119 O 5
Grove City (OH.) 128 H 2
Grove City (PA.) 125 O 8
Grove Hill (AL.) 130 G 3
Grover (CO.) 115 N 3
Grover (UT.) 114 F 4
Grover City (CA.) 113 E 7
Groves (TX.) 123 K 6
Groveton (N.H.) 126 H 4
Groveton (TX.) 123 H 4
Grovﬁord 150 G 2
Growler (AZ.) 116 C 5
Growler Peak 116 C 5
Groznyy 155 G 2
Grubišno Polje 153 G 2
Grudziądz 149 G 4
Gruesa, Punta 140 B 5
Grums 151 F 4
Grünau 200 B 5
Grundy (VA.) 129 J 4
Grundy Center (IA.) 119 Q 8
Gruñidera 132 B 3
Gruppo di Brenta 153 F 2
Gruver (TX.) 117 P 1
Gruziya 155 F 2
Gryada Khara-Tas 170 J 1
Gryazi 158 H 5
Gryazovets 158 G 4

Grycksbo 151 G 3
Grygla (MN.) 119 N 2
Grythyttan 151 F 4
Grytviken 203
Gßkçe Ada 154 C 3
Guacamayas 138 D 3
Guacanayabo, Golfo de 133 G 3
Guacara 138 E 1
Gu Achi (AZ.) 116 DE 5
Guadalajara (Mexico) 132 B 3
Guadalajara (Spain) 152 C 3
Guadalcanal 185 G 3
Guadalcanal 186 B 4
Guadalén 152 C 4
Guadalmena 152 C 4
Guadalquivir 152 C 4
Guadalupe (AZ.) 116 E 4
Guadalupe (CA.) 113 E 7–8
Guadalupe (Mexico) 132 C 2
Guadalupe (Mexico) 132 B 3
Guadalupe, Isla de 106 C 6
Guadalupe, Sierra de 152 B 4
Guadalupe Bravos 106 E 5
Guadalupe Mountains 117 M 5–6
Guadalupe Mountains National Park 117 M 6
Guadalupe Peak 117 M 6
Guadalupe River 122 FG 7
Guadalupita (N.M.) 117 L 1
Guadarrama, Sierra de 152 C 3
Guadelope (Spain) 152 C 3
Guadeloupe (Lesser Antilles) 133 K 4
Guadeloupe Passage 133 K 4
Guadiana 152 B 4
Guadiana 152 B 4
Guadiana 152 C 4
Guadix 152 C 4
Guafo, Boca del 143 AB 7
Guafo, Isla 143 AB 7
Guafba 142 F 5
Guaina 139 F 2
Guainia 138 E 3
Guaiquinima, Cerro 139 F 2
Guaíra 141 F 5
Guaiúba 141 J 1
Guajará Mirim 140 CD 3
Guajataruba 139 F 5
Guajira, Península de 138 D 1
Guala (CA.) 112 B 4
Gualaquiza 138 C 4
Gualeguay 142 DE 5
Gualeguaychú 142 E 5
Gualicho, Salina del 143 D 7
Guallatiri 140 C 4
Guam 186 A 2
Guamá 138 J 4
Guamblin, Isla 143 A 7
Guaminí 143 D 6
Guamo 133 G 3
Guampi, Sierra de 138 E 2
Guamúchil 106 E 6
Gua Musang 176 B 3
Gu'an 173 G 3
Guanajibo, Punta 130 B 8
Guanajuato 132 B 3
Guanambi 141 H 3
Guanape, Isla 138 C 5
Guanare 138 E 2
Guanare 138 E 2
Guanarito 138 E 2
Guandacol 142 C 4
Guane 132 F 3
Guang'an 172 E 4
Guangchang 172 G 5
Guangde 173 G 4
Guangdong 172 F 6
Guanghan 172 D 4
Guanghe 172 D 3
Guanghua 172 F 4
Guangji 172 G 5
Guangling 172 F 3
Guangnan 172 DE 6
Guangning 172 F 6
Guangshan 172 F 4
Guangxi Zhuangzu Zizhiqu 172 E 6
Guangyuan 172 E 4
Guangze 173 G 5
Guangzhou 172 F 6
Guanhães 141 H 4
Guánica (P.R.) 130 C 9
Guanling 172 E 5
Guano Island 130 E 8
Guantánamo 133 H 4
Guantao 172 G 3
Guan Xian 172 D 4
Guanyun 173 G 4
Guapí 138 C 3
Guapó 141 G 4
Guaporé (Río Grande do Sul, Brazil) 142 F 4
Guaporé (Rondônia, Brazil) 140 D 3
Guaqui 140 C 4
Guarabira 141 J 2
Guaranda 138 C 4
Guarapari 141 H 5
Guarapuava 142 F 4
Guaratuba 142 G 4
Guarda 152 B 3
Guardafui, Cape 199 J 2

Guardal 152 C 4
Guardia Mitre 143 D 7
Guardo 152 C 3
Guarenas 138 E 1
Guárico 138 E 2
Guárico, Embalse del 138 E 2
Guascama, Punta 138 C 3
Guasdualito 138 D 2
Guasipati 139 F 2
Guasopa 185 F 3
Guatemala 132 D 4
Guatemala City 132 DE 5
Guaviare 138 E 3
Guaxupé 141 G 5
Guayabal 138 E 2
Guayabero 138 D 3
Guayama (P.R.) 130 C 8–9
Guayaneco, Archipiélago 143 A 8
Guayanilla (P.R.) 130 C 8
Guayaquil 138 C 4
Guayaquil, Golfo de 138 B 4
Guayaramerin 140 C 3
Guaymallén 142 C 5
Guaymas 106 D 6
Guba (U.S.S.R.) 158 F 3
Guba (Zaire) 200 D 2
Guba Buorkhaya 171 O 1
Guba Gusinaya 171 RS 1
Gubakha 159 L 4
Guban 199 GH 2
Gubba 198 F 2
Gubbio 153 F 3
Gubin 149 F 4
Gubio 197 G 3
Gubkin 158 G 5
Guchin-Us 172 D 1
Gudar, Sierra de 152 C 3
Gudauta 155 F 2
Gudbrandsdalen 150 EF 3
Guddu Barrage 169 HJ 5
Gudená 151 E 4
Gudermes 155 G 2
Gudivada 174 D 4
Gudiyattam 174 C 5
Gudur 174 C 5
Gudvangen 150 E 3
Guebwiller 153 E 2
Guékédou 196 B 4
Guelb er Richât 192 C 4
Guélengdeng 197 H 3
Guelma 193 G 1
Guelph 105 L 7
Guelta Zemmur 192 C 3
Guem 196 D 2
Guémar 193 G 2
Guéné 196 E 3
Guénéné-Penfao 152 C 2
Güera 192 B 4
Guéra 194 B 6
Guera 197 H 3
Guéra, Massif de 197 H 3
Guérande 152 C 2
Guéret 152 D 2
Guerneville (CA.) 112 B 4
Guernsey 148 C 5
Guernsey (WY.) 118 D 8
Guernsey Reservoir 118 D 8
Guérou 192 C 5
Guerra (TX.) 122 E 9
Guerrero 132 B 4
Guerzim 192 E 3
Gueydan (LA.) 123 L 5
Guffey (CO.) 115 M 5
Guﬀy Peak 111 S 7
Guga 171 P 5
Gügerd, Küh-e (Iran) 157 F 2
Gughe 199 F 3
Guguan 186 A 1
Guiana Highlands 139 FH 3
Guibes 200 B 5
Guichi 173 G 4
Guide 172 D 3
Guider 197 G 4
Guiding 172 E 5
Guidimouni 197 F 3
Guidjiba (Ngaoundéré) 197 G 4
Guidong 172 F 5
Guiers, Lac de 196 A 2
Guiglo 196 C 4
Guiguinto 177 F 1
Guijá 201 E 4
Guijuelo 152 B 3
Guildford 148 C 4
Guildhall (VT.) 126 H 4
Guilford (ME.) 126 K 3
Guilin 172 F 5
Guillaume Delisle, Lac 105 M 4
Guilvinec 152 C 2
Guimarães 152 B 3
Guimaras 177 F 1
Guin (AL.) 128 D 8
Guinan 172 D 3
Guinea 196 B 3
Guinea, Gulf of 197 EF 5

Guinea Basin 208 A 3
Guinea-Bissau 196 AB 3
Guinea Equatorial 197 F 5
Güines 133 F 3
Guingamp 152 C 2
Guinguinéo 196 A 3
Guir 196 D 2
Guiratinga 141 F 4
Guiria 139 F 1
Guisanbourg 139 H 3
Guita Koulouba 198 C 3
Guitiriz 152 B 3
Guitri 196 C 4
Guiuan 177 G 1
Guixi 173 G 5
Gui Xian 172 E 6
Guiyang 172 E 5
Guizhou 172 E 5
Gujarat 174 B 3
Gujar Khan 169 J 4
Gujranwala 169 J 4
Gujrat 169 J 4
Gu Komelik (AZ.) 116 E 5
Gukovo 155 F 1
Gulang 172 D 3
Gulbarga 174 C 4
Gulbene 151 J 4
Gul'cha 169 J 2
Gülek Boğazı 155 D 3
Gulf Breeze (FL.) 130 G 4
Gulf Islands National Seashore 130 GH 4
Gulf of Aden 195 H 6
Gulf of Alaska 102 HJ 4
Gulf of Aqaba → Khalīj al 'Aqa-bah 194 E 3
Gulf of Boothia 103 T 1
Gulf of Bothnia 150 GH 3
Gulf of Carpentaria 183 F 1
Gulf of Chihli 173 GH 3
Gulf of Danzig 149 G 4
Gulf of Guinea 197 EF 5
Gulf of Khambhat 174 B 3–4
Gulf of Kutch 174 A 3
Gulf of Maine 126 KM 6
Gulf of Mannar 174 C 6
Gulf of Martaban 175 C 4
Gulf of Mexico 132 DE 2
Gulf of Ob 159 O 2
Gulf of Oman 195 K 4
Gulf of Papua 184 DE 3
Gulf of Papua 186 A 3
Gulf of Riga 151 H 4
Gulf of Saint Lawrence 105 P 6
Gulf of Santa Catalina 113 GH 9
Gulf of Sirt 193 J 2
Gulf of Suez 156 A 3
Gulf of Thailand 175 H 5
Gulf of Tonking 175 J 3–4
Gulf of Venice 153 F 2
Gulfport (FL.) 131 M 6
Gulfport (MS.) 130 E 4
Gulf Saint Vincent 183 F 6
Gulf Shores (AL.) 130 G 4
Gulgong 183 H 5
Gulian 171 M 5
Gulin 172 E 5
Gulistan 169 H 2
Guliya Shan 171 M 6
Gulkana 102 H 3
Gulkhari (Iran) 157 F 3
Gullﬁoss 150 B 3
Gullivan Bay 131 N 9
Gullkrona fjärd 151 H 4
Gull Lake (MN.) 119 O 4
Gull Lake (Sask., Can.) 103 Q 5
Gullspång 151 F 4
Güllük 154 C 3
Gülnar 155 D 3
Gulnare (CO.) 115 N 6
Gülşehir 155 D 3
Gul'shad 159 O 6
Gulu 198 E 4
Gülübovo 154 C 2
Guluguba 183 HJ 4
Gulwe 199 F 6
Gulya 170 M 5
Gulyaypole 155 E 1
Gumbiri 198 E 4
Gumbira 201 F 2
Gümbet 155 E 2
Gumel 197 F 3
Gummi 197 F 3
Gumuru 198 E 3
Gümüşane Dağları 155 E 2
Gümüshane 155 E 2
Guna (Ethiopia) 199 F 2
Guna (India) 174 C 3
Gunda 170 K 5
Gundagai 183 H 6
Gundji 198 C 3
Gundoğmus 155 D 3
Güneydoğu Toros lar 155 EF 3
Gungu 198 B 6
Guni 197 F 3
Gunib 168 D 2
Gunnar 103 Q 4
Günnariyn 172 D 1
Gunnarn 150 G 3
Gunnedah 183 HJ 5
Gunnison (CO.) 115 L 5

Gunnison (UT.) 114 F 4
Gunnison, Mount 115 K 5
Gunnison River 115 JK 5
Guntakal 174 C 4
Guntersville (AL.) 128 E 7
Guntersville Lake 128 E 7
Guntur 174 D 4
Gunung Abong Abong 176 A 3
Gunung Agung 176 E 5
Gunung Angemuk 177 J 4
Gunung Api 177 E 5
Gunung Bakayan 176 E 3
Gunung Balikpapan 176 E 4
Gunung Bandahara 176 A 3
Gunung Batai 176 BC 5
Gunung Batulantee 176 E 5
Gunung Batu Puteh 176 B 3
Gunung Besar 176 E 4
Gunung Binaiya 177 G 4
Gunung Boliohutu 177 F 3
Gunung Ceremai 176 C 5
Gunung Dempo 176 B 4
Gunung Gamkunoro 177 G 3
Gunung Gueredong 176 A 3
Gunung Kaubalatmada 177 G 4
Gunung Kerinci 176 B 4
Gunung Kinabalu 176 E 2
Gunung Klabat 177 G 3
Gunung Kongkemul 176 E 3
Gunung Kwoka 177 H 4
Gunung Lawit 176 D 3
Gunung Leuser 176 A 3
Gunung Lewotobi 177 F 5
Gunung Liangpran 176 D 3
Gunung Lokilalaki 177 F 4
Gunung Lompobatang 177 F 5
Gunung Maling 177 F 3
Gunung Marapi 176 B 4
Gunung Mekongga 177 F 4
Gunung Menyapa 176 E 3
Gunung Mulu 176 DE 3
Gunung Mutis 177 F 5
Gunung Niut 176 CD 3
Gunung Ogoamas 177 F 3
Gunung Pangrango 176 C 5
Gunung Peuetsagu 176 A 3
Gunung Rinjani 176 E 5
Gunung Saran 176 D 4
Gunung Sarempaka 176 E 4
Gunung Sinabung 176 A 3
Gunung Sitoli 176 A 3
Gunung Slamet 176 C 5
Gunung Sombang 176 E 3
Gunung Sorikmerapi 176 A 3
Gunungsugih 176 C 4
Gunung Tahan 176 B 3
Gunung Talakmau 176 B 3
Gunung Tambora 177 E 5
Gunung Tentolomatinan 177 F 3
Gunung Wanggameti 177 EF 6
Gunung Waukara 177 E 4
Gu Oidak (AZ.) 116 D 6
Guoiret es Soud 193 F 3
Guoyang 172 G 4
Gurais 169 K 4
Guran 170 H 5
Gurara 197 F 4
Gurban Obo 172 F 2
Gurbantünggüt Shamo 169 M 1–2
Gurdaspur 174 C 1
Gurdim 168 FG 5
Gurdon (AR.) 121 M 9
Gurdzhaani 155 G 2
Gurgan (Iran) 157 G 1
Gurgaon 174 C 2
Gurgei, Jabal 194 C 6
Gürgen Tepe 155 E 2
Gurgueia 141 H 2
Gurha 174 B 2
Guri Dam 139 F 2
Gurimatu 184 D 3
Gürlevik Daği 155 E 3
Gurley (NE.) 118 F 9
Guro 201 E 3
Gürpınar 155 F 3
Gurskoye 171 P 5
Gúruè 201 F 3
Gürun 155 E 3
Gurupá 139 H 4
Gurupá, Ilha Grande do 139 H 4
Gurupi (Brazil) 139 J 4
Gurupí (Goiás, Brazil) 141 G 3
Gurupi, Cabo 139 J 4
Gurupi, Serra do 139 J 4–5
Guru Sikhar 174 B 3
Guruve 201 E 3
Guruzala 174 C 4
Gurvanbulag 170 H 6
Gurvan Sayhan Uul 172 D 2
Gur'yev 168 E 1
Gur'yevsk 159 R 5
Gusau 197 F 3
Gusave 106 E 6
Güselyurt (Cyprus) 156 A 2
Gusev 151 H 5
Gushi 172 G 4
Gushiago 196 D 4
Gusikha 170 J 1
Gusinaya Zemlya, Poluostrov 158 K 1
Gusinoozersk 170 J 5
Gusinoye Ozero 170 J 5
Gus'Khrustal'nyy 158 GH 4
Gusmp, Ostrov 171 U 1–2
Guspini 153 E 4
Güssing 153 G 2
Gustavus 102 K 4
Gustine (CA.) 112 D 5
Gustine (TX.) 122 E 4
Güstrow 149 F 4
Guthrie (KY.) 128 D 5
Guthrie (OK.) 120 H 7
Guthrie (TX.) 117 Q 4
Guthrie Center (IA.) 119 O 9
Gutian 173 G 5
Gutii, Virful 154 B 1
Guttenberg (IA.) 119 R 8
Guyana 139 G 3
Guyenne 152 CD 3
Guymon (OK.) 120 D 6
Guyra 183 J 5
Guyuan 172 E 3
Guyuan 173 G 2
Guzar 169 H 3
Güzelhisar 154 C 3
Güzelyurt 155 D 3
Güzhān (Iran) 157 E 2
Guzhang 172 EF 5
Guzhen 173 G 4
Gvardeysk 151 H 5
Gvardeyskoye 155 D 1
Gvarv 151 E 4
Gwa 175 F 4
Gwadabawa 197 F 3
Gwadar 169 G 5
Gwai 200 D 3
Gwalior 174 C 2
Gwanda 200 D 4
Gwane 198 D 4
Gwatar Bay 169 G 5–6
Gwda 149 G 4
Gwebin 175 F 3
Gweru 200 D 3
Gweta 200 D 4
Gwinn (MI.) 124 G 3
Gwinner (N.D.) 119 L 4
Gyaca 172 B 5
Gya La 174 E 2
Gyangzê 174 E 2
Gyaring 172 C 3
Gyaring Co 174 E 1
Gyaring Hu 172 C 4
Gyda 159 P 1
Gydanskaya Guba 159 P 1
Gydanskiy Poluostrov 159 P 1–2
Gyirong 174 E 2
Gyitang 172 C 4
Gympie 183 J 4
Gyöngyös 154 A 1
Győr 154 A 1
Győr 154 A 1
Gypsum (CO.) 115 KL 4
Gypsum (KS.) 120 H 4
Gypsum Hills 120 F 6
Gypsum Point 103 O 3
Gypsumville 103 S 5
Gyula 154 B 1
Gyurgyan 168 E 2

H

Haanhöniy Uul 170 F 6
Haanja Kõrgustik 151 J 4
Ha'apai Group 186 D 4
Haapajärvi 150 HJ 3
Haapavesi 150 J 3
Haapsalu 151 H 4
Haarlem 148 D 4
Haast 184 P 9
Haast 186 C 5
Habahe 169 M 1
Habarūt 195 J 5
Habas 192 C 3
Ḥabashīyah, Jabal 195 J 5
Habaswein 199 FG 4
Habay (Alb., Can.) 103 O 4
Habay (Somalia) 199 G 4
Ḥabbān 195 H 6
Ḥabbānīyah (Iraq) 156 D 2
Ḥabbānīyah, Hawral (Iraq) 156 D 2
Habiganj 175 F 3
Habīt Awlād Muḥammad 193 H 2
Ḥabshān (United Arab Emirates) 157 F 5
Hachijō-jima 173 LM 4
Hachinohe 173 M 2
Hachita (N.M.) 116 H 6
Hacıbektaş 155 D 3
Hackamore (CA.) 112 D 1
Hackberry (LA.) 123 K 5–6
Hackbery (AZ.) 116 C 2
Hackleburg (AL.) 128 D 7
Hackney (KS.) 120 H 5
Haḍabat al Jilf al Kabīr 194 D 4
Ḥadada, Jabal 194 D 4
Ḥaḍan, Ḥarrat 195 G 4
Ḥadāribah, Ra's al 194 F 4
Ḥadd, Ra's al 195 KL 4
Ḥaddā' 195 F 4
Haddam (KS.) 120 H 3
Ḥadded 199 H 2
Hadejia 197 F 3
Hadejia 197 G 3
Hadeland 151 F 3
Hadera (Israel) 156 B 2
Haderslev 151 E 4
Ḥādh Banī Zaynān 195 H 4
Hadīboh 199 J 2
Hadid, Jabal 193 K 4
Hadilik 169 M 3
Hadım 155 D 3
Hadım (Turkey) 156 A 1
Hadjer el Hamis 197 GH 3
Hadjer Kamaran 197 J 3
Hadjer Mardi 197 J 3
Hadjer Mornou 197 J 2
Hadjer Telfane 197 H 3
Hadjout 152 D 4
Hadley Bay 103 Q 1
Hadlock (WA.) 110 C 2
Ha Dong 175 J 3
Ḥaḍramawt 195 H 5
Hadrian's Wall 148 C 3–4
Hadsund 151 F 4
Haeju 173 J 3
Haena (HI.) 113 C 9
Ḥafar al 'Atk (Saudi Arabia) 157 E 4
Ḥafar al Bāṭin (Saudi Arabia) 157 E 3
Hafik 155 E 3
Ḥafīrat al 'Aydā (Saudi Arabia) 156 C 4
Ḥafīt (Oman) 157 G 4–5
Ḥafīt, Jabal (United Arab Emirates) 157 G 4
Hafnarfjörður 150 A 3
Haft Gel (Iran) 157 E 3
Ḥāfūn 199 J 2
Ḥāfūn, Ra's 199 J 2
Hag 'Abdullah 194 E 6
Hagadera 199 G 4
Hagari 174 C 5
Hagemeister 102 E 4
Hagen 149 E 4
Hagerhill (KY.) 128 J 4
Hagerman (ID.) 111 KL 8
Hagerman (N.M.) 117 M 4
Hagerstown (MD.) 129 O 2
Hagewood (LA.) 123 K 4
Hagfors 151 F 3
Häggenås 150 G 3
Haggin, Mount 111 M 4
Ha Giang 175 J 3
Hags Head 148 AB 4
Hague (ND.) 118 J 4
Hague, Cap de la 152 C 2
Haguenau 153 E 2
Hagues Peak 115 M 3
Hagunia 192 C 3
Hahira (GA.) 131 L 3
Hai'an 173 H 4
Haicheng 173 H 2
Hai Duong 175 J 3
Haifa (Israel) 156 B 2
Haifeng 172 G 6
Haig (NE.) 118 E 9
Haigler (NE.) 120 D 3
Haigler (NE.) 120 D 3
Hai He 173 G 3
Haikang 172 EF 6
Haikou 172 F 6–7
Ḥā'il (Saudi Arabia) 156 C 4
Hailakandi 175 F 3
Hailar 170 L 6
Hailar He 170 M 6
Hailey (ID.) 111 L 7
Hailin 173 J 2
Hailing Dao 172 F 6
Hailong 173 HJ 2
Hailun 171 N 6
Hailuoto 150 H 2
Haimen 173 H 4
Hainan Dao 172 F 7
Haines (AK.) 102 K 4
Haines (OR.) 110 H 6
Haines City (FL.) 131 N 6
Haines Junction 102 K 3
Hai Phong 175 J 3
Haiqing 171 O 6
Haïti 133 H 4
Haivare 184 D 3
Haiwee Reservoir 112 H 6
Haiyan 172 D 3
Haiyang 173 H 3
Haiyuan 172 E 3
Haizhou Wan 173 G 4
Hajar, Tall al (Syria) 156 B 2
Ḥajārah, Saḥrā' al 195 GH 2–H 3
Hajdúböszormény 154 B 1
Hajdúság 154 B 1
Hajhir, Jabal 199 J 2
Hajipur 174 E 2
Ḥājjīābād (Iran) 157 G 3
Ḥājjīābād (Iran) 157 G 3
Ḥajjīābād-e Māsīleh (Iran) 157 F 2
Hajmah 195 K 4–5
Haka 175 F 3
Hakkâri 155 F 3
Hakkâri Dağları 155 F 3
Hakkas 150 H 2
Hakksund 151 E 4
Hakodate 173 M 2
Haku-san 173 L 3
Halab (Iran) 157 E 1
Halab (Syria) 156 B 1
Ḥalabjah (Iraq) 157 DE 2
Ḥalā'ib 194 F 4
Halali 200 B 3
Halawa (HI.) 113 F 10
Halawa, Cape 113 F 10
Ḥalbā (Lebanon) 156 B 2
Halberstadt 149 F 4
Halcon, Mount 177 F 1
Halden 151 F 4
Haldia 174 E 3
Haldia 174 E 3
Haldwani 174 C 2
Hale (MO.) 121 M 3
Hale, Mount 182 B 4
Haleakala National Park 113 F 11
Hale Center (TX.) 117 P 3
Haletown (TN.) 128 F 6
Haley (ND.) 118 E 5
Haleyville (AL.) 128 D 7
Halfeti 155 E 3
Ḥalī 195 G 5
Halia 174 D 3
Halicarnassus 154 C 3
Halifax 105 P 7
Halifax (N.C.) 129 O 5
Halifax (Queensland, Austr.) 183 H 2
Halifax (U.K.) 148 C 4
Halifax (VA.) 129 M 5
Halifax, Mount 183 H 2
Halifax Bay 183 H 2
Hālil 168 F 5
Ḥalin 199 H 3
Halkett, Cape 102 G 1
Hall (AK.) 102 C 3
Hall (MT.) 111 M 4
Halland 151 F 4
Ḥallat 'Ammār 194 F 3
Hallat' Ammār (Saudi Arabia) 156 B 3
Hall Beach 103 V 2
Halle 149 F 4
Halleberg 151 F 4
Halleck (NV.) 112 K 2
Hällefors 151 F 4
Hallettsville (TX.) 122 FG 6
Halley Bay 203
Halliday (ND.) 118 F 3
Halligan Reservoir 115 M 3
Hallingdalselva 151 E 3
Hallingskarvet 151 E 3
Hall Islands 186 B 2
Hall Lake 103 V 2
Hällnäs 150 G 3
Hallock (MN.) 119 M 2
Hall Peninsula 105 O 3
Hallsberg 151 G 4
Halls Creek 182 D 2
Hallstahammar 151 G 4
Hallstatt 153 F 2
Hallstavik 151 G 3
Hallstead (PA.) 126 D 7
Hall Summit (LA.) 123 K 3
Halmahera 177 G 3
Halmahera, Laut 177 G 4
Halmstad 151 F 4
Hals 151 F 4
Halsey (NE.) 118 H 9
Halsey (OR.) 110 B 6
Hälsingeskogen 150 G 3
Hälsingland 150 G 3
Halsön 150 H 3
Halstad (MN.) 119 LM 3
Haltia 150 H 2
Haltom City (TX.) 122 F 3
Ḥālūl (Qatar) 157 F 4
Ham 197 H 3
Hamab 200 B 5
Hamada de Tindouf 192 D 3
Hamada de Tinrhert 193 G 3
Hamada du Drâa 192 D 3
Hamada du Guir 192 E 2
Hamada el Haricha 192 E 4
Hamada Mangueni 197 G 1
Hamadān (Iran) 157 E 2
Hamada Safia 192 E 4
Hamada Tounassine 192 DE 3
Ḥamādat Tingharat 193 H 3
Hamāh (Syria) 156 B 2
Hamamatsu 173 L 4
Hamar 151 F 3
Hamarro Hadad 199 G 3
Hămașu Mare, Virful 154 C 1
Hamātah, Jabal (Egypt) 156 B 4
Hambantota 174 D 6
Hamberg (ND.) 118 J 3
Hamburg 149 F 4
Hamburg (AR.) 121 O 9
Hamburg (CA.) 112 C 1
Hamburg (IA.) 119 N 10
Hamburg (N.Y.) 125 Q 7
Hamburg (PA.) 127 D 8
Hamd, Wādī al (Saudi Arabia) 156 B 4
Ḥamḍah 195 G 5
Ḥamdānah 195 G 5
Hamden (CT.) 127 G 7
Häme 150 HJ 3
Hämeenlinna (Tavastehus) 150 HJ 3
Hämeenselkä 150 H 3
Hamelin Pool 182 A 4
Hamelin Pool 182 A 4
Hameln 149 E 4
Hamer (ID.) 111 N 7
Hamersley Range 182 B 3
Hamersley Range National Park 182 B 3
Hamgyŏng-sanmaek 173 J 2
Hamhŭng 173 J 3
Hami 172 B 2
Ḥamīd (Iran) 157 E 3
Ḥamīdīyeh (Iran) 157 E 3
Hamill (SD.) 118 J 7
Hamilton (AK.) 108 F 3
Hamilton (AL.) 128 D 7
Hamilton (Bermuda Is.) 133 K 1
Hamilton (CO.) 115 K 3
Hamilton (GA.) 131 K 2
Hamilton (IL.) 124 C 9
Hamilton (KS.) 120 J 5
Hamilton (MI.) 124 J 7
Hamilton (MO.) 121 LM 3
Hamilton (MT.) 111 L 4
Hamilton (N.D.) 119 L 2
Hamilton (New Zealand) 185 R 8
Hamilton (New Zealand) 186 C 5
Hamilton (OH.) 128 G 2
Hamilton (Ontario, Can.) 105 M 7
Hamilton (Queensland, Austr.) 183 G 3
Hamilton (TX.) 122 E 4
Hamilton (Victoria, Austr.) 183 G 6
Hamilton, Mount (AK.) 108 G 3
Hamilton, Mount (NV.) 112 K 3
Hamilton Acres 109 J 3
Hamilton City (CA.) 112 D 3
Hamilton Dorne (WY.) 111 R 7
Hamilton River 183 G 3
Hamiltons Fort (UT.) 114 D 6
Ḥamīm, Wādī 193 K 2
Hamina (Fredrikshamn) 151 J 3
Hamirpur 174 D 2
Hamlin (TX.) 122 C 3
Hamlin (W.V.) 129 J 3
Hamm 149 E 4
Ḥammādat Mānghīnī 193 H 4
Ḥammām al 'Alīl 195 G 1
Ḥammam al 'Alīl (Iraq) 156 D 1
Hammām al Anf 193 H 1
Ḥammāmāt 193 H 1
Hammami 192 C 4
Hammar, Hawr al (Iraq) 157 E 3
Hammarstrand 150 G 3
Hammerdal 150 FG 3
Hammerfest 150 H 1
Hammon (OK.) 120 F 7
Hammond (LA.) 123 N 5
Hammond (MT.) 118 D 5
Hammondsport (N.Y.) 126 B 6
Hammonton (N.J.) 127 E 9
Hammur Koke 199 F 3
Hamodji 197 G 2
Hamoyet, Jabal 194 F 5
Hampden 185 Q 10
Hampden (N.D.) 119 K 2
Hampton (AR.) 121 N 9
Hampton (FL.) 131 M 5
Hampton (GA.) 128 G 8
Hampton (IA.) 119 P 8
Hampton (N.H.) 126 J 6
Hampton (OR.) 110 E 7
Hampton (S.C.) 129 K 9
Hampton (VA.) 129 P 4
Hampton Bays (N.Y.) 127 G 8
Hampton Butte 110 E 7
Hamra 150 G 3
Hamrān (Iran) 157 D 1
Ḥamrat ash Shaykh 194 D 6
Hamrīn, Jabal (Iraq) 156–157 D 2
Hamuku 177 HJ 4
Hamum i Mashkel 169 G 5
Hāmun-e Hīrmand 169 G 4
Hāmūn-e Jaz Mūriān 168 F 5
Han 196 D 3
Hana (HI.) 113 G 11
Hanahan (S.C.) 129 LM 9
Hanak (Saudi Arabia) 156 B 4
Hanalei (HI.) 113 C 9
Hanamaki 173 M 3
Hanang 198 EF 5
Hanapepe (HI.) 113 C 10
Hanbogd 172 E 2
Hanceville 103 N 5
Hanceville (AL.) 128 E 7
Hancheng 172 F 3
Hanchuan 172 F 4
Hancock (MD.) 129 NO 2
Hancock (MI.) 124 F 2
Hancock (MN.) 119 N 5
Hancock (N.Y.) 126 D 7
Hancock, Mount 111 P 6
Handan 172 F 3
Handen 151 G 4
Handeni 199 F 6
Hanegev (Israel) 156 B 3
Haney (TX.) 117 P 2
Hanford (CA.) 112 F 6
Hanford (WA.) 110 F 4
Hangay 170 G 6
Hangayn Nuruu 170 GH H 6

Han – Hei

Hanggin Houqi 172 E 2
Hanggin Qi 172 E 3
Hangö (Hanko) 151 H 4
Hangu (China) 173 G 3
Hangu (Pakistan) 169 J 4
Hangya 172 C 3
Hangzhou 173 H 4
Hangzhou Wan 173 H 4
Hanh 170 H 5
Han Jiang 172 G 6
Ḥanjūrah, Ra's (United Arab Emirates) 157 G 4
Hankasalmi 150 J 3
Hankinson (N.D.) 119 M 4
Hanko 151 H 4
Hankoniemi 151 H 4
Hanksville (UT.) 114 G 5
Hanle 169 K 4
Hanna (Alberta, Can.) 103 P 5
Hanna (UT.) 114 G 3MO
Hanna (WY.) 118 B 9
Hannaford (N.D.) 119 K 3
Hannah (N.D.) 119 K 2
Hannah Bay 105 LM 5
Hannibal (MO.) 121 O 3
Hannibal (N.Y.) 126 C 5
Hannover (F.R.G.) 149 E 4
Hannover (ND.) 118 G 3
Hanöbukten 151 FG 4
Ha Noi 175 J 3
Hanover (F.R.G.) 149 E 4
Hanover (MT.) 111 Q 3
Hanover (NE.) 120 J 3
Hanover (N.H.) 126 G 5
Hanover (PA.) 127 C 9
Hanover (South Africa) 200 C 6
Hanover (VA.) 129 O 4
Hanover, Islas 143 AB 9
Hansboro (N.D.) 118 J 2
Han Shui 172 F 4
Hanska (MN.) 119 O 6
Hanstholm 151 E 4
Hanston (KS.) 120 F 4
Hantengri Feng 169 L 2
Hantzsch 105 N 2
Han-Uul 170 L 6
Hanuy Gol 170 H 6
Hanyuan 172 D 5
Hanzhong 172 E 4
Hao 187 F 4
Haouach 197 J 2
Haoud el Hamra 193 G 2
Haparanda 150 H 2
Hapo 177 G 3
Happy (TX.) 117 P 3
Happy Camp (CA.) 112 B 1
Happy Jack (AZ.) 116 E 3
Hapur 174 C 2
Ḥaql (Saudi Arabia) 156 B 3
Ḥaql (Saudi Arabia) 156 B 3
Hara 170 J 6
Haraa Gol 170 J 6
Ḥaraḍ 195 G 5
Hara Fanna 199 G 3
Haraiki 187 F 4
Harand (Iran) 157 F 2
Harar 199 G 3
Hararge 199 G 3
Harāsīs, Jiddat al 195 K 4–5
Harāwah 193 J 2
Har-Ayrag 172 E 1
Harāzah, Jabal 194 E 6
Haraz Djoumba 197 H 3
Harazé 197 J 4
Harbel 196 B 4
Harbin 173 J 1
Harbor Beach (MI.) 125 M 6
Harbor Springs (MI.) 125 K 4
Harbour Breton 105 Q 6
Harbour Grace 105 R 6
Harcuvar Mountains 116 C 3–4
Harda 174 C 3
Hardangerfjorden 151 E 3–4
Hardangerjökulen 151 E 3
Hardangervidda 151 E 3
Hardap Dam 200 B 4
Hardaway (FL.) 131 K 4
Hardeeville (S.C.) 129 KL 9
Hardesty (OK.) 120 D 6
Hardin (IL.) 121 P 3
Hardin (MT.) 111 S 5
Hardin (TX.) 123 J 5
Harding (SD.) 118 E 5
Harding, Lake 131 J 2
Hardinsburg (KY.) 128 E 4
Hardman (OR.) 110 F 5
Hardoi 174 D 2
Hardtner (KS.) 120 G 5
Hardwar 174 C 2
Hardwick (GA.) 128 H 8
Hardwick (VT.) 126 G 4
Hardy (AR.) 121 O 6
Hardy (IA.) 119 OP 8
Hardy (MT.) 111 O 3
Hardy (OK.) 120 J 6
Hardy Dam Pond 124 J 6

Harēri Mālin Warfā 199 H 4
Harga 198 C 3
Hargeysa 199 G 3
Hargill (TX.) 122 EF 9
Har Hu 172 C 3
Hari, Batang 176 B 4
Ḥarib 195 H 6
Harihari 185 Q 9
Harike Barrage 174 C 1
Hari Kurk 151 H 4
Ḥārim 156 B 1
Haringhat 175 F 3
Haripur 169 J 4
Hari Rud 169 G 4
Harjavalta 150 H 3
Härjedalen 150 F 3
Harlan (IA.) 119 N 9
Harlan County Lake 120 F 2
Harlem (MT.) 111 R 2
Harlingen (Netherlands) 148 E 4
Harlingen (TX.) 122 F 9
Harlow 148 D 4
Harlow (ND.) 118 J 2
Harlowton (MT.) 111 Q 4
Harmak 169 G 4
Harmalīyah (Saudi Arabia) 157 E 4
Harman (W.V.) 129 M 3
Harmancık 154 C 3
Harmånger 150 G 3
Harmony (MN.) 119 Q 7
Harnai 169 H 4
Harney (NV.) 112 J 2
Harney (OR.) 110 G 7
Harney Basin 110 EG 7
Harney Lake 110 F 7
Harney Peak 118 E 7
Härnön 150 G 3
Härnösand 150 G 3
Har Nuur 170 F 6
Haröyfjorden 150 E 3
Harper 196 C 5
Harper (KS.) 120 GH 5
Harper (OR.) 110 H 7
Harper (TX.) 122 D 5
Harper Lake 113 H 7
Harpers Ferry (MD.) 129 O 2
Harpster (ID.) 111 K 4
Harqin Qi 173 G 2
Harquahala Mountain 116 C 4
Ḥarrat al Buqūm 195 G 4
Ḥarrat al Kishb 195 G 4
Ḥarrat al ‘Uwayrid (Saudi Arabia) 156 B 4
Ḥarrat ar Rahāh (Saudi Arabia) 156 B 4
Ḥarrat Ḥaḍan 195 G 4
Ḥarrat Ithnayn (Saudi Arabia) 156 C 4
Ḥarrat Khaybar (Saudi Arabia) 156 C 4
Ḥarrat Kuramā (Saudi Arabia) 156 C 4
Ḥarrat Lunayyir (Saudi Arabia) 156 B 4
Ḥarrat Nawāṣīf 195 G 4
Ḥarrat Rahaṭ 195 G 4
Harricana 105 M 5
Harriman (WY.) 118 C 9
Harrington (ME.) 126 M 4
Harrington (PA.) 127 D 10
Harrington (SD.) 118 G 7
Harrington (WA.) 110 G 3
Harrington Harbour 105 Q 5
Harris 148 B 3
Harris (MN.) 119 PQ 5
Harris, Lake 131 N 6
Harrisburg (AR.) 121 P 7
Harrisburg (IL.) 121 R 5
Harrisburg (NE.) 118 E 9
Harrisburg (OR.) 110 B 6
Harrisburg (PA.) 127 C 8
Harrismith 200 D 5
Harrison (AR.) 121 M 6
Harrison (ID.) 110 J 3
Harrison (MI.) 125 K 5
Harrison (NE.) 118 E 8
Harrison, Cape 105 Q 5
Harrison Bay 102 G 1
Harrisonburg (LA.) 123 M 4
Harrisonburg (VA.) 129 MN 3
Harrisonville (MO.) 121 L 4
Harriston (MS.) 130 CD 3
Harrisville (N.Y.) 126 D 4
Harrisville (W.V.) 129 KL 2
Harrodsburg (KY.) 128 FG 4
Harrogate 148 C 4
Harrold (ID.) 118 J 6
Harrold (TX.) 122 D 1
Harry S. Truman Dam 121 M 4
Harry S. Truman Reservoir 121 M 4
Harry Strunk Lake 120 E 2
Har Sai Shan 172 C 3
Harshō 199 H 2
Harsim (Iran) 157 E 2
Harsin (Iran) 157 E 2
Harşit 155 E 2
Harsprånget 150 GH 2
Harstad 150 G 2
Harsvik 150 E 3
Hart (MI.) 124 H 6
Hart (TX.) 117 O 3
Hartbees 200 C 5
Hartford (AL.) 131 J 3
Hartford (CT.) 126 G 7
Hartford (IA.) 119 P 9

Hartford (KY.) 128 E 4
Hartford (MI.) 124 H 7
Hartford (S.D.) 119 M 7
Hartford (WI.) 124 F 6
Hartford City (IN.) 124 J 9
Hartington (NE.) 119 L 8
Hart Lake 110 F 8
Hartland Point 148 BC 4
Hartlepool 148 C 4
Hartley (IA.) 119 N 7
Hartley (TX.) 117 O 2
Hartley → Chegutu 200 DE 3
Hartman (CO.) 115 P 5
Hartola 200 B 4
Hartsel (CO.) 115 M 4
Hartselle (AL.) 128 E 7
Hartshorne (OK.) 121 K 8
Harts Range 182 E 3
Hartsville (S.C.) 129 L 7
Hartsville (TN.) 128 E 5
Hartville (MO.) 121 N 5
Hartville (WY.) 118 D 8
Hartwell (GA.) 128 J 8
Hartwell Lake 128 J 7
Hartz Mountains National Park 184 L 9
Haruchas 200 B 4
Har Us Nuur 170 F 6
Ḥarūṭ 195 J 5
Harvard (ID.) 110 J 4
Harvard (IL.) 124 F 7
Harvard (NE.) 120 G 2
Harvard, Mount 115 L 5
Harvey (MI.) 124 G 3
Harvey (N.D.) 118 J 3
Harvey (Western Australia) 182 B 5
Harwich 148 D 4
Harwood (N.C.) 129 P 7
Haryana 174 C 2
Harz 149 F 4
Hasalbag 169 K 3
Hasanābād (Iran) 157 EF 1
Hasanābād (Iran) 157 FG 3
Hasançelebi 155 E 3
Hasan Langi 168 F 5
Hasār 168 F 5
Hasekiyata 154 C 2
Haseré Vokré 197 G 4
Haskell (OK.) 121 K 7
Haskell (TX.) 122 D 2
Haslet (TX.) 122 F 2–3
Hassan 174 C 5
Hassayampa River 116 D 3–4
Hasse 149 E 4
Hassela 150 G 3
Hassi Barouda 193 F 3
Hassi Bel Guebbour 193 G 3
Hassi Bou Akba 192 D 3
Hassi Bou Krechba 193 G 3
Hassi Bou Zid 193 F 2
Hassi Chaamba 192 E 3
Hassi Djafou 193 F 2
Hassi el Hadadra 193 F 2
Hassi el Krenig 193 F 3
Hassi Erg Sedra 193 F 2
Hassi Fokra 192 E 2
Hassi Habadra 193 F 3
Hassi Imoulaye 193 G 3
Hassi Inifel 193 F 2
Hassi Insokki 193 F 3
Hassi Krezrez 193 F 3
Hassi Marroket 193 F 2
Hassi Messaoud 193 G 2
Hassi Ouchen 192 F 2
Hassi R'Mel 193 F 2
Hassi Serouenout 193 G 4
Hassi Tartrat 193 G 2
Hassi Timellouline 193 G 3
Hassi Tin Fouchaye 193 G 3
Hassi Zemmoul 192 D 3
Hassi Zirara 193 F 2
Hässleholm 151 F 4
Hassman (MN.) 119 P 4
Hastings (FL.) 131 N 5
Hastings (MI.) 124 J 7
Hastings (MN.) 119 Q 6
Hastings (NE.) 120 G 2
Hastings (New Zealand) 185 R 8
Hastings (U.K.) 148 D 4
Hasty (CO.) 115 OP 5
Hasvik 150 H 1
Haswell (CO.) 115 OP 5
Ḥasy Hague 193 H 3
Hatanbulag 172 E 2
Hatch (N.M.) 117 J 5
Hatch (UT.) 114 E 6
Hat Creek (CA.) 112 D 2
Ḥaṭeg 154 B 1
Hatgal 170 G H 5
Hathaway (MT.) 118 B 4
Hat Hin 175 H 3
Hathras 174 C 2
Ḥāṭībah, Ra's 194 F 4
Ha Tien 175 H 5
Ha Tinh 175 J 4
Hatisar 175 F 2
Hatta 174 C 3
Hattah 183 G 5
Hatteras (N.C.) 129 Q 6
Hatteras, Cape 129 Q 6
Hatteras Island 129 Q 6
Hattfjelldal 150 F 2

Hattiesburg (MS.) 130 E 3
Hatton (AL.) 128 D 7
Hatton (N.D.) 119 L 3
Hatton Bank 208 A 2
Hatutu 187 F 3
Hat Yai 175 H 6
Hauberg Mountains 203
Haud 199 GH 3
Hauge 151 E 4
Hauge (N.Y.) 126 F 5
Haugesund 151 DE 4
Haugsdorf 153 G 2
Haukeligrend 151 E 4
Haukipudas 150 HJ 2
Haukivesi 150 J 3
Haukivuori 150 J 3
Hauraki Gulf 185 R 8
Hausa 192 C 3
Hauser (OR.) 110 A 7
Hausruck 153 F 2
Haut, Isle au 126 L 4
Hauterive 105 O 6
Haute-Saône, Plateau de 153 E 2
Hauts Plateaux 192 EF 2
Haut-Zaïre 198 CD 4
Hauula (HI.) 113 E 10
Havana 133 F 3
Havana (AR.) 121 M 7
Havana (Cuba) 107 K 7
Havana (FL.) 131 K 4
Havana (IL.) 124 E 8
Havasu, Lake 116 B 3
Havasupai Indian Reservation 116 D 1
Havel 149 F 4
Havelock 175 F 5
Havelock (N.C.) 129 P 7
Havensville (NE.) 120 J 3
Haverhill (MA.) 126 H 6
Haviland (KS.) 120 FG 5
Haviřov 149 G 5
Havličkův Brod 149 G 5
Havöysund 150 H 1
Havran 154 C 3
Havre (MT.) 111 Q 2
Havre de Grace (MD.) 129 PQ 2
Havre-Saint-Pierre 105 P 5
Havsa 154 C 2
Havza 155 E 2
Haw 128 GH 6
Hawaii 113 G 12
Hawaii 187 E 1
Hawaiian Islands 187 E 1
Hawaiian Ridge 209 D 3
Hawaii Volcanoes National Park 113 G 12
Ḥawallī (Kuwait) 157 E 3
Ḥawār (Qatar) 157 F 4
Hawarden (IA.) 119 M 8
Hawera 185 Q 8
Hawesville (KY.) 128 E 4
Hawi 187 E 1
Hawi (HI.) 113 G 11
Hawick 148 C 3
Hawke Bay 185 R 8
Hawke Harbour 105 Q 5
Hawker 183 F 5
Hawkers Gate 183 G 4
Hawkins (WI.) 124 D 4
Hawkinsville (GA.) 131 L 2
Hawksbill Mountain 129 K 6
Hawk Springs (WY.) 118 D 9
Hawkwood 183 J 4
Hawley (CO.) 115 O 6
Hawley (MN.) 119 M 4
Hawmat as Sūq 193 H 2
Hawng Luk 175 G 3
Ḥawrā' 195 H 5
Hawr al Ḥabbānīyah (Iraq) 156 D 2
Hawr al Hammar (Iraq) 157 E 3
Hawrān, Wadī (Iraq) 156 C 2
Hawr as Sʿadīyah (Iraq) 157 E 2
Hawr as Suwayqīyāh (Iraq) 157 E 2
Hawr Dalmaj (Iraq) 157 D 2
Hawthorne (FL.) 131 MN 5
Hawthorne (NV.) 112 G 4
Haxby (MT.) 118 B 3
Haxtun (CO.) 115 P 3
Hay 103 O 4
Hay (N.S.W., Austr.) 183 G 5
Haybān 194 E 6
Hayban, Jabal 194 E 6
Hayden (AZ.) 116 F 4–5
Hayden (CO.) 115 K 3
Hayden Lake 110 J 3
Hayden Peak 110 J 8
Hayes (Manitoba, Can.) 103 T 4
Hayes (SD.) 118 GH 6
Hayes, Mount 102 H 3
Hayes Center (NE.) 120 E 2
Hayesville (N.C.) 128 H 6
Hayesville (OR.) 110 C 6
Hayfield Lake 113 K 9
Hayford Peak 112 K 6
Hayfork Bally 112 B 2
Hayjān 195 G 5
Hayl (Oman) 157 G 4
Hayl, Wādi al (Syria) 156 C 2
Haymana 155 D 3
Haymana Platosu 155 D 3

Haynes (AR.) 121 P 8
Hayneville (AL.) 131 H 2
Hayraboly 154 C 2
Ḥayrān 195 G 5
Hay River (N.T., Austr.) 183 F 3
Hay River (N.W.T., Can.) 103 O 3
Hays (KS.) 120 F 4
Hays (MT.) 111 R 2
Hay Springs (NE.) 118 F 8
Haystack Mountain 112 K 1
Haystack Peak 114 D 4
Haysville (KS.) 120 H 5
Hayti (MO.) 121 Q 6
Hayti (S.D.) 119 L 6
Hayward (CA.) 112 CD 5
Hayward (WI.) 124 C 3
Haywood, Mount 103 N 3
Hayyā 194 F 5
Hazarajat 169 H 4
Hazard (KY.) 128 H 4
Hazard (NE.) 120 F 1
Hazar Gölü 155 E 3
Hazaribagh 174 E 3
Hazaribagh Range 174 D 3
Hazebrouck 152 D 1
Hazel (W.V.) 124 D 7
Hazelhurst (WI.) 124 E 4
Hazelton (Br. Col., Can.) 103 M 4
Hazelton (ID.) 111 L 8
Hazelton (KS.) 120 G 5
Hazelton (ND.) 118 H 4
Hazelton Peak 118 AB 6
Hazen (ND.) 118 G 3
Hazen (NV.) 112 FG 3
Hazen Bay 108 E 3
Ḥazeva (Israel) 156 B 3
Hazhdanahr 169 H 3
Hazlehurst (GA.) 131 M 3
Hazlehurst (MS.) 130 D 3
Hazleton (PA.) 127 D 8
Hazlett, Lake 182 D 3
Ḥazrah, Ra's al (United Arab Emirates) 157 F 4
Hazro 155 F 3
Headland (AL.) 131 J 3
Head of Bight 182 E 5
Headquarters (ID.) 111 K 4
Heafford Junction (WI.) 124 E 4
Healdsburg (CA.) 112 BC 4
Healdton (OK.) 120 H 8
Heales-ville 183 H 6
Healy (KS.) 120 E 4
Healy, Mount 109 HJ 3
Healy Fork 109 J 3
Hearne (TX.) 122 G 5
Hearst 104 L 6
Heart Lake 111 P 6
Heart River 118 F 4
Heartwell (NE.) 120 G 2
Heath (MT.) 111 Q 3
Heathsville (VA.) 129 P 4
Heavener (OK.) 121 L 8
Hebbronville (TX.) 122 E 8
Hebei 173 G 3
Hebel 183 H 4
Heber (AZ.) 116 F 3
Heber City (UT.) 114 F 3
Heber Springs (AR.) 121 NO 7
Hebgen Lake 111 O 6
Hebi 172 F 3
Hebian 172 F 3
Hebo (OR.) 110 B 5
Hebrides, Inner 148 B 3
Hebrides, Outer 148 B 3
Hebrides, Sea of the 148 B 3
Hebron (IN.) 124 G 8
Hebron (ND.) 118 FG 4
Hebron (NE.) 120 H 2
Hebron (Newfoundl., Can.) 105 P 4
Hebron (N.M.) 117 M 1
Heby 151 G 4
Hecate Strait 102 L 5
Hechi 172 E 6
Hechuan 172 E 4
Hecla (S.D.) 119 K 5
Hector (MN.) 119 O 6
Hede 150 F 3
Hedemora 151 G 3
Hedgesville (MT.) 111 Q 4
Hedley (TX.) 117 Q 3
Hedmark 150 F 3
Hedwigs Hill (TX.) 122 D 5
Heerenveen 148 E 4
Hefa (Israel) 156 B 2
Hefei 173 G 4
Heflin (AL.) 128 F 8
Hefner, Lake 120 H 7
Hegang 171 NO 6
Heglar (ID.) 111 M 8
Hegura-jima 173 L 3
Heide (F.R.G.) 149 E 4
Heide (Namibia) 200 B 4
Heidelberg 149 E 5
Heidelberg (MS.) 130 EF 3
Heidenheim 149 F 5
Heilbron 200 D 5
Heilbronn 149 E 5
Heiligenblut 153 F 2
Heiligenstadt 149 F 4
Heilong Jiang 171 O 6

Heilongjiang 173 JK 1
Heimaey 150 A 3
Heimahe 172 C 3
Heimdal 150 EF 3
Heinola 150 J 3
Heirnkut 175 FG 2
Heishan 173 H 2
Heishui 172 D 4
Heizer (KS.) 120 FG 4
Hejaz (Saudi Arabia) 156 B 4
Hejian 173 G 3
Hejiang 172 E 5
Hejing 169 M 2
Heka 172 C 3
Hekimhan 155 E 3
Hekla 150 B 3
Helagsfjället 150 F 3
Helan 172 E 3
Helan Shan 172 E 3
Helena (AR.) 121 P 8
Helena (CA.) 112 B 2
Helena (MT.) 111 N 4
Helena (OK.) 120 G 6
Helendale (CA.) 113 H 8
Helen Reef 177 H 3
Helensville 185 Q 8
Helgeland 150 F 2
Helgoland 149 E 4
Helgoländer Bucht 149 E 4
Helikarnassos 154 C 3
Heliotrope Mountain 114 F 4
Hella 150 A 3
Hellas 154 B 3
Hellin 152 C 4
Hells Canyon 110 J 5
Hells Canyon Dam 110 J 5
Hell-Ville 201 H 2
Helm (CA.) 112 EF 6
Helmand 169 G 4
Helmeringhausen 200 B 5
Helmsdale 148 C 3
Helmstedt 149 F 4
Helmville (MT.) 111 N 4
Helong 173 J 2
Helper (UT.) 114 G 4
Helsingborg 151 F 4
Helsingfors 151 J 3
Helsingör 151 F 4
Helsinki (Helsingfors) 151 J 3
Helwan → Ḥulwān 194 E 3
Hemet (CA.) 113 J 9
Hemingford (NE.) 118 E 8
Hemingway (S.C.) 129 M 8
Hemlock (OR.) 110 B 5
Hemnesberget 150 F 2
Hempstead (TX.) 122 G 5
Hemse 151 G 4
Hemsö 150 G 3
Henan 172 D 4
Henan 172 F 4
Henares 152 C 3
Henbury 182 E 3
Hendek 154 D 2
Henderson (IA.) 119 N 9
Henderson (KY.) 128 D 4
Henderson (MN.) 119 P 6
Henderson (N.C.) 129 N 5
Henderson (NV.) 112 KL 6
Henderson (Pacific Ocean, U.K.)
187 G 4
Henderson (TN.) 128 C 6
Henderson (TX.) 123 J 3
Hendijan (Iran) 157 E 3
Hendorābi (Iran) 157 F 4
Hendriktop 139 G 3
Hendrik Verwoerd Dam 200 D 6
Henefer (UT.) 114 F 4
Hengām (Iran) 157 G 4
Henganon 184 E 3
Hengduan Shan 172 C 5
Hengshan 172 E 3
Heng Shan 172 F 3
Hengshan 172 F 5
Heng Shan 172 F 5
Hengshui 172 G 3
Hengue 200 B 2
Heng Xian 172 E 6
Hengyang 172 F 5
Henik Lakes 103 S 3
Henlopen, Cape 127 DE 10
Henly (TX.) 122 E 5
Hennan 150 G 3
Hennepin (IL.) 124 E 8
Hennessey (OK.) 120 H 6
Henniker (N.H.) 126 H 5
Henrietta (TX.) 122 E 2
Henrietta Maria, Cape 105 L 4
Henry (ID.) 111 O 8
Henry (IL.) 124 E 8
Henry (NV.) 112 L 1
Henry (S.D.) 119 L 6
Henry, Cape 129 Q 5
Henryetta (OK.) 120 JK 7
Henry Kater Peninsula 105 O 2
Henry Mountains 114 G 5
Henrys Lake 111 O 6
Henshaw, Lake 113 J 9
Henties Bay 200 A 4
Hentiy 170 J 6
Hentiyn Nuruu 170 J 6

Henzada 175 G 4
Hephzibah (GA.) 129 J 8
Heppner (OR.) 110 F 5
Hepu 172 E 6
Hequ 172 F 3
Heraklia 194 F 1
Herakol Dağı 155 F 3
Herald Cays 183 H 2
Herat 169 G 4
Herber (CA.) 113 K 10
Herberton 181
Herbert 103 Q 5
Herbert River 183 F 3
Hercegnovi 154 A 2
Hercegovina 153 G 3
Herd (OK.) 120 J 6
Herðubreið 150 B 2
Heredia 132 F 5
Hereford (AZ.) 116 F 6
Hereford (SD.) 118 F 6
Hereford (TX.) 117 O 3
Hereford (U.K.) 148 C 4
Hereheretue 187 F 4
Herford 149 E 4
Herington (KS.) 120 J 4
Herlen Gol 170 K 6
Herlen He 170 L 6
Herluf Trolle, Cape 105 T 3
Herman (MN.) 119 M 5
Herman (NE.) 119 M 9
Hermanas 132 B 2
Hermann (MO.) 121 O 4
Hermanos, Islas los 139 F 1
Hermansville (MI.) 124 G 4
Hermanus 200 B 6
Hermidale 183 H 5
Hermiston (OR.) 110 F 5
Hermitage (AR.) 121 N 9
Hermitage (MO.) 121 M 5
Hermit Islands 184 E 2
Hermit Islands 186 A 3
Hermleigh (TX.) 122 C 4
Hermon, Mount (Lebanon) 156 B 2
Hermosa (SD.) 118 E 7
Hermosa (TX.) 121 N 6
Hermosillo 106 D 6
Hernandarias 142 EF 4
Hernandez (N.M.) 117 K 1
Hernando (MS.) 121 Q 8
Hernani 152 C 3
Herndon (KS.) 120 E 3
Herndon (PA.) 127 C 8
Herning 151 E 4
Heroica Alvarado 132 C 4
Heroica Tlapacoyan 132 C 4
Heron (MT.) 111 K 2
Heron Bay (AL.) 130 F 4
Heron Lake (MN.) 119 N 7
Herreid (SD.) 118 HJ 5
Herrera 142 D 4
Herrera de Pisuerga 152 C 3
Herrin (IL.) 121 Q 5
Herrington Lake 128 G 4
Herrljunga 151 F 4
Herschel 102 K 2
Hershey (NE.) 120 E 1
Hershey (PA.) 127 C 8
Hertford (N.C.) 129 P 5
Hervey Bay 183 J 3
Herzliyya (Israel) 156 B 2
Hesāmābād (Iran) 157 E 2
Heşār (Iran) 157 F 3
Heshun 172 F 3
Hesperia (CA.) 113 H 8
Hesperia (MI.) 124 H 6
Hesperus (CO.) 115 J 6
Hesperus Mountain 115 JK 6
Hess 102 L 3
Hessen 149 E 4
Hetch Hetchy Reservoir 112 F 5
Hettinger (ND.) 118 F 5
Hewitt (MN.) 119 N 4
He Xian 172 F 6
Hexigten Qi 173 G 2
Hext (TX.) 122 D 5
Heyburn (ID.) 111 M 8
Heyburn, Lake 120 J 7
Heydarābād (Iran) 157 D 1
Heydarābād (Iran) 157 G 3
Heyuan 172 F 6
Heywood (Victoria, Austr.) 183 G 6
Heyworth (IL.) 124 F 9
Heze 172 G 3
Hezheng 172 D 3
Hiawassee (GA.) 128 H 7
Hiawatha (CO.) 114 J 3
Hiawatha (KS.) 120 J 2
Hiawatha (UT.) 114 G 4
Hibbing (MN.) 119 Q 3
Hibernia Reef 182 C 1
Hickman (KY.) 128 BC 5
Hickman (NE.) 120 J 2
Hickok (KS.) 120 D 5
Hickory (N.C.) 129 K 6
Hickory, Lake 129 K 6
Hickory Valley (TN.) 128 B 6
Hicksville (OH.) 125 K 8

Hico (TX.) 122 E 3–4
Hidaka-sammyaku 173 M 2
Hidalgo 132 C 3
Hidalgo (TX.) 122 E 9
Hidalgo del Parral 106 E 6
Hidcolândia 141 G 4
Hierro 192 B 3
Higgins (TX.) 117 QR 1
Higgins Lake 125 K 5
Higginsville 182 C 5
Higginsville (MO.) 121 M 3
High Island 124 J 4
High Island (TX.) 123 J 6
Highland Home (AL.) 131 H 3
Highland Park (IL.) 124 G 7
Highland Peak 112 F 4
Highlands (N.C.) 128 H 6
High Level 103 O 4
Highmore (SD.) 118 J 6
High Point 127 E 7
High Point (N.C.) 129 LM 6
High Prairie 103 O 4
High River 103 P 5
High Rock (N.C.) 129 L 6
High Rock Lake (N.C.) 129 L 6
High Rock Lake (NV.) 112 F 1
Highrock Lake (Sask., Can.) 103 Q 4
High Springs (FL.) 131 M 5
Highway (N.M.) 117 N 4
Highwood (MT.) 111 P 3
Highwood Baldy 111 P 3
Highwood Mountains 111 P 3
Higüero, Punta 130 B 8
Higuerote 138 E 1
Higüey 133 J 4
Hiitola 150 J 3
Hiiumaa 151 H 4
Hijar 152 C 3
Hiko (NV.) 112 K 5
Hikurangi 185 R 8
Hila 177 G 5
Hiland (WY.) 111 S 7
Hildesheim 149 EF 4
Hildreth (NE.) 120 F 2
Hilger (MT.) 111 Q 3
Hill (IL.) 121 P 3
Hill (MT.) 111 O 2
Hilland (SD.) 118 G 6
Hill Bank 132 E 4
Hill City (ID.) 111 K 7
Hill City (KS.) 120 F 3
Hill City (MN.) 119 P 4
Hill City (SD.) 118 E 7
Hillcrest Center (CA.) 113 G 7
Hilleröd 151 F 4
Hill Grove 183 H 2
Hilliard (FL.) 131 N 4
Hilliards (PA.) 125 P 8
Hill Island Lake 103 Q 3
Hillister (TX.) 123 J 5
Hillman (MI.) 125 K 4
Hillrose (CO.) 115 O 3
Hills (MN.) 119 M 7
Hillsboro (GA.) 128 H 8
Hillsboro (IL.) 121 Q 3
Hillsboro (KS.) 120 H 4
Hillsboro (MO.) 121 P 4
Hillsboro (MT.) 111 R 3
Hillsboro (N.D.) 119 LM 3
Hillsboro (N.H.) 126 H 5
Hillsboro (OH.) 128 H 2
Hillsboro (OR.) 110 C 5
Hillsboro (TX.) 122 F 3
Hillsboro (WI.) 124 D 6
Hillsboro Canal 131 O 8
Hillsborough (N.C.) 129 M 5
Hills Creek Lake 110 C 6
Hillsdale (MI.) 125 K 8
Hillsdale (WY.) 118 D 9
Hillside (AZ.) 116 D 3
Hillside (CO.) 115 M 5
Hillston 183 H 5
Hillsville (VA.) 129 L 5
Hillswick 148 C 2
Hilo 187 E 1
Hilo (HI.) 113 G 12
Hilo Bay 113 GH 12
Hilt (CA.) 112 C 1
Hilton Head Island 129 L 9
Hilvan 155 E 3
Hilversum 148 DE 4
Himā' 149 F 4
Himachal Pradesh 174 C 1
Himanka 150 H 3
Himara 154 A 2
Himatnagar 174 B 3
Himes (WY.) 111 R 6
Himi 173 L 3
Himmerland 151 E 4
Himmetdede 155 E 3
Himo 199 F 5
Hims (Syria) 156 B 2
Hinchin Brook 102 H 3
Hinchinbrook Island 183 H 2
Hinckley (MN.) 119 Q 4
Hinckley (UT.) 114 E 4
Hindarun 174 C 2
Hindman (KY.) 128 H 4
Hindmarsh, Lake 183 G 6
Hindubagh 169 H 4

Hindu Kush 169 HJ 3
Hindupur 174 C 5
Hindustan 162 FG 4
Hines (OR.) 110 F 7
Hinesville (GA.) 131 N 3
Hinganghat 174 C 3
Hingol 169 H 5
Hingoli 174 C 4
Hin Heup 175 H 4
Hinkley (CA.) 113 H 8
Hinnöya 150 G 2
Hinobaan 177 F 2
Hinsdale (MT.) 111 S 2
Hinton (Alberta, Can.) 103 O 5
Hinton (KY.) 128 G 3
Hinton (OK.) 120 G 7
Hinton (W.V.) 129 L 4
Hirado 173 J 4
Hirakud Reservoir 174 D 3
Hirara 173 J 6
Hirfanlı Barajı 155 D 3
Hiriyur 174 C 5
Hirosaki 173 LM 2
Hiroshima 173 K 4
Hirson 152 D 2
Hirtshals 151 E 4
Hirvensalmi 150 J 3
Hisle (SD.) 118 G 7
Hismâ (Saudi Arabia) 156 B 3
Ḥiṣn al 'Abr 195 H 5
Hispaniola 133 H 4
Hissar 174 C 2
Hīt (Iraq) 156 D 2
Hita 173 K 4
Hitachi 173 M 3
Hitchcock (OK.) 120 G 7
Hitchcock (S.D.) 119 K 6
Hitchland (OK.) 120 D 6
Hitra 150 E 3
Hiva Oa 187 F 3
Hiwassee Lake 128 G 6
Hjälmaren 151 G 4
Hjelmsöya 150 H 1
Hjerkinn 150 E 3
Hjo 151 F 4
Hjörring 151 E 4
Hlatikulu 201 E 5
Ho 196 E 4
Hoa Binh 175 HJ 3
Hoachanas 200 B 4
Hoai Nhon 175 J 5
Hoan (TX.) 117 N 6
Hoare Bay 105 P 2
Hoaseb Store 200 B 4
Hoban (TX.) 117 N 6
Hobart (Tasmania, Austr.) 184 L 9
Hobart (Tasmania, Austr.) 186 A 5
Hobbs (N.M.) 117 N 5
Hobbs Island (AL.) 128 E 7
Hobergs (CA.) 112 C 4
Hobe Sound (FL.) 131 O 7
Hobgood (N.C.) 129 O 5
Hobo 138 C 3
Hoboksar 169 M 1
Hobo Shamo 172 E 2
Hobro 151 EF 4
Hobson (MT.) 111 Q 3
Hoburgen 151 G 4
Hobyä 199 H 3
Hochfeld 200 B 4
Hochheim (TX.) 122 F 6
Ho Chi Minh 175 J 5
Hochschwab 153 G 2
Hodal 174 C 2
Hodda 199 J 2
Hodge (CA.) 113 H 8
Hodgenville (KY.) 128 F 4
Hodges (MT.) 118 D 4
Hodgson River 182 E 2
Hodh 192 C 3
Hódmezővásárhely 154 B 1
Hodna, Chott el 193 F 1
Hodna, Monts du 193 F 1
Hodonin 149 G 5
Hodzana River 109 J 2
Hoehne (CO.) 115 N 6
Hof 149 F 4
Höfðakaupstaður 150 AB 2
Hoffman (MN.) 119 N 5
Höfn 150 B 3
Hofors 151 G 3
Hofsá 150 B 2
Hofsjökull 150 B 3
Höfu 173 K 4
Höganäs 151 F 4
Hogansville (GA.) 128 FG 8
Hogback Mountain 111 N 6
Hogeland (MT.) 111 R 2
Hoggar 193 F 4
Hoggar → Ahaggar 193 G 4
Hog Island 129 Q 4
Högstegia 150 EF 3
Hŏhang-nyŏng 173 J 2
Hohe Acht 153 E 1
Hohenwald (TN.) 128 D 6

Hohes Venn 148 E 4
Hohe Tauern 153 F 2
Hohhot 172 F 2
Hohoe 196 E 4
Hohokam Pima National Monument
116 E 4
Hoh Sai Hu 172 B 3
Hoh Xil Hu 172 B 3
Hoi An 175 J 4
Hoima 198 E 4
Hoisington (KS.) 120 G 4
Hoi Xuan 175 J 3
Hokah (MN.) 119 R 7
Hokitika 185 Q 9
Hokitika 186 C 5
Hokkaidō 173 M 2
Hokmābād 168 F 3
Hol 151 E 3
Holanda 140 C 3
Holbæk 151 F 4
Holbox, Isla 132 E 3
Holbrook (ID.) 111 N 8
Holbrook (NE.) 120 E 2
Holcomb (KS.) 120 E 4
Holcut (MS.) 121 R 8
Holdbrook (AZ.) 116 F 3
Holden (UT.) 114 E 4
Holdenville (OK.) 120 J 7
Holdrege (NE.) 120 F 8
Hole in the Mountain Peak 112 K 2
Hole Narcipur 174 C 5
Holgate (OH.) 125 K 8
Holguín 133 G 3
Hol Hol 199 G 2
Holitna 102 F 3
Höljes 151 F 3
Hollabrunn 153 G 2
Holladay (UT.) 114 F 3
Holland (MI.) 124 H 7
Holland (TX.) 122 F 5
Hollandale (MS.) 130 D 1
Hollandsbird 200 A 4
Hollick-Kenyon Plateau 203
Holliday (TX.) 122 E 2
Hollidaysburg (PA.) 125 Q 9
Hollis (AR.) 121 M 8
Hollis (OK.) 120 F 8
Hollister (CA.) 112 D 6
Hollister (ID.) 111 L 8
Holly (CO.) 115 P 5
Holly (MI.) 125 L 7
Holly Beach (LA.) 123 K 6
Holly Grove (AR.) 121 O 8
Holly Hill (S.C.) 129 L 8
Holly Springs (GA.) 128 G 7
Holly Springs (MS.) 121 Q 8
Hollywood (FL.) 131 OP 8
Hollywood (N.M.) 117 L 4
Holman Island 103 O 1
Hólmavik 150 A 2
Holmes, Mount 111 P 6
Holmes Reefs 183 H 2
Holmestrand 151 EF 4
Holmön 150 H 3
Holmsjön 150 FG 3
Holmsund 150 H 3
Holmudden 151 G 4
Holoog 200 B 5
Holopaw (FL.) 131 NO 6
Holstebro 151 E 4
Holstein (IA.) 119 N 8
Holsteinsborg 105 R 2
Holston River 128 J 5
Holt (MT.) 111 L 2
Holter Lake 111 O 4
Holton (KS.) 121 K 3
Holtville (CA.) 113 K 10
Holualoa (HI.) 113 G 12
Holy Cross 102 E 3
Holyhead 148 C 4
Holyoke (CO.) 115 P 3
Holyoke (MA.) 126 G 6
Holyoke (MN.) 119 Q 4
Holyrood (KS.) 120 G 4
Homā (Iran) 157 E 2
Homa Bay 198 E 5
Homalin 175 G 3
Homāyūnshahr (Iran) 157 F 2
Hombori 196 D 2
Hombori, Monts du 196 D 2
Hombori Tondo 196 D 3
Hombre Muerto, Salar de 142 C 4
Home Bay 105 O 2
Homedale (ID.) 110 HJ 7
Home Hill 183 H 2
Homer (AK.) 102 G 4
Homer (GA.) 128 H 7
Homer (LA.) 123 K 3
Homer (N.Y.) 126 C 6
Homerville (GA.) 131 M 3
Homer Youngs Peak 111 M 5
Homestead (FL.) 131 O 9
Homestead (MT.) 118 D 2
Homestead (OK.) 120 G 6
Homestead (OR.) 110 HJ 5
Homestead (Queensland, Austr.)
183 H 3
Homestead National Monument 120 J 2
Homewood (AL.) 128 E 8
Hominy (OK.) 120 J 6

Hommelstö 150 F 2
Homnabad 174 C 4
Homoine 201 E 4
Homoljske Planina 154 B 2
Homosassa Springs (FL.) 131 M 6
Homs 194 F 2
Homs → Al Khums 193 H 2
Honaker (VA.) 129 K 4
Honaunau (HI.) 113 G 12
Honavar 174 B 5
Hon Chong 175 H 5
Honda 138 D 2
Hondeklip Baai 200 B 6
Hondo (N.M.) 117 L 4
Hondo (TX.) 122 D 6
Honduras 132 E 5
Honea Path (S.C.) 129 J 7
Honea Reservoir 123 H 5
Hönefoss 151 F 3
Honesdale (PA.) 126 D 7
Honeydew (CA.) 112 A 2
Honey Lake 112 E 2
Honeyville (UT.) 114 E 2
Hon Gai 175 J 3
Honghe 172 D 6
Hong Kong 172 FG 6
Hongliuhe 172 B 2
Hongliuyuan 172 BC 2
Hongor 172 F 1
Hongqizhen 172 E 7
Hongsa 175 H 4
Hongshui He 172 E 6
Honguedo, Détroit d' 105 P 6
Hongyuan 172 D 4
Hongze 173 G 4
Hongze Hu 173 G 4
Honiara 185 G 3
Honjara 186 B 3
Honkajoki 150 H 3
Hon Khoci 175 J 6
Honnali 174 C 5
Honningsvåg 150 J 1
Honokaa (HI.) 113 G 11
Honokahua (HI.) 113 F 10–11
Honolulu 187 E 1
Honolulu (HI.) 113 E 10
Honomu (HI.) 113 G 12
Hon Panjang 175 H 6
Honrubia 152 C 4
Honshū 173 KL 3
Honuapo (HI.) 113 G 12
Hood, Mount 110 D 5
Hood Canal 110 B 3
Hoodoo Peak 110 E 2
Hood Point 182 B 5
Hood River (OR.) 110 D 5
Hoodsport (WA.) 110 B 3
Hoogeveen 148 E 4
Hooghly 174 E 3
Hooker (OK.) 120 D 6
Hooker Creek 182 E 2
Hook Island 183 H 3
Hoolehua (HI.) 113 E 10
Hoonah 102 K 4
Hoopa (CA.) 112 B 1
Hoopa Valley Indian Reservation
   112 B 1
Hooper (CO.) 115 LM 6
Hooper (NE.) 119 M 9
Hooper (WA.) 110 G 4
Hooper, Cape 105 O 2
Hooper Bay 102 D 3
Hoopeston (IL.) 124 G 9
Hoople (N.D.) 119 L 2
Hoorn 148 E 4
Hoosick Falls (N.Y.) 126 F 6
Hoosier Pass 115 L M 4
Hoover (SD.) 118 E 5
Hoover Dam 116 B 1–2
Hoover Reservoir 125 M 9
Hopa 155 F 2
Hope (AK.) 109 J 3
Hope (AR.) 121 M 9
Hope (AZ.) 116 C 4
Hope (IN.) 128 F 2
Hope (N.D.) 119 L 3
Hope (N.M.) 117 M 5
Hope, Cape 103 O 2
Hope, Point 102 D 2
Hopedale (LA.) 123 O 6
Hopedale (Newfoundl., Can.) 105 P 4
Hopes Advance, Cap 105 O 3
Hopetoun (Victoria, Austr.) 183 G 6
Hopetoun (Western Australia) 182 C 5
Hopetown 200 C 5
Hopewell (KS.) 120 G 5
Hopewell (VA.) 129 O 4
Hopewell Islands 105 M 4
Hopi Buttes 116 F 2
Hopi Indian Reservation 116 F 2
Hopin 175 G 3
Hopkins (MO.) 121 L 2
Hopkins, Lake 182 D 3
Hopkinsville (KY.) 128 D 5
Hopland (CA.) 112 BC 4
Hoquiam (WA.) 110 AB 4
Horace Mountain 109 J 2
Hora Kalifo 199 G 3
Horasan 155 F 2
Hordaland 151 E 3

Hordio → Hurdiyo 199 J 2
Horgen 153 E 2
Horgos 154 A 1
Hörh Uul 172 E 2
Horinger 172 F 2
Horizon Deep 186 D 4
Horlick Mountains 203
Hormoz (Iran) 157 G 4
Hormoz (Iran) 157 G 4
Hormoz, Küh-e (Iran) 157 G 4
Hormuz, Strait of 157 G 4
Horn (Austria) 153 G 2
Horn (Iceland) 150 A 2
Horn, Cape 143 C 10
Hornad 149 H 5
Hornavan 150 G 2
Hornbrock (CA.) 112 C 1
Hornby Bay 103 O 2
Horncut (CA.) 112 D 3
Hörnefors 150 G 3
Hornell (N.Y.) 126 B 6
Hornepayne 104 K 6
Horn Island 130 F 4
Horn Islands 186 D 3
Hornos, Cabo de 143 C 10
Hornos, Falso Cabo de 143 C 10
Horn Plateau 103 O 3
Hornslandet 150 G 3
Hornsens 151 EF 4
Horqin Youyi Qianqi 173 H 1
Horqin Youyi Zhongqi 173 H 1
Horqin Zuoyi Houqi 173 H 2
Horqin Zuoyi Zhongqi 173 H 2
Horqueta 140 E 5
Horred 151 F 4
Horse Creek (WY.) 118 CD 9
Horsehead Lake 118 J 3
Horse Heaven Hills 110 F 4
Horse Lake 112 E 2
Horsens 151 EF 4
Horseshoe Bend (ID.) 110 J 7
Horseshoe Reservoir 116 E 3
Horsetooth Reservoir 115 M 3
Horsham 183 G 6
Hortobágy 154 B 1
Horton (MT.) 118 B 4
Horton (N.W.T., Can.) 103 N 2
Hosalay 155 D 2
Hose Mountains 176 D 3
Hosenofu 193 K 4
Hoseynābād (Iran) 157 E 2
Hoseynābād (Iran) 157 F 2
Hoseynīyeh (Iran) 157 E 2
Hosford (FL.) 131 K 4
Hoshab 169 G 5
Hoshangabad 174 C 3
Hoskins 185 F 3
Hoskins (TX.) 123 H 6
Hosmer (SD.) 118 J 5
Hospet 174 C 4
Hospitalet de Llobregat 152 D 3
Hosseina 199 F 3
Hosta Butte 116 H 2
Hoste, Isla 143 C 10
Hot 175 G 4
Hotagen 150 F 3
Hotan 169 K 3
Hotan He 169 L 2–3
Hotazel 200 C 5
Hotchkiss (CO.) 115 K 5
Hot Creek Range 112 J 4
Hotevilla (AZ.) 116 F 2
Hoting 150 G 3
Hot Spring (ID.) 111 K 8
Hot Springs (AR.) 121 MN 8
Hot Springs (MT.) 111 L 3
Hot Springs (SD.) 118 E 7
Hot Springs (VA.) 129 LM 3
Hot Springs Peak (CA.) 112 E 2
Hot Springs Peak (NV.) 112 H 1
Hot Sulphur Springs (CO.) 115 LM 3
Hottah Lake 103 O 2
Houei Sai 175 H 3
Hough (OK.) 120 D 6
Houghton (KS.) 120 D 5
Houghton (MI.) 124 F 2
Houghton (N.Y.) 125 Q 7
Houghton Lake 125 K 5
Houghton Lake (MI.) 125 K 5
Houlka (MS.) 121 Q 8
Houlton (ME.) 126 LM 2
Houma (China) 172 F 3
Houma (LA.) 123 N 6
Houndé 196 D 3
Hourtin, Étang d' 152 C 2
House (N.M.) 117 N 3
House, Mount 182 D 2
Houston (MO.) 121 O 5
Houston (MS.) 121 QR 9
Houston (TX.) 123 H 6
Houston, Lake 123 H 5–6
Houtman Abrolhos 182 A 4
Houxia 169 M 2
Hovd 170 F 6
Hovd 172 D 2
Hovd Gol 170 F 6
Hoven (SD.) 118 J 5
Hovenweep National Monument
   114 H 6
Hoveyzeh (Iran) 157 E 3
Hövsgöl 172 E 2

Hövsgöl Nuur 170 H 5
Howar 194 D 5
Howard 183 J 4
Howard (CO.) 115 M 5
Howard (KS.) 120 J 5
Howard (OH.) 125 M 9
Howard (PA.) 127 B 7
Howard (S.D.) 119 L 6
Howard (WI.) 124 F 5
Howard City (MI.) 124 J 6
Howard Lake (MN.) 119 OP 5
Howard Prairie Lake 110 C 8
Howe (ID.) 111 N 7
Howe (OK.) 121 L 8
Howe (TX.) 122 G 2
Howe, Cape 183 J 6
Howell (MI.) 125 L 7
Howell (UT.) 114 E 2
Howes (SD.) 118 G 6
Howland (Pacific Ocean, U.S.A.)
   186 D 2
Howrah 174 E 3
Hoxie (AR.) 121 OP 6
Hoxie (KS.) 120 E 3
Hoxud 172 A 2
Hox Xil Shan 172 AB 3
Hoy 148 C 3
Höyanger 150 E 3
Hoyos 152 B 3
Hoyt (CO.) 115 NO 3
Hoyt (MT.) 118 D 4
Höytiäinen 150 J 3
Hozat 155 E 3
Hpunhpu 175 G 2
Hradec Králové 149 G 4
Hraun 150 BC 3
Hron 149 H 5
Hrubieszow 149 H 4
Hrvatska 153 G 2
Hsi-hseng 175 G 3
Hsinchu 173 H 6
Hsinying 173 H 6
Hsipaw 175 G 3
Hua'an 173 G 5
Huachinango 132 C 3
Huacho 138 C 6
Huachuan 171 O 6
Huacrachuco 138 C 5
Huade 172 F 2
Huadian 173 J 2
Hua Hin 175 GH 5
Huahine 187 EF 4
Huahuapán 132 A 3
Huai'an 172 F 2
Huaibei 173 G 4
Huaibin 172 G 4
Huaide 173 H 2
Huaihua 172 E 5
Huaiji 172 F 6
Huailai 172 G 2
Huainan 173 G 4
Huairen 172 F 2
Huaiyin 173 G 4
Huajuapan de León 132 C 4
Hualapai Indian Reservation 116 C 2
Hualapai Mountains 116 C 3
Hualapai Peak 116 C 2
Hualien 173 H 6
Huallaga 138 C 5
Huallanca 138 C 5
Hualong 172 D 3
Huambo 200 B 2
Huambo 200 B 2
Huanan 173 K 1
Huancabamba 138 C 5
Huancané 140 C 4
Huancavelica 140 A 3
Huancayo 140 A 3
Huanchaca, Serranía de 140 D 3
Huanchasa 140 C 5
Huangchuan 172 G 4
Huang Hai 173 H 3
Huanghe Kou 173 G 3
Huanghetan 172 C 3
Huanghua 173 G 3
Huangling 172 E 3
Huangliu 172 E 7
Huanglong 172 EF 3
Huang Shan 173 G 4
Huangshi 172 G 4
Huang Shui 172 D 3
Huang Xian 173 H 3
Huangyan 173 H 5
Huangyangzhen 172 D 3
Huangyuan 172 D 3
Huangzhong 172 D 3
Huanren 173 HJ 3
Huanta 140 B 3
Huánuco 138 C 5
Huan Xian 172 E 3
Huanzo, Cordillera de 140 B 3
Huaping 172 D 5
Huara 140 C 4
Huaral 140 A 3
Huaraz 138 C 5
Huariaca 140 A 3
Huarmey 138 C 6
Huasago 138 C 4
Hua Sai 175 H 6

Huascarán, Nevado 138 C 5
Huasco 142 B 4
Huashixia 172 C 3
Huatabampo 106 E 6
Huating 172 E 3
Huautla 132 C 3
Hua Xian (Guangdong, China) 172 F 6
Hua Xian (Shanxi, China) 172 F 3
Hua Xian (Shanxi, China) 172 E 4
Huayllay 140 A 3
Huayuri, Pampa de 140 A 3
Huazhou 172 F 6
Hubbard (IA.) 119 P 8
Hubbard (TX.) 122 G 4
Hubbard Creek Lake 122 DE 3
Hubbard Lake 125 L 5
Hubbart Point 103 T 4
Hubei 172 F 4
Hubli 174 C 4
Hucal 143 D 6
Huckitta 182 F 3
Huckleberry Mountain 110 C 7
Hudat 199 F 4
Huddersfield 148 C 4
Huddur 199 H 3
Huddur Hadama 199 G 4
Huder 171 M 6
Hudiksvall 150 G 3
Hudson (FL.) 131 M 6
Hudson (IA.) 119 Q 8
Hudson (KS.) 120 G 4
Hudson (MI.) 125 K 8
Hudson (N.Y.) 126 F 6
Hudson (WY.) 111 R 8
Hudson, Cerro 143 B 8
Hudson Bay 104 KL 3–4
Hudson Bay (Sask., Can.) 103 R 5
Hudson Falls (N.Y.) 126 F 5
Hudson River 126 F 6
Hudson's Hope 103 N 4
Hudson Strait 105 N 3
Hue 175 J 4
Hueco Mountains 117 KL 6
Huehuetenango 132 D 4
Huelma 152 C 4
Huelo Point 113 F 11
Huelva 152 B 4
Huercal-Overá 152 C 4
Huerfano River 115 N 6
Huesca 152 C 3
Huéscar 152 C 4
Hufrat an Naḥās 198 C 3
Hugh Butler Lake 120 E 2
Hughenden 183 G 3
Hughes (AK.) 102 G 2
Hughes (AR.) 121 P 8
Hughes (South Australia) 182 D 5
Hughson (CA.) 112 E 5
Hugo (CO.) 115 O 4
Hugo (OK.) 121 K 8
Hui'an 173 G 5
Huiarau Range 185 R 8
Huib High Plateau 200 B 5
Huichang 172 G 5
Huicholes, Sierra de los 132 B 3
Hūich'on 173 J 2
Huidong 172 F 6
Huihe 170 L 6
Huila 138 C 3
Huíla 200 AB 2
Huilai 172 G 6
Huili 172 D 5
Huimin 173 G 3
Huinan 173 J 2
Huishui 172 E 5
Huiten Nur 172 B 3
Huittinen 150 H 3
Hui Xian 172 E 4
Huixtla 132 D 4
Huize 172 D 5
Hūksan-chedo 173 HJ 4
Hukuntsi 200 C 4
Hulah Lake 120 J 6
Hulahula River 109 K 2
Hulan 173 J 1
Ḥulayfā' 195 G 3
Ḥulayfī' (Saudi Arabia) 156 C 4
Huld 172 E 1
Hulett (WY.) 118 D 6
Hulin 173 K 1
Hull 105 M 6
Hultsfred 151 G 4
Hulun Buir Meng 170 LM 6
Hulun Nur 170 L 6
Ḥulwän 194 E 3
Huma 171 N 5
Humacao (P.R.) 130 D 8
Huma He 171 M 5
Humahuaca 140 C 5
Humaitá (Amazonas, Brazil) 139 F 5
Humaitá (Paraguay) 142 E 4
Humansdorp 200 C 6
Humansville (MO.) 121 M 5
Humara, Jabal al 194 E 5
Humay 171 O 6
Humber 148 C 4
Humboldt (AZ.) 116 D 3
Humboldt (NE.) 120 K 2
Humboldt (NV.) 112 G 2
Humboldt (Sask., Can.) 103 R 5

Humboldt (TN.) 128 C 6
Humboldt Bay 112 A 2
Humboldt Peak 115 M 6
Humboldt River 112 G 2
Humboldt Salt Marsh 112 H 3
Humboldt Sink 112 G 2–3
Humeburn 183 H 4
Hu Men 172 F 6
Humenné 149 H 5
Humeston (IA.) 119 P 10
Humpata 200 A 2
Humphrey (AR.) 121 O 8
Humphrey (ID.) 111 N 6
Humphrey (NE.) 119 L 9
Humphreys Peak 116 E 2
Hūn 193 J 3
Húnaflói 150 A 2
Hunan 172 F 5
Hunchun 173 K 2
100 Mile House 103 N 5
Hunedoara 154 B 1
Hungary 154 A 1
Hungerford (Queensland, Austr.)
   183 G 4
Hungerford (TX.) 122 G 6
Hūngnam 173 J 3
Hungry Horse Reservoir 111 M 3
Hun He 173 H 2
Huni Valley 196 D 4
Hunjiang 173 J 2
Hunnebostrand 151 F 4
Huns Mountains 200 B 5
Hunsrück 149 E 5
Hunsur 174 C 5
Hunte 149 E 4
Hunter 184 K 9
Hunter 186 C 4
Hunter (KS.) 120 G 3
Hunter (N.D.) 119 L 3
Hunter, Ile 185 K 6
Hunterdon (OH.) 129 JK 2
Hunter's Bay 175 F 3–4
Hunter's Range 175 F 3–4
Huntingburg (IN.) 128 E 3
Huntingdon (PA.) 127 B 8
Huntingdon (TN.) 128 C 5–6
Huntington (IN.) 124 J 9
Huntington (OR.) 110 H 6
Huntington (TX.) 123 J 4
Huntington (UT.) 114 G 4
Huntington (W.V.) 129 J 3
Huntington Beach (CA.) 113 GH 9
Huntley (MT.) 111 R 5
Huntley (NE.) 120 F 2
Huntly 148 C 3
Hunt Mountain 111 S 6
Huntsville (AL.) 128 E 7
Huntsville (AR.) 121 M 6
Huntsville (MO.) 121 N 3
Huntsville (Ontario, Can.) 105 M 6
Huntsville (TN.) 128 G 5
Huntsville (TX.) 123 H 5
Huntsville (UT.) 114 F 2
Hun Xiang Hung 175 H 3
Hunyani 201 E 3
Hunyuan 172 F 3
Huocheng 169 L 2
Huolongmen 171 N 6
Huon 185 H 5
Huon 186 B 4
Huong Khe 175 J 4
Huong Thuy 175 J 4
Huon Gulf 184 E 3
Huon Peninsula 184 E 3
Huoshan 172 G 4
Huo Xian 172 F 3
Hur 168 F 4
Huraymilāh (Saudi Arabia) 157 E 4
Hurdiyo 199 J 2
Hure Qi 173 H 2
Huri Hills 199 F 4
Hurley (N.M.) 116 H 5
Hurley (S.D.) 119 LM 7
Huron (CA.) 112 EF 6
Huron (OH.) 125 M 8
Huron (S.D.) 119 K 6
Huron Beach (MI.) 125 KL 4
Huron Mountains 124 FG 3
Hurricane(AK.) 109 J 3
Hurricane (UT.) 114 D 6
Hurricane Cliffs 116 C 1
Hurtsboro (AL.) 131 J 2
Húsavík 150 B 2
Huşi 154 C 1
Huskvarna 151 F 4
Huslia 102 F 2
Hustisford (WI.) 124 F 6
Husum (F.R.G.) 149 E 4
Husum (Sweden) 150 G 3
Hutag 170 H 6
Hutchinson (KS.) 120 H 4
Hutchinson (MN.) 119 O 6
Hutch Mountain 116 E 3
Ḥuth 195 G 5
Huthi 173 K 1
Hutou 173 K 1
Hutsonville (IL.) 121 S 3
Huttig (AR.) 121 N 9
Hutton, Mount 183 H 4
Huttonsville (W.V.) 129 M 3

Hutubi 169 M 2
Huxford (AL.) 130 G 3
Hu Xian 172 E 4
Huzhou 173 H 4
Hvammstangi 150 AB 2
Hvar 153 G 3
Hvarski Kanal 153 G 3
Hveragerði 150 A 3
Hveravellir 150 B 3
Hvide Sande 151 E 4
Hvíta 150 A 3
Hvitá 150 B 3
Hvítárvatn 150 AB 3
Hwange 200 D 3
Hwange National Park 200 D 3
Hwang Ho 173 G 3
Hyampom (CA.) 112 B 2
Hyannis (MA.) 126 J 7
Hyannis (NE.) 118 G 9
Hyargas Nuur 170 F 6
Hyattville (WY.) 111 S 6
Hybart (AL.) 130 G 3
Hyden 182 B 5
Hyden (KY.) 128 H 4
Hyde Park (VT.) 126 G 4
Hyder (AZ.) 116 C 4
Hyder(Br. Col., Can.) 109 M 4
Hyderabad (India) 174 C 4
Hyderabad (Pakistan) 169 H 5
Hye (TX.) 122 E 5
Hyères 153 E 3
Hyères, Iles d' 153 E 3
Hyesan 173 J 2
Hyland River 109 N 3
Hyltebruk 151 F 4
Hyndman (PA.) 125 Q 10
Hyndman Peak 111 L 7
Hyrra Banda 198 C 3
Hyrum (UT.) 114 F 2
Hyrynsalmi 150 J 3
Hysham (MT.) 111 S 4
Hyūga 173 K 4
Hyvinge 151 H 3
Hyvinkää (Hyvinge) 151 H 3

I

Iacó 140 C 3
Iaçu 141 H 3
Iaeger (W.V.) 129 K 4
Iakora 201 H 4
Ialomiţa 154 C 2
Iaripo 139 H 3
Iaşi 154 C 1
Iauaretê 138 E 3
Iba 177 HJ 1
Ibadan 197 E 4
Ibagué 138 C 3
Ibaiti 141 F 5
Ibapah (UT.) 114 D 3
Ibar 154 B 2
Ibarra 138 C 3
Ibb 195 G 6
Ibba 198 D 4
Ibembo 198 C 4
Ibenga 197 H 5
Iberá, Esteros del 142 E 4
Iberia 140 C 3
Iberville, Lac d' 105 N 4
Ibestad 150 G 2
Ibi 197 F 4
Ibiapaba, Serra da 141 H 1–2
Ibiara 141 J 2
Ibicaraí 141 J 4
Ibicui 142 E 4
Ibicuy 142 E 5
Ibipetuba 141 H 3
Ibitiara 141 H 3
Íbiza 152 D 4
Ibiza 152 D 4
Ibn Qawrah 195 J 5
Ibo 201 G 2
Ibonma 177 H 4
Ibotirama 141 H 3
Iboundji, Mont 197 G 6
Ibrã' 195 K 4
Ibrah, Wādī 194 C 6
Ibrāhīm, Jabal 195 G 4
'Ibrī 195 K 4
Ibrīm 194 E 4
Icá (Amazonas, Brazil) 138 E 4
Ica (Peru) 140 A 3
Içana 138 E 3
Içana (Amazonas, Brazil) 138 E 3
Icapuí 141 J 1
Icatu 141 H 1
Iceberg Pass 115 M 3
Ice Harbor Dam 110 G 4
Içel 155 D 3
Iceland 150 A 3
Icepê 141 F 5
Icha 171 T 4
Ichaf 192 D 3
Ichalkaranji 174 B 4
Ichchapuram 174 D 4
Ichera 170 J 4
Ichibusa-yama 173 K 4

Ichig → Chegga 192 D 3
Ichigemskiy Khrebet 171 UV 3
Ichinskaya Sopka 171 T 4
Ichnya 158 F 5
Ichourad 196 D 1
Ico 141 J 2
Icoca 200 B 1
Icoraci 139 J 4
Icy Bay 109 K 3
Icy Cape 102 E 1
Ida Grove (IA.) 119 N 8
Idah 197 F 4
Idaho City (ID.) 111 K 7
Idaho Falls (ID.) 111 N 7
Idalia (CO.) 115 P 4
Idalou (TX.) 117 P 4
Idân 199 H 3
Idanha (OR.) 110 CD 6
Idavada (ID.) 111 L 8
Íday 197 G 3
'Idd al Ghanam 194 C 6
Idd el Shargi (Qatar) 157 F 4
Ideal (SD.) 118 J 7
Idel 150 K 3
Idelès 193 G 4
Idélimen 196 E 2
Idfū (Egypt) 156 A 4
Idhân Awbārī 193 H 3
Idhân Murzuq 193 H 4
Ídhi Óros 154 BC 3
Ídhra 154 B 3
Idikel 197 F 2
Idil 155 F 3
Idiofa 198 B 5
Iditarod River 108 G 3
Idleyld Park (OR.) 110 C 7
Idre 150 F 3
Idrī 193 H 3
Idria (CA.) 112 E 6
Idrija 153 F 2
Idutywa 200 D 6
Idyum 171 O 4
Iema 197 E 3
Ierápetra 154 C 3
Ierisós 154 B 2
Ierisoú, Kólpos 154 B 2
Iesi 153 F 3
Iet 199 G 4
Iezerul, Virful 154 B 1
Ifag 199 F 2
Ifakara 199 F 6
Ifalik 186 A 2
Ifanadiana 201 H 4
Ife 197 E 4
Iférouane 197 F 2
Ifetesene 193 F 3
Ifinga 198 F 6
Ifjord 150 J 1
Ifon 197 F 4
Iganga 198 E 4
Igara Paraná 138 D 4
Igarapava 141 G 4
Igarapé-Açu 139 J 4
Igarka 159 R 2
Igatimí 140 E 5
Igatpuri 174 B 4
Igbetti 197 E 4
Igdet, Jbel 192 D 2
Igdir (Iran) 168 D 3
Iğdır (Turkey) 155 F 3
Ige 172 B 3
Iggesund 150 G 3
Iglesia 142 C 5
Iglesias 153 E 4
Igli 192 E 2
Ignace 104 J 6
Ignacio (CO.) 115 K 6
Ignashino 171 M 5
Iğneada 154 C 2
Igoumenitsá 154 B 3
Igra 158 K 4
Igrim 159 M 3
Iguaçu 142 F 4
Iguaçu, Parque Nacional do 142 F 4
Iguala 132 C 4
Igualada 152 D 3
Igualdade 138 E 4
Iguassú Falls 142 F 4
Iguatu 141 J 2
Iguazú, Cataratas del 142 F 4
Iguéla 197 F 6
Iguetti, Sebkha 192 D 3
Iguidi, Erg 192 DE 3
Iguigik 102 F 4
Igusi 200 D 3
Ih Bogd Uul 172 CD 2
Ihirene 193 F 4
Ihosy 201 H 4
Ihsaniye 154 D 3
Ihtamir 170 H 6
Ii 150 J 2
Iijoki 150 J 2
Iisalmi 150 J 3
Iivaara 150 J 3
Ijebu Ode 197 E 4
Ijuí 142 F 4
Ikaalinen 150 H 3

Ikalamavony 201 H 4
Ikali 198 C 5
Ikanda 198 C 5
Ikaría 154 C 3
Ikatan 108 F 5
Ikatskiy Khrebet 170 K 5
Ikeda 173 M 2
Ikeja 196 E 4
Ikela 198 C 5
Ikerre 197 F 4
Ikey 170 H 5
Iki Burul 155 F 1
Ikom 197 F 4
Ikomba 201 E 1
Ikongo 199 F 6
Ikot Ekpene 197 F 4
Ikryanoye 155 G 1
Ikuktlitlik Mountain 108 F 4
Ikungi 198 E 6
Ikungu 198 E 6
Ila 197 EF 4
Ilabaya 140 B 4
Ilad 199 H 2
Ilaferh 193 F 4
Ilaferh 193 F 4
Ilagan 177 J 1
Ilam (Iran) 157 E 2
Ilan 173 H 6
Ilanskiy 170 G 4
Ilaro 196 E 4
Ilatan 197 E 2
Ilawa 149 G 4
Ilbenge 171 M 3
Ile-à-la-Crosse 103 Q 4
Ilebo 198 C 5
Île d'Anticosti 105 P 6
Ile de France 152 D 2
Ile de France, Côte de l' 152 D 2
Ile de Groix 152 C 2
Ile de la Gonâve 133 H 4
Île de la Madeleine 105 P 6
Ile de la Tortue 133 H 3
Île de Ré 152 C 2
Île de Sable 186 B 4
Iles des Noefs 199 J 6
Île des Pins 185 J 6
Île des Pins 186 C 4
Ile d'Oléron 152 C 2
Île d'Ouessant 152 B 2
Île du Diable 139 H 2
Ile d'Yeu 152 C 2
Ile Hunter 185 K 6
Ile Matthew 185 K 6
Ilemera 198 E 5
Îles Belep 185 H 5
Îles Belep 186 B 4
Iles Chesterfield 186 B 4
Îles de Los 196 B 4
Îles d'Hyères 153 E 3
Îles du Désappointement 187 F 3
Îles du Duc de Gloucester 187 F 4
Îles du Roi Georges 187 F 3
Iles Glorienses (Réunion) 201 H 2
Ilesha 196 E 4
Iles Loyauté 185 J 6
Îles Palliser 187 F 4
Ile Tidra 192 B 5
Ile Walpole 185 J 6
Ilford 103 S 4
Ilfracombe 148 C 4
Ilgaz 155 D 2
Ilgaz Dağları 155 D 2
Ilgin 155 D 3
Ilha Bailique 139 J 3
Ilha Caçumba 141 J 4
Ilha Caviana 139 HJ 3
Ilha Curuá (Amapá, Brazil) 139 J 3
Ilha da Inhaca 201 E 5
Ilha de Maracá 139 HJ 3
Ilha de Marajó 139 HJ 4
Ilha de Orango 196 A 3
Ilha de Santa Catarina 142 G 4
Ilha de São Sebastião 141 GH 5
Ilha de Tinharé 141 J 3
Ilha do Bananal 141 F 3
Ilha Grande 141 H 5
Ilha Grande (Brazil) 138 E 4
Ilha Grande do Gurupá 139 H 4
Ilha Janaucu 139 HJ 3
Ilha Mexiana 139 J 3
Ilha Queimada 141 G 5
Ilhas, Cachoeira das 139 G 4
Ilha Santa Carolina 201 F 4
Ilhas de São João 139 K 4
Ilhas Selvagens (Portugal) 192 B 2
Ilha Tupinambaranas 139 G 4
Ilha Vamizi 201 G 2
Ilhéa Point 200 A 4
Ilhéus 141 J 3
Ili 169 L 2
Ilia 154 B 1
Iliad (MT.) 111 Q 3
Iliamna 102 G 4
Iliamna Lake 102 F 4
Íliç 155 E 3
Il'ich 169 H 2
Ilidza 153 G 3
Iliff (CO.) 115 O 3

Iligan 177 F 2
Iligan Bay 177 F 2
Ili He 169 L 2
Ilim 170 H 4
Ilimniir 171 S 2
Ilimsk 170 H 4
Ilimskiy, Ust'-, Vodokhrani-
 lishche 170 H 4
Ilinskiy 171 Q 6
Ilinsky 150 K 3
Ilio Point 113 E 10
Ilir 170 H 4
Ilirgytkin, Ozero 171 T 1
Ilirney 171 V 2
Ilirska Bistrica 153 F 2
Il'ka 170 J 5
Illana Bay 177 F 2
Illapel 142 B 5
Illéla 197 F 3
Illescas 152 C 3
Illimani, Nevado 140 C 4
Illinois (North) 124
Illinois (South) 121
Illinois City (IL.) 124 D 8
Illinois River 121 P 3
Illizi 193 G 3
Illo 196 E 3
Ilmajoki 150 H 3
Il'men, Ozero 151 K 4
Ilmuvye 171 W 3
Ilo 140 B 4
Ilo, Lake 118 F 3
Iloilo 177 F 1
Ilok 153 G 2
Ilomantsi 150 K 3
Ilorin 197 E 4
Ilots de Bass 187 F 4
Il'pi 171 W 3
Il'pyrskiy 171 U 4
Ilskiy 155 E 2
Ilubabor 198 EF 3
Ilunde 198 E 6
Ilwaco (WA.) 110 AB 4
Ilwaki 177 G 5
Ilych 158 L 3
Ilyichovsk 154 D 1
Ima 170 L 4
Imabari 173 K 4
Imám al Hamzah (Iraq) 157 D 3
Iman 173 L 1
Imandra, Ozero 150 K 2
Imari 173 JK 4
Imasa 194 F 5
Imataca, Serranía de 139 F 2
Imatra 150 K 3
Imbituba 142 G 4
Imbler (OR.) 110 H 5
Imenas 196 D 2
Imeni 26 Bakinskikh Komissarov
 168 DE 3
Iméni Gastello 171 R 3
Iméni Lazo 171 S 3
Iméni Mariny 171 R 3
Imese 198 B 4
Imgytskoye Boloto 159 O 4
Imi 199 G 3
Imilac 140 C 5
Imilili 192 B 5
Imi n'Tanoute 192 D 2
Imishli 168 D 3
Imlay (SD.) 118 F 7
Immokalee (FL.) 131 N 8
Iméni Poliny Osipenko 171 P 5
Imola 153 F 3
Imonda 184 D 2
Imotski 153 G 3
Impenekuim, Gora 108 B 2
Imperatriz (Amazonas, Brazil) 138 E 5
Imperatriz (Maranhão, Brazil) 139 J 5
Imperia 153 E 3
Imperial (CA.) 113 K 10
Imperial (NE.) 120 D 2
Imperial (NE.) 120 D 2
Imperial, Point 116 E 1
Imperial Beach (CA.) 113 H 10
Imperial Valley 113 K 10
Impfondo 197 H 5
Imphal 175 F 3
Imphy 152 D 2
Imralı 154 C 2
Imranlı 155 E 3
İmroz 154 C 2
İmroz 154 C 2
Imst 153 F 2
Imtän (Syria) 156 B 2
Imtonzha 171 N 2
Imuruk Lake 108 F 2
In Abalene 196 E 2
Inagua Island, Great 133 H 3
Inagua Island, Little 133 H 3
Inajá 141 J 2
In Akhmed 196 D 2
In Alay 196 D 2
In Allarène Gérigéri 197 F 2
Inanwatan 177 H 4
Inanya 171 S 3
Iñapari 140 C 3

Inari 150 J 2
Inarigda 170 J 3
Inarijärvi 150 J 2
In Azaoua 197 F 1
In Belbel 193 F 3
In Beriem 196 DE 2
Inca 152 D 4
Inca de Oro 142 C 4
Ince Burnu 155 D 2
İncekum Burnu 155 D 3
Inchiri 192 C 5
Inch'ŏn 173 J 3
Inchôpe 201 E 3
Inchoun 108 D 2
In Dagouber 196 D 1
Indalsälven 150 G 3
Indargarh 174 C 2
Independence (CA.) 112 G 6
Independence (IA.) 119 R 8
Independence (KS.) 121 K 5
Independence (KY.) 128 G 3
Independence (LA.) 123 N 5
Independence (MO.) 121 L 3
Independence (OR.) 110 B 6
Independence (VA.) 129 L 5
Independence Mountains 112 J 1–2
Independence Pass 115 L 4
Independencia, Isla 140 A 3
Independenta 154 C 1
Inderagiri, Sungai 176 B 4
Inderapura 176 B 4
Inderborskiy 168 E 1
Index (WA.) 110 D 3
India 174 CD 3
Indialantic (FL.) 131 O 6
Indiana (North) 124–125
Indiana 125 P 9
Indiana (South) 128 HJ 2
Indianapolis (IN.) 128 E 2
Indian Harbour 105 Q 5
Indian Lake (MI.) 124 H 3
Indian Lake (N.Y.) 126 E 5
Indian Lake (N.Y.) 126 E 5
Indian Lake (OH.) 125 L 9
Indian Ocean 205
Indianola (IA.) 119 P 9
Indianola (MS.) 121 P 9
Indianola (NE.) 120 E 2
Indianola (TX.) 122 G 7
Indianola (UT.) 114 F 4
Indian Peak (UT.) 114 D 5
Indian Peak (WY.) 111 Q 6
Indian River (MI.) 125 K 4
Indian River Inlet 127 DE 10
Indian Rocks Beach (FL.) 131 M 6
Indian Springs (NV.) 112 K 6
Indian Valley (ID.) 110 J 6
Indiaroba 141 J 3
Indias Occidentales 133 H 3
Indiga 158 J 2
Indigirka 171 R 2
Indigirskaya Nizmennost' 171 QR 2
Indija 154 B 1
Indio (CA.) 113 J 9
Índios, Cachoeira dos 139 F 3
Indispensable Reefs 186 B 3
Indispensable Strait 185 H 3
Indonesia 176–177 DG 4
Indore 174 C 3
Indramayu 176 C 5
Indravati 174 D 4
Indre 152 D 2
Indus 169 H 6
Indus (MN.) 119 P 2
Indus Cone 208 B 3
Industry (TX.) 122 G 5–6
Inebolu 155 D 2
İnecik 154 C 2
İnecik 154 C 2
In Edek 197 E 2
İnegöl 154 C 2
Inez (KY.) 128 J 4
Inez (TX.) 122 G 7
Inezgane 192 D 2
Infermo, Cachoeira do 139 G 4
Inga 198 A 6
In Gall 197 F 2
Ingalls (KS.) 120 E 5
Ingawa 197 F 3
Ingelstad 151 F 4
Ingende 197 H 6
Ingham 183 H 2
Inglewood 183 J 4
Inglewood (CA.) 113 G 9
Inglis (FL.) 131 M 5
Ingoda 170 K 5
Ingólfshöfði 150 B 3
Ingolstadt 149 F 5
Ingomar (MT.) 111 S 4
Ingomer 182 E 4
Ingot (CA.) 112 C 2
Ing-Puta-Yaun-Pugol 159 O 3
Ingram (TX.) 122 D 5
Ingrid Christensen Coast 203
Inguisivi 140 C 4
Ingul 155 D 1
Ingulets 155 D 1

Ingulets 155 D 1
Inguri 155 F 2
Inhaca, Ilha de 201 E 5
Inhambane 201 F 4
Inhaminga 201 F 3
Inharrime 201 F 4
Inhassôro 201 F 4
Inhaúmas 141 GH 3
Inhumas 141 G 4
Inirida 138 E 3
Inishowen Peninsula 148 B 3
Injune 183 H 4
Inkerman 183 G 2
Inkisi-Kisantu 198 B 6
Inklin 102 L 4
Inkster (N.D.) 119 L 2
Inlay City (MI.) 125 L 6
Inle, Lake 175 G 3
Inman (S.C.) 129 J 6
Inn 149 F 5
Innamincka 183 G 4
Inner Hebrides 148 B 3
Inner Mongolia 172 E 2–3
Innisfail (Queensland, Austr.) 183 H 2
Innokent'evka 171 O 6
Innokent'yevka 171 P 6
Innoko River 108 G 3
Innsbruck 153 F 2
Innset 150 G 2
Inobonto 177 F 3
Inola (OK.) 121 K 6
Inongo 198 B 5
Inoni 197 H 6
Inorunie 183 G 2
In Ouagar 197 F 2
Inoucdjouac 105 M 4
In Ouelene 197 F 2
Inowrocław 149 G 4
In Rhar 193 F 3
In Salah 193 F 3
Insein 175 G 4
Insiza 200 D 3
Insulă Sacalin 154 CD 2
Inta 159 LM 2
In Tadreft 197 F 2
Intake (MT.) 118 D 3
In Talak 196 E 2
In Tebezas 196 E 2
Intepe 154 C 2–3
Interior (SD.) 118 G 7
Interlaken 153 E 2
International Falls (MN.) 119 P 2
Interview 175 F 5
Intletovy 159 P 3
Intracoastal City (LA.) 123 L 6
Intuto 138 D 4
Inuvik 102 L 2
Inuvik, District of 102 LM 2
Inveraray 148 B 3
Invercargill (New Zealand) 184 P 10
Inverell 183 J 4
Inverness 148 C 3
Inverness (CA.) 112 BC 4
Inverness (FL.) 131 M 6
Inverway 182 D 2
Investigator Shoal 176 D 2
Investigator Strait 183 F 6
Inwood (IA.) 119 M 7
Inya 159 Q 4
Inya 159 R 5
Inya 171 R 3
Inyanga 201 E 3
Inyangani 201 E 3
Inyan Kara Mountain 118 D 6
Inyati 200 D 3
Inyo, Mount 112 H 6
Inyokern (CA.) 113 H 7
Inyo Mountains 112 GH 6
Inyonga 198 E 6
Inza 158 J 5
In Zekouane 196 E 2
Ioánnina 154 B 3
Iola (CO.) 115 K 5
Iola (KS.) 121 K 5
Iolotan 169 G 3
Ioma 184 E 3
Iona (Angola) 200 A 3
Iona (SD.) 118 J 7
Iona (U.K.) 148 B 3
Iona National Park 200 A 3
Iona Peres 139 HJ 4
Ione (CA.) 112 DE 4
Ione (OR.) 110 F 5
Ione (WA.) 110 H 2
Iongo 200 B 1
Ionia (KS.) 120 G 3
Ionia (MI.) 124 J 7
Ionian Islands 154 A 3
Ionian Sea 154 AB 3
Ionioi Nísoi 154 A 3
Iónion Pélagos 154 AB 3
Iony, Ostrov 171 Q 4
Íos 154 C 3
Íos 154 C 3
Iō-shima 173 K 4
Iosser 158 K 3
Iowa 119
Iowa City (IA.) 119 R 9
Iowa Falls (IA.) 119 P 8

Iowa Park (TX.) 122 E 2
Ipala 198 E 5
Ipameri 141 G 4
Ipatinga 141 H 4
Ipatovo 155 F 1
Ipava (IL.) 124 D 9
Ipiales 138 C 3
Ipiaú 141 J 3
Ipiranga 138 E 4
Ipixuna (Amazonas, Brazil) 138 D 5
Ipixuna (Amazonas, Brazil) 139 F 5
Ipoh 176 B 3
Iporá 141 F 4
Ippy 198 C 3
Ipsala 154 C 2
Ipswich (Australia) 183 J 4
Ipswich (SD.) 118 JK 5
Ipswich (U.K.) 148 D 4
Ipu 141 H 1
Ipun, Isla 143 B 7
Iquapé 141 G 5
Iquique 140 B 5
Iquitos 138 D 4
Ira (TX.) 117 PQ 5
Iraan (TX.) 117 P 7
Iracoubo 139 H 2
Irafshan 169 G 5
Iraí 142 F 4
Iráklion 154 C 3
Iran 168 EF 4
Iran, Pegunungan 176 D 3
Iränshahr 169 G 5
Irapa 139 F 1
Irapuato 132 B 3
Iraq 156 D 2
Irati 142 F 4
Īrawān, Wādī 193 H 3
Irbeni Väin 151 H 4
Irbid (Jordan) 156 B 2
Irbit 159 M 4
Irebu 198 B 5
Irecê 141 H 3
Irene (S.D.) 119 L 7
Iret' 171 S 3
Irgiz 158 J 5
Irgiz 169 G 1
Irharen 193 F 4
Irharhar 193 G 3
Irharharene 193 G 3
Irharrhar 193 G 4
Irhazer Ouan Agadez 197 F 2
Irherm 192 D 2
Irian Jaya 177 J 4
Iriba 197 J 2
Iriklinskiy 159 L 5
Iringa 199 F 6
Iriomote-jima 173 H 6
Iriona 152 EF 4
Iriri 139 H 4
Irish, Mount 112 K 5
Irish Sea 148 BC 4
Iritsoka 201 H 4
Irkeneyeva 170 G 4
Irkutsk 170 H 5
Irkutsk 170 H 5
Irmasan Geçidi 154 D 3
Irminger Basin 208 A 2
Irnijärvi 150 J 2
Iroise 152 BC 2
Ironaton (AL.) 128 F 8
Iron Belt (WI.) 124 D 3
Iron City (TN.) 128 D 6
Irondequoit (N.Y.) 126 B 5
Iron gate → Portile de Fier 154 B 2
Iron Knob 183 F 5
Iron Mountain (AZ.) 116 E 4
Iron Mountain (MI.) 124 G 4
Iron Mountain (WA.) 110 D 2
Iron Mountains 148 B 4
Iron Mountains (N.C.) 129 K 5
Iron Range 183 G 1
Iron River (MI.) 124 F 3
Iron River (WI.) 124 C 3
Ironside (OR.) 110 GH 6
Ironside (OR.) 110 H 6
Iron Springs (UT.) 114 D 6
Ironton (MO.) 121 P 5
Ironton (OH.) 128 J 3
Ironwood (MI.) 124 D 3
Iroquois (S.D.) 119 L 6
Iroquois River 124 G 9
Irosin 177 F 1
'Irq al Idrīsī 193 K 4–5
'Irq al Maẕḥūr 195 G 3
'Irq al Maẕḥur (Saudi Arabia) 156 D 4
Irq Jahām 195 H 3
Irq Jahām (Saudi Arabia) 157 E 4
Irrawaddy 175 G 3
Irrawaddy, Mouths of the 175 FG 4
Irrigi 196 CD 2
Irrigon (OR.) 110 F 5
Irtuia 139 H 4
Irtysh 159 N 4
Irtysh 159 O 5
Irtyshskoye 159 O 5
Irumu 198 D 4
Irún 152 C 2
Irves Šaurums 151 H 4
Irvine (KY.) 128 H 4

Irving (TX.) 122 G 3
Irvington (KY.) 128 E 4
Irwinton (GA.) 131 L 2
Is, Jabal 194 EF 4
Isa 197 F 3
Īsā, Ra's 195 G 5
Isabel (SD.) 118 G 5
Isabela (Ecuador) 138 B 6
Isabela (P.R.) 130 B 8
Isabella Lake 113 G 7
Isabel Segunda 130 D 8
Isahaya 173 K 4
Isaka 198 E 5
Isá Khel 169 J 4
Isakogorka 158 GH 3
Isalo, Massif de l' 201 H 4
Isandja 198 C 5
Isanga 198 C 5
Isangi 198 C 4
Isanlu Makatu 197 F 4
Isanti (MN.) 119 P 5
Isaouane N-Irharharene 193 G 3
Isar 149 F 5
Isayevskiy 170 G 1
Ischia 153 F 3
Ischodnaya, Gora 108 D 3
Iscia Baidoa → Isha Bayḏabo 199 G 4
Ise 173 L 4
Isefjord 151 F 4
Isere 153 DE 2
Iséo, Lago d' 153 F 2
Isere 153 F 3
Isernia 153 F 3
Iset' 159 M 4
Ise-wan 173 L 4
Iseyin 196 E 4
Isfahan (Iran) 157 F 2
Isfendiyar Dağlari 155 D 2
Isha Bayḏabo 199 G 4
Isherim, Gora 159 L 3
Isherton 139 G 3
Ishigaki 173 H 6
Ishikari-wan 173 M 2
Ishikawa 173 J 5
Ishikhly 168 D 3
Ishim 159 N 4
Ishim 159 O 4
Ishimbay 158 L 5
Ishimskaya Step' 159 O 5
Ishinomaki 173 M 3
Ishkamish 169 H 3
Ishkashim 169 J 3
Ishpeming (MI.) 124 G 3
Ishull i Sazanit 154 A 2
Isiboro 140 C 4
Isigny-sur-Mer 152 C 2
Işikli Gölü 154 CD 3
Isil'kul 159 O 5
Isinga 170 K 5
Isiolo 199 F 4
Isipingo Beach 201 E 5–6
Isiro 198 D 4
Isisford 183 G 3
Isit' 171 N 3
Iskamen', Khrebet 102 B 2
Iskander 169 H 2
İskenderun 155 E 3
İskenderun (Turkey) 156 B 1
İskenderun Körfezi 155 E 3
İskenderun Körfezi (Turkey) 156 B 1
İskilip 155 D 2
Iskitim 159 Q 5
Iskup 159 R 3
Iskŭr 154 B 2
Iskushuban 199 J 2
Iskut River 102 L 4
Isla Ángel de la Guarda 106 D 6
Isla Aruba 138 E 1
Isla Bonaire 138 E 1
Isla Byron 143 A 8
Isla Caja de Muertos 130 C 9
Isla Campana 143 A 8
Isla Carmen 106 D 6
Isla Cedros 106 C 6
Isla Cerralvo 106 E 7
Isla Chao 138 C 5
Isla Clarence 143 B 9
Isla-Cristina 152 B 4
Isla Curaçao 138 E 1
Isla Darwin 138 B 6
Isla Dawson 143 B 9
Isla de Altamura 106 E 7
Isla de Aves 133 K 4
Isla de Chiloé 143 B 7
Isla de Coiba 138 B 2
Isla de Cozumel 132 E 3
Isla de Culebra 130 D 8
Isla de Guadelupe 106 C 6
Isla de la Juventud 132 F 3
Isla del Maíz 132 F 5
Isla de los Estados 143 D 9
Isla del Rey 138 C 2
Isla de Margarita 139 F 1
Isla de Ometepe 132 EF 5
Isla de Providencia 133 F 5
Isla de San Ignacio 106 E 6
Isla de Santa Margarita 106 D 7
Isla Desecheo 130 B 8
Isla Desolación 143 AB 9

Isla de Vieques 130 D 8
Isla de Vieques 133 JK 4
Isla Esmeralda 143 A 8
Isla Española 138 B 6
Isla Fernandina 138 B 6
Isla Genovesa 138 B 6
Isla Gorgona (Colombia) 138 C 3
Isla Grande de Tierra del Fuego 143 C 9
Isla Guafo 143 AB 7
Isla Guamblin 143 A 7
Isla Guañape 138 C 5
Isla Holbox 132 E 3
Isla Hoste 143 C 10
Isla Independencia 140 A 3
Isla Ipun 143 B 7
Isla Isabela (Ecuador) 138 B 6
Isla Jicarón 138 B 2
Isla Jorge Montt 143 AB 9
Isla La Blanquilla 139 F 1
Isla La Orchila 138 E 1
Isla La Tortuga 138 E 1
Isla Lennox 143 C 10
Isla Lobos de Tierra 138 B 5
Isla Los Roques 138 E 1
Islamabad 169 J 4
Isla Madre de Dios 143 AB 9
Isla Magdalena (Chile) 143 B 7
Isla Magdalena (Mexico) 106 D 7
Isla Malpelo 138 B 3
Isla Marchena 138 B 6
Isla Melchor 143 B 8
Isla Mocha 143 B 6
Isla Mona 130 B 8
Isla Mona 133 J 4
Isla Monito 130 B 8
Isla Montague 106 D 5
Islamorada (FL.) 131 O 10
Isla Mornington 143 A 8
Ísland 150 AB 3
Island City (KY.) 128 H 4
Island Falls (ME.) 126 L 2
Island Lake (Manitoba, Can.) 103 T 5
Island Lake (Manitoba, Can.) 103 T 5
Island Lake Reservoir 119 Q 3
Island Mountain (CA.) 112 B 2
Island Park (ID.) 111 O 6
Island Park Reservoir 111 O 6
Island Pond (VT.) 126 H 4
Islands, Bay of 105 Q 6
Isla Noir 143 B 9
Isla Nueva 143 C 10
Isla Picton 143 C 10
Isla Pinta 138 B 6
Isla Puna 138 B 4
Isla Riesco 143 B 9
Isla San Cristóbal 138 B 6
Isla Sangayán 140 A 3
Isla San José 106 DE 6
Isla San Marcos 106 D 6
Isla San Salvador 138 B 6
Isla Santa Cruz 138 B 6
Isla Santa Inés 143 B 9
Isla Santa María 138 B 6
Islas Baleares 152 D 3–4
Islas Canarias 192 B 3
Islas de la Bahía 132 E 4
Islas del Cisne (Honduras) 132 F 4
Islas de los Riachos 143 D 6
Islas de Sotavento 133 JK 5
Islas de Sotavento 138 E 1
Islas Diego Ramírez 143 BC 10
Islas Grafton 143 B 9
Islas Hanover 143 AB 9
Islas las Aves 138 E 1
Islas Lobos de Afuera 138 B 5
Islas los Hermanos 139 F 1
Islas los Monjes 138 D 1
Islas los Testigos 139 F 1
Islas Malvinas 143 DE 9
Islas Malvinas → Falkland Islands 143 DE 9
Islas Rennell 143 B 9
Islas Stewart (Chile) 143 B 9
Islas Wollaston 143 C 10
Isla Tiburon 106 D 6
Isla Tobago 139 F 1
Isla Trinidad (Argentina) 143 D 6
Isla Trinidad (Trinidad and Tobago) 139 F 1
Isla Vista (CA.) 113 E 8
Isla Wellington 143 AB 8
Isla Wolf 138 B 6
Islay 148 B 3
Isle 152 D 2
Isle (MN.) 119 P 4
Isle au Haut 126 L 4
Islen (NV.) 112 L 5
Isle of Man 148 C 4
Isle of Wight 148 C 4
Isle Royale 124 F 1
Isle Royale National Park 124 F 1
Islesboro Island 126 L 4
Isles Dernieres 123 N 6
Isles of Scilly 148 B 5
Ísles Tristao 196 A 3
Isleta (N.M.) 117 K 3
Isleta Indian Reservation 117 K 3
Isleton (CA.) 112 D 4
Isluga 140 C 4

Ismailia → Al Ismā'īlīyah 194 E 2
Ismay (MT.) 118 D 4
Isnä 194 E 3
Isoka 201 E 2
Isola (MS.) 130 D 1
Isole Egadi 153 F 4
Isole Eolie o Lipari 153 F 4
Isole Ponziane 153 F 3
Isole Tremiti 153 G 3
Isosyöte 150 J 2
Isparta 154 D 3
İspir 155 F 2
Israel 156 B 3
Issano 139 G 2
Issia 196 C 4
Issoire 152 D 2
Issoudun 152 D 2
Issyk-Kul, Ozero 169 K 2
Istabŭlat (Iraq) 156 D 2
İstanbul 154 C 2
İstanbul 154 C 2
İstanbul Boğazi 154 C 2
Isteren 150 F 3
Isthmus of Kra 175 G 5
Istiaía 154 B 3
Istmina 138 C 2
Istmo de Panamá 138 C 2
Istmo de Tehuantepec 132 D 4
Isto, Mount 109 K 2
Istokpoga, Lake 131 N 7
Istra 153 F 2
Istria 154 C 2
Itabaiana (Paraíba, Brazil) 141 J 2
Itabaiana (Sergipe, Brazil) 141 J 3
Itabapoana 141 H 5
Itabira 141 H 4
Itaboca 139 F 4
Itabuna 141 J 3
Itacaiúna 141 F 2
Itacajá 139 J 5
Itacarambi 141 H 3–4
Itacaré 141 J 3
Itacoatiara 139 G 4
Itaete 141 H 3
Itaguajé 141 F 5
Itagüí 138 C 2
Itaituba 139 G 4
Itajaí 142 G 4
Itaka 170 L 5
Italia 153 FG 3
Italy 153 F 3
Italy (TX.) 122 G 3
Itamataré 139 J 4
Itambé 141 H 4
Itambé, Pico de 141 H 4
Itampolo 201 G 4
Itapaci 141 G 3
Itaparica 141 J 3
Itaparica, Ilha 141 J 3
Itapemirim 141 H 5
Itaperucu Mirim 141 H 1
Itaperuna 141 H 5
Itapetim 141 J 2
Itapetinga 141 HJ 4
Itapetininga 141 G 5
Itapicuru 141 H 2
Itapinima 139 F 5
Itapipoca 141 J 1
Itapiranga (Amazonas, Brazil) 139 G 4
Itapiranga (Santa Catarina, Brazil) 142 F 4
Itapiúna 141 J 1
Itaporã 139 J 5
Itaporanga 141 J 2
Itaquari 141 H 5
Itaqui 142 E 4
Itaquyry 141 EF 5
Itararé 141 G 5
Itarsi 174 C 3
Itaruma 141 F 4
Itasca (TX.) 122 F 3
Itatupá 139 H 4
Itaum 141 EF 5
Itaúna 141 H 5
Itaúnas 141 J 4
Itbāy 194 EF 3–4
Itchen Lake 103 P 2
Iténez 140 D 3
Iteshi-Teshi, Lake 200 D 3
Ithaca (N.Y.) 126 C 6
Ithaka (MI.) 125 K 6
Itháki 154 B 3
Ithnayn, Harrat 195 FG 3
Ithra (Saudi Arabia) 156 BC 3
Itigi 198 E 6
Itiquira 140 E 4
Itirucu 141 H 3
Itiúba, Serra de 141 HJ 3
Itivdleg 105 R 2
Itkillik River 109 H 2
Itoigawa 173 L 3
Itoko 198 C 5
Itongafeno 201 H 3
Itta Bena (MS.) 121 P 9
Itu 197 G 4
Itu Aba 176 D 1
Itubera (Bahía, Brazil) 141 J 3
Ituí 138 D 5

Ituiutaba 141 G 4
Itula 198 D 5
Itumbiara 141 G 4
Itungi 198 E 6
Itupiranga 139 J 5
Iturama 141 F 4
Iturbe 140 C 5
Ituri 198 D 4
Iturup, Ostrov 171 R 6–7
Ituxi 138 E 5
Itzehoe 149 E 4
Iuka (KS.) 120 G 5
Iuka (MS.) 121 R 8
Iul'tin 102 B 2
Iva (S.C.) 128 J 7
Ivaí 141 F 5
Ivaiporã 141 F 5
Ivakoany, Massif de l' 201 H 4
Ivalo 150 J 2
Ivalojoki 150 J 2
Ivan (TX.) 122 E 3
Ivangrad 151 J 4
Ivangrad 154 A 2
Ivanhoe 183 G 5
Ivanhoe (CA.) 112 F 6
Ivanhoe (MN.) 119 N 6
Ivanhoe (VA.) 129 K 5
Ivaničgrad 153 G 2
Ivanjska 153 G 3
Ivankov 158 E 5
Ivano-Frankovsk 158 D 6
Ivanovka 155 D 1
Ivanovka 158 K 5
Ivanovka 159 Q 6
Ivanovka 171 N 5
Ivanovo 158 H 4
Ivanpah (CA.) 113 K 7
Ivao, Gora 171 RS 6
Ivashka 171 U 4
Ivdel' 159 M 3
Ivigtut 105 S 3
Ivindo 197 G 5
Ivinheima 141 F 5
Ivohibe 201 H 4
Ivory Coast 196 CD 4
Ivory Coast 196 CD 5
Ivrea 153 E 2
Ivujivik 105 M 3
Iwaki 173 M 4
Iwakuni 173 K 4
Iwanai 173 M 2
Iwo 197 E 4
Iwo Jima 161 R 7
Iwōn 173 J 2
Ixiamas 140 C 3
Iya 170 G 5
'Iyāl Bakhīt 194 D 6
Izamal Balankanche 132 E 3
Izberbash 168 D 2
Īzeh (Iran) 157 F 3
Izhevsk 158 K 4
Izhma 158 K 3
Izhorskaya Vozvyshennost' 151 J 4
Izkī 195 K 4
Izmail 154 C 1
Izmir 154 C 3
Izmir Körfezi 154 C 3
Izmit 154 C 2
Izmit Körfezi 154 C 2
Iznik Gölü 154 C 2
Izobil'noye 155 F 1
Izozog, Bañados de 140 D 4
Iztočni Rodopi 154 C 2
Izuhara 173 J 4
Izu-shotō 173 M 4
Izyndy 168 F 1
Izyum 158 G 6

J

Jaala 150 J 3
Jaama 151 J 4
Jääsjärvi 150 J 3
Jabal Abadab 194 F 5
Jabal 'Abd al 'Azīz 155 EF 3
Jabal 'Abd al 'Azīz 195 F 1
Jabal Abū Ḥasan 195 G 5
Jabal Abū Rujmayn (Syria) 156 BC 2
Jabal Abyaḍ 194 D 5
Jabal ad Dayr 194 E 6
Jabal ad Durūz (Syria) 156 B 2
Jabal Adhan (United Arab Emirates) 157 G 4
Jabal Ajā' (Saudi Arabia) 156 C 4
Jabal al 'Ajmah (Egypt) 156 A 3
Jabal al Akhḍar 195 K 4
Jabal al Ansariye (Syria) 156 B 2
Jabal al Awliyā' 194 E 5
Jabal al Bishrī (Syria) 156 C 2
Jabal al Bishrī (Syria) 156 C 2
Jabal al Farāyid (Egypt) 156 B 5
Jabal al Ghurāb (Syria) 156 C 2
Jabal al Humara 194 E 5
Jabal al Kū' (Saudi Arabia) 157 E 4
Jabal al Lawz (Saudi Arabia) 156 B 3
Jabal al Ung 153 E 4
Jabal al 'Urf (Egypt) 156 A 4

Jabal al 'Uwaynāt 194 D 4
Jabal 'Anazah (Iraq) 156 C 2
Jabal an Nabī Shu'ayb 195 G 5
Jabal an Nāmūs 193 J 3–4
Jabal an Nīr 195 G 4
Jabal an Nir (Saudi Arabia) 156 D 4–5
Jabal Aqrin (Saudi Arabia) 156 C 3
Jabal Arkanū 193 K 4
Jabal as Ḥasāwinah 193 H 3
Jabal ash Shargī (Syria) 156 B 2
Jabal ash Shaykh (Lebanon) 156 B 2
Jabal ash Shifā' (Saudi Arabia) 156 B 3
Jabal ask Shām (Oman) 195 H 4
Jabal Asoteriba 194 F 4
Jabal as Sawdā 193 HJ 3
Jabal as Sibā'ī (Egypt) 156 AB 4
Jabal at Tanf (Syria) 156 C 2
Jabal at Tarhūnī 193 K 4
Jabal at Tubayq (Saudi Arabia) 156 B 3
Jabal az Ẓannah (United Arab Emirates) 157 F 4
Jabal Bartazuga 194 E 4
Jabal Batrā (Saudi Arabia) 156 B 4
Jabal Bin Ghanīmah 193 J 3–4
Jabal Dabbāgh (Saudi Arabia) 156 B 4
Jabal Eigat 194 EF 4
Jabal Eigrim 194 F 5
Jabal Erba 194 F 4
Jabal Ghārib (Egypt) 156 A 3
Jabal Ghemi 198 E 3
Jabal Gumbiri 198 E 4
Jabal Gurgei 194 C 6
Jabal Ḥabashīyah 195 J 5
Jabal Ḥadada 194 D 4
Jabal Hadid 193 K 4
Jabal Ḥafīt (United Arab Emirates) 157 G 4
Jabal Hajhir 199 J 2
Jabal Hamātah (Egypt) 156 B 4
Jabal Hamoyet 194 F 5
Jabal Hamrīn (Iraq) 156–157 D 2
Jabal Harāzah 194 E 6
Jabal Haybān 194 F 5
Jabal Ḥimā Ḍarīyah (Saudi Arabia) 156 C 4
Jabal Ibrāhīm 195 G 4
Jabal Is 194 EF 4
Jabal Kātrīna (Egypt) 156 AB 3
Jabal Katul 194 D 6
Jabal Kinyeti 198 E 4
Jabal Kissū 194 D 4
Jabal Kurur 194 E 4
Jabal Lado 198 E 3
Jabal Lotuke 198 E 4
Jabal Lubnān (Lebanon) 156 B 2
Jabal Mahrāt 195 J 5
Jabal Manda 198 C 3
Jabal Marrah 194 C 6
Jabal Nafūsah 193 H 2
Jabal Natītyāy 194 E 4
Jabal Nuqay 193 J 4
Jabal Nuqras (Egypt) 156 B 4
Jabal Oda 194 F 4
Jabalón 152 C 4
Jabalpur 174 CD 3
Jabal Qarā' 195 J 5
Jabal Radwā (Saudi Arabia) 156 BC 4
Jabal Rāf (Saudi Arabia) 156 C 3
Jabal Rahib 194 D 5
Jabal Ramm (Jordan) 156 B 3
Jabal Sabidana 194 F 5
Jabal Ṣabīr 195 G 6
Jabal Sāq (Saudi Arabia) 156 D 4
Jabal Shā'ib al Banāt (Egypt) 156 A 4
Jabal Shammar (Saudi Arabia) 156 CD 4
Jabal Sharshar 194 E 4
Jabal Sinjār (Iraq) 156 C 1
Jabal Tageru 194 D 5
Jabal Teljo 194 D 6
Jabal Thāmir 195 H 6
Jabal Thanīyah 195 H 5
Jabal Tlētē Ouate Gharbī (Syria) 156 C 2
Jabal Ṭuwayq (Saudi Arabia) 157 D 4
Jabal Waddān 193 J 3
Jabālyah (Gaza Strip) 156 B 3
Jabal Yu 'Alliq (Egypt) 156 A 3
Jabjabah, Wādī 194 E 4
Jablah (Syria) 156 B 2
Jablanica 153 G 3
Jablaničko Jezero 153 G 3
Jablonec 149 G 4
Jaboatão 141 J 2
Jaboticabal 141 G 5
Jabrīn (Iran) 157 F 4
Jabung, Tanjung 176 B 4
Jaburu 139 F 5
Jaca 152 C 3
Jacaré 139 H 4
Jacareacanga 139 G 5
Jacaretinga 139 G 5
Jacarézinho 141 G 5
Jaciara 141 F 4
Jaciparaná 139 F 5
Jack Mountain (MT.) 111 N 4
Jack Mountain (WA.) 110 E 2
Jackpot (NV.) 112 L 1
Jacksboro (TN.) 128 G 5
Jacksboro (TX.) 122 E 2

Jackson (AL.) 130 G 3
Jackson (CA.) 112 E 4
Jackson (GA.) 128 GH 8
Jackson (KY.) 128 H 4
Jackson (MI.) 125 K 7
Jackson (MN.) 119 O 7
Jackson (MO.) 121 Q 5
Jackson (MS.) 130 D 2
Jackson (MT.) 111 M 5
Jackson (N.C.) 129 O 5
Jackson (OH.) 128 J 2
Jackson (TN.) 128 C 6
Jackson (WY.) 111 P 7
Jackson, Mount (Antarctica) 203
Jackson, Mount (Western Australia) 182 B 5
Jackson Head 184 P 9
Jackson Junction (IA.) 119 QR 7
Jackson Lake (GA.) 128 H 8
Jackson Lake (WY.) 111 P 7
Jackson Reservoir 115 NO 3
Jacksonville (AR.) 121 N 8
Jacksonville (FL.) 131 N 4
Jacksonville (IL.) 121 P 3
Jacksonville (N.C.) 129 O 7
Jacksonville (OR.) 110 BC 8
Jacksonville (TX.) 123 H 4
Jacksonville Beach (FL.) 131 N 4
Jacobabad 169 H 4
Jacobina 141 H 3
Jacob Lake (AZ.) 116 D 1
Jacona 132 B 4
Jacques, Lac 109 N 2
Jacques Cartier, Détroit de 105 P 6
Jacuí 142 F 4
Jacuipe 141 HJ 3
Jacundá (Pará, Brazil) 139 H 4
Jacundá (Pará, Brazil) 139 J 4
Jada 197 G 4
Jadal 197 E 2
Jadīd Ra's al Fīl 194 D 6
J.A.D. Jensens Nunatakker 105 S 3
J. A. D. Jensens Nunatakker 202
Jādū 193 H 2
Jaén 152 C 4
Jæren 151 E 4
Jærens rev 151 DE 4
Jaffa, Cape 183 F 6
Jaffa → Tel Aviv-Yafo 194 E 2
Jaffna 174 D 6
Jafjaf aş Şaghīr 193 K 4
Jagdalpur 174 D 4
Jagdaqi 171 M 5
Jagersfontein 200 CD 5
Jaggang 174 C 1
Jagged Mountain 108 F 4
Jagtial 174 C 4
Jaguaquara 141 J 3
Jaguarão 142 F 5
Jaguarari 141 HJ 3
Jaguari 142 F 4
Jaguariaíva 141 FG 5
Jaguaribe 141 J 2
Jaguaribe 141 J 2
Jagué 142 C 4
Jahām, 'Irq 195 H 3
Jahrom (Iran) 157 F 3
Jaice 153 G 3
Jailolo 177 G 3
Jailolo, Selat 177 G 4
Jaina 132 D 3
Jainca 172 D 3
Jaipur 174 C 2
Jaisalmer 174 B 2
Jājarm (Iran) 157 G 1
Jakarta 176 C 5
Jake Creek Mountain 112 J 1
Jakhan 174 A 3
Jakobshavn 202
Jakobstad 150 H 3
Jakpa 197 EF 4
Jakupica 154 B 2
Jal (N.M.) 117 N 5
Jalaid Qi 173 H 1
Jalājil (Saudi Arabia) 157 D 4
Jalalabad 169 J 4
Jalalpur Pirwala 169 J 5
Jalapa 132 E 5
Jalapa Enríquez 132 C 4
Jalasjärvi 150 H 3
Jalaun 174 C 2
Jales 141 F 5
Jalgaon 174 C 4
Jālībah (Iraq) 157 E 3
Jalib Shahab (Iraq) 157 DE 3
Jalingo 197 G 4
Jalisco 132 B 3
Jālitah 193 G 1
Jalkot 169 J 3
Jalna 174 C 4
Jalón 152 C 3
Jalo Oasis → Wāḥāt Jālū 193 K 3
Jalor 174 B 2
Jalostotitlán 132 B 3
Jalpa 132 B 3
Jalpaiguri 174 E 2
Jālū 193 K 3
Jālū, Wāḥāt 193 K 3
Jaluit 186 C 2

Jalūlā' (Iraq) 157 D 2
Jam (Iran) 157 G 2
Jam (Iran) 157 F 4
Jama 138 B 4
Jamaica 133 G 4
Jamaica (IA.) 119 O 9
Jamaica (VT.) 126 G 5
Jamaica Channel 133 GH 4
Jamalpur 175 F 3
Jamame 199 G 4
Jamanxim 139 G 5
Jamari 139 F 5
Jamari 139 F 5
Jamba 200 B 2
Jambi 176 B 4
Jamboaye 176 A 3
Jambuair, Tanjung 176 A 2
Jambusar 174 B 3
James, Lake 129 K 6
James River 129 OP 4
James River (S.D.) 119 L 7
James Ross Strait 103 S 1–2
Jamestown (CA.) 112 E 5
Jamestown (KS.) 120 GH 3
Jamestown (KY.) 128 F 5
Jamestown (N.C.) 129 M 5–6
Jamestown (N.D.) 119 K 4
Jamestown (N.Y.) 125 P 7
Jamestown (PA.) 125 O 8
Jamestown (S.C.) 129 M 8
Jamestown (South Australia) 183 F 5
Jamestown (TN.) 128 G 5
Jamieson (OR.) 110 H 6
Jamiltepec 132 C 4
Jamkhandi 174 C 4
Jamkhed 174 C 4
Jammer Bugt 151 E 4
Jammu 169 K 4
Jammu and Kashmir 169 K 4
Jamnagar 174 B 3
Jampur 169 J 5
Jämsä 150 HJ 3
Jämsänkoski 150 HJ 3
Jamshedpur 174 E 3
Jämtland 150 F 3
Jamuna 174 E 2–3
Jamundí 138 C 3
Janā' 157 EF 4
Janakpur 174 E 2
Janaúba 141 H 4
Janaucu, 139 HJ 3
Jandaia 141 FG 4
Jandaq (Iran) 157 G 2
Jándula 152 C 4
Jane Lew (W.V.) 129 L 2
Janesville (CA.) 112 E 2
Janesville (MN.) 119 P 6
Janesville (WI.) 124 E 7
Janīn (Westbank) 156 B 2
Janjira 174 B 4
Jan Mayen Island 202
Jan Mayen Ridge 208 A 1
Jannatabad 169 G 3
Janney (MT.) 111 N 5
Janos 106 E 5
Jansen (CO.) 115 N 6
Jansenville 200 C 6
Januária 141 H 4
Jaora 174 C 3
Japan 173 L 3
Japan, Sea of 173 KL 3
Japan Trench 209 C 2
Japiim 138 D 5
Japurá 138 E 4
Japurá 138 E 4
Japvo Mountain 175 F 2
Jaqué 138 C 3
Jarābulus (Syria) 156 C 1
Jaraguá 141 G 4
Jaramillo 143 C 8
Jarandilla 152 B 3
Jaranwala 169 J 4
Jarash (Jordan) 156 B 2
Jarbah 193 H 2
Jardim 140 E 5
Jardine River National Park 183 G 1
Jardines de la Reina, Archipiélago de los 133 FG 3
Jargalant 172 FG 1
Jargalant→Hovd 170 F 6
Jari 139 H 3
Jarjis 193 H 2
Jarny 153 E 2
Jarocin 149 G 4
Jarosław 149 H 4
Järpen 150 F 3
Jarrahdale 181
Jarratt (VA.) 129 O 5
Jartai 172 E 3
Jaru 140 D 3
Jarud Qi 173 H 2
Järvenpää 151 J 3
Jarvis 187 E 2–3
Jarvisburg (N.C.) 129 Q 5
Järvsö 150 G 3
Jashpurnagar 174 D 3
Jasikan 196 E 4

Jasīra 199 H 4
Jāsk 168 F 5
Jaslo 149 H 5
Jason Islands 143 D 9
Jasper 103 O 5
Jasper (AL.) 128 D 8
Jasper (AR.) 121 M 6–7
Jasper (FL.) 131 M 4
Jasper (GA.) 128 G 7
Jasper (IN.) 128 E 3
Jasper (MN.) 119 M 7
Jasper (TN.) 128 F 6
Jasper (TX.) 123 JK 5
Jasper National Park 103 O 5
Jaşşan (Iraq) 157 D 2
Jastrzebie Zdrój 149 G 5
Jászberény 154 A 1
Jászság 154 AB 1
Jataí 141 F 4
Jatapu 139 G 4
Jatisiri, Pulau 176 E 4
Játiva 152 C 4
Jatobá 138 H 4
Jatobal 139 HJ 4
Jatuarana 139 F 5
Jaú (Amazonas, Brazil) 139 F 4
Jaú (São Paulo, Brazil) 141 G 5
Jaua, Meseta del Cerro 139 F 2–3
Jauaperi 139 F 3
Jauja 140 A 3
Jaumave 132 C 3
Jaunjelgava 151 J 4
Jaunpur 174 D 2
Jaupaci 141 F 4
Java 176 C 5
Java (SD.) 118 J 5
Javānrūd (Iran) 157 E 2
Javari 138 D 5
Java Sea 176 C 5
Java Trench 209 C 4
Jávea 152 D 4
Javhlant→Uliastay 170 G 6
Javor 154 A 2
Javorie 149 G 5
Javorie 154 A 1
Javorová skála 149 F 5
Jävre 150 H 2
Jawa 176 C 5
Jawi 176 C 4
Jay (FL.) 130 G 4
Jay (OK.) 121 L 6
Jaya, Puncak 177 J 4
Jayapura 184 D 2
Jayawijaya, Pegunungan 177 J 4
Jay Em (WY.) 118 D 8
Jayton (TX.) 117 Q 4
Jazā'ir Farasān 195 G 5
Jazā'ir Khurīyā Murīyā 195 K 5
Jazīrat (Egypt) 156 B 4
Jazvān (Iran) 157 E 1
Jbel Ayachi 192 E 2
Jbel Bani 192 D 3
Jbel Igdet 192 D 2
Jbel Ighil Mgoun 192 D 2
Jbel Lekst 192 D 3
Jbel Mousaaou Salah 192 E 2
Jbel Ouarkziz 192 D 3
Jbel Sarhro 192 D 2
Jbel Tidirhine 192 E 2
Jbel Toubkal 192 D 2
Jean (NV.) 113 K 7
Jeanerette (LA.) 123 M 6
Jebba 197 E 4
Jebel 193 K 3
Jeberos 138 C 5
Jeci 201 EF 2
Jedda → Jiddah 195 F 4
Jedrzejów 149 H 4
Jeffers (MN.) 119 N 6
Jefferson (GA.) 128 H 7
Jefferson (IA.) 119 O 8
Jefferson (N.C.) 129 K 5
Jefferson (OH.) 125 O 8
Jefferson (OR.) 110 B 6
Jefferson (TX.) 123 J 3
Jefferson (WI.) 124 F 7
Jefferson, Mount (ID.) 111 O 6
Jefferson, Mount (NV.) 112 J 4
Jefferson, Mount (OR.) 110 D 6
Jefferson City (MO.) 121 N 4
Jefferson City (MT.) 111 O 4
Jefferson City (TN.) 128 H 5
Jefferson River 111 N 5
Jeffersonville (GA.) 131 L 2
Jeffersonville (IN.) 128 F 3
Jeffersonville (OH.) 128 H 2
Jeffrey City (WY.) 111 S 8
Jega 197 E 3
Jēkabpils 151 J 4
Jekyll Island 131 N 3
Jelenia Góra 149 G 4
Jelgava 151 H 4
Jelica 154 B 2
Jelling 151 E 4
Jelow Gir (Iran) 157 E 2
Jemaja, Pulau 176 C 3
Jember 176 D 5

Jembongan 176 E 2
Jemez Indian Reservation 117 K 2
Jemez Mountains 117 K 2
Jemez Pueblo (N.M.) 117 K 2
Jemez Springs (N.M.) 117 K 2
Jen 197 G 4
Jena 149 F 4
Jena (FL.) 131 L 5
Jena (LA.) 123 L 4
Jeneponto 177 E 5
Jenifer (AL.) 128 F 8
Jenison (MI.) 124 J 7
Jenner (CA.) 112 B 4
Jennings (FL.) 131 L 4
Jennings (KS.) 120 E 3
Jennings (LA.) 123 L 5
Jenny 139 G 2
Jenny Lind Island 103 R 2
Jensen Beach (FL.) 131 O 7
Jens Munk Island 105 L 2
Jenson (UT.) 114 H 3
Jequié 141 H 3
Jequitinhonha 141 H 4
Jequitinhonha 141 H 4
Jerada 192 E 2
Jérémie 133 H 4
Jeremoabo 141 J 3
Jerez de Garcia Salinas 132 B 3
Jerez de la Frontera 152 B 4
Jerez de los Caballeros 152 B 4
Jericho (TX.) 117 Q 2
Jericho (UT.) 114 E 4
Jerik 177 H 4
Jerimoth Hill 126 H 7
Jerisjärvi 150 H 2
Jerome (AZ.) 116 D 3
Jerome (ID.) 111 L 8
Jerruck 169 H 5
Jersey 148 C 5
Jersey City (N.J.) 127 EF 8
Jersey Mountain 111 K 5
Jerseyville (IL.) 121 P 3
Jerumenha 141 H 2
Jerusalem 156 B 3
Jervis Bay 183 J 6
Jesenice 153 F 2
Jesenice 153 G 3
Jessore 174 E 3
Ještěd 149 F 4
Jesup (GA.) 131 N 3
Jesup (IA.) 119 Q 8
Jesus Carranza 132 C 4
Jesús María 142 D 5
Jet (OK.) 120 G 6
Jetmore (KS.) 120 EF 4
Jevnaker 151 F 3
Jewell (IA.) 119 P 8
Jewell (KS.) 120 G 3
Jewell Cave National Monument 118 E 7
Jewett (TX.) 122 G 4
Jeyḥūn (Iran) 157 G 4
Jeypore 174 D 4
Jezercës 154 A 2
Jezioro Drawsko 149 G 4
Jezioro Gardno 149 G 4
Jezioro Gopło 149 G 4
Jezioro Jeziorak 149 G 4
Jezioro Koronowski 149 G 4
Jezioro Łebsko 149 G 4
Jezioro Mamry 149 H 4
Jezioro Miedwie 149 F 4
Jezioro Sniardwy 149 H 4
Jhabua 174 B 3
Jhalawar 174 C 3
Jhang Sadar 169 J 4
Jhansi 174 C 2
Jhelum 169 J 4
Jhelum 169 J 4
Jhunjhunu 174 C 2
Jiahe 172 F 5
Jialing Jiang 172 E 4
Jiamusi 173 K 1
Ji'an 172 F 5
Ji'an (N. Korea) 173 J 2
Jianchang 173 GH 2
Jianchuan 172 CD 5
Jiande 173 G 5
Jiang'an 172 DE 5
Jiangao Shan 172 C 5
Jiangbiancun 172 G 5
Jiangcheng 172 D 6
Jiangchuan 172 D 6
Jiange 172 E 4
Jianghua 172 F 5
Jiangjin 172 E 5
Jiangle 173 G 5
Jiangling 172 F 4
Jiangmen 172 F 6
Jiangsu 173 GH 4
Jiangxi 172 G 5
Jiangyin 173 H 4
Jiangyong 172 F 5
Jiangyou 172 D 4
Jianli 172 F 5
Jianning 172 G 5
Jian'ou 173 G 5
Jianshi 172 E 4
Jianshui 172 D 6

Jianyang 172 D 4
Jianyang 173 G 5
Jiaocheng 172 F 3
Jiaohe 173 J 2
Jiaonan 173 H 3
Jiaozuo 172 F 3
Jiashan 173 G 4
Jiashi 169 K 3
Jia Xian 172 F 3
Jiaxing 173 H 4
Jiayin 171 O 6
Jiayu 172 F 5
Jiayuguan 172 C 3
Jibāl ash Sharāh (Jordan) 156 B 3
Jibāl ash Sharāh (Jordan) 156 B 3
Jibiya 197 F 3
Jicarilla Indian Reservation 117 J 1
Jicarón, Isla 138 B 2
Jiddah 195 F 4
Jiddat al Ḥarāsīs 195 K 4–5
Jidong 173 K 1
Jiekkevarre 150 GH 2
Jiešjavrre 150 HJ 2
Jiexi 172 G 6
Jiexiu 172 F 3
Jieyang 172 G 6
Jieznas 151 H 5
Jifārah Plain 193 H 2
Jiftūn (Egypt) 156 AB 4
Jigzhi 172 D 4
Jihlava 149 G 5
Jijel 193 G 1
Jijiga 199 G 3
Jijona 152 C 4
Jilib 199 G 4
Jilin 173 J 2
Jilin Hada Ling 173 J 2
Jiloca 152 C 3
Jimāl, Wādi (Egypt) 156 B 4
Jimbolia 154 B 1
Jimena de la Frontera 152 B 4
Jiménez 132 B 2
Jimma 199 F 3
Jimo 173 H 3
Jimsar 169 M 2
Jim Thorpe (PA.) 127 D 8
Jim Woodruff Dam 131 K 4
Jinan 173 G 3
Jincheng 172 F 3
Jinchuan 172 D 4
Jind 174 C 2
Jingbian 172 E 3
Jingde 173 G 4
Jingdezhen 173 G 5
Jinggu 172 D 6
Jinghai 173 G 3
Jinghe 169 L 2
Jinghong 172 D 6
Jingle 172 F 3
Jingmen 172 F 4
Jingning 172 E 3
Jingpo Hu 173 J 2
Jingtai 172 D 3
Jing Xian 172 E 5
Jing Xian 173 G 4
Jingyu 173 J 2
Jingyuan 172 D 3
Jinhua 173 H 5
Jining 172 F 2
Jining 173 G 3
Jinja 198 E 4
Jinkouhe 172 D 5
Jinotega 132 E 5
Jinotepe 132 E 5
Jinping 172 E 5
Jinping 172 D 6
Jinsha 172 E 5
Jinsha Jiang 172 D 5
Jinshan 173 H 4
Jinshi 172 F 5
Jinst 172 D 1
Jinta 172 C 3
Jinxi 173 H 2
Jin Xian 172 G 3
Jin Xian 173 H 2
Jin Xian 173 H 3
Jinxiang 173 G 3–4
Jinyang 172 D 5
Jinzhai 172 G 4
Jinzhou 173 H 2
Jiparaná 139 F 5
Jipijapa 138 B 4
Jirjā 141 HJ 4
Jirwān (Saudi Arabia) 157 F 5
Jishan 172 F 3
Jishou 172 E 5
Jishui 172 G 5
Jiu 154 B 2
Jiujiang 172 G 5
Jiulong 172 D 5
Jiuquan 172 C 3
Jiutai 173 J 2
Jiwani, Ras 169 G 6
Jiwen 171 M 5
Jixi 173 K 1
Jīzān 195 G 5
Jize 172 FG 3
Joaçaba 142 F 4

Joal-Fadiout 196 A 3
Joanes 139 J 4
Joanésia 141 H 4
João Pessoa 141 K 2
João Pinheiro 141 G 4
Joaquin (TX.) 123 J 4
Joaquín V. González 142 D 4
Job Peak 112 H 3
Jocassee, Lake 128 J 6–7
Jódar 152 C 4
Jodhpur 174 B 2
Joensuu 150 JK 3
Joes (CO.) 115 P 4
Joe Ward Camp 109 K 2
Joffre 197 F 3
Jõgeva 151 J 4
Joghatāy (Iran) 157 G 1
Joghatāy, Kūh-e (Iran) 157 G 1
Johannesburg 200 D 5
Johannesburg (CA.) 113 H 7
John, Mount 182 D 2
John Day (OR.) 110 G 6
John Day Fossil Buttes National Monument 110 E 6
John Day River 110 E 5
John F. Kennedy Space Center 131 O 6
John H. Kerr Reservoir 129 N 5
John Martin Reservoir 115 OP 5
John O'Groat's 148 C 3
John Redmond Reservoir 120 K 4
Johnson (KS.) 120 D 5
Johnson City (N.Y.) 126 D 6
Johnson City (TN.) 129 J 5
Johnson City (TX.) 122 E 5
Johnsondale (CA.) 112 G 7
Johnsons Crossing 102 L 3
Johnston (S.C.) 129 K 8
Johnstone (TX.) 122 C 6
Johnstown (NE.) 118 H 8
Johnstown (N.Y.) 126 E 5–6
Johnstown (PA.) 125 Q 9
John W. Flannigan Reservoir 129 J 4
Johor Baharu 176 B 3
Joigny 152 D 2
Joinvile 142 G 4
Joinville 153 DE 2
Joinville Island 203
Jokk 150 H 2
Jokkmokk 150 GH 2
Jökulsá 150 B 2–3
Jökulsá á Dal 150 BC 2
Jökulsá á Fjöllum 150 B 2
Jolfa 168 D 3
Joliet (IL.) 124 F 8
Joliet (MT.) 111 QR 5
Joliette 105 N 6
Jolly (TX.) 122 E 2
Jolo 177 F 2
Jolo Island 177 F 2
Jombang 176 D 5
Jomda 172 C 4
Jonava 151 H 4
Jonê 172 D 4
Jones (OK.) 120 H 7
Jones, Cape 103 T 3
Jonesboro (AR.) 121 P 7
Jonesboro (GA.) 128 G 3
Jonesboro (IL.) 121 Q 5
Jonesboro (LA.) 123 L 3
Jonesboro (TN.) 128 J 5
Jonesboro (TX.) 122 F 4
Jonestown (MS.) 121 P 8
Jonesville (MI.) 125 K 8
Jonesville (S.C.) 129 K 7
Jonesville (VA.) 128 H 5
Jonglei 198 E 3
Jonglei Canal 198 E 3
Jonk 174 D 3
Jönköping 151 F 4
Jonquière 105 N 6
Jontoy 199 G 5
Jonuta 132 D 4
Joplin (MO.) 121 L 5
Joplin (MT.) 111 P 2
Joppa (IL.) 121 R 5
Jordan 156 B 2–3
Jordan 156 B 3
Jordan (MN.) 119 P 6
Jordan (MT.) 118 B 3
Jordânia 141 HJ 4
Jordan Lake 131 H 2
Jordan Valley (OR.) 110 H 7
Jorge Montt, Isla 143 AB 9
Jorhat 175 F 2
Jörn 150 H 2
Jornado del Muerto 117 K 4–5
Joroinen 150 J 3
Jørpeland 151 E 4
Jos 197 F 4
José de San Martín 143 B 7
Joseph (OR.) 110 H 5
Joseph Bonaparte Gulf 182 D 1
Joseph City (AZ.) 116 F 2–3
Joseph Lake 105 O 5
Josephstaal 184 E 2
Joshua Tree (CA.) 113 J 8

Joshua Tree National Monument 113 JK 9
Jos Plateau 197 F 4
Josselin 152 C 2
Jos Sodarso, Pulau 177 J 5
Jostedalen 150 E 3
Jostedalsbreen 150 E 3
Jotunheimen 150 E 3
Jourdanton (TX.) 122 E 7
Joutsa 150 J 3
Joutseno 150 J 3
Jõwhar 199 H 4
Joy (IL.) 124 D 8
Joy, Mount 109 M 3
J. Percy Priest Reservoir 128 E 5
Jreïda 192 B 5
Juaba 139 J 4
Juan Aldama 132 B 3
Juancheng 172 G 3
Juan de Fuca, Strait of 110 AB 2
Juan de Nova 201 G 3
Juan Fernández Islands 135 B 6
Juan José 142 D 4
Juanjuí 138 C 5
Juankoski 150 J 3
Juan L. Lacaze 142 E 5
Juárez 143 E 6
Juarzon 196 C 4
Juàzeiro 141 H 2
Juàzeiro do Norte 141 J 2
Jubaland 199 G 4
Jubany 203
Jubayl (Egypt) 156 A 3
Jubayl (Lebanon) 156 B 2
Jubayt 194 F 4
Jubayt 194 F 5
Jubbah (Saudi Arabia) 156 C 3
Jubilee Lake 182 D 4
Jubileo 142 E 5
Juby, Cap 192 C 3
Júcar 152 C 4
Juçara 141 F 4
Juchitan de Zaragoza 132 D 4
Jucurucú 141 J 4
Judayyīdat al Hamīr (Saudi Arabia) 156 C 3
Judayyidat 'Ar'ar (Saudi Arabia) 156 C 3
Judith Gap (MT.) 111 Q 4
Judith Mountains 111 QR 3
Judith River 111 Q 3
Jugoslavija → Yugoslavia 153 G 3
Juhaym (Iraq) 157 D 3
Juigalpa 132 E 5
Juiz de Fora 141 H 5
Juktân 150 G 2
Julaca 140 C 5
Julesburg (CO.) 115 P 3
Julesburg Reservoir 115 P 3
Juli 140 C 4
Juliaca 140 B 4
Julia Creek 183 G 3
Julian (CA.) 113 J 9
Julianatop 139 G 3
Julianehåb 105 S 3
Julimes 106 C 3
Jullundur 174 D 1
Jumanggoin 172 C 4
Jumayrah (United Arab Emirates) 157 G 4
Jumbo 199 G 5
Jumilla 152 C 4
Jumla 174 D 2
Junagadh 174 B 3
Junagarh 174 D 4
Junan 173 G 3
Jun Bulen 173 G 1
Juncos (P.R.) 133 D 8
Junction (TX.) 122 D 5
Junction (UT.) 114 E 5
Junction City (KS.) 120 J 3
Junction City (KY.) 128 G 4
Junction City (LA.) 123 L 2–3
Junction City (OR.) 110 B 6
Jundah 183 G 3
Jundiaí 141 G 5
Jundūbah 193 G 1
Juneau 102 L 4
Junee 183 H 5
Jungar Qi 172 F 3
Junggar Pendi 169 M 1
Jungo (NV.) 112 G 2
Junín (Argentina) 142 D 5
Junín (Chile) 140 B 4
Junín (Peru) 140 A 3
Junín, Lago de 140 A 3
Junín de los Andes 143 B 6–7
Junipero Serra Peak 112 D 6
Juniyah (Lebanon) 156 B 2
Junlian 172 D 5
Juno (TX.) 117 P 7
Juno Beach (FL.) 131 OP 8
Junosuando 150 H 2
Junqueiro 141 J 2
Junsele 150 G 3
Juntura (OR.) 110 G 7

Jun Xian 172 F 4
Juoksengi 150 H 2
Jupiá, Reprêsa de 141 F 5
Jupiter (FL.) 131 O 8
Juquiá 141 G 5
Jura (Switzerland) 153 E 2
Jura (U.K.) 148 B 3
Jurado 138 C 2
Juratishki 151 J 5
Juraybī'āt (Iraq) 157 D 3
Juraybī'at (Saudi Arabia) 157 E 4
Jurbarkas 151 H 4
Jurhen Ul Shan 172 B 4
Jurien Bay 182 A 5
Jurm 169 J 2
Jürmala 151 H 4
Juruá 138 E 4
Juruá (Amazonas, Brazil) 138 E 4
Juruena 140 E 3
Juruena 140 E 3
Jurumirim, Reprêsa de 141 G 5
Juruti 139 G 4
Justo Daract 142 C 5
Jutaí (Amazonas, Brazil) 138 E 4
Jutaí (Amazonas, Brazil) 138 E 5
Jutiapa 132 E 5
Juticalpa 132 E 5
Jutland 151 E 4
Juuka 150 J 3
Juva 150 J 3
Juventud, Isla de la 132 F 3
Ju Xian 173 G 3
Jüybār (Iran) 157 F 1
Jüyom (Iran) 157 FG 3
Južni Rodopi 154 C 2
Juzna Morava 154 B 2
Juzur Qarqannah 193 H 2
Jylland 151 E 4
Jyväskylä 150 J 3

K

Kaabong 198 E 4
Kaakhka 168 F 3
Kaala 113 D 10
Kaamanen 150 J 2
Kaarta 196 C 3
Kaba 177 J 5
Kabaena, Pulau 177 F 5
Kabakly 169 G 3
Kabala 196 B 4
Kabale 198 D 5
Kabalebo Reservoir 139 G 3
Kabali 177 H 4
Kabalo 198 D 6
Kabambare 198 D 5
Kabanjahe 176 A 3
Kabanovka 158 K 5
Kaban'ya 171 P 6
Kabardinka 155 E 2
Kabare 198 B 4
Kabarega Falls 198 E 4
Kabasalan 177 F 2
Kābāw 193 H 2
Kabba 197 F 4
Kābdalis 150 G 2
Kaberamaido 198 E 4
Kabetogama Lake 119 P 2
Kabinakagami Lake 104 L 6
Kabinda 198 C 6
Kabīr Kūh (Iran) 157 E 2
Kabkābīyah 194 C 6
Kabna 194 E 5
Kabo 198 B 3
Kabompo 200 C 2
Kabompo 200 C 2
Kabondo Dianda 198 D 6
Kabongo 198 D 6
Kabūd (Iran) 157 E 2
Kabūdiyāh, Ra's 193 H 1
Kabul 169 H 4
Kabuli 184 E 2
Kabunda 200 D 2
Kabushiya 194 E 5
Kabwe 200 D 2
Kabwe Katanda 198 C 6
Kabylie 193 G 1
Kacha 155 D 2
Kacha Kuh 169 G 5
Kachalinskaya 158 H 6
Kaché 197 H 3
Kachess Lake 110 D 3
Kachia 197 F 4
Kachikattsy 171 NO 3
Kachikau 200 C 3
Kachin 175 G 2
Kachkanar 159 L 4
Kachreti 155 G 2
Kachug 170 J 5
Kaçkar Daği 155 F 2
Kada 197 H 2
Kadali 170 K 4
Kadan Kyun 175 G 5
Kade 196 D 4
Kadeï 198 B 4
Kadiana 196 C 3

Kadina 183 F 5
Kadınhanı 155 D 3
Kadiolo 196 C 3
Kadiri 174 C 5
Kadiyevka 155 E 1
Kadmat 174 B 5
Kadoka (SD.) 118 G 7
Kadoma 200 D 3
Kadonkani 175 G 4
Käduglī 194 D 6
Kaduna 197 F 3
Kadur 174 C 5
Kadusam 175 G 2
Kadyr-Egi-Tayga, Khrebet 170 G 5
Kadzherom 158 L 3
Kaédi 192 C 5
Kaélé 197 G 3
Kaeleku (HI.) 113 FG 11
Kaena Point (HI.) 113 D 10
Kaena Point (HI.) 113 E 11
Kaesŏng 173 J 3
Kāf (Saudi Arabia) 156 B 3
Kafakumba 198 C 6
Kafan 168 D 3
Kafanchan 197 F 4
Kaffir (TX.) 117 P 3
Kaffrine 196 A 3
Kafia Kingi 198 C 3
Kafta 199 F 2
Kafu 198 E 4
Kafue 200 D 3
Kafue Dam 200 D 3
Kafue National Park 200 D 2–3
Kafue [River] 200 D 2
Kafulwe 200 D 1
Kafura 198 E 5
Kaga 173 L 3
Kaga Bandoro 198 B 3
Kagalaska 102 B 5
Kagal'nitskaya 155 EF 1
Kagaluk 105 P 4
Kagan 169 G 3
Kagera 198 E 5
Kağızman 155 F 2
Kagmar 194 E 6
Kagoshima 173 JK 4
Kagua 184 D 3
Kagul 154 C 1
Kahak (Iran) 157 E 1
Kahal Tabelbala 192 E 3
Kahama 198 E 5
Kahan 169 H 5
Kahe 199 F 5
Kahemba 198 B 6
Kahia 198 D 6
Kahlotus (WA.) 110 G 4
Kahoka (MO.) 121 O 2
Kahoolawe 113 F 11
Kahoolawe 187 E 1
Kahramanmaras 155 E 3
Kahrūyeh (Iran) 157 F 3
Kahuku Point 113 E 10
Kai, Kepulauan 177 H 5
Kaiama 197 E 4
Kaibab Indian Reservation 116 D 1
Kaibab Plateau 116 D 1
Kai Besar, Pulau 177 H 5
Kaibito Plateau 116 E 1
Kaibobo 177 G 4
Kaidu He 169 M 2
Kaieteur Falls 139 G 2
Kaifeng 172 FG 4
Kaikohe 185 Q 8
Kaikoura 185 Q 9
Kailahun 196 B 4
Kaili 172 E 5
Kailu 173 H 2
Kailua (HI.) 113 E 10
Kailua (HI.) 113 FG 12
Kaimana 177 H 4
Kaimur Range 174 D 3
Kainantu 184 E 3
Kainji Dam 197 EF 4
Kainji Reservoir 197 E 3
Kaintragarh 174 D 3
Kaipara Harbour 185 Q 8
Kaiparowits Plateau 114 F 6
Kaiping 172 F 6
Kairouan → Al Qayrawān 193 GH 1
Kairuku 184 E 3
Kaiserslautern 149 E 5
Kaitaia 185 Q 8
Kaithal 174 C 2
Kaiti 199 F 5
Kaitumälven 150 G 2
Kaiwatu 177 G 5
Kaiwi Channel 113 E 10
Kai Xian 172 E 4
Kaiyang 172 E 5
Kaiyuan 172 D 6
Kaiyuan 173 H 2
Kaiyuh Mountains 102 F 3
Kajaani 150 J 3
Kajabbi 183 G 3
Kajaki Dam 169 H 4
Kajiado 199 F 5
Kajo Kaji 198 E 4

Kaju (Iran) 157 E 1
Kajura 197 F 3
Kaka (Ethiopia) 199 F 3
Kākā (Sudan) 194 E 6
Kakada 197 H 2
Kakamas 200 C 5
Kakamega 198 EF 4
Kakana 175 F 6
Kaka Point 113 F 11
Kakata 196 BC 4
Kakdwip 174 E 3
Kake 109 M 4
Kakenge 198 C 5
Kakhonak 102 G 4
Kakhovka 155 D 1
Kakhovskoye Vodokhranilishche 155 D 1
Kākī (Iran) 157 F 3
Kakinada 174 D 4
Kakisa 103 O 3
Kakisa Lake 103 O 3
Kakonko 198 E 5
Kakpin 196 D 4
Kaktovik 102 J 1
Kakuma 198 F 4
Kakumbi 201 E 2
Kakya 199 F 5
Kala 198 E 6
Kalabagh 169 J 4
Kalabahi 177 F 5
Kalabáka 154 B 3
Kalabakan 176 E 3
Kalabana 196 C 3
Kalabo 200 C 3
Kalach 158 H 5
Kalachinsk 159 O 4
Kalach-na-Donu 158 H 6
Kalahari 200 C 4
Kalahari Gemsbok National Park 200 C 5
Kalahasti 174 CD 5
Kalaheo (HI.) 113 C 10
Kalai-Khumb 169 J 3
Kalai-Mor 169 G 3
Kalajoki 150 H 3
Kalakan 170 L 4
Kalaloch (WA.) 110 A 3
Kalama (WA.) 110 C 4
Kalámai 154 B 3
Kalamazoo (MI.) 124 J 7
Kalambo Falls 198 E 6
Kalamitskiy Zaliv 155 D 2
Kalampising 176 E 3
Kalanchak 155 D 1
Kalanshiyū 193 K 3
Kalao, Pulau 177 F 5
Kalaoa (HI.) 113 G 12
Kalaong 177 F 2
Kalaotoa, Pulau 177 F 5
Kalapana (HI.) 113 H 12
Kalar 170 L 4
Kalar 170 L 4
Kalarash 154 C 1
Kalasin (Indonesia) 176 D 3
Kalasin (Thailand) 175 H 4
Kalat 174 A 2
Kalāteh (Iran) 157 G 1
Kalaupapa (HI.) 113 F 10
Kalaus 155 F 1
Kalavárdha 154 C 3
Kalávrita 154 B 3
Kalaw 175 G 3
Kalbarri 182 A 4
Kalbarri National Park 182 A 4
Kalbinskiy Khrebet 159 Q 6
Kaldbakur 150 A 2
Kaldfarnes 150 G 2
Kale 154 C 3
Kale (Turkey) 154 D 3
Kale (Turkey) 155 E 2
Kale (Turkey) 155 E 3
Kalecik 155 D 2
Kalegauk 175 G 4
Kalehe 198 D 5
Kalemyo 175 F 3
Kalene Hill 200 C 2
Kāl-e Shūr 168 F 3
Kalevala 150 K 2
Kalewa 175 F 3
Kálfshamarsvik 150 AB 2
Kalga 170 L 5
Kalgoorlie 182 C 5
Kali 174 D 2
Kalianda 176 C 5
Kaliganj 175 F 3
Kalima 198 D 5
Kálimnos 154 C 3
Kálimnos 154 C 3
Kalingapatam 174 D 4
Kalinin 158 G 4
Kalinin 168 F 2
Kaliningrad 151 H 5
Kalinino 155 F 2
Kalinkovichi 151 J 5

Kalinovik 153 G 3
Kaliro 198 E 4
Kalis 199 H 3
Kalispel Indian Reservation 110 H 2
Kalispell (MT.) 111 L 2
Kalisz 149 G 4
Kaliua 198 E 5–6
Kalix 150 H 2
Kalixälven 150 H 2
Kalkah 183 G 1
Kalkan 154 C 3
Kalkaska (MI.) 124 J 5
Kalkfeld 200 B 4
Kalkfontein 200 C 4
Kalkrand 200 B 4
Kall 150 F 3
Kallaktjåkkå 150 G 2
Kallavesi 150 J 3
Kallinge 151 F 4
Kallonis, Kólpos 154 C 3
Kallsjön 150 F 3
Kalmar 151 G 4
Kalmarsund 151 G 4
Kal'mius 155 E 1
Kalmykovo 168 E 1
Kalni 175 F 3
Kalnik 153 G 2
Kalohi Channel 113 EF 11
Kaloko 198 D 6
Kalol 174 B 3
Kalole 198 D 5
Kalolio 177 F 4
Kalomo 200 D 3
Kalona (IA.) 119 R 9
Kalpa 174 C 1
Kalpákion 154 B 3
Kalpeni 174 B 5
Kalpi 174 C 2
Kalpin 169 K 2
Kalskag 102 E 3
Kalsubai 174 B 4
Kaltag 102 F 3
Kaltungo 197 G 4
Kaluga 158 G 5
Kalukalukuang, Pulau 176 E 5
Kalulushi 200 D 2
Kalumburu 182 D 3
Kalundborg 151 F 4
Kalush 158 D 6
Kalutara 174 C 6
Kalvarija 151 H 5
Kalvesta (KS.) 120 E 4
Kalya 159 L 3
Kalya 198 D 6
Kalyazin 158 G 4
Kama (U.S.S.R.) 158 K 4
Kama (Zaire) 198 D 5
Kamaï 193 J 4
Kamaishi 173 M 3
Kamakou 113 F 10
Kamal 176 D 5
Kamalampa 198 E 6
Kamalia 169 J 4
Kamalo (HI.) 113 F 10
Kamamaung 175 G 4
Kaman 155 D 3
Kamanjab 200 B 3
Kamanyola 198 D 5
Kamarān 195 G 5
Kamaran, Hadjer 197 J 3
Kamard 169 H 3
Kamareddi 174 C 4
Kamaria Falls 139 G 2
Kamas (UT.) 114 F 3
Kamashi 169 H 3
Kambalda 182 C 5
Kambal'naya Sopka 171 T 5
Kambanós, Ákra 154 BC 3
Kambia 196 B 4
Kambove 200 D 2
Kambuno, Bukit 177 EF 4
Kambūt 193 K 2
Kamchatka 171 TU 4
Kamchatka, Poluostrov 171 T 4–5
Kamchatskiy Poluostrov 171 U 4
Kamchatskiy Zaliv 171 U 4
Kamčija 154 C 2
Kamčiyska Plato 154 C 2
Kamela (OR.) 110 G 5
Kamen, Gora 170 F 2
Kamende 198 C 6
Kamenets-Podolskiy 154 C 1
Kamenjak, Rt 153 F 3
Kamenka 158 H 2
Kamenka 158 H 5
Kamenka 158 H 5
Kamenka 170 G 4
Kamen-na-Obi 159 Q 5
Kamennogorsk 150 J 3
Kamennomostskiy 155 F 2
Kamennoye, Ozero 150 K 3
Kamennyy, Khrebet 171 UV 3
Kamenolomni 155 EF 1
Kamensk 170 J 5
Kamenskoye 171 V 3
Kamensk-Shakhtinskiy 155 F 1
Kamensk-Ural'skiy 159 M 4
Kameshki 171 U 3
Kamiah (ID.) 110 J 4

Kamiak Mountain 110 H 4
Kamieskroon 200 B 6
Kamileroi (Queensland, Austr.) 183 H 2
Kamina 198 D 6
Kaminak Lake 103 S 3
Kaminuriak Lake 103 S 3
Kamituga 198 D 5
Kamla 174 E 2
Kamloops 103 N 5
Kamnik 153 F 2
Kamnrokan 170 K 4
Kamo 155 FG 2
Kamoa Mountains 139 G 3
Kampala 198 E 4
Kampanda 200 C 2
Kampar 176 B 3
Kampar, Sungai 176 B 3
Kampen 148 E 4
Kampene 198 D 5
Kamphaeng Phet 175 G 4
Kampot 175 H 5
Kampsville (IL.) 121 P 3
Kamptee 174 C 3
Kampti 196 D 3
Kampuchea 175 HJ 5
Kampungtengah 176 D 4
Kamsack 103 R 5
Kamskoye Vodokhranilishche 158 L 4
Kam Summa 199 G 4
Kamundan 177 H 4
Kāmyārān (Iran) 157 E 2
Kamyshevatskaya 155 E 1
Kamyshin 158 HJ 5
Kamyshlov 159 M 4
Kamyshnyy 159 M 5
Kamyshovaya Bukhta 155 D 2
Kamyzyak 168 D 1
Kan (Burma) 175 F 3
Kan (Iran) 157 F 2
Kan (Sudan) 198 E 3
Kan (U.S.S.R.) 170 G 4
Kanaaupscow 105 M 5
Kanab (UT.) 114 E 6
Kanaga 102 B 5
Kanairiktok 105 P 5
Kananga 198 C 6
Kanangra Boyd National Park 183 H 5
Kanarraville (UT.) 114 D 6
Kanawha (IA.) 119 P 8
Kanawha River 129 K 3
Kanayka 159 Q 6
Kanazawa 173 L 3
Kanbalu 175 G 3
Kanchanaburi 175 G 5
Kanchenjunga 174 E 2
Kanchipuram 174 CD 5
Kandagach 168 F 1
Kandahar 169 H 4
Kandalaksha 150 K 2
Kandalakshskaya Guba 150 K 2
Kandale 198 B 6
Kandangan 176 DE 4
Kandavu 186 C 4
Kande 196 E 4
Kandi 196 E 3
Kandi, Tanjung 177 F 3
Kandıra 154 D 2
Kandla 174 B 3
Kandovān, Gardaneh-ye (Iran) 157 F 1
Kandreho 201 H 3
Kandrian 185 EF 3
Kandukur 174 CD 4
Kandy 174 D 6
Kandychan 171 RS 3
Kane (PA.) 125 Q 8
Kane (WY.) 111 R 6
Kane Fracture Zone 208 A 2–3
Kanem 197 GH 3
Kaneohe (HI.) 113 E 10
Kánestron, Ákra 154 B 3
Kanevskaya 155 E 1
Kang 200 C 4
Kanga 199 F 6
Kangaba 196 C 3
Kangal 155 E 3
Kangalassy 171 N 3
Kangâmiut 105 R 2
Kangan (Iran) 157 F 4
Kangan (Iran) 157 F 4
Kangar 176 B 2
Kangare 196 C 3
Kangaroo Island 183 F 6
Kangasala 150 H 3
Kangasniemi 150 J 3
Kangávar 168 D 4
Kangāvar (Iran) 157 E 2
Kangaz 154 C 1
Kangbao 172 F 2
Kangding 172 D 5
Kangean, Kepulauan 176 E 5
Kangeeak Point 105 P 2
Kangen 198 E 3
Kangerlussuaq 105 RS 2
Kangetet 199 F 4
Kanggup'o 173 J 2
Kanggye 173 J 2

Kangle 172 D 3
Kangmar 174 E 1
Kangmar 174 E 2
Kangnŭng 173 J 3
Kango 197 G 5
Kangping 173 H 2
Kangrinboqe Feng 174 D 1
Kangto 175 F 2
Kang Xian 172 E 4
Kangynin 102 B 2
Kanhan 174 C 3
Kani 174 C 4
Kaniama 198 C 6
Kaniet Islands 184 E 2
Kaniet Islands 186 A 3
Kanigiri 174 C 4
Kanin, Poluostrov 158 HJ 2
Kaningo 199 F 5
Kanin Nos 158 H 2
Kanin Nos, Mys 158 H 2
Kaninskiy Bereg 158 H 2
Kanioumé 196 D 2
Kanjiža 154 B 1
Kankaanpää 150 H 3
Kankakee (IL.) 124 G 8
Kankakee River 124 G 8
Kankan 196 C 3
Kanker 174 D 3
Kankesanturai 174 D 6
Kankossa 192 C 5
Kankunskiy 171 N 4
Kanmaw Kyun 175 G 5
Kannapolis (N.C.) 129 L 6
Kannauj 174 CD 2
Kannonkoski 150 J 3
Kannus 150 H 3
Kano 197 F 3
Kanona 201 E 2
Kanopolis (KS.) 120 GH 4
Kanopolis Lake 120 H 4
Kanorado (KS.) 120 D 3
Kanosh (UT.) 114 E 5
Kanovlei 200 B 3
Kanowit 176 D 3
Kanoya 173 K 4
Kanozero, Ozero 150 K 2
Kansanshi 200 D 2
Kansas 120–121
Kansas City (KS.) 121 L 3
Kansas City (MO.) 121 L 3
Kansas River 120 J 3
Kansk 170 G 4
Kansŏng 173 J 3
Kantang 175 G 6
Kantaralak 175 H 5
Kantchari 196 E 3
Kantche 197 F 3
Kantemirovka 158 G 6
Kantishna 102 G 3
Kantishna River 109 H 3
Kanturk 148 B 4
Kanuku Mountains 139 G 3
Kanuti River 109 H 2
Kanye 200 CD 4
Kanyu 200 C 4
Kanzenze 200 D 2
Kaohsiung 173 GH 6
Kaolack 196 A 3
Kaoma 200 C 2
Kaouadja 198 C 3
Kaouar 197 G 2
Kapaa (HI.) 113 C 9
Kapanga 198 C 6
Kapar (Iran) 157 E 1
Kaparhā (Iran) 157 E 3
Kap Arkona 149 E 1
Kapatu 201 E 1
Kap Brewster 202
Kapchagay 169 K 2
Kapchagayskoye Vodokhranilishche 169 K 2
Kap Cort Adelaer 105 T 3
Kap Farvel 105 T 4
Kapfenberg 153 G 2
Kapıdağı Yarımadası 154 C 2
Kapili 175 F 2
Kapingamarangi 186 B 2
Kapingamaringi 185 F 1
Kapiri Moposhi 200 D 2
Kapisigdlit 105 RS 3
Kapiskau 104 L 5
Kapit 176 D 3
Kapitanskaya Zaseka 171 PQ 3
Kapitonovka 158 F 6
Kapka, Massif du 197 J 2
Kaplan (LA.) 123 L 5–6
Kapoe 175 G 6
Kapoeta 198 E 4
Kapombo 200 C 2
Kapona 198 D 2
Kaposvár 154 A 1
Kapowsin (WA.) 110 C 3
Kapp 151 F 3
Kapsukas 151 H 5
Kapterko 197 J 2
Kapuas, Sungai 176 C 4
Kapuas, Sungai 176 D 4
Kapuskasing 104 L 6
Kapustoye 150 J 2
Kaputir 198 F 4

Kara 159 MN 2
Kara 159 MN 2
Kara-Balty 169 J 2
Karabas 159 O 6
Karabas 159 P 6
Karabekaul 169 G 3
Karabiga 154 C 2
Karabil', Vozvyshennost' 169 G 3
Kara-Bogaz-Gol 168 E 2
Karabük 155 D 2
Karabulak 159 Q 6
Karabutak 168 G 1
Karaca Dağ 155 E 3
Karacaköy 154 C 2
Karacapey 154 C 2
Karacasu 154 C 3
Karachayevsk 155 F 2
Karachev 158 FG 5
Karachi 169 H 6
Karad 174 B 4
Kara Dağ 155 D 3
Kara Dağı 155 EF 3
Karadoruk 155 E 3
Karadzha 155 D 1
Karaftit 170 K 5
Karaga 171 U 4
Karagan 170 M 5
Karaganda 159 O 6
Karagayly 159 P 6
Karaginskiy, Ostrov 171 U 4
Karaginskiy Zaliv 171 U 4
Karagüney Dağları 155 DE 2
Karaikkudi 174 C 5
Karaisalı 155 E 3
Karaitivu 174 C 6
Karaj (Iran) 157 F 2
Kara-Kala 168 F 3
Karakax He 169 K 3
Karakeçi 155 E 3
Karakelong, Pulau 177 G 3
Karakoçan 155 F 3
Karakoin, Ozero 169 H 1
Karakolka 169 K 2
Karakoram 169 JK 3–4
Karakore 199 G 2
Karakorum 170 H 6
Karakorum Shankou 169 K 3
Karaköse 155 F 3
Karakuduk 159 P 5
Karakul' 169 G 3
Karakul' 169 J 3
Karakum, Peski 168 E 1
Karakumskiy Kanal 169 G 3
Karakumy, Peski 168–169 FG 3–4
Karakuwisa 200 B 3
Karalundi 182 B 4
Karam 170 J 4
Karamagay 169 M 1
Karaman 155 D 3
Karamay 169 L 1
Karamea 185 Q 9
Karamea Bight 185 Q 9
Karamet Niyaz 169 G 3
Karamıkbataklığı 154 D 3
Karamiran He 169 M 3
Karamiran Shankou 169 M 3
Karamysheva 170 GH 4
Karān (Saudi Arabia) 157 EF 4
Karand (Iran) 157 E 2
Karanj (Iran) 157 EF 3
Karapınar 155 D 3
Karasburg 200 B 5
Kara Sea 159 M 1
Kara Sea 202
Karashoky 159 P 5
Karasjåkka 150 H 2
Karasjok 150 HJ 2
Karasu (Turkey) 154 D 2
Karasu (Turkey) 155 F 3
Karasu-Aras Dağları 155 F 3
Karasuk 159 P 5
Karatal 159 P 6
Karatan 159 R 6
Karataş 155 E 3
Karataş (Turkey) 156 B 1
Karataş Burnu 155 DE 3
Karatau 169 J 2
Karatau, Khrebet 169 H 2
Kara Tepe 155 D 3
Karatepe 155 E 3
Karathuri 175 G 5
Karatj 150 G 2
Karatobe 150 E 1
Karatogay 168 F 1
Karaton 168 E 1
Karaul 159 Q 1
Karauli 174 C 2
Karaulkel'dy 168 F 1
Karavat 185 F 2
Karawa 198 C 4
Karawang 176 C 5
Karayulgun 169 L 2
Karazhal 159 O 6
Karazhingil 159 O 6
Karbalā' (Iraq) 156 D 2
Kårböle 150 FG 3
Karcag 154 B 1
Karchyk, Poluostrov 171 V 2
Kardhámila 154 C 3
Kardhitsa 154 B 3

Kärdla 151 H 4
Kareliya 150 K 3
Karema 198 E 6
Karen 175 G 4
Karen 175 F 5
Karenga 170 L 5
Karepino 158 L 3
Karesuando 150 H 2
Karet 192 D 4
Kargalinskaya 155 G 2
Karganay 171 X 2
Kargasok 159 Q 4
Kargat 159 Q 4
Kargı 155 D 2
Kargil 169 K 4
Kargopol' 158 G 3
Karhijärvi 150 H 3
Kari 197 G 3
Kariai 154 B 2
Kariba 200 D 3
Kariba, Lake 200 D 3
Kariba Dam 200 D 3
Karibib 200 B 4
Karigasniemi 150 J 2
Karikal 174 C 5
Karimata, Pulau 176 C 4
Karimata, Selat 176 C 4
Karimganj 175 F 3
Karimnagar 174 C 4
Karimunjawa, Pulau 176 D 5
Karin 199 H 2
Karin 199 H 2
Karis (Karjaa) 151 H 3
Karisimbi 198 D 5
Káristos 154 B 3
Karjaa 151 H 3
Karkabat 199 F 1
Karkär 199 H 3
Karkaralinsk 159 OP 6
Karkar Island 184 E 2
Karkar Island 186 A 3
Karkas, Küh-e (Iran) 157 F 2
Karkheh (Iran) 157 E 2
Karkinitskiy Zaliv 155 D 1
Karkūmā, Ra's (Saudi Arabia) 156 B 4
Karla Marksa, Pik 169 J 3
Karleby 150 H 3
Karlik Shan 172 B 2
Karlino 149 G 4
Karliova 155 F 3
Karl-Marx-Stadt 149 F 4
Karlobag 153 G 3
Karlovac 153 G 2
Karlovy Vary 149 F 4
Karlsborg 151 F 4
Karlshamn 151 FG 4
Karlskoga 151 FG 4
Karlskrona 151 G 4
Karlsöarna 151 G 4
Karlsruhe 149 E 5
Karlsruhe (ND.) 118 H 2
Karlstad (MN.) 119 M 2
Karlstad (Sweden) 151 F 4
Karluk 102 F 4
Karma 196 E 3
Karmah 194 E 5
Karmala 174 C 4
Karmøy 151 DE 4
Karnafuli Reservoir 175 F 3
Karnal 174 C 2
Karnali 174 D 2
Karnataka 174 C 4
Karnes City (TX.) 122 F 7
Karnobat 154 C 2
Karokpi 175 G 4
Karong 175 F 2
Karonga 201 E 1
Karonie 182 C 5
Karora 194 F 5
Karossa, Tanjung 177 E 5
Karoy 159 O 6
Kárpathos 154 C 3
Kárpathos 154 C 3
Karpenision 154 B 3
Kars 155 F 2
Karsakpay 169 H 1
Kärsämäki 150 J 3
Kärsava 151 J 4
Karshi 169 H 3
Karskiye Vorota, Proliv 158–159 L 1
Karskoye More 159 M 1
Kars Platosu 155 F 2
Karstula 150 HJ 3
Kartal 154 C 2
Kartaly 159 LM 5
Karthago 193 H 1
Karthaus (PA.) 125 Q 8
Katerini 173 K 1
Kartula 173 K 1
Karufa 177 H 4
Karuma National Park 198 E 4
Karumba 183 G 2
Kārun (Iran) 157 E 3
Kārūn (Iran) 157 F 3
Karungi 150 H 2
Karungu 198 E 5
Karunjie 182 D 2
Karunki 150 H 2
Karur 174 C 5
Karval (CO.) 115 O 5
Karvia 150 H 3

Karvina 149 G 5
Karwar 174 B 5
Karwi 174 D 2
Karym 159 N 3
Karymskoye 170 K 5
Karzala 158 K 5
Kas (Sudan) 194 C 6
Kaş (Turkey) 154 C 3
Kas (U.S.S.R.) 159 R 4
Kasaan 109 M 4
Kasai 198 B 5
Kasai Occidental 198 C 6
Kasai Oriental 198 C 5–6
Kasaji 200 C 2
Kasama 201 E 2
Kasane 200 CD 3
Kasanga 198 E 6
Kasangulu 198 B 5
Kasaragod 174 B 5
Kasba Lake 103 R 3
Kas'bi 169 GH 3
Kasempa 200 D 2
Kasenga 200 D 2
Kasenye 198 E 4
Kasese (Uganda) 198 E 4
Kasese (Zaire) 198 D 5
Kasganj 174 C 2
Kāshān (Iran) 157 F 2
Kashanuk River 108 F 3
Kashegelok 108 G 3
Kashi 169 K 3
Kashin 158 G 4
Kashipur 174 C 2
Kashitu 200 D 2
Kashiwazaki 173 L 3
Kashken Teniz 159 O 6
Kāshmar 168 F 3
Kashmor 169 H 5
Kashyukulu 198 D 6
Kasimov 158 H 5
Kasindi 198 D 4
Kasiruta, Pulau 177 G 4
Kasisty 170 K 1
Kaskaskia River 121 Q 4
Kaskelen 169 K 2
Kaskö (Kaskinen) 150 H 3
Kas Kong 175 H 5
Kasli 159 M 4
Kasongo 198 D 5
Kasongo-Lunda 198 B 6
Kásos 154 C 3
Kaspi 155 F 2
Kaspiysk 168 D 2
Kaspiyskiy 155 G 1
Kaspiyskoye More 168 E 1
Kasr, Ra's 194 F 5
Kas Rong 175 H 5
Kassalā 194 F 5
Kassándra 154 B 2
Kassándras, Kólpos 154 B 2–3
Kasserine → Al Qaşrayn 193 G 1
Kastamonu 155 D 2
Kastaneaí 154 C 2
Kastéllion 154 B 3
Kastellós, Ákra 154 C 3
Kastoria 154 B 2
Kástron 154 BC 3
Kasuku 198 D 5
Kasulu 198 E 5
Kasumbalesa 200 D 2
Kasumkent 168 D 2
Kasungan 176 D 4
Kasungu 201 E 2
Kasungu National Park 201 E 2
Kasur 169 J 4
Kata 170 H 4
Kataba 200 C 3
Kataeregi 197 F 4
Katagum 197 G 3
Katahdin, Mount 126 L 3
Katako-Kombe 198 CD 5
Katalla 109 K 3
Katangli 171 Q 5
Katanga 198 D 6
Katangi 171 Q 5
Katanning 182 B 5
Katav-Ivanovsk 159 L 5
Katawaz 169 H 4
Katchall 175 F 6
Katchiungo 200 B 2
Katea 198 D 6
Katende Falls 198 C 6
Katenga 198 D 6
Katesh 198 F 5
Katete 201 E 2
Katha 175 G 3
Katherine 182 E 1
Katherine Gorge National Park 182 E 1
Katherine River 182 E 1
Kathiawar 174 B 3
Kāthiri 195 H 5
Kathleen Falls 182 E 1
Kathmandu 174 E 2
Kathua 169 K 4
Kati 196 C 3

Katihar 174 E 2
Katima Mulilo 200 C 3
Katima Rapids 200 C 3
Katiola 196 CD 4
Katla 150 B 3
Katlanovo 154 B 2
Katmai, Mount 102 FG 4
Katmai National Park and Preserve 102 G 4
Katompi 198 D 6
Katondwe 201 E 3
Katonga 198 E 4
Katon-Karagay 159 R 6
Katoomba 183 J 5
Katowice 149 G H 4
Kātrīna, Jabal (Egypt) 156 AB 3
Katrineholm 151 G 4
Katshi 198 D 6
Katsina 197 F 3
Katsina 197 F 3
Kattaktoc, Cape 105 O 4
Kattakurgan 169 H 3
Kattavia 154 C 3
Kattegat 151 F 4
Katul, Jabal 194 D 6
Katulu 199 G 4
Katumba 198 D 6
Katun' 159 R 5
Katunskiy Khrebet 159 R 5–6
Katyl'ga 159 P 4
Katyryk 170 G 1
Kau, Teluk 177 G 3
Kauai 113 C 9
Kauai 187 E 1
Kauai Channel 113 D 10
Kaubalatmada, Gunung 177 G 4
Kaufbeuren 149 F 5
Kaufman (TX.) 122 G 3
Kauhajoki 150 H 3
Kauhava 150 H 3
Kauhola Point 113 G 11
Kaukauna (WI.) 124 F 5
Kaukkwe Hills 175 G 3
Kaukonen 150 J 2
Kaukura 187 F 4
Kaula 187 E 1
Kaula Island 113 B 10
Kaulakahi Channel 113 C 10
Kaulishishi 200 D 3
Kaumalapau (HI.) 113 EF 11
Kauna Point 113 G 12
Kaunas 151 H 5
Kaunispää 150 J 2
Kauno Marios 151 H 5
Kaura Namoda 197 F 3
Kaustinen 150 H 3
Kautokeino 150 H 2
Kavacha 171 V 3
Kavadarci 154 B 2
Kavaja 154 A 2
Kavak (Turkey) 154 C 2
Kavak (Turkey) 155 E 3
Kavak (Turkey) 155 E 3
Kavak Dağı 154 C 3
Kavála 154 B 2
Kavalerovo 173 KL 2
Kavali 174 D 5
Kaval'kan 171 P 4
Kavar (Iran) 157 F 3
Kavendou, Mont 196 B 3
Kavieng 185 F 2
Kavieng 186 B 3
Kavīr (Iran) 157 F 2
Kavīr, Dasht-e (Iran) 157 FG 2
Kavir-e Abarqu (Iran) 157 F 3
Kavir-e Marvast (Iran) 157 G 3
Kavir-e Namak 168 F 3
Kavīr-e Namak (Iran) 157 G 1
Kavir-e Sirjan (Iran) 157 G 3
Kavkaz 155 E 1
Kawa 194 E 5
Kawaihae (HI.) 113 G 11
Kawaihae Bay 113 FG 12
Kawaihoa Point 113 B 10
Kawalusu, Pulau 177 F 3
Kawambwa 200 D 1
Kawardha 174 D 3
Kaw City (OK.) 120 J 6
Kaweah, Lake 112 G 6
Kawerau 185 R 8
Kawich Peak 112 J 4–5
Kawich Range 112 J 5
Kawio, Kepulauan 177 F 3
Kawkareik 175 G 4
Kawm Umbū (Egypt) 156 A 4
Kawthaung 175 G 5
Kaxgar He 169 K 3
Kax He 169 L 2
Kaya 196 D 3
Kayah 175 G 4
Kayak (AK, U.S.A.) 102 J 4
Kayak (U.S.S.R.) 170 H 1
Kayambi 201 E 1
Kayan 176 E 3
Kayan, Sungai 176 E 3
Kayankulam 174 C 6
Kaycee (WY.) 118 B 7
Kayenta (AZ.) 116 F 1
Kayes 196 B 3

Kayf, Tall (Iraq) 156 D 1
Kaygy 159 M 5
Kaymysovy 159 OP 4
Kaynar 159 P 6
Kayoa, Pulau 177 G 3
Kayseri 155 E 3
Kaysvile (UT.) 114 EF 2
Kayuagung 176 BC 4
Kayyerkan 159 R 2
Kazachinskoye 170 F 4
Kazachinskoye 170 J 4
Kazach'ye 171 P 1
Kazakh 155 G 2
Kazakhskiy Melkosopochnik 159 NP 6
Kazakhstan 169 FH 1
Kazalinsk 169 G 1
Kazan (N.W.T., Can.) 103 S 3
Kazandzik 168 F 3
Kazan Islands (Japan) 161 QR 7
Kazanka 155 D 1
Kazanlı 155 D 3
Kazanlŭk 154 C 2
Kazanskoye 159 NO 4
Kazan' 158 J 4
Kazan (N.W.T., Can.) 103 S 3
Kazantip, Mys 155 E 1
Kazantsevo 159 Q 1–2
Kazarman 169 J 2
Kazatin 158 E 6
Kazbek 155 F 2
Kaz Dağı 154 C 3
Käzerūn (Iran) 157 F 3
Kazgorodok 159 N 5
Kazhim 158 K 3
Kazi Magomed 168 D 2
Kâzımkarabekir 155 D 3
Kazincbarcika 154 B 1
Kaztalovka 158 J 6
Kazungula 200 D 3
Kazym 159 N 3
Kazymskaya 159 N 3
Kazymskiy Mys 159 N 3
Kazzān ar Ruşayriş 194 E 6
Kéa 154 B 3
Kéa 154 B 3
Keaau (HI.) 113 G 12
Keahole Point 113 F 12
Kealaikahiki Channel 113 F 11
Kealaikahiki Point 113 F 11
Kealakekua (HI.) 113 G 12
Kealia (HI.) 113 G 12
Keams Canyon (AZ.) 116 F 2
Kearney (NE.) 120 F 2
Kearns (UT.) 114 EF 3
Kearny (AZ.) 116 F 4
Keatchie (LA.) 123 K 3
Keating (OR.) 110 H 6
Keauhou (HI.) 113 FG 12
Keban Gölü 155 E 3
Ke Bao 175 J 3
Kebbi 197 E 3
Kébémer 196 A 2
Kebnekaise 150 G 2
Kebumen 176 C 5
Kecskemét 154 AB 1
Keda 155 F 2
Kédainiai 151 H 4
Keddie (CA.) 112 E 2
Kediet Idjil 192 C 4
Kediri 176 D 5
Kedjaman 176 D 3
Kedong 171 N 6
Kédougou 196 B 3
Kedva 158 K 3
Kedzierzyn Koźle 149 G 4
Keele 103 M 3
Keele Peak 109 M 3
Keele Peak (Yukon, Can.) 102 LM 3
Keeler (CA.) 112 H 6
Keelung 173 H 5
Keene (CA.) 113 G 7
Keene (ND.) 118 F 3
Keene (N.H.) 126 G 6
Keenesburg (CO.) 115 N 3
Keer-Weer, Cape 183 G 1
Keestekraal 200 D 5
Keetmanshoop 200 B 5
Keewatin (MN.) 119 P 3
Keewatin (Ontario, Can.) 104 HJ 6
Keewatin, District of 103 TU 2–3
Kefa 199 F 3
Kefallinía 154 B 3
Kéfalos 154 C 3
Kefamanau 177 F 5
Keffi 197 F 4
Kefken 154 D 2
Keflavík 150 A 3
Kegalla 174 CD 6
Kégashka 105 P 5
Kegen' 169 K 2
Kegulta 155 F 1
Kehl 149 E 5
Kehsi Mansam 175 G 3
Keila 151 H 4
Keimoes 200 C 5
Keitele 150 J 3
Keith (South Australia) 183 G 6
Keith Arm 103 N 2
Keithsburg (IL.) 124 D 8
Keizer (OR.) 110 B 5

Kekaha (HI.) **113** C 10
Keketa **184** D 3
Keke Usun, Ozero **155** G 1
Kekurnaya, Gora **171** V 3
Kel' **171** N 2
Kelam **199** F 4
Kelan **172** F 3
Kelang **176** B 3
Kelang, Pulau **177** G 4
Kelantan **176** B 2
Kelcyra **154** B 2
Kele **171** O 3
Kélekam **197** G 3
Keles **154** C 3
Keli Hāji Ibrāhīm (Iraq) **157** D 1
Kelil'vun, Gora **171** V 2
Kelkit **155** E 2
Kelkit **155** E 2
Kellé **197** G 6
Keller (WA.) **110** G 2
Kellerberrin **182** B 5
Kellerville (TX.) **117** Q 2
Kellett, Cape **103** M 1
Kelleys Island **125** M 8
Kellog (U.S.S.R.) **159** R 3
Kellogg (ID.) **110** J 3
Kellogg (MN.) **119** Q 6
Kelloselkä **150** J 2
Kelly (WY.) **111** P 7
Kelly Lake **109** N 2
Kelo **197** H 4
Kelolokan **176** E 3
Kelowna **103** O 6
Kelsey **103** S 4
Kelsey Bay **103** M 5
Kelso (CA.) **113** K 7
Kelso (WA.) **110** C 4
Kel'terskiy Khrebet **171** N 3
Keluang **176** B 3
Kelvin (AZ.) **116** EF 4
Kelvin (ND.) **118** J 2
Kelyeḥed **199** H 3
Kem' **150** K 3
Ké Macina **196** C 3
Kemah **155** E 3
Kemalpaşa (Turkey) **154** C 3
Kemalpaşa (Turkey) **155** F 2
Kembé **198** C 4
Kemboma **197** G 5
Kemer **154** C 3
Kemer **154** D 3
Kemer Barajı **154** C 3
Kemerovo **159** R 4
Kemi **150** H 2
Kemijärvi **150** J 2
Kemijoki **150** J 2
Kemkra **171** P 4
Kemmerer (WY.) **111** P 9
Kemp (TX.) **122** G 3
Kemp, Lake **122** D 2
Kempele **150** HJ 3
Kempendyayi **170** L 3
Kempner (TX.) **122** EF 4
Kemps Bay **133** G 3
Kempsey **183** J 5
Kempt, Lac **105** N 6
Kempten **149** F 5
Kempton (IL.) **124** F 9
Ken **174** D 3
Kenadsa **192** E 2
Kenai **102** G 3
Kenai Fjords National Park **102** H 4
Kenai Mountains **102** G 4
Kenai Peninsula **102** GH 4
Kenaliasam **176** B 4
Kenansville (FL.) **131** O 7
Kenansville (N.C.) **129** O 7
Kenbridge (VA.) **129** NO 5
Kencha **171** P 3
Kendall (FL.) **131** O 9
Kendall (KS.) **120** D 5
Kendall (N.Y.) **125** Q 6
Kendall, Cape **103** U 3
Kendari **177** F 4
Kendawangan **176** CD 4
Kendigué **197** H 3
Kendrick (ID.) **110** J 4
Kendyrlik **159** R 6
Kenedy (TX.) **122** F 7
Kenel (SD.) **118** H 5
Kenema **196** B 4
Kenesaw (NE.) **120** G 2
Kenga **159** Q 4
Kenge **198** B 5
Kengere **200** D 2
Kengtung **175** G 3
Kenhardt **200** C 5
Kéniéba **196** B 3
Kenitra **192** D 2
Keniut **171** X 3
Kenkeme **171** N 3
Kenly (N.C.) **129** N 6
Kenmare (ND.) **118** FG 2
Kenmare (Rep. of Ireland) **148** B 4
Kenna (N.M.) **117** N 4MO
Kennaday Peak **118** B 9
Kennard (NE.) **119** M 9
Kennard (TX.) **123** H 4
Kennebec (SD.) **118** J 7
Kennebec River **126** K 3–4
Kennebunk (ME.) **126** J 5
Kennebunkport (ME.) **126** J 5
Kennedy (AL.) **128** D 8
Kennedy (NE.) **118** H 8
Kennedy, Mount **109** L 3
Kennedy Entrance **109** H 4
Kennedy Peak **175** F 3
Kennedy Range National Park **182** B 3
Kenner (LA.) **123** N 5
Kennet **148** C 4
Kennett (MO.) **121** P 6
Kennewick (WA.) **110** F 4
Kenn Reef **183** K 3
Kennya **171** P 3
Kenogami **104** K 5
Keno Hill **102** K 3
Kenora **104** J 6
Kenosha (WI.) **124** G 7
Kensal (N.D.) **119** K 3
Kensington (KS.) **120** F 3
Kent (OR.) **110** E 5
Kent (Sierra Leone) **196** B 4
Kent (TX.) **117** M 6
Kent (WA.) **110** C 3
Kentau **169** H 2
Kent City (MI.) **124** J 6
Ken Thao **175** H 4
Kentland (IN.) **124** G 9
Kenton (OH.) **125** L 9
Kenton (OK.) **120** C 6
Kenton (TN.) **128** BC 5
Kent Peninsula **103** Q 2
Kentucky **128** HJ 2
Kentucky Lake **128** C 5
Kentucky River **128** G 3
Kenya **199** F 4
Kenya, Mount **199** F 5
Kenyon (MN.) **119** Q 6
Keokea (HI.) **113** F 11
Keokuk (IA.) **119** R 10
Keonihargarh **174** E 3
Keosauqua (IA.) **119** R 10
Keota (CO.) **115** NO 3
Keota (OK.) **121** L 7
Keowee, Lake **128** J 7
Kepahiang **176** B 4
Kepe **150** K 2
Kepi **177** J 5
Kep i Gjuhës **154** A 2
Kep i Rodonit **154** A 2
Kepno **149** G 4
Keppyul'skaya **171** P 4
Keptin **171** M 3
Kepulauan Aju **177** H 3
Kepulauan Anambas **176** C 3
Kepulauan Aru **177** HJ 5
Kepulauan Asia **177** H 3
Kepulauan Babar **177** G 5
Kepulauan Balabalangan **176** E 4
Kepulauan Banda **177** G 4
Kepulauan Banggai **177** F 4
Kepulauan Kai **177** H 5
Kepulauan Kangean **176** E 5
Kepulauan Kawio **177** FG 3
Kepulauan Leti **177** G 5
Kepulauan Lingga **176** B 3–4
Kepulauan Mapia **177** HJ 3
Kepulauan Mentawai **176** A 4
Kepulauan Nanusa **177** G 3
Kepulauan Natuna **176** C 3
Kepulauan Obi **177** G 4
Kepulauan Palau **177** H 2
Kepulauan Riau **176** B 3
Kepulauan Sangihe **177** G 3
Kepulauan Seram Laut **177** H 4
Kepulauan Sula **177** FG 4
Kepulauan Talaud **177** G 3
Kepulauan Tambelan **176** C 3
Kepulauan Tanimbar **177** H 5
Kepulauan Tenggara **177** G 5
Kepulauan Togian **177** F 4
Kepulauan Tukangbesi **177** F 5
Kepulauan Watubela **177** H 4
Kerala **174** C 5
Kerama-rettō **173** J 5
Kerandin **176** BC 4
Kerang **183** G 6
Kerava **151** J 3
Kerch **155** E 1
Kerchel' **159** M 4
Kerchenskiy Proliv **155** E 1–2
Kerchevskiy **158** L 4
Kerekhtyakh **171** N 3
Kerema **184** E 3
Kerempe Burnu **155** D 2
Keren **199** F 1
Keret', Ozero **150** K 2
Kerets, Mys **158** G 2
Kerewan **196** A 3
Kerguelen-Gaussberg Ridge **208** B 5
Kericho **198** F 5
Kerick (TX.) **117** O 1
Keri Kera **194** E 6
Kerimäki **150** J 3
Kerimbas, Archipelago **201** G 2
Kerinci, Gunung **176** B 4
Kerion **154** B 3
Keriske **171** O 2
Keriya He **169** L 3
Keriya Shankou **169** L 3
Kerkennah Islands → Juzur Qarqannah **193** H 2
Kerkhoven (MN.) **119** N 5
Kerki **158** K 3
Kerki **169** GH 3
Kérkira **154** A 3
Kérkira **154** A 3
Kerkour Nourene, Massif du **197** J 2
Kermadec Islands **186** D 4–5
Kermadec Trench **209** D 5
Kermān **168** F 4
Kerman (CA.) **112** E 6
Kermanshāh (Iran) **157** E 2
Kermānshāhān (Iran) **157** G 3
Kerme Körfezi **154** C 3
Kermit (TX.) **117** N 6
Kermit (W.V.) **129** J 4
Kern River **113** G 7
Kernville (CA.) **113** G 7
Kérouané **196** C 4
Kerrick (MN.) **119** Q 4
Kerrobert **103** PQ 5
Kerrville (TX.) **122** D 5
Kersey (CO.) **115** N 3
Kershaw (S.C.) **129** L 7
Kertamulia **176** C 4
Kerteh **176** B 3
Kerulen **170** K 6
Kerzaz **192** E 3
Kesagami Lake **105** L 5
Kesälahti **150** J 3
Keşan **154** C 2
Kesen'numa **173** M 3
Keshan **171** N 6
Keshena (WI.) **124** F 5
Keshvar (Iran) **157** E 2
Keskin **155** D 3
Kestenga **150** K 2
Keswick **148** C 4
Keszthely **154** A 1
Ket' **159** Q 4
Ket' **170** F 4
Keta **196** E 4
Keta, Ozero **170** F 2
Ketanda **171** Q 3
Ketapang **176** CD 4
Ketchikan **102** L 4
Ketchum (ID.) **111** L 7
Ketchum Mountain **122** C 4
Kete **196** E 4
Ket-Kap, Khrebet **171** O 4
Ketmen', Khrebet **169** KL 2
Ketou **196** E 4
Ketoy, Ostrov **171** S 6
Ketrzyn **149** H 4
Kettering (OH.) **128** G 2
Kettle Falls (WA.) **110** G 2
Kettleman City (CA.) **112** F 6
Kettle River Range **110** G 2
Keuka Lake **126** B 6
Keul' **170** H 4
Keurusselkä **150** HJ 3
Keuruu **150** H 3
Kevin (MT.) **111** N 2
Kew **133** H 3
Kewa (WA.) **110** G 2
Kewagama **105** M 6
Kewanee (IL.) **124** E 8
Kewaunee (WI.) **124** G 5
Keweenaw Bay **124** F 2–3
Keweenaw Peninsula **124** FG 2
Keweenaw Point **124** G 2
Key (TX.) **117** P 5
Keyano **105** N 5
Keyapaha (SD.) **118** HJ 7
Key Colony Beach (FL.) **131** NO 10
Keyes (OK.) **120** C 6
Keyhole Reservoir **118** D 6
Key Largo (FL.) **131** O 9
Key Largo (FL.) **131** O 9
Keystone (MN.) **119** Q 9
Keystone (NE.) **118** G 9
Keystone (SD.) **118** E 7
Keystone Heights (FL.) **131** MN 5
Keystone Lake **120** J 6
Keystone Peak **116** E 6
Keysville (VA.) **129** N 4
Key West (FL.) **131** N 10
Kezhma **170** H 4
Kezi **200** D 4
Kghoti **200** C 4
Kgun Lake **108** F 3
Khabalakh **170** K 3
Khabarikha **158** K 2
Khabarovsk **171** P 6
Khabary **159** P 5
Khabr, Kūh-e (Iran) **157** G 3
Khabūr (Syria) **156** C 1
Khachmas **168** D 2
Khadki **174** B 4
Khafji (Saudi Arabia) **157** E 3
Khafjī, Ra's al (Saudi Arabia) **157** E 3
Khafs Banbān (Saudi Arabia) **157** E 4
Khaipur **169** J 5
Khairagarh **174** D 3
Khairpur **169** J 5
Khaishi **155** F 2
Khāīz, Kūh-e (Iran) **157** F 3
Khajuri Kach **169** H 4
Khakh (Iran) **157** F 2
Khakhar **171** P 4
Khakhea **200** C 4
Khakhsyn **171** M 2
Khakriz **169** H 4
Khalach **169** G 3
Khalatse **169** K 4
Khalesavoy **159** P 3
Khalīj al Aqabah **156** B 3
Khalīj al Bahrayn (Saudi Arabia) **157** F 4
Khalīj as Suways **156** A 3
Khalīj Foul (Egypt) **156** B 5
Khalīj Maṣīrah **195** K 5
Khalīj Qābis **193** H 2
Khalīj Sirt **193** J 2
Khalkhāl **168** D 3
Khálki **154** C 3
Khalkidhiki **154** B 2
Khalkis **154** B 3
Khal'mer-Yu **159** M 2
Khalturin **158** J 4
Khalygras **171** N 2
Khamaky **170** K 3
Khamar Daban, Khrebet **170** HJ 5
Khambhat **174** B 3
Khambhat, Gulf of **174** B 3–4
Khambi Yakha **159** O 2
Khamgaon **174** C 3
Khamir **195** G 5
Khamīs Mushayṭ **195** G 5
Kham Keut **175** H 4
Khammam **174** D 4
Khampa **170** L 3
Khampa **171** M 3
Khamra **170** K 3
Khamsara **170** G 5
Khamseh (Iran) **157** E 1
Khanabad **169** H 3
Khān al Baghdādī (Iraq) **156** CD 2
Khanapur **174** B 4
Khānaqīn (Iraq) **157** D 2
Khandagayty **170** F 5
Khandwa **174** C 3
Khandyga **171** P 3
Khangarh **169** J 5
Khanglasy **159** M 3
Khangokurt **159** M 3
Khanh Hung **175** J 6
Khani **170** M 4
Khánia **154** B 3
Khaniadhana **174** C 2
Khanion, Kólpos **154** B 3
Khanka, Ozero **173** K 1–2
Khannya **170** L 2
Khanovey-Sede **159** P 2
Khanpur **169** J 5
Khān Ruhābah (Iraq) **156** D 3
Khān Shaykhūn (Syria) **156** B 2
Khanskoye Ozero **155** E 1
Khantau **169** J 2
Khantayka **159** R 2
Khantayskoye, Ozero **170** F 2
Khantayskoye Vodokhranilishche **159** RS 2
Khanty-Mansiysk **159** N 3
Khanu **175** G 4
Khanyangda **171** Q 4
Khanyardakh **171** N 3
Khānzīr, Ra's **199** H 2
Khao Lang **175** G 6
Khao Luang **175** G 6
Khao Sai Dao Tai **175** H 5
Khapa **174** C 3
Khapalu **169** K 3
Khapcheranga **170** K 6
Khappyrastakh **171** M 4
Khara **170** G 5
Khara-Aldan **171** O 3
Khara Astakh **170** K 3
Kharabali **155** G 1
Kharagpur **174** E 3
Kharagun **170** K 5
Kharakas **154** BC 4
Khar al Amaya (Iraq) **157** E 3
Kharampur **159** P 3
Khārān (Iran) **168** F 5
Kharan (Pakistan) **169** G 5
Kharan (Pakistan) **169** H 5
Kharānaq (Iran) **157** G 2
Kharānaq, Kūh-e (Iran) **157** G 2
Kharanor **170** L 5
Khara-Tala **171** ST 2
Khara-Tas, Gryada **170** J 1
Kharaulakhskiy Khrebet **171** N 1
Kharauz **170** J 5
Kharga Oasis → Wāḥāt al Khārijah **194** E 3–4
Kharik **170** H 5
Kharimkotan, Ostrov **171** ST 6
Kharīt, Wādī al (Egypt) **156** B 4–5
Khārk (Iran) **157** F 3
Khārk (Iran) **157** F 3
Kharkov **158** G 6
Khār Kūh (Iran) **157** F 3
Kharlovka**158** G 2
Kharlu **150** K 3
Kharmanli **154** C 2
Kharoti **169** H 4
Kharovsk **158** H 4
Kharstan **171** Q 1
Kharsysk **155** E 1
Khartaksho **169** K 4
Khartoum**194** E 5
Khartoum North → Al Kharṭūm Baḥrī **194** E 5
Kharutayuvam **159** LM 2
Kharwar **169** H 4
Khasan **173** K 2
Khasavyurt **155** G 2
Khash (Afghanistan) **169** G 4
Khāsh (Iran) **169** G 5
Khash Desert **169** G 4
Khashgort **159** N 2
Khashm al Qirbah **194** F 6
Khashm Mishraq (Saudi Arabia) **157** DE 4
Khash Rud **169** G 4
Khashuri **155** F 2
Khasi Jaintia **175** F 2
Khaskovo **154** C 2
Khatanga **170** H 1
Khatangskiy Zaliv **170** JK 1
Khataren **171** T 3
Khatyngnakh **171** O 3
Khatyrka **171** X 3
Khatystakh **170** M 4
Khāvar (Iran) **157** E 3
Khawr Abū Habl **194** E 6
Khawr al Fakkān (United Arab Emirates) **157** G 4
Khawr āl Juḥaysh **195** J 4
Khawr al Mufattaḥ (Saudi Arabia) **157** E 3
Khaya **171** P 3
Khaybar (Saudi Arabia) **156** C 4
Khaybar, Ḥarrat **195** FG 3
Khaydarken **169** J 3
Khaylino **171** V 3
Khaylyulya **171** U 4
Khaypudyrskaya Guba **159** LM 2
Khayryuzovka **170** H 5
Khayryuzovo **171** T 4
Khayyr **171** O 1
Khazzān Jabal al Awliyā' **194** E 5–6
Khe Bo **175** HJ 4
Kheda **174** B 3
Khelyulya **150** K 3
Khemchik **170** F 5
Khemis Miliana **193** F 1
Khemisset **192** D 2
Khemmarat **175** H 4
Khenchela **193** G 1
Khenifra **192** D 2
Kheri **174** D 2
Kherpuchi **171** P 5
Khersan (Iran) **157** F 3
Kherson **155** D 1
Khe Sanh **175** J 4
Khesh **169** H 4
Kheta **159** Q 2
Kheta **170** G 1
Kheta **170** H 1
Khetta, Levaya **159** O 3
Kheyrābād (Iran) **157** E 3
Kheyrābād (Iran) **157** G 3
Khibiny **150** K 2
Khilchipur **174** C 3
Khil'mi, Gora **171** S 1
Khilok **170** J 5
Khilok **170** K 5
Khimki **158** G 4
Khíos **154** C 3
Khíos **154** C 3
Khirbat Isriyah (Syria) **156** BC 2
Khlong Makham **175** H 5
Khmelev **158** F 5
Khmel'nik **158** E 6
Khmel'nitskiy **158** E 6
Khobol'chan **171** Q 2
Khodzha Mubarek **169** H 3
Khodzheyli **168** F 2
Khoe **171** Q 5
Khogali **198** D 3
Khokhropar **169** J 5
Khokiley **159** Q 2
Khok Kloi **175** G 6
Kholm (Afghanistan) **169** H 3
Kholm (U.S.S.R.) **151** K 4
Kholmogory **158** H 3
Kholmsk **171** Q 6
Kholodnoye **159** M 3
Kholzun, Khrebet **159** Q 5
Khomān **168** DE 3
Khomas Highland **200** B 4
Khomeyn (Iran) **157** F 2
Khomeyni, Bandar-e (Iran) **157** E 3
Khomokashevo **170** HJ 3
Khong **175** J 5
Khongkhoyuku **171** O 3
Khongo **171** S 3
Khong Sedone **175** J 4
Khonj (Iran) **157** F 4
Khon Kaen **175** H 4
Khonsār (Iran) **157** F 2
Khonu **171** O 2
Khonu **171** Q 2
Khoper **158** H 5
Khoppuruo **170** L 4
Khor **171** P 6
Khor **171** P 6
Khora **154** B 3

Khor Anghar 199 G 2
Khorāsān 168 F 4
Khorat Plateau 175 H 4
Khorb el Ethel 192 D 3
Khordogoy 170 L 3
Khorgo 170 K 1
Khorinsk 170 J 5
Khorintsy 170 M 3
Khorixas 200 A 4
Khorog 169 J 3
Khoronkhu 171 O 3
Khoronnokh 170 LM 2
Khorram (Iran) 157 E 1
Khorramābād (Iran) 157 E 2
Khorramshahr (Iran) 157 E 3
Khorsābād (Iraq) 156 D 1
Khosheutovo 155 G 1
Khoshyeylaq (Iran) 157 G 1
Khosrowābād (Iran) 157 E 3
Khosta 155 EF 2
Khotin 154 C 1
Khouribga 192 D 2
Khovu-Aksy 170 F 5
Khowrjān (Iran) 157 F 3
Khowst 169 H 4
Khoydype, Gora 159 N 2
Khoyniki 158 F 5
Khrami 155 F 2
Khrebet, Katunski 159 R 5–6
Khrebet Bol'shoy Balkhan 168 EF 3
Khrebet Borong 171 P 2
Khrebet Bureinskiy 171 O 5
Khrebet Chayatyn 171 P 5
Khrebet Cherskogo 170 KL 5
Khrebet Cherskogo 171 P 1–2
Khrebet Chingiz-Tau 159 P 6
Khrebet Dygdy-Sise 171 O 4
Khrebet Dzhagdy 171 O 5
Khrebet Dzhaki-Unakhta Yak-
  byyana 171 OP 5–6
Khrebet Dzhugdzhur 171 OP 4
Khrebet Dzhungarskiy Alatau 159 Q 6
Khrebet Genkanyy 108 D 2
Khrebet Iskaten' 102 B 2
Khrebet Kadyr-Egi-Tayga 170 G 5
Khrebet Kamennyy 171 UV 3
Khrebet Karatau 169 H 2
Khrebet Ket-Kap 171 O 4
Khrebet Ketmen' 169 KL 2
Khrebet Khamar Daban 170 HJ 5
Khrebet Kholzun 159 Q 5
Khrebet Khugdyungda 170 G 2
Khrebet Kivun 171 P 5
Khrebet Kodar 170 L 4
Khrebet Kolymskiy 171 SU 3
Khrebet Kopet-Dag 168 F 3
Khrebet Koryakskiy 171 VW 3
Khrebet Kungey Alatau 169 K 2
Khrebet Mayskiy 171 O 4–5
Khrebet Narymskiy 159 QR 6
Khrebet Nuratau 169 H 2
Khrebet Orulgan 171 N 2
Khrebet Pay-Khoy 159 M 2
Khrebet Pekul'ney 171 WX 2
Khrebet Pribrezhnyy 171 P 4
Khrebet Rarytkin 171 WX 3
Khrebet Saur 159 QR 6
Khrebet Semme-Dahan 171 P 3
Khrebet Sette-Daban 171 P 3
Khrebet Suntar Khayata 171 PQ 3
Khrebet Taaga 171 N 4
Khrebet Talasskiy Alatau 169 J 2
Khrebet Tarbagatay 159 Q 6
Khrebet Taskyl 170 G 5
Khrebet Tas-Kystabys 171 QR 3
Khrebet Terskey Alatau 169 K 2
Khrebet Tukuringra 171 N 5
Khrebet Turana 171 O 5
Khrebet Udokan 170 L 4
Khrebet Ulakhan-Chistay 171 QR 2–3
Khrebet Ulan-Burgasy 170 J 5
Khrebet Umnyn Syverma 170 GH 2
Khrebet Verkhoyanskiy 171 N 2–3
Khrebet Yam-Alin' 171 OP 5
Khrebet Yankan 170 L 4
Khrebet Yuzhno Chuyskiy 159 R 6
Khroma 171 Q 1
Khromskaya Guba 171 R 1
Khrom-Tau 159 L 5
Khrustal'nyy 173 KL 2
Khudoseya 159 Q 2–3
Khudumelapye 200 C 4
Khudzhakh 171 R 3
Khuff 193 J 3
Khuff (Saudi Arabia) 156 B 4
Khugdyungda, Khrebet 170 G 2
Khugiani 169 H 4
Khuis 200 C 5
Khulga 159 N 2
Khulkhuta 155 G 1
Khulna 174 D 3
Khulo 155 F 2
Khummi, Ozero 171 P 5
Khūrāb (Iran) 157 F 3
Khurai 174 C 3
Khūran (Iran) 157 G 4
Khuray$ (Saudi Arabia) 157 E 4
Khurayt 194 D 6
Khurchan 171 S 4
Khurda 174 E 3

Khuren 171 R 3
Khurīyā Murīya, Jazā'ir 195 K 5
Khurja 174 C 2
Khurmalik 169 G 4
Khurr, Wādī al (Saudi Arabia) 156 C 3
Khurram shahr (Iran) 157 E 3
Khursanīyah (Saudi Arabia) 157 E 4
Khushab 169 J 4
Khust 154 B 1
Khutse 200 C 4
Khuwayy 194 D 6
Khuzdar 169 H 5
Khūzestān (Iran) 157 E 3
Khuzhir 170 J 5
Khvāf 168 FG 4
Khvāf 168 G 4
Khvalynsk 158 J 5
Khvojeh, Kūh-e (Iran) 157 E 2
Khvor (Iran) 157 G 2
Khvormūj (Iran) 157 F 3
Khvormūj, Kūh-e (Iran) 157 F 3
Khvoy 168 D 3
Khwaja Amran 169 H 4
Khyber Pass 169 J 4
Kia 185 G 3
Kiama 198 B 6
Kiamba 177 F 2
Kiambi 198 D 6
Kiana 102 E 2
Kiantajärvi 150 J 2
Kiapulka 198 D 6
Kiāseh (Iran) 157 F 1
Kibaha 199 F 6
Kibamba 198 D 5
Kibangou 197 G 6
Kibau 198 F 6
Kibaya 199 F 6
Kiberege 199 F 6
Kiberg 150 K 1
Kiboko 199 F 5
Kibombo 198 D 5
Kibondo 198 E 5
Kibre Mengist 199 F 3
Kibris → Cyprus 155 D 3
Kibungo 198 E 5
Kibuye 198 D 5
Kibwezi 199 F 5
Kicevo 154 B 2
Kichiga 171 U 4
Kickapoo, Lake 122 E 2
Kickapoo Indian Reservation 121 J 3
Kicking Horse Pass 103 O 5
Kidal 196 E 2
Kidatu 199 F 6
Kidepo National Park 198 E 4
Kidira 196 B 3
Kidnappers, Cape 185 R 8
Kiel 171 F 4
Kiel (WI.) 124 F 6
Kielce 149 H 4
Kieler Bucht 149 F 4
Kienge 200 D 2
Kieta 185 G 3
Kieta 186 B 3
Kiffa 192 C 5
Kifissós 154 B 3
Kifrī (Iraq) 156 D 2
Kifri (Iraq) 157 D 2
Kigali 198 E 5
Kiği 155 F 3
Kigille 198 E 3
Kigilyakh 171 Q 1
Kignan 196 C 3
Kigoma 198 D 5
Kihelkonna 151 H 4
Kihnu 151 H 4
Kiholo Bay 113 FG 12
Kii-hantō 173 L 4
Kiik 159 O 6
Kiiminki 150 J 2
Kii-suidō 173 KL 4
Kikai-jima 173 JK 5
Kikiakki 159 Q 3
Kikinda 154 B 1
Kikladhes 154 C 3
Kikori 184 D 3
Kikori 186 A 3
Kikwit 198 B 6
Kil 151 F 4
Kilafors 150 G 3
Kilakkarai 174 C 6
Kilambé 132 E 5
Kīlan (Iran) 157 F 2
Kilauea (HI.) 113 C 9
Kilauea Crater 113 G 12
Kilbuck Mountains 102 F 3
Kilchu 173 J 2
Kilcoy 183 J 4
Kildare 148 B 4
Kildare (GA.) 131 N 2
Kil'din, Ostrov 150 K 2
Kilembe 198 C 6
Kilgore (ID.) 111 NO 6
Kilgore (NE.) 118 GH 8
Kilgore (TX.) 123 J 3
Kili 186 C 2
Kiliç Dağları 154 C 3
Kilifi 199 F 5

Kilimanjaro 199 F 5
Kilimanjaro National Park 199 F 5
Kilinailau Islands 185 G 2
Kilindini 199 F 5
Kilindoni 199 F 6
Kilis (Turkey) 156 B 1
Kilitbahir 154 C 2
Kilkee 148 B 4
Kilkenny 148 B 4
Kilkenny (N.C.) 129 P 6
Kilkis 154 B 2
Killarney 148 B 4
Killdeer (ND.) 118 F 3
Killeen (TX.) 122 F 4
Killelu 199 G 2
Killen (AL.) 128 D 7
Killik River 109 H 2
Killinek 105 O 3
Killington Peak 126 G 5
Killini Óros 154 B 3
Kilmarnock 148 C 2
Kilmarnock (VA.) 129 P 4
Kil'mez' 158 K 4
Kilmez 158 K 4
Kilmichael (MS.) 121 Q 9
Kilmore 183 H 6
Kilombero 199 F 6
Kilosa 199 F 6
Kilpisjärvi 150 H 2
Kilp-Javr 150 K 2
Kilur Karim (Iran) 157 F 3
Kilwa 198 D 6
Kilwa Kisiwani 199 F 6
Kilwa Kivinje 199 F 6
Kilwa Masoko 199 F 6
Kilyos 154 C 2
Kim (CO.) 115 O 6
Kimaan 177 J 5
Kimba 183 F 5
Kimball (NE.) 118 E 9
Kimball (SD.) 118 K 7
Kimball, Mount 102 J 3
Kimbe Bay 185 F 3
Kimberley 103 O 6
Kimberley (South Africa) 200 CD 5
Kimberley (Western Australia) 182 D 2
Kimberley Downs 182 C 2
Kimberley Plateau 182 D 2
Kimberly (ID.) 111 L 8
Kimberly (OR.) 110 F 6
Kimbrough (AL.) 130 E 7
Kimch'aek 173 J 2
Kimch'on 173 J 3
Kimhandu 199 F 6
Kimi (Cameroon) 197 G 4
Kimi (Greece) 154 B 3
Kimito 151 H 3
Kimongo 197 G 6
Kimovsk 158 G 5
Kimparana 196 C 3
Kimpese 198 A 6
Kimry 158 G 4
Kimvula 198 B 6
Kinabalu, Gunung 176 E 2
Kinabatangan 176 E 2
Kincaid, Lake 121 Q 3
Kinchang 175 G 2
Kinchega National Park 183 G 5
Kinda (Sweden) 151 G 4
Kinda (Zaire) 198 C 6
Kindamba 197 G 6
Kindambi 198 C 6
Kindat 175 F 3
Kinder (LA.) 123 L 5
Kindersley 103 Q 5
Kindia 196 B 4
Kindred (N.D.) 119 LM 4
Kindu 198 D 5
Kineshma 158 H 4
King 184 K 8
King and Queen Court House (VA.)
  129 P 4
Kingaroy 183 J 4
King Christian IX Land 202
King Christian X Land 202
King City (CA.) 112 DE 6
King City (MO.) 121 L 2
King Cove 108 F 4–5
Kingdom City (MO.) 121 O 4
King Edward VII Falls 139 G 3
King Frederik VIII Land 202
King George (VA.) 129 O 3
King George Islands 105 M 4
King George Sound 182 B 6
King Hill (ID.) 111 K 7
Kingisepp (U.S.S.R.) 151 J 4
King Island 183 G 6
King Island (AK.) 108 E 3
Kingissepp (Estoniya, U.S.S.R.) 151 H 4
King Lear Peak 112 G 1
King Leopold Ranges 182 CD 2
Kingman (AZ.) 116 B 2
Kingman (KS.) 120 G 5
Kingman (Pacific Ocean, U.S.A.)
  186 E 2
King Mountain(Br. Col., Can.)
  109 MN 4
King Mountain (OR.) 110 G 7

King Mountain (OR.) 110 B 8
Kingombe 198 D 5
Kingombe 198 D 5
Kingoonya 183 F 5
King Salmon 108 G 4
Kings Beach (CA.) 112 E 3
Kingsburg (CA.) 112 F 6
Kingsburg (S.D.) 119 K 8
Kingsbury Lake 111 P 3
Kings Canyon (CO.) 115 LM 3
Kings Canyon National Park 112 G 6
Kingscote 183 F 6
Kingsford (WI.) 124 F 4
Kingsland (GA.) 131 N 4
Kingsland (TX.) 122 E 5
Kingsley (IA.) 119 N 8
Kingsley (MI.) 124 J 5
Kingsley Dam 120 D 1
King's Lynn 148 D 4
Kings Peak (CA.) 112 A 2
Kings Peak (UT.) 114 G 3–H 4
Kings River 112 F 6
King Sound 182 C 2
Kingsport (TN.) 128 J 5
Kings River 112 F 6
Kingston (Jamaica) 133 G 4
Kingston (MO.) 121 LM 3
Kingston (N.M.) 116 J 5
Kingston (Norfolk Is., Austr.) 186 C 4
Kingston (N.Y.) 126 EF 7
Kingston (OH.) 128 J 2
Kingston (OH.) 128 J 2
Kingston (OK.) 120 J 8–9
Kingston (Ontario, Can.) 105 M 7
Kingston (PA.) 127 D 7
Kingston (South Australia) 183 F 6
Kingston-upon-Hull 148 C 4
Kingstown 133 K 5
Kingstree (S.C.) 129 M 8
Kingsville (TX.) 122 F 8
Kinguji 198 B 6
King William (VA.) 129 O 4
King William Island 103 S 2
King Williams Town 200 D 6
Kingwood (W.V.) 129 M 2
Kiniama 200 D 2
Kinkala 197 G 6
Kinmaw 175 F 4
Kinmundy (IL.) 121 R 4
Kinna 175 F 4
Kinnairds Head 148 C 3
Kinnekulle 151 F 4
Kinoosao 103 R 4
Kinsale 148 B 4
Kinsale (VA.) 129 P 3
Kinsarvik 151 E 3
Kinsey (MT.) 118 C 4
Kinshasa 198 B 5
Kinsley (KS.) 120 F 5
Kinston (N.C.) 129 O 6
Kinta (OK.) 121 K 7
Kintampo 196 D 4
Kintap 176 E 4
Kinter (AZ.) 116 B 5
Kintinku 198 EF 6
Kintyre 148 B 3
Kinyangiri 198 E 5
Kinyeti, Jabal 198 E 4
Kinzia 198 B 5
Kinzua (OR.) 110 EF 5
Kiowa (CO.) 115 N 4
Kiowa (KS.) 120 G 5
Kipahulu (HI.) 113 F 11
Kipaka 198 D 5
Kiparissiakós Kolpós 154 B 3
Kipawa, Lac 105 M 6
Kipembawe 198 E 6
Kipengere Range 198 E 6
Kipili 198 E 6
Kipini 199 G 5
Kipnuk 102 E 4
Kipushi 200 D 2
Kirakira 185 H 4
Kirakira 186 B 3
Kirané 196 B 2
Kiraz 154 C 3
Kirbey 170 H 2
Kirbey 170 K 2
Kirby (AR.) 121 M 8
Kirbyville (TX.) 123 K 5
Kirdimi 197 H 2
Kirenga 170 J 4
Kirensk 170 J 4
Kirghiz Steppe 168–169 FG 1
Kirgiziya 169 JK 2
Kirgizskiy Khrebet 169 J 2
Kirgiz Step' 168–169 FH 1
Kiri 198 B 5
Kiribati 186 DE 3
Kırıkhan 185 G 2
Kırıkhan (Turkey) 156 B 1
Kırıkkale 155 D 3
Kirillovka 155 E 1
Kirimati 187 E 2
Kiritimati 187 E 2
Kiritimati 187 E 2
Kirk (OR.) 110 D 8

Kırkağaç 154 C 3
Kirkby (MT.) 118 B 5
Kirkcaldy 148 C 3
Kirkcudbright 148 C 4
Kirkee → Khadki 174 B 4
Kirkenes 150 K 2
Kirkjubæjarklaustur 150 B 3
Kirkland (AZ.) 116 D 3
Kirkland (TX.) 117 QR 3
Kirkland (WA.) 110 C 3
Kirkland Lake 105 L 6
Kırklareli 154 C 2
Kirklin (IN.) 124 H 9
Kirkmansville (KY.) 128 D 4
Kirkpatrick, Mount 203
Kirksville (MO.) 121 N 2
Kirkwall 148 C 3
Kirkwood (MO.) 121 P 4
Kirkwood (South Africa) 200 D 6
Kırlangıç Burun 154 D 3
Kirov 158 J 4
Kirov 158 F 5
Kirovabad 168 D 2
Kirovakan 155 F 2
Kirovo Chepetsk 158 K 4
Kirovograd 155 D 1
Kirovsk 150 K 2
Kirovsk 151 K 4
Kirovsk 168 E 3
Kirovskiy 169 K 2
Kirovskiy 171 T 5
Kirovskiy 173 K 1
Kirs 158 K 4
Kırşehir 155 D 3
Kirtachi 196 E 3
Kirthar Range 169 H 5
Kiruna 150 H 2
Kirundu 198 D 5
Kirwin (KS.) 120 F 3
Kirwin Reservoir 120 F 3
Kir'yanovskaya Kontora 170 H 4
Kisa 151 G 4
Kisabi 198 D 6
Kisaki 199 F 6
Kisalföld 154 A 1
Kisambo 198 B 6
Kisangani 198 D 4
Kisangire 199 F 6
Kisar, Pulau 177 G 5
Kiselevsk 159 R 5
Kishangarh 174 B 2
Kishangarh 174 BC 2
Kishb, Ḥarrat al 195 G 4
Kishi 196 E 4
Kishinev 154 C 1
Kishorganj 175 F 3
Kishtwar 169 K 4
Kisii 198 E 5
Kisiju 199 F 6
Kısılırmak 155 D 2
Kısır Dağı 155 F 2
Kiska 196 B 4
Kiska Volcano 102 A 5
Kiskőrei Víztároló 154 B 1
Kiskőrös 154 A 1
Kiskunfélegyháza 154 A 1
Kiskunhalas 154 AB 1
Kislovodsk 155 F 2
Kismāyu 199 G 5
Kismet (KS.) 120 E 5
Kisoro 198 DE 5
Kissidougou 196 B 4
Kissimmee (FL.) 131 N 6
Kissimmee, Lake 131 N 6
Kissimmee River 131 NO 7
Kissü, Jabal 194 D 4
Kisumu 198 E 5
Kisvárda 154 B 1
Kita 196 B 3
Kitab 169 H 3
Kita-daitō-jima 173 K 5
Kitai, Ozero 154 C 1
Kitakyushū 173 JK 4
Kitale 198 F 4
Kitami 173 M 2
Kitami-sanchi 173 M 2
Kitanda 198 D 6
Kitangari 201 F 2
Kitangiri, Lake 198 E 5
Kit Carson (CO.) 115 P 5
Kitchener 105 L 7
Kitee 150 K 3
Kiteiyab 194 E 4
Kitete 198 E 5
Kitgum 198 E 4
Kíthira 154 B 3
Kíthira 154 B 3
Kithnos 154 B 3
Kitimat 102 M 5
Kitimat Ranges 102–103 M 5
Kitinen 150 J 2
Kitoboynyy 171 S 6
Kitoy 170 H 5
Kitsman 154 C 1
Kittanning (PA.) 125 P 9
Kittery (ME.) 126 J 5
Kittilä 150 H 2
Kittitas (WA.) 110 E 3

Kitty Hawk (N.C.) 129 Q 5
Kitui 199 F 5
Kitunda 198 E 6
Kitwe 200 D 2
Kitzbühel 153 F 2
Kitzbüheler Alpen 153 F 2
Kiunga (Kenya) 199 G 5
Kiunga (Papua New Guinea) 184 D 3
Kiuruvesi 150 J 3
Kivak 102 C 3
Kivalina 102 E 2
Kivijärvi 150 HJ 3
Kivik 151 F 4
Kiviõli 151 J 4
Kivu 198 D 5
Kivu, Lake 198 D 5
Kivun, Khrebet 171 P 5
Kiwaba N'zogi 200 B 1
Kiwalik 108 F 2
Kiya 159 R 4
Kiyāmakī Dāgh 168 D 3
Kiyeng-Kyuyel' 171 S 2
Kiyeng-Kyuyel', Ozero 170 JK 1
Kiyev 158 F 5
Kiyevka 159 O 5
Kiyevka 173 K 2
Kiyevskoye Vodokhranilishche 158 F 5
Kıyıköy 154 C 2
Kiyma 159 N 5
Kizel 159 L 4
Kizema 158 H 3
Kizha 170 J 5
Kizhinga 170 J 5
Kızılcahamam 155 D 2
Kızıl Dağ 155 D 3
Kızıl Dağ (Turkey) 156 A 1
Kızılırmak 155 E 2
Kizilirmak 155 E 3
Kizil'skoye 159 L 5
Kızıl Tepe 154 D 2
Kızıltepe 155 F 3
Kızıltepe (Turkey) 156 C 1
Kizimen, Sopka 171 U 4
Kizimi 197 H 2
Kizlyar 155 G 2
Kizlyarskiy Zaliv 155 G 2
Kizyl-Arvat 168 F 3
Kizyl-Atrek 168 E 3
Kizyl-Su 168 E 3
Kjöllefjord 150 J 1
Kjölur 150 B 3
Kjöpsvik 150 G 2
Klabat, Gunung 177 G 3
Kladanj 153 G 3
Kladno 149 F 4
Klagan 176 E 2
Klagenfurt 153 F 2
Klaipėda 151 H 4
Klamath (CA.) 112 B 1
Klamath Falls (OR.) 110 D 8
Klamath Marsh 110 D 7–8
Klamath Mountains 112 B 1
Klamath River 112 B 1
Klamono 177 H 4
Klarälven 151 F 3
Klatovy 149 F 5
Klatt Road 109 J 3
Klawer 200 B 6
Klea → Abū Tulayh 194 E 5
Klein (MT.) 111 R 4
Klein Aub 200 B 4
Kleinsee 200 B 5
Klerksdorp 200 D 5
Klevan' 151 J 5
Klichka 170 L 5
Klickitat (WA.) 110 D 5
Klin 158 G 4
Klina 154 B 2
Kline (CO.) 115 J 6
Klintehamn 151 G 4
Klintsovka 158 J 5
Klintsy 158 F 5
Klipgat 200 C 4
Klippan 151 F 4
Klit 151 E 4
Kłodzko 149 G 4
Kłomnice 149 G 4
Klondike Plateau 102 K 3
Klondike River 109 L 3
Klosi 154 B 2
Klotz, Lac 105 N 3
Klotz, Mount 102 K 2
Klowa (MT.) 111 M 2
Kluane Lake 102 K 3
Kluane National Park 102 K 3
Kluczbork 149 G H 4
Klukhorskiy Pereval 155 F 2
Klyavlino 158 K 5
Klyazma 158 H 4
Klyuchevaya 158 H 2
Klyuchevskaya Sopka 171 U 4
Klyuchi 170 K 5
Klyuchr 171 U 4
Kneža 154 B 2
Knife River 118 G 3
Knin 153 G 3
Knippa (TX.) 122 D 6
Knittelfeld 153 FG 2
Knjaževac 154 B 2
Knob 128 GH 6
Knob Noster (MO.) 121 M 4
Knolls (UT.) 114 D 3
Knösen 151 EF 4
Knosós 154 C 3
Knowles (OK.) 120 E 6
Knowlton (MT.) 118 C 4
Knox (IN.) 124 H 8
Knox, Cape 102 L 5
Knox City (MO.) 121 NO 2
Knox City (TX.) 122 D 2
Knox Coast 203
Knoxville (GA.) 131 KL 2
Knoxville (IA.) 119 P 9
Knoxville (IL.) 124 D 9
Knoxville (TN.) 128 H 6
Knud Rasmussen Land 202
Knyazhevo 158 H 4
Knysna 200 C 6
Koal 197 H 3
Koartac 105 N 3
Koba 176 C 4
Koba 177 J 5
Kobar Sink 199 G 2
Kobbo 199 F 2
Kobdo→Hovd 170 F 6
Kōbe 173 KL 4
København 151 F 4
Kobenni 192 D 5
Koblenz 149 E 4
Koboldo 171 O 5
Kobrin 151 H 5
Kobroor, Pulau 177 H 5
Kobuk (AK.) 102 EF 2
Kobuk (AK.) 102 F 2
Kobuk Valley National Park (AK.) 102 F 2
Kobuleti 155 F 2
Kobyai 171 N 3
Koca Çal 155 D 3
Koca Çay 154 C 3
Kocaeli 154 CD 2
Kočani 154 B 2
Kocasu 154 C 3
Koch 105 M 2
Ko Chan 175 G 6
Ko Chang 175 H 5
Kochechum 170 G 2
Kochegarovo 170 L 4
Kochenga 170 H 4
Kochevo 158 K 4
Kōchi 173 K 4
Kochikha 170 G 1
Koçhisar Ovası 155 D 3
Kochkorka 169 K 2
Kočhmar 154 C 2
Kochmes 159 M 2
Koch Peak 111 O 5
Kochubey 155 G 2
Kock 149 H 4
Kodar, Khrebet 170 L 4
Kodi 177 E 5
Kodiak 102 G 4
Kodiak Island 102 G 4
Kodima 158 H 3
Kodino158 GH 3
Kodok 198 E 3
Kodori, Mys 155 F 2
Kodyma 154 D 1
Kodžha Balkan 154 C 2
Koehler (N.M.) 117 M 1
Koehn Dry Lake 113 H 7
Koel 174 D 3
Kōes 200 B 5
Kofa (AZ.) 116 C 5
Kofa Mountains 116 C 4
Kofçaz 154 C 2
Koffiefontein 200 C 5
Köflach 153 G 2
Koforidua 196 D 4
Koggala 174 D 6
Kogil'nik 154 C 1
Kogon 196 B 3
Kohala Mountains 113 G 11
Kohat 169 J 4
Koh-Hisar 169 H 3–4
Koh-i-Baba 169 H 4
Kohima 175 F 2
Koh-i-Mazar 169 H 4
Koh-i-Pantar 169 H 5
Koh i Qaisar 169 G 4
Koh-i-Sangan 169 GH 4
Kohistan 169 J 3
Kohlu 169 H 5
Kohtla-Järve 151 J 4
Kohunlich 132 E 4
Koidern 109 K 3
Koitere 150 K 3
Kojonup 182 B 5
Kojūr (Iran) 157 F 2
Kokadio (ME.) 126 K 3
Kokalaat 169 G 1
Kokand 169 J 2
Kökar 151 H 4
Kokaral, Ostrov 168 FG 1
Kokas 177 H 4
Kokcha 169 H 3
Kokchetav 159 N 5
Kokemäenjoki 150 H 3
Kokemäki 150 H 3
Kokkola 150 H 3
Koko 198 F 2
Kokoda 184 E 3
Kokolik River 108 F 2
Kokomo (IN.) 124 H 9
Kokonau 177 J 4
Kokong 200 C 4
Koko Nor 172 D 3
Kokora, Ozero 170 H 1
Kokpekty 159 Q 6
Koksaray 169 H 2
Kokshaga 158 J 4
Koksoak 105 O 4
Kokstad 200 D 6
Koktuma 159 Q 6
Kokuora 171 Q 1
Ko Kut 175 H 5
Kok-Yangak 169 J 2
Kola 150 K 2
Kolahun 196 BC 4
Kolai 169 J 3
Kolaka 177 F 4
Ko Lanta 175 G 6
Kola Peninsula 158 G 2
Kolar 174 C 5
Kolar Gold Fields 174 C 5
Kolari 150 H 2
Kolbachi 171 M 5
Kolbio 199 G 5
Kolda 196 B 3
Kolding 151 E 4
Kole 198 D 4
Kole 198 C 5
Koléa 152 D 4
Kolepom Island 177 J 5
Kolesnoye 154 D 1
Kolesovo 171 S 1
Kolff, Tanjung 177 J 5
Kolguyev, Ostrov 158 J 2
Kolhapur 174 B 4
Koli 150 J 3
Koliganek 102 F 4
Kolin (MT.) 111 Q 3
Kolka 151 H 4
Kolkasrags 151 H 4
Kollegal 174 C 5
Kollumúli 150 C 2
Kolmanskop 200 AB 5
Kolmården 151 G 4
Kolmogorovo 170 F 4
Köln 149 E 4
Kolo 149 G 4
Koloa (HI.) 113 C 10
Kołobrzeg 149 G 4
Kologi 194 E 6
Kolokani 196 C 3
Koloko 196 C 3
Kololo 199 G 3
Kolombangara 185 G 3
Kolomna 158 G 4
Kolomyya 154 C 1
Kolondieba 196 C 3
Kolonia 186 E 1
Kolonodale 177 F 4
Kolosovka 159 O 4
Kolozero, Ozero 150 K 2
Kolpakovo 171 T 5
Kolpashevo 159 Q 4
Kolpino 151 K 4
Kólpos Ierisou 154 B 2
Kólpos Kallonis 154 C 3
Kólpos Kassándras 154 B 2–3
Kólpos Khanion 154 B 3
Kol'skiy, Poluostrov 158 G 2
Koluton 159 N 5
Kolva 158 L 2
Kolvitskoye, Ozero 150 K 2
Kolwa 169 G 5
Kolwezi 200 D 2
Kolyma 171 T 2
Kolyma Range 171 U 3
Kolymskaya 171 T 2
Kolymskaya 171 V 2
Kolymskaya Nizmennost' 171 ST 2
Kolymskiy, Khrebet 171 SU 3
Kolymskoye Nagor'ye 171 S 3
Kolyshley 158 H 5
Kolyuchinskaya Guba 102 C 2
Kolyvan' 159 Q 5
Koma 199 F 3
Komadugu Gana 197 G 3
Komadugu Yobe 197 G 3
Komandorski Islands 161 TU 4
Komandorskije Ostrova 161 TU 4
Komarichi 158 F 5
Komárno 149 G 5
Komarom 154 A 1
Komati Poort 201 E 5
Komatsu 173 L 3
Komba 198 C 4
Kombat 200 B 3
Kombissiguiri 196 D 3
Kombolchia 199 FG 2
Komdi 175 G 2
Kome 198 E 5
Kome Island 198 E 5
Komelek 171 O 3
Komfane 177 HJ 5
Komló 154 A 1
Kommunarka 159 R 2
Kommunarsk 155 E 1
Kommunist 171 X 3
Kommunizma, Pik 169 J 3
Komodo, Pulau 177 E 5
Komoé 196 D 4
Komoé, Parc National de la 196 D 4
Komono 197 G 6
Komoran, Pulau 177 J 5
Komotini 154 C 2
Kompas Berg 200 C 6
Kompong Cham 175 J 5
Kompong Chhnang 175 H 5
Kompong Som 175 H 5
Kompong Speu 175 H 5
Kompong Sralao 175 J 5
Kompong Thom 175 J 5
Kompot 177 F 3
Komrat 154 C 1
Komsa 159 R 3
Komsomolets 159 M 5
Komsomol'sk 169 G 3
Komsomolskiy 155 G 1
Komsomol'skiy 159 M 2
Komsomol'skiy 168 E 1
Komsomol'sk-na-Amure 171 P 5
Komusan 173 JK 2
Kona 196 D 3
Konakovo 158 G 4
Konarak 174 E 4
Konawa (OK.) 120 J 8
Konda 159 M 3
Konda 177 H 4
Kondagaon 174 D 4
Kondakova 171 T 2
Kondakovo 171 S 2
Kondinin 182 B 5
Kondoa 199 F 5
Kondon 171 P 5
Kondopoga 158 F 3
Kondor 168 F 3
Kondut 182 B 5
Konetsbor 158 L 3
Konevits, Ostrov 150 K 3
Konevo158 G 3
Kong 196 D 4
Kong Frederik VI-Kyst 105 T 3
Konginskiye Gory 171 T 3
Kongkemul, Gunung 176 E 3
Kongola 200 C 3
Kongolo 198 D 6
Kongor 198 E 3
Kongsberg 151 EF 4
Kongsvinger 151 F 3
Kongur Shan 169 K 3
Kongwa 199 F 6
Koni, Poluostrov 171 ST 4
Koniakar 196 B 3
Konin 149 G 4
Konitsa 154 B 2
Konjed Jān (Iran) 157 F 2
Könkämä älv 150 H 2
Konkan 174 B 4
Konko 200 D 2
Konkouré 196 B 3
Konkudera 170 K 4
Konnarock (VA.) 129 K 5
Konosha 158 H 3
Konoshchel'ye 159 R 2
Konotop 158 F 5
Kon Plong 175 J 5
Konqi He 172 A 2
Końskie 149 H 4
Konstantinovka 155 E 1
Konstantinovskiy 155 F 1
Konstanz 149 E 5
Kontagora 197 F 3
Kontcha 197 G 4
Kontiomäki 150 J 3
Kontum 175 J 5
Konus, Gora 108 B 2
Konus, Gora 171 O 4
Konya 155 D 3
Konya Ovası 155 D 3
Konza 199 F 5
Konzaboy 171 T 2
Konzhakovskiy Kamen', Gora 159 L 4
Koocanusa, Lake 111 K 2
Kookynie 182 C 4
Kooline 182 B 3
Koolivoo, Lake 183 F 3
Koonalda 182 D 5
Koör 177 H 4
Koorda 182 B 5
Koosharem (UT.) 114 EF 5
Kooskia (ID.)(MT.) 111 K 4
Kootenai River 111 K 2
Kootenay 103 O 5–6
Kootenay National Park 103 O 5
Kooussa 196 C 4
Kopanovka 155 G 1
Kópasker 150 B 2
Kópavogur 150 A 3
Koper 153 F 2
Kopervik 151 DE 4
Kopet-Dag, Khrebet 168 F 3
Kopeysk 159 M 5
Kop Geçidi 155 F 2
Ko Phangan 175 H 6
Ko Phuket 175 G 6
Köping 151 G 4
Koplik 154 A 2
Köpmanholmen 150 G 3
Koppang 150 F 3
Kopparberg 151 FG 4
Koprivnića 153 G 2
Kopychintsy 158 E 6
Kop'yevo 159 R 5
Kopylovka 159 Q 4
Kor (Iran) 157 F 3
Koralpe 153 FG 2
Koramlik 169 M 3
Korangi 169 H 6
Koraput 174 D 4
Korarou, Lac 196 D 2
Korba 174 D 3
Korbach 149 E 4
Korbel (CA.) 112 B 2
Korbol 197 H 3
Korça 154 B 2
Korchino 159 Q 5
Korčula 153 G 3
Korčulanski Kanal 153 G 3
Kordān (Iran) 157 F 2
Kordestān (Iran) 157 E 2
Kord Kūy (Iran) 157 G 1
Kordofan → Kurdufān 194 DE 6
Kords 168 FG 5
Kord Sheykh (Iran) 157 F 3
Korea Strait 173 J 4
Korelaksha 150 K 2
Korennoye 170 J 1
Korenovsk 155 E 1
Korenshty 154 C 1
Korets 151 J 5
Korf 171 V 3
Korfa, Zaliv 171 V 3–4
Korfovskiy 171 P 6
Korgen 150 F 2
Korhogo 196 C 4
Korienza 196 D 2
Korim 177 J 4
Korinthiakos Kólpos 154 B 3
Kórinthos 154 B 3
Koriolei 199 G 4
Kōriyama 173 M 3
Korkino 159 M 5
Korkino 170 J 5
Korkodon 171 ST 3
Korkodon 171 T 3
Korkut 155 F 3
Korkuteli 154 D 3
Korla 169 M 2
Korliki 159 Q 3
Kormakiti Bur (Cyprus) 156 A 2
Kormakiti Burnu 155 D 3
Kornat 153 FG 3
Kornegay (N.M.) 117 N 5
Korneuburg 153 G 2
Kórnik 149 G 4
Kornilovo 159 Q 5
Koro (Fiji) 186 C 4
Koro (Ivory Coast) 196 C 4
Koro (Mali) 196 D 3
Korobovskiy 159 P 6
Köroğlu Dağları 155 D 2
Köroğlu Tepe 155 D 2
Korogwe 199 F 6
Koroit 183 G 6
Koro Kidinga 197 H 2
Korongo 198 E 6
Koror 177 H 2
Kőrös 154 B 1
Korosten 151 J 5
Korostyshev 151 J 5
Korostyshev 158 E 5
Koro Toro 197 H 2
Korovin Volcano 102 C 5
Korpilahti 150 J 3
Korpilombolo 150 H 2
Korsakov 171 Q 6
Korsfjorden 151 DE 3
Korshunovo 170 K 4
Korskrogen 150 G 3
Korsnäs 150 H 3
Korsör 151 F 4
Kort Creek 174 A 3
Kortes Dam (WY.) 118 B 8
Koryak Range 171 W 3
Koryakskaya Sopka 171 T 5
Koryakskiy Khrebet 171 VW 3
Koryazhma 158 J 3
Kos 154 C 3
Kos 154 C 3
Kosa (Mauritania) 192 D 5
Kosa (U.S.S.R.) 170 J 5
Kosa Fedotova 155 E 1
Ko Samui 175 G 6
Ko Samui 175 H 6
Koschagyl 168 E 1
Kościan 149 G 4
Kosciusko (MS.) 130 E 1
Kosciusko, Mount 183 H 6
Kose 151 J 4
Köse Dağı 155 E 2
Kosha 194 E 4
Kosh-Agach 159 R 6
Koshkonong (MO.) 121 O 6
Koshkonong, Lake 124 EF 7
Kosi 174 C 2
Košice 149 H 5
Koskuduk 169 K 2

Kosmaj 154 B 2
Kosŏng 173 J 3
Kosovo Polje 154 B 2
Kosovska Mitrovica 154 B 2
Kosse (TX.) 122 G 4
Kossou, Lac de 196 C 4
Kossovo 151 J 5
Kostajnica 153 G 2
Kostamus 150 K 3
Koster 200 D 5
Kostino 159 R 2
Kostomuksa 150 K 3
Kostopol' 151 J 5
Kostroma 158 H 4
Kostroma 158 H 4
Kostrzyn 149 F 4
Kos'yu 159 L 2
Koszalin 149 G 4
Kota 174 C 2
Kotaagung 176 B 5
Kotabaharu (Indonesia) 176 D 4
Kota Baharu (Malaysia) 176 B 2
Kotabaru 176 E 4
Kota Belud 176 E 2
Kotabumi 176 BC 4
Kota Kinabalu 176 E 2
Kotamobagu 177 F 3
Ko Tao 175 G 4
Kotapad 174 D 4
Ko Tarutao 175 G 6
Kota Tinggi 176 B 3
Kotchandpur 174 E 3
Kotcho, Lake 101
Koteasro 169 H 4
Kotel'nich 158 J 4
Kotel'nikovo 155 F 1
Kotel'nyy, Ostrov 171 P 1
Kotido 198 E 4
Kotikovo 171 Q 6
Kotik River 108 G 1
Kotka 151 J 3
Kot Kapura 174 B 1
Kotkino 159 P 4
Kotlas 158 J 3
Kotli 169 J 4
Kotlik 102 E 3
Kotlina Sandomierska 149 H 4
Koto 171 P 6
Koton Karifi 197 F 4
Kotor 154 A 2
Kotor Varoš 153 G 3
Kotovsk 154 C 1
Kotovsk 154 C 1
Kotovsk 158 H 5
Kotri Allahrakhio 169 H 6
Kotr-Tas 168 F 1
Kötschach 153 F 2
Kottagudem 174 D 4
Kottayam 174 C 6
Kotto 198 C 3
Kotton 199 J 3
Kotturu 174 C 5
Kotu Group 186 D 4
Kotuy 170 H 1
Kotuykan 170 HJ 1
Kotzebue 102 E 2
Kotzebue Sound 102 E 2
Kouango 198 C 3
Kouba Modounga 197 H 2
Koudougou 196 D 3
Kouéré 196 D 3
Koufey 197 G 3
Kougaberge 200 C 6
Kouilou 197 G 6
Koukdjuak 105 N 2
Kouki 198 B 3
Koukourou 198 C 3
Koulamoutou 197 G 6
Koulen 175 H 5
Koulikoro 196 C 3
Koumac 185 H 6
Koumac 186 B 4
Koumala 183 H 3
Koumameyong 197 G 5
Koumbia 196 B 3
Koumbi-Saleh 192 D 5
Koumongou 196 E 3
Koumra 197 H 4
Koundara 196 B 3
Koundian 196 B 3
Koundougou 196 D 3
Koungheul 196 AB 3
Koungou, Monts 197 G 6
Kounradskiy 159 O 6
Kountze (TX.) 123 J 5
Koupéla 196 DE 3
Kourou 139 H 2
Kouroussa 196 B 3
Koussanar 196 B 3
Kousseri 197 G 3
Koutiala 196 C 3
Koutous 197 FG 3
Kouvola 150 J 3
Kova 170 H 4
Kova 170 H 4
Kovac 154 A 2
Kovdor 150 K 2
Kovdozero, Ozero 150 K 2
Kovel' 151 HJ 5

Kovgarok, Mount 108 E 2
Kovinskaya Gora 170 H 4
Kovriga, Gora 158 J 2
Kovrizhka 171 U 3
Kovrov 158 H 4
Kovylkino 158 H 5
Kowares 200 A 3
Ko Way 175 H 6
Kowloon 172 FG 6
Kowt-e Ashrow 169 HJ 4
Koyandy 159 P 6
Köyceğiz 154 C 3
Koyda 158 H 2
Koyuk 102 E 3
Koyuk River 108 F 2
Koyukuk (AK.) 102 F 2
Koyukuk (AK.) 102 FG 3
Koyulhisar 155 E 2
Kozaklı 155 D 3
Kozan 155 E 3
Kozáni 154 B 2
Kozel'sk 158 G 5
Kozhevnikovo 159 Q 4
Kozhevnikovo 170 K 1
Kozhim 159 L 2
Kozhozero, Ozero 158 G 3
Kozhva 158 L 2
Kozlu 154 D 2
Kozul'ka 170 F 4
Kozyrevsk 171 T 4
Kpandu 196 DE 4
Kpessi 196 E 4
Kra 196 E 4
Kra, Isthmus of 175 G 5
Kra Buri 175 G 5
Kraemer (LA.) 123 N 6
Krafla 150 B 2
Kragerö 151 E 4
Kragujevac 154 B 2
Krak des Chevaliers (Syria) 156 B 2
Krakor 175 H 5
Kraków 149 GH 4
Kralendijk 138 E 1
Kraljevica 153 F 2
Kraljevo 154 B 2
Kramatorsk 155 E 1
Kramer (ND.) 118 H 2
Kramer Junction (CA.) 113 H 7–8
Kramfors 150 G 3
Kranj 153 F 2
Kranzburg (S.D.) 119 M 6
Krapina 153 G 2
Krasilov 158 E 6
Krasino 158 K 1
Kraskino 173 K 2
Kráslava 151 J 4
Krasnaya Polyana 155 F 2
Krasnaya Yaranga 102 C 2
Krasnaya Yaranga 171 X 3
Krasneno 171 W 3
Kraśnik 149 H 4
Krasnoarmeysk 155 E 1
Krasnoarmeysk 158 HJ 5
Krasnoarmeysk 159 N 5
Krasnoarmeyskiy 155 F 1
Krasnodar 155 E 2
Krasnogorsk 171 Q 6
Krasnograd 158 G 6
Krasnogvardeyskoye 155 D 1
Krasnogvardeyskoye 155 F 1
Krasnogvardeyskoye 155 F 1
Krasnoje Selo 151 J 4
Krasnokamsk 158 KL 5
Krasnokutskoye 159 OP 5
Krasnoperekopsk 155 D 1
Krasnosel'kup 159 Q 2
Krasnoslobodsk 158 HJ 6
Krasnoturansk 170 F 5
Krasnotur'insk 159 M 4
Krasnoufimsk 159 L 4
Krasnoural'sk 159 M 4
Krasnousol'skiy 158 L 5
Krasnovishersk 158 L 3
Krasnovodsk 168 E 2
Krasnovodskoye Poluostrov 168 E 2
Krasnoyarovo 171 N 5
Krasnoyarsk 170 F 4
Krasnoyarskiy 159 L 5
Krasnoyarskoye Vodokhrani-
  lishche 170 F 5
Krasnoye 158 F 5
Krasnoye, Ozero 171 W 3
Krasnoye Znamya 169 G 3
Krasnozatonskiy 158 K 3
Krasnozerskoye 159 PQ 5
Krasnoznamenskoye 159 N 5
Krasnystaw 149 H 4
Krasnyy Chikoy 170 J 5
Krasnyy Kut 158 J 5
Krasnyy Luch 155 E 1
Krasnyy Sulin 155 EF 1
Krasnyy Yar 158 HJ 5
Krasnyy-Yar 159 O 4
Krasnyy Yar 159 N 5
Krasnyy Yar 168 D 1
Kratie 175 J 5
Kratovo 154 B 2
Krayište 154 B 2
Kray Lesov 171 U 2

Krebs (OK.) 121 K 8
Krefeld 148 E 4
Kremastá, Limni 154 B 3
Kremenchug 158 F 6
Kremenchugskoye Vodokhrani-
  lishche 158 F 6
Kremenets 151 J 5
Kremmling (CO.) 115 L 3
Krems 153 G 2
Kreshchenka 159 Q 4
Kress (TX.) 117 P 3
Kresta, Zaliv 102 B 2
Kresti 158 F 4
Krest-Khal'dzhayy 171 O 3
Krestovaya 170 K 4
Krestovka 158 K 2
Krestovskiy, Ostrov 171 U 1
Krestovyy Pereval 155 F 2
Kresty 170 E 1
Kretinga 151 H 4
Kreuztal 149 E 4
Kribi 197 F 5
Krichev 158 F 5
Kričim 154 B 2
Krider (N.M.) 117 N 3
Kril'on, Mys 171 Q 6
Krimml 153 F 2
Krishna 174 C 4
Krishna, Mouths of the 174 D 4
Krishnagiri 174 C 5
Krishnanagar 174 E 3
Kristiansand 151 E 4
Kristianstad 151 F 4
Kristiansund 150 E 3
Kristiinankaupunki 150 H 3
Kristineberg 150 G 2
Kristinehamn 151 F 4
Kristinestad (Kristiinankaupunki)
  150 H 3
Kristinovka 154 C 1
Kríti 154 BC 3
Kritikón Pélagos 154 BC 3
Kriva Palanka 154 B 2
Krivoy Rog 155 D 1
Krk 153 F 2
Krnov 149 G 4
Kroken 150 F 2
Krokodil River 200 D 4
Krokom 150 F 3
Kroměříž 149 G 5
Kronotskaya Sopka 171 T 5
Kronotski 171 U 5
Kronotskiy, Mys 171 U 4–5
Kronotskiy Poluostrov 171 U 5
Kronotskiy Zaliv 171 U 5
Kronotskoye Ozero 171 TU 5
Kronshtadt 151 J 4
Kroonstad 200 D 5
Kropotkin 155 F 1
Kropotkin 170 L 4
Kroppefjäll 151 F 4
Krosno 149 H 5
Krotoszyn 149 G 4
Krotovka 158 K 5
Kroviga, Gora 170 F 3
Krško 153 G 2
Krstača 154 B 2
Krueng Geumpang 176 A 3
Kruger National Park 201 E 4
Krugersdorp 200 D 5
Krugloye 155 E 1
Krui 176 B 5
Krung Thep 175 H 5
Kruså 151 E 5
Krusenstern, Cape 108 F 2
Kruševac 154 B 2
Krusne Hory 149 F 4
Krutinka 159 O 4
Kruzenshterna, Proliv 171 S 6
Kruzof 102 K 4
Kryazh Chernycheva 159 LM 2
Kryazh Kula 171 O 2
Kryazh Polousnyy 171 PQ 2
Kryazh Ulakhan-Sis 171 S 1–2
Krym 155 E 1
Krym (Ukraine, U.S.S.R.) 155 D 1
Krym (Ukraine, U.S.S.R.) 155 E 1
Krymsk 155 E 1–2
Krymskiye Gory 155 D 2
Krzyż 149 G 4
Ksabi 192 E 3
Ksar Chellala 193 F 1
Ksar el Barka 192 C 5
Ksar el Boukhari 193 F 1
Ksar el Kebir 192 D 2
Ksar Torchane 192 C 4
Ksen'yevka 170 L 5
Ksour, Monts des (Algeria) 192 EF 2
Ksour, Monts des (Tunisia) 193 GH 2
Kū', Jabal al (Saudi Arabia) 157 E 4
Kuala Belait 176 D 3
Kuala Dungun 176 B 3
Kuala Kangsar 176 B 3
Kuala Kapuas 176 D 4
Kuala Kerai 176 B 2
Kualakeriau 176 D 3
Kualakurun 176 D 4
Kuala Lipis 176 B 3
Kuala Lumpur 176 B 3
Kualamanjual 176 D 4

Kualapembuang 176 D 4
Kuala Pilah 176 B 3
Kuala Rompin 176 B 3
Kuala Selangor 176 B 3
Kualasimpang 176 A 3
Kuala Terengganu 176 B 2
Kualatungkal 176 B 4
Kuamut 176 E 2
Kuancheng 173 G 2
Kuandian 173 H 2
Kuantan 176 B 3
Kuba 155 F 2
Kuba (Azerbaydzhan, U.S.S.R.)
  168 D 2
Kuban' 155 E 1
Kubaysah (Iraq) 156 D 2
Kubbe 150 G 3
Kubbum 194 C 6
Kubenskoye, Ozero 158 G 4
Kubkain 184 D 2
Kubumesaäi 176 E 3
Kuching 176 D 3
Kudara 169 J 3
Kudat 176 E 2
Kudaw 176 G 3
Kudremukh 174 BC 5
Kudryashevo 159 Q 4
Kudu-Kyuyel't 170 LM 4
Kudus 176 D 5
Kudymkar 158 K 4
Kuee Ruins 113 G 12
Kufra Oases 193 K 4
Kufstein 153 F 2
Kugmallit Bay 102 L 2
Kugul'ta 155 F 1
Kuhayli 194 E 5
Kūhbonān (Iran) 157 G 3
Kūh-e Ālādāgh 168 F 3
Kūh-e 'Aliābād (Iran) 157 F 2
Kūh-e Alijūq (Iran) 157 F 3
Kūh-e Alvano (Iran) 157 E 2
Kūh-e Bāfq (Iran) 157 G 3
Kūh-e Bārān 168 G 4
Kūh-e Bazmān 168 F 5
Kūh-e Biābān 168 F 5
Kūh-e Bozqūsh 168 D 3
Kūh-e Būl (Iran) 157 F 3
Kūh-e Chehel Dokhtarān 169 G 4
Kūh-e Chelleh Khāneh (Iran) 157 E 1
Kūh-e Darband 168 E 4
Kūh-e Dāvarān (Iran) 157 G 3
Kūh-e Dīnār (Iran) 157 F 3
Kūh-e Dom (Iran) 157 F 2
Kūh-e Garbosh (Iran) 157 EF 2
Kūh-e Garri (Iran) 157 E 2
Kūh-e Gāvbūs (Iran) 157 FG 4
Kūh-e Gügerd (Iran) 157 F 2
Kūh-e Hormoz (Iran) 157 G 4
Kūh-e Jebal Bārez 168 F 5
Kūh-e Joghatāy (Iran) 157 G 1
Kūh-e Kalat 168 F 4
Kūh-e Karkas (Iran) 157 F 2
Kūh-e Khabr (Iran) 157 G 3
Kūh-e Khāiz (Iran) 157 F 3
Kūh-e Kharānaq (Iran) 157 G 2
Kūh-e Khormūj 168 E 5
Kūh-e Khvojeh (Iran) 157 E 2
Kūh-e Khvormūji (Iran) 157 F 3
Kūh-e Kūhrān 168 F 5
Kūh-e Kūkalār (Iran) 157 F 3
Kūh-e Lāleh Zār 168 F 5
Kūh-e Malek Sīāh 169 G 5
Kūh-e Masāhīm (Iran) 157 G 3
Kūh-e Nāy Band 168 F 4
Kūh-e Safīd (Iran) 157 E 2
Kūh-e Shah Jahān 168 F 3
Kūh-e Sorkh 168 F 3
Kūh-e Sorkh (Iran) 157 G 2
Kūhestak 168 F 5
Kūh-e Tābask (Iran) 157 F 3
Kūh-e Taftān 169 G 5
Kūhhā-ye Bashākerd 168 F 5
Kūhhā-ye Genū (Iran) 157 G 4
Kūhhā-ye Qorūd (Iran) 157 F 2–3
Kūhhā-ye-Sabalān 168 D 3
Kūhha ye Zagros (Iran) 157 EF 2–F 3
Kuhmo 150 J 3
Kuhmoinen 150 J 3
Kūhpāyeh (Iran) 157 F 2
Kuikkavaara 150 J 3
Kui Nua 175 GH 5
Kuiseb 200 B 4
Kuito 200 B 2
Kuiu 102 L 4
Kuivaniemi 150 J 2
Kujani Game Reserve 196 D 4
Kujawy 149 G 4
Kuji 173 M 3
Kukalek Lake 108 G 4
Kukan 171 O 6
Kukawa 197 G 3
Kukësi 154 B 2
Kukhtuy 171 Q 4
Kukushka 171 N 5
Kula 171 O 5
Kulagino 168 E 1
Kulakovo 170 F 4

Kulakshi 168 F 1
Kulaneh 169 G 5
Kulanoy 168 F 1
Kulbus 194 C 6
Kul'chi 171 P 5
Kuldīga 151 H 4
Kuldja 169 L 2
Kul'dzhuktau, Gory 169 G 2
Kule 200 C 4
Kulenjin (Iran) 157 E 2
Kulen Vakuf 153 G 3
Kulgera 182 E 4
Kulinda 170 H 3
Kulinda 170 J 3
Kullen 151 F 4
Kulm (ND.) 118 K 4
Kulmasa 196 D 4
Kulmbach 149 F 4
Kulp 155 F 3
Kul'sary 168 E 1
Kul'skiy 170 J 5
Kultay 168 E 1
Kultsjön 150 G 3
Kulu (Turkey) 155 D 3
Kulu (U.S.S.R.) 171 R 3
Kuludzhun 159 Q 6
Kululli 199 G 2
Kululu 198 E 6
Kulunda 159 P 5
Kulundinskaya Step' 159 P 5
Kulundinskoye, Ozero 159 PQ 5
Kulyab 169 HJ 3
Kuma (Russia, U.S.S.R.) 150 K 2
Kuma (Russia, U.S.S.R.) 155 G 2
Kumagaya 173 L 3
Kumai 176 D 4
Kumai, Teluk 176 D 4
Kumak 159 M 5
Kumakh-Surt 171 N 1
Kumakhta 170 K 5
Kumamoto 173 K 4
Kumanovo 154 B 2
Kumara 171 N 5
Kumasi 196 D 4
Kumawa, Pegunungan 177 H 4
Kumba 197 F 5
Kumbakonam 174 C 5
Kumbe 184 CD 3
Kumbo 197 G 4
Kum-Dag 168 E 4
Kumdah 195 H 4
Kume-jima 173 J 5
Kumertau 158 KL 5
Kuminskiy 159 N 4
Kum Kuduk 172 B 2
Kumla 151 F 4
Kumluca 154 D 3
Kumo 197 G 3
Kumonda 170 G 4
Kumon Range 175 G 2
Kumora 170 K 4
Kumta 174 B 5
Kumu 198 D 4
Kumukahi, Cape 113 H 12
Kümüx 172 A 2
Kuna (ID.) 110 J 7
Kunar 169 J 4
Künas 169 L 2
Kunashak 159 M 4
Kunda 151 J 4
Kunda-dia-Baze 200 B 1
Kunda Hills 174 C 5
Kundelungu, Monts 198 D 6–7
Kundelungu National Park 200 D 2
Kundur, Pulau 176 B 3
Kunduz 169 H 3
Kunene 200 A 3
Kunes 150 J 1
Künes He 169 L 2
Kungälv 151 F 4
Kungasalakh, Ozero 170 JK 1
Kungey Alatau, Khrebet 169 K 2
Kungrad 168 F 2
Kungsbacka 151 F 4
Kungu 198 B 4
Kungur 158 L 4
Kungurri 183 H 3
Kungur Tuk 170 G 5
Kunhing 175 G 3
Kunjirap Daban 169 K 3
Kunlong 175 G 3
Kunlun Shan 169 KM 3
Kunlun Shankou 172 B 3
Kunming 172 D 5
Kunsan 173 J 3
Kuntshankoi 198 C 5
Kuntuk 171 R 4
Kununurra 182 D 2
Kunwak 103 S 3
Kunya 197 G 3
Kunya-Urgench 168 F 2
Kuocang Shan 173 H 5
Kuonamka 170 J 2
Kuonara 170 M 2
Kuop 186 B 2
Kuopio 150 J 3
Kuoqiang 172 A 3

Kuorboaivi 150 J 2
Kuoyka 170 M 1
Kupa 153 G 2
Kupang 177 F 6
Kupang, Teluk 177 F 5–6
Kuparuk River 109 J 2
Kupiano 184 E 4
Kupino 159 P 5
Kupiškis 151 J 4
Kupreanof 102 L 4
Kupyansk 158 G 6
Kuqa 169 L 2
Kura 155 F 2
Kura 155 G 2
Kura (Nigeria) 197 F 3
Kura (U.S.S.R.) 168 D 2
Kuragino 170 F 5
Kuramã, Harrat 195 G 4
Kurashasayskiy 158 L 5
Kurashiki 173 K 4
Kuraymah 194 E 5
Kurayn 157 EF 4
Kurbatovo 170 F 4
Kurbulik 170 J 5
Kurchum 159 Q 6
Kurdufãn 194 DE 6
Kürdžhali 154 C 2
Küre 155 D 2
Kure 173 K 4
Kureyka 159 RS 2
Kurgaldzhino 159 O 5
Kurgalski, Mys 151 J 4
Kurgan 159 N 4
Kurganinsk 155 F 2
Kurgan-Tyube 169 H 3
Kurgasyn 169 H 1
Kuria 186 C 2
Kuria Muria Islands 195 K 5
Kurikka 150 H 3
Kuril Islands 171 S 6
Kurilovka 158 J 5
Kuril'sk 171 R 6
Kuril'skiye Ostrova 171 RS 6
Kuril Trench 209 C 2
Kurkure-Bazhi, Gora 159 R 5
Kurleya 170 L 5
Kurmuk 194 E 6
Kurnool 174 C 4
Kuroiso 173 M 3
Kuro-shima 173 J 4
Kurovskiy 171 N 5
Kurram 169 J 4
Kursavka 155 F 2
Kuršenai 151 H 4
Kursk 158 G 5
Kurskaja Kosa Neringa 151 H 4
Kurskaya 155 F 2
Kurski Zaliv 151 H 4
Kursu 150 J 2
Kuršumlija 154 B 2
Kurşunlu 155 D 2
Kurşunlu Daği 155 E 3
Kurtalan 155 F 3
Kurtamysh 159 M 5
Kurten (TX.) 122 G 5
Kürtï 194 E 5
Kurtistown (HI.) 113 G 12
Kuru 198 D 3
Kurucaşile 155 D 2
Kuruçay 155 E 3
Kuru Daği 154 C 2
Kuruktag 172 A 2
Kurum 184 E 2
Kuruman 200 C 5
Kuruman 200 C 5
Kurume 173 K 4
Kurumkan 169 M 5
Kurunegala 174 CD 6
Kurung 170 L 3
Kurupka 102 C 3
Kurur, Jabal 194 E 4
Kur'ya 158 L 3
Kur'ya 159 Q 5
Kur'ya 170 E 1
Kurzeme 151 H 4
Kuşada Körfezi 154 C 3
Kusadasi 154 C 3
Kusaie 186 B 2
Kuş Gölü 154 C 2
Kushchevskaya 155 E 1
Kusheriki 197 F 3
Küshik, Tall (Syria) 156 C 1
Kushimoto 173 L 4
Kushiro 173 M 2
Kushka 169 G 3
Kushkushara 158 H 3
Kushmurun 159 MN 5
Kushmurun, Ozero 159 M 5
Kushva 159 L 4
Kuskokwim 102 E 3
Kuskokwim Bay 102 E 4
Kuskokwim Mountains 102 F 3
Kusma 174 D 2
Kussharo-ko 173 M 2
Kustanay 159 M 5
Küstï 194 E 6
Kut (Iran) 157 E 3
Kuta 197 F 4
Küt Abdollah (Iran) 157 E 3

Kütahya 154 C 3
Kutai, Sungai 176 E 4
Kutaisi 155 F 2
Kutan 155 G 2
Kutana 171 O 4
Kutch 174 AB 3
Kutch, Gulf of 174 A 3
Kutch, Rann of 174 AB 3
Kutima 170 J 4
Kutina 153 G 2
Kutno 149 G 4
Kutop'yegan 159 NO 2
Kutru 174 D 4
Kuttusvaara 150 J 2
Kutu 198 B 5
Kutulik 170 H 5
Kutum 194 C 6
Kuuli-Mayak 168 E 2
Kuusamo 150 J 2
Kuusankoski 150 J 3
Kuusivaara 150 H 2
Kuutse Mägi 151 J 4
Kuvango 200 B 2
Kuwait 157 E 3
Kuwait (Kuwait) 157 E 3
Kuya 158 H 2
Kuybyshev 158 K 5
Kuybyshev 159 P 4
Kuybyshevo 171 R 6
Kuybyshevskiy 159 N 5
Kuybyshevskoye Vodokhrani-
lishche 158 JK 5
Kuygan 159 O 6
Kuytun 169 M 2
Kuytun, Gora 159 R 6
Kuytun (U.S.S.R.) 170 H 5
Kuytun, Gora 159 R 6
Kuytun He 169 L 2
Kuyucuk Daği 154 D 3
Kuyumba 170 G 3
Kuzitrin River 108 F 2
Kuznetsk 158 J 5
Kuznetsk Basin 165
Kuznetskiy Alatau 159 R 4–5
Kuzomen158 G 2
Kvabé 197 H 4
Kvænangen 150 H 1
Kvalöy 150 G 2
Kvalöya 150 H 1
Kvalsund 150 H 1
Kvareli 155 G 2
Kvarner 153 F 2–3
Kvarnerič 153 F 3
Kverkfjöll 150 B 3
Kvichak 102 F 4
Kvichak Bay 102 F 4
Kvikkjokk 150 G 2
Kvinesdal 151 E 4
Kvissleby 150 G 3
Kviteseid 151 E 4
Kwa 198 B 5
Kwahu Plateau 196 D 4
Kwaja Ali 169 G 4
Kwajalein 186 C 2
Kwakoegron 139 G 2
Kwale (Kenya) 199 F 5
Kwale (Nigeria) 197 F 4
Kwamisa 196 D 4
Kwamouth 198 B 5
Kwa Mtoro 198 EF 6
Kwangju 173 J 3
Kwango 198 B 5
Kwangsi Chuang 172 E 6
Kwanmo-bong 173 JK 2
Kwatisore 177 HJ 4
Kwekwe 200 D 3
Kwenge 198 B 6
Kwethluk 102 E 3
Kwidzyn 149 G 4
Kwiguk 102 E 4
Kwikila 184 E 3
Kwilu 198 B 5
Kwilu 198 B 6
Kwitaro 139 G 3
Kwoka, Gunung 177 H 4
Kyabram 183 GH 5
Kyaikkami 175 G 4
Kyaikto 175 G 4
Kyaka 198 E 5
Kyakhta 170 H 5
Kyancutta 183 F 5
Kyango 198 D 3
Kyaukkyi 175 G 4
Kyaukme 175 G 3
Kyaukpyu 175 F 4
Kyaukse 175 G 3
Kyauktaw 175 F 3
Kybartai 151 H 5
Kyburz (CA.) 112 E 4
Kycham-Kyuyel' 171 R 2
Kychema 158 H 2
Kyeintali 175 F 4
Kyela 198 E 6
Kyelang 174 C 1
Kyenjojo 198 E 4
Kyffhäuser 149 F 4
Kyjov 149 G 5
Kyle (SD.) 118 F 7

Kyle (TX.) 122 F 6
Kyle of Lochalsh 148 B 3
Kyll 153 E 1
Kymijoki 151 J 3
Kynnefjell 151 F 4
Kynuna 183 G 3
Kyoga, Lake 198 E 4
Kyong 175 G 3
Kyŏnggi-man 173 HJ 3
Kyŏngju 173 J 3
Kyōto 173 L 3
Kypros → Cyprus 155 D 3
Kyrbykan 171 N 3
Kyren 170 H 5
Kyrenia → Girne 155 D 3
Kyrgyday 171 M 3
Kyrkheden 151 F 3
Kyröŋjoki 150 H 3
Kyrönjärvi 150 H 3
Kyrta 158 L 3
Kyrynniky 170 L 3
Kyshtovka 159 P 4
Kyshtym 159 M 4
Kystatam 170 M 2
Kytalyktakh 171 OP 2
Kyuekh-Bulung 170 KL 2
Kyungyaung 175 G 4
Kyushe 168 F 1
Kyūshū 173 K 4
Kyustendil 154 B 2
Kyusyur 171 N 1
Kyzas 159 R 5
Kyzyk 168 E 2
Kyzyl 159 R 5
Kyzyl 170 F 5
Kyzylart, Pereval 169 J 3
Kyzyldyykan 169 H 1
Kyzylkiya 159 P 6
Kyzyl-Kiya 169 J 2
Kyzylkoga 168 E 1
Kyzyl-Kommuna 169 H 1
Kyzylkum, Peski 169 G 2
Kyzylrabot 169 J 3
Kyzyl-Suluo 171 P 3
Kyzyl-Syr 171 NO 3
Kyzyltau 159 O 6
Kyzyluy 169 H 1
Kyzyl-Yllyk 170 K 3
Kyzylzhar 169 G 1
Kzyl-Dzhar 169 H 1
Kzyl-Orda 169 H 2
Kzyltu 159 O 5

L

Laa an der Thaya 153 G 2
La Asunción 139 F 1
Laau Point 113 E 10
Laba 155 F 2
La Babia 132 B 2
La Banda 142 D 4
Labang 176 D 3
La Barca 132 B 3
La Barge (WY.) 111 P 8
Labaz, Ozero 170 G 1
Labazhskoye 158 K 2
Labbezenga 196 E 2
Labe (Czechoslovakia) 149 F 4
Labé (Guinea) 196 B 3
La Belle (FL.) 131 N 8
Labelle (Quebec, Can.) 105 N 6
Labengke, Pulau 177 F 4
Labenne 152 C 3
Laberge, Lake 102 K 3
Labinsk 155 F 2
Labis 176 B 3
La Blanquilla, Isla 139 F 1
Labota 177 F 4
Labouheyre 152 C 3
Laboulaye 142 D 5
Labrador 105 NO 4
Labrador, Coast of 105 PQ 4–5
Labrador Basin 208 A 2
Labrador City 105 O 5
Labrador Sea 105 QR 4
Labrieville 105 O 6
Labuan (Indonesia) 176 C 5
Labuan (Malaysia) 176 DE 2
Labuha 177 G 4
Labuhanbajo 177 EF 5
Labuhanbilik 176 B 3
La Bureba 152 C 3
Labutta 177 F 4
Labuya 171 S 2
Labytnangi 159 N 2
Lac 154 A 2
La Cadena 132 B 2
Lac Alaotra 201 H 3
Lac Albanel 105 N 5
Lac à l'Eau-Claire 105 MN 4
Lac Allard 105 P 5
La Campina 152 BC 4
La Canada (CA.) 113 G 8
Lacanau 152 C 2
La Canourgue 152 D 3

Lacantún, Rio 132 D 4
La Carlota 142 D 5
La Carlota 177 F 1
La Carolina 152 C 4
Lacaune, Monts de 152 D 3
Lac aux Goélands 105 P 4
Lac Aux Mortes 118 J 2
Lac Belot 103 M 2
Lac Bermen 105 O 5
Lac Bienville 105 N 4
Lac Brochet 103 R 4
Lac Burton 105 M 5
Laccadive Islands 174 B 5
Lac Caniapiscau 105 O 5
Lac Champdoré 105 O 4
Lac Chibougamau 105 N 6
Lac Courte Oreilles Indian Reservation
124 C 4
Lac Couture 105 N 3
Lac Débo 196 D 2
Lac de Grand Lieu 152 C 2
Lac de Gras 103 P 3
Lac de Guiers 196 A 2
Lac de Kossou 196 C 4
Lac Delcommune 200 D 2
Lac Delorme 105 O 5
Lac de Neuchâtel 153 E 2
Lac des Allemands 123 N 6
Lac des Bois 103 N 2
Lac d'Iberville 105 N 4
Lac Dô 196 D 2
Lac du Bourget 153 E 2
Lac du Der 153 D 2
Lac du Flambeau Indian Reservation
124 E 3–4
La Cebollera 152 C 3
La Ceiba (Honduras) 132 E 4
La Ceiba (Venezuela) 138 D 2
Lacepede Bay 183 F 6
Lacepede Islands 182 C 2
Lacerdónia 201 F 3
Lac Evans 105 M 5
Lacey (WA.) 110 C 3
Lac Faguibine 196 D 2
Lac Faribault 105 N 4
Lac Fitri 197 H 3
Lac Guillaume Delisle 105 M 4
Lacha, Ozero 158 G 3
La Charité-sur-Loire 152 D 2
La Châtre 152 D 2
La Chaux-de-Fonds 153 E 2
Lachay, Punta 138 C 6
Lachine (MI.) 125 KL 4
Lachlan River 183 GH 5
La Chorrera 138 BC 2
La Chorrera 138 D 4
La Ciotat 153 E 3
Lac Jacques 109 N 2
Lackawanna (N.Y.) 125 Q 7
Lac Kempt 105 N 6
Lac Kipawa 105 M 6
Lac Klotz 105 N 3
Lac Korarou 196 D 2
Lac la Croix 119 R 2
Lac La Biche 103 P 5
Lac la Martre (N.W.T., Can.) 103 O 3
Lac la Martre (N.W.T., Can.) 103 O 3
Lac la Ronge 103 R 4
Lac Léman 153 E 2
Lac Le Moyne 105 O 4
Lac Mai-Ndombe 198 B 5
Lac Manouane 105 N 5
Lac Maunoir 103 MN 2
Lac Mégantic 105 N 6
Lac Minto 105 N 4
Lac Mistassini 105 N 5
Lac Moero 198 D 6
Lac Musquaro 105 P 5
Lac Nantais 105 N 3
Lac Naococane 105 NO 5
Lac Niangay 196 D 2
Lac Nichicum 105 N 5
La Cocha 142 C 4
La Colorada 106 D 6
Lacombe 103 P 5
La Concepción 138 D 1
Laconia (N.H.) 126 H 5
Lacoochee (FL.) 131 M 6
Lac Opiscotéo 105 O 5
La Cordillera 130 C 8
La Coronilla 142 F 5
La Coruña 152 B 3
Lac Payne 105 N 4
Lac Peribonca 105 N 5
Lac Plétipi 105 N 5
Lacq 146
Lac qui Parle 119 M 5
La Crescent (MN.) 119 R 7
La Crosse (KS.) 120 F 4
La Crosse (VA.) 129 N 5
La Crosse (WA.) 110 GH 4
La Crosse (WI.) 124 C 6
La Cruz (Argentina) 142 E 4
La Cruz (Costa Rica) 132 E 5
La Cruz (Mexico) 106 E 7
La Cruz (Uruguay) 142 E 5
Lac Sakami 105 M 5

Lacs des Loups Marins 105 N 4
Lac Seul 104 J 5
Lac Tassilouc 105 N 4
Lac Tshangalele 200 D 2
Lac Tumba 198 B 5
La Cuesta 132 B 2
La Cueva 143 B 6
La Cueva (N.M.) 117 L 2
Lacul Razelm 154 C 2
Lacul Sinoe 154 C 2
Lac Upemba 198 D 6
Lac Wakuach 105 O 4
Ladakh Range 169 K 4
Ladário 140 E 4
Laddicea 154 C 3
Laddonia (MO.) 121 O 3
La Digue 199 K 5
Lâdik 155 D 2
Ladismith 200 C 6
Lâdïz 169 G 5
Ladner (SD.) 118 E 5
Lado, Jabal 198 E 3
Ladoga, Lake 150 K 3
Ladong 172 E 6
La Dorada 138 D 2
Ladozhskoye Ozero 150 K 3
Ladrillero, Golfo 143 A 8
Ladu 175 F 2
Ladybrand 200 D 5
Ladyga 159 R 2
Ladysmith (WI.) 124 CD 4
Ladyzhenka 159 N 5
Ladzhanur 155 F 2
Lae (Marshall Is.) 186 C 2
Lae (Papua New Guinea) 184 E 3
Lae (Papua New Guinea) 186 A 3
Laea 177 F 4
Laem Ngop 175 H 5
Lærdalsöyri 150 E 3
La Escala 152 D 3
La Esmeralda 140 D 5
Læsö 151 F 4
La Esperanza (Argentina) 143 C 6
La Esperanza (Bolivia) 140 D 3
La Estrada 152 B 3
La Estrella 140 D 5
Lafayette (AL.) 131 J 2
La Fayette (GA.) 128 F 7
Lafayette (IN.) 124 H 9
Lafayette (LA.) 123 LM 5
Lafayette (MN.) 119 O 6
Lafayette (TN.) 128 EF 5
La Feria (TX.) 122 F 9
Laffan, Ra's (Qatar) 157 F 4
Lafia 197 F 4
Lafiagi 197 EF 4
La Flèche 152 CD 2
La Flor 132 F 5
La Follette (TN.) 128 G 5
La Forestière 139 H 2
La Fría 138 D 2
Läft (Iran) 157 G 4
La Fuente de San Esteban 152 B 3
Laful 175 F 6
Laga Hida 199 G 3
Lagan 151 F 4
La Garita (CO.) 115 L 6
Lagarto 141 F 3
Lagash (Iraq) 157 E 3
Lågen 150 E 3
Laghouat 193 F 2
La Glória 138 D 2
Lagoa dos Patos 142 F 5
Lagoa Feia 141 H 5
Lago Agrio 138 C 4
Lago Amanã 139 F 4
Lagoa Mangueira 142 F 5
Lagoa Mirim 142 F 5
Lago Arapa 140 B 4
Lago Argentino 143 B 9
Lago Badajós 139 F 4
Lago Blanco 143 C 9
Lago Buenos Aires 143 B 8
Lago Cabora Bassa 201 E 3
Lago Cardiel 143 B 8
Lago Chilwa 201 F 2
Lago Chiuta 201 F 2
Lago Colhué Huapí 143 C 8
Lago da Pedra 139 J 4
Lago de Chapala 132 B 3
Lago de Erepecu 139 G 4
Lago de Junín 140 A 3
Lago del Coghinas 153 E 3
Lago del Toro 143 B 9
Lago de Manacapuru 139 F 4
Lago de Managua 132 E 5
Lago de Maracaibo 138 D 1–2
Lago de Nicaragua 132 E 5
Lago de Poopó 140 C 4
Lago de San Luis 140 D 3
Lago de Yojoa 132 E 5
Lago di Bolsena 153 F 3
Lago di Bracciano 153 F 3
Lago di Como 153 E 2
Lago di Garda 153 F 2
Lago di Lesina 153 G 3
Lago d'Iséo 153 E 2
Lago di Varano 153 G 3
Lago d'Ortà 153 E 2

Lago Fagnano **143** C 9
Lago General Carrera **143** B 8
Lago Llanquihue **143** B 7
Lago Maggiore **153** E 2
Lago Mandioré **140** E 4
Lago Musters **143** C 8
Lago Nahuel Huapi **143** B 7
Lago Novo **139** H 3
Lagonoy Gulf **177** F 1
Lago O'Higgins **143** B 8
Lago Omodeo **153** E 3
Lago Piorini **139** F 4
Lago Posadas **143** B 8
Lago Pueyrredón **143** B 8
Lago Rogagua **140** C 3
Lagos (Greece) **154** C 2
Lagos (Nigeria) **196** E 4
Lagos (Portugal) **152** B 4
Lagosa **198** E 6
Lago San Martín **143** B 8
Lagos de Moreno **132** B 3
Lago Titicaca **140** C 4
Lago Trasimeno **153** F 3
Lago Uiñaimarca **140** C 4
Lago Viedma **143** B 8
La Grand-Combe **152** D 3
La Grande (OR.) **110** G 5
La Grande (WA.) **110** C 4
La Grande Rivière **105** MN 5
Lagrange **182** C 2
La Grange (GA.) **128** FG 8
Lagrange (IN.) **124** J 8
La Grange (KY.) **128** F 3
La Grange (N.C.) **129** O 6
La Grange (TX.) **122** G 6
La Grange (WY.) **118** DE 9
La Granja **152** C 3
La Gran Sabana **139** F 2–3
La Gruta **142** F 4
La Guaira **138** E 1
La Guardia (Argentina) **142** C 4
La Guardia (Bolivia) **140** D 4
La Guardia (Spain) **152** B 3
Laguiole **152** D 3
Laguna **142** G 4
Laguna (N.M.) **117** J 2
Laguna Beach (CA.) **113** H 9
Laguna Beach (FL.) **131** HJ 4
Laguna Blanca **143** B 9
Laguna Concepción **140** D 4
Laguna de Antela **152** B 3
Laguna de Brus **132** F 4
Laguna de Caratasca **132** F 4
Laguna de Chiriquí **138** B 2
Laguna del Perro **117** KL 3
Laguna de Perlas **132** F 5
Laguna de Santa Maria **106** E 5
Laguna de Tamiahua **132** C 3
Laguna de Términos **132** D 4
Laguna Indian Reservation **117** J 2–3
Laguna Madre **122** F 9
Laguna Madre (Mexico) **132** C 2–3
Laguna Mar Chiquita **142** D 5
Laguna Merín **142** F 5
Laguna Morales **132** C 3
Laguna Mountains **113** J 9–10
Laguna Park (TX.) **122** F 4
Lagunas (Chile) **140** BC 5
Lagunas (Peru) **138** C 5
Laguna Uberaba **140** E 4
Laguna Veneta **153** F 2
Lagune Aby **196** D 4
Lagune Ndogo **197** G 6
Lagune Nkomi **197** F 6
Lagunillas **138** D 1
Lagunillas **140** D 4
Lagunitos **138** B 4
Laha **171** M 6
La Habana **133** F 3
Lahad Datu **177** E 2
Lahaina (HI.) **113** F 11
La Harpe (IL.) **124** D 9
Lahat **176** B 4
Lahe **175** G 2
Lahewa **176** A 3
Lahij **195** G 6
Lāhījān (Iran) **157** F 1
Laholm **151** F 4
Laholmsbukten **151** F 4
Lahontan Reservoir **112** F 3
Lahore **169** J 4
Lahr **149** E 5
Lahti **150** J 3
La Huacan **132** B 4
Lai **197** H 4
Laiagam **184** D 3
Laibin **172** E 6
Lai Chau **175** H 3
Laie (HI.) **113** E 10
Laihia **150** H 3
Lainioälven **150** H 2
Lairi **197** H 3
Lais **176** B 4
Laisamis **199** F 4
Laisvall **150** G 2
Laitila **151** H 3
Laiwu **173** G 3
Laiwui **177** G 4

Laixi **173** H 3
Laiyang **173** H 3
Laiyuan **172** F 3
Laizhou Wan **173** G 3
La Japonesa **143** C 6
La Jara (CO.) **115** M 6
La Jara (N.M.) **117** JK 1
Lajes (Rio Grande do Norte, Brazil) **141** J 2
Lajes (Santa Catarina, Brazil) **142** F 4
Lajitas (TX.) **117** M 8
La Joya (N.M.) **117** K 3
La Junta (Bolivia) **140** D 4
La Junta (CO.) **115** O 6
La Junta (Mexico) **106** E 6
Lak Boggal **199** F 4
Lak Bor **199** G 4
Lak Dera **199** FG 4
Lake (WY.) **111** P 6
Lake Abaya **199** F 3
Lake Abbe **199** G 2
Lake Abitibi **105** M 6
Lake Afrēra **199** G 2
Lake Albert **110** E 8
Lake Albert (Zaire/Uganda) **198** E 4
Lake Alexandrina **183** F 6
Lake Almanor **112** D 2
Lake Altus **120** F 8
Lake Amadeus **182** E 3
Lake Andes (S.D.) **119** K 7
Lake Andes (S.D.) **119** K 7
Lake Anna **129** O 3
Lake Annean **182** B 4
Lake Apopka **131** N 6
Lake Arbuckle **131** N 7
Lake Argyle **182** D 2
Lake Arrowhead **122** E 2
Lake Arthur (N.M.) **117** M 4–5
Lake Artur (LA.) **123** L 5
Lake Ashtabula **119** L 3
Lake Assale **199** G 2
Lake Athabasca **103** Q 4
Lake Aubry **103** M 2
Lake Auld **182** C 3
Lake Austin **182** B 4
Lake Avalon **117** M 5
Lake Baikal **170** J 5
Lake Ballard **182** C 4
Lake Bangweulu **200** D 2
Lake Baringo **199** F 4
Lake Barkley **128** D 5
Lake Barlee **182** B 4
Lake Benton (MN.) **119** M 6
Lake Berryessa **112** C 4
Lake Billy Chinook **110** D 6
Lake Bistineau **123** K 3
Lake Blackshear **131** KL 3
Lake Blanche (South Australia) **183** F 4
Lake Blanche (Western Australia) **182** C 3
Lake Borgne **123** O 5
Lake Bowdoin **111** S 2
Lake Breaden **182** D 4
Lake Bridgeport **122** F 2
Lake Brownwood **122** D 4
Lake Buchanan (Queensland, Austr.) **183** H 3
Lake Buchanan (Western Australia) **182** C 4
Lake Buck **182** E 2
Lake Burton **128** H 7
Lake Butler(FL.) **131** M 4–5
Lake Cachuma **113** F 8
Lake Callabonna **183** F 4
Lake Carey **182** C 4
Lake Cargelligo **183** H 5
Lake Carl Blackwell **120** H 6
Lake Carnegie **182** C 4
Lake Chad **197** G 3
Lake Chamo **199** F 3
Lake Champlain **126** F 4
Lake Charles (LA.) **123** K 5
Lake Chelan **110** E 2
Lake Chippewa **124** J 3
Lake City (AR.) **121** P 7
Lake City (CA.) **112** E 1
Lake City (CO.) **115** K 5
Lake City (FL.) **131** M 4
Lake City (KS.) **120** G 5
Lake City (MI.) **124** J 5
Lake City (MN.) **119** Q 6
Lake City (S.C.) **129** M 8
Lake City (S.D.) **119** L 5
Lake City (TN.) **128** G 5
Lake Claire **103** P 4
Lake Clark **108** H 3
Lake Clark National Park and Preserve **108** H 3
Lake Conway **121** N 7–8
Lake Cormorant (MS.) **121** P 8
Lake Corpus Christi **122** F 7
Lake Cowal **183** H 5
Lake Cowan **182** C 5
Lake Creek (TX.) **123** H 2
Lake Crowley **112** G 5
Lake Crystal (MN.) **119** O 6
Lake Cumberland **128** G 5
Lake Darling **118** G 2
Lake Darlot **182** C 4
Lake Davis **112** E 3

Lake Deborah **182** B 5
Lake Delton (WI.) **124** E 6
Lake De Smet **118** B 6
Lake Dey Dey **182** E 4
Lake Disappointment **182** C 3
Lake District **148** C 4
Lake Dora **182** C 3
Lake Dundas **182** C 5
Lake Earl **112** A 1
Lake Eaton **182** E 3
Lake Edward **198** D 5
Lake Ell **182** D 4
Lake Elsinore **113** H 9
Lake Elsworth **120** H 8
Lake Erie **125** NO 7–8
Lake Erling **121** M 9
Lake Everard **183** F 5
Lake Eyasi **198** E 5
Lake Eyre **183** F 4
Lake Eyre Basin **183** F 4
Lakefield **183** G 1
Lake Fort Phantom Hill **112** D 3
Lake Frances **111** N 2
Lake Francis Case **118** J 7
Lake Frome **183** F 5
Lake Gairdner **183** F 5
Lake Galilee **183** H 3
Lake Gamarri **199** G 2
Lake Gaston **129** N 5
Lake Geneva (WI.) **124** F 7
Lake George (CO.) **115** M 4
Lake George (FL.) **131** N 5
Lake George (N.D.) **118** J 4
Lake George (N.Y.) **126** F 5
Lake George (N.Y.) **126** F 5
Lake George (Uganda) **198** E 5
Lake George (Western Australia) **182** C 3
Lake Gidgi **182** D 4
Lake Gillen **182** C 4
Lake Gillian **105** M 2
Lake Gogebic **124** E 3
Lake Grace **182** B 5
Lake Granbury **122** F 3
Lake Granby **115** M 3
Lake Grandin **103** O 3
Lake Greenwood **129** JK 7
Lake Greeson **121** M 8
Lake Gregory **182** B 4
Lake Gregory (South Australia) **183** F 4
Lake Gregory (Western Australia) **182** D 3
Lake Gregory (Western Australia) **182** B 4
Lake Hamilton **121** M 8
Lake Harbor (FL.) **131** O 8
Lake Harbour **105** O 3
Lake Harding **131** J 2
Lake Harris **131** N 6
Lake Havasu **116** B 3
Lake Havasu City (AZ.) **116** B 3
Lake Hazlett **182** D 3
Lake Hefner **120** H 7
Lake Henshaw **113** J 9
Lake Heyburn **120** J 7
Lake Hickory **129** K 6
Lake Hopkins **182** D 3
Lake Houston **123** H 5–6
Lake Hughes (CA.) **113** G 8
Lake Huron **125** L 4–5
Lakehurst (N.J.) **127** E 9
Lake Ilo **118** F 3
Lake Inle **175** G 3
Lake Isabella (CA.) **113** G 7
Lake Istokpoga **131** N 7
Lake Itasca (MN.) **119** N 3
Lake Itchen **103** P 2
Lake Iteshi-Teshi **200** D 3
Lake Jackson (TX.) **123** H 6
Lake James **129** K 6
Lake Jocassee **128** J 6–7
Lake Kariba **200** D 3
Lake Kaweah **112** G 6
Lake Kemp **122** D 2
Lake Keowee **128** J 7
Lake Kickapoo **122** E 2
Lake Kincaid **121** Q 3
Lake King **182** B 5
Lake Kissimmee **131** N 7
Lake Kitangiri **198** E 5
Lake Kivu **198** D 5
Lake Koocanusa **111** K 2
Lake Koolivoo **183** F 3
Lake Kopiago **184** D 3
Lake Koshkonong **124** EF 7
Lake Kotcho **101**
Lake Kutubu **184** D 3
Lake Kyoga **198** E 4
Lake Laberge **102** K 3
Lakeland (FL.) **131** N 6
Lakeland (GA.) **131** LM 3
Lake Lapage **182** C 5
Lake Lefroy **182** C 5
Lake Lenore **110** F 3
Lake Linden (WI.) **124** F 2
Lake Livingston **123** H 5
Lake Louise **109** J 3
Lake Lowell **110** J 7
Lake Lucas **182** D 3
Lake Lucero **117** K 5

Lake Lyndon B. Johnson **122** E 5
Lake Macdonald **182** D 3
Lake Machattie **183** FG 3
Lake Mackay **182** D 3
Lake Magenta **182** B 5
Lake Maitland **182** C 4
Lake Malawi (Lake Nyasa) **201** E 2
Lake Maloney **120** E 1
Lake Manitoba **103** S 5
Lake Manyara **199** F 5
Lake Marion **129** L 8
Lake Mason **182** B 4
Lake Mattamuskeet **129** P 6
Lake Maurepas **123** N 5
Lake Maurice **182** E 4
Lake Maxinkuckee **124** H 8
Lake Mburu **198** E 5
Lake McClure **112** E 5
Lake McConaughy **120** D 1
Lake McDonald **111** M 2
Lake Mc Leod **182** A 3
Lake McMillan **117** M 5
Lake Mead **112** L 6
Lake Mean National Recreation Area **112** L 6
Lake Melville **105** Q 5
Lake Mendocino **112** B 3
Lake Mendota **124** E 6
Lake Meredith (CO.) **115** O 5
Lake Meredith (TX.) **117** P 2
Lake Meredith National Recreation-Area **117** P 2
Lake Merwin **110** C 4–5
Lake Michigamme **124** F 3
Lake Michigan **124** EG 2
Lake Mills (IA.) **119** P 7
Lake Minchumina **102** G 3
Lake Minigwal **182** C 4
Lake Mitchell **131** H 2
Lake Mohave **116** B 2
Lake Monger **182** B 4
Lake Moore **182** B 4
Lake Moultrie **129** L 8
Lake Murray (OK.) **120** H 8
Lake Murray (Papua New Guinea) **184** D 3
Lake Murray (Papua New Guinea) **184** D 3
Lake Murray (S.C.) **129** K 7
Lake Mweru **198** D 6
Lake Nabberu **182** C 4
Lake Nash **183** F 3
Lake Nasser **194** E 4
Lake Natron **199** F 5
Lake Neale **182** E 3
Lake Ngami **200** C 4
Lake Ngina **104** K 6
Lake Nipigon **104** K 6
Lake Nipissing **105** LM 6
Lake Norden (S.D.) **119** L 6
Lake Norman **129** KL 6
Lake Nyanga **182** D 4
Lake Nyasa **201** E 2
Lake Oahe **118** H 5
Lake of the Ozarks **121** N 4
Lake of the Woods **119** NO 1
Lake Okeechobee **131** O 7–8
Lake Oliver **131** J 2
Lake Onega **158** G 3
Lake Ontario **125** QR 6
Lake Oroville **112** D 3
Lake Osakis **119** N 5
Lake Oswego (OR.) **110** C 5
Lake O' The Cherokees **121** L 6
Lake O' The Pines **123** J 3
Lake Ouachita **121** M 8
Lake Owyhee **110** H 7
Lake Oxford **103** S 4–5
Lake Park (FL.) **131** OP 8
Lake Park (IA.) **119** N 7
Lake Park (MN.) **119** M 4
Lake Peipus **151** J 4
Lake Pend Oreille **110** J 2
Lake Peter, **103** T 3
Lake Philippi **183** F 3
Lake Pillsbury **112** C 3
Lake Placid (FL.) **131** N 7
Lake Placid (N.Y.) **126** F 4
Lake Pleasant (AZ.) **116** D 4
Lake Pleasant (N.Y.) **126** E 5
Lake Poinsett **119** LM 6
Lake Pontchartrain **123** N 5
Lakeport (CA.) **112** BC 3
Lakeport (MI.) **125** M 6
Lake Powell **114** FG 6
Lake Poygan **124** F 5
Lake Providence (LA.) **123** M 3
Lake Raeside **182** C 4
Lake Rason **182** C 4
Lake Ray Hubbard **122** G 3
Lake Rebecca **182** C 5
Lake Red Rock **119** P 9
Lake River **105** L 5
Lake Rosa **133** H 3
Lake Rudolf **199** F 4
Lake Rukwa **198** E 6
Lake Rutanzige **198** D 4
Lake Rutanzige → Lake Edward **198** D 5
Lakes, Eskimo **102** L 2
Lake Sacajawea **110** G 4

Lake Saint Clair **125** M 7
Lake Saint-Jean,**105** N 6
Lake Saint Joseph **104** J 5
Lake Saint Lucia **201** E 5
Lake Sakakawea **118** F 2
Lake Salvador **123** N 6
Lake Sara **121** R 3
Lake Scugog **105** M 7
Lake Seabrook **182** B 5
Lake Seminole **131** K 4
Lakes Entrance **183** H 6
Lake Shafer **124** H 9
Lake Shala **199** F 3
Lake Shannon **110** D 2
Lake Sharpe **118** J 6
Lake Shelbyville **121** R 3
Lake Shepperd **182** D 3
Lakeshore (CA.) **112** F 5
Lakeside (AZ.) **116** G 3
Lakeside (MT.) **111** L 2
Lakeside (OH.) **125** M 8
Lakeside (OR.) **110** A 7
Lakeside (UT.) **114** E 2
Lake Sidney Lanier **128** H 7
Lake Simcoe **105** M 7
Lake Simtustus **110** D 6
Lake Sinclair **128** H 8
Lakes National Park **185** Q 9
Lake Springfield **121** Q 3
Lake Stamford **122** D 2
Lake Stefanie **199** F 4
Lake Stevens (WA.) **110** CD 2
Lake Success **112** G 6
Lake Sumner **117** M 3
Lake Superior **124** EG 2
Lake Tahiryuak, **103** P 1
Lake Tahoe **112** EF 3
Lake Talquin **131** K 4
Lake Tana **199** F 2
Lake Tanganyika **198** DE 6
Lake Taupo **185** R 8
Lake Tawakoni **122** GH 3
Lake Te Anau **184** P 10
Lake Texarkana **123** J 2
Lake Texoma **120** J 9
Lake Throssel **182** C 4
Lake Thunderbird **120** H 7
Lake Tillery **129** L 6
Lake Timagami **105** L 6
Lake Timiskaming **105** M 6
Lake Tobin **182** D 3
Lake Tohopekaliga **131** N 6
Laketon (TX.) **117** Q 2
Lake Torrens **183** F 5
Laketown (UT.) **114** F 2
Lake Traverse **119** M 5
Lake Travis **122** E 5
Lake Tschida **118** G 4
Lake Turkana (Lake Rudolf) **199** F 4
Lake Umatilla **110** F 5
Lake Verret **123** M 6
Lake Victoria **198** E 5
Lakeview (MI.) **124** J 6
Lakeview (MI.) **124** J 7
Lakeview (MT.) **111** O 6
Lakeview (OR.) **110** E 8
Lakeview (TX.) **117** Q 3MO
Lake Village (AR.) **121** O 9
Lake Volta **196** DE 4
Lake Waccamaw **129** N 7
Lake Wakatinu **184** P 10
Lake Walcott **111** M 8
Lake Walk **122** C 6
Lake Wallenpaupack **127** D 7
Lake Wallula **110** FG 4
Lake Wanaka **184** P 9
Lake Wappapello **121** P 5–6
Lake Washington **110** C 3
Lake Waukarlycarly **182** C 3
Lake Wawasee **124** J 8
Lake Way **182** C 4
Lake Whatcom **110** C 2
Lake White **182** D 3
Lake Whitney **122** F 3–4
Lake Wichita **122** E 2
Lake Wills **182** D 3
Lake Wilson (MN.) **119** N 7
Lake Windermere **148** C 4
Lake Winnebago **124** F 5–6
Lake Winnibigoshish **119** OP 3
Lake Winnipeg **103** S 5
Lake Winnipegosis **103** RS 5
Lake Winnipesaukee **126** H 5
Lake Wissota **124** C 5
Lakewood (CO.) **115** M 4
Lakewood (N.J.) **127** E 8
Lakewood (N.M.) **117** M 5
Lakewood (N.Y.) **125** P 7
Lakewood (OH.) **125** N 8
Lakewood (WI.) **124** F 4
Lakewood Center **110** C 3
Lake Woods **182** E 2
Lake Worth (FL.) **131** OP 8
Lake Wylie **129** K 6
Lake Xau **200** C 4
Lake Yamma Yamma **183** G 4
Lake Yeo **182** C 4
Lake Zwai **199** F 3
Lakhdenpokh **150** K 3
Lakhimpur **174** D 2

Lakhnadon 174 C 3
Lakhpat 174 A 3
Lakin (KS.) 120 D 5
Lakki 169 J 4
Lakon 185 J 4
Lakon 186 C 3
Lakonikos Kólpos 154 B 3
Lakota 196 C 4
Lakota (IA.) 119 O 7
Lakota (N.D.) 119 K 2
Laksefjorden 150 J 1
Lakselv 150 J 1
Lakshadweep 174 B 5
Lakuramau 185 F 2
Lalago 198 E 5
Lala Musa 169 J 4
Lalara 197 G 5
Lâleli Geçidi 155 E 3
Lalereh, Tanjung 177 E 4
Lālī (Iran) 157 E 2
Lalibela 199 F 2
La Libertad 132 E 5
La Ligua 142 B 5
Lalin 152 B 3
La Linea 152 B 4
Lalitpur 174 C 3
La Loche 103 Q 4
Lama, Ozero 170 F 2
La Maddalena 153 E 3
La Maiella 153 F 3
Lama Kara 196 E 4
La Malbaie 105 N 6
La Mancha 152 C 4
Lamar (CO.) 115 P 5
Lamar (MO.) 121 L 5
Lamar (TX.) 122 G 7
La Marina 152 C 4
La Mariscala 142 F 5
La Marmora 153 E 4
Lamarque 143 C 6
La Marque (TX.) 123 HJ 6
Lamas 138 C 5
Lama Shillindi 199 G 4
La Mauricie National Park 105 N 6
Lamballe 152 C 2
Lambaréné 197 F 6
Lambay 148 B 4
Lambayeque 138 B 5
Lambert (MT.) 118 D 3
Lambert, Cape 185 F 2
Lambert Glacier 203
Lamberts Bay 200 B 6
Lambon 185 F 2
Lam Chi 175 H 4
Lamé 197 G 4
Lame Deer (MT.) 118 B 5
Lamego 152 B 3
La Merced 142 C 4
La Mesa (CA.) 113 HJ 10
La Mesa (N.M.) 117 K 5
Lamesa (TX.) 117 P 5
Lamezia Terme 153 G 4
Lamia 146
Lamía 154 B 3
Lamington National Park 183 J 4
Lammermoor 183 G 3
La Moille (IL.) 124 E 8
Lamoille (NV.) 112 K 2
Lamoine (CA.) 112 C 2
Lamon Bay 177 F 1
Lamoni (IA.) 119 O 9
Lamont (CA.) 113 G 7
Lamont (FL.) 131 L 4
Lamont (ID.) 111 O 7
Lamont (OK.) 120 H 6
Lamont (WA.) 110 GH 3
Lamont (WY.) 111 S 8
La Montaña 140 B 2–3
La Mosquitia 132 F 4–5
Lamotrek 186 A 2
Lamotte-Beuvron 152 D 2
La Moure (N.D.) 119 K 4
Lampang 175 G 4
Lam Pao Reservoir 175 H 4
Lampasas (TX.) 122 E 4
Lampazos de Naranjo 132 BC 2
Lamphun 175 G 4
Lamu 199 G 5
Lamud 138 C 5
Lamy (N.M.) 117 L 2
Lanagan (MO.) 121 L 6
Lanai 113 EF 11
Lanai 187 E 1
Lanai City (HI.) 113 F 11
Lanaihale 113 F 11
Lanare (CA.) 112 EF 6
Lanark (N.M.) 117 K 5–6
Lanbi Kyun 175 G 5
Lancang 172 C 6
Lancang Jiang 172 D 6
Lancaster (CA.) 113 G 8
Lancaster (KY.) 128 G 4
Lancaster (MN.) 119 M 2
Lancaster (MO.) 121 N 2
Lancaster (OH.) 128 J 2
Lancaster (PA.) 127 C 8
Lancaster (S.C.) 129 L 7
Lancaster (TX.) 122 G 3
Lancaster (U.K.) 148 C 4
Lancaster (VA.) 129 P 4

Lancaster (VT.) 126 H 4
Lancaster (WI.) 124 D 7
Lance Creek (WY.) 118 D 7
Lancelin 182 B 5
Lanchkhuti 155 F 2
Lanciano 153 F 3
Lanco 143 B 6
Łańcut 149 H 4
Landa (ND.) 118 H 2
Landau 149 F 5
Landeck 153 F 2
Landegode 150 F 2
Landete 152 C 4
Landfall 175 F 5
Land O'Lakes (WI.) 124 E 3
Landsdale (PA.) 127 D 8
Land's End 148 B 4
Landshut 149 F 5
Landskrona 151 F 4
Landsort 151 G 4
Landsortsdjupet 151 G 4
Landusky (MT.) 111 R 3
Lane (OK.) 120 JK 8
Lane (S.D.) 119 K 6
Lane City (TX.) 122 GH 6
La Negra 140 B 5
La'nga Co 174 D 1
Langa Langa 198 C 2
Lângan 150 F 3
Langanes 150 BC 2
Langarfoss 150 C 2
Langdon (N.D.) 119 K 2
Lange Berg 200 B 6
Langeberg 200 BC 6
Langeland 151 F 5
Längelmävesi 150 H 3
Langenhagen 149 E 4
Langesund 151 E 4
Langford (S.D.) 119 L 5
Langjökull 150 B 3
Langkawi 176 A 2
Langkon 176 E 2
Langlade 105 M 6
Langley (WA.) 110 C 2
Langlois (OR.) 110 A 8
Langlo River 183 H 4
Langogne 152 D 3
Langon 152 C 3
Langøya 150 F 2
Langreo 152 B 3
Langres 153 E 2
Langres, Plateau de 153 E 2
Langry 171 Q 5
Langsa 176 A 3
Lângsele 150 G 3
Lângseleån 150 G 3
Lang Shan 172 E 2
Lang Son 175 J 3
Lang Suan 175 G 6
Langtry (TX.) 122 B 6
Languedoc 152 D 3
Langzhong 172 E 4
Lan Hsu 173 H 6
Lanji 174 D 3
Lannemezan 152 D 3
Lannion 152 C 2
Lannion, Baie de 152 C 2
Lanping 172 C 5
Lansdowne House 104 K 5
L'Anse (MI.) 124 F 3
L'Anse Indian Reservation 124 F 3
Lansford (N.D.) 118 G 2
Lanshan 172 F 5
Lansing (IA.) 119 N 7
Lansing (MI.) 125 K 7
Lansing (N.W.T., Can.) 102 L 3
Lansjärv 150 H 2
Lanxi 173 G 5
Lanzarote 192 C 3
Lanzhou 172 D 3
Laoag 177 J 1
Laoang 177 G 3
Lao Cai 175 H 3
Laodikeia 154 C 3
Laoha He 173 G 2
Laohekou 172 F 4
Lao Ling 173 J 2
Laon 152 D 2
Laona (WI.) 124 F 4
La Orchila, Isla 138 E 1
La Oroya 140 A 3
Laos 175 HJ 4
Laouni 193 G 4
Laoye Ling 173 J 2
Lapa 142 G 4
Lapage, Lake 182 C 5
Lapai 197 F 4
Lapalisse 152 D 2
La Palma (Canary Islands) 192 B 3
La Palma (Panamá) 138 C 2
La Palma del Condado 152 B 4
La Paloma 142 F 5
La Paloma (TX.) 122 F 9
La Paragua 139 F 2
La Paz (Argentina) 142 C 5
La Paz (Argentina) 142 E 5

La Paz (Bolivia) 140 C 4
La Paz (Mexico) 106 D 7
La Paz, Bahia de 106 D 7
La Pedrera 138 DE 4
Lapeer (MI.) 125 L 6
La Pelada 142 D 5
La Perouse Strait 171 Q 6
La Pesca 132 C 3
La Piedad 132 B 3
La Pine (OR.) 110 D 7
Lapinig 177 G 1
Lapinlahti 150 J 3
Lápithos 155 D 3
Lápithos (Cyprus) 156 A 2
Lapland 150 H 2
La Plant (SD.) 118 H 5
La Plata 142 E 5–6
La Plata (MD.) 129 P 3
La Plata (MO.) 121 N 2–3
La Plata (N.M.) 116 H 1
La Porte (IN.) 124 H 8
Laporte (PA.) 126 C 7
La Porte City (IA.) 119 Q 8
Lappajärvi 150 H 3
Lappeenranta (Villmanstrand) 150 J 3
Lappi 150 J 2
Lapri 171 MN 4
Laprida (Argentina) 142 D 4
Laprida (Argentina) 143 D 6
Lapseki 154 C 2
Lapteva 158 G 5
Laptev Sea 171 NO 1
Laptev Sea 202
Laptevykh, More 170 MN 1
Lapua 150 H 3
La Puebla de Cazalla 152 B 4
La Puerta 142 D 5
La Puntilla 138 B 4
La Push (WA.) 110 A 3
Lapwai (ID.) 110 L 4
Laqiyat al Arba'in 194 D 4
Laqiyat 'Umran 194 D 5
La Quemada 132 B 3
La Quiaca 140 C 5
L'Aquila 153 F 3
Lär (Iran) 157 G 4
Larache 192 D 1
Laragne 153 E 3
Lārak (Iran) 157 G 4
Laramate 140 B 3
Laramie (WY.) 118 C 9
Laramie Mountains 118 C 8–9
Laramie Peak 118 C 8
Laramie River 118 C 9
Laranjal 139 G 4
Larantuka 177 F 5
Larat 177 H 5
La Raya Abra 140 B 3
Lärbro 151 G 4
Larche, Col de 153 E 3
Larde 201 F 3
Laredo (MT.) 111 Q 2
Laredo (Spain) 152 C 3
Laredo (TX.) 122 D 8
La Réole 152 CD 3
Larimore (N.D.) 119 L 3
La Rioja (Argentina) 142 C 4
La Rioja (Spain) 152 C 3
La Ribera 152 C 3
Larisa 154 B 3
Larkana 169 H 5
Lar Koh 169 G 4
Larkspur (CO.) 115 N 4
Larlomkriny 159 O 4
Larnaca 155 D 4
Larnaca (Cyprus) 156 A 2
Lárnax → Larnaca 155 D 4
Larne 148 B 4
Larned (KS.) 120 FG 4
La Robla 152 B 3
La Roche 185 J 6
La Rochelle 152 C 2
La Roche-sur-Yon 152 C 2
La Roda 152 C 4
La Romana 133 J 4
Larose (LA.) 123 N 6
Larrey Point 182 B 2
Larrimah 182 E 2
Larsa (Iraq) 157 D 3
Larsen Bay 108 M 4
Larsen Ice Shelf 203
Larslan (MT.) 118 B 2
Larvik 151 F 4
Lar'yak 159 Q 3
Larzac, Causse du 152 D 3
La Sabana (Argentina) 142 D 4
La Sabana (Colombia) 138 E 3
La Sal (UT.) 114 H 5MO
La Salina 106 D 5
La Salle (CO.) 115 N 3
La Salle (IL.) 124 E 8
La Sal Mountains 114 H 5
Las Animas (CO.) 115 O 5
Lãs 'Änöd 199 H 3
La Sarre 105 M 6
Las Bonitas 138 E 2

Lascaux, Grotte de 152 D 2
Las Cejas 142 D 4
Las Coloradas 143 B 6
Las Cruces (N.M.) 117 K 5
Las Cruces (NV.) 113 E 8
Lãs Dãred 199 H 2
Lãs Dawa 199 H 2
La Serena (Chile) 142 B 4
La Serena (Spain) 152 B 4
La Seyne-sur-Mer 153 E 3
Las Flores 143 E 6
Lãsh-e Joveyn 169 G 4
Lashio 155 G 3
Lashkar 174 C 2
Lashkar Gãh 169 G 4
Lasia, Pulau 176 A 3
Lãsjerd (Iran) 157 F 2
Las Lajas 143 BC 6
Las Lanjitas 140 D 5
Las Lomitas 140 D 5
Las Marismas 152 B 4
Las Martinetas 143 C 8
Las Mestenas 132 B 2
La Solana 152 C 4
Lasolo 177 F 4
La Souterraine 152 D 2
Las Palmas 192 B 3
Las Palomas 106 C 5
La Spezia 153 EF 3
Las Piedras 142 E 5
Las Pipinas 142 E 6
Las Plumas 143 C 7
Lãs Qoray 199 H 2
Lassen Peak 112 D 2
Lassen Volcanic National Park 112 D 2
Las Tablas 138 B 2
Last Chance(CO.) 115 O 4
Las Tinajas 142 D 4
Last Mountain Lake 103 R 5
Las Tórtolas 142 C 4
Lastoursville 197 G 6
Lastovo 153 G 3
Latacunga 138 C 4
Latady Island 203
La Tagua 138 CD 3
Latakia (Syria) 156 B 2
Latakia (Syria) 156 B 2
Latgales Augstiene 151 J 4
Latham (KS.) 120 J 5
Lathrop (CA.) 112 D 5
Lathrop Wells (NV.) 112 J 5
Lãtiã'ân (Iran) 157 G 4
Latimer (IA.) 119 P 8
Latimer (UT.) 114 D 5
Latina 153 F 3
Laton (CA.) 112 F 6
La Tortuga, Isla 138 E 1
Latouche Treville, Cape 182 C 2
Latouma 197 G 1
Latronico 153 G 3
Latta (S.C.) 129 M 7
La Tuque 105 N 6
Latur 174 C 4
Latviya 151 J 4
Lau 197 G 4
Lauderdale (MS.) 130 F 2
Lauenburg 149 F 4
Laughlin Peak 117 M 1
Lau Group 186 D 4
Lauhanvuori 150 H 3
Laukaa 150 J 3
Launceston 186 A 5
Launceston (Tasmania, Austr.) 184 L 9
Launggyaung 175 G 2
La Unión 138 C 3
La Unión (Chile) 143 B 7
La Unión (El Salvador) 132 E 5
La Union (Mexico) 132 B 4
La Union (Spain) 152 C 4
Laura 183 G 2
La Urbana 138 E 2
Laurel (MS.) 130 E 3
Laurel (MT.) 111 R 5
Laurel (NE.) 119 L 8
Laurel Bay (S.C.) 129 L 9
Laurens (S.C.) 129 JK 7
Laurentian Scarp 105 M 6
Lauria 153 G 3–4
Laurier (WA.) 110 G 2
Laurie River 103 R 4
Laurinburg (N.C.) 129 M 7
Laurium (WI.) 124 F 2
Lauro Retiro 142 G 4
Lausanne 153 E 2
Lausitz 149 F 4
Laut, Pulau 176 E 4
Laut, Selat 176 E 4
Laut Arafura 177 HJ 5
Laut Bali 176 E 5
Laut Banda 177 G 5
Laut Flores 177 E 5
Laut Halmahera 177 G 4
Laut Jawa 176 CD 4
Laut Maluku 177 G 4
Laut Seram 177 G 4

Laut Sulawesi 177 F 3
Laut Timor 177 G 6
Lautz 117 OP 1
Lava Beds National Monument 112 D 1
Lavaca River 122 G 6
Lava Hot Springs (ID.) 111 O 8
Laval (France) 152 C 2
Laval (Quebec, Can.) 105 N 6
Lavalle 142 C 5
Lävän (Iran) 157 F 4
Lavapié, Punta 143 B 6
Laveen (AZ.) 116 D 4
La Vega 133 H 4
La Venta 132 D 4
La Ventana 132 B 3
La Ventura 132 B 3
La Verkin (UT.) 114 D 6
Laverne (OK.) 120 F 6
La Vernia (TX.) 122 E 6
Laverton 182 C 4
La Veta (CO.) 115 N 6
Lavezares 171 F 1
Lavia 150 H 3
Lavic Lake 113 J 8
La Viña 138 C 5
Lavina (MT.) 111 R 4
Lavka Integralsoyuza 171 V 2
Lavonia (GA.) 128 H 7
Lavon Lake 122 G 2
Lavras 141 G 5
Lavrentiya 102 C 2
Lávrion 154 B 3
Lavumisa 201 E 5
Läw 198 E 3
Läw 198 E 3
Lawas 176 E 3
Lawdar 195 H 6
Lawele 177 F 5
Lawit, Gunung 176 D 3
Lawksawk 175 G 3
Lawn (TX.) 122 D 3
Lawndale (N.C.) 129 K 6
Lawn Hill (Queensland, Austr.) 183 F 2
Lawn Hill Creek (Queensland, Austr.) 183 F 2
Lawqah (Saudi Arabia) 156 D 3
Lawra 196 D 3
Lawrence (IN.) 128 F 2
Lawrence (KS.) 121 K 4
Lawrence (MA.) 126 H 2
Lawrence (NE.) 119 L 8
Lawrenceburg (IN.) 128 FG 2
Lawrenceburg (KY.) 128 F 3
Lawrenceburg (TN.) 128 D 6
Lawrenceville (GA.) 128 H 8
Lawrenceville (IL.) 121 S 4
Lawrenceville (VA.) 129 O 5
Laws (CA.) 112 G 5
Lawson (MO.) 121 L 3
Lawtey (FL.) 131 M 4
Lawton (MI.) 124 J 7
Lawton (N.D.) 119 K 2
Lawton (OK.) 120 G 8
Lawz, Jabal al (Saudi Arabia) 156 B 3
Laxå 151 F 4
Lay (CO.) 115 K 3
Layar, Tanjung 176 E 4
Laydennyy, Mys 158 J 2
Laylã 195 H 4
Layton (FL.) 131 O 10
Layton (UT.) 114 F 2
Laytonville (CA.) 112 B 3
La Zarca 132 B 3
Lazare (TX.) 122 CD 1
Lazarev 171 Q 5
Lazarevac 154 B 2
Lazarevskoye 155 F 2
Läzeh (Iran) 157 F 4
Lazo, Iméni 171 S 3
Lazo Dolinovka 171 T 4
Leaburg (OR.) 110 C 6
Leachville (AR.) 121 P 7
Leadbetter Point 110 A 4
Lead Hill (AR.) 121 N 6
Leadore (ID.) 111 M 6
Leadville (CO.) 115 L 4
Leaf River 130 E 3
League City (TX.) 123 H 6
Leake, Mount 182 D 2
Leakesville (MS.) 130 F 3
Leakey (TX.) 122 D 4
Le'an 172 G 5
Leary (GA.) 131 K 3
Leatherwood (KY.) 128 H 4
Leavenworth (KS.) 121 L 3
Leavenworth (WA.) 110 E 3
Łeba 149 G 4
Lebak 177 F 2
Lebam (WA.) 110 B 4
Lebanon (IN.) 124 H 9
Lebanon (KS.) 120 G 3
Lebanon (KY.) 128 F 4
Lebanon (Lebanon) 156 B 2
Lebanon (MO.) 121 N 5
Lebanon (N.H.) 126 G 3
Lebanon (OH.) 128 G 2
Lebanon (OR.) 110 C 6
Lebanon (PA.) 127 C 8
Lebanon (SD.) 118 J 5

Lebanon (TN.) **128** E 5
Lebanon (VA.) **129** JK 5
Lebeau (LA.) **123** M 5
Lebec (CA.) **113** G 8
Lebedin **158** F 5
Lebedyan' **158** G 5
Le Blanc **152** D 2
Lebo **198** C 4
Lebombo Mountains **201** E 4–5
Lębork **149** G 4
Lebrija **152** B 4
Lebu **143** B 6
Lebyazh'ye **159** P 5
Lecce **153** G 3
Lecco **153** E 2
Le Center (MN.) **119** P 6
Lech **149** F 5
Lechang **172** F 5
Lechkhumskiy Khrebet **155** F 2
Lecompte (LA.) **123** L 4
Léconi **197** G 6
Le Creusot **153** D 2
Ledesma **152** B 3
Ledger (MT.) **111** O 2
Ledger (N.C.) **129** J 6
Ledo, Cabo **200** A 1
Leduc **103** P 5
Ledyanaya, Gora **171** W 3
Lee (NV.) **112** K 2
Leech Lake **119** O 3
Leech Lake Indian Reservation **119** O 3
Leedey (OK.) **120** F 7
Leeds **148** C 4
Leeds (AL.) **128** E 8
Leeds (ND.) **118** J 2
Leeds (UT.) **114** D 6
Leer **149** E 4
Leesburg (FL.) **131** N 6
Leesburg (GA.) **131** K 3
Leesburg (VA.) **129** O 2
Lees Summit (MO.) **121** L 4
Leesville (LA.) **123** K 4
Leesville (TX.) **122** F 6
Leesville Lake **125** N 9
Leesville Lake **129** M 4
Leeuwarden **148** E 4
Leeuwin, Cape **182** A 5
Le Vining (CA.) **112** FG 5
Leeward Islands (French Polynesia) **187** E 4
Leeward Islands (West Indies) **133** K 4
Léfini **197** H 6
Léfini Reserve **197** H 6
Lefke → Levka **155** D 3
Lefkoniko **155** D 3
Lefkoniko (Cyprus) **156** A 2
Lefkosa → Nicosia **155** D 3
Lefor (ND.) **118** F 4
Lefors (TX.) **117** Q 2
Leganés **152** C 3
Legaspi **177** F 1
Legges Tor **184** L 9
Leggett (CA.) **112** B 3
Legnago **153** F 2
Legnano **153** E 2
Legnica **149** G 4
Le Grand (CA.) **112** E 5
Legune **182** D 2
Leh **169** K 4
Léhamba **197** G 6
Le Havre **152** CD 2
Lehi (UT.) **114** F 3
Lehr (ND.) **118** J 4
Lehua Island **113** B 9
Lehututu **200** C 4
Leibnitz **153** G 2
Leicester **148** C 4
Leichardt River (Queensland, Austr.) **183** F 2
Leiden **148** D 4
Leidy, Mount **111** P 7
Leigh (NE.) **119** L 9
Leigh Creek **183** F 5
Leikanger **150** E 3
Leila Lake (TX.) **117** Q 3
Leine **149** E 4
Leipzig **149** F 4
Leiria **152** B 4
Leirvik **151** E 4
Leisler, Mount **182** D 3
Leitchfield (KY.) **128** E 4
Leiter (WY.) **118** B 6
Leiyang **172** F 5
Leizhou Bandao **172** E 6
Leizhou Wan **172** F 6
Leje **148** D 4
Lejia, Cerro **140** C 5
Lek **148**E 4
Leka **150** F 2
Lékana **197** G 6
Lekemti → Nekemt **199** F 3
Lekey **197** G 6
Lekhainá **154** B 3
Lekitobi **177** F 4
Lekki Lagoon **197** E 4
Leknes **150** F 2
Lekrisovo **159** P 3
Leksand **151** F 3
Leksozero, Ozero **150** K 3

Lekst, Jbel **192** D 3
Leksvik **150** F 3
Lela (TX.) **117** Q 2
Le Lamentin **133** K 5
Leland (MI.) **124** J 4
Leland (MS.) **121** P 9
Lelång **151** F 4
Lelekovka **155** D 1
Leleque **143** B 7
Lelewau **177** F 4
Leling **173** G 3
Lelinta **177** GH 4
Le Locle **153** E 2
Le Maire, Estrecho de **143** CD 9–10
Léman, Lac **153** E 2
Le Mans **152** D 2
Le Mars (IA.) **119** M 8
Lembolovskaya Vozvyshennost' **151** JK 3
Lemesós → Limassol **155** D 4
Lemgo **149** E 4
Lemhi (ID.) **111** M 6
Lemhi Range **111** M 6
Lemhi River **111** M 6
Lemieux Islands **105** P 3
Leming (TX.) **122** E 6
Lemitar (N.M.) **117** K 3
Lemluia **192** C 3
Lemmenjoki **150** J 2
Lemmon (SD.) **118** F 5
Lemmon (SD.) **118** FG 5
Lemmon, Mount **116** F 5
Lemoncove (CA.) **112** FG 6
Le Mont-Saint-Michel **152** C 2
Lemoore (CA.) **112** F 6
Lemoro **177** F 4
Lemos **139** H 4
Le Moyne, Lac **105** O 4
Lempa, Rio **132** E 5
Lempäälä **150** H 3
Lemtybozh **158** L 3
Lemvig **151** E 4
Lena **171** N 1
Lena (WI.) **124** G 5
Lendava **153** G 2
Lendery **150** K 3
Lengeh, Bandar-e (Iran) **157** G 4
Lenger **169** H 2
Lengshuijiang **172** F 5
Lengua de Vaca, Punta **142** B 5
Lenina, Pik **169** J 3
Leninabad **169** HJ 2
Leninakan **155** F 2
Leningrad **151** K 4
Leningradskaya **155** E 1
Leningradskaya **203**
Leninka **171** X 3
Lenino **155** E 1
Leninogorsk **158** K 5
Leninogorsk **159** Q 5
Leninsk **155** F 1
Leninskiy **171** N 4
Leninsk-Kuznetskiy **159** QR 5
Leninskoye **171** O 6
Len'ki **159** Q 5
Lenkoran' **168** D 3
Len Malaäs **177** H 4
Lennard River **182** C 2
Lennep (MT.) **111** P 4
Lennox (S.D.) **119** M 7
Lennox, Isla **143** C 10
Leno-Angarskoye Plato **170** HJ 4
Lenoir (NC.) **129** K 6
Lenoir City (TN.) **128** G 6
Lenorah (TX.) **117** P 5
Lenore (ID.) **110** J 4
Lenore, Lake **110** F 3
Lenox (GA.) **131** L 3
Lenox (MA.) **126** F 6
Lensk **170** K 3
Lentekhi **155** F 2
Lentiira **150** J 3
Lentini **153** F 4
Lentua **150** JK 3
Léo **196** D 3
Leo (TX.) **122** F 2
Leo (TX.) **122** F 2
Leoben **153** F 2
Leola (SD.) **118** K 5
Leon (IA.) **119** P 10
Leon (KS.) **120** J 5
Leon (Mexico) **132** B 3
León (Nicaragua) **132** E 5
León (Spain) **152** B 3
León, Cerro **140** D 5
Leon, Montes de **152** B 3
Leonard (N.D.) **119** L 4
Leonard (TX.) **122** G 2
Leonardtown (MD.) **129** P 3
Leonardville (KS.) **120** J 3
León Nuevo (Mexico) **132** C 2
Leonora **182** C 4
Leonora (KS.) **120** E 3
Leon River **122** F 4
Leon Valley (TX.) **122** E 6
Leopold and Astrid Coast **203**
Leopoldina **141** H 5

Leopoldo de Bulhões **141** G 4
Leoti (KS.) **120** D 4
Leovo **154** C 1
Le Palais **152** C 2
Lepar, Pulau **176** C 4
Lepe **152** B 4
Lepel' **151** J 5
Lephepe **200** D 4
Leping **173** G 5
Lepini, Monti **153** F 3
Lepiske **171** N 2
Lepsy **159** P 6
Leptis Magna **193** H 2
Le Puy **152** D 2
Lercara Friddi **153** F 4
Léré (Chad) **197** G 4
Lere (Nigeria) **197** F 3
Lerfroy, Lake **182** C 5
Léros **154** C 3
Lerma **152** C 3
Lermontovskiy **155** F 2
Lermoos **153** F 2
Lérida (Colombia) **138** D 3
Lérida (Spain) **152** D 3
Lerum **151** F 4
Lerwick **148** C 2
Les Cayes **133** H 4
Les Coëvrons **152** C 2
Les Escoumins **105** O 6
Lesina, Lago di **153** G 3
Lesjöfors **151** F 4
Leskino **170** C 1
Leskovac **154** B 2
Les Landes **152** C 3
Leslie (AR.) **121** N 7
Lesnaya **171** TU 4
Lesnoy **159** N 4
Lesogorsk **171** Q 6
Lesosibirsk **170** F 4
Lesosavodsk **173** K 1
Lesozavodskiy **150** K 2
Lesparre-Médoc **152** C 2
L'Esperance Rock **186** D 5
Les Sables-d'Olonne **152** C 2
Lessebo **151** G 4
Lesser Antilles **133** K 4–5
Lesser Khingan Mountains **171** N 6
Lesser Slave Lake **103** OP 4
Lesser Sunda Islands **177** FG 5
Lester (WA.) **110** D 3
Lestijärvi **150** H 3
Lestijoki **150** H 3
Le Sueur (MN.) **119** P 6
Lesueur, Mount **182** B 5
Lésvos **154** C 3
Leszno **149** G 4
Le Tanargue **152** D 3
Letcher (S.D.) **119** KL 7
Letha Range **175** F 3
Lethbridge **103** P 6
Lethem **139** G 3
Le Thillot **153** E 2
Leti, Kepulauan **177** G 5
Leticia **138** D 4
Leting **173** G 3
Letlhakane **200** D 4
Letlhakeng **200** C 4
Letnerechenskiy **150** K 3
Letnyaya Zolotitsa **158** G 3
Letong **176** C 3
Letovice **149** G 5
Le Tréport **152** D 1
Letsok-aw Kyun **175** G 5
Lettsworth (LA.) **123** M 5
Léua **200** C 2
Leuca **153** G 4
Leucadia (CA.) **113** H 9
Leucate, Étang de **152** D 3
Leunovo **198** B 4
Leuser, Gunung **176** A 3
Levadhia **154** B 3
Levan (UT.) **114** F 4
Levanger **150** F 3
Levante, Riviera di **153** E 3
Levanzo **153** F 4
Levas **168** D 2
Levaya Khetta **159** O 2–3
Levelland (TX.) **117** O 4
Leveloch **108** G 4
Lévêque, Cape **182** C 2
Le Verdon-sur-Mer **152** C 2
Leverkusen **149** E 4
Lévézou **152** D 3
Levice **149** G 5
Levin **185** R 9
Levis **105** N 6
Levittown (PA.) **127** E 8
Levka **155** D 3
Levka (Cyprus) **156** A 2
Levká Óri **154** B 3
Levkás **154** B 3
Levkosia → Nicosia **155** D 3
Levokumskoye **155** F 2
Levski **154** C 2
Levy (N.M.) **117** M 1
Lewe **175** G 4

Lewellen (NE.) **118** F 9
Lewes (PA.) **127** D 10
Lewis **148** B 3
Lewis (CO.) **114** J 6
Lewis (KS.) **120** F 5
Lewis, Mount **112** J 2
Lewis and Clark Lake **119** L 8
Lewisburg (KY.) **128** E 5
Lewisburg (PA.) **127** B 8
Lewisburg (TN.) **128** E 6
Lewisburg (W.V.) **129** L 4
Lewisetta (VA.) **129** P 3
Lewis Lake **111** P 6
Lewis Range **111** M 2
Lewis Smith Lake **128** D 7–8
Lewis Springs (AZ.) **116** F 6
Lewiston (ID.) **110** HJ 4
Lewiston (ME.) **126** J 4
Lewiston (MI.) **125** K 5
Lewiston (N.C.) **129** O 5
Lewiston (N.Y.) **125** Q 6
Lewiston (UT.) **114** F 2
Lewistown (IL.) **124** D 9
Lewistown (MO.) **121** O 2
Lewistown (MT.) **111** Q 3
Lewistown (PA.) **127** B 8
Lewisville (AR.) **121** M 9
Lewisville (ID.) **111** N 7
Lewisville (TX.) **122** FG 2
Lewotobi, Gunung **177** F 5
Lexa (AR.) **121** P 8
Lexington (GA.) **128** H 8
Lexington (KY.) **128** G 3
Lexington (MO.) **121** M 3
Lexington (MS.) **130** DE 1
Lexington (N.C.) **129** L 6
Lexington (NE.) **120** F 2
Lexington (OK.) **120** H 7–8
Lexington (OR.) **110** F 5
Lexington (S.C.) **129** K 7–8
Lexington (TN.) **128** C 6
Lexington (TX.) **122** FG 5
Lexington (VA.) **129** M 4
Leye **172** E 6
Leyte **177** F 1
Lezha **154** A 2
Lezhi **172** DE 4
Lézignan-Corbieres **152** D 3
L'gov **158** G 5
Lhari **172** B 4
Lhasa **175** F 2
Lhasa He **175** F 1
Lhazê **174** E 2
Lhazhong **174** E 1
Lhok Seumawe **176** A 2
Lhoksukon **176** A 2–3
Lhorong **172** C 4
Lhozhag **175** F 2
Lhünze **172** B 5
Lhünzhub **175** F 1
Lia **198** B 3
Liancheng **172** G 5
Lianga **172** G 4
Lianghe **172** C 6
Liangpran, Gunung **176** D 3
Lianhua Shan **172** G 6
Lianjiang **172** EF 6
Lianjiang **173** G 5
Lianping **172** F 6
Lian Xian **172** F 6
Lianyin **171** M 5
Lianyungang **173** GH 4
Liaodong Bandao **173** H 3
Liaodong Wan **173** H 2
Liao He **173** H 2
Liaoning **173** H 2
Liaoyang **173** H 2
Liaoyuan **173** HJ 2
Liard River **103** M 4
Liard River **109** N 4
Libby Dam **111** K 2
Libenge **198** B 4
Liberal (KS.) **120** E 5
Liberal (MO.) **121** L 5
Liberec **149** G 4
Liberia **196** BC 4
Liberia (Costa Rica) **132** E 5
Libertade **141** F 3
Libertador General San Martín **140** D 5
Liberty (IL.) **121** O 3
Liberty (IN.) **128** FG 2
Liberty (KY.) **128** F 4
Liberty (MO.) **121** L 3
Liberty (MS.) **130** D 3
Liberty (N.C.) **129** M 6
Liberty (NE.) **120** J 2
Liberty (N.Y.) **126** E 7
Liberty (TN.) **128** F 5
Liberty (TX.) **123** J 5
Liberty Center (OH.) **125** L 8
Liberty Hill (TX.) **122** F 5
Liberty Reservoir **129** OP 2
Libo **172** E 5
Libobo, Tanjung **177** G 4
Liboi **199** G 4
Libourne **152** CD 3
Librazhdi **154** B 3
Libreville **197** F 5
Libro Point **177** E 1

Libya **193** HK 3
Libyan Desert **194** CD 3–4
Licata **153** F 4
Lice **155** F 3
Lichinga **201** F 2
Lichinga, Planalto de **201** F 2
Lichtenburg **200** D 5
Lichuan **172** E 4
Licking (MO.) **121** O 5
Licking River **128** H 3
Licosa, Punta **153** F 3
Lida (Japan) **173** L 3
Lida (NV.) **112** H 5
Lida (U.S.S.R.) **151** J 5
Liden **150** G 3
Lidgerwood (N.D.) **119** LM 4
Lidhorikion **154** B 3
Lidköping **151** F 4
Lido di Ostia **153** F 3
Lidzbark Wármiński **149** H 4
Liebenthal (KS.) **120** F 4
Liebig, Mount **182** E 3
Liechtenstein **153** EF 2
Liége **148** E 4
Lieksa **150** K 3
Lielupe Musa **151** H 4
Lienart **198** D 4
Lienz **153** F 2
Liepāja **151** H 4
Lierne **150** F 3
Liestal **153** E 2
Lievestuoreenjärvi **150** J 3
Lievre **105** M 6
Lifou **185** J 6
Lifou **186** C 4
Ligatne **151** H 4
Ligeni Shkodrës **154** A 2
Lighthouse Point (FL.) **131** O 8
Lignite (ND.) **118** F 2
Ligonha **201** F 3
Ligure, Appennino **153** E 3
Ligurian Sea **153** E 3
Ligurta (AZ.) **116** B 5
Ligwera **201** F 2
Lihir Group **185** F 2
Lihir Group **186** B 3
Lihou Reef and Cays **183** J 2
Lihue (HI.) **113** C 10
Liinahamari **150** K 2
Lijiang **172** D 5
Likasi **200** D 2
Likati **198** C 4
Likely (CA.) **112** E 1
Likenäs **151** F 3
Likhapani **175** G 2
Likiep **186** C 2
Likoma Islands **201** E 2
Likoro **197** F 3
Likoto **198** C 5
Likouala **197** H 5
Likouala **197** H 5
Likouala aux Herbes **197** GH 5
Likwangoli **198** E 3
Liling **172** F 5
Lilla Edet **151** F 4
Lille **152** D 1
Lille Bælt **151** EF 4
Lillebonne **152** D 2
Lillehammer **150** F 3
Lillesand **151** E 4
Lilleström **151** F 4
Lillhärdal **150** F 3
Lillington (N.C.) **129** N 6
Lilongwe **201** E 2
Liloy **177** F 2
Lim **154** A 2
Lima (MT.) **111** N 6
Lima (OH.) **125** K 9
Lima (Peru) **140** A 3
Lima (Portugal) **152** B 3
Limache **142** B 5
Limah **193** E 5
Limah (Oman) **157** G 4
Limal **140** D 5
Lima Reservoir **111** N 6
Limassol **155** D 4
Limassol (Cyprus) **156** A 2
Limay **143** C 6
Limay Mahuida **143** C 6
Limbaži **151** H 4
Limbe **201** F 3
Limboto **177** F 3
Limburg **149** E 4
Lime (OR.) **110** H 6
Limedsforsen **151** F 3
Limeira **141** G 5
Limerick **148** B 4
Limeston (ME.) **126** LM 2
Limestone (MT.) **111** Q 5
Lime Village **108** GH 3
Limfjorden **151** E 4
Liminka **150** HJ 3
Limmen Bight **182** F 1
Límni **154** B 3
Limni Kremastá **154** B 3
Límni Mikre Prèspa **154** B 2
Limningen **150** F 3
Limni Trikhonis **154** B 3
Limni Vegorritis **154** B 2

Limni Zistonis 154 C 2
Limnos 154 C 3
Limoeiro 141 J 2
Limoges 152 D 2
Limogne, Causse de 152 D 3
Limon (CO.) 115 O 4
Limón (Costa Rica) 132 F 5
Limone Piemonte 153 E 3
Limoquije 140 CD 4
Limousin 152 D 2
Limoux 152 D 3
Limpopo 200 D 4
Limpopo 201 E 4
Limuru 199 F 5
Linaälven 150 H 2
Linah (Saudi Arabia) 156 D 3
Lin'an 173 G 4
Linapacan Strait 177 E 1
Linares (Chile) 143 B 6
Linares (Mexico) 132 C 3
Linares (Spain) 152 C 4
Linaro, Capo 153 F 3
Lincang 172 D 6
Linch (WY.) 118 B 7
Lincoln (AR.) 121 L 7
Lincoln (Argentina) 142 D 5
Lincoln (CA.) 112 D 4
Lincoln (ID.) 111 O 7
Lincoln (IL.) 124 E 9
Lincoln (KS.) 120 G 3
Lincoln (ME.) 126 L 3
Lincoln (MI.) 125 L 5
Lincoln (MO.) 121 M 4
Lincoln (MT.) 111 N 4
Lincoln (NE.) 120 J 2
Lincoln (N.M.) 117 L 4
Lincoln (TX.) 122 FG 5
Lincoln (U.K.) 148 C 4
Lincoln City (IN.) 128 E 3
Lincoln Park (MI.) 125 L 7
Lincoln Sea 202
Lincolnton (GA.) 128 J 8
Lincolnton (N.C.) 129 K 6
Lincoln Village (CA.) 112 D 4
Lincoln Wolds 148 CD 4
Lind (WA.) 110 G 4
Linda (CA.) 112 D 3
Lindale (TX.) 123 H 3
Lindau 149 E 5
Linde 170 M 2
Linden 139 G 2
Linden (AL.) 130 G 2
Linden (AZ.) 116 F 3
Linden (CA.) 112 DE 4
Linden (TN.) 128 D 6
Linden (TX.) 123 J 2
Lindenows Fjord 105 T 3
Linderödsåsen 151 F 4
Lindesberg 151 FG 4
Lindesnes 151 E 4
Lindhos 154 C 3
Lindi (Tanzania) 199 F 6–7
Lindi (Zaire) 198 D 4
Lindon (CO.) 115 O 4
Lindsay (CA.) 112 FG 6
Lindsay (MT.) 118 CD 3
Lindsay (NE.) 119 L 9
Lindsay (OK.) 120 H 8
Lindsborg (KS.) 120 H 4
Line Islands 187 E 2–3
Lineville (AL.) 128 F 8
Lineville (IA.) 119 P 10
Linfen 172 F 3
Lingao 172 E 7
Lingayan Gulf 177 H 1
Lingayen 177 H 1
Lingen 149 E 4
Lingga, Kepulauan 176 B 3–4
Lingga, Pulau 176 B 4
Lingle (WY.) 118 D 8
Lingling 172 F 5
Lingomo 198 C 4
Lingqiu 172 F 3
Lingshan 172 E 6
Lingshi 172 F 3
Lingshui 172 F 7
Lingsugur 174 C 4
Linguère 196 AB 2
Lingwu 172 E 3
Lingyuan 173 G 2
Linhai 173 H 5
Linhares 141 J 4
Linh Cam 175 J 4
Linhe 172 E 2
Linhpa 175 G 2
Linjanti 200 C 3
Linköping 151 G 4
Linkou 173 K 1
Linn (KS.) 120 H 3
Linn (MO.) 121 O 4
Linn (TX.) 122 E 9
Linneus (MO.) 121 M 3
Linosa 153 F 4
Linquan 172 G 4
Lins 141 G 5
Linshu 173 G 4
Lintan 172 D 4
Lintao 172 D 3
Linton (IN.) 128 D 2
Linton (KY.) 128 D 5

Linton (ND.) 118 H 4
Lintong 172 E 4
Linxi 173 G 2
Linxia 172 D 3
Lin Xian 172 F 3
Linyi (Shandong, China) 173 G 3
Linyi (Shanxi, China) 172 F 3
Linz 153 F 2
Linze 172 CD 3
Lion, Golfe du 152–153 D 3
Liondo 198 C 5
Lioppa 177 G 5
Liouesso 197 H 5
Lipa 177 F 1
Lipari 153 FG 4
Lipatkain 176 B 3
Lipéité 197 H 5
Lipetsk 158 GH 5
Lipin Bor 158 G 3
Liping 172 E 5
Lipkany 154 C 1
Lipno 149 G 4
Lipova 154 B 1
Lipovtsy 173 K 2
Lipscomb (TX.) 117 Q 1
Lipu 172 F 6
Liquica 177 FG 5
Lira 198 E 4
Liranga 197 H 6
Lircay 140 B 3
Lisa 154 A 2
Lisabata 177 G 4
Lisakovskiy 159 M 4
Lisala 198 C 4
Lisboa 152 B 4
Lisbon (N.D.) 119 L 4
Lisbon (N.M.) 116 H 5
Lisbon (OH.) 125 O 9
Lisbon (Portugal) 152 B 4
Lisburn 148 B 4
Lisburne, Cape 102 D 2
Lisco (NE.) 118 F 9
Lishi 172 F 3
Lishu 173 H 2
Lishui 173 G 5
Lisichansk 158 G 6
Lisieux 152 D 2
L'Isle-Jourdain 152 D 3
L'Isle-sur-la-Sorgue 153 E 3
Lismanovy 159 P 3
Lismore (MN.) 119 N 7
Lismore (N.S.W., Austr.) 183 J 4
Listafjorden 151 E 4
Lištica 153 G 3
Litang 172 CD 4
Litang 172 E 6
Litang Qu 172 D 5
Litchfield (IL.) 121 Q 3
Litchfield (MN.) 119 O 5
Litchfield (NE.) 120 FG 1
Litchville (N.D.) 119 K 4
Lithgow 183 HJ 5
Lithinon, Ákra 154 B 4
Lithuania 151 H 4
Litke 158 L 1
Litke 171 Q 5
Litoměřice 149 F 4
Litovko 171 P 6
Little Abaco Island 133 G 2
Little Aden 195 G 6
Little America (WY.) 111 Q 9
Little Andaman 175 F 5
Little Belt Mountains 111 P 4
Little Blue River 120 H 2
Little Cayman 133 F 4
Little Colorado River 116 E 2
Little Creek (TN.) 128 G 5
Little Desert National Park 183 G 6
Little Eagle (SD.) 118 GH 5
Little Falls (MN.) 119 O 4–5
Littlefield (AZ.) 116 C 1
Littlefield (TX.) 117 O 4
Littlefork (MN.) 119 P 2
Little Goose Dam 110 H 4
Little Grand Rapids 103 ST 5
Little Humboldt River 112 H 1
Little Inagua Island 133 H 3
Little Karroo 200 C 6
Little Lake (CA.) 112 H 7
Little Lake (MI.) 124 G 3
Little Minch 148 B 3
Little Missouri Badlands 118 E 3–4
Little Missouri River 118 E 3
Little Nicobar 175 F 6
Little Pamir 169 J 3
Little Powder River 118 C 5–6
Little River (KS.) 120 G 4
Little River (OK./AR.) 121 L 9
Little Rock (AR.) 121 N 8
Little Rocky Mountains 111 QR 3
Little Sable Point 124 H 4
Little Salt Lake 114 E 6
Little Sioux River 119 N 8
Little Sitkin 102 A 9
Little Smoky River 103 O 5
Littlestown (PA.) 127 BC 9
Little Tanaga 102 BC 5
Littleton (CO.) 115 MN 4
Littleton (N.H.) 126 H 4
Littleton(W.V.) 129 L 2

Little Traverse Bay 124 J 4
Little Valley (N.Y.) 125 Q 7
Litva 151 H 4
Liuhe 173 J 2
Liujia Xia 172 D 3
Liuku 172 C 5
Liupanshui 172 D 5
Liushuquan 172 B 2
Liuwa Plain 200 C 2
Liuyuan 172 C 2
Liuzhou 172 E 6
Līvāni 151 J 4
Live Oak (CA.) 112 C 3
Live Oak (CA.) 112 D 3
Live Oak (FL.) 131 M 4
Live Oak Springs (CA.) 113 J 10
Liveringa 182 C 2
Livermore (CA.) 112 D 5
Livermore (CO.) 115 M 3
Livermore (IA.) 119 O 8
Livermore (KY.) 128 DE 4
Livermore, Mount 117 M 7
Livermore Falls (ME.) 126 J 4
Liverpool 148 C 4
Liverpool (Nova Scotia, Can.) 105 P 7
Liverpool (TX.) 123 H 6
Liverpool Bay 102 LM 1–2
Liverpool Range 183 J 5
Livingston (AL.) 130 F 2
Livingston (CA.) 112 E 5
Livingston (KY.) 128 G 4
Livingston (LA.) 123 N 5
Livingston (MT.) 111 P 5
Livingston (Newfoundl., Can.) 105 O 5
Livingston (TN.) 128 F 5
Livingston, Lake 123 H 5
Livingstone 200 D 3
Livingstone Falls 197 G 7
Livingstone Memorial 201 E 2
Livingstone Mountains 198 E 6
Livingstonia 201 E 2
Livington (TX.) 123 J 5
Livny 158 G 5
Livona (ND.) 118 H 4
Livonia (LA.) 123 M 5
Livonia (MI.) 125 L 7
Livonia (N.Y.) 126 B 6
Livoniya 151 J 4
Livornia (N.Y.) 126 B 6
Livorno 153 EF 3
Livradois, Monts du 152 D 2
Liwale 199 F 6
Liwonde 201 F 2–3
Li Xian 172 D 4
Li Xian 172 E 4
Li Xian 172 F 5
Liyang 173 G 4
Lizard 148 BC 5
Lizarda 139 J 5
Lizard Head Peak 111 Q 8
Ljig 154 B 2
Ljubeli 153 F 2
Ljubinje 153 G 3
Ljubljana 153 F 2
Ljubovija 154 A 2
Ljugarn 151 G 4
Ljungan 150 F 3
Ljungaverk 150 G 3
Ljungby 151 F 4
Ljungdalen 150 F 3
Ljungskile 151 F 4
Ljusdal 150 G 3
Ljusnan 150 F 3
Ljusne 150 G 3
Ljusterö 150 H 3
Llaima, Volcán 143 B 6
Llallagua 140C 4
Llandovery 148 C 4
Llanelli 148 C 4
Llanes 152 C 3
Llano (TX.) 122 E 5
Llano Estacado 117 NO 4
Llano River 122 DE 5
Llanos 138 DE 2
Llanos de Chiquitos 140 D 4
Llanos de Moxos 140 CD 4
Llanos de Tabasco y Campeche 132 D 4
Llanos de Tamaulipas 132 C 2
Llanos de Urgel 152 D 3
Llanquihue, Lago 143 B 7
Llanta 142 C 4
Lleyn 148 C 4
Llica 140 C 5
Llico 143 B 5
L'lle Rousse 153 E 3
Lloyd (MT.) 111 Q 2
Lluchmayor 152 D 4
Llullaillaco, Volcán 140 C 5
Loa 140 C 5
Loa (UT.) 114 F 5
Loaita Island 176 D 1
Loanda 197 F 6
Loandjili 197 G 6
Loange 198 C 6
Loano 153 E 3
Lobatse 200 D 5
Lobaye 198 B 4
Lobecks Pass 113 L 8
Loberia 143 E 6

Lobito 200 A 2
Lobitos 138 B 4
Lobo (TX.) 117 M 7
Lobos 142 E 6
Lobos de Afuera, Islas 138 B 5
Lobos de Tierra, Isla 138 B 5
Lobva 159 M 4
Locarno 153 E 2
Locate (MT.) 118 C 4
Loch Awe 148 B 3
Lochboisdale 148 B 3
Loch Fyne 148 B 3
Lochiel (AZ.) 116 F 6
Lochinver 148 B 3
Loch Lomond 148 C 3
Lochmaddy 148 B 3
Lochnagar 148 C 3
Loch Ness 148 C 3
Lochsa River 111 K 4
Loch Shin 148 C 3
Loch Tay 148 C 3
Lock 183 F 5
Locke (N.Y.) 126 C 6
Lockeford (CA.) 112 DE 4
Lockhart (TX.) 122 F 6
Lockhart River Mission 183 G 1
Lock Haven (PA.) 127 B 7
Lockney (TX.) 117 P 3
Lockout (CA.) 112 D 1
Lockport (N.Y.) 125 Q 6
Lockwood (CA.) 112 DE 7
Locminé 152 C 2
Locri 153 G 4
Lod (Israel) 156 B 3
Loddon River 183 G 6
Lodève 152 D 3
Lodeynoye Pole 158 F 3
Lodge Grass (MT.) 111 S 5
Lodgepole (MT.) 111 R 2
Lodgepole (NE.) 118 F 9
Lodge (pole (SD.) 118 F 5
Lodi (CA.) 112 D 4
Lodi (OH.) 125 MN 9
Lodi (WI.) 124 E 6
Lödingen 150 G 2
Lodja 198 C 5
Lodoga (CA.) 112 C 3
Lödöse 151 F 4
Lodwar 198 F 4
Łodz 153 EF 3
Loelli 198 E 3
Loeriesfontein 200 B 6
Lofa 196 B 4
Lofgreen (UT.) 114 E 3
Lofoten 150 F 2
Lofsdalen 150 F 3
Lofty Ranges, Mount 183 F 5
Loga 196 E 3
Logan (IA.) 119 N 9
Logan (KS.) 120 F 3
Logan (MT.) 111 O 5
Logan (N.M.) 117 N 2
Logan (OH.) 129 J 2
Logan (OK.) 120 E 6
logan (UT.) 114 F 2
Logan (W.V.) 129 K 4
Logan, Mount (WA.) 110 E 2
Logan, Mount (Yukon, Can.) 102 J 3
Logandale (NV.) 112 L 6
Logan Martin Reservoir 128 E 8
Logan Mountains 102 M 3
Logan Pass 111 M 2
Logansport (IN.) 124 H 9
Logansport (LA.) 123 K 3–4
Logone 197 H 3–4
Logone Birni 197 G 3
Logoualé 196 C 4
Logroño 152 C 3
Logrosán 152 B 4
Lögstör 151 E 4
Lögurinn 150 C 2
Lohardaga 174 D 3
Lohit 175 G 2
Lohja (Lojo) 151 H 3
Lohjanjärvi 151 H 3
Lohjanselkä 151 H 3
Lohrville (IA.) 119 O 8
Loholoho 177 F 4
Lohrville (IA.) 119 O 8
Loikaw 175 G 4
Loimaa 151 H 3
Loimijoki 151 H 3
Loir 152 C 2
Loir, Vaux du 152 D 2
Loire 158 G 5
Loire, Val de 152 D 2
Loíza Aldea (P.R.) 130 D 8
Loja (Ecuador) 138 B 4
Loja 152 C 4
Loji 177 G 4
Lojo 151 H 3
Loka (Sudan) 198 E 4
Loka (Zaire) 198 B 4
Lokan tekojärvi 150 J 2
Lokaw 198 C 5
Löken 151 F 4
Lokgwabe 200 C 4
Lokhpodgort 159 N 2

Lokichar 199 F 4
Lokichokio 198 E 4
Lokilalaki, Gunung 177 F 4
Lokka 150 J 2
Lökken (Denmark) 151 E 4
Lökken (Norway) 150 E 3
Loknya 151 K 4
Loko (Centr. Afr. Rep.) 198 B 4
Loko (Nigeria) 197 F 4
Lokoja 197 F 4
Lokomo 197 H 5
Lokoro 198 C 5
Lokosovo 159 O 3
Loksa 151 J 4
Lokshak 171 O 5
Loks Land 105 P 3
Lokwa-Kangole 199 F 4
Lol 198 D 3
Lola 196 C 4
Lola, Mount 112 E 3
Loleta (CA.) 112 A 2
Loliondo 199 F 5
Lolita (TX.) 122 G 7
Lolland 151 F 5
Lolo 112 A 1
Lolo (MT.) 111 L 4
Loloda 177 G 3
Lolodorf 197 G 5
Lolo Hot Springs (MT.) 111 L 4
Lolo Peak 111 L 4
Lolowau 176 A 3
Lom (Bulgaria) 154 B 2
Lom (Cameroon) 197 G 4
Loma (CO.) 114 J 4MO
Loma (MT.) 111 P 3
Loma Alta (TX.) 122 C 6
Loma Bonita 132 C 4
Lomami 197 G 6
Loma Mountains 196 B 4
Loma Negra, Planicie de la 143 C 6
Loma Prieta 112 C 5
Lomas 140 B 4
Lomas Colorados 143 C 7
Lomas de Zamora 142 E 6
Lomax (IL.) 124 C 9
Lombarda, Serra 139 H 3
Lomblen, Pulau 177 F 5
Lombok 176 E 5
Lombok, Selat 176 E 5
Lomé 196 E 4
Lomela 198 C 5
Lomela 198 C 5
Lomététi 185 J 5
Lometa (TX.) 122 E 4
Lomié 197 G 5
Lomonosov 151 J 4
Lomonosovka 159 N 5
Lomovoye 158 GH 3
Lomphat 175 J 5
Lompobatang, Gunung 177 F 5
Lompoc (CA.) 113 E 8
Lom Sak 175 H 4
Łomz'a 149 H 4
Lo Nakpo 175 F 2
Loncoche 143 B 6
Loncopue 143 B 6
Londiani 198 F 5
London (KY.) 128 G 4
London (OH.) 128 H 2
London (Ontario, Can.) 105 L 7
London (TX.) 122 D 5
London (U.K.) 148 CD 4
Londonderry 143 B 10
Londonderry 148 B 4
Londonderry, Cape 182 D 1
Londonderry, Isla (Chile) 143 B 9
Londrina 141 F 5
Lone 112 H 4–5
Lone Mountain 118 E 5
Lone Mountains 112 H 4–5
Lone Pine (CA.) 112 GH 6
Lone Wolf (OK.) 120 F 7–8
Longa (Angola) 200 A 2
Longa (Angola) 200 B 2
Longa (Brazil) 141 H 1
Long Akah 176 DE 3
Long Bay 129 N 8
Long Beach (CA.) 113 G 9
Long Beach (MS.) 130 E 4
Long Beach (N.Y.) 127 F 8
Long Beach (WA.) 110 A 4
Longbleh 176 E 3
Long Branch (N.J.) 127 F 8
Longchuan 172 C 6
Long Creek (OR.) 110 F 6
Longde 172 E 3
Longfellow (TX.) 117 O 7
Longford (KS.) 120 H 3
Longford (Tasmania, Austr.) 184 L 9
Longford (U.K.) 148 B 4
Longhai 173 G 4
Longhua 173 G 2
Longhui 172 F 5
Long Island (KS.) 120 F 3
Long Island (N.Y.) 127 FG 8
Long Island (Papua New Guinea) 184 E 3
Long Island (Quebec, Can.) 105 M 5
Long Island (The Bahamas) 133 G 3
Long Island Sound 127 G 7

Longitudinal, Valle 143 B 6
Longjiang 171 M 6
Longkou 173 GH 3
Longlac 104 K 6
Long Lake (ME.) 126 L 1
Long Lake (ME.) 126 K 2
Long Lake (MI.) 125 L 4
Long Lake (N.D.) 118 H 4
Long Lake (N.Y.) 126 E 5
Long Lake (Ontario, Can.) 104 K 6
Long Lake (WA.) 110 H 3
Long Lake (WA.) 110 H 3
Longleju 176 E 3
Longlin 172 E 6
Longling 172 C 6
Longmen 172 F 6
Longmont (CO.) 115 M 3
Longnan 172 FG 6
Long Pine (NE.) 118 J 8
Long Prairie (MN.) 119 O 5
Longquan 173 G 5
Long Range Mountaines 105 Q 5–6
Longreach 183 G 3
Longsegah 176 E 3
Longshan 172 E 5
Longsheng 172 F 5
Longshou Shan 172 D 3
Longs Peak 115 M 3
Long Tom Reservoir 111 K 7
Longton (KS.) 120 J 5
Longvalley (SD.) 118 G 7
Long Valley Wash 112 K 2–3
Longview (TX.) 123 J 3
Longview (WA.) 110 BC 4
Longwy 153 E 2
Longxi 172 D 3
Long Xian 172 E 4
Long Xuyen 175 J 5
Longyan 172 G 5
Longyao 172 G 3
Longzhou 172 E 6
Lonkin 175 G 2
Lons-le-Saunier 153 E 2
Lonton 175 G 2
Lontra 139 H 4
Lontree (WY.) 111 P 9
Loo 155 E 2
Looc 177 F 1
Lookout, Cape (N.C.) 129 P 7
Lookout, Cape (OR.) 110 A 5
Lookout Mountain 110 E 6
Lookout Point Lake 110 C 7
Lookout Ridge 102 F 2
Loolmalasin 199 F 5
Loomis (NE.) 120 F 2
Loongana 182 D 5
Loon Lake (WA.) 110 H 2
Loop (TX.) 117 O 5
Loop Head 148 AB 4
Lop 169 L 3
Lopari 198 C 4
Lopatin 168 D 2
Lopatina, Gora 171 Q 5
Lopatka 171 T 5
Lopatka, Mys 171 T 5
Lopatki 159 N 5
Lop Buri 175 H 5
Lopcha 171 M 4
Lopeno (TX.) 122 D 9
Lopez, Cap 197 F 6
Lopez Point 112 D 6
Lop Nur 172 B 2
Lopphavet 150 H 1
Loppi 151 H 3
Lopud 153 G 3
Lopydino 158 K 3
Lora 169 H 4
Lora del Río 152 B 4
Lorain (OH.) 125 M 8
Loraine (TX.) 122 C 3
Loralai 169 H 4
Lorca 152 C 4
Lordegän (Iran) 157 F 3
Lord Howe Island 183 K 5
Lord Mayor Bay 103 TU 2
Lordsburg (N.M.) 116 H 5
Lorengau 184 E 2
Lorent 152 C 2
Lorenzo (ID.) 111 O 7
Lorenzo (NE.) 118 EF 9
Lorequville (LA.) 123 M 5
Lorestan (Iran) 157 E 2
Loreto 106 D 6
Loreto 138 D 4
Loreto (Maranhão, Brazil) 139 JK 5
Loreto (Mexico) 132 B 3
Loretta (WI.) 124 CD 4
Loretto (TN.) 128 D 6
Lorica 138 C 2
Lorida (FL.) 131 N 7
Loring (MT.) 111 S 2
Loris (S.C.) 129 N 7
Lorman (MS.) 130 CD 3
Lörrach 149 E 5
Lorraine 153 E 2
Lorraine (Queensland, Austr.) 183 F 2
Los 150 G 3
Los, Îles de 196 B 4
Los Alamos (CA.) 113 E 8

Los Alamos (N.M.) 117 K 2
Los Andes 142 B 5
Los Angeles (CA.) 113 G 9
Los Ángeles (Chile) 143 B 6
Los Antiguos 143 B 8
Losap 186 B 2
Los Banos (CA.) 112 E 5
Los Blancos 140 D 4
Los Coyotes Indian Reservation 113 J 9
Los Frentones 142 D 4
Los Fresnos (TX.) 122 F 9
Los Gatos (CA.) 112 CD 5
Lošinj 153 F 3
Losinoborskaya 159 R 4
Los Juríes 142 D 4
Los Lagos 143 B 6
Los Lavaderos 132 C 3
Los Lunas (N.M.) 117 K 3
Los Menucos 143 C 7
Los Mochis 106 E 6
Los Molinos (CA.) 112 CD 2
Los Monegros 152 C 3
Los Palacios 132 F 3
Los Pozos 142 BC 4
Los Reyes de Salgado 132 B 4
Los Roques, Islas 138 E 1
Lost Cabin (WY.) 111 S 7
Lost City (VA.) 129 N 3
Los Teques 138 E 1
Lost Hills (CA.) 113 F 7
Lost Peak 114 D 6
Lost Springs (WY.) 118 D 8
Lost Sprs (KS.) 120 H 4
Lost Trail Pass 111 M 5
Lostwood (ND.) 118 F 2
Losuia 185 F 3
Losuwo 177 G 3
Los Vilos 142 B 5
Lot 152 D 3
Lota 143 B 6
Loto 198 C 5
Lott (TX.) 122 F 4
Lotta 150 J 2
Lotuke, Jabal 198 E 4
Lou 184 E 2
Loubomo 197 G 6
Loubuzhuang 172 A 3
Loudéac 152 C 2
Loudon (TN.) 128 G 6
Loudonville (OH.) 125 M 9
Loudun 152 D 2
Loué 152 C 2
Louga 196 A 2
Lough Conn 148 B 4
Lough Neagh 148 B 4
Lough Ree 148 B 4
Lough Sheelin 148 B 4
Louhans 153 E 2
Louisa (KY.) 128 J 3
Louisa (VA.) 129 N 3
Louisa Reef 176 D 2
Louisburg (KS.) 121 L 4
Louisburg (N.C.) 129 N 5
Louise (MS.) 130 D 2
Louise (TX.) 122 G 6
Louise, Lake 109 J 3
Louisiade Archipelago 183 J 1
Louisiade Archipelago 185 F 4
Louisiana 123
Louisiana (MO.) 121 O 3
Louis Trichardt 200 DE 4
Louisville (CO.) 115 M 4
Louisville (GA.) 131 J 8
Louisville (IL.) 121 R 4
Louisville (KY.) 128 EF 3
Louisville (MS.) 130 EF 1
Louisville (NE.) 120 J 2
Loukhi 150 K 2
Loukolela 197 H 6
Loulan Yiji 172 A 2
Loum 197 FG 5
Loup City (NE.) 120 F 1
Loup River 120 GH 1
Loups Marins, Lacs des 105 N 4
Lourdes 152 C 3
Loústin 149 F 4
Louth (Australia) 183 H 5
Loutrá Killinis 154 B 3
Louviers 152 D 2
Louviers (CO.) 115 N 4
Louwater 200 B 4
Lövånger 150 H 3
Lovat 151 K 4
Loveči 154 B 2
Lovelady (TX.) 123 H 4
Loveland (CO.) 115 M 3
Loveland Pass 115 M 4
Lovell (WY.) 111 R 6
Lovelock (NV.) 112 G 2
Loves Park (IL.) 124 EF 7
Lovewell Reservoir 120 G 3
Loviisa 151 J 3
Loving (N.M.) 117 M 5
Loving (TX.) 122 E 2
Lovingston (VA.) 129 N 4
Lovington (IL.) 121 R 3
Lovington (N.M.) 117 N 4–5
Lovisa (Loviisa) 151 J 3
Lovozero 150 L 2

Lovozero, Ozero 150 L 2
Lóvua 200 C 1
Lóvua 200 C 2
Low (UT.) 114 E 3
Low, Cape 103 UV 3
Lowa 198 D 5
Lowa 198 D 5
Lowell (MA.) 126 H 6
Lowell (OR.) 110 C 7
Lowell, Lake 110 J 7
Lowelltown (ME.) 126 J 3
Lowemont (KS.) 121 K 3
Lowemont (MO.) 119 K 3
Lower Brule (SD.) 118 J 6
Lower Brule Indian Reservation 118 HJ 6
Lower California 106 D 6
Lower Goose Creek Reservoir 111 M 8
Lower Hutt 185 R 9
Lower Kalskag 108 F 3
Lower Klamath Lake 112 D 1
Lower Lake (CA.) 112 C 4
Lower Lake (CA./NV.) 112 EF 1
Lower Lough Erne 148 B 4
Lower Monumental Dam 110 G 4
Lower Post 102 M 4
Lower Red Lake 119 NO 3
Lower Tunguska River 170 F 3
Lower Ugashik Lake Wide Bay 108 G 4
Lowestoft 148 D 4
Lowicz 149 G 4
Lowman (ID.) 111 K 6
Lowry City (MO.) 121 M 4
Lowshān (Iran) 157 E 1
Lowville (N.Y.) 126 D 5
Loxton (South Africa) 200 C 6
Loxton (South Australia) 183 G 5
Loyalton (CA.) 112 E 3
Loyalton (SD.) 118 J 5
Loyalty Islands 185 J 6
Loyalty Islands 186 C 4
Loyal Valley (TX.) 122 DE 5
Loyauté, Iles 185 J 6
Loyoro 198 E 4
Lozeau (MT.) 111 L 3
Lozére, Mont 152 D 3
Loznica 154 A 2
Lozovaya 159 P 5
Loz'va 159 M 4
Lua 198 B 4
Luacano 200 C 2
Luahasibuka 176 A 4
Luala 201 F 3
Lualaba 198 D 5
Luama 198 D 6
Lua Makiki 113 F 11
Lu'an 173 G 4
Luanda 200 A 1
Luando 200 B 2
Luando 200 B 2
Luando Reserve 200 B 2
Luanginga 200 C 2
Luang Prabang 175 H 4
Luangue 200 B 1
Luangwa 201 E 2
Luangwa Valley Game Reserve 201 E 2
Luan He 173 G 2
Luanping 173 G 2
Luanshya 200 D 2
Luán Toro 143 D 6
Luan Xian 173 G 3
Luanza 198 D 6
Luapala 200 D 2
Luarca 152 B 3
Luashi 200 C 2
Luau 200 C 2
Luba 197 F 5
Lubalo 200 B 1
Lubāns Ezers 151 J 4
Lubang Islands 177 EF 1
Lubang Islands 177 EF 1
Lubango 200 A 2
Lubao 198 D 6
Lubartów 149 H 4
Lübbenau 149 F 4
Lubbock (TX.) 117 P 4
Lübeck 149 F 4
Lubec (ME.) 126 M 4
Lubefu 198 C 5
Lubefu 198 C 5
Lubero 198 D 5
Lubika 198 D 6
Lubilash 198 C 6
Lubin 149 G 4
Lublin 149 H 4
Lubnān, Jabal (Lebanon) 156 B 2
Lubny 158 F 5
Luboń 149 G 4
Lubondaie 198 D 6
Lubuagan 177 J 1
Lubudi 198 D 6
Lubue 198 B 5
Lubuklinggau 176 B 4
Lubumbashi 200 D 2
Lubwe 200 D 2
Lucala 200 B 1
Lucala 200 B 1
Lucania, Mount 102 J 3

Lucano, Appenino 153 G 3
Lucapa 200 C 1
Lucas 140 E 3
Lucas (KS.) 120 G 3
Lucas (KY.) 128 F 5
Lucas (SD.) 118 J 7
Lucas, Lake 182 D 3
Lucasville (OH.) 128 H 3
Lucca 153 F 2
Lucca (N.D.) 119 L 4
Lucea 133 G 4
Luce Bay 148 C 4
Lucedale (MS.) 130 F 4
Lucena (Philippines) 177 F 1
Lucena (Spain) 152 C 4
Lucenec 149 G 5
Lucera 153 G 3
Lucerne (CA.) 112 C 3
Lucerne (WA.) 110 E 2
Lucerne (WY.) 111 RS 7
Lucerne Lake 113 J 8
Lucerne Valley (CA.) 113 J 8
Lucero (Mexico) 106 E 5
Lucero (N.M.) 117 L 1
Lucero, Lake 117 K 5
Luchulingo 201 F 2
Lüchun 172 D 6
Lucile (ID.) 110 J 5
Lucin (UT.) 114 D 2
Lucira 200 A 2
Luck (WI.) 124 J 4
Luckenwalde 149 F 4
Lucknow 174 D 2
Lucksta 150 G 3
Lucky Peak Lake 111 J 7
Lucon 152 C 2
Lucusse 200 C 2
Lucy (N.M.) 117 KL 3
Lucy Creek 183 F 3
Lüda 173 H 3
Ludbreg 153 G 2
Ludden (N.D.) 119 K 5
Ludhiana 174 C 1
Ludian 172 D 5
Ludington (MI.) 124 H 6
Ludlow 148 C 4
Ludlow (CA.) 113 J 8
Ludlow (CO.) 115 N 6
Ludlow (MS.) 130 E 2
Ludlow (SD.) 118 E 5
Ludlowville (N.Y.) 126 C 6
Ludogorie 154 C 2
Ludovici (GA.) 131 N 3
Luduș 154 B 1
Ludvika 151 G 3
Ludwigsburg 149 E 5
Ludwigshafen 149 E 5
Ludwigslust 149 F 4
Ludza 151 J 4
Luebo 198 C 6
Lueders (TX.) 122 D 3
Lueki 198 D 5
Luena (Angola) 200 B 2
Luena (Angola) 200 C 2
Luena (Zaire) 198 D 6
Luena (Zambia) 201 E 2
Luena Flats 200 C 2
Luengue 200 C 3
Luepa 198 E 2
Lüeyang 172 E 4
Lufeng 172 D 5
Lufeng 172 G 6
Lufico 200 A 1
Lufira 198 D 6
Lufira, Chutcs de la 198 D 6
Lufira Falls 198 D 6
Lufkin (TX.) 123 J 4
Luga 151 J 4
Lugano 153 E 2
Lugansk → Voroshilovgrad 155 E 1
Luganville 186 C 4
Lugards Falls 199 F 5
Lugela 201 F 3
Lugenda 201 F 2
Lugnaquillia 148 B 4
Lugnvik 150 G 3
Lugo 152 B 3
Lugoj 154 B 1
Lugovoy 169 J 2
Lugovskiy 170 K 4
Luhin Sum 173 G 1
Luhuo 172 D 4
Lui 200 B 1
Luia 200 C 1
Luiana 200 C 3
Luiana 200 C 3
Luilaka 198 C 5
Luimneach 148 B 4
Luino 153 E 2
Luiro 150 J 2
Luís Correia 141 H 1
Luis d'Abreu → Calchaguí 142 D 4
Luishia 200 D 2
Luiza 198 C 6
Luizi 198 D 6
Lujiang 173 G 4

Lukachukai (AZ.) 116 G 1
Lukanga Swamp 200 D 2
Lukashkin Yar 159 P 3
Lukenie 198 B 5
Lukeville (AZ.) 116 D 6
Lukolela (Congo) 198 B 5
Lukolela (Zaire) 198 C 6
Lukonzolwa 198 D 6
Lukovit 154 B 2
Lukoyanov 158 H 4
Lukuga 198 D 6
Lukuka 197 G 7
Lukumburu 198 F 6
Lukuni 198 B 6
Lukusashi 201 E 2
Lula (MS.) 121 P 8
Luleå 150 H 2
Luleälven 150 H 2
Lüleburgaz 154 C 2
Luliang 172 D 5
Lüliang Shan 172 F 3
Lulimba 198 D 5
Luling (TX.) 122 F 6
Lulonga 198 B 4
Lulonga 198 B 4
Lulu (Saudi Arabia) 157 E 3
Lulua 198 C 6
Luma Cassai 200 B 2
Lumajangdong Co 174 D 1
Lumbala Kaquengue 200 C 2
Lumbala N'guimbo 200 C 2
Lumberton (MS.) 130 E 3–4
Lumberton (N.C.) 129 MN 7
Lumbo 201 G 3
Lumbovka 158 H 2
Lumbrales 152 B 3
Lumding 175 F 2
Lummi Indian Reservation 110 C 2
Lumpkin (GA.) 131 K 2
Lumsden 184 P 10
Lumuna 198 D 5
Lumut, Tanjung 176 C 4
Luna Pier (MI.) 125 L 8
Lunayyir, Harrat 194 F 3
Lund 151 F 4
Lund (UT.) 114 D 5
Lunda Norte 200 C 1
Lunda Sul 200 C 2
Lundazi 201 E 2
Lundevatn 151 E 4
Lundi → Runde 201 E 4
Lundu 176 C 3
Lundy 148 BC 4
Lüneburg 149 EF 4
Lüneburger Heide 149 EF 4
Lunel 152 D 3
Lunenburg (VA.) 129 N 5
Lunéville 153 E 2
Lunga 200 D 2
Lunggar 174 D 1
Lungleh 175 F 3
Lungue-Bungo 200 B 2
Luni 174 B 2
Luninets 151 J 5
Luning (NV.) 112 G 4
Lunkho 169 J 3
Lunovayam 171 U 3
Lunsar 196 B 4
Lunsemfwa 200 D 2
Luntai 169 L 2
Luobei 171 O 6
Luocheng 172 E 6
Luochuan 172 E 3
Luodian 172 E 5
Luoding 172 F 6
Luofu 198 D 5
Luo He 172 E 3
Luohe 172 F 4
Luoisiade 186 B 3
Luonan 172 F 4
Luong Nam Tha 175 H 3
Luonteri 150 J 3
Luoshan 172 FG 4
Luoxiao Shan 172 F 5
Luoyang 172 F 4
Luoyuan 173 GH 5
Luozi 197 G 6
Lupane 200 D 3
Lupan Shan 172 E 3
Lupeni 154 B 1
Luperón 133 H 4
Lupire 200 B 2
Lupton (AZ.) 116 G 2
Luputa 198 C 6
Lüq 199 G 4
Luqu 172 D 4
Luquan 172 D 5
Luquembo 200 B 2
Luquillo (P.R.) 130 D 8
Luquillo, Sierra de 130 D 8
Luray (KS.) 120 G 3
Luray (VA.) 129 N 3
Lure, Montagne de 153 E 3
Lurgan 148 B 4
Luribay 140 C 4
Lurín 140 A 3
Lurio 201 G 2
Lurio 201 G 2
Lusaka 200 D 3

Lusambo 198 C 5
Lusanga 198 B 5
Lusangi 198 D 5
Lush, Mount 182 D 2
Lushan 172 D 4
Lushi 172 F 4
Lushnja 154 A 2
Lushoto 199 F 5
Lushton (NE.) 120 H 2
Lushui 172 C 5
Lüshun 173 H 3
Lusitano 200 B 1
Lusk (WY.) 118 D 8
Lussanvira 141 F 5
Lustrafjorden 150 E 3
Lustre (MT.) 118 BC 2
Lūt, Dasht-e (Iran) 157 G 2
Lu Tao 173 H 6
Lutembo 200 C 2
Luther (IA.) 119 P 9
Luther (MI.) 124 J 5
Luther (MT.) 111 Q 5
Luther (OK.) 120 H 7
Lutie (TX.) 117 Q 2
Luton 148 C 4
Lutong 176 D 3
Lutshima 198 B 6
Lutsk 151 J 5
Lutuai 200 B 2
Luusua 150 J 2
Luverne (AL.) 131 H 3
Luverne (IA.) 119 O 8
Luverne (MN.) 119 M 7
Luvua 198 D 6
Luvuei 200 C 2
Luwegu 199 F 6
Luwingu 200 D 2
Luwuk 177 F 4
Luxembourg 148 E 5
Luxi 172 C 6
Luxi 172 D 6
Luxor 194 E 3
Luxora (AR.) 121 Q 7
Luza 158 J 3
Luza 158 J 3
Luzern 153 E 2
Luzhai 172 E 6
Luzhou 172 E 5
Luzhskaya Vozvyshennost' 151 J 4
Luziânia 141 G 4
Luzilândia 141 H 1
Luzino 159 QR 2
Luzon 177 J 1
Luzon Strait 177 J 1
Lvov 158 D 6
L'vovka 159 P 4
Lyady 151 J 4
Lyakhovskiy, Bol'shoy, Ostrov 171 Q 1
Lyakhovskiy, Malyy, Ostrov 171 Q 1
Lyakhovskiye Ostrova 171 P 1
Lyamin 159 O 3
Lycksele 150 G 3
Lydenburg 200 DE 5
Lygyy, Mys 170 LM 1
Lyle (MN.) 119 Q 7
Lyman (IA.) 119 O 9
Lyman (WY.) 111 P 9
Lyman Lake 116 G 3
Lyme Bay 148 C 4
Lynch (NE.) 119 K 8
Lynchburg (MO.) 121 N 5
Lynchburg (S.C.) 129 LM 7
Lynchburg (TN.) 128 E 6
Lynchburg (VA.) 129 M 4
Lynches River 129 L 7
Lynd 183 G 2
Lynden (WA.) 110 C 2
Lyndhurst (Queensland, Austr.) 183 G 2
Lyndon (KS.) 121 K 4
Lyndon B. Johnson, Lake 122 E 5
Lyndon River 182 A 3
Lyndonville (VT.) 126 G 4
Lynd River 183 G 2
Lyngdal 151 E 4
Lyngen 150 H 2
Lyngseidet 150 H 2
Lynn (AL.) 128 D 7
Lynn (IN.) 125 K 9
Lynn (MA.) 126 J 6
Lynn (UT.) 114 D 2
Lynn Canal 102 K 4
Lynndyl (UT.) 114 E 4
Lynn Lake 103 R 4
Lynnwood (WA.) 110 C 3
Lynx Lake 103 Q 3
Lyon 153 DE 2
Lyon Inlet 103 V 2
Lyon Mountain (N.Y.) 126 E 4
Lyonnais, Monts du 153 D 2
Lyons (GA.) 131 M 2
Lyons (KS.) 120 G 4
Lyons (NE.) 119 M 9
Lyons (TX.) 122 G 5
Lyons Falls (N.Y.) 126 D 5
Lyons River 182 B 3
Lysefjorden 151 E 4
Lysekil 151 F 4
Lysite (WY.) 111 S 7
Lyskovo 158 H 4
Łyso Gory 149 H 4

Lys'va 159 L 4
Lysye Gory 158 H 5
Lytle (TX.) 122 E 6
Lytton 103 N 5
Lyuban' 151 K 4
Lyubar 151 J 6
Lyubertsy 158 G 4
Lyubeshov 151 J 5
Lyuboml 151 H 5
Lyucha 170 G 3
Lyudinovo 158 FG 5
Lyuri 171 W 3

M

Maalaea (HI.) 113 F 11
Ma'āmīr (Iraq) 157 E 3
Ma'ān (Jordan) 156 B 3
Maanselkä 150 J 3
Ma'anshan 173 G 4
Maarianhamina (Mariehamn) 151 H 3
Ma'arrat an Nu'mān (Syria) 156 B 2
Maas 148 E 4
Maasin 177 F 1
Maastricht 148 E 4
Maaza Plateau → Al Haḍabat al Ma'āzah 194 E 3
Mabaia 200 A 1
Mabalane 201 E 4
Mabank (TX.) 122 G 3
Ma'bar 195 G 6
Mabaruma 139 G 2
Mabelle (TX.) 122 D 2
Mableton (GA.) 128 G 8
Mabote 201 E 4
Mabrous 197 G 1
Mabrūk 193 J 3
Mabton (WA.) 110 EF 4
Mabuasehube 200 C 5
Mabuki 198 E 5
Ma'būs Yūsuf 193 K 3
Maca, Monte 143 B 8
Macaé 141 H 5
Macaíba 141 J 2
Macalister River 183 H 6
Macaloge 201 F 2
MacAlpine Lake 103 R 2
Macao 172 F 6
Macapá 139 H 3
Macará (Peru) 138 B 4
Macarena, Parque Nacional de la 138 D 3
Macas 138 C 4
Macau 141 J 2
Macaúba 141 F 3
Macauley 186 D 4–5
Macclenny (FL.) 131 M 4
Macclesfield 148 C 4
Macdoel (CA.) 112 D 1
Macdonald, Lake 182 D 3
MacDonald Pass 111 N 4
Macdonnell Ranges 182 E 3
Macedo de Cavaleiros 152 B 3
Maceió 141 J 2
Macenta 196 C 4
Macerata 153 F 3
Mach 169 H 5
Macha 170 L 4
Machacamarca 140 C 4
Machachi 138 C 4
Machaíla 201 E 4
Machakos 199 F 5
Machala 138 C 4
Machar Marshes 198 E 3
Machattie, Lake 183 FG 3
Machaze 201 E 4
Machece 201 F 3
Macheke 201 E 3
Macheng 172 FG 4
Machera 155 D 4
Machevna 171 W 3
Machias (ME.) 126 M 4
Machilipatnam 174 D 4
Machiques 138 D 1
Machupicchu 140 B 3
Macia 201 E 5
Măcin 154 C 1
Macina 196 D 3
Mack (CO.) 114 J 4
Maçka 155 E 2
Mackay 183 H 3
Mackay (ID.) 111 M 7
Mackay, Lake 182 D 3
Mackay Reservoir 111 M 7
Mackenzie 102 LM 2
Mackenzie Bay 102 K 2
Mac Kenzie Bay 203
Mackenzie King Island 202
Mackenzie Mountains 102–103 LM 2–3
Mackenzie River 183 H 3
Mackinac, Stratis of 125 K 4
Mackinac Island (MI.) 125 K 4
Mackinaw City (MI.) 125 K 4
Mackinaw River 124 E 9
Mac Kinlay River 183 G 3

Mackinnon Road 199 F 5
Macksville (KS.) 120 G 5
Maclean 183 J 4
Macmillan 102 L 3
Macmillan Pass 102 L 3
Macocola 200 B 1
Macomb (IL.) 124 D 9
Macomer 153 E 3
Macomia 201 FG 2
Macondo 200 C 2
Mac Pherson Range 183 J 4
Macquarie Harbour 184 L 9
Macquarie Island 203
Macquarie River 183 H 5
Mac Robertson Land 203
Macujer 138 D 3
Macumba 183 F 4
Macusani 140 B 3
Macuze 201 F 3
Mačva Podluzje 154 A B 2
Macwahoc (ME.) 126 L 3
Ma'dabā (Jordan) 156 B 3
Madadi 197 J 2
Madagali 197 G 3
Madagascar 201 G 3
Madā'in Sālih (Saudi Arabia) 156 C 4
Madama 197 G 1
Madan 146
Madang 184 E 3
Madang 186 A 3
Madanīyīn 193 H 2
Madaoua 197 F 3
Madarounfa 197 F 3
Madau 185 F 3
Madawaska (ME.) 126 L 1
Madawaska Highlands 105 M 6
Madaya 175 G 3
Madd, Ra's Abū (Saudi Arabia) 156 B 4
Maddaloni 153 F 3
Maddock (ND.) 118 J 3
Madeir 198 D 3
Madeira (Brazil) 139 F 4–5
Madeira (Portugal) 192 B 2
Madeleine, Île de la 105 P 6
Madelia (MN.) 119 O 6
Madeline (CA.) 112 E 1
Madeline Island 124 D 3
Maden 155 F 2
Maden 155 E 3
Madeniyet 159 P 6
Madeniyet 168 F 2
Madera (CA.) 112 EF 6
Madero, Puerto del 152 C 3
Madesimo 153 E 2
Madetkoski 150 J 2
Madhipura 174 E 2
Madhubani 174 E 2
Madhupur Jungle 175 F 3
Madhya Pradesh 174 CD 3
Madidi 140 C 3
Madill (OK.) 120 J 8
Madimba 198 B 5
Madina 196 B 3
Madīnat ash Sha'b 195 G 6
Madingo-Kayes 197 G 6
Madingou 197 G 6
Madirovalo 201 H 3
Madison (AL.) 131 H 2
Madison (FL.) 131 L 4
Madison (GA.) 128 H 8
Madison (IN.) 128 F 3
Madison (KS.) 120 J 4
Madison (ME.) 126 K 4
Madison (MN.) 119 M 5
Madison (MS.) 130 D 2
Madison (N.C.) 129 M 5
Madison (NE.) 119 L 9
Madison (S.D.) 119 L 7
Madison (VA.) 129 N 3
Madison (WI.) 124 E 6
Madison (W.V.) 129 K 3
Madison Range 111 O 5
Madison River 111 O 5
Madisonville (KY.) 128 D 4
Madisonville (TN.) 128 G 6
Madisonville (TX.) 122 H 5
Madiun 176 D 5
Madjingo 197 G 5
Mad Lake 111 N 7
Mado Gashi 199 F 4
Madoi 197 J 4
Madonie 153 F 4
Madrakah 195 FG 4
Madrakah, Ra's al 195 K 5
Madras (India) 174 D 5
Madras (OR.) 110 D 6
Madre, Sierra 132 D 4
Madre de Dios 140 C 3
Madre de Dios 140 C 3
Madre de Dios, Isla 143 AB 9
Madre del Sur, Sierra 132 B 4
Madre Oriental, Sierra 132 BC 2–3
Madrid 152 C 3
Madrid (AL.) 131 J 3
Madrid (IA.) 119 P 9
Madrid (NE.) 120 D 2

Madrid (NE.) 120 D 2
Madridejos 152 C 4
Mad River 125 L 9
Madrona, Sierra 152 C 4
Mādrūsah 193 H 4
Madura, Pulau 176 D 5
Madura, Selat 176 D 5
Madurai 174 C 6
Madurantakam 174 C 5
Madyan (Saudi Arabia) 156 B 4
Madzha 158 K 3
Maebashi 173 L 3
Mae Hong Son 175 G 4
Mae Nam Mun 175 H 4
Mae Nam Nan 175 H 4
Mae Nam Yom 175 G 4
Mae Rim 175 G 4
Mae Sariang 175 G 4
Mae Sot 175 G 4
Maevatanana 201 H 3
Mafeking 200 D 5
Mafeteng 200 D 5
Mafia Island 199 FG 6
Mafikeng [Mmbatho] 200 D 5
Mafra 142 FG 4
Magadan 171 S 4
Magadi 199 F 5
Magallanes, Estrecho de 143 B 9
Magalo 199 G 3
Maganja 201 F 3
Magaria 197 F 3
Magarida 185 E 4
Magazine Mountain 121 M 7
Magburaka 196 B 4
Magdagachi 171 N 5
Magdala 199 F 2
Magdalena (Bolivia) 140 D 3
Magdalena (Colombia) 138 D 1–2
Magdalena (Mexico) 106 D 5
Magdalena (N.M.) 117 J 3
Magdalena, Bahia 106 D 7
Magdalena, Isla (Chile) 143 B 7
Magdalena, Isla (Mexico) 106 D 7
Magdalena, Punta 138 C 3
Magdeburg 149 F 4
Magee (MS.) 130 E 3
Magelang 176 C 5
Magellan, Strait of 143 BC 9
Magenta 153 E 2
Magenta, Lake 182 B 5
Magerøya 150 J 1
Maggiorasca 153 E 3
Maggiore, Lago 153 E 2
Maghāgha 194 E 3
Maghama 192 C 5
Maghnia 192 E 2
Magic Reservoir 111 L 7
Maglaj 153 G 3
Maglie 153 G 3
Magma (AZ.) 116 E 4
Magnitogorsk 159 L 5
Magnolia (AR.) 121 M 9
Magnolia (KY.) 128 F 4
Magnolia (MS.) 130 D 3
Magnolia (TX.) 123 H 5
Magnor 151 F 4
Mago 171 Q 5
Mágoè 201 E 3
Magosa → Famagusta 155 D 3
Magpie 105 P 5
Magruder Mountain 112 H 5
Magta Lahjar 192 C 5
Maguarinho, Cabo 139 J 4
Magude 201 E 5
Magumeri 197 G 3
Măgura Priei 154 B 1
Magwalt (TX.) 117 N 6
Magwe 175 G 3
Magyarország 154 A 1
Magyichaung 175 F 3
Mahābād (Iran) 157 D 1
Mahabalipuram 174 D 5
Mahabe 198 D 4
Mahabharat Range 174 E 2
Mahabo 201 G 4
Mahadday Wēyne 199 H 4
Mahadeo Hills 174 C 3
Mahadeo Range 174 B 4
Mahagi 198 E 4
Mahajamba 201 H 3
Mahajan 174 B 2
Mahajanga 201 H 3
Mahakam, Sungai 176 E 3
Mahalapye 200 D 4
Mahalevona 201 J 3
Mahallāt (Iran) 157 F 2
Mahān 168 F 4
Mahanadi 174 DE 3
Mahanoro 201 H 3
Maharashtra 174 BC 4
Mahārlū, Daryāchēh-ye (Iran) 157 F 3
Maḥas 199 H 4
Mahasamund 174 D 3
Maha Sarakham 175 H 4
Mahaska (KS.) 120 H 2
Mahatalaky 201 H 4
Mahatsanary 201 G 5
Mahavavy 201 H 3

Madrid (NE.) 120 D 2
Mahbés 192 D 3
Mahbubnagar 174 C 4
Mahd adh Dhahab 195 G 4
Mahd adh Dhahab (Saudi Arabia) 156 C 5
Mahdah (Oman) 157 G 4
Mahdia (Algeria) 193 F 1
Mahdia (Guyana) 139 G 2
Mahè 174 C 5
Mahébourg 201 K 6
Mahendragirii 174 D 4
Mahenge 199 F 6
Mahesana 174 B 3
Maheshwar 174 C 3
Mahi 174 B 3
Mahi 174 B 3
Mahia Peninsula 185 R 8
Mahin 197 E 4
Mahkene 150 F 3
Mahmudiye 154 D 3
Mahmūdābād (Iran) 157 F 1
Mahmudiye 154 D 3
Mähneshān (Iran) 157 E 1
Mahmud-Raqi 169 HJ 3
Mahnomen (MN.) 119 N 3
Mahogany Mountain 110 H 7
Mahón 152 F 4
Mahony Lake 109 O 2
Mahrāṭ, Jabal 195 J 5
Māh Shahr, Bandar (Iran) 157 E 3
Mahuva 174 B 3
Mahwa 174 C 2
Mahyār (Iran) 157 F 2
Maiana 186 C 2
Maïao 187 F 4
Maicao 138 D 1
Maicurú 139 H 4
Maida (N.D.) 119 K 2
Maiduguri 197 G 3
Maigudo 197 F 3
Maihar 174 D 3
Maijdi 175 F 3
Maikala Range 174 D 3
Maiko 198 D 5
Maiko National Park 198 D 5
Maimana 169 G 3
Mai Munene 198 C 6
Main 149 E 5
Maínalon Óros 154 B 3
Main Barrier Range 183 G 5
Mai-Ndombe, Lac 198 B 5
Maine 126
Maine, Gulf of 126 KM 6
Mainland (Orkney Is., U.K.) 148 C 3
Mainland (Shetland Is., U.K.) 148 C 2
Mainling 172 B 5
Mainoru 182 E 1
Mainpuri 174 C 2
Maintirano 201 G 3
Mainz 149 E 5
Maio 196 B 6
Maipo, Volcán 142 C 5
Maipú (Argentina) 143 E 6
Maipú (Chile) 142 B 5
Maipuco 138 C 4
Maiquetía 138 E 1
Maisi, Punta 133 H 3
Maiskhal 175 F 3
Maitengwe 200 D 4
Maitland (CO.) 115 N 6
Maitland (N.S.W., Austr.) 183 J 5
Maitland (South Australia) 183 F 5
Maitland, Lake 182 C 4
Maiyu, Mount 182 D 2
Maíz, Isla del 132 F 5
Maizhokunggar 172 B 5
Maizuru 173 L 3
Majaagual 138 D 2
Majardah 153 EF 4
Majdanpek 154 B 2
Majene 177 E 4
Majērtēn 199 HJ 3
Maji 198 F 3
Majune 201 F 2
Majuriã 138 E 5
Majuro 186 C 2
Maka 196 B 3
Makabana 197 G 6
Makah Indian Reservation 110 A 2
Makahuena Point 113 C 10
Makalamabedi 200 C 4
Makale (Ethiopia) 199 F 2
Makale (Indonesia) 177 E 4
Makalu, Mount 174 E 2
Makambako 198 EF 6
Makanchi 159 Q 6
Makanrushi, Ostrov 171 S 6
Makanza 198 C 4
Makapuu Point 113 E 10
Makari 197 G 3
Makarikari 200 D 4
Makarov 171 Q 6
Makarova 170 D 1
Makarovo 158 H 5
Makarovo 170 J 4
Makā Rūd (Iran) 157 F 1

Makaryev 158 H 4
Makassar 177 E 4–5
Makassar, Selat 176 E 4
Makassar Strait 176 E 4
Makat 168 E 1
Makatea 187 F 4
Makaw 175 G 2
Makay, Massif du 201 H 4
Makedhonía 154 B 2
Makedonia 154 B 2
Makemo 187 F 4
Makeni 196 B 4
Makeyevka 155 E 1
Makgadikgadi Pan 200 D 4
Makgadikgadi Pans Game Reserve 200 CD 4
Makhachkala 168 D 2
Makharadze 155 F 2
Makhfar al Buşayyah (Iraq) 157 D 3
Makhfar al Ḥammām (Syria) 156 C 2
Makhmūr (Iraq) 156 D 2
Maki 177 H 4
Makian, Pulau 177 G 3
Makinsk 159 O 5
Makkah 195 FG 4
Makkovik 105 Q 4
Maknassy 193 G 2
Makó 154 B 1
Makokou 197 G 5
Makoli 200 D 3
Makongolosi 198 E 6
Makopse 155 E 2
Makorako 185 R 8
Makoua 197 H 6
Makovskoye 159 R 2
Makrai 174 C 3
Makran 168–169 FG 5
Makri 174 D 4
Maksimkiy Yar 159 R 4
Maksimovka 173 L 1
Makteir 192 C 4
Makū (Iran) 157 F 3
Makumbi 198 C 6
Makung 173 G 6
Makunza 198 C 6
Makurazaki 173 JK 4
Makurdi 197 F 4
Makushino 159 N 4
Makushin Volcano 102 D 5
Makuyuni 199 F 5
Makwa 185 J 2
Mal 192 C 5
Mala 140 A 3
Malá 150 G 2
Malabang 177 F 2
Malabar Coast 174 BC 5–6
Malabo 197 F 5
Malacacheta 139 FG 3
Malacca, Strait of 176 B 3
Malacky 149 G 5
Malá Fatra 149 G 5
Málaga 152 C 4
Málaga (N.M.) 117 M 5
Malagarasi 198 E 5–6
Malagasy Republic 201 G 3
Malagón 152 C 4
Malaimbandy 201 H 4
Malaita 185 H 3
Malaita 186 B 3
Malakāl 198 E 3
Malakanagiri 174 D 4
Malakand 169 J 4
Mala Kapela 153 G 2–3
Malakoff (TX.) 122 G 3
Malakula 186 C 4
Malam 184 D 3
Malang 176 D 5
Malanje 200 B 1
Malanville 196 E 3
Malao 185 J 5
Mälaren 151 G 4
Malargue 143 C 6
Malaripo 139 H 3
Malaspina (Argentina) 143 C 7
Malaspina Glacier 102 J 4
Malatayur, Tanjung 176 D 4
Malatya 155 E 3
Malatya Dağları 155 E 3
Malawi 201 E 2
Malāwī (Iran) 157 E 2
Malawi, Lake 201 E 2
Malawi National Park 201 E 2
Malawiya 194 F 5
Malax 150 H 3
Malaya 176 D 4
Malaya Baranikha 171 V 2
Malaya Sos'va 159 M 3
Malaya Vishera 154 E 3
Malaya Viška 154 D 1
Malaybalay 177 G 2
Malāyer (Iran) 157 E 2
Malaysia 176 CD 2
Malazgirt 155 F 3
Malbon 183 G 3
Malbork 149 G 4
Malbrán 142 D 4
Malcolm 182 C 4
Malda 174 E 2

Malden 187 E 3
Malden (MO.) 121 P 6
Maldives 174 B 6
Maldonado 142 F 5
Malé 153 F 2
Maleás, Ákra 154 B 3
Malegaon 174 B 3
Maléha 196 C 3
Malei 201 F 3
Malek 198 E 3
Malekābād (Iran) 157 EF 2
Malé Karpaty 149 G 5
Malek Kandī (Iran) 157 DE 1
Malekula 185 J 5
Malema 201 F 2
Maleta 170 J 5
Maleyevo 170 G 4
Maleza 138 E 3
Malgobek 155 F 2
Malgomaj 150 G 3
Malha 194 D 5
Malhada 141 H 3
Malheur Lake 110 G 7
Malheur Reservoir 110 H 6
Malheur River 110 H 7
Mali 196 CD 2–3
Mali (Guinea) 196 B 3
Maliana 177 G 5
Malianjing 172 C 2
Mali Hka 175 G 2
Mali i Gribës 154 A 2
Mali i Ostroviçës 154 B 2
Mali i Tomorit 154 B 2
Malik 177 F 4
Malik, Wādī al 194 D 5
Mali Kanal 154 A 1
Malik Naro 169 G 5
Mali Kyun 175 G 5
Malili 177 F 4
Mali Lošinj 153 F 3
Malimba, Monts 198 D 6
Malin 151 J 5
Malin (OR.) 110 D 8
Malindi 199 G 5
Maling, Gunung 177 F 3
Malin Head 148 B 3
Malinovka 159 R 4
Malinovoye Ozero 159 PQ 5
Malinyi 199 F 6
Malipo 172 D 6
Malita 177 G 2
Maljamar (N.M.) 117 N 5
Malka 155 F 2
Malkachan 171 S 4
Malkaïli (Iran) 157 E 2
Malkara 154 C 2
Malkhanskiy Khrebet 170 JK 5
Mallacoota 183 H 6
Mallaig 148 B 3
Mallani 174 B 2
Mallawī 194 E 3
Mallery Lake 103 S 3
Mallorca 152 D 4
Malm 150 F 3
Malmberget 150 H 2
Malmesbury (South Africa) 200 B 6
Malmö 151 F 4
Malmo (MN.) 119 P 4
Malo (WA.) 110 G 2
Maloca 139 G 3
Maloca 139 H 5
Maloca de Indios 140 E 3
Maloca do Gonçalo 139 G 5
Maloelap 186 C 2
Malole 201 E 2
Malolos 177 F 1
Malone (FL.) 131 J 4
Malone (N.Y.) 126 E 4
Maloney, Lake 120 E 1
Malonga 200 C 2
Malorita 151 H 5
Maloshuyka 158 G 3
Malosofiyevka 155 D 1
Malott (WA.) 110 F 2
Mâløy 150 D 3
Malozemel'skaya Tundra 158 JK 2
Malpelo, Isla 138 B 3
Malpura 174 C 2
Malta 153 F 4
Malta (ID.) 111 M 8
Malta (MT.) 111 S 2
Maltahöhe 200 B 4
Maluku 177 G 4
Maluku, Laut 177 G 3
Malunda 177 E 4
Malung 151 F 3
Malūṭ 194 E 6
Malvan 174 B 4
Malvern (AR.) 121 N 8
Malvern (IA.) 119 N 9–10
Malvinas, Islas → Falkland Islands 143 DE 9
Malwa 174 C 3
Malya 198 E 5
Maly Kavkaz 155 FG 2
Malykay 170 L 3
Malyovitsa 154 B 2
Malyshevka 159 QR 2

Malyy Anyuy 171 U 2
Malyye Derbety 155 FG 1
Malyye Derbety 168 CD 1
Malyy Lyakhovskiy, Ostrov 171 Q 1
Malyy Yenisey 170 FG 5
Mama 170 K 4
Mamagota 185 G 3
Mamaia 154 C 2
Mamakan 170 K 4
Mamara 140 B 3
Mamberamo, Sungai 177 J 4
Mambéré 198 B 4
Mambili 197 H 5
Mambrui 199 G 5
Mamburao 177 F 1
Mamfe 197 F 4
Mamiña 140 C 4
Mamlyutka 159 N 5
Mammamattawe 104 L 5
Mammoth (AZ.) 116 F 5
Mammoth Cave (KY.) 128 E 4
Mammoth Cave National Park 128 E 4
Mammoth Hot Springs (WY.) 111 P 6
Mammoth Lakes (CA.) 112 G 5
Mammoth Pool Reservoir 112 F 5
Mammoth Spring (AR.) 121 O 6
Mamonovo 151 H 5
Mamonta, Poluostrov 170 C 1
Mamoré 140 C 3
Mamou 196 B 3
Mamou (LA.) 123 L 5
Mamoun 198 C 2
Mampikony 201 H 3
Mampodre 152 BC 3
Mampong 196 D 4
Mamry, Jezioro 149 H 4
Mamué 200 A 2
Mamuju 177 E 4
Mamuno 200 C 4
Man 196 C 4
Man, Isle of 148 C 4
Mana (French Guiana) 139 H 3
Mana (HI.) 113 C 9
Mana (U.S.S.R.) 170 F 4
Manacacías 138 D 3
Manacapuru 139 F 4
Manacapuru, Lago de 139 F 4
Manacor 152 D 4
Manado 177 F 3
Managua 132 E 5
Managua, Lago de 132 E 5
Manakara 201 H 4
Manakau 185 Q 9
Manākhah 195 G 6
Manama (Qatar) 157 F 4
Manambao 201 G 3
Manam Island 184 E 2
Manam Island 186 A 3
Manan ara 201 H 3
Mananara [River] 201 H 4
Manandréa 201 G 4
Manangoora 183 F 2
Mananjary 201 H 4
Manankoro 196 C 3
Manantenina 201 H 4
Manantiales 142 D 4
Manapouri 184 P 10
Manapouri 186 C 6
Manāqīsh (Kuwait) 157 E 3
Manas (Bhutan) 175 F 2
Manas (China) 169 M 2
Manas He 169 M 2
Manas Hu 169 M 1
Manaslu 174 D 2
Manassas (VA.) 129 O 3
Manatí (P.R.) 130 C 8
Manatuto 177 G 5
Manaua Loa 187 E 1
Manaus 139 FG 4
Manavgat 154 D 3
Manbij (Syria) 156 BC 1
Mancelona (MI.) 124 J 5
Mancha Blanca 143 C 7
Mancheng 172 FG 3
Manchester 148 C 4
Manchester (CA.) 112 B 4
Manchester (CT.) 126 G 7
Manchester (GA.) 131 K 2
Manchester (IA.) 119 R 8
Manchester (KS.) 120 H 3
Manchester (KY.) 128 H 4
Manchester (N.H.) 126 H 6
Manchester (OH.) 128 H 3
Manchester (TN.) 128 EF 6
Manchester (VT.) 126 F 5
Manchuria 173 HJ 2
Manciano 153 F 3
Mancinik 155 E 3
Mancınık Dağı 154 C 3
Mancınık Dağı 154 C 3
Máncora 138 B 4
Mancos (CO.) 115 J 6
Mand (Iran) 157 F 3
Mand (Iran) 157 F 3
Manda 201 E 2
Manda, Jabal 198 C 3

Mandabe 201 G 4
Manda Hills 174 B 3
Manda Island 199 G 5
Mandal (Mongolia) 170 H 6
Mandal (Norway) 151 E 4
Mandalay 175 G 3
Mandalgovı̆ 172 E 1
Mandalī (Iraq) 157 D 2
Mandal-Ovoo 172 D 2
Mandalya Körfezi 154 C 3
Mandan (N.D.) 118 H 4
Mandaon 177 F 1
Mandaree (N.D.) 118 F 3
Mandas 153 E 4
Mandasor 174 B 3
Mandawa 199 F 6
Mandera 199 G 4
Manderson (WY.) 111 S 6
Mandeville 133 G 4
Mandeville (LA.) 123 NO 5
Mandi 174 C 1
Mandiana 196 C 3
Mandimba 201 F 2
Mandinga 138 C 2
Mandingues, Monts 196 B 3
Mandioli, Pulau 177 G 4
Mandioré, Lago 140 E 4
Mandjafa 197 H 3
Mandji 197 G 6
Mandla 174 D 3
Mandö 151 E 4
Mandor 176 C 3
Mandora 182 C 2
Mandoúdhion 154 B 3
Mandritsara 201 H 3
Mandurah 182 B 5
Manduria 153 G 3
Mandvi 174 A 3
Mandya 174 C 5
Manendragarh 174 D 3
Maneromango 199 F 6
Manevichi 151 J 5
Manfalut 194 E 3
Manfredonia 153 G 3
Manfredonia, Golfo di 153 G 3
Manga (Minas Gerais, Brazil) 141 H 3
Manga (Niger/Chad) 197 GH 3
Mangabeiras, Chapada das 141 G 2–3
Mangai 198 B 5
Mangaia 187 E 4
Mangalia 154 C 2
Mangalmé 197 H 3
Mangalore 174 B 5
Mangareva 187 G 4
Manggawitu 177 H 4
Mangit 168 G 2
Mangkalihat, Tanjung 177 E 3
Manglar Alto 138 B 4
Manglares, Cabo 138 C 3
Mangnai 172 B 3
Mangoche 201 EF 2
Mangoky 201 G 4
Mangole, Pulau 177 G 4
Mangueigne 197 J 3
Mangueira, Lagoa 142 F 5
Mangui 171 M 5
Manguredjipa 198 D 4
Mangut 170 K 6
Mangyshlak, Poluostrov 168 E 2
Manhan 170 F 6
Manhattan (KS.) 120 J 3
Manhattan (MT.) 111 O 5
Manhica 201 E 5
Manhuacu 141 H 5
Maní (Colombia) 138 D 3
Mani (Zaire) 198 D 6
Manianko 196 C 3
Manica 201 E 3
Manicaland 201 E 3
Manicore 139 F 5
Manicouagan 105 O 5
Manicouagan, Réservoir 105 O 5
Maniema 191
Manifa (Saudi Arabia) 157 E 4
Maniganggo 172 C 4
Manihi 187 F 3
Manihiki 186 E 3
Manila 177 F 1
Manila (AR.) 121 P 7
Manila (UT.) 114 H 3
Manilla (IA.) 119 N 9
Manimbaya, Tanjung 177 E 4
Maningrida 182 E 1
Manipa 201 F 4
Manipa, Selat 177 G 4
Manipur 175 F 3
Manipur 175 F 3
Manisa 154 C 3
Manises 152 C 4
Manistee (MI.) 124 H 5
Manistee River 124 J 5
Manistique (MI.) 124 H 4
Manistique Lake 124 J 3

Manitoba 103 S 5
Manitoba, Lake 103 S 5
Manitou Island 124 G 2
Manitoulin Island 104 L 6
Manitou Springs (CO.) 115 N 5
Manitowish (WI.) 124 E 3
Manitowoc (WI.) 124 G 5
Maniwaki 105 M 6
Manizales 138 C 2
Manja 201 G 4
Manjacaze 201 E 4
Manjakandriana 201 H 3
Manjil (Iran) 157 E 1
Manjimup 182 B 5
Manjra 174 C 4
Mankato (KS.) 120 G 3
Mankato (MN.) 119 P 6
Mankhere 174 D 3
Mankim 197 G 5
Mankins (TX.) 122 E 2
Mankono 196 C 4
Manlay 172 E 2
Manlleu 152 D 3
Manly (IA.) 119 P 7
Manmad 174 BC 3
Man Na 175 G 3
Manna 176 B 4
Mannahill 183 F 5
Mannar 174 C 6
Mannar, Gulf of 174 C 6
Mannheim 149 E 5
Manning (Alberta, Can.) 103 O 4
Manning (IA.) 119 NO 9
Manning (ND.) 118 F 3
Manning (S.C.) 129 L 8
Mannington (W.V.) 129 L 2
Manns Harbor (N.C.) 129 Q 6
Mannu, Capo 153 E 3
Manoa 138 E 5
Manokotek 108 G 4
Manokwari 177 H 4
Manombo 201 G 4
Manompana 201 HJ 3
Manonga 198 E 5
Manono 198 D 6
Manor (TX.) 122 F 5
Manoron 175 G 5
Manosque 153 E 3
Manouane 105 N 6
Manouane, Lac 105 N 5
Manp'ojin 173 J 2
Manra 186 B 3
Manresa 152 D 3
Mansa 200 D 2
Mansa Konko 196 A 3
Mansehra 169 J 4
Mansel Island 105 L 3
Mansfield (AR.) 121 L 7
Mansfield (GA.) 128 H 8
Mansfield (LA.) 123 K 3–4
Mansfield (MO.) 121 N 5
Mansfield (OH.) 125 M 9
Mansfield (PA.) 126 BC 7
Mansfield (U.K.) 148 C 4
Mansfield (WA.) 110 F 3
Mansfield, Mount 126 G 4
Mansfield Lake 128 D 2
Mansi 175 G 3
Mansle 152 D 2
Mansôa 196 A 3
Manson (IA.) 119 O 8
Manson (WA.) 110 E 3
Mansura (LA.) 123 LM 4
Mansūri (Iran) 157 E 3
Mansūri (Iran) 157 E 3
Manta 138 B 4
Mantalingajan, Mount 176 E 2
Mantaro 140 B 3
Manteca (CA.) 112 D 5
Mantecal 138 E 2
Manteo (N.C.) 129 Q 6
Mantes-la-Jolie 152 D 2
Manti (UT.) 114 F 4
Mantiqueira, Serra da 141 GH 5
Manton (CA.) 112 D 2
Manton (MI.) 124 J 5
Mantova 153 E 2
Mäntsälä 151 J 3
Mänttä 150 H 3
Mantua (OH.) 125 N 8
Mäntyharju 150 J 3
Manú 140 B 3
Manuae 187 E 4
Manua Islands 186 E 3
Manuangi 187 F 4
Manuel Benavides 132 B 2
Manuelito (N.M.) 116 GH 2
Manuel Urbano 138 E 5
Manuelzinho 139 H 5
Manui, Pulau 177 F 4
Mānūk, Tall (Iraq) 156 C 2
Manukau 185 Q 8
Manukau 186 C 5
Manu Ranipur 174 C 2
Manus 184 E 2
Manus 186 A 3
Manvel (N.D.) 119 L 2
Manville (WY.) 118 D 8
Manwat 174 C 4

Many (LA.) **123** K 4
Man'ya **159** M 3
Manyara, Lake **199** F 5
Manych **155** F 1
Manych Gudilo, Ozero **155** F 1
Manychskaya Vpadina **155** F 1
Manyoni **198** E 6
Manzanares **152** C 4
Manzanillo (Cuba) **133** G 3
Manzanillo (Mexico) **132** B 4
Manzanita (OR.) **110** A 5
Manzanola (CO.) **115** O 5
Manzano Mountains **117** K 3
Manzano Peak **117** K 3
Manzariyeh (Iran) **157** F 2
Manzhouli **170** L 6
Manzil Bū Ruqaybah **193** GH 1
Manzini **201** E 5
Manzurka **170** J 5
Mao **133** H 4
Maoke, Pegunungan **177** J 4
Maoke Mountains **184** D 2
Maoming **172** F 6
Maowen **172** D 4
Mapaga **177** EF 4
Mapam Yumco **174** D 1
Mapanza **200** D 3
Maper **198** DE 3
Mapi **177** J 5
Mapia, Kepulauan **177** HJ 3
Mapinhane **201** F 4
Mapire **139** F 2
Mapireme **139** H 3
Mapiripana **138** D 2
Maple Creek **103** Q 6
Maple Peak **116** G 4
Maple River **119** L 4
Maplesville (AL.) **130** H 2
Mapleton (IA.) **119** N 8
Mapleton (MN.) **119** P 7
Mapleton (OR.) **110** B 6
Mapmakers Seamounts **209** C 3
Maprik **184** D 2
Mapuera **139** G 4
Maputo **201** E 5
Maputo **201** E 5
Maputo, Baía de **201** E 5
Māqām, Bandar-e (Iran) **157** F 4
Maqar an Na'am (Iraq) **156** C 3
Maqên **172** D 4
Maqên Gangri **172** C 4
Maqu **172** D 4
Maquan He **174** D 2
Maquela do Zombo **200** B 1
Maquinchao **143** C 7
Maquoketa (IA.) **119** S 8
Maquon (IL.) **124** D 9
Mar, Serra do **142** G 4
Mara **198** E 5
Mara **198** E 5
Maraá **138** E 4
Marabá **139** J 5
Marabahan **176** DE 4
Mara Bridge **198** E 5
Maracá, Ilha de **139** HJ 3
Maracaçume **139** J 4
Maracá **139** J 4
Maracaibo **138** D 1
Maracaibo, Lago de **138** D 1–2
Maracaju **141** F 5
Maracaju, Serra de **140–141** EF 5
Maracanã **139** J 4
Maracanaquará, Planalto **139** H 3–4
Maracás **141** H 3
Maracay **138** E 1
Marādah **193** J 3
Maradi **197** F 3
Marāgheh **168** D 3
Maragogipe **141** J 3
Marāh (Saudi Arabia) **157** D 4
Marahuaca, Cerro **138** E 3
Marais Breton **152** C 2
Marajó, Baía de **139** J 4
Marajó, Ilha de **139** HJ 4
Marakei **186** C 2
Maralal **199** F 4
Maralaleng **200** C 5
Marali **198** B 3
Maralik **155** F 2
Maralinga **182** E 5
Maramasike **185** H 3
Maramba **200** D 3
Maran **176** B 3
Marana (AZ.) **116** E 5
Maranã (Iraq) **157** D 2
Marānd **168** D 3
Marandellas → Marondera **201** E 3
Marang **176** B 2
Maranguape **141** J 1
Maranhão (Brazil) **141** GH 2
Maranhão (Goiás, Brazil) **141** G 3
Maranhão, Cachoeira **139** G 4
Maranoa River **183** H 4
Marañón **138** C 4
Marão **201** E 4
Marão, Serra do **152** B 3
Maraoue **196** C 4
Marapi, Gunung **176** B 4
Marargiu, Capo **153** E 3
Marari **138** E 5

Mărăşeşti **154** C 1
Maratea **153** G 4
Marathon **154** B 3
Marathon (Ontario, Can.) **104** K 6
Marathon (TX.) **117** N 7
Maraú **141** J 3
Marauá **138** E 4
Marávia, Planalto de **201** E 2
Maravovo **185** G 3
Marāwah **193** K 2
Marawi (Philippines) **177** F 2
Marawī (Sudan) **194** E 5
Marāwiḥ (United Arab Emirates) **157** F 4
Maraxó Paiá **139** G 3
Maraza **168** D 2
Marbella **152** C 4
Marble (CO.) **115** K 4
Marble (N.C.) **128** H 6
Marble (WA.) **110** GH 2
Marble Bar **182** B 3
Marble Canyon **116** E 1
Marble City (OK.) **121** L 7
Marble Falls (TX.) **122** E 5
Marble Hall **200** D 4
Marble Hill (MO.) **121** Q 5
Marblemount (WA.) **110** D 2
Marble Rock (IA.) **119** Q 8
Marbleton (WY.) **111** P 8
Marburg **149** E 4
Marcala **132** E 5
Marcelino Ramos **142** F 4
Marcellus (WA.) **110** G 3
March (Austria) **153** G 2
Marche **153** F 3
Marche, Plateaux de la **152** D 2
Marchena **153** E 3
Marchena, **138** B 6
Mar Chiquita, Laguna **142** D 5
Marcigny **152** D 2
Marco (FL.) **131** N 9
Marcola (OR.) **110** BC 6
Marcos Juárez **142** D 5
Marcus (IA.) **119** N 8
Marcus Baker, Mount **102** H 3
Marcy, Mount **126** F 4
Mardan **169** J 4
Mar del Plata **143** E 6
Mardi, Hadjer **197** J 3
Mardin **155** F 3
Mardin Eşigi **155** F 3
Maré **185** J 6
Maré **186** C 4
Marechal Deodoro **141** J 2
Mareeba (Queensland, Austr.) **183** GH 2
Marêg **199** H 4
Marell (AR.) **121** OP 8
Maréna **196** C 3
Marendego **199** F 6
Marengo (IA.) **119** Q 9
Marengo (WA.) **110** G 3
Marengo (WI.) **124** D 3
Marenisco (MI.) **124** E 3
Marennes **152** C 2
Marettimo **153** F 4
Marfa (TX.) **117** M 7
Marganets **155** D 1
Margaret River (Western Australia) **182** D 2
Margaret River (Western Australia) **182** A 5
Margaretville (N.Y.) **126** E 6
Margarida **140** E 5
Margarita, Isla de **139** F 1
Margaritovo **173** K 2
Margate (South Africa) **200** DE 6
Margherita di Savona **153** G 3
Margherita → Jamāme **199** G 4
Margie **103** P 4
Margilan **169** J 2
Margyang **174** E 2
Marhoum **192** E 2
Mari (Burma) **175** G 2
Mari (Papua New Guinea) **184** D 3
Mari (Syria) **156** C 2
Mari (Syria) **195** G 2
Maria (Tuamotu Is.) **187** F 4
Maria (Tubai Is.) **187** E 4
Maria Island **183** F 1
Mariakani **199** F 5
Mariana Islands **186** A 1
Marianao **133** F 3
Mariana Trench **209** C 3
Marianna (AR.) **121** P 8
Marianna (FL.) **131** J 4
Marias Pass **111** M 2
Marias River **111** O 2
María Teresa (Argentina) **142** D 5
Maria Theresa (Pacific Ocean) **187** E 5
Mariato, Punta **138** B 2
Maria van Diemen, Cape **185** Q 7
Mariazell **153** G 2
Maricao (P.R.) **130** C 8
Marico **200** D 4
Maricopa (AZ.) **116** DE 4
Maricopa (CA.) **113** F 7
Marīdī **198** D 4

Marie Byrd Land **203**
Marie-Galante **133** K 4
Mariehamn **151** H 3
Mariental **200** B 4
Marienthal (KS.) **120** D 4
Marienville (PA.) **125** P 8
Mariestad **151** F 4
Marietta (GA.) **128** G 8
Marietta (OH.) **129** K 2
Marietta (OK.) **120** H 9
Mariga **197** F 3
Marignane **153** E 3
Mariinsk **159** R 4
Mariinskoye **171** Q 5
Marília **141** G 5
Marillana **182** B 3
Marimba **200** B 1
Marina Gorka **151** J 5
Marinduque **177** F 1
Marine City (MI.) **125** M 7
Marineland (FL.) **131** N 5
Marinette (WI.) **124** G 4
Maringá (Paraná, Brazil) **141** F 5
Maringa (Zaire) **198** C 4
Marinjab (Iran) **157** F 2
Marinuma **138** E 3
Mariny, Iméni **171** R 3
Marion (AL.) **130** G 2
Marion (AR.) **121** P 7
Marion (IA.) **119** R 8
Marion (ID.) **111** LM 8
Marion (IL.) **121** R 5
Marion (IN.) **124** J 9
Marion (KS.) **120** J 4
Marion (KY.) **128** C 4
Marion (LA.) **123** L 3
Marion (MT.) **111** L 2
Marion (N.C.) **129** JK 6
Marion (N.D.) **119** K 4
Marion (OH.) **125** L 9
Marion (S.C.) **129** M 7
Marion (S.D.) **119** L 7
Marion (WI.) **124** E 5
Marion, Lake **129** L 8
Marion Downs **183** F 3
Marion Junction (AL.) **130** G 2
Marion Lake **120** H 4
Marion Reef **183** J 2
Maripa **138** E 2
Mariposa (CA.) **112** F 5
Mariscal Estigarribia **140** D 5
Maritsa **154** C 2
Maritime, Alpi **153** E 3
Mariu **184** D 3
Marīvān (Iran) **157** E 2
Marka (Saudi Arabia) **157** E 3
Marka **199** GH 4
Markagunt Plateau **114** E 6
Markakol', Ozero **159** R 6
Markam **172** C 5
Markapur **174** C 4
Markaryd **151** F 4
Marked Tree (AR.) **121** P 7
Markesan (WI.) **124** F 6
Markha **170** K 2
Markha **170** L 3
Markha **171** M 3
Markham (TX.) **122** G 7
Markham Bay **105** N 3
Markham Ferry Reservoir **121** K 6
Markit **169** K 3
Markleeville (CA.) **112** F 4
Marko **150** G 2
Markounda **198** B 4
Markovo **159** R 3
Markovo **171** W 3
Marks (MS.) **121** P 8
Marksville (LA.) **123** LM 4
Marland (OK.) **120** H 6
Marlborough (Guyana) **139** G 2
Marlborough (Queensland, Austr.) **183** HJ 3
Marlette (MI.) **125** LM 6
Marlin (TX.) **122** G 4
Marlin (WA.) **110** G 3
Marlinton (W.V.) **129** LM 3
Marlow (OK.) **120** GH 8
Marmagao **174** B 4
Marmande **152** D 3
Marmara **154** C 2
Marmara, Sea of **154** C 2
Marmara Denizi **154** C 2
Marmara Gölü **154** C 3
Marmaris **154** C 3
Marmarth (N.D.) **118** E 4
Marmelos **139** F 5
Mar Menor **152** D 4
Marmolada **153** F 2
Marmot Bay **109** H 4
Marmot Peak **111** K 3
Marne **152** D 2
Marne à la Sane, Canal de la **153** E 2
Mârnes **150** J 1
Maro **197** H 2
Maro **197** H 4
Maroa **138** E 3

Maroantsetra **201** H 3
Marolambo **201** H 4
Maromandia **201** H 2
Maromokotro **201** H 2
Marondera **201** E 3
Maroni **139** H 3
Maros **177** E 4
Marovoay **201** H 3
Marowijne **139** H 3
Marqab, Qal 'at al (Syria) **156** B 2
Marqādah (Syria) **156** C 2
Marquesas Islands **187** F 3
Marquesas Keys **131** M 10
Marquette (KS.) **120** GH 4
Marquette (MI.) **124** G 3
Marquette Island **125** K 4
Marquez (N.M.) **117** J 2
Marquez (TX.) **122** G 4
Marracuene **201** E 5
Marradi **153** F 3
Marrah, Jabal **194** C 6
Marrakech **192** D 2
Marrawah **184** K 9
Marree **183** F 4
Marrero (LA.) **123** N 6
Marromeu **201** F 3
Marrupa **201** F 2
Marsa al' Alam (Egypt) **156** B 4
Marsa al Uwayjah **193** J 2
Marsabit **199** F 4
Marsabit National Reserve **199** F 4
Marsa Fatma **199** G 2
Marsala **153** F 4
Marsa Sha'b **194** F 4
Marsa Taklai **199** F 1
Marsa 'Umm Ghayj (Egypt) **156** B 4
Marsden **183** H 5
Marseille **153** E 3
Marseilles (IL.) **124** F 8
Marsfjällen **150** G 2
Marsh (TX.) **117** OP 2
Marshall (AK.) **102** E 3
Marshall (AR.) **121** N 7
Marshall (IL.) **121** S 3
Marshall (IN.) **128** D 2
Marshall (Liberia) **196** B 4
Marshall (MI.) **125** K 7
Marshall (MN.) **119** N 6
Marshall (MO.) **121** M 3
Marshall (N.D.) **118** F 3
Marshall (TX.) **123** J 3
Marshall (VA.) **129** O 3
Marshall (WA.) **110** H 3
Marshall (WY.) **118** C 8
Marshall Islands **186** BC 2
Marshall River **183** F 3
Marshalltown (IA.) **119** Q 8
Marshfield (MO.) **121** N 5
Marshfield (WI.) **124** D 5
Marsh Harbour **133** G 2
Mars Hill (ME.) **126** L 2
Mars Hill (N.C.) **128** J 6
Marsh Island **123** M 6
Marsh Peak **114** H 3
Marsing (ID.) **110** J 7
Marsland (NE.) **118** E 8
Märsta **151** G 4
Marstrand **151** F 4
Mart (TX.) **122** G 4
Marta **153** F 3
Martaban **175** G 4
Martaban, Gulf of **175** G 4
Martap **197** G 4
Martapura **198** B 4
Martapura **176** DE 4
Martés, Sierra de **152** C 4
Martha's Vineyard **127** J 7
Martigny **153** E 2
Martigues **153** DE 3
Martin (Czechoslovakia) **149** G 5
Martin (N.D.) **118** H 3
Martin (S.D.) **118** G 7
Martin (TN.) **128** C 5
Martin Dam **131** J 2
Martín de Loyola **143** C 6
Martínez (CA.) **112** C 4
Martínez de la Torre **132** C 3
Martinez Lake **113** L 10
Martinique **133** K 5
Martinique Passage **133** K 5
Martin Lake **131** J 2
Martinsburg (PA.) **125** Q 9
Martinsburg (W.V.) **129** NO 2
Martinsdale (MT.) **111** P 4
Martins Ferry (W.V.) **125** O 9
Martinsville (IL.) **121** R 3
Martinsville (IN.) **128** E 2
Martinsville (VA.) **129** M 5
Martin Vaz Islands **135** H 5
Marton **185** R 9
Martos **152** C 4
Martre, Lac la **103** O 3
Martūbah **193** K 2
Martuk **158** L 5

Martuni **155** G 2
Martyn **159** L 2
Marudi **176** D 3
Mārūn (Iran) **157** E 3
Marunga **185** F 3
Marungu, Monts **198** D 6
Marusthali **174** B 2
Marutea **187** F 4
Marvast (Iran) **157** G 3
Marvast, Kavīr-e (Iran) **157** G 3
Marv Dasht (Iran) **157** F 3
Marvejols **152** D 3
Marvine, Mount **114** F 5
Marwar Junction **174** B 2
Mary **169** G 3
Maryborough (Queensland, Austr.) **183** J 4
Maryborough (Victoria, Austr.) **183** G 6
Marydale **200** C 5
Mar'yevka **159** N 5
Maryhill (WA.) **110** E 5
Maryland **129**
Maryneal (TX.) **122** C 3
Marys Igloo **108** F 2
Marys River **112** K 1
Marystown **105** R 6
Marysvale (UT.) **114** E 5
Marysville (CA.) **112** D 3
Marysville (NE.) **120** J 3
Marysville (OH.) **125** L 9
Marysville(WA.) **110** C 2
Maryville (MI.) **125** M 7
Maryville (MO.) **121** L 2
Maryville (TN.) **128** H 6
Marzafal **196** D 2
Marzo, Cabo **138** C 2
Masaguru **201** J 3
Masāhīm, Kūh-e (Iran) **157** G 3
Masai Steppe **199** F 5
Masaka **198** E 5
Masākin **193** H 1
Masalasef **197** H 3
Masalembo, Pulau **176** D 5
Masally **168** D 3
Masamba **177** F 4
Masan **173** J 3
Masardis (ME.) **126** L 2
Masasi **201** F 2
Masaya **132** E 5
Masbate **177** F 1
Masbate Island **177** F 1
Mascara **192** EF 1
Mascarene Islands **201** K 6
Mascota **132** B 3
Masela, Pulau **177** GH 5
Maseru **200** D 5
Masfinto **199** F 2
Mashaba **201** E 4
Mashābī (Saudi Arabia) **156** B 4
Mashaki **169** J 4
Mashala **198** C 6
Mashan **172** E 6
Mashewa **199** F 5
Mashhad **168** F 3
Mashīz (Iran) **157** G 3
Mashkel **169** G 5
Mäshkid **169** G 5
Mashonaland **201** E 3
Mashoro **200** D 4
Mashra'ar Raqq **198** D 3
Ma'shur, Bandar (Iran) **157** E 3
Masīlah, Wādī al **195** J 5
Masi-Manimba **198** B 5
Masimbu **177** E 4
Maṣīrah **195** K 4
Maṣīrah, Khalīj **195** K 5
Masisea **138** D 5
Masisi **198** D 5
Masjed Soleymān (Iran) **157** E 3
Maskanah (Syria) **156** B 2
Maslovare **153** G 3
Maslovo **159** M 3
Maslyanskoye **159** O 4
Maso **196** D 4
Masoala, Cap **201** J 3
Masohi **177** G 4
Mason (TN.) **128** B 6
Mason (TX.) **122** D 5
Mason, Lake **182** B 4
Mason City (IA.) **119** P 7
Mason City (IL.) **124** E 9
Mason City (NE.) **120** F 1
Masqat **195** K 4
Massa **153** F 3
Massachusetts **126**
Massachusetts Bay **126** J 6
Massacre Lake **112** F 1
Massadona (CO.) **114** J 3
Massafra **153** G 3
Massaguet **197** H 3
Massakori **197** H 3
Massa Marittima **153** F 3
Massangena **201** E 4
Massango **200** B 1
Massapé **141** H 1
Massau **185** E 2
Massava **159** M 3
Massawa **199** F 1

Massawarat es Sufra → Al Mu-
  sawwarāt aṣ Ṣafra' **194** E 5
Massena (N.Y.) **126** E 4
Massénya **197** H 3
Masset **102** L 5
Massif Central **152** D 2–3
Massif d'Abo **197** H 1
Massif de Guéra **197** H 3
Massif de l'Adamoua **197** G 4
Massif de l'Aurès **193** G 1
Massif de l'Isalo **201** H 4
Massif de l'Ivakoany **201** H 4
Massif de l'Ouarsenis **193** F 1
Massif des Bongos **198** C 3
Massif de Takolokouzet **197** F 2
Massif de Tarazit **197** F 1
Massif de Termit **197** G 2
Massif du Chaillu **197** G 6
Massif du Diois **153** E 3
Massif du Kapka **197** J 2
Massif du Kerkour Nourene **197** J 2
Massif du Makay **201** H 4
Massif du Pelvoux **153** E 3
Massif du Tamgué **176** B 3
Massif du Tondou **198** C 3
Massif du Tsaratanana **201** H 2
Massif du Yadé **198** B 3
Massigui **196** C 3
Massillon (OH.) **125** N 9
Massinga **201** F 4
Massingir **201** E 4
Masslo **199** F 3
Mastābah **195** F 4
Masteksay **168** E 1
Masters (CO.) **115** N 3
Masterson (TX.) **117** OP 2
Masterton **185** R 9
Mastuj **169** J 3
Mastung **169** H 5
Mastūrah **194** F 4
Masuda **173** K 4
Masuika **198** C 6
Māsüleh (Iran) **157** E 1
Masulipatnam → Machilipatnam
  174 D 4
Masurai, Bukit **176** B 4
Masvingo **201** E 4
Maṣyāf (Syria) **156** B 2
Mata Amarilla **143** B 8
Matabeleland **200** D 3–4
Matachewan **105** L 6
Matachic **106** E 6
Matadi **198** A 6
Matador (TX.) **117** Q 3
Matagalpa **132** E 5
Matagalpa, Rio Grande de **132** F 5
Matagami **105** M 6
Mata Gassile **199** G 4
Matagorda (TX.) **122** GH 7
Matagorda Bay **122** G 7
Matagorda Island **122** G 7
Matagorda Peninsula **122** GH 7
Mataiva **187** F 3
Matakana **183** H 5
Matala **200** B 2
Matale **174** D 6
Matam **196** B 2
Matameye **197** F 3
Matamoros **132** B 2
Matamoros **132** C 2
Ma'ṭan as Sārah **193** K 4
Ma'ṭan Bishārah **193** K 4
Ma'ṭan Bū at Tifl **193** K 3
Matancita **106** D 6
Matandu **199** F 6
Matane **105** O 6
Matankari **197** E 3
Matanuska River **109** J 3
Matanzas **133** F 3
Matanzilla, Pampa de la **143** C 6
Matão, Serra do **139** H 5
Maṭār (Saudi Arabia) **157** E 4
Matara (Ethiopia) **199** F 2
Matara (Peru) **138** C 5
Matara (Sri Lanka) **174** D 6
Mataram **176** E 5
Matarani **140** B 4
Mataranka **182** E 1
Matarca **138** D 4
Matārimah, Ra's (Egypt) **156** A 3
Mataró **152** D 3
Matatiele **200** D 6
Matatila Dam **174** C 2
Mata-Utu **186** D 3
Matay **159** P 6
Mategua **140** D 3
Matehuala **132** B 3
Matera **153** G 3
Mátészalka **154** B 1
Matetsi **200** D 3
Matfield Green (KS.) **120** J 4
Matfors **150** G 3
Mather (CA.) **112** F 5
Matheson (CO.) **115** O 4
Matheson (Ontario, Can.) **105** L 6
Mathews (VA.) **129** P 4
Mathis (TX.) **122** F 7
Mathiston (MS.) **121** Q 9
Mathura **174** C 2

Mati **177** G 2
Matiakouali **196** E 3
Matimbuka **201** F 2
Matinha **139** J 4
Matinicus Island **126** L 5
Maṭir **193** G 1
Matla **174** E 3
Mato, Cerro **138** E 2
Mato Grosso **140–141** EF 3
Mato Grosso (Mato Grosso, Brazil)
  140 E 3
Mato Grosso do Sul **140–141** EF 4
Matopo Hills **200** D 4
Matozinhos **152** B 3
Mátra **154** AB 1
Maṭrāḥ **195** K 4
Matru **196** B 4
Matrūh **194** D 2
Matseses **155** EF 2
Matsu (Japan) **173** M 2
Matsu (Taiwan) **173** H 5
Matsudo **173** M 3
Matsue **173** K 3
Matsumoto **173** L 3
Matsusaka **173** L 4
Matsuyama **173** K 4
Mattamuskeet, Lake **129** P 6
Mattancheri **174** C 6
Mattawamkeag (ME.) **126** L 3
Matterhorn (NV.) **112** H 1
Matterhorn (Switzerland) **153** E 2
Matthew **186** C 4
Matthews (N.C.) **129** L 6
Matthews Range **199** F 4
Matthew's Ridge **139** G 2
Matthew Town **133** H 3
Maṭṭī, Sabkhat **195** J 4
Mattoon (IL.) **121** R 3
Mattydale (N.Y.) **126** C 5
Matu **176** D 3
Matua, Ostrov **171** S 6
Matucana **140** A 3
Maturín **139** F 2
Matveyev-Kurgan **155** E 1
Matyl'ka **159** R 3
Matyshevo **158** H 5
Matyushkinskaya **159** P 4
Mau **174** D 3
Maúa **201** F 2
Maubeuge **152** D 1
Maubin **175** G 4
Maud (OK.) **120** J 7
Maud (TX.) **123** J 2
Maude **183** G 5
Maudlow (MT.) **111** O 4
Maués **139** G 4
Maués Açu **139** G 4
Maug **186** A 1
Mauganj **174** D 3
Maui **113** F 11
Maui **113** F 11
Mauke **187** E 4
Maula (Saudi Arabia) ...
Maulvi Bazar **175** F 3
Maumee (OH.) **125** L 8
Maumee River **125** K 8
Maumere **177** F 5
Maun **200** C 4
Mauna Kea **113** G 12
Mauna Kea **187** E 1
Mauna Loa **113** G 12
Maunaloa (HI.) **113** E 10
Maunoir, Lac **103** MN 2
Maupin (OR.) **110** D 5
Maupihaa **187** E 4
Maupiti **187** E 4
Mauralasan **176** E 3
Mau Range **199** F 5
Maurepas, Lake **123** N 5
Maurice, Lake **182** E 4
Mauriceville (TX.) **123** K 5
Maurine (SD.) **118** F 5
Mauritania **192** CD 5
Mauritius **201** K 6
Mauron **152** C 2
Mauston (WI.) **124** D 6
Mavasjaure **150** G 2
Mavinga **200** BC 3
Mavue **201** E 4
Mavume **201** E 4
Mavuradonha Mountains **201** E 3
Mawa, Bukit **176** D 3
Mawa'afaq **195** JK 5
Mawei **173** G 5
Mawkmai **175** G 3
Mawlaik **175** F 3
Mawqaq (Saudi Arabia) **156** C 4
Mawson **203**
Mawson Coast **203**
Max (ND.) **118** G 4
Maxbass (ND.) **118** G 2
Maxcanu **132** DE 3
Maxie (MS.) **130** E 4
Maxinkuckee, Lake **124** H 8
Maxixe **201** F 4
Maxville (MT.) **111** M 4
Maxwell (NE.) **120** E 1
Maxwell (N.M.) **117** M 1

May (OK.) **120** F 6
May (TX.) **122** E 3–4
May, Cape **127** E 10
Maya **171** O 4
Maya, Pulau **176** C 4
Mayaguana Island **133** H 3
Mayaguana Passage **133** H 3
Mayagüez **133** J 4
Mayagüez (P.R.) **130** B 8
Mayahi **197** F 3
Mayahi **197** F 3
Mayakan **171** S 3
Mayama **197** GH 6
Mayāmey (Iran) **157** G 1
Maya Mountains **132** E 4
Mayang **172** E 5
Mayapán **132** E 3
Maybell (CO.) **115** JK 3
Maybeury (W.V.) **129** K 4
Mayd **199** H 2
Maydān (Iraq) **157** D 2
Maydī **195** G 5
Mayenne **152** C 2
Mayenne **152** C 2
Mayer (AZ.) **116** D 3
Mayfield (ID.) **111** K 7
Mayfield (KY.) **128** C 5
Mayfield (OK.) **120** F 7
Mayfield (UT.) **114** F 4
Mayfield Reservoir **110** C 4
Mayhill (N.M.) **117** L 5
Maykain **159** P 5
Maykop **155** F 2
Maylykum **169** H 1
Maymak **169** J 2
Maymakan **171** P 4
Maymecha **170** H 1
Maymyo **175** G 3
Mayn **171** W 3
Mayna **170** F 5
Maynardville (TN.) **128** H 5
Maynas **138** C 4
Mayno-Amamkut **171** X 3
Mayno-Gytkino **108** B 3
Maynopil'gyno **171** X 3
Mayo (FL.) **131** L 4
Mayo (Yukon, Can.) **102** K 3
Mayo, Mountains of **148** B 4
Mayo Daga **197** G 4
Mayoko **197** G 6
Mayo Lake **109** M 3
Mayo Mayo **140** C 3
Mayon **177** F 1
Mayor Buratovich **143** D 6
Mayor-Krest **171** Q 2
Mayotte **201** H 2
May Pen **133** G 4
Mayraira Point **177** HJ 1
May River **184** D 2
Maysk **159** P 4
Mayskiy **155** F 2
Mayskiy **171** N 5
Mayskiy, Khrebet **171** O 4–5
Mayskoye **159** P 5
Mays Landing (N.J.) **127** E 9
Maysville (MO.) **121** L 3
Maysville (N.C.) **129** O 7
Mayumba **197** G 6
Mayum La **174** D 1
Mayvale **183** H 4
Mayville (N.D.) **119** L 3
Mayville (N.Y.) **125** P 7
Mayville (WI.) **124** F 6
Maywood (NE.) **120** E 2
Mayworth (WY.) **118** B 7
Mayya **171** O 3
Maza **143** D 6
Mazabuka **200** D 3
Mazagão **139** H 4
Mazalet **197** F 2
Mazalij (Saudi Arabia) **157** E 4
Mazama (WA.) **110** E 2
Mazamet **152** D 3
Mazar **169** K 3
Mazara dell Vallo **153** F 4
Mazar-i-Sharif **169** H 3
Mazarredo **143** C 8
Mazaruni **139** FG 2
Mazatenango **132** D 5
Mazatlán **132** A 3
Mazatzal Mountains **116** E 3–4
Mažeikiai **151** H 4
Mazirbe **151** H 4
Mazoe **201** E 3
Mazomanie (WI.) **124** E 6
Mazomeno **198** D 5
Mazong Shan **172** C 2
Mazowe **201** E 3
Mazowsze **149** H 4
Mazrub **194** D 6
Māzū (Iran) **157** E 2
Mazunga **200** D 4
Mazury **149** H 4
Mbabane **201** E 5
Mbahiakro **196** D 4
Mbaiki **198** B 4
Mbakaou Reservoir **197** G 4
Mbaké **196** A 3
Mbala (Centr. Afr. Rep.) **198** C 3
Mbala (Zambia) **201** E 1
Mbale **198** E 4

Mbalmayo **197** G 5
Mbamba Bay **201** E 2
Mbandaka **198** B 4
Mbang, Monts **197** G 4
Mbanga **197** F 5
M'banza Congo **200** A 1
Mbanza-Ngungu **198** B 6
Mbarara **198** E 5
Mbari **198** C 3
Mbé **197** G 4
Mbengwi **197** F 4
Mberengwa **200** D 4
Mbeya **198** E 6
Mbigou **197** G 6
Mbinda **197** G 6
Mbinga **201** F 2
Mbini **197** F 5
Mbini **197** G 5
Mbini **197** G 5
Mbizi **201** E 4
M'Boi **198** C 6
Mbokou **198** D 3
M'Boli **198** C 4
Mboma **197** G 5
Mbomou **198** C 4
Mbouda **197** FG 4
Mbour **196** A 3
Mbout **196** C 5
Mbozi **198** E 6
Mbrés **198** BC 3
M'bridge **200** A 1
Mbuji-Mayi **198** C 6
Mbulu **198** F 5
Mburu, Lake **198** E 5
Mburucuyá **142** E 4
Mbuyuni **199** F 6
McAlester (OK.) **121** K 8
McAlister (N.M.) **117** N 3
McAllen (TX.) **122** E 9
McAllister (MT.) **111** O 5
Mc Arthur (OH.) **128** J 2
McArthur River **182** F 2
Mc Arthur River **182–183** F 2
Mc Bain (MI.) **124** J 5
McBaine (MO.) **121** N 4
McBee (S.C.) **129** L 7
McBeth Fjord **105** O 2
Mc Cabe (MT.) **118** D 2
McCall (ID.) **110** J 6
McCamey (TX.) **117** O 6
Mc Cammon (ID.) **111** N 8
McCarthy **102** J 3
McCartys (N.M.) **116** J 2
Mc Clave (CO.) **115** P 5
McCleary (WA.) **110** B 3
McClellanville (S.C.) **129** M 8
Mc Cloud (CA.) **112** C 1
McClure, Lake **112** E 5
Mc Clusky (N.D.) **118** H 3
McComb (MS.) **130** D 3
McConaughy, Lake **120** D 1
McConnellsburg (PA.) **125** Q 10
McConnelsville (OH.) **129** K 2
Mc Cook (NE.) **120** E 2
McCormick (S.C.) **129** J 8
Mc Coy (CO.) **115** L 4
Mc Cracken (KS.) **120** F 4
McCredie Springs (OR.) **110** C 7
McCullough Mountain **113** K 7
McCurtain (OK.) **121** L 7
McDade (TX.) **122** F 5
McDame **104** M 4
McDavid (FL.) **130** G 4
McDonald (KS.) **120** D 3
McDonald (N.M.) **117** N 4
McDonald, Lake **111** M 2
McDonough (GA.) **128** G 8
McDougall, Mount **111** P 8
Mc Fadden (WY.) **118** BC 9
McFarland (CA.) **113** F 7
Mc Gill (NV.) **112** L 3
Mc Grath (AK.) **102** F 3
McGrath (MN.) **119** P 4
McGregor (MN.) **119** P 4
Mc Gregor (ND.) **118** F 2
Mc Gregor (TX.) **122** F 4
McGuire, Mount **111** L 5
Mc Henry (N.D.) **119** K 3
McKay Reservoir **110** G 5
McKean **186** D 3
McKeand **105** O 3
Mc Kee (KY.) **128** G 4
McKeesport (PA.) **125** P 9
McKenzie (AL.) **130** H 3
McKenzie (TN.) **128** C 5
McKenzie Bridge (OR.) **110** C 6
McKenzie Island **104** J 5
McKinley, Mount **102** G 3
McKinley Park **102** H 3
Mc Kinleyville (CA.) **112** A 2
McKinney (TX.) **122** G 2
McKinney Mountain **117** N 8
Mc Kinnon (WY.) **111** Q 9

McKittrick (CA.) **113** F 7
McKittrick Summit **113** F 7
McLain (MS.) **130** F 4
Mc Laughlin (SD.) **118** H 5
McLaurin (MS.) **130** E 3
Mc Lean (IL.) **124** E 9
Mc Lean (TX.) **117** Q 2
McLeansboro (IL.) **121** R 4
McLeod (MT.) **111** P 5
Mc Leod (N.D.) **119** L 4
McLeod, Lake **182** A 3
McLeod Bay **103** P 3
Mc Leod Lake **103** N 5
M'Clintock **103** T 4
M'Clintock Channel **103** R 1
McLoughlin, Mount **110** C 8
M'Clure Strait **103** O 1
McMillan (MS.) **130** E 1
McMillan, Lake **117** M 5
McMinnville (OR.) **110** B 5
McMinnville (TN.) **128** F 6
Mc Murdo **203**
Mc Murdo Sound **203**
McNab (AR.) **121** M 9
McNary (AZ.) **116** G 3
McNary (TX.) **117** L 6
McNary Dam **110** F 5
McNeal (AZ.) **116** G 6
McNeil (AR.) **121** M 9
McNeil (TX.) **122** F 5
McPherson (KS.) **120** H 4
McRae (GA.) **131** M 2
Mc Roberts (KY.) **128** J 4
McVeigh (KY.) **129** J 4
McVicar Arm **103** O 2
Mc Ville (N.D.) **119** K 3
Mdandu **198** EF 6
Mdennah **192** D 4
Mead, Lake **112** L 6
Meade (AK.) **102** F 1–2
Meade (KS.) **120** E 5
Meaden Peak **115** K 3
Meade Peak **111** O 8
Meadow **182** A 4
Meadow (SD.) **118** F 5
Meadow (TX.) **117** O 4
Meadow (UT.) **114** E 5
Meadowdale (WY.) **118** D 8
Meadow Lake **103** Q 5
Meadow Valley Wash **112** L 5
Meadville (PA.) **125** O 8
Mealhada **152** B 3
Mealy Mountains **105** Q 5
Meander River **103** O 4
Meath (AZ.) **116** D 2
Meaux **152** D 2
Mecanhelas **201** F 3
Mecca **195** FG 4
Mecca (CA.) **113** JK 9
Mechanicville (N.Y.) **126** F 6
Mecheria **192** E 2
Mechigmen **108** D 2
Mechigmenskiy Zaliv **102** C 2
Mecklenburg **149** F 4
Mecklenburger Bucht **149** F 4
Meconta **201** F 3
Mecrihan **155** E 3
Mecsek **154** A 1
Mecuburi **201** F 2
Mecúfi **201** G 2
Mecula **201** F 2
Mecumbura **201** E 3
Medaguine **193** F 2
Medak **174** C 4
Médala **192** D 5
Medan **176** A 3
Medano **142** C 5
Médanos **142** E 5
Medanos **143** D 6
Medanosa, Punta **143** CD 8
Médéa **193** F 1
Medellín **138** CD 2
Medelpad **150** G 3
Mederdra **192** B 5
Medétsiz **155** D 3
Medford (MA.) **126** H 6
Medford (OK.) **120** H 6
Medford (OR.) **110** C 8
Medford (WI.) **124** D 4
Medgidia **154** C 2
Medi **198** E 3
Mediapolis (IA.) **119** R 9–10
Mediaş **154** B 1
Medical Lake (WA.) **110** H 3
Medical Springs (OR.) **110** H 5
Medicine Bow (WY.) **118** B 9
Medicine Bow Mountains **118** B 9
Medicine Hat **103** P 5
Medicine Lake (MT.) **118** D 2
Medicine Lake (MT.) **118** D 2
Medicine Lodge (KS.) **120** G 5
Medicine Mound (TX.) **122** D 1
Medigan **159** R 5
Medina (ND.) **118** J 4
Medina (N.Y.) **125** Q 6
Medina (OH.) **125** N 8
Medina (Saudi Arabia) **156** C 4
Medina (TX.) **122** D 6
Medina del Campo **152** C 3

Medina Lake 122 E 6
Medina River 122 D 6
Medinipur 174 E 3
Medira 108 G 3
Mediterranean Sea 145 HL 8–9
Medje 198 D 4
Mednogorsk 159 L 5
Mêdog 172 C 5
Medora (KS.) 120 H 4
Medora (ND.) 118 E 4
Médouneu 197 G 5
Medveditsa 158 H 5
Medvezh'i, Ostrova 171 U 1
Medvezhiy Var 170 F 1
Medvezh'ya, Gora 171 P 6
Medvezh'yegorsk 158 FG 3
Meeberrie 182 B 4
Meekatharra 182 B 4
Meeker (CO.) 115 K 3
Meeker (OK.) 120 J 7
Meeks Bay (CA.) 112 E 3
Meerut 174 C 2
Meeteetse (WY.) 111 R 6
Mega (Ethiopia) 199 F 4
Mega (Indonesia) 177 H 4
Mega, Pulau 176 B 3
Megalopolis 154 B 3
Meganom, Mys 155 E 2
Mégara 154 B 3
Megargel (TX.) 122 DE 2
Megasani Hill 174 E 3
Megève 153 E 2
Meggett (S.C.) 129 L 9
Meghalaya 175 F 2
Megid 193 K 3
Megion 159 P 3
Megra 158 H 2
Megra 158 G 3
Meguidene 193 F 3
Meguinenza, Embalse de 152 CD 3
Mehadia 154 B 2
Mehar 169 H 5
Mehdīshahr (Iran) 157 F 2
Meherrin River 129 O 5
Mehrābād (Iran) 157 E 1
Mehrān (Iran) 157 E 2
Mehrān (Iran) 157 G 4
Mehrīz (Iran) 157 G 3
Mehtar Lam 169 J 4
Meia Meia 199 F 6
Meiganga 197 G 4
Meigs (GA.) 131 K 3
Meiktila 175 G 3
Meissen 149 F 4
Meissner 149 E 4
Meitan 172 E 5
Mei Xian 172 G 6
Mejillones 140 B 5
Mékambo 197 G 5
Mekerrhane, Sebkha 193 F 3
Mekhé 196 A 2
Mekinock (N.D.) 119 L 3
Meknès 192 D 2
Meko 196 E 4
Mekong 175 J 5
Mekong, Mouths of the 175 J 6
Mekongga, Gunung 177 F 4
Mekoryuk 102 D 3
Mekrou 196 E 3
Mel'nichnaya 159 R 2
Melo 142 F 5
Melolo 177 F 5
Melrhir, Chott 193 G 2

Melrose (MT.) 111 N 5
Melrose (N.M.) 117 N 3
Melrose (WI.) 124 D 5
Melsetter → Chimanimani 201 E 3
Melstone (MT.) 111 S 4
Melsungen 149 E 4
Meltaus 150 HJ 2
Meluco 201 F 2
Melun 152 D 2
Melvern (KS.) 121 K 4
Melville (MT.) 111 Q 4
Melville (Sask., Can.) 103 R 5
Melville, Cape 183 G 1
Melville, Lake 105 Q 5
Melville Bay 202
Melville Fracture Zone 208 B 5
Melville Hills 103 N 2
Melville Island 182 E 1
Melville Island 202
Melville Peninsula 103 V 2
Melville Sound 103 Q 2
Melvin (TX.) 122 D 4
Melyuveyem 171 W 3
Meman 175 J 5
Mêmar Co 174 D 1
Memba 201 G 2
Memboro 177 E 5
Memmingen 149 EF 5
Mempawah 176 C 3
Memphis (Egypt) 194 E 3
Memphis (MO.) 121 N 2
Memphis (TN.) 128 AB 6
Memphis (TX.) 117 Q 3
Mena (AR.) 121 L 8
Mena (U.S.S.R.) 158 F 5
Menahga (MN.) 119 N 4
Ménaka 196 E 2
Menard (MT.) 111 O 4
Menard (TX.) 122 D 4
Menasha (WI.) 124 F 5
Menawashei 194 D 6
Mencué 143 C 7
Mendawai, Sungai 176 D 4
Mende 152 D 3
Mendenhall (MS.) 130 E 3
Mendi (Ethiopia) 198 F 3
Mendi (Papua New Guinea) 184 D 3
Mendocino (CA.) 112 B 3
Mendocino, Cape 112 A 2
Mendocino, Lake 112 B 3
Mendota (CA.) 112 E 6
Mendota (IL.) 124 E 8
Mendota (TX.) 117 Q 2
Mendota (VA.) 129 J 7
Mendota, Lake 124 E 6
Mendoza (Argentina) 142 C 5
Mendoza (Peru) 138 C 5
Mendoza (TX.) 122 F 5
Mene Grande 138 D 2
Menemen 154 C 3
Menentor (KY.) 128 G 3
Menez Hom 152 C 2
Mengcheng 173 G 4
Méngen 155 D 2
Mengene Dağı 155 F 3
Menghai 172 D 6
Mengla 172 D 6
Menglian 172 C 6
Mengzi 172 D 6
Meniet 193 F 3
Menihek Lakes 105 O 5
Menindee 183 G 5
Meningie 183 F 6
Menkere 170 M 2
Menkere 171 MN 2
Menno (S.D.) 119 L 7
Meno (OK.) 120 G 6
Menominee (MI.) 124 G 4
Menominee Indian Reservation 124 F 4–5
Menominee River 124 G 4
Menomonee Falls (WI.) 124 F 6
Menomonie (WI.) 124 C 5
Menongue 200 B 2
Menorca 152 D 3
Menouarar 192 E 2
Men'shikova, Mys 159 LM 1
Men'shikova, Ostrov 171 PQ 5
Mentasta Lake 102 J 3
Mentawai, Kepulauan 176 A 4
Mentawai, Selat 176 A 4
Mentese 154 C 3
Mentok 176 C 4
Mentone (TX.) 117 N 6
Mentor (OH.) 125 N 8
Menyamya 184 E 3
Menyapa, Gunung 176 E 3
Menyuan 172 D 3
Menzel Bourgiba → Manzil Bū Ruquaybah 193 GH 1
Menzelinsk 158 K 4
Menzies 182 C 4
Menzies, Mount 203
Meoqui 106 E 6
Mepistskaro 155 F 2
Meponda 201 E 2
Meppel 148 E 4
Meppen 149 E 4
Mepuze 201 E 4
Merak 176 C 5

Meråker 150 F 3
Meramec River 121 O 4
Meranggau 176 D 4
Merano 153 F 2
Merauke 184 D 3
Mercadal 152 D 4
Mercara 174 C 5
Merced (CA.) 112 E 5
Mercedario, Cerro 142 BC 5
Mercedes 142 C 5
Mercedes (Argentina) 142 E 4
Mercedes (TX.) 122 EF 9
Mercedes (Uruguay) 142 E 5
Merceditas 142 BC 4
Mercer (ND.) 118 H 3
Mercer (PA.) 125 O 8
Mercersburg (PA.) 127 B 9
Mercury (NV.) 112 K 6
Mercy, Cape 105 P 3
Mercy Bay 103 O 1
Meredith (N.H.) 126 H 5
Meredith, Cape 143 D 9
Meredith, Lake (CO.) 115 O 5
Meredith, Lake (TX.) 117 P 2
Meredosia (IL.) 121 P 3
Merefa 158 G 6
Merenga 171 T 3
Merga → Nukhaylak 194 D 5
Mergenevo 168 E 1
Mergui 175 G 5
Mergui Archipelago 175 G 5
Meriç 154 C 2
Mérida (Mexico) 132 E 3
Mérida (Spain) 152 B 4
Mérida (Venezuela) 138 D 2
Mérida, Cordillera de 138 D 2
Meriden (CT.) 126 G 7
Meriden (WY.) 118 D 9
Meridian (GA.) 131 N 3
Meridian (MS.) 130 F 2
Meridian (TX.) 122 F 4
Meridja 192 E 2
Mérignac 152 C 3
Merikarvia 150 H 3
Merín, Laguna 142 F 5
Meringur 183 G 5
Merinos 142 E 5
Merir 177 H 3
Merivale River 183 H 4
Merkel (TX.) 122 C 3
Merkushino 159 N 4
Merkushura Strelka 171 R 1
Merlin (OR.) 110 B 8
Merna (NE.) 120 F 1
Merna (WY.) 111 P 8
Meroe 194 E 5
Merouane, Chott 193 G 2
Merredin 182 B 5
Merriam (IN.) 124 J 8
Merrick 148 C 3
Merrill (IA.) 119 M 8
Merrill (MI.) 125 K 6
Merrill (OR.) 110 D 8
Merrill (WI.) 124 E 4
Merrillan (WI.) 124 D 5
Merrimack River 126 H 5
Merriman (NE.) 118 G 8
Merritt 103 N 5
Merritt Island (FL.) 131 O 6
Merritt Island (FL.) 131 O 6
Merritt Reservoir 118 H 8
Merseburg 149 F 4
Mersin 155 D 3
Mersin (Turkey) 156 B 1
Mersing 176 B 3
Mêrsrags 151 H 4
Merta 174 C 2
Merthyr Tydfil 148 C 4
Merti 199 F 4
Mértola 152 B 4
Mertole Maryam 199 F 2
Mertzon (TX.) 122 C 4
Meru (Kenya) 199 F 4
Meru (Tanzania) 199 F 5
Meru Game Reserve 199 F 4
Merutai 176 E 3
Merwin, Lake 110 C 4–5
Merzifon 155 E 2
Merzig 149 E 5

Merāker 150 F 3
Meseta del Cerro Jaua 139 F 2–3
Meseta de Somuncurá 143 C 7
Mesetas de las Vizcachas 143 B 9
Mesick (MI.) 124 J 5
Mesilla (N.M.) 117 K 5
Meskou 197 H 2
Mesmiyah (Syria) 156 B 2
Mesolóngion 154 B 3
Mesopotamia (Iraq) 156–157 D 2–3
Mesquite (N.M.) 117 K 5
Mesquite (TX.) 122 G 3
Mesquite Flat 112 J 6
Mesquite Lake 113 K 7
Mesquite Lake 113 J 8
Messaad 193 F 2
Messalo 201 F 2
Messengue 201 E 4
Messerian 168 E 3
Mercês 138 E 5
Messina (Italy) 153 FG 4
Messina (South Africa) 200 D 4
Messina, Stretto di 153 G 4
Messiniakós Kolpós 154 B 3
Messo 159 P 2
Messoyakha 159 PQ 2
Mesta 154 B 2
Mesters Vig 202
Meszah Peak 109 M 4
Meta Incognita Peninsula 105 O 3
Metairie (LA.) 123 N 6
Metal, Mont du 193 G 4
Metaline (WA.) 110 H 2
Metaline Falls (WA.) 110 H 2
Metán 142 D 4
Metangula 201 EF 2
Metapan 132 E 5
Metaponto 153 G 3
Metcalf (GA.) 131 KL 4
Metcalf (KS.) 120 H 5
Meteghan 105 O 7
Metemma 198 F 2
Meter (GA.) 131 MN 2
Meteor Depth 208 A 5
Meteran 185 F 2
Méthana 154 B 3
Metković 153 G 3
Metlakatla 109 M 4
Metlika 153 G 2
Metlili Chaamba 193 F 2
Metro 176 C 5
Metropolis (IL.) 121 R 5
Métsevon, Zigos 154 B 3
Metter (GA.) 131 MN 2
Metu 198 F 3
Metz 153 E 2
Meulaboh 176 A 3
Meureudu 176 A 2
Meuse 153 E 2
Mexia (TX.) 122 G 4
Mexiana, 139 J 3
Mexicali 106 CD 5
Mexican Springs (N.M.) 116 H 2
Mexican Water (AZ.) 116 G 1
Mexico 132 C 3
Mexico (ME.) 126 J 4
Mexico (MO.) 121 O 3
Mexico, Gulf of 132 DE 2
Mexico Beach (FL.) 131 J 5
México City 132 BC 4
Meyanobab 177 H 5
Meybod (Iran) 157 F 2
Meydān-e Gel (Iran) 157 G 3
Meyeihido 192 B 4
Meyers Chuck 109 M 4
Meyersdale (PA.) 125 Q 10
Meyísti (NV.) 154 C 3
Meymeh (Iran) 157 E 2
Meymeh (Iran) 157 F 2
Meyo Centre 197 G 5
Mezada (Israel) 156 B 3
Mezcalapa, Rio 132 D 4
Mezdra 154 B 2
Mezen' 158 HJ 2
Mezen' 158 HJ 2
Mezenskaya Guba 158 H 2
Mezenskiy 170 G 1
Mezhdurechensk 159 R 5
Mezhdurechenskiy 159 M 2
Mezhdusharskiy, Ostrov 158 K 1
Mezhevaya 155 E 1
Mežica 153 F 2
Mezőtúr 154 B 1
Mezraa 155 E 2
Mfanganu 198 E 5
Mgachi 171 Q 5
Mgera 199 F 6
Mgori 198 EF 5
Mhow 174 C 3
Miajadas 152 B 4
Miaméré 198 C 3
Miami (AZ.) 116 F 4
Miami (FL.) 131 OP 9
Miami (OK.) 121 L 6
Miami (TX.) 117 Q 2
Miami Beach (FL.) 131 OP 9
Miami Canal 131 O 8
Miami Springs (FL.) 131 O 9
Miān Āb (Iran) 157 E 2–3
Miancaowan 172 C 3
Mianchi 172 F 4
Miāndarreh (Iran) 157 F 2
Miāndowāb (Iran) 157 D 1

Miandrivazo 201 H 3
Mianduhe 171 M 6
Mīāneh (Iran) 157 E 1
Mīāneh (Iran) 157 E 1
Miani Hor 169 H 5
Mian Kalai 169 J 4
Mianning 172 D 5
Mianwali 169 J 4
Mianyang 172 D 4
Mianzhu 172 D 4
Miaodao Qundao 173 H 3
Miao'ergou 169 L 1
Miarinarivo 201 H 3
Miaru 184 E 3
Miass 159 M 4
Miass 159 LM 5
Miastko 149 G 4
Micaune 201 F 3
Micay 138 C 3
Michalovce 149 H 5
Micheweni 199 FG 5
Michelson, Mount 102 H 2
Michigamme, Lake 124 F 3
Michigan 124–125
Michigan (N.D.) 119 KL 2
Michigan Center (MI.) 125 K 7
Michigan City (IN.) 124 H 8
Michigan Island 124 D 3
Michipicoten Bay 104 K 6
Michipicoten Island 104 K 6
Michoacán 132 B 4
Mičurin 154 C 2
Michurinsk 158 G 5
Micronesia 186 A–C 2
Midai, Pulau 176 C 3
Midas (NV.) 112 J 1
Mid-Atlantic Ridge 208 A 2–5
Middelburg 148 D 4
Middelburg (South Africa) 200 D 5
Middelburg (South Africa) 200 D 6
Middelfart 151 EF 4
Middelwit 200 D 4
Middle Alkali Lake 112 E 1
Middle America Trench 209 D 3
Middle Andaman 175 F 5
Middlebourne (W.V.) 129 L 2
Middleburg (N.Y.) 126 E 6
Middleburg (PA.) 127 B 8
Middleburry (VT.) 126 F 5
Middle Fork (AK.) 109 H 2
Middle Fork (AK.) 109 J 2
Middle Fork (ID.) 111 L 5–6
Middle Fork (KS.) 120 D 3
Middle Loup River 118 J 9
Middleport (OH.) 129 J 3
Middle River (MN.) 119 M 2
Middlesboro (KY.) 128 H 5
Middlesbrough 148 C 4
Middleton (ID.) 110 J 7
Middleton (TN.) 128 C 6
Middleton Island 109 H 4
Middletown (CA.) 112 C 4
Middletown (CT.) 126 G 7
Middletown (IN.) 124 E 9
Middletown (N.Y.) 126 E 7
Middletown (OH.) 128 G 2
Middletown (PA.) 127 D 9
Middletown (W.V.) 129 N 2
Middleville (MI.) 124 J 7
Middle Water (TX.) 117 O 2
Midelt 192 E 2
Midfield (TX.) 122 G 7
Midford (N.J.) 127 E 9
Miðsandur 150 A 3
Midi, Canal du 152 D 3
Mid-Indian Ridge 208 B 4
Midland (CA.) 113 L 9
Midland (MI.) 125 K 6
Midland (Ontario, Can.) 105 M 7
Midland (S.D.) 118 G 6
Midland (TX.) 117 O 5–6
Midlothian (TX.) 122 FG 3
Midongy Atsimo 201 H 4
Midpines (CA.) 112 F 5
Midvales (ID.) 110 J 6
Midville (GA.) 131 M 2
Midway (AL.) 131 J 2
Midway (AZ.) 116 D 5
Midway (GA.) 131 N 3
Midway (TX.) 123 H 4
Midway (UT.) 114 F 3
Midwest (WY.) 118 B 7
Midwest City (OK.) 120 H 7
Midyat 155 F 3
Midžor 154 B 2
Miedwie, Jezioro 149 F 4
Międzyrzec Podlaski 149 H 4
Międzyrzecz 149 G 4
Miekojärvi 150 HJ 2
Mielan 152 C 3
Mielec 149 H 4
Mielno 149 G 4
Miesso 199 G 3
Miffin (OH.) 125 M 9
Migiurtinia 199 HJ 2
Miguel Alves 141 H 1

Mihăilesti 154 C 2
Mihalıççık 154 D 3
Mihuru 201 F 2
Mijares 152 C 3
Mjdaḥah 195 H 6
Mikelumne Hill (CA.) 112 E 4
Mikhalkino 171 U 2
Mikha Tskhakaya 155 F 2
Mikhaylov 158 G 5
Mikhaylovgrad 154 B 2
Mikhaylovka 155 G 1
Mikhaylovka 158 H 5
Mikhaylovka 168 D 1
Mikhaylovskiy 159 PQ 5
Mikinai 154 B 3
Mikindani 201 FG 2
Mikino 171 U 3
Mikkeli (Sankt Michel) 150 J 3
Míkonos 154 C 3
Mikré Prëspa, Límni 154 B 2
Mikumi 199 F 6
Mikumi National Park 199 F 6
Mikun' 158 JK 3
Mikuni-sanmyaku 173 L 3
Mila 153 E 4
Milaca (MN.) 119 P 5
Miladunmadulu Atoll 174 B 6
Milagro 138 C 4
Mīlājerd (Iran) 157 E 2
Milan 153 EF 2
Milan (GA.) 131 L 2–3
Milan (MI.) 125 L 7
Milan (MN.) 119 N 5
Milan (MO.) 121 M 2
Milan (N.M.) 116 J 2
Milan (TN.) 128 C 6
Milando Reserve 200 B 1
Milange 201 F 3
Milano 153 E 2
Milano (TX.) 122 G 5
Milás 154 C 3
Milazzo 153 FG 4
Milbank (S.D.) 119 M 5
Milburn (OK.) 120 J 8
Milcan Tepe 155 E 3
Mildred (MT.) 118 D 4
Mildura 183 G 5
Miléai 154 B 3
Miles 183 HJ 4
Miles (TX.) 122 C 4
Miles (WA.) 110 G 3
Miles City (MT.) 118 C 4
Milesville (S.D.) 118 G 6
Milet 154 C 3
Milford (CA.) 112 E 2
Milford (CT.) 127 FG 7
Milford (IA.) 119 N 7
Milford (MA.) 126 H 6
Milford (NE.) 120 H 2
Milford (N.H.) 126 H 6
Milford (PA.) 127 D 10
Milford (PA.) 127 E 7
Milford (UT.) 114 E 5
Milford (WY.) 111 R 8
Milford Center (OH.) 125 L 9
Milford Haven 148 B 4
Milford Lake 120 J 3
Milford Sound 184 P 9
Milgun 182 B 4
Mili 186 C 2
Milk, Bahr al (Iraq) 156 D 2
Milk River 118 B 2
Mill 105 M 3
Millau 152 D 3
Mill City (NV.) 112 GH 2
Mill City (OR.) 110 C 6
Milledgeville (GA.) 128 H 8
Mille Lacs Lake 119 P 4
Millen (GA.) 131 N 2
Miller (AL.) 130 G 2
Miller (NE.) 120 F 2
Miller (S.D.) 118 K 6
Miller House 109 J 2
Millerovo 158 H 6
Miller Peak 116 F 6
Millersburg (OH.) 125 M 9
Millers Ferry (AL.) 130 G 2
Millersview (TX.) 122 D 4
Millerton Lake 112 F 5
Millevaches, Plateau de 152 D 2
Mill Hall (PA.) 127 B 7
Millicent 183 FG 6
Millington (TN.) 128 B 6
Millinocket (ME.) 126 L 3
Millinocket Lake 126 L 3
Mill Iron (MT.) 118 D 5
Millry (AL.) 130 F 3
Mills (NE.) 118 J 8
Mills (N.M.) 117 M 1
Mills (UT.) 114 E 4
Mills (WY.) 118 B 8
Mills Lake 103 O 3
Millstatt 153 F 2
Millstone (W.V.) 129 KL 3
Millstream 182 B 3
Millville (N.J.) 127 E 9
Millwood Lake 121 M 9

Milner (CO.) 115 K 3
Milnesand (N.M.) 117 N 4
Milnor(N.D.) 119 L 4
Milo 196 C 3
Milolii (HI.) 113 G 12
Mílos 154 B 3
Milparinka 183 G 4
Milroy (PA.) 127 B 8
Milton (FL.) 130 G 4
Milton (N.D.) 119 K 2
Milton (N.S.W., Austr.) 183 J 6
Milton (PA.) 127 C 7
Milton (VT.) 126 F 4
Milton (W.V.) 129 J 3
Milton Freewater (OR.) 110 G 5
Milton Reservoir 115 N 3
Miltonvale (KS.) 120 H 3
Miltou 197 H 3
Miluo 172 F 5
Mil'utke, Gora 108 C 2
Milwaukee (WI.) 124 G 6
Milwaukie (OR.) 110 C 5
Milyatino 158 F 5
Mimbres Mountains 116 J 5
Mimizan 152 C 3
Mimongo 197 G 6
Mims (FL.) 131 O 6
Mina 170 F 5
Mina (NV.) 112 G 4
Mina (S.D.) 119 K 5
Mina, Mont 196 C 3
Mīnā' 'Abd Allāh (Kuwait) 157 E 3
Mīnā' al 'Aḥmadī (Kuwait) 157 E 3
Mīnāb 168 F 3
Mīnā' Baranīs (Egypt) 156 B 5
Minahassa Peninsula 177 F 3
Mina Jabal 'Ālī (United Arab Emirates) 157 G 4
Minam (OR.) 110 H 5
Minamata 173 JK 4
Minami-daitō-jima 173 K 5
Minas (Indonesia) 176 B 3
Minas (Uruguay) 142 EF 5
Minas, Sierra de las 132 E 4
Mīnā' Sa'ūd (Saudi Arabia) 157 E 3
Minas Gerais 141 GH 4
Minas Novas 141 H 4
Minatare (NE.) 118 E 9
Minatitlán 132 D 4
Minbu 175 F 3
Minbya 175 F 3
Mincha 142 B 5
Mincio 153 F 2
Minco (OK.) 120 H 7
Mindanao 177 FG 2
Mindelo 196 B 6
Minden (F.R.G.) 149 E 4
Minden (LA.) 123 K 3
Minden (NE.) 120 FG 2
Minden (NV.) 112 F 4
Minden City (MI.) 125 L 6
Mindenmines (MO.) 121 L 5
Minderoo 182 B 3
Mindif 197 G 3
Mindoro 177 F 1
Mindoro Strait 177 F 1
Mindorou 197 G 5
Mindyak 159 L 5
Mine Head 148 B 4
Mineiros 141 F 4
Mineola (TX.) 123 H 3
Miner (MT.) 111 P 5
Mineral (CA.) 112 D 2
Mineral (VA.) 129 O 3
Mineral (WA.) 110 C 4
Mineral'nyye Vody 155 F 2
Mineral Point (WI.) 124 D 7
Mineral Springs (AR.) 121 M 9
Mineral Wells (TX.) 122 E 3
Minersville (UT.) 114 DE 5
Minerva (OH.) 125 N 9
Minerva (TX.) 122 FG 5
Minerva Reefs 186 D 4
Minfeng 169 L 3
Minga 200 D 2
Mingan 105 P 5
Mingary 183 G 5
Mingechaur 168 D 2
Mingechaurskoye Vodokhrani-
lishche 168 D 2
Mingenew 182 B 4
Mingin Range 175 G 3
Mingo Lake 105 N 3
Mingon 175 G 3
Mingrel'skaya 155 E 1
Mingshui 172 C 2
Mingshui 173 J 1
Mingteke 169 K 3
Mingxi 173 G 5
Minhe 172 D 3
Minho 152 B 3
Minicoy 174 B 6
Minidoka (ID.) 111 M 8
Minigwal, Lake 182 C 4
Minilya 182 A 3
Minilya River 182 A 3
Ministro João Alberto 141 F 3
Min Jiang 172 D 5
Min Jiang 173 G 5
Mink Creek (ID.) 111 O 8

Minle 172 D 3
Minna 197 F 4
Minneapolis (KS.) 120 H 3
Minneapolis (MN.) 119 P 5–6
Minnedosa 103 S 5
Minnehaha Sprs (W.V.) 129 M 3
Minneola (KS.) 120 E 5
Minnesota 119
Minnesota City (MN.) 119 R 6
Minnesota River 119 NO 6
Minnewaukan (ND.) 118 J 2
Miño 152 B 3
Minong (WI.) 124 C 3
Minonk (IL.) 124 F 9
Minot (N.D.) 118 G 2
Minqin 172 D 3
Minqing 173 G 5
Min Shan 172 D 4
Minsin 175 G 2
Minsk 151 J 5
Minster (OH.) 125 K 9
Minter (AL.) 130 GH 2
Mintle (NE.) 118 E 9
Minto (Fed. States of Micronesia) 186 B 2
Minto (N.D.) 119 L 2
Minto, Lac 105 N 4
Minto (Yukon, Can.) 102 K 3
Minto Inlet 103 O 1
Minturn (CO.) 115 L 4
Minūdasht 168 F 3
Minusinsk 170 F 5
Minvoul 197 G 5
Minwakh 195 H 5
Min Xian 172 D 4
Mio (MI.) 125 K 5
Miquan 169 M 2
Miquelon (Quebec, Can.) 105 M 6
Miquelon (Saint Pierre et Miquelon) 105 Q 6
Miquelon et Saint Pierre 105 Q 6
Mir 197 G 3
Mira 153 F 2
Mirabad 169 G 4
Miracle Hot Springs (CA.) 113 G 7
Mirador 141 H 2
Miraflores 138 D 3
Miraj 174 B 4
Miramar 143 E 6
Mirambeau 152 C 2
Miramichi Bay 105 P 6
Miramont-de-Guyenne 152 D 3
Miran 172 A 3
Miraña 138 D 2
Miranda 140 E 5
Miranda 140 E 5
Miranda (CA.) 112 B 2
Miranda de Ebro 152 C 3
Mirandela 152 B 3
Mirandola 153 F 3
Mirapinima 139 F 4
Miravalles, Volcán 132 F 5
Miravete, Puerto de 152 B 4
Mirbāt 195 J 5
Mirdita 154 AB 2
Mirgorod 158 F 6
Miri 176 D 3
Miriam Vale 183 J 3
Mirim, Lagoa 142 F 5
Mirina 154 C 3
Mirnoye 159 R 3
Mirnyy 170 K 3
Mirnyy 203
Mirpur 169 J 4
Mirpur Khas 169 H 5
Mirria 197 F 3
Mirsäle 199 H 3
Mirsali 169 M 2
Mirtna 183 H 3
Mirtóon Pélagos 154 B 3
Mirzapur 174 D 2
Misenheimer (N.C.) 129 L 6
Misgar 169 J 3
Mish'āb, Ra's al (Saudi Arabia) 157 E 3
Mishan 173 K 1
Mishawaka (IN.) 124 H 8
Misheguk Mountains 108 C 2
Mishicot (WI.) 124 G 5
Mishkino 158 L 4
Misima Island 183 J 1
Misima Island 185 F 4
Misión Cavinas 140 C 3
Miskah (Saudi Arabia) 156 D 4
Miskitos, Cayos 132 F 5
Miskolc 154 B 1
Mismār 194 F 5
Misool, Pulau 177 H 4
Miṣr 194 DE 4
Miṣrātah 193 HJ 2
Miṣrātah, Ra's 193 J 2
Missinaibi 104 L 5
Mission (SD.) 118 H 7
Mission (TX.) 122 E 9
Mission Range 111 N 3
Mission Ridge (SD.) 118 GH 6
Missisa Lake 104 K 5
Mississinewa River 124 J 9
Mississippi (North) 121
Mississippi (South) 130
Mississippi River 123 M 4

Mississippi River Delta 123 OP 6
Mississippi Sound 130 F 4
Missoula (MT.) 111 LM 4
Missour 192 E 2
Missouri 121
Missouri Buttes 118 D 6
Missouri River 121 O 4
Missouri Valley (IA.) 120 K 1
Mist (OR.) 110 B 4
Mistassini, Lac 105 N 5
Misti, Volcán 140 B 4
Mistrás 154 B 3
Misty Fjords National Monument 102 L 4
Mitchell (IN.) 128 E 3
Mitchell (NE.) 118 E 9
Mitchell (OR.) 110 E 6
Mitchell (Queensland, Austr.) 183 H 4
Mitchell (S.D.) 119 K 7
Mitchell, Lake 131 H 2
Mitchell, Mount 129 J 6
Mitchell River 183 G 2
Mitchell River (Queensland, Austr.) 183 G 2
Mitchell River (Victoria, Austr.) 183 H 6
Miteja 199 F 6
Mithimna 154 C 3
Mitiaro 187 E 4
Mitilini 154 C 3
Mitina 158 J 2
Mitla 132 C 4
Mito 173 M 3
Mitomoni 201 EF 2
Mitra 197 F 5
Mitsinjo 201 H 3
Mitsiwa 195 G 5
Mittelland kanal 149 E 4
Mittersill 153 F 2
Mitú 138 D 3
Mitumba 198 E 6
Mitumba, Monts 198 D 5–6
Mitwaba 198 D 6
Mityayevo 159 M 3
Mitzic 197 G 5
Mius 155 E 1
Mivec 192 C 4
Miyāh, Wādi al (Syria) 156 C 2
Miyake-jima 173 LM 4
Miyako 173 M 3
Miyako-jima 173 J 6
Miyakonojō 173 K 4
Miyako-rettō 173 H 6
Miyaly 168 E 1
Miyazaki 173 K 4
Miyi 172 D 5
Miyun 173 G 2
Mizan Teferi 198 F 3
Mizdah 193 H 2
Mize (MS.) 130 E 3
Mizen Head 148 AB 4
Mizhi 172 F 3
Mizil 154 C 2
Mizoram 175 F 3
Mizque 140 D 4
Mizuho 203
Mizusawa 173 M 3
Mjölby 151 FG 3
Mjøndalen 151 E 4
Mjøsa 151 F 3
Mkangira 199 F 6
Mkasu 199 F 6
Mkata 199 F 6
Mkoani 199 F 6
Mkokotoni 199 F 6
Mkomazi 199 F 5
Mkomazi Game Reserve 199 F 5
Mkuku 200 D 2
Mkulwe 198 E 6
Mkushi 200 D 2
Mladá Boleslav 149 F 4
Mladenovac 154 B 2
Mlala Hills 198 E 6
Mleihas 192 D 4
Mljet 153 G 3
Mljetski kanal 153 G 3
Mlnta 197 G 5
Mława 149 H 4
Mleti 155 F 2

Mocajuba 139 J 4
Moçambique 201 G 3
Mocambique Basin 208 B 5
Moccasin (AZ.) 116 D 1
Moccasin (CA.) 112 E 5
Moccasin (MT.) 111 P 3
Moccasin Gap (VA.) 128 J 5
Mocha, Isla 143 B 6
Mocha → Al Mukhā 195 G 6
Mochudi 200 D 4
Mocímboa da Praia 201 G 2
Mockfjärd 151 FG 3
Mocksville (N.C.) 129 L 6
Moclips (WA.) 110 A 3
Môco, Morro de 200 AB 2
Mocoa 138 C 3
Mococa 141 G 5
Moctezuma 106 E 6
Moctezuma 132 B 3
Mocuba 201 F 3
Modane 153 E 2
Moddersville (MI.) 125 K 5
Model (CO.) 115 N 6
Model Town 169 J 4
Modena (Italy) 153 F 3
Modena (UT.) 114 D 6
Modesto (CA.) 112 DE 5
Modica 153 F 4
Modjamboli 198 C 4
Modoc (S.C.) 129 J 8
Modoc Point (OR.) 110 D 8
Modowi 177 H 4
Modra 197 H 1
Modriča 153 G 3
Modur Dağı 155 F 3
Moe 183 H 6
Moengo 139 H 2
Moenkopi (AZ.) 116 E 1
Moero, Lac 198 D 6
Moffat (CO.) 115 K 3
Moffat (CO.) 115 LM 6
Moffit (ND.) 118 H 4
Moga 198 D 5
Mogadiscio → Muqdisho 199 H 4
Mogadishu 199 H 4
Mogadouro, Serra do 152 B 3
Mogäl (Iran) 157 F 1
Mogaung 175 G 2
Mogdy 171 O 5
Moghüyeh, Bandar-e (Iran) 157 FG 4
Mogi das Cruzes 141 G 5
Mogilev 151 JK 5
Mogilev Podol'skiy 154 C 1
Mogil-Mogil 183 H 4
Mogi-Mirim 141 G 5
Mogincual 201 G 3
Mogocha 170 LM 5
Mogochin 159 Q 4
Mogogh 198 E 3
Mogok 175 G 3
Mogollon Baldy Peck 116 H 4
Mogollon Range 116 H 4
Mogollon Rim 116 F 3
Mogotoyevo, Ozero 171 R 1
Mogoyn 170 G 6
Mogoytui 170 KL 5
Mogu 199 G 4
Moguqi 171 M 6
Mogzon 170 K 5
Mohács 154 A 1
Mohall (ND.) 118 G 2
Moḥammadābād (Iran) 157 G 3
Mohammedia 192 D 2
Mohave, Lake 116 B 2
Mohawk (AZ.) 116 C 5
Mohawk (N.Y.) 126 D 5
Mohawk (WI.) 124 F 2
Mohawk Valley 116 C 5
Mohe 171 M 5
Moheda 151 F 4
Moheli 201 G 2
Mohenjo Daro 169 H 5
Mohikan, Cape 102 D 3
Mohnyin 175 G 3
Mohona 174 C 2
Mohon Peak 116 C 3
Mohoro 199 F 6
Mointy 159 O 6
Mo i Rana 150 F 2
Moisака 105 O 5
Moise 105 O 5
Moisie 105 O 5
Moissac 152 D 3
Moissala 197 H 4
Moitaco 139 F 2
Mojácar 152 C 4
Mojave (CA.) 113 G 7
Mojave Desert 113 HK 8
Mojave River 113 J 8
Mojiang 172 D 6
Mojjo 199 F 3
Moju 139 J 4
Mokambo 200 D 2
Mokhotlong 200 D 5
Mokhovaya 171 T 5
Mokil 186 B 2
Moklakan 170 L 4
Mokokchung 175 F 2
Mokolo 197 G 3
Mokp'o 173 J 4
Mokra Gora 154 B 2

Mokwa 197 E 4
Mol 148 E 4
Mola di Bari 153 G 3
Molagno 132 C 3
Molalla (OR.) 110 C 5
Molat 153 F 3
Molchanovo 159 Q 4
Moldava 154 C 1
Moldaviya 154 C 1
Molde 150 E 3
Moldefjorden 150 E 3
Moldes 142 D 5
Moldova Nouă 154 B 2
Moldoveanu, Vîrful 154 B 1
Mole Game Reserve 196 D 4
Molegbe 198 C 4
Moleke 198 B 5
Molepolole 200 D 4
Molfetta 153 G 3
Molina (Argentina) 142 C 5
Molina (Chile) 143 B 6
Molina de Aragón 152 C 3
Molina de Segura 152 C 4
Moline (IL.) 124 D 8
Moline (KS.) 120 J 5
Moling 175 F 2
Molino (FL.) 130 G 4
Moliro 198 E 6
Molkäbäd (Iran) 157 F 2
Molkom 151 F 4
Mollendo 140 B 4
Molochansk 155 E 1
Molochnyy Liman 155 E 1
Molodechno 151 J 5
Molodezhnaya 203
Molodo 170 M 2
Molodogvardeyskaya 159 O 5
Molokai 113 EF 10
Molokai 187 E 1
Molokai Fracture Zone 209 D 2
Molong 183 H 5
Molopo 200 C 5
Molotovo 155 F 2
Moloundou 197 H 5
Molt (MT.) 111 R 5
Molteno 200 D 6
Moluccas 177 G 4
Molus Ridge 208 A 1
Molybdenite Mountain 110 H 2
Moma (Mozambique) 201 F 3
Moma (U.S.S.R.) 171 QR 2
Mombaça 141 J 2
Mombasa 199 FG 5
Mombetsu 173 M 2
Mombi New 175 F 3
Mombo 199 F 5
Mombotuta Falls 200 D 2
Momboyo 198 B 5
Momence (IL.) 124 G 8
Momi 198 D 5
Mompono 198 C 4
Mompós 138 D 2
Momskiy Khrebet 171 QR 1–2
Mön 151 F 5
Mon 175 G 4–5
Mona (UT.) 114 F 4
Mona, Canal de la 133 J 4
Mona, Isla 130 B 8
Mona, Isla 133 J 4
Monaco 153 E 3
Monadhliath Mountains 148 C 3
Monadnock Mountain 126 G 6
Monaghan 148 B 4
Monahans (TX.) 117 O 6
Monango (N.D.) 119 K 4
Monapo 201 G 2
Mona Quimbundo 200 B 1
Monarch (MT.) 111 P 3
Monarch Mountain 103 M 5
Monarch Pass 115 L 5
Mona Reservoir 114 F 4
Monashee Mountains 103 O 5
Monastery of Saint Catherine (Egypt)
  156 AB 3
Monatélé 197 G 5
Monbetsu 173 M 2
Moncalieri 153 E 2–3
Moncayo, Sierra del 152 C 3
Monchegorsk 150 J 2
Mönchen-Gladbach 148 E 4
Moncks Corner (S.C.) 129 LM 8
Monclova 132 B 2
Moncton 105 O 6
Mondego 152 B 3
Mondego, Cabo 152 B 3
Mondjuko 198 C 5
Mondo 197 H 3
Mondoñedo 152 B 3
Mondovi 153 E 3
Mondovi (WI.) 124 C 5
Mondragone 153 F 3
Mondy 170 H J 5
Monero (N.M.) 117 K 1
Monessen (PA.) 125 P 9
Moneta (WY.) 111 S 7
Monett (MO.) 121 M 6
Money 175 K 4
Monfalcone 153 F 2
Monforte 152 B 4
Monga 198 C 4

Mongala 198 C 4
Mongalla 198 E 3
Mongbwalu 198 D 4
Mong Cai 175 J 3
Monger, Lake (Western Australia)
  182 B 4
Mong Hang 175 G 3
Mong Hpayak 175 G 3
Monghyr 174 E 2
Mong La 175 G 3
Mong Lin 175 H 3
Mong Loi 175 H 3
Mongo (Chad) 197 H 3
Mongo (Sierra Leone) 196 B 4
Mongol Ard Uls 170 GH 6
Mongolia 170 GH 6
Mongolo 170 J 2
Mongono 197 G 5
Mongonu 197 G 3
Mongororo 197 J 3
Mongu 200 C 3
Môngua 200 B 3
Monguel 192 C 5
Mong Yai 175 G 3
Monhegan Island 126 K 5
Mönnhaan 172 F 1
Monichkirchen 153 G 2
Monida (MT.) 111 N 6
Monida Pass 111 N 6
Monigotes 142 D 5
Monito, Isla 130 B 8
Monitor Range 112 J 4
Monjes, Islas los 138 D 1
Monkey Bay 201 EF 2
Monkey River 132 E 4
Monkira 183 G 3
Monkoto 198 C 5
Monmouth (IL.) 124 D 9
Monmouth (OR.) 110 B 6
Mono (Solomon Is.) 185 G 3
Mono (Togo) 196 E 4
Mono Lake (CA.) 112 FG 4
Mono Lake (CA.) 112 FG 4
Monolithos 154 C 3
Monomoy Island 126 K 7
Monon (IN.) 124 G 9
Monona (WI.) 124 E 6
Monong 200 C 4
Monopoli 153 G 3
Monor 154 A 1
Monou 197 J 2
Monreal del Campo 152 C 3
Monreale 153 F 4
Monroe (GA.) 128 H 8
Monroe (IA.) 119 P 9
Monroe (LA.) 123 L 3
Monroe (MI.) 125 L 8
Monroe (N.C.) 129 L 7
Monroe (OR.) 110 B 6
Monroe (WA.) 110 C 3
Monroe (WI.) 124 E 7
Monroe City (MO.) 121 O 3
Monroe Lake 128 E 2
Monroeville (AL.) 130 G 3
Monrovia 196 B 4
Mons 148 D 4
Monsanto 152 B 3
Monse (WA.) 110 F 2
Monsefú 138 C 5
Mönsterås 151 G 4
Mont Afao 193 G 3
Montagne d'Ambre 201 H 2
Montagne de Lure 153 E 3
Montagne Pelée 133 K 5
Montague (AK.) 102 H 4
Montague (CA.) 112 C 1
Montague (MI.) 124 H 6
Montague (MT.) 111 Q 3
Montague (TX.) 122 F 2
Mont Aigoual 152 D 3
Mont Ajir 197 F 2
Montalbán 152 C 3
Montalegre 152 B 3
Montana (AK.) 109 HJ 3
Montana (East) 118
Montana (West) 118
Montana City (MT.) 111 O 4
Montargis 152 D 2
Montauban 152 C 2
Montauban 152 D 3
Montauk (N.Y.) 127 H 8
Mont aux Sources 200 D 5
Montbard 153 D 2
Montbeliard 153 E 2
Mont Belvieu (TX.) 123 J 6
Mont Blanc 153 E 2
Montbrison 152 D 2
Mont Cameroun 197 F 5
Mont-de-Ganga 197 G 4
Mont Deinguéri 197 F 5
Mont du Metal 193 G 4
Monte Alban 132 C 4
Monte Alegre 139 H 4
Monte Azul 141 H 4
Monte Bello Islands 182 AB 3
Monte Binga 201 E 3
Monte Carlo 153 E 3

Monte Carmelo 141 G 4
Monte Caseros 142 E 5
Montech 152 D 3
Monte Cinto 153 E 3
Monte Clare (S.C.) 129 M 7
Monte Claros 141 H 4
Monte Común 142 C 5
Montecristi 133 H 4
Monte Cristo 140 D 3
Monte d'Oro 153 E 3
Monte Dourado 139 H 4
Monte Fitz Roy 143 B 8
Montego Bay 133 G 4
Mont Ei Loutone 197 G 1
Montejinnie 182 E 2
Monte Lindo 140 E 5
Montello (NV.) 112 L 1
Montello (WI.) 124 E 6
Monte Maca 143 B 8
Monte Melimoyo 143 B 7
Montemoreos 132 C 2
Montemor-o-Novo 152 B 4
Montenegro 142 F 4
Monte Negro Falls 200 A 3
Monte Pascoal, Parque Nacio-
  nal de 141 J 4
Montepuez 201 F 2
Montepulciano 153 F 3
Monte Quemado 142 D 4
Monterado 176 C 3
Monterey (CA.) 112 D 6
Monterey (TN.) 128 F 5
Monterey (VA.) 129 M 3
Monterey Bay 112 CD 6
Monteria 138 C 2
Montero 140 D 4
Monte Rosa 153 E 2
Monterotondo 153 F 3
Monterrey 132 BC 2
Montes Altos 139 J 5
Monte Santo 139 J 5
Monte Sarmiento 143 B 9
Montes de Leon 152 B 3
Montes de Toledo 152 C 4
Montesilvano 153 F 3
Montes Universales 152 C 3
Montes Vascos 152 C 3
Monte Tronador 143 B 7
Montevallo (AL.) 128 E 8
Montevideo (MN.) 119 N 6
Monteview (ID.) 111 N 7
Monte Vista (CO.) 115 LM 6
Monte Zeballos 143 B 8
Montezuma (IA.) 119 Q 9
Montezuma (KS.) 120 E 5
Montezuma Castle National
  Monument 116 E 3
Montgomery (AL.) 131 H 2
Montgomery (MN.) 119 P 6
Montgomery (TX.) 123 H 5
Montgomery City (MO.) 121 O 3–4
Montgomery Creek (CA.) 112 D 2
Mont Gréboun 197 F 1
Monthey 153 E 2
Monti Aurunci 153 F 3
Mont Iboundji 197 G 6
Monticello (AR.) 121 O 9
Monticello (FL.) 131 L 4
Monticello (GA.) 128 H 8
Monticello (IA.) 119 R 8
Monticello (IL.) 124 F 9
Monticello (IN.) 124 H 9
Monticello (KY.) 128 G 5
Monticello (MO.) 121 O 2
Monticello (MS.) 130 D 3
Monticello (N.M.) 117 J 4
Monticello (N.Y.) 126 E 7
Monticello (UT.) 114 H 6
Monticello (WI.) 124 E 7
Monti dei Frentani 153 FG 3
Monti di Ala 153 E 3
Montiel, Campo de 152 C 4
Montigny-le-Roi 153 E 2
Montigny-les-Metz 153 E 2
Monti Iblei 153 F 4
Monti Lepini 153 F 3
Montilla 152 C 4
Monti Peloritani 153 FG 4
Monti Sabini 153 F 3
Monti Volsini 153 F 3
Mont Jacques-Cartier 105 OP 6
Mont Joli 105 O 6
Mont Kavendou 196 B 3
Mont-Louis 152 D 3
Mont Lozère 152 D 3
Montluçon 152 D 2
Montmagny 105 NO 6
Mont Mézenc 152 D 3
Mont Mina 196 C 3
Mont Mpelé 197 G 6
Mont Ngoua 198 C 3
Mont Niéndkoué 196 C 4
Monto 183 J 3
Montoro 152 C 4
Montour (ID.) 110 J 7

Montour Falls (N.Y.) 126 C 6
Mont Panié 185 H 6
Mont Pelat 153 E 3
Montpelier (CA.) 112 E 5
Montpelier (ID.) 111 O 8
Montpelier (MS.) 121 R 9
Montpelier (VT.) 126 G 4
Montpéllier 152 D 3
Mont Pinçon 152 C 2
Montréal 105 N 6
Montreal Lake 103 QR 5
Montréjeau 152 D 3
Montreux 153 E 2
Montrose (AR.) 121 O 9
Montrose (CO.) 115 JK 5
Montrose (MS.) 130 E 2
Montrose (PA.) 126 D 7
Montrose (S.D.) 119 LM 7
Montrose (U.K.) 148 C 3
Montross (VA.) 129 P 3
Montsalvy 152 D 3
Montsant, Sierra de 152 D 3
Monts Bagzane 197 F 2
Monts Bambouto 197 G 4
Monts Bleus 198 E 4
Monts Chic-Chocs 105 O 6
Monts d'Amain 152 C 2
Monts d'Arrée 152 C 2
Monts d'Aubrac 152 D 3
Monts de Cristal 197 G 5
Monts de Lacaune 152 D 3
Monts de la Medjerda 193 G 1
Monts des Ksour (Algeria) 192 EF 2
Monts des Ksour (Tunisia) 193 GH 2
Monts des Oulad Naïl 193 F 2
Monts de Toura 196 C 4
Monts Dore 152 D 2
Monts du Beaujolais 153 D 2
Monts du Hodna 193 FG 1
Monts du Hombori 196 D 2
Monts du Livradois 153 D 2
Monts du Lyonnais 153 D 2
Montseck, Sierra del 152 D 3
Montseny, Sierra de 152 D 3
Montserrat 133 K 4
Monts Koungou 197 G 6
Monts Kundelungu 198 D 6–7
Monts Malimba 198 D 6
Monts Mandingues 196 B 3
Monts Marungu 198 D 6
Monts Mbang 197 G 4
Monts Mitumba 198 D 5–6
Monts Moukandé 197 G 6
Monts Mugila 198 D 6
Monts Nimba 196 C 4
Monts Notre-Dame 105 O 6
Monts Otish 105 N 5
Monts Tamgak 197 F 2
Monts Tarouadji 197 F 2
Monts Timétrine 196 D 2
Mont Tahat 193 G 4
Mont Tembo 197 G 5
Mont Tonkou 196 C 4
Mont Ventoux 153 E 3
Mont Zedness 192 C 4
Monument (OR.) 110 F 6
Monument Peak (CO.) 115 K 4
Monument Peak (ID.) 111 L 8
Monument Valley 114 H 6
Monveda 198 C 4
Monviso 153 E 3
Mon Yul 175 F 2
Monywa 175 G 3
Monza 153 E 2
Monzón 152 D 3
Monze 200 D 3
Moody (TX.) 122 F 4
Moonie 183 J 4
Moonie River 183 H 4
Moon Lake 112 E 1
Moon Reservoir 110 F 7
Moonta 183 F 5
Moora 182 B 5
Mooraberree 183 G 4
Moorcroft (WY.) 118 D 6
Moore (ID.) 111 M 7
Moore (OK.) 120 H 7
Moore (TX.) 122 DE 6
Moore, Lake 182 B 4
Moorea 187 EF 4
Moorefield (W.V.) 129 N 2
Moore Haven (FL.) 131 N 8
Mooreland (OK.) 120 F 6
Mooresville (IN.) 128 E 2
Mooresville (N.C.) 129 L 6
Moorhead (MN.) 119 M 4
Moorhead (MT.) 118 C 4
Moorlands 183 F 6
Moor of Rannoch 148 BC 3
Moorreesburg 200 B 6
Moose (Ontario, Can.) 105 L 5
Moose (WY.) 111 P 7
Moosehead Lake 126 K 3
Moose Jaw 103 Q 5
Moose Lake (MN.) 119 Q 4
Mooselookmeguntic Lake 126 J 4
Moose Pass 102 H 3
Moose River (ME.) 126 J 3
Moosomin 103 R 5

Moosonee 105 L 5
Mopeia 201 F 3
Mopipi 200 CD 4
Mopti 196 D 3
Moqokorei 199 H 4
Moquegua 140 B 4
Mora (Cameroon) 197 G 3
Mora (MN.) 119 P 5
Mora (N.M.) 117 L 1–2
Mora (Spain) 152 C 4
Mora (Sweden) 151 F 3
Moraca 154 A 2
Moradabad 174 C 2
Mora de Ebro 152 D 3
Morado, Cerro 140 CD 5
Morafenobe 201 G 3
Morąg 149 H 3
Moraleda, Canal 143 B 7
Morales (TX.) 122 G 6
Moraleya 152 B 3
Moramanga 201 H 3
Moran (KS.) 121 K 5
Moran (MI.) 125 K 3
Moran (TX.) 122 D 3
Moran (WY.) 111 P 7
Morane 187 F 4
Morant Cays 133 G 4
Morata, Puerto de 152 C 3
Moratuwa 174 C 6
Morava (Czechoslovakia) 149 G 5
Morava (Western Australia) 182 B 4
Morava (Yugoslavia) 154 B 2
Moravia (IA.) 119 Q 10
Moravia (N.Y.) 126 C 6
Moraviţa 154 B 1
Morawhanna 139 G 2
Moray Firth 148 C 3
Morbi 174 B 3
Mordaga 170 M 5
Morden (Manitoba, Can.) 103 S 6
Morden (N.D.) 119 K 1
Mordovo 158 H 5
Möre 151 G 4
Moreau River 118 F 5
Morecambe Bay 148 C 4
Moree 183 H 4
Morehead 184 D 3
Morehead (KY.) 128 H 3
Moreira 139 F 4
Moreland (GA.) 128 G 8
Moreland (KY.) 128 FG 4
More Laptevykh 170 MN 1
Morelia 132 B 4
Morelos 132 C 4
Morena 174 C 2
Morena, Sierra 152 BC 4
Morenci (AZ.) 116 G 4
Morenci (MI.) 125 K 8
Moreni 154 C 1–2
Moreno (Argentina) 143 B 6
Moreno (Peru) 138 C 5
Moreno, Parque Nacional 143 B 8
Moreno National Park 143 B 8
Moresby 102 L 5
Moreton 183 G 1
Moreton Island 183 J 4
Morey Peak 112 J 4
Morgan 183 F 5
Morgan (GA.) 131 K 3
Morgan (MN.) 119 O 6
Morgan (MT.) 111 S 2
Morgan (UT.) 114 F 2
Morgan, Mount 112 G 5
Morgan City (AL.) 128 E 7
Morgan City (LA.) 123 M 6
Morganfield (KY.) 128 D 4
Morgan Hill (CA.) 112 D 5
Morgan Lake 116 H 1
Morgan Mill (TX.) 122 E 3
Morganton (N.C.) 129 K 6
Morgantown (KY.) 128 E 4
Morgantown (W.V.) 129 M 2
Morges 153 E 2
Morges 155 E 2
Mori (China) 172 B 2
Mori (Japan) 173 M 2
Moriah, Mount 112 L 3
Moriarty (N.M.) 117 K 2
Morichal 138 D 3
Moriki 197 F 3
Morin Dawa 171 M 6
Morioka 173 M 3
Morjärv 150 H 2
Morkoka 170 K 2
Morlaix 152 C 2
Morland (KS.) 120 EF 3
Morley (MI.) 124 J 6
Morley (MO.) 121 Q 5
Mormanno 153 G 4
Mormon Lake 116 E 3
Mormon Mountains 112 L 5
Mormon Reservoir 111 L 7
Morne Diablotin 133 K 4
Mornington, Isla 143 A 8
Mornington Abyssal Plain 209 D 5
Mornington Island (Queensland, Austr.)
  183 F 2
Morno 196 D 4

Mornou, Hadjer 197 J 2
Moro (OR.) 110 E 5
Morobe 184 E 3
Morobe 186 A 3
Morocco 192 D 2
Moroga 158 G 4
Morogoro 199 F 6
Moro Gulf 177 F 2
Moroleón 132 B 3
Morombe 201 G 4
Mörön 170 H 6
Morón (Kuba) 133 G 3
Morón (Spain) 152 B 4
Morón (Venezuela) 138 E 1
Morona 138 C 4
Morondava 201 G 4
Morondo 196 C 4
Morongo Indian Reservation 113 J 9
Moroni 201 G 2
Moroni (CO.) 114 F 4
Moroshechnoye 171 T 4
Morotai, Pulau 177 G 3
Morotai, Selat 177 G 3
Moroto 198 E 4
Moroto, Mount 198 EF 4
Morovis (P.R.) 130 C 8
Morozovsk 155 F 1
Morpará 141 H 3
Morphou → Güzelyurt 155 D 3
Morrill (NE.) 118 E 9
Morrinhos 141 H 1
Morrinhos 141 G 4
Morris (IL.) 124 F 8
Morris (Manitoba, Can.) 103 S 6
Morris (MN.) 119 N 5
Morris (N.D.) 119 L 1
Morrison (IL.) 124 DE 8
Morrisonville (IL.) 121 Q 3
Morristown (AZ.) 116 D 4
Morristown (N.J.) 127 E 8
Morristown (N.Y.) 126 D 4
Morristown (SD.) 118 G 5
Morristown (TN.) 128 H 5
Morro, Punta 142 B 4
Morro Bay (CA.) 113 E 7
Morro de Chapéu 141 H 3
Morro de Môco 200 AB 2
Morro do Sinal 141 G 3
Morrow (LA.) 123 L 5
Mörrum 151 F 4
Morrumbala 201 F 3
Morrumbene 201 F 4
Mors 151 E 4
Morse (TX.) 117 P 1
Morshansk 158 H 5
Mörsil 150 F 3
Morskaya 171 X 3
Mortagne-sur-Sèvre 152 C 2
Mortain 152 C 2
Morteros 142 D 5
Mortesoro 194 E 6
Mortlake 183 G 6
Mortlock Islands 186 B 2
Morton (IL.) 124 E 9
Morton (MN.) 119 O 6
Morton (MS.) 130 E 2
Morton (TX.) 117 O 4
Morton (WA.) 110 C 4
Moruya 183 J 6
Morven 183 H 4
Morven (GA.) 131 L 4
Morwell 183 H 6
Moryakovskiy Zaton 159 Q 4
Morzelândia 141 F 3
Morzhovel 108 F 5
Mosby 151 E 4
Mosby (MT.) 111 S 4
Moscow 158 G 4
Moscow (ID.) 110 HJ 3
Moscow (KS.) 120 D 5
Mosel 149 E 4
Moselle 148 E 5
Moselle 153 E 2
Moselle (MS.) 130 E 3
Moses Lake (WA.) 110 F 3
Moses Lake (WA.) 110 F 3
Moses Point 102 E 3
Moseyevo 158 J 2
Mosgiel 184 Q 10
Moshchnyy, Ostrov 151 J 4
Mosher (SD.) 118 H 7
Moshi 199 F 5
Mosina 149 G 4
Mosinee (WI.) 124 E 5
Mosjöen 150 F 2
Moskal'vo 171 Q 5
Moskenesöya 150 F 2
Moskosel 150 G 2
Moskva 158 G 4
Moskva, Gora 170 F 5
Mosomane 200 D 4
Mosonmagyaróvár 154 A 1
Mosquera 138 C 3
Mosquero (N.M.) 117 MN 2
Mosquito, Baie 105 M 3
Mosquito Creek Lake 125 O 8
Mosquitos, Costa de 132 F 5
Mosquitos, Golfo de los 138 B 2
Moss 151 F 4

Mossaka 197 H 6
Mosselbaai 200 C 6
Mossendjo 197 G 6
Mossoró 141 J 2
Moss Point (MS.) 130 F 4
Mossuril 201 G 2
Most 149 F 4
Mostaganem 192 EF 1
Mostar 153 G 3
Mostardas 142 F 5
Mosty 151 H 5
Mostyn 177 E 3
Mosul 195 G 1
Mota 199 F 2
Motajica 153 G 2–3
Motala 151 G 4
Motherwell 148 C 3
Motihari 174 DE 2
Motley (MN.) 119 O 4
Motilla del Palancar 152 C 4
Motoursville (PA.) 127 C 7
Motovskiy Zaliv 150 K 2
Motril 152 C 4
Motru 154 B 2
Mott (ND.) 118 F 4
Motueka 185 Q 9
Motu 132 E 3
Motu One 187 E 4
Mototunga 187 F 4
Motykleyka 171 R 4
Mouchard 153 E 2
Moudjéria 192 C 5
Mouila (Algeria) 192 E 3
Mouila (Gabon) 197 G 6
Mouka 198 C 3
Moukandé, Monts 197 G 6
Moul 197 G 2
Moulhoulé 199 G 2
Moulins 152 D 2
Moulmein 175 G 4
Moulouya 192 E 2
Moulton (AL.) 128 D 7
Moulton (IA.) 119 Q 10
Moulton Heights (AL.) 128 DE 7
Moultrie (GA.) 131 L 3
Moultrie, Lake 129 L 8
Mound City (IL.) 121 Q 5
Mound City (KS.) 121 L 4
Mound City (MO.) 121 K 2
Mound City (SD.) 118 HJ 5
Mound City Group National Monument
    128 HJ 2
Moundou 197 H 4
Moundridge (KS.) 120 H 4
Mounds (OK.) 120 J 7
Mounds (UT.) 114 G 4
Moundsville (W.V.) 129 L 2
Moundville (AL.) 130 G 1—2
Mount Adal 109 LM 4
Mount Adam 143 DE 9
Mount Adams 110 D 4
Mountain (WI.) 124 F 4
Mountainair (N.M.) 117 K 3
Mountain Brook (AL.) 128 E 8
Mountain City (GA.) 128 H 7
Mountain City (NV.) 112 K 1
Mountain City (TN.) 129 K 5
Mountain Creek (AL.) 131 H 2
Mountain Grove (MO.) 121 N 5
Mountain Home (AR.) 121 N 6
Mountain Home (ID.) 111 K 7
Mountain Home (TX.) 122 D 5
Mountain Meadows Reservoir 112 E 2
Mountain Pass 113 K 7
Mountain Pine (AR.) 121 M 8
Mountain Point 109 M 4
Mountain River 109 N 3
Mountains of Connemara 148 AB 4
Mountains of Mayo 148 B 4
Mountain View (AR.) 121 N 7
Mountain View (CA.) 112 C 5
Mountain View (MO.) 121 O 5
Mountainview (WY.) 111 P 9
Mountain Village 102 E 3
Mountain Wiew (WY.) 118 B 8
Mount Airy (N.C.) 129 L 5
Mount Amundsen 203
Mount Anglem 184 P 10
Mount Antero 115 L 5
Mount Apo 177 G 2
Mount Ararat 155 F 3
Mount Armstrong 109 M 3
Mount Arrowsmith 185 Q 9
Mount Ascutney 126 G 5
Mount Aspiring 184 P 9
Mount Assiniboine 103 O 5
Mount Augustus 182 B 3
Mount Ayr (IA.) 119 O 10
Mount Baker 110 D 2
Mount Balbi 185 F 3
Mount Bangeta 184 E 3
Mount Bangs 116 C 1
Mount Barker 183 F 6
Mount Barker 182 B 5
Mount Bendeleben 108 F 2
Mount Bimberi 183 H 6
Mount Blackburn 102 J 3
Mount Blackmore 111 OP 5
Mount Bona 102 J 3

Mount Bonaparte 110 F 2
Mount Brassey 182 E 3
Mount Brockman 182 B 3
Mount Broome 182 D 2
Mount Brown 111 O 2
Mount Brukkaros 200 B 5
Mount Bruce 182 B 3
Mount Cabot 126 H 4
Mount Callaghan 112 J 3
Mount Calm (TX.) 122 G 4
Mount Carmel (IL.) 121 S 4
Mount Carmel (UT.) 114 E 6
Mount Carter 183 G 1
Mount Casuarina 182 D 1
Mount Chiginagak 108 G 4
Mount Christie 109 M 3
Mount Christie 182 E 5
Mount Churchill 109 K 3
Mount Clark 103 N 3
Mount Clemens (MI.) 125 M 7
Mount Clere 182 B 4
Mount Cleveland 111 M 2
Mount Columbia 103 O 5
Mount Connor 182 D 1
Mount Constance 110 B 3
Mount Cook 185 Q 9
Mount Cook 186 C 5
Mount Coolon 183 H 3
Mount Cowen 111 P 5
Mount Crillon 109 L 4
Mount Crosby 111 Q 7
Mount Curious 182 A 4
Mount Curwood 124 F 3
Mount Cushing 103 M 4
Mount Dalrymple 183 H 3
Mount Darwin 201 E 3
Mount Davies 182 D 4
Mount Davis 125 P 10
Mount Deering 182 D 3
Mount Dellenbaugh 116 C 1
Mount Demavend (Iran) 157 F 2
Mount Denison 102 G 4
Mount Desert Island 126 L 4
Mount Doonerak 102 H 2
Mount Dora (N.M.) 117 N 1
Mount Douglas 183 H 3
Mount Eagle 130 E 9
Mount Eba 183 F 5
Mount Edith 111 O 4
Mount Eduni 109 N 3
Mount Egerton 182 B 3
Mount Egmont 185 Q 8
Mount Elbert 115 L 4
Mount Eldridge 109 K 3
Mount Elgon 198 E 4
Mount Elizabeth 182 D 2
Mount Elliot (Queensland, Austr.)
    183 H 2
Mount Enterprise (TX.) 123 J 4
Mount Erebus 203
Mount Essendon 182 C 3
Mount Evans 115 M 4
Mount Everest 174 E 2
Mount Fairweather 102 K 4
Mount Feathertop 183 H 6
Mount Finke 182 E 5
Mount Foraker 102 G 3
Mount Forel 202
Mount Forest 105 L 7
Mount Foster 102 K 4
Mount Fraser (Western Australia)
    182 B 4
Mount Frere 200 D 6
Mount Gambier 183 FG 6
Mount Gilead (OH.) 125 M 9
Mount Giluwe 184 D 3
Mount Gimie 133 K 5
Mount Glottof 102 G 4
Mount Godwin Austen 169 K 3
Mount Gould 182 B 4
Mount Graham 116 G 5
Mount Grant 112 G 4
Mount Grayback 108 M 4
Mount Greenough 109 K 2
Mount Greylock 126 F 6
Mount Groodenough 109 L 2
Mount Gunnison 115 K 5
Mount Hagen 184 D 3
Mount Haggin 111 M 4
Mount Halcon 177 F 1
Mount Hale (Western Australia) 182 B
Mount Halifax (Queensland, Austr.)
    183 H 2
Mount Hamilton (AK.) 108 G 3
Mount Hamilton (NV.) 112 K 3
Mount Hancock 111 P 6
Mount Harper 102 J 3
Mount Harvard 115 L 5
Mount Hawkes 203
Mount Hayes 102 H 3
Mount Haywood 103 N 3
Mount Healy 109 HJ 3
Mount Hermon (Lebanon) 156 B 2
Mount Hillaby 139 G 1
Mount Holly Springs (PA.) 127 B 8
Mount Holmes 111 O 4
Mount Hood 110 D 5
Mount Hope 183 F 5
Mount Hope (KS.) 120 H 5

Mount Hope (W.V.) 129 K 4
Mount Horeb (WI.) 124 E 7
Mount House 182 D 2
Mount Hutton 183 H 4
Mount Ida (AR.) 121 M 8
Mount Inyo 112 H 6
Mount Irish 112 K 5
Mount Isa 183 F 3
Mount Isto 109 K 2
Mount Jackson 182 B 5
Mount Jackson 203
Mount Jefferson (ID.) 111 O 6
Mount Jefferson (NV.) 112 J 4
Mount Jefferson (OR.) 110 D 6
Mount Jewett (PA.) 125 Q 8
Mount John 182 D 2
Mount Joy 109 M 3
Mount Katahdin 126 L 3
Mount Katmai 102 G 4
Mount Kennedy 109 L 3
Mount Kenya 199 F 5
Mount Kenya National Park 199 F 5
Mount Kimball 102 J 3
Mount Kirkpatrick 203
Mount Klotz 102 K 2
Mount Kosciusko 183 H 6
Mount Kovgarok 108 E 2
Mount Leake 182 D 2
Mount Leidy 111 P 7
Mount Leisler 182 D 3
Mount Lemmon 116 F 5
Mount Lesueur 182 B 5
Mount Lewis 112 J 2
Mount Liebig 182 E 3
Mount Livermore 117 M 7
Mount Lofty Ranges 183 F 5
Mount Logan (WA.) 110 E 2
Mount Logan (Yukon, Can.) 102 J 3
Mount Lola 112 E 3
Mount Lucania 102 J 3
Mount Lush 182 D 2
Mount Makalu 174 E 2
Mount Mansfield 126 G 4
Mount Mantalingajan 176 E 2
Mount Marcus Baker 102 H 3
Mount Marcy 126 F 4
Mount Marvine 114 F 5
Mount McDougall 111 P 8
Mount McGuire 111 L 5
Mount McKinley 102 G 3
Mount McLoughlin 110 C 8
Mount Menzies 203
Mount Michelson 102 H 2
Mount Mitchell 129 J 6
Mount Molloy (Queensland, Austr.)
    183 GH 2
Mount Montgomery (NV.) 112 GH 5
Mount Morgan 112 G 5
Mount Morgan 183 J 3
Mount Moriah 112 L 3
Mount Moroto 198 EF 4
Mount Mowbullan 183 J 4
Mount Muir 109 J 3
Mount Murchison (Western Australia)
    182 B 4
Mount Murray 109 N 3
Mount Nebo 114 F 4
Mount Nesselrode 109 M 4
Mount Nurri 183 H 5
Mount Nyiru 199 F 4
Mount Ogden 109 M 4
Mount Olga 182 E 4
Mount Olive (MS.) 130 E 3
Mount Olivet (KY.) 128 H 3
Mount Olympos → Kato Olimbos
    154 B 3
Mount Olympus 110 B 3
Mount Omatupa 200 B 4
Mount Orab (OH.) 128 H 2
Mount Ord 182 D 2
Mount Ossa 184 L 9
Mount Ossa 186 A 5
Mount Ouray 115 L 5
Mount Owen 185 Q 9
Mount Patterson 109 M 3
Mount Pattullo 102 LM 4
Mount Peale 114 H 5
Mount Pennell 114 G 6
Mount Perkins 116 B 2
Mount Pinos 113 F 8
Mount Pleasant (IA.) 119 R 10
Mount Pleasant (MI.) 125 K 6
Mount Pleasant (PA.) 125 P 9
Mount Pleasant (S.C.) 129 M 9
Mount Pleasant (TN.) 128 D 6
Mount Pleasant (TX.) 123 J 2
Mount Pleasant (UT.) 114 F 4
Mount Pleasant (WA.) 110 B 2–3
Mount Pulaski (IL.) 121 Q 3
Mount Pulog 177 F 1
Mount Queen Bess 103 N 5
Mount Ragang 177 F 2
Mount Rainier 110 D 4
Mount Rainier National Park 110 D 4
Mount Ratz 102 L 4
Mount Redcliffe 182 C 4
Mount Ritter 112 F 5
Mount Robe 183 G 5

Mount Roberts 183 J 4
Mount Robson 103 NO 5
Mount Rogers 129 K 5
Mount Roosevelt 103 M 4
Mount Rushmore 118 E 7
Mount Russel 109 H 3
Mount Saint Elias 102 J 3
Mount Saint Helens 110 C 4
Mount Saint Nicholas 111 M 2
Mount Samuel 182 E 2
Mount San Antonio 113 H 8
Mount Sandiman 182 B 3
Mount Sanford 102 J 3
Mount Scott (OR.) 120 FG 8
Mount Scott (OR.) 110 CD 8
Mount Sedgewick 116 H 2
Mount Selous 109 M 3
Mount Shasta 112 C 1
Mount Shasta (CA.) 112 C 1
Mount Shenton 182 C 4
Mount Singleton 182 B 4
Mount Sir Alexander 103 N 5
Mount Sir James MacBrien 109 N 3
Mount Sir Thomas 182 D 4
Mount Smythe 103 MN 4
Mount Spokane 110 H 3
Mount Springer 105 N 6
Mount Squires 182 D 4
Mount Steele 118 B 9
Mount Steller 109 K 3
Mount Sterling (IL.) 121 P 3
Mount Sterling (KY.) 128 H 3
Mount Sterling (OH.) 128 H 2
Mount Storm (W.V.) 129 M 2
Mount Storm Lake 129 M 2
Mount Sulen 184 D 2
Mount Sunflower 120 CD 3
Mount Tama 200 A 2
Mount Taylor 116 J 2
Mount Tazi 109 H 2
Mount Thuillier 175 F 6
Mount Tipton 116 B 2
Mount Tobin 112 H 2
Mount Tom White 102 J 3
Mount Torbert 102 G 3
Mount Travers 185 Q 9
Mount Trumbull 116 C 1
Mount Turnbull 116 F 4
Mount Union (PA.) 127 B 8
Mount Usborne 143 E 9
Mount Veniaminof 102 EF 4
Mount Vernon (AL.) 130 FG 3
Mount Vernon (Australia) 182 B 3
Mount Vernon (GA.) 131 M 2
Mount Vernon (IL.) 121 R 4
Mount Vernon (KY.) 128 G 4
Mount Vernon (MO.) 121 M 5
Mount Vernon (OH.) 125 M 9
Mount Vernon (OR.) 110 F 6
Mount Vernon (TX.) 123 H 2
Mount Vernon (WA.) 110 C 2
Mount Victoria (Burma) 175 F 3
Mount Victoria (Papua New Guinea)
    184 E 3
Mount Vsevidof 102 D 5
Mount Waddington 103 M 5
Mount Warner 110 F 8
Mount Washington 126 H 4
Mount Whitney 112 G 6
Mount Wilhelm 184 D 3
Mount Will 109 N 4
Mount Willoughby 182 E 4
Mount Wilson (AZ.) 116 B 2
Mount Wilson (NV.) 112 L 4
Mount Wilson (OK.) 115 JK 6
Mount Withington 117 J 4
Mount Wolf (PA.) 127 C 8
Mount Wood 111 Q 5
Mount Woodroffe 182 E 4
Mount Wrightson 116 F 6
Mount Zirkel 115 L 3
Moura 139 F 4
Mourão 152 B 4
Mourdi, Dépression du 197 J 2
Mourdiah 196 C 3
Mourenx 152 C 3
Mournei 194 C 6
Mourne Mountains 148 B 4
Mourra 197 J 3
Mousaaou Salah, Jbel 192 E 2
Mouscron 148 D 4
Moussoro 197 H 3
Mouths of the Amazon 139 J 3
Mouths of the Danube 154 CD 1
Mouths of the Ganges 174–175 EF 3
Mouths of the Godavari 174 D 4
Mouths of the Irrawaddy 175 FG 4
Mouths of the Krishna 174 D 4
Mouths of the Mekong 175 J 6
Mouths of the Orinoco 139 FG 2
Moûtiers 153 E 2
Moutong 177 F 3
Mouydir 193 F 2
Mouyondzi 197 G 6
Movas 106 E 6
Mowbullan, Mount 183 J 4
Möwe Bay 200 A 3
Moxee City (WA.) 110 E 4
Moxico 200 BC 2
Moxico 200 C 2

Moxos, Llanos de 140 CD 4
Moyahua 132 B 3
Moyale 199 F 4
Moyamba 196 B 4
Moyeni 200 D 6
Moyero 170 H 2
Moyie Spring (ID.) 110 J 2
Moyo, Pulau 176 E 5
Moyobamba 138 C 5
Moyowosi 198 E 5
Moyto 197 H 3
Moyu 169 K 3
Mozambique 201 EF 3
Mozambique Channel 201 FG 3–4
Mozdok 155 FG 2
Mozharka 170 F 5
Mozhga 158 K 4
Mozyr' 151 J 5
Mpala 198 D 6
Mpanda 198 E 6
Mpé 197 G 6
Mpelé, Mont 197 G 6
Mpika 201 E 2
Mporokosa 200 DE 1
Mpouya 197 H 6
Mpui 198 E 6
Mpulungu 201 E 1
Mpwapwa 199 F 6
Mragowa 149 H 4
Mrakovo 158 L 5
Mrewa 201 E 3
Msāk Mallat 193 H 3–5
Msāk Mastāfat 193 H 3
Msata 199 F 6
M'Sila 193 F 1
Msoro 201 E 2
Mstislavl' 158 F 5
Mtabatuba 201 E 5
Mtakuja 198 E 6
Mtama 201 F 2
Mtandi 199 F 6
Mtegere 199 F 6
Mtera 199 F 6
Mtito Andei 199 F 5
Mtoko 201 E 3
Mtsensk 158 G 5
Mtskheta 155 F 2
Mtwara 201 G 2
Mualang 176 D 3
Muanā 139 J 4
Muang 175 H 5
Muang Loei 175 H 4
Muang Long 175 G 4
Muang Moc 175 H 4
Muang Nan 175 H 4
Muang Ngao 175 G 4
Muang Oi 175 H 4
Muang Phayao 175 G 4
Muang Phrae 175 H 4
Muanza 201 EF 3
Muar 176 B 3
Muara 176 E 2–3
Muaraaman 176 B 4
Muarabenangin 176 E 4
Muarabungo 176 B 4
Muaraenim 176 B 4
Muaramawai 176 E 4
Muarapangean 176 E 3
Muarapayang 176 E 4
Muarasiberut 176 A 4
Muaratebo 176 B 4
Muara Teweh 176 D 4
Muarawahau 176 E 3
Muari, Ras 169 H 6
Muaro 176 B 4
Mubaraki (Iran) 157 G 4
Mubende 198 E 4
Mubi 197 G 3
Mucajaí 141 F 3
Muchinga Escarpment 201 E 2
Mucojo 201 G 2
Muconda 200 C 2
Mucubela 201 F 3
Mucur 155 D 3
Mucura 139 F 4
Mucuri 141 H 4
Mucurici 141 H 4
Mucusso 200 C 3
Muda 201 E 3
Mudan Jiang 173 J 1–2
Mudanjiang 173 JK 2
Mudanya 154 C 2
Mud Butte (SD.) 118 F 6
Muddy Creek (UT.) 114 F 5
Muddy Creek Reservoir 115 O 6
Muddy Gap (WY.) 111 S 8
Muddy River 112 L 6
Mudgee 183 H 5
Mudhol 174 C 4
Mud Lake 112 HJ 5
Mud Lake Reservoir 119 K 5
Mudon 175 G 4
Mudug 199 H 3
Mudurnu 154 C 2
Muecate 201 F 2
Mueda 201 F 2
Mufulira 200 D 2
Mufu Shan 172 F 5
Muganskaya Step' 168 D 3
Mugatta 194 F 6

Mugila, Monts 198 D 6
Muğla 154 C 3
Mugodzhary 168 F 1
Muhagiriya 194 D 6
Muhaiwir (Iraq) 156 C 2
Muhammad, Ra's (Egypt) 156 B 4
Muhammadgarh 174 C 3
Muhammad Qawl 194 F 4
Mühlhausen 149 F 4
Mühlig-Hofmann Mountains 203
Muhos 150 J 3
Muhu 151 H 4
Muhulu 198 D 5
Muhuwesi 201 F 2
Mui Bai Bung 175 H 6
Mui Ca Mau 175 H 6
Muié 200 C 2
Muir, Mount 109 J 3
Muiron Islands 182 A 3
Muite 201 F 2
Mujimbeji 200 C 2
MukacheVo 154 B 1
Mukah 176 D 3
Mukdahan 175 H 4
Mukden 173 J 2
Mukhino 171 N 5
Mukho 173 J 3
Mukhomornoye 171 W 2
Mukhor-Shibir' 170 J 5
Mukilteo (WA.) 110 C 3
Mukinbudin 182 B 5
Mukoba 198 C 6
Mukomuko 176 B 4
Muktinath 174 D 2
Mukur 168 E 1
Mukur (Afghanistan) 169 H 4
Mukwe 200 C 3
Mula 152 C 4
Mulainagiri 174 C 5
Mulaly 159 P 6
Mulan 173 J 1
Mulanje 201 F 3
Mulata 199 G 3
Mulberry (TN.) 128 E 6
Mulchatna 102 F 3
Mulchén 143 B 6
Mulde 149 F 4
Muldoon (TX.) 122 F 6
Mule Creek (N.M.) 116 GH 4
Mulegé 106 D 6
Mulegé, Sierra de 106 D 6
Mulenda 198 D 5
Muleshoe (TX.) 117 O 3
Mulevala 201 F 3
Mulga Park 182 E 4
Mulgrave Hills 108 F 2
Mulgrave Island 184 D 4
Mulhacén 152 C 4
Mulhall (OK.) 120 H 6
Mulhouse 153 E 2
Muli 172 D 5
Muling 173 K 2
Muling He 173 K 1
Mull 148 B 3
Mullaittivu 174 D 6
Mullaley 183 HJ 5
Mullan (ID.) 111 K 3
Mullen (NE.) 118 G 8
Mullens (W.V.) 129 K 4
Muller, Pegunungan 176 D 3
Mullet Peninsula 148 A 4
Mullett Lake 125 K 4
Mullewa (Western Australia) 182 B 4
Müllheim 149 E 5
Mulligan River 183 F 4
Mullin (TX.) 122 E 4
Mullingar 148 B 4
Mullinville (KS.) 120 F 5
Mulobezi 200 D 3
Mulonga 198 D 6
Multan 169 J 4
Multanovy 159 O 3
Multia 150 H 3
Mulu, Gunung 176 DE 3
Mulvane (KS.) 120 H 5
Mulym'ya 159 M 3
Mumbué 200 B 2
Mumbwa 200 D 2
Mumena 200 D 2
Mumford (TX.) 122 G 5
Mumra 168 D 1
Muna 170 M 2
Muna, Pulau 177 F 5
Munabao 174 B 2
Munamägi 151 J 4
München 149 F 4
Munchique, Cerro 138 C 3
Muncho Lake 103 M 4
Muncie (IN.) 124 J 9
Muncy (PA.) 127 C 7
Mundar 171 R 2
Munday (TX.) 122 D 2
Mundelein (IL.) 124 FG 7
Münden 149 E 4
Mundo Nôvo 141 H 3
Mundra 174 A 3
Mundrabilla 182 D 5
Munducurus 139 G 4
Mundurushuchu 171 N 3

Mundybash 159 R 5
Munford (TN.) 128 B 6
Munfordville (KY.) 128 EF 4
Mungar 183 J 4
Mungbere 198 D 4
Mungo 200 B 2
Munhango 200 B 2
Munich 149 F 5
Munīfah (Saudi Arabia) 157 E 4
Munising (MI.) 124 H 3
Munkedal 155 F 4
Munkfors 151 F 4
Munkhafad al Qattārah 194 D 3
Munku-Sardyk, Gora 170 GH 5
Munster 148 B 4
Münster 149 E 4
Muntenia 154 C 2
Munţii Almājului 154 B 1–2
Muntii Apuseni 154 B 1
Muntii Bihorului 154 B 1
Muntii Calimanului 154 BC 1
Munţii Harghita 154 C 1
Muntii Metaliferi 154 B 1
Muntii Poiana Ruscă 154 B 1
Muntii Rodnei 154 B 1
Muntii Sebeşului 154 B 1
Muntii Zărandului 154 B 1
Munugudzhak 171 U 3
Munzur Silsilesi 155 E 3
Muodoslompolo 150 H 2
Muojärvi 150 J 2
Muong Hiem 175 H 3
Muong Khoua 175 H 3
Muong Khuong 175 H 3
Muong Lam 175 HJ 4
Muong Nong 175 J 4
Muong Sai 175 H 3
Muong Sen 175 H 4
Muong Sing 175 H 3
Muong Son 175 H 3
Muong Te 175 H 3
Muonio 150 H 2
Muonioälven 150 H 2
Muonionjoki 150 H 2
Mupa National Park 200 B 3
Muqaddam 194 E 5
Muqayshit 195 F 4
Muqdisho 199 H 4
Muqshin 195 J 5
Mur 153 G 2
Mura 153 G 2
Muradiye 155 F 3
Murakami 173 L 3
Murallón, Cerro 143 B 8
Murana 177 H 4
Muranga 199 F 5
Murashi 158 J 4
Murat (France) 152 D 2
Murat (Turkey) 155 F 3
Murat Dağı 154 C 3
Muratlı 154 C 2
Muratlı 154 C 2
Murau 153 F 2
Muravera 153 E 4
Mürcheh Khvort (Iran) 157 F 2
Murchison, Mount 182 B 4
Murchison Falls 198 E 4
Murchison River 182 AB 4
Murcia 152 C 4
Murdo (SD.) 118 H 7
Murdock (FL.) 131 M 6
Mureş 154 B 1
Muret 152 D 3
Murfreesboro (AR.) 121 M 8
Murfreesboro (N.C.) 129 O 5
Murfreesboro (TN.) 128 E 6
Murgab 169 G 3
Murgash 154 B 2
Murgāsh 154 B 2
Murghab 169 G 3
Murgon 183 J 4
Murgoo 182 B 4
Murguba 197 G 3
Murguz 153 G 2
Muriaé 141 H 5
Murici 141 J 2
Muriége 200 C 1
Murilo 186 B 2
Murin'ya 170 J 5
Muritz 149 F 4
Mūrjān (Iran) 157 F 3
Murjek 150 H 2
Murkong Selek 175 FG 3
Murmansk 150 K 2
Murmashi 150 K 2
Murmino 158 H 5
Murnau 149 F 5
Murom 158 H 4
Muromtsevo 159 P 4
Muroran 173 M 2
Muros 152 B 3
Muros y Noya, Rio de 152 B 3
Muroto 173 K 4
Murphy (ID.) 110 J 7
Murphy (OR.) 110 B 8
Murphysboro (IL.) 121 Q 5
Murrah 194 E 4
Murray (KY.) 128 C 5
Murray (UT.) 114 F 3
Murray, Lake (OK.) 120 HJ 8

Murray, Lake (Papua New Guinea) 184 D 3
Murray, Lake (S.C.) 129 K 7
Murray, Mount 109 N 3
Murray Bridge 183 F 6
Murray Downs 182 E 3
Murray Fracture Zone 209 D 2
Murray Islands 184 D 3
Murray River 183 G 5
Murraysburg 200 C 6
Murrayville (IL.) 121 P 3
Murrumbidgee River 183 H 5
Murrupula 199 F 3
Mursala, Pulau 176 A 3
Murshidabad 174 E 3
Murska Sobota 153 G 2
Murtaugh (ID.) 111 L 8
Murtazat Lake 111 L 8
Murten 153 E 2
Murtoa 183 F 6
Murukta 170 H 2
Mururoa 187 F 4
Murwara 174 D 3
Murwillumbah 183 J 4
Murzuq 193 H 3
Muş 155 F 3
Muša 151 H 4
Mūsā, Wādi (Jordan) 156 B 3
Musadi 198 C 5
Musala 154 B 2
Musallah (Iraq) 156 D 2
Musallam (Iraq) 157 E 3
Musan 173 J 2
Musandam Peninsula (Oman) 157 G 4
Musao 198 D 6
Musa Qala 169 G 4
Musay'īd (Iran) 195 J 4
Musayid (Qatar) 157 F 4
Musaymir 195 G 6
Muscat 195 K 4
Muscatine (IA.) 119 R 9
Muscoda (WI.) 124 D 6
Musgrave 183 G 1
Musgrave Ranges 182 E 4
Mushāsh (Saudi Arabia) 157 E 4
Mushāsh al 'Ashāwī (Saudi Arabia) 157 E 4
Mushayrib, Ra's (United Arab Emirates) 157 F 4
Mushie 198 B 5
Musi, Air 176 B 4
Mūsiān (Iran) 157 E 2
Muskegon (MI.) 124 H 6
Muskegon Heights (MI.) 124 H 6
Muskegon River 124 J 6
Muskogee (OK.) 121 K 7
Musoma 198 E 5
Musquaro, Lac 105 P 5
Mussa Ali 199 G 2
Mussafah (United Arab Emirates) 157 G 4
Musselshell (MT.) 111 RS 4
Musselshell River 111 S 3
Mussende 200 B 2
Mussidan 152 D 2
Mustafa 171 P 3
Mustafakemalpaşa 154 C 3
Mustahil 199 G 3
Mustang 174 D 2
Mustang Island 122 F 8
Musters, Lago 143 C 8
Mustla 151 J 4
Mustvee 151 J 4
Muswellbrook 183 J 5
Mūt (Egypt) 194 D 3
Mut (Turkey) 155 D 3
Mut (Turkey) 156 A 1
Mutá, Ponta de 141 J 3
Mūtaf, Ra's al (Iran) 157 F 4
Mutanda 200 D 2
Mutarara 201 F 3
Mutare 201 E 3
Mutayyin 195 G 5
Mutha 199 F 5
Mutis, Gunung 177 F 5
Mutnovskaya Sopka 171 T 5
Mutoray 170 H 3
Mutriba (Kuwait) 157 E 3
Mutsamudu 201 G 2
Mutshatsha 200 C 2
Mutsu-wan 173 M 2
Muttaburra 183 G 3
Mutual (UT.) 114 F 4
Mutuşjärvi 150 J 2
Mu Us Shamo 172 E 3
Muwale 198 E 6
Muxaluando 200 A 1
Muxima 200 A 1
Muya 170 K 4
Muya 170 L 4
Muyezerskiy 150 K 3
Muyinga 198 E 5
Muynak 168 F 2
Muyumba 198 D 6
Muzaffarabad 169 J 4
Muzaffargarh 169 J 4–5
Muzaffarnagar 174 C 2
Muzaffarpur 174 DE 2

Muzhi 159 M 2
Muzillac 152 C 2
Muztag 169 L 3
Muztag 169 M 3
Muztagata 169 K 3
Mvolo 198 D 3
Mvomero 199 F 6
Mvoung 197 G 5
Mwadingusha 200 D 2
Mwanga 201 E 2
Mwangalala 200 D 2
Mwanya 201 E 2
Mwanza (Tanzania) 198 E 5
Mwanza (Zaire) 198 D 6
Mwatate 199 F 5
Mweelrea 148 B 4
Mweka 199 C 5
Mwene Biji 198 C 6
Mwene Ditu 198 C 6
Mwenesi 201 E 4
Mwenezi 201 E 4
Mwenga 198 D 5
Mweru, Lake 200 D 1
Mwimba 198 C 6
Mwinilunga 200 C 2
Mya 193 F 2
Myakit 171 S 3
Myakka City (FL.) 131 M 6
Myaksa 158 G 4
Myanaung 175 F 4
Myaundzha 171 R 3
Myaungmya 175 F 4
Mycenae 154 B 3
Mydaburg 109 M 4
Myingyan 175 G 3
Myinmoletkat 175 G 5
Myinmu 175 G 3
Myitkyina 175 G 2
Myitta 175 G 5
Myittha 175 G 3
Mymensingh 175 F 3
Myn-Aral 159 O 6
Mynbulak 169 G 2
Myndagayy 171 O 3
Mynydd Prescelly 148 BC 4
Mýrar 150 A 3
Mýrdalsjökull 150 B 3
Myre 150 F 2
Myrtle Beach (S.C.) 129 N 8
Myrtle Creek (OR.) 110 B 7
Myrtle Point (OR.) 110 A 7
Mys Aniva 171 Q 6
Mys Bolvanskiy Nos 159 M 1
Mys Buorkhaya 171 O 1
Mys Chukotskiy 102 C 3
Mys Dezhneva 102 D 2
Mys Duga-Zapadnaya 171 R 4
Mys Dzenzik 155 E 1
Mysen 151 F 4
Mys Enkan 171 Q 4
Mys Kanin Nos 158 H 2
Mys Kazantip 155 E 1
Mys Kerets 158 G 2
Mys Kril'on 171 Q 6
Mys Kodori 155 F 2
Mys Kronotskiy 171 U 4–5
Mys Kurgalski 151 J 4
Mys Laydennyy 158 J 2
Mys Lopatka 171 T 5
Mys Lygyy 170 LM 1
Mys Meganom 155 E 2
Mys Men'shikova 159 LM 1
Mys Navarin 108 B 3
Mys Olyutorskiy 171 VW 4
Mysore 174 C 5
Mys Ostrovnoy 171 T 3
Mysovaya 171 T 2
Mys Peschanyy 168 E 2
Mys Pitsunda 155 F 2
Mys Ratmanova 158–159 L 1
Mys Sarych 155 D 2
Mys Sengiri 168 E 2
Mys Shipunskiy 171 TU 5
Mys Shmidta 108 C 2
Mys Svatoy Nos 171 P 1
Mys Svyatoy Nos 158 J 2
Mys Svyatoy Nos 158 GH 3
Mys Taran 151 GH 4–5
Mys Tarkhankut 155 C 1
Mys Taygonos 171 U 3
Mys Terpeniya 171 Q 6
Mys Tolstoy 171 T 4
Mys Uengan 159 N 1
Mys Yelizavety 171 Q 5
Mys Yuzhnyy 171 T 4
Myszków 149 G 4
My Tho 175 J 5
Myton (UT.) 114 GH 3
My Trach 175 J 5
Mývatn 150 B 2
Myylybulak 159 P 6
Mze 149 F 5
Mzenga 199 F 6
Mziha 199 F 6
Mzimba 201 E 2
Mzuzu 201 E 2

N

Naab 149 F 5
Naalehu (HI.) 113 G 12
Naama 192 EF 2
Naandi 198 D 3
Naantali 151 H 3
Naas 148 B 4
Näätämöjoki 150 J 2
Näätämöjoki 150 J 2
Naba 175 G 3
Nabadid 199 G 3
Na Baek 175 H 4
Nabberu, Lake 182 C 4
Naberera 199 F 5
Nabesna 109 K 3
Nabesna River 109 K 3
Nabha 174 C 1
Nabire 177 J 4
Nabī Shuʿayb, Jabal an 195 G 5
Nabk al Gharbī (Saudi Arabia) 156 B 3
Nabou 196 D 3
Nabq (Egypt) 156 B 3
Nābul 193 H 1
Nābulus (Westbank) 156 B 2
Nacala 201 G 2
Nacala 201 G 2
Nacaroña 201 F 2
Nachana 174 B 2
Naches (WA.) 110 E 4
Naches River 110 E 4
Nachikinskaya, Gora 171 U 4
Nachingwea 201 F 2
Nachod 149 G 4
Nachuge 175 F 5
Nachvak Fiord 105 P 4
Naco (AZ.) 116 FG 6
Nacogdoches (TX.) 123 J 4
Nacozari 106 E 5
Nacunday 142 EF 4
Nådendal 151 H 3
Nadiad 174 B 3
Nådlac 154 B 1
Nador 192 E 1
Nadvoitsy 150 K 3
Nadvornaya 154 B 1
Nadym 159 O 2
Nadym 159 O 3
Nærbö 151 E 4
Nærbö 151 E 4
Næstved 151 F 4
Nafada 197 G 3
Naft-e Safid (Iran) 157 E 3
Naft-e Shah (Iran) 157 D 2
Naft Khāneh (Iraq) 157 D 2
Naftshahr (Iran) 157 D 2
Nafuce 197 F 3
Nafūd ad Daḥy 195 GH 4
Nafūd al ʿUrayq (Saudi Arabia) 156 D 4
Nafūd as Sirr (Saudi Arabia)
   156–157 D 4
Nafūd as Surrah 195 G 4
Nafud Qunayfidhah (Saudi Arabia)
   157 D 4
Nafūsah, Jabal 193 H 2
Nafy (Saudi Arabia) 156 D 4
Nag 169 G 5
Naga 177 F 1
Naga Hills 175 FG 2
Nagai 102 E 5
Nagaland 175 F 2
Nagano 173 L 3
Nagaoka 173 L 3
Nagappattinam 174 CD 5
Nagarzê 175 F 2
Nagasaki 173 J 4
Nagato 173 K 4
Nagaur 174 B 2
Nagavati 174 D 4
Nagda 174 C 3
Nageezi (N.M.) 116 J 1
Nagercoil 174 C 6
Nagichot 198 E 4
Nago 173 J 5
Nagornyy 171 N 4
Nagorʾye Sangilen 170 G 5
Nagoya 173 L 3
Nagpur 174 C 3
Nagqu 172 E 3
Nagyatád 154 A 1
Nagykanizsa 154 A 1
Nagykőrös 154 AB 1
Naha 173 J 5
Nahan 174 C 1
Nahang 169 G 5
Nahanni Butte 103 N 3
Nahanni National Park 103 M, 3
Nahariyya (Israel) 156 B 2
Nahāvand (Iran) 157 E 2
Naʾhīmābād (Iran) 157 G 3
Nahma (MI.) 124 H 4
Nahr ad Dindar 194 EF 6
Nahr al Liṭānī (Lebanon) 156 B 2
Nahr an Nīl 194 E 3
Nahr ʿUm (Iraq) 157 E 3
Nahuel Huapi, Lago 143 B 7
Nahuel Niyeu 143 C 7
Nahunta (GA.) 131 N 3
Nai 185 E 2
Nai Ga 175 G 2

Naikliu 177 F 5
Naʿīmābād (Iran) 157 G 1
Naiman Qi 173 H 2
Nain 105 P 4
Nã'ın (Iran) 157 F 2
Naini Tal 174 C 2
Nairobi 199 F 5
Naissaar 151 H 4
Naita 198 F 3
Naivasha 199 F 5
Najafābād (Iran) 157 F 2
Najd (Saudi Arabia) 156 CD 4
Najera 152 C 3
Najʾ Ḥammādi 194 E 3
Najibabad 174 C 2
Najin 173 K 2
Najmah (Saudi Arabia) 157 F 4
Najrān 195 G 5
Nakalele Point 113 F 10
Nakamti → Nekemt 199 F 3
Nakanno 170 J 3
Naka-no-shima 173 K 3
Nakasongola 198 E 4
Nakatsu 173 L 3
Nakfa 199 F 1
Nakhichevanʾ 155 FG 3
Nakhichevanʾ 168 CD 3
Nakhodka 159 O 2
Nakhodka 159 P 2
Nakhodka 173 K 2
Nakhon Nayok 175 H 5
Nakhon Pathom 175 G 5
Nakhon Phanom 175 H 4
Nakhon Ratchasima 175 H 5
Nakhon Sawan 175 GH 4
Nakhon Si Thammarat 175 G 6
Nakina 104 K 5
Nakło 149 G 4
Naknek 102 F 4
Naknek Lake 108 G 4
Nako 196 D 3
Nakonde 201 E 1
Nakop 200 B 5
Nakskov 151 F 5
Näkten 150 F 3
Näkten 150 F 3
Nakuru 199 F 5
Nalayh 170 J 6
Nalázi 201 E 4
Nalʾchik 155 F 2
Näldsjön 150 F 3
Näldsjön 150 F 3
Nalgimskaya 171 VW 3
Nalgonda 174 C 4
Nallamala Range 174 C 4
Nallıhan 154 D 2
Nālūt 193 H 2
Namaacha 201 E 5
Namacunde 200 B 3
Namacurra 201 F 3
Namak, Daracheh-ye (Iran) 157 F 2
Namak, Kavir-e (Iran) 157 G 1
Namakan Lake 119 Q 2
Namaki (Iran) 157 G 3
Namakzar-e Shadad 168 F 4
Namaland 200 B 5
Namanga 199 F 5
Namanyere 198 E 6
Namapa 201 G 2
Namaponda 201 G 3
Namaqualand 200 B 5
Namarrói 201 F 3
Namasagali 198 E 4
Namatanai 185 F 2
Nambe Indian Reservation 117 L 2
Nambour 183 J 4
Nam Ca Dinh 175 H 4
Nam Can 175 J 6
Namche Bazar 174 E 2
Nam Co 175 F 1
Namdalen 150 F 3
Nam Dinh 175 J 3
Nametil 201 F 3
Namib Desert 200 AB 3–5
Namib Desert Park 200 AB 4
Namibe 200 A 3
Namibe Reserve 200 A 3
Namibia 200 B 4
Namiquipa 106 E 6
Namjagbarwa Feng 172 C 5
Namkham 175 G 3
Namlan Pan 175 G 3
Namlea 177 G 4
Namling 174 E 2
Namoi River 183 H 5
Namoluk 186 B 2
Namonuito 186 A 2
Namorik 186 C 2
Nam Ou 175 H 3
Namoya 198 D 5
Nampa (ID.) 110 J 7
Nampala 196 C 2
Nam Phang 175 H 3
Nam Phong 175 H 4
Namʾpo 173 HJ 3
Nampula 201 F 3
Namrole 177 G 4
Namru 174 D 1
Namsang 175 G 3

Namsê La 174 D 2
Namsen 150 F 2–3
Namsos 150 F 3
Namsvattnet 150 F 2
Nam Teng 175 G 3
Namton 175 G 3
Namtsy 171 N 3
Namtu 175 G 3
Namu 186 C 2
Namuli 201 F 3
Namuno 201 F 2
Namur 148 DE 4
Namutoni 200 B 3
Namwala 200 D 3
Namwŏn 173 J 3
Namy 171 O 2
Namya Ra 175 G 2
Namyit Island 176 D 1
Nanaimo 103 N 6
Nanakuli (HI.) 113 D 10
Nanam 173 JK 2
Nancha 171 N 6
Nanchang 172 G 5
Nancheng 172 G 5
Nanchong 172 E 4
Nanchuan 172 E 5
Nancowry 175 F 6
Nancy 153 E 2
Nancy (KY.) 128 G 4
Nanda Devi 174 C 1
Nandan 172 E 6
Nander 174 C 4
Nandod 174 B 3
Nandu Jiang 172 E 7
Nandurbar 174 B 3
Nandyal 174 C 4
Nanfeng 172 G 5
Nanga Emboko 197 G 5
Nangakelawit 176 D 3
Nanga Parbat 169 J 3
Nangapinoh 176 D 4
Nangatayap 176 D 4
Nangin 175 G 5
Nangnim-sanmaek 173 J 2
Nangong 172 G 3
Nangqên 172 C 4
Nanguneri 174 C 6
Nang Xian 172 B 5
Nanhua 172 D 5
Nanhui 173 H 4
Nan Hulsan Hu 172 C 3
Nanjian 172 D 5
Nanjiang 172 E 4
Nanjing 173 G 4
Nankang 172 F 5
Nanking → Nanjing 173 G 4
Nankova 200 B 3
Nanle 172 G 3
Nan Ling 172 EF 5
Nannine 182 B 4
Nanning 172 E 6
Nannup 182 B 5
Nanortalik 105 S 3
Nanpan Jiang 172 D 6
Nanpara 174 D 2
Nanpi 173 G 3
Nanping 172 D 4
Nanping 173 G 5
Nansei-shotō 173 J 5
Nanshan Islands 176 D 2
Nansha Qundao 176 D 2
Nansikan, Ostrov 171 PQ 4
Nansio 198 E 5
Nantais, Lac 105 N 3
Nantes 152 C 2
Nanticoke (PA.) 127 CD 7
Nanton 103 P 5
Nantong 173 H 4
Nantou 173 H 6
Nantucket (N.Y.) 127 J 8
Nantucket Island 127 K 7
Nantucket Sound 126 J 7
Nantulo 201 F 2
Nanumanga 186 C 3
Nanumea 186 C 3
Nanuque 141 HJ 4
Nanusa, Kepulauan 177 G 3
Nanwei Dao 176 D 2
Nanxiong 172 F 5
Nanyang 172 F 4
Nanyuki 199 F 5
Nanzhang 172 F 4
Nanzhao 172 F 4
Nanzhil 201 F 2
Nao, Cabo de la 152 D 4
Naococane, Lac 105 N 5
Naoli He 171 O 6
Naomi Peak 114 F 2
Náousa 154 B 2
Napa (CA.) 112 C 4
Napaku 154 B 2
Napalkovo 159 OP 1
Napamute 108 G 3
Napana 171 T 4
Napas 159 Q 4
Napassoq 105 R 2
Napata 194 E 5

Napavine (WA.) 110 BC 4
Nape 175 J 4
Naper (NE.) 118 J 8
Naperville (IL.) 124 F 8
Napido 177 J 4
Napier 185 R 8
Napier 186 C 5
Napier Mountains 203
Naples (FL.) 131 N 8
Naples (ID.) 110 J 2
Naples (Italy) 153 F 3
Naples (N.Y.) 126 B 6
Naples (TX.) 123 J 2
Naples Park (FL.) 131 N 8
Napo 172 E 6
Napo (Peru) 138 D 4
Napoleon (ND.) 118 J 4
Napoleon (OH.) 125 K 8
Napoleonville (LA.) 123 M 6
Napoli 153 F 3
Napperby 182 E 3
Napuka 187 F 3
Naqa 194 E 5
Naqadeh (Iran) 157 D 1
Naqb, Raʾs an (Jordan) 156 B 3
Naqsh-e Rostam (Iran) 157 F 3
Naquabo (P.R.) 130 D 8
Nara (Japan) 173 L 4
Nara (Mali) 196 C 2
Nara (Pakistan) 169 H 6
Naracoorte 183 G 6
Naran 170 G 6
Naran 172 F 1
Naranjos 132 C 3
Narasapur 174 D 4
Narasun 170 K 5
Nara Visa (N.M.) 117 N 2
Narathiwat 175 H 6
Narayanganj 175 F 3
Narbonne 152 D 3
Nares Strait 202
Naretha 182 C 5
Narew 149 H 4
Narlı 155 E 3
Narman 155 F 2
Narnaul 174 C 2
Naroch 151 J 5
Narodnaya, Gora 159 LM 2
Naro-Fominsk 158 G 4
Narok 199 F 5
Narooma 183 J 6
Narowal 169 J 4
Narrabri 183 HJ 5
Narrandera 183 H 5
Narrogin 182 B 5
Narromine 183 H 5
Narrowsburg (N.Y.) 126 E 7
Narsimhapur 174 C 3
Narsinghgarh 174 C 3
Narsinghpur 174 E 3
Narssalik 105 S 3
Narssaq 105 R 3
Narssaq 105 S 3
Narssarssuaq 105 ST 3
Naruja 154 C 1
Narungombe 199 F 6
Narva 151 J 4
Narvik 150 G 2
Narvski Zaliv 151 J 4
Narwietooma 182 E 3
Narʾyan Mar 158 K 2
Narym 159 Q 4
Narymskiy Khrebet 159 QR 6
Naryn 169 JK 2
Naryn 169 K 2
Naryn 170 G 5
Narynkolʾ 169 KL 2
Nås 151 F 3
Nås 151 F 3
Nåsåker 150 G 3
Nåsåker 150 G 3
Na San 175 G 6
Nasarawa 197 F 4
Nåsåud 154 B 1
Nash (OK.) 120 GH 6
Nashua (IA.) 119 Q 8
Nashua (MN.) 119 M 4
Nashua (N.H.) 126 H 6
Nashva (MT.) 118 B 2
Nashville (AR.) 121 M 9
Nashville (GA.) 131 L 3
Nashville (IL.) 121 Q 4
Nashville (IN.) 128 E 2
Nashville (KS.) 120 G 5
Nashville (N.C.) 129 NO 6
Nashville (TN.) 128 E 5
Našice 153 G 2
Näsijärvi 150 H 3
Näsijärvi 150 H 3
Nasik 174 B 3
Nåşir 198 E 3
Nasirabad (India) 174 B 2
Nasirabad (Pakistan) 169 H 5
Naskaupi 105 P 5
Nasmah 193 H 2
Nasmgani 174 D 3

Nasrābād (Iran) 157 F 2
Nass 102 M 4
Nassau (Cook Is.) 186 D 3
Nassau (The Bahamas) 133 G 2
Nasser, Birkat 194 E 4
Nassian 196 D 4
Nässjö 151 FG 4
Nastapoka Islands 105 M 4
Nasukoin Mountain 111 L 2
Nasva 151 K 4
Nata 200 D 4
Nata 200 D 4
Natal 141 JK 3
Natal (Amazonas, Brazil) 139 F 5
Natal (Indonesia) 176 A 3
Natal (South Africa) 200–201 E 5
Natanes Plateau 116 F 2
Natara 171 MN 2
Natashquan 105 P 5
Natchez (MS.) 130 C 3
Natchitoches (LA.) 123 K 4
Nathdwara 174 B 3
Nathrop (CO.) 115 LM 5
Natīḥ 195 K 4
National City (CA.) 113 H 10
Natitingou 196 E 3
Natityãy, Jabal 194 E 4
Natividade 141 G 3
Natkyizin 175 G 5
Natoma (KS.) 120 G 3
Natron, Lake 199 F 5
Natrona (WY.) 118 B 7
Natrona Heights (PA.) 125 P 9
Natrūn, Wādī an 194 DE 2
Nattaung 175 G 4
Nattavaara 150 H 2
Natuna, Kepulauan 176 C 3
Natuna Utara 176 C 3
Natural Bridge (AL.) 128 D 7
Natural Bridges National Monument
   114 G 6
Naturaliste, Cape 182 A 5
Naturaliste Channel 182 A 4
Naturita (CO.) 114 J 5
Naturno 153 F 2
Natwick (WY.) 118 C 9
Nauchas 200 B 4
Naugatuck (CT.) 126 F 7
Nauja Bay 105 M 2
Naujoji-Akmene 151 H 4
Naukluft 200 B 4
Naumburg 149 F 4
Naungpale 175 G 4
Naupe 138 C 5
Nāʾūr (Jordan) 156 B 3
Naurskaya 155 G 2
Nauru 185 J 2
Nauru 186 C 3
Naurzum 159 M 5
Naushahro Firoz 169 H 5
Naushki 170 J 5
Nauta 138 D 4
Nautanwa 174 D 2
Nava 132 B 2
Navahermosa 152 C 4
Navajo (AZ.) 116 G 2
Navajo-Hopi Indian Reservation
   116 F 1
Navajo Indian Reservation 116 F 1
Navajo Mountain 114 G 6
Navajo National Monument 116 F 1
Navajo Reservoir 117 J 1
Naval 177 F 1
Navalmoral de la Mata 152 B 4
Navarin, Mys 108 B 3
Navarino 143 C 10
Navarra 152 C 3
Navarro Head 112 B 3
Navarro Mills Lake 122 G 4
Navasota (TX.) 122 GH 5
Navasota River 122 G 4–5
Navassa 133 G 4
Navia (Argentina) 142 C 5
Navia (Spain) 152 B 3
Navidad 142 B 5
Navidad River 122 G 6
Naviraí 141 F 5
Navlya 158 F 5
Nåvodari 154 C 2
Navoi 169 H 2
Navojoa 106 E 6
Navoloto 106 E 7
Navolok 158 G 3
Navplion 154 B 3
Navrongo 196 D 3
Navsari 174 B 3
Navtlug 155 G 2
Nawabganj 174 D 2
Nawabshah 169 H 5
Nāwah 169 H 4
Nawalgarh 174 C 2
Nawāşif, Ḥarrat 195 G 4
Naws, Raʾs 195 K 5
Náxos 154 C 3
Nayakhan 171 T 3
Nayarit 132 B 3
Nayarit, Sierra 132 B 3
Nãy Banḍ (Iran) 157 F 4
Nãy Band, Raʾs-e (Iran) 157 F 4
Nayoro 173 M 2

Naystenyarvi 150 K 3
Nazaré 152 B 4
Nazaré (Bahía, Brazil) 141 J 3
Nazaré (Goiás, Brazil) 139 J 5
Nazareth (Peru) 138 C 5
Nazarovka 158 H 5
Nazarovo 170 F 4
Nazas 132 B 2
Nazca 140 B 3
Nazca Ridge 209 E 4
Naze 173 J 5
Nazerat (Israel) 156 B 2
Nazilli 154 C 3
Nazimovo 170 F 4
Nazina 159 P 3
Nazira 175 F 2
Nazmiye 155 EF 3
Nazran' 155 F 2
Nazwa 195 K 4
Nchelenge 200 D 1
Ncheu 201 E 2
Ndala 198 E 5
N'dalatando 200 A 1
Ndali 196 E 4
Ndandawala 199 F 6
Ndélé 198 C 3
Ndélélé 197 G 5
Ndendé 197 G 6
Ndeni 185 J 4
Ndindi 197 G 6
N'Djamena 197 H 3
Ndjolé 197 G 6
Ndogo, Lagune 197 G 6
Ndola 200 D 2
Ndoro 197 G 6
Ndrhamcha, Sebkha de 192 BC 5
Ndu 198 C 4
Nea (Norway) 150 F 3
Nea (Solomon Is.) 185 J 4
Nea Filippías 154 B 3
Neagh, Lough 148 B 4
Neagh, Lough 148 B 4
Neale, Lake 182 E 3
Neápolis 154 B 2
Neápolis 154 B 3
Near Islands 102 A 5
Néa Zikhni 154 B 2
Nebbou 196 D 3
Nebine River 183 H 4
Nebit-Dag 168 E 3
Neblina, Pico da 138 E 3
Nebo 183 H 3
Nebo, Mount 114 F 4
Nebolchi 158 F 4
Nebraska (North) 118–119
Nebraska (South) 120
Nebraska City (NE.) 120 K 2
Necedah (WI.) 124 D 5
Nechako 103 N 5
Nechako Plateau 103 N 5
Nechako Reservoir 103 M 5
Neche (N.D.) 119 L 2
Neches (TX.) 123 H 4
Nechi 138 D 2
Neckar 149 E 5
Necochea 143 E 6
Nédéley 197 H 2
Nederland (TX.) 123 JK 6
Nedong 175 F 2
Neebish Island 125 K 3
Needle Mountain 111 Q 6
Needle Range 114 D 5
Needles (CA.) 113 L 8
Needmore (PA.) 125 Q 10
Needmore (TX.) 117 O 3
Needmore (TX.) 117 O 4
Neelville (MO.) 121 P 6
Neely Henry Lake 128 E 8
Neenah (WI.) 124 F 5
Nefedovo 159 O 4
Neftah 193 G 2
Neftegorsk 155 EF 2
Neftegorsk 158 K 5
Neftekamsk 158 K 4
Neftekumsk 155 F 2
Neftelensk 170 J 4
Nefteyugansk 159 O 3
Negage 200 B 1
Negala 196 C 3
Neganili Lake 103 S 4
Negaunee (MI.) 124 G 3
Negelli 199 F 3
Negomano 201 F 2
Negombo 174 C 6
Negonengo 187 F 4
Negotin 154 B 2
Negotka 159 Q 4
Negra (N.M.) 117 KL 3
Negra, Cordillera 138 C 5
Negra, Punta 138 B 5
Negra, Serra 139 J 5
Negrais, Cape 175 F 4
Négrine 193 G 2
Negritos 138 B 4
Negro, Cerro 143 C 7
Negro, Río (Brazil) 139 F 4
Negro, Rio (Uruguay) 142 EF 5
Negros 177 F 2
Negru Vodă 154 C 2
Nehalem River 110 B 5

Nehävand (Iran) 157 E 2
Nehbandan 168 FG 4
Nehe 171 MN 6
Nehoiu 154 C 1
Nehone 200 B 3
Neiba, Crêt de la 153 E 2
Neihart (MT.) 111 P 4
Neijiang 172 E 5
Neillsville (WI.) 124 D 5
Neilton (WA.) 110 B 3
Nei Monggol Zizhiqu 172 DG 2
Neiqiu 172 F 3
Neiva 138 CD 3
Nejo 198 F 3
Neka (Iran) 157 F 1
Nekemt 199 F 3
Nekoma (N.D.) 119 K 2
Nekoosa (WI.) 124 D 5
Nekrasovka 173 L 2
Neksikan 171 R 3
Neksö 151 G 4
Nelemnoye 171 S 2
Nel'gese 171 O 2
Nelichu 198 E 3
Nelidovo 158 F 4
Neligh (NE.) 119 K 8
Nel'kan 171 P 4
Nel'keskan 170 M 2
Nellore 174 D 5
Nel'ma 171 P 6
Nelson 186 C 5
Nelson (AZ.) 116 C 2
Nelson (Br. Col., Can.) 103 O 6
Nelson (Man., Can.) 103 S 5
Nelson (NE.) 120 G 2
Nelson (New Zealand) 185 Q 9
Nelson (NV.) 113 L 7
Nelson, Cape 183 G 6
Nelson, Estrecho 143 AB 9
Nelson Head 103 N 1
Nelson Island 102 D 3
Nelson Reservoir 111 S 2
Nelspruit 201 E 5
Nelyaty 170 L 4
Néma 192 D 5
Nemah (WA.) 110 B 4
Neman 151 HJ 5
Nembrala 177 F 6
Nemira, Virful 154 C 1
Némiscau 105 M 5
Nemours → Ghazaouet 192 E 1
Nemrutdağı 155 E 3
Nemunas 151 H 4
Nemuro 170 H 4
Nemuy 171 P 4
Nenana (AK.) 102 H 3
Nenana (AK.) 102 H 3
Nendo 185 J 4
Nene 148 C 4
Nenjiang 171 N 6
Nen Jiang 173 H 1
Neodesha (KS.) 121 K 5
Neola (IA.) 119 N 9
Neola (UT.) 114 GH 3
Néon Karlovásion 154 C 3
Neopit (WI.) 124 F 5
Neosho (MO.) 121 L 6
Neosho River 121 K 5
Nepa 170 J 4
Nepa 170 J 4
Nepal 174 D 2
Nepalganj 174 D 2
Nepeña 138 C 5
Nephi (UT.) 114 F 4
Nepoko 198 D 4
Neptune (N.J.) 127 E 8
Nera 171 Q 3
Nérac 152 D 3
Nercha 170 L 5
Nerchinsk 170 L 5
Nerchinskiy Khrebet 170 L 5
Nerekhta 158 H 4
Neretva 153 G 3
Neringa-Nida 151 H 4
Neriquinha 200 C 3
Neris 151 HJ 5
Neroy 170 G 5
Nerpich'ye, Ozero 171 T 2
Nerpio 152 C 4
Nerva 152 B 4
Nes' 158 H 2
Nesbyen 151 E 3
Nesebŭr 154 C 2
Neshkan 108 D 2
Nesika Beach (OR.) 110 A 8
Nesjöen 150 F 3
Neskaupstaður 150 C 2
Nesna 150 F 3
Nespelem (WA.) 110 G 2
Ness City (KS.) 120 EF 4
Nesselrode, Mount 109 M 4
Nesterov 151 H 5
Nesterovo 170 J 5
Nestoria (MI.) 124 F 3
Néstos 154 B 2
Nesvizh 151 J 5
Netanya (Israel) 156 B 2
Netcong (N.J.) 127 E 8

Netherlands 148 D–E 4
Netherlands Antilles 133 K 4
Netherlands Antilles 138 E 1
Net Lake Indian Reservation 119 P 2
Netrakona 175 F 3
Nettilling Lake 105 N 2
Nett Lake (MN.) 119 P 2
Nettleton (MS.) 121 R 8
Nettuno 153 F 3
Neubrandenburg 149 F 4
Neuces Plains 122 D 7
Neuchâtel 153 E 2
Neuchâtel, Lac de 153 E 2
Neufchâteau 153 E 2
Neufchâtel-en-Bray 152 D 2
Neum 153 G 3
Neumarkter Sattel 153 F 2
Neumünster 149 F 4
Neunkirchen (Austria) 153 G 2
Neuquén 143 C 6
Neuquén 143 C 6
Neuruppin 149 F 4
Neuse River 129 O 6
Neusiedler See 153 G 2
Neustrelitz 149 F 4
Nevada 112
Nevada (IA.) 119 P 8
Nevada (MO.) 121 L 5
Nevada, Cerro el 138 D 3
Nevada, Sierra (Spain) 152 C 4
Nevada City (CA.) 112 D 3
Nevado, Cerro 143 C 6
Nevado, Sierra del 143 C 6
Nevado Ausangate 140 B 3
Nevado Chachani 140 B 4
Nevado Citac 140 AB 3
Nevado Cololo 140 C 4
Nevado Coropuna 140 B 4
Nevado de Cachi 140 C 5
Nevado de Colima 132 B 4
Nevado Huascarán 138 C 5
Nevado Illimani 140 C 4
Nevado Sajama 140 C 4
Nevado Salcantay 140 B 3
Nevado Salluyo 140 C 3
Nevado Yerupajá 140 A 3
Neve, Serra da 200 A 2
Nevel' 151 K 4
Nevel'sk 171 Q 6
Nevel'skogo, Proliv 171 Q 5
Never 171 M 5
Nevers 152 D 2
Nevesinje 153 G 3
Nevinnomyssk 155 F 2
Nevis 133 K 4
Nevon 170 H 4
Nevşehir 155 D 3
Nev'yansk 159 M 4
Newala 201 F 2
New Albany (IN.) 128 F 3
New Albany (MS.) 121 QR 8
New Amsterdam 139 G 2
Newark (AR.) 121 O 7
Newark (DE.) 127 D 9
Newark (N.J.) 127 E 8
Newark (N.Y.) 126 B 5
Newark (OH.) 125 M 9
Newark Lake 112 K 3
Newark-on-Trent 148 C 4
Newark Valley (N.Y.) 126 C 6
New Athens (IL.) 121 Q 4
Newaygo (MI.) 124 J 6
New Bedford (MA.) 126 J 7
Newberg (OR.) 110 C 5
New Berlin (N.Y.) 126 D 6
New Bern (N.C.) 129 OP 6
Newberry (FL.) 131 M 5
Newberry (MI.) 124 J 3
Newberry (S.C.) 129 K 7
Newberry Springs (CA.) 113 J 8
New Bloomfield (PA.) 127 B 8
New Braunfels (TX.) 122 E 6
New Britain 185 F 3
New Britain (CT.) 126 G 7
New Brunswick (Canada) 105 O 6
New Brunswick (N.J.) 127 E 8
New Buffalo (MI.) 124 H 8
Newburgh (N.Y.) 126 E 7
Newburyport (MA.) 126 J 6
New Busuanga 177 E 1
New Caledonia 185 H 6
New Caledonia 186 B 4
New Canton (VA.) 129 N 4
Newcastle (CA.) 112 D 4
New Castle (CO.) 115 K 4
New Castle (IN.) 128 F 2
New Castle (KY.) 128 E 1
Newcastle (New Brunsw., Can.) 105 O 6
Newcastle (N.S.W., Austr.) 183 J 5
New Castle (PA.) 125 O 8
Newcastle (South Africa) 200 D 5
Newcastle (TX.) 122 E 2
New Castle (UT.) 114 D 6
New Castle (VA.) 129 L 4
Newcastle (WY.) 118 D 7
Newcastle River 182 E 2
Newcastle-upon-Tyne 148 C 3
Newcastle Waters 182 E 2
New City (N.Y.) 127 EF 7
Newcomb (N.M.) 116 H 1

Newcomerstown (OH.) 125 N 9
New Creek (W.V.) 129 M 2
New Delhi→Delhi 174 C 2
New Edinburg (AR.) 121 N 9
New Effington (S.D.) 119 LM 5
Newell (SD.) 118 E 6
Newellton (LA.) 123 M 3
New England 126 JL 4
New England 126 M 4
New England (ND.) 118 F 4
New England Range 183 J 5
Newenham, Cape 102 E 4
New Florence (MO.) 121 O 4
Newfoundland 105 Q 5
Newfoundland 105 Q 6
Newfoundland Mountains 114 D 2–3
New Franklin (MO.) 121 N 3
New Georgia 185 G 3
New Georgia Sound 185 G 3
New Glarus (WI.) 124 E 7
New Glasgow 105 P 6
New Guinea 177 J 4
New Guinea 179 CD 3
New Guinea 186 A 3
Newhalem (WA.) 110 D 2
Newhall (CA.) 113 G 8
New Hampshire 126
New Hampton (IA.) 119 Q 7
New Hanover 185 F 2
New Hanover 186 B 3
New Haven (CT.) 127 G 7
New Haven (IN.) 125 K 8
Newhaven (U.K.) 148 CD 4
New Haven (W.V.) 129 K 3
New Haven (WY.) 118 D 6
New Hebrides 185 J 5
New Hebrides 186 C 4
New Hogan Lake 112 E 4
New Hradec (ND.) 118 F 3
New Iberia (LA.) 123 M 5
New Ireland 185 F 2
New Ireland 186 B 3
New Jersey 127 H 7
New Kensington (PA.) 125 P 9
New Kent (VA.) 129 O 4
Newkirk (N.M.) 117 M 2
Newkirk (OK.) 120 HJ 6
Newland (N.C.) 129 K 5
New Leipzig (ND.) 118 G 4
New Lexington (OH.) 129 J 2
Newlin (TX.) 117 Q 3MO
New Lisbon (WI.) 124 D 6
New London (CT.) 127 G 7
New London (IA.) 119 R 10
New London (MN.) 119 NO 5
New London (MO.) 121 O 3
New London (WI.) 124 EF 5
New Madrid (MO.) 121 Q 6
Newman 182 B 3
Newman (CA.) 112 D 5
Newman (N.M.) 117 K 5
Newman Gr (NE.) 119 L 9
New Market (AL.) 128 E 7
New Market (VA.) 129 N 3
New Martinsville (W.V.) 129 L 2
New Meadows (ID.) 110 J 6
New Melones Lake 112 E 5
New Mexico 116–117
Newnan (GA.) 128 G 8
New Norcia 182 B 5
New Norfolk 184 L 9
New Orleans (LA.) 123 O 5–6
New Paris (OH.) 128 G 2
New Philadelphia (OH.) 125 N 9
New Pine Creek (OR.) 110 E 8
New Plymouth 185 Q 8
New Plymouth 186 C 5
New Plymouth (ID.) 110 J 6–7
Newport (AR.) 121 O 7
Newport (IN.) 121 S 3
Newport (ME.) 126 K 4
Newport (NE.) 118 J 8
Newport (N.H.) 126 G 5
Newport (OR.) 110 B 6
Newport (PA.) 127 B 8
Newport (R.I.) 126 H 7
Newport (TN.) 128 H 6
Newport (TX.) 122 E 2
Newport (U.K.) 148 C 4
Newport (VT.) 126 G 4
Newport (WA.) 110 H 2
Newport Beach (CA.) 113 GH 9
Newport News (VA.) 129 P 4–5
New Port Richey (FL.) 131 M 6
New Prague (MN.) 119 P 6
New Providence Island 133 G 3
Newquay 148 B 4
New Raymer (CO.) 115 O 3
New Richmond (OH.) 128 G 3
New Richmond (Quebec, Can.) 105 O 6
New River 129 K 3–4
New River (Guyana) 139 G 3
New Roads (LA.) 123 M 5
New Rochelle 127 F 8
New Rockford (ND.) 118 JK 3
Newry (N.T., Austr.) 182 D 2
New Salem (ND.) 118 G 4
New Sharon (IA.) 119 Q 9
New Siberian Islands 202

New Smyrna Beach (FL.) 131 O 5
New South Wales 183 GH 5
New Stuvahok 102 F 4
New Taiton (TX.) 122 G 6
Newtok 108 F 3
Newton (GA.) 131 K 3
Newton (IA.) 119 P 9
Newton (IL.) 121 R 4
Newton (KS.) 120 H 4
Newton (MA.) 126 H 6
Newton (MS.) 130 E 2
Newton (N.C.) 129 K 6
Newton (N.J.) 127 E 7
Newton (TX.) 123 K 5
Newton (UT.) 114 E 2
Newtonabbey 148 B 4
Newton Falls (N.Y.) 126 D 4
Newton Grove (N.C.) 129 N 6
Newtown 148 C 4
New Town (ND.) 118 F 2
New Ulm (MN.) 119 O 6
New Vienna (OH.) 128 H 2
Newville (CA.) 112 C 3
Newville (PA.) 127 B 8
New Waverly (TX.) 123 H 5
New Westminster 103 N 6
New York (City) 127 EF 8
New York (State) 126–127
New York Mills (MN.) 119 N 4
New Zealand 185 R 9
New Zealand 185 R 9
New Zealand 186 C 5
Neya 158 H 4
Neyestänak (Iran) 157 F 2
Neyriz (Iran) 157 G 3
Neyshäbür 168 F 3
Nezhin 158 F 5
Nezperce (ID.) 110 J 4
Nez Perce Indian Reservation 110 J 4
Ngabé 197 H 6
Ngala 197 G 3
Ngambé 197 G 5
Ngami, Lake 200 C 4
Ngamiland 200 C 3
Ngangala 198 E 4
Ngangerabeli Plain 199 G 5
Nganglong Kangri 174 D 1
Ngangze Co 174 E 1
Ngaoundal 197 G 4
Ngaoundéré → Guidjiba 197 G 4
Ngara 198 E 5
Ngathainggyaung 175 F 4
Ngatik 186 B 2
Nggatokae 185 G 3
Ngidinga 198 B 6
Ngo 197 H 6
Ngoc Linh 175 J 4
Ngoïla 197 G 5
Ngoko 197 H 5
Ngomeni, Ras 199 G 5
Ngom Qu 172 C 4
Ngong 199 F 5
Ngoring 172 C 3
Ngoring Hu 172 C 4
Ngorongoro Crater 198 F 5
Ngoua, Mont 198 C 3
Ngoui 196 B 2
Ngouiéié 197 G 6
Ngouri 197 H 3
Ngourti 197 G 2
Ngoussi 193 G 2
Ngoywa 198 E 6
Nguara 197 H 3
Ngudu 198 E 5
Nguigmi 197 G 3
Ngum 175 H 4
Nguni 197 F 5
Nguru 197 G 3
Nguyen Binh 175 J 3
Ngwale 201 F 2
Ngwane 201 E 5
Nhachengue 201 F 4
Nhambiquara 140 E 3
Nhamundá 139 G 4
Nhamundá 139 G 4
N'harea 200 B 2
Nha Trang 175 J 5
Nhill 183 H 6
Nhoma 200 C 3
Nhommarath 175 J 4
Nhulunbuy 183 F 1
Niafounke 196 D 2
Niagara Falls (N.Y.) 125 PQ 6
Niagassola 196 C 3
Niah 176 D 3
Niakaramandougou 196 C 4
Niamey 196 E 3
Niaming 196 C 3
Niandan Koro 196 C 3
Niangara 198 D 3
Niangay, Lac 196 D 2
Niangoloko 196 D 3
Nia-Nia 198 D 3
Nianzishan 171 M 6
Niarada (MT.) 111 L 3
Niari 197 G 6

Nias, Pulau 176 A 3
Niassa 201 F 2
Niau 187 F 4
Nibâk (Saudi Arabia) 157 F 4
Nicaragua 132 EF 5
Nicaragua, Lago de 132 E 5
Nicatous Lake 126 L 3
Nice 153 E 3
Niceville (FL.) 131 H 4
Nichalakh 171 QR 1
Nichicun, Lac 105 N 5
Nicholas Channel 133 G 3
Nicholasville (KY.) 128 G 4
Nicholls Town 133 G 2
Nichols (S.C.) 129 M 7
Nicholson (MS.) 130 E 4
Nicholson River 183 F 2
Nickel Creek (TX.) 117 M 6
Nickerie 139 G 2
Nickerson (KS.) 120 G 4
Nickol Bay 182 B 3
Nicobar Islands 175 F 6
Nicocli 138 C 2
Nicodemus (KS.) 120 F 3
Nicosia 155 D 3
Nicosia (Cyprus) 156 A 2
Nicotera 153 G 4
Nicoya 132 E 5
Nicoya, Golfo de 132 F 6
Nicoya, Península de 132 E 6
Nicuadala 201 F 3
Nida 149 H 4
Nidelva 151 E 4
Nido, Sierra del 106 E 6
Nidym 170 G 3
Nidzica 149 H 4
Niebüll 149 E 4
Niecka Sieradzka 149 G 4
Nieddu 153 E 3
Niedersachsen 149 E 4
Niedre Tauern 153 F 2
Niefang 197 G 5
Niellé 196 C 3
Niellim 197 H 4
Niemba 198 D 6
Niemba 198 D 6
Niemisel 150 H 2
Nienburg 149 E 4
Niéndkoué, Mont 196 C 4
Niéré 197 J 3
Niete Mountains 196 C 4
Nieuw Amsterdam 139 H 2
Nieuw Nickerie 139 G 2
Nieuwoudtville 200 B 6
Nieves 140 C 3
Niğde 155 D 3
Nigenän 168 F 4
Niger 197 FG 2
Niger (River) 197 F 4
Niger Delta 197 F 5
Nigeria 197 F 4
Nighasan 174 D 2
Nihau 187 E 1
Nihiru 187 F 4
Nihoa 186 E 1
Niigata 173 L 3
Niihama 173 K 4
Niihau 113 B 10
Niitsu 173 L 3
Nîjar 152 C 4
Nijmegen 148 E 4
Nikel 150 K 2
Nikk 196 E 4
Nikkaluokta 150 G 2
Nikolaos, Ayios 154 C 3
Nikolayev 154 D 1
Nikolayevka 155 D 1
Nikolayevka 159 N 5
Nikolayevo 151 J 4
Nikolayevskiy 158 J 5
Nikolayevskiy 159 M 5
Nikolayevskiy 171 N 5
Nikolayevsk-na-Amure 171 Q 5
Nikol'sk 158 J 4
Nikol'sk 158 J 5
Nikol'sk 170 F 4
Nikolski 102 D 5
Nikol'skiy 169 H 1
Nikol'skoye 155 G 1
Nîkpey (Iran) 157 E 1
Niksar 155 E 2
Nikshahr 169 G 5
Nikšic 154 A 2
Nikumaroro 186 D 3
Nila, Pulau 177 G 5
Nilakka 150 J 3
Niland (CA.) 113 K 9
Nile 194 E 3
Niles (MI.) 124 H 8
Nili 193 F 2
Nilka 169 L 2
Nilo Peçanha 139 H 5
Nilsiä 150 J 3
Nimach 174 B 3
Nimba, Monts 196 C 4
Nimbe 197 F 5
Nimes 152 D 3
Nimmitable 183 H 6

Nimrod Lake 121 M 8
Nimrûd (Iraq) 156 D 1
Nimule 198 E 4
Nin 153 G 3
Ninaview (CO.) 115 O 6
Nincheng 173 G 2
Ninda 200 C 2
Nine Degree Channel 174 B 6
Ninety East Ridge 208 B 5
Ninety Mile Beach 183 H 6
Nineveh (Iraq) 156 D 1
Ninfas, Punta 143 D 7
Ningaloo 182 A 3
Ningbo 173 H 5
Ningde 173 G 5
Ningdu 172 G 5
Ninghai 173 H 5
Ningi 197 F 3
Ningjing Shan 172 C 4
Ninglang 172 D 5
Ningming 172 E 6
Ningnan 172 D 5
Ningshan 172 E 4
Ningwu 172 F 3
Ningxia Huizu Zizhiqu 172 E 3
Ning Xian 172 E 3
Ningxiang 172 F 5
Ninh Binh 175 J 3
Ninhue 143 B 6
Ninigo Group 186 A 3
Ninigo Islands 184 D 2
Ninyako-Vogumma 159 P 1
Niobrara (NE.) 119 K 8
Niobrara River 118 J 8
Nioki 198 B 5
Niokolo Koba, Parc National du 196 B 3
Niono 196 C 3
Niordenskiold River 109 L 3
Nioro 196 A 3
Nioro du Sahel 196 C 2
Niort 152 C 2
Niou 196 D 3
Niout 192 D 5
Nipa 139 F 2
Nipani 174 B 4
Nipawin 103 R 5
Nipigon 104 K 6
Nipigon, Lake 104 K 6
Nipissing, Lake 105 LM 6
Nippur (Iraq) 157 D 2
Nipton (CA.) 113 K 7
Nir, Jabal an (Saudi Arabia) 156 D 4–5
Nirmal 174 C 4
Nirmal Range 174 C 4
Nis 154 B 2
Nisâb (S. Yemen) 195 H 6
Nişâb → Ansâb 195 G 3
Nišava 154 B 2
Niscemi 153 F 4
Nishino'omote 173 K 4
Nísiros 154 C 3
Nisko 149 H 4
Nisland (SD.) 118 E 6
Nisling River 109 L 3
Nisser 151 E 4
Nissum Bredning 151 E 4
Nissum Fjord 151 E 4
Nisswa (MN.) 119 O 4
Nisutlin River 109 M 3
Nitchequon 105 N 5
Niterói 141 H 5
Nitiya 171 P 4
Nitra 149 G 5
Nitsa 159 M 4
Niuafo'ou 186 D 4
Niuato Putapu 186 D 4
Niue 186 D 4
Niulakita 186 C 3
Niut, Gunung 176 D 3
Niutao 186 C 3
Niutoushan 173 G 4
Nivala 150 H 3
Nivernais 152 D 2
Nivskiy 150 K 2
Nixon (TX.) 122 F 6
Niyabâd (Iran) 157 E 2
Niza (Iran) 157 G 3
Nizamabad 174 C 4
Nizhmozero 158 G 3
Nizhnaya Pesha 158 J 2
Nizhneangarsk 170 J 4
Nizhnegorskiy 155 D 1
Nizhne-Kamchatsk 171 U 4
Nizhne-Ozernaya 171 U 4
Nizhneshadrino 170 F 4
Nizhneudinsk 170 G 4
Nizhnetambovskoye 171 P 5
Nizhnevartovskoye 159 P 3
Nizhneyansk 171 P 1
Nizhneye Bugayevo 158 K 2
Nizhneye Karelina 170 J 4
Nizhniy Baskunchak 158 J 6
Nizhniy Chir 158 H 6
Nizhniye Kresty 171 U 2
Nizhniy Kholtoson 170 H J 5
Nizhniy Kuranakh 171 MN 4
Nizhniy Lomov 158 H 5
Nizhniy Pyandzh 169 H 3

Nizhniy Tagil 159 M 4
Nizhniy Tsasuchey 170 L 5
Nizhniy Yenangsk 158 J 4
Nizhnyaya Mgla 158 HJ 2
Nizhnyaya Omka 159 O 4
Nizhnyaya Poyma 170 G 4
Nizhnyaya Tavda 159 N 4
Nizhnyaya Tunguska 170 F 3
Nizhnyaya Voch' 158 K 3
Nizhnyaya Zolotitsa 158 H 2
Nizina Podlaska 149 H 4
Nizip 155 E 3
Nizip (Turkey) 156 B 1
Nízke Tatry 149 G 5
Njinjo 199 F 6
Njombe 198 EF 6
Njonbe 198 E 6
Njudung 151 F 4
Njunes 150 G 2
Njurunda 150 G 3
Njutånger 150 F 3
Nkai 200 D 3
Nkambe 197 G 4
Nkawkaw 196 D 4
Nkayi 197 G 6
Nkhata Bay 201 E 2
Nkhotka-Kota 201 E 2
Nkolabona 197 G 5
Nkomi, Lagune 197 F 6
Nkongsamba 197 G 5
Nkurenkuru 200 B 3
Nkusi 198 E 4
Nkwalini 201 E 5
Nmai Hka 175 G 2
Noakhali 175 F 3
Noanamá 138 C 2
Noatak (AK.) 102 E 2
Noatak (AK.) 102 EF 2
Noatak National Preserve 102 F 2
Nobel 105 L 6
Nobeoka 173 K 4
Nobéré 196 D 3
Noblesville (IN.) 124 H 9
Nobres 140 E 3
Noccundra 183 G 4
Nocona (TX.) 122 F 2
Node (WY.) 118 D 8
Noefs, Ile des 199 J 6
Noelke (TX.) 122 C 4
Nogales (AZ.) 116 F 6
Nogales (Mexico) 106 D 3
Nogal Valley → Dôhô Nugâlêd 199 H 3
Nogayskiye Step' 155 G 2
Nogent-le-Rotrou 152 D 2
Noginsk 158 G 4
Noginskiy 170 F 3
Nogliki 171 Q 5
Nogoya 142 D 5
Nogueira, Serra da 152 B 3
Nohar 174 B 2
Nohili Point 113 C 9
Nohly (MT.) 118 D 3
Noir, Isla 143 B 9
Noirmoutier 152 C 2
Nojane 200 C 4
Nokaneng 200 C 3
Nokia 150 H 3
Nok Kundi 169 G 5
Nokou 197 G 3
Nokra 199 F 1
Nokrek 175 F 2
Nola 198 B 4
Nolan 109 H 2
Nolanville (TX.) 122 F 4
Nolin Lake 128 E 4
Nolinsk 158 J 4
Noma (FL.) 131 J 4
Nomad 184 D 3
Nomad 186 A 3
Nomans Land 127 J 7
Nombre de Dios 132 B 3
Nome 102 D 3
Nomgon 172 D 2
Nomhon 172 C 3
Nömrög 170 G 6
Nomtsas 200 B 4
Nomwin 186 B 2
Nonacho Lake 103 Q 3
Nonburg 158 K 2
Nondalton 108 G 3
Nondugl 184 D 3
Nong Khai 175 H 4
Nongoma 201 E 5
Nonoava 106 E 6
Nonouti 186 C 3
Nonuianuk Lake 108 G 4
Noonan (ND.) 118 E 2
Noonkanbah 182 C 2
Noordoewer 200 B 5
Noordzeekanaal 148 D 4
Noorvik 102 E 2
Nora 151 F 4
Nora Springs (IA.) 119 PQ 7
Norberg 151 G 3
Norcatur (KS.) 120 E 3
Nordaustlandet 202
Norden 149 E 4
Norden (NE.) 118 H 8
Nordenham 149 E 4

Norderstedt 149 E 4
Nordfjord 150 E 3
Nordfjordeid 150 E 3
Nordfold 150 FG 2
Nordfriesische Inseln 149 E 4
Nordhausen 149 F 4
Norðoyar 148 A 1
Nordkapp 150 J 1
Nordkinn 150 J 1
Nordkinnhalvöya 150 J 1
Nordkjosbotn 150 GH 2
Nordland 150 F 2
Nordmaling 150 GH 3
Nordman (WA.) 110 H 2
Nordostrundingen 202
Nord-Ostsee-Kanal 149 E 4
Norðöyane 150 E 3
Nordreisa 150 H 2
Nordre Strømfjord 105 R 2
Nord-Trøndelag 150 F 3
Nordvik 170 K 1
Norefjell 151 E 3
Norfolk (CO.) 115 M 3
Norfolk (NE.) 119 L 8
Norfolk (VA.) 129 P 5
Norfolk Islands 186 C 4
Norfork (AR.) 121 N 6
Norfork Lake 121 N 6
Norge 150 F 2
Nori 159 O 2
Norias (TX.) 122 F 9
Noril'sk 159 R 2
Norlina (N.C.) 129 N 5
Normal (AL.) 128 E 7
Normal (IL.) 124 F 9
Norman (AR.) 121 M 8
Norman (NE.) 120 G 2
Norman (OK.) 120 H 7
Norman, Lake 129 KL 6
Normanby Island 183 J 1
Normanby Island 185 F 4
Normandie 152 CD 2
Normangee (TX.) 122 G 4
Norman Island 130 E 8
Norman River 183 G 2
Normanton 183 G 2
Norman Wells 109 N 2
Norquin 143 B 6
Norquinco 143 B 7
Norrahammar 151 F 4
Norråker 150 G 3
Norra Kvarken 150 H 3
Norra Storfjället 150 G 2
Norrbotten 150 GH 2
Norresundby 151 F 4
Norris (MT.) 111 O 5
Norris City (IL.) 121 R 5
Norris Lake 128 H 5
Norristown (PA.) 127 D 8
Norrköping 151 G 4
Norrland 150 FG 3
Norrtälje 151 G 4
Norseman 182 C 5
Norsjö (Norway) 151 E 4
Norsjö (Sweden) 150 G 3
Norsk 171 O 5
Norsoup 185 J 5
Norte, Cabo 139 J 3
Norte, Canal do 139 H 3
Norte, Punta 143 E 6
North (S.C.) 129 K 8
North, Cape (Nova Scotia, Can.) 105 P 6
North Adams (MA.) 126 F 6
Northam (Australia) 182 B 5
Northam (South Africa) 200 D 4
Northampton (MA.) 126 G 6
Northampton (U.K.) 148 C 4
Northampton (Western Australia) 182 A 4
North Andaman 175 F 5
North Arm 103 P 3
North Augusta (S.C.) 129 J 8
North Aulatsivik Island 105 P 4
North Battleford 103 Q 5
North Battle Mountain (NV.) 112 J 2
North Bay 105 M 6
North Beach Peninsula 110 A 4
North Belcher Islands 105 L 4
North Bend (NE.) 119 M 9
North Bend (OR.) 110 A 7
North Bonneville (WA.) 110 C 5
North Branch (MN.) 119 O 5
North Branch (MO/W.V.) 129 M 2
North Canadian River 120 G 7
North Canton (OH.) 125 N 9
North Cape (New Zealand) 185 Q 7
North Cape (New Zealand) 186 C 5
North Cape (Norway) 150 J 1
North Caribou Lake 104 J 5
North Carolina 129
North Cascades National Park 110 D 2
North Channel 104 L 6
North Channel (U.K.) 148 B 3–4
North Charleston (S.C.) 129 M 9
North Chicago (IL.) 124 G 7
Northcliff 182 B 5
North College Hill (OH.) 128 G 2

North Creek (N.Y.) 126 F 5
North Dakota 118–119
North Dam 110 FG 3
North Danger Reef 176 D 1
North East (MD.) 129 Q 2
North East (PA.) 125 OP 7
Northeast Cape 102 D 3
Northeast Providence Channel 133 G 2
Northeim 149 F 4
North English (IA.) 119 QR 9
Northern Cheyenne Indian Reservation 118 B 5
Northern Cook Islands 186 E 3
Northern Dvina River 158 H 3
Northern Indian Lake 103 S 4
Northern Ireland 148 B 4
Northern Light Lake 119 S 2
Northern Mariana Islands 186 B 1
Northern Perimeter Highway 138 D 4–5
Northern Territory 182 E 2–3
Northfield (MA.) 126 G 6
Northfield (MN.) 119 P 6
Northfield (TX.) 117 Q 3
Northfield (VT.) 126 G 4
North Fork (AK.) 109 H 3
North Fork (ID.) 111 L 5
North Fork (KS.) 120 F 3
North Fork (NV.) 112 K 1
North Fork (OK./TX.) 120 EF 7
North Fork (S.C.) 129 K 8
North Fox Pass 102 K 3
North Fort (CO.) 115 M 4
North Fort Myers (FL.) 131 N 8
North Fox Island 124 J 4
Northgate (ND.) 118 F 2
North Geomagnetic Pole 202
North Hero (VT.) 126 G 4
North Highlands (CA.) 112 D 4
North Horr 199 F 4
North Island 185 Q 8
North Island 186 C 5
North Island (S.C.) 129 M 8
North Judson (IN.) 124 H 8
North Korea 173 K 2
North Lakhimpur 175 F 2
Northland (MI.) 124 G 3
North Las Vegas (NV.) 112 K 6
North La Veta Pass 115 M 6
North Little Rock (AR.) 121 N 8
North Loon Mountain 111 K 5
North Loup River 118 J 9
North Magnetic Pole 202
North Mamm Peak 115 K 4
North Manchester (IN.) 124 J 9
North Manitou Island 124 H 4
North Miami Beach (FL.) 131 O 9
North Minch 148 B 3
Northome (MN.) 119 O 3
North Pacific Basin 209 D 2
North Pack (IL.) 124 E 7
North Peak 116 E 3
North Platte (NE.) 120 E 1
North Platte River 118 F 9
North Point 125 L 4
North Point 184 L 8
North Pole 202
North Pole (AK.) 109 J 3
Northport (AL.) 128 D 8
Northport (MI.) 124 J 4
Northport (WA.) 110 H 2
North Powder (OR.) 110 GH 5
North Richland Hills (TX.) 122 F 3
North Rim (AZ.) 116 D 1
North River 103 T 4
North Roby (TX.) 122 C 3
North Rona 148 B 3
North Ronaldsay 148 C 3
North Salt Lake (UT.) 114 F 3
North Saskatchewan 103 PQ 5
North Schell Peak 112 L 3
North Sea 148 D 3
North Sentinel 175 F 5
North Shoshone Peak 112 H 3
North Slope 102 FH 2
North Stradbroke Island 183 J 4
North Stratford (VT.) 126 H 4
North Syracuse (N.Y.) 126 CD 5
North Taranaki Bight 185 Q 8
North Thompson 103 O 5
North Uist 148 B 3
Northumberland Islands 183 J 3
Northumberland Strait 105 P 5
North Umpqua River 110 C 7
Northville (N.Y.) 126 E 5
Northville (S.D.) 119 K 5
Northway Junction 102 J 3
North West Cape 182 A 3
North West Highlands 148 C 3
Northwest Pacific Basin 209 C 2
North West River 105 P 5
Northwest Territories (Canada) 103 NT 2
Northwood (IA.) 119 P 7
Northwood (N.D.) 119 L 3
Northwood (N.H.) 126 H 5
North Zulch (TX.) 122 G 5
Norton (KS.) 120 F 3
Norton (W.V.) 129 L 3
Norton (Zimbabwe) 201 E 3
Norton Bay 102 E 3

Norton Reservoir 120 F 3
Norton Sound 102 E 3
Nortonville (KS.) 121 K 3
Nortonville (KY.) 128 D 4
Nortonville (N.D.) 119 K 4
Nortport (NE.) 118 E 9
Norvegia, Cape 203
Norwalk (CT.) 127 F 7
Norwalk (OH.) 125 M 8
Norway 150 F 2
Norway (KS.) 120 H 3
Norway (MI.) 124 G 4
Norway Bay 103 R 1
Norway House 103 S 5
Norwegian Basin 208 A 1
Norwich 148 D 4
Norwich (CT.) 126 G 7
Norwich (KS.) 120 H 5
Norwich (N.Y.) 126 D 6
Norwood (CO.) 115 J 5
Norwood (N.C.) 129 L 6
Norwood (N.Y.) 126 E 4
Norwood (OH.) 128 G 2
Noshiro 173 L 2
Noshul' 158 J 3
Nosok 159 Q 1
Nosovaya 158 K 2
Nosovka 158 F 5
Nosovshchina158 G 3
Nosratābād 168 F 5
Nossa Senhora da Glória 138 D 5
Nossob 200 B 4
Nossob 200 C 5
No. 5 Station 194 E 4
No. 10 Station 194 E 5
Nosy Barren 201 G 3
Nosy-Bé 201 H 2
Nosy Boraha 201 J 3
Nosy Mitsio 201 H 2
Nosy-Varika 201 H 4
Nota 104 J 2
Notch Peak 114 D 4
Noteć 149 G 4
Nótioi Sporádhes 154 C 3
Noto 153 FG 4
Notodden 151 E 4
Noto-hantō 173 L 3
Notorskoye 171 O 3
Notre Dame, Monts 105 O 6
Notre Dame Bay 105 QR 6
Notrees (TX.) 117 O 6
Nottawasaga Bay 105 L 7
Nottaway 105 M 5
Nottingham (Ontario, Can.) 105 M 3
Nottingham (U.K.) 148 C 4
Nottoway River 129 O 5
Nouadhibou 192 B 4
Nouadhibou, Dakhlet 192 B 4
Nouakchott 192 B 5
Nouamrhar 192 B 5
Nouméa 185 J 6
Nouméa 186 C 4
Noumin He 171 M 6
Nouna 196 D 3
Noupoort 200 D 6
Nouveau Comptoir 105 M 5
Nouvelle-Calédonie 185 H 6
Nouvelle Calédonie 186 B 4
Nouvelle France, Cap de 105 N 3
Nova 141 H 2
Nova, Serra 139 F 5
Nova Andradina 141 F 5
Novabad 169 HJ 3
Nova Caipemba 200 A 1
Nova Cruz 141 J 2
Nova Friburgo 141 H 5
Nova Gorica 153 F 2
Nova Gradiška 153 G 2
Nova Iguaçu 141 H 5
Nova Lamego 196 B 3
Nova Lima 141 H 5
Nova Mambone 201 F 4
Nova Olinda do Norte 139 G 4
Novara 153 E 2
Nova Scotia 105 P 7
Nova Sento Sé 141 H 2
Nova Sofala 201 EF 4
Novato (CA.) 112 C 4
Nova Varoš 154 A 2
Nova Venécia 141 H 4
Nova Vida 140 D 3
Novaya Igirma 170 H 4
Novaya Kakhovka 155 D 1
Novaya Kazanka 158 J 6
Novaya Lyalya 159 M 4
Novaya Odessa 154 D 1
Novaya Ushitsa 154 C 1
Novaya Ussuri 171 P 6
Novaya Zemlya 158 L 1
Novaya Zemlya 202
Nova Zagora 154 C 2
Novelda 152 E 2
Novembro, Cachoeira dois de 139 F 5
Nové Zámky 149 G 5
Novgorod 151 K 4
Novgorodka 151 J 4
Novgorodka 155 D 1
Novgorod Severskiy 158 F 5
Novice (TX.) 122 D 3–4
Novigrad 153 F 2

Novikovo 171 Q 6
Novi Ligure 153 E 3
Novillero 132 A 3
Novi Pazar (Bulgaria) 154 C 2
Novi Pazar (Yugoslavia) 154 B 2
Novi Sad 154 AB 1
Novi Vinodolski 153 FG 2
Novo, Lago 139 H 3
Novo Acôrdo 139 H 4
Novoaleksandrovsk 155 F 1
Novoalekseyevka 155 D 1
Novoaltaysk 159 Q 5
Novoanninskiy 158 H 5
Novo Aripuanã 139 FG 5
Novo Arkhangelsk 154 D 1
Novoazovskoye 155 E 1
Novobiryusinskiy 170 G 4
Novobogatinskoye 168 E 1
Novobogdanovka 155 DE 1
Novocherkassk 155 E 1
Novodolinka 159 O 5
Novogeorgiyevka 171 N 5
Novograd-Volynskiy 151 J 5
Novogrudok 151 J 5
Novo Hamburgo 142 F 4
Novo Horizonte 141 G 5
Novokazalinsk 169 G 1
Novokhoperskiy 158 H 5
Novokocherdyk 159 M 5
Novokubansk 155 F 1
Novokuybyshevsk 158 J 5
Novokuznetsk 159 R 5
Novolazarevskaya 203
Novoletov'ye 170 H 1
Novoluzino 159 R 2
Novolynsk 149 H 4
Novomariinka 170 G 4
Novomikhaylovskoye 155 E 2
Novomirgorod 154 D 1
Novomoskovsk 155 E 1
Novomoskovsk 158 G 5
Novonikolskoye 159 NO 4
Novonikol'skoye 159 P 4
Novoorsk 159 L 5
Novopavlovskoye 170 K 5
Novopokrovskaya 155 F 1
Novopolotsk 151 J 4
Novo Pskov 158 G 6
Novorossiysk 155 E 2
Novorybnoye 170 HJ 1
Novo Sagres 177 G 5
Novo-selitsa 154 C 1
Novoselovo 170 F 4
Novo Sergeyevka 158 K 5
Novoshakhtinsk 155 E 1
Novosibirsk 159 Q 4
Novosibirskiye Ostrova → New Siberi-
    an Islands 161 QR 2
Novosibirskoye Vodokhrani-
    lishche 159 Q 5
Novosokol'niki 151 JK 4
Novotroitsk 159 L 5
Novotroitskoye 169 J 2
Novotsimlyanskiy 155 F 1
Novo Ukrainka 154 D 1
Novo Uzensk 158 J 5
Novoveselyy 155 F 1
Novovorontsovka 155 D 1
Novovoskresenovka 171 N 5
Novo-Vyatsk 158 J 4
Novoyeniseysk 170 FG 4
Novoyerudinskiy 170 F 4
Novoye Ust'ye 171 Q 4
Novoyugino 159 PQ 4
Novozhilovskaya 158 K 3
Novozybkov 158 F 5
Novvy Bug 155 D 1
Nový Jičín 149 G 5
Novyy 159 R 4
Novyy 170 J 1
Novyy Afon 155 F 2
Novyy Bor 158 K 2
Novyy Karymkary 159 N 3
Novyy Oskol 158 G 5
Novyy Port 159 O 2
Novyy Tanguy 170 H 4
Novyy Vasyugan 159 P 4
Nowa Ruda 149 G 4
Nowa Sól 149 G 4
Nowata (KS.) 121 K 6
Now Bandegān (Iran) 157 FG 3
Nowbarān (Iran) 157 E 2
Nowdesheh (Iran) 157 E 2
Nowfel low Shātow (Iran) 157 F 2
Now Gombād (Iran) 157 F 2
Nowgong 175 F 2
Nowitna 102 FG 3
Nowlin (SD.) 118 G 6
Nowogard 149 G 4
Nowo Korczyn 149 H 4
Nowood River 111 S 6–7
Nowra 183 J 5
Nowrangapur 174 D 4
Now Shahr (Iran) 157 F 1
Nowshera 169 J 4
Nowy Dwór 149 H 4
Nowy Sacz 149 H 5
Nowy Targ 149 H 5

Noxapater (MS.) 130 EF 1
Noxon Reservoir 111 K 3
Noya 152 B 3
Noyek (Iran) 157 G 1
Noyon 172 D 2
Nozay 152 C 2
Nsa 193 F 2
Nsanje 201 F 3
Nsawam 196 D 4
Nsok 197 G 5
Nsombo 200 D 2
Nsukka 197 F 4
Nsuta 196 D 4
Ntadembele 198 B 5
Ntakat 192 C 5
Ntem 197 G 5
Ntui 197 G 5
Nuaib 192 D 3
Nuanetsi → Mwenezi 201 E 4
Nuatja 196 E 4
Nuba Mountains → Dar Nūbah
    194 DE 6
Nubia 194 E 5
Nubian Desert → Aş Şaḥrā' an Nūbiyah
    194 E 4
Nubieber (CA.) 112 D 1
Nūbiyah 194 DE 5
Nūbiyah, Aş Şaḥrā' an 194 E 4
Nucla (CO.) 114 J 5
Nueces River 122 DE 7
Nueifed 192 C 4
Nueltin Lake 103 S 3
Nueva, Isla 143 C 10
Nueva Alejandría 138 D 5
Nueva Antioqia 138 E 2
Nueva Esperanza 140 D 4
Nueva Galia 142 C 5–6
Nueva Gerona 132 F 3
Nueva Imperial 143 B 6
Nueva León 132 BC 2
Nueva Lubecka 143 BC 7
Nueva Rosita 132 B 2
Nueva San Salvador 132 DE 5
Nueve de Julio 142 D 6
Nuevitas 133 G 3
Nuevo, Golfo 143 D 7
Nuevo Año, Point 112 C 5
Nuevo Berlin 142 E 5
Nuevo Casas Grandes 106 E 5
Nuevo Laredo 132 BC 2
Nuevo Mundo, Cerro 140 C 5
Nuevo Rocafuerte 138 C 4
Nugāl 199 H 3
Nuguria Islands 185 FG 2
Nuguria Islands 186 B 3
Nui 186 C 3
Nuiqsut 102 G 1
Nujiang 172 C 4–5
Nu Jiang 172 C 5–6
Nukey Bluff 183 F 5
Nukhayb (Iraq) 156 D 2
Nukhaylak 194 D 5
Nuku'alofa 186 D 4
Nukufetau 186 C 3
Nuku Hiva 187 F 3
Nukuhu 185 E 3
Nukulaelae 186 C 3
Nukunonu 186 D 3
Nukunau 186 C 3
Nukuoro 186 B 2
Nukus 168 F 2
Nulato 102 F 3
Nulepel'men 108 D 2
Nullagine 182 C 3
Nullarbor 182 E 5
Nullarbor Plain 182 D 5
Nulloocha 183 F 3
Num, Pulau 177 J 4
Numan 197 G 4
Numancia 177 G 2
Numazu 173 L 4
Numbulwar Mission 182 F 1
Numedal 151 E 3
Numfor, Pulau 177 H 4
Numkaub 200 B 3
Numto 159 O 3
Numurkah 183 H 6
Nunda (S.D.) 119 M 6
Nundle 183 J 5
Nundu 198 D 5
Nunelly (TN.) 128 D 6
Nungo 201 F 2
Nunivak Island 102 D 3
Nunkun 169 K 4
Nunlygran 102 B 3
Nunn (CO.) 115 N 3
Nunthergie 183 G 5
Nunyamo 102 C 2
Nuorajärvi 150 K 3
Nuorgam 150 J 1
Nuoro 153 E 3
Nūq (Iran) 157 G 3
Nuqay, Jabal 193 J 4
Nuqrah (Saudi Arabia) 156 C 4
Nuqrus, Jabal (Egypt) 156 B 4
Nuquí 138 C 2
Nūr (Iran) 157 G 3

Nura 159 O 5
Nura 159 O 6
Nūrabād (Iran) 157 F 3
Nurata 169 H 2
Nuratau, Khrebet 169 H 2
Nur Dağları 155 E 3
Nurek 169 H 3
Nuremberg 149 F 5
Nurhak Dağı 155 E 3
Nurī 194 E 5
Nuristan 169 J 3
Nurlat 158 K 5
Nurmes 150 J 3
Nurpur 174 C 1
Nurri, Mount 183 H 5
Nursery (TX.) 122 F 7
Nusaybin 155 F 3
Nusaybin (Turkey) 156 C 1
Nushagak 102 F 4
Nushagak Bay 108 G 4
Nushagale (NE.) 118 G 4
Nushagak Peninsula 108 G 4
Nu Shan 172 C 5
Nushki 169 H 5
Nutak 105 P 4
Nutepel'men 108 C 2
Nutrioso (AZ.) 116 G 3–4
Nutt (N.M.) 117 J 5
Nuuk 105 R 3
Nuupas 150 J 2
Nuwara Eliya 174 D 6
Nuwaybi'al Muzayyinah (Egypt) 156 B 3
Nuweveldreekes 200 C 6
Nxai Pan National Park 200 C 3
Nyaake 196 C 5
Nyabéssan 197 G 5
Nyabing 182 B 5
Nyac 108 F 3
Nyahanga 198 E 5
Nyahua 198 E 6
Nyahururu 199 F 5E◊
Nyainqentanglha Shan 172 B 4
Nyainrong 172 B 4
Nyakakangaga 198 E 5
Nyakanazi 198 E 5
Nyåker 150 G 3
Nyaksimvol' 159 M 3
Nyala 194 D 6
Nyalam 174 E 2
Nyalikungu 198 E 5
Nyamandhlovu 200 D 3
Nyamboma Rapids 200 C 2
Nyamboyto 159 Q 2
Nyamirembe 198 E 5
Nyamlell 198 D 3
Nyamtumbo 201 F 2
Nyanda Rua 199 F 5
Nyandoma 158 H 3
Nyanga 197 FG 6
Nyanga 197 G 6
Nyanga, Lake 182 D 4
Nyangana 200 C 3
Nyanza 198 D 5
Nyasa, Lake 201 E 2
Nyassa (OR.) 110 H 7
Nyaungu 175 F 3
Nyayba 171 O 1
Nyazepetrovsk 159 L 4
Nyborg 151 F 4
Nybro 151 G 4
Nyda 159 O 2
Nyêmo 175 F 2
Nyeri 199 F 5
Nyerol 198 E 3
Nyika Plateau 201 E 2
Nyima 174 E 1
Nyimba 201 E 2
Nyingchi 172 B 5
Nyiregyháza 154 B 1
Nyiri Desert 199 F 5
Nyiru, Mount 199 F 4
Nykarleby 150 H 3
Nyköbing (Denmark) 151 E 4
Nyköbing (Denmark) 151 F 4
Nyköbing (Denmark) 151 F 5
Nyköping (Sweden) 151 G 4
Nylstroom 200 D 4
Nymagee 183 H 5
Nynäshamn 151 G 4
Nyngan 183 H 5
Nyon 153 E 3
Nyong 197 G 5
Nyrob 158 L 3
Nysa 149 G 4
Nyslott 150 J 3
Nystad 151 H 3
Nytva 158 L 4
Nyuk, Ozero 150 K 3
Nyuksenitsa 158 H 3
Nyukzha 171 M 4
Nyunzu 198 D 6
Nyurba 170 L 3
Nyurol'skiy 159 P 4
Nyuya 170 K 3
Nyuya 170 L 3
Nyvrovo 171 Q 5
Nyyiskiy Zaliv 171 Q 5
Nzambi 197 G 6
Nzara 198 D 4

Nzébéla 196 C 4
Nzega 198 E 5
Nzerékoré 196 C 4
N'zeto 200 A 1

O

Oahe, Lake 118 H 5
Oahe Dam 118 H 6
Oahu 113 DE 10
Oahu 187 E 1
Oakbank 183 G 5
Oak City (UT.) 114 E 4
Oak Creek (CO.) 115 L 3
Oak Creek Reservoir 122 C 3
Oakdale (CA.) 112 E 5
Oakdale (LA.) 123 L 5
Oakdale (NE.) 119 K 8
Oakes (N.D.) 119 KL 4
Oakesdale (WA.) 110 H 3
Oakey 183 J 4
Oak Grove (LA.) 123 M 3
Oak Harbor (WA.) 110 C 2
Oak Hill (FL.) 131 O 6
Oak Hill (KY.) 128 J 3
Oak Hill (TN.) 128 E 5
Oak Hill (TX.) 122 F 5
Oak Hill (W.V.) 129 K 4
Oak Hills 183 G 5
Oakhurst (CA.) 112 F 5
Oakland (CA.) 112 C 5
Oakland (IA.) 119 N 9
Oakland (IL.) 121 S 3
Oakland (MD.) 129 M 2
Oakland (ME.) 126 K 4
Oakland (MS.) 121 N 8
Oakland (NE.) 119 M 9
Oakland (OR.) 110 B 7
Oakland City (IN.) 128 D 3
Oakland Park (FL.) 131 O 8
Oak Lawn (IL.) 124 G 8
Oakley (ID.) 111 M 8
Oakley (KS.) 120 E 3
Oakley (MI.) 125 K 6
Oakover River 182 C 3
Oak Park Reservoir 114 H 3
Oak Ridge (OR.) 110 C 7
Oak Ridge (TN.) 128 G 3
Oaktown (IN.) 128 D 3
Oakville 105 M 7
Oakwood (TX.) 122 H 4
Oamaru 185 Q 10
Oasis (CA.) 112 H 4
Oasis (NV.) 112 L 1
Oates Coast 203
Oatlands 184 L 9
Oaxaca 132 C 4
Oaxaca de Juárez 132 C 4
Ob 159 N 2
Oba 104 L 6
Obala 197 G 5
Oban (New Zealand) 184 P 10
Oban (U.K.) 148 B 3
Obanazawa 173 LM 3
Obando 138 E 3
Oban Hills 197 F 4
Obar (N.M.) 117 N 2
Obbia 199 H 3
Obeh 169 G 4
Obeliai 151 J 4
Oberlin (KS.) 120 E 3
Oberlin (LA.) 123 L 5
Oberlin (OH.) 125 M 8
Oberon (ND.) 118 J 3
Oberovaca 154 AB 2
Oberpfälzer Wald 149 F 5
Obervellach 153 F 2
Obi 197 F 4
Obi, Selat 177 G 4
Óbidos 139 G 4
Obihiro 173 M 2
Obil'noye 155 F 1
Obion (TN.) 128 B 5
Oblivskaya 158 H 6
Obluch'ye 171 O 6
Oblukovino 171 T 4
Obninsk 158 G 4
Obo 172 D 3
Obo 198 D 3
Obock 199 G 2
Obodovka 154 C 1
Obokote 198 D 5
Oborniki 149 G 4
Obouya 197 H 6
Oboyan' 158 G 5
Obozerskiy 158 H 3
O'Brien (OR.) 110 B 8
O'Brien (TX.) 122 D 1
Obruk Platosu 155 D 3
Observation Peak 112 E 2
Obshchiy Syrt 158 KL 5
Obskaya Guba 159 O 1–2
Obuasi 196 D 4
Obubra 197 F 4
Obudu 197 F 4
Obzor 154 C 2
Ocala (FL.) 131 M 5

Ocampo 106 E 6
Ocaña (Colombia) 138 D 2
Ocaña (Spain) 152 C 4
Ocate (N.M.) 117 LM 1MO
Occidental, Cordillera 140 BC 3–4
Occidental, Cordillera (Colombia) 138 C 2–3
Oceana (W.V.) 129 K 4
Ocean City (MD.) 129 R 3
Ocean City (N.J.) 127 E 9
Ocean Falls 103 M 5
Ocean Island 185 J 2
Ocean Lake 111 R 7
Oceano (CA.) 113 E 7
Ocean Park (WA.) 110 A 4
Oceanside (CA.) 113 H 9
Ocean Springs (MS.) 130 F 4
Ochakov 154 D 1
Ochamchire 155 F 2
Ocher 158 K 4
Ochlockonee River 131 K 4
Ochoa (TX.) 117 M 8
Ocilla (GA.) 131 L 3
Ockelbo 151 G 3
Ocmulgee River 131 L 2
Ocoña 140 B 4
Oconee River 131 M 2
Oconto (NE.) 120 F 1
Oconto (WI.) 124 G 5
Ocotlán 132 B 3
Ocotlán de Morelos 132 C 4
Ocracoke (N.C.) 129 Q 6
Ocracoke Island 129 Q 6
Ocreza 152 B 4
Ocumare del Tuy 138 E 1
Oda 196 D 4
Oda, Jabal 194 F 4
Ódáðahraun 150 B 2–3
Odalen 151 F 3
Ódate 173 M 2
Odawara 173 L 3–4
Odda 151 E 3
Odder 151 F 4
Odell (NE.) 120 J 2
Odell (TX.) 122 D 1
Odell Lake 110 D 7
Odem (TX.) 122 F 8
Odemira 152 B 4
Ödemiş 154 C 3
Odendaalsrus 200 D 5
Odense 151 F 4
Oder 149 F 4
Ödeshög 151 FG 4
Odessa (TX.) 117 O 6
Odessa (U.S.S.R.) 154 D 1
Odessa (WA.) 110 F 2
Odgers Ranch Indian Reservation 112 KL 2
Odiel 152 B 4
Odienné 196 C 4
Ödmården 151 G 3
O'Donnell (TX.) 117 OP 5
Odra 149 FG 4
Ódwěyne 199 H 3
Odžak 153 G 2
Odzala National Park 197 GH 5
Oeiras 141 H 2
Oelrichs (SD.) 118 E 7
Oelwein (IA.) 119 R 8
Oeno 187 G 4
Oenpelli 182 E 1
Of 155 F 2
Ofanto 153 G 3
Ofeigsfjarðarheiði 150 A 2
Offenbach 149 E 4
Offenburg 149 E 5
Offerle (KS.) 120 F 5
Oficina 139 F 2
Ofotfjorden 150 G 2
Oga 173 L 3
Ogaden 199 GH 3
Og Aguelt Abd el Jebar 192 D 4
Oga-hanto 173 L 3
Ögaki 173 L 3
Ogala (SD.) 118 F 7
Ogallah (KS.) 120 F 4
Ogallala (NE.) 118 G 9
Ogbomosho 197 E 4
Ogden (KS.) 120 J 3
Ogden (UT.) 114 F 2
Ogden, Mount 109 M 4
Ogdensburg (N.Y.) 126 D 4
Ogeechee River 131 N 2
Ogg (TX.) 117 P 3
Oghroud 193 G 2
Ogilby (CA.) 113 L 10
Ogilvie (MN.) 119 P 5
Ogilvie Mountains 102 JK 2
Ogilvie River 109 L 2
Oginskiy Kanal 151 J 5
Oglanly 168 E 3
Oglat Beraber 192 E 2
Oglat el Fersig 192 D 4
Oglethorpe (GA.) 131 K 2
Oglio 153 F 2
Ogmore 183 H 3
Ognev Yar 159 P 4
Ognon 153 E 2
Ogoamas, Gunung 177 F 3

Ogoja 197 F 4
Ogoki 104 K 5
Ogoki Reservoir 104 K 5
Ogooué 197 G 6
Ogoron 171 N 5
Ogradžen 154 B 2
Ogre 151 H 4
Ogr → Sharafah 194 D 6
Ogulin 153 G 2
Oguma 197 F 4
Ogun 196 E 4
Oguossoc (ME.) 126 J 4
Ogurchinskiy, Ostrov 168 E 3
Ogwashi Uku 197 F 4
Ohakune 185 R 8
Ohanet 193 G 3
O'Higgins, Cerro 143 B 8
O'Higgins, Lago 143 B 8
Ohio (North) 125
Ohio (South) 128–129
Ohio (OH.) 125 K 9
Ohio River 128 C 4
Ohopoho 200 A 3
Ohře 149 F 4
Ohrid 154 B 2
Ohridskojezero 154 B 2
Oiapoque 139 H 3
Oiapoque 139 H 3
Oijärvi 150 J 2
Oil City (LA.) 123 K 3
Oil City (PA.) 125 P 8
Oil City (TX.) 117 P 2
Oildale (CA.) 113 FG 7
Oilmont (MT.) 111 O 2
Oilton (OK.) 120 J 6
Oise 152 D 2
Óita 173 K 4
Ojai (CA.) 113 F 8
Ojebyn 150 H 2
Ojibwa (WI.) 124 CD 4
Ojinaga 132 B 2
Ojo de Agua 142 D 4
Ojos del Salado, Cerro 142 C 4
Oka 158 H 4
Oka 170 H 5
Okaba 177 J 5
Okahao 200 A 3
Okahumpka (FL.) 131 N 6
Okakarara 200 B 4
Okak Islands 105 P 4
Okanagan Lake 103 NO 6
Okanogan (WA.) 110 F 2
Okanogan River 110 F 2
Okapa 184 E 3
Okaputa 200 B 4
Okara 169 J 4
Okarche (OK.) 120 GH 7
Okaukuejo 200 B 3
Okavango 200 C 3
Okavango Swamp 200 C 3
Okavarumendu 200 B 4
Okaya 173 L 3
Okayama 173 K 3–4
Okazaki 173 L 4
Okazize 200 B 4
Okeanskoye 171 T 5
Okeechobee (FL.) 131 O 7
Okeechobee, Lake 131 O 7–8
Okeene (OK.) 120 G 6
Okefenokee Swamp 131 M 4
Okemah (OK.) 120 J 7
Okene 197 F 4
Okha (India) 174 A 3
Okha (U.S.S.R.) 171 Q 5
Ókhi Oros 154 B 3
Okhota 171 Q 3
Okhotsk 171 Q 4
Okhotsk, Sea of 171 R 4
Okhotskiy Perevoz 171 P 3
Okhotskoye More 171 QS 4
Okhthonia, Ákra 154 B 3
Okinawa-jima 173 J 5
Okinoerabu-jima 173 J 5
Oki-shotó 173 K 3
Okitipupa 197 EF 4
Oklahoma 120–121
Oklahoma City (OK.) 120 H 7
Oklee (MN.) 119 N 3
Okmulgee (OK.) 120 JK 7
Oknitsa 154 C 1
Okollo 198 E 4
Okolona (KY.) 128 F 3
Okolona (MS.) 121 R 8–9
Okombahe 200 B 4
Okondja 197 G 6
Okonogan 103 O 6
Okorukambe 200 B 4
Okoyo 197 H 6
Öksfjord 150 H 1
Oksino 158 K 2
Okstindan 150 F 2
Oktemberyan 155 F 2
Oktwin 175 G 4
Oktyabr'skiy 155 F 1
Oktyabrskiy 158 K 5
Oktyabr'skiy 159 M 5
Oktyabr'skiy 170 G 4
Oktyabr'skiy 170 F 1
Oktyabr'skiy 171 N 4

Oktyabrskiy 171 N 5
Oktyabr'skiy 171 Q 5
Oktyabr'skiy 171 T 5
Oktyabr'skoye 158 GH 5
Oktyabr'skoye 159 N 3
Okurchan 171 S 4
Okushiri-tó 173 L 2
Okuta 171 S 4
Ola 171 S 4
Ola (ID.) 110 J 6
Ólafsfjörður 150 B 2
Ólafsvík 150 A 3
Ola Grande, Punta 130 C 9
Olancha (CA.) 112 H 6
Olancha Peak 112 G 6
Olanchito 132 E 4
Öland 151 G 4
Olanga 150 K 2
Olary 183 G 5
Olathe (CO.) 115 K 5
Olathe (KS.) 121 L 4
Olavarría 143 DE 6
Oława 149 G 4
Olbia 153 E 3
Old Bahama Channel 133 G 3
Old Cherrabun 182 D 2
Old Crow (N.W.T., Can.) 102 K 2
Old Crow (N.W.T., Can.) 102 K 2
Old Dominion Mountain 110 H 2
Oldenburg (F.R.G.) 149 E 4
Old Forge(N.Y.) 126 E 5
Old Fort (N.C.) 129 J 6
Old Gidgee 182 B 4
Old Glory (TX.) 117 QR 4
Oldham 148 C 4
Oldham (S.D.) 119 L 6
Old Harbor 102 G 4
Old Hickory Lake 128 E 5
Old Mines (MO.) 121 P 4—5
Old Mkushi 200 D 2
Old Orchard Beach (ME.) 126 J 5
Olds 103 P 5
Old Speck Mountain 126 J 4
Old Town (FL.) 131 LM 5
Old Wives Lake 103 Q 5
Olean (N.Y.) 125 Q 7
Olekma 170 M 4
Olekminsk 170 LM 3
Olekminskiy Stanovik 170 LM 5
Olekmo-Charskoye Nagor'ye 170 LM 4
Olema 158 J 3
Olene (OR.) 110 D 8
Olenegorsk 150 K 2
Oleněk 170 M 1
Oleněk 170 K 2
Olenëkskiy Zaliv 170 M 1
Olenevod 171 WX 3
Olenevod 171 T 4
Olenitsa 150 KL 2
Olen'ya Rechka 170 F 5
Oléron, Ile d' 152 C 2
Oleśnica 149 G 4
Olevsk 151 J 5
Olex (OR.) 110 E 5
Ol'ga 173 KL 2
Olga, Mount 182 E 4
Ol'ginka 155 E 1
Ólgiy 170 F 6
Ol'gopol 154 C 1
Ol'gopol' 155 D 1
Olhão 152 B 4
Oliana 152 D 3
Olib 153 F 3
Olifants 201 E 4
Olifantshoek 200 C 5
Olimarao 186 C 2
Olimbia 154 B 3
Olímbos 154 B 2–3
Olímbos 154 C 3
Olímpia 141 G 5
Olinda 141 K 5
Olindina 141 J 3
Olite 152 C 3
Oliva (Argentina) 142 D 5
Oliva (Spain) 152 C 4
Olive (MT.) 118 C 5
Olive Branch (MS.) 121 Q 8
Olive Hill (KY.) 128 H 3
Olivehurst (CA.) 112 D 3
Oliveira 141 H 5
Olivença 201 EF 2
Oliver, Lake 131 J 2
Oliver Springs (TN.) 128 G 5
Olivet (S.D.) 119 L 7
Olivia (MN.) 119 O 6
Olkusz 149 G 4
Ollagüe 140 C 5
Ollagüe, Volcán 140 C 5
Olmos 138 C 5
Olney (IL.) 121 R 4
Olney (MT.) 111 L 2
Olney (TX.) 122 E 2
Olochi 170 L 5
Olofström 151 F 4
Olomouc 149 G 5
Olonets 151 K 2
Olongapo 177 H 1
Oloron-Sainte-Marie 152 C 3
Olot 152 D 3
Olov Annaya 108 C 2

Olovo 153 G 3
Olowalu (HI.) 113 F 11
Oloyskiye 171 U 2
Olpe (KS.) 120 J 4
Olshammar 151 F 4
Olsonville (SD.) 118 H 7
Olsztyn 149 H 4
Olsztynek 149 H 4
Olt 154 B 2
Olten 153 E 2
Oltenia 154 B 2
Olteniţa 154 C 2
Olton (TX.) 117 O 3
Oltu 155 F 2
Olustee (FL.) 131 M 4
Olustee (OK.) 120 F 8
Olvera 152 B 4
Olympia (WA.) 110 BC 3
Olympia → Olimbia 154 B 3
Olympic Mountains 110 B 3
Olympic National Park 110 B 3
Olympus 154 B 3
Olympus, Mount 110 B 3
Olyutorka 171 V 3
Olyutorskiy VW 3
Olyutorskiy, Mys 171 V 4
Olyutorskiy Gory 171 W 3
Olyutorskiy Poluostrov 171 W 3
Olyutorskiy Zaliv 171 V 3
Om' 159 Q 4
Omagh 148 B 4
Omaguas 138 D 4
Omaha (NE.) 120 J 1
Omaha Indian Reservation 119 M 8
Omak (WA.) 110 F 2
Omak Lake 110 F 2
Omak Mountain 110 F 2
Oman 157 G 4
Oman 157 G 5
Oman, Gulf of 195 K 4
Omarama 184 P 9
Omaruru 200 A 4
Omaruru 200 B 4
Omatako 200 B 4
Omatako, Mount 200 B 4
Omate 140 B 4
Omatjete 200 B 4
Ombai, Selat 177 G 5
Ombombo 200 A 3
Ombone 153 F 3
Ombu 174 E 1
Omchali 168 E 2
Omdurman194 E 5
Omeleut 171 W 3
Omemee (ND.) 118 H 2
Omeo 183 H 6
Ometepe, Isla de 132 E 5
Ometepec 132 C 4
Omili 153 G 2
Omineca Mountains 103 M 4
Omiš 153 G 3
Omitara 200 B 4
Ōmiya 173 L 3
Ommanney Bay 103 R 1
Omnödelger 170 K 6
Omnögovi 172 D 2
Omo 199 F 3
Omodeo, Lago 153 E 3
Omolon 171 T 2
Omolon 171 U 2
Omoloy 170 J 4
Omoloy 171 O 1
Omo Ranch (CA.) 112 E 4
Omro (WI.) 124 F 5
Omsk 159 O 4–5
Omsukchan 171 T 3
Omsukchanskiy Gory 171 T 3
Omu, Virful 154 C 1
Omulew 149 H 4
Ōmuta 173 K 4
Omutinskiy 159 N 4
Omutninsk 158 K 4
Ona Dikonde 198 C 5
Onaga (NE.) 120 J 3
Onaka (SD.) 118 J 5
Onamia (MN.) 119 P 4
Onancock (VA.) 129 Q 4
Onang 177 E 4
Onarga (IL.) 124 G 9
Onava (N.M.) 117 L 2
Onawa (IA.) 119 M 8
Onaway (MI.) 125 K 4
Onayena 200 B 3
Oncócua 200 A 3
Ondangwa 200 B 3
Ondaruza Falls 200 A 3
Ondava 149 H 5
Ondekaremba 200 B 4
Ondjiva 200 B 3
Ondo 197 E 4
Öndörhaan 170 K 6
Ondorkara 169 M 1
Öndörshireet 170 H 6
Ondor Sum 172 F 2
Ondozero, Ozero 150 K 3
O'Neals (CA.) 112 F 5

Onega 158 G 3
Onega 158 G 3
Oneida (IL.) 124 D 8
Oneida (N.Y.) 126 D 5
Oneida (TN.) 128 G 5
Oneida Indian Reservation 124 F 5
Oneida Lake 126 CD 5
Oneill (MT.) 118 C 4
O'Neill (NE.) 119 K 8
Onekotan, Ostrov 171 ST 6
Oneonta (AL.) 128 E 8
Oneonta (N.Y.) 126 D 6
Onesi 200 A 3
Onezhskaya Guba158 G 3
Onezhskoye, Ozero158 G 3
Ongiyn Gol 172 D 1
Ongjin 173 J 3
Ongniud Qi 173 G 2
Ongole 174 D 4
Onguday 159 R 5
Oni 155 F 2
Onida (SD.) 118 J 6
Onilahy 201 G 4
Onitsha 197 F 4
Onk,Djebel 193 G 2
Onkuchakh 170 KL 2
Ono (CA.) 112 C 2
Ono-i-Lau Islands 186 CD 4
Onomichi 173 K 4
Onon 170 L 5
Onondaga Indian Reservation 126 C 6
Onon Gol 170 K 6
Onotoa 186 C 3
Onovgay 171 T 4
Onsala 151 F 4
Onseepkans 200 B 5
Onslow 182 B 3
Onslow Bay 129 O 7
Ontario (CA.) 113 H 8
Ontario (Canada) 104 JL 5
Ontario (OR.) 110 H 6
Ontario, Lake 125 QR 6
Onteniente 152 C 4
Ontojärvi 150 J 3
Ontonagon (MI.) 124 E 3
Ontong Java 185 G 3
Ontong Java 186 B 3
Onyx (CA.) 113 G 7
Oodnadatta 183 F 4
Ookiep 200 B 5
Ooldea 182 E 5
Oologah Lake 121 K 6
Oorindi 183 G 3
Oostburg (WI.) 124 G 6
Oostende 148 D 4
Ootacamund 174 C 5
Opal (SD.) 118 F 6
Opala (U.S.S.R.) 171 T 5
Opala (Zaïre) 198 C 5
Opanake 174 D 6
Opari 198 E 4
Opasatika 104 L 6
Opatija 153 F 2
Opava 149 G 5
Opelika (AL.) 131 J 2
Opelousas (LA.) 123 L 5
Opheim (MT.) 118 B 2
Ophir (AK.) 102 F 3
Ophir (OR.) 110 A 8
Opienge 198 D 4
Opihikao (HI.) 113 H 12
Opis (Iraq) 156 D 2
Opiscotéo, Lac 105 O 5
Opobo 197 F 5
Opochka 151 J 4
Opoczno 149 GH 4
Opole 149 G 4
Oporto 152 B 3
Oposhnya 158 F 6
Opotiki 185 R 8
Opp (AL.) 131 H 3
Oppland 150 E 3
Opportunity (MT.) 111 N 4
Opportunity (WA.) 110 H 3
Optima (OK.) 120 D 6
Optimo (N.M.) 117 M 2
Oputo 106 E 2
Or, Côte d' 153 D 2
Oracle (AZ.) 116 F 5
Oracle Junction (AZ.) 116 EF 5
Oradea 154 B 1
Oraibi (AZ.) 116 F 2
Orai 174 C 2
Orahovica 153 G 2
Orai 174 C 2
Orange (Australia) 183 H 5
Orange (France) 153 D 3
Orange (Namibia) 200 B 5
Orange (TX.) 123 K 5
Orange (VA.) 129 N 3
Orange, Cabo 139 H 3
Orangeburg (S.C.) 129 L 8
Orange City (FL.) 131 N 6
Orange City (IA.) 119 M 7
Orange Free State 200 D 5
Orange Grove (TX.) 122 EF 8
Orange Lake (FL.) 131 M 5
Orange Love (CA.) 112 F 6

Orange Park (FL.) 131 N 4
Orange Walk 132 E 4
Orango, Ilha de 196 A 3
Orangville (UT.) 114 F 4
Oranienburg 149 F 4
Oranje 200 B 5
Oranje Gebergte 139 GH 3
Oranjemund 200 B 5
Oranjestad 138 E 1
Oranzherei 155 G 1
Orapa 200 D 4
Orbetello 153 F 3
Orbigo 152 B 3
Orbisonia (PA.) 127 B 8
Orbost 183 H 6
Orcadas 203
Orcas Island 110 C 2
Orchard (ID.) 110 J 7
Orchard (NE.) 119 K 8
Orchard City (CO.) 115 J 5
Orchard Homes (MT.) 111 L 4
Orchard Valley (WY.) 118 D 9
Orcutt (CA.) 113 E 8
Ord (NE.) 118 JK 9
Ord, Mount 182 D 2
Ordenes 152 B 3
Ord Mountain 113 J 8
Ordoquí 143 D 2
Ordos Plateau 172 E 3
Ord River 182 D 2
Ord River Dam 182 D 2
Ordu 155 E 2
Ordway (CO.) 115 O 5
Ordynskoye 159 Q 5
Ordzhonikidze 155 E 2
Ordzhonikidze 155 FG 2
Ordzhonikidzeabad 169 HJ 3
Orealla 139 G 2
Oreana (IL.) 121 QR 3
Oreana (NV.) 112 G 2
Orebić 153 G 3
Örebro 151 G 4
Ore City (TX.) 123 J 3
Oregon 110
Oregon (IL.) 124 E 7
Oregon (MO.) 121 K 3
Oregon (OH.) 125 L 8
Oregon Butte 110 H 4
Oregon Caves National Monument 110 B 8
Oregon City (OR.) 110 C 5
Öregrund 151 G 3
Orekhov 155 E 1
Orekhovo 154 B 2
Orekhovo Zuyevo 158 G 4
Orel' 155 D 1
Orel 158 G 5
Orel', Ozero 171 P 5
Orellana (Peru) 138 C 4
Orellana (Peru) 138 C 5
Orem (UT.) 114 F 3
Oren 154 C 3
Orenburg 158 K 5
Orense 152 B 3
Orestiás 154 C 2
Öresund 151 F 4
Organ (TX.) 117 K 5
Organá 152 D 3
Organ Peak 117 K 5
Organ Pipe Cactus National Monument 116 D 5–6
Orgeyev 154 C 1
Órgiva 152 C 4
Orhaneli 154 C 3
Orhangazi 154 C 2
Orhon Gol 170 H 6
Ori 141 J 2
Orick (CA.) 112 A 1
Orient (IA.) 119 O 9
Orient (SD.) 118 J 6
Orient (WA.) 110 G 2
Orienta (OK.) 120 G 6
Oriental (N.C.) 129 P 6
Oriental, Cordillera 140 BC 3–5
Oriental, Cordillera (Colombia) 138 CD 2–3
Oriente 143 D 6
Orihuela 152 C 4
Orillia 105 M 7
Orimattila 151 J 3
Orin (WY.) 118 C 8
Orinduik 139 F 3
Orinoco (Colombia) 138 E 2
Orion (IL.) 124 D 8
Oriskany (N.Y.) 126 D 5
Orissa 174 DE 3
Orissaare 151 H 4
Oristano 153 E 4
Orivesi 150 H 3
Oriximiná 139 G 4
Orizaba 132 C 4
Orjen 154 A 2
Orkadalen 150 EF 3
Orkanger 150 E 3
Örkelljunga 151 F 4
Orkla 150 E 3
Orkney (South Africa) 200 D 5
Orkney Islands 148 C 3
Orla (TX.) 117 N 6
Orland (CA.) 112 C 3

Orlando (FL.) 131 N 6
Orlando (OK.) 120 H 6
Orléans 152 D 2
Orleans (CA.) 112 B 1
Orleans (MA.) 126 K 7
Orleans (NE.) 120 F 2
Orleans (VT.) 126 G 4
Orlik 170 G 5
Orlinnaya, Gora 108 B 3
Orlovskaya 171 V 3
Orlu 197 F 4
Ormara 169 G 5
Ormoc 177 F 1
Ormond Beach (FL.) 131 NO 5
Ormond-by-the-Sea (FL.) 131 NO 5
Órmos Almiroú 154 B 3
Orne 152 C 2
Ornö 151 G 4
Örnsköldsvik 150 G 3
Oro, Monte d' 153 E 3
Orobie, Alpi 153 EF 2
Orocué 138 D 3
Orodara 196 CD 3
Orofino (ID.) 110 J 4
Oron (Nigeria) 197 F 5
Oron (U.S.S.R.) 170 L 4
Orona 186 D 3
Orono (ME.) 126 L 4
Oropesa 152 CD 3
Oropesa 152 B 4
Oroqen Zizhiqi 171 M 5
Oroquieta 177 F 2
Orosei 153 E 3
Óros Ossa 154 B 3
Oroszlány 154 A 1
Orotukan 171 S 3
Orovada (NV.) 112 H 1
Oroville (CA.) 112 C 3
Oroville (WA.) 110 F 2
Oroville, Lake 112 D 3
Oroville Dam 112 D 3
Oroyëk 171 S 3
Orpha (WY.) 118 C 8
Orqohan 171 M 6
Orrefors 151 G 4
Orrin (ND.) 118 H 2
Orroroo 183 F 5
Orsa 150 F 3
Orsa Finnmark 150 F 3
Orsasjön 150 F 3
Orsha 151 K 5
Orsk 159 L 5
Orşova 154 B 2
Örsta 150 E 3
Orta 155 D 2
Ortà, Lago d' 153 E 2
Ortaca 154 C 3
Ortegal, Cabo 152 B 3
Orthez 152 C 3
Ortigueira 152 B 3
Orting (WA.) 110 C 3
Ortiz 106 D 6
Ortles 153 F 2
Ortona 153 F 3
Ortonville (MN.) 119 M 5
Orto-Ayan 171 NO 1
Oruhito 200 A 3
Orulgan, Khrebet 171 N 2
Orungo 198 E 4
Oruro 140 C 4
Orust 151 F 4
Orvault 152 C 2
Orvieto 153 F 3
Orvyn, Gora 108 CD 2
Orwell (OH.) 125 O 8
Osa 158 L 4
Osa 170 H 5
Osa, Península de 132 F 6
Osage (IA.) 119 Q 7
Osage (WY.) 118 D 7
Osage City (KS.) 120 K 4
Osage Indian Reservation 120 J 6
Osage River 121 N 4
Ōsaka 173 L 4
Osakarovka 159 O 5
Ōsaka-wan 173 L 4
Osakis (MN.) 119 N 5
Osakis, Lake 119 N 5
Osam 154 B 2
Osawatomie (KS.) 121 KL 4
Osborne (KS.) 120 G 3
Osby 151 F 4
Oscarville 108 F 3
Osceola (AR.) 121 PQ 7
Osceola (IA.) 119 P 9–10
Osceola (MO.) 121 L 4
Osceola (NE.) 120 H 1
Osceola (S.D.) 119 L 6
Oschiri 153 E 3
Oscoda (MI.) 125 L 5
Oscura (N.M.) 117 KL 4
Osen 150 F 3

Osgood (IN.) 128 F 2
Osh 169 J 2
Osha 159 O 4
Oshakati 200 B 3
Oshawa 105 M 7
Oshikango 200 B 3
Ō-shima 173 L 2
Oshivelo 200 B 3
Oshkosh (NE.) 118 F 9
Oshkosh (WI.) 124 F 5
Oshmarino 170 D 1
Oshmyany 151 J 5
Oshnavīyeh (Iran) 157 D 1
Oshogbo 197 EF 4
Oshoto (WY.) 118 CD 6
Oshtoran Kūh (Iran) 157 E 2
Oshtorīnān (Iran) 157 E 2
Oshwe 198 B 5
Osijek 153 G 2
Osimo 153 F 3
Osinniki 159 R 5
Osinovka 159 Q 6
Osinovo 159 R 3
Osipovichi 151 J 5
Osire 200 B 4
Oskaloosa (IA.) 119 Q 9
Oskaloosa (MO.) 119 K 3
Oskarshamn 151 G 4
Oskarström 151 F 4
Oskino 170 J 3
Öskjuuvatn 150 B 2
Oskoba 170 H 3
Oslo 151 F 4
Oslob 177 F 2
Oslofjorden 151 F 4
Osmanabad 174 C 4
Osmancık 155 DE 2
Osmaneli 154 D 2
Osmaniye 155 E 3
Osmaniye (Turkey) 156 B 1
Os'mino 151 J 4
Osmond (NE.) 119 L 8
Osmyanskaya Vozvyshennost' 151 J 5
Osnabrück 149 E 4
Osor 153 F 3
Osorno 143 M 2
Osoyoos 103 NO 6
Osöyra 151 E 3
Ospito 138 E 2
Ossa, Mount 184 L 9
Ossa, Mount 186 A 5
Ossa, Óros 154 B 3
Ossabaw Island 131 NO 3
Osse 197 F 4
Osseo (WI.) 124 C 5
Ossineke (MI.) 125 L 5
Ossining (N.Y.) 127 F 7
Ossipee (N.H.) 126 H 5
Ossjöen 150 F 3
Ossora 171 U 4
Ostashkov 158 F 4
Östavall 150 G 3
Österdalälven 150 F 3
Österdalen 150 F 3
Östergötland 151 G 4
Östersund 150 FG 3
Ostfriesische Inseln 148–149 E 4
Östhammar 151 G 3
Östhavet 150 JK 1
Östmark 151 F 3
Ostrava 149 G 5
Ostroda 149 GH 4
Ostrogozhsk 158 GH 5
Ostrołeka 149 H 4
Ostroshitski Gorodok 151 J 5
Ostrov (Czechoslovakia) 149 F 4
Ostrov (Romania) 154 C 2
Ostrov (Russia, U.S.S.R.) 151 J 4
Ostrova Chernyye Brat'ya 171 S 6
Ostrova Diomida 102 D 2
Ostrova Medvezh'i 171 U 1
Ostrova Arakamchechen 108 D 3
Ostrova Solovetskiye 158 G 2
Ostrova Srednego 171 S 6
Ostrov Atlasova 171 ST 5
Ostrov Tyuleni'i 168 E 1–2
Ostrov Barsa-Kel'mes 168 F 1
Ostrov Beringa 161 T 4
Ostrov Bol'shoy Begichev 170 KL 1
Ostrov Bol'shoy Lyakhovskiy 171 Q 1
Ostrov Bol'shoy Shantar 171 P 4–5
Ostrov Broutona 171 S 6
Ostrov Chirinkotan 171 S 6
Ostrov Dolgiy 159 LM 2
Ostrov Ekarma 171 S 6
Ostrov Feklistova 171 P 4–5
Ostrov Gusmp 171 U 1–2
Ostrov Iony 171 Q 4
Ostrov Iturup 171 R 6–7
Ostrov Karaginskiy 171 U 4
Ostrov Ketoy 171 S 6
Ostrov Kharimkotan 171 ST 6
Ostrov Kil'din 150 KL 2
Ostrov Kokaral 168 FG 1
Ostrov Kolguyev 158 J 2
Ostrov Konevits 150 K 3
Ostrov Kotel'nyy 171 P 1
Ostrov Krestovskiy 171 U 1

Ostrov Makanrushi 171 S 6
Ostrov Malyy Lyakhovskiy 171 Q 1
Ostrov Matua 171 S 6
Ostrov Mednyy 161 TU 4
Ostrov Men'shikova 171 PQ 5
Ostrov Mezhdusharskiy 158 K 1
Ostrov Moshchnyy 151 J 4
Ostrov Nansikan 171 Q 4
Ostrovnoy 171 U 4
Ostrovnoy, Mys 171 T 3
Ostrovnoye 171 U 2
Ostrovnoye 171 TU 5
Ostrov Ogurchinskiy 168 E 3
Ostrov Onekotan 171 ST 6
Ostrov Paramushir 171 T 5
Ostrov Peschanyy 170 L 1
Ostrov Rasshua 171 S 6
Ostrov Raykoke 171 S 6
Ostrov Semenovskiy 171 O 1
Ostrov Shiashkotan 171 S 6
Ostrov Shumshu 171 T 5
Ostrov Simushir 171 S 6
Ostrov Stolbovoy 171 P 1
Ostrov Urup 171 S 6
Ostrov Valaam 150 K 3
Ostrov Vaygach 159 L 1
Ostrov Vozrozhdeniya 168 F 1
Ostrov Zav'yalova 171 RS 4
Ostrovul Letea 154 C 1
Ostrovul Sfintu Gheorghe 154 C 1–2
Ostrowiec Świetokrzyski 149 H 4
Ostrow Mazowiecka 149 H 4
Ostrow Wielkopolski 149 G 4
Ostryak, Gora 171 W 3
Ostrzeszow 149 G 4
Ostuni 153 G 3
O'Sullivan Dam 110 F 4
Ōsumi-shotō 173 JK 4
Osuna 152 BC 4
Os'van' 158 L 2
Otar 169 K 2
Otaru 173 M 2
Otautau 184 P 10
Otava 149 F 5
Otavalo 138 C 3
Otavi 200 B 3
Otchinjau 200 A 3
Otgon 170 G 6
Othello (WA.) 110 F 4
O' The Cherokees, Lake 121 KL 6
O' The Pines, Lake 123 J 3
Othonoí 154 A 3
Oti 196 E 4
Oti-daitō-jima 173 K 6
Otis (CO.) 115 P 3
Otis (KS.) 120 FG 4
Otish, Monts 105 N 5
Otjiha'vara 200 B 4
Otjikondo 200 B 3
Otjimbingwe 200 B 4
Otjinene 200 B 4
Otjinoko 200 B 4
Otjipatera Mountains 200 B 4
Otjitambi 200 AB 3
Otjituuo 200 B 3
Otjiwarongo 200 B 4
Otjivazandu 200 AB 3
Otjozondjou 200 B 4
Otjozondu 200 B 4
Otkrytyy 171 M 4
Otočac 153 G 3
Otoe (NE.) 120 J 2
Otog Qi 172 E 3
Otoño 143 D 6
Otoskwin 104 JK 5
Otra 151 E 4
Otradnaya 155 F 2
Otradnoye 171 T 5
Otranto 154 A 2
Otsego (MI.) 124 J 7
Otsego Lake 126 E 6
Otshandi 200 A 3
Otshikuku 200 B 3
Otsu 173 L 4
Otta 150 E 3
Otta 151 E 4
Ottadalen 150 E 3
Ottawa (IL.) 124 F 8
Ottawa (KS.) 121 K 4
Ottawa (OH.) 125 KL 9
Ottawa (, Can.) 105 MN 6
Ottawa Islands 105 L 4
Ottawa River 105 M 6
Ottenby 151 G 4
Otter (MT.) 118 B 5
Otter Creek (FL.) 131 M 5
Otter Creek Reservoir 114 F 5
Otter Lake (MI.) 125 L 6
Ottertail (MN.) 119 N 4
Otter Tail Lake 119 N 4
Ottumwa (IA.) 119 Q 9
Ottumwa (SD.) 118 G 6
Oturkpo 197 F 4
Otuwe 200 B 4
Otway, Bahía 143 B 9

Otway, Cape 183 G 6
Otwock 149 H 4
Ötz 153 F 2
Ouachita Mountains 121 KL 8
Ouachita River 123 L 3
Ouadane 192 C 4
Ouadda 198 C 3
Ouaddaï 197 J 3
Ouad Naga 192 B 5
Ouagadougou 196 D 3
Ouahigouya 196 D 3
Ouahran → Oran 192 E 1
Ouaka 198 C 3
Oualam 196 E 3
Oualata 192 D 5
Oualidia 192 D 2
Ouallene Bordj 193 F 4
Ouanary 193 H 3
Ouanda-Djallé 198 C 3
Ouando 198 D 3
Ouango 197 H 5
Ouangolodougou 196 CD 4
Ouani 197 H 2
Ouan Taredert 193 G 3
Ouaqui 139 H 3
Ouarane 192 CD 4
Ouargaye 196 DE 3
Ouargla 193 G 2
Ouarkziz, Jbel 192 D 3
Ouarsenis, Massif de l' 193 F 1
Ouarzazate 192 D 2
Ouassou 196 B 3
Ouatcha 197 F 3
Oubangui 197 H 5
Oudeïka 196 D 2
Oudje 193 G 2
Oudong 175 H 5
Oudtshoorn 200 C 6
Oued Rhiou 193 F 1
Oued Zem 192 D 2
Oueïta 197 J 2
Ouéllé 196 D 4
Ouémé 196 E 4
Ouessant, Ile de 152 B 2
Ouesso 197 H 5
Ouezzane 192 D 2
Ougarou 196 E 3
Ouham 197 H 4
Ouidah 196 E 4
Ouiriguó 192 D 5
Ouistreham 152 C 2
Oujaf 192 D 5
Oujda 192 E 2
Oujeft 192 C 4
Oulad Naïl, Monts des 193 F 2
Oulainen 150 HJ 3
Oulankajoki 150 J 2
Ould Yenjé 192 C 5
Ouled Djellal 193 G 2
Oulossébougou 196 C 3
Oulu 150 J 2
Oulujärvi 150 J 3
Oulujoki 150 J 3
Oum Chalouba 197 J 2
Oumé 196 E 4
Oum el Asell 192 E 4
Oum el Bouaghi 193 G 1
Oum er Rbia 192 D 2
Oum Hadjer 197 H 3
Oumm ed Droûs Guebli, Sebkhet 192 C 4
Oumm ed Droûs Telli, Sebkha 192 C 4
Ounane, Djebel 193 G 3
Ounasjoki 150 H 2
Ou Neua 175 H 3
Ounianga Kebir 197 J 2
Ounianga Serir 197 J 2
Ounissoui Baba 197 G 2
Ouray (CO.) 115 K 5
Ouray (UT.) 114 H 3
Ouray, Mount 115 L 5
Ouricuri 141 J 5
Ourinhos 141 G 5
Ouro Prêto 141 H 5
Ourthe 148 E 4
Ōu-sanmyaku 173 M 2–3
Ouse 148 D 4
Oust 152 C 2
Outagouna 196 E 2
Outaouais 105 M 6
Outapi 200 A 3
Outardes, Rivière aux 105 O 5–6
Outat Oulad el Haj 192 E 2
Outer Hebrides 148 B 3
Outer Island 124 D 2
Outer Santa Barbara Passage 113 G 9–10
Outjo 200 B 4
Outlook 103 Q 5
Outlook (MT.) 118 D 2
Outokumpu 150 J 3
Outpost Mountain 109 H 2
Ouvéa 185 J 6
Ouvéa 186 C 4
Ouyen 183 G 5–6
Ovacık 155 D 3
Ovacık 155 E 3
Ovacık (Turkey) 156 A 1

Ovada 153 E 3
Ovalle 142 B 5
Ovamboland 200 B 3
Ovando (MT.) 111 M 3
Oveng 197 G 5
Överbygd 150 G 2
Overhalla 150 F 3
Överkalix 150 H 2
Overton (NE.) 120 F 2
Overton (NV.) 112 L 6
Overton (TX.) 123 HJ 3
Övertorneå 150 H 2
Överuman 150 FG 2
Ovett (MS.) 130 E 3
Ovid (MI.) 125 K 6
Oviedo (Haiti) 133 H 4
Oviedo (Spain) 152 B 3
Oviksfjällen 150 F 3
Övre Årdal 150 E 3
Övre Fryken 151 F 3
Övre Soppero 150 H 2
Ovruch 151 J 5
Ovsyanka 171 N 5
Ovul 185 F 3
Owando 197 H 6
Owanka (SD.) 118 F 6
Owasco Lake 126 C 6
Owasso (OK.) 121 K 6
Owatonna (MN.) 119 P 6
Owego (N.Y.) 126 C 6
Owego (TX.) 117 O 6
Owen (WI.) 124 D 5
Owen, Mount 185 Q 9
Owensboro (KY.) 128 D 4
Owens Lake 112 H 6
Owen Sound 105 L 7
Owens River 112 G 5
Owen Stanley Range 184 E 3
Owensville (MO.) 121 O 4
Owenton (KY.) 128 G 3
Owerri 197 F 4
Owingsville (KY.) 128 H 3
Owl Creek Mountains 111 QR 7
Owo 197 F 4
Owosso (MI.) 125 K 6–7
Owyhee (NV.) 112 J 1
Owyhee, Lake 110 H 7
Owyhee Mountains 110 J 7–8
Owyhee River 110 H 7
Oxberg 150 F 3
Oxbow (ME.) 126 L 2
Oxbow Dam 110 J 6
Oxelösund 151 G 4
Oxford (KS.) 120 H 5
Oxford (MI.) 125 L 7
Oxford (MS.) 121 Q 8
Oxford (N.C.) 129 N 5
Oxford (NE.) 120 F 2
Oxford (OH.) 128 G 2
Oxford (TX.) 122 E 5
Oxford (U.K.) 148 C 4
Oxford (WI.) 124 E 6
Oxford Junction (IA.) 119 S 9
Oxford Lake 103 S 4–5
Oxford Peak 111 N 8
Ox Mountains 148 B 4
Oxnard (CA.) 113 F 8
Oyapock 139 H 3
Oyem 197 G 5
Öyeren 151 F 4
Oymyakon 171 Q 3
Oyo (Nigeria) 196 E 4
Oyo (Sudan) 194 F 4
Oyón 140 A 3
Oyonnax 153 E 2
Oyotung 171 R 1
Oyshilik 159 Q 6
Oyster Cliffs 200 A 5
Oysterville (WA.) 110 A 4
Öystese 151 E 3
Oysurdakh 171 S 2
Oytal 169 J 2
Oyun-Khomoto 171 P 2
Ozamiz 177 F 2
Ozark (AL.) 131 J 3
Ozark (AR.) 121 M 7
Ozark (MO.) 121 M 6
Ozark Plateau 121 LM 5–6
Ozark Reservoir 121 LM 7
Ozarks, Lake of the 121 N 4
Ózd 154 B 1
Ozernaya 171 U 4
Ozernovskiy 171 T 5
Ozernoy, Zaliv 171 U 4
Ozero Akzhaykyn 169 H 1–2
Ozero Alakol' 159 Q 6
Ozero Alibey 154 D 1
Ozero Arys 169 H 1
Ozero Aschikol' 169 H 1
Ozero Ayaturku 170 EF 1
Ozero Balkhash 159 OP 6
Ozero Baykal 170 J 5
Ozero Biylikol' 169 J 2
Ozero Bolon' 171 P 5
Ozero Bol'shoy Yeravnoye 170 K 5
Ozero Bustakh 171 Q 1
Ozero Chany 159 P 5
Ozero Chatyrkel' 169 JK 2

Ozero Chervonoye 151 J 5
Ozero Chukchagirskoye 171 P 5
Ozero Dadynskoye 155 FG 1
Ozero Donuzlav 155 D 1
Ozero El'gygytgyn 171 W 2
Ozero Engozero 150 K 2
Ozero Gimolskoye 150 K 3
Ozero Ilirgytkin 171 T 1
Ozero Il'men 151 K 4
Ozero Imandra 150 K 2
Ozero Issyk-Kul 169 K 2
Ozero Kamennoye 150 K 3
Ozero Kanozero 150 K 2
Ozero Karakoin 169 H 1
Ozero Keke Usun 155 G 1
Ozero Keret' 150 K 2
Ozero Keta 170 F 2
Ozero Khanka 173 K 1–2
Ozero Khantayskoye 170 F 2
Ozero Khummi 171 P 5
Ozero Kitai 154 C 1
Ozero Kiyeng-Kyuyel' 170 JK 1
Ozero Kokora 170 H 1
Ozero Kolozero 150 K 2
Ozero Kovdozero 150 K 2
Ozero Kozhozero 158 G 3
Ozero Krasnoye 171 W 3
Ozero Kubenskoye 158 G 4
Ozero Kulundinskoye 159 PQ 5
Ozero Kungasalakh 170 JK 1
Ozero Kushmurun 159 M 5
Ozero Labaz 170 G 1
Ozero Lacha 158 G 3
Ozero Lama 170 F 2
Ozero Leksozero 150 K 3
Ozero Lovozero 150 L 2
Ozero Manych Gudilo 155 F 1
Ozero Markakol' 159 R 6
Ozero Mogotoyevo 171 R 1
Ozero Nerpich'ye 171 T 2
Ozero Nyuk 150 K 3
Ozero Ondozero 150 K 3
Ozero Onezhskoye 158 G 3
Ozero Orel' 171 P 5
Ozero Osvejskoje 151 J 4
Ozero Ozhogino 171 R 2
Ozero Paravani 155 F 2
Ozero Portnyagino 170 HJ 1
Ozero Purinskoye 170 G 2
Ozero Pyaozero 150 K 2
Ozero Pyasino 159 R 2
Ozero Rovkulskoye 150 K 3
Ozero Sadochye 168 F 2
Ozero Sartlan 159 PQ 4–5
Ozero Sarykamysh 168 F 2
Ozero Sasyk 154 C 1
Ozero Sasykkol' 159 Q 6
Ozero Segozero 150 K 3
Ozero Seletyteniz 159 O 5
Ozero Sevan 155 G 2
Ozero Sonkel' 169 K 2
Ozero Sovetskoje 159 Q 2
Ozero Sredneye Kuyto 150 K 2–3
Ozero Sukhodolskoye 150 K 3
Ozero Svetloye 155 G 1
Ozero Syamozero 150 K 3
Ozero Taymyr 170 H 1
Ozero Teletskoye 159 R 5
Ozero Tengiz 159 N 5
Ozero Tikhtoozero 150 K 2
Ozero Tikshozero 150 K 2
Ozero Tulos 150 K 3
Ozero Ubinskoye 159 Q 4
Ozero Udyl' 171 P 5
Ozero Umbozero (Umbozero) 150 KL 2
Ozero Verkhneye Kuyto 150 K 3
Ozero Vodlozero 158 G 3
Ozero Vozhe 158 G 3
Ozero Vuoksa 150 JK 3
Ozero Vyalozero 150 L 2
Ozero Vygozero 158 G 3
Ozero Yalpukh 154 C 1
Ozero Yambuto 159 PQ 1
Ozero Yanis'yarvi 150 K 3
Ozero Yessey 170 H 2
Ozero Zaysan 159 Q 6
Ozero Zhamanakkal' 169 G 1
Ozero Zvoron 171 P 5
Ozette Lake 110 A 2
Ozhogina 171 R 2
Ozhogino 171 R 2
Ozhogino, Ozero 171 R 2
Ozinki 158 J 5
Ozona (TX.) 117 P 7
Ozorków 149 G 4

P

Paamiut 105 R 3
Pa-an 175 G 4
Paarl 200 B 6
Paauilo (HI.) 113 G 11
Paavola 150 J 3
Pabianice 149 G 4
Pablo (MT.) 111 L 3
Pabna 174 E 3
Pabradé 151 J 4

Pab Range 169 H 5
Pacaás Novos, Serra dos 140 D 3
Pacaraima, Sierra 139 F 3
Pacasmayo 138 BC 5
Pachacamac 140 A 3
Pachakshiri 175 F 2
Pachbhadra 174 B 2
Pacheco Pass 112 D 5
Pachino 153 G 4
Pachitea 138 D 5
Pachiza 138 C 5
Pacho 138 D 2
Pachuca 132 C 3–4
Pachuta (MS.) 130 F 2
Pacific (MO.) 121 P 4
Pacifica (CA.) 112 C 5
Pacific City (OR.) 110 A 5
Pacific Grove (CA.) 112 CD 6
Pacific Ocean 204
Pacific Ranges 103 M 5
Packaway Lake 124 E 6
Packwood (WA.) 110 D 4
Pacora 138 C 2
Padam 169 K 4
Padang 176 C 3
Padang 176 B 4
Padang 176 C 4
Padang, Pulau 176 B 3
Padangpanjang 176 AB 4
Padangsidempuan 176 A 3
Padany 150 K 2
Padauari 139 F 3
Paddle Prairie 103 O 4
Paderborn 149 E 4
Padilla 140 D 4
Padova 153 F 2
Padrão, Ponta do 200 A 1
Padrauna 174 D 2
Padre Island 122 F 8
Padre Island National Seashore 122 F 9
Padroni (CO.) 115 O 3
Padua 153 G 3
Paengnyŏng-do 173 H 3
Paestum 153 FG 3
Pafuri 201 E 4
Pag 153 F 3
Paga Centa 139 H 4
Pagadian 177 F 2
Pagai 197 F 6
Pagan 186 A 1
Pagasitikós Kólpos 154 B 3
Pagatan 176 E 4
Page (AZ.) 116 E 1
Page (N.D.) 119 L 3
Page (NE.) 119 K 8
Page City (KS.) 120 D 3
Pageland (S.C.) 129 L 7
Pagoda Peak 115 K 3
Pago Mission 182 D 1
Pago-Pago 186 D 3
Pagosa Springs (CO.) 115 L 6
Pagri 174 E 3
Pagwi 184 D 2
Pahala (HI.) 113 G 12
Paharpur 169 J 4
Pahkaing Bum 175 G 2
Pahlavi Dezh (Iran) 157 E 2
Pahoa (HI.) 113 H 12
Pahute Mesa 112 J 5
Pahute Peak 112 F 1
Pai 197 G 4
Paicines (CA.) 112 D 6
Paide 151 J 4
Paige (TX.) 122 F 5
Paiguás 140 E 4
Päijänne 150 J 3
Páikon Oros 154 B 2
Paikot 171 J 2
Pailin 175 H 5
Pailolo Channel 113 F 10
Paimio 151 H 3
Paimpol 152 C 2
Painan 176 B 4
Paine Medio, Cerro 143 B 9
Painesdale (MI.) 124 F 2
Painesville (OH.) 125 N 8
Painesville (Western Australia) 182 B 4
Painted Desert 116 E 1–F 2
Painted Rock Dam 116 C 4
Paint Rock (TX.) 122 D 4
Paintsville (KY.) 128 J 4
Paisano (TX.) 117 N 7
Paisley 148 C 3
Paisley (OR.) 110 E 8
Paita 138 B 5
Paithan 174 C 4
Pajala 150 H 2
Pajares, Puerto de 152 B 3
Pájaros Point 130 E 8
Pajatén 138 C 5
Pakala 174 C 5
Pakaraima Mountains 139 FG 2–3
Pak Beng 175 H 4
Pakhacha 171 V 3
Paki 197 F 3
Pakima 198 C 5

Pakin 186 B 2
Pakistan 169 H 5
Pak Lay 175 H 4
Pak Neun 175 H 4
Pakokku 175 F 3
Pakpattan 169 J 4
Pak Phanang 175 H 6
Pakse 175 J 4
Pakrac 153 G 2
Paks 154 A 1
Pakwach 198 E 4
Pala 175 H 4
Pala (Centr. Afr. Rep.) 198 C 3
Pala (Chad) 197 H 4
Palacios (TX.) 122 G 7
Palafrugell 152 D 3
Palagruža 153 G 3
Pala Indian Reservation 113 H 9
Palaiokhóra 154 B 3
Palakollu 174 D 4
Palamau 174 D 3
Palamós 152 D 3
Palana 171 T 4
Palanan Point 177 J 1
Palanga 151 H 4
Palangkaraya 176 D 4
Palanpur 174 B 3
Palaoa Point 113 EF 11
Palapye 200 D 4
Palatka 171 S 3
Palatka (FL.) 131 N 5
Palau 153 E 3
Palauk 175 G 5
Palaw 175 G 5
Palawan 176–177 E 2
Palawan Passage 176–177 E 1–2
Palayankottai 174 C 6
Palazzo, Punta 153 E 3
Palca 140 C 4
Palco (KS.) 120 F 3
Paldiski 151 H 4
Pale 175 F 3
Palel 175 F 3
Paleleh 177 F 3
Palembang 176 BC 4
Palencia 152 C 3
Palen Dry Lake 113 K 9
Palenque 132 D 4
Palermo 153 F 4
Palestine 156 B 2–3
Palestine (TX.) 123 H 4
Paletwa 175 F 3
Palghat 174 C 5
Palgrave Point 200 A 4
Pali 174 B 2
Palimé 196 E 4
Palinuro, Capo 153 FG 3
Palisade (CO.) 115 J 4
Palisade (NE.) 120 D 2
Palisade (NV.) 112 J 2
Palisades (ID.) 111 O 7
Palisades (WA.) 110 F 3
Palisades Reservoir 111 O 7
Palitana 174 B 3
Paljakka 150 J 3
Paljenik 153 G 2
Palkonda Range 174 C 5
Palk Strait 174 C 5–6
Palla Bianca 153 F 2
Pal Lahara 174 E 3
Pallasovka 158 J 5
Pallastunturit 150 H 2
Palliser, Cape 185 R 9
Palliser, Îles 187 F 4
Palma (Mozambique) 201 G 2
Palma (Spain) 152 D 4
Palma del Río 152 B 4
Pal Malmal 185 F 3
Palmares 141 J 2
Palmares do Sul 142 FG 5
Palmarito 138 DE 2
Palmarola 153 F 3
Palmar Sur 132 F 6
Palmas, Cape 196 C 5
Palmas, Golfo di 153 E 4
Palmas Bellas 138 B 2
Palma Soriano 133 G 3
Palm Bay (FL.) 131 O 6
Palmdale (CA.) 113 G 8
Palmdale (FL.) 131 N 8
Palmeira 142 F 4
Palmeirais (Piauí, Brazil) 141 H 2
Palmeiras (Goiás, Brazil) 141 G 3
Palmer (AK, U.S.A.) 109 H 3
Palmer (Antarctica) 203
Palmer (NE.) 120 G 2
Palmer (TN.) 128 F 6
Palmer Archipelago 203
Palmer Lake (CO.) 115 N 4
Palmer Land 203
Palmerston 185 Q 10
Palmerston 186 E 4
Palmerston North 185 R 9
Palmerston North 186 C 5
Palmerton (PA.) 127 D 8
Palmi 153 G 4
Palmira 138 C 3

Palm Springs (CA.) 113 J 9
Palmyra (MO.) 121 O 3
Palmyra (PA.) 127 C 8
Palmyra (Pacific Ocean, U.S.A.) 186 E 2
Palmyra (Syria) 194 F 2
Palmyra (VA.) 129 N 4
Palmyras Point 174 E 3
Palmyra Tudmur As Suknah (Syria) 156 C 2
Palni 174 C 5
Paloemeu 139 G 3
Palo Flechado Pass 117 L 1
Paloh (Indonesia) 176 C 3
Paloh (Malaysia) 176 D 3
Paloich 194 E 6
Palomar Mountain 113 J 9
Palomas (N.M.) 117 N 2
Palo Pinto (TX.) 122 E 3
Palo Pinto Creek Reservoir 122 E 2
Palopo 177 F 4
Palos, Cabo de 152 C 4
Palo Santo 142 E 4
Palouse (WA.) 110 H 4
Palo Verde (AZ.) 116 D 4
Palo Verde (CA.) 113 L 9
Palpa 140 A 3
Pal-Pal, Gora 171 VW 3
Palpala 140 C 5
Palpetu, Tanjung 177 G 4
Paltamo 150 J 3
Palu 177 E 4
Palu (Turkey) 155 EF 3
Palwal 174 C 2
Pama 196 E 3
Pamanukan 176 C 5
Pamban Channel 174 C 6
Pamekasan 176 D 5
Pameungpeuk 176 C 5
Pamiers 152 D 3
Pamir 169 J 3
Pamlico Sound 129 PQ 6
Pampa (TX.) 117 Q 2
Pampa de Huayuri 140 A 3
Pampa de la Matanzilla 143 C 6
Pampa de las Salinas 142 C 5
Pampa del Castillo 143 C 8
Pampa del Tamarugal 140 C 5
Pampa Grande 140 D 4
Pampas (Argentina) 142–143 D 5–6
Pampas (Peru) 140 B 3
Pamplin (VA.) 129 N 4
Pamplona (Colombia) 138 D 2
Pamplona (Spain) 152 C 3
Pamukan, Teluk 176 E 4
Pamukova 154 CD 2
Pamyati 170 F 4
Pan, Tierra del 152 B 3
Pana 197 G 6
Pana (IL.) 121 Q 3
Panaca (NV.) 112 L 5
Panacea (FL.) 131 K 4–5
Panagjurište 154 B 2
Panahan 176 D 4
Panaitan, Pulau 176 BC 5
Panaitolikón Óros 154 B 3
Panaji 174 B 4
Panakhaikón Óros 154 B 3
Panama 138 C 2
Panama 138 C 2
Panama (OK.) 121 L 7
Panamá, Golfo de 138 C 2
Panamá, Istmo de 138 C 2
Panama Canal 138 B 2
Panama City (FL.) 131 J 4
Panama City Beach (FL.) 131 J 4
Panamint Range 112 H 6
Panarea 153 F 4
Panay 177 F 1
Pancake Range 112 JK 4
Pančevo 154 B 2
Pančićev vrh 154 B 2
Panda (Mozambique) 201 E 4
Panda (Zaire) 198 B 4
Pandamatenga 200 D 3
Pandan 177 F 1
Pandan 177 F 1
Pandaria 174 D 3
Pan de Azúcar 142 B 4
Pandharpur 174 BC 4
Pandivere Kõrgustik 151 J 4
Pando 142 E 5
Pandokrátor 154 A 3
Pandrup 151 E 4
Panevėžys 151 H 4
Panga 198 D 4
Pangala 197 G 6
Pangani 199 F 5
Pangani 199 F 6
Panggoe 185 G 3
Panggoe 186 B 3
Panghkam 175 G 3
Pangi 198 D 5
Pangi Range 169 JK 4
Pangkajene 177 E 4
Pangkalanbrandan 176 A 3
Pangkalanbuun 176 D 4
Pangkalpinang 176 C 4
Panglang 175 G 2
Pangnirtung 105 OP 2

Pango Aluquém 200 A 1
Pangrango, Gunung 176 C 5
Panguitch (UT.) 114 E 6
Panguitch Lake 114 E 6
Pangururan 176 A 3
Pangutaran Group 177 F 2
Panhandle (TX.) 117 P 2
Pania Mutombo 198 C 6
Paniau 113 B 10
Panié, Mont 185 H 6
Panipat 174 C 2
Panjang 176 C 5
Panjao 169 H 4
Panjbarar (Iran) 157 E 2
Panjim 174 B 4
Panjgur 169 G 5
Panjnad 169 J 5
Panjshir 169 H 3
Panjwïn (Iraq) 157 D 2
Pankshin 197 F 4
P'anmunjŏm 173 J 3
Panna 174 D 3
Panola (AL.) 130 F 2
Panopah 176 D 4
Panora (IA.) 119 O 9
Panorama 141 F 5
Panovo 159 O 4
Panshan 173 H 2
Panshi 173 J 2
Pantanal de São Lourénço 140 E 4
Pantanal do Río Negro 140 E 4
Pantano (AZ.) 116 F 5
Pantar, Pulau 177 F 5
Pantego (N.C.) 129 P 6
Pantelleria 153 F 4
Pantemakassar 177 F 5
Pantiacolla, Cadena del 140 B 3
Panuco 132 C 3
Panuco, Rio 132 C 3
Pan Xian 172 DE 5
Panyam 197 F 4
Panzi 198 B 6
Paola 153 G 4
Paola (KS.) 121 L 4
Paoli (IN.) 128 E 3
Paonia (CO.) 115 K 5
Paoua 198 B 3
Pap 198 E 3
Pápa 154 A 1
Papa (HI.) 113 G 12
Papaaloa (HI.) 113 G 12
Papagayo, Golfo del 132 E 5
Papago Indian Reservation 116 DE 5
Papaikou (HI.) 113 G 12
Papalote (TX.) 122 F 7
Papantla de Olarte 132 C 3
Papar 176 E 2
Papeete 187 F 4
Papenburg 149 E 4
Papey 150 C 3
Paphos 155 D 4
Paphos (Cyprus) 156 A 2
Papikion Óros 154 C 2
Papillon (NE.) 120 J 1
Paposo 142 B 4
Papua, Gulf of 184 DE 3
Papua, Gulf of 186 A 3
Papua New Guinea 184 E 2–3
Papua New Guinea 186 A 3
Papun 175 G 4
Pará (Brazil) 139 GH 5
Parabel 159 Q 4
Parabel' 159 Q 4
Pará → Belém 139 J 4
Pará (AR.) 121 M 7
Paraburdoo 182 B 3
Paracatu 141 G 4
Paracel Islands 163 K 5
Paracel Islands 175 K 4
Paracuru 141 J 2
Parade (SD.) 118 GH 5
Paradise (CA.) 112 D 3
Paradise (KS.) 120 FG 3
Paradise (MI.) 124 J 3
Paradise (MT.) 111 KL 3
Paradise (TX.) 122 F 2
Paradise Beach (FL.) 130 G 4
Paradise Valley (AZ.) 116 E 3
Paradise Valley (NV.) 112 H 1
Paragonah (UT.) 114 E 6
Paragould (AR.) 121 P 6
Paragua 139 F 2
Paraguaçu 141 J 3
Paraguai 140 E 5
Paraguái (Bolivia) 140 D 3
Paraguaná, Península de 138 E 1
Paraguari 142 E 4
Paraguay 140 DE 5
Paraguay 142 E 4
Paraíba 141 J 2
Paraíba do Sul 141 H 5
Parainen 151 H 3
Paraiso, Serra do 141 F 3–4
Parakhino Poddubye 158 F 4
Parakou 196 E 4
Paramaribo 139 GH 2
Paramillo 138 C 2
Paramirim 141 H 3
Paramonga 138 C 6
Paramore Island 129 Q 4
Paramushir, Ostrov 171 T 5

Paraná 141 G 3
Paraná 142 E 5
Paraná (Argentina) 142 D 5
Paraná (Brazil) 141 F 5
Paraná (Goiás, Brazil) 141 G 3
Paranaguá 142 G 4
Paranaguá, Baia de 142 G 4
Paranaíba 141 F 4
Paranam 139 G 2
Paranapanema 141 F 5
Paranapiacaba, Serra do 141 G 5
Paranavai 141 F 5
Parandak (Iran) 157 F 2
Paranéstion 154 B 2
Parangaba 141 J 1
Paranhos 141 E 5
Paraoa 187 F 4
Parapetí 140 D 4
Parapol'skiy Dolina 171 V 3
Parara 177 F 4
Parati 141 H 5
Paratinga 141 H 3
Paratunka 171 T 5
Paravani, Ozero 155 F 2
Paray-le-Monial 152 D 2
Parbati 174 C 2
Parbhani 174 C 4
Parbig 159 Q 4
Parc National de la Boucle De Baoule 196 C 3
Parc National de la Komoé 196 D 4
Parc National de la Pendjari 196 E 3
Parc National de Sinianka-Minia 197 H 3
Parc National de Taï 196 C 4
Parc National de Wonga Wongué 197 FG 6
Parc National de Zakouma 197 H 3
Parc National du Bamingui-Bangoran 198 BC 3
Parc National du Niokolo Koba 196 B 3
Parcs Nationaux du ''W'' 196 E 3
Pardo 141 H 4
Pardubice 149 G 4
Parecis 140 E 3
Parecis, Serra dos 140 D 3
Pareditas 142 C 5
Pǎreh (Iran) 157 E 1
Pare Mountains 199 F 5
Paren 171 U 3
Paren 171 U 3
Parent 105 N 6
Parepare 177 E 4
Parera 142 E 5
Párga 154 B 3
Pargas (Parainen) 151 H 3
Parguaza 138 E 2
Parguera (P.R.) 130 B 9
Pari 155 F 2
Paria, Golfo de 139 F 1
Paria, Península de 139 F 1
Pariaguán 139 F 2
Pariaman 176 B 4
Paria Plateau 116 DE 1
Paricatuba 139 F 4
Parichi 151 J 5
Pariçuti'n, Volcán 132 B 4
Parigi 177 F 4
Parika 139 G 2
Parikkala 150 J 3
Parima, Sierra 139 F 3
Parinari 138 D 4
Pariñas, Punta 138 B 4
Parintins 139 G 4
Paris (AR.) 121 M 7
Paris (France) 152 D 2
Paris (ID.) 111 O 8
Paris (IL.) 121 S 3
Paris (KY.) 128 G 3
Paris (MO.) 121 N 3
Paris (TN.) 128 C 5
Paris (TX.) 123 H 2
Parismina 132 F 5
Pariti 177 F 6
Parkano 150 H 3
Park City (KS.) 120 H 5
Park City (KY.) 128 F 4
Park City (MT.) 111 R 5
Parkdale (CO.) 115 M 5
Parkdale (OR.) 110 D 5
Parker (AZ.) 116 B 3
Parker (WA.) 110 E 4
Parker Dam 116 B 3
Parkersburg (IA.) 119 Q 8
Parkersburg (IL.) 121 R 4
Parkersburg (W.V.) 129 K 2
Parkers Prairie (MN.) 119 N 4
Parkes 183 H 5
Park Falls (WI.) 124 D 4
Park Grove (MT.) 118 B 2
Parkhar 169 H 3
Parkin (AR.) 121 P 7
Parkland (WA.) 110 C 3
Parkman (WY.) 111 S 6
Park Range 115 L 3–4
Park Rapids (MN.) 119 NO 4
Park River (N.D.) 119 L 2
Parks (AZ.) 116 DE 2
Parkston (S.D.) 119 L 7
Park Valley (UT.) 114 D 2

Park View (N.M.) 117 K 1
Parlakimidi 174 D 4
Parlakote 174 D 4
Parle, Lac qui 119 M 5
Parma (ID.) 110 J 7
Parma (Italy) 153 F 3
Parma (MO.) 121 Q 6
Parma (OH.) 125 N 8
Parmelee (SD.) 118 H 7
Parnaguá 141 H 3
Parnaíba 141 H 1
Parnaíba 141 H 1
Parnamirim 141 J 2
Parnarama 141 H 2
Parnassós Óros 154 B 3
Parnell (TX.) 117 Q 3
Parnon Óros 154 B 3
Pärnu 151 H 4
Pärnu Jõgi 151 HJ 4
Parola 150 H 3
Paromay 171 Q 5
Paroo River 183 GH 4
Paropamisus 169 G 4
Parowan (UT.) 114 E 6
Parpaillon 153 E 3
Parque Arqueológico 138 C 3
Parque Nacional Canaima 139 F 2
Parque Nacional da Quiçama 200 A 1
Parque Nacional de Chaco 142 E 4
Parque Nacional de la Macarena 138 D 3
Parque Nacional de Monte Pascoal 141 J 4
Parque Nacional do Araguaia 141 FG 3
Parque Nacional do Brasília 141 G 4
Parque Nacional do Chapada dos Veadeiros 141 G 3
Parque Nacional do Emas 141 F 4
Parque Nacional do Iguaçu 141 F 5
Parque Nacional el Tuparro 138 E 2
Parque Nacional Lanin 143 B 6
Parque Nacional Los Alerges 143 B 6
Parque Nacional los Glaciares 143 B 8
Parque Nacional los Paraguas 143 B 6
Parque Nacional Moreno 143 B 8
Parque Nacional Nahuel Huapi 143 B 7
Parque Nacional Simón Bolivar 138 D 2
Parral 143 B 6
Parran (NV.) 112 G 3
Parras, Sierra de 132 B 2
Parras de la Fuente 132 B 2
Parrish (AL.) 128 D 8
Parrish (FL.) 131 M 6
Parris Island 129 L 9
Parrita 132 F 6
Parry Bay 103 V 2
Parry Islands 202
Parry Peninsula 103 MN 2
Parseta 149 G 4
Parshall (CO.) 115 L 3
Parshall (ND.) 118 F 3
Parshino 170 K 4
Parsons (KS.) 121 K 5
Parsons (TN.) 128 C 6
Parsons (W.V.) 129 M 2
Partabpur 174 D 3
Pårtetjåkkå 150 G 2
Parthenay 152 CD 2
Partille 151 H 1
Partinico 153 F 4
Partizansk 173 K 2
Partizanske 149 G 5
Partizanskoye 170 F 4
Partridge (KS.) 120 GH 5
Paru 139 H 4
Paru de Oeste 139 G 3
Paruro 140 B 3
Parvatipuram 174 D 4
Paryang 174 D 2
Parys 200 D 5
Pasadena (CA.) 113 G 8
Pasadena (TX.) 123 H 6
Pasado, Cabo 138 B 4
Pasaje 138 C 4
Pasangkayu 177 E 4
Pãsãrgãd (Iran) 157 F 3
Pasarwajo 177 F 5
Pasawng 175 G 4
Pascagoula (MS.) 130 F 4
Pascagoula River 130 F 4
Pasco (WA.) 110 F 4
Pas de Calais 148 D 4
Pasekudah 174 D 6
Pashkovo 171 O 6
Pashshkiy-Perevoz 158 F 3
Pashtun Zarghün 169 G 4
Pasinler 155 F 3
Pasir Mas 176 B 2
Pasirpengarayan 176 AB 3
Paskenta (CA.) 112 C 3
Pasni 169 G 5
Paso de Indios 143 C 7
Paso del Limay 143 BC 7
Paso de los Libres 142 E 4
Paso de los Toros 142 E 5
Paso de los Vientos 133 H 3–4
Paso de Pino Hachado 143 B 6
Paso de San Francisco 142 C 4
Paso Río Mayo 143 B 8

Paso Robles (CA.) 113 E 7
Paso Socompa 140 C 5
Passage Keys 131 M 7
Passagem 141 H 3
Passage of Tiree 148 B 3
Passaic (N.J.) 127 E 8
Passau 149 F 5
Passero, Capo 153 G 4
Passo della Futa 153 F 3
Passo della Spluga 153 E 2
Passo dello Stelvio 153 F 2
Passo dello Scalone 153 G 4
Passo di Resia 153 F 2
Passo Fundo 142 F 4
Passos 141 G 5
Pastaza 138 C 4
Pasto 138 C 3
Pasto Grande 139 F 5
Pastol Bay 108 F 3
Pastora Peak 116 G 1
Pastos Bons 141 H 2
Paštrik 154 B 2
Pasul Mestecănis 154 C 1
Pasul Predeal 154 C 1
Pasul Turnu Roşu 154 B 1
Pasuruan 176 D 5
Pasvalys 151 H 4
Pasvikelva 150 J 2
Patacamaya 140 C 4
Patagonia 143 BC 7–9
Patagonia (AZ.) 116 F 6
Pataha City (WA.) 110 H 4
Patan (India) 174 B 3
Patan (Nepal) 174 E 2
Patani 177 G 3
Patãven (Iran) 157 F 3
Pate 199 G 5
Pategi 197 F 4
Pate Island 199 G 5
Patensie 200 C 6
Paterno 153 F 4
Paterson (N.J.) 127 E 8
Pathankot 174 C 1
Pathfinder Reservoir 118 B 8
Pathiu 175 G 5
Pathrump (NV.) 112 K 6
Patía 138 C 3
Patiala 174 C 1
Pativilca 138 C 6
Patkaglik 169 M 3
Pat Mayse Lake 123 H 2
Pátmos 154 C 3
Patna 174 E 2
Patnagarh 174 D 3
Patnos 155 F 3
Patomskoye Nagor'ye 170 KL 4
Patonga 198 E 4
Patos 141 J 2
Patos, Cachoeira dos 139 FG 5
Patos, Lagoa dos 142 F 5
Patos de Minas 141 G 4
Patquía 142 C 5
Patras 154 B 3
Patras 154 B 3
Patricia (TX.) 117 OP 5
Patricio Lynch 143 A 8
Patrĩkos Kólpos 154 B 3
Patrocínio 141 G 4
Patroon (TX.) 123 K 4
Patsville (NV.) 112 K 1
Pattani 175 H 6
Pattaya 175 H 5
Patten (ME.) 126 L 3
Patten Escaprment 209 D 2
Patterson (CA.) 112 DE 5
Patterson (ID.) 111 M 6
Patterson, Mount 109 M 3
Pattison (MS.) 130 D 3
Pattle 175 K 4
Patton (MO.) 121 P 5
Patton (PA.) 125 Q 9
Pattonsburg (MO.) 121 L 2
Pattullo, Mount 102 LM 4
Patú 141 J 2
Patuakhali 175 F 3
Patuca, Rio 132 F 4
Patvinsuo 150 K 3
Pau 152 C 3
Pau d'Arco 139 J 5
Pauillac 152 C 2
Pauini 138 E 5
Pauini 138 E 5
Pauksa Taung 175 F 4
Paul (ID.) 111 M 8
Paulatuk 103 N 2
Paulden (AZ.) 116 D 3
Paulding (MS.) 130 E 2
Paulding (OH.) 125 K 8
Paulina (OR.) 110 EF 6
Paulina Marsh 110 DE 7
Paulina Peak 110 D 7
Paulistana 141 H 2
Paulo Afonso 141 J 2
Paulo Afonso, Cachoeira de 141 J 2
Pauloff Harbour 108 F 5
Paul Spur (AZ.) 116 G 6
Pauls Valley (OK.) 120 H 8
Paungde 175 G 4

Paunsaugunt Plateau 114 E 6
Pausa 140 B 4
Pauto 138 D 2
Pauwela (HI.) 113 F 11
Pavant Range 114 E 4–5
Pǎveh (Iran) 157 E 2
Pavia 153 E 2
Pǎvilosta 151 H 4
Pavlikeni 154 C 2
Pavlodar 159 P 5
Pavlof Bay 108 F 4
Pavlof Islands 102 E 5
Pavlof Volcano 102 E 4
Pavlograd 155 E 1
Pavlovka 159 O 5
Pavlovo 158 H 4
Pavlovsk 159 Q 5
Pavlovskaya 155 E 1
Pavlysh 158 F 6
Pavo (GA.) 131 L 4
Pavón 138 D 3
Pavullo nel Frignano 153 F 3
Pawahku 175 G 2
Pawan, Sungai 176 D 4
Pawhuska (OK.) 120 J 6
Pawnee (OK.) 120 J 6
Pawnee City (NE.) 120 J 3
Pawnee River 120 EF 4
Pawnee Rock (KS.) 120 F 4
Paw Paw (MI.) 124 J 7
Paw Paw (W.V.) 129 N 2
Paw Paw Lake (MI.) 124 H 7
Pawtucket (R.I.) 126 H 7
Pawut 175 G 5
Paxoí 154 AB 3
Paxson 102 H 3
Paxton (IL.) 124 F 9
Paxton (NE.) 118 G 9
Payakumbuh 176 B 4
Pay-Khoy, Khrebet 159 M 2
Payne, Baie 105 O 4
Payne, Lac 105 N 4
Paynes Find 182 B 4
Paynesville (MN.) 119 O 5
Paysandú 142 E 5
Payson (AZ.) 116 E 3
Payson (UT.) 114 F 3
Payturma 170 F 3
Payún, Cerro 143 C 6
Pay-Yer, Gora 159 M 2
Pǎzanãn (Iran) 157 EF 3
Pazar 155 F 2
Pazarcik 155 E 3
Pazardžik 154 B 2
Pazaryeri 154 C 3
Paz de Ariporo 138 D 2
Pazña 140 C 4
Peabody (KS.) 120 H 4
Peace Point 103 P 4
Peace River 103 P 4
Peach Springs (AZ.) 116 C 2
Peacock (TX.) 117 Q 4
Peacock Hills 103 PQ 2
Peaima Falls 139 F 2
Peaked Mountain 126 K 2
Peale, Mount 114 H 5
Pearce (AZ.) 116 G 6
Pearisburg (VA.) 129 L 4
Pea River 131 H 3
Pearl (IL.) 121 P 3
Pearland (TX.) 123 H 6
Pearl Harbor 113 E 10
Pearl Peak 112 K 2
Pearl River 139 E 3–4
Pearl River (LA.) 123 O 5
Pearsall (TX.) 122 D 7
Pearsoll Peak 110 B 8
Pearson (GA.) 131 M 3
Peary Land 202
Pease River 122 D 1
Pebane 201 F 3
Pebas 138 D 4
Pebble Beach (CA.) 112 C 6
Pebble Island 143 E 9
Peć 154 B 2
Peca 153 F 2
Pech de Bugarach 152 D 3
Pechenga 150 K 2
Pecherakh 159 M 3
Pechora 158 L 2–3
Pechora 158 L 2
Pechorskaya Guba 158 KL 2
Pechorskoye More 158 KL 2
Pechory 151 J 4
Peckerwood Lake 121 O 8
Pecos (N.M.) 117 L 2
Pecos (TX.) 117 N 6
Pecos National Monument 117 L 2
Pecos Plains 117 M 4
Pecos River 117 P 7
Pécs 154 A 1
Pededze 151 J 4
Pedernales (Ecuador) 138 B 3
Pedernales (Venezuela) 139 F 2
Pedirka 182 F 4
Pedo La 174 D 2

Pedra Lume 196 B 6
Pedras Negras 140 D 3
Pedreiras 141 GH 1
Pedriceña 132 B 2
Pedro (SD.) 118 F 6
Pedro Afonso 139 J 5
Pedro Cays 133 G 4
Pedro de Valdivia 140 BC 5
Pedro Gomes 141 F 4
Pedro Juan Caballero 140 E 5
Pedro Luro 143 D 6
Pedro R. Fernández 142 E 4
Pedroso, Sierra del 152 B 4
Peebles (OH.) 128 H 3
Pee Dee River 129 M 7
Peekskill (N.Y.) 127 F 7
Peel (N.W.T., Can.) 102 L 2
Pe Ell (WA.) 110 B 4
Peera Peera Poolanna Lake 183 F 4
Peerless (MT.) 118 BC 2
Peetz (CO.) 115 O 3
Peever (S.D.) 119 M 5
Pegasus Bay 185 Q 9
Pegu 175 G 4
Pegunungan Barisan 176 B 4
Pegunungan Charles Louis 177 J 4
Pegunungan Gauttier 177 J 4
Pegunungan Iran 176 D 3
Pegunungan Jayawijaya 177 J 4
Pegunungan Kumawa 177 H 4
Pegunungan Maoke 177 J 4
Pegunungan Muller 176 D 3
Pegunungan Sudirman 177 J 4
Pegunungan Tamrau 177 H 4
Pegunungan van Rees 177 J 4
Pegunungan Weyland 177 J 4
Pegu Yoma 175 G 4
Pegysh 158 K 3
Pehastin (WA.) 110 E 3
Pehuajó 143 D 6
Peine 149 F 4
Peipus, Lake 151 J 4
Peixe (Goiás, Brazil) 141 G 3
Peixe (São Paulo, Brazil) 141 F 5
Pei Xian 173 G 4
Pejantan, Pulau 176 C 3
Pekalongan 176 C 5
Pekanbaru 176 B 3
Pekin (IL.) 124 E 9
Pekin (IN.) 128 F 3
Pekin (N.D.) 119 K 3
Peking 173 G 2
Pekkala 150 J 2
Pekon 175 G 4
Pekornica 154 A 2
Pekul'ney, Khrebet 171 WX 2
Pekul'veyem 171 X 3
Pelabuanratu 176 C 5
Pelabuanratu, Teluk 176 C 5
Pelagonija 154 B 2
Pélagos 154 B 3
Pelaihari 176 D 4
Pelat, Mont 153 E 3
Peleaga, Virful 154 B 1
Peleduy 170 K 4
Peleliu 177 H 2
Peleng, Pulau 177 F 4
Peleng, Selat 177 F 4
Peleniya 154 C 1
Pelia (KS.) 120 K 3
Pelican 102 K 4
Pelican Island 131 O 7
Pelican Lake (MN.) 119 Q 2
Pelican Lake (WI.) 124 E 4
Pelican Narrows 103 R 4
Pelican Rapids (MN.) 119 M 4
Pelinaion Óros 154 C 3
Peliny Osipenko, Iméni 171 P 5
Pelion (S.C.) 129 K 4
Pelješac 153 G 3
Pelkosenniemi 150 J 2
Pella (IA.) 119 Q 9
Pellegrini 143 D 6
Pello 150 H 2
Pellston (MI.) 125 K 4
Pelly 102 L 3
Pelly Bay (N.W.T., Can.) 103 T 2
Pelly Bay (N.W.T., Can.) 103 U 2
Pelly Crossing 102 K 3
Pelly Mountains 102 L 3
Peloncillo Mountains 116 H 5
Peloponnese 154 B 3
Pelopónnisos 154 B 3
Peloritani, Monti 153 FG 4
Pelotas (Rio Grande do Sul, Brazil) 142 F 5
Pelotas (Santa Catarina, Brazil) 142 F 4
Pelvoux, Massif du 153 E 3
Pelym 159 M 3
Pemadumcook Lake 126 L 3
Pemalang 176 C 5
Pemangkat 176 C 3
Pemarung, Pulau 176 E 4
Pematangsiantar 176 A 3
Pemba (Mozambique) 201 G 2
Pemba (Zambia) 200 D 3
Pemba Island (Tanzania) 199 FG 6
Pemberton 182 B 5
Pembina (N.D.) 119 L 2

Pembina Mountains 119 K 1
Pembina River 119 KL 2
Pembine (WI.) 124 F 4
Pembroke 148 BC 4
Pembroke (GA.) 131 N 2
Pembroke (Ontario, Can.) 105 M 6
Pembroke, Cape 143 E 9
Pembroke, Cape (N.W.T., Can.) 105 L 3
Pembuang 176 D 4
Peña, Sierra de la 152 C 3
Peñafiel 152 C 3
Peñaranda de Bracamonte 152 BC 3
Penarie 183 G 5
Peñarroya Pueblonuevo 152 B 4
Peñas, Cabo de 152 B 3
Penas, Golfo de 143 B 8
Penasco (N.M.) 117 L 1
Pendembu 196 B 4
Pender 182 C 2
Pender (NE.) 119 M 8
Pendjari, Parc National de la 196 E 3
Pendleton (IN.) 124 J 9
Pendleton (OR.) 110 G 5
Pend Oreille, Lake 110 J 2
Pend Oreille River 110 HJ 2
Pendroy (MT.) 111 N 2
Pendzhikent 169 H 3
Penedo 141 J 3
Pene Mende 198 D 5
Penfield (PA.) 125 Q 8
Peng'an 172 E 4
Penge 198 C 6
Penghu Liedaoo 173 G 6
Pengilly (MN.) 119 P 3
Penglai 173 H 3
Pengshui 172 E 5
Pengze 172 G 5
Penida, Pulau 176 E 5
Península Brecknock 143 B 9
Península de Azuero 138 B 2
Península de Brunswick 143 B 9
Península de Guajira 138 D 1
Península de Nicoya 132 E 6
Península de Osa 132 F 6
Península de Paraguaná 138 DE 1
Península de Paria 138 E 1
Península de Taitao 143 AB 8
Península de Yucatán → Yucatán Penin-sula 132 E 3–4
Península Tres Montes 143 A 8
Península Valdés 143 D 7
Péninsule de Gaspé 105 O 6
Peninsule d'Ungava 105 MN 4
Penisola Salentina 153 G 3
Penitente, Serra do 139 J 5
Pénjamo 132 B 3
Pennell, Mount 114 G 6
Penner 174 C 5
Penninechain (U.K.) 148 C 4
Pennsylvania (East) 126–127
Pennsylvania, West 125
Penn Yan (N.Y.) 126 B 6
Penny Ice Cap 105 O 2
Penobscot Bay 126 L 4
Penobscot River 126 L 3
Penola 183 G 6
Peñón Blanco 132 B 3
Penong 182 E 5
Penonomé 138 B 2
Penrhyn 187 E 3
Penrith 148 C 4
Penrose (CO.) 115 MN 5
Penrose (UT.) 114 E 2
Pensacola (FL.) 130 G 4
Pensacola Bay 130 G 4
Pensacola Mountains 203
Pensiangan 176 E 3
Pentecost 185 J 5
Pentecôte 186 C 4
Penticton 103 O 6
Pentland 183 H 3
Pentland Firth 148 C 3
Pentwater (MI.) 124 H 6
Penukonda 174 C 5
Penwegon 175 G 4
Penwell (TX.) 117 O 6
Penza 158 H 5
Penzance 148 B 4
Penzance (AZ.) 116 F 3
Penzhino 171 V 3
Penzhinskaya Guba 171 U 3
Penzhinskiy Khrebet 171 VW 3
Peoa (UT.) 114 F 3
Peoria (IL.) 124 E 9
Peoria Heights (IL.) 124 E 9
Peotone (IL.) 124 G 8
Pepa 198 DE 6
Pepacton Reservoir 126 E 6
Pepel 196 B 4
Pequizeiro 139 J 5
Pequop (NV.) 112 L 1
Pequop Mountains 112 L 2
Pequot Lakes (MN.) 119 O 4
Perabumulih 176 B 4
Perales, Puerto de 152 B 3
Percé 105 P 6
Perche, Collines du 152 D 2
Percival Lakes 182 C 3

Perdido (AL.) 130 G 3
Perdido River 130 G 4
Pereira, Cachoeira 139 G 4
Pereira Barreto 141 F 5
Pereirinha 139 G 5
Pereshchepino 158 FG 6
Pereval Akbaytal 169 J 3
Pereval Dolon 169 K 2
Pereval Kyzylyart 169 J 3
Pereval Torugart 169 K 2
Pereval Yablonitse 154 BC 1
Perevolotskiy 158 K 5
Pérez 142 C 4
Perez (CA.) 112 D 1
Pergamino 142 D 5
Pergamon 154 C 3
Perge 154 D 3
Perham (MN.) 119 N 4
Perho 150 H 3
Péribonca 105 N 6
Peribonca, Lac 105 N 5
Pericos 106 E 6
Peridot (AZ.) 116 F 4
Périgueux 152 D 2
Perijá, Sierra de 138 D 1–2
Perim Island → Barîm 195 G 6
Perito Moreno 143 B 8
Peritoró 141 H 1
Perkins (OK.) 120 H 7
Perkins, Mount 116 B 2
Perković 153 G 3
Perlas, Laguna de 132 F 5
Perm 158 L 4
Perma (MT.) 111 L 3
Përmeti 154 B 2
Pernambuco 141 J 2
Pernambuco → Recife 141 K 2
Pernell (OK.) 120 H 8
Pernik 154 B 2
Pèronne 152 D 2
Perote 132 C 4
Perpignan 152 D 3
Perrin (TX.) 122 E 2
Perrine (FL.) 131 O 9
Perris (CA.) 113 H 9
Perro, Laguna del 117 KL 3
Perros-Guirec 152 C 2
Perry (FL.) 131 L 4
Perry (GA.) 131 L 2
Perry (IA.) 119 O 9
Perry (LA.) 123 L 6
Perry (MI.) 125 K 7
Perry (MO.) 121 O 3
Perry (N.Y.) 126 B 6
Perry (OK.) 120 H 6
Perry (UT.) 114 EF 2
Perry Island 103 R 2
Perry Lake 121 K 3
Perryton (TX.) 117 Q 1
Perryville (AK.) 102 F 4
Perryville (AR.) 121 N 7–8
Perryville (MO.) 121 Q 5
Persembe 155 E 2
Persepolis (Iran) 157 F 3
Perseverancia 140 D 3
Persia 168 EF 4
Persia (IA.) 119 N 9
Persian Gulf 157 EF 3–4
Pertek 155 E 3
Perth (Australia) 182 B 5
Perth (U.K.) 148 C 3
Perth Amboy (N.J.) 127 E 8
Perth-Andover 105 O 6
Perthus, Col de 152 D 3
Pertuis 153 E 3
Pertuis Breton 152 C 2
Pertuis d'Antioche 152 C 2
Peru 138 C 5
Peru (IL.) 124 E 8
Peru (IN.) 124 H 9
Peru (WY.) 111 Q 9
Peru Basin 209 E 4
Peru-Chile Trench 208 A 4–5
Perugia 153 F 3
Peruíbe 141 G 5
Perušić 153 G 3
Pervari 155 F 3
Pervomaysk (Russiya, U.S.S.R.) 154 D 1
Pervomaysk (Russiya, U.S.S.R.) 158 H 5
Pervomayskiy (Kazakhstan, U.S.S.R.) 159 Q 5
Pervomayskiy (Russiya, U.S.S.R.) 158 H 3
Pervoural'sk 159 L 4
Pervoye Pole 108 B 3
Pervyy Kamen' 171 U 2
Pesaro 153 F 3
Pescadero (CA.) 112 C 5
Pescadores 173 G 6
Pescara 153 F 3
Pescara 155 F 3
Peschanyy, Mys 168 E 2
Peschanyy, Ostrov 170 L 1
Peschici 153 G 3
Pescoraro 153 G 4

Peshawar 169 J 4
Peshawbestown (MI.) 124 J 5
Peshchanopskoye 155 F 1
Peshkopi 154 B 2
Peshtigo (WI.) 124 G 4
Peski 169 G 3
Peski Karakum 168 E 1
Peski Karakumy 168–169 FG 3
Peski Karynzharyk 168 E 2
Peski Kyzylkum 169 GH 2
Peski Muyunkum 169 J 2
Peski Priaral'skiye Karakumy 169 G 1
Peski Sary Ishikotrau 159 P 6
Pesochny 151 K 3
Peso da Régua 152 B 3
Pesqueira 141 J 2
Pessac 152 C 3
Pestovo 154 G 3
Pestravka 158 J 5
Petacalco, Bahia de 132 B 4
Petäjävesi 150 J 3
Petal (MS.) 130 E 3
Petaluma (CA.) 112 C 4
Petare 138 E 1
Petatlán 132 B 4
Petén 132 D 4
Petenwell Lake 124 E 5
Peterborough (Ontario, Can.) 105 M 7
Peterborough (South Australia) 183 F 5
Peterborough (U.K.) 148 C 4
Peterhead 148 C 3
Peter I Island 203
Peter Island 130 E 8
Peter Lake 103 T 3
Petermann Ranges 182 D 4
Peteroa 143 BC 6
Peter Pond Lake 103 Q 4
Petersburg (AK.) 102 L 4
Petersburg (IL.) 124 E 9
Petersburg (IN.) 128 D 3
Petersburg (NE.) 119 KL 9
Petersburg (TN.) 128 E 6
Petersburg (TX.) 117 P 3
Petersburg (VA.) 129 M 3
Petersburg (W.V.) 129 L 2
Peterstown (W.V.) 129 L 4
Petilia Policastro 153 G 4
Petites Pyrénées 152 D 3
Petit-Mécatina, Rivière du 105 PQ 5
Petitot 103 N 4
Petitsikapau Lake 105 O 5
Petkula 150 J 2
Petlad 174 B 3
Peto 132 E 3
Petorca 142 B 5
Petoskey (MI.) 125 K 4
Petra (Jordan) 156 B 3
Petra Azul 141 H 4
Petra Velikogo, Zaliv 173 K 2
Petrel 203
Petrela 154 A 2
Petrified Forest National Park 116 F 3
Petrified Forest National Park 143 C 8
Petrikov 151 J 5
Petrikovka 155 DE 1
Petrila 154 B 1
Petrinja 153 G 2
Petrodvorets 151 J 4
Petrolândia 141 J 2
Petrolia (CA.) 112 A 2
Petrolia (TX.) 122 E 1
Petrolina 141 H 2
Petronell 153 G 2
Petropavlovka 170 J 5
Petropavlovsk 159 NO 5
Petropavlovsk 159 O 4
Petropavlovskoye 159 QR 5
Petropavlovskoye 170 J 4
Petropayelovka 159 Q 6
Petrópolis 141 H 5
Petroşeni 154 B 1
Petroso 153 F 3
Petrovac 154 A 3
Petrova Gora 153 G 2
Petrovsk 158 J 5
Petrovskaya 155 E 1
Petrovskiy Yam 158 G 3
Petrovsk-Zabaykal'skiy 170 J 5
Petrozavodsk 158 FG 3
Petsamo 150 K 2
Pettibore (ND.) 118 J 3
Pettus (TX.) 122 F 7
Petukhovo 159 N 4
Peuetsagu, Gunung 176 A 3
Peureulah 176 A 3
Pevek 202
Peyton (CO.) 115 N 4
Peza 158 J 2
Pezas 159 R 5
Pézenas 152 D 3
Pfaffenhofen 149 F 5
Pforzheim 149 E 5
Phalaborwa 201 E 4
Phalodi 174 B 2
Phaltan 174 B 4

Phangnga 175 G 6
Phanom Dang Raek 175 H 5
Phan Rang 175 J 5
Phan Thiet 175 J 5
Pharr (TX.) 122 E 9
Phatthalung 175 H 6
Pheba (MS.) 121 R 9
Phelps (WI.) 124 E 3
Phelps Lake 129 O 5
Phenix City (AL.) 131 J 2
Phet Buri 175 G 5
Phetchabun 175 H 4
Phiafay 175 J 5
Phichit 175 H 4
Philadelphia (MS.) 130 E 2
Philadelphia (N.Y.) 126 D 4
Philadelphia (PA.) 127 DE 8
Philae (Egypt) 156 A 5
Phil Campbell (AL.) 128 D 7
Philip (SD.) 118 G 6
Philipp (MS.) 121 P 9
Philippeville → Skikda 193 G 1
Philippi 154 B 2
Philippi (W.V.) 129 M 2
Philippi, Lake 183 F 3
Philippine Basin 209 C 3
Philippines 177 F 1
Philipsburg (MT.) 111 M 4
Philipsburg (PA.) 125 Q 9
Philip Smith Mountains 102 H 2
Philipstown 200 C 6
Phillips (ME.) 126 J 4
Phillips (TX.) 117 P 2
Phillips (WI.) 124 D 4
Phillipsburg (KS.) 120 F 3
Phillipsburg (N.J.) 127 D 8
Philo (CA.) 112 B 3
Philomath (OR.) 110 B 6
Phippsburg (CO.) 115 L 3
Phitsanulok 175 H 4
Phnom Aural 175 H 5
Phnom Penh 175 H 5
Phoenix (AZ.) 116 D 4
Phoenix Islands 186 D 3
Phoenixville (PA.) 127 D 8
Phong Nha 175 J 4
Phong Saly 175 H 3
Phrao 175 G 4
Phu Dien Chau 175 J 4
Phuket 175 G 6
Phulbani 174 D 3
Phu Ly 175 J 3
Phum Khvao 175 HJ 5
Phum Siem 175 H 5
Phu My 175 J 5
Phung Hiep 175 J 6
Phuoc Le 175 J 5
Phu Set 175 J 4
Phu Tho 175 J 3
Phu Vinh 175 J 6
Piacá 139 J 5
Piacenza 153 EF 2–3
Piana Mwanga 198 D 6
Pianguan 172 F 3
Pianosa 153 F 3
Pianosa 153 F 3
Piara Açu 139 H 5
Piatra Neamţ 154 C 1
Piauí 141 H 2
Piauí 141 H 2
Piave 153 F 2
Pibor Post 198 E 3
Pica 140 C 5
Pica (AZ.) 116 C 2
Picabo (ID.) 111 L 7
Picacho (AZ.) 116 E 5
Picacho (N.M.) 117 L 4
Picacho del Centinela 132 B 2
Picardie 152 D 2
Picayune (MS.) 130 E 4
Pic Baumann 196 E 4
Pic Boby 201 H 4
Pic de la Selle 133 H 4
Pic de Macaya 133 H 4
Pic d'Estats 152 D 3
Pichanal 140 D 5
Pichilemu 143 B 5
Pichilingue 106 DE 7
Pichimá 138 C 3
Pick City (ND.) 118 G 3
Pickens (MS.) 130 DE 2
Pickens (S.C.) 129 J 3
Pickens (W.V.) 129 L 3
Pickford (MI.) 125 K 3
Pickle Lake 104 J 5
Pickstown (S.D.) 119 K 7
Pickwick Lake 128 CD 7
Pico 192 A 1
Pico Aitana 152 C 4
Pico Atalaya 130 B 8
Pico Bolívar 138 D 2
Pico Bonito 132 E 4
Pico Colorado 142 C 4
Pico Cristóbal Colón 138 D 1
Pico da Neblina 138 E 3
Pico das Agulhas Negras 141 H 5
Pico de Aneto 152 D 3
Pico de Aroche 152 B 4
Pico de Itambé 141 H 4
Pico de Santa Isabel 197 F 5

Pico de Teide 192 B 3
Pico de Tio 196 C 4
Pico de Tomé 197 F 5
Pico Rondón 139 F 3
Picos 141 H 2
Pico San Juan 133 F 3
Picota 138 C 5
Pico Tamacuarí 138 E 3
Pico Truncado 143 C 8
Picton, Isla 143 C 6
Pictou 105 P 6
Pic Tousside 197 H 1
Pictured Rocks National Lakeshore 124 H 3
Picún Leufú 143 C 6
Picuris Indian Reservation 117 L 1
Pidurutalagala 174 D 6
Piedecuesta 138 D 2
Piedmont (AL.) 128 F 8
Piedmont (MO.) 121 P 5
Piedmont (OH.) 125 N 9
Piedmont (SD.) 118 E 6
Piedra (AZ.) 116 D 5
Piedra, Cerro 143 B 6
Piedrabuena 152 C 4
Piedrahita 152 B 3
Piedras Blancas, Point 113 D 7
Piedras Negras 132 B 2
Piedra Sola 142 E 5
Pieksämäki 150 J 3
Pielavesi 150 J 3
Pielinen 150 J 3
Pierce (CO.) 115 N 3
Pierce (NE.) 119 L 8
Pierce City (MO.) 121 L 6
Pierceville (KS.) 120 E 5
Pierpont (S.D.) 119 L 5
Pierre (S.D.) 118 H 6
Pierrelatte 153 D 3
Pierz (MN.) 119 O 5
Piesapa 177 J 4
Pieskehaure 150 G 2
Piešťany 149 G 5
Pietarsaari 150 H 3
Pietermaritzburg 200 E 5
Pietersburg 200 D 4
Pie Town (N.M.) 116 H 3
Piet Retief 201 E 5
Pietrosu, Virful 154 BC 1
Pietroşul, Virful 154 BC 1
Pigawasi 198 E 5
Pigeon (MI.) 125 L 6
Pigeon Hole 182 E 2
Piggott (AR.) 121 P 6
Pigué 143 D 6
Pihlajavesi 150 J 3
Pihtipudas 150 J 3
Pik Aborigen 171 R 3
Pikangikum 104 J 5
Pikelot 186 A 2
Pikes Peak 115 MN 5
Pikesville (MD.) 129 P 2
Piketberg 200 B 6
Piketon (OH.) 128 H 2
Pikeville (KY.) 128 J 4
Pikeville (TN.) 128 F 6
Pik Grandioznyy 170 G 5
Pikhtovka 159 Q 4
Pik Karla Marksa 169 J 3
Pik Kommunizma 169 J 3
Pikounda 197 H 5
Pik Pobedy 169 KL 2
Pik Revolyutsii 169 J 3
Pila (Argentina) 143 E 6
Piła (Poland) 149 G 4
Pila, Sierra de la 152 C 4
Pilão Arcado 141 H 3
Pilar 142 E 4
Pilar (Alagoas, Brazil) 141 J 2
Pilar (Argentina) 142 D 5
Pilas Group 177 F 2
Pilatus 153 E 2
Pilcaniyeu 143 BC 7
Pilcomayo 140 DE 4
Pilger (NE.) 119 LM 8
Pilica 149 H 4
Pilion Óros 154 B 3
Pilis 154 A 1
Pillar Point 112 C 5
Pillsbury (N.D.) 119 L 3
Pillsbury, Lake 112 C 3
Pilos 154 B 3
Pilot Grove (MO.) 121 MN 4
Pilot Hill (CA.) 112 E 4
Pilot Knob (MT.) 111 K 5
Pilot Knob (TN.) 128 E 5
Pilot Mountain (N.C.) 129 L 5
Pilot Peak (NV.) 112 L 1–2
Pilot Peak (NV.) 112 H 4
Pilot Point (AK.) 108 G 4
Pilot Point (TX.) 122 G 2
Pilot Rock (OR.) 110 G 5
Pilot Station 108 F 3
Pilottown (LA.) 123 O 6
Pil'tun 171 Q 5
Pil'tun, Zaliv 171 Q 5
Pim 159 O 3
Pimenta, Cachoeira do 139 F 3

Pimenta Bueno 140 D 3
Pimental 139 G 4
Pimentel (Peru) 138 B 5
Pinaki 187 F 4
Pinang, Pulau 176 B 2
Pınarbaşi 155 E 3
Pínar del Rio 132 F 3
Pinarello 153 E 3
Pınarhisar 154 C 2
Piñas 142 C 5
Pincher Creek 103 P 6
Pinchincha 138 C 3
Pinckneyville (IL.) 121 Q 4
Pinçon, Mont 152 C 2
Pinconning (MI.) 125 K 6
Pindaíba 141 F 3
Pindaré 141 G 1
Pindaré Mirim 141 G 1
Pindhos Óros 154 B 2–3
Pindi Gheb 169 J 4
Pindobal 139 J 4
Pindorama 141 G 3
Pine (AZ.) 116 E 3
Pine (ID.) 111 K 7
Pine Apple (AL.) 130 GH 3
Pine Bluff (AR.) 121 N 8
Pine Bluffs (WY.) 118 DE 9
Pine Bush (N.Y.) 126 E 7
Pine City (WA.) 110 H 3
Pine Creek 182 E 1
Pine Creek (NV.) 112 J 2
Pine Creek (PA.) 126 B 7
Pine Creek Lake 121 K 8
Pinedale (N.M.) 116 H 2
Pinedale (WY.) 111 Q 8
Pine Falls 103 S 5
Pine Flat Dam 112 F 6
Pine Flat Lake 112 F 6
Pinega 158 H 3
Pinega 158 J 3
Pine Grove (CA.) 112 E 4
Pine Grove (OR.) 110 D 5
Pine Grove (W.V.) 129 L 2
Pinehurst (ID.) 110 J 3
Pine Island 131 M 8
Pine Island Bay 203
Pineland (TX.) 123 K 4
Pinellas Park (FL.) 131 M 7
Pine Mountain 113 D 7
Pine Mountain (OR.) 110 E 7
Pine Mountain (WY.) 111 QR 9
Pine Pass 103 N 4
Pine Peak 116 C 3
Pine Point 103 P 3
Pine Ridge (SD.) 118 F 7
Pine Ridge Indian Reservation 118 FG 7
Pine River (MN.) 119 O 4
Pine Springs (TX.) 117 M 6
Pinetop (AZ.) 116 G 3
Pinetown 201 E 5
Pineville (KY.) 128 H 5
Pineville (MO.) 121 L 6
Pineville (N.C.) 129 L 6
Pineville (W.V.) 129 K 4
Piney Buttes 118 B 3
Piney Point 131 L 5
Ping'anyi 172 D 3
Pingbian 172 D 6
Pingchang 172 E 4
Pingdingshan 172 F 4
Pingdu 173 H 3
Pingelap 186 B 2
Pingelly 182 B 5
Pingguo 172 E 6
Pinghu 173 H 4
Pingjiang 172 F 5
Pingle 172 F 6
Pingli 172 E 4
Pingliang 172 E 3
Pinglu 172 F 4
Pingluo 172 E 3
Pingnan 172 F 6
Pingquan 173 G 2
Pingshan 172 F 3
Pingtan 173 GH 5
Pingtung 173 H 6
Pingwu 172 D 4
Pingxiang 172 F 5
Pingxiang 172 E 6
Pingyang 173 H 5
Pingyao 172 F 3
Pingyuan 173 G 3
Pinheiro Machado 142 F 5
Pinhel 152 B 3
Pini, Pulau 176 A 3
Piniós 154 B 3
Pinjang 177 F 3
Pink Mountain 103 N 4
Pinlebu 175 G 3
Pinnacle Buttes 111 Q 7
Pinnacle Peak 111 P 7
Pinnacles National Monument 112 D 6
Pinnaroo 183 G 6
Pinnes, Akra 154 B 2
Pino Hachado, Paso de 143 B 6
Pinola (MS.) 130 E 3
Pinon (AZ.) 116 F 1
Pinos, Mount 113 F 8

Pinos Altos Range 116 H 4
Pinos-Puente 152 C 4
Pinrang 177 E 4
Pins, Île des 186 C 4
Pinsk 151 J 5
Pinta (AZ.) 116 G 2
Pinta 140 C 4
Pinta,138 B 6
Pintados 140 BC 5
Pinto 142 D 4
Pintura (UT.) 114 D 6
Pinyug 158 J 3
Pio 185 H 4
Pioche (NV.) 112 L 5
Pio IX 141 H 2
Piombino 153 F 3
Pioneer (OH.) 125 K 8
Pioneer Mountains 111 MN 5
Pioner 159 R 4
Pionki 149 H 4
Piorini, Lago 139 F 4
Piotrków Trybunalski 149 G 4
Pipar 174 B 2
Pipe Creek (TX.) 122 E 6
Pipe Spring National Monument 116 D 1
Pipestone (MN.) 119 M 6
Pipmouacan, Réservoir 105 N 6
Piqua (OH.) 125 K 9
Piquiá 138 E 4
Piquiri 141 F 5
Piracicaba 141 G 5
Piracuruca 141 H 1
Piran 153 F 2
Piranhas 141 J 2
Piranhas 141 F 4
Pirapemas 141 H 1
Pirapora 141 H 4
Pires do Río 141 G 4
Pirgos 154 B 3
Piriá 139 H 4
Pirimapuan 177 J 5
Pirin 154 B 2
Piripiri 141 H 1
Pirmasens 141 E 5
Pirna 149 F 4
Pirot 154 B 2
Pirovano 143 D 6
Pir Panjal Range 169 J 4
Pir Tãj (Iran) 157 E 2
Piru 177 G 4
Piryatin 158 F 5
Pisa 153 F 3
Pisac 140 B 3
Pisagua 140 B 4
Pisco 140 A 3
Pishan 169 K 3
Pishin 169 H 4
Pishvä (Iran) 157 F 2
Pisinimo (AZ.) 116 D 5
Pismo Beach (CA.) 113 E 7
Piso Firme 140 D 3
Pissila 196 D 3
Pisté 132 E 3
Pisticci 153 G 3
Pistoia 153 F 3
Pistol River (OR.) 110 A 8
Pisuerga 152 C 3
Pita 196 B 3
Pitaga 105 O 5
Pitalito 138 C 3
Pitcairn 187 G 4
Piteå 150 H 2
Piteälven 150 H 2
Piterka 158 J 5
Piteşti 154 B 2
Pit-Gorodoko 170 F 4
Pithapuram 174 D 4
Pithara 182 B 5
Pithiviers 152 D 2
Pitibhit 174 C 2
Pitkin (CO.) 115 L 5
Pitkul' 150 K 2
Pitkyaranta 150 K 3
Pitlyar 159 N 2
Pitomača 153 G 2
Pit River 112 D 2
Pitrufquén 143 B 6
Pitsunda, Mys 155 F 2
Pitt 185 S 9
Pitt 186 D 5
Pitt Island (Br. Col., Canada) 102 L 5
Pittsboro (MS.) 121 Q 9
Pittsboro (N.C.) 129 M 6
Pittsburg (KS.) 121 L 5
Pittsburg (TX.) 123 J 2–3
Pittsburgh (PA.) 125 OP 9
Pittsfield (MA.) 126 F 6
Pittsfield (ME.) 126 K 4
Pittston (PA.) 127 D 7
Pittsview (AL.) 131 J 2
Pittsville (WI.) 124 D 6
Pituri River 183 F 3
Piùí 141 G 5
Pium 141 G 3
Plaza (ND.) 118 FG 2

Piura 138 B 5
Piute Peak 113 G 7
Piute Reservoir 114 E 5
Pivan' 171 P 5
Pixley (CA.) 112 F 7
Pizacoma 140 C 4
Pizzo Calabro 153 G 4
Placentia 105 R 6
Placentia Bay 105 R 6
Placer 177 F 1
Placerville (CA.) 112 E 4
Placerville (CO.) 115 JK 5
Placetas 133 G 3
Placidia (FL.) 131 M 8
Placitas (N.M.) 117 K 2
Plaguemine (LA.) 123 M 5
Plain City (UT.) 114 E 2
Plain Dealing (LA.) 123 K 3
Plaine de Garar 197 J 3
Plaine des Flandres 152 D 1
Plaine du Forez 152 D 2
Plaines et Seuil du Poitou 152 D 2
Plainfield (IN.) 128 E 2
Plainfield (N.J.) 127 E 8
Plainfield (WI.) 124 E 5
Plains (KS.) 120 E 5
Plains (MT.) 111 KL 3
Plains (TX.) 117 O 4
Plains of San Agustin 116 HJ 4
Plainview (MN.) 119 Q 6
Plainview (NE.) 119 L 8
Plainview (TX.) 117 P 3
Plainville (KS.) 120 F 3
Plainwell (MI.) 124 J 7
Plaistow (Haiti) 154 B 3
Plake 154 B 2
Plakhino 159 R 2
Plameira dos Indios 141 J 2
Plampang 176 E 5
Planada (CA.) 112 E 5
Planalto 141 H 3
Planalto Central 141 G 4
Planalto da Borborema 141 J 2
Planalto de Angónia 201 E 2
Planalto de Chimoio 201 E 3
Planalto de Lichinga 201 F 2
Planalto de Marávia 201 E 2
Planalto do Brasil 141 H 4
Planalto do Mato Grosso 140–141 EF 3–4
Planalto Maracanaquará 139 H 3–4
Planeta Rica 138 C 2
Planicie de la Loma Negra 143 C 6
Plankinton (S.D.) 119 K 7
Plano (TX.) 122 G 2
Plantation (FL.) 131 O 8
Plant City (FL.) 131 M 6
Plantersville (AL.) 130 H 2
Plasencia 152 B 3
Plaster City (CA.) 113 K 10
Plastun 173 L 2
Plastunka 155 E 2
Plata (TX.) 117 M 8
Platanal 139 F 3
Plateau (TX.) 117 M 6
Plateau de Basso 197 J 2
Plateau de Haute-Saône 153 E 2
Plateau de l'Androna 201 H 3
Plateau de Langres 153 D 2
Plateau de Millevaches 152 D 2
Plateau des Achikouya 197 GH 6
Plateau du Bemaraha 201 GH 3
Plateau du Djado 197 G 1
Plateau du Tademaït 193 D 3
Plateau du Tchigai 197 G 1
Plateau Laurentien 105 NQ 5
Plateau of Tibet 174 DE 1
Plateaux 197 H 6
Plateaux de la Marche 152 D 2
Plati 154 B 2
Platina (CA.) 112 C 2
Platinum 108 F 4
Plato 138 D 2
Plato Syverma 170 G 3
Plato Ustyurt 168 F 2
Plato Yagtali 170 G 2
Platte 199 K 6
Platte (SD.) 118 K 7
Platte Center (NE.) 119 L 9
Platte City (MO.) 121 L 3
Platte River 120 H 1
Platte River (MO.) 121 L 3
Platteville (CO.) 115 MN 3
Platteville (WI.) 124 D 7
Platt National Park 120 J 8
Plattsburg (MO.) 121 L 3
Plattsburgh (N.Y.) 126 F 4
Plattsmouth (NE.) 120 K 2
Plau 149 F 4
Plauen 149 F 4
Plavigas 151 J 4
Plavsk 158 G 5
Playa Azul 132 B 4
Playas 138 B 4
Playas Lake 116 H 6
Playitas 138 D 2
Plaza (ND.) 118 FG 2

Plaza (WA.) 110 H 3
Plaza Huincul 143 C 6
Pleasant, Lake 116 D 4
Pleasant, Mount 110 B 2–3
Pleasant Grove (UT.) 114 F 3
Pleasant Hill (LA.) 123 K 4
Pleasant Hill (MO.) 121 L 4
Pleasant Hill (N.M.) 117 N 3
Pleasanton (KS.) 121 L 4
Pleasanton (TX.) 122 E 7
Pleasant View (CO.) 114 HJ 6
Pleasant View (UT.) 114 F 2
Pleasantville (N.J.) 127 E 9
Pleiku 175 J 5
Plenty, Bay of 186 C 5
Plentywood (MT.) 118 D 2
Plesetsk 158 H 3
Pleshchenitsy 151 J 5
Pleşu, Virful 154 B 1
Pleszew 149 G 4
Plétipi, Lac 105 N 5
Pleven 154 C 2
Plevna (MT.) 118 D 4
Plevlja 154 A 2
Plibo 196 C 5
Plitvice 153 G 3
Pljevlja 154 A 2
Ploča, Rt 153 G 3
Ploče 153 G 3
Płock 149 GH 4
Ploiești 154 C 2
Plomárion 154 C 3
Plomb du Cantal 152 D 2
Plouguerneau 152 BC 2
Plovdiv 154 BC 2
Plum Island 127 G 7
Plummer (ID.) 110 HJ 3
Plumridge Lake 182 D 4
Plumtree 200 D 4
Plunge 151 H 4
Plush (OR.) 110 EF 8
Plymouth (CA.) 112 E 4
Plymouth (IL.) 124 D 9
Plymouth (IN.) 124 H 8
Plymouth (MA.) 126 J 7
Plymouth (Montserrat) 133 K 4
Plymouth (N.C.) 129 P 6
Plymouth (NE.) 120 H 2
Plymouth (N.H.) 126 H 5
Plymouth (U.K.) 148 C 4
Plymouth (WA.) 110 F 5
Plymouth (WI.) 124 F 6
Plyussa 151 J 4
Plyussa 151 J 4
Plzeň 149 F 5
Plzeňská Pahorkatina 149 F 5
Pô (Burkina) 196 D 3
Po (Italy) 153 F 3
Pobè (Benin) 196 E 4
Pobé (Burkina) 196 D 3
Pobeda, Gora 171 R 2
Pobedino 171 Q 6
Pobedy, Pik 169 KL 2
Pobežhiye 154 C 2
Pocahontas (AR.) 121 P 6
Pocahontas (IA.) 119 O 8
Pocasset (OK.) 120 GH 7
Pocatello (ID.) 111 N 8
Pochala 198 E 3
Pochinok 158 F 5
Pochtovaya 171 R 3
Pocklington Reef 185 G 4
Poçoes 141 H 3
Pocoma 140 B 4
Pocomoke City (MD.) 129 Q 3
Poconé 140 E 4
Pocono Mountains 127 D 7
Poços de Caldas 141 G 5
Podgornoye 159 Q 4
Podgornyy 171 R 6
Podkagernoye 171 U 3
Podkamennaya Tunguska 170 FG 3
Podlesnoye 158 J 5
Podluzje 154 B 2
Podol'sk 158 G 4
Podor 196 B 2
Podosinovets 158 J 3
Podporozh'ye 158 FG 3
Podravska Slatina 153 G 2
Podresovo 159 N 4
Podtesovo 170 F 4
Pod'yelanka 170 H 4
Podyuga 158 H 3
Pofadder 200 B 5
Poggibonsi 153 F 3
Pogibi 171 Q 5
Pogórze Karpackie 149 H 5
Pogoso 198 B 6
Pogradeci 154 B 2
Pogranichnoye 171 Q 5
P'ohang 173 J 3
Pohjanmaa 150 J 3
Poi 175 F 2
Poiana Mare 154 B 2
Poie 198 C 5
Poinsett, Cape 203
Poinsett, Lake 119 LM 6
Point Año Nuevo 112 C 5
Point Arena (CA.) 112 B 4
Point Arguello 113 E 8
Point au Fer Island 123 M 6

Point aux Barques 125 M 5
Point Baker 102 L 4
Pointblank (TX.) 123 H 5
Point Barrow 102 F 1
Point Brown 110 A 4
Point Buchon 113 E 7
Point Cabrillo 112 B 3
Point Calimere 174 C 5
Point Carmel 112 CD 6
Point Cloates 182 A 3
Point Conception 113 E 8
Point Culver 182 C 5
Point Delgada 112 A 2
Point D'Entrecasteaux 182 B 5
Pointe-à-Pitre 133 K 4
Pointe a la Hache (LA.) 123 O 6
Pointe aux E'cueils 105 M 4
Pointe aux Pins (MI.) 125 K 4
Pointe de Barfleur 152 C 2
Pointe de Grave 152 C 2
Pointe de la Coubre 152 C 2
Pointe de l'Est 105 P 6
Pointe de Penmarch 152 BC 2
Pointe de Saint-Gildas 152 C 2
Pointe de Saint-Mathieu 152 BC 2
Pointe des Monts 105 O 6
Pointe du Croisic 152 C 2
Pointe du Raz 152 BC 2
Pointe Louis-XIV 105 L 5
Pointe Noire 197 G 6
Point Estero 113 D 7
Point Harbor (N.C.) 129 Q 5
Point Hope 102 D 2
Point Imperial 116 E 1
Point Kadami 198 E 4
Point Lake 103 P 2
Point Marion (PA.) 125 P 10
Point of Rocks (WY.) 111 R 9
Point Piedras Blancas 113 D 7
Point Pleasant (N.J.) 127 EF 8
Point Pleasant (W.V.) 129 J 3
Point Reyes 112 B 5
Point Reyes National Seashore
   112 BC 4
Point Saint George 112 A 1
Point Sal 113 E 8
Points of Rocks (MD.) 129 O 2
Point Stuart 182 E 1
Point Sur 112 D 6
Poissonnier Point 182 B 2
Poitiers 152 D 2
Poitou 152 CD 2
Poitou, Plaines et seeuil du 152 D 2
Poivre Islands 199 J 6
Pojeierze Pomorskie 149 G 4
Pojezierze Mazurskie 149 H 4
Pojoaque (N.M.) 117 K 2
Pokaran 174 B 2
Pokegama Lake 119 P 3
Pokhara 174 D 2
Pokhodsk 171 TU 2
Pokhvistnevo 158 K 5
Poko 198 D 4
Pokontopugol 159 Q 3
Pokrovsk 171 N 3
Pokrovskoye 155 E 1
Polacca (AZ.) 116 F 2
Pola de Siero 152 B 3
Poland 149 G 4
Poland (N.Y.) 126 D 5
Polaris (MT.) 111 MN 5
Polar Plateau 203
Polatlı 155 D 3
Polcura 143 B 6
Polei Monu 175 J 5
Pole Mountain 118 C 9
Pole of Inaccessibility 203
Polesie Lubelskie 149 H 4
Polessk 151 H 5
Polesskoye 151 J 5
Polevskoy 159 M 4
Polewali 177 E 4
Polgovskoye 159 N 4
Pólgyo 173 J 4
Poli 197 G 4
Policastro, Golfo di 153 G 4
Policoro 153 G 3
Poligus 170 F 3
Polillo Islands 177 J 1
Polillo Strait 177 J 1
Pólis 155 D 3
Pólis (Cyprus) 156 A 2
Polist' 151 K 4
Polistena 153 G 4
Poliyiros 154 B 2
Polk (NE.) 120 H 1
Polk City (FL.) 131 N 6
Pollachi 174 C 5
Pollensa 152 D 4
Pollock (ID.) 110 J 5
Pollock (SD.) 118 H 5
Polnovat 159 N 3
Polo (IL.) 124 E 8
Polo (MO.) 121 LM 3
Pologi 155 E 1
Polonio, Cabo 142 F 5
Polonnaruwa 174 D 6
Polonnoye 151 J 5
Polotsk 151 J 4

Polousnyy, Kryazh 171 PQ 2
Polovniki 158 K 3
Polska 149 G 4
Polson (MT.) 111 L 3
Poltava 158 F 6
Poltavka 159 O 5
Põltsamaa 151 J 4
Polunochnoye 159 MN 3
Poluostrov Buzachi 168 E 1–2
Poluostrov Govena 171 V 4
Poluostrov Gusinaya Zemlya 158 JK 1
Poluostrov Kamchatka 171 T 4–5
Poluostrov Kanin 158 HJ 2
Poluostrov Karchyk 171 V 2
Poluostrov Kol'skiy 158 G 2
Poluostrov Koni 171 S 4
Poluostrov Mamonta 170 C 1
Poluostrov Mangyshlak 168 E 2
Poluostrov Pyagina 171 S 4
Poluostrov Rybachiy 150 K 2
Poluostrov Shirokostan 171 PQ 1
Poluostrov Shmidta 171 Q 5
Poluostrov Taygonos 171 U 3
Poluostrov Taymyr 170 K 5
Poluostrov Yamal 159 NO 1
Polūr (Iran) 157 F 2
Polūr (Iran) 157 F 2
Poluy 159 N 2
Polvijärvi 150 J 3
Pol'yanovo 159 N 3
Polyarnik 102 B 2
Polyarnyy (Kamchatka, U.S.S.R.)
   171 R 1
Polyarnyy (Kola Pen., U.S.S.R.)
   150 K 2
Polyarnyy Ural 159 MN 2
Polynesia 187 EG 2–4
Poman 142 C 4
Pombal (Bahía, Brazil) 141 J 3
Pombal (Paraíba, Brazil) 141 J 2
Pombal (Portugal) 152 B 4
Pomerania 149 FG 4
Pomeroy (OH.) 129 K 2
Pomeroy (TX.) 117 P 2
Pomeroy (WA.) 110 H 4
Pomio 186 B 3
Pomme de Terre Lake 121 M 5
Pomme de Terre River 121 M 5
Pommersche Bucht 149 F 4
Pomona (CA.) 113 H 8
Pomona (KS.) 121 K 4
Pomona (MO.) 121 N 5
Pomona Lake 121 K 4
Pomorie 154 C 2
Pomoshnaya 154 D 1
Pomozdino 158 K 3
Pompano Beach (FL.) 131 O 8
Pompei 153 F 3
Pompeyevka 171 O 6
Pompeys Pillar (MT.) 111 S 5
Pompton Lakes (N.J.) 127 E 7
Ponape 186 B 2
Ponca (NE.) 119 M 8
Ponca City (OK.) 120 HJ 6
Ponce 133 J 4
Ponce (P.R.) 130 C 8
Ponce de Leon (FL.) 131 J 4
Ponce de Leon Bay 131 N 9
Poncha Springs (CO.) 115 LM 5
Ponchatoula (LA.) 123 N 5
Pond (CA.) 113 F 7
Pond Creek (OK.) 120 H 6
Pondicherry 174 CD 5
Pondosa (CA.) 112 D 1
Ponente, Rivera di 153 E 3
Ponérihouen 185 J 6
Ponferrada 152 B 3
Pongkolaero 177 F 5
Pongo 198 D 3
Pongola 201 E 5
Pongo Manserichi 138 C 4
Ponnani 174 C 5
Ponnyadaung Range 175 F 3
Ponomarevka 158 KL 5
Ponoy 158 G 2
Ponoy 158 H 2
Pons (France) 152 C 2
Pons (Spain) 152 D 3
Ponta da Baleia 141 J 4
Ponta das Salinas 200 A 2
Ponta Delgada 192 A 1
Ponta de Mutá 141 J 3
Ponta do Manguinho 141 J 3
Ponta do Padrão 200 A 1
Ponta Grossa 142 F 4
Ponta Porã 141 E 5
Pontant 143 D 6
Pontarlier 153 E 2
Pontassieve 153 F 3
Pont-Audemer 152 D 2
Pontchartrain, Lake 123 N 5
Pontchâteau 152 C 2
Pont de Suert 152 D 3
Ponte de Pedra 140 E 3
Ponte do Lima 152 B 3
Ponte Nova 141 H 5
Pontes-e-Lacerda 140 E 4
Pontevedra 152 B 3
Pontiac (IL.) 124 F 9
Pontiac (MI.) 125 L 7

Pontianak 176 C 4
Pontine Mountains 155 F 2
Pont-l'Abbé 152 C 2
Pontotoc (MS.) 121 QR 8
Pontotoc (TX.) 122 DE 5
Pontremoli 153 E 3
Pony (MT.) 111 O 5
Ponza 153 F 3
Ponzari 158 H 5
Ponziane, Isola 153 F 3
Poochera 182 E 5
Pool 197 H 6
Poole 148 C 4
Pool Maleb 198 B 5
Poona 174 B 4
Poopó 140 C 4
Poopó, Lago de 140 C 4
Poorman 102 F 3
Popacatepetl, Volcan 132 C 4
Popar Hill 104 J 5
Popa Taung 175 G 3
Popayán 138 C 3
Pope (MS.) 121 PQ 8
Pope Valley (CA.) 112 C 4
Poperechnoye 170 FH 1
Popigay 170 J 1
Popigay 170 K 1
Poplar (MT.) 118 BC 2
Poplar (WI.) 124 C 3
Poplar Bluff (MO.) 121 P 6
Poplar River 118 C 2
Poplarville (MS.) 130 E 4
Popokabaka 198 B 6
Popondetta 184 E 3
Popovo 154 C 2
Poprad 149 H 5
Poptún 132 E 4
Poquis 140 C 5
Porahat 174 E 3
Porangatu 141 G 3
Porbandar 174 A 3
Porcuna 152 C 4
Porcupine (AK.) 102 J 2
Porcupine (SD.) 118 F 7
Porcupine Plain 102 K 2
Pordenone 153 F 2
Poretta 153 E 3
Pórfido, Punta 143 D 7
Pori (Björneborg) 150 H 3
Porirua 185 R 9
Porjus 150 H 2
Porkhov 151 J 4
Porkkala 151 H 4
Porlamar 139 F 1
Pornic 152 C 2
Porog 158 G 3
Porog 158 L 3
Porog Bol'shoy 170 H 1
Poronaysk 171 Q 6
Porosozero 150 K 3
Porphyry Peak 111 Q 3
Porpoise Bay 203
Porrentruy 153 E 2
Porsangen 150 J 1
Porsangerhalvøya 150 HJ 1
Porsgrunn 151 EF 4
Porsuk 154 D 3
Porsuk Barajı 154 D 3
Portachuelo 140 D 4
Portadown 148 B 4
Portage (MI.) 124 J 7
Portage (MT.) 111 O 3
Portage (UT.) 114 E 2
Portage (WI.) 124 E 6
Portage la-Prairie 103 S 5
Portageville (MO.) 121 Q 6
Portageville (N.Y.) 125 Q 7
Portal (AZ.) 116 G 6
Portal (ND.) 118 F 1
Port Alberni 103 N 6
Portalegre 152 B 4
Portales (N.M.) 117 N 3
Port Alfred 200 D 6
Port Alice 103 M 5
Port Allegany (PA.) 125 Q 8
Port Allen (LA.) 123 M 5
Port Angeles (WA.) 110 B 2
Port Antonio 133 G 4
Port Arthur (Tasmania, Austr.) 184 L 9
Port Arthur (TX.) 123 K 6
Port Arthur → Lüshun 173 H 3
Port Augusta 183 F 5
Port au Prince 133 H 4
Port Austin (MI.) 125 L 5
Port-Bergé-Vao Vao 201 J 4
Port Blair 175 F 5
Port Blandford 105 R 6
Port Bolivar (TX.) 123 J 6
Port-Bou 152 D 3
Port Burwell 105 P 3
Port-Cartier 105 O 5
Port Chalmers 185 Q 10
Port Charlotte (FL.) 131 M 8
Port Chilkoot 109 L 4
Port Clarence 108 Z 2
Port Clements 109 N 4
Port Clinton (OH.) 125 L 8
Port Darwin (Falkland Is., U.K.) 143 E 9

Port Darwin (N.T., Austr.) 182 E 1
Port Davey 184 L 9
Port Douglas 183 H 2
Port Edward 200 DE 6
Port Edwards (WI.) 124 E 5
Porteira 139 G 4
Portel 139 H 4
Portel 152 B 4
Port Elgin 105 L 7
Port Elizabeth 200 D 6
Port Ellen 148 B 3
Porter (WA.) 110 B 4
Porterville (CA.) 112 FG 6
Porterville (MS.) 130 F 2
Portes d'Enfer 198 D 6
Port Étienne → Nouadhibou 192 B 4
Port Fairy 183 G 6
Port Gamble (WA.) 110 C 3
Port Gentil 197 F 6
Port Gibson (MS.) 130 CD 3
Port Graham 102 G 4
Port Harcourt 197 F 5
Port Hardy 103 M 5
Port Hawkesbury 105 P 6
Port Hedland 182 B 3
Port Heiden 102 F 4
Port Henry (N.Y.) 126 F 4
Porthill (ID.) 110 J 2
Port Hope (MI.) 125 M 6
Port Hope Simpson 105 QR 5
Port Hueneme (CA.) 113 F 8
Port Huron (MI.) 125 M 6–7
Portile de Fier 154 B 2
Portimão 152 B 4
Portis (KS.) 120 G 3
Port Isabel (TX.) 122 F 9
Portiţa 154 C 2
Port Jackson 185 R 8
Port Jefferson (N.Y.) 127 F 8
Port Jervis (N.Y.) 127 E 7
Port Katon 155 E 1
Port Keats 182 D 1
Port Láirge 148 B 4
Portland (IN.) 125 K 9
Portland (ME.) 126 J 5
Portland (MI.) 125 K 7
Portland (N.D.) 119 L 3
Portland (N.S.W., Austr.) 183 H 5
Portland (OR.) 110 C 5
Portland (TN.) 128 E 5
Portland (TX.) 122 F 8
Portland (Victoria, Austr.) 183 G 6
Portland, Cape 184 L 9
Portland Bill 148 C 4
Port-la-Nouvelle 152 D 3
Portlaoise 148 B 4
Port Lavaca (TX.) 122 G 7
Port Lincoln 183 F 5
Port Loko 196 B 4
Port-Louis (Guadeloupe) 133 K 4
Port-Louis (Mauritius) 201 K 6
Port Macquarie 183 J 5
Portmadoc 148 C 4
Port Mansfield (TX.) 122 F 9
Port Matilda (PA.) 125 Q 9
Port Mayaca (FL.) 131 O 8
Port Moller 102 E 5–6
Port Moresby 184 E 3
Port Moresby 186 A 3
Port Neches (TX.) 123 K 6
Port Nelson 103 T 4
Port Nelson 104 J 4
Portneuf Range 111 NO 8
Portneuf Reservoir 111 O 8
Portnyagino, Ozero 170 HJ 1
Port Nolloth 200 B 5
Port Norris (N.J.) 127 E 9
Port-Nouveau-Québec 105 O 4
Port of Ness 148 B 3

Port of Spain 139 F 1
Pôrto Grande 139 H 3
Portogruaro 153 F 2
Pôrto Jofre 140 E 4
Portola (CA.) 112 E 3
Pôrto Lucena 142 EF 4
Pörtom 150 H 3
Pôrto Mendes 141 F 5
Pôrto Murtinho 140 E 5
Pôrto Nacional 141 G 3
Porto Novo (Benin) 196 E 4
Porto Novo (India) 174 CD 5
Port Orange (FL.) 131 NO 5
Port Orchard (WA.) 110 C 3
Port Orford (OR.) 110 A 8
Pôrto Santana 139 H 3
Pôrto Santo 192 B 3
Porto Santo Stefano 153 F 3
Pôrto São José 141 F 5
Pôrto Seguro 141 J 4
Porto Tolle 153 F 3
Porto Torres 153 E 3
Pôrto União 142 F 4
Pôrto Valter 138 D 5
Porto-Vecchio 153 E 3
Pôrto Velho 139 F 3
Portoviejo 138 BC 4
Port Pegasus 184 P 10
Port Phillip Bay 183 GH 6
Port Pirie 183 F 5
Port Radium 103 O 2
Portree 148 B 3
Port Royal (PA.) 127 B 8
Port Royal (VA.) 129 O 3
Port Royal Sound 129 L 9
Port Said (Egypt) 156 A 3
Port Saint Joe (FL.) 131 J 5
Port Saint Johns 200 DE 6
Port Sanilac (MI.) 125 M 6
Port Saunders 105 Q 5
Port Shepstone 200 DE 6
Port Simpson 102 LM 5
Portsmouth (N.H.) 126 J 5
Portsmouth (OH.) 128 HJ 3
Portsmouth (U.K.) 148 C 4
Portsmouth (VA.) 129 P 5
Portsmouth Island 129 PQ 6
Port Sudan → Bur Sudan 194 F 5
Port Sulphur (LA.) 123 O 6
Port Talbot 148 C 4
Porttipahdan tekojärvi 150 J 2
Port Townsend (WA.) 110 C 2
Portugal 152 B 3
Portugalete 152 C 3
Port Victoria 198 E 4–5
Portville (N.Y.) 125 Q 7
Port Wakefield 109 H 4
Port Wakefield 183 F 5
Port Washinton (WI.) 124 G 6
Port Wing (WI.) 124 C 3
Porum (OK.) 121 K 7
Porvenir 143 BC 9
Porvoo 151 J 3
Posadas 142 E 4
Poschiavo 153 F 2
Posen (MI.) 125 KL 4
Posht-e Badam 168 F 4
Posht-e Badam (Iran) 157 G 2
Posio 150 J 2
Positos 140 D 5
Poso 177 F 4
Posof 155 F 2
Pospelikha 159 Q 5
Pos Poluy 159 N 2
Posse 141 G 3
Possel 198 B 3
Possesion 200 AB 5
Possum Kingdom Lake 122 E 2
Post (OR.) 110 E 6
Post (TX.) 117 P 4
Postavy 151 J 4
Post Bobonazo 138 C 4
Post Creek (MT.) 111 L 3
Poste Maurice Cortier 193 F 4
Poste Weygand 192 EF 4
Post Falls (ID.) 110 J 3
Postmasburg 200 C 5
Pôsto Alto Manissauá 141 F 3
Posto Cunambo 138 C 4
Postojna 153 F 2
Poston (S.C.) 129 M 8
Postville (IA.) 119 R 7
Postville (Newfoundl., Can.) 105 Q 5
Potapovo 159 R 2
Potato Creek (SD.) 118 G 7
Potawatomi Indian Reservation 120 J 3
Potchefstroom 200 D 5
Poteau (OK.) 121 L 7
Poteet (TX.) 122 E 6
Potenza 153 G 3
Potes 152 C 3
Potgietersrus 200 D 4
Poth (TX.) 122 E 6
Potholes Reservoir 110 F 3
Poti (Brazil) 141 H 2
Poti (Gruziya, U.S.S.R.) 155 F 2
Potiskum 197 G 3
Potlatch (ID.) 110 J 4
Pot Mountain 111 K 4

Potnarhvin 185 J 5
Potomac (IL.) 124 G 9
Potomac River 129 P 3
Potosi (Bolivia) 140 C 4
Potrerillos 142 C 4
Potsdam 149 F 4
Potsdam (N.Y.) 126 E 4
Potter (NE.) 118 E 9
Potter Valley (CA.) 112 B 3
Potts Camp (MS.) 121 Q 8
Pottstown (PA.) 127 D 8
Pottsville (PA.) 127 C 8
Pou Bia 175 H 4
Poughkeepsie (N.Y.) 126 F 7
Poulaphuca Reservoir 148 B 4
Pou Loi 175 H 3
Poulsbo (WA.) 110 C 3
Pou Miang 175 H 4
Pound (WI.) 124 F 4
Pou San 175 H 4
Pouso Alegre (Mato Grosso, Brazil) 140 E 3
Pouso Alegre (Minas Gerais, Brazil) 141 G 5
Povenets 158 F 3
Poverty Mountain 116 C 1
Povlen 154 A 2
Póvoa de Varzim 152 B 3
Povungnituk 105 M 3
Powassan 105 M 6
Poway (CA.) 113 H 10
Powderhorn (CO.) 115 KL 5
Powderly (TX.) 123 H 2
Powder River (MT.) 118 C 4
Powder River (OR.) 110 H 6
Powder River (WY.) 118 B 7
Powder River Pass 111 S 6
Powderville (MT.) 118 CD 5
Powder Wash (CO.) 115 J 3
Powell (WY.) 111 R 6
Powell, Lake 114 FG 6
Powell Butte (OR.) 110 D 6
Powell Creek 182 E 2
Powell River 103 N 6
Power (MT.) 111 O 3
Powers (MI.) 124 G 4
Powers (OR.) 110 AB 8
Powers Lake (ND.) 118 F 2
Powhatan (LA.) 123 K 4
Powhatan (VA.) 129 O 4
Powhatan Pt (OH.) 129 K 2
Poxoreu 141 F 4
Poya 185 J 6
Poyang, Lake 124 F 5
Pozanti 155 DE 3
Požarevac 154 B 2
Poza Rica de Hidalgo 132 C 3
Pozdeyevka 171 N 5
Pozega 154 AB 2
Pozharskoye 173 K 1
Poznan 149 G 4
Pozo Almonte 140 C 5
Pozo del Molle 142 D 5
Pozo del Tigre 140 D 5
Pozzuoli 153 F 3
Prabuty 149 G 4
Prachuap Khiri Khan 175 GH 5
Praděd 149 G 4
Pradera 138 C 3
Prades 152 D 3
Prado 141 J 4
Prague 149 FG 4
Prague (NE.) 120 J 1
Prague (OK.) 120 J 7
Praha → Prague 149 FG 4
Praia 196 B 7
Praia Albandão 142 F 5
Praia Azul 200 A 3
Prainha 139 H 4
Prainha 139 F 5
Praire (ID.) 111 K 7
Prairie City (OR.) 110 G 6
Prairie City (SD.) 118 F 5
Prairie Dog Creek 120 E 3
Prairie du Chien (WI.) 124 C 6
Prairie View (KS.) 120 F 3
Prairie View (TX.) 122 GH 5
Prairie Village (KS.) 121 L 4
Prakhon Chai 175 H 5
Prapat 176 A 3
Praslin 199 K 5
Prat 152 D 3
Prata 141 G 4
Pratapgarh 174 B 3
Prato 153 F 3
Pratt (KS.) 120 G 5
Prattville (AL.) 131 H 2
Praya 176 E 5
Prechistoye 158 F 4
Predgornoye 155 G 2
Predivinsk 170 F 4
Pregolya 151 H 1
Prek Kak 175 J 5
Premont (TX.) 122 E 8
Premuda 153 F 3
Prenjsi 154 B 2
Prentice (WI.) 124 D 4
Prentiss (MS.) 130 E 3

Prenzlau 149 F 4
Preobrazhenka 170 J 3
Prepansko jezero 154 B 2
Preparis 175 F 5
Preparis Nourth Channel 175 F 4
Preparis South Channel 175 F 5
Přerov 149 G 5
Presa de la Boquilla 106 EF 6
Presa Falcon 132 C 2
Presa Miguel Alemán 132 C 4
Presa Netzahualcyótl 132 D 4
Prescott (AR.) 121 M 9
Prescott (AZ.) 116 D 3
Presho (SD.) 118 HJ 7
Presidencia Roque Sáenz-Peña 142 D 4
Presidente Dutra 141 H 2
Presidente Epitácio 141 F 5
Presidente Murtinho 141 F 4
Presidente Prudente 141 F 5
Preslav 154 C 2
Presnogor'kovka 159 N 5
Presnovka 159 N 5
Prešov 149 H 5
Presque Isle (ME.) 126 L 2
Presque Isle (MI.) 125 KL 4
Presque Isle (WI.) 124 E 3
Prestea 196 D 4
Preston (GA.) 131 K 2
Preston (ID.) 111 O 8
Preston (KS.) 120 G 5
Preston (MN.) 119 QR 7
Preston (NV.) 112 KL 4
Preston (U.K.) 148 C 4
Prestonsburg (KY.) 128 HJ 4
Prestwick 148 C 3
Prêto 141 G 4
Prêto do Igapó Açu 139 F 4
Pretoria 200 D 5
Prettyboy Reservoir 129 P 2
Pretty Prairie (KS.) 120 G 5
Prévesa 154 B 3
Prewitt (N.M.) 116 HJ 2
Prewitt Reservoir 115 O 3
Prey Veng 175 J 5
Priangarskoye Plato 170 G 4
Priaral'skiye Karakumy, Peski 169 G 1
Priazovskaya Vozvyshennost' 155 E 1
Pribilof Islands 102 D 4
Priboj 154 A 2
Přibram 149 F 5
Pribrezhnyy, Khrebet 171 P 4
Price (UT.) 114 G 4MO
Prichard (AL.) 130 F 4
Prichernomorskaya Nizmennost' 155 D 1
Priddy (TX.) 122 E 4
Priekule 151 H 4
Priene 154 C 3
Prieska 200 C 5
Priest Lake 110 J 2
Priest Rapids Dam 110 F 4
Priest River (ID.) 110 J 2
Prievidza 149 G 5
Prijedor 153 G 3
Prikaspiyskaya Nizmennost 168 DE 1
Prikubanskaya Nizmennost' 155 E 1
Prilep 154 B 2
Priluki 158 H 3
Priluki 158 F 5
Primavera 203
Primeira Cruz 141 H 1
Primghar (IA.) 119 N 7
Primorsk 151 J 3
Primorsk 155 E 1
Primorskiy 155 E 1
Primorskiy Khrebet 170 HJ 5
Primorsko-Akhtarsk 155 E 1
Primorskoye 155 E 1
Primošten 153 G 3
Primrose Lake 103 Q 4–5
Prince (NV.) 112 L 5
Prince Albert 103 Q 5
Prince Albert (South Africa) 200 C 6
Prince Albert Mountains 203
Prince Albert National Park 103 Q 5
Prince Albert Peninsula 103 O 1
Prince Albert Road 200 C 6
Prince Albert Sound 103 OP 1
Prince Alfred, Cape 103 M 1
Prince Charles Island 105 M 2
Prince Charles Mountains 203
Prince-de-Galles, Cap 105 N 3
Prince Edward Island (Canada) 105 P 6
Prince Edward Islands (Antarctica) 203
Prince Frederik (MD.) 129 P 3
Prince George 103 N 5
Prince George (VA.) 129 O 4
Prince of Wales, Cape 102 D 2
Prince of Wales Island (AK.) 102 L 4
Prince of Wales Island (N.W.T., Can.) 103 S 1
Prince of Wales Island (Queensland, Austr.) 183 G 1
Prince of Wales Strait 103 O 1
Prince Patrick Island 202
Prince Rupert 102 L 5
Princess Anne (MD.) 129 Q 3
Princess Astrid Coast 203

Princess Charlotte Bay 183 G 1
Princess Martha Coast 203
Princess Ragnhild Coast 203
Princess Royal Island 102 M 5
Princeton (AR.) 121 N 8–9
Princeton (Br. Col., Can.) 103 N 6
Princeton (CA.) 112 D 3
Princeton (IL.) 124 E 8
Princeton (IN.) 128 D 3
Princeton (KY.) 128 D 4
Princeton (ME.) 126 M 3
Princeton (MI.) 124 G 3
Princeton (MN.) 119 P 5
Princeton (MO.) 121 M 2
Princeton (N.J.) 127 E 8
Princeton (OR.) 110 G 7
Prince William Sound 102 H 3
Príncipe 197 F 5
Príncipe da Beira 140 D 3
Prineville (OR.) 110 E 6
Prineville Reservoir 110 E 6
Pringle (SD.) 118 E 7
Pringle (TX.) 117 P 2
Priozersk 150 K 3
Pripet Marshes 151 J 5
Pripolyarnyy Ural 159 LM 3
Pripyat 151 J 5
Prirechnyy 150 K 2
Pristina 154 B 2
Pritchett (CO.) 115 OP 6
Pritzwalk 149 F 4
Privas 153 D 3
Privolzhskaya Vozvyshennost' 158 J 5
Privolzhskiy 168 D 1
Priyutnoye 155 F 1
Priyutovo 158 K 5
Prizren 154 B 2
Proberta (CA.) 112 C 2
Proctor (NV.) 112 L 2
Proctor (TX.) 122 E 3—4
Proctor Lake 122 E 3—4
Proddatur 174 C 3
Progreso 132 E 3
Progreso (TX.) 122 F 9
Prohod Vráška čuka 154 B 2
Prokhladnyy 155 F 2
Prokhorkino 159 P 4
Prokop'yevo 170 H 4
Prokop'yevsk 159 R 5
Prokuplje 154 B 2
Proletariy 151 K 4
Proletarskaya 155 F 1
Proletarskiy 158 G 5
Proliv Bussol' 171 S 6
Proliv Dmitriya Lapteva 171 Q 1
Proliv Fritsa 171 R 6
Proliv Karskiye Vorota 158–159 L 1
Proliv Kruzenshterna 171 S 6
Proliv Nevel'skogo 171 Q 5
Proliv Sannikova 171 PQ 1
Proliv Yugorskiy Shar 159 LM 2
Prome 175 G 4
Promissão, Reprêsa 141 G 5
Promontoire Portland 105 LM 4
Promontorio del Gargano 153 G 3
Promontory Mountains 114 E 2
Promontory Point (UT.) 114 E 2
Promyshlennaya 159 R 5
Pronto (NV.) 112 G 2
Prophetstown (IL.) 124 E 8
Propria 141 J 3
Propriano 153 E 3
Proserpine 183 H 3
Prosna 149 G 4
Prospect (OR.) 110 C 8
Prosper (TX.) 122 G 2
Prosperidad 177 G 2
Prosperity (WA.) 110 F 4
Prosser (WA.) 110 F 4
Prostějov 149 G 5
Prospikhino 170 G 4
Protection (KS.) 120 F 5
Protochnoye 159 N 3
Provadija 154 C 2
Provence 153 E 3
Providence (KY.) 128 D 4
Providence (R.I.) 126 H 7
Providence (Seychelles) 199 J 6
Providence, Cape 184 P 10
Providencia, Isla de 133 F 5
Providência, Serra da 140 D 3
Provideniya 102 C 3
Provincetown (MA.) 126 J 6
Provincias Vascongadas 152 C 3
Provins 152 D 2
Provo (SD.) 118 E 7
Provo (UT.) 114 F 3
Prozor 153 G 3
Prudhoe Bay 102 H 1
Pruess Lake 114 D 5
Pruszków 149 H 4
Prut 154 C 1
Pruzhany 151 H 5
Pryazha 158 F 3
Prydz Bay 203
Pryor (MT.) 111 R 5
Pryor(OK.) 121 K 6
Przemyśl 149 H 5
Przeworsk 149 H 4

Przheval'sk 169 K 2
Psará 154 C 3
Pshada 155 E 2
Pshino Ob 159 Q 4
Pshish 155 E 2
Pshish, Gora 155 F 2
Pskov 151 J 4
Pskovskoye Ozero 151 J 4
Ptich 151 J 5
Ptolemaïs (Greece) 154 B 2
Ptolemais → Tulmaythah (Libya) 193 K 2
Ptuj 153 G 2
Puako (HI.) 113 G 12
Puán 143 D 6
Pubei 172 E 6
Pucallpa 138 CD 5
Pucará 140 D 4
Pucheng 173 G 5
Pucheveem 171 W 2
Pucioasa 154 C 1
Puckett (MS.) 130 E 2
Pudasjärvi 150 J 2
Pudino 159 P 4
Pudozh158 G 3
Pudukkottai 174 C 5
Puebla 132 C 4
Puebla de Alcocer 152 BC 4
Pueblo (CO.) 115 N 5
Pueblo Hundido 142 C 4
Pueblo Mountain 110 G 8
Puelches 143 C 6
Puelén 143 C 6
Puente Alto 142 BC 5
Puente-Genil 152 C 4
Pueo Point 113 B 10
Pu'er 172 D 6
Puerca, Punta 130 D 8
Puerto Acosta 140 C 4
Puerto Adela 141 EF 5
Puerto Aisén 143 B 8
Puerto Alegre 140 D 3
Puerto Angel 132 C 4
Puerto Arista 132 D 4
Puerto Armuelles 138 B 2
Puerto Asis 138 C 3
Puerto Ayacucho 138 E 2
Puerto Baquerizo Moreno 138 B 6
Puerto Barrios 132 E 4
Puerto Bermúdez 140 B 3
Puerto Berrio 138 D 2
Puerto Boyacá 138 D 2
Puerto Caballas 140 A 3
Puerto Cabello 138 E 1
Puerto Cabezas 132 F 5
Puerto Carreño 138 E 2
Puerto Casade 140 E 5
Puerto Chicama 138 BC 5
Puerto Cisnes 143 B 7
Puertocito Indian Reservation 117 J 3
Puerto Coig 143 C 9
Puerto Colombia 138 C 1
Puerto Cortés 132 E 4
Puerto Cumarebo 138 E 1
Puerto de Contreras 152 C 4
Puerto del Escudo 152 C 3
Puerto del Madeiro 152 C 3
Puerto del Rosario 192 C 3
Puerto de Mazarrón 152 C 4
Puerto de Miravete 152 B 4
Puerto de Morata 152 C 3
Puerto de Pajares 152 B 3
Puerto de Perales 152 B 3
Puerto Deseado 143 C 8
Puerto de Somport 152 C 3
Puerto de Torre Miró 152 C 3
Puerto de Villatoro 152 B 3
Puerto Escondido 132 C 4
Puerto Esperanza 142 F 4
Puerto Estrella 138 D 1
Puerto Etén 138 BC 5
Puerto Grether 140 D 4
Puerto Guaraní 140 E 5
Puerto Harberton 143 C 9
Puerto Heath 140 C 3
Puerto Huitoto 138 D 3
Puerto Iguazu 142 EF 4
Puerto Juárez 132 E 3
Puerto la Concordia 138 D 3
Puerto la Cruz 139 F 1
Puerto la Paz 140 D 5
Puerto Leguizamo 138 D 4
Puerto Leigue 140 D 3
Puerto Lempira 132 F 4
Puerto Libertad 106 D 6
Puerto Limón 138 D 3
Puertollano 152 C 4
Puerto Lobos 143 C 7
Puerto López 138 D 1
Puerto Madero 132 D 5
Puerto Madryn 143 C 7
Puerto Magdalena 106 D 7
Puerto Maldonado 140 C 3
Puero Montt 143 B 7
Puerto Nariño 138 E 3
Puerto Natales 143 B 9
Puerto Nuevo 138 E 2
Puerto Ordaz 139 F 2
Puerto Padilla 140 B 3
Puerto Páez 138 E 2

Puerto Patillos 140 B 5
Puerto Patiño 140 C 4
Puerto Pinasco 140 E 5
Puerto Pirámides 143 D 7
Puerto Portillo 138 D 5
Puerto Plata 133 HJ 4
Puerto Princesa 177 E 2
Puerto Reyes 138 D 4
Puerto Rico 130 CD 8
Puerto Rico 131
Puerto Rico (Argentina) 142 F 4
Puerto Rico (Bolivia) 140 C 3
Puerto Rico (Colombia) 138 CD 3
Puerto Rico (U.S.A.) 133 J 4
Puerto Rico Trench 208 A 3
Puerto Rondón 138 D 2
Puerto Sastre 140 E 5
Puerto Siles 140 C 3
Puerto Suárez 140 E 4
Puerto Tejada 138 C 3
Puerto Umbría 138 C 3
Puerto Vallarta 132 AB 3
Puerto Varas 143 B 7
Puerto Verlarde 140 D 4
Puerto Victoria 138 D 5
Puerto Villamizar 138 D 2
Puerto Villazón 140 D 3
Puerto Visser 143 C 8
Puerto Wilches 138 D 2
Puerto Williams 143 C 10
Puerto Ybapobó 140 E 5
Pueyrredón, Lago 143 B 8
Pugachev 158 J 5
Pugal 174 B 2
Puget Sound 110 C 3
Puigmal 152 D 3
Puig Mayor 152 D 4
Puisaye, Collines de la 152 D 2
Pujehun 196 B 4
Puka 154 AB 2
Pukapuka (Cook Is.) 186 DE 3
Pukapuka (French Polynesia) 187 F 3
Pukaruha 187 F 4
Pukaskwa National Park 104 K 6
Pukatawagan 103 R 4
Pukch'ŏng 173 J 2
Puketeraki Range 185 Q 9
Puksoozero 158 H 3
Pula 153 F 3
Pula, Capo di 153 E 4
Pulap 186 A 2
Pulaski (N.Y.) 126 C 5
Pulaski (TN.) 128 D 6
Pulaski (VA.) 129 L 4
Pulaski (WI.) 124 F 5
Pulau, Sungai 177 J 5
Pulau Adi 177 H 4
Pulau Alor 177 F 5
Pulau Alor 177 F 5
Pulau Ambon 177 G 4
Pulau Atauro 177 G 5
Pulau Babi 176 A 3
Pulau Bacan 177 G 4
Pulau Bangka 176 C 4
Pulau Bangkaru 176 A 3
Pulau Baso 176 B 4
Pulau Batam 176 B 3
Pulau Batanta 177 H 4
Pulau Bawean 176 D 5
Pulau Belitung 176 C 4
Pulau Bengkalis 176 B 3
Pulau Besar 177 F 5
Pulau Biak 177 J 4
Pulau Biaro 177 G 3
Pulau Binongko 177 F 5
Pulau Bintan 176 B 3
Pulau Boano 177 G 4
Pulau Breueh 176 A 2
Pulau Buru 177 G 4
Pulau Butung 177 F 4
Pulau Damar (L. Sunda Is.) 177 G 5
Pulau Damar (Moluccas) 177 G 4
Pulau Enggano 176 B 5
Pulau Gag 177 H 4
Pulau Gebe 177 G 4
Pulau Jatisiri 176 E 4
Pulau Jemaja 176 C 3
Pulau Jos Sodarso 177 J 5
Pulau Kabaena 177 F 5
Pulau Kai Besar 177 H 5
Pulau Kai Kecil 177 H 5
Pulau Kalao 177 F 5
Pulau Kalaotoa 177 F 5
Pulau Kalukalukuang 176 E 5
Pulau Karakelong 177 G 3
Pulau Karimata 176 C 4
Pulau Karimunjawa 176 D 5
Pulau Kasiruta 177 G 4
Pulau Kawalusu 177 F 3
Pulau Kayoa 177 G 3
Pulau Kelang 177 G 4
Pulau Kisar 177 G 5
Pulau Kobroor 177 H 5
Pulau Kofiau 177 GH 4
Pulau Komodo 177 E 5
Pulau Komoran 177 J 5
Pulau Komoran 184 C 3
Pulau Kundur 176 B 3
Pulau Labengke 177 F 4

Pulau Lasia 176 A 3
Pulau Laut 176 E 4
Pulau Lepar 176 C 4
Pulau Lingga 176 B 4
Pulau Lomblen 177 F 5
Pulau Madura 176 D 5
Pulau Makian 177 G 3
Pulau Mandioli 177 G 4
Pulau Mangole 177 G 4
Pulau Manipa 177 G 4
Pulau Manui 177 F 4
Pulau Mao 177 G 5
Pulau Masalembo 176 D 5
Pulau Masela 177 GH 5
Pulau Maya 176 C 4
Pulau Mega 176 B 4
Pulau Midai 176 C 3
Pulau Misool 177 H 4
Pulau Morotai 177 G 3
Pulau Moyo 176 E 5
Pulau Muna 177 F 5
Pulau Mursala 176 A 3
Pulau Nias 176 A 3
Pulau Nila 177 G 5
Pulau Num 177 J 4
Pulau Numfor 177 H 4
Pulau Obi 177 G 4
Pulau Padang 176 B 3
Pulau Panaitan 176 B 5
Pulau Pantar 177 F 5
Pulau Pejantan 176 C 3
Pulau Peleng 177 F 4
Pulau Pemarung 176 E 4
Pulau Penida 176 E 5
Pulau Pinang 176 B 2
Pulau Pini 176 A 3
Pulau Rakata 176 C 5
Pulau Rangsang 176 B 3
Pulau Rinja 177 E 5
Pulau Romang 177 G 5
Pulau Roti 177 F 6
Pulau Rupat 176 B 3
Pulau Salawati 177 H 4
Pulau Samosir 176 A 3
Pulau Sanana 177 G 4
Pulau Sanding 176 B 4
Pulau Sangeang 177 E 5
Pulau Sangihe 177 G 3
Pulau Sawu 177 F 6
Pulau Sayang 177 G 3
Pulau Sebanka 176 BC 3
Pulau Sebatik 176–177 E 3
Pulau Sebuku 176 E 4
Pulau Selaru 177 H 5
Pulau Selatan 176 B 4
Pulau Selayar 177 F 5
Pulau Semau 177 F 6
Pulau Sepanjang 176 E 5
Pulau Serasan 176 C 3
Pulau Sermata 177 G 5
Pulau Siberut 176 A 4
Pulau Sibutu 177 E 3
Pulau Simeulue 176 A 3
Pulau Simuk 176 A 3
Pulau Singkep 176 B 4
Pulau Sipora 176 A 4
Pulau Subi 176 C 3
Pulau Supiori 177 J 4
Pulau Tahulandang 177 FG 3
Pulau Taliabu 177 FG 4
Pulau Tanahbala 176 A 4
Pulau Tanahjampea 177 F 5
Pulau Tanahmasa 176 A 4
Pulau Tebingtinggi 176 B 3
Pulau Terentang 176 E 4
Pulau Trangan 177 H 5
Pulau Tuangku 176 A 3
Pulau Tubelai 177 G 4
Pulau Utara 176 B 4
Pulau Waigeo 177 H 4
Pulau Wangiwangi 177 F 5
Pulau Weh 176 A 2
Pulau Wetar 177 G 5
Pulau Wokam 177 H 5
Pulau Workai 177 HJ 5
Pulau Wowoni 177 F 4
Pulau Yamdena 177 H 5
Pulau Yapen 177 J 4
Puławy 149 H 4
Pulicat 174 D 5
Pulkkila 150 J 3
Pullman (WA.) 110 H 4
Pulo Anna 177 J 1
Pulog, Mount 177 J 1
Pulonga 158 H 2
Pulozero 150 K 2
Pułtusk 149 H 4
Pulusuk 186 A 2
Puluwat 186 A 2
Puma Yumco 175 F 2
Pumpkin Buttes 118 C 7
Pumpville (TX.) 117 P 8
Puná, Isla 138 B 4
Puna de Atacama 140 C 5–6
Punakha 174 E 2
Punaluu (HI.) 113 G 12
Puncak Jaya 177 J 4
Puncak Trikora 177 J 4
Punda Milia 201 E 4
Punduga 158 H 3

Pune 174 B 4
Pungo Lake 129 P 6
Punia 198 D 5
Puning 172 G 6
Punjab 174 BC 1
Punkaharju 150 J 3
Puno 140 B 4
Punta, Cerro de 133 J 4
Punta, Ninfas 143 D 7
Punta Alegre 133 G 3
Punta Almina 192 D 1
Punta Alta 143 D 6
Punta Angamos 140 B 5
Punta Arenas 130 D 8
Punta Arenas 143 B 9
Punta Ballenita 142 B 4
Punta Bermeja 143 D 7
Punta Borinquen 130 B 8
Punta Brea 130 C 9
Punta Burica 132 F 6
Punta Cachos 142 B 4
Punta Carreta 140 A 3
Punta Catalina 143 C 9
Punta Colorada 142 B 4
Punta de Arenas 143 C 9
Punta de Chilca 140 A 3
Punta de Europa 152 BC 4
Punta del Diamante 132 BC 4
Punta Delgada 143 D 7
Punta Delgado 143 C 9
Punta dell' Alice 153 G 4
Punta de Mata 139 F 2
Punta Desengaño 143 C 8
Punta Este 130 D 8
Punta Eugenia 106 C 6
Punta Falcone 153 E 3
Punta Fijo 138 D 1
Punta Galera 143 B 7
Punta Gallinas 138 D 1
Punta Gorda (Belize) 132 E 4
Punta Gorda (CA.) 112 A 2
Punta Gorda (FL.) 131 MN 8
Punta Gorda (Nicaragua) 132 F 5
Punta Gorda, Bàhia de 132 F 5
Punta Gruesa 140 B 5
Punta Guanajibo 130 B 8
Punta Guascama 132 C 3
Punta Guayanés 130 D 8
Punta Higüero 130 B 8
Punta Lachay 138 C 6
Punta Lavapié 143 B 6
Punta Lengua de Vaca 142 B 5
Punta Licosa 153 F 3
Punta Magdalena 138 C 3
Punta Maisí 133 H 3
Punta Mala 138 C 2
Punta Mariato 138 B 2
Punta Medanosa 143 CD 8
Punta Morro 142 B 4
Punta Negra 138 B 5
Punta Norte 143 E 6
Punta Ola Grande 130 C 9
Punta Palazzo 153 E 3
Punta Pariñas 138 B 4
Punta Pórfido 143 D 7
Punta Poro 142 E 4
Punta Prieta 106 D 6
Punta Puerca 130 D 8
Punta Rasa 143 D 7
Punta Rieles 140 E 5
Punta Roja 143 CD 7
Punta Rotja 152 D 4
Punta Sarga 192 B 4
Punta Stilo 153 G 4
Punta Sur 143 E 6
Punta Topocalma 142 B 5
Punta Verde 132 F 5
Punto, Cerro de 130 C 8
Punxsutawney (PA.) 125 P 9
Puolanka 150 J 3
Puolo Point 113 C 10
Puper 177 H 4
Puqi 172 F 5
Puquio 140 B 3
Puquios 142 C 4
Pur 159 P 2
Pura 170 E 1
Pura 170 E 1
Puracé 138 C 3
Purcell (OK.) 120 H 7
Purcell Mountains (Br. Col., Can.)
  103 O 5
Purcell Mount (MT.) 111 K 2
Purdum (NE.) 118 E 3
Purdy (OK.) 120 H 8
Purdy Islands 184 E 2
Purdy Islands 186 A 3
Purgatoire Peak 115 M 6
Purgatoire River 115 O 6
Puri 174 E 4
Puri 200 B 1
Purificación 138 D 3
Purikari Neem 151 J 4
Purinskoye, Ozero 170 E 1
Purisima Point 113 E 8
Purna 174 C 3
Purnea 174 E 2
Pursat 175 H 5
Purtuniq 105 N 3

Purukcahu 176 D 4
Purulia 174 E 3
Purus 139 F 4
Puruvesi 150 J 3
Purvis (MS.) 130 E 3
Purwakarta 176 C 5
Pusan 173 J 3
Pushchino 171 T 5
Pushkin 151 K 4
Pushkino 158 J 5
Pusht-i-Rud 169 G 4
Pusteci 154 B 2
Pustoretsk 171 U 3
Pustoshka 151 J 4
Puszcza Notecka 149 G 4
Putao 175 G 2
Putian 173 G 5
Putina 140 C 3
Put-in-Bay (OH.) 125 LM 8
Puting, Tanjung 176 D 4
Putla de Guerrero 132 C 4
Putnam (CT.) 126 GH 7
Putnam (OK.) 120 FG 7
Putnam (TX.) 122 D 3
Putney (S.D.) 119 K 5
Putnok 154 B 1
Putorana, Gory 170 FH 2
Puttalam 174 C 6
Puttgarden 149 F 4
Putumayo 138 D 4
Putussibau 176 D 3
Puuanahulu (HI.) 113 G 12
Puukolii (HI.) 113 F 11
Puulavesi 150 J 3
Puu o Keokeo 113 G 12
Puuwai (HI.) 113 B 10
Puxico (MO.) 121 P 6
Puyallup (WA.) 110 C 3
Puyang 172 G 3
Puy Crapaud 152 C 2
Puy de Dôme 152 D 2
Puy de Sancy 152 D 2
Puyo 138 C 4
Puzla 168 K 3
Pwani 199 F 6
Pweto 198 D 6
Pwllheli 148 C 4
Pyagina, Poluostrov 171 S 4
Pyakupur 159 P 2–3
Pyal'ma 158 F 3
Pyaozero, Ozero 150 K 2
Pyapon 175 G 4
Pyasina 170 E 1
Pyasino, Ozero 159 R 2
Pyatigorsk 155 F 2
Pyatigory 158 B 2
Pyatikhatki 155 D 1
Pyatistennoy 171 TU 2
Pyat'kovende, Gora 171 T 2
Pyawbwe 175 G 3
Pygmalion Point 175 F 6
Pyhäjärvi 150 J 3
Pyhäjärvi 151 H 3
Pyhäjoki 150 HJ 3
Pyhäntä 150 J 3
Pyhäselkä 150 JK 3
Pyhätunturi 150 J 2
Pyinmana 175 G 4
Pyl'karamo 159 Q 3
Pym 159 O 3
Pymatuning Reservoir 125 O 8
Pymta 171 T 5
P'yönggang 173 J 3
P'yöngyang 173 HJ 3
Pyramid Head 113 G 10
Pyramid Lake 112 F 2–3
Pyramid Lake Indian Reservation
  112 F 2
Pyramids 194 E 3
Pyrénées 152 CD 3
Pyshchug 158 H 4
Pytalovo 151 J 4
Pyu 175 G 4

Q

Qābis 193 H 2
Qābis, Khalīj 193 H 2
Qabr Hūd 195 H 5
Qaderābād (Iran) 157 F 3
Qādir Karam (Iraq) 157 D 2
Qādub 199 J 2
Qā'emshahr (Iran) 157 F 1
Qafşah 193 G 2
Qagan (Nei Monggul Zizhiqu, China)
  170 L 6
Qagan Nur (Nei Monggul Zizhiqu, Chi-
  na) 172 F 2
Qagan Nur (Qinghai, China) 172 C 3
Qagan Tohoi 172 B 3
Qagcaka 174 D 1
Qahar Youyi Houqi 172 F 2
Qahar Youyi Qianqi 172 F 2
Qahremānshahr (Iran) 157 E 2
Qaidam He 172 C 3
Qaidam Pendi 172 BC 3

Qala'an Naḥl 194 E 6
Qala-Nau 169 G 4
Qālat 169 H 4
Qal'at Abū Ghār (Iraq) 157 DE 3
Qal'at al Akhdar (Saudi Arabia) 156 B 4
Qal 'at al Husn (Syria) 156 B 2
Qal 'at al Marqab (Syria) 156 B 2
Qal'at al Mu'azam (Saudi Arabia)
  156 BC 4
Qal'at Bīshah 195 G 4
Qal' at Dīzah (Iraq) 157 D 1
Qal'at Şāliḥ (Iraq) 157 E 3
Qal 'at Sukkar (Iraq) 157 E 3
Qal'eh (Iran) 157 G 1
Qal'eh Asgar (Iran) 157 G 3
Qal'eh-ye Now (Iran) 157 E 2
Qalīb ash Shuyūkh (Kuwait) 157 E 3
Qallābāt 194 F 6
Qamalung 172 C 4
Qamar, Ghubbat al 195 J 5
Qamata 200 D 6
Qamdo 172 C 4
Qamīnis 193 J 2
Qamsar (Iran) 157 F 2
Qanāt as Suways (Egypt) 156 A 3
Qandala 199 H 2
Qapqal 169 L 2
Qaqortoq 105 S 3
Qarā', Jabal 195 J 5
Qārah 194 D 3
Qarah Dāgh (Iraq) 156 D 1
Qarānqū 168 D 3
Qar'at al Ashkal 153 E 4
Qara Tarai 169 H 4
Qārat Dalmā' 193 K 3
Qārawah (Saudi Arabia) 157 E 3
Qardo 199 H 3
Qareh Āghāj (Iran) 157 E 1
Qareh Sū (Iran) 157 G 1
Qarhan 172 B 3
Qarnayn (United Arab Emirates) 157 F 4
Qarqan He 169 M 3
Qarqannah, Juzur 193 H 2
Qarqi 169 M 2
Qārūn, Birkat 194 E 3
Qar Wagēr 199 H 2
Qaryat al Gharab (Iraq) 157 D 3
Qaryat al 'Ulyā (Saudi Arabia)
  157 E 4
Qasa Murg 169 G 4
Qaşr Aḥmad 193 J 2
Qaşr al Azraq (Jordan) 156 B 3
Qaşr al Ḥayr (Syria) 156 BC 2
Qaşr al Khūbbaz (Iraq) 156 D 2
Qaşr Āmij (Iraq) 156 C 2
Qaşr aş Şabīyah (Kuwait) 157 E 3
Qaşr bū Hādī 193 J 2
Qasr Burqu' (Jordan) 156 BC 2
Qasr-e Qand 169 G 5
Qasr-e Shīrīn (Iran) 157 DE 2
Qaşr Farāfirah 194 D 3
Qaşr Ḥamām 195 H 4
Qatar 157 F 4
Qatif (Saudi Arabia) 157 E 4
Qatlīsh 168 F 3
Qatrūyeh (Iran) 157 G 3
Qattara Depression 194 D 3
Qawām al Hamzah (Iraq) 157 D 3
Qawz Abū ulū' 194 E 5
Qawz Rajab 194 F 5
Qāyen 168 F 4
Qaysān 194 E 6
Qayyārah (Iraq) 156 D 2
Qazvīn (Iran) 157 F 1
Qeshm (Iran) 157 G 4
Qeshm (Iran) 157 G 4
Qeydār (Iran) 157 E 1
Qeydū (Iran) 157 F 2
Qeys (Iran) 157 F 4
Qezel Owzan (Iran) 157 E 1
Qezi'ot (Israel) 156 B 3
Qian'an 173 H 1
Qian Gorlos 173 H 2
Qianjiang 172 E 5
Qianning 172 D 4
Qian Shan 173 H 2–3
Qianwei 172 D 5
Qianxi 172 E 5
Qianyang 172 F 5
Qiaojia 172 D 5
Qiaowan 172 C 2
Qichun 172 G 4
Qidong 173 H 4
Qiemo 169 M 3
Qift (Egypt) 156 A 4
Qijiang 172 E 5
Qijiaojing 172 B 2
Qila Ladgasht 169 G 5
Qila Saifullah 169 H 4
Qilian 172 D 3
Qilian Shan 172 CD 3
Qimantag 172 B 3
Qimen 173 G 5
Qinā (Egypt) 156 A 4
Qina, Wādī (Egypt) 156 A 4
Qin'an 172 E 4
Qingchuan 172 E 4
Qingdao 173 H 3
Qinggang 173 J 1
Qinghai 172 C 3

Qinghai Hu 172 D 3
Qinghe 169 N 1
Qing He 172 E 3
Qing Jiang 172 F 4
Qingjiang (Jiangsu, China) 173 G 4
Qingjiang (Jiangxi, China) 172 G 5
Qinglong 172 DE 5
Qinglong (Hebei, China) 173 G 2
Qingshen 172 D 5
Qingshuihe 172 F 3
Qingxu 172 F 3
Qingyang 172 E 3
Qing Zang Gaoyuan 174 DE 1
Qinhuangdao 173 GH 3
Qinling Shan 172 EF 4
Qinliu 172 G 5
Qin Xian 172 F 3
Qinzhou 172 E 6
Qionghai 172 F 7
Qionglai 172 D 4
Qionglai Shan 172 D 4
Qiongshan 172 F 7
Qiongzhou Haixia 172 EF 6
Qiqihar 170 M 5
Qira 169 L 3
Qirdi (Saudi Arabia) 157 E 4
Qiryat Shemona (Israel) 156 B 2
Qiryat Yam (Israel) 156 B 2
Qiryat Gat (Israel) 156 B 3
Qirzah 193 H 2
Qishn 195 J 5
Qishrān 195 FG 4
Qitai 169 M 2
Qitaihe 173 K 1
Qitbit, Wādī 195 J 5
Qiyang 172 F 5
Qog Qi 172 E 2
Qog Ul 173 G 2
Qolleh-ye Damāvand (Iran) 157 F 2
Qoltag 172 A 2
Qom (Iran) 157 F 2
Qom (Iran) 157 F 2
Qomdo 172 C 4
Qomolangma Feng 174 E 2
Qomrūd (Iran) 157 F 2
Qomsheh (Iran) 157 F 2–3
Qonggyai 175 F 2
Qôrnoq 105 R 3
Qorveh (Iran) 157 E 2
Qoşbeh-ye Naşşār (Iran) 157 E 3
Qotbābād (Iran) 157 F 3
Qotbābād (Iran) 157 G 4
Qotur 168 C 3
Quaboin Reservoir 126 G 6
Quairading 182 B 5
Quajará 139 G 5
Quakertown (PA.) 127 D 8
Quanah (TX.) 122 D 1
Quan Dao Nam Du 175 H 6
Quang Ngai 175 J 4
Quang Tri 175 J 4
Quang Yen 175 J 3
Quan Long 175 J 4
Quan Phu Quoc 175 H 5
Quanshuigou 169 K 3
Quantico (VA.) 129 O 3
Quanzhou (Fujian, China) 173 G 6
Quanzhou (Guangxi Zhuangzu Zizhiqu,
  China) 172 F 5
Qu'Appelle 103 R 5
Quaraí 142 E 5
Quarryville (PA.) 127 C 9
Quartu Sant' Elena 153 E 4
Quartz Hill (CA.) 113 G 8
Quartz Mountain 110 C 7
Quartzsite (AZ.) 116 B 4
Quatro Ciénegas 132 B 2
Quay (N.M.) 117 N 3
Quayti 195 H 5
Qūchān 168 F 3
Queanbeyan 183 H 6
Québec (Canada) 105 N 5
Québec (Quebec, Can.) 105 N 6
Quebec (TX.) 117 M 7
Quebeck (TN.) 128 F 6
Quebracho 142 E 5
Quebracho Coto 142 D 4
Quebradillas (P.R.) 130 C 8
Quedal, Cabo 143 B 7
Queen, Cape 105 M 3
Queen Anne (MD.) 129 Q 3
Queen Charlotte Islands 102 KL 5
Queen Charlotte Sound 102 LM 5
Queen Charlotte Strait 102–103 M 5
Queen City (MO.) 121 N 2
Queen Elizabeth Islands 202
Queen Fabiola Mountains 203
Queen Mary Coast 203
Queen Maud Gulf 103 R 2
Queen Maud Land 203
Queen Maud Mountains 203
Queens Channel 182 D 1
Queensland 183 GH 3
Queenstown (New Zealand) 184 P 9
Queenstown (South Africa) 200 D 6
Queenstown (Tasmania, Austr.) 184 L 9

Queets (WA.) 110 A 3
Quehue 143 D 6
Queimada, Ilha 141 G 5
Queimadas 141 HJ 3
Quela 200 B 1
Quelimane 201 F 3
Quellón 143 B 7
Quemado (N.M.) 116 H 3
Quemado (TX.) 122 C 7
Quembo 200 B 2
Quemchi 143 B 7
Quemoy 173 G 6
Quemu Quemu 143 D 6
Quen Bess, Mount 103 N 5
Quequén 143 E 6
Querétaro 132 BC 3
Quesada 132 F 5
Queshan 172 F 4
Quesnel 103 N 5
Quesnel Lake 103 N 5
Questa (N.M.) 117 L 1
Quetena 140 C 5
Quetta 169 H 4
Quevedo 138 C 4
Quezaltenango 132 D 5
Quezon City 177 J 1
Quibala 200 B 2
Quibaxe 200 A 1
Quibdó 138 C 2
Quiberon 152 C 2
Quibilī 193 G 2
Quicabo 200 A 1
Quiçama National Park 200 A 1
Quiches 138 C 5
Quiculungo 200 B 1
Quienha 200 B 2
Quietus (MT.) 118 B 5
Quiha 199 F 2
Quihita 200 A 3
Quijotoa (AZ.) 116 D 5
Quila 106 E 7
Quilán, Cabo 143 B 7
Quilberry 183 H 4
Quilca 140 B 4
Quilco 143 D 6
Quilenda 200 A 2
Quilengues 200 A 2
Quilino 142 D 5
Quillabamba 140 B 3
Quillacollo 140 C 4
Quillagua 140 BC 5
Quillaicillo 142 B 5
Quillota 142 B 5
Quilon 174 C 6
Quilpie 183 H 4
Quimbele 200 B 1
Quimby (IA.) 119 N 8
Quimilí 142 D 4
Quimper 152 C 2
Quinault Indian Reservation 110 A 3
Quince Mil 140 B 3
Quincy (CA.) 112 DE 3
Quincy (FL.) 131 K 4
Quincy (IL.) 121 O 3
Quincy (MA.) 126 J 4
Quincy (WA.) 110 F 3
Quines 142 C 5
Quingey 153 E 2
Quinhagak 102 E 4
Qui Nhon 175 J 5
Quinlan (OK.) 120 FG 6
Quinn River 112 H 1
Quiñones 106 D 7
Quintanar de la Orden 152 C 4
Quintana Roo 132 E 3–4
Quinter (KS.) 120 E 3
Quinto 142 D 5
Quinton (OK.) 121 K 7
Quionga 201 G 2
Quipapá 141 J 2
Quipungo 200 A 2
Quirima 200 B 2
Quirinopólis 141 F 4
Quissanga 201 G 2
Quissico 201 EF 4
Quitaque (TX.) 117 P 3
Quitasueño, Banco 133 F 5
Quiterajo 201 G 2
Quitman (GA.) 131 L 4
Quitman (MS.) 130 F 2
Quitman (TX.) 123 H 3
Quitman Mountains 117 L 6–7
Quito 138 C 4
Quivero (AZ.) 116 D 2
Quivilla 138 C 5
Quixadá 141 J 1
Quixeramobim 141 J 2
Qujing 172 D 5
Qulansiyah 199 J 2
Qulaybiah 193 H 1
Qulbān Layyah (Iraq) 157 E 3
Qulin (MO.) 121 P 6
Qumarlēb 172 C 4
Qumarrabdūn 172 B 4
Qumbu 200 D 6
Qunayfidhah, Nafūd 195 GH 4
Qu'nyido 172 C 4
Quoich 103 T 3

Quorn 183 F 5
Qūr al Hulwāt (Saudi Arabia) 156 C 3
Qurdūd 194 D 6
Qurnat aṣ Ṣawdā' (Lebanon) 156 B 2
Qūs (Egypt) 156 A 4
Qusaybah (Iraq) 156 C 2
Quṣayr ad Daffah 193 K 2
Qusum 172 B 5
Qu Xian 173 G 5
Qūxū 175 F 2
Quyang 172 F 3
Quynh Luu 175 J 4
Qyteti Stalin 154 B 2

R

Raab 153 G 2
Raahe 150 H 3
Rääkkylä 150 J 3
Rab 153 F 3
Rába 154 A 1
Raba 177 E 5
Rabak 194 E 6
Rabal 177 HJ 5
Rabalou 152 D 4
Rabat (Malta) 153 F 4
Rabat (Morocco) 192 D 2
Rabaul 185 F 2
Rabaul 186 B 3
Rabbit Ears Pass 115 L 3
Rabiah (Iraq) 156 D 1
Rābigh 195 F 4
Rabka 149 H 5
Rabocheostrovsk 150 K 2
Rabyānah 193 K 4
Rabyānah, Ramlat 193 JK 4
Racconigi 153 E 3
Race, Cape 105 R 6
Raceland (LA.) 123 N 6
Race Point 126 J 6
Racepond (GA.) 131 M 3–4
Rachal (TX.) 122 E 9
Rach Gia 175 HJ 5–6
Rachid 192 C 5
Racine (WI.) 124 G 7
Raco (MI.) 125 K 3
Radā' 195 GH 6
Rădăuți 154 C 1
Radebeul 149 F 4
Radeče 153 G 2
Radekhov 151 HJ 5
Radersburg (MT.) 111 O 4
Radford (VA.) 129 L 4
Radhanpur 174 B 3
Radisson 105 M 5
Radium Springs (N.M.) 117 K 5
Radom 149 H 4
Radom (Sudan) 198 C 3
Radomir 154 B 2
Radomsko 149 G 4
Radöy 150 D 3
Radun 151 J 5
Radviliškis 151 H 4
Radville 103 R 6
Radwā, Jabal (Saudi Arabia) 156 BC 4
Radzyń Podlaski 149 H 4
Rae 103 O 3
Rae Bareli 174 D 2
Ra's-e Barkan (Iran) 157 E 3
Raeford (N.C.) 129 M 7
Ra's-e Nāy Band (Iran) 157 F 4
Raeside, Lake 182 C 4
Raevavae 187 F 4
Rāf, Jabal (Saudi Arabia) 156 C 3
Rafael, Cachoeira do 140 D 3
Rafaela 142 D 5
Rafah 156 B 3
Rafaï 198 C 3
Raffili Rapids 198 D 3
Rafḥā (Saudi Arabia) 156 D 3
Rafsanjān (Iran) 157 G 3
Raft River Mountains 114 D 2
Raga 198 D 3
Ragam 197 F 3
Ragan (WY.) 111 P 9
Ragang, Mount 177 F 2
Ragay Gulf 177 F 1
Ragged Island Range 133 G 3
Ragged Top Mountain 118 C 9
Ragland (N.M.) 117 N 3
Rago (KS.) 120 GH 5
Raha 177 F 4
Rahad al Bardī 194 C 6
Raḥāh, Ḥarrat ar 194 F 3
Rāhang (Iran) 157 E 2
Rahaṭ, Ḥarrat 195 G 4
Raheita 199 G 2
Rahib, Jabal 194 D 5
Rahimyar Khan 169 J 5
Raia 198 D 3
Raiatea 187 E 4
Raichur 174 C 4
Raiganj 174 E 2
Raigarh 174 D 3
Raimangal 174 E 3

Rainbow Bridge National Monument
  114 G 6
Rainbow Plateau 116 EF 1
Rainelle (W.V.) 129 L 4
Rainier, Mount 110 D 4
Rains (S.C.) 129 M 7
Rainy Lake (MN.) 119 P 2
Rainy Lake (Ontario, Can.) 104 J 6
Rainy River 119 OP 2
Raipur 174 D 3
Raisen 174 C 3
Raisio 151 H 3
Raiwind 169 J 4
Rajabasa 176 B 5
Rajada 141 H 2
Rajahmundry 174 D 4
Rajakoski 150 J 2
Rajang 176 D 3
Rajanpur 169 J 5
Rajapalaiyam 174 C 6
Rajapur 174 B 4
Rajasthan 174 BC 2
Rajasthan Canal 174 B 2
Rajgarh 174 C 2
Rajgarh 174 C 3
Rajinac 153 FG 3
Rajkot 174 B 3
Rajmahal Hills 174 E 3
Raj Nandgaon 174 D 3
Rajshahi 174 E 3
Rajura 174 C 4
Raka 174 E 2
Rakahanga 186 E 3
Rakan, Ra's (Qatar) 157 F 4
Rakata, Pulau 176 C 5
Raka Zangbo 174 E 2
Rakhmanoviskoye 159 R 6
Rakhsh (United Arab Emirates) 157 F 4
Rakitnoye 151 J 5
Rakkestad 151 F 4
Rakoko 200 C 3
Rakops 200 C 4
Rakshan 169 G 5
Rakulka 158 HJ 3
Råkvåg 150 E 3
Rakvere 151 J 4
Raleigh (MS.) 130 E 2
Raleigh (N.C.) 129 N 6
Raleigh (ND.) 118 G 4
Raleigh Bay 129 Q 6–7
Ralik Chain 186 C 2
Ralls (TX.) 117 P 4
Ralph (SD.) 118 EF 5
Ralston (PA.) 126 C 7
Ralston (WA.) 110 G 4
Ralston (WY.) 111 QR 6
Rama 132 F 5
Ramādah 193 H 2
Ramah Indian Reservation 116 H 3
Ramalho, Serra do 141 H 3
Rām Allāh (Westbank) 156 B 3
Ramallo 142 D 5
Ramanathapuram 174 C 6
Ramapo Deep 161 R 6
Ramatlabama 200 CD 5
Ramblon 142 C 5
Rambouillet 152 D 2
Rambutyo 184 E 2
Rambutyo 186 A 3
Ramea 105 Q 6
Ramer (AL.) 131 H 2
Rameswaram 174 C 6
Ramgarh (Bangla Desh) 175 F 3
Ramgarh (India) 174 E 3
Ramgul 169 J 3
Rāmhormoz (Iran) 157 E 3
Ramirez (TX.) 122 E 8
Ramkola 174 D 3
Ramlān (Saudi Arabia) 157 E 4
Ramlat al Wīgh 193 J 4
Ramlat as Sab'atayn 195 H 5
Ramlat Dahm 195 H 5
Ramlat Hagolan 156 B 2
Ramlat Rabyānah 193 JK 4
Ramlat Yām 195 H 5
Ramlu 199 G 2
Ramm, Jabal (Jordan) 156 B 3
Ramnagar 174 D 3
Ramo 199 G 3
Ramokgwebana 200 D 4
Ramona (CA.) 113 J 9
Ramona (S.D.) 119 L 6
Ramotswa 200 D 4
Rampart 102 F 2
Rampur 174 C 2
Rampur 174 D 3
Ramree 175 F 4
Rams (United Arab Emirates) 157 G 4
Rāmsar (Iran) 157 F 1
Ramsay (MT.) 111 N 4
Ramsele 150 G 3
Ramsey (IL.) 121 QR 3
Ramsey (Ontario, Can.) 104 L 6
Ramsey (U.K.) 148 C 4
Ramsgate 148 D 4
Rāmshīr (Iran) 157 E 3
Ramsjö 150 G 3
Ramsund 150 G 2

Ramu 199 G 4
Ramu River 184 D 2
Ramvik 150 G 3
Rañadoiro, Sierra de 152 B 3
Rancagua 142 B 5
Rancharia 141 F 5
Rancheria 109 M 3
Ranchester (WY.) 111 S 6
Ranchi 174 E 3
Ranchos de Taos (N.M.) 117 L 1
Rancul 142 D 6
Rand (CO.) 115 L 3
Randers 151 F 4
Randijaure 150 G 2
Randleman (N.C.) 129 M 6
Randlett (OK.) 120 G 8
Randolph (AZ.) 116 E 5
Randolph (IA.) 119 N 10
Randolph (NE.) 120 J 3
Randolph (UT.) 114 F 2
Randolph (VT.) 126 G 5
Random Lake (WI.) 124 G 6
Rand Rifles 200 A 4
Randsfjorden 151 F 3
Råneå 150 H 2
Råneälven 150 H 2
Ranelva 150 F 2
Ranérou 196 B 2
Rangamati 175 F 3
Rangantamiang 176 D 4
Rangeley (ME.) 126 J 3
Rangeley (CO.) 114 J 3
Ranger (TX.) 122 E 3
Rangia 175 F 2
Rangiroa 187 F 3
Rangkasbitung 176 C 5
Rangoon 175 G 4
Rangpur 174 E 2
Rangsang, Pulau 176 B 3
Rania 174 B 2
Ranibennur 174 C 5
Ranikhet 174 C 2
Rāniyah (Iraq) 157 D 1
Ranken River 183 F 3
Ranken Store 183 F 2
Rankin (TX.) 117 OP 6
Rankin Inlet 103 T 3
Rannes 183 HJ 3
Rannoch, Moor of 148 BC 3
Rann of Kutch 174 AB 3
Ranohira 201 H 4
Ranon 185 J 5
Ranong 175 G 6
Ranongga 185 G 3
Ransaren 150 G 2
Ransiki 177 H 4
Ransom (KS.) 120 F 4
Rantabe 201 H 3
Rantasalmi 150 J 3
Rantau 176 E 4
Rantauprapat 176 AB 3
Rantoul (IL.) 124 F 9
Ranua 150 J 2
Raohe 171 O 6
Rapadalen 150 G 2
Rapallo 153 E 3
Rapa Nui 187 H 4
Rapelje (MT.) 111 Q 5
Raper, Cabo 143 A 8
Raper, Cape 105 O 2
Rapid City (MI.) 124 J 5
Rapid City (S.D.) 118 E 6
Rapid River (MI.) 124 H 4
Rappahannock River 129 P 3–4
Rappang 177 EF 4
Rapulo 140 C 3
Raraka 187 F 4
Raroïa 187 F 4
Rarotonga 187 E 4
Rarytkin, Khrebet 171 WX 3
Rasa, Punta 143 D 7
Ra's Abū Madd (Saudi Arabia) 156 B 4
Ra's Abū Qumayyis (United Arab Emir-
  ates) 157 F 4
Ra's Abū Sawmah (Egypt) 156 B 4
Ra's Abū Shajarah 194 F 4
Ra's ad Daqm 195 K 5
Ra's Ajdir 193 H 2
Ra's al Abyad (Saudi Arabia) 156 BC 5
Ra's al Abyaḍ (Tunisia) 193 G 1
Ra's 'Alam al Rūm 194 D 2
Ra's al 'Ayn (Syria) 156 C 1
Ra's al Ḥadārībah 194 F 4
Ra's al Ḥadd 195 K 4
Ra's al Ḥazrah (United Arab Emirates)
  157 F 4
Ra's al Kanā'is 194 D 2
Ra's al Khafjī (Saudi Arabia) 157 E 3
Ra's al Khaymah (United Arab Emir-
  ates) 157 G 4
Ra's al Kūh 195 K 3
Ra's al Madrakah 195 K 5
Ra's al Milḥ 193 L 2

Ra's al Mish'āb (Saudi Arabia) 157 E 3
Ra's al Mūtaf (Iran) 157 F 4
Ra's an Naqb (Jordan) 156 B 3
Ra's ash Shaykh (Saudi Arabia) 156 B 3
Ra's ash Shaykh Ḥumayd 194 EF 3
Ra's Asir 199 J 2
Ra's as Saffānīyah (Saudi Arabia)
  157 E 3
Ra's as Sidr (Egypt) 156 A 3
Ra's as Saffānīyah (Saudi Arabia)
  157 E 3
Ra's at Tanāqīb (Saudi Arabia) 157 E 4
Ra's at Tannūrah (Saudi Arabia) 157 F 4
Ra's aṭ Ṭīb 193 H 1
Ra's at Tin 193 K 2
Ra's az Zawr (Saudi Arabia) 157 E 4
Ra's Ba'labakk (Syria) 156 B 2
Ra's Banās (Egypt) 156 B 5
Ra's Barīdī (Saudi Arabia) 156 B 4
Ra's Chiamboni 199 G 5
Ras Dashan 199 F 2
Ra's Durbat 'Alī 195 J 5
Ra's el Cheil 199 HJ 3
Ras el Ma 196 D 2
Ra's Fartak 195 J 5
Ra's Ghanadah (United Arab Emirates)
  157 G 4
Ra's Ghārib (Egypt) 156 A 3
Rashād 194 E 6
Ra's Ḥāfūn 199 J 2
Ra's Ḥanjūrah (United Arab Emirates)
  157 G 4
Ra's Ḥāṭībah 194 F 4
Rashīd 192 E 2
Rasht (Iran) 157 E 1
Ra's Īsā 195 G 5
Ras Jiwani 169 G 6
Ra's Kabūdīyah 193 H 1
Ra's Karkūmā (Saudi Arabia) 156 B 4
Ra's Kasr 194 F 5
Ra's Khānzīr 199 H 2
Raskoh 169 G 5
Ra's Laffān (Qatar) 157 F 4
Ra's Lānūf 193 J 2
Ra's Matārimah (Egypt) 156 A 3
Ra's Miṣrātah 193 J 2
Ras Muari 169 H 6
Ra's Muhammad (Egypt) 156 B 4
Ra's Mushayrib (United Arab Emirates)
  157 F 4
Rasmussen Basin 103 ST 2
Ra's Naws 195 K 5
Ras Ngomeni 199 G 5
Rason, Lake 182 C 4
Ra's Qaṭṭārah 194 D 2
Ra's Rakan (Qatar) 157 F 4
Ras Rawura 201 G 2
Ra's Sharbithāt 195 K 5
Rasshevatskaya 155 F 1
Rasshua, Ostrov 171 S 6
Rasskazovo 158 H 5
Rassokha 171 S 2
Ra's Sura 199 H 2
Rastigaissa 150 J 1
Råstojaure 150 H 2
Rasul (Iran) 157 G 4
Ra's Zayt (Egypt) 156 A 4
Rat 102 A 5
Ratak Chain 186 C 2
Ratangarh 174 B 2
Rat Buri 175 G 5
Rath 174 C 2
Rathbun Lake 119 PQ 10
Rathenow 149 F 4
Rathlin Island 148 B 3
Ráth Luirc 148 B 4
Rat Islands 102 A 5
Ratlam 174 C 3
Ratliff City (OK.) 120 H 8
Ratmanova, Mys 158–159 L 1
Ratmanova, Ostrov 102 D 2
Ratnagiri 174 B 4
Ratnapura 174 D 6
Ratno 151 H 4
Raton (N.M.) 117 M 1
Ratqah, Wadi ar (Iraq) 156 C 2
Ratta 129 Q 3
Rattray Head 148 C 3
Rättvik 151 F 3
Ratz, Mount 102 L 4
Raub 176 B 3
Raub (ND.) 118 F 3
Rauch 143 E 6
Rauchua 171 V 2
Raufarhöfn 150 B 2
Raufoss 151 F 3
Raukela 174 D 3
Raúl Leoni, Represa 139 F 2
Rauma (Norway) 150 E 3
Rauma (Raumo) (Finland) 150 H 3
Raumo 150 H 3
Raupelyan 102 C 2
Ravahere 187 F 4
Ravalli (MT.) 111 L 3
Ravānsar (Iran) 157 E 2
Rāvar (Iran) 157 G 3
Rava-Russkaya 151 H 5
Ravelsbach 153 G 2
Ravena (N.Y.) 126 F 6
Ravendale (CA.) 112 E 2
Ravenna 153 F 3
Ravenna (MT.) 111 M 4

Ravenna (NE.) 120 FG 1
Ravenna (OH.) 125 N 8
Ravensburg 149 EF 5
Ravenshoe (Queensland, Austr.) 183 GH 2
Ravensthorpe 182 C 5
Ravenwood (MO.) 121 L 2
Ravi 169 J 4
Ravia (OK.) 120 J 8
Ravinia (S.D.) 119 K 7
Ravnina 169 G 3
Rāwah (Iraq) 156 CD 2
Rawaki 186 D 3
Rawalpindi 169 J 4
Rawandūz (Iraq) 157 D 1
Rawas 177 H 4
Rawdah (Iraq) 156 C 2
Rawicz 149 G 4
Rawlinna 182 D 5
Rawlins (WY.) 111 S 9
Rawson 143 D 7
Rawura, Ras 201 G 2
Ray (MN.) 119 P 2
Ray (ND.) 118 E 2
Ray, Cape 105 Q 6
Raya, Bukit 176 D 4
Rayachoti 174 C 5
Rayadrug 174 C 5
Rayagada 174 D 4
Rayak (Lebanon) 156 B 2
Rāyāt (Iraq) 157 D 1
Raychikhinsk 171 N 6
Ray City (GA.) 131 L 3
Ray Hubbard, Lake 122 G 3
Raykoke, Ostrov 171 S 6
Raymond (CA.) 112 F 5
Raymond (IL.) 121 Q 3
Raymond (KS.) 120 G 4
Raymond (MN.) 119 N 5
Raymond (MS.) 130 D 2
Raymond (MT.) 118 D 2
Raymond (WA.) 110 B 4
Raymondville (TX.) 122 F 9
Ray Mountains 109 H 2
Raynesford (MT.) 111 P 3
Rayón 132 C 3
Rayong 175 H 5
Raytown (MO.) 121 L 3–4
Rayville (LA.) 123 M 3
Răzân (Iran) 157 E 2
Razan (Iran) 157 E 2
Razdan 155 F 2
Razdel'naya 154 D 1
Razdolinsk 170 F 4
Razdol'noye 155 D 1
Razdolnoye 171 S 3
Razeh (Iran) 157 E 2
Razgrad 154 C 2
Razlog 154 B 2
Razmak 169 J 4
Ré, Ile de 152 C 2
Read 103 P 2
Reading 148 C 4
Reading (KS.) 120 K 4
Reading (MI.) 125 K 8
Reading (OH.) 128 G 2
Reading (PA.) 127 D 8
Readlyn (IA.) 119 Q 8
Readstown (WI.) 124 D 6
Reagan (TN.) 128 C 6
Real, Cordillera 138 C 4
Real del Padre 142 C 5
Realico 142 D 6
Realitos (TX.) 122 E 8
Rèalmont 152 D 3
Reao 187 FG 4
Reardan (WA.) 110 H 3
Reata 132 B 2
Rebbenesöy 150 G 1
Rebecca, Lake 182 C 5
Rebi 177 H 5
Rebiana Sand Sea → Ramlat Ra-
byânah 193 JK 4
Rebojo, Cachoeira do 139 G 5
Reboly 150 K 3
Rebun-tō 173 M 1
Recalde 143 D 6
Recaş 154 B 1
Rechitsa 158 F 5
Rechna Doab 169 J 4
Recife 141 K 2
Récifs de l'Astrolabe 185 J 5
Récifs de l'Astrolabe 186 C 4
Récifs d'Entrecasteaux 185 H 5
Récifs d'Entrecasteaux 186 B 4
Récifs et Iles Chesterfield 183 K 2
Reconquista 142 DE 4
Recreio 139 G 5
Recreo 142 D 4
Rector (AR.) 121 P 6
Recuay 138 C 5
Red Bank (N.J.) 127 E 8
Red Bank (TN.) 128 F 6
Red Bank (TN.) 128 F 6
Red Basin 172 E 4
Red Bay (Newfoundl., Can.) 105 Q 5
Redbird (WY.) 118 D 7
Red Bluff (CA.) 112 C 2
Red Bluff Lake 117 N 6
Red Boiling Spring (TN.) 128 F 5

Red Bud (IL.) 121 Q 4
Red Buttes (WY.) 118 C 9
Red Cliff (CO.) 115 L 4
Red Cliff (WI.) 124 D 3
Redcliffe 183 J 4
Redcliffe, Mount 182 C 4
Red Cliff Indian Reservation 124 D 3
Red Cloud (NE.) 120 G 2
Red Deer 103 P 5
Red Deer River (Alb., Can.) 103 P 5
Red Deer River (Sask., Can.) 103 R 5
Red Devil 102 F 3
Redding (CA.) 112 C 2
Red Elm (SD.) 118 G 5
Redenção da Gurguéia 141 H 2
Red Feather Lakes (CO.) 115 M 3
Redfield (S.D.) 119 K 6
Redford (TX.) 117 M 8
Red Hill 113 F 11
Red Hill (New Zealand) 185 Q 9
Red Hill (South Australia) 183 F 5
Red Hills 120 FG 5
Red House (NV.) 112 H 1—2
Redig (SD.) 118 E 5
Redington (NE.) 118 E 9
Redkey (IN.) 124 J 9
Red Lake (AZ.) 116 C 2
Redlake (MN.) 119 N 3
Red Lake (Ontario, Can.) 104 J 5
Red Lake (S.D.) 118 J 7
Red Lake Falls (MN.) 119 M 3
Red Lake Indian Reservation 119 N 2–3
Red Lake River 119 M 3
Redlands (CA.) 113 H 8
Red Level (AL.) 131 H 3
Red Lodge (MT.) 111 Q 5
Redmesa (CO.) 115 J 6
Redmond (OR.) 110 D 6
Redmond (UT.) 114 F 4
Red Mountain (CA.) 113 H 7
Red Mountain (MT.) 111 N 3
Red Mountain Pass 115 K 6
Red Oak (IA.) 119 N 9
Red Oak (OK.) 121 KL 8
Redon 152 C 2
Redoubt Volcano 102 G 3
Redowl (SD.) 118 F 6
Red River (LA.) 123 LM 4
Red River (MN/N.D.) 119 L 2
Red River Hot Springs (ID.) 111 KL 5
Red River Valley 119 M 2–3
Red Rock (AZ.) 116 G 1
Red Rock (MT.) 111 N 6
Redrock (N.M.) 116 H 5
Red Rock (TX.) 122 F 5–6
Red Rock, Lake 119 P 9
Red Rock Lakes 111 O 6
Redruth 148 B 4
Red Sea 194 F 3–4
Red Shirt (SD.) 118 F 7
Red Springs (N.C.) 129 M 7
Redstar (AR.) 121 M 7
Redstone (CO.) 115 K 4
Redstone (MT.) 118 D 2
Redstone Arsenal (AL.) 128 E 7
Redstone River 109 N 3
Red Water 103 P 5
Redwater River 118 C 3
Red Wing (MN.) 119 Q 6
Redwood (MS.) 130 D 2
Redwood City (CA.) 112 C 5
Redwood Falls (MN.) 119 N 5
Redwood National Park 112 A 1
Redwood Valley (CA.) 112 B 3
Reece (KS.) 120 J 5
Reed City (MI.) 124 J 6
Reedley (CA.) 112 F 6
Reed Point (MT.) 111 Q 5
Reedsburg (WI.) 124 D 6
Reeds Peak 116 J 4
Reedsport (OR.) 110 AB 7
Reedville (VA.) 129 P 4
Reef Islands 185 J 4
Reef Islands 186 BC 3
Reelfoot Lake 128 B 5
Reese (MI.) 125 L 6
Reese River 112 H 2
Refahiye 155 E 3
Reform (AL.) 128 CD 8
Refresco 142 C 4
Refugio (TX.) 122 F 7
Regar 169 H 3
Regencia 141 J 4
Regensburg 149 F 5
Regent (ND.) 118 F 4
Reggane 192 EF 3
Reggio di Calabria 153 G 4
Reggio nell'Emilia 153 F 3
Reghin 154 B 1
Regina 103 R 5
Regina 139 H 3
Registan 169 GH 4
Regocijo 132 AB 3
Rehoboth 200 B 4
Rehoboth Beach (N.J.) 127 DE 10
Reidsville (GA.) 131 M 2
Reidsville (N.C.) 129 M 5
Reims 152 D 2
Reina Adelaida, Archipiélago-
de la 143 A 9

Reindeer 103 R 4
Reindeer Lake 103 R 4
Reindeer Station 109 M 2
Reine 150 F 2
Reinoksfjellet 150 G 2
Reinosa 152 C 3
Reisaelva 150 H 2
Reistertown (MD.) 129 OP 2
Reitoru 187 F 4
Reitz 200 D 5
Relizane 192 F 1
Reliance (N..W.T., Can.) 103 Q 3
Reliance (WY.) 111 Q 9
Remanso 141 H 2
Remansão 139 HJ 4
Rembang 176 D 5
Remer (MN.) 119 P 3
Remeshk 168 F 5
Remington (VA.) 129 O 3
Rémire 139 H 3
Remiremont 153 E 2
Remontnoye 155 F 1
Remus (MI.) 124 J 6
Rena 150 F 3
Renascença 138 E 4
Rend Lake 121 Q 4
Rendova 185 G 3
Rendsburg 149 EF 4
Renfrew 105 M 6
Rengat 176 B 4
Rengma Hills 175 F 2
Rengo 142 B 5
Reni 154 C 1
Renick (W.V.) 129 L 3
Renmark 183 G 5
Rennell 185 H 4
Rennell 186 B 3
Rennell, Islas 143 B 9
Rennes 152 C 2
Rennie Lake 103 Q 3
Reno (Italy) 153 F 3
Reno (NV.) 112 F 3
Renovo (PA.) 127 B 7
Renqiu 173 G 3
Renshou 172 D 5
Renton (WA.) 110 C 3
Ren Xian 172 FG 3
Reo 177 F 5
Repartição 139 G 4
Repartimento 139 G 4
Replot 150 H 3
Repolovo 159 N 3
Reprêsa Agua Vermelha 141 FG 4–5
Reprêsa Bariri 141 G 5
Reprêsa Boa Esperança 141 H 2
Reprêsa da Capivara 141 F 5
Reprêsa de Furnas 141 G 5
Reprêsa de Jupi 141 F 5
Reprêsa de Jurumirim 141 G 5
Reprêsa de Xavantes 141 FG 5
Reprêsa do Estreito 141 G 4–5
Reprêsa Promissão 141 G 5
Represa Raúl Leoni 139 F 2
Reprêsa Três Marias 141 G 4
Repton (AL.) 130 G 3
Republic (KS.) 120 H 3
Republic (MO.) 121 M 5
Republican City (NE.) 120 F 2
Republican River 120 G 2
Republic of Ireland 148 B 4
Repulse Bay 103 U 2
Repulse Bay 103 U 2
Repvåg 150 J 1
Requena 138 C 4
Requena 152 C 4
Requina (CA.) 112 A 1
Reşadiye 155 E 2
Reşadiye Yarımadası 154 C 3
Reserve (MT.) 118 D 2
Reserve (N.M.) 116 H 4
Réservoir Baskatong 105 MN 6
Réservoir Cabonga 105 M 6
Réservoir Decelles 105 M 6
Réservoir Dozois 105 M 6
Réservoir Gouin 105 MN 6
Réservoir Manicouagan 105 O 5
Réservoir Pipmouacan 105 N 6
Reservoir Rocklands 183 G 6
Resheth-ye Esfarâyeh 168 F 3
Reshteh-ye Kûhhã-ye Alborz 168 E 3
Reshteh-ye Kûhhã-ye Alborz (Iran) 157 F 1
Resia, Passo di 153 F 2
Resistencia 142 DE 4
Reşita 154 B 1
Resolution 184 P 10
Resolution Island 205 P 3
Resplendor 141 H 4
Retalhuleu 132 D 5
Rethel 153 D 2
Rethimnon 154 B 3
Retkucha 171 W 2
Retz 153 G 2
Reut 154 C 1
Reutlingen 149 E 5

Reutte 153 F 2
Reva (SD.) 118 EF 5
Revantazón 138 B 5
Revda (MT.) 111 K 2
Revda 159 L 4
Revelstoke 103 O 5
Revilla Gigedo 102 L 4
Revilla Gigedo Islands 99 G 8
Revillo (S.D.) 119 M 5
Revin 153 D 2
Revolyutsii, Pik 169 J 3
Revsundssjön 150 FG 3
Revue 201 E 3
Rewa 174 D 3
Rewari 174 C 2
Rexburg (ID.) 111 O 7
Rexford (KS.) 120 E 3
Rexford (MT.) 111 K 2
Rexton (MI.) 124 J 3
Rey (Iran) 157 F 2
Rey, Isla del 138 C 2
Rey Bouba 197 G 4
Reyes 140 C 3
Reyes, Point 112 B 5
Reyhanli 155 E 3
Reyhanli (Turkey) 156 B 1
Reykjahlö 150 B 2
Reykjanes 150 A 3
Reykjavik 150 A 3
Reynaldo Cullen 142 D 5
Reynolds (N.D.) 119 L 3
Reynosa 132 C 2
Rezé 152 C 2
Rēzekne 151J 4
Rezovo 154 C 2
Rezvãn (Iran) 157 G 4
Rhages (Iran) 157 F 2
Rhallamane 192 CD 4
Rhallamane, Sebkha de 192 D 4
Rhame (ND.) 118 CD 5
Rharis 193 F 3
Rharsa, Chott el 193 G 2
Rhein 148 E 4
Rhemilès 192 E 3
Rhinelander (WI.) 124 E 4
Rhinmal 174 B 2
Rhino Camp 198 E 4
Rhir, Cap 192 CD 2
Rhode Island 126 H 7
Rhode Island Sound 127 H 7
Rhodes 154 C 3
Rhodes Grave 200 D 4
Rhodesia → Zimbabwe 200–201 DE 3
Rhodhiss Lake 129 K 6
Rhodope Mts 154 BC 2
Rhondda 148 C 4
Rhône 153 D 3
Rhourde el Baguel 193 G 2
Rhuis 152 C 2
Rhum 148 B 3
Ri-Aba 197 F 5
Riachão 121 J 5
Riachão do Jacuípe 141 J 3
Riacho de Santana 141 H 3
Riachos, Islas de los 143 D 6
Ria de Muros y Noya 152 B 3
Ría de Santa Marta 152 B 3
Ría de Vigo 152 B 3
Rianápolis 141 G 4
Riangnom 198 E 3
Rías Altas 152 B 3
Rías Bajas 152 B 3
Riasi 169 J 4
Ribadeo 152 B 3
Ribamar 141 H 1
Ribas do Río Pardo 141 F 5
Ribáuè 201 F 2
Ribe 151 E 4
Ribeira 141 G 5
Ribeira Brava 196 B 6
Ribeira Grande 196 A 6
Ribeirão Prêto 141 G 5
Ribeiro Gonçalves 141 G 2
Ribera 153 F 4
Riberalta 140 C 3
Rib Lake (WI.) 124 D 4
Ribnica 153 F 2
Ricardo (N.M.) 117 M 3
Ricardo (TX.) 122 8
Riccione 153 F 3
Rice (CA.) 113 L 8
Rice (TX.) 122 G 3
Rice (WA.) 110 G 2
Rice Lake (WI.) 124 C 4
Riceville (IA.) 119 Q 7
Rich 192 E 2
Richard Collinson Inlet 103 P 1
Richard's Bay 201 E 5
Richards Mountain 111 K 2
Richardson (TX.) 122 G 3
Richardson Lakes 126 J 4
Richardson Mountains 102 K 2
Richard Toll 196 A 2
Richardton (ND.) 118 F 4
Rich Bar (CA.) 112 D 2
Richey (MT.) 118 C 3
Richfield (ID.) 111 LM 7
Richfield (KS.) 120 D 5

Richfield (PA.) 127 B 8
Richfield (UT.) 114 EF 5
Richfield Springs (N.Y.) 126 E 6
Richford (VT.) 126 G 4
Rich Hill (MO.) 121 L 4
Richland (GA.) 131 K 2
Richland (MI.) 124 J 7
Richland (MO.) 121 N 5
Richland (MT.) 118 BC 2
Richland (OR.) 110 H 6
Richland (TX.) 122 G 4
Richland (WA.) 110 F 4
Richland Center (WI.) 124 D 6
Richlands (N.C.) 129 O 7
Richlands (VA.) 129 K 4
Richlands Springs (TX.) 122 E 4
Richmond (CA.) 112 C 5
Richmond (IN.) 128 G 2
Richmond (KS.) 121 K 4
Richmond (KY.) 128 G 4
Richmond (ME.) 126 K 4
Richmond (MO.) 121 M 3
Richmond (Queensland, Austr.) 183 G 3
Richmond (South Africa) 200 C 6
Richmond (TX.) 123 H 6
Richmond (UT.) 114 EF 2
Richmond (VA.) 129 O 4
Richmond Hill (GA.) 131 N 3
Richmond Hill (Ontario, Can.) 105 M 7
Rich Square (N.C.) 129 O 5
Richton (MS.) 130 F 3
Richwood (W.V.) 129 L 3
Rickleån 150 H 3
Rico (CO.) 115 K 6
Ricobayo, Embalse de 152 B 3
Riddle (ID.) 110 J 8
Riddle (OR.) 110 B 8
Riddle Mountain 110 G 7
Ridge (MT.) 118 CD 5
Ridgecrest (CA.) 113 H 7
Ridgeland (S.C.) 129 KL 9
Ridgely (TN.) 128 B 5
Ridgeview (SD.) 118 H 5
Ridgeway (CO.) 115 K 5
Ridgeway (MO.) 121 LM 2
Ridgeway (S.C.) 129 L 7
Ridgway (PA.) 125 Q 8
Riding Mountain National Park 103 R 5
Ried 153 F 2
Rienzi (MS.) 121 R 8
Riesa 149 F 4
Riesco, Isla 143 B 9
Rietavas 151H 4
Rietfontein (Namibia) 200 C 4
Rietfontein (South Africa) 200 C 5
Rieth (OR.) 110 G 5
Rieti 153 F 3
Rifle (CO.) 115 K 4
Rifstangi 112 B 2 Riga 150 H 4
Rig, BAndar-e (Iran) 157 F 3
Riga 151 H 4
Riga, Gulf of 151 H 4
Rigachikun 197 F 3
Rigby (ID.) 111 O 7
Riggins (ID.) 110 J 5
Rigolet 105 Q 5
Rig Rig 197 G 3
Rihand Dam 174 D 3
Riihimäki 151 HJ 3
Riiser-Larsen Ice Shelf 203
Riiser-Larsen Peninsula 203
Rijau 197 F 3
Rijeka 153 F 2
Riley (KS.) 120 J 3
Riley (OR.) 110 F 7
Rillito (AZ.) 116 E 5
Rimatara 187 E 4
Rimavská Sobota 149 H 5
Rimbo 151 G 4
Rimini 153 F 3
Rimnicu Sărat 154 C 1
Rimnicu Vilcea 154 B 1–2
Rimouski 105 O 6
Rinbung 174 E 2
Rinchinlhümbe 170 G 5
Rinconada 140 C 5
Rincon Indian Reservation 113 J 9
Ringe 151 F 4
Ringerike 151 EF 3
Ringgold (GA.) 128 F 7
Ringgold (LA.) 123 K 3
Ringgold (NE.) 120 E 1
Ringgold Isles 186 D 4
Ringhkung 175 G 2
Ringim 197 F 3
Ringköbing 151 E 4
Ringköbing Fjord 151 E 4
Ringládes 154 AB 3
Ringling (MT.) 111 P 4
Ringling (OK.) 120 H 8
Ringsted (IA.) 119 O 7
Ringvassöy 150 G 2
Ringwood (OK.) 120 G 6
Rinihue 143 B 6
Rinja, Pulau 177 E 5
Rinjani, Gunung 176 E 5
Rio Balsas 132 B 4
Ríobamba 138 C 4
Rio Blanco (CO.) 115 JK 4
Río Branco 138 E 5

Río Branco 139 F 3
Río Branco (Uruguay) 142 F 5
Río Branco do Sul 142 G 4
Río Bravo del Norte106 EF 5–6
Río Bravo del Norte 132 C 2
Río Brilhanter141 EF 5
Río Bueno 143 B 7
Río Casca 141 H 5
Río Chico (Argentina) 143 C 8
Río Chico (Venezuela) 138 E 1
Río Claro 141 G 5
Río Coco o Segovia 132 F 5
Río Colorado (Argentina) 143 D 6
Río Conchos 106 EF 6
Río Cuarto 142 CD 5
Rio das Mortes 141 F 3
Río de Janeiro 141 H 5
Río de la Plata 143 EF 6
Río de las Piedras 140 B 3
Río Dell (CA.) 112 A 2
Río del Rey 197 F 5
Río de Oro 192 BC 4
Río do Sul 142 G 4
Río Gallegos 143 C 9
Río Grande (Argentina) 143 C 9
Río Grande (Bahía, Brazil) 141 H 3
Río Grande (Brazil) 141 G 4
Río Grande (P.R.) 130 D 8
Río Grande Río Grande do Sul, Brazil)
142 F 5
Rio Grande (TX./Mexico) 122 E 9
Río Grande City (TX.) 122 E 9
Río Grande de Matagalpa 132 F 5
Río Grande de Santiago 132 B 3
Río Grande de Tarija 140 D 5
Río Grande do Norte 141 J 2
Río Grande do Sul 142 EF 4
Río Grande Fracture Zone 208 A 5
Río Grande o'Guapay 140 D 4
Ríohacha 138 D 1
Río Hondo 142 D 4
Río Hondo (TX.) 122 F 9
Rioja 138 C 5
Río Lacantún 132 D 4
Río Lagartos 132 E 3
Río Largo 141 J 2
Río Lempa 132 E 5
Riom 152 D 2
Riomedina (TX.) 122 E 6
Río Mezcalapa 132 D 4
Río Muerto 142 D 4
Río Mulatos 140 C 4
Rion 154 B 3
Río Negrinho 142 FG 4
Río Negro (Argentina) 143 D 6–7
Río Negro (Brazil) 139 F 4
Río Negro (Uruguay) 142 EF 5
Río Negro, Pantanal do 140 E 4
Rioni 155 F 2
Río Pardo 142 F 4
Rio Patuca 132 F 4
Río Pecos (TX.) 117 O 6
Río Pedras (P.R.) 130 C 8
Río Real 141 J 3
Rios (TX.) 122 E 8
Rio San Juan 132 F 5
Rio Siquia 132 F 5
Río Sonora 106 D 6
Ríosucio 138 C 2
Río Tercero 142 D 5
Río Tinto 141 J 2
Rio Turbio Mines 143 B 9
Río Usumacinta 132 D 4
Ríoverde (Ecuador) 138 C 3
Rioverde (Goiás, Brazil) 141 F 4
Rio Verde (Mato Grosso do Sul, Brazil)
141 F 5
Rioverde (Mexico) 132 BC 3
Rio Verde de Mato Grosso 141 F 4
Rio Viejo 132 E 5
Rio Vista (CA.) 112 D 4
Rio Vista (TX.) 122 F 3
Rio Yaqui 106 E 6
Ríozinho 138 E 4
Ripley (CA.) 113 L 9
Ripley (MS.) 121 R 8
Ripley (OH.) 128 H 3
Ripley (TN.) 128 B 6
Ripley (W.V.) 129 K 3
Ripoll 152 D 3
Ripon (CA.) 112 D 5
Ripon (WI.) 124 F 6
Ririe (ID.) 111 O 7
Risan 154 A 2
Risasi 198 D 5
Risbäck 150 G 3
Risco (MO.) 121 Q 6
Rī shahr (Iran) 157 F 3
Rishiri-tō 173 M 1
Rīshmūk (Iran) 157 F 3
Rising Star (TX.) 122 E 3
Rising Sun (IN.) 128 FG 3
Rison (AR.) 121 N 9
Risør 151 E 4
Risøyhamn 150 FG 2
Risti 151H 4
Ristiina 150 J 3
Ristijärvi 150 J 3
Ristna Neem 151 H 4

Ritchie's Archipelago 175 F 5
Rito 200 B 3
Ritsa 155 F 2
Ritter, Mount 112 F 5
Ritzville (WA.) 110 G 3
Rivadavia (Argentina) 140 D 5
Rivadavia (Chile) 142 B 4
Rivas 132 E 5
River, Cape 183 H 3
River, Niordenskiold 109 L 3
Rivera (Argentina) 143 D 6
Rivera (Uruguay) 142 E 5
Riverbank (CA.) 112 E 5
River Cess 196 BC 4
Riverdale (CA.) 112 F 6
Riverdale (ND.) 118 G 3
River Falls (WI.) 124 B 5
Riverhead (N.Y.) 127 G 8
Riverina 183 GH 5
Riversdale 200 C 6
Riverside (CA.) 113 H 9
Riverside (OR.) 110 G 7
Riverside (TX.) 123 H 5
Riverside (WA.) 110 F 2
Riverside Reservoir 115 N 3
Rivers Inlet 103 M 5
Riverton (Man., Can.) 103 S 5
Riverton (New Zealand) 184 P 10
Riverton (WY.) 111 R 7
Riverview (WY.) 118 D 7
Rives (TN.) 128 BC 5
Rivesaltes 152 D 3
Rives Junction (MI.) 125 K 7
Riviera (TX.) 122 F 8
Riviera Beach (FL.) 131 OP 8
Riviera di Levante 153 E 3
Riviera di Ponente 153 E 3
Rivière à la Baleine 105 O 4
Rivière aux Feuilles 105 N 4
Rivière aux Mélèzes 105 N 4
Rivière aux Outardes 105 O 5
Rivière-du-Loup 105 O 6
Rivière du Petit-Mécatina 105 PQ 5
Rivoli 153 E 2
Rivungo 200 C 3
Riwoqê 172 C 4
Riyādh (Saudi Arabia) 157 E 4
Riyān 195 H 6
Riza (Iran) 157 G 2
Rize 155 F 2
Rize Dağları 155 F 2
Rizhao 173 G 3
Rizhskiy Zaliv 151 H 4
Rizokárpasso → Dipkarpas 155 D 3
Rjukan 151 E 4
Rjuven 151 E 4
Rkiz 192 B 5
Ro 175 J 4
Roach (NV.) 113 K 7
Roachdale (IN.) 128 DE 2
Roach Lake 113 K 7
Roads End (CA.) 112 G 7
Roanne 152 D 2
Roanoke (AL.) 128 F 8
Roanoke (VA.) 129 M 4
Roanoke Rapids (N.C.) 129 O 5
Roanoke Rapids Lake 129 O 5
Roanoke River 129 O 5
Roan Plateau 114 HJ 4
Roaring Springs (TX.) 117 Q 4
Roatán 132 E 4
Robât-e Khān (Iran) 157 G 2
Robât-e Kord (Iran) 157 G 2
Robat-e Tork (Iran) 157 F 2
Robat Karīm (Iran) 157 F 2
Robbah 193 G 2
Robben Island 200 B 6
Robbins (CA.) 112 D 4
Robe 183 F 6
Robert Butte 203
Robert Lee (TX.) 122 C 4
Robert Lee Reservoir 122 C 4
Roberts (ID.) 111 N 7
Roberts (MT.) 111 Q 5
Roberts, Mount 183 J 4
Roberts Creek Mountain 112 J 3
Robertsdale (AL.) 130 G 4
Robertsfield 196 BC 4
Robertsfors 150 H 3
Robert S. Kerr Reservoir 121 KL 7
Roberts Mountain 108 E 3–4
Robertsport 196 B 4
Robi 199 F 3
Robinson (IL.) 121 S 3
Robinson (TX.) 122 F 4
Robinson Crusoe 143 A 5
Robinson Mountain 111 K 2
Robinson Ranges (Western Australia)
182 B 4
Robinson River 183 F 2
Robles Junction (AZ.) 116 E 5
Robore 140 E 4
Robson, Mount 103 O 5
Robstown (TX.) 122 F 8
Roby (TX.) 122 C 3

Rocha 142 F 5
Rocha de Galé, Barragem da 152 B 4
Rochefort 152 C 2
Rochelle (IL.) 124 E 8
Rochelle (TX.) 122 D 4
Rocher River 103 P 3
Rocher Thomasset 187 F 3
Rochester (IN.) 124 H 8
Rochester (MN.) 119 Q 6
Rochester (N.H.) 126 H 5
Rochester (N.Y.) 126 B 5
Rochester (TX.) 122 D 2
Rochester (U.K.) 148 D 4
Rochester (WA.) 110 B 4
Rochford (SD.) 118 E 6
Rochlitzer Berg 149 F 4
Rocigalgo 152 BC 4
Rock (MI.) 124 G 3
Rock Candy Mountain 111 K 2
Rock Cave (W.V.) 129 L 3
Rock Creek (NV.) 112 J 1–2
Rock Creek (OR.) 110 E 5
Rock Creek Butte 110 G 6
Rockdale (TX.) 122 FG 5
Rockefeller Plateau 203
Rock Falls (IL.) 124 E 8
Rockford (AL.) 131 H 2
Rockford (ID.) 111 N 7
Rockford (IL.) 124 E 7
Rock Hall (MD.) 129 P 2
Rockham (SD.) 118 K 6
Rockhampton 183 HJ 3
Rockhampton Downs 182 F 2
Rock Hill (S.C.) 129 K 7
Rockingham (N.C.) 129 M 7
Rockingham (Western Australia)182 B 5
Rockinstraw Mountain 116 F 4
Rock Lake 110 H 3
Rocklake (ND.) 118 J 2
Rockland (ID.) 111 MN 8
Rockland (ME.) 126 K 4
Rockland (MI.) 124 E 3
Rocklands Reservoir 183 G 6
Rockledge (FL.) 131 O 6
Rockmart (GA.) 128 FG 7
Rockport (CA.) 112 B 3
Rockport (IN.) 128 D 4
Rockport (MA.) 126 J 6
Rockport (MO.) 121 K 2
Rockport (TX.) 122 F 7
Rock Rapids (IA.) 119 M 7
Rock River(IL.) 124 E 8
Rock River (WY.) 118 C 9
Rock Springs (AZ.) 116 D 3
Rock Springs (MT.) 118 B 4
Rocksprings (TX.) 122 C 5
Rock Springs (WY.) 111 Q 9
Rockstone 139 G 2
Rockton (IL.) 124 E 7
Rock Valley (IA.) 119 M 7
Rockville (IN.) 128 D 2
Rockville (MD.) 129 O 2
Rockville (UT.) 114 DE 6
Rockwell (IA.) 119 P 7–8
Rockwell City (IA.) 119 O 8
Rockwood (ME.) 126 K 3
Rockwood (MI.) 125 L 7
Rockwood (PA.) 125 P 10
Rockwood (TX.) 122 D 4
Rocky (OK.) 120 FG 7
Rocky Boy (MT.) 111 Q 2
Rocky Boys Indian Reservation 111 Q 2
Rocky Dam 117 M 4
Rocky Island Dam 110 E 3
Rocky Mount (N.C.) 129 O 6
Rocky Mount (VA.) 129 M 5
Rocky Mountain (MT.) 111 N 3
Rocky Mountain House 103 O 5
Rocky Mountain National Park 115 M 3
Rocky Mountains 99 FH 4–6
Rocky Point (AK.) 108 F 3
Rocky Point (CA.) 112 A 1
Rockypoint (WY.) 118 CD 6
Rocky Reach Dam 110 E 3
Rocky Top 110 C 6
Rodanthe (N.C.) 129 Q 6
Rödby Havn 151 F 5
Roddickton 105 Q 5
Rodeo (Mexico) 132 B 2
Rodeo (N.M.) 116 GH 6
Rodez 152 D 3
Rodholivos 154 B 2
Rodhopi, Dytike 154 B 2
Ródhos 154 C 3
Ródhos 154 C 3
Rodina 170 G 4
Rodionovo 158 L 2
Rodney, Cape (AK.) 102 D 3
Rodopi 154 BC 2
Rodrigues 138 D 5
Roe (N.C.) 129 P 6—7
Roebourne 182 B 3
Roebuck Bay 182 C 2
Roeselare 148 D 4
Roes Welcome Sound 103 U 2–3
Roff (OK.) 120 J 8
Rogachev 151 J 5
Rogagua, Lago 140 C 3
Rogaland 151 E 4

Rogaška Slatina 153 G 2
Rogatica 153 G 3
Rogen 150 F 3
Rogers (N.D.) 119 K 3
Rogers (TX.) 122 F 5
Rogers, Mount 129 K 5
Rogers City (MI.) 125 L 4
Rogers Lake (AK.) 113 H 8
Rogers Lake (AZ.) 116 E 2
Rogerson (ID.) 111 L 8
Rogersville (AL.) 128 D 7
Rogersville (MO.) 121 M 5
Rogersville (TN.) 128 HJ 5
Roggeveld Berge 200 BC 6
Rognan 150 FG 2
Rogovskaya 155 E 1
Rogozhina 154 A 2
Rogue River 110 B 8
Rogue River (OR.) 110 B 8
Rohrbach 155 F 2
Rohri 169 H 5
Rohtak 174 C 2
Roi Et 175 H 4
Roi Georges, Îles du 187 F 3
Roja, Punta 143 CD 7
Rojas 142 D 5
Rojo, Cabo 130 B 9
Rojo, Cabo 133 J 4
Rokan, Sungai 176 B 3
Rokeby 183 G 1
Rokel 196 B 4
Roland (IA.) 119 P 8
Rolândia 141 F 5
Rolette (ND.) 118 J 2
Rolfe (IA.) 119 O 8
Roll (AZ.) 116 BC 5
Roll (OK.) 120 F 7
Rolla (KS.) 120 D 5
Rolla (MO.) 121 O 5
Rolla (N.D.) 118 J 2
Rolleston 183 H 3
Rolling Fork (MS.) 130 D 2
Rollins (MT.) 111 L 3
Rolvsøya 150 H 1
Roma (Queensland, Austr.) 183 H 4
Roma (Rome) 153 F 3
Romain, Cape 129 M 9
Romaine 105 P 5
Roma - Los Saenz (TX.) 122 DE 9
Roman 154 C 1
Romang, Pulau 177 G 5
Romania 154 BC 1
Roman Kosh 155 D 2
Roman Nose Mountain 110 B 7
Romano, Cape 131 N 9
Romanova 170 H 4
Romanovka 158 H 5
Romanovka 170 K 5
Romans-sur-Isère 153 E 2
Romanzof, Cape 102 D 3
Romanzof Mountains 102 J 2
Romblon 177 F 1
Rome (GA.) 128 F 7
Rome (Italy) 153 F 3
Rome (N.Y.) 126 D 5
Rome (TN.) 128 E 5
Romeo (CO.) 115 LM 6
Romeo (MI.) 125 M 7
Romerike 151 F 3
Romero (TX.) 117 O 2
Romeroville (N.M.) 117 L 2
Romilly-sur-Seine 152 D 2
Rommani 192 D 2
Romney (TX.) 122 DE 3
Romney (W.V.) 129 N 2
Romny 158 F 5
Römö 151 E 4
Romoland (CA.) 113 H 9
Romont 153 E 2
Romorantin-Lanthenay 152 D 2
Romsdal 150 E 3
Ronan (MT.) 111 L 3
Ronas Hill 148 C 2
Roncador 185 G 3
Roncador 186 B 3
Roncador, Cayos de 133 G 5
Roncador, Serra do 141 F 3
Roncesvalles 152 C 1
Ronda (China) 169 K 3
Ronda (Spain) 152 BC 4
Rondane 150 EF 3
Rondas das Salinas 140 D 4
Rönde 151 F 4
Rondón, Pico 139 F 3
Rondônia 140 D 3
Rondonópolis 141 F 4
Ronge, Lac la 103 R 4
Rongcheng 173 H 3
Rongelap 186 C 2
Rongerik 186 C 2
Rongjiang 172 E 5
Rongklang Range 175 F 3
Rongshui 172 E 5
Rong Xian 172 D 5
Rong Xian 172 F 6
Rönne 151 F 4
Ronneby 151 G 4

Ronne Ice Shelf 203
Roof Butte 116 G 1
Rooikop 200 AB 4
Roorkee 174 C 2
Roosevelt 140 D 3
Roosevelt (AZ.) 116 E 4
Roosevelt (MN.) 119 N 2
Roosevelt (OK.) 120 F 8
Roosevelt (UT.) 114 H 3
Roosevelt, Mount 103 M 4
Roosvelt (MT.) 111 KL 2
Roosville 203
Roper River 182 E 1
Roper River 182 EF 1
Ropesville (TX.) 117 O 4
Ropi 150 H 2
Roquetas de Mar 152 C 4
Roraima (Brazil) 139 F 3
Roraima (Venezuela) 139 F 2
Rori 174 C 2
Røros 150 F 3
Rørvik 150 F 3
Rosa 201 E 1
Rosa, Lake 133 H 3
Rosalia (WA.) 110 H 3
Rosamond (CA.) 113 G 8
Rosamond Lake 113 G 8
Rosamorada 132 A 3
Rosanky (TX.) 122 F 6
Rosario 132 A 3
Rosario (Argentina) 142 D 5
Rosario (Chile) 140 B 5
Rosário (Maranhão, Brazil) 141 H 1
Rosario (Paraguay) 140 E 5
Rosario, Bahía 106 C 6
Rosario de la Frontera 142 D 4
Rosario de Lerma 142 C 4
Rosario del Tala 142 E 5
Rosário do Sul 142 F 5
Rosário Oeste 140 E 3
Rosarito 106 D 6
Rosas, Golfo de 152 D 3
Roscoe (SD.) 118 J 5
Roscoe (TX.) 122 C 3
Roscoff 152 C 2
Roscommon 148 B 4
Roscommon (MI.) 125 K 5
Roscrea 148 B 4
Rose (NE.) 118 J 8
Roseau 133 K 4
Roseau (MN.) 119 N 2
Roseau River 119 M 2
Roseboro (N.C.) 129 N 7
Rosebud (MT.) 118 B 4
Rosebud (SD.) 118 H 7
Rosebud (FX.) 122 FG 4
Rosebud Indian Reservation 118 H 7
Roseburg (OR.) 110 B 7
Rose City (MI.) 125 K 5
Rosedale (MS.) 121 OP 9
Roseglen (ND.) 118 G 3
Rose Hill (N.C.) 129 NO 7
Rose Hill (VA.) 128 H 5
Rosenheim 149 F 5
Rose Peak 116 G 4
Rosetown 103 Q 5
Rosetta → Rashīd 194 E 2
Rosette (UT.) 114 D 2
Roseville (CA.) 112 D 4
Roseville (IL.) 124 D 9
Roseville (MI.) 125 M 7
Roseworth (ID.) 111 KL 8
Rosholt (S.D.) 119 M 5
Rosholt (WI.) 124 E 5
Rosh Pinah 200 B 5
Rosignol 139 G 2
Roşiori de Vede 154 C 2
Rosita (TX.) 122 E 8
Roslagen 151 G 4
Roslavl' 158 F 5
Roslyn (S.D.) 119 L 5
Roslyn (WA.) 110 E 3
Rosman (N.C.) 128 J 6
Ross (ID.) 118 F 2
Ross (Senegal) 196 A 2
Ross (Yukon, Can.) 102 L 3
Rossano 153 G 4
Rossan Point 148 B 4
Rossel Island 185 F 4
Rossell y Rius 142 E 5
Ross Ice Shelf 203
Rössing 200 A 4
Ross Island 203
Ross Lake 110 DE 2
Rosslare 148 B 4
Rosso 192 B 5
Rossön 150 G 3
Rossosh 158 G 5
Ross R. Barnett Reservoir 130 E 2
Ross River 102 L 3
Ross Sea 203
Rosston (OK.) 120 EF 6
Rössvatn 150 F 2
Röst 150 F 2
Rosta 150 G 2
Rostam (United Arab Emirates) 157 F 4
Rostami (Iran) 157 F 3
Rostam Kalā (Iran) 157 F 1

Rostāq (Iran) 157 FG 4
Rosthern 103 Q 5
Rostock 149 F 4
Rostonsölkä 150 H 2
Rostov 158 G 4
Rostov-na-Donu 155 EF 1
Roswell (GA.) 128 G 7
Roswell (N.M.) 117 M 4
Rota 152 B 4
Rota 186 A 2
Rotan (TX.) 122 C 3
Rothenburg 149 EF 5
Rothera 203
Rothiemay (MT.) 111 Q 4
Rothsay (MN.) 119 M 4
Roti, Pulau 177 F 6
Roti, Selat 177 F 6
Rotja, Punta 152 D 4
Roto 183 H 5
Rotorua 185 R 8
Rotterdam 148 D 4
Rottweil 149 E 5
Rotuma 186 C 3
Roubaix 152 D 1
Rouen 152 D 2
Rougemont (N.C.) 129 MN 5
Rough River Lake 128 E 4
Round Mound 120 F 4
Round Mountain (NV.) 112 HJ 4
Round Mountain (TX.) 122 E 5
Round Rock (AZ.) 116 G 1
Round Rock (TX.) 122 F 5
Roundup (MT.) 111 R 4
Round Valley Indian Reservation 112 B 3
Rousay 148 C 3
Rouyn 105 M 6
Rovaniemi 150 J 2
Rovdino 158 H 3
Rovereto 153 F 2
Rovigo 153 F 2
Rovinj 153 F 2
Rovkulskoye, Ozero 150 K 3
Rovno 151 J 5
Rovnoye 158 J 5
Rovuma 201 F 2
Rowe (N.M.) 117 L 2
Rowena (TX.) 122 C 4
Rowland (N.C.) 129 M 7
Rowland (NV.) 112 K 1
Rowley 105 M 2
Rowley Shoals 182 B 2
Roxas (Philippines) 177 E 1
Roxas (Philippines) 177 F 1
Roxboro (N.C.) 129 MN 5
Roxboro Lake 129 MN 5
Roxburgh 184 P 10
Roxen 151 G 4
Roxie (MS.) 130 C 3
Roxo, Cap 196 A 3
Roy (ID.) 111 N 8
Roy (MT.) 111 R 3
Roy (N.M.) 117 M 2
Roy (UT.) 114 E 2
Roy (WA.) 110 C 3
Royal City (WA.) 110 F 4
Royale, Isle 124 F 2
Royalton (MN.) 119 O 5
Royalty (TX.) 117 O 6
Royan 152 C 2
Roy Hill 182 C 4
Royse City (TX.) 122 G 2–3
Royston (GA.) 128 H 7
Rozel (KS.) 120 F 4
Rozet (WY.) 118 C 6
Rozhdestvenskoye 158 J 4
Rozhkao 155 F 2
Rožňava 149 H 5
Rozovka 155 E 1
Roztocze 149 H 4
Rtanj 154 B 2
Rtishchevo 158 H 5
Rt Kamenjak 153 F 3
Rt Ploča 153 G 3
Ruacana Falls 200 AB 3
Ruaha National Park 198 E 6
Ruahine Range 185 R 8–9
Ruapehu 185 R 8
Ruapuke 184 P 10
Ruawai 185 Q 8
Rubeho Mountains 199 F 6
Rubi 198 D 4
Rubiku 154 A 2
Rubinéia 141 F 5
Rubio 138 D 2
Rubondo 198 E 5
Rubonia (FL.) 131 M 6
Rubtsovsk 159 Q 5
Ruby (AK.) 102 F 3
Ruby (WA.) 110 H 2
Ruby Lake 112 K 2
Ruby Mountains 112 K 2–3
Ruby Range 111 N 5
Rubys Inn (UT.) 114 E 6
Ruby Valley (NV.) 112 K 2
Ruch (OR.) 110 BC 8
Rūdak (Iran) 157 F 3
Rudall River National Park 182 C 3
Rudao 173 H 4
Rudauli 174 D 2

Rūdbār (Iran) 157 E 1
Rudkøbing 151 F 5
Rudnaya Pristan' 173 L 2
Rudnik 154 B 2
Rudnya 158 F 4–5
Rudnyy 159 M 5
Rudolf, Lake 199 F 4
Rudolph (TX.) 122 F 9
Rudong 173 H 4
Rūd Sar (Iran) 157 F 1
Rudyard (MI.) 125 K 3
Rudyard (MT.) 111 P 2
Rudy Dome 112 K 2
Rufā'ah 194 E 6
Ruff (WA.) 110 G 3
Ruffec 152 D 2
Ruffin (S.C.) 129 L 8–9
Ruffling Point 130 E 8
Rufiji 199 F 6
Rufino 142 D 5
Rufisque 196 A 3
Rufunsa 200 D 3
Rufus (OR.) 110 E 5
Rugby (ND.) 118 J 2
Rügen 149 F 4
Ruhea 174 E 2
Ruhengeri 198 DE 5
Ruhnu 151 H 4
Ruhr 149 E 4
Ruhuhu 201 EF 2
Rui'an 173 H 5
Rui Barbosa 141 H 3
Ruidosa (TX.) 117 M 7–8
Ruidoso (N.M.) 117 L 4
Ruijin 172 G 5
Ruili 172 C 6
Rujm al Mudhari (Iraq) 156 C 2
Rujmayn, Jabal Abū (Syria) 156 BC 2
Rukumkot 174 D 2
Rukwa, Lake 198 E 6
Rule (TX.) 122 D 2
Ruleville (MS.) 121 P 9
Rulo (NE.) 121 K 2
Ruma 154 A 2
Rumādah 195 G 6
Rumaïla (Iraq) 157 E 3
Rumaylah 194 E 6
Rumbalara 182 E 4
Rumbek 198 DE 3
Rum Cay 133 H 3
Rumia 149 G 4
Rum Jungle 182 E 1
Rummah, Wādī ar (Saudi Arabia) 156 D 4
Rumoi 173 M 2
Rumphi 201 E 2
Runan 172 F 4
Runaway, Cape 185 R 8
Runde 201 E 4
Rundu 200 B 3
Rungu 198 D 4
Rungwa 198 E 6
Rungwa 198 E 6
Rungwa West 198 E 6
Rungwe 198 E 6
Runn 151 G 3
Ruokolahti 150 J 3
Ruo Shui 172 C 2
Ruovesi 150 H 3
Rupanco 143 B 7
Rupara 200 B 3
Rupat, Pulau 176 B 3
Rupert (GA.) 131 K 2
Rupert (ID.) 111 M 8
Rupert (Quebec, Can.) 105 M 5
Rupert (W.V.) 129 L 4
Rupert, Baie de 105 LM 5
Rupnagar 174 B 2
Ruponda 201 F 2
Rural Hall (N.C.) 129 L 5
Rurrenabaque 140 C 3
Rurutu 187 E 4
Rusakovo 171 U 4
Rusanovo 158 L 1
Rusape 201 E 3
Ruse 154 C 2
Ruşeţu 154 C 2
Rush (CO.) 115 N 5
Rushan 173 H 3
Rushan (U.S.S.R.) 169 J 3
Rush Center (KS.) 120 F 4
Rush City (MN.) 119 Q 5
Rushford (MN.) 119 R 7
Rushi (Iraq) 157 E 3
Rushmore, Mount 118 E 7
Rush Springs (OK.) 120 GH 8
Rushville (IL.) 124 D 9
Rushville (IN.) 128 F 2
Rushville (NE.) 118 F 8
Rusinga 198 E 5
Rusk (TX.) 123 H 4
Ruskin (FL.) 131 M 6
Ruso (ND.) 118 H 3
Russas 141 J 1
Russel (KS.) 120 G 4
Russel, Mount 109 H 3
Russell (Manitoba, Can.) 103 R 5
Russell (MN.) 119 N 6
Russell (New Zealand) 185 Q 8

Russell Cave National Monument 128 F 7
Russell Islands 185 G 3
Russell Range 182 C 5
Russellville (AL.) 128 D 7
Russellville (AR.) 121 M 7
Russellville (KY.) 128 D 5
Russel Springs (KS.) 120 DE 4
Russel Springs (KY.) 128 FG 4
Russian Mission 108 F 3
Russian River 112 C 4
Russkaya 173 L 1
Russkaya 203
Rustak 169 H 3
Rustavi 155 G 2
Rustburg (VA.) 129 MN 4
Rustenburg 200 D 5
Ruston (LA.) 123 L 3
Rutana 198 E 5
Ruteng 177 F 5
Rutenga 201 E 4
Ruth (MS.) 130 D 3
Ruth (NV.) 112 K 3
Rutherfordton (N.C.) 129 J 6
Ruther Glen (VA.) 129 O 4
Ruthton (MN.) 119 M 6
Ruthven (IA.) 119 O 7
Rutland 175 F 5
Rutland (N.D.) 119 L 4
Rutland (VT.) 126 G 5
Rutledge (TN.) 128 H 5
Rutog 174 C 1
Rutshuru 198 D 5
Ruvu 199 F 6
Ruvuma 201 F 2
Ruvuma 201 F 2
Ruwaybah 194 D 5
Ruwenzori National Park 198 DE 5
Ruwenzori Range 198 E 4
Ruzayevka 158 H 5
Ruzayevka 159 N 5
Ruzhnikova 171 T 2
Ruzitgort 159 N 3
Ruzizi 198 D 5
Ružomberok 149 G 5
Rwanda 198 DE 5
Ryābād (Iran) 157 G 1
Ryan (OK.) 120 GH 8
Ryan (TX.) 117 M 7MO
Ryan Park (WY.) 118 B 9
Ryan Peak 111 L 7
Ryazan' 158 G 5
Ryazhsk 158 G 5
Rybachiy, Poluostrov 150 K 2
Rybach'ye 169 K 2
Rybinsk → Andropov 158 G 4
Rybinskoye Vodokhranilishche 158 G 4
Rybnik 149 G 4
Rybnitsa 154 C 1
Rybnovsk 171 Q 5
Ryde 148 C 4
Ryder (ND.) 118 G 3
Ryderwood (WA.) 110 BC 4
Rye (CO.) 115 N 6
Ryegate (MT.) 111 Q 4
Rye Patch Reservoir 112 G 2
Ryfylke 151 E 4
Ryl'sk 158 F 5
Ryn Peski 158 J 6
Ryōtsu 173 L 3
Rytterknegten 151 G 4
Ryukyu Islands 173 J 5
Rzepin 149 FG 4
Rzeszów 149 H 4
Rzhev 158 F 4

S

Sa'ādatābād (Iran) 157 F 3
Sa'ādatābād (Iran) 157 F 3
Sa'ādatābād (Iran) 157 G 3
Saale 149 F 4
Saalfeld 149 F 4
Saanen 153 E 2
Saarbrücken 149 E 5
Sääre 151 H 4
Saaremaa 151 H 4
Saarijärvi 150 J 3
Saariselkä 150 J 2
Saarlouis 148 E 5
Saavedra 143 D 6
Šabac 154 A 2
Sabadell 152 D 3
Sabah 176 E 2
Sabak 176 B 3
Sabán 138 E 2
Sabana 138 D 3
Sabanalarga 138 C 1
Sabang 176 A 2
Sabang 177 E 3
Sabanözü 155 D 2
Săbăoani 154 C 1
Sabará 141 H 4

Sabari 174 D 4
Sabaya 140 C 4
Şabāyā 195 G 5
Sabderat 198 F 1
Sabetha (KS.) 120 K 3
Şabḥā (Jordan) 156 B 2
Sabhā (Libya) 193 H 3
Şabḥā' (Saudi Arabia) 195 G 4
Sabhā, Wāhāt 193 H 3
Sabi 201 E 3
Sabidana, Jabal 194 F 5
Sabinal (N.M.) 117 K 3
Sabinal (TX.) 122 D 6
Sabinas 132 B 2
Sabinas Hidalgo 132 B 2
Sabina Shoal 176 E 2
Sabine (TX.) 123 K 6
Sabine Lake 123 K 6
Sabine Pass (TX.) 123 K 6
Sabine River 123 K 5
Sabini, Monti 153 F 3
Şabīr, Jabal 195 G 6
Şābirīyah (Kuwait) 157 E 3
Sabkhat al Bardawīl (Egypt) 156 A 3
Sabkhat Albū Gharz (Iraq) 156 C 2
Sabkhat Maţţi (United Arab Emirates) 157 F 5
Sable, Cape (FL.) 131 N 9
Sable, Cape (Nova Scotia, Can.) 105 O 7
Sable, Île de 186 B 4
Sable Island 105 P 7
Sablinskoye 155 F 2
Sabon 159 Q 3
Sabonkafi 197 F 3
Sábor 152 B 3
Sabou 196 D 3
Sabozo 197 G 1
Sabrātah 193 H 2
Sabres 152 C 3
Sabrina Coast 203
Sabun 159 Q 3
Şabyā 195 G 5
Sabyndy 159 O 5
Sabzevār (Iran) 157 G 1
Saca, Vîrful 154 C 1
Sacagawea Peak 111 OP 5
Sacajawea, Lake 110 G 4
Sacajawea Peak 110 H 5
Sacanana 143 C 7
Sacandaga Reservoir 126 E 5
Sac and Fox Indian Reservation 121 J 3
Sacavém 152 B 4
Sac City (IA.) 119 NO 8
Sacco 153 F 3
Sacedón 152 C 3
Săcele 154 C 1
Sachkhere 155 F 2
Sachsen 149 F 4
Sachs Harbour 103 N 1
Saco (ME.) 126 J 5
Saco (MT.) 111 S 2
Sacramento (CA.) 112 D 4
Sacramento (N.M.) 117 L 5
Sacramento Mountains 117 L 4–5
Sacramento River 112 D 3
Sacramento Valley 112 C 3–D 4
Sacuriuiná 140 E 3
Sadabá 152 C 3
Sad ad Darbandī Khān (Iraq) 157 D 2
Sad ad Dūkān (Iraq) 157 D 1–2
Şa'dah 195 G 5
Sadani 199 F 6
Sad Bi'Ar (Syria) 156 B 2
Saddajaure 150 G 2
Sadd al Aswān (Egypt) 156 A 4
Saddle Mountain (WA.) 110 B 5
Saddle Mountain (WY.) 111 Q 6
Saddle Mountains (WA.) 110 EF 4
Saddle Peak 110 E 2
Saddle Peak 175 F 5
Saddlestring (WY.) 118 B 6
Sa Dec 175 J 5
Sadiya 175 G 2
S'adīyah, Hawr as (Iraq) 157 E 2
Sad Kharv (Iran) 157 G 1
Sado 152 B 4
Sadochye, Ozero 168 F 2
Sadon 155 F 2
Sadovoye 155 F 1
Sæböl 150 A 2
Sæby 151 F 4
Safané 196 D 3
Safed Khirs 169 J 3
Safed Koh 169 GH 4
Saffānīyah, Ra's as (Saudi Arabia) 157 E 3
Säffle 151 F 4
Safford (AL.) 130 G 2
Safford (AZ.) 116 G 5
Safi 192 D 2
Safid, Kūh-e (Iran) 157 E 2
Safid Dasht (Iran) 157 E 2
Safid Rūd (Iran) 157 E 1

Safonovo 158 F 4
Safonovo 171 X 3
Safrā' al Asyāḥ (Saudi Arabia) 156 D 4
Safrā' as Sark (Saudi Arabia) 156 D 4
Safranbolu 155 D 2
Şafwān (Iraq) 157 E 3
Saga (China) 174 E 2
Saga (Japan) 173 K 4
Saga (U.S.S.R.) 159 M 5
Sagaing 175 G 3
Sagala 196 C 3
Sagan 169 K 3
Sagar 174 C 3
Sagar 174 E 3
Sagastyr 171 N 1
Sagavanirktok 102 H 2
Sage (WY.) 111 P 9
Sagerton (TX.) 117 QR 4
Sagerton (TX.) 122 CD 2
Saghād (Iran) 157 F 3
Saginaw (MI.) 125 L 6
Saginaw Bay 125 L 6
Sagiz 168 E 1
Sagleipie 196 C 4
Saglek Bay 105 P 4
Saglouc 105 M 3
Sagres 152 B 4
Sagu (Indonesia) 177 F 5
Sagu (Romania) 154 B 1
Sague de Tánamo 133 H 3
Saguache (CO.) 115 LM 5
Sagua la Grande 133 G 3
Saguaro National Monument 116 E-F 5
Saguenay 105 NO 6
Saguia el Hamra 192 C 3
Saguia el Hamra 192 C 3
Sagunto 152 C 4
Sagwon 102 H 2
Sahagún (Colombia) 138 C 2
Sahagún (Spain) 152 B 3
Sahara 192–193 EG 4
Saharanpur 174 C 2
Saharsa 174 E 2
Sahiwal 169 J 4
Sahlābad 158 F 4
Sahl Rakbah 195 G 4
Şahneh (Iran) 157 E 2
Şaḥrā' al Hajārah (Iraq) 156–157 D 3
Şaḥrā' Bayyūdah 194 E 5
Sahuaripa 106 E 6
Sahuarita (AZ.) 116 F 6
Sahuayo de Diaz 132 B 4
Sahul Shelf 209 C 4
Sa Huynh 175 J 5
Saiapoun 175 H 4
Saibai 184 D 3
Saïda 192 F 2
Sa'īdābād (Iran) 157 G 3
Said Bundas 198 C 3
Saīdīyeh (Iran) 157 E 1
Saidor 184 E 3
Saidpur 174 E 2
Saigon 175 J 5
Saihan Toroi 172 D 2
Saiki 173 K 4
Saimaa 150 J 3
Saimaan kanava 150 J 3
Sain Alto 132 B 3
Saindak 169 G 5
Sāïn Dezh (Iran) 157 E 1
Saint Alban's (Newfoundl., Can.) 105 Q 6
St. Albans (U.K.) 148 CD 4
St. Albans (VT.) 126 F 4
Saint Albans (W.V.) 129 K 3
Saint Albert 103 P 5
Saint-Amand-Mont-Rond 152 D 2
Saint-André, Cap 201 G 3
St. Andrews 148 C 3
Saint Andrew Sound 131 N 3–4
St. Anne (IL.) 124 G 8
Saint Ann's Bay 133 G 4
Saint Anthony 105 QR 5
St. Anthony (ID.) 111 O 7
St. Anthony (ND.) 118 H 4
Saint Arnaud 183 G 6
St. Augustine (FL.) 131 N 5
Saint Augustin Saguenay 105 Q 5
St. Austell 148 C 4
Saint-Avold 153 E 2
Saint-Barthélemy 133 K 4
Saint-Brieuc 152 C 2
St.-Calais 152 D 2
St. Catherines Island 131 N 3
Saint-Chamond 153 D 2
St. Charles (ID.) 111 O 8
St. Charles (MI.) 125 K 6
Saint Charles (MN.) 119 QR 7
Saint Charles (MO.) 121 P 4
Saint Charles (SD.) 118 J 7
St. Christopher 133 K 4
St. Clair (MI.) 125 M 7
Saint Clair (MN.) 119 P 6
Saint Clair (MO.) 121 P 4
Saint Clair, Lake 125 M 7
Saint Clair River 125 M 7

Saint Clair Shores (MI.) **125** M 7
St. Clairsville (OH.) **125** N 9
Saint-Claude **153** E 2
Saint Cloud (FL.) **131** N 6
St. Cloud (MN.) **119** O 5
Saint Croix **130** E 9
Saint Croix **133** JK 4
St. Croix falls (WI.) **124** B 4
Saint Croix River (ME.) **126** M 3
Saint Croix River (MN./WI.)
 119 Q 5
Saint-Cyr-sur-Loire **152** D 2
Saint David (AZ.) **116** F 6
Saint David's Head **148** B 4
Saint-Denis (France) **152** D 2
Saint-Denis (Réunion) **201** K 6
Saint-Denis-d'Oléron **152** C 2
Saint-Dié **153** E 2
St. Dizier **153** DE 2
St. Edward (NE.) **119** L 9
Sainte Genevieve (MO.) **121** P 4–5
Saint Elias, Mount **102** J 3
Saint Elias Mountains **102** K 3
Saint-Elie **139** H 3
St. Elmo (IL.) **121** R 3
Sainte Lucie, Canal de **133** K 5
Sainte Marie, Cap **201** GH 5
Saintes **152** C 2
Saintes-Maries-de-la Mer **153** D 3
Sainte-Thérèse **105** MN 6
Saint-Étienne **152** D 2
Saint Félicien **105** N 6
Saint-Florent, Golfe de **153** E 3
Saint Flores National Park **198** C 3
Saint-Flour **152** D 2
St. Francis (KS.) **120** D 3
St. Francis (KS.) **120** D 3
St. Francis (ME.) **126** M 3
St. Francis (SD.) **118** H 7
Saint Francis, Cape **200** CD 6
Saint Francis Bay **200** A 5
Saint Francisville (LA.) **123** M 5
Saint Francois **199** J 6
Saint Francois Mountains **121** P 5
Saint Froid Lake **126** L 2
St. Gallen **153** E 2
Saint-Gaudens **152** D 3
Saint George (AK.) **102** D 4
Saint George (GA.) **131** M 4
Saint George (Queensland, Austr.)
 183 H 4
Saint George (S.C.) **129** L 8
St. George (UT.) **114** D 4
St. George, Cape **105** PQ 6
Saint George, Cape (Papua New
 Guinea) **185** F 2
Saint George, Point **112** A 1
St. George Island **131** K 5
Saint-Georges **105** NO 6
Saint George's **133** K 5
Saint Georges **139** H 3
Saint George's Bay **105** Q 6
Saint George's Channel **148** B 4
Saint George's Channel **185** F 2–3
Saint-Gildas, Pointe de **152** C 2
Saint Helena **188** B 3
St. Helena (CA.) **112** C 4
Saint Helena Bay **200** B 6
Saint Helena Sound **129** L 9
St. Helens, Mount **110** C 4
St. Helier **152** C 5
St. Ignace (MI.) **125** K 4
Saint Ignace Island **104** K 6
Saint Ignatius (MT.) **111** L 3
St. James (MI.) **124** J 4
Saint James (MN.) **119** O 7
Saint James (MO.) **121** O 4–5
Saint Jean **105** N 6
Saint-Jean, Lake **105** N 6
Saint-Jean-d'Angély **152** C 2
Saint-Jean-de-Luz **152** C 2
Saint-Jean-de-Monts **152** C 2
Saint Jérôme **105** N 6
Saint Jo (TX.) **122** F 2
St. Joe (ID.) **110** J 3
Saint Joe River **110** J 3
St. John (KS.) **120** G 4
Saint John (Liberia) **196** C 4
Saint John (ND.) **118** J 2
Saint-John (New Brunsw., Can.)
 105 O 6
Saint John (P.R.) **130** E 8
Saint John (WA.) **110** H 3
Saint John River **105** O 6
Saint John's (Antigua) **133** K 4
Saint Johns (AZ.) **116** G 3
St. Johns (MI.) **125** K 6
Saint John's (Newfoundl., Can.)
 105 R 6
St. Johnsbury (VT.) **126** H 4
Saint Johns River **131** N 4–5
Saint Joseph (LA.) **123** M 4
Saint Joseph (MI.) **124** H 7
St. Joseph (MO.) **121** M 3
Saint Joseph (Seychelles) **199** J 6
Saint Joseph, Lake **104** J 5
St. Joseph Island **122** G 7–8
Saint Joseph Point **131** J 5
Saint Joseph River **124** J 8
Saint-Junien **152** D 2

Saint Kilda **148** B 3
Saint Kitts-Nevis **133** K 4
Saint Kitts [Saint Christopher]
 133 K 4
Saint Landry (LA.) **123** L 5
Saint Laurent **139** H 2
Saint Lawrence **183** H 3
Saint Lawrence, Gulf of **105** P 6
Saint Lawrence Island **102** C 3
Saint Lawrence River **105** O 6
Saint Léonard **105** O 6
St. Louis (MO.) **121** P 4
St.-Louis (Senegal) **196** A 2
Saint Louis River **119** Q 3
Saint Lucia **133** K 5
Saint Lucia, Cape **201** E 5
Saint Lucia, Lake **201** E 5
Saint Magnus Bay **148** C 2
Saint-Malo **152** C 2
Saint-Marc **133** H 4
St. Margaret's Hope **148** C 3
St. Maries (ID.) **110** J 3
Saint Marks (FL.) **131** K 4
Saint-Martin **133** K 4
Saint Martin, Cape **112** L 6
Saint Martin Island **124** H 4
Saint-Martin-Vésubie **153** E 3
Saint Martinville (LA.) **123** M 5
Saint Mary (MT.) **111** M 2
Saint Mary Lake **111** M 2
Saint Mary Peak **183** F 5
Saint Marys **184** L 9
St. Marys (AK.) **102** E 3
Saint Marys (GA.) **131** N 4
St. Marys (KS.) **120** J 3
St. Marys (OH.) **125** K 9
St. Marys (PA.) **125** Q 8
St. Marys(W.V) **129** K 2
Saint Mary's **105** R 6
Saint Mary's Bay **105** R 6
Saint Marys River **131** N 4
Saint Matthew **102** C 3
Saint Matthews (S.C.) **129** L 8
Saint Matthias Group **185** E 2
Saint Matthias Group **186** AB 3
Saint Maurice **105** N 6
Saint Michael **102** E 3
Saint Michaels (AZ.) **116** G 2
St. Michales (MD.) **129** P 3
St Moritz **153** E 2
Saint-Nazaire **152** C 2
Saint Nicholas, Mount **111** M 2
St. Niklaas **148** D 4
Saint-Omer **152** D 1
Saint Onge (SD.) **118** E 6
Saint Patrick Peak **111** L 4
Saint Paul (AK., U.S.A.) **102** D 4
Saint Paul (Alb., Can.) **103** P 5
St. Paul (KY.) **128** HJ 3
St. Paul (MN.) **119** Q 6
St. Paul (Liberia) **196** B 4
St. Paul (NE.) **120** G 1
Saint-Paul (Réunion) **201** K 6
St. Paul (VA.) **129** J 5
Saint Pauls (N.C.) **129** MN 7
Saint-Péray **153** D 3
Saint Peter (KS.) **120** EF·3
Saint Peter (MN.) **119** OP 6
St. Peter and St. Paul Rocks
 135 G 2
St. Peter Port **148** C 5
St. Petersburg (FL.) **131** M 7
Saint Petersburg Beach (FL.)
 131 M 6
St. Phillip (MT.) **118** D 4
Saint Pierre **105** Q 6
Saint-Pierre (Réunion) **201** K 6
Saint Pierre (Seychelles) **199** J 6
Saint Pierre et Miquelon **105** Q 6
Saint-Pons **152** D 3
Saint-Quentin **152** D 2
Saint Regis (MT.) **111** K 3
St. Regis Falls (N.Y.) **126** E 4
Saint Regis Indian Reservation
 126 E 4
St. Roch Basin **103** ST 2
Saint-Savin **152** D 2
Saint-Seine-l'Abbaye **153** DE 2
St. Simons Island **131** N 3
Saint Stephen (New Brunsw., Can.)
 105 O 6
Saint Stephen (S.C.) **129** M 8
Saint Teresa Beach (FL.) **131** K 5
Saint-Thomas (Ontario, Can.)
 105 L 7
Saint Thomas(P.R.) **130** E 8
Saint-Thomas (Puerto Rico)
 133 JK 4
St. Tomas (N.D.) **119** L 2
Saint-Tropez **153** E 3
Saint Vincent **133** K 5
St. Vincent (MN.) **119** L 2
Saint Vincent, Gulf **183** F 6
Saint Vincent Island **131** J 5
Saint Vincent Passage **133** K 5
St. Walburg **103** Q 5
St. Xavier (MT.) **111** S 5
Saint-Yrieix-la-Perche **152** D 2
Saipal **174** D 2
Saipan **186** A 1

Sai Yok **175** G 5
Sajama **140** C 4
Sajama, Nevado **140** C 4
Sajānan **153** E 4
Sajid **195** G 5
Sajó **154** B 1
Sajzī (Iran) **157** F 2
Saka **199** F 5
Sakabinda **200** CD 2
Sakai **173** L 4
Sakākah (Saudi Arabia) **156** C 3
Sakakawea, Lake **118** F 2
Sakala Kõrgustik **151** J 4
Sakami **105** M 5
Sakami, Lac **105** M 5
Sakami River **105** N 5
Sakania **200** D 2
Sakar **154** C 2
Sakaraha **201** G 4
Sakarat Dağı **155** E 2
Sakaraya **154** D 3
Sakarya **154** D 2
Sakashima-guntō **173** HJ 6
Sakata **173** L 3
Sakçagöz **155** E 3
Sakchu **173** J 2
Sakété **196** E 4
Sakevare **150** G 2
Sakha **154** C 3
Sakhalin **171** Q 5
Sakhalinskiy Zaliv **171** Q 5
Sakhandzha **171** N 2
Sakht Sar (Iran) **157** F 1
Saki **155** D 1
Sakoli **174** D 3
Sakon Nakhon **175** H 4
Sakrivier **200** C 6
Sakti **174** D 3
Saksaul'skiy **169** G 1
Säkylä **150** H 3
Sal **155** F 1
Sal (Cape Verde) **196** B 6
Sal, Point **113** E 8
Sala **151** H 4
Sala Andong Tuk **175** H 5
Salaca **151** H 4
Salacgrîva **151** H 4
Sala Consilina **153** G 3
Salada **132** B 2
Salada, Gran Laguna **143** C 7
Saladillo **143** E 6
Salado **142** C 4
Salado **143** C 6
Salaga **196** D 4
Salagle **199** G 4
Salair **159** R 5
Salairskiy Kryazh **159** R 5
Salal **197** H 3
Salālah (Oman) **195** J 5
Salālah (Sudan) **194** F 4
Salamá **132** D 4
Salamanca (Mexico) **132** B 3
Salamanca (Spain) **152** B 3
Salamat **197** J 3
Salamina **138** C 2
Salamis (Cyprus) **155** D 3
Salamis (Cyprus) **156** AB 2
Salamis (Greece) **154** B 3
Salar de Antofalla **142** C 4
Salar de Arizaro **140** C 5
Salar de Atacama **140** C 5
Salar de Coipasa **140** C 4
Salar de Hombre Muerto **142** C 4
Salar de Uyuni **140** C 5
Salas **152** B 3
Salatiga **176** D 5
Salavat **155** E 2
Salaverry **138** C 5
Salavina **142** D 4
Salawati, Pulau **177** H 4
Sala y Gómes **187** H 4
Salbris **152** D 2
Salcantay, Nevado **140** B 3
Salchininkai **151** J 5
Saldanha **200** B 6
Salduro (UT.) **114** D 3
Saldus **151** H 4
Sale (Australia) **183** H 6
Salé (Morocco) **192** D 2
Sale Creek (TN.) **128** F 6
Sālehābād (Iran) **157** E 2
Salekhard **159** N 2
Salem (AR.) **121** O 6
Salem (FL.) **131** L 5
Salem (IA.) **119** R 10
Salem (IL.) **121** R 4
Salem (IN.) **128** E 3
Salem (India) **174** C 5
Salem (MA.) **126** J 6
Salem (MO.) **121** O 5
Salem (N.Y.) **126** F 5
Salem (OR.) **110** BC 6
Salem (PA.) **127** D 9
Salem (S.D.) **119** L 7
Salem (VA.) **129** L 4
Salem (W.V.) **129** L 2
Salemi **153** E 4
Sälen **150** F 3
Salentina, Penisola **153** G 3–4
Salerno **153** FG 3
Salerno, Golfo di **153** F 3

Sales **139** H 5
Salesville (TX.) **122** E 3
Saletekri **174** D 3
Salgótarján **154** AB 1
Salgueiro **141** J 2
Salhus **151** E 3
Sali (Algeria) **192** E 3
Sali (Argentina) **142** C 4
Sali (Yugoslavia) **153** FG 3
Salida (CO.) **115** M 5
Salihli **154** C 3
Salima **201** E 2
Salīmah, Wāhāt **194** D 4
Salin **175** F 3
Salina (AZ.) **116** G 1
Salina (Italy) **153** F 4
Salina (KS.) **120** H 4
Salina (UT.) **114** F 5
Salina del Gualicho **143** D 7
Salina Grande **143** C 6
Salinas (CA.) **112** D 6
Salinas (Ecuador) **138** B 4
Salinas (Minas Gerais, Brazil)
 141 H 4
Salinas (P.R.) **130** C 9
Salinas, Cabo de **152** D 4
Salinas, Ponta das **200** A 2
Salinas de Hidalgo **132** B 3
Salinas Peak **117** K 4
Salinas River **112** D 6
Saline (LA.) **123** L 3
Saline Lake **123** L 4
Salineno (TX.) **122** D 9
Saline River (AR.) **121** N 9
Saline River (KS.) **120** F 3
Salinitas **140** B 5
Salinópolis **139** J 4
Salisbury (MD.) **129** Q 3
Salisbury (N.C.) **129** L 6
Salisbury (N.W.T., Can.) **105** M 3
Salisbury (PA.) **125** PQ 10
Salisbury (U.K.) **148** C 4
Salisbury → Harare **201** E 3
Salkhad (Syria) **156** B 2
Salkum (WA.) **110** C 4
Salla **150** J 2
Salling **151** E 4
Sallisaw (OK.) **121** L 7
Sallūm **194** F 5
Salluyo, Nevado **140** C 3
Sallyana **174** D 2
Salmās **168** C 3
Salmi **150** K 3
Salmon (ID.) **111** LM 5
Salmon Arm **103** O 5
Salmon Creek Reservoir **111** L 8
Salmon Mountains **112** B 1–2
Salmon River **110** J 5
Salmon River Mountains **111** K 5–6
Salo (Centr. Afr. Rep.) **198** B 4
Salo (Finland) **151** H 3
Saló (Italy) **153** F 2
Salome (AZ.) **116** C 4
Salon-de-Provence **153** E 3
Salong, Tünel-e- **169** H 3
Salonga National Park **198** C 5
Salonica **154** B 2
Salon Springs (WI.) **124** C 3
Salonta **154** B 1
Salor **152** B 4
Salou **152** D 3
Salpausselkä **150** J 3
Sal-Rei **196** B 6
Salsbruket **150** F 3
Sal'sk **155** F 1
Salso **153** F 4
Salsomaggiore Terme **153** E 3
Salt **152** D 3
Salta **140** C 5
Saltdale (CA.) **113** H 7
Saltdalselva **150** G 2
Salten **150** G 2
Saltfjellet **150** G 2
Saltfjorden **150** F 2
Salt Flat (TX.) **117** L 6
Salt Fork (OK.) **120** GH 6
Salt Fork (OK.) **120** F 8
Salt Fork (TX.) **117** Q 4
Salt Gap (TX.) **122** D 4
Saltillo **132** B 2
Saltillo (MS.) **121** R 8
Saltillo (TN.) **128** C 6
Salt Lake (N.M.) **117** MN 5
Salt Lake (Queensland, Austr.)
 183 F 3
Salt Lake City (UT.) **114** F 3
Salt Lakes **182** C 3
Salt Lakes **182** B 4
Salt Marsh Lake **114** D 4
Salto (Uruguay) **142** E 5
Salto Angostura **138** D 3
Salto da Divisa **141** J 4
Salto das Sete Quedas **141** F 5
Salto del Guaira **141** EF 5
Salton Sea **113** K 9
Salt Range **169** J 4
Salt River **116** F 4
Salt River (South Africa) **200** C 6

Salt Springs (FL.) **131** N 5
Saltville (VA.) **129** K 5
Salt Wells (NV.) **112** G 3
Saluda (S.C.) **129** K 7–8
Saluda (VA.) **129** P 4
Saluda River **129** K 7
Salue Timpaus, Selat **177** F 4
Salumbar **174** B 3
Salur **174** D 4
Salvador (Brazil) **141** J 3
Salvador (Libya) **197** G 1
Salvador, Lake **123** N 6
Salvatierra (Mexico) **132** B 3
Salvatierra (Spain) **152** C 3
Salwā (Qatar) **157** F 4
Salwá Baḥrī (Egypt) **156** A 4
Salween **175** G 4
Sal'yany **168** D 3
Salyer (CA.) **112** B 2
Salyersville (KY.) **128** J 4
Salzach **153** F 2
Salzburg **153** F 2
Salzgitter **149** F 4
Salzwedel **149** F 4
Sa Madre Occidental **132** AB 2–3
Samagaltay **170** G 3
Samāh (Libya) **193** J 3
Samāh (Saudi Arabia) **157** D 3
Samaipata **140** D 4
Samak, Tanjung **176** C 4
Samales Group **177** F 2
Samalga Pass **102** D 5
Samālūt **194** E 3
Samaná **133** J 4
Samandağ **155** E 3
Samandgi (Turkey) **156** B 1
Samangan **169** H 3
Samani **173** M 2
Samar **177** G 1
Samara (Russiya, U.S.S.R.)
 158 K 5
Samara (Ukraine, U.S.S.R.)
 155 E 1
Samarai **185** F 4
Samaria (ID.) **111** N 8
Samaríapo **138** E 2
Samarinda **176** E 4
Samarkand **169** H 3
Samar Sea **177** F 1
Samarskoye **159** Q 6
Samastipur **174** E 2
Samate **177** H 4
Samaūma **138** E 5
Samba **198** C 4
Samba **198** D 5
Samba Caju **200** B 1
Sambaliung **176–177** E 3
Sambalpur **174** D 3
Sambar, Tanjung **176** CD 4
Sambas **176** C 3
Sambava **201** J 2
Sambhar **174** C 2
Samboja **176** E 4
Sambor (Kampuchea) **175** J 5
Samborombón, Bahía **143** E 6
Samborondón **138** B 4
Sambre **152** D 1–2
S. Ambrosio Island **135** C 5
Sambu **176** B 3
Sambuan **196** E 4
Samburg **159** P 2
Samch'ŏnp'o **173** N 4
Same (Indonesia) **177** G 5
Same (Tanzania) **199** F 5
Samfya **200** D 2
Sámi **154** B 3
Sami Ghar **169** H 4
Samīrah (Saudi Arabia) **156** C 4
Samka **175** G 3
Sam Neua **175** H 3
Samoa (CA.) **112** A 2
Samoa Islands **186** D 3
Samo Alto **142** B 5
Samobor **153** G 2
Samokov **154** B 2
Sámos **154** C 3
Samosir, Pulau **176** A 3
Samothraki **154** C 2
Samothraki **154** C 2
Sampaga **177** E 4
Sampit **176** D 4
Sampit, Teluk **176** D 4
Sampun **185** F 2
Sampwe **198** D 6
Sam Rayburn Dam **123** JK 4
Sam Rayburn Reservoir **123** J 4
Samrong **175** H 5
Samsang **174** D 1
Samsö **151** F 4
Sam Son **175** J 4
Samson (AL.) **131** HG 3
Samsun **155** E 2
Samthar **174** C 2
Samtredia **155** F 2
Samuel, Mount **182** E 2
Samus' **159** QR 4

Samut Prakan 175 H 5
Samut Songkhram 175 H 5
San (Mali) 196 D 3
San (Poland) 149 H 4
Sana 153 G 3
San'ā' 195 G 5
Sanaba 196 D 3
San Acacia (N.M.) 117 K 3
Sanae 203
Sanāfir (Saudi Arabia) 156 B 3–4
Sanaga 197 G 5
Sanagir 174 C 2
San Agustin, Cape 177 G 2
San Agustin, Plains of 116 HJ 4
San Agustin de Valle Fértil 142 C 5
Sanain 155 F 2
Sanak Islands 102 E 5
Sanana 177 G 4
Sanana, Pulau 177 G 4
Sanandaj (Iran) 157 E 2
San Andreas (CA.) 112 E 4
San Andrés 133 F 5
San Andrés del Rabanedo 152 B 3
San Andres Mountains 117 K 4–5
San Andres Peak 117 K 5
San Andrés Tuxtla 132 D 4
Sananduva 142 F 4
San Angelo (TX.) 122 C 4
San Angelo Lake 122 C 4
San Anselmo (CA.) 112 C 4
San Antonia de Cortés 132 E 4–5
San Antonio 138 E 3
San Antonio (Chile) 142 B 5
San Antonio (CO.) 115 M 6
San Antonio (N.M.) 117 K 4
San Antonio (Portugal) 192 A 1
San Antonio (TX.) 122 E 6
San Antonio (Uruguay) 142 E 5
San Antonio, Cabo (Argentina)
  143 E 6
San Antonio, Cabo (Cuba) 132 F 3
San Antonio, Mount 113 H 8
San Antonio Abad 152 D 4
San Antonio Bay 122 G 7
San Antonio de Caparo 138 D 2
San Antonio de los Cobres 140 C 5
San Antonio del Tachira 138 D 2
San Antonio Mountain 117 KL 1
San Antonio Oeste 143 D 7
San Antonio Reservoir 113 DE 7
San Antonio River 122 F 7
San Ardo (CA.) 112 E 6
San Augstin Pass 117 K 5
San Augustine (TX.) 123 J 4
San Augustin Pass (TX.) 122 F 9
Sanāw 195 J 5
San Barnardino (CA.) 113 H 8
San Benito (CA.) 112 D 6
San Benito Mountain 112 E 6
San Bernadetto del Tronto 153 F 3
San Bernardino Mountains
  113 J 8–9
San Bernardo (Chile) 142 BC 5
San Bernardo (Mexico) 106 D 6
San Blas 106 E 6
San Blas 132 B 2
San Blas 132 A 3
San Blas, Cape 131 J 5
San Borja 140 C 3
San Borjas, Sierra de 106 D 6
Sanborn (MN.) 119 N 6
Sanborn (N.D.) 119 K 4
San Buenaventura 132 B 2
SanCarlos 138 BC 2
Sancarlos 138 E 2
San Carlos (Argentina) 142 C 4
San Carlos (Argentina) 142 C 5
San Carlos (AZ.) 116 F 4
San Carlos (Chile) 143 B 6
San Carlos (Mexico) 132 C 3
San Carlos (Nicaragua) 132 F 5
San Carlos (Philippines) 177 F 1
San Carlos (Uruguay) 142 EF 5
San Carlos (Venezuela) 138 E 2
San Carlos de Bariloche 143 B 7
San Carlos del Zulia 138 D 2
San Carlos de Río Negro 138 E 3
San Carlos Indian Reservation
  116 FG 4
San Carlos Lake 116 F 4
San Casme 142 E 4
San Cataldo 153 F 4
Sancerrois, Collines du 152 D 2
Sánchez 133 J 4
Sanchez (N.M.) 117 M 2
Sanchor 174 B 3
San Clemente (CA.) 113 H 9
San Clemente Island 113 G 10
San Cristóbal (Argentina) 142 D 5
San Cristóbal (Dominican Rep.)
  133 HJ 4
San Cristobal (Galápagos Is.)
  138 B 6
San Cristobal (Solomon Is.)
  185 H 4
San Cristóbal (Solomon Is.) 186 B 3
San Cristóbal (Venezuela) 138 D 2
San Cristóbal de las Casas 132 D 4
Sancti Spíritus 133 G 3
San Custodio 138 E 3

Sand 151 E 4
Sandai 176 D 4
Sandakan 176 E 2
Sandanski 154 B 2
Sandaré 196 B 3
Sandarne 150 E 3
Sanday 148 C 3
Sand Cay 174 B 5
Sand Creek 118 C 7
Sand Draw (WY.) 111 R 8
Sandefjord 151 EF 4
Sanders (AZ.) 116 G 2
Sanders (MT.) 111 S 4
Sanderson (TX.) 117 O 7
Sandersville (GA.) 131 M 2
Sandersville (MS.) 130 EF 3
Sand Hills 118 G 9
Sandia 140 C 3
Sandia Crest 117 K 2
Sandia Pueblo (N.M.) 117 K 2
San Diego (CA.) 113 H 10
San Diego (TX.) 122 E 8
San Diego, Cabo 143 C 9
Sandıklı 154 D 3
Sandila 174 D 2
Sandiman, Mount 182 B 3
San Dimitri Point 153 F 4
Sanding, Pulau 176 B 4
Sand Island 124 CD 3
Sandnes 151 E 4
Sandnessjöen 150 F 2
Sandoa 198 C 6
Sandomierz 149 H 4
San Dona di Piave 153 F 2
Sandow (TX.) 122 F 5
Sandoway 175 F 4
Sandoy 148 A 1
Sand Pass (NV.) 112 F 2
Sand Point 102 EF 4
Sands Key 131 O 9
Sandspit 102 L 5
Sand Springs (MT.) 111 S 3
Sand Springs (OK.) 120 J 6
Sandstone (MN.) 119 Q 4
Sandstone (Western Australia)
  182 B 4
Sandur 148 A 1
Sandusky (MI.) 125 M 6
Sandusky (OH.) 125 M 8
Sandvig 151 FG 4
Sandvika 151 F 4
Sandviken 151 G 3
Sandwich (MA.) 126 J 7
Sandwich Bay (Namibia) 200 A 4
Sandwich Bay (Newfoundl., Can.)
  105 Q 5
Sandwip 175 F 3
Sandy (OR.) 110 C 5
Sandy (TX.) 122 E 5
Sandy Cape 183 J 3
Sandy Desert, Great 182 C 3
Sandy Hook (KY.) 128 H 3
Sandy Hook (MS.) 130 E 3
Sandykachi 169 G 3
Sandy Lake 104 J 5
Sandy Point 175 F 5
Sandy Springs (GA.) 128 G 8
San Estanislao 140 E 5
San Esteban de Gormaz 152 C 3
San Felípe (Chile) 142 B 5
San Felípe (Colombia) 138 E 3
San Felipe (Mexico) 106 D 5
San Felipe (Mexico) 132 B 3
San Felipe (Venezuela) 138 E 1
San Felipe, Cerro de 152 C 3
San Feliu 152 D 3
San Feliú de Guixols 152 D 3
San Fernando (CA.) 113 G 8
San Fernando (Chile) 143 B 5
San Fernando (Mexico) 132 C 3
San Fernando (Philippines) 177 J 1
San Fernando (Spain) 152 B 4
San Fernando (Trinidad and
  Tobago) 139 F 1
San Fernando de Apure 138 E 2
San Fernando de Atabapo
  138 E 3
Sånfjället 150 F 3
Sanford (FL.) 131 N 6
Sanford (KS.) 120 F 4
Sanford (ME.) 126 J 3
Sanford (MI.) 125 K 6
Sanford (N.C.) 129 M 6
Sanford, Mount 102 J 3
Sanford River 182 B 4
San Francisco (Argentina) 142 D 5
San Francisco (CA.) 112 C 5
San Francisco, Cabo de 138 B 3
San Francisco, Paso de 142 C 4
San Francisco Bay 112 C 5
San Francisco de Arriba 132 B 2
San Francisco del Chanar 142 D 4
San Francisco del Monte de Oro
  142 C 5
San Francisco del Oro 106 E 6
San Francisco del Rincón 132 B 3
San Francisco de Macorís 133 HJ 4
San Francisco Javier 152 D 4
San Francisco Mountains (AZ.)
  116 DE 2

San Francisco Mountains (N.M.)
  116 H 3–4
Sanga 201 F 2
San Gabriel Mountains 113 GH 8
Sanga-Kyuyel' 171 Q 3
Sangamner 174 B 4
Sangamon River 121 Q 3
Sangar 171 N 3
Sangar (Iran) 157 E 1
Sangareddipet 174 C 4
Sangatolon 171 R 3
Sangay, Volcán 138 C 4
Sangayán, Isla 140 A 3
Sangbe 197 G 4
Sange 198 D 6
Sangeang, Pulau 177 E 5
Sanger (CA.) 112 F 6
Sanger (TX.) 122 F 2
Sangerfield (N.Y.) 126 D 6
San Germán (P.R.) 130 C 8
Sanggan He 172 F 2
Sanggau 176 D 3
Sangha 197 GH 5
Sangha 197 H 5
Sangihe, Kepulauan 177 G 3
Sangihe, Pulau 177 G 3
San Gil 138 D 2
San Giovanni in Fiore 153 G 4
Sangiyn Dalay Nuur 170 GH 6
Sangin 169 F 2
Sangju 173 J 3
Sangkhla Buri 175 G 5
Sangkulirang, Teluk 177 E 3
Sangli 174 B 4
Sangmélima 197 G 5
San Gorgonio Mountain 113 J 8
San Gregorio (Chile) 143 B 9
San Gregorio (Uruguay) 142 E 5
Sangre Grande 139 F 1
Sangri 172 B 5
Sangrur 174 C 1
Sangue 140 E 3
Sangüesa 152 C 3
Sangzhi 172 F 5
Sanhala 196 C 4
Sanhe 170 M 5
San Hilario 106 D 7
Sanibel Island 131 M 8
San Ignacio 140 D 4
San Ignacio (Argentina) 143 E 4
San Ignacio (Belize) 132 E 4
San Ignacio (Bolivia) 140 C 3
San Ignacio (Mexico) 106 D 6
San Ignacio (Paraguay) 142 E 4
San Ignacio, Isla de 106 E 6
Sanikiluaq 105 M 4
San Isidro (Argentina) 142 DE 5
San Isidro (Costa Rica) 132 F 6
San Isidro (Peru) 138 C 4
San Isidro (TX.) 122 E 9
San Jacinto 138 C 2
San Jacinto (NV.) 112 L 1
San Jacinto Mountains 113 J 9
San Jacinto Peak 113 J 9
San Javier (Argentina) 142 D 5
San Javier (Bolivia) 140 D 4
San Javier (Chile) 143 B 6
San Javier (Spain) 152 C 4
San Javier (Uruguay) 142 E 5
Sanjawi 169 H 4
Sanjiang 172 E 5
Sanjō 173 L 3
San Joaquín 140 D 3
San Joaquin (CA.) 112 EF 6
San Joaquin River 112 E 5
San Joaquin Valley 112 D 5–6
San Jon (N.M.) 117 N 2
San Jorge (Colombia) 138 C 2
San Jorge (Solomon Is.) 185 G 3
San Jorge, Bahia de 106 D 5
San Jorge, Golfo 143 C 8
San Jorge, Golfo de 152 D 3
San Jose (CA.) 112 D 5
San José (Costa Rica) 132 F 6
San José (Guatemala) 132 D 5
San Jose (N.M.) 117 L 2
San Jose (Philippines) 177 F 1
San Jose (Philippines) 177 J 1
San José, Isla 106 DE 6
San José de Amacuro 139 F 2
San Jose de Buenavista 177 F 1
San José de Chiquitos 140 D 4
San José de Feliciano 142 E 5
San José de Gracia 106 E 6
San José de Guanipa 139 F 2
San José de Jáchal 142 C 4
San José del Cabo 106 E 7
San José del Guaviare 138 D 3
San José de Mayo 142 E 5
San José de Ocuné 138 DE 3
San Juan (Argentina) 142 C 5
San Juan (Argentina) 142 C 5
San Juan (Dominican Rep.) 133 H 4
San Juan (Peru) 140 A 4
San Juan (P.R.) 130 C 8
San Juan (Puerto Rico) 133 J 4
San Juan (Venezuela) 138 E 2

San Juan, Cabo 197 F 5
San Juan, Pico 133 F 3
San Juan, Rio 132 F 5
San Juana (Venezuela) 138 E 2
San Juan Basin 116 HJ 1
San Juan Bautista (Paraguay)
  142 E 4
San Juan Bautista (Spain) 152 D 4
San Juan Bautista Tuxtepec
  132 C 4
San Juan de Guadalupe 132 B 3
San Juan del Norte 132 F 5
San Juan de los Cayos 138 E 1
San Juan del Rio 132 B 3
San Juan del Rio 132 BC 3
San Juan Indian Reservation
  117 K 1
San Juan Island 110 B 2
San Juan Mountains 115 KL 6
San Juan River 114 G 6
San Julián 143 C 8
San Justo 142 D 5
Sankarani 196 C 3
Sankosh 174 E 2
Sankt Gotthard-Pass 153 E 2
Sankt Martin 153 G 2
Sankt Michel 150 J 3
Sankt Pölten 153 F 2
Sankt Veit an der Glan 153 F 2
Sankuru 198 C 5
San Lázaro, Sierra de 106 C 7
San Leandro (CA.) 112 C 5
San Lorenzo (Argentina) 142 D 5
San Lorenzo (Ecuador) 138 C 3
San Lorenzo (Mexico) 106 E 7
San Lorenzo, Cabo 138 B 4
San Lorenzo, Cerro 143 B 8
Sanlúcar de Barrameda 152 B 4
San Lucas (Bolivia) 140 C 5
San Lucas (CA.) 112 E 6
San Lucas (Mexico) 106 D 7
San Lucas, Cabo 106 E 7
San Luis (Argentina)142 C 5
San Luis (AZ.) 116 B 5
San Luis (CO.) 115 M 6
San Luis (Mexico) 106 D 6
San Luís (Venezuela) 138 E 1
San Luis, Lago de 140 D 3
San Luis de la Paz 132 BC 3
San Luis Gonzaga, Bahía 106 D 5
San Luis Obispo (CA.) 113 E 7
San Luis Obispo Bay 113 E 7
San Luis Peak 115 L 6
San Luis Potosi 132 B 3
San Luis Reservoir 112 D 5
San Luis Rio Colorado 106 D 5
San Manuel (AZ.) 116 F 5
San Marcial (N.M.) 117 K 4
San Marco, Capo 153 E 4
San Marcos (Colombia) 138 C 2
San Marcos (Mexico) 132 B 3
San Marcos (Mexico) 132 C 4
San Marcos (TX.) 122 F 6
San Marcos, Isla 106 D 6
San Marino 153 F 3
San Martín (Bolivia) 140 D 3
San Martín (Colombia) 138 D 3
San Martín (Spain) 152 C 3
San Martín, Lago 143 B 8
San Martín de los Andes 143 B 7
San Mateo (CA.) 112 C 5
San Mateo (N.M.) 116 J 2
San Matías 140 E 4
San Matías, Golfo 143 D 7
Sanmen 173 H 5
Sanmenxia 172 F 4
San Miguel (AZ.) 116 E 6
San Miguel (Bolivia) 140 D 3
San Miguel (CA.) 113 E 7
San Miguel (El Salvador) 132 E 5
San Miguel (N.M.) 117 K 1
San Miguel (Peru) 140 B 3
San Miguel de Allende 132 BC 3
San Miguel de Horcasitas 106 D 6
San Miguel de Huachi 140 C 4
San Miguel del Padrón 133 F 3
San Miguel de Tucumán 142 C 4
San Miguel Island 113 E 8
San Miguel Islands 177 E 2
San Miguel Sole de Vega 132 C 4
Sanming 173 G 5
Sannār 194 E 6
Sannikova 202
Sannikova, Proliv 171 PQ 1
Sanniquellie 196 C 4
Sanok 149 H 4
San Onofre 138 C 2
Sa-Nos-tee (N.M.) 116 H 1
San Pablo (Argentina) 143 C 9
San Pablo (Bolivia) 140 C 5
San Pablo (CO.) 115 M 6
San Pablo (Philippines) 177 F 1
San Pablo Bay 112 C 4
San Pedro (Argentina) 140 D 5
San Pedro (Argentina) 142 DE 5
San Pedro (CO.) 115 M 6

San Pedro (Dominican Rep.)
  133 J 4
San Pédro (Ivory Coast) 196 C 5
San Pedro (Mexico) 132 B 2
San Pedro (Paraguay) 140 E 5
San Pedro (TX.) 122 F 8
San Pedro, Sierra de 152 B 4
San Pedro Channel 113 G 9
San Pedro de Arimena 138 D 3
San Pedro de Atacama 140 C 5
San Pedro de las Bôcas 139 F 2
San Pedro de Lloc 138 BC 5
San Pedro Pochutla 132 C 4
San Pedro River 116 F 5
San Pedro Sula 132 E 4
San Pietro 153 E 4
Sanpoil River 110 G 2
San Quintin 106 C 5
San Quintin, Bahia de 106 C 5
San Rafael (Argentina) 142 C 5
San Rafael (Bolivia) 140 D 4
San Rafael (CA.) 112 C 5
San Rafael (Chile) 143 B 6
San Rafael (Mexico) 132 B 2
San Rafael (N.M.) 116 J 2
San Rafael, Cabo 133 J 4
San Rafael Mountains 113 EF 8
San Rafael River 114 G 5
San Rafael Swell 114 G 5
San Ramón 140 AB 3
San Ramón de la Nueva Orán
  140 D 5
Remo 153 E 3
San Remo 152 B 4
San Roque 152 B 4
San Saba (TX.) 122 E 4
San Saba River 122 D 4–5
San Salvador (El Salvador) 132 E 5
San Salvador (Spain) 152 D 4
San Salvador (Watling Is.)
  133 GH 3
San Salvador, Isla138 B 6
San Salvador de Jujuy 140 C 5
Sansanding 196 C 3
Sansanné Mango 196 E 3
San Sebastian (Argentina) 143 C 9
San Sebastián (P.R.) 130 C 8
San Sebastián (Spain) 152 C 3
San Severo 153 G 3
San Silvestre 138 D 2
San Simeon (CA.) 113 D 7
San Simon (AZ.) 116 G 5
San Simon Valley 116 G 5
Santa 138 C 5
Santa (ID.) 110 J 3
Santa Ana 106 D 5
Santa Ana (Bolivia) 140 C 3
Santa Ana (CA.) 113 H 9
Santa Ana (Ecuador) 138 BC 4
Santa Ana (El Salvador) 132 DE 5
Santa Ana (Solomon Is.) 185 H 4
Santa Ana, Cuchilla de 142 EF 5
Santa Ana Mountains 113 H 9
Santa Ana Pueblo (N.M.) 117 K 2
Santa Anna (TX.) 122 D 4
Santa Barbara (CA.) 113 F 8
Santa Barbara (Mexico) 106 E 6
Santa Barbara Channel 113 EF 8
Santa Bárbara do Sul 142 F 4
Santa Barbara Island 113 F 9
Santa Carolina, Ilha 201 F 4
Santa Catalina (Argentina) 140 C 5
Santa Catalina (Chile) 142 C 4
Santa Catalina, Gulf of 113 GH 9
Santa Catalina Island 113 G 9
Santa Catarina (Brazil) 142 F 4
Santa Catarina, Ilha de 142 G 4
Santa Clara (CA.) 112 CD 5
Santa Clara (Colombia) 138 E 4
Santa Clara (Cuba) 133 F 3
Santa Clara (Mexico) 106 E 6
Santa Clara (UT.) 114 G 5
Santa Clara Indian Reservation
  117 K 2
Santa Clara Valley 112 D 5–6
Santa Clotilde 138 D 4
Santa Comba 152 B 3
Santa Cruz (Amazonas, Brazil)
  138 D 5
Santa Cruz (Argentina) 143 B 9
Santa Cruz (Argentina) 143 C 9
Santa Cruz (Bolivia) 140 D 4
Santa Cruz (CA.) 112 C 6
Santa Cruz (Chile) 143 B 5
Santa Cruz (Costa Rica) 132 E 5
Santa Cruz (Espírito Santo, Brazil)
  141 HJ 5
Santa Cruz (Pará, Brazil) 139 H 4
Santa Cruz (Peru) 138 C 5
Santa Cruz (Philippines) 177 F 1
Santa Cruz (Philippines) 177 H 1
Santa Cruz, Isla (Galápagos Is.)
  138 B 6
Santa Cruz de la Palma 192 B 3
Santa Cruz de la Zarza 152 C 4
Santa Cruz del Sur 133 G 3
Santa Cruz de Mudela 152 C 4
Santa Cruz de Tenerife 192 B 3
Santa Cruz do Río Pardo 141 G 5
Santa Cruz do Sul 142 F 4
Santa Cruz Island 113 F 8–9

Santa Cruz Islands (Solomon Is.) 185 J 4
Santa Cruz Islands (Solomon Is.) 186 C 3
Santa Cruz River 116 E 5
Santa Cruz Wash 116 D 4
Santa Elena 138 B 4
Santa Elena, Bahía de 132 E 5
Santa Elena, Cabo 132 E 5
Santa Elena de Uairén 139 F 3
Santa Fé (Argentina) 142 D 5
Santa Fé (Goiás, Brazil) 141 F 4
Santa Fe (N.M.) 117 KL 2
Santafé (Spain) 152 C 4
Santa Fe Baldy 117 L 2
Santa Fe River 131 M 5
Santa Filomena 141 G 2
Sant' Agata di Militello 153 F 4
Santa Helena 139 JK 4
Santai 172 E 4
Santa Inés 139 J 4
Santa Ines, Bahía 106 D 6
Santa Inés, Isla 143 B 9
Santa Isabel 139 G 5
Santa Isabel 140 D 3
Santa Isabel 186 B 3
Santa Isabel (Argentina) 143 C 6
Santa Isabel (P.R.) 130 C 9
Santa Isabel (Solomon Is.) 185 G 3
Santa Isabel, Pico de 197 F 5
Santa Isabel do Araguaia 139 J 5
Santa Juana 138 E 2
Santa Júlia 139 G 5
Santa Lucía (Uruguay) 142 E 5
Santa Lucia Range 112D 6–7
Santa Luzia 196 AB 6
Santa Margarita (CA.) 113 E 7
Santa Margarita, Isla de 106 D 7
Santa Margarita Lake 113 E 7
Santa Maria (Amazonas, Brazil) 139 F 4
Santa María (Amazonas, Brazil) 139 G 4
Santa María (Argentina) 142 C 4
Santa Maria (CA.) 113 E 8
Santa María (Portugal) 192 A 1
Santa María (Río Grande do Sul, Brazil) 142 F 4
Santa Maria, Bahia de 106 E 6
Santa Maria, Cabo de 152 B 4
Santa Maria, Cabo de 201 E 5
Santa Maria, Isla 138 B 6
Santa María de Ipire 138 E 2
Santa María del Oro 132 B 3
Santa Maria del Río 132 B 3
Santa Maria di Leuca, Capo 153 G 4
Santa Maria dos Marmelos 139 F 5
Santa Maria River 116 C 3
Santa Marta 138 D 1
Santa Marta, Cabo de 200 A 2
Santa Marta, Ría de 152 B 3
Santa Marta Grande, Cabo de 142 G 4
Santa Monica (CA.) 113 G 8
Santa Monica Bay 113 G 9
Santan 176 E 4
Santana 141 H 3
Santana do Livramento 142 EF 5
Santander (Colombia) 138 C 3
Santander (Spain) 152 C 3
Sant' Antioco 153 E 4
Santañy 152 D 4
Santa Olalla del Cala 152 B 4
Santa Paula (CA.) 113 F 8
Santaquin (UT.) 114 F 4
Santarém (Pará, Brazil) 139 H 4
Santarém (Portugal) 152 B 4
Santaren Channel 133 G 3
Santa Rita (Colombia) 138 D 3
Santa Rita (N.M.) 116 F 3
Santa Rita (Venezuela) 138 E 2
Santa Rita do Araguaia 141 F 4
Santa Rosa (Argentina) 142 C 5
Santa Rosa (Argentina) 143 C 6
Santa Rosa (Argentina) 143 CD 6
Santa Rosa (Bolivia) 140 C 4
Santa Rosa (CA.) 112 C 4
Santa Rosa (Colombia) 138 E 3
Santa Rosa (N.M.) 117 M 3
Santa Rosa (Peru) 138 C 5
Santa Rosa (Río Grande do Sul, Brazil) 142 F 4
Santa Rosa (TX.) 122 F 9
Santa Rosa Beach (FL.) 131 H 4
Santa Rosa de Cabal 138 C 3
Santa Rosa de Copán 132 E 4–5
Santa Rosa de la Roca 140 D 4
Santa Rosa Island (CA.) 113 E 9
Santa Rosa Island (FL.) 130 H 4
Santa Rosalia 106 D 6
Santa Rosa Mountains 113 JK 9
Santa Rosa Range 112 H 1
Santa Sylvina 142 D 4
Santa Teresa (Espírito Santo, Brazil) 141 H 5
Santa Teresa (Goiás, Brazil) 141 G 3
Santa Teresinha 141 F 3
Santa Vitória do Palmar 142 F 5

Santa Ynez (CA.) 113 E 8
Santa Ynez Mountains 113 EF 8
Santa Ysabel (CA.) 113 J 9
Santa Ysabel Indian Reservation 113 J 9
Santee Indian Reservation 119 L 8
Santee River 129 M 8
Santeh (Iran) 157 E 1
San Telmo 106 C 5
Santiago (Chile) 142 BC 5
Santiago (Haiti) 133 H 4
Santiago (Panamá) 138 B 2
Santiago (Rio Grande de Sul, Brazil) 142 F 4
Santiago, Cerro 133 F 6
Santiago, Rio Grande de 132 A 3
Santiago da Cacém 152 B 4
Santiago de Compostela 152 B 3
Santiago de Cuba 133 G 4
Santiago del Estero 142 CD 4
Santiago de Papasquiaro 132 AB 2
Santiago Mountains 117 N 8
Santiam Pass 110 D 6
Santo (TX.) 122 E 3
Santo Amaro 141 J 3
Santo André 141 G 5
Santo Ângelo 142 F 4
Santo Antão 196 A 6
Santo Antonio 142 F 4
Santo Antonio (São Tomé) 197 F 5
Santo António de Jesus 141 J 3
Santo Antônio do Içá 138 E 4
Santo Domingo (Argentina) 142 D 4
Santo Domingo (Cuba) 133 F 3
Santo Domingo (Dominican Rep.) 133 J 4
Santo Domingo (Mexico) 106 D 6
Santo Domingo Pueblo (N.M.) 117 K 3
Santo Felipe Pueblo (N.M.) 117 K 2
Santoña 152 C 3
Santopitar 152 C 4
Santoríni 154 B 3
Santos 141 G 5
Santos Dumont (Amazonas, Brazil) 138 E 5
Santos Dumont (Minas Gerais, Brazil) 141 H 5
Santo Tomás (Nicaragua) 132 F 5
Santo Tomás (Peru) 140 B 3
Santo Tomé (Argentina) 142 E 4
Santo Tomé de Guayana 139 F 2
San Valentin, Cerro 143 B 8
San Vicente (Mexico) 106 C 5
San Vicente (Philippines) 177 J 1
San Vicente de Cañete 140 A 3
San Vicente de la Barquerq 152 C 3
San Vicente del Raspeig 152 CD 4
San Xavier Indian Reservation 116 EF 5
San Ygnacio (TX.) 122 D 8
Sanza Pombo 200 B 3
São Antônio 139 H 5
São Bente do Norte 141 J 1–2
São Bento (Maranhão, Brazil) 141 GH 1
São Bento (Roraima, Brazil) 139 F 3
São Bernardo 141 H 1
São Borja 142 E 4
São Brás, Cabo de 200 A 1–2
São Carlos (Santa Catarina, Brazil) 142 F 4
São Carlos (São Paulo, Brazil) 141 G 5
São Christóvão 141 J 3
São Domingos 141 G 3
São Domingos 196 A 3
São Felix 141 F 3
São Felix do Xingu 139 H 5
São Francisco (Brazil) 141 J 2
São Francisco (Minas Gerais, Brazil) 141 H 4
São Francisco do Sul 142 G 4
São Gabriel 142 F 5
São Gabriel de Goiás 141 G 4
São Geraldo do Araguaia 139 J 5
Sao Hill 198 F 6
São Jerônimo, Serra de 141 EF 4
São João 141 G 5
São João, Ilhas de 139 K 4
São João da Barra 141 H 5
São João da Madeira 152 B 3
São João de Aliança 141 G 3
São João del Rei 141 H 5
São João do Araguaia 139 J 5
São João do Paraíso 141 H 4
São João do Piauí 141 H 2
São João dos Patos 141 H 2
São Joaquim (Amazonas, Brazil) 138 E 4
São Joaquim (Santa Catarina, Brazil) 142 F 4
São Jorge 192 A 1
São José (Amazonas, Brazil) 138 E 4
São José do Anauá 139 F 3
São José do Norte 142 F 5

São José do Peixe 141 H 2
São José do Rio Pardo 141 G 5
São José do Río Prêto 141 FG 5
São José dos Campos 141 G 5
São Leopoldo 142 F 4
São Lourénço 140 E 4
Sao Lourénço, Pantanal de 140 E 4
São Lourénço do Sul 142 F 5
São Luís (Maranhão, Brazil) 141 H 1
São Luis de Cassianã 138 E 5
São Luis Gonzaga 142 E 4
São Mamede, Serra de 152 B 4
São Manuel 139 G 5
São Marcelino 138 E 3
São Mateus 141 J 4
São Miguel 192 A 1
São Miguel do Araguaia 141 F 3
Saône 153 D 2
São Nicolau 196 B 6
São Paulo 141 FG 5
São Paulo 141 G 5
São Paulo de Olivença 138 E 4
São Pedro do Sul 142 F 4
São Pedro do Sul 152 B 3
São Raimundo das Mangabeiras 141 G 2
São Raimundo Nonato 141 H 2
São Romão (Amazonas, Brazil) 138 E 5
São Romão (Minas Gerais, Brazil) 141 G 4
São Roque, Cabo de 141 J 2
São Sebastião (Pará, Brazil) 139 H 5
São Sebastião (São Paulo, Brazil) 141 GH 5
São Sebastião, Ilha de 141 GH 5
São Sebastião do Paraíso 141 G 5
São Sepé 142 F 5
São Tiago 196 B 6
São Tomé (São Tomé) 197 F 5
São Tomé, Cabo de 141 H 5
São Tomé and Principe 197 F 5
Sa Oui 175 H 5
Saoura 192 E 3
São Vicente 141 G 5
São Vicente 196 A 6
São Vicente, Cabo de 152 B 4
Sápai 154 C 2
Sapanca Gölü 154 D 2
Sapé (Brazil) 141 J 2
Sape (Indonesia) 177 E 5
Sape, Selat 177 E 5
Sapele 197 F 4
Sapelo Island 131 N 3
Sapiéntza 154 B 3
Saponé 196 D 3
Saposoa 138 C 5
Sappa Creek 120 E 3
Sapphire Mountains 111 M 4
Sappho (WA.) 110 A 2
Sappington (MT.) 111 O 5
Sapporo 173 M 2
Sapri 153 G 3
Sapulpa (OK.) 120 J 6–7
Sapulut 176 E 3
Sapwe 200 D 2
Sâq, Jabal (Saudi Arabia) 156 D 4
Sâqand (Iran) 157 G 2
Saqqez (Iran) 157 E 1
Sara, Lake 121 R 3
Saráb 168 D 3
Sara Buri 175 H 5
Sarafére 196 D 2
Sarafjagār (Iran) 157 F 2
Saragosa (TX.) 117 N 6
Saraguro 138 C 4
Sarajevo 153 G 3
Sarakhs 169 G 3
Saraktash 158 L 5
Saraland (AL.) 130 FG 4
Saralzhin 168 E 1
Saramati 175 FG 2
Saran' 159 O 6
Saran, Gunung 176 D 4
Saranac Lake (N.Y.) 126 E 4
Saranda 154 B 3
Sarandï do Yï 142 EF 5
Sarandí Grande 142 E 5
Sarangani Bay 177 G 2
Sarangani Islands 177 G 2
Sarangarh 174 D 3
Saranley 199 G 3
Saranpaul' 159 M 3
Saransk 158 J 3
Sarapul 158 K 4
Sarapul'skoye 171 P 6
Sarare 138 E 2
Sarasota (FL.) 131 M 7
Sarata 154 C 1
Saratoga (CA.) 112 C 5
Saratoga (TX.) 123 J 5
Saratoga (WY.) 118 B 9
Saratoga Springs (N.Y.) 126 F 5
Saratok 176 D 3
Saratov 158 HJ 5
Saravan 169 G 5
Saravane 175 J 4
Sarawak 176 D 3

Saray 154 C 2
Saraya 196 B 3
Sârâya (Syria) 156 B 2
Saraykōy 154 C 3
Sarbâz 169 G 5
Sarca 153 F 2
Sarco 142 B 4
Sarcoxie (MO.) 121 L 5
Sardalas → Al 'Awaynât 193 H 3
Sardarshahr 174 B 2
Sar Dasht (Iran) 157 D 1
Sar Dasht (Iran) 157 E 2
Sardegna 153 E 3
Sardina 138 E 3
Sardinia 153 E 3
Sardis (AL.) 130 H 2
Sardis (GA.) 131 N 2
Sardis (MS.) 121 Q 8
Sardis Lake 121 Q 8
Sarek National Park 150 G 2
Sarektjåkkå 150 G 2
Sarempaka, Gunung 176 E 4
Sarenga 199 F 2
Sarepta (LA.) 123 K 3
Sar-e Yazd (Iran) 157 G 3
Sarga, Punta 192 B 4
Sargasso Sea 133 JK 2
Sargatskoye 159 O 4
Sargent (NE.) 118 J 9
Sargento Lores 138 CD 4
Sargento Paixão, Serra do 140 DE 3
Sargents (CO.) 115 L 5
Sargodha 169 J 4
Sarh 197 H 4
Sarhro, Jbel 192 D 2
Sârï (Iran) 157 F 1
Saría 154 C 3
Sarıbuğday 155 E 2
Sarigan 186 A 1
Sarıkamış 155 F 2
Sarikaya 155 E 3
Sarikei 176 D 3
Sarila 174 C 2
Sarıoğlan 155 E 3
Sarıkışla 155 E 3
Şarköy 154 C 2
Sarir al Qaṭṭûsah 193 J 3
Sarir Kalanshiyū 193 K 3
Sarir Tibisti 193 J 4
Sarita (TX.) 122 F 8
Sariwon 173 J 3
Sariyar Barajı 154 D 2–3
Sariyer 154 C 2
Sark 148 C 5
Sark, Safrã' as 195 G 3
Sarkand 159 P 6
Şarkikáraağaç 154 D 3
Şarkışla 155 E 3
Şarköy 154 C 2
Sarlat-la-Canéda 152 D 3
Sarles (ND.) 118 K 2
Sarmi 177 J 4
Sarmiento 143 C 8
Sarmiento, Monte 143 BC 9
Särna 150 F 3
Sarneh (Iran) 157 E 2
Sarnia 104 L 7
Sarny 151 J 5
Saroako 177 F 4
Sarobi 169 H 4
Sarolangun 176 B 4
Saronikos Kólpos 154 B 3
Saronno 153 E 2
Saros Körfezi 154 C 2
Saroto 159 N 2
Sarpa 155 G 1
Sarpinskaya Nizmennost' 155 G 1
Sarpsborg 151 F 4
Sarralbe 153 E 2
Sarrebourg 153 E 2
Sarreguemines 153 E 2
Sars 158 L 4
Sartang 171 O 2
Sartène 153 E 3
Sarthe 152 C 2
Sartlan, Ozero 159 PQ 4–5
Sarto 138 D 3
Sartyn'ya 159 M 3
Saruhanli 154 C 3
Sârûq (Iran) 157 E 2
Sarvestân (Iran) 157 F 3
Saryassiya 169 H 3
Sarych, Mys 155 D 2
Saryg 197 G 3
Sary Ishikotrau, Peski 159 P 6
Sarykamysh, Ozero 168 F 2
Saryoba 199 FG 1
Sary-Ozek 169 K 2
Sary-Shagan 159 O 6
Sarysu 159 N 2
Sary-Tash 169 J 3
Sasa Baneh 199 G 3
Sasabe (AZ.) 116 E 6
Sasamungga 185 G 3
Sasar, Tanjung 177 E 5
Sasaram 174 D 3
Sasebo 173 J 4
Saskatchewan 103 Q 5

Saskatchewan 103 R 5
Saskatoon 103 Q 5
Saskylakh 170 KL 1
Saslaya 132 F 5
Sason Dağları 155 F 3
Sasovo 158 H 5
Sassafras Mountain 128 J 6
Sassan (United Arab Emirates) 157 F 4
Sassandra 196 C 5
Sassandra (River) 196 C 4
Sassari 153 E 3
Saßnitz 149 F 4
Sassuolo 153 F 3
Sas-Tobe 169 J 2
Sastre 149 D 4
Sasyk, Ozero (Ukraine, U.S.S.R.) 154 C 1
Sasykkol', Ozero 159 Q 6
Sasyk Ozero (Russia, U.S.S.R.) 155 D 1
Satadougou 196 B 3
Satanta (KS.) 120 D 5
Satara (India) 174 B 4
Satara (U.S.S.R.) 171 NO 2
Satawal 186 A 2
Satawan 186 B 2
Satellite Beach (FL.) 131 O 6
Säter 151 G 3
Satilla River 131 M 3
Satipo 140 B 3
Satka 159 L 4
Satmala Range 174 C 4
Satna 174 D 3
Satolah (GA.) 128 H 7
Satoou 197 F 3
Sátoraljaujhely 154 B 1
Satpura Range 174 C 3
Sattahip 175 H 5
Satthwa 175 G 4
Sattur 174 C 6
Satun 175 H 6
Sauce 142 E 5
Sauceda Mountains 116 E 5
Saucier (MS.) 130 E 4
Saucillo 106 EF 6
Sauda Nathil (Saudi Arabia) 157 F 4
Sauðarkrókur 150 B 2
Saudi Arabia 195 GH 4
Saugatuck (MI.) 124 H 7
Saugerties (N.Y.) 126 E 6
Saugus (CA.) 113 G 8
Sauiá 139 G 4
Sauk Centre (MN.) 119 O 5
Sauk City (WI.) 124 E 6
Sauk Rapids (MN.) 119 O 5
Saúl 139 H 3
Saulieu 152 D 2
Sault Sainte Marie (MI.) 125 K 3
Sault Sainte Marie (Ontario, Can.) 104 L 6
Saumarez Reef 183 J 3
Saumlaki 177 F 5
Saumur 152 C 2
Saunders (KS.) 120 D 5
Saur, Khrebet 159 QR 6
Saura 168 E 2
Saurimo 200 C 1
Sautar 200 B 2
Sauwald 155 F 2
Sava 154 AB 2
Savage (MT.) 118 D 3
Savageton (WY.) 118 C 7
Savai'i 186 D 3
Savalou 196 E 4
Savanna (WI.) 124 D 7
Savannah (GA.) 131 N 2
Savannah (MO.) 121 L 3
Savannah (TN.) 128 C 6
Savannah Beach (GA.) 131 O 2–3
Savannah River 129 K 9
Savannakhet 175 HJ 4
Savanna la Mar 133 G 4
Savanne 104 K 6
Savant Lake 104 JK 5
Savantvadj 174 B 4
Savanur 174 C 5
Sävar 150 H 3
Savaştepe 154 C 3
Savé (Benin) 196 E 4
Save (Mozambique) 201 F 3
Sâveh (Iran) 157 F 2
Savelugu 196 D 3
Saverdun 152 D 3
Saverne 153 E 2
Savigliano 153 E 3
Savino 158 K 2
Sävirşin 154 B 1
Savitaipale 150 J 3
Savo 150 J 3
Savoie 153 E 2
Savona 153 E 3
Savonlinna 150 J 3
Savonselkä 150 J 3
Savoonga 102 C 3
Savoy (MT.) 111 R 2
Şavşat 155 F 2
Sävsjö 151 F 4
Savukoski 150 J 2

Savur 155 F 3
Saw 175 F 3
Sawah 176 E 3
Sawahlunto 176 B 4
Sawai Madhopur 174 C 2
Sawang 176 B 3
Sāwānī Fassānū 193 H 2
Sawankhalok 175 G 4
Sawatch Range 115 L 4–5
Sawbā 198 E 3
Sawdirī 194 D 6
Sawek 177 J 4
Saweyrs Bar (CA.) 112 B 1
Sawhāj 194 E 3
Sawmah, Ra's Abū (Egypt) 156 B 4
Sawmill Bay 103 O 2
Şawqirah 195 K 5
Sawtayr 194 E 5
Sawtooth Mountains 119 RS 3
Sawtooth Range 111 K 6–7
Sawu, Pulau 177 F 6
Sawu Laut 177 F 5
Şawwān, Arḍ aş 194 F 2
Sawyer (KS.) 120 G 5
Sawyer (ND.) 118 G 2
Saxton (PA.) 125 Q 9
Say 196 E 3
Sayaboury 175 H 4
Sayak 195 K 5
Sayakskaya Pristan' 159 P 6
Sayán 140 A 3
Sayan, Zapadnyy 170 F 5
Sayang, Pulau 177 GH 3
Sayan Vostochnyy 170 G 5
Sayat 169 G 3
Saydā (Lebanon) 156 B 2
Saydy 171 O 2
Sayhūt 195 J 5
Saynshand 172 F 2
Sayram Hu 169 L 2
Sayre (OK.) 120 F 7
Sayreville (N.J.) 127 E 8
Saywūn 195 H 5
Sázava 149 F 5
Sazdy 168 D 1
Sazin 169 J 3
Sbaa 192 E 3
Scaër 152 C 2
Scafell Pike 148 C 4
Scaife Mountains 203
Scalea 153 G 4
Scalone, Passo dello 153 G 4
Scammon Bay 102 D 3
Scandia (KS.) 120 H 3
Scapa Flow 148 C 3
Scappoose (OR.) 110 BC 5
Ščara 149 H 4
Scaramia, Capo 153 F 4
Scarborough (Trinidad and Tobago) 139 F 1
Scarborough (U.K.) 148 C 4
Scarface Peak 111 M 3
Scar Hill 110 B 4
Scenic (WA.) 110 D 3
Schärding 153 F 2
Schefferville 105 O 5
Scheibbs 153 FG 2
Schelde 148 D 4
Schell City (MO.) 121 L 4–5
Schell Creek Range 112 L 3–4
Schenectady (N.Y.) 126 F 4
Schiltigheim 153 E 2
Schio 153 F 2
Schklov 151 K 5
Schladming 153 F 2
Schleswig 149 E 4
Schleswig (IA.) 119 N 8
Schleswig-Holstein 149 E 4
Schneeberg 149 F 4
Schoenchen (KS.) 120 F 4
Scholle (N.M.) 117 K 3
Schönebeck 149 F 4
Schouten Islands 184 D 2
Schouten Islands 186 A 3
Schrag (WA.) 110 G 3
Schriever (LA.) 123 N 6
Schroon Lake 126 F 5
Schuchk (AZ.) 116 E 5
Schuls → Scuol 153 F 2
Schultz Lake 103 S 3
Schulenburg (TX.) 122 G 6
Schurz (NV.) 112 G 4
Schuyler (NE.) 120 H 1
Schwabach 149 F 5
Schwäbisch Hall 149 EF 5
Schwaner, Pegunungan 176 D 4
Schwarzwald 149 E 5
Schwatka Mountains 102 F 2
Schwaz 153 F 2
Schwedt 149 F 4
Schweinfurt 149 F 4
Schweizer Reneke 200 CD 5
Schwenningen 149 E 5
Schwerin 149 F 4
Schwyz 153 E 2
Sciacca 153 F 4
Scicli 153 F 4
Scilly, Isles of 148 B 5
Scio (OR.) 110 C 6

Scioto River 125 L 9
Scipio (UT.) 114 E 4
Scobey (MT.) 118 BC 2
Scofield Reservoir 114 F 4
Scooba (MS.) 130 F 2
Scoresby Sound 202
Scoresbysund 202
Scotia (NE.) 120 G 1
Scotia Ridge 208 A 5
Scotia Sea 203
Scotland 148 C 3
Scotland (MD.) 129 P 3
Scotland (S.D.) 118 L 7
Scotland (TX.) 122 E 2
Scotlandville (LA.) 123 M 5
Scott (Antarctica) 203
Scott (MS.) 121 OP 9
Scott (Sask., Can.) 103 Q 5
Scott, Cape 102 M 5
Scott, Cape (N.T., Austr.) 182 D 1
Scott, Mount 110 CD 8
Scott City (KS.) 120 DE 4
Scott Island 203
Scott Mountain 111 K 6
Scott Peak 111 N 6
Scott Reef 182 C 1
Scottsbluff (NE.) 118 E 9
Scotts Bluff National Monument 118 E 9
Scottsboro (AL.) 128 E 7
Scottsburg (IN.) 128 F 3
Scottsdale (AZ.) 116 E 4
Scottsdale (Tasmania, Austr.) 184 L 9
Scottsville (KY.) 128 E 5
Scottville (MI.) 124 H 6
Scranton (ND.) 118 E 4
Scranton (PA.) 126 D 7
Screven (GA.) 131 MN 3
Scribner (NE.) 119 M 9
Scugog, Lake 105 M 7
Scuol 153 F 2
Scutari, Lake → Skardarsko Jezero 154 A 2
Seabra 141 H 3
Seabrook, Lake 182 B 5
Seadrift (TX.) 122 G 7
Seaford (PA.) 127 D 10
Seagraves (TX.) 117 O 5
Seagrove (N.C.) 129 M 6
Seahorse Point 103 V 3
Sea Island (GA.) 131 N 3
Sea Isle City (N.J.) 127 E 9
Seal 103 S 4
Seal Island 126 L 5
Sealy (TX.) 122 G 6
Sea of Azov 155 E 1
Sea of Crete 154 BC 3
Sea of Japan 173 KL 3
Sea of Marmara → Marmara Denizi 154 C 2
Sea of Okhotsk 171 R 4
Sea of the Hebrides 148 B 3
Sea Pines (S.C.) 129 L 9
Searchlight (NV.) 113 L 7
Searcy (AR.) 121 O 7
Searles (CA.) 113 H 7
Searles Lake 113 H 7
Seaside (CA.) 112 D 6
Seaside (OR.) 110 AB 4
Seaside Park (N.J.) 127 E 9
Seattle (WA.) 110 C 3
Seba 177 F 6
Sebago Lake 126 J 5
Sebanka, Pulau 176 BC 3
Sebastian (TX.) 122 F 9
Sebastián Vizcaino, Bahía 106 D 6
Sebatik, Pulau 176 E 3
Sebba 196 E 3
Sebec Lake 126 K 3
Sebeka (MN.) 119 N 4
Sébékoro 196 C 3
Sebewaing (MI.) 125 L 6
Sebezh 151 J 4
Sebha Oasis → Wāhāt Sabhā 193 H 3
Sebha → Sabhā 193 H 3
Şebinkarahisar 155 E 2
Sebjet Agsumal 192 C 4
Sebjet Aridal 192 C 3
Sebkha Azzel Matti 192 F 3
Sebkha de Ndrhamcha 192 B 5
Sebkha de Rhallamane 192 D 4
Sebkha de Timimoun 192–193 F 3
Sebkha de Tindouf 192 D 3
Sebkha Iguetti 192 D 3
Sebkha Mekerrhane 193 F 3
Sebkha Oumm ed Droûs Telli 192 C 4
Sebkha Tah 192 C 3
Sebkhet Oumm ed Droûs Guebli 192 C 4
Seboeis Lake 126 L 3
Seboomook Lake 126 K 3
Sebou 192 D 2
Seboyeta (N.M.) 117 J 2
Sebree (KY.) 128 D 4

Sebring (FL.) 131 N 7
Sebuku, Pulau 176 E 4
Secchia 153 F 3
Sechura 138 B 5
Sechura, Bahía de 138 B 5
Sechura, Desierto de 138 B 5
Second Baku 146
Secunderabad 174 C 4
Seda 152 B 4
Sedah 177 F 6
Sedalia (MO.) 121 M 4
Sedan 153 DE 2
Sedanka 102 D 5
Sedano 152 C 3
Seddenga 194 DE 4
Sededema 171 S 2
Sedel'nikovo 159 P 4
Sedgewick, Mount 116 H 2
Sedgwick (CO.) 115 P 3
Sedgwick (KS.) 120 H 5
Sédhiou 196 A 3
Sedom (Israel) 156 B 3
Sedona (AZ.) 116 E 3
Seeley Lake (MT.) 111 M 3
Sées 152 D 2
Seesen 149 F 4
Şefaatli 155 D 3
Sefadu 196 B 4
Sefīd Dasht (Iran) 157 F 2
Sefrou 192 E 2
Segag 199 G 3
Segamat 176 B 3
Segantur 176 E 3
Segbana 196 E 3
Segesta 153 F 4
Seget 177 H 4
Segeza 150 K 3
Seghe 185 G 3
Seghnān 169 J 3
Segine I-yy 177 P 3
Segorbe 152 C 4
Ségou 196 C 3
Segovia 152 C 3
Segozero, Ozero 150 K 3
Segré (France) 152 C 2
Segre (Spain) 152 D 3
Seguam 102 C 5
Séguédine 197 G 1
Séguéla 196 C 4
Seguin (KS.) 120 E 3
Seguin (TX.) 122 F 6
Segula 102 A 5
Segura 152 C 4
Segura, Sierra de 152 C 4
Sehithwa 200 C 4
Sehore 174 C 3
Sehwan 169 H 5
Seibert (CO.) 115 P 4
Seiland 150 H 1
Seiling (OK.) 120 G 6
Seinäjoki 150 H 3
Seine 152 D 2
Seine, Baie de la 152 C 2
Sekayu 176 B 4
Seke 198 E 5
Sekena 154 B 3
Sekenke 198 E 5
Seki 154 C 3
Sekkemo 150 H 2
Sekoma 200 C 4
Sekondi-Takoradi 196 D 5
Sekondya 171 MN 2
Se Kong 175 J 4
Selaru, Pulau 177 H 5
Selassi 177 H 4
Selat Alas 176 E 5
Selat Alor 177 F 5
Selatan, Pulau 176 B 4
Selatan, Tanjung 176 D 4
Selat Bangka 176 B 4
Selat Berhala 176 B 4
Selat Dampier 177 H 4
Selat Gaspar 176 C 4
Selat Jailolo 177 G 3–4
Selat Karimata 176 C 4
Selat Laut 176 E 4
Selat Lombok 176 E 5
Selat Madura 176 D 5
Selat Makassar 176 E 4
Selat Manipa 177 G 4
Selat Mentawai 176 A 4
Selat Morotai 177 G 3
Selat Obi 177 G 4
Selat Ombai 177 G 5
Selat Peleng 177 F 4
Selat Roti 177 F 6
Selat Salue Timpaus 177 F 4
Selat Sape 177 E 5
Selat Selayar 177 F 5
Selat Serasan 177 D 3
Selat Sumba 177 EF 5
Selat Sunda → Sunda Strait 176 BC 5
Selat Tiworo 177 F 4
Selat Wetar 177 G 5
Selat Yapen 177 J 4
Selawik 102 F 2
Selawik Lake 102 F 2
Selayar, Pulau 177 F 5

Selayar, Selat 177 F 5
Selbu 150 F 3
Selbusjöen 150 F 3
Selby (SD.) 118 HJ 5
Selbyville (PA.) 127 D 10
Selçuk 154 C 3
Selden (KS.) 120 E 3
Seldovia 102 G 4
Selebi-Pikwe 200 D 4
Selebir 171 O 2
Selemdzha 171 O 5
Selemdzhinsk 171 O 5
Selendi 154 C 3
Selenduma 170 J 5
Selenge 170 H 6
Selenge (Mongolia) 170 J 6
Selenge (Zaire) 198 B 5
Selennyakh 171 Q 2
Sélestat 153 E 2
Selety 159 O 5
Seletyteniz, Ozero 159 O 5
Selfjord 151 E 4
Selfoss 150 A 3
Selfridge (ND.) 118 H 4
Selgon 171 P 6
Sélibaby 192 C 5
Seligman (AZ.) 116 D 2
Seligman (MO.) 121 L 6
Selim 155 F 2
Selima Oasis → Wāhāt Salīmah 194 D 4
Selinunte 153 F 4
Seliyarovo 159 O 3
Selizharovo 158 F 4
Selkirk (KS.) 120 D 4
Selkirk Mountains (Br. Col., Can.) 103 O 5
Selkirk Mountains (ID.) 110 J 2
Sella di Conza 153 G 3
Selle, Pic de la 133 H 4
Sellersburg (IN.) 128 F 3
Sells (AZ.) 116 E 6
Sellyakhskaya Guba 171 P 1
Selma (AL.) 130 GH 2
Selma (CA.) 112 F 6
Selma (OR.) 110 B 8
Selmer (TN.) 128 C 6
Selong 176 E 5
Selous, Mount 109 M 3
Selous Game Reserve 199 F 6
Selukwe → Shurugwi 200 DE 3
Selva 142 D 4
Selvagens, Ilhas 192 B 2
Selvänä 168 C 3
Selvas 138–139 EF 5
Selway River 111 K 4
Selwyn 183 G 3
Selwyn Lake 103 R 3–4
Selwyn Mountains 102 LM 3
Selz (ND.) 118 J 3
Semani 154 A 2
Semara 192 C 3
Semarang 176 D 5
Sematan 176 C 3
Semau, Pulau 177 F 6
Sembakung, Sungai 176 E 3
Sembé 197 G 5
Şemdinli 155 F 3
Semenovskiy, Ostrov 171 O 1
Semichi Islands 102 A 5
Semidi Islands 108 G 4
Semikarakorskiy 155 F 1
Semiluki 158 G 5
Seminoe Dam (WY.) 118 AB 8
Seminoe Reservoir 118 B 8
Seminole (FL.) 131 M 7
Seminole (OK.) 120 J 7
Seminole (TX.) 117 O 5
Seminole, Lake 131 K 4
Semiozeṛnoye 159 N 5
Semipalatinsk 159 Q 5
Semirara Islands 177 F 1
Semīrom (Iran) 157 F 3
Semisopochnoi 102 AB 5
Semitau 176 D 3
Semium 176 C 3
Semiyarka 159 P 5
Semiz-Bugu 159 OP 5
Semliki 198 DE 4
Semme Dahan, Khrebet 171 P 3
Semmering 153 G 2
Semmes (AL.) 130 F 4
Semnān (Iran) 157 F 2
Semporna 177 E 3
Sem Tripa 139 H 4
Semuda 176 D 4
Sena (Bolivia) 140 C 3
Sena (Mozambique) 201 E 3
Senador Canedo 141 G 4
Senador Pompeu 141 J 2
Senaja 176 E 2
Sena Madureira 138 E 5
Senanga 200 C 3
Senatobia (MS.) 121 PQ 8
Sendai 173 M 3
Sendai 173 JK 4
Sendai-wan 173 M 3
Sendelingsdrif 200 B 5
Sêndo 172 C 4

Seneca (MO.) 121 L 6
Seneca (NE.) 118 H 8
Seneca (N.E.) 120 J 3
Seneca (N.Y.) 125 Q 7
Seneca (N.Y.) 126 C 6
Seneca (OR.) 110 FG 6
Seneca (SD.) 118 J 5
Senecaville Lake 129 K 2
Senegal 196 AB 3
Sénégal (River) 196 B 2
Senekal 200 D 5
Seney (MI.) 124 J 3
Senftenberg 149 F 4
Sênggê Zangbo 174 D 1
Sengiri, Mys 168 E 2
Sengkang 177 F 4
Senhor do Bonfim 141 H 3
Senigallia 153 F 3
Senjavin Grop 186 B 2
Senja 150 G 2
Senkaku-shotō 173 H 5
Şenkaya 155 F 2
Senkyabasa 170 K 2
Sennaya 155 E 1
Senneterre 105 M 6
Senno 151 J 5
Seno de Otway 143 B 9
Senoia (G.A.) 128 G 8
Senorbi 153 E 4
Seno Skyring 143 B 9
Sens 152 D 2
Senta 154 B 1
Sentani 184 D 2
Sentinel (AZ.) 116 C 5
Sentinel (OK.) 120 F 7
Sentinel Butte (N.D.) 118 E 4
Sentinel Peak 103 N 5
Sentinel Plain 116 C 5
Şenyurt 155 F 3
Şenyurt (Turkey) 156 C 1
Seo de Urgel 152 D 3
Seoni 174 C 3
Seoul 173 J 4
Sepanjang, Pulau 176 E 5
Separ (N.M.) 116 H 5
Separation Point 105 Q 5
Sepasu 176 E 3
Sepik 186 A 3
Sepik River 184 D 2
Sepone 175 J 4
Sept-Îles 105 O 5
Sequillo 152 B 3
Sequim (WA.) 110 B 2
Sequoia National Park 112 G 6
Şerafettin Dağları 155 F 3
Seraing 148 E 4
Serakhs 169 G 3
Seram 177 G 4
Seram, Laut 177 GH 4
Seram Laut, Kepulauan 177 H 4
Serang 176 C 5
Serasan, Pulau 176 C 3
Serasan, Selat 176 C 3
Serbia 154 B 2
Serdo 199 G 2
Serdobsk 158 HJ 5
Serebryansk 159 Q 6
Serebryanskiy 150 L 2
Sered 149 G 5
Seredka 151 J 4
Şereflikoçhisar 155 D 3
Seremban 176 B 3
Serengeti National Park 198 EF 5
Serengeti Plain 198 EF 5
Serenje 201 E 2
Sergach 158 J 4
Sergant Bluff (IA.) 119 M 8
Sergelen 170 J 6
Sergeyevo 159 R 4
Sergino 159 N 3
Sergipe 141 J 3
Sergiyevka 155 F 2
Seria 176 D 3
Serian 176 D 3
Sérifos 154 B 3
Serifou, Sténon 154 B 3
Serik 154 C 3
Seringa, Serra da 139 H 5
Seringapatam Reef 182 C 1
Serkovo 159 R 2
Sernovodsk 158 K 5
Sernyy-Zavod 168 F 2
Séro 196 B 3
Seroglazovka 155 G 1
Serov 159 M 4
Serowe 200 D 4
Serpa 152 B 4
Serpentine Lakes 182 D 4
Serpiente, Boca de la 139 F 2
Serpukhov 158 G 5
Serra Acarai 139 G 3
Serra Bonita 141 G 4
Serra da Bodoquena 140 E 5
Serra da Canastra 141 G 4
Serra da Chela 200 A 3
Serra da Estrela (Mato Grosso, Brazil) 141 F 4
Serra da Estrêla (Portugal) 152 B 3

Serra da Gorongosa 201 E 3
Serra da Ibiapaba 141 H 1–2
Serra da Mantiqueira 141 GH 5
Serra da Neve 200 A 2
Serra da Providência 140 D 3
Serra das Alpercatas 139 JK 5
Serra das Araras 141 F 4
Serra das Cordilheiras 139 J 5
Serra da Seringa 139 H 5
Serra da Tabatinga 141 H 3
Serra de Alvelos 152 B 4
Serra de Caldeirão 152 B 4
Serra de Grândola 152 B 4
Serra de Itiúba 141 HJ 3
Serra de Maracaju 140–141 EF 5
Serra de Nogueira 152 B 3
Serra de São Jerônimo 141 EF 4
Serra de São Mamede 152 B 4
Serra do Aguapeí 140 E 4
Serra do Apiaú 139 F 3
Serra do Cachimbo 139 G 5
Serra do Caiapó 141 F 4
Serra do Caramulo 152 B 3
Serra do Chifre 141 H 4
Serra do Divisor 138 D 5
Serra do Escorial 152 B 4
Serra do Espinhaço 141 H 4
Serra do Estrondo 139 J 5
Serra do Gerâs 152 B 3
Serra do Gurupi 139 J 4–5
Serra Dois Irmãos 141 H 2
Serra do Jibão 141 G 4
Serra do Mar 142 G 4
Serra do Marêo 152 B 3
Serra do Matão 139 H 5
Serra do Mogadouro 152 B 3
Serra do Navio 139 H 3
Serra do Paraiso 141 H 4
Serra do Paranapiacaba 141 G 5
Serra do Penitente 139 J 5
Serra do Ramalho 141 H 3
Serra do Roncador 141 F 3
Serra dos Aimorés 141 HJ 4
Serra dos Apiacás 140 E 2–3
Serra do Sargento Paixão 140 DE 3
Serra dos Caiabis 140 E 3
Serra dos Carajás 139 H 4–5
Serra dos Gradaús 139 H 5
Serra dos Pacaás Novos 140 D 3
Serra dos Parecis 140 D 3
Serra dos Xavantes 141 G 3
Serra do Tiracambu 141 G 1
Serra do Tombador 140 E 3
Serra Dourada 141 G 3
Serra do Uruçui 141 H 2
Serra Formosa 141 E 3
Serra Geral 142 F 4
Serra Geral de Goiás 141 G 3
Serra Geral do Paraná 141 G 3
Serra Geral ou Grande 141 G 3
Serra Grande 141 H 2
Serrai 154 B 2
Serra Lombarda 139 H 3
Serrana, Banco de 133 G 5
Serra Negra 139 J 5
Serranía de Baudó 138 C 2
Serranía de Huanchaca 140 D 3
Serranía de Imataca 139 F 2
Serranía del Darién 138 C 2
Serranía de Santiago 140 DE 4
Serranía de Tabasara 138 B 2
Serranías Turagua 139 F 2
Serranilla, Banco 133 G 4
Serra Nova 139 F 5
Serra Talhada 141 J 2
Serra Tumucumaque 139 H 3
Serra Urubuquara 139 H 4
Serres 153 E 3
Serrezuela 142 C 5
Serrinha 141 J 3
Serrota 152 BC 3
Sertã 152 B 4
Sêrtar 172 D 4
Sertavul Geçidi 155 D 3
Seruai 177 J 4
Serule 200 D 4
Seruyan, Sungai 176 D 4
Servia 154 B 2
Serwaru 177 G 5
Sêrxü 172 C 4
Seryshevo 171 N 5
Sesao 197 E 2
Sesayap 176 E 3
Seseganaga Lake 104 K 5
Sese Islands 198 E 5
Sesfontein 200 A 3
Seshachalam Hills 174 C 5
Seshan 108 D 2
Sesheke 200 C 3
Seshia Mountains 199 F 3
Sesibi 194 E 4
Sesimbra 152 B 4
Seskarö 150 H 2
Sessa Aurunca 153 F 3
Sesto Fiorentino 153 F 3
Sestri Levante 153 E 3
Sesupé 151 H 5
Sesvete 153 G 2
Setana 173 L 2

Séte 152 D 3
Sete Lagoas 141 H 4
Sete Quedas, Cachoeira das 139 G 5
Sete Quedas, Salto das 141 F 5
Setermoen 150 G 2
Setesdal 151 E 4
Seth Ward (TX.) 117 P 3
Sétif 193 G 1
Seto-naikai 173 K 4
Settat 192 D 2
Setté Cama 197 F 6
Sette-Daban, Khrebet 171 P 3
Setúbal 152 B 4
Setúbal, Baía de 152 B 4
Seui 153 E 4
Seul Choix Point 124 J 4
Seumanyam 176 A 3
Sevan 155 F 2
Sevan, Ozero 155 G 2
Sevarujo 140 C 4
Sevastopol' 155 D 2
Seven Devils Mountains 110 J 5
Seven Pagodas → Mahabalipuram 174 D 5
Seven Sisters (TX.) 122 E 7
Sever 171 V 3
Severino Ribeiro 142 E 5
Severn 148 C 4
Severnaya 159 S 2
Severnaya Bruingra 171 N 4
Severnaya Dvina 158 H 3
Severnaya Sos'va 159 M 3
Severnaya Zemlya 202
Severnayy 158 J 2
Severn Lake 104 JK 5
Severnoye 158 K 5
Severnoye 159 P 4
Severn River (Ontario, Can.) 104 K 4
Severnykh 168 E 2
Severnyy 159 MN 2
Severnyy Anyuyskiy Khrebet 171 UW 2
Severnyy Ural 159 L 3
Severo Baykal'skoye Nagor'ye 170 K 4
Severodvinsk 158 G 3
Severo-Kuril'sk 171 ST 5
Severomorsk 150 K 2
Severo Sibirskaya Nizmennost' 170 FK 1
Severoural'sk 159 L 3
Severo-Yeniseyskiy 170 F 3
Severskiy Donets 155 F 1
Severskiy Donets 158 G 6
Severy (KS.) 120 J 5
Sevier (UT.) 114 E 5
Sevier Bridge Reservoir 114 F 4
Sevier Desert 114 E 4
Sevier Lake 114 D 5
Sevier Plateau 114 E 5
Sevier River 114 E 5
Sevierville (TN.) 128 H 6
Sevilla 152 B 4
Seville (FL.) 131 N 5
Sevlijevo 154 BC 2
Sevola 154 B 1
Sevrey 172 D 2
Seward (AK.) 102 H 3
Seward (KS.) 120 G 4
Seward (NE.) 120 HJ 2
Seward Peninsula 102 E 2
Sewell 142 B 5
Seyah Band Koh 169 G 4
Sëyakha 159 NO 1
Sëyakha 159 O 1
Seychelles 199 J 4
Seychelles Bank 208 B 4
Seydān (Iran) 157 F 3
Seyðisfjörður 150 N 1
Seydişehir 155 D 3
Seyfe Gölü 155 D 3
Seyf Tāleh (Iran) 157 E 2
Seyhan 155 E 3
Seyhan (Turkey) 156 B 1
Seyhan Barajı 155 E 3
Seyitgazi 154 D 3
Seymchan 171 S 3
Seymour (IN.) 128 F 3
Seymour (MO.) 121 N 5
Seymour (South Africa) 200 D 6
Seymour (TX.) 122 D 2
Seymour (Victoria, Austr.) 183 H 6
Seyyedābād 169 H 4
Sežana 153 F 2
Sfax 193 H 2
S. Félix Island 135 B 5
Sferracavallo, Capo 153 E 4
Sfîntu Gheorghe 154 C 1
Sfîntu Gheorghe 154 CD 2
Sfîntu Gheorghe, Bratul 154 C 1
Sfîntu Gheorghe, Ostruvul 154 C 1
Shaanxi 172 E 4
Shaartuz 169 H 3
Shaba 198 CD 6
Shabani → Zvishavane 200 D 4
Shābelle, Webi 199 G 4
Shabelsk 155 E 1
Shabunda 198 D 5

Shabwah 195 H 5
Shache 169 K 3
Shackleton Ice Shelf 203
Shackleton Range 203
Shaddādī (Syria) 156 C 1
Shādegān (Iran) 157 E 3
Shadehill (SD.) 118 F 5
Shadehill (SD.) 118 FG 5
Shadehill Reservoir 118 F 5
Shadrinsk 159 M 4
Shadwān 194 E 3
Shadwān (Egypt) 156 B 4
Shady Cove (OR.) 110 C 8
Shady Dale (GA.) 128 H 8
Shady Grove (FL.) 131 L 4
Shadzud 169 J 3
Shafer, Lake 124 H 9
Shafer Butte 110 J 7
Shafter (CA.) 113 F 7
Shafter (TX.) 117 M 8
Shageluk 102 F 3
Shāghir (Syria) 156 C 1
Shagonar 170 F 5
Shāh ʻAbbas (Iran) 157 F 2
Shah Alam 176 B 3
Shahba (Syria) 156 B 2
Shahbandar 169 H 6
Shahdol 174 D 3
Shah Fuladi 169 H 4
Shaḥḥāt 193 K 2
Shahin Dezh 168 D 3
Shahjahanpur 174 C 2
Shahjahanpur 174 CD 2
Shāh Kūh 168 F 4
Shahmīrzad (Iran) 157 F 2
Shahpur 169 J 4
Shahpura 174 B 2
Shahpura 174 C 2
Shahrak 169 G 4
Shahr-e Bābak (Iran) 157 G 3
Shahr-e Khafr (Iran) 157 F 3
Shahr Kord (Iran) 157 F 2
Shahtinsk 169 J 1
Shāh Zeyd (Iran) 157 F 1
Shā'ib al Banāt, Jabal (Egypt) 156 A 4
Sha'ib Hasb (Saudi Arabia) 156 D 3
Sha'ib Nisāh (Saudi Arabia) 157 E 4
Shaikh Bazit Dāgh 168 C 3
Shaim 159 M 3
Sha'it, Wādī (Egypt) 156 A 4
Shajapur 174 C 3
Shakawe 200 C 3
Shaker Heights (OH.) 125 N 8
Shakhrisyabz 169 H 3
Shakhtersk 159 Q 6
Shakhtersk 171 Q 6
Shakhterskiy 171 X 3
Shakhtinsk 159 O 6
Shakhty 155 F 1
Shakhun'ya 158 J 4
Shaki 196 E 4
Shaksgam 169 K 3
Shaktoolik 102 E 3
Shāl (Iran) 157 E 2
Shala, Lake 199 F 3
Shalakusha 158 H 3
Shalamzār (Iran) 157 F 2
Shalānbod 199 GH 4
Shaler Mountains 103 P 1
Shalgachëva 158 G 3
Shalgiya 159 O 6
Shali 155 G 2
Shalkar 158 K 5
Shallotte (N.C.) 129 N 8
Shallowater (TX.) 117 OP 4
Shallow Water (KS.) 120 E 4
Shaluli Shan 172 C 4–5
Shalunti 175 G 2
Shalya 159 L 4
Shalym 159 R 5
Shām, Jabal ash (Oman) 195 K 4
Shām, Jabal ash (Oman) 195 JK 5
Shamattawa 103 T 4
Shambār (Iran) 157 E 2
Shambe 198 E 3
Shambo 199 F 3
Shāmīyah 156 C 2
Shammar, Jabal (Saudi Arabia) 156 CD 4
Shamokin (PA.) 127 C 8
Shamrock (TX.) 117 Q 2
Shams (Iran) 157 G 3
Shamsī 194 D 5
Shamuhombo 198 B 6
Shamva 201 E 3
Shan 175 G 3
Shandan 172 D 3
Shandī 194 E 5
Shandong 173 G 3
Shandong Bandao 173 H 3
Shangaly 158 H 3
Shangani 200 D 3
Shangcai 172 F 4
Shangcheng 172 FG 4
Shangchuan Dao 172 F 6
Shangdu 172 F 2
Shanghai 173 H 4
Shanghang 172 G 5
Shanglin 172 E 6

Shangnan 172 F 4
Shangombo 200 C 3
Shangqiu 172 G 4
Shangrao 173 G 5
Shangsi 172 E 6
Shang Xian 172 E 4
Shangyi 172 F 2
Shangzhi 173 J 1
Shanh 170 H 6
Shani 197 G 3
Shaniko (OR.) 110 E 5
Shankou 172 B 2
Shannon (GA.) 128 F 7
Shannon (MS.) 121 R 8
Shannon (Rep. of Ireland) 148 B 4
Shannon, Lake 110 D 2
Shannon, Mouth of the 148 AB 4
Shano 199 F 3
Shanshan 172 B 2
Shantarskiye Ostrova 171 P 4
Shantou 172 G 6
Shantung Peninsula → Shandong Bandao 173 H 3
Shanxi 172 F 3
Shanyin 172 F 3
Shaodong 172 F 5
Shaoguan 172 F 6
Shaoshan 172 F 5
Shaowu 173 G 5
Shaoxing 173 H 5
Shaoyang 172 F 5
Shapkina 158 K 2
Shāpūr (Iran) 157 F 3
Shaqlāwah (Iraq) 156 D 1
Shaqrā' 195 H 6
Shaqū (Iran) 157 G 4
Sharaf (Iraq) 156 D 3
Sharafah 194 D 6
Sharāh, Jibāl ash 194 F 2
Sharā ʻIwah (Qatar) 157 F 4
Sharak (Iran) 157 F 1
Sharan 158 K 4
Sharbithāt, Ra's 195 K 5
Shargī, Jabal ash (Syria) 156 B 2
Sharīfābād (Iran) 157 F 2
Sharjah → Ash Shāriqah 195 K 3
Shark Bay 182 A 4
Sharlauk 168 F 3
Sharlyk 158 K 5
Sharon (N.D.) 119 L 3
Sharon (PA.) 125 O 8
Sharon Springs (KS.) 120 D 4
Sharonville (OH.) 128 G 2
Sharpe, Lake 118 J 6
Sharpsburg (Iowa) 119 N 10
Sharpsville (PA.) 125 O 8
Sharshar, Jabal 194 E 4
Shary (Saudi Arabia) 156 D 4
Sharypovo 159 R 4
Shar'ya 158 J 4
Shashamanna 199 F 3
Shashe 200 D 4
Shashe 200 D 4
Shashi 172 F 4
Shasta (CA.) 112 C 2
Shasta, Mount 112 C 1
Shasta Dam 112 C 2
Shasta Lake 112 C 2
Shatsk 158 H 5
Shatt al Arab (Iraq) 157 E 3
Shatt al Gharrāf (Iraq) 157 DE 3
Shatt al Jarīd 193 G 2
Shattuck (OK.) 120 F 6
Shaunavon 103 Q 6
Shaviklde 155 G 2
Shaw (MS.) 121 P 9
Shawan 169 M 2
Shawano (WI.) 124 F 5
Shawāq (Saudi Arabia) 156 B 4
Shawinigan 105 N 6
Shawmut (MT.) 111 Q 4
Shawnee (OH.) 129 J 2
Shawnee (OK.) 120 J 7
Shawneetown (IL.) 121 R 5
Sha Xian 173 G 5
Shaybārā (Saudi Arabia) 156 B 4
Shaykh, Jabal Shaykh (Lebanon) 156 B 2
Shaykh, Ra's ash 156 B 3
Shaykh Ahmad (Iraq) 157 E 2
Shaykh Sa'd (Iraq) 157 DE 2
Shaykh ʻUthmān 195 H 6
Shchara 151 J 5
Shcherbakty 159 P 5
Shchigry 158 G 5
Shchuchin 151 H 5
Shchuch'ya 159 N 2
Shchuchinsk 159 N 5
Shchuch'ye 159 M 4
Shea Ghimirra 198 F 3
Shebalino 155 F 1
Shebekino 158 G 5
Sheboygan (WI.) 124 G 6
Shebshi Mountains 197 G 4

Shebunino 171 Q 6
Sheckler Reservoir 112 G 3
Shedgum (Saudi Arabia) 157 E 4
Shedin Peak 103 M 4
Shedok 155 F 2
Sheenjek 102 J 2
Sheep Mountain 116 B 5
Sheep Peak 117 M 6
Sheep Range 112 K 6
Sheep Springs (N.M.) 116 H 1
Sheet Harbour 105 P 7
Sheffield (AL.) 128 D 7
Sheffield (IA.) 119 P 8
Sheffield (PA.) 125 P 8
Sheffield (TX.) 117 P 7
Sheffield (U.K.) 148 C 4
Shegarka 159 Q 4
Shehong 172 E 4
Sheikh Idris 194 E 6
Shekhawati 174 C 2
Shekhupura 169 J 4
Sheki 168 D 2
Shelār (Iran) 157 E 2
Shelbina (MO.) 121 NO 3
Shelburne 105 OP 7
Shelby (MI.) 124 H 6
Shelby (MS.) 121 P 9
Shelby (MT.) 111 O 2
Shelby (N.C.) 129 K 6
Shelby (NE.) 120 H 1
Shelby (OH.) 125 M 9
Shelbyville (IL.) 121 R 3
Shelbyville (IN.) 128 F 2
Shelbyville (KY.) 128 F 3
Shelbyville (MO.) 121 N 3
Shelbyville (TN.) 128 E 6
Shelbyville (TN.) 128 E 6
Shelbyville, Lake 121 R 3
Sheldon (IA.) 119 N 7
Sheldon (MO.) 121 L 5
Sheldon Point 102 D 3
Shelekhov 170 H 5
Shelekhova 171 T 5
Shelikhova, Zaliv 171 T 3–4
Shelikof Strait 102 G 4
Shell (WY.) 111 S 6
Shell Beach (LA.) 123 O 6
Shellbrook 103 Q 5
Shelley (ID.) 111 N 7
Shellharbour 183 J 5
Shell Island 131 J 4
Shell Keys 123 M 6
Shell Lake (N.D.) 118 F 2
Shell Lake (WI.) 124 C 4
Shell Lakes 182 D 4
Shelopugino 170 L 5
Shelton (WA.) 110 B 3
Shemakha 168 D 2
Shemonaikha 159 Q 5
Shenandoah (IA.) 119 N 10
Shenandoah (PA.) 127 C 8
Shenandoah (VA.) 129 N 3
Shenandoah Mountain 129 M 3
Shenandoah National Park 129 N 3
Shenandoah River 129 O 2
Shenber 199 H 1
Shenchi 172 F 3
Shendam 197 F 4
Shenge 196 B 4
Shengsi Liedao 173 H 4
Sheng Xian 173 H 5
Shenkursk 158 H 3
Shenmu 172 F 3
Shenqiu 172 G 4
Shenton, Mount 182 C 4
Shenyang 173 H 2
Shenze 172 G 3
Sheopur 172 E 3
Shepetovka 151 J 5
Shepherd (MI.) 125 K 6
Shepherd (MT.) 111 R 5
Shepherd (TX.) 123 HJ 5
Shepherdsville (KY.) 128 F 4
Shepparton 183 H 6
Shepperd, Lake 182 C 4
Sherbro Island 196 B 4
Sherburn (MN.) 119 O 7
Sherburne (N.Y.) 126 D 6
Sherda 197 H 1
Shere Hill 197 F 4
Sheridan (AR.) 121 N 8
Sheridan (MT.) 111 N 5
Sheridan (OR.) 110 B 5
Sheridan (TX.) 122 G 6
Sheridan (WY.) 118 B 5
Sheridan Lake (CO.) 115 P 5
Sheringham 148 D 4
Sherkaly 159 N 3
Sherlovaya Gora 170 L 5
Sherman (N.M.) 116 J 5
Sherman (N.Y.) 125 P 7
Sherman (TX.) 122 G 2
Sherman Reservoir 120 G 1
Sherman Station (ME.) 126 L 3
Sherpur 174 E 3
Sherridon 103 R 4
Sherwood (AR.) 121 N 8
Sherwood (N.D.) 118 D 2
Sherwood (OH.) 125 K 8

Shetland Islands 148 D 2
Shevchenko 168 E 2
Shevli 171 O 5
Shevykan 170 J 5
Sheya 170 L 3
Sheyang 173 H 4
Sheyenne (ND.) 118 JK 3
Sheyenne River 119 L 4
Shiashkotan, Ostrov 171 S 6
Shibām 195 H 5
Shibarghan 169 H 3
Shibazhan 171 N 5
Shibeli, Webbe 199 G 3
Shibīn al Kawm 194 E 2
Shibogama Lake 104 K 5
Shicheng Dao 173 H 3
Shickley (NE.) 120 H 2
Shidao 173 H 3
Shidian 172 C 6
Shidler (OK.) 120 J 6
Shields (KS.) 120 E 4
Shields (ND.) 118 GH 4
Shifā', Jabal ash (Saudi Arabia)
  156 B 3
Shihezi 169 M 2
Shijiazhuang 172 F 3
Shikarpur 169 H 5
Shikoku 173 K 4
Shila 170 F 4
Shilabo 199 G 3
Shilikarym 159 Q 6
Shilka 170 L 5
Shilka 170 L 5
Shilkan 171 R 4
Shilla 174 C 1
Shillong 175 F 2
Shilovo 158 H 5
Shimanovsk 171 N 5
Shimian 172 D 5
Shimizu 173 L 4
Shimoga 174 C 5
Shimo la Tewa 199 FG 5
Shimoni 199 F 5
Shimonoseki 173 JK 4
Shinak Pass 157 D 1
Shinās 195 K 4
Shindand 169 G 4
Shiner (TX.) 122 F 6
Shingbwiyang 175 G 2
Shinghar 169 H 4
Shingleton (MI.) 124 H 3
Shingletown (CA.) 112 CD 2
Shingozha 159 Q 6
Shingshal 169 K 3
Shingū 173 L 4
Shinjō 173 M 3
Shinkafi 197 F 3
Shinnston (W.V.) 129 L 2
Shinyanga 198 E 5
Shiocton (WI.) 124 F 5
Ship Bottom (N.J.) 127 E 9
Shiping 172 D 6
Shippegan 105 P 6
Shippensburg (PA.) 127 B 8
Shippenville (PA.) 125 P 8
Ship Rock (CO.) 116 H 1
Shiprock (N.M.) 116 H 1
Shipunovo 159 Q 5
Shipunskiy, Mys 171 TU 5
Shiquan 172 E 4
Shiquanhe 174 C 1
Shira 159 R 5
Shirabad 169 H 3
Shirase Glacier 203
Shīrāz (Iran) 157 F 3
Shire 201 F 2
Shīrgāh (Iran) 157 F 1
Shirikrabat 169 G 2
Shīrīn Sū (Iran) 157 E 2
Shiriya-zaki 173 M 2
Shīr Kūh (Iran) 157 FG 3
Shirley Mountain 118 B 8
Shirokaya Pad 171 Q 5
Shirokostan, Poluostrov 171 PQ 1
Shirokovo 170 G 4
Shirokoye 155 D 1
Shīrvān 168 F 3
Shīrvān (Iran) 157 E 2
Shisanzhan 171 MN 5
Shishaldin Volcano 102 E 5
Shishaldin Volcano 108 F 5
Shishmaref 102 D 2
Shishou 172 F 5
Shithāthah (Iraq) 156 D 2
Shiveluch, Sopka 171 U 4
Shively (CA.) 112 B 2
Shively (KY.) 128 F 3
Shivpuri 174 C 2
Shivwits (UT.) 114 D 6
Shivwits Plateau 116 C 1
Shiwan Dashan 172 E 6
Shiwa Ngandu 201 E 2
Shiyan 172 F 4
Shizong 172 D 6
Shizuishan 172 E 3
Shizuoka 173 L 4
Shkodra 154 A 2
Shlyuz 159 R 4
Shmidta, Poluostrov 171 Q 5

Shnezhnoye 155 E 1
Shoa 199 F 3
Shoals (IN.) 128 E 3
Sholapur 174 C 4
Shonkin (MT.) 111 P 3
Shoptykul' 159 P 5
Shorapur 174 C 4
Shorawak 169 H 4
Shortandy 159 O 5
Shoshone (CA.) 112 J 6
Shoshone (ID.) 111 L 8
Shoshone Basin 111 RS 8
Shoshone Lake 111 P 6
Shoshone Mountains 112 H 3–4
Shoshone Peak 112 J 5–6
Shoshone River 111 R 6
Shoshoni (WY.) 111 RS 7
Shoshong 200 D 4
Shostka 158 F 5
Shouguang 173 G 3
Shoup (ID.) 111 L 5
Shou Xian 172 G 4
Showa 203
Show Low (AZ.) 116 F 3
Show Low Lake 116 FG 3
Shoyna 158 H 2
Shpakovskoye 155 F 1
Shqiperia 154 AB 2
Shreveport (LA.) 123 K 3
Shrewsbury 148 C 4
Shuangcheng 173 J 1
Shuangjiang 172 CD 6
Shuangliao 173 H 2
Shuangyang 173 J 2
Shuangyashan 173 K 1
Shu'ayt 195 J 5
Shubar-Kuduk 168 F 1
Shublik Mountains 109 J 2
Shubuta (MS.) 130 F 3
Shucheng 173 G 4
Shufu 169 K 3
Shuga 159 O 2
Shuga 159 P 5
Shugualak (MS.) 130 F 2
Shugur 159 N 3
Shuguri Falls 199 F 6
Shulan 173 J 2
Shule 169 K 3
Shule He 172 C 2
Shulehe 172 C 2
Shulu 172 G 3
Shumagin Islands 102 F 4–5
Shuman House 109 K 2
Šumen 154 C 2
Shumerlya 158 J 4
Shumikha 159 M 4
Shumshu, Ostrov 171 T 5
Shumskiy 170 G 5
Shunak, Gora 169 J 1
Shunchang 173 G 5
Shungnak 102 F 2
Shuolong 172 E 6
Shuo Xian 172 F 3
Shūr (Iran) 157 F 3
Shur (Iran) 157 G 3
Shūrāb (Iran) 157 G 2
Shūr Gaz 168 F 5
Shurinda 170 K 4
Shūr Kūl 168 F 5
Shurugwi 200 DE 3
Shushenskoye 170 F 5
Shūshtar (Iran) 157 E 2
Shuwak 194 F 6
Shuya 150 K 3
Shuya 158 H 4
Shuyak 102 G 4
Shuyang 173 G 4
Shwābische Alb 149 E 5
Shwebo 175 G 3
Shwegun 175 G 4
Shwegyin 175 G 4
Shweli 175 G 3
Shyok 169 K 4
Sia 177 H 5
Siahan Range 169 H 5
Siah-Chashmeh 168 C 3
Sīāh-Kūh (Iran) 157 F 2
Siak Sri Indrapura 176 B 3
Sialk (Iran) 157 F 2
Sialkot 169 J 4
Siam 175 H 4
Sian → Xi'an 172 E 4
Siapa 138 E 3
Siargao 177 G 2
Siasconset (N.Y.) 127 K 8
Siassi 184 E 3
Siau 177 G 3
Šiauliai 151 H 4
Siavonga 200 D 3
Siazan' 168 D 2
Sibā'ī, Jabal as 194 E 3
Sibay 159 L 5
Šibenik 153 G 3
Siberut, Pulau 176 A 4
Sibi 169 H 5
Sibigo 176 A 3
Sibirskiye Uvaly 159 NO 3
Sibirsko
Sibsagar 175 FG 2

Sibu 176 D 3
Sibuguey Bay 177 F 2
Sibut 198 B 3
Sibutu, Pulau 177 E 3
Sibuyan 177 F 1
Sibuyan Sea 177 F 1
Sicasica 140 C 4
Sichon 175 G 6
Sichuan 172 CE 4
Sichuan Pendi 172 E 4
Sicilia 153 F 4
Sicilia, Canale de 153 F 4
Sicily 153 F 4
Sicily Island (LA.) 123 M 4
Sicuani 140 B 3
Sidamo 199 F 4
Sidaouet 197 F 2
Side 154 D 3
Sidéradougou 196 D 3
Siderno 153 G 4
Sīdī Barrānī 194 D 2
Sidi-bel-Abbès 192 E 1
Sidi Bennour 192 D 2
Sidi Ifni 192 C 3
Sidi Kacem 192 D 2
Sidikalang 176 A 3
Sidi Krelil 193 D 2
Sidnaw (MI.) 124 F 3
Sidney (Br. Col., Can.) 103 N 6
Sidney (IA.) 119 N 10
Sidney (IL.) 124 F 9
Sidney (MT.) 118 D 3
Sidney (NE.) 118 F 9
Sidney (N.Y.) 126 D 6
Sidney (OH.) 125 K 9
Sidney Lanier, Lake 128 H 7
Sidon (Lebanon) 156 B 2
Sidorovsk 159 Q 2
Sidr, Ra's as (Egypt) 156 A 3
Siedlce 149 H 4
Siegburg 149 E 4
Siegen 149 E 4
Siegen-Kyuyel' 171 NO 3
Siem Reap 175 H 5
Siena 153 F 3
Sieradz 149 G 4
Sierpo 149 G 4
Sierra Alamos 132 B 2
Sierra Añueque 143 C 7
Sierra Auca Mahuida 143 C 6
Sierra Bermeja 152 B 4
Sierra Blanca 117 L 4
Sierra Blanca Peak 117 L 4
Sierra Chauchaiñeu 143 C 7
Sierra Cimaltepec 132 C 4
Sierra City (CA.) 112 E 3
Sierra Colorada 143 C 7
Sierra de Agalta 132 E 4
Sierra de Alcaraz 152 C 4
Sierra de Alfabia 152 D 3
Sierra de Ancares 152 B 3
Sierra de Ancasti 142 C 4
Sierra de Aracena 152 B 4
Sierra de Coalcoman 132 B 4
Sierra de Córdoba 142 D 5
Sierra de Curupira 138–139 EF 3
Sierra de Famatina 142 C 4
Sierra de Gata 152 B 3
Sierra de Gredos 152 B 3
Sierra de Guadalupe 152 B 4
Sierra de Guadarrama 152 C 3
Sierra de Guampi 138 E 2
Sierra de Gúdar 152 C 3
Sierra de Juarez 106 C 5
Sierra de la Almenara 152 C 4
Sierra de la Cabrera 152 B 3
Sierra de la Demanda 152 C 3
Sierra de la Encantada 132 B 2
Sierra de la Giganta 106 D 6
Sierra de la Peña 152 C 3
Sierra de la Pila 152 C 4
Sierra de las Estancias 152 C 4
Sierra de las Minas 132 E 4
Sierra de las Tunas 106 E 6
Sierra de la Tasajera 106 E 6
Sierra del Cadí 152 D 3
Sierra del Castañar 152 C 4
Sierra del Chorito 152 C 4
Sierra del Faro 152 B 3
Sierra del Moncayo 152 C 3
Sierra del Nevado 143 C 6
Sierra del Nido 106 E 6
Sierra de los Alamitos 132 B 2
Sierra de los Cuchumatanes
  132 D 4
Sierra de los Huicholes 132 B 3
Sierra del Pedroso 152 B 4
Sierra de Luquillo 130 D 8
Sierra de Martés 152 C 4
Sierra de Montsant 152 D 3
Sierra de Montsech 152 D 3
Sierra de Montseny 152 D 3
Sierra de Mulegé 106 D 6
Sierra de Parras 132 B 2
Sierra de Perijá 138 D 1–2
Sierra de Rañadoiro 152 B 3

Sierra de San Borjas 106 D 6
Sierra de San Lázaro 106 E 7
Sierra de San Pedro 152 B 4
Sierra de San Vicente 152 C 3
Sierra de Segura 152 C 4
Sierra Espinazo del Diablo 132 A 3
Sierra Gorda 140 C 5
Sierra Grande (Argentina) 143 C 7
Sierra Grande (Mexico) 106 F 6
Sierra Grande (Mexico) 132 B 2
Sierra Leone 196 B 4
Sierra Madre (Mexico) 132 D 4
Sierra Madre (Philippines) 177 J 1
Sierra Madre (WY.) 118 AB 9
Sierra Madre del Sur 132 BC 4
Sierra Madre Oriental 132 BC 2–3
Sierra Madrona 152 C 4
Sierra Maestra 133 G 3
Sierra Mojada 132 B 2
Sierra Morena 152 BC 4
Sierra Nayarit 132 B 3
Sierra Nevada 112 E 3–6
Sierra Nevada (Spain) 152 C 4
Sierra Nevada del Cocuy 138 D 2
Sierra Pacaraima 139 F 3
Sierra Parima 138 E 3
Sierra Prieta 106 D 5
Sierra Tarahumara 106 E 6
Sierra Velasco 142 C 4
Sierra Vieja 117 M 7
Sierra Vista (AZ.) 116 F 6
Sierra Vizcaíno 106 D 6
Sierre 153 E 2
Sifani 199 G 2
Sifié 196 C 4
Sífnos 154 B 3
Sig 150 K 2
Sig 192 EF 1
Sığacık 154 C 3
Sigean, Étang de 152 D 3
Sighetul Marmaţiei 154 B 1
Sighişoara 154 B 1
Sigli 176 A 2
Sigiri 196 C 3
Sigiriya 174 D 6
Siglufjörður 150 B 2
Signakhi 155 G 4
Signal Peak (AZ.) 116 B 4
Signal Peak (UT.) 114 D 6
Signy Island 203
Sigoisoinan 176 A 4
Sigourney (IA.) 119 Q 9
Sigovo 159 R 3
Sigsig 138 C 4
Sigtuna 151 G 4
Siguiri 196 C 3
Sigulda 151 HJ 4
Sigurd (UT.) 114 F 5
Sihaung Myauk 175 F 3
Sihui 172 F 6
Siikajoki 150 J 3
Siilinjärvi 150 J 3
Siin 171 P 6
Siirt (Turkey) 155 F 3
Sikanni Chief 103 N 4
Sikar 174 C 2
Sikaram 169 H 4
Sikariman 176 BA 4
Sikasso 196 C 3
Sikéa 154 B 2
Sikéa 154 B 3
Sikerin 171 Q 2
Sikes (LA.) 123 L 3
Sikeston (MO.) 121 Q 6
Sikfors 150 H 2
Sikhote-Alin 171 P 6
Síkinos 154 BC 3
Sķinos 154 C 3
Sikkim 174 E 2
Siklós 154 A 1
Sikonge 198 E 6
Sikosi 200 C 3
Siktemey 171 S 2
Siktyakh 171 N 2
Sil 172 B 3
Silagui 176 A 4
Silas (AL.) 130 F 3
Silba 153 F 3
Silchar 175 F 3
Sildagapet 150 D 3
Sile 154 C 2
Siler City (N.C.) 129 M 6
Silesia 149 G 4
Silesia (MT.) 111 R 5
Silet 193 F 4
Silgarhi-Doti 174 D 2
Silhouette 199 J 5
Sili 196 D 3
Silicon Valley 112 D 5
Silife (Turkey) 156 AB 1
Siligir 170 K 2
Siliguri 174 E 2
Siling Co 174 E 1
Silio (N.M.) 117 KL 3
Silistra 154 C 2
Silivri 154 C 2
Siljan 151 F 3
Silkeborg 151 E 4
Sillajhuay → Cerro Toroni 140 C 4

Sillamäe 151 J 4
Sille 155 D 3
Sillian 153 F 2
Sillil 199 G 2
Sillustani 140 B 4
Sil Nakya (AZ.) 116 E 5
Siloam Springs (AR.) 121 L 6
Siloana Plains 200 C 3
Silom 185 F 2
Silonga 200 C 3
Silsbee (TX.) 123 J 5
Siltcoos (OR.) 110 AB 7
Siltou 197 H 2
Silup 169 G 5
Silvan 155 F 3
Silvassa 174 B 3
Silver (TX.) 122 C 3
Silver Bank Passage 133 HJ 3
Silver Bow Park (MT.) 111 N 5
Silver City (ID.) 110 J 7
Silver City (MI.) 124 E 3
Silver City (N.M.) 116 H 5
Silver City (SD.) 118 E 6
Silver City (UT.) 114 E 4
Silver Cliff (CO.) 115 M 5
Silver Creek (MS.) 130 DE 3
Silver Creek (NE.) 120 H 1
Silver Creek (N.Y.) 125 P 7
Silver Island Mountains 114 D 2–3
Silver Lake (CA.) 113 J 7
Silver Lake (OR.) 110 D 7
Silver Lake (OR.) 110 E 7
Silver Lake (OR.) 110 F 7
Silver Lake (WA.) 110 C 4
Silver Peak Range 112 H 5
Silver Spring 129 OP 3
Silver Springs (NV.) 112 F 3
Silver Star Mountain 110 E 2
Silvertip Mountain 111 M 3
Silverton (CO.) 115 K 6
Silverton (N.S.W., Austr.) 183 G 5
Silverton (OR.) 110 C 5
Silverton (TX.) 117 P 3
Silverton (WA.) 110 D 2
Silver Valley (TX.) 122 D 4
Silves 139 G 4
Silvies (OR.) 110 G 6
Silvies River 110 F 7
Silyānah 193 G 1
Sil'yeyaki 171 Q 1
Simaleke Hilir 176 A 4
Simanggang 176 D 3
Simao 172 D 6
Simareh (Iran) 157 E 2
Simav 154 C 2
Simav 154 C 3
Simav 154 C 3
Simba 198 C 4
Simbo (Solomon Is.) 185 G 3
Simbo (Tanzania) 198 DE 5
Simcoe, Lake 105 M 7
Simenga 170 J 3
Simeulue, Pulau 176 A 3
Simferopol' 155 D 2
Sími 154 C 3
Simití 138 D 2
Simi Valley (CA.) 113 G 8
Simla 174 C 1
Simla (CO.) 115 N 4
Şimleu Silvaniei 154 B 1
Simms (MT.) 111 NO 3
Simnasho (OR.) 110 D 6
Simo 150 H 2
Simojärvi 150 J 2
Simojoki 150 J 2
Simojovel de Allende 132 D 4
Simón Bolivar, Parque Nacional
  138 D 2
Simonstown 200 B 6
Simpele 150 J 3
Simplicio Mendes 141 H 2
Simplon Pass 153 E 2
Simpson (LA.) 123 KL 4
Simpson (MN.) 119 Q 7
Simpson (MT.) 111 P 2
Simpson Desert 183 F 3
Simpson Desert National Park
  183 F 4
Simpson Hill 182 D 4
Simpson Peak 109 M 4
Simpson Peninsula 103 U 2
Simrishamn 151 F 4
Sims (IL.) 121 R 4
Simson Lake 109 N 2
Simtustus, Lake 110 D 6
Simuk, Pulau 176 A 3
Simushir, Ostrov 171 S 6
Sinā' (Egypt) 156 A 3
Sinabang 176 A 3
Sinabung, Gunung 176 A 3
Sinadaqo 199 H 3
Sinai (Egypt) 156 A 3
Sinaloa 106 E 6–7
Sinalunga 153 F 3
Sinamaica 138 D 1
Sinan 172 E 5
Sināwan 193 H 2
Sinazongwe 200 D 3
Sinbo 175 G 3

Sincé 138 C 2
Sincelejo 138 C 2
Sinch'am 173 J 2
Sinch'ang-ni 173 J 2
Sinclair (WY.) 118 AB 9
Sinclair, Lake 128 H 8
Sinclair Mine 200 B 5
Sin Cow 176 D 2
Sind 169 H 5
Sinda 171 P 6
Sindangbarang 176 C 5
Sindara 197 G 6
Sindeh, Teluk 177 F 5
Sindèr 196 E 3
Sindgi 174 C 4
Sindhuli Garhi 174 E 2
Sindor 158 K 3
Sinegorskiy 155 F 1
Sinelnikovo 155 E 1
Sines, Cabo de 152 B 4
Sinettä 150 J 2
Sinfra 196 C 4
Singako 197 H 4
Singapore 176 B 3
Singapore, Strait of 176 B 3
Singaraja 176 E 5
Sing Buri 175 GH 5
Singen 149 E 5
Singer (LA.) 123 K 5
Singida 198 E 5
Singitikós Kólpos 154 B 2–3
Singkaling Hkamti 175 G 2
Singkawang 176 C 3
Singkep, Pulau 176 B 4
Singkilbaru 176 A 3
Singleton 183 J 5
Singleton (TX.) 122 GH 5
Singleton, Mount (Western
    Australia) 182 B 4
Singö 151 G 3
Singu 175 G 3
Sinhailien 173 GH 4
Si Nho 175 J 4
Sinianka-Minia, Parc National du
    197 H 3
Siniscola 153 E 3
Siniy-Shikhan 159 M 5
Sinj 153 G 3
Sinjai 177 F 5
Sinjaja 151 J 4
Sinjār (Iraq) 156 C 1
Sinjār, Jabal 195 G 1
Sinkan 175 G 3
Sinkät 194 F 5
Sinkiang Uighur 169 L 3
Sinn al Kadhdhāb 194 E 4
Sinnamary 139 H 2
Sinnar 174 B 4
Sinnicolau Mare 154 B 1
Sinnüris 194 E 3
Sinop 155 E 2
Sinp'o 173 J 2–3
Sinskoye 171 N 3
Sintana 154 B 1
Sintang 176 D 3
Sinton (TX.) 122 F 7
Sintra 152 B 4
Sinú 138 C 2
Sinüiju 173 HJ 2
Sinujif 199 H 3
Sinyaya 171 M 3
Sinyukha 154 D 1
Siocon 177 F 2
Siófok 154 A 1
Sioma 200 C 3
Sion 153 E 2
Sioux Center (IA.) 119 M 7
Sioux City (IA.) 119 M 8
Sioux Falls (S.D.) 119 M 7
Sioux Lookout 104 J 5
Sioux Pass (MT.) 118 D 3
Sioux Rapids (IA.) 119 N 8
Sipalay 177 F 2
Siping 173 H 2
Sipiwesk 103 S 4
Sipiwesk Lake 103 S 4
Siple Station 203
Sipolilo → Guruve 201 E 3
Sipora 176 A 4
Sipora, Pulau 176 A 4
Sipsey River 128 D 8
Siquia, Rio 132 F 5
Siquijor 177 F 2
Siquisique 138 DE 1
Sira (India) 174 C 5
Sira (Norway) 151 E 4
Sīr Abū Nu'ayr (United Arab
    Emirates) 157 G 4
Si Racha 175 H 5
Siracusa 153 G 4
Sirajganj 174 E 3
Sir Alexander, Mount 103 N 5
Şir Banī Yās (United Arab
    Emirates) 157 F 4
Sirdalen 151 E 4
Sirdalsvatn 151 E 4
Sirdān (Iran) 157 E 1
Sire 199 F 3
Sir Edward Pellew Group 183 F 2
Siren (WI.) 124 B 4

Sireniki 102 C 3
Siret 154 C 1
Sirevåg 151 E 4
Sirgän 169 G 5
Sirhān, Wādi as (Saudi Arabia)
    156 BC 3
Siri 199 F 3
Sīrīk 168 F 5
Sirino 153 G 3
Siris 174 D 3
Sirja 169 G 5
Sir James MacBrien, Mount
    109 N 3
Sirjan, Kavir-e (Iran) 157 G 3
Sirkka 150 H 2
Sirnak 155 F 3
Sirohi 174 B 3
Sironj 174 C 3
Siros 154 B 3
Sirotskiy 155 F 1
Sirpur 174 C 4
Sirr, Nafūd as (Saudi Arabia)
    156–157 D 4
Sīrrī (Iran) 157 G 4
Sirsa 174 C 2
Sirt 193 J 2
Sirt, Gulf of 193 J 2
Sir Thomas, Mount 182 D 4
Sisak 153 G 2
Si Sa Ket 175 H 4
Sisakht (Iran) 157 F 3
Sishen 200 C 5
Sisimiut 105 R 2
Siskiyou (OR.) 110 C 8
Siskiyou Mountains 112 B 1
Sisophon 175 H 5
Sisselton (S.D.) 119 L 5
Sisseton Indian Reservation
    119 LM 5
Sissonville (W.V.) 129 K 3
Sistema Iberico 152 C 3
Sistemas Béticos 152 C 4
Sisteron 153 E 3
Sisters (OR.) 110 D 6
Sister Bay (WI.) 124 G 4
Sistig-Khem 170 FG 5
Sistranda 150 E 3
Sitalike 198 E 6
Sitamarhi 174 E 2
Sitapur 174 D 2
Sitasjaure 150 G 2
Sitges 152 D 3
Sithonia 154 B 2
Sitka 102 K 4
Sitkalidak 102 G 4
Sitkinak Strait 108 M 4
Sitoli, Gunung 176 A 3
Sitrah 194 D 3
Sittang 175 G 4
Sittona 199 F 2
Sittwe 175 F 3
Situbondo 176 D 5
Siuna 132 F 5
Siuri 174 E 3
Sivaki 171 N 5
Sivas 155 E 3
Sivash 155 D 1
Sivaslı 154 C 3
Sivé 192 C 5
Siverek 155 E 3
Siverskiy 151 K 4
Sivrice 155 E 3
Sivrihisar 154 D 3
Siwah 194 D 3
Siwalik Range 174 CD 1–2
Siwan 174 D 2
Siwana 174 B 2
Siwa Oasis → Wāḥāt Sīwah
    194 D 3
Sixes (OR.) 110 A 8
Si Xian 173 G 4
Sixin 172 D 3
Sixteen (MT.) 111 P 4
Sixth Cataract → Ash Shallāl as
    Sablūkah 194 E 5
Siya 158 H 3
Siziwang 172 F 2
Sjælland 151 F 4
Sjaunja 150 GH 2
Sjövegan 150 G 2
Sjürjestan (Iran) 157 F 3
Skäckerfjällen 150 F 3
Skadarsko Jezero 154 A 2
Skadovsk 155 D 1
Skærbæck 151 E 4
Skaftá 150 B 3
Skagatá 150 A 2
Skagen 151 F 4
Skagern 151 F 4
Skagerrak 151 E 4
Skagit River 110 D 2
Skagway 102 K 4
Skaidi 150 H 1
Skaland 150 G 2
Skala Podolskaya 154 C 1
Skaliskaya, Gora 170 D 1
Skamokawa (WA.) 110 B 4
Skanderborg 151 E 4
Skåne 151 F 4

Skaneateles Lake 126 C 6
Skanör 151 F 4
Skara 151 F 4
Skärblacka 151 G 4
Skardu 169 K 3
Skärhamn 151 F 4
Skarsöy 150 E 3
Skarstind 150 E 3
Skarsvåg 150 E 3
Skarżysko-Kamienna 149 H 4
Skeena 102 M 5
Skeena Mountains 102 M 4
Skeggöxl 150 A 2
Skegness 148 D 4
Skeiðárarsandur 150 B 3
Skeldon 139 G 2
Skeleton Coast Park 200 A 3
Skellefteå 150 H 3
Skellefteälven 150 G 2
Skelleftehamn 150 H 3
Skellytown (TX.) 117 P 2
Ski 151 F 4
Skíathos 154 B 3
Skiatook (OK.) 120 JK 6
Skibbereen 148 B 4
Skibotn 150 H 2
Skidegate 102 L 5
Skidel' 151 H 5
Skidmore (TX.) 122 F 7
Skien 151 E 4
Skierniewice 149 H 4
Skiftet 151 H 3
Skíros 154 B 3
Skikda 193 G 1
Skime (MN.) 119 N 2
Skíros 154 B 3
Skive 151 E 4
Skjálfandafljót 150 B 2
Skjálfandi 150 B 2
Skjern 151 E 4
Skjervöy 150 H 1
Skjoldungen 105 T 3
Sklad 170 M 1
Škofja Loka 153 F 2
Skoghall 151 F 4
Skokie (IL.) 124 G 7–8
Skokomish Indian Reservation
    110 B 3
Skópelos 154 B 3
Skopi 154 C 3
Skopje 154 B 2
Skorodum 159 O 4
Skorovatn 150 F 3
Skörping 151 EF 4
Skövde 151 F 4
Skovorodino 171 M 5
Skowhegan (ME.) 126 K 4
Skradin 153 G 3
Skrekken 151 E 3
Skudeneshavn 151 DE 4
Skull Valley (AZ.) 116 D 3
Skull Valley Indian Reservation
    114 E 3
Skunk River 119 R 9
Skurup 151 F 4
Skutskär 151 G 3
Skvira 158 E 6
Skwentna 109 H 3
Skwentna River 109 H 3
Skye 148 B 3
Slagnäs 150 G 2
Slamet, Gunung 176 C 5
Slannik 154 C 2
Slano 153 G 3
Slantsy 151 J 4
Slapout (OK.) 120 E 6
Slashchevskaya 158 H 6
Śląsk 149 G 4
Slater (MO.) 121 M 3
Slater (WY.) 118 D 9
Slatina 154 B 2
Slaton (TX.) 117 P 4
Slaty Fork (W.V.) 129 L 3
Slaughter (LA.) 123 M 5
Slautnoye 171 V 3
Slave Coast 196 E 4
Slave Lake 103 P 4
Slave River 103 P 3–4
Slavgorod 155 E 1
Slavgorod 159 P 5
Slavnoye 171 R 6
Slavonska Požega 153 G 2
Slavonski Brod 153 G 2
Slavuta 151 J 5
Slavyanka 173 K 2
Slavyansk 158 G 6
Slavyansk-na-Kubani 155 E 1
Sławno 149 G 4
Slayton (MN.) 119 N 6–7
Sledge (MS.) 121 P 8
Sleeper Islands 105 L 4
Sleeping Bear Dunes National
    Lakeshore 124 H 5
Sleepy Eye (MN.) 119 O 6
Sleetmute 108 G 3
Slettuheiði 150 B 2
Slick Rock (CO.) 114 J 5
Slidell (LA.) 123 O 5
Slide Mountain 126 E 7
Sliderock Mountain 111 M 4

Sligo 148 B 4
Sligo (PA.) 125 P 8
Slim Buttes 118 E 5
Slite 151 G 4
Sliven 154 C 2
Sloan (IA.) 119 M 8
Sloan (NV.) 112 K 7
Sloat (CA.) 112 E 3
Slobodchikovo 158 J 3
Slobodka 154 C 1
Slobodskoy 158 K 4
Slobodzeya 154 C 1
Slobozia 154 C 2
Slochteren 146
Slonim 151 J 5
Slough 148 C 4
Slovakia 149 H 5
Slovechno 151 J 5
Slovenija 153 FG 2
Slovenske Gorice 153 G 2
Slovensko 149 GH 5
Sluch' 151 J 5
Slünchev Bryag 154 C 2
Slunj 153 G 2
Słupia 149 G 4
Słupsk 149 G 4
Slutsk 151 J 5
Slyudyanka 170 HJ 5
Småland 151 G 4
Smålandsstenar 151 F 4
Small (TX.) 117 L 6
Small, Cape 126 K 5
Smallwood Réservoir 105 P 5
Smederevo 154 B 2
Smedjebacken 151 G 3
Smela 158 F 6
Smethport (PA.) 125 Q 8
Smidovich 171 O 6
Smidovich 202
Smiley (TX.) 122 F 6
Smirnovskiy 159 N 5
Smirnykh 171 Q 6
Smith (Alberta, Can.) 103 P 4
Smith (NV.) 112 F 4
Smith Arm 103 N 2
Smith Bay 102 G 1
Smith Center (KS.) 120 G 3
Smithers 103 M 5
Smith Falls 105 M 7
Smithfield (N.C.) 129 N 6
Smithfield (UT.) 114 F 2
Smithfield (VA.) 129 P 5
Smith Island (N.C.) 129 O 8
Smith Island (VA.) 129 Q 4
Smith Mountain Lake 129 M 4
Smith Peak 110 J 2
Smith River (CA.) 112 A 1
Smith River (MT.) 111 O 3
Smiths Ferry (ID.) 110 J 6
Smithton 184 L 9
Smithtown-Gladstone 183 J 5
Smithville (GA.) 131 K 3
Smithville (OK.) 121 L 8
Smithville (TN.) 128 F 6
Smithville (TX.) 122 F 5
Smithwick (SD.) 118 E 7
Smjörfjöll 150 C 2
Smögen 151 F 4
Smoke Creek (NV.) 112 F 2
Smoke Creek Desert 112 F 2
Smoke Creek Reservoir 112 F 2
Smoky Cape 183 J 5
Smoky Dome 111 L 7
Smoky Falls 104 L 5
Smoky Hill River 120 G 4
Smoky Hills 120 FG 3
Smoky River 103 O 5
Smøla 150 E 3
Smolensk 158 F 5
Smólikas Óros 154 B 2
Smolyan 154 B 2
Smooth Rock Falls 105 L 6
Smorgon' 151 J 5
Smygehamn 151 F 4
Smyrna (PA.) 127 D 9
Smyrna (TN.) 128 E 6
Smyrna → İzmir 154 C 3
Smyrna Mills (ME.) 126 L 2
Smythe, Mount 103 MN 4
Snæfell 150 B 3
Snæfellsjökull 150 A 3
Snæfellsnes 150 A 3
Snag 102 J 3
Snake Bay 182 E 1
Snake Range 112 L 3–4
Snake River (NE.) 118 G 8
Snake River (WA.) 110 H 4
Snake River (Yukon, Can.) 109 M 2
Snare 103 O 3
Snåsa 150 F 3
Snåsvattnet 150 F 3
Sneedville (TN.) 128 H 5
Snelling (CA.) 112 E 5
Snezhnogorsk 159 R 2
Snezhnoye 171 W 2
Snežnik 153 F 2
Śnieżka 149 G 4
Śnieżnik 149 G 4
Snigirevka 155 D 1

Snøhetta 150 E 3
Snohomish (WA.) 110 CD 3
Snoqualmie (WA.) 110 D 3
Snoqualmie Pass 110 D 3
Snoul 175 J 5
Snover (MI.) 125 L 6
Snowbird Lake 103 R 3
Snowdon 148 C 4
Snowdoun (AL.) 131 H 2
Snowdrift 103 P 3
Snowflake (AZ.) 116 F 3
Snow Hill (MD.) 129 Q 3
Snow Hill (N.C.) 129 O 6
Snow Lake 103 R 5
Snowmass Mountain 115 K 4
Snow Mountain (NV.) 112 C 3
Snow Peak 110 G 2
Snowshoe Peak 111 K 2
Snowside Peak 111 L 7
Snowville (ID.) 111 N 8
Snow Water Lake 112 L 2
Snowy Mountains 183 H 6
Snowy River 183 H 6
Snyatyn 154 C 1
Snyder (CO.) 115 O 3
Snyder (OK.) 120 FG 8
Snyder (TX.) 122 C 4
Soacha 138 D 3
Soahanina 201 G 3
Soalala 201 H 3
Soanierana-Ivongo 201 H 3
Soap Lake (WA.) 110 F 3
Soasiu 177 G 3
Soavinandriana 201 H 3
Soba 197 F 3
Sobat → Sawbā 198 E 3
Sobolevo 171 T 5
Sobolokh Mayan 171 MN 2
Sobopol 171 N 2
Sobradinho, Barragem de 141 H 3
Sobral 141 H 1
Socaire 140 C 5
Sochaczew 149 GH 4
Sochi 155 E 2
Society Hill (S.C.) 129 M 7
Society Islands 187 EF 4
Socorro (Colombia) 138 D 2
Socorro (N.M.) 117 K 3
Socorro (TX.) 117 K 6
Sócota 138 C 5
Socotra 199 J 2
Soda Lake (CA.) 113 JK 7
Sodankylä 150 J 2
Soda Plains 169 K 3
Soda Springs (CA.) 112 E 3
Soda Springs (ID.) 111 O 8
Soddu 199 F 3
Soddy - Daisy (TN.) 128 F 6
Söderhamn 150 G 3
Söderköping 151 G 4
Södermanland 151 G 4
Södertälje 151 G 4
Södra Kvarken 151 G 3
Sodus Pt (N.Y.) 126 B 5
Soe 177 F 5
Soela Väin 151 H 4
Soest 149 E 4
Sofádhes 154 B 3
Sofala, Baía de 201 EF 4
Sofia (Madagascar) 201 H 3
Sofia (N.M.) 117 N 1
Sofia → Sofiya 154 BC 2
Sofiya 154 B 2
Sofiyevka 155 D 1
Sofiysk 171 O 5
Sofiysk 171 PQ 5
Sofporog 150 K 2
Söfu-gan 173 LM 5
Sogamoso 138 D 2
Soğanlı 155 D 2
Sogda 171 O 5
Sogeri 184 E 3
Sogndalsfjöra 150 E 3
Sognefjorden 150 E 3
Sognesjöen 150 D 3
Sogn og Fjordane 150 E 3
Sogod 177 F 1
Sogo Hills 199 F 4
Sogolle 197 H 2
Sogom 159 N 3
Sogo Nur 172 D 2
Sögüt 154 D 3
Sögüt Gölü 154 CD 3
Sog Xian 172 B 4
Sohag → Sawhāj 194 E 3
Sohano 185 FG 3
Sohm Abyssal Plain 208 A 2
Sohŭksan-do 173 J 4
Soila 172 C 4
Soissons 152 D 2
Sojat 174 B 2
Söjosŏn-man 173 H 3
Sokal' 151 H 5
Sokch'o 173 J 3
Söke 154 C 3
Sokele 198 C 6
Sokhondo, Gora 170 K 6
Sokhor, Gora 170 J 5
Sokna 151 E 3
Sokodé 196 E 4

Sokol 154 A 2
Sokółka 149 H 4
Sokolo 196 C 3
Sokolov 149 F 4
Sokolozero 150 K 2
Sokone 196 A 3
Sokosti 150 J 2
Sokota 199 F 2
Sokoto 197 EF 3
Söl 199 H 3
Sola 151 E 4
Solai 199 F 4
Solano (N.M.) 117 M 2
Solbad Hall 153 F 2
Solberg 150 G 3
Soldatovo 171 V 3
Sölden 153 F 2
Soldier Pond (ME.) 126 L 1
Soldotna 102 G 3
Soledad (CA.) 112 D 6
Soledad (Colombia) 138 D 1
Soledad (Venezuela) 139 F 2
Soledade (Amazonas, Brazil)
138 E 5
Soledade (Río Grande do Sul,
Brazil) 142 F 4
Solen (ND.) 118 H 4
Solenoye (Russia, U.S.S.R.)
155 F 1
Solenoye (Ukraine, U.S.S.R.)
155 D 1
Solenzara 153 E 3
Solferino 153 F 2
Solhan 155 F 3
Soligorsk 151 J 5
Solikamsk 158 L 4
Sol'-Iletsk 158 L 5
Soliman 153 F 4
Solimões 138 E 4
Solingen 149 E 4
Solita 138 D 2
Solitaire 200 B 4
Solleftea 150 G 3
Sollerön 151 FG 3
Solling 149 E 4
Sologne Bourbonnais 152 D 2
Solok 176 B 4
Solomon (AZ.) 116 G 5
Solomon (KS.) 120 H 4
Solomon Islands 185 GH 3
Solomon Islands 186 B 3
Solomon Islands 186 BC 3
Solomon River 120 GH 3
Solomon Sea 185 F 3
Solomon Sea 186 B 3
Solon 173 H 1
Solon (IA.) 119 R 9
Solon (ME.) 126 K 4
Solontsovo 170 KL 5
Solör 151 F 3
Solothurn 153 E 2
Solov'yevsk 170 L 5
Solov'yevsk 171 MN 5
Solta 153 G 3
Soltānābād 168 F 3
Soltānābād (Iran) 157 E 3
Soltau 149 E 4
Sol'tsy 151 K 4
Solvang (CA.) 113 E 8
Sölvesborg 151 FG 4
Solway Firth 148 C 4
Solwezi 200 D 2
Solyanka 170 M 3
Soma 154 C 3
Somabula 200 D 3
Somalia 199 GH 3–4
Somali Basin 208 B 3
Sombang, Gunung 176 E 3
Sombo 200 C 1
Sombor 154 A 1
Sombrerete 132 B 3
Sombrero Channel 175 F 6
Sombrero Peak 116 F 4
Somcuţa Mare 154 B 1
Somero 151 H 3
Somers (IA.) 119 O 8
Somers (MT.) 111 L 2
Somerset (Australia) 183 G 1
Somerset (CO.) 115 K 5
Somerset (KY.) 128 G 4
Somerset (OH.) 129 J 2
Somerset (PA.) 125 PQ 9
Somerset (TX.) 122 E 6
Somerset East 200 CD 6
Somerton (AZ.) 116 B 5
Somerville (N.J.) 127 E 8
Somerville (TN.) 128 B 6
Somerville (TX.) 122 G 5
Somerville Lake 122 G 5
Someş 154 B 1
Somes Bar (CA.) 112 B 1
Someşu Mare 154 B 1
Somme 152 D 1
Sommen 151 G 4
Somnath 174 B 3
Somnitel'nyy 171 P 5
Somontano 152 C 3
Somoto 132 E 5
Somport, Puerto de 152 C 3
Somuncurá, Meseta de 143 C 7

Son 174 D 3
Soná 138 B 2
Sonakh 171 P 5
Sonaly 159 O 6
Sönch'ön 173 H 3
Sonda de Vieques 130 D 8
Sönderborg 151 EF 5
Sondershausen 149 F 4
Söndre Strömfjord 105 R 2
Söndre Strömfjord 105 RS 2
Sondrio 153 E 2
Sonepur 174 D 3
Sonequera 140 C 5
Sonestown (PA.) 127 C 7
Song 197 G 4
Song Cau 175 J 5
Song Da 175 H 3
Songea 201 F 2
Song Hong 175 H 3
Songhua Hu 173 J 2
Songhua Jiang 173 J 1
Songjiang 173 H 4
Songjiang 173 H 4
Songkhla 175 H 6
Songling 171 M 6
Song Ma 175 H 3
Songnim 173 J 3
Songo 201 E 3
Songolo 198 A 6
Songpan 172 D 4
Songwe 198 E 6
Songxi 173 G 5
Son Ha 175 J 4
Sonid Youqi 172 F 2
Sonid Zuoqi 172 F 2
Sonipat 174 C 2
Sonkel', Ozero 169 K 2
Son La 175 H 3
Sonmiani 169 H 5
Sonmiani Bay 169 H 5
Sonneberg 149 F 4
Sonnette (MT.) 118 C 5
Sono 139 J 5
Sonoita (AZ.) 116 F 6
Sonoita (Mexico) 106 D 5
Sonoma (CA.) 112 C 4
Sonoma Peak 112 H 2
Sonora (AZ.) 116 EF 4
Sonora (CA.) 112 E 5
Sonora (Mexico) 106 D 6
Sonora (TX.) 122 C 5
Sonora, Rio 106 D 6
Sonora Desert 116 AC 4
Sonqor (Iran) 157 E 2
Sonsón 138 CD 2
Sonsonate 132 DE 5
Sonsorol Islands 177 H 2
Sop Bau 175 H 3
Sopchoppy (FL.) 131 K 4
Soperton (GA.) 131 M 2
Sopka Anangravnen 171 U 4
Sopka Kizimen 171 U 4
Sopka Shiveluch 171 U 4
Sopochnaya Karga 170 DE 1
Sopochnoye 171 T 4
Sopot 149 G 4
Sopron 154 A 1
Sopur 169 J 4
Sor 152 B 4
Sora 153 F 3
Sorada 174 D 4
Söräker 150 G 3
Sorata 140 C 4
Sordoginskiy Khrebet 171 OP 3
Sorel 105 N 6
Sorell 184 L 9
Sörfold 150 G 2
Sorgues 153 D 3
Sorgun 155 E 3
Soria 152 C 3
Soriano 142 E 5
Sorikmerapi, Gunung 176 A 3
Sor Kaydak 168 E 1–2
Sorkh, Küh-e (Iran) 157 G 2
Sorkheh 168 E 3
Sorkheh (Iran) 157 F 2
Sor Mertvyy Kultuk 168 E 1
Sorocaba 141 G 5
Sorochinsk 158 K 5
Sorok 170 H J 5
Soroki 154 C 1
Sorolen 159 P 6
Sorong 177 H 4
Soroti 198 E 4
Söröya 150 H 1
Söröyane 150 E 3
Sorraia 152 B 4
Sörreisa 150 G 2
Sorrento 153 F 3
Sör Rondane Mountains 203
Sorsatunturi 150 J 2
Sorsele 150 G 2
Sorso 153 E 3
Sorsogon 177 F 1
Sort 152 D 3
Sortavala 150 K 3
Sortland 150 FG 2
Sör-Tröndelag 150 F 3
Sorum (SD.) 118 F 5
Sörværöy 150 F 2
Sörvagur 148 A 1

Sösan 173 J 3
Sosna 170 J 3
Sosnogorsk 158 KL 3
Sosnovka 173 JK 3
Sosnovka 158 H 2
Sosnovka 158 J 4
Sosnovka 170 J 5
Sosnovo-Ozerskoye 170 K 5
Sosnovy Bor 151 J 4
Sosnovyy Bor 159 Q 3
Sosnovyy Mys 159 N 3
Sosnowiec 149 G 4
Sos'va, Malaya 159 MN 3
Sos'va, Severnaya 159 MN 3
Sos'vinskaya Kul'tbaza 159 M 3
Sosyka 155 EF 1
Sotavento, Islas de 138 E 1
Sotik 198 F 5
Sotkamo 150 J 3
Sotnikovskoye 155 F 1
Sotonera, Embalse de la 152 C 3
Sotouboua 196 E 4
Sotra 153 E 1
Sotsial 159 P 6
Souanké 197 G 5
Soubré 196 C 4
Soudan 183 F 3
Souf 139 G 2
Souflion 154 C 2
Soufrière (Guadeloupe) 133 K 4
Soufrière (St. Vincent) 133 K 5
Souillac 152 D 3
Souilly 153 E 2
Souk Ahras 193 G 1
Souk el Arbaa du Rharb 192 D 2
Soukouralla 196 C 4
Soumenselkä 150 H 3
Sound of Harris 148 B 3
Sound of Jura 148 B 3
Sound of Raasay 148 B 3
Sounfat 196 E 1
Soúnion, Ákra 154 B 3
Sountellane 197 G 2
Soure 139 J 4
Souris (Manitoba, Can.) 103 R 6
Souris (Prince Edw. Isl., Can.)
105 P 6
Souris Plain 118 HJ 2
Souris River (N.D.) 118 H 2
Sour Lake (TX.) 123 J 5
Sous 192 D 2
Sousa 141 J 2
Sousel 139 H 4
Sousse → Süsah (Tunisia) 193 H 1
Soutbeach (OR.) 110 A 6
South Africa 200 CD 6
South Alligator River 182 E 1
Southampton 148 C D 4
Southampton (N.Y.) 127 G 8
Southampton, Cape 103 U 3
Southampton Island 103 UV 3
South Andaman 175 F 5
South Aulatsivik 105 P 4
South Australia 182–183 E 4
South Australian Basin 209 C 5
South Baldy 117 J 3–4
South Bay (FL.) 131 O 8
South Bay (N.W.T., Can.) 103 V 3
South Bend (IN.) 124 H 8
South Bend (WA.) 110 B 4
South Boston (VA.) 129 M 5
South Branch 129 N 2
South Burlington (VT.) 126 F 4
South Carolina 129
South China Sea 176 CD 2
South Dakota 118–119
South East Cape 184 L 9
Southeast Indian Rise 208 BC 5
South East Point 183 H 6
Southend 103 R 4
Southend-on-Sea 148 D 4
Southern Alps 185 Q 9
Southern Alps 186 C 5
Southern Cook Islands 187 E 4
Southern Cross 182 C 5
Southern Indian Lake 103 S 4
Southern Uplands 148 C 3
Southern Ute Indian Reservation
115 JK 6
South Fork (AK.) 109 H 2
South Fork (AK.) 109 H 3
South Fork (CO.) 115 L 6
South Fork (CO./KS.) 115 P 4
South Fork (KS.) 120 H 3
South Fork (KS.) 120 F 5
South Fork (MT.) 111 K 5
South Fork (S.C.) 129 K 8
South Fork Indian Reservation
112 K 2
South Fox Island 124 J 4
South Garcia (N.M.) 117 J 3
South Geomagnetic Pole 203
South Georgia 203
South Haven (KS.) 120 H 5
South Haven (MI.) 124 H 7
South Holston Lake 129 JK 5
South Horr 199 F 4
South Indian Lake 103 S 4

South Island 184 P 9
South Island 186 C 5
South Island (S.C.) 129 M 8
South Korea 173 JK 3
South Lake Tahoe (CA.) 112 EF 4
Southland (TX.) 117 P 4
South Loup River 120 F 1
South MacMillan River 109 M 3
South Magnetic Pole 203
South Manitou Island 124 H 4
South Milwaukee (WI.) 124 G 7
South Mountain 110 J 8
South Nahanni 103 M 3
South Orkney Islands 203
South Paris (ME.) 126 J 4
South Pass (CA.) 113 L 8
South Pass (WY.) 111 R 8
South Pass City (WY.) 111 R 8
South Patrick Shores (FL.) 131 O 6
South Plains (TX.) 117 P 3
South Platte River 115 OP 3
South Pole 203
South Ponte Vedra Beach (FL.)
131 N 4
Southport (FL.) 131 J 4
Southport (N.C.) 129 NO 8
South Portland (ME.) 126 J 5
South Punta Gorda Heights (FL.)
131 MN 8
South Ronaldsay 148 C 3
South St. Paul (MN.) 119 PQ 6
South Sandwich Islands 203
South Saskatchewan 103 PQ 5
South Shetland Islands 203
South Shields 148 C 3–4
South Shore (S.D.) 119 M 5
South Sioux City (IA.) 119 M 8
South Taranaki Bight 185 Q 8
South Tasman Rise 209 C 5
South Torrington (WY.) 118 D 8
South Uist 148 B 3
South Umpqua River 110 B 7
South Ventana Cone 112 D 6
South Wellesley Islands
(Queensland, Austr.) 183 F 2
Southwest Cape 184 P 10
Southwest Cape 186 C 5
Southwest Cape (P.R.) 130 E 9
Southwestern Pacific Basin 209 D 5
Southwest Harbor (ME.) 126 L 4
Southwest Indian Ridge 208 B 5
South Yemen 195 HJ 5–6
Soutpansberg 200 D 4
Soutra Hill 184 P 10
Soven 142 C 5
Soverato 153 G 4
Soveria 151 H 4
Sovetsk 158 J 4
Sovetskaya 155 F 2
Sovetskaya Gavan' 171 PQ 6
Sovetskaya Rechka 159 Q 2
Sovetskiy 155 D 1
Sovetskoje, Ozero 159 Q 2
Sovetskoye 155 G 2
Soya Strait 161 R 5
Soyatita 106 E 6
Soyo 200 A 1
Sozh 158 F 5
Sozimskiy 158 K 4
Sozopol 154 C 2
Spade (TX.) 117 PQ 5
Spain 152 BC 4
Spalding (ID.) 110 J 4
Spalding (NE.) 119 K 9
Spanish Fork (UT.) 114 F 3
Spanish Fork Peak 114 F 3
Spanish Peak 110 F 6
Spanish Town 130 E 9
Spanish Town 133 G 4
Sparbu 150 F 3
Sparks (NE.) 118 H 8
Sparks (NV.) 112 F 3
Sparta (GA.) 128 J 8
Sparta (IL.) 121 Q 4
Sparta (N.C.) 129 K 5
Sparta (TN.) 128 F 6
Sparta (WI.) 124 D 6
Sparta → Spartí 154 B 3
Spartel, Cap 192 D 1
Spartí 154 B 3
Spartivento, Capo 153 E 4
Spassk Dal'niy 173 K 2
Spátha, Ákra 154 B 3
Spearfish (SD.) 118 E 6
Spearman (TX.) 117 P 1
Spearville (KS.) 120 F 5
Speedway (IN.) 128 E 2
Speight (KY.) 128 J 4
Speke Gulf 198 E 5
Spenard 102 G 3
Spence Bay 103 T 2
Spencer (IA.) 119 N 7
Spencer (ID.) 111 N 6
Spencer (IN.) 128 E 2
Spencer (NE.) 119 K 8
Spencer (N.Y.) 126 C 6
Spencer (S.D.) 119 L 7
Spencer (TN.) 128 F 6
Spencer (W.V.) 129 K 3

Spencer, Cape 183 F 6
Spencer Bay 200 A 5
Spencer Gulf 183 F 5
Sperryville (VA.) 129 N 3
Spétsai 154 B 3
Spey 148 C 3
Speyer 149 E 5
Spicer Islands 105 M 2
Spickard (MO.) 121 M 2
Spiez 153 E 2
Spirit Lake (IA.) 119 N 7
Spirit Lake (IA.) 119 N 7
Spirit Lake (ID.) 110 J 2–3
Spirit Lake (WA.) 110 CD 4
Spirit River 103 O 4
Spišská-Nová Ves 149 H 5
Spitsbergen 202
Spittal 153 F 2
Spjelkavik 150 E 3
Split 153 G 3
Split Lake 103 S 4
Spluga, Passo della 153 E 2
Spofford (TX.) 122 C 6
Spogi 151 J 4
Spokane (WA.) 110 H 3
Spokane, Mount 110 H 3
Spokane Indian Reservation
110 GH 3
Spokane River 110 GH 3
Spoleto 153 F 3
Spong 175 J 5
Spooner (WI.) 124 C 4
Spoon River 124 D 9
Sportsmans Lake 120 H 3
Spotsylvania (VA.) 129 O 3
Spotted Horse (WY.) 118 C 6
Spraberry (TX.) 117 P 6
Sprague (AL.) 131 H 2
Sprague (WA.) 110 GH 3
Sprague River (OR.) 110 D 8
Spratly Island 176 D 2
Spray (OR.) 110 F 6
Spree 149 F 4
Sprengisandur 150 B 3
Spring (TX.) 123 H 5
Spring Branch (TX.) 122 E 6
Spring Butte 111 R 9
Spring City (TN.) 128 G 6
Spring City (UT.) 114 F 4
Springdale (AR.) 121 L 6
Springdale (MT.) 111 P 5
Springdale (Newfoundl., Can.)
105 Q 6
Springdale (WA.) 110 GH 2
Springer (N.M.) 117 M 1
Springer, Mount 105 N 6
Springerville (AZ.) 116 G 3
Springfield (CO.) 115 P 6
Springfield (FL.) 131 J 4
Springfield (GA.) 131 N 2
Springfield (ID.) 111 N 7
Springfield (IL.) 121 Q 3
Springfield (KY.) 128 FG 4
Springfield (MA.) 126 G 6
Springfield (MN.) 119 O 6
Springfield (MO.) 121 M 5
Springfield (OH.) 128 H 2
Springfield (OR.) 110 C 6
Springfield (S.C.) 131 M 3
Springfield (S.D.) 119 K 8
Springfield (TN.) 128 E 5
Springfield, Lake 121 Q 3
Springfontein 200 D 5–6
Spring Green (WI.) 124 D 6
Spring Grove (MN.) 119 R 7
Springhill (LA.) 123 K 2–3
Springhill (Nova Scotia, Can.)
105 P 6
Spring Lake (N.C.) 129 N 6
Springlake (TX.) 117 O 3
Springlands 139 G 2
Spring Mountains 112 K 6–7
Springs 200 D 5
Springs Junction 185 Q 9
Springsure 183 H 3
Springvale (Queensland, Austr.)
183 GH 2
Spring Valley (MN.) 119 Q 7
Spring Valley (NV.) 112 L 3–4
Springview (NE.) 118 J 8
Springville (CA.) 112 G 6
Springville (N.Y.) 125 Q 7
Spruce Mountain (AZ.) 116 D 3
Spruce Mountain (NV.) 112 L 2
Spud Rock 116 F 5
Spur (TX.) 117 Q 4
Spurn Head 148 D 4
Squamish 103 N 6
Squa Pan Lake 126 L 2
Square Butte (MT.) 111 P 3
Square Islands 105 QR 5
Squaw Hill 118 C 9
Squaw Lake (MN.) 119 O 3
Squaw Peak 111 L 3
Squaw Valley (CA.) 112 F 6
Squillace, Golfo di 153 G 4
Squinzano 153 G 3
Squires, Mount 182 D 4
Srbija 154 B 2

Sredinnyy Khrebet 171 TU 4–5
Sredna Gora 154 B 2
Srednebelaya 171 N 5
Srednego, Ostrova 171 S 6
Sredne-Kamchatsk 171 U 4
Srednekolymsk 171 S 2
Sredne Russkaya Vozvyshennost' 158 G 5
Sredne Sibirskoye Ploskogor'ye 170 FK 2–3
Sredne Yegorlyk 155 F 1
Sredneye Kuyto, Ozero 150 K 2–3
Sredniy 171 S 4
Sredniy Kalar 170 L 4
Sredniy Ural 159 L 4
Sredniy Vasyugan 159 P 4
Srednyaya Itkana 171 U 3
Srednyaya Nyukzha 171 M 4
Srednyaya Olekma 170 M 4
Šrem 149 G 4
Sremska Mitrovica 154 A 2
Sretensk 170 L 5
Sriharikota 174 D 5
Srikakulam 174 D 4
Sri Lanka 174 D 6
Sri Madhopur 174 C 2
Srinagar 169 K 4
Środa Wielkopolska 149 G 4
Staaten River 183 G 2
Staaten River National Park 183 G 2
Stack Skerry 148 BC 3
Stadhavet 150 DE 3
Städjan 150 F 3
Stadlandet 150 DE 3
Stafford 148 C 4
Stafford (KS.) 120 G 5
Stafford (VA.) 129 O 3
Stagno di Cabras 153 E 4
Stainach 153 F 2
Ställdalen 151 F 4
Stallo (MS.) 130 E 2
Stalowa Wola 149 H 4
Stamford (CT.) 127 F 7
Stamford (NE.) 120 F 2
Stamford (N.Y.) 126 E 6
Stamford (TX.) 122 D 3
Stamford, Lake 122 D 2
Stampede Reservoir 112 E 3
Stampriet 200 B 4
Stamps (AR.) 121 M 9
Stamsund 150 F 2
Stanardsville (VA.) 129 N 3
Stanchik 171 S 1
Standerton 200 D 5
Standing Rock (N.M.) 116 H 2
Standing Rock Indian Reservation 118 GH 5
Standish (CA.) 112 E 2
Standish (MI.) 125 L 6
Stanfield (AZ.) 116 E 5
Stanfield (OR.) 110 F 5
Stanford (KY.) 128 G 4
Stanford (MT.) 111 P 3
Stanger 201 E 5
Stanke Dimitrov 154 B 2
Stanley (Falkland Is., U.K.) 143 E 9
Stanley (ID.) 111 L 6
Stanley (ND.) 118 F 2
Stanley (N.M.) 117 L 2
Stanley (VA.) 129 N 3
Stanley Falls 198 D 4
Stanley Mission 103 R 4
Stanley Reservoir 174 C 5
Stannakh-Khocho 170 M 1
Stanovaya 171 T 2
Stanovka 159 O 4
Stanovoy Khrebet 170 LM 4
Stanovoy Nagor'ye 170 KL 4
Stanovoy Range 171 N 4
Stanraer 148 B 4
Stans 153 E 2
Stansberry (MO.) 121 L 2
Stanthorpe 183 J 4
Stanton (KY.) 128 H 4
Stanton (MI.) 124 J 6
Stanton (ND.) 118 G 3
Stanton (NE.) 119 L 9
Stanton (TN.) 128 B 6
Stanton (TX.) 117 P 5
Stanwood (WA.) 110 C 2
Staples (MN.) 119 O 4
Stapleton (AL.) 130 G 4
Stapleton (NE.) 120 E 1
Star (N.C.) 129 M 6
Starachowice 149 H 4
Stara Pazova 154 B 2
Stara Planina 154 BC 2
Staraya Russa 151 K 4
Staraya Vorpavla 159 N 3
Stara Zagora 154 C 2
Starbuck 187 I 3
Starbuck (MN.) 119 N 5
Starbuck (WA.) 110 G 4
Star City (AR.) 121 O 9
Star City (IN.) 124 H 9
Stargard Szczecinski 149 G 4
Starichkova 171 V 2
Starigrad 153 G 3
Staritsa 171 Q 6

Starke (FL.) 131 M 5
Starkville (MS.) 121 R 9
Starkweather (ND.) 118 JK 2
Starnberg 149 F 5
Starobel'sk 158 G 6
Starodub 158 F 5
Starogard Gdanski 149 G 4
Starominskaya 155 E 1
Staromlinovka 155 E 1
Starovercheskaya 158 J 4
Staroye Linde 170 M 2
Star Peak 112 G 2
Start Point 148 C 4
Starvation Reservoir 114 G 3
Staryy Dom 171 Q 3
Staryy Krym 155 DE 1
Staryy Oskol 158 G 5
State Bridge (CO.) 115 L 4
State College (MS.) 121 R 9
State College (PA.) 127 B 8
State Line (MS.) 130 F 3
Staten Island 127 E 8
Staten Island 143 D 9
Statenville (GA.) 131 L 4
Statesboro (GA.) 131 N 2
Statesville (N.C.) 129 L 6
Statford-upon-Avon 148 C 4
Statland 150 F 3
Staunton (IL.) 121 Q 3
Staunton (VA.) 129 MN 3
Stavanger 151 DE 4
Stavern 151 F 4
Stavropol' 155 F 1
Stavropol' 155 F 2
Stavropolka 159 N 5
Stavropol'skaya Vozvyshennost' 155 F 1
Stavrós 154 B 2
Stavroupolis 154 B 2
Stawell 183 G 6
Stawiski 149 H 4
Stayton (OR.) 110 C 6
Stead (N.M.) 117 N 1
Steamboat Canyon (AZ.) 116 G 2
Steamboat Springs (CO.) 115 L 3
Stearns (KY.) 128 G 5
Stebbins 108 F 3
Steele (MO.) 121 Q 6
Steele (ND.) 118 J 4
Steele, Mount 118 B 9
Steele City (NE.) 120 J 2
Steelport 200 DE 4
Steelville (IL.) 121 Q 5
Steelville (MO.) 121 O 5
Steen River 103 O 4
Steensby Inlet 105 M 1
Steens Mountain 110 G 8
Ştefăneşti 154 C 1
Stefanie, Lake 199 F 4
Stefansson Island 103 Q 1
Stegi 201 E 5
Stehekin (WA.) 110 E 2
Steilrand Steinach 153 F 2
Steinaker Reservoir 114 H 3
Steinauer (NE.) 120 J 2
Steinbach 103 S 6
Steinfeld 200 B 4
Steinfurt 149 E 4
Steinhatchee (FL.) 131 L 5
Steinkjer 150 F 3
Steinkopf 200 B 5
Steins (N.M.) 116 GH 5
Stekol'nyy 171 S 4
Stella 200 C 5
Stellenbosch 200 B 6
Steller, Mount 109 K 3
Stello 153 E 3
Stelvio, Passo della 153 F 2
Stenay 153 DE 2
Stendal 149 F 4
Stende 151 H 4
Stenfjället 150 F 3
Stenhouse Bay 183 F 6
Stenon 154 C 3
Sténon Serifou 154 B 3
Stenungsund 151 F 4
Stepanakert 168 D 3
Stephan (SD.) 118 J 6
Stephen (MN.) 119 M 2
Stephens City (VA.) 129 N 2
Stephens Knob 128 G 5
Stephens Passage 102 L 4
Stephenson (MI.) 124 G 4
Stephenville (Newfoundl., Can.) 105 Q 6
Stephenville (TX.) 122 E 3
Stepnoye 155 F 2
Stepnyak 159 O 5
Step' Shaidara 169 H 2
Steptoe (WA.) 110 H 3
Steptoe Valley 112 L 2
Sterkstroom 200 D 6
Sterling (AK.) 109 H 3
Sterling (CO.) 115 O 3
Sterling (IL.) 124 E 8
Sterling (KS.) 120 G 4
Sterling (MI.) 125 K 5
Sterling (ND.) 118 H 4
Sterling (NE.) 120 J 2

Sterling City (TX.) 117 PQ 6
Sterling Reservoir 115 O 3
Sterlington (LA.) 123 L 3
Sterlitamak 158 KL 5
Sternberk 149 G 5
Stettiner Haff 149 F 4
Stettler 103 P 5
Steuben (MI.) 124 H 3
Steubenville (OH.) 125 N 9
Stevenson (WA.) 110 CD 5
Stevenson Entrance 102 G 4
Stevens Pass 110 DE 3
Stevens Peak 111 K 3
Stevens Point (WI.) 124 E 5
Stevens Village 109 J 2
Stevensville (MT.) 111 L 4
Stewardson (IL.) 121 R 3
Stewart 186 C 6
Stewart (AK.) 102 M 4
Stewart (New Zealand) 184 P 10
Stewart (Yukon, Can.) 102 KL 3
Stewart, Isla 143 B 9
Stewart Crossing 102 K 3
Stewart Island 186 B 3
Stewart Islands 185 H 3
Stewart River 102 K 3
Stewart Sound 175 F 5
Stewarts Point (CA.) 112 B 4
Stewartstown (PA.) 127 C 9
Stewartsville (MO.) 121 L 3
Stewartville (MN.) 119 Q 7
Steynsburg 200 D 6
Steyr 153 F 2
Stickney (S.D.) 119 K 7
Stigler (OK.) 121 K 7
Stikine 102 L 4
Stikine Ranges 102 L 4
Stikine River 109 M 4
Stiles (TX.) 117 P 6
Stílis 154 B 3
Stillhouse Hollow Reservoir 122 F 4
Stillwater (MN.) 119 Q 5
Stillwater (NV.) 112 G 3
Stillwater (OK.) 120 HJ 6
Stillwater (WI.) 124 B 4
Stillwater Range 112 G 3
Stillwater Reservoir 126 D 5
Stilo, Punta 153 G 4
Stilwell (OK.) 121 L 7
Stine Mountain 111 M 5
Stinnett (TX.) 117 P 2
Stip 154 B 2
Stirling 148 C 3
Stirling City (CA.) 112 D 3
Stirling Creek 182 D 2
Stirling Range 182 B 5
Stirling Range National Park 182 B 5
Stirrat (W.V.) 129 K 4
Štit 149 H 5
Stjernöya 150 H 1
Stjördal 150 F 3
Stockbridge (MI.) 125 K 7
Stockbridge Indian Reservation 124 F 5
Stockdale (TX.) 122 EF 6
Stockerau 153 G 2
Stockett (MT.) 111 O 3
Stockholm 151 G 4
Stockholm (ME.) 126 L 1
Stockport (IA.) 119 R 10
Stockton (AL.) 130 G 3–4
Stockton (CA.) 112 D 3
Stockton (GA.) 131 L 4
Stockton (IL.) 124 E 7
Stockton (KS.) 120 F 3
Stockton (MO.) 121 M 5
Stockton Island 124 D 3
Stockton Lake 121 M 5
Stockton Plateau 117 O 7
Stockville (NE.) 120 E 2
Stöde 150 G 3
Stoffberg 200 D 5
Stoke-on-Trent 148 C 4
Stokksnes 150 C 3
Stokmarknes 150 F 2
Stol 154 B 2
Stolbovoy, Ostrov 171 P 1
Stolbtsy 151 J 5
Stolin 151 J 5
Ston 153 G 3
Stone City (CO.) 115 N 5
Stoneham (CO.) 115 O 3
Stone Harbor (N.J.) 127 E 9
Stonehenge 148 C 4
Stoner (CO.) 115 J 6
Stonewall (OK.) 120 J 8
Stonington (CO.) 115 PQ 6
Stonington (ME.) 126 L 4
Stony 102 F 3
Stonyford (CA.) 112 C 3
Stony Gorge Reservoir 112 C 3
Stony Point 126 C 5
Stony Point (N.C.) 129 K 6
Stony Rapids 103 Q 4
Stony River 102 F 3
Stony Tunguska River 170 GH 3
Storå 151 E 4
Stora Björkvattnet 150 FG 2

Stora Lu[e]vatten 150 G 2
Storån 150 G 3
Stora Sjöfallet 150 G 2
Storavan 150 G 2
Stord 151 E 4
Store Bælt 151 F 4
Storfjorden 150 E 3
Storis Passage 103 S 2
Storkerson Bay 103 M 1
Storkerson Peninsula 103 Q 1
Storla (S.D.) 119 K 7
Storli 150 F 3
Storlien 150 F 3
Storm Bay 184 L 9
Storm King Mountain 110 C 4
Storm Lake (IA.) 119 N 8
Storm Mountain 109 H 4
Stormy Mountain 110 E 3
Stornoway 148 B 3
Storozhevsk 158 K 3
Storozhinets 154 C 1
Storsjöen 150 F 3
Storsjön 151 F 3
Storsjön 150 F 3
Storsjön (Sweden) 150 F 3
Storstenfjellet 150 G 2
Storuman 150 G 2
Storvigelen 150 F 3
Storvindeln 150 G 2
Story (WY.) 118 AB 6
Story City (IA.) 119 P 8
Stöttingfjället 150 G 3
Stoughton (WI.) 124 E 7
Stoun Lake (WI.) 124 C 4
Stövring 151 E 4
Stoyba 171 O 5
Strabane 148 B 4
Stradbroke Island, North 183 J 4
Strahan 184 L 9
Strait of Belle Isle 105 Q 5
Strait of Bonifacio 153 E 3
Strait of Canso 105 P 6
Strait of Dover 148 D 4
Strait of Gibraltar 152 B 4
Strait of Hormuz 157 G 4
Strait of Juan de Fuca 110 AB 2
Strait of Magellan 143 BC 9
Strait of Makassar 176 B 3
Strait of Malacca 176 B 3
Strait of Singapore 176 B 3
Straits of Mackinac 125 K 4
Strakonice 149 F 5
Stralsund 149 F 4
Strand 200 B 6
Strangford Lough 148 BC 4
Strängnäs 151 G 4
Strasbourg 153 E 2
Strasburg (CO.) 115 N 4
Strasburg (ND.) 118 HJ 4
Strasswalchen 153 F 2
Strat (New Zealand) 185 Q 8
Stratford (CA.) 112 F 6
Stratford (IA.) 119 P 8
Stratford (OK.) 120 HJ 8
Stratford (TX.) 117 OP 1
Stratford (Victoria, Austr.) 183 H 6
Stratford (WA.) 110 F 3
Stratford (WI.) 124 D 5
Strathmay 183 G 1
Strathmore (Australia) 183 G 2
Strathmore (CA.) 112 F 6
Strathy Point 148 C 3
Stratton (CO.) 115 P 4
Stratton (ME.) 126 J 3
Stratton (NE.) 120 D 2
Straubing 149 F 5
Straumnes 150 A 2
Straumsjöen 150 F 2
Strauss (N.M.) 117 K 6
Strawberry Daniels Pass 114 F 3
Strawberry Mountain 110 G 6
Strawberry Point (IA.) 119 R 8
Strawberry Reservoir 114 F 3
Strawn (TX.) 122 E 3
Streaky Bay 182 E 5
Streator (IL.) 124 F 8
Streeter (ND.) 118 J 4
Strehaia 154 B 2
Strelka 170 F 4
Strelka 171 S 3
Strelka-Chunya 170 H 3
Stretto di Messina 153 G 4
Stretton 182 B 5
Streymoy 148 A 1
Strfbro 149 F 5
Strickland River 184 D 3
Strimón 154 B 2
Strimonikós Kólpos 154 B 2
Strizhovo 159 O 4
Stroeder 143 D 7
Strofádhes, Nísoi 154 B 3
Strogonof Point 108 G 4
Stromboli 153 FG 4
Strömfjord, Norde 105 R 2
Strömfjord, Söndre 105 R 2
Strömsbruk 150 G 3
Strömsnäsbruk 151 F 4
Strömstad 151 F 4
Ströms Vattudal 150 F 3

Strong (AR.) 121 N 9
Strong City (KS.) 120 J 4
Strong City (OK.) 120 F 7
Strongsville (OH.) 125 N 8
Stronsay 148 C 3
Struer 151 E 4
Struga 154 B 2
Struma 154 B 2
Strumica 154 B 2
Strydenburg 200 C 5
Stryker (MT.) 111 L 2
Strynsvatn 150 E 3
Strzyzów 149 H 5
Stuart (FL.) 131 O 7
Stuart (IA.) 119 O 9
Stuart (NE.) 118 J 8
Stuart (VA.) 129 L 5
Stuart, Lake 103 MN 5
Stuart, Point 182 E 1
Stuarts Draft (VA.) 129 N 3
Stump Lake 119 K 3
Stung Treng 175 J 5
Sturgeon (MO.) 121 N 3
Sturgeon Bay (WI.) 124 G 5
Sturgeon Lake 104 J 6
Sturgis (KY.) 128 D 4
Sturgis (MO.) 120 C 6
Sturgis (SD.) 118 E 6
Sturt Creek 182 D 2
Sturt Desert 183 G 4
Sturt National Park 183 G 4
Sturt Plain 182 E 2
Stutterheim 200 D 6
Stuttgart 149 E 5
Stuttgart (AR.) 121 O 8
Stykkishólmur 150 A 2
Styr' 151 J 5
Suai 177 G 5
Suao 173 H 6
Subã'il (Iraq) 156 D 2
Subay', Uruq as 195 G 4
Subayhah (Saudi Arabia) 156 C 3
Subei Monggolzu Zizhixian 172 C 3
Subeita (Israel) 156 B 3
Subi, Pulau 176 B 3
Sublette (KS.) 120 DE 5
Sublett Range 111 N 8
Subotica 154 A 1
Success, Lake 112 G 6
Suceava 154 C 1
Suck 148 B 4
Sucre 140 CD 4
Sucuaro 138 E 3
Sućúraj 153 G 3
Sucuriju 139 J 3
Sudak 155 D 2
Sudan 194 DE 6
Sudbury 105 L 6
Sudd 198 E 3
Sudden (CA.) 113 E 8
Suddie 139 G 2
Sudety 149 G 4
Sudirman, Pegunungan 177 J 4
Sue 198 D 3
Suez 156 A 3
Suez Canal (Egypt) 156 A 3
Süf Ajjin, Wädi 193 H 2
Şufaynah 195 G 4
Suffolk (VA.) 129 P 5
Sufiän 168 D 3
Sugar City (CO.) 115 O 5
Sugar City (ID.) 111 O 7
Sugar Island 125 K 3
Sugarville (UT.) 114 E 4
Sugla Gölü 155 D 3
Sugoy 171 T 3
Suguta 199 F 4
Suhai Hu 172 B 3
Şuḩār 195 K 4
Sühbaatar 170 J 5
Sühbaatar 172 F 1
Suhl 149 F 4
Suiá-Missu 141 F 3
Suibin 171 O 6
Suichang 173 G 5
Suichuan 172 F 5
Suide 172 F 3
Suifenhe 173 K 2
Suihua 173 J 1
Suijiang 172 D 5
Suileng 173 J 1
Suining 172 E 4
Suining 173 G 4
Suipacha 140 C 5
Suir 148 B 4
Suisun Bay 112 CD 4
Suixi 172 F 6
Suixi 173 G 4
Sui Xian 172 F 4
Suizhong 173 H 2
Suizhou 172 F 4
Sujangarh 174 B 2
Sukabumi 176 C 5
Sukadana 176 CD 4
Sukagawa 173 LM 3
Sukaraja 176 D 4
Sukau 177 E 2
Sukeva 150 J 3

Sukhana 170 L 2
Sukhodolskoye, Ozero 150 K 3
Sukhona 158 H 4
Sukhothai 175 G 4
Sukhotinskiy 155 F 1
Sukhoy 155 F 1
Sukhumi 155 F 2
Sukkertoppen 105 R 2
Sukkozero 150 K 3
Sukkur 169 H 5
Sukma 174 D 4
Süknah 193 J 3
Sukses 200 B 4
Suksukan 171 S 3
Suksun 159 L 4
Sul, Canal do 139 HJ 4
Sula (MT.) 111 M 5
Sula (Norway) 150 D 3
Sula (U.S.S.R.) 158 JK 2
Sula, Kepulauan 177 FG 4
Sulaimāniya (Iraq) 157 D 2
Sulaiman Range 169 H 4–5
Sulak 168 D 2
Sulanheer 172 E 2
Sülär (Iran) 157 F 3
Sularya Dağları 154 C 3
Sula Sgeir 148 B 3
Sulat, Bukit 177 G 3
Sulawesi 177 EF 4
Sulawesi, Laut 177 F 3
Sulb 194 E 4
Süldeh (Iran) 157 F 1
Sulechów 149 G 4
Sulen, Mount 184 D 2
Sule Skerry 148 BC 3
Sulima 196 B 4
Sulina 154 C 1
Sulina 154 C 1
Sulitelma 150 G 2
Sulkava 150 J 3
Sullana 138 B 4
Sulligent (AL.) 128 C 8
Sullivan (IL.) 121 R 3
Sullivan (IN.) 121 S 3
Sullivan (MO.) 121 O 4
Sulmona 153 F 3
Sulphur (LA.) 123 K 5
Sulphur (NV.) 112 G 2
Sulphur (OK.) 120 J 8
Sulphur(Yukon, Can.) 109 L 3
Sulphurdale (UT.) 114 E 5
Sulphur Springs (TX.) 123 H 2
Sulṭān 193 JK 2
Sultan (WA.) 110 D 3
Sultan Dağları 154–155 D 3
Sultanhanı 155 D 3
Sultanpur 174 C 1
Sultanpur 174 D 2
Sulu Archipelago 177 F 2
Sulūq 193 K 2
Sulu Sea 177 EF 2
Suly 159 N 5
Sulyukta 169 H 3
Sumalata 177 F 3
Sümar (Iran) 172 D 2
Sumarokovo 159 R 3
Sumas (WA.) 110 C 2
Sumatera 176 A 3
Sumatra (FL.) 131 K 4–5
Sumatra (MT.) 111 S 4
Sumaúma 139 G 5
Šumava 149 F 5
Sumba 177 EF 5
Sumba, Selat 177 EF 5
Sumba Game Reserve 201 E 1
Sumbawa 176 E 5
Sumbawa Besar 176 E 5
Sumbawanga 198 E 6
Sumbe 200 A 2
Sümber 172 E 1
Sumbu 201 E 1
Sumburgh Head 148 C 3
Sumedang 176 C 5
Sumenep 176 D 5
Sumesar Range 174 D 2
Sumgait 168 DE 2
Sumisu-jima 173 L 4
Sumkino 159 N 4
Summel (Iraq) 156 D 1
Summerfield (N.C.) 129 M 5
Summerhaven (AZ.) 116 F 5
Summer Island 124 H 4
Summer Lake (OR.) 110 E 8
Summerland Key (FL.) 131 N 10
Summer Strait 109 M 4
Summersville (MO.) 121 O 5
Summersville (W.V.) 129 L 3
Summerside (S.C.) 129 L 8
Summerton (S.C.) 129 L 8
Summertown (TN.) 128 D 6
Summerville (GA.) 128 F 7
Summerville (S.C.) 129 L 8
Summit(AK.) 109 J 3
Summit (MS.) 130 D 3
Summit (N.M.) 116 H 5
Summit (S.D.) 119 LM 5
Summit Lake 112 F 1
Summit Lake (Br. Col., Can.)
   103 N 4

Summit Lake (WI.) 124 E 4
Summit Lake Indian Reservation
   112 G 1
Summit Mountain 112 J 3
Summit Peak 115 L 6
Sumner (IA.) 119 Q 8
Sumner (MO.) 121 M 3
Sumner (MS.) 121 P 9
Sumner (OK.) 120 H 6
Sumner, Lake 117 M 3
Sumperk 149 G 5
Sumprabum 175 G 2
Sumrall (MS.) 130 E 3
Sumter (S.C.) 129 L 8
Sumuma 170 G 3
Sumy 158 G 5
Sumzom 172 C 5
Suna 150 K 3
Suna 198 E 6
Sunamganj 175 F 2
Sunan 172 C 3
Sunayşilah (Iraq) 156 CD 2
Sunbeam (ID.) 111 L 6
Sunburst (MT.) 111 O 2
Sunbury (N.C.) 129 P 5
Sunbury (PA.) 127 C 8
Suncho Corral 142 D 4
Sunch'ŏn (N. Korea) 173 J 3
Sunch'ŏn (S. Korea) 173 J 3
Sun City (AZ.) 116 D 4
Suncook (N.H.) 126 H 5
Sundance (WY.) 118 D 6
Sundarbans 174–175 EF 3
Sundargarh 174 D 3
Sunday Creek 182 E 2
Sunday Strait 182 C 2
Sundbron 150 G 3
Sunde 151 E 4
Sunderland 148 C 4
Sündiren Dağları 154 D 3
Sundsvall 150 G 3
Sunduyka 170 K 6
Sunflower (AZ.) 116 E 4
Sunflower (MS.) 121 P 9
Sunflower, Mount 120 CD 3
Sungaianyar 176 E 4
Sungai Barito 176 D 4
Sungaidareh 176 B 4
Sungai Digul 177 J 5
Sungaigerong 176 BC 4
Sungaiguntung 176 B 3
Sungai Inderagiri 176 B 4
Sungai Kampar 176 B 3
Sungai Kapuas 176 C 4
Sungai Kapuas 176 D 4
Sungai Kayan 176 E 3
Sungai Kutai 176 E 4
Sungailiat 176 C 4
Sungai Mahakam 176 E 3
Sungai Mamberamo 177 J 4
Sungai Melawi 176 D 4
Sungai Mendawai 176 D 4
Sungai Pahang 176 B 3
Sungai Pawan 176 D 4
Sungaipenuh 176 B 4
Sungai Pulau 177 J 5
Sungai Rokan 176 B 3
Sungai Sembakung 176 E 3
Sungai Seruyan 176 D 4
Sungai Tariku 177 J 4
Sungai Taritatu 177 J 4
Sungai Wama 177 J 4
Sungai Warenai 177 J 4
Sungei Patani 176 B 2
Sungguminasa 177 E 5
Sungurlu 155 D 2
Suning 173 G 3
Sunja 153 G 2
Sunjikäy 195 D 6
Sun Kosi 174 E 2
Sunnan 150 F 3
Sunndalen 150 E 3
Sunndalsfjorden 150 E 3
Sunndalsöra 150 E 3
Sunnfjord 150 DE 3
Sunnyside (NV.) 112 L 4
Sunnyside (TX.) 117 O 3
Sunnyside (UT.) 114 G 4
Sunnyside (WA.) 110 F 4
Sunnyvale (CA.) 112 CD 5
Sun Prairie (MT.) 111 S 3
Sun Prairie (WI.) 124 E 6
Sunray (TX.) 117 P 1
Sun River 111 N 3
Sun River (MT.) 111 O 3
Sunset (LA.) 123 L 5
Sunset (TX.) 122 F 2
Sunset Crater National Monument
   116 E 2
Suntar 170 L 3
Suntar Khayata, Khrebet 171 PQ 3
Suntrana 109 J 3
Sun Valley (ID.) 111 L 7
Sun Valley (NV.) 112 F 3
Sunwu 171 N 6
Sunyani 196 D 4
Suokonmäki 150 H 3
Suolahti 150 J 3
Suomenselkä 150 J 3
Suomi 150 J 3

Suomussalmi 150 J 3
Suomutunturi 150 J 2
Sūo-nada 173 K 4
Suonenjoki 150 J 3
Suoyarvi 150 K 3
Superior (AZ.) 116 EF 4
Superior (MT.) 111 L 3
Superior (NE.) 120 GH 2
Superior (WI.) 124 B 3
Superior (WY.) 111 R 9
Supetar 153 G 3
Suphan Buri 175 GH 5
Süphan Dağı 155 F 3
Supiori, Pulau 177 J 4
Süq Suwayq (Saudi Arabia) 156 C 4
Suquṭrā 199 J 2
Şūr (Lebanon) 156 B 2
Şūr (Oman) 195 K 4
Sur, Point 112 D 6
Sur, Punta 143 E 6
Sura 158 J 4
Sura, Ra's 199 H 2
Surabaya 176 D 5
Surahammar 151 G 4
Sürak 168 F 5
Surakarta 176 CD 5
Surar 199 G 3
Surat (India) 174 B 3
Surat (Queensland, Austr.) 183 H 4
Suratgarh 174 B 2
Surat Thani 175 GH 6
Surazh 151 K 4
Surendranagar 174 B 3
Surf City (N.C.) 129 O 7
Surgut 159 O 3
Surgutikha 159 R 3
Suriapet 174 C 4
Surigao 177 G 2
Surigao Strait 177 G 1
Surin 175 H 5
Suring (WI.) 124 F 5
Sürīyah 156 BC 2
Surkhab 169 H 3
Sürmag (Iran) 157 F 3
Surmān 193 H 2
Sürmene 155 F 2
Surovikino 158 H 6
Surrah, Nafūd as 195 G 4
Surrency (GA.) 131 M 3
Surrey (ND.) 118 G 2
Surry (VA.) 129 P 4
Sursee 153 E 2
Surskoye 158 J 5
Surte 151 F 4
Surtsey 150 A 3
Surud Ad 199 H 2
Surulangun 176 B 4
Survey Pass 102 G 2
Susa 153 E 2
Susa (Iran) 157 E 2
Sušac 153 G 3
Süsah (Libya) 193 K 2
Süsah (Tunisia) 193 H 1
Susak 153 F 3
Susan (VA.) 129 P 4
Süsangerd (Iran) 157 E 3
Susanino 171 Q 5
Susanville (CA.) 112 E 2
Suşehri 155 E 2
Sušice 149 F 5
Susitna 109 H 3
Susquehanna (PA.) 126 D 7
Susquehanna River 127 C 7
Susques 140 C 5
Sussex (New Brunswick, Can.)
   105 O 6
Sussex (VA.) 129 O 5
Sussex (WY.) 118 B 7
Sussundenga 201 E 3
Susuman 171 R 3
Susunu 177 H 4
Susurluk 154 C 3
Sutam 171 N 4
Sutcliffe (NV.) 112 F 3
Sutgun 171 S 2
Sutherland (IA.) 119 N 8
Sutherland (NE.) 118 G 9
Sutherland Reservoir 120 D 1
Sutherlin (OR.) 110 B 7
Sutlej 169 J 4
Sut Ta 175 G 4
Sutter (CA.) 112 D 3
Sutter Buttes 112 D 3
Sutton (AK.) 109 J 3
Sutton (N.D.) 119 K 3
Sutton (NE.) 120 H 2
Sutton (W.V.) 129 L 3
Sutton Lake 129 L 3
Suttor River 183 H 3
Sutun'ya 171 O 2
Sutwik 102 F 4

Suvasvesi 150 J 3
Suvorov 186 E 3
Suwa 173 L 3
Suwalki 149 H 4
Suwannaphum 175 H 4
Suwannee (FL.) 131 L 5
Suwannee River 131 M 5
Suwannee Sound 131 L 5
Suwanose-jima 173 JK 5
Suwayqīyah, Hawr as (Iraq)
   157 E 2
Suwon 173 J 3
Su Xian 173 G 4
Suzhou 173 GH 4
Suzu 173 L 3
Suzun 159 Q 5
Svaerholthalvöya 150 J 1
Svalbard 202
Svalyava 154 B 1
Svappavaara 150 H 2
Svartisen 150 F 2
Svatay 171 S 2
Svatovo 158 G 6
Svatoy Nos, Mys 171 P 1
Svay Rieng 175 J 5
Svealand 151 FG 4
Sveg 150 F 3
Svegsjön 150 F 3
Svendborg 151 F 4
Svenljunga 151 F 4
Šventoji 151 J 4
Sverdlovsk 159 M 4
Sverige 150 G 3
Svetac 153 G 3
Svetlaya 171 P 6
Svetlogorsk (Belorussiya,
   U.S.S.R.) 151 J 5
Svetlogorsk (Russia, U.S.S.R.)
   151 GH 5
Svetlograd 155 F 1
Svetloye, Ozero 155 G 1
Svetly 151 H 5
Svetlyy 159 M 5
Svetlyy 171 L 4
Svetlyy 171 N 4
Svetogorsk 150 J 3
Svetozarevo 154 B 2
Svidnik 149 FG 5
Svir' 158 F 3
Svirsk 170 H 5
Svishtov 154 C 2
Svitavy 149 G 5
Svobodnyy 171 N 5
Svobodnyy Port 154 D 1
Svolvær 150 FG 2
Svrljig 154 B 2
Svullrya 151 F 3
Svyatoy Nos, Mys 158 G 2
Svyatoy Nos, Mys 158 J 2
Swain Reefs 183 J 3
Swains 186 D 3
Swainsboro (GA.) 131 M 2
Swakop 200 B 4
Swakopmund 200 A 4
Swale 148 C 4
Swallow Reef 176 D 2
Swan Hill 183 G 6
Swan Islands → Islas del Cisne
   132 F 4
Swan Lake (MO.) 121 M 3
Swan Lake (MT.) 111 M 3
Swan Lake (S.D.) 118 J 5
Swan Peak 111 M 3
Swanquarter (N.C.) 129 P 6
Swan Range 111 M 3
Swan River (Manitoba, Can.)
   103 R 5
Swan River (MN.) 119 P 3
Swansboro (NC.) 129 O 7
Swansea 148 C 4
Swansea (S.C.) 129 K 8
Swans Island 126 L 4
Swanson Lake 120 D 2
Swanton (VT.) 126 F 4
Swan Valley (ID.) 111 O 7
Swartberge 200 C 6
Swasey Peak 114 D 4
Swatara (MN.) 119 P 4
Swatow → Shantou
Swaziland [Ngwane] 201 E 5
Swea City (IA.) 119 O 7
Swearingen (TX.) 117 Q 3
Sweden 150 G 3
Sweeny (TX.) 123 H 6
Sweetgrass (MT.) 111 N 2
Sweetgrass Hills 111 O 2
Sweet Home (OR.) 110 C 6
Sweet Springs (MO.) 121 M 4
Sweet Springs (W.V.) 129 L 4
Sweetwater (OK.) 120 F 7
Sweetwater (TN.) 128 G 6
Sweetwater (TX.) 122 C 3
Sweetwater Lake 119 K 2
Sweetwater River 111 R 8
Swellendam 200 C 6
Swenson (TX.) 117 Q 4
Świdnica 149 G 4
Świdnik 149 H 4
Świdwin 149 G 4
Świebodzin 149 G 4
Świecie 149 G 4

Swift Current 103 Q 5
Swift Reservoir 110 CD 4
Swift River 102 L 4
Swinburne, Cape 103 RS 1
Swindon 148 C 4
Swinomish Indian Reservation
   110 C 2
Swinoujście 149 F 4
Switzerland 153 E 2
Syadaykharvuta 159 OP 2
Syagannakh 171 Q 2
Syalakh 171 MN 2
Syamozero, Ozero 150 K 3
Syangannakh 171 R 2
Sycamore (GA.) 131 L 3
Sycan Marsh 110 D 8
Syðri-Hagangur 150 B 2
Sydney (N.D.) 119 K 4
Sydney (New Brunswick, Canada)
   105 P 6
Sydney (N.S.W., Austr.) 183 J 5
Sydney Mines 105 PQ 6
Sydpröven 105 S 3
Syktyvkar 158 JK 3
Sylacauga (AL.) 128 E 8
Sylarna 150 F 3
Sylhet 175 F 3
Sylt 151 E 5
Sylva (NC.) 128 H 6
Sylvan Grove (KS.) 120 G 3
Sylvan Hills (AR.) 121 N 8
Sylvania (GA.) 131 N 2
Sylvania (OH.) 125 L 8
Sylvan Pass 111 P 6
Sylvester (GA.) 131 L 3
Sylvester (TX.) 122 C 3
Sylvia (KS.) 120 G 5
Sym 159 R 3
Sym 159 R 3
Synegey 171 OP 2
Syracuse (KS.) 120 D 4
Syracuse (MO.) 121 N 4
Syracuse (NE.) 120 J 2
Syracuse (N.Y.) 126 C 5
Syrdar'ya 169 H 2
Syr-Dar'ya 169 H 2
Syria 156 BC 2
Syriam 175 G 4
Syrian Desert 156 C 2
Sysmä 150 J 3
Sysola 158 K 3
Systengnakh 171 P 1
Sytomino 159 O 3
Syuge-Khaya, Gora 171 P 2
Syurkum 171 Q 5
Syuryakh-Dzhangy, Vozvyshen-
   ost' 170 M 1
Syuryun-Kyuyel' 171 O 2
Syväri 150 J 3
Syverma, Plato 170 G 3
Syzran 158 J 5
Szamotuły 149 G 4
Szczecin 149 F 4
Szczecinek 149 G 4
Szczytno 149 H 4
Szechwan 172 D 5
Szeged 154 A 1
Székesfehérvár 154 A 1
Szekszárd 154 A 1
Szentes 154 B 1
Szolnok 154 B 1
Szombathely 154 A 1
Szprotawa 149 G 4

T

Ṭa'ām 195 G 5
Taarom 183 HJ 4
Tabacal 140 D 5
Tābah (Saudi Arabia) 156 CD 4
Tabaí 142 E 4
Tabajara 139 F 5
Tabankort 196 E 2
Tabaqah (Syria) 156 C 2
Tabar Islands 185 F 2
Tabar Islands 186 B 3
Tab arja (Lebanon) 156 B 2
Tabarqah 193 G 1
Tabarsuq 153 E 4
Tabas 168 G 4
Tabas (Iran) 157 G 2
Tabasara, Serranía de 138 B 2
Tabasco 132 D 4
Tābask, Kūh-e (Iran) 157 F 3
Tabatinga 138 E 4
Tabatinga, Serra da 141 H 3
Tabelbala 192 E 3
Tabelbala, Kahal 192 E 3
Tabelbalet 193 G 3
Tabelkoza 192 F 3
Tabeng 175 H 5
Taber 103 P 6
Taberg 151 F 4
Tabernas 152 F 4
Tabernes de Valldigna 152 CD 4

Tabiteuea 186 C 3
Tabla 196 E 3
Tablas 177 F 1
Table Mountain 116 F 5
Table Mountain 200 B 6
Table Rock (WY.) 111 R 9
Table Rock Lake 121 M 6
Table Top 116 D 5
Tábor 149 F 5
Tabor 171 R 1
Tabor (S.D.) 119 L 8
Tabora 198 E 6
Tabor City (N.C.) 129 N 7
Tabou 196 C 5
Tabrīz 168 D 3
Tabuaeran 187 E 2
Tabūk (Saudi Arabia) 156 B 3
Tabuleiro 139 G 5
Tabuleiro de Norte 141 J 2
Täby 151 G 4
Tacámbaro 132 B 4
Tacheng 169 L 1
Tachiumet 193 GH 3
Tachov 149 F 5
Tacloban 177 F 1
Tacna 140 B 4
Tacna (AZ.) 116 BC 5
Tacoma (CO.) 115 K 6
Tacoma (WA.) 110 C 3
Taco Pozo 142 D 4
Tacora 140 C 4
Tacuarembó 142 E 5
Tademaït, Plateau du 193 F 3
Tadjakant 192 C 5
Tadjemout 193 F 3
Tadjetaret 193 G 4
Tadjourah 199 G 2
Tadjourah, Golfe de 199 G 2
Tadoule Lake 103 S 4
Tad Park (UT.) 114 E 3
Tadpatri 174 C 3
Tadzhikistan 169 HJ 3
Taebaek-Sanmaek 173 J 3
Taegu 173 J 3
Taejŏn 173 J 3
Tafahi 186 D 4
Tafalla 152 C 3
Tafanlieh 173 H 6
Tafassasset 193 G 4
Tafassasset, Ténéré du 197 G 1
Tafermaar 177 H 5
Tafihān (Iran) 157 F 3
Tafihān (Iran) 157 F 3
Tafiré 196 CD 4
Tafí Viejo 142 CD 4
Tafo 196 D 4
Tafraoute 192 D 3
Tafresh (Iran) 157 E 2
Taft (CA.) 113 F 7
Taft (Iran) 157 G 3
Taft (OK.) 121 K 7
Taftanās (Syria) 156 B 2
Tagama 197 F 2
Tagan 184 D 3
Taganrog 155 E 1
Taganrogskiy Zaliv 155 E 1
Tagaung 175 G 3
Tagbilaran 177 F 2
Tageru, Jabal 194 D 5
Taggafadi 197 F 2
Taghit 192 E 2
Taghrīfat 193 J 3
Tagish Lake 102 L 3
Tagliamento 153 F 2
Tagounite 192 D 3
Taguá 141 H 3
Taguatinga 141 G 3
Tagudin 177 H 1
Taguenout Haggueret 196 D 1
Taguersimet 192 B 4
Taguienout 193 G 4
Tagula 185 F 4
Tagula Island 183 J 1
Tagula Island 185 F 4
Tagum 177 G 2
Tagus 152 B 4
Tagus (ND.) 118 G 2
Tahan, Gunung 176 B 3
Tahanea 187 F 4
Tahat, Mont 193 G 4
Tahe 171 M 5
Tāheri (Iran) 157 F 4
Tahifet 193 G 4
Tahiryuak Lake 103 P 1
Tahiti 187 F 4
Tahkuna Neem 151 H 4
Tahlequah (OK.) 121 L 7
Tahoe, Lake 112 EF 3
Tahoe City (CA.) 112 E 3
Tahoka (TX.) 117 P 4
Tahoua 197 EF 3
Tahrūd 168 F 5
Ta Hsai 175 G 3
Ṭahṭā 194 E 3
Tahtali Dağlari 155 E 3
Tahuamanu 140 C 3
Tahuata 187 F 3
Tahuna 177 G 3
Taï 196 C 4
Taï, Parc National de 196 C 4
Tai'an 173 H 2
Tai'an 173 G 3
Taibai Shan 172 E 4
Taiban (N.M.) 117 MN 3
Taibus Qi 172 FG 2
Taichung 173 H 6
Taigu 172 F 3
Taihang Shan 172 F 3
Taihe 172 F 5
Taihu 172 G 4
Tai Hu 173 H 4
Taikang 172 FG 4
Tailai 173 H 1
Taimani 169 G 4
Taimba 170 G 3
Tainan 173 GH 6
Taínaron, Ákra 154 B 3
Taining 173 G 5
Taipei 173 H 6
Taiping 173 G 4
Taiping (Malaysia) 176 B 3
Taiping Ling 170 M 6
Taipu 141 J 2
Taisetsu-zan 173 M 2
Taishan 172 F 6
Tai Shan 173 G 3
Taishun 173 G 5
Taitao, Península de 143 AB 8
Taitung 173 H 6
Taivalkoski 150 J 2
Taiwan 173 H 6
Taiwan Haixia 173 GH 5–6
Taiwan Shan 173 H 6
Taiyetos Óros 154 B 3
Taiyuan 172 F 3
Taizhou 173 GH 4
Ta'izz 195 G 6
Tājābād (Iran) 157 G 3
Tajarhī 193 H 4
Tajito 106 D 5
Tajo 152 C 3
Tájo 152 B 4
Tajrīsh (Iran) 157 F 2
Tajumulco, Volcán 132 D 4
Tak 175 G 4
Takāb (Iran) 157 E 1
Takabba 199 G 4
Takalar 177 E 5
Takamatsu 173 K 4
Takaoka 173 L 3
Takara-jima 173 J 5
Takasaki 173 L 3
Takatshwane 200 C 4
Takaungu 199 FG 5
Takazze 199 F 2
Takengon 176 A 3
Takeo 175 H 5
Takestan (Iran) 157 E 1
Taketa 198 B 5
Takhādīd (Iraq) 157 D 3
Ta Khli 175 H 4
Takhta 155 F 1
Takhta-Bazar 169 G 3
Takhtabrod 159 N 5
Takhtakupyr 168 FG 2
Takhtamygda 171 M 5
Takhtayamsk 171 ST 3
Takht-e Soleiman (Iran) 157 F 1
Takht-i-Sulaiman 169 HJ 4
Taki 185 G 3
Takijuq Lake 103 P 2
Takikawa 173 M 2
Takket → Aïn el Hadjadj 193 G 3
Takla Lake 103 M 4
Takla Landing 103 M 4
Takla Makan 169 L 3
Taklaun, Gora 171 Q 3
Taklimakan Shamo 169 LM 3
Takolokouzet, Massif de 197 F 2
Takoradi → Sekondi-Takoradi 196 D 5
Takotra 108 G 3
Takpa Shiri 175 F 2
Takslesluk Lake 108 F 3
Takua Pa 175 G 6
Takum 197 F 4
Takume 187 F 4
Takutea 187 E 4
Tala 132 B 3
Talagante 142 B 5
Talagapa 143 C 7
Tālah 193 G 1
Talak 197 F 2
Talakan 171 O 6
Talakmau, Gunung 176 B 3
Talandzha 171 O 6
Talara 138 B 4
Talar-i-Band 169 G 5
Talas 169 J 2
Talasea 185 EF 3
Talasskiy Alatau, Khrebet 169 J 2
Talata Mafara 197 F 3
Tala-Tumsa 171 O 2
Talaud, Kepulauan 177 G 3
Talavera de la Reina 152 C 4
Talawdī 194 E 6
Talaya 170 G 4
Talaya 171 S 3
Talbotton (GA.) 131 K 2
Talca 143 B 6
Talcahuano 143 B 6
Talcher 174 E 3
Talco (TX.) 123 H 2
Taldora 183 G 2
Taldy-Kurgan 159 P 6
Talēh 199 H 3
Taleh Zang (Iran) 157 E 2
Tal-e Khosravi (Iran) 157 F 3
Talence 152 C 3
Tālesh 168 D 3
Talgar 169 K 2
Taliabu, Pulau 177 FG 4
Talihina (OK.) 121 KL 8
Talima 139 G 3
Talimardzhan 169 H 3
Taliqan 169 H 3
Talitsa 159 M 4
Taliwang 176 E 5
Talkalakh (Syria) 156 B 2
Talkeetna 102 G 3
Talkeetna Mountains 102 H 3
Talladega (AL.) 128 E 8
Tall Afar (Iraq) 156 D 1
Tallahassee (FL.) 131 K 4
Tall al Hajar (Syria) 156 B 2
Tallapoosa River 131 J 2
Tall as Asfar (Jordan) 156 B 2
Tall aş Şuwār (Syria) 156 C 2
Tall Birāk at Tahtānī (Syria) 156 C 1
Tall Fajāmi (Syria) 156 C 2
Tallinn 151 J 4
Tall Kayf (Iraq) 156 D 1
Tall Kūshik (Syria) 156 CD 1
Tallmadge (OH.) 125 N 8
Tall Mānūk (Jordan) 156 C 2
Tall Tamīr (Syria) 156 C 1
Tallulah (LA.) 123 M 3
Tall 'Uwaynāt (Iraq) 156 D 1
Tălmaciu 154 B 1
Tal'menka 159 Q 5
Talmine 192 E 3
Talnakh 159 R 2
Tal'nik 171 T 4
Tal'noye 154 D 1
Talo 199 F 2
Taloda 174 B 3
Taloga (OK.) 120 FG 6
Talok 177 E 3
Talovka 155 G 2
Talovka 171 UV 3
Talpa (TX.) 122 D 4
Talquin, Lake 131 K 4
Talsi 151H 4
Talsinnt 192 E 2
Taltal 142 B 4
Taltson 103 P 3
Taluma 171 M 4
Talvik 150 H 1
Tama (IA.) 119 Q 9
Tama, Mount 200 A 2
Tamabo Range 176 E 3
Tamada 193 F 4
Tamaia 197 F 2
Tamala 182 A 4
Tamale 196 D 4
Taman 155 E 1
Tamana 186 C 3
Tamani Desert 182 E 2
Tamanrasset (Algeria) 193 F 4
Tamanrasset (Algeria) 193 G 4
Tamaqua (PA.) 127 D 8
Tamar 148 C 4
Tamar 174 E 3
Támara (Colombia) 138 D 2
Tamara (Yugoslavia) 154 A 2
Tamaroa (IL.) 121 Q 4
Tamarugal, Pampa del 140 C 5
Tamaské 197 F 3
Tamaulipas 132 C 3
Tamaya 142 B 5
Tamazunchale 132 C 3
Tamba 196 B 3
Tambacounda 196 B 3
Tambalan 176 E 3
Tambara 201 E 3
Tambelan, Kepulauan 176 C 3
Tambisan 177 E 2
Tambo (Peru) 140 B 3
Tambo (Queensland, Austr.) 183 H 3
Tambo de Mora 140 A 3
Tambohorano 201 G 3
Tambor 200 A 3
Tambora, Gunung 177 E 5
Tamboril 141 H 1
Tambov 158 H 5
Tambovka 171 N 5
Tambre 152 B 3
Tambura 198 D 3
Tamburi 141 H 3
Tamch 170 F 6
Tamchaket 192 C 5
Tamdybulak 169 GH 2
Tame 138 D 2
Tamel Aike 143 B 8
Tamesguidat 193 F 3
Tamgak, Monts 197 F 2
Tamgué, Massif du 196 B 3
Tamil Nadu 174 C 5
Tamīr, Tall (Syria) 156 C 1
Tamis 154 B 1
Tam Ky 175 J 4
Tammerfors 150 H 3
Tammisaari 151 H 4
Tampa (FL.) 131 M 6–7
Tampa Bay 131 M 7
Tampere (Tammerfors) 150 H 3
Tampico 132 C 3
Tampico (MT.) 118 B 2
Tamrau, Pegunungan 177 H 4
Tamri 192 CD 2
Tamsagbulag 173 G 1
Tamshiyacu 138 D 4
Tamsu 200 C 3
Tamu 175 F 3
Tamuin 132 C 3
Tamworth (N.S.W., Austr.) 183 J 5
Tana 185 J 5
Tana (Kenya) 199 F 5
Tana (Norway) 150 J 1
Tana, Lake 199 F 2
Tana bru 150 J 1
Tanacross 102 J 3
Tanafjorden 150 J 1
Tanaga 102 B 5
Tanahbala, Pulau 176 A 4
Tanahgrogot 176 E 4
Tanahjampea, Pulau 177 F 5
Tanahmasa, Pulau 176 A 4
Tanah Merah 176 B 2
Tanahmerah 184 CD 3
Tanakpur 174 D 2
Tanam, Cape 103 T 4
Tanama 159 PQ 1
Tanami 182 D 2
Tanami Desert Wildlife Sanctuary 182 E 3
Tan An 175 J 5
Tanana 102 G 2
Tanana River 109 K 3
Tanāqīab, Ra's at (Saudi Arabia) 157 E 4
Tanaro 153 E 3
Tanch'ŏn 173 J 2
Tanda 196 D 4
Tandag 177 G 2
Tandaho 199 G 2
Tandaltī 194 E 6
Tăndărei 154 C 2
Tandil 143 E 6
Tandsjöborg 150 F 3
Tanḍubāyah 194 D 5
Tane-ga-shima 173 K 4
Tan Emellel 193 G 3
Tanezrouft 192 E 4
Tanezrouft N-Ahenet 192–193 F 4
Tanf, Jabal at (Syria) 156 C 2
Tang 168 F 5
Tanga 199 F 5–6
Tangail 174 E 3
Tanga Islands 185 F 2
Tanga Islands 186 B 3
Tangalla 174 D 6
Tanganyika, Lake 198 DE 6
Tang-e Karam (Iran) 157 F 3
Tanger 192 D 1
Tangerang 176 C 5
Tanggula Shan 172 BC 4
Tanggula Shankou 172 B 4
Tanghe 172 F 4
Tangier Island 129 PQ 4
Tangier → Tanger 192 D 1
Tangmai 172 C 4
Tangra Yumco 174 E 1
Tangshan 173 G 3
Tanguiéta 196 E 3
Tangwanghe 171 N 6
Tangyin 172 F 3
Tangyuan 173 J 1
Tani 175 H 5
Taniantaweng Shan 172 C 4–5
Tanimbar, Kepulauan 177 H 5
Tanimbar Islands 184 B 3
Tanjung 176 E 4
Tanjung, Jabung 176 B 4
Tanjung Api 176 C 3
Tanjung Aru 176 E 4
Tanjung Arus 177 F 3
Tanjungbalai 176 AB 3
Tanjungbatu 176 E 3
Tanjung Blitung 176 C 3
Tanjung Bugel 176 D 5
Tanjung Cangkuang 176 BC 5
Tanjung Cina 176 BC 5
Tanjung De Jong 177 J 5
Tanjung Jambuair 176 A 2
Tanjung Kandi 177 F 3
Tanjung Karossa 177 E 5
Tanjung Kolff 177 J 5
Tanjung Lalereh 177 E 4
Tanjung Layar 176 E 4
Tanjung Libobo 177 G 4
Tanjung Lumut 176 C 4
Tanjung Malatayur 176 D 4
Tanjung Mangkalihat 177 E 3
Tanjung Manimbaya 177 E 4
Tanjung Palpetu 177 G 4
Tanjungpandan 176 C 4
Tanjungpinang 176 B 3
Tanjungpusu 176 D 4
Tanjung Puting 176 D 4
Tanjungredeb 176 E 3
Tanjung Samak 176 C 4
Tanjung Sambar 176 CD 4
Tanjung Sasar 177 E 5
Tanjung Selatan 176 D 4
Tanjungselor 176 E 3
Tanjung Vals 177 J 5
Tanjung Waka 177 G 4
Tan Kena Bordj 193 G 3
Tankersley (TX.) 122 C 4
Tankhoy 170 H 5
Tankovo 159 R 3
Tankse 169 K 4
Tanlovo 159 O 2
Tanna 186 C 4
Tännäs 150 F 3
Tannu Ola 170 F 5
Tannūrah, Ra's at (Saudi Arabia) 157 F 4
Tanoucherte 192 C 4
Tanout 197 F 3
Tanque (AZ.) 116 G 5
Tanque Verde (AZ.) 116 F 5
Ṭanṭā 194 E 2
Tan Tan 192 C 3
Tanto Adam 169 H 5
Tantoyuca 132 C 3
Tanuku 174 D 4
Tanyurer 171 X 2
Tanzania 198 EF 6
Tao'an 173 H 1
Taoghe 200 C 3
Taolanaro 201 H 5
Taongi 186 C 2
Taormina 153 FG 4
Taos Indian Reservations 117 L 1
Taos Pueblo (N.M.) 117 L 1
Taoudenni 196 D 1
Taoujafet 192 C 5
Taounate 192 E 2
Taourirt (Algeria) 192 F 3
Taourirt (Morocco) 192 E 2
Taouz 192 E 2
Taoyuan 173 H 5
Tapachula 132 D 5
Tapah 176 B 3
Tapajós 139 G 4
Tapaktuan 176 A 3
Tapan 176 B 4
Tapauá 138 E 5
Tapauá 139 F 5
Tapes 142 F 5
Tapeta 196 C 4
Tapiche 138 D 5
Tapini 184 E 3
Tapirapua 140 E 3
Tappahannock (VA.) 129 OP 4
Tappan Lake 125 N 9
Tappen (ND.) 118 J 4
Tapti 174 B 3
Tapul Group 177 F 2
Tapurucuara 138 E 4
Taqbostān (Iran) 157 E 2
Ṭaqṭaq (Iraq) 157 D 2
Taquara 142 F 4
Taquari 140 E 4
Taquari 141 F 4
Tara 159 P 4
Tara (Rep. of Ireland) 148 B 4
Tara (U.S.S.R.) 159 O 4
Tara (Yugoslavia) 154 A 2
Tara (Yugoslavia) 154 A 2
Tara (Zambia) 200 D 3
Taraba 197 G 4
Tarābulus (Lebanon) 156 B 2
Ṭarābulus (Libya) 193 H 2
Taracua 138 E 3
Tarahouahout 193 G 4
Tarahumara, Sierra 106 E 6
Tarai 174 E 2
Tarakan 176 E 3
Tarakki 169 H 4
Tarakliya 154 C 1
Taran 159 O 1
Taran, Mys 151 G H 5
Tarançón 152 C 3
Tarangire National Park 199 F 5
Taranto 153 G 3
Taranto, Golfo di 153 G 3–4
Tarapacá 138 DE 4
Tarapoto 138 C 5
Tararua Range 185 R 9
Tarascon 153 D 3
Tarasovo 158 J 2
Tarat 193 G 3
Tarata (Bolivia) 140 C 4
Tarata (Peru) 140 C 4
Tarauacá 138 D 5
Tarauacá 138 D 5
Tarawa 186 C 2
Tarazi (Iran) 157 E 3
Tarazit 197 F 1
Tarazit, Massif de 197 F 1
Tarazona 152 C 3
Tarazona de la Mancha 152 C 4
Tarbagatay, Khrebet 159 Q 6
Tarbagatay Shan 169 L 1
Tarbert 148 B 3
Tarbes 152 D 3

Tarboro (N.C.) 129 O 6
Tarbū 193 J 3
Tarcoola (N.S.W., Austr.) 183 G 5
Tarcoola (South Australia) 182 E 5
Tarcutta 183 H 6
Tardoki Yani, Gora 171 P 6
Taree 183 J 5
Tareina 199 G 2
Tärendö 150 H 2
Tareya 170 F 1
Tarfaya 192 C 3
Targhee Pass 111 O 6
Tarhūnah 193 H 2
Tarīf (United Arab Emirates) 157 F 4
Tarifa 152 B 4
Tarija 140 D 5
Tariku, Sungai 177 J 4
Tarim 169 L 2
Tarīm (S. Yemen) 195 H 5
Tarim Basin 162 FG 3
Tarime 198 E 5
Tarim He 169 L 2
Tarim Liuchang 172 A 2
Tarin Kowt 169 K 4
Tarin Kowt 169 H 4
Taritatu, Sungai 177 J 4
Tarka 197 F 3
Tarkhankut, Mys 155 D 1
Tarkio (MO.) 121 K 2
Tarkio (MT.) 111 L 3
Tarko-Zale 159 P 3
Tarkwa 196 D 4
Tarlac 177 J 1
Tarma 140 A 3
Tarn 152 D 3
Tärnaby 150 G 2
Tarnobrzeg 149 H 4
Tarnów 149 H 4
Tarnowskie Góry 149 G 4
Taron 185 F 2
Tarou 197 H 1
Tarouadji, Monts 197 F 2
Taroudant 192 D 2
Tarpon Springs (FL.) 131 M 6
Tarquí 138 CD 4
Tarquinia 153 F 3
Tarradalen 150 G 2
Tarrafal 196 B 6
Tarrasa 152 D 3
Tárrega 152 D 3
Tar River 129 O 6
Tarryall (CO.) 115 M 4
Tarso Taro 197 H 1
Tarso Tiéroko 197 H 1
Tarsū Mūsā 193 J 4
Tarsus 155 G 2
Tarsus (Turkey) 156 B 1
Tart 172 B 3
Tartagal 140 D 5
Tartas 152 C 3
Tartu 151 J 4
Tartuke 196 C 4
Tartus (Syria) 156 B 2
Ta Ruang 175 H 5
Tarumovka 155 G 2
Tārūt (Saudi Arabia) 157 F 4
Tarutino 154 C 1
Tarutung 176 A 3
Tarvo 140 D 4
Tarzan (TX.) 117 OP 5
Tasajera, Sierra de la 106 E 6
Tas-Buget 169 H 2
Tasco (KS.) 120 E 3
Tascosa (TX.) 117 O 2
Tasedjibest 193 G 3
Tashanta 159 R 6
Tashauz 168 F 2
Tashigang 175 F 2
Tashk, Daryācheh-ye (Iran) 157 F 3
Tashkent 169 H 2
Tashkepri 169 G 3
Tash-Kumyr 169 J 2
Tashkurghan 169 H 3
Tashtagol 159 R 5
Tashtyp 159 R 5
Tasikmalaya 176 C 5
Tåsjön 150 G 3
Taskan 171 S 3
Tasker 197 G 2
Taşköprü 155 D 2
Taskyl, Khrebet 170 G 5
Tas-Kystabys, Khrebet 171 Q 2
Taşlıçay 155 F 3
Tasman Basin 209 C 5
Tasman Bay 185 Q 9
Tasmania 184 L 9
Tasmania 186 A 5
Tasman Peninsula 184 L 9
Tasman Sea 184 NO 8
Tasman Sea 186 B 5
Tasova 155 E 2
Tassara 197 F 2
Tassiast 192 B 4
Tassialouc, Lac 105 N 4
Tassili N-Ajjer 193 G 3
Tassili Oua-n Ahaggar 193 FG 4
Tas-Tumus 171 O 1
Tas-Tumus 171 N 3

Tastūr 153 E 4
Taşucu 155 D 3
Taşucu (Turkey) 156 A 1
Tasūj 168 D 3
Tas-Yuryakh 170 K 3
Tata 192 D 3
Tatabánya 154 A 1
Tatakoto 187 F 4
Tatarbunary 154 C 1
Tatarsk 159 P 4
Tatarskiy Proliv 171 Q 6
Tatau 176 D 3
Tataurovo 170 J 5
Tathlina Lake 103 O 3
Tathlīth 195 G 5
Tatos Dağları 155 F 2
Tatry 149 H 5
Tatsinskaya 155 F 1
Tatta 169 H 6
Tatty 169 J 2
Tatum (N.M.) 117 N 4
Tatum (TX.) 123 J 3
Tatvan 155 F 3
Tauá 141 H 2
Tauapeçaçu 139 F 4
Tauariã 139 F 5
Taubaté 141 GH 5
Tauchik 168 E 2
Tauere 187 F 4
Taumarunui 185 R 8
Taumaturgo 138 D 5
Taum Sauk Mountain 121 P 5
Taung 200 CD 5
Taungdwingyi 175 G 3
Taunggon 175 G 3
Taung-gyi 175 G 3
Taunglau 175 G 3
Taungnyo Range 175 G 4
Taungup 175 F 4
Taunton 148 C 4
Taunton (MA.) 126 H 7
Taunus 149 E 4
Taupo 185 R 8
Taupo, Lake 185 R 8
Tauragė 151 H 4
Tauranga 185 R 8
Tauranga 186 C 5
Taurisano 153 G 4
Taurus Mountains (Turkey) 156 A 1
Taurus Mountains→Toros Dağlari 155 D 3
Tauu Island 186 B 3
Tauu Islands 185 G 2
Tauysk 171 R 4
Tauz 155 G 2
Tavaputs Plateau 114 GH 4
Tavas 154 C 3
Tavastehus 150 H 3
Tavatuma 171 T 3
Tavda 159 M 4
Tavda 159 N 4
Taverner Bay 105 N 2
Tavernier (FL.) 131 O 9–10
Taveta 199 F 5
Taviano 153 G 4
Tavolara 153 E 3
Tavoy 175 G 5
Tavşanlı 154 C 3
Tavvaskaite 150 H 2
Tavyskaya Guba 171 RS 4
Tawakoni, Lake 122 GH 3
Tāwarghā' 193 J 2
Tawas City (MI.) 125 L 5
Tawau 176 E 3
Tawfīqīyah 198 E 3
Tawīlah (Egypt) 156 AB 4
Tawkar 197 F 5
Tawūq (Iraq) 156 D 2
Tawzar 193 G 2
Taxco de Alarcón 132 C 4
Taxi, Mount 109 H 2
Taxkorgan 169 K 3
Tay 148 C 3
Tayabamba 138 C 5
Tayakhtakh 171 N 4
Tayandu 177 H 5
Taybola 159 K 2
Tayègle 199 G 4
Tayga 159 QR 4
Taygonos, Mys 171 U 3
Taygonos, Poluostrov 171 U 3
Taylor (AK.) 102 DE 2
Taylor (AR.) 121 M 9
Taylor (AZ.) 116 F 3
Taylor (NE.) 118 J 9
Taylor (TX.) 122 F 5
Taylor, Mount 116 J 2
Taylor Mountain 111 L 6
Taylor Mountains 108 G 3
Taylor Park Reservoir 115 L 5
Taylorsville (CA.) 112 E 2
Taylorsville (KY.) 128 F 3
Taylorsville (MS.) 130 E 3
Taylorsville (N.C.) 129 K 6
Taylorville (IL.) 121 Q 3
Taymā' 194 F 3
Taymā' (Saudi Arabia) 156 C 4
Taymura 170 G 3
Taymylyr 170 M 1

Taymyr 170 F 2
Taymyr, Ozero 170 H 1
Taymyr, Poluostrov 170 FH 1
Taymyra, Verkhnyaya 170 G 1
Taymyr Peninsula 170 GH 1
Tay Ninh 175 J 5
Tayshet 170 G 4
Tayshir 170 G 6
Taytay 177 E 1
Tayura 170 J 4
Taz 159 P 2
Taz 159 Q 2
Taza 192 E 2
Tāzah Khurmātū (Iraq) 156 D 2
Tazdağ 154 C 2
Tazenakht 192 D 2
Tazerbo Oasis → Wāhāt al Tā-zirbū 193 K 3
Tazewell (TN.) 128 H 5
Tazewell (VA.) 129 K 4
Tazovskaya Guba 159 P 2
Tazovskij 159 P 2
Tazumal 132 DE 5
Tazungdam 175 G 2
Tbilisi 155 F 2
Tbilisskaya 155 F 1
Tchabal Mbabo 197 G 4
Tchamba (Cameroon) 197 G 4
Tchamba (Togo) 196 E 4
Tchaourou 196 E 4
Tchibanga 197 G 6
Tchié 197 H 2
Tchien 196 C 4
Tchigai, Plateau du 197 G 1
Tcholliré 197 G 4
Tchula (MS.) 130 D 1
Tczew 149 G 4
Tea (S.D.) 119 M 7
Teague (N.M.) 117 N 5
Teague (TX.) 122 G 4
Teahwhit Head 110 A 3
Te Anau, Lake 184 P 10
Teapa 132 D 4
Teasdale (UT.) 114 F 5
Tea Tree 182 E 3
Teba 177 J 4
Tebahalet 196 E 2
Teberda 155 F 2
Tébessa 193 G 1
Tebingtinggi 176 A 3
Tebingtinggi 176 B 4
Tebingtinggi, Pulau 176 B 3
Tebulos Mta 155 G 2
Tecalitlán 132 B 4
Tecate (CA.) 113 J 10
Tecer Dağları 155 E 3
Tecka 143 B 7
Tecolote (CA.) 113 K 3
Tecomán 132 B 4
Tecopa (CA.) 113 J 7
Tecuala 132 A 3
Tecuci 154 C 1
Tecumseh (NE.) 120 J 2
Tecumseh (OK.) 120 HJ 7
Tedzhen 168 FG 3
Tedzhenstroy 169 G 3
Teec Nos Pas (AZ.) 116 GH 1
Tees 148 C 4
Tefé 138 E 4
Tefé 139 F 4
Tefenni 154 C 3
Tegal 176 C 5
Tegarden (OK.) 120 G 6
Tegguidda In Tessoum 197 F 2
Tegina 197 F 3
Tegre 199 FG 2
Tegucigalpa 132 E 5
Tegul'det 159 R 4
Tegyul'te-Tërde 171 O 3
Tehachapi (CA.) 113 G 7
Tehachapi Mountains 113 G 7–8
Tehamiyam 194 F 5
Te Hapua 185 Q 7
Teheran → Tehrān 157 F 2
Téhini 196 D 4
Tehi-n Isser 193 G 4
Tehoru 177 G 4
Tehrān 157 F 2
Tehuacán 132 C 4
Tehuantepec 132 C 4
Tehuata 187 F 4
Teide, Pico de 192 B 3
Teiga Plateau 194 D 5
Teiga Plateau → Hadabat Tayga 194 D 5
Teigen (MT.) 111 R 3
Teixeira Pinto 196 A 3
Tejo 152 B 4
Tejon Pass 113 G 8
Teju 175 G 2
Tekamah (NE.) 119 M 9
Tekeli 169 K 2
Tekes 169 L 2
Tekes He 169 L 2
Tekija 154 B 2
Tekin 171 O 6
Tekirdağ 154 C 2
Tekman 155 F 3
Teknaf 175 F 3
Tekoa (WA.) 110 H 3

Tekonsha (MI.) 125 K 7
Tekro 197 J 2
Tekro 197 J 2
Te Kuiti 185 R 8
Tel 174 D 3
Telavåg 151 D 3
Telavi 155 G 2
Tel Aviv-Yafo (Israel) 156 B 2–3
Telč 149 G 5
Telefomin 184 D 3
Telegraph (TX.) 122 CD 5
Telegraph Creek 109 M 4
Telemaco Borba 141 F 5
Telemark 151 E 4
Telén 197 G 2
Teleneshty 154 C 1
Telerhteba, Djebel 193 G 4
Telescope Peak 112 H 6
Teles Pires 139 G 5
Teletskoye, Ozero 159 R 5
Telfane, Hadjer 197 H 3
Telfel 196 D 2
Teli 197 F 5
Telida 109 H 3
Télimélé 196 B 3
Teljo, Jabal 194 D 6
Tell al 'Amārna 194 E 3
Tell al Ubaid (Iraq) 157 D 3
Tell City (IN.) 128 E 4
Teller 102 D 2
Teller Mission 108 E 2
Tellicherry 174 C 5
Tell Mān 194 F 2
Tello 142 C 5
Telluride (CO.) 115 K 6
Telma (WA.) 110 E 3
Telmen Nuur 170 G 6
Telmest 192 D 2
Telocaset (OR.) 110 H 5
Telok Anson 176 B 3
Teloloapan 132 C 4
Tel'pos-Iz, Gora 159 L 3
Telsen 143 C 7
Telšiai 151 H 4
Telton (ID.) 111 O 7
Teluk Adang 176 E 3
Teluk Balikpapan 176 E 4
Telukbatang 176 CD 4
Teluk Berau 177 H 4
Teluk Bintuni 177 H 4
Teluk Bone 177 F 4
Teluk Buli 177 G 3
Telukbutun 176 C 3
Teluk Cendrawasih 177 HJ 4
Telukdalam 176 A 3
Teluk Darvel 177 E 3
Teluk Datu 176 D 3
Teluk Kau 177 G 3
Teluk Kuantan 176 B 4
Teluk Kumai 176 D 4
Teluk Kupang 177 F 5–6
Teluk Mandar 177 E 4
Teluk Pamukan 176 E 4
Teluk Pelabuanratu 176 C 5
Teluk Sampit 176 D 4
Teluk Sangkulirang 177 E 3
Teluk Sindeh 177 F 5
Teluk Tolo 177 F 4
Teluk Tomini 177 F 4
Teluk Weda 177 G 3
Téma 196 E 4
Temangi 187 F 4
Tembenchi 170 F 2
Tembenchi 170 G 3
Tembilahan 176 B 4
Temblador 139 F 2
Tembleque 152 C 4
Temblor Range 113 EF 7
Tembo 198 B 6
Tembo, Mont 197 G 5
Tembo Falls 198 B 6
Tembué 200 B 2
Temecula (CA.) 113 H 9
Temerin 154 AB 1
Temerloh 176 B 3
Temir 168 F 1
Temirgoyevskaya 155 EF 1
Temirtau 159 O 5
Temirtau 159 R 5
Temiscaming 105 M 6
Temki 197 H 3
Temoe 187 G 4
Temora 183 H 5
Tempa 202
Tempe (AZ.) 116 E 4
Temperanceville (VA.) 129 Q 4
Tempio Pausania 153 E 3
Tempiute (NV.) 112 K 5
Temple (OK.) 120 G 8
Temple (TX.) 122 F 4
Tempué 200 B 2
Temryuk 155 E 1
Temryukskiy Zaliv 155 E 1
Temuco 143 B 6
Temvik (ND.) 118 H 4
Tena 138 C 3
Tenaha (TX.) 123 J 4
Tenali 174 D 4
Tenasserim 175 G 5

Tenasserim 175 G 5
Tende, Col di 153 E 3
Ten Degree Channel 175 F 6
Tendel 192 C 5
Tendoy (ID.) 111 M 6
Tendrara 192 E 2
Tendrovskaya Kosa 154–155 D 1
Tendürek Dağı 155 F 3
Tenekert 196 C 3
Tenenkou 196 C 3
Ténéré 197 G 2
Ténéré, Erg de 197 G 2
Ténéré du Tafassasset 197 G 1
Tenerife 192 B 3
Ténès 193 F 1
Tengchong 172 C 5
Tenggara, Kepulauan 177 G 5
Tenggarong 176 E 4
Tengger Shamo 172 D 3
Tengiz, Ozero 159 N 5
Tengushevo 158 H 5
Teng Xian 172 F 6
Teng Xian 173 G 3
Tenialig 192 C 4
Teniente Marsh 203
Teniente Matienzo 203
Tenino (WA.) 110 C 4
Tenkasi 174 C 6
Tenke (U.S.S.R.) 170 L 3
Tenke (Zaire) 200 D 2
Tenkiller Ferry Lake 121 L 7
Tenkodogo 196 D 3
Tenmile (OR.) 110 B 7
Tennant Creek 182 E 2
Tennessee 128 HJ 2
Tennessee Pass 115 L 4
Tennessee River 128 D 6
Tennyson (TX.) 122 C 4
Teno 143 B 5
Tenojoki 150 J 2
Tenom 176 E 2
Tenosique de Pino Suárez 132 D 4
Tensas River 123 M 3
Tensed (ID.) 110 J 3
Tensleep (WY.) 111 S 6
Tenterfield 183 J 4
Ten Thousand Islands 131 N 9
Tentolomatinan, Gunung 177 F 3
Tentugal 139 J 4
Teocaltiche 132 B 3
Teófilo Otoni 141 H 4
Teotihuacan 132 C 4
Teouit 193 G 2
Tepa 177 G 5
Tepa 184 A 3
Tepache 106 E 6
Tepatitlán 132 B 3
Tepe Gawra → Khorsābād 195 G 1
Tepelena 154 A 2
Tepic 132 B 3
Teplice 149 F 4
Teplik 154 C 1
Teplogorka 158 K 3
Teplogorka 158 K 3
Tequila 132 B 3
Ter 152 D 3
Téra (Niger) 196 E 3
Tera (Portugal) 152 B 4
Teraina 187 E 2
Terakeka 198 E 3
Teramo 153 F 3
Tercan 155 F 3
Terceira 192 A 1
Terek 155 F 2
Terek 168 D 2
Terekhovka 158 F 5
Terempa 176 C 3
Terenni 192 D 5
Terenos 141 E 5
Terentang, Pulau 176 E 4
Tereraimbu, Cachoeira do 139 H 5
Teresina 141 H 2
Teresinha 139 H 3
Teresita 138 E 3
Teressa 175 F 6
Terhazza 192 D 4
Terhir 193 F 2
Teriberka 150 K 2
Teriberka 150 L 2
Terkezi 197 J 2
Terlingua (TX.) 117 M 8
Terme 155 F 2
Termelli 155 D 3
Termez 169 H 3
Termini Imerese 153 F 4
Termit, Massif de 197 G 2
Termit Kaoboul 197 G 2
Termo (CA.) 112 E 2
Termoli 153 F 3
Ternate 177 G 3
Terneuzen 148 D 4
Terney 173 L 1
Terni 153 F 3
Ternopol' 158 E 6
Terpeniya, Mys 171 QR 6
Terpeniya, Zaliv 171 Q 6
Terpugovo 159 N 4
Terra Bella (CA.) 112 FG 7
Terrace 102 M 5
Terracina 153 F 3
Terracy Bay 104 K 6

Terra de Basto 152 B 3
Terra di Bari 153 G 3
Terra Firma 200 C 5
Terråk 150 F 2
Terral (OK.) 120 H 9
Terralba 153 E 4
Terra Prêta 139 G 4–5
Terra Santa 139 G 4
Terrebonne (OR.) 110 D 6
Terrebonne Bay 123 N 6
Terre Haute (IN.) 128 D 2
Terrell (TX.) 122 G 3
Terre Plaine 152 D 2
Terreton (ID.) 111 N 7
Terry (MT.) 118 C 4
Terry Peak 118 E 6
Tersakan Gölü 155 D 3
Terskey Alatau, Khrebet 169 K 2
Terskiy Bereg 158 GH 2
Teruel 152 C 3
Tervola 150 H 2
Teshekpuk Lake 102 G 1
Teslin 102 L 3
Teslin Lake 102 L 3–4
Teslin River 109 M 4
Tesocoma 106 E 6
Tessalit 196 E 1
Tessaoua 197 F 3
Tessenei 199 F 1–2
Tessenei 199 F 2
Testa, Capo 153 E 3
Testigos, Islas los 139 F 1
Tesuque (N.M.) 117 KL 2
Tetari, Cerro 138 D 2
Tete 201 E 3
Tetepare 185 G 3
Tetere 185 H 3
Teteven 154 B 2
Tetiaroa 187 F 4
Tetonia (ID.) 111 O 7
Teton Pass 111 P 7
Teton Range 111 P 6–7
Teton River 111 O 3
Tétouan 192 D 1
Tetovo 154 B 2
Tetrino 158 G 2
Tetuan → Tétouan 192 D 1
Teuini 138 E 5
Teulada 153 E 4
Tevere 153 F 3
Teverya (Israel) 156 B 2
Teviot 148 C 3
Tevriz 159 O 4
Tëwo 172 D 4
Texarkana (AR.) 121 LM 9
Texarkana (TX.) 123 J 2
Texarkana, Lake 123 J 2
Texas (East) 122–123
Texas (Queensland, Austr.) 183 J 4
Texas (West) 117
Texas City (TX.) 123 J 6
Texas Creek (CO.) 115 M 5
Texel 148 D 4
Texhoma (TX.) 117 P 1
Texico (N.M.) 117 N 3
Texline (TX.) 117 NO 1
Texoma, Lake 120 J 9
Texon (TX.) 117 P 6
Teya 170 F 3
Teykovo 158 GH 4
Teyuareh 169 G 4
Teziutlán 132 C 4
Tezpur 175 F 2
Tha-anne 103 S 3
Thabana Ntlenyana 200 D 5
Thabazimbi 200 D 4
Thackerville (OK.) 120 H 9
Thādíq (Saudi Arabia) 157 DE 4
Thagyettaw 175 G 5
Thai Binh 175 J 3
Thailand 175 GH 4
Thailand, Gulf of 175 H 5
Thai Nguyen 175 J 3
Thakhek 175 HJ 4
Thal 169 J 4
Thalabarivat 175 J 5
Thal Desert 169 J 4
Thale Luang 175 H 6
Thalia (TX.) 122 D 1
Thallon 183 H 4
Thamad Bū Hashishah 193 J 3
Thamarīd 195 J 5
Thames (New Zealand) 185 R 8
Thames (U.K.) 148 C 4
Thāmir, Jabal 195 H 6
Tham Krabok 175 J 4
Thamūd 195 H 5
Thana 174 B 4
Thaneta Pass 109 J 3
Thangoo 182 C 2
Thangool 183 J 3
Thanh Hoa 175 J 4
Thanīyah, Jabal 195 H 5
Thanjavur 174 C 5
Thann 153 E 2
Thano Bula Khan 169 H 5
Tha Pla 175 H 4
Thap Sakae 175 GH 5
Tharad 174 B 3
Thar Desert 174 B 2

Thargomindah 183 G 4
Tharrawaddy 175 G 4
Tharrawaw 175 G 4
Tharthār, Bahr ath (Iraq) 156 D 2
Tharthār, Wādī ath (Iraq) 156 D 2
Thásos 154 B 2
Thásos 154 B 2
Thásos 154 B 2
Tha Tako 175 H 4
Thatcher (AZ.) 116 G 5
Thatcher (CO.) 115 NO 6
Thatcher (ID.) 111 O 8
Thateng 175 J 4
Thaton 175 G 4
Tha Tum 175 H 4
Thau, Bassin de 152 D 3
Thaungdut 175 FG 3
Thayer (MO.) 121 O 4
Thayer Junction (WY.) 111 QR 9
Thayetchaung 175 G 5
Thayetmyo 175 G 4
Thayne (WY.) 111 P 8
Thazi 175 F 4
The Alps 153 EF 2
The Bahamas 133 GH 2
Thebes 154 B 3
Thebes 194 E 3
The Brothers → Al Ikhwān 199 J 2
The Cheviot 148 C 3
The Dalles (OR.) 110 D 5
Thedford (NE.) 118 H 9
The Everglades 131 O 8–9
The Fens 148 CD 4
The Gambia 196 A 3
The Granites 182 E 3
The Granites 182 E 3
The Great Oasis→Wāhāt al
  Khārijah 194 E 3–4
The Grove (TX.) 122 F 4
The Gulf 157 EF 3–4
The Hague 148 D 4
The Heads 110 A 8
Theinkun 175 G 5
The Johnston Lakes 182 C 5
Thelon 103 S 3
The Monument 183 G 3
Thénia 152 D 4
Theodore (AL.) 130 F 4
Theodore Roosevelt Lake 116 E 4
Theologos 154 B 2
The Pas 103 R 5
Theresa (N.Y.) 126 D 4
Theriot (LA.) 123 N 6
Thermaïkos Kólpos 154 B 2–3
Thermalito (CA.) 112 D 3
Thermopílai 154 B 3
Thermopolis (WY.) 111 RS 7
Theronsvalley 200 BC 4
Thesiger Bay 103 MN 1
Thessalía 154 B 3
Thessaloníki 154 B 2
The Teeth 177 E 2
Thetford 148 D 4
Thetford Mines 105 N 6
The Twins 185 Q 9
The Valley 133 K 4
The Village (OK.) 120 H 7
The Wash 148 D 4
Thibodaux (LA.) 123 N 6
Thief Lake 119 N 2
Thief River Falls (MN.) 119 M 2
Thiel Mts. 203
Thiers 152 D 2
Thiès 196 A 3
Thiesi 153 E 3
Thika 199 F 5
Thiladummathi Atoll 174 B 6
Thimphu 174 E 2
Þingvallavatn 150 A 3
Þingvellir 150 A 3
Thio (Ethiopia) 199 G 2
Thio (New Caledonia) 185 J 6
Thionville 153 E 2
Thiou 196 D 3
Thira 154 B 3
Thíra 154 C 3
Third Cataract → Ash Shallāl ath
  Thālith 194 E 5
Thirsk 148 C 4
Thisted 151 E 4
Thistle (UT.) 114 F 4
Thitu Island 176 D 1
Thivai 154 B 3
Thiviers 152 D 2
Þjórsá 150 B 3
Thlewiaza 103 S 3
Thoen 175 G 4
Thoeng 175 H 4
Thohoyandou 201 E 4
Thomas (OK.) 120 G 7
Thomas (W.V.) 129 M 2
Thomas Hill Reservation 121 N 3
Thomas Shoal 176 E 2
Thomaston (GA.) 131 K 2
Thomasville (AL.) 130 G 3
Thomasville (GA.) 131 L 4
Thomasville (N.C.) 129 L 6
Thompson (Manitoba, Can.)
  103 S 4
Thompson (N.D.) 119 L 3

Thompson (UT.) 114 H 5
Thompson Falls (MT.) 111 K 3
Thompson Peak 112 B 1–2
Thompson Reservoir 110 D 8
Thompson River 121 M 2
Thompsons Station (TN.) 128 E 6
Thompsonville (MI.) 124 J 5
Thomson (GA.) 128 J 8
Thomson (IL.) 124 D 8
Thomson River 183 G 3
Thon Buri 175 GH 5
Thongwa 175 G 4
Thonon 153 E 2
Thoreau (N.M.) 116 H 2
Þórisvatn 150 B 3
Þorlákshöfn 150 A 3
Thorne (NV.) 112 G 4
Thornton (CO.) 115 N 4
Thornton (TX.) 122 G 4
Thorp (WA.) 110 E 3
Thorsby (AL.) 130 H 2
Þórshöfn 150 B 2
Thousand Lake Mountain 114 F 5
Thousand Oaks (CA.) 113 G 8
Thowa 199 F 5
Thraki 154 BC 2
Thrakion Pélagos 154 BC 2
Three Forks (MT.) 111 O 5
Three Hummock Island 184 L 9
Three Kings Island 186 C 5
Three Kings Islands 185 Q 7
Three Lakes (WI.) 124 E 4
Three Pagodas Pass 175 G 4
Three Points, Cape 196 D 5
Three Rivers (CA.) 112 G 6
Three Rivers (MI.) 124 J 8
Three Rivers (N.M.) 117 K 4
Three Rivers (TX.) 122 E 7
Three Sisters 110 D 6
Three Springs 182 B 4
Throckmorton (TX.) 122 D 2
Throssel, Lake 182 C 4
Thuillier, Mount 175 F 6
Thule 202
Thun 153 E 2
Thundelarra 182 B 4
Thunder Bay (Canada) 104 K 6
Thunder Bay (MI.) 125 L 4–5
Thunderbird, Lake 120 H 7
Thunder Butte (SD.) 118 FG 5
Thung Luang 175 G 5
Thung Song 175 G 6
Thung Wa 175 G 6
Thüringen 149 F 4
Thüringer Wald 149 F 4
Thurles 148 B 4
Thurso 148 C 3
Thurston Island 203
Thusis 153 E 2
Thy 151 E 4
Thylungra 183 G 4
Tiago 139 G 4
Tianchang 173 G 4
Tiandong 172 E 6
Tian'e 172 E 6
Tiangua 141 H 1
Tianjin 173 G 3
Tianjin Xingang 173 G 3
Tianjun 172 C 3
Tianlin 172 E 6
Tianmen 172 F 4
Tianmu Shan 173 G 4
Tianshifu 173 H 2
Tianshui 172 E 4
Tiantai 173 H 5
Tianyang 172 E 6
Tianzhu 172 D 3
Tiaret 193 F 1
Tiassalé 196 D 4
Tibaradine 193 F 3
Tibati 197 G 4
Tibbie (AL.) 130 F 3
Tiber 153 F 3
Tiberias → Teverya 194 F 2
Tiber Reservoir 111 O 2
Tibesti 197 H 1
Tibet 174 E 1
Tibet, Plateau of 174 DE 1
Tibiri 197 E 3
Tibiri 197 E 3
Tibistī, Sarīr 193 J 4
Tibnah (Syria) 156 B 2
Tibni (Syria) 156 C 2
Tibro 151 F 4
Tiburon, Isla 106 D 6
Ticao 177 F 1
Tichla 192 B 4
Ticino 153 E 2
Ticonderoga (N.Y.) 126 F 5
Ticul 132 E 3
Tidaholm 151 F 4
Tiddim 175 F 3
Tidikelt 193 F 3
Tidioute (PA.) 125 P 8
Tidjettaouine 193 F 4
Tidjkdja 192 C 5
Tidra, Ile 192 B 5
Tiebissou 196 CD 4

Tiel 196 A 3
Tieli 173 J 1
Tieling 173 H 2
Tielongtan 169 K 3
Tiéme 196 C 4
Tienba 196 C 4
Tientsin 173 G 3
Tierra Amarilla (N.M.) 117 K 1
Tierra Blanca 132 C 4
Tierra Colorada 132 C 4
Tierra de Barros 152 B 3
Tierra de Campos 152 BC 3
Tierra del Fuego, Isla Grande de
  143 C 9
Tierra del Pan 152 B 3
Tierra del Vino 152 B 3
Tie Siding (WY.) 118 C 9
Tieté 141 F 5
Tieton (WA.) 110 E 4
Tifariti 192 C 3
Tiffany (CO.) 115 K 6
Tiffany Mountain 110 F 2
Tiffin (OH.) 125 L 8
Tiflis → Tbilisi 155 F 2
Tifton (GA.) 131 L 3
Tiftona (TN.) 128 F 6–7
Tifu 177 G 4
Tiga 185 J 6
Tigalda 102 E 5
Tigil 171 T 4
Tigil 171 T 4
Tignall (GA.) 128 J 8
Tignère 197 G 4
Tigre 138 C 4
Tigres, Baía dos 200 A 3
Tigris (Iraq) 157 D 2
Tiguent 192 B 5
Tigui 197 H 2
Tiguidit, Falaise de 197 F 2
Tihāmat 195 G 5
Tijeras (N.M.) 117 K 2
Tiji 193 H 2
Tijuana 106 C 5
Tijucas 142 G 4
Tikal 132 E 4
Tikamgarh 174 C 3
Tikanlik 172 A 2
Tikaré 196 D 3
Tikchik Lakes 102 F 3
Tikhoretsk 155 F 1
Tikhtoozero, Ozero 150 K 2
Tikhvin 158 F 4
Tikkakoski 150 J 3
Tikopia 185 J 5
Tikopia 186 C 3
Tikrīt 195 G 2
Tikshozero, Ozero 150 K 2
Tiksi 171 N 1
Tilaiya Reservoir 174 E 3
Tilbeşar Ovası 155 E 3
Tilbooroo 183 H 4
Tilburg 148 E 4
Tilbury 148 E 4
Tilcara 140 C 5
Tilden (NE.) 119 L 8
Tilden (TX.) 122 E 7
Tilemsi, Vallée du 196 E 2
Tilemsi el Fasi 192 E 3
Tilia 192 F 3
Tilichiki 171 V 3
Tilin 175 F 3
Tillabéri 196 E 3
Tillamook (OR.) 110 B 5
Tillamook Bay 110 A 5
Tillamook Head 110 A 5
Tillanchong 175 F 6
Tillery, Lake 129 L 6
Tillia 197 E 2
Tiloa 196 E 2
Tilogne 196 B 2
Tílos 154 C 3
Tilpa 183 G 5
Til'tim 159 M 2
Tilton (N.H.) 126 H 5
Timä 194 E 3
Timagami, Lake 105 L 6
Timanskiy Kryazh 158 J 2–K 3
Timar 155 F 3
Timaru 185 Q 9
Timaru 186 C 5
Timashevskaya 155 E 1
Timbákion 154 B 3
Timber Lake (SD.) 118 GH 5
Timber Peak 113 EF 7
Timbio 138 C 3
Timbo 196 BC 4
Timbuktu → Tombouctou 196 D 2
Timeiaouine 193 F 4
Timétrine 196 D 2
Timétrine, Monts 196 D 2
Timfi Óros 154 B 3
Timg'aouine 193 F 4
Timia 197 F 2

Timimoun 192 F 3
Timimoun, Sebkha de 192–193 F 3
Timir-Atakh-Tas 171 S 2
Timiris, Cap 192 B 5
Timiş 154 B 1
Timiskaming, Lake 105 M 6
Timişoara 154 B 1
Timkapaul' 159 M 3
Timmins 105 L 6
Ti-m Missao 193 F 4
Timmoudi 192 E 3
Timms Hill 124 D 4
Timon 141 H 2
Timor 177 G 5
Timor, Laut 177 G 6
Timor Sea 177 G 6
Timoshino 158 G 3
Timote 142 D 6
Timpanogos Cave National
  Monument 114 F 3
Timpas (CO.) 115 O 6
Timpson (TX.) 123 J 4
Timpton 171 N 4
Timrå 150 G 3
Tims Ford Lake 128 E 6
Timur 169 H 2
Tinaca Point 177 G 2
Tinaco 138 E 2
Tinaja (TX.) 117 N 7
Ti-n Amzi 193 F 4
Tin Asaguid 196 E 2
Tindalo 198 K 3
Tindivanam 174 CD 5
Tindouf 192 D 3
Tindouf, Hamada de 192 D 3
Tindouf, Sebkha de 192 D 3
Tinef 193 F 4
Tineldjame 193 F 3
Tineo 152 B 3
Tinerhir 192 D 2
Tin Ethisane 196 D 2
Tinfouchy 192 D 3
Tin Fouye 193 G 3
Tingharat, Hamādat 193 H 3
Tingkawk Sakan 175 G 2
Tingmerkpuk Mountains 108 F 2
Tingmiarmiut 105 T 3
Tingo María 138 C 5
Tingréla 196 C 3
Tingri 194 F 2
Tingsryd 151 FG 4
Tinguiririca 143 BC 5
Tingvoll 150 E 3
Tinharé, Ilha de 141 J 3
Tinh Gia 175 J 4
Tinian 186 A 2
Tini Wells 194 C 6
Tinnsjö 151 E 4
Tinogasta 142 C 4
Tinombo 177 F 3
Tínos 154 C 3
Ti-n Rerhoh 193 F 4
Tinrhert, Hamada de 193 G 3
Tinsley (MS.) 130 D 2
Tinsukia 175 G 2
Tintane 192 C 5
Ti-n Taoundi 193 G 4
Ti-n Tarabine 193 G 4
Tintina 142 D 4
Ti-n-Toumma 197 G 2
Tin Tounannt 196 D 1
Ti-n Zaouâtene 193 F 4
Tio, Pico de 196 C 4
Tioga (ND.) 118 F 2
Tioga (PA.) 126 B 7
Tioga Pass 112 F 5
Tioman 176 B 3
Tione di Trento 153 F 2
Tionesta (CA.) 112 F 6
Tionesta (PA.) 125 P 8
Tiongui 196 C 3
Tiouardiouine Aguelman 193 G 4
Tiouilit Anagoum 192 B 5
Tipler (WI.) 124 F 4
Tipperary 148 B 4
Tippett (NV.) 112 L 3
Tipton (CA.) 112 F 6
Tipton (IA.) 119 R 9
Tipton (IN.) 124 J 9
Tipton (KS.) 120 G 3
Tipton (OK.) 120 F 8
Tipton, Mount 116 B 2
Tiquisate 132 D 5
Tiracambu, Serra do 141 G 1
Tirah 169 J 4
Tirān (Egypt) 156 B 4
Tirān (Iran) 157 F 2
Tirana 154 AB 2
Tirano 153 F 2
Tiras Mountains 200 B 5
Tiraspol' 154 C 1
Tirat Karmel (Israel) 156 B 2
Tire 154 C 3
Tirebolu 155 E 2
Tiree 148 B 3
Tirgelir 171 Q 3
Tîrgu Frumos 154 C 1
Tîrgovişte 154 C 2

Tirgu Bujor **154** C 1
Tirgu Cărbuneşti **154** B 2
Tîrgu Jiu **154** B 1
Tîrgu Mureş **154** BC 1–2
Tîrgu Neamţ **154** C 1
Tirgu Ocna **154** C 1
Tirgu Secuiesc **154** C 1
Tirich Mir **169** J 3
Tiririne **193** G 4
Tiris **192** C 4
Tîrnăveni **154** B 1
Tirnavos **154** B 3
Tiro **196** B 4
Tirol **153** F 2
Tirso **153** E 3
Tiruchchirappalli **174** C 5
Tiruchendur **174** C 6
Tirunelveli **174** C 6
Tiruntán **138** D 5
Tirupati **174** C 5
Tiruppur **174** C 5
Tiruvannamalai **174** C 5
Tisa **154** A 1
Tisdale **103** R 5
Tishomingo (MS.) **121** R 8
Tishomingo (OK.) **120** J 8
Tisisat Falls **199** F 2
Tissemsilt **193** F 1
Tista **174** E 2
Tisul' **159** R 4
Tisza **154** B 1
Tiszafüred **154** B 1
Tiszántúl **154** B 1
Tit **193** F 3
Titaf **192** E 3
Tit-Ary **171** N 1
Titicaca, Lago **140** C 4
Titlagarh **174** D 3
Titley (TX.) **117** N 7
Titograd **154** A 2
Titonka (IA.) **119** OP 7
Titonville (TN.) **128** B 5
Titova Korenica **153** G 3
Titovo Užice **154** A 2
Titov Veles **154** B 2
Titov vrh **154** B 2
Titran **150** E 3
Titule **198** D 4
Titusville (FL.) **131** O 6
Titusville (PA.) **125** P 8
Tiui **139** GH 3
Tivaouane **196** A 3
Tiveden **151** F 4
Tiverton **148** C 4
Tivoli (TX.) **122** G 7
Tiwī **195** K 4
Tiworo, Selat **177** F 4
Tizatlan **132** C 4
Tizimín **132** E 3
Tizi n'Test **192** D 2
Tizi Ouzou **193** F 1
Tiznit **192** D 3
Tjåhumas **150** G 2
Tjeggelvas **150** G 2
Tjidtjak **150** G 2
Tjörn **151** F 4
Tjotta **150** F 2
Tjust **151** G 4
Tkhach **155** F 2
Tkibuli **155** F 2
Tkvarcheli **155** F 2
Tlalnepantla **132** C 4
Tlapa de Comonfort **132** C 4
Tlaxcala **132** C 4
Tlemcen **192** E 2
Tlemcès **197** E 2
Tlētē Ouate Gharbi, Jabal (Syria) **156** C 2
Tlyarata **155** G 2
Tmassah **193** J 3
Tni Haïa **192** E 4
Toaca, Vîrful **154** C 1
Toamasina **201** H 3
Toana Range **112** L 1–2
Toay **143** D 6
Toba, Danau **176** A 3
Tobacco Root Mountains **111** N 5
Tobago, Isla **139** F 1
Toba & Kakar Ranges **169** H 4
Tobarra **152** C 4
Tobermorey **183** F 3
Tobermory **105** L 6
Tobermory **148** B 3
Tobi **177** H 3
Tobias (NE.) **120** H 2
Tobin, Lake **182** D 3
Tobin, Mount **112** H 2
Tobo **177** H 4
Toboali **176** C 4
Tobol **159** N 4
Tobol **159** M 5
Tobol'sk **159** N 4
Tobruk → Ţubruq **193** K 2
Tobseda **158** K 2
Tobyhanna (PA.) **127** D 7
Tobysh **158** K 3
Tocantinia **139** J 5
Tocantinópolis **139** J 5 Tocantins **139** J 4
Tocapilla **140** B 5

Toccoa (GA.) **128** H 7
Tocito (N.M.) **116** H 1
Töcksfors **151** F 4
Toco **140** C 5
Toconao **140** C 5
Tocorpuri, Cerro de **140** C 5
Toddville (MD.) **129** P 3
Todenyang **199** F 4
Todi **153** F 3
Todos os Santos, Baia de **141** J 3
Todos Santos **106** D 7
Tofino **103** M 6
Tofte **151** F 4
Togatax **169** L 3
Togiak **102** E 4
Togiak Bay **108** F 4
Togian, Kepulauan **177** F 4
Togni **194** F 5
Togo **196** E 4
Togo (MN.) **119** P 3
Togqên **174** D 1
Togtoh **172** F 2
Toguchin **159** Q 4
Togur **159** Q 4
Togwottee Pass **111** P 7
Togyz **169** G 1
Tohakum Peak **112** F 2
Tohatchi (N.M.) **116** H 2
Tohen **199** J 2
Tohma **155** E 3
Tohopekaliga, Lake **131** N 6
Toibalewe **175** F 5
Toijala **150** H 3
Toisvesi **150** J 3
Toiyabe Range **112** HJ 3
Tok (AK, U.S.A.) **102** J 3
Tok (Czechoslovakia) **149** F 5
Tokaj **154** B 1
Tokara-kaikyō **173** JK 4–5
Tokara-rettō **173** J 5
Tokat **155** E 2
Tok-do **173** K 3
Tokeland (WA.) **110** B 4
Tokelau Islands **186** D 3
Tokio (TX.) **117** O 4
Tokko **170** L 4
Tokma **170** J 4
Tokmak **155** E 1
Tokmak **169** K 2
Tokomaru Bay **185** R 8
Toksun **169** M 2
Toktamysh **169** JK 3
Toktogul **169** J 2
Tokur **171** O 5
Tokushima **173** K 4
Tōkyō **173** L 3
Tolbazy **158** L 5
Tolbonuur **170** F 6
Tolbukhin **154** C 2
Toledo (Chile) **140** B 4
Toledo (IA.) **119** Q 8–9
Toledo (IL.) **121** R 3
Toledo (OH.) **125** L 8
Toledo (OR.) **110** B 6
Toledo (Spain) **152** C 4
Toledo, Montes de **152** C 4
Toledo Bend Dam **123** K 4
Toledo Bend Reservoir **123** K 4
Tolga (Algeria) **193** G 2
Tolga (Norway) **150** F 3
Toli **169** L 1
Toliara **201** G 4
Tolima **138** C 3
Tolitoli **177** F 3
Tol'ka **159** Q 3
Tollarp **151** F 4
Tolley (ND.) **118** G 2
Tollhouse (CA.) **112** F 6
Tolmezzo **153** F 2
Tolmin **153** F 2
Tolo **198** B 5
Tolo, Teluk **177** F 4
Tolochin **151** J 5
Tolon **170** K 4
Tolon **171** R 4
Tolono (IL.) **124** F 9
Tolstoe **154** C 1
Tolstoy, Mys **171** T 4
Toltén **143** B 6
Toluca **132** C 4
Tol'yatti **158** J 5
Tolybay **159** M 5
Tom' **159** QR 4
Tom (OK.) **121** L 9
Tomahawk (WI.) **124** E 4
Tomakomai **173** M 2
Tomales Bay **112** C 4
Tomales Point **112** BC 4
Tomar (Portugal) **152** B 4
Tomari **171** Q 6
Tómaros **154** B 3
Tomaszów Lubelski **149** H 4
Tomaszów Mazowiecki **149** H 4
Tomatlán **132** AB 4
Tombador, Serra do **140** E 3
Tombe **198** E 3
Tomboco **200** A 1

Tombouctou **196** D 2
Tombstone (AZ.) **116** FG 6
Tombstone Mountain **109** L 3
Tômbua **200** A 3
Tomé **143** B 6
Tomé, Pico de **197** F 5
Tomé Açu **139** J 4
Tomelilla **151** F 4
Tomelloso **152** C 4
Tomini, Teluk **177** F 4
Tominian **196** D 3
Tomkinson Ranges **182** D 4
Tomma **150** F 2
Tommot **171** N 4
Tomo **138** E 2
Tompa **170** J 4
Tompkinsville (KY.) **128** F 5
Tompo **171** P 3
Tompo (Indonesia) **177** F 3
Tompo (U.S.S.R.) **171** P 3
Tom Price **182** B 3
Tomsa **199** G 3
Tomsk **159** R 4
Toms Place (CA.) **112** G 5
Toms River (N.J.) **127** E 9
Tomtor **171** O 2
Tom White, Mount **102** J 3
Tonalea (AZ.) **116** F 1
Tonantins **138** E 4
Tonasket (WA.) **110** F 2
Tonate **139** H 3
Tonawanda (N.Y.) **125** Q 6
Tonb-e Bozorg (Iran) **157** G 4
Tondano **177** FG 3
Tondela **152** B 3
Tønder **151** E 5
Tondibi **196** D 2
Tondou, Massif du **198** C 3
Tonekābon (Iran) **157** F 1
Tonga **186** D 4
Tonga (Sudan) **198** E 3
Tongaat **201** E 5
Tonga Islands **186** D 4
Tongariro National Park **185** R 8
Tongatapu Group **186** D 4
Tonga Trench **209** J 4
Tongbai Shan **172** F 4
Tongcheng **173** G 4
Tongchuan **172** E 3
Tongdao **172** EF 5
Tongde **172** D 3
Tonghai **172** D 6
Tonghe **173** J 1
Tonghua **173** J 2
Tongjiang **171** O 6
Tongjoson-man **173** J 3
Tongliao **173** H 2
Tongling **173** G 4
Tongliong **172** E 5
Tonglu **173** GH 5
Tongoy **142** B 5
Tongren **172** D 3
Tongren **172** E 3
Tongsa **175** F 2
Tongshan **172** F 5
Tongta **175** G 3
Tongtian He **172** C 4
Tongue **148** C 3
Tongue of the Ocean **133** G 3
Tongue River (MT.) **118** B 5
Tongue River (WY.) **118** L 2
Tongue River Reservoir **118** B 5
Tongulakh **171** M 3
Tong Xian **173** G 3
Tongxin **172** E 3
Tongyu **173** H 2
Tongzi **172** E 5
Tonhil **170** F 6
Tonichí **106** E 6
Tonj **198** D 3
Tonk **174** C 2
Tonkawa (OK.) **120** H 6
Tonkou, Mont **196** C 4
Tonle Sap **175** H 5
Tonneins **152** D 3
Tonnerre **152** D 2
Tonopah (AZ.) **116** D 4
Tonopah (NV.) **112** H 4
Tonosí **138** B 2
Tönsberg **151** F 4
Tonstad **151** E 4
Tonto National Monument **116** EF 4
Tonya **155** E 2
Tonzang **175** F 3
Tooday **182** B 5
Tooele (UT.) **114** E 3
Toolik River **109** J 2
Toompine **183** G 4
Toonerville (CO.) **115** OP 6
Topano (VA.) **129** P 4
Topawa (AZ.) **116** E 6
Topaz Lake **112** F 4
Topchikha **159** Q 5
Topeka (KS.) **121** J 3
Topki **159** R 4
Topko, Gora **171** P 4
Topliţa **154** C 1

Topocalma, Punta **142** B 5
Topock (AZ.) **116** B 3
Topoli **168** E 1
Topolinyy **171** P 3
Topolobampo **106** E 6
Topolobampo, Bahia de **106** E 6
Toponas (CO.) **115** L 3
Topozero, Ozero **150** K 2
Toppenish (WA.) **110** E 4
Toprak-Kala **169** G 2
Topsail Beach (N.C.) **129** O 7
Topsfield (ME.) **126** M 3
Topton (N.C.) **128** H 6
Tora-Khem **170** G 5
Toranggekuduk **169** N 2
Toraya **140** B 3
Torbalı **154** C 3
Torbat-e Heydarīyeh **168** FG 3
Torbat-e Jām **168** G 3
Torbay **148** C 4
Torbino **158** F 4
Torch Lake **124** J 4
Tordesillas **152** BC 3
Töre **150** H 2
Töreboda **151** F 4
Torekov **151** F 4
Torenberg **148** E 4
Torey **170** H J 5
Torez **155** E 1
Torgau **149** F 4
Torgovoye **155** F 1
Tori **198** E 3
Toribulu **177** F 4
Torino **153** E 2
Tori-shima **173** LM 4
Torit **198** E 4
Torkeman, Bandar-e (Iran) **157** G 1
Torkovichi **151** K 4
Tormes **152** B 3
Torneå **150** H 2
Torneälven **150** H 2
Torneträsk **150** H 2
Torngat Mountains **105** P 4
Tornillo (TX.) **117** KL 6
Tornio **150** H 2
Tornionjoki **150** H 2
Tornquist **143** D 6
Toro, Cerro del **142** C 4
Toro, Lago del **143** B 9
Torodi **196** E 3
Toro Doum **197** H 2
Torokina **185** FG 3
Torom **171** P 5
Toroni, Cerro **140** C 4
Toronto (Ontario, Can.) **105** M 7
Toronto (S.D.) **119** M 6
Toronto (W.V.) **125** O 9
Toronto Lake **120** JK 5
Toro Peak **113** J 9
Tororo **198** E 4
Toropets **158** F 4
Toros Dağlari **155** D 3
Toros Dağlari (Turkey) **156** A 1
Torquato Severo **142** F 5
Torra Bay **200** A 4
Torra Miro, Puerto de **152** C 3
Torrance (CA.) **113** G 9
Torre Annunziata **153** F 3
Torre del Greco **153** F 3
Torre de Moncorvo **152** B 3
Torrejón de Ardoz **152** C 3
Torrelavega **152** C 3
Torre City (N.D.) **119** L 4
Torremolinos **152** C 4
Torrens, Lake **183** F 5
Torrens Creek **183** H 3
Torrens River **183** H 3
Torrente **152** C 4
Torreón **132** B 2
Tôrres **142** G 4
Torres Islands **185** J 4
Torres Islands **186** BC 3
Torres Martinez Indian Reservation **113** J 9
Torres Strait **183** G 1
Torres Strait **186** A 3
Torres Vedras **152** B 4
Torrijos **152** C 4
Torrington **183** J 4
Torrington (CT.) **126** F 7
Torrington (WY.) **118** D 8
Torröjen **150** F 3
Torsby **151** F 3
Torshälla **151** G 4
Tórshavn **148** A 1
Torsken **150** G 2
Torsö **151** F 4
Tortilla Flat (AZ.) **116** E 4
Tortkuduk **159** O 5
Tortola **130** E 8
Tortola **133** K 4
Tortona **153** E 3
Tortosa **153** D 3
Tortosa, Cabo de **152** D 3
Tortue, Ile de la **133** H 3
Tortuguero **132** F 5
Tortum **155** F 2

Torud (Iran) **157** G 2
Torugart, Pereval **169** K 2
Torul **155** E 2
Toruń **149** G 4
Torup **151** F 4
Torzhok **158** F 4
Tosashimizu **173** K 4
Tosa-wan **173** K 4
Toscana **153** F 3
Toscanini **200** A 4
Tosenfjorden **150** F 2
Tosno **151** K 4
Toson Hu **172** C 3
Tosontsengel **170** G 6
Tossa **152** D 3
Tostado **142** D 4
Tõstamaa **151** H 4
Toston (MT.) **111** O 4
Tostuya **170** K 1
Tosya **155** D 2
Totak **151** E 4
Totana **152** C 4
Toten **151** F 3
Toteng **200** C 4
Tõtias **199** G 4
Totma **158** H 4
Totness **139** G 2
Totonicapan **132** D 4–5
Totoras **142** D 5
Totota **196** C 4
Totson Mountain **108** G 3
Totten Glacier **203**
Tottori **173** K 3
Touat Oases **192** E 3
Touba (Ivory Coast) **196** C 4
Touba (Senegal) **196** A 3
Toubkal, Jbel **192** D 2
Toufourine **192** DE 4
Tougan **196** D 3
Touggourt **193** G 2
Tougué **196** B 3
Touila **192** D 3
Toukoto **196** C 3
Toul **153** E 2
Toulépleu **196** C 4
Toulon **153** E 3
Toulon (IL.) **124** E 8
Toulon Lake **112** G 2
Toulouse **152** D 3
Toumodi **196** C 4
Tounassine **192** E 3
Tounassine, Hamada **192** DE 3
Toungo **197** G 4
Toungoo **175** G 4
Toura, Monts de **196** C 4
Touraine **152** D 2
Tourassine **192** C 4
Tourcoing **152** D 1
Touriñán, Cabo **152** B 3
Tourine **192** C 4
Tournai **148** D 4
Tournavista **138** CD 5
Tournon **153** E 2
Tournus **153** DE 2
Touros **141** J 2
Tours **152** D 2
Toury **152** D 2
Tousside, Pic **197** H 1
Toussoro **198** C 3
Touws River **200** C 6
Towada **173** M 2
Towakaima **139** G 2
Towanda (PA.) **126** C 7
Towaoc (CO.) **114** J 6
Tower (WY.) **111** P 6
Tower City (N.D.) **119** L 4
Tower City (PA.) **127** C 8
Tower Hill **183** G 3
Towerhill River **183** G 3
Towne Pass **112** H 6
Towner (CO.) **115** PQ 5
Towner (ND.) **118** J 2
Townsend (MT.) **111** O 4
Townshend Island **183** J 3
Townsville **183** H 2
Towot **198** E 3
Towson (MD.) **129** P 2
Towuti, Danau **177** F 4
Towy **148** C 4
Toxkan He **169** K 2
Toy (NV.) **112** G 2
Toyah (TX.) **117** N 6
Toyahvale (TX.) **117** N 7
Toyama **173** L 3
Toygunen **102** C 2
Toyohashi **173** L 4
Toyota **173** L 3
Trabzon **155** EF 2
Tracy (CA.) **112** D 5
Tracy (MN.) **119** N 6
Tracy (MT.) **111** O 3
Trafalgar, Cabo **152** B 4
Trâghan **193** H 3
Traiguén **143** B 6
Trail **103** O 6
Trail City (SD.) **118** H 5
Trairi **141** J 1
Tralee **148** B 4
Tralee Bay **148** AB 4
Tranås **151** F 4

Trancas 142 C 4
Trancoso 152 B 3
Tranemo 151 F 4
Trang 175 G 6
Trangan, Pulau 177 H 5
Trani 153 G 3
Trans-Amazon Highway 138 D 5
Transantarctic Mountains 203
Transilvania 154 B 1
Transkei 200 D 6
Transtrand 150 F 3
Transtrandsfjällen 150 F 3
Transvaal 200 D 5
Transylvanian Alps 154 B 1–2
Trapani 153 F 4
Trapper Peak 111 L 5
Traralgon 183 H 6
Trarza 192 BC 5
Trasimeno, Lago 153 F 3
Trask Mountain 110 B 5
Trat 175 H 5
Traun 153 F 2
Traunsee 153 F 2
Travers, Mount 185 Q 9
Traverse, Lake 119 M 5
Traverse City (MI.) 124 J 5
Traverse Peak 108 G 2
Travesia 132 E 4
Travesia Puntana 142 C 5
Travis, Lake 122 E 5
Travnik 153 G 3
Trayning 182 B 5
Trbovlje 153 FG 2
Třebíč 149 G 5
Trebinje 153 G 3
Trebisacce 153 G 4
Trebišov 149 H 5
Treblinka 149 H 4
Třebon 149 F 5
Trego (NV.) 112 F 2
Trego (WI.) 124 C 4
Tregosselslets and Reefs 183 J 2
Treinta y Tres 142 EF 5
Trélazé 152 C 2
Trelew 143 CD 7
Trelleborg 151 F 4
Trementina (N.M.) 117 M 2
Tremiti, Isole 153 G 3
Tremont (PA.) 127 C 8
Tremonton (UT.) 114 EF 2
Tremp 152 D 3
Trenary (MI.) 124 H 3
Trenčín 149 G 5
Trenel 143 D 6
Trenque Lauquen 143 D 6
Trent 148 C 4
Trento 153 F 2
Trenton (FL.) 131 M 5
Trenton (GA.) 128 F 7
Trenton (MO.) 121 M 2
Trenton (N.C.) 129 O 6
Trenton (ND.) 118 E 2
Trenton (NE.) 120 D 2
Trenton (NE.) 120 D 2
Trenton (N.J.) 127 E 8
Trenton (TN.) 128 C 6
Trenton (TX.) 122 G 2
Trepassey 105 R 6
Tres Arobles 142 E 5
Tres Arroyos 143 D 6
Tres Cerros 143 C 8
Três Corações 141 GH 5
Tres Esquinas 138 CD 3
Tres Forcas, Cap 192 E 1
Três Lagoas 141 F 5
Tres Lagos 143 B 8
Tres Marías Dam 141 G 4
Tres Montes, Península 143 A 8
Tres Montosas 116 J 4
Tres Picos 132 D 4
Tres Picos, Cerro 143 D 6
Tres Piedras (N.M.) 117 L 1
Tres Puentes 142 BC 4
Três Ríos 141 H 5
Tres Zapotes 132 CD 4
Treuchtlingen 149 F 5
Treviglio 153 E 2
Treviso 153 F 2
Treze Quedas 139 G 4
Trgovište 154 B 2
Triabunna 184 L 9
Trialetskiy Khrebet 155 F 2
Tribeč Vtácnik 149 G 5
Tribune (KS.) 120 D 4
Trichur 174 C 5
Trident Peak 112 G 1
Trident Shoal 176 D 1
Trier 148 E 5
Trieste 153 F 2
Triglav 153 F 2
Trigo Mountains 116 B 4
Trikala 154 B 3
Trikhonis Limni 154 B 3
Trikomo 155 D 3
Trikomo (Cyprus) 156 AB 2
Trikomon → Trikomo 155 D 3
Trikora, Puncak 177 J 4
Trimble (CO.) 115 K 6
Trimmer (CA.) 112 F 6
Trimont (MN.) 119 O 7

Trinchera (CO.) 115 N 6
Trincomalee 174 D 6
Trindade Island 135 G 5
Třinec 149 G 5
Trinidad (Bolivia) 140 D 3
Trinidad (CA.) 112 A 1
Trinidad (CO.) 115 N 6
Trinidad (Colombia) 138 D 2
Trinidad (Cuba) 133 G 3
Trinidad (TX.) 122 G 3
Trinidad (Uruguay) 142 E 5
Trinidad, Golfo 143 A 8
Trinidad, Isla 139 F 1
Trinidad, Isla (Argentina) 143 D 6
Trinidad and Tobago 139 FG 1
Trinity (TX.) 123 H 5
Trinity Bay 105 R 6
Trinity Bay (Australia) 183 H 2
Trinity Center (CA.) 112 C 2
Trinity Dam 112 C 2
Trinity Islands 102 G 4
Trinity Mountain 111 K 7
Trinity Mountains 112 C 2
Trinity Peak 112 G 2
Trinity Range 112 G 2
Trinity River 112 B 2
Trinity River 123 J 5
Trinkitat 194 F 5
Trinway (OH.) 125 N 9
Tripoli (Lebanon) 156 B 2
Tripoli (Libya) 193 J 2
Tripolis 154 B 3
Tripolitania 193 HJ 2
Tripp (S.D.) 119 K 7
Tripura 175 F 3
Tristao, Îles 196 A 3
Trivandrum 174 C 6
Trnava 149 G 5
Trobriand Islands 186 B 3
Trobriand or Kiriwina Islands 185 F 3
Trofimov 155 F 1
Trofimovsk 171 NO 1
Trofors 150 F 2
Trogir 153 G 3
Troglav 153 G 3
Trois-Pistoles 105 O 6
Trois Rivières 105 N 6
Troitsk 159 M 5
Troitsk 170 F 4
Troitskiy 158 K 5
Troitskiy 159 O 5
Troitskiy 170 K 5
Troitsko-Pechorsk 158 L 3
Troitskoye 154 D 1
Troitskoye 158 L 5
Troitskoye 159 Q 5
Troitskoye 171 P 6
Trolla 197 G 2
Trollhättan 151 F 4
Trollheimen 150 E 3
Trollhetta 150 E 3
Trolltindane 150 E 3
Trombetas 139 G 3–4
Tromelin 189 H 6
Tromöya 151 E 4
Troms 150 G 2
Tromsö 150 G 2
Tronador, Monte 143 B 7
Trondheim 150 F 3
Trondheimsfjorden 150 F 3
Troodos 155 D 4
Troodos (Cyprus) 156 A 2
Trosa 151 G 4
Trosh 158 L 2
Trostyanets 154 C 1
Trotters (ND.) 118 E 3
Troup (TX.) 123 H 3
Trout Creek (MI.) 124 F 3
Trout Creek (MT.) 111 K 3
Trout Creek (UT.) 114 D 4
Trout Creek Pass 115 L 5
Trout Lake (MI.) 124 J 3
Trout Lake (N.W.T., Can.) 103 N 3
Trout Lake (Ontario, Can.) 104 J 5
Trout Lake (WA.) 110 D 4
Trout Peak 111 Q 6
Trout River 105 Q 6
Trout Run (PA.) 126 B 7
Troy 154 C 3
Troy (AL.) 131 J 3
Troy (ID.) 110 J 4
Troy (KS.) 121 K 3
Troy (MT.) 111 K 2
Troy (N.C.) 129 M 6
Troy (N.Y.) 126 F 6
Troy (OH.) 125 K 9
Troy (OR.) 110 H 4
Troy (PA.) 126 C 7
Troy (TX.) 122 F 4
Troyan 154 B 2
Troyanski Manastir 154 B 2
Troyekurovo 158 G 5
Troyes 152 D 2
Troy Lake 113 J 8
Troy Peak 112 JK 4
Trubchevsk 158 F 5
Truc Giang 175 J 5
Truchas (N.M.) 117 L 1

Trucial Coast (United Arab Emirates) 157 FG 4
Truckee (CA.) 112 E 3
Trudovoye 173 K 2
Trujillo (Honduras) 132 E 4
Trujillo (N.M.) 117 M 2
Trujillo (Peru) 138 C 5
Trujillo (Spain) 152 B 4
Trujillo (Venezuela) 138 D 2
Truk Islands 186 B 2
Truman (MN.) 119 O 7
Trumann (AR.) 121 P 7
Trumbull, Mount 116 C 1
Truro 105 P 6
Trusovo 158 K 2
Trussville (AL.) 128 E 8
Trust Territory of the Pacific Islands 186 AB 2
Truth or Consequences (N.M.) 117 J 4
Trutnov 149 G 4
Truva 154 C 3
Truxton (AZ.) 116 C 2
Truyére 152 D 3
Tryavna 154 C 2
Tryon (NE.) 118 GH 9
Trysil 150 F 3
Trysilelva 150 F 3
Trysilfjellet 150 F 3
Trzcianka 149 G 4
Tsagaannuur 170 E 6
Tsagaan-Uul 170 G 6
Tsagaan Üür 170 H 5
Tsagan-Nur 155 G 1
Tsageri 155 F 2
Tsaidam Basin 172 BC 3
Tsaidam Basin → Qaidam Pendi 172 BC 3
Tsala Apopka Lake 131 M 6
Tsalka 155 F 2
Tsangpo 172 B 5
Tsapelka 151 J 4
Tsaratanana 201 H 3
Tsaratanana, Massif du 201 H 2
Tsaris Mountains 200 B 4
Tsatsana 200 C 3
Tsau 200 C 4
Tsaukaib 200 B 5
Tsavo 199 F 5
Tsavo National Park 199 F 5
Tsäwah 193 H 3
Tsawisis 200 B 5
Tschida, Lake 118 G 4
Tselina 155 F 1
Tselinnoye 159 R 5
Tselinograd 159 O 5
Tsenhermandal 170 JK 6
Tsenogora 158 J 3
Tsentralno Yakutskaya Nizmen-nost' 171 MN 3
Tsentral'nyy 159 R 4
Tses 200 B 5
Tsetseg 170 F 6
Tsetserleg 170 G 6
Tsetserleg 170 H 6
Tsévié 196 E 4
Tshabong 200 C 5
Tshabuta 198 D 4
Tshane 200 C 4
Tshangalele, Lac 200 D 2
Tshela 197 G 6
Tshele 198 D 5
Tshesebe 200 D 4
Tshibamba 198 C 6
Tshikapa 198 C 6
Tshilenge 198 C 6
Tshimbulu 198 C 6
Tshkudu 200 C 4
Tshofa 198 D 6
Tshuapa 198 C 5
Tshwane 200 C 4
Tsiafajavona 201 H 3
Tsiazonano 201 H 3
Tsihombe 201 H 5
Tsimlyansk 155 F 1
Tsimlyanskoye Vodokhranilishche 155 F 1
Tsimlyanskoye Vodokhranilishche 155 F 1
Tsineng 200 C 5
Tsinghai 172 C 4
Tsingtao 173 H 3
Tsintsabis 200 B 3
Tsipa 170 L 4
Tsipanda 171 P 4
Tsipikan 170 K 5
Tsiroanomandidy 201 H 3
Tsitondroina 201 H 3
Tskhaltubo 155 F 2
Tskhinvali 155 F 2
Tsna 151 J 5
Tsna 158 H 5
Tsodilo Hills 200 C 3
Tsu 173 L 4
Tsuchiura 173 M 3
Tsugaru-kaikyō 173 M 2
Tsumeb 200 B 3
Tsumis Park 200 B 4

Tsumkwe 200 C 3
Tsuruga 173 L 3
Tsuruoka 173 L 3
Tsushima 173 JK 4
Tsuyama 173 K 3
Tsyurupinsk 155 D 1
Tua (Portugal) 152 B 3
Tua (Zaire) 198 B 5
Tual 177 H 5
Tuamotu Archipelago 187 F 4
Tuan 175 H 3
Tuangku, Pulau 176 A 3
Tuapse 155 E 2
Tuaran 176 E 2
Tuba 170 H 4
Tuba 170 F 5
Tubac (AZ.) 116 E 6
Tuba City (AZ.) 116 E 1
Tubal, Wâdi aṭ (Iraq) 156 C 2
Tuban 176 D 5
Tubarão 142 G 4
Tubayq, Jabal at (Saudi Arabia) 156 B 3
Tubbataha Reefs 177 E 2
Tubelai, Pulau 177 G 4
Tübingen 149 E 5
Tubruq 193 K 2
Tubuaï 187 F 4
Tubuai Islands 187 EF 4
Tucacas 138 E 1
Tucano 141 J 3
Tucavaca 140 E 4
Tuchola 149 G 4
Tucker (GA.) 128 G 8
Tucson (AZ.) 116 EF 5
Tucumán 117 N 2
Tucumcari (N.M.) 117 N 2
Tucunaré 139 G 5
Tucupita 139 F 2
Tucurui 139 HJ 4
Tudela 152 C 3
Tudmur (Syria) 156 C 2
Tuensang 175 F 2
Tufi 184 E 3
Tufi 186 A 3
Tugela 200 E 5
Tuguegarao 177 J 1
Tugur 171 P 5
Tuim 159 R 5
Tukangbesi, Kepulauan 177 F 5
Tukayyid (Iraq) 157 D 3
Tükrah 193 K 2
Tuktoyaktuk 102 L 2
Tukums 151 H 4
Tukuringra, Khrebet 171 N 5
Tukuyu 198 E 6
Tukzar 169 H 3
Tula (Mexico) 132 C 3
Tula (Mexico) 132 C 4
Tula (U.S.S.R.) 158 G 5
Tulai 172 C 3
Tulalip Indian Reservation 110 C 2
Tulancingo 132 C 4
Tulare (CA.) 112 F 6
Tulare (S.D.) 119 K 6
Tulare Lake Bed 112 F 6–7
Tularosa (N.M.) 117 KL 4
Tularosa Valley 117 K 5
Tulasi 178 D 4
Tulay-Kiryaka-Tas, Vozvyshen-nost' 170 JK 1
Tulbagh 200 B 6
Tulcán 138 C 3
Tulcea 154 C 1
Tulchin 154 C 1
Tule Lake 112 D 1
Tulelake (CA.) 112 D 1
Tulemalu Lake 103 RS 3
Tule River Indian Reservation 112 G 6–7
Tule Valley 114 D 4
Tuli 200 D 4
Tulia (TX.) 117 P 3
Tulihe 171 M 5
Tullahoma (TN.) 128 E 6
Tullamore 148 B 4
Tulle 152 D 2
Tullner Becken 153 G 2
Tulloch Reservoir 112 E 5
Tullus 194 C 6
Tully 183 H 2
Tulmaythah 193 K 2
Tuloma 150 K 2
Tulos, Ozero 150 K 3
Tulpan 158 L 3
Tulsa (OK.) 120 JK 6
Tuluá 138 C 3
Tulum 132 E 3
Tulun 170 H 5
Tulungagung 176 D 5
Tumacacori National Monument 116 E 6
Tumaco 138 C 3
Tumalo (OR.) 110 D 6
Tumannaya, Gora 108 B 2
Tumanovo 158 F 4
Tumanskiy 171 X 3

Tumany 171 T 3
Tumatumari 139 G 2
Tumba 151 G 4
Tumba, Lac 198 B 5
Tumbarumba 183 H 6
Tumbes 138 B 4
Tumble Mountain 111 P 5
Tumbling Waters 182 E 1
Tumcha 150 K 2
Tumd Youqi 172 F 2
Tumd Zuoqi 172 F 2
Tumen 173 J 2
Tumeremo 139 F 2
Tumkur 174 C 5
Tumnin 171 PQ 6
Tump 169 G 5
Tumpat 176 B 2
Tumtum Lake 110 G 8
Tümü 193 H 4
Tumu 196 D 3
Tumucumaque, Serra 139 H 3
Tumupasa 140 C 3
Tumwater (WA.) 110 BC 4
Tunari, Cerro 140 C 4
Tunago Lake 109 N 2
Tunas 141 G 4
Tunas, Sierra de las 106 E 6
Tunceli 155 E 3
Tundla 174 C 2
Tunduma 198 E 6
Tunduru 201 F 2
Tundzha 154 C 2
Tünel-e-Salong 169 H 3
Tunga 197 F 5
Tungabhadra 174 C 4
Tungaru 194 E 6
Tungku 177 E 2
Tungnaá 150 B 3
Tungokochen 170 KL 5
Tungsten 102 M 3
Tunguska, Nizhnyaya 170 F 2
Tunguska, Podkamennaya 170 FG 3
Tungus-Khaya 171 N 3
Tünhel 170 J 6
Tuni 174 D 4
Tunica (MS.) 121 P 8
Tūnis 193 GH 1
Tunisia 193 GH 2
Tunja 138 D 2
Tunkhannock (PA.) 126 C 7
Tunnhovdfjorden 151 E 3
Tununak 102 D 3
Tununguayualok 105 P 4
Tunuyan 142 C 5
Tunxi 173 G 5
Tuolumne (CA.) 112 E 5
Tuóroyri 148 A 1
Tuostakh 171 P 2
Tuotuo He 172 B 4
Tuotuo Heyan 172 B 4
Tupá 141 F 5
Tupaciguara 141 G 4
Tupancireitá 142 F 4
Tupelo (MS.) 121 R 8
Tupelo (OK.) 120 J 8
Tupik 170 L 5
Tupinambaranas, Ilha 139 G 4
Tupirama 139 J 5
Tupirantins 139 J 5
Tupiza 140 C 5
Tupper Lake (N.Y.) 126 E 4
Tuquan 173 H 1
Túquerres 138 C 3
Tura (India) 175 F 2
Tura (Tanzania) 198 E 6
Tura (U.S.S.R.) 159 M 4
Tura (U.S.S.R.) 170 H 3
Turabah 193 H 4
Turabah (Saudi Arabia) 156 D 3
Turagua, Serranías 139 F 2
Turakh 170 M 1
Turallin 183 J 4
Turama 170 G 3
Turan 170 F 5
Türän (Iran) 157 G 2
Turana, Khrebet 171 O 5
Turanskaya Nizmennost 168–169 FG 2
Turbaco 138 C 1
Turbat 169 G 5
Turbeville (S.C.) 129 L 8
Turbo 138 C 2
Turda 149 B 2
Türeh (Iran) 157 E 2
Tureia 187 F 4
Turek 149 G 4
Turell (AR.) 121 P 7
Turen 138 E 2
Turfan Depression 172 A 2
Turgay 169 G 1
Turgay 169 G 1
Turgayskaya Dolina 159 M 5–6
Turgayskaya Stolovaya Strana 159 M 5
Türgen Uul 170 F 6
Türgovishte 154 C 2
Turgutlu 154 C 2
Turhal 155 E 2
Türi 151 J 4

Turia 152 C 4
Turiaçu 139 J 4
Turin 153 E 2–3
Turinsk 159 M 4
Turiy Rog 173 K 1
Turka 170 J 5
Turkana 198 F 4
Turkana, Lake 199 F 4
Turkannakh 170 MN 1
Turkestan 169 H 2
Turkestanskiy Khrebet 169 H 3
Turkey 155 DE 3
Turkey (TX.) 117 Q 3
Turkey Mountain 122 C 6
Turkey Ridge 119 L 7
Turkey River 119 R 7–8
Türkiiye 155 DE 3
Türkoğlu 155 E 3
Turks and Caicos Islands 133 HJ 3
Turks Island Passage 133 H 3
Turks Islands 133 H 3
Turku (Åbo) 151 H 3
Turkwel 198 F 4
Turley (N.M.) 116 J 1
Turley (OK.) 120 JK 6
Turlock (CA.) 112 E 5
Turlock Lake 112 E 5
Turmus, Wādī aṭ (Saudi Arabia) 156 D 4
Turnbull, Mount 116 F 4
Turneffe Islands 132 E 4
Turner (MT.) 111 R 2
Turner (WA.) 110 H 4
Turner River 182 D 2
Turnu Măgurele 154 BC 2
Turnu Roşu, Pasul 154 B 1
Turobay 159 P 6
Turochak 159 R 5
Turon (KS.) 120 G 5
Turpan 172 A 2
Turpan Pendi 172 A 2
Turpan Zhan 169 M 2
Turpin (OK.) 120 E 6
Turret Peak 116 E 3
Tursha 158 J 4
Turtkul' 169 G 2
Turtle Flambeau Flowage 124 D 3
Turtle Islands 196 B 4
Turtle Lake (ND.) 118 H 3
Turtle Lake (WI.) 124 B 4
Turtle Mountain Indian Reservation 118 J 2
Turtle Mountains 118 H 2
Turugart Shankou 169 K 2
Turukhan 159 QR 2
Turukhansk 159 R 2
Turukta 170 L 3
Tusayan (AZ.) 116 D 1—2
Tuscaloosa (AL.) 128 D 8
Tuscarawas River 125 N 9
Tuscarora (NV.) 112 J 1
Tuscarora Mountain (PA.) 127 B 8
Tuscarora Mountains (NV.) 112 J 1–2
Tuscola (IL.) 121 R 3
Tuscola (TX.) 122 D 3
Tuscumbia (AL.) 128 D 7
Tuscumbia (MO.) 121 N 4
Tuskegee (AL.) 131 J 2
Tustumena Lake 109 H 3
Tutak 155 F 3
Tutayev 158 G 4
Tuticorin 174 C 6
Tutóia 141 H 1
Tutonchana 170 F 2
Tutonchana, Vozvyshennost' 170 FG 2–3
Tutonchany 170 F 3
Tutrakan 154 C 2
Tuttle (ND.) 118 J 3
Tuttle Creek Lake 120 J 3
Tüttlingen 149 E 5
Tutubu 198 E 6
Tutuila 186 D 3
Tutupaca, Volcán 140 BC 4
Tututalak Mountains 108 F 2
Tutuwang 177 GH 5
Tutuwawang 184 A 3
Tutwiler (MS.) 121 P 8
Tuul Gol 170 H 6
Tuvalu 186 D 3
Tuwayq, Jabal 195 H 4
Ṭuwayq, Jabal (Saudi Arabia) 157 D 4
Tuxedo (TX.) 122 CD 3
Tuxpán 132 A 3
Tuxpan de Rodríguez Cano 132 C 3
Tuxtla Gutiérrez 132 D 4
Tuy 152 B 3
Tuyen Quang 175 J 3
Tuy Hoa 175 J 5
Tuymazy 158 K 5
Tüyserkān (Iran) 157 E 2
Tuz Gölü 155 D 3
Tuzigoot National Monument 116 E 3
Tuzla 153 G 3
Tuzla 155 DE 3

Tuzluca 155 F 2
Tuzly 154 CD 1
Tvedestrand 151 E 4
Twain (CA.) 112 D 2
Twain Harte (CA.) 112 E 4
Tweed 148 C 3
Tweedsmuir Hills 148 C 3
Tweedy Mountain 111 N 5
Twee Rivieren 200 BC 5
Twentynine Palms (CA.) 113 JK 8
Twichell (TX.) 117 Q 1
Twin Bridges (MT.) 111 N 5
Twin Buttes 110 C 6
Twin Buttes Reservoir 122 C 4
Twin City (GA.) 131 M 2
Twin Falls (ID.) 111 L 8
Twin Falls (Newfoundl., Can.) 105 P 5
Twin Islands 105 L 5
Twin Lake (MI.) 124 H 6
Twin Lakes (CO.) 115 L 4
Twin Mills 108 F 4
Twin Peaks 111 L 6
Twin Valley (MN.) 119 M 3
Twitchell Reservoir 113 E 7–8
Twitty (TX.) 117 Q 2
Twitya River 109 N 3
Two Buttes (CO.) 115 P 6
Two Buttes Reservoir 115 P 6
Twodot (MT.) 111 P 4
Two Guns (AZ.) 116 E 2
Two Rivers (WI.) 124 G 5
Two Rivers Reservoir 117 M 4
Tyan'-Shan' 169 JK 2
Tyatino 173 N 2
Tychkino 159 P 4
Tychy 149 G 4
Tydal 150 F 3
Tygart Lake 129 M 2
Tygda 171 N 5
Tygh Valley (OR.) 110 D 5
Tyk 171 Q 5
Tyler (MN.) 119 M 6
Tyler (TX.) 123 H 4
Tyler (WA.) 110 H 3
Tylertown (MS.) 130 D 3
Tylkhoy 171 U 3
Tylösand 151 F 4
Tym 159 Q 4
Tymovskoye 171 Q 5
Tynda 171 M 4
Tyndall (S.D.) 119 L 7
Tyne 148 C 4
Tynset 150 F 3
Tyonek 109 H 3
Tyräjärvi 150 J 2
Tyre (Lebanon) 156 B 2
Tyrifjorden 151 F 4
Tyrma 171 O 5
Tyrma 171 O 5
Tyrone (CO.) 115 N 6
Tyrone (OK.) 120 D 6
Tyrone (PA.) 125 Q 9
Tyrrell Lake 103 QR 3
Tyrrhenian Sea 153 F 3–4
Tyry 171 P 3
Tysnesöy 151 E 3–4
Tysse 151 E 3
Tyssedal 151 E 3
Tyubelyakh 171 Q 2
Tyugene 171 N 3
Tyugene 171 N 3
Tyuguren 171 Q 2
Tyukalinsk 159 O 4
Tyukhtet 159 R 4
Tyul'-Bannovka 169 J 2
Tyulen'i, Ostrova 168 E 1–2
Tyul'gan 158 L 5
Tyumen' 159 N 4
Tyumsyu 171 Q 3
Tyung 170 L 2
Tyungulyu 171 O 3
Tyuntyugur 159 MN 5
Tzaneen 200 DE 4

U

Uad el Jat 192 C 3
Ua Huka 187 F 3
Ua Pu 187 F 3
Uatumá 139 G 4
Uauá 141 J 2
Uaupés 138 E 3
Uaupés 138 E 4
Uaxactún 132 D 4
Ubá 141 H 5
Ubagan 159 N 5
Ubā'ila (Iraq) 156 C 2
Ubaitaba 141 J 3
Ubangi 198 B 4
'Ubayyid, Wādī al (Iraq) 156 CD 2
Ube 173 K 4
Ubeda 152 C 4
Uberaba 141 G 4

Uberaba, Laguna 140 E 4
Uberlândia 141 G 4
Ubiaja 197 F 4
Ubinskoye, Ozero 159 Q 4
Ubiyenka 171 W 2
Ubolratna Dam 175 H 4
Ubombo 201 E 5
Ubon Ratchathani 175 HJ 4
Ubort' 151 J 5
Ubundi 198 D 5
Ucayali 138 D 5
Uch 169 J 5
Uchaly 159 L 5
Uchami 170 F 3
Uch-Aral 159 Q 6
Uchiura-wan 173 M 2
Uch Kuduk 169 G 2
Uchkulan 155 F 2
Uchur 171 O 4
Učka 153 F 2
Ucolo (UT.) 114 HJ 6
Uda 171 O 5
Udachnaya 170 K 2
Udaipur 174 B 3
Udamalpet 174 C 5
Udanna 171 Q 2
Udaquilla 143 E 6
Udayagiri 174 C 5
Udbina 153 G 3
Uddevalla 151 F 4
Uddjaure 150 G 2
Udgir 174 C 4
Udhampur 169 K 4
Udialla 182 C 2
Udine 153 F 2
Udipi 174 B 5
Udokan, Khrebet 170 L 4
Udon Thani 175 H 4
Udskaya Guba 171 P 5
Udskoye 171 O 5
Udyl', Ozero 171 P 5
Udzha 170 L 1
Uebi Scebeli → Webi Shābelle 199 G 4
Uebonti 177 F 4
Ueda 171 L 3
Uele 198 C 4
Uelen 102 CD 2
Uel'kal' 102 AB 2
Uelzen 149 F 4
Uengan, Mys 159 N 1
Uere 198 D 4
Ufa 158 L 4
Ufa 158 L 5
Ugab 200 A 4
Ugagli 171 N 5
Ugalla 198 E 6
Ugalla 198 E 6
Ugalla River Game Reserve 198 E 6
Uganda 198 E 4
Ugarit (Syria) 156 B 2
Ugashik 102 F 4
Ughelli 197 F 4
Uglegorsk 171 Q 6
Uglekamensk 173 K 2
Uglich 158 G 4
Uglovoya 171 NO 5
Ugol'naya 171 X 3
Ugolnyy 108 B 3
Ugoyan 171 N 4
Ugulan 171 T 3
Ugumun 170 L 2
Ugun 171 N 4
Ugut 159 O 3
Uherské Hradiště 149 G 5
Uig 148 B 3
Uíge 200 B 1
Uil 158 E 1
Uilpata 155 F 2
Uiñaimarca, Lago 140 C 4
Uinta and Ouray Indian Reservation 114 G 3–H 4
Uinta Mountains 114 GH 3
Uis Mine 200 AB 4
Uitenhage 200 D 6
Ujae 186 C 2
Ujarrás 132 F 6
Ujelang 186 B 2
Ujiji 198 D 6
Ujjain 174 C 3
Ujung 177 F 5
Ujunglamuru 177 F 4
Ujungpandang 177 E 4–5
Uk 170 G 4
Uka 171 U 4
Ukara 198 E 5
Ukelayat 171 W 3
Ukerewe 198 E 5
Ukhaydir (Iraq) 156 D 2
Ukholovo 158 H 5
Ukhta 158 K 3
Ukiah (CA.) 112 B 3
Ukiah (OR.) 110 G 5
Ukivok 108 E 3
Ukmergé 151 HJ 4
Ukm 158 J 3

Uku 200 A 2
Ukuma 200 B 2
Ukwaa 198 E 3
Ula 154 C 3
Ulaanbaatar 170 J 6
Ulaangom 170 F 6
Ulaanhus 170 E 6
Ulaga 171 O 2
Ulakhan Botuobuya 170 K 3
Ulakhan-Cistay, Khrebet 171 QR 2–3
Ulakhan-Kyugel' 170 KL 3
Ulakhan-Sis, Kryazh 171 S 1–2
Ulakhe 173 K 2
Ulamba 198 C 6
Ulan 172 C 3
Ulan Bator 170 J 6
Ulanbel 169 J 2
Ulan-Burgasy, Khrebet 170 J 5
Ulan-Khol 155 G 1
Ulansuhai Nur 172 E 2
Ulan-Ude 170 J 5
Ulan Ul Hu 172 B 4
Ularunda 183 H 4
Ulaş 155 E 3
Ulastay 169 M 2
Ulawa 185 H 3
Ul'ba 159 Q 5
Ul'beya 171 Q 3
Ulchin 173 J 3
Ulcinj 154 A 2
Uleåborg 150 HJ 3
Ulefoss 151 E 4
Ulety 170 K 5
Ulga, Jabal al 153 E 4
Ulhasnagar 174 B 4
Uliastay 170 G 6
Uliga 186 C 2
Ulindi 198 D 5
Ullapool 148 B 3
Ullared 151 F 4
Ullatti 150 H 2
Ulldecona 152 D 3
Ullen (MN.) 119 M 3
Ullin (IL.) 121 Q 5
Ullsfjorden 150 G 2
Ullūng-do 173 K 3
Ulm 149 E 5
Ulm (MT.) 111 O 3
Ulm (WY.) 118 B 6
Ulmeni 154 C 1
Ulmer (S.C.) 129 K 8
Ulovo 171 S 1
Ulongué 201 E 2
Ulu 177 G 3
Ulu 194 E 6
Ulubat Gölü 154 C 2
Uludağ 154 C 2–3
Ulugqat 169 J 3
Ulukişla 155 D 3
Ulunga 171 P 6
Ulungur He 169 M 1
Ulungur Hu 169 M 1
Ulunkhan 170 K 5
Ulupalakua (HI.) 113 F 11
Ulus 155 D 2
Ulutau, Gory 169 H 1
Ulvön 150 G 3
Ul'ya 171 Q 4
Ulya 171 Q 4
Ul'yankovo 158 J 4
Ul'yanovsk 158 J 5
Ul'yanovskoye 159 O 5
Ulysses (KS.) 120 D 5
Ulysses (NE.) 120 H 1
Uma 170 M 5
Uman' 154 D 1
Umanak 202
Ūmánaq 105 T 3
Umari 177 J 4
Umarkot 169 HJ 5
Umatilla (OR.) 110 F 5
Umatilla, Lake 110 F 5
Umatilla Indian Reservation 110 G 5
Umba 150 K 2
Umbagog Lake 126 H 4
Umbarger (TX.) 117 O 3
Umboi 184 E 3
Umboi 186 A 3
Umbozero, Ozero 150 KL 2
Umbria 153 F 3
Umeå 150 H 3
Umeälven 150 G 3
Umiat 102 G 2
Umikoa (HI.) 113 G 12
Umma (Iraq) 157 D 3
Umm al 'Abīd 193 J 3
Umm al Arānib 193 H 3
'Umm al Armad (Qatar) 157 F 4
Umm al Birak (Saudi Arabia) 156 C 5
Umm al Ḥayt, Wādī 195 J 5
Umm al Jamājim (Saudi Arabia) 157 D 4

Umm al Qaywayn (United Arab Emirates) 157 G 4
'Umm al Sheif (United Arab Emirates) 157 F 4
Umm as Samīm 195 K 4
'Umm aṭ Ṭūz (Iraq) 156 D 2
Umm az Zumūl (United Arab Emirates) 157 G 5
Umm Bāb (Qatar) 157 F 4
Umm Badr 194 D 6
Umm Bel 194 D 6
Umm Buru 194 C 5
Umm Dafok 194 C 6
Umm Dhibbān 194 DE 6
Umm Durmān 194 E 5
Umm Hagar 199 F 2
Umm Haraz 194 C 6
Umm Inderaba 194 E 5
Umm Kaddādah 194 D 6
Umm Lahai 194 D 5
Umm Lajj (Saudi Arabia) 156 B 4
Umm Qawzayn 194 D 6
Umm Rumaylah 194 E 5
Umm Ruwābah 194 E 6
'Umm Saïd (Qatar) 157 F 4
Umm Sayyālah 194 E 6
Umm Urūmah (Saudi Arabia) 156 B 4
Umnak 108 E 5
Umnak Passage 108 E 5
Umnyn Syverma, Khrebet 170 GH 2
Umpilua 201 F 2
Umpqua (OR.) 110 B 7
Umpqua River 110 B 7
Umpulo 200 B 2
Umraniye 154 D 3
Ums 200 B 4
Umtali → Mutare 201 E 3
Umtata 200 D 6
Umuarama 141 F 5
Umvuma 201 E 3
Una 141 J 4
Una (Yugoslavia) 153 G 2
Unadilla (GA.) 131 L 2
Unaí 141 G 4
Unai Pass 169 H 4
Unalakleet 108 F 3
Unalakleet River 108 FG 3
Unalaska 108 E 5
Unari 150 J 2
Unayzah (Jordan) 156 B 3
'Unayzah (Saudi Arabia) 156 D 4
Uncompahgre Peak 115 K 5
Uncompahgre Plateau 115 JK 5
Underberg 200 D 5
Underwood (ND.) 118 GH 3
Underwood (TX.) 117 P 3–4
Undva Neem 151 H 4
Undyulyung 171 N 2
Unecha 158 E 5
Uneiuxi 138 E 4
Ung, Jabal al 153 E 4
Unga 108 F 4
Ungava, Péninsule d' 105 MN 4
Ungava Bay 105 O 4
Ungwatiri 194 F 5
Uniabmund 200 A 4
União (Acre, Brazil) 138 D 5
União (Maranhão, Brazil) 141 H 1
União dos Palmares 141 J 2
União do Vitória 142 F 4
Unije 153 F 3
Unimak 102 E 5
Unimak Pass 102 E 5
Unini 139 F 4
Unión 143 C 6
Union (LA.) 123 N 5
Union (MO.) 121 O 4
Union (MS.) 130 E 2
Union (N.J.) 127 E 8
Union (OR.) 110 H 5
Union (S.C.) 129 K 7
Union (TX.) 117 PQ 5
Union (W.A.) 110 B 3
Union (W.V.) 129 L 4
Union Center (SD.) 118 F 6
Union Church (MS.) 130 D 3
Union City (GA.) 128 G 8
Union City (OH.) 125 K 9
Union City (PA.) 125 P 8
Union City (TN.) 128 BC 5
Union Creek (OR.) 110 C 8
Uniondale 200 C 6
Union Gap (WA.) 110 E 4
Union of Soviet Socialist Republics 158–171
Union Point (GA.) 128 HJ 8
Union Springs (AL.) 131 J 2
Uniontown (AL.) 130 G 2
Uniontown (KY.) 128 D 4
Uniontown (PA.) 125 P 10
Uniontown (WA.) 110 H 4
Union Valley Reservoir 112 E 4
Unionville (MI.) 125 L 6
Unionville (MO.) 121 MN 2
Unionville (NV.) 112 GH 2
United Arab Emirates 157 FG 5

United Kingdom 148 DC 3–4
United States 106–107
Unitsa 158 FG 3
Unity 103 Q 5
Unity (ME.) 126 K 4
Unity (OR.) 110 G 6
Universal City (TX.) 122 E 6
Universales, Montes 152 C 3
University City (MO.) 121 P 4
Unkyur 171 O 2
'Unnab, Wādi al (Jordan) 156 B 3
Unnao 174 D 2
Unst 148 C 2
Unuli Horog 172 B 3
Ünye 155 E 2
Unzba 158 H 4
Unzha 158 H 4
Uoyan 170 K 4
Upalco (UT.) 114 G 3
Upanu 171 X 3
Upar Ghat 174 D 3
Upata 139 F 2
Upemba, Lac 198 D 6
Upemba National Park 198 D 6
Upernavik 202
Upham (ND.) 118 H 2
Upham (N.M.) 117 JK 5
Upi 177 F 2
Upington 200 C 5
Upolu 186 D 3
Upolu Point 113 G 11
Upper Arlington (OH.) 125 L 9
Upper Klamath Lake 110 D 8
Upper Lake 112 E 1
Upper Lake (CA.) 112 C 3
Upper Liard 109 N 3
Upper Lough Erne 148 B 4
Upper Marlboro (MD.) 129 P 3
Upper Red Lake 119 O 2
Upper Ugashik Lake 108 G 4
Uppland 151 G 3
Uppsala 151 G 4
Upshi 169 K 4
Upton (WY.) 118 D 6
'Uqlat aṣ Ṣuqūr (Saudi Arabia) 156 C 4
Ur 195 H 2
Uracoa 139 F 2
Urad Qianqi 172 E 2
Urad Zhonghou Lianheqi 172 E 2
Ura Guba 150 K 2
Urak 171 Q 4
Ural 168 E 1
Ural Mountains 159 LM 2–4
Uralovka 171 N 5
Ural'sk 158 K 5
Urambo 198 E 6
Urandangie 183 F 3
Urandi 141 H 3
Urangan 183 J 4
Uranium City 103 Q 4
Uraricoera 139 F 3
Uraricoera 139 F 3
Ura-Tyube 169 H 3
Uravan (CO.) 114 J 5
'Uray'irah (Saudi Arabia) 157 E 4
'Urayq, Nafūd al 195 G 3–4
Urbana (IL.) 124 F 9
Urbana (OH.) 125 L 9
Urbandale (IA.) 119 P 9
Urbano Santos 141 H 1
Urbino 153 F 3
Urco 138 D 4
Urcos 140 B 3
Urdzhar 159 Q 6
Uré 138 C 2
Ureki 155 F 2
Uren 158 J 4
Urengoy 159 P 2
Urewera National Park 185 R 8
Urez 159 P 4
'Urf, Jabal al (Egypt) 156 A 4
Urfa 155 E 3
Urfa Platosu 155 E 3
Urgamal 170 F 6
Urgench 168 FG 2
Urgel, Llano de 152 D 3
Ürgüp 155 D 3
Urgut 169 H 3
Urho 169 M 1
Ürī 193 J 4
Uribe 138 D 3
Uribia 138 D 1
Urich (MO.) 121 LM 4
Urimán 139 F 2
Uritskoye 159 N 5
Uritskoye 171 M 3
Urjala 150 H 3
Urkan 171 N 5
Urla 154 C 3
Urlu Dağ 155 D 2
Urluk 170 J 5
Urmannyy 159 N 3
Urmi 171 O 5
Urmia, Lake → Daryācheh-ye Orūmīyeh 168 D 3
Urninskoye Boloto 159 O 4
Uromi 197 F 4
Uroševac 154 B 2
Urrao 138 C 2

Ursa (IL.) 124 C 9
Urshult 151 FG 4
Ursine (NV.) 112 L 5
Ur Suq ash Shuyūkh (Iraq) 157 DE 3
Ursus 149 H 4
Uruaçu 141 G 3
Uruana 141 FG 4
Uruapan 132 B 4
Urubamba 140 B 3
Urubamba 140 B 3
Urubu 139 G 4
Urubupunga Dam 141 F 5
Urubuquara, Serra 139 H 4
Urucará 139 G 4
Urucu 139 F 4
Uruçuca 141 J 3
Uruçuí 141 H 2
Uruçui, Serra do 141 H 2
Urucuia 141 G 4
Uruçui Prêto 141 GH 2
Urucurituba 139 G 4
Uruguaiana 142 E 4
Uruguay 142 E 5
Uruguay 142 E 5
Uruk (Iraq) 157 D 3
Urul'ga 170 KL 5
Urumchi 169 M 2
Urumkuveem 108 A 2
Ürümqi 169 M 2
Urup 155 F 2
Urup, Ostrov 171 S 6
Urusha 171 M 5
Urutágua 141 G 3
Uruwira 198 E 6
Uruzgan 169 H 4
Uryung-Khaya 170 KL 1
Uryupinsk 158 H 5
Urzhum 158 J 4
Urziceni 154 C 2
Usa 159 M 2
Uşak 154 C 3
Usakos 200 B 4
Usal'gin 171 P 5
Usambara Mountains 199 F 5
Usborne, Mount 143 E 9
Ušče 154 B 2
Usedom 149 F 4
'Ushayrah 195 G 4
'Ushayrah (Saudi Arabia) 157 DE 4
Ushirombo 198 E 5
Ushkan'iy, Gory 171 X 2
Ushki 171 U 4
Ushki, Zaliv 171 R 4
Ushuaia 143 C 9
Ushumun 171 N 5
Ushurakchan, Gory 171 U 2
Usibelli 109 J 3
Usina 139 H 5
Usinge 198 E 6
Usk (WA.) 110 H 2
Uska 174 D 2
Üsküdar 154 C 2
Usman 158 GH 5
Usmas ezers 151 H 4
Usoke 198 E 6
Usol'ye 152 L 4
Usol'ye-Sibirskoye 170 H 5
Uspenka 159 P 5
Uspenskiy 159 O 6
Uspenskoye 155 F 2
U.S.S.R. 155 F 1
Ussuri 171 O 6
Ussuriysk 173 K 2
Ust'-Allakh 171 T 4
Ust'-Amginskoye 171 O 3
Ust'-Barguzin 170 JK 5
Ust'-Bokhapcha 171 S 3
Ust'-Bol'sheretsk 171 ST 5
Ust'-Charky 171 P 2
Ust'-Chayka 170 J 3
Ust'-Chernaya 158 K 3
Ust'-Chona 170 G 3
Ust'-Dzhegutinskaya 155 F 2
Uster 153 E 2
Usti 149 F 4
Ustica 153 F 4
Ust'-Ilimpeya 170 HJ 3
Ust'-Ilimsk 170 H 4
Ust'-Ilimskiy Vodokhranilishche 170 H 4
Ustinovka 155 D 1
Ust'-Ishim 159 O 4
Ustka 149 G 4
Ust-Kada 170 H 4
Ust'-Kamchatsk 171 U 4
Ust'-Kamenogorsk 159 Q 6
Ust'-Kamo 170 G 3
Ust'-Kan 170 F 4
Ust'-Karabula 170 G 4
Ust'-Karenga 170 L 5
Ust'-Karsk 170 L 5
Ust'-Katav 158 K 4
Ust'-Khayryuzovo 171 T 4
Ust'-Kolik'yegan 159 P 3

Ust'-Kulom 158 K 3
Ust'-Kut 170 J 4
Ust'-Kuyga 171 P 2
Ust-Labinsk 155 EF 1
Ust'-Luga 151 J 4
Ust'-Lyzha 158 L 2
Ust'-Maya 171 O 3
Ust'-Mayn 171 W 3
Ust'-Mil' 171 O 4
Ust'-Nem 158 K 3
Ust'-Nera 171 Q 3
Ust'-Olenëk 170 L 1
Ust'-Omchug 171 R 3
Ust'-Ordynskiy 170 HJ 5
Ust'-Ozernoye 159 R 4
Ust'-Paden'ga 158 H 3
Ust'-Penzhino 171 V 3
Ust'-Pit 170 F 4
Ust'-Port 159 Q 2
Ust'-Reka 158 J 3
Ust'-Shchugor 158 L 3
Ust'-Sopochnoye 171 T 4
Ust'-Sugoy 171 S 3
Ust'-Tatta 171 O 3
Ust'-Tigil 171 T 4
Ust'-Tsil'ma 158 K 2
Ust'-Tym 159 Q 4
Ust'-Ulagan 159 R 5
Ust'-Umal'ta 171 O 5
Ust'-Un'ya 171 N 5
Ust'-Ura 158 H 3
Ust'-Urgal 171 O 5
Ust'Urov 170 M 5
Ust'-Us 170 F 5
Ust'-Usa 158 L 2
Ust Usa 158 J 5
Ust'-Uyskoye 159 M 5
Ust'-Vaga 158 H 3
Ust'-Voyampolka 171 T 4
Ust'-Vym' 158 K 3
Ust'-Vyyskaya 158 J 3
Ust'-Yudoma 171 P 4
Ust'-Yuribey 159 N 2
Usu 169 L 2
Usulután 132 E 5
Usumacinta, Rio 132 D 4
Utah 114
Utah Lake 114 F 3
Utajärvi 150 J 3
Utara, Pulau 176 B 4
Utata 170 H J 5
Ute (IA.) 119 N 8
Ute Mountain Indian Reservation 114 J 6
Utena 151 J 4
Ute Reservoir 117 N 2
Utës 159 P 5
Utesiki 171 W 2
Utete 199 F 6
Uthai Thani 175 H 4
Uthal 169 H 5
Uthumphon Phisai 175 H 5
Utiariti 140 E 3
Utica (KS.) 120 E 4
Utica (MS.) 130 D 4
Utica (MT.) 111 P 4
Utica (N.Y.) 126 D 5
Utica (OH.) 125 M 9
Utiel 152 C 4
Utik 159 P 5
Utirik 186 C 2
Utkholok 171 T 4
Utlängan 151 G 4
Utleyville (CO.) 115 OP 6
Utopia 182 E 3
Utopia (TX.) 122 D 6
Utorgosh 151 K 4
Utrecht 148 E E 4
Utrera 152 B 4
Utsjoki 150 J 2
Utsunomiya 173 L 3
Utta 158 J 5
Uttaradit 175 H 4
Uttar Pradesh 174 D 2
Uttyakh 171 O 2
Utukok 102 E 2
Utulik 170 H J 5
Utupua 185 J 4
Utupua 186 C 3
Uulbayan 172 F 1
Uuldza 170 K 6
Uuldza Gol 170 K 6
Uusikaarlepyy 150 H 3
Uusikaupunki (Nystad) 151 H 3
Uusimaa 151 H 3
Uva 158 K 4
Uvá (Goiás, Brazil) 141 F 4
Uvada (NV.) 112 LM 5
Uvak 108 M 4
Uvalda (GA.) 131 M 2
Uvalde (TX.) 122 D 6
Uvarovo 158 H 5
Uvdal 151 E 3
Uvéa 186 D 3
Uvinza 198 E 6
Uvira 198 D 5
Uvs Nuur 170 F 5
Uwajima 173 K 4

Uwayl 198 D 3
'Uwaynāt, Jabal al 194 D 4
'Uwaynāt, Tall (Iraq) 156 D 1
'Uwayrid, Ḥarrat al 194 F 3
Uxin Qi 172 E 3
Uxituba 139 G 4
Uxmal 132 E 3
Uy 159 M 5
Uyandi 171 Q 2
Uyandina 171 QR 2
Uyar 170 F 4
Uyĕdey 159 P 1
Uyega 171 Q 3
Uyo 197 F 4
Üyönch 170 F 6
Uyuk 169 J 2
Uyuni 140 C 5
Uyuni, Salar de 140 C 5
Uzbekistan 169 GH 2
Uzbel Shankou 169 J 3
Uzen 168 E 2
Uzerche 152 D 2
Uzh 151 J 5
Uzhgorod 154 B 1
Uzhur 159 R 4
Üzī 193 J 4
Uzlovaya 158 G 5
Üzü 193 J 4
Uzungwa 199 F 6
Uzunköprü 154 C 2
Uzynkair 169 G 2

V

Vääksy 150 J 3
Vaal 200 C 5
Vaala 150 J 3
Vaal Dam 200 D 5
Vaalwater 200 D 4
Vaasa (Vasa) 150 H 3
Vác 154 A 1
Vacaria 142 F 4
Vacaville (CA.) 112 CD 4
Vadodara 174 B 3
Vadsø 150 J 1
Vadstena 151 FG 4
Vaduz 153 E 2
Vaga 158 H 3
Vågåmo 150 E 3
Vågar 148 A 1
Vågåvatn 150 E 3
Vaggeryd 151 F 4
Vaghena 185 G 3
Vågsøy 150 D 3
Váh 149 G 5
Vahitahi 187 F 4
Vaiden (MS.) 121 Q 9
Vaigai 174 C 6
Vail (AZ.) 116 F 5
Vail (IA.) 119 N 8
Vailjapur 174 B 4
Vainikkala 150 J 3
Vairaatea 187 F 4
Vaitupu 186 C 3
Vakarevo 171 W 3
Vakh 159 P 3
Vaknavolok 150 JK 3
Vaku 197 G 7
Valaam 150 K 3
Valaam, Ostrov 150 K 3
Valachia 154 BC 2
Valasské Meziříčí 149 G 5
Valchelta 143 C 7
Valday 158 F 4
Valdayskaya Vozvyshennost' 158 F 4
Valdecañas, Embalse de 152 B 4
Val de Loire 152 D 2
Valdemarsvik 151 G 4
Valdepeñas 152 C 4
Valderaduey 152 BC 3
Valdés, Península 143 D 7
Valdez (AK.) 102 H 3
Valdez (N.M.) 117 L 1
Val-d'Isère 153 E 2
Valdivia (Chile) 143 B 6
Valdivia (Colombia) 138 C 2
Val-d'Or 105 M 6
Valdosta (GA.) 131 L 4
Vale 155 F 2
Vale (OR.) 110 H 7
Vale (SD.) 118 E 6
Valea lui Mihai 154 B 1
Valença 141 J 3
Valença do Piauí 141 H 2
Valence 153 DE 3
Valence-d'Apen 152 D 3
Valencia 138 E 1–2
Valencia (Spain) 152 C 4
Valencia, Golfo de 152 D 4
Valencia de Alcántara 152 B 4
Valenciennes 152 D 1
Vălenii de Munte 154 C 1

Valentin 173 K 2
Valentine (AZ.) 116 C 2
Valentine (MT.) 111 R 3
Valentine (NE.) 118 H 8
Valentine (TX.) 117 M 7
Valera 138 D 2
Valga 151 J 4
Valier (MT.) 111 N 2
Valjevo 154 B 2
Valkeakoski 150 H 3
Valladolid (Mexico) 132 E 3
Valladolid (Spain) 152 C 3
Vall de Uxó 152 C 4
Vallecito (CO.) 115 K 6
Vallecito Reservoir 115 K 6
Valle de la Pascua 138 E 2
Valle de Topia 132 A 2
Valle de Zaragoza 106 E 6
Valledupar 138 D 1
Vallée de l'Azaouak 196 E 2
Valle Edén 142 E 5
Vallée du Tilemsi 196 E 2
Valle Grande 140 D 4
Valle Hermoso 132 C 2
Vallejo (CA.) 112 C 4
Valle Longitudinal 143 B 6
Vallenar 142 B 4
Valle Salado 132 B 3
Valletta 153 F 4
Valley (NE.) 120 J 1
Valley (WA.) 110 H 2
Valley (WY.) 111 Q 6
Valley Center (CA.) 113 HJ 9
Valley Center (KS.) 120 H 5
Valley City (N.D.) 119 K 4
Valley Falls (KS.) 121 K 3
Valley Falls (OR.) 110 E 8
Valley Farm (TX.) 117 N 6
Valleyfield 105 N 6
Valley Head (W.V.) 129 L 3
Valley Mills (TX.) 122 F 4
Valley Springs (CA.) 112 E 4
Valley Springs (S.D.) 119 M 7
Valley Station (KY.) 128 EF 3
Valleyview (Alberta, Can.) 103 O 4
Valley View (TX.) 122 F 2
Vallgrund 150 H 3
Vallorbe 153 E 2
Valls 152 D 3
Valmiera 151 J 4
Valmont (N.M.) 117 L 5
Valmy (NV.) 112 H 2
Valparaíso (Chile) 142 B 5
Valparaiso (FL.) 131 H 4
Valparaiso (IN.) 124 G 8
Valparaíso (Mexico) 132 B 3
Valparaiso (NE.) 120 J 1
Valpovo 153 G 2
Vals, Tanjung 177 J 5
Valsetz (OR.) 110 B 6
Valsjöbyn 150 F 3
Valtimo 150 J 3
Valuyevka 155 F 1
Valuyki 158 G 5
Vamizi, Ilha 201 G 2
Vammala 150 H 3
Van 155 F 3
Vanajavesi 150 H 3
Vanak (Iran) 157 F 3
Vanak (Iran) 157 F 3
Vananda (MT.) 118 B 4
Vanavana 187 F 4
Vanavara 170 H 3
Van Blommestein Reservoir 139 G 3
Van Buren (AR.) 121 L 7
Van Buren (MO.) 121 P 6
Van Canh 175 J 5
Vance (TX.) 122 CD 6
Vanceboro (ME.) 126 M 3
Vanceboro (N.C.) 129 O 6
Vanceburg (KY.) 128 H 3
Vancleave (MS.) 130 F 4
Vancorum (CO.) 114 J 5
Vancouver (Br. Col., Can.) 103 N 6
Vancouver (WA.) 110 C 5
Vancouver Island 103 M 6
Vanda 203
Vandalia (IL.) 121 QR 4
Vandalia (MO.) 121 O 3
Vandalia (MT.) 118 B 2
Vandalia (OH.) 128 G 2
Vanderbijlpark 200 D 5
Vanderbilt (TX.) 122 G 7
Vanderhoof 103 N 5
Vanderlin Island 183 F 2
Vanderpool (TX.) 122 D 6
Vandervoort (AR.) 121 L 8
Van Diemen, Cape 182 D 1
Van Diemen Gulf 182 E 1
Vanduzi 201 E 3
Vänern 151 F 4
Vänersborg 151 F 4
Väneshän (Iran) 157 F 2
Vang 150 E 3
Vangaindrano 201 H 4
Van Gölü 155 F 3
Vangou 173 K 2
Vangunu 185 G 3

Vangunu 186 B 3
Vang Vieng 175 H 4
Van Horn (TX.) 117 M 6
Vanikolo Islands 186 C 3
Vanikoro Islands 185 J 4
Vanillas 140 B 5
Vanimo 184 D 2
Vanino 171 P 6
Vankarem 108 C 2
Van Meter (IA.) 119 P 9
Van Metre (SD.) 118 GH 6
Vanna 150 G 1
Vännäs 150 G 3
Vannes 152 C 2
Van Ninh 175 J 5
Van Norman (MT.) 118 B 3
Vanoua Lava 185 J 4
Vanoua Lava 186 C 3
van Rees, Pegunungan 177 J 4
Vanrhynsdorp 200 B 6
Vansant (VA.) 129 J 4
Vansbro 151 F 3
Vansittart 103 V 2
Vantage (WA.) 110 E 4
Van Tassell (WY.) 118 D 8
Vanua Levu 186 C 4
Vanuatu 185 J 5
Vanuatu 186 B 3
Van Wert (OH.) 125 K 9
Vanwyksvlei 200 C 6
Vanzevat 159 N 3
Vanzhil'kynak 159 QR 3
Vapnyarka 154 C 1
Var 153 E 3
Varämïn (Iran) 157 F 2
Varanasi 174 D 2
Varandey 158 L 2
Varangerfjorden 150 K 1–2
Varangerhalvöya 150 JK 1
Varano, Lago di 153 G 3
Varävi (Iran) 157 F 4
Varaždin 153 G 2
Varberg 151 F 4
Varcheh (Iran) 157 E 2
Vardar 154 B 2
Varde 151 E 4
Vardö 150 K 1
Vardofjällen 150 FG 2
Värend 151 FG 4
Varenikovskaya 155 E 1
Varese 153 E 2
Vårgårda 151 F 4
Vargas 142 C 5
Vargashi 159 N 4
Varginha 141 GH 5
Varkaus 150 J 3
Värmland 151 F 4
Varna (Bulgaria) 154 C 2
Varna (U.S.S.R.) 159 M 5
Värnamo 151 F 4
Varnenski zaliv 154 C 2
Varnya 159 O 2
Varsinais Suomi 151 H 3
Värska 151 J 4
Varto 155 F 3
Värtsilä 150 K 3
Var'yegan 159 P 3
Varzaneh (Iran) 157 F 2
Várzea Grande 140 E 4
Varzi 153 E 3
Varzino 158 G 2
Varzy 152 D 2
Vasa 150 G 3
Vasai 174 B 4
Vascos, Montes 152 C 3
Vashnel 159 N 3
Vasil'kov 158 F 5
Vasilyevka 155 E 1
Vasiss 159 O 4
Vaslui 154 C 1
Väsman 151 F 3
Vass (N.C.) 129 M 6
Vassar (MI.) 125 L 6
Vassdalsegga 151 E 4
Vasta 168 D 1
Vastenjaure 150 G 2
Västerås 151 G 4
Västerbotten 150 GH 3
Västerdalälven 151 F 3
Västergötland 151 F 4
Västervik 151 G 4
Vasto 153 F 3
Västra Granberget 150 H 2
Vasyugan 159 P 4
Vasyuganskaya Step' 159 PQ 4
Vatan 152 D 2
Vaticano, Capo 153 G 4
Vaticano, Citta Del 153 F 3
Vatican State 153 F 3
Vatnajökull 150 B 3
Vatneyri 150 A 2
Vatoa 186 D 4
Vatomandry 201 H 3
Vatra Dornei 154 C 1
Vättern 151 F 4
Vatyna 171 W 3
Vaudémont, Butte de 153 E 2
Vaughn (MT.) 111 O 3
Vaughn (N.M.) 117 KL 3

Vaupés 138 D 3
Vaux du Loir 152 D 2
Vavatenina 201 H 3
Vava'u Group 186 D 4
Vavoua 196 C 4
Vavuniya 174 D 6
Vaxholm 151 G 4
Växjö 151 FG 4
Vayalpad 174 C 5
Vayegi 171 W 3
Vaygach 159 L 1
Vaygach, Ostrov 159 L 1
Vayvida 170 F 3
Vaza Barris 141 J 2–3
Vazhgort 158 J 3
Veadeiros 141 G 3
Veal Renh 175 H 5
Veblen (S.D.) 119 L 5
Vecht 148 E 4
Vedeno 155 G 2
Vedia 142 D 5
Vefsna 150 F 2
Vega 150 F 2
Vega (TX.) 117 O 2
Vega Baja (P.R.) 130 C 8
Vegorritis, Limni 154 B 2
Vegreville 103 P 5
Veguita (N.M.) 117 K 3
Veijo, Cerro 138 C 4
Veinticinco del Mayo 143 C 6
Veiros 139 H 4
Vejen 151 E 4
Vejle 151 E 4
Velasco, Sierra 142 C 4
Velbäždski prohod 154 B 2
Velenje 153 G 2
Velestínon 154 B 3
Velež 153 G 3
Vélez-Málaga 152 C 4
Vélez Rubio 152 C 4
Velhas 141 H 4
Velichayevskoye 155 G 2
Velika Plana 154 B 2
Velikaya 108 B 3
Velikaya 151 J 4
Velikaya 171 X 3
Velikaya Kema 173 L 1
Veliki Kanal 154 A 1
Velikiye Luki 151 K 4
Velikiy Ustyug 158 J 3
Velikonda Range 174 C 4–5
Veliko Tŭrnovo 154 C 2
Veli Lošinj 153 F 3
Vélingara 196 B 3
Velingrad 154 B 2
Vella Lavella 185 G 3
Velletri 153 F 3
Vellore 174 C 5
Velsk 158 H 3
Vel't 158 K 2
Velva (ND.) 118 H 2
Vemdalen 150 F 3
Vemor'ye 171 Q 6
Venado Tuerto 142 D 5
Vena Park 183 G 2
Venafro 153 F 3
Venango (NE.) 120 D 2
Venda 201 E 4
Venda Nova 141 H 4
Vendas Novas 152 B 4
Vendôme 152 D 2
Vendrell 152 D 3
Vendsyssel 151 EF 4
Veneta (OR.) 110 B 6
Veneta, Laguna 153 F 2
Venetie 102 H 2
Venezia 153 F 2
Venezuela 138–139 EF 2
Venezuela, Golfo de 138 D 1
Vengerovo 159 P 4
Vengurla 174 B 4
Venice 153 F 2
Venice (FL.) 131 M 6
Venice (LA.) 123 O 6
Vénissieux 153 DE 2
Venjan 151 F 3
Venkatapuram 174 CD 4
Vennesla 151 E 4
Venta 151 H 4
Venta de Baños 152 C 3
Ventersdorp 200 D 5
Ventimiglia 153 E 3
Ventotene 153 F 3
Ventuari 138 E 3
Ventura (CA.) 113 F 8
Venturia (ND.) 118 J 5
Venus (FL.) 131 N 7
Venus Bay 183 H 6
Veon (ID.) 111 O 7
Vera (Argentina) 142 D 4
Vera (IL.) 121 Q 3
Vera (Spain) 152 C 4
Vera (TX.) 122 D 2
Veracruz (Mexico) 132 C 4
Veraval 174 B 3
Verbania 153 E 2

Vercelli 153 E 2
Vercors 153 E 2–3
Verdalsöra 150 F 3
Verde, Cape (Senegal) 192 B 6
Verde, Costa 152 B 3
Verde River (IN.) 116 E 3
Verdigre (NE.) 119 K 8
Verdon (NE.) 121 K 2
Verdun 153 E 2
Vereeniging 200 D 5
Vereshchagino 158 K 4
Verga, Cap 196 B 3
Vergara 142 F 5
Vergennes (VT.) 126 F 4
Verhalen (TX.) 117 N 6
Verhnedvinsk 151 J 4
Verkhn'aya Salda 159 M 4
Verkhnearshinskiy 159 L 5
Verkhne-Avzyan 159 L 5
Verkhnebakanskiy 155 E 2
Verkhne Dneprovsk 155 D 1
Verkhneimbatskoye 159 RS 3
Verkhne-Ozernaya 171 U 4
Verkhnetulomskiy 150 K 2
Verkhnetulomskoye Vodokhranilishche 150 K 2
Verkhneural'sk 159 L 5
Verkhnevilyuysk 170 M 3
Verkhneye Kuyto,Ozero 150 K 3
Verkhneye Nil'dno 159 M 3
Verkhneye Skoblino 159 M 4
Verkhniy Ufaley 159 M 4
Verkhnyaya Amga 171 N 4
Verkhnyaya Angara 170 K 4
Verkhnyaya Baikha 159 Q 2
Verkhnyaya Chunku 170 G 3
Verkhnyaya Pakhacha 171 V 3
Verkhnyaya Taymyra 170 G 1
Verkhnyaya Toyma 158 J 3
Verkhnyaya Vol'dzha 159 P 4
Verkholensk 170 J 5
Verkhoyansk 171 O 2
Verkhoyanskiy Khrebet 171 N 2–P 3
Verkhoyansk Range 171 O 3
Verme Falls 199 G 2
Vermilion Bay 123 LM 6
Vermilion Bay (Ontario, Can.) 104 J 5–6
Vermilion Lake 119 Q 3
Vermillion (OH.) 125 M 8
Vermillion (S.D.) 119 M 8
Vermion Óros 154 B 2
Vermont 126
Vernal (UT.) 114 H 3
Verneuk Pan 200 C 5
Vernon (AL.) 128 C 8
Vernon (Br. Col., Can.) 103 O 5
Vernon (CO.) 115 P 4
Vernon (FL.) 131 J 4
Vernon (France) 152 D 2
Vernon (IN.) 128 F 3
Vernon (TX.) 122 D 1
Vernon (UT.) 114 E 3
Vernon, Mount (Western Australia) 182 B 3
Vernonia (OR.) 110 B 5
Vero Beach (FL.) 131 O 7
Verona 153 F 2
Verona (N.D.) 119 K 4
Verona (WI.) 124 E 7
Verret, Lake 123 M 6
Vérroia 154 B 2
Versailles 152 D 2
Versailles (IN.) 128 F 2
Versailles (KY.) 128 G 3
Versailles (MO.) 121 N 4
Verse (WY.) 118 C 7
Vershina 159 M 3
Vershino-Darasunskiy 170 L 5
Vershino-Shakhtaminskiye 170 L 5
Vert, Cap 196 A 3
Vertikoss Óros 154 B 2
Vérviers 148 E 4
Vescovato 153 E 3
Veselovskoye Vodokhranilishche 155 F 1
Veseloye 155 DE 1
Veseloye 155 E 1
Veselyy 155 F 1
Veshenskaya 158 H 6
Vesoul 153 E 2
Vest-Agder 151 E 4
Vestbygd 151 E 4
Vesterålen 150 FG 2
Vesterö Havn 151 F 4
Vestfirðir 150 A 2
Vestfjorden 150 FG 2
Vestmannaeyjar 150 A 3
Vestre Jakobselv 150 J 1
Vestvågöy 150 F 2
Vesuvio 153 F 3
Vet 200 D 5
Vetal (SD.) 118 G 7
Vétaounde 185 J 4
Vétaoundé 186 C 3
Veteran (WY.) 118 D 9
Vetlanda 151 G 4
Vetluga 158 J 4

Vetluzhskiy 158 J 4
Vetrenyy 171 R 3
Vettore 153 F 3
Vetvey 171 V 3
Veurne 148 D 4
Vevay (IN.) 128 F 3
Vevey 153 E 2
Veyo (UT.) 114 D 6
Vézhen 154 B 2
Vezh'yudor 158 K 3
Vezirköprü 155 E 2
Viacha 140 C 4
Viamonte 142 D 5
Viamonte 143 C 9
Vian (OK.) 121 L 7
Viana 139 J 4
Viana (Angola) 200 A 1
Viana do Castelo 152 B 3
Viang Chan 175 H 4
Viar 152 B 4
Viareggio 153 EF 3
Viboras (TX.) 122 E 9
Viborg (S.D.) 119 LM 7
Vibo Valentia 153 G 4
Vicari 153 F 4
Vicecommodoro Marambio 203
Vicenza 153 F 2
Vichada 138 E 3
Vichy 152 D 2
Vici (OK.) 120 F 6
Vick (TX.) 122 C 4
Vicksburg (AZ.) 116 C 4
Vicksburg (MI.) 124 J 7
Vicksburg (MS.) 130 D 2
Victor (CO.) 115 M 5
Victor (ID.) 111 O 7
Victor (MT.) 111 L 4
Victor Harbour 183 F 6
Victoria (Argentina) 142 DE 5
Victoria (Australia) 183 G 6
Victoria (Br. Col., Can.) 103 N 6
Victoria (Chile) 143 B 6
Victoria (Guinea) 196 B 3
Victoria (Hong Kong) 172 F 6
Victoria (KS.) 120 F 4
Victoria (Malaysia) 176 E 2
Victoria (Malta) 153 F 4
Victoria (Seychelles) 199 K 5
Victoria (TX.) 122 FG 7
Victoria, Lake 198 E 5
Victoria, Mount (Burma) 175 F 3
Victoria, Mount (Papua New Guinea) 184 E 3
Victoria, Mount (Papua New Guinea) 186 A 3
Victoria de Durango 132 B 3
Victoria de las Tunas 133 G 3
Victoria Falls 200 D 3
Victoria Falls 200 D 3
Victoria Island 103 PQ 1
Victoria Land 203
Victoria Nile 198 E 4
Victoria River 182 E 2
Victoria River Downs 182 E 2
Victoria Strait 103 R 2
Victoriaville 105 N 6
Victoria West 200 C 6
Victorica 143 CD 6
Victorino de la Plaza 143 D 6
Victorville (CA.) 113 H 8
Victory Downs 182 E 4
Vicuña Mackenna 142 D 5
Vida (MT.) 118 C 3
Vidal (CA.) 113 L 8
Vidalia (GA.) 131 M 2
Vidal Junction (CA.) 113 L 8
Vidauri (TX.) 122 F 7
Vidin 154 B 2
Vidisha 174 C 3
Vidra 154 C 2
Vidsel 150 H 2
Viduša 153 G 3
Vidzemes Augstiene 151 J 4
Vidzy 151 J 4
Viedma 143 D 7
Viedma 143 D 8
Viedma, Lago 143 B 8
Viejo, Rio 132 E 5
Vienna (Austria) 153 G 2
Vienna (GA.) 131 L 2
Vienna (IL.) 121 R 5
Vienna (MD.) 129 Q 3
Vienna (MO.) 121 O 4
Vienna (S.D.) 119 L 6
Vienna (W.V.) 129 K 2
Vienne 152 D 2
Vienne 153 DE 2
Vientiane 175 H 4
Vientos, Paso de los 133 H 3–4
Vieques, Isla de 130 D 8
Vieques, Isla de 133 JK 4
Vierwaldstätter See 153 E 2
Vierzon 152 D 2
Viesca 132 B 2
Vieste 153 G 3
Vietas 150 G 2
Vietnam 175 J 5
Viet Tri 175 J 3

Vieux-Fort 105 Q 5
Viewfield (SD.) 118 F 6
Vigan 177 J 1
Vigevano 153 E 2
Vigia 139 J 4
Vignola 153 F 3
Vigo 152 B 3
Vigo, Ría de 152 B 3
Vigo Park (TX.) 117 P 3
Vihanti 150 H 3
Vihoflat 149 H 5
Viiala 150 H 3
Viitasaari 150 J 3
Vijayadurg 174 B 4
Vijayawada 174 CD 4
Vijosa 154 A 2
Vik 150 B 3
Vikersund 151 E 4
Vikhorevka 170 H 4
Viking 103 P 5
Vikna 150 F 3
Vila 185 J 5
Vila 186 C 4
Vila Bittencourt 138 E 4
Vila Conceição 139 F 3
Vila do Porto 192 A 1
Vila Franca de Xira 152 B 4
Vila Gamito 201 E 2
Vilaine 152 C 2
Vilanculo 201 F 4
Viljäni 153 J 4
Vila Nova de Gaia 152 B 3
Vila Pouca de Aquiar 152 B 3
Vila Real 152 B 3
Vilas (CO.) 115 P 6
Vila Velha (Amapá, Brazil) 139 H 3
Vila Velha (Espírito Santo, Brazil) 141 HJ 5
Vila Velha (Portugal) 152 B 4
Vilcabamba 140 B 3
Vilcabamba, Cordillera 140 B 3
Vıldız Dağları 154 C 2
Vileyka 151 J 5
Vil'gort 118 L 3 158 L 3
Vilhelmina 150 G 3
Vilhena 140 D 3
Viliga-Kushka 171 T 3
Viliya 151 J 5
Viljandi 151 J 4
Vilkija 151 H 4
Vilkovo 154 C 1
Villa Abecia 140 C 5
Villa Ahumada 106 E 5
Villa Ángela 142 D 4
Villa Bella 140 C 3
Villablino 152 B 3
Villacarrillo 152 C 4
Villacastin 152 C 3
Villach 153 F 2
Villacidro 153 E 4
Villa Colón 142 C 5
Villa Constitución 142 D 5
Villa Coronado 132 B 2
Villa de Cos 132 B 3
Villa de Guadalupe 132 B 3
Villa del Rosario (Argentina) 142 D 5
Villa del Rosario (Venezuela) 138 D 1
Villa de Reyes 132 B 3
Villa Dolores 142 C 5
Villa Federal 142 E 5
Villa Flores 132 D 4
Villafranca del Cid 152 C 3
Villafranca di Verona 153 F 2
Villa Frontera 132 B 2
Villagarcia de Arosa 152 B 3
Villa General Roca 142 C 5
Villa Grove (CO.) 115 M 5
Villa Grove (IL.) 121 R 3
Villaguay 142 E 5
Villa Guillermina 142 DE 4
Villa Hayes 140 E 5
Villahermosa 132 D 4
Villa Hidalgo 132 B 2
Villa Huidobro 142 D 5
Villa Ingavi 140 D 5
Villa Iris 143 D 6
Villajoyosa 152 C 4
Villalba 152 B 3
Villaldama 132 B 2
Villalón de Campos 152 B 3
Villalpando 152 B 3
Villa María 142 D 5
Villa Martín (Bolivia) 140 C 5
Villamartin (Spain) 152 B 4
Villa Matoque 142 D 4
Villa Mazán 142 C 4
Villa Minetti 142 D 4
Villa Montes 140 D 5
Villanova y Geltrú 152 D 3
Villanueva 132 B 3
Villanueva (N.M.) 117 L 2
Villanueva de Córdoba 152 BC 4
Villanueva de la Serena 152 B 4
Villanueva del Fresno 152 B 4
Villa Ocampo 132 AB 2
Villa Ocampo 142 DE 4
Villa Oliva 142 E 4

Villa Regina 143 C 6
Villa Rey 140 E 5
Villarreal de los Infantes 152 C 3–4
Villarrica (Chile) 143 B 6
Villarrica (Paraguay) 142 E 4
Villarrobledo 152 C 4
Villa S. Giovanni 153 G 4
Villa S. Giovanni 153 G 4
Villatoro, Puerto de 152 B 3
Villa Unión (Argentina) 142 C 4
Villa Union (Mexico) 132 A 3
Villa Valeria 142 CD 5
Villavicencio 138 D 3
Villaviciosa 152 B 3
Villazón 140 C 5
Villefranche 153 DE 2
Villegreen (CO.) 115 O 6
Villena 152 C 4
Villeneuve-sur-Lot 152 D 3
Ville Platte (LA.) 123 L 5
Villmanstrand 150 J 3
Villupuram 174 C 5
Vil'mo 170 F 3
Vilnius 151 J 5
Vilppula 150 H 3
Vilsandi 151 H 4
Vilusi 154 A 2
Vilyuy 171 MN 3
Vilyuyskoye Plato 170 J 2
Vilyuyskoye Vodokhranilishche
  170 JK 3
Vilyuyskt 170 M 3
Vimmerby 151 G 4
Vina 197 G 4
Vina (CA.) 112 D 3
Viña del Mar 142 B 5
Vinalhaven (ME.) 126 L 4
Vinalhaven Island 126 KL 4
Vinaroz 152 E 4
Vincennes (IN.) 128 D 3
Vincent (AL.) 128 E 8
Vincent (TX.) 117 P 5
Vinces 138 C 4
Vinchina 142 C 4
Vindelälven 150 G 2
Vindeln 150 G 3
Vindhya Range 174 C 3
Vinegar Hill 110 G 6
Vineland (N.J.) 127 D 9
Vinemont (AL.) 128 E 7
Vineyards Haven (MA.) 126 J 7
Vineyard Sound 126 J 7
Vingåker 151 G 4
Vinh 175 J 4
Vinh Giat 175 J 5
Vinh Linh 175 J 4
Vinh Loi 175 J 6
Vinh Long 175 J 5
Vinica (Yugoslavia) 153 G 2
Vinica (Yugoslavia) 154 B 2
Vinita (KS.) 121 K 6
Vinkovci 153 G 2
Vino, Tierra del 152 B 3
Vinson (OK.) 120 F 8
Vinson Massif 203
Vinstervatn 150 E 3
Vinstra 150 E 3
Vinton (CA.) 112 E 3
Vinton (IA.) 119 Q 8
Viola (CA.) 112 D 2
Viola (IL.) 124 D 8
Viqueque 177 G 5
Virac 177 F 1
Viramgam 174 B 3
Virandozero158 FG 3
Viranşehir 155 D 3
Viranşehir 155 EF 3
Virarajendrapet 174 C 5
Virden (Manitoba, Can.) 103 R 6
Virden (N.M.) 116 H 5
Vire 152 C 2
Virei 200 A 3
Virful Balota 154 B 1
Virful Bivolu 154 C 1
Virful Budacu 154 C 1
Virful Ciucasu 154 C 1
Virful Curcubăta 154 B 1
Virful Farcău 154 B 1
Virful Gogu 154 B 1
Virful Goru 154 C 1
Virful Gutii 154 B 1
Virful Hămaşu Mare 154 C 1
Virful Iezerul 154 B 1
Virful Moldoveanu 154 B 1
Virful Nemira 154 C 1
Virful Omu 154 C 1
Virful Peleaga 154 B 1
Virful Pietrosu 154 B 1
Virful Pietroşul 154 BC 1
Virful Pleşu 154 B 1
Virful Saca 154 C 1
Virful Toaca 154 C 1
Virful Vlădeasa 154 B 1
Virful Vulcan 154 B 1
Virgelle (MT.) 111 P 2
Virgem da Lapa 141 H 4
Virgenes, Cabo 143 C 9
Virgil (KS.) 120 J 4
Virgil (S.D.) 119 K 6

Virgin Gorda 130 E 8
Virginia 129
Virginia (ID.) 111 N 8
Virginia (IL.) 121 P 3
Virginia (MN.) 119 Q 3
Virginia (South Africa) 200 D 5
Virginia Beach (VA.) 129 Q 5
Virginia City (MT.) 111 O 5
Virginia City (NV.) 112 F 3
Virginia Falls 103 N 3
Virginia Peak 112 F 3
Virgin Islands 130 E 8–9
Virgin Islands 133 K 4
Virgin River 112 L 6
Virihaure 150 G 2
Virojoki 151 J 3
Viroqua (WI.) 124 C 6
Virovitica 153 G 2
Virrat 150 H 3
Virserum 151 G 4
Virsko More 153 FG 3
Virtsu 151 H 4
Virú 138 C 5
Virudunagar 174 C 6
Vis 153 G 3
Visalia (CA.) 112 F 6
Visayan Sea 177 F 1
Visby 151 G 4
Viscount Melville Sound 103 P 1
Visegrad 154 A 2
Viseu 153 C 3
Viseu 152 B 3
Vişeu de Sus 154 B 1
Vishakhapatnam 174 D 4
Vishera 158 L 3
Vishnevka 159 O 5
Visingsö 151 F 4
Viskafors 151 F 4
Visoko 153 G 3
Visp 153 E 2
Vista (CA.) 113 H 9
Vista Alegre (Amazonas, Brazil)
  138 E 3
Vista Alegre (Amazonas, Brazil)
  138 E 5
Vista Alegre (Roraima, Brazil)
  139 F 3
Vistula 149 G 4
Vitarte 140 A 3
Vitebsk 151 K 4
Viterbo 153 F 3
Vitiaz Strait 184 E 3
Vitim 170 K 4
Vitim 170 K 4
Vitimskiy 170 K 4
Vitimskoye Ploskogor'ye 170 K 5
Vitolište 154 B 2
Vitoria 152 C 3
Vitória (Espírito Santo, Brazil)
  141 HJ 5
Vitória (Pará, Brazil) 139 H 4
Vitória da Conquista 141 H 3
Vitré 152 C 2
Vitry-le-François 153 D 2
Vittangi 150 H 2
Vittoria 153 F 4
Vittorio d'Africa → Shalänböd
Vittorio Veneto 153 F 2
Viver 152 C 4
Vivero 152 B 3
Vivi 170 G 3
Vivian (LA.) 123 K 3
Vivian (SD.) 118 H 7
Viviers 153 D 3
Vivonne 183 F 6
Vivorata 143 E 6
Vizagapatam → Vishakhapatam
  174 D 4
Vizcachas, Meseta de las 143 B 9
Vizcaino, Cape 112 B 3
Vizcaino, Sierra 106 D 6
Vize 154 C 2
Vizianagaram 174 D 4
Vizinga 158 JK 3
Vlădeasa, Virful 154 B 1
Vladimir 158 H 4
Vladimir 173 L 2
Vladimirovka 158 K 5
Vladimirovskiy 159 M 5
Vladimir-Volynskiy 151 H 5
Vladislavovka 155 E 1
Vladivostok 173 K 2
Vlakhina 154 B 2
Vlasenica 153 G 3
Vlissingen 148 D 4
Vlorë 154 A 2
Vltava 149 F 4
Voca (TX.) 122 D 4–5
Vöcklabruck 153 F 2
Vodice 153 G 3
Vodla 158 G 3
Vodlozero, Ozero 158 G 3
Vodnjan 153 F 3
Vœune Sai 175 J 5
Vogan 196 E 4
Vogel Peak 197 G 4
Vogelsberg 149 E 4
Voghera 153 E 2–3

Vohimarina 201 J 2
Vohipeno 201 H 4
Voi 199 F 5
Voinjama 196 C 4
Voiron 153 E 2
Voitsberg 153 G 1
Vojens 151 E 4
Vojmån 150 G 3
Vojmsjön 150 G 2–3
Vojnić 153 G 2
Vojvodina 154 AB 1
Volborg (MT.) 118 C 5
Volcán Antofalla 142 C 4
Volcán Barú 138 B 2
Volcán Ceboruco 132 B 3
Volcán Citlaltépetl 132 C 4
Volcán Corcovado 143 B 7
Volcán Domuyo 143 BC 6
Volcan Irazu 132 F 5–6
Volcán Lanin 143 B 6
Volcán Las Tres Virgenes
  106 D 6
Volcán Llaima 143 B 6
Volcán Llullaillaco 140 C 5
Volcán Maipo 142 C 5
Volcán Miravalles 132 EF 5
Volcán Misti 140 B 4
Volcano House (HI.) 113 G 12
Volcán Ollagüe 140 C 5
Volcán Paricutín 132 B 4
Volcán Popocatéptl 132 C 4
Volcán Sangay 138 C 4
Volcán San Juan 132 AB 3
Volcán Tajumulco 132 D 4
Volcán Tutupaca 140 BC 4
Volcán Wolf 138 B 6
Volchikha 159 Q 5
Volchya 155 E 1
Volda 150 E 3
Voldafjorden 150 E 3
Volga 155 G 1
Volga-Balt (I.V. Lenin) Kanal
  158 G 3
Volgodonsk 155 F 1
Volgograd 158 H 6
Volgogradskoye Vodokhrani-
  lishche 158 J 6
Volikovisochnoye 158 K 2
Volin (S.D.) 119 L 8
Volkhov 151 K 4
Volkovysk 151 H 5
Volksrust 200 DE 5
Vollmar (CO.) 115 MN 3
Volna, Gora 171 T 3
Volnovakha 155 E 1
Volochanka 170 F 1
Volochayevka 171 O 6
Volodarskoye 159 N 5
Volodorsk 158 GH 4
Vologda 158 G 4
Volokon 170 J 4
Volokovaya 158 J 2
Volonga 158 J 2
Volos 154 B 3
Volosovo 151 J 4
Volovets 158 K 5
Volozhin 151 J 5
Volsini, Monti 153 F 3
Vol'sk 158 J 5
Volt (MT.) 118 BC 2
Volta, Lake 196 DE 4
Volta (CA.) 112 E 5
Volta Blanche 196 D 3
Volta Noire 196 D 3
Volta Redonda 141 H 5
Volta Rouge 196 D 3
Volterra 153 F 3
Volteva 158 H 3
Volturino 153 G 3
Volupai 185 E 3
Volynskaya Vozvyshennost'
  151 HJ 5
Volynskye Polesye 151 J 5
Volzhsk 158 J 4
Volzhskiy 158 J 6
Vondrozo 201 H 4
Von Frank Mountain 108 GH 3
Vónitsa 154 B 3
Voodbine (IA.) 119 N 9
Vopnafjörður 150 BC 2
Vopnafjörður 150 C 2
Vora 154 A 2
Vorau 153 G 2
Vordingborg 151 F 4
Vórioi Sporádhes 154 B 3
Vorjing 175 F 2
Vorkuta 159 MN 2
Vormsi 151 H 4
Vorman 159 P 4
Vorob'yevo 159 P 4
Vorob'yevo 170 H 4
Vorogovo 159 R 3
Voronezh 158 GH 5
Voronovo 159 Q 4
Vorontsovka 158 H 5
Vorontsovka 170 K 4
Vorontsovo 170 D 1
Voron'ya 150 L 2
Voroshilovgrad 155 EF 1
Vörts Järv 151 J 4
Võru 151 J 4

Vor'yapaul' 159 M 3
Vosges 153 E 2
Voskhod 155 F 1
Voss 150 E 3
Vostochnaya Litsa158 G 2
Vostochno-Kounradskiy 159 P 6
Vostochno-Sakhalinskiy Khrebet
  171 Q 5–6
Vostochnyy 171 Q 5
Vostochnyy 171 Q 6
Vostochnyy Sayan 170 G 5
Vostok (Antarctica) 203
Vostok (Kiribati) 187 E 3
Vostok Manych 155 F 1
Vostykhoy 159 N 3
Votkinsk 158 K 4
Votkinskoye Vodokhranilishche
  158 L 4
Vourinos Oros 154 B 2
Vouziers 153 D 2
Voxnan 150 F 3
Voyageors National Park 119 Q 2
Voyampolka 171 T 4
Voyvozh 158 L 3
Vozhe, Ozero 158 G 3
Vozhega 158 H 3
Vozhgora 158 J 3
Voznesensk 154 D 1
Vozrozhdeniya, Ostrov 168 F 1
Vozvrashcheniye 171 Q 6
Vozvyshennost' Byraya-Tas
  170 M 1
Vozvyshennost' Gabrey 170 F 1
Vozvyshennost' Karabil' 169 G 3
Vozvyshennost' Syuryakh-Dahangy
  170 M 1
Vozvyshennost' Tulay-Kiryaka-Tas
  170 J 1
Vozvyshennost' Tutonchana
  170 FG 2–3
Vradiyevka 154 D 1
Vran 153 G 3
Vranje 154 B 2
Vratnica 154 B 2
Vratsa 154 B 2
Vrbas 153 G 3
Vrbovsko 153 G 2
Vrede 200 D 5
Vreed en Hoop 139 G 2
Vriddhachalam 174 C 5
Vrigstad 151 F 4
Vršac 154 B 1
Vryburg 200 CD 5
Vryheid 201 E 5
Vsetin 149 G 5
Vsevidof, Mount 102 D 5
Vsevolozhsk 151 K 3
Vucitrn 154 B 2
Vukovar 153 G 2
Vulcan, Virful 154 B 1
Vulcano 153 F 4
Vung Tau 175 J 5
Vuohijärvi 150 J 3
Vuokkijärvi 150 J 3
Vuoksa 150 J 3
Vuollerim 150 H 2
Vuotso 150 J 2
Vya (NV.) 112 F 1
Vyalozero, Ozero 150 L 2
Vyaltsevo 158 H 4
Vyartsilya 150 K 3
Vyatka 158 K 4
Vyatskiye Polyany 158 K 4
Vyazemskiy 171 P 6
Vyaz'ma 158 F 4
Vyazovka 158 J 5
Vyborg 150 J 3
Vychegda 158 J 3
Vydrino 170 G 4
Vygoda 154 D 1
Vygozero, Ozero 158 G 3
Vyksa 158 H 4
Vym' 158 K 3
Vyngapur 159 P 3
Vyritsa 151 K 4
Vyselki 155 E 1
Vyshniy-Volochek 158 FG 4
Vysokaya Parma 159 L 3
Vysokogornyy 171 P 5
Vysokoye 158 F 4
Vysotsk 151 J 3
Vytegra 158 G 3
V'yuny 159 Q 4
Vyvenka 171 V 3

Vosges 153 E 2

W

"W", Parcs Nationaux, du 196 E 3
Wa 196 D 3
Waal 148 DE 4
Wabag 184 D 3
Wabana 105 R 6
Wabara 199 G 3

Wabasca 103 P 4
Wabasca River 103 O 4
Wabash (IN.) 124 J 9
Wabasha (MN.) 119 Q 6
Wabash River 128 D 3
Wabasso (FL.) 131 O 7
Wabeno (WI.) 124 F 4
Wäbirī 193 J 3
Wabowden 103 S 5
Wabrah (Saudi Arabia) 157 E 4
Wąbrzeźno 149 G 4
Wabuska (NV.) 112 F 3
Waccamaw, Lake 129 N 7
Waccasassa Bay 131 M 5
Waco (Quebec, Can.) 105 O 5
Waco (TX.) 122 F 4
Waco Lake 122 F 4
Waconda Reservoir 120 G 3
Wad 169 H 5
Wad al Ḥaddad 194 E 6
Wad Bandah 194 D 6
Waddän 193 J 3
Waddän, Jabal 193 J 3
Waddeneilanden 148 D E 4
Waddenzee 148 E 4
Waddington (N.Y.) 126 D 4
Waddington, Mount 103 M 5
Wadena (MN.) 119 N 4
Wadesboro (N.C.) 129 L 7
Wad Ḥāmid 194 E 5
Wādī al Dawāsir 195 G 4
Wādī al Akhḍar (Saudi Arabia)
  156 B 4
Wādī al 'Allāqī 194 E 4
Wādī al 'Arabah (Jordan) 156 B 3
Wādī al Bāṭin (Iraq) 157 DE 3
Wādī al Ghudāf (Iraq) 156 D 2
Wādī al Hamd (Saudi Arabia)
  156 B 4
Wādī al Hayl (Syria) 156 C 2
Wādī al Kharīt (Egypt) 156 B 4–5
Wādī al Khurr (Saudi Arabia)
  156 C 3
Wādī al Malik 194 D 5
Wādī al Masīlah 195 J 5
Wādī al Miyāh (Syria) 156 C 2
Wādī al 'Ubayyid (Iraq) 156 CD 2
Wādī al 'Unnab (Jordan) 156 B 3
Wādī an Natrūn 194 DE 2
Wādī 'Ar 'ar (Saudi Arabia) 156 C 3
Wadi ar Ratqah (Iraq) 156 C 2
Wādī ar Rummah (Saudi Arabia)
  156 D 4
Wādī ash Shāṭi' 193 H 3
Wādi as Sirhān (Saudi Arabia)
  156 BC 3
Wādī ath Tharthār (Iraq) 156 D 2
Wādī at Ṭubal (Iraq) 156 C 2
Wādī at Ṭurmus (Saudi Arabia)
  156 D 4
Wādī Bayy al Kabīr 193 H 2
Wadi Drāa 192 D 3
Wādī Fajr (Saudi Arabia) 156 BC 3
Wādī Färigh 193 K 2
Wādī Ḥalfa' 194 E 4
Wādī Ḥamīm 193 K 2
Wādī Hawrān (Iraq) 156 C 2
Wādī Ibrah 194 C 6
Wādī Īrāwan 193 H 3
Wādī Jabjabah 194 E 4
Wādī Jimāl (Egypt) 156 B 4
Wādī Mūsā (Jordan) 156 B 3
Wādī Qina (Egypt) 156 A 4
Wādī Qitbīt 195 J 5
Wādī Sha'īt (Egypt) 156 A 4
Wādī Şūf Ajjin 193 H 2
Wādī Umm al Ḥayt 195 J 5
Wadley (AL.) 128 F 8
Wadley (GA.) 131 M 2
Wad Madanī 194 E 6
Wad Nimr 194 E 6
Wad Rawa 194 E 5
Wadsworth (NV.) 112 F 3
Wadsworth (OH.) 125 N 8
Wadsworth (TX.) 122 GH 7
Waelder (TX.) 122 F 6
Wafrah (Saudi Arabia) 157 E 3
Wagarville (AL.) 130 F 3
Wager Bay 103 U 2
Waggabundi (Queensland, Austr.)
  183 F 2
Wagga Wagga 183 H 6
Wagin 182 B 5
Wagner (S.D.) 119 K 7
Wagoner (OK.) 121 K 7
Wagon Mound (N.M.) 117 M 1
Wagontire (OR.) 110 F 7
Wagontire Mountain 110 F 7
Wagon Wheel Gap (CO.) 115 L 6
Wągrowiec 149 G 4
Wah 169 J 4
Wahai 177 G 4
Wāhāt ad Dākhilah 194 D 3
Wāhāt al Baḥarīyah 194 D 3
Wāhāt al Farāfirah 194 D 3
Wāhāt al Jufrah 193 J 3
Wāhāt al Khārijah 194 E 3–4
Wāhāt al Kufrah 193 K 4
Wāhāt al Rabyānah 193 K 4
Wāhāt al Tāzirbū 193 K 3

Wāhāt Jālū 193 K 3
Wāhāt Sabhā 193 H 3
Wāhāt Salīmah 194 D 4
Wāhāt Sīwah 194 D 3
Wāhāt Zīghan 193 K 3
Wahiawa (HI.) 113 DE 10
Waḥībah 195 K 4
Waḥidī 195 H 6
Wahni 199 F 2
Wahoo (NE.) 120 J 1
Wahpeton (N.D.) 119 M 4
Wah Wah Mountains 114 D 5
Wai 174 B 4
Waialeale 113 C 9
Waialee (HI.) 113 D 10
Waialua (HI.) 113 D 10
Waianae (HI.) 113 D 10
Waibeem 177 H 4
Waidhofen 153 F 2
Waidhofen 153 F 2
Waigama 177 G 4
Waigeo, Pulau 177 H 4
Waihi 185 R 8
Waikabubak 177 E 5
Waikato 185 R 8
Waikouaiti 185 Q 10
Wailua (HI.) 113 F 11
Wailuku (HI.) 113 F 11
Waimate 185 Q 9
Waimea (HI.) 113 G 11
Wainganga 174 C 3
Waingapu 177 F 5
Wainwright (AK.) 102 E 1
Wainwright (Alb., Can.) 103 P 5
Waipara 185 Q 9
Waipukuran 185 R 8
Wairoa 185 R 8
Waisai 177 H 4
Waitaki River 185 Q 9
Waitara 185 Q 8
Waite Park (MN.) 119 O 5
Waitsburg (WA.) 110 G 4
Wājid 199 G 4
Wajir 199 G 4
Waka (Ethiopia) 199 F 3
Waka (TX.) 117 PQ 1
Waka (Zaire) 198 C 4
Waka, Tanjung 177 G 4
Wakasa-wan 173 KL 3
Wakatinu, Lake 184 P 10
Wakayama 173 L 4
Wake 186 C 1
Wakeeney (KS.) 120 F 3
Wakefield (KS.) 120 H 3
Wakefield (MI.) 124 E 3
Wakefield (R.I.) 126 GH 7
Wake Forest (N.C.) 129 N 5–6
Wakenaam Island 139 G 2
Wakita (OK.) 120 H 6
Wakkanai 173 M 1
Wakpala (S.D.) 118 H 5
Wakre 177 H 4
Wakuach, Lac 105 O 4
Waku Kungo 200 B 2
Wakulla (FL.) 131 K 4
Walaga 198 F 3
Walapai (AZ.) 116 C 2
Wałbrzych 149 G 4
Walcott (N.D.) 119 M 4
Walcott (WY.) 118 B 9
Walcott, Lake 111 M 8
Wałcz 149 G 4
Walden (CO.) 115 L 3
Waldenburg (AR.) 121 OP 7
Walden Reservoir 115 L 3
Waldia 199 F 2
Waldo (FL.) 131 M 5
Waldo Lake 110 C 7
Waldorf (MD.) 129 P 3
Waldport (OR.) 110 A 6
Waldron (AR.) 121 L 8
Waldron (MI.) 125 K 8
Wales (AK.) 102 D 2
Wales (U.K.) 148 C 4
Wales Island (N.W.T., Can.) 103 U 4
Walewale 196 D 3
Walgett 183 H 4–5
Walgreen Coast 203
Walhalla (N.D.) 119 KL 2
Walhalla (TN.) 128 H 7
Walikale 198 D 5
Walinga 184 E 3
Walk, Lake 122 C 6
Walker (IA.) 119 R 8
Walker (MN.) 119 O 3
Walker (SD.) 118 G 5
Walker Lake 112 G 4
Walker River Indian Reservation 112 G 3–4
Walkers Point 125 J 5
Walkersville (W.V.) 129 L 3
Walkerton (IN.) 124 H 8
Walkite 199 F 3
Wall (SD.) 118 F 6
Wallaby Island 183 G 2
Wallace (ID.) 111 K 3
Wallace (KS.) 120 D 4
Wallace (N.C.) 129 NO 7
Wallace (NE.) 120 D 2

Wallaceburg (MI.) 125 M 7
Wallaceburg (Ontario, Can.) 104 L 7
Wallal Downs 182 C 2
Wallaroo 183 F 5
Walla Walla (WA.) 110 G 4
Wall Creek 182 E 4
Wallel 198 E 3
Wallendbeen 183 H 5
Wallenpaupack, Lake 127 D 8
Wallinford (VT.) 126 F 5
Wallis 186 D 3
Wallis (TX.) 122 G 6
Wallis and Futuna 186 CD 3
Wallisville Lake 123 J 6
Wall Lake (IA.) 119 N 8
Wallowa (OR.) 110 H 5
Wallowa Mountains 110 H 5
Walls (MS.) 121 P 8
Wallsend 183 J 5
Wallula (WA.) 110 G 4
Wallula, Lake 110 FG 4
Walnut (IL.) 124 E 8
Walnut (KS.) 121 KL 5
Walnut (MS.) 121 R 8
Walnut (N.C.) 128 J 6
Walnut Canyon National Monument 116 E 2
Walnut Grove (CA.) 112 D 4
Walnut Grove (MS.) 130 E 2
Walnut Ridge (AR.) 121 P 6
Walnut Springs (TX.) 122 F 3
Walpole (N.H.) 126 G 5
Walpole, Ile 185 J 6
Walrus Islands 102 EF 4
Walsenburg (CO.) 115 N 6
Walsh 183 G 2
Walsh (CO.) 115 P 6
Walsingham, Cape 105 P 2
Walt Disney World 131 N 6
Walterboro (S.C.) 129 L 8
Walter F. George Dam 131 JK 3
Walter F. George Reservoir 131 J 3
Walters (LA.) 123 M 4
Walters (OK.) 120 G 8
Waltersville (MS.) 130 D 2
Walthall (MS.) 121 Q 9
Walthill (NE.) 119 M 8
Waltman (WY.) 111 S 7
Walton (KY.) 128 G 3
Walton (N.Y.) 126 D 6
Walvis Bay 200 A 4
Walvis Ridge 208 B 5
Wama, Sungai 177 J 4
Wamba (Kenya) 199 F 4
Wamba (Nigeria) 197 F 4
Wamba (Zaire) 198 D 4
Wamba (Zaire) 198 B 6
Wamego (KS.) 120 J 3
Wamena 177 J 4
Wami 199 F 6
Wamsisi 177 G 4
Wamsutter (WY.) 111 S 9
Wan 177 J 5
Wana 169 H 4
Wanaaring 183 G 4
Wanaka 184 P 9
Wanaka 186 C 5
Wanaka, Lake 184 P 9
Wanapiri 177 J 4
Wanapum Dam 110 F 4
Wanblee (SD.) 118 G 7
Wandel Sea 202
Wandinzhen 172 C 6
Wanganella 183 GH 6
Wanganui 185 R 8
Wangaratta 183 H 6
Wangcang 172 E 4
Wanggameti, Gunung 177 EF 6
Wangi 199 G 5
Wangiwangi, Pulau 177 F 5
Wangka 175 G 4
Wang Kai 198 D 3
Wangkui 173 J 1
Wangmo 172 E 5
Wangqing 173 J 2
Wan Hsa-la 175 G 3
Wanie Rukula 198 D 4
Wanigela 184 E 3
Wanilla (MS.) 130 D 3
Wankaner 174 B 3
Wanle Wēyn 199 G 4
Wannaska (MN.) 119 N 2
Wanneroo 182 B 5
Wanning 172 F 7
Wanor 197 G 4
Wanship (UT.) 114 F 3
Wanxian 172 E 4
Wanyuan 172 E 4
Wanzai 172 F 5
Wapakoneta (OH.) 125 K 9
Wapamoiwa 185 F 3
Wapanucka (OK.) 120 J 8
Wapato (WA.) 110 E 4
Wapello (IA.) 119 R 9
Wapinitia Pass 110 D 5
Wapiti (WY.) 111 Q 6
Wappapello, Lake 121 P 5–6
Wapsipinicon River 119 Q 8
War (W.V.) 129 K 4

Warangal 174 CD 4
Waratah 184 L 9
Waratah Bay 183 H 6
Warbumi 177 H 4
Warburg 149 E 4
Warburton Bay 103 P 3
Warburton Mission 182 D 4
Warburton Range 182 D 4
Warburton River 183 F 4
Warden (WA.) 110 FG 4
Wardensville (W.V.) 129 N 2
Warder 199 H 3
Wardha 174 C 3
Ward Hunt Strait 185 EF 3
Ward Mountain 111 L 4
Ware (Br. Col., Can.) 103 M 4
Ware (TX.) 117 O 1
Wareham (MA.) 126 J 7
Waren 177 J 4
Warenai, Sungai 177 J 4
Warenda 183 G 3
Warialda 183 J 4
Warin Chamrap 175 HJ 4
Warmbad (Namibia) 200 B 5
Warmbad (South Africa) 200 D 4
Warmfontein 200 B 5
Warminster 148 C 4
Warm Springs (NV.) 112 L 3
Warm Springs (OR.) 110 D 6
Warm Springs (VA.) 129 L 3
Warm Springs Indian Reservation 110 D 6
Warm Springs Reservoir 110 G 7
Warnemünde 149 F 4
Warner (OK.) 121 K 7
Warner (S.D.) 119 K 5
Warner, Mount 110 F 8
Warner Lakes 110 F 8
Warner Mountains 112 E 1
Warner Robins (GA.) 131 L 2
Warner Springs (CA.) 113 J 9
Waroona 182 B 5
Warora 174 C 3
Warragul 183 H 6
Warrawagine 182 C 3
Warrego River 183 H 4
Warren (AR.) 121 N 9
Warren (Australia) 183 H 5
Warren (ID.) 111 K 5
Warren (IL.) 124 E 7
Warren (IN.) 124 J 9
Warren (MI.) 125 L 7
Warren (MT.) 111 R 4
Warren (OH.) 125 O 8
Warren (PA.) 125 P 8
Warren Peaks 118 D 6
Warrens (WI.) 124 D 5
Warrensburg (MO.) 121 M 4
Warrensburg (N.Y.) 126 F 5
Warrenton 200 C 5
Warrenton (GA.) 128 J 8
Warrenton (MO.) 121 O 4
Warrenton (N.C.) 129 N 5
Warrenton (OR.) 110 AB 4
Warrenton (VA.) 129 O 3
Warri 197 F 4
Warrington (FL.) 130 G 4
Warrior (AL.) 128 E 8
Warrnambool 183 G 6
Warroad (MN.) 119 N 2
Warrow 183 F 5
Warrumbungle Range 183 H 5
Warsaw 149 H 4
Warsaw (IN.) 124 HJ 8
Warsaw (MO.) 121 M 4
Warsaw (N.C.) 129 N 6–7
Warsaw (N.Y.) 125 Q 7
Warsaw (VA.) 129 P 4
Warshīkh 199 H 4
Warszawa → Warsaw 149 H 4
Warta 149 G 4
Wartburg (TN.) 128 G 5
Warthen (GA.) 128 J 8
Wartrace (TN.) 128 E 6
Waru 177 H 4
Warwick (N.D.) 119 K 3
Warwick (Queensland, Austr.) 183 J 4
Warwick (R.I.) 126 H 7
Warwick Channel 183 F 1
Wasagu 197 F 3
Wasatch Range 114 F 2–4
Wasco (CA.) 113 F 7
Wasco (OR.) 110 E 5
Wase 197 FG 4
Waseca (MN.) 119 P 6
Washburn (ND.) 118 GH 3
Washburn (TX.) 117 P 2
Washburn (WI.) 124 CD 3
Washburn Lake 103 Q 2
Washim 174 C 3
Washington (D.C.) 129 OP 3
Washington (GA.) 128 J 8
Washington (IA.) 119 R 9
Washington (IN.) 128 D 3
Washington (Kiribati) → Teraina 187 E 2
Washington (KS.) 120 H 3
Washington (MO.) 121 O 4

Washington (N.C.) 129 O 6
Washington (PA.) 125 O 9
Washington (State) 110
Washington (VA.) 129 N 3
Washington 1(WI.) 124 H 4
Washington, Lake 110 C 3
Washington, Mount 126 H 4
Washington Court House (OH.) 128 H 2
Washington Island 124 H 4
Washington Terrace (UT.) 114 F 2
Washita River 120 H 8
Washoe City (NV.) 112 F 3
Washoe Lake 112 F 3
Washtucna (WA.) 110 G 4
Washuk 169 G 5
Wasian 177 H 4
Wasior 177 H 4
Wāsit (Iraq) 157 E 2
Waskish (MN.) 119 O 2
Waspám 132 F 5
Wassaw Island 131 O 3
Wasserburg 149 F 5
Wassuk Range 112 G 4
Wasta (SD.) 118 F 6
Wasua 184 D 3
Wasum 185 E 3
Watampone 177 F 4
Watan Soppeng 177 E 3–4
Watauga (SD.) 118 G 5
Watauga Lake 129 JK 5
Waterberg 200 B 4
Waterbury (CT.) 126 F 7
Waterbury (VT.) 126 G 5
Wateree (S.C.) 129 L 8
Wateree Lake 129 L 7
Wateree River 129 L 7–8
Waterflow (N.M.) 116 H 1
Waterford 148 B 4
Waterford (CA.) 112 E 5
Waterford (WI.) 124 F 7
Waterhouse River 182 E 1
Waterloo (AR.) 121 M 9
Waterloo (Belgium) 148 D 4
Waterloo (IA.) 119 Q 8
Waterloo (IL.) 124 D 10
Waterloo (Sierra Leone) 196 B 4
Waterman (IL.) 124 F 8
Watersmeet (MI.) 124 E 3
Waterton Lakes National Park 103 OP 6
Watertown (FL.) 131 M 4
Watertown (N.Y.) 126 D 5
Watertown (S.D.) 119 L 6
Watertown (WI.) 124 F 6
Water Valley (MS.) 121 Q 8
Water Valley (TX.) 122 C 4
Waterville (ME.) 126 K 4
Waterville (MN.) 119 P 6
Waterville (NE.) 120 J 3
Waterville (WA.) 110 E 3
Watford City (ND.) 118 E 3
Wa'th 198 E 3
Watheroo 182 B 5
Watkins Glen (N.Y.) 126 C 6
Watkinsville (GA.) 128 H 8
Watonga (OK.) 120 G 7
Watrous 103 Q 5
Watsa 198 D 4
Watseka (IL.) 124 G 9
Watsi Kengo 198 C 5
Watson (TX.) 122 EF 5
Watson Lake 102 M 3
Watsonville (CA.) 112 D 6
Watts Bar Lake 128 G 6
Wattsville (AL.) 128 E 8
Watubela, Kepulauan 177 H 4
Waubay (S.D.) 119 L 5
Waubay Lake 119 L 5
Wauchope 182 E 3
Wauchope 183 J 5
Wauchula (FL.) 131 N 7
Waucoba Mountain 112 GH 5
Waugh Mountain 111 L 5
Waukara, Gunung 177 E 4
Waukarlycarly, Lake 182 C 3
Waukegan (IL.) 124 G 7
Waukesha (WI.) 124 F 6–7
Waukon (IA.) 119 R 7
Wauneta (NE.) 120 D 2
Waupaca (WI.) 124 E 5
Waupun (WI.) 124 F 6
Waurika (OK.) 120 GH 8
Wausa (NE.) 119 L 8
Wausau (WI.) 124 E 5
Wausaukee (WI.) 124 F 4
Wauseon (OH.) 125 K 8
Wautoma (WI.) 124 E 5
Wauwatosa (WI.) 124 F 6
Wau → Wāw 198 D 3
Wave Hill 182 E 2
Waveland (AR.) 121 M 7
Waveland (MS.) 130 E 4
Waverley (N.Y.) 126 C 6
Waverly (OH.) 128 H 2
Waverly (IA.) 119 Q 8
Waverly (IL.) 121 P 3
Waverly (KS.) 121 K 4
Waverly (MO.) 121 M 3
Waverly (TN.) 128 D 5

Waverly (VA.) 129 O 4
Wāw 198 D 3
Wawa (MI.) 125 K 2
Wawa (Nigeria) 197 E 4
Wawa (Ontario, Can.) 104 L 6
Wāw al Kabīr 193 J 3
Wāw an Nāmūs 193 J 4
Wawasee, Lake 124 J 8
Wawona (CA.) 112 F 5
Wawotobi 177 F 4
Waxahachie (TX.) 122 G 3
Waxxari 169 M 3
Way, Lake 182 C 4
Wayabula 197 G 3
Wayamli 177 G 3
Wayao 172 C 5
Waycross (GA.) 131 M 3
Wayland (MI.) 124 J 7
Wayland (N.Y.) 126 B 6
Wayne (KS.) 120 H 3
Wayne (NE.) 119 LM 8
Wayne (OK.) 120 H 8
Wayne (W.V.) 128 J 3
Waynesboro (GA.) 129 JK 8
Waynesboro (MS.) 130 F 3
Waynesboro (PA.) 127 B 9
Waynesboro (TN.) 128 D 6
Waynesboro (VA.) 129 N 3
Waynesburg (PA.) 125 O 10
Waynesville (MO.) 121 N 5
Waynesville (N.C.) 128 J 6
Waynoka (OK.) 120 G 6
Waza (Burma) 175 G 2
Waza (Cameroon) 197 G 3
Waza National Park 197 G 3
Wāzīn 193 H 2
Wazirabad 169 J 4
Wda 149 G 4
Wé 185 J 6
Weagamow Lake 104 J 5
Weatherford (OK.) 120 G 7
Weatherford (TX.) 122 F 3
Weaubleau (MO.) 121 M 5
Weaverville (N.C.) 128 J 6
Webb (TX.) 122 F 6
Webb City (MO.) 121 L 5
Webbe Gestro 199 G 3
Webbe Shibeli 199 G 3
Weber City (N.M.) 117 N 3
Webi Shābelle 199 G 3
Webster (MA.) 126 H 6
Webster (MT.) 118 D 4
Webster (ND.) 118 JK 2
Webster (S.D.) 119 L 5
Webster (WI.) 124 B 4
Webster City (IA.) 119 P 8
Webster Reservoir 120 F 3
Webster Springs (TX.) 123 H 6
Webster Sprs (W.V.) 129 L 3
Weda 177 G 3
Weda, Teluk 177 G 3
Weddell 143 D 9
Weddel Sea 203
Wedel 149 E 4
Wedowee (AL.) 128 F 8
Weed (CA.) 112 C 1
Weed (N.M.) 117 L 5
Weed Heights (NV.) 112 F 3
Weeks (LA.) 123 M 6
Weert 148 E 4
Weh, Pulau 176 A 2
Weichang 173 G 2
Weiden 149 F 5
Weifang 173 G 3
Weihai 173 H 3
Wei He 172 E 4
Weimar (CA.) 112 D 3
Weimar (TX.) 122 G 6
Weinan 172 E 4
Weining 172 D 5
Weipa 183 G 1
Weippe (ID.) 111 K 4
Weir (KS.) 121 L 5
Weirsdale (FL.) 131 N 6
Weirton (W.V.) 125 O 9
Weiser (OR.) 110 HJ 6
Weiser River 110 J 6
Weishan 173 G 4
Weishan Hu 173 G 4
Weishi 172 F 4
Weiss Lake 128 F 7
Weitra 153 FG 2
Weixi 172 C 5
Wei Xian 172 G 3
Weiyuan 172 D 5
Weiyuan 172 D 5
Weizhou Dao 172 E 6
Wejherowo 149 G 4
Welbourn Hill 182 E 4
Welch (KS.) 121 K 6
Welch (TX.) 117 O 5
Welch (W.V.) 129 K 4
Welcome Kop 200 B 6
Weldon (MT.) 118 C 3
Weldon (N.C.) 129 O 5
Welkom 200 D 5

Wellborn (TX.) **122** G 5
Wellesley Islands (Queensland, Austr.) **183** F 2
Wellesley Islands, South (Queensland, Austr.) **183** F 2
Wellfleet (MA.) **126** K 7
Wellfleet (NE.) **120** E 2
Wellington (KS.) **120** H 5
Wellington (New Zealand) **185** R 9
Wellington (New Zealand) **186** C 5
Wellington (N.S.W., Austr.) **183** H 5
Wellington (NV.) **112** F 4
Wellington (OH.) **125** M 8
Wellington (TX.) **117** Q 3
Wellington (UT.) **114** G 4
Wellington, Isla (Chile) **143** AB 8
Wellman (TX.) **117** O 4
Wells (MN.) **119** P 7
Wells (NV.) **112** KL 1
Wells (N.Y.) **126** E 5
Wellsboro (PA.) **126** B 7
Wells Dam **110** F 3
Wellston (OH.) **128** J 2
Wellsville (MO.) **121** O 3
Wellsville (UT.) **114** F 2
Wellton (AZ.) **116** B 5
Welo **199** FG 2
Wels **153** F 2
Welty (OK.) **120** J 7
Wema **198** C 5
Wembere **198** E 5
Wenatchee (WA.) **110** E 3
Wenatchee Mountains **110** E 3
Wenchang **172** F 7
Wenchi **196** D 4
Wenchuan **172** D 4
Wendel (CA.) **112** E 2
Wendell (ID.) **111** L 8
Wenden (AZ.) **116** C 4
Wendeng **173** H 3
Wendover (NV.) **112** L 2
Wendte (SD.) **118** H 6
Wengshui **172** CD 5
Wengyuan **172** F 6
Wenjiang **172** D 4
Wenling **173** H 5
Wenlock River **183** G 1
Wenona (IL.) **124** F 8
Wenquan **169** L 2
Wenquan **172** CD 3
Wenshan **172** D 6
Wenshang **173** G 3
Wenslay **148** C 4
Wensu **169** L 2
Wentworth **183** G 5
Wentworth (S.D.) **119** M 6
Wen Xian **172** DE 4
Wen Xian **172** F 4
Wenzhou **173** H 5
Weott (CA.) **112** AB 2
Wepener **200** D 5
Werda **200** C 5
Weri **177** H 4
Werribee **183** G 6
Werris Creek **183** J 5
Wesel **148** E 4
Weser **149** E 4
Wesiri **177** G 5
Weskan (KS.) **115** PQ 5
Weslaco (TX.) **122** E 9
Wesley (IA.) **119** OP 7
Wesley (ME.) **126** M 4
Wesleyville **105** R 6
Wessel, Cape **183** F 1
Wessel Islands **183** F 1
Wessington (S.D.) **119** K 6
Wessington Springs (S.D.) **119** K 6
West (MS.) **130** E 1
West (TX.) **122** F 4
West Allis (WI.) **124** G 6–7
West Antarctica **203**
Westbank **156** B 2
Westbay (FL.) **131** J 4
West Bay (LA.) **123** O 6
West Bay (TX.) **123** HJ 6
West Bend (IA.) **119** O 8
West Bend (WI.) **124** F 6
West Bengal **174** E 3
Westboro (MO.) **121** K 2
West Branch (IA.) **119** R 9
West Branch (MI.) **125** K 5
West Bromwich **148** C 4
Westbrook (ME.) **126** J 5
Westbrook (TX.) **117** PQ 5
Westby (MT.) **118** DE 2
Westby (WI.) **124** D 6
West Cape **186** C 6
West Cape Howe **182** B 6
West Channel **109** L 2
Westcliffe (CO.) **115** M 5
West Des Moines (IA.) **119** P 9
West Elk Mountains **115** K 5
Westend (CA.) **113** H 7
Westerland **149** E 4
Westerly (R.I.) **127** H 7
Western (NE.) **120** H 2
Western Australia **182** C 3
Western Desert → Aş Şahrā' al Gharbīyah **194** D 3
Western Dvina **151** J 4
Western Ghats **174** BC 4–5
Western Grove (AR.) **121** N 6
Western Port **183** GH 6
Westernport (MD.) **129** N 2
Western Sahara **192** C 4
Western Samoa **186** D 3
Westerville (NE.) **120** F 1
Westerville (OH.) **125** L 9
West Falkland **143** D 9
Westfall (OR.) **110** H 7
West Fayu **186** A 2
Westfield (MA.) **126** G 6
Westfield (ND.) **118** H 4
Westfield (N.Y.) **125** P 7
Westfield (PA.) **126** B 7
Westfield (TX.) **123** H 5
West Fork **118** C 2
West Frankfort (IL.) **121** R 5
Westgate **183** H 4
West Glacier (MT.) **111** L 2
West Grand Lake **126** M 3
West Helena (AR.) **121** P 8
Westhoff (TX.) **122** F 6
Westhope (ND.) **118** G 2
West Ice Shelf **203**
West Indies **133** G, H 3
West Irian **184** C 2
West Lafayette (IN.) **124** H 9
West Lake Wales (FL.) **131** N 7
Westley (CA.) **112** D 5
West Liberty (IA.) **119** R 9
West Liberty (KY.) **128** H 4
Westlock **103** P 5
West Memphis (AR.) **121** P 7
Westminster (CO.) **115** M 4
Westminster (MD.) **129** P 2
Westminster (S.C.) **128** H 7
West Monroe (LA.) **123** L 3
Westmoreland (KS.) **120** J 3
Westmoreland (Queensland, Austr.) **183** F 2
Westmoreland (TN.) **128** E 5
Westmorland (CA.) **113** K 9
West Nicholson **200** D 4
West Nishnabotna River **119** N 9
Weston (CO.) **115** N 6
Weston (ID.) **111** N 8
Weston (OR.) **110** G 5
Weston (W.V.) **129** L 2
Weston (WY.) **118** C 6
Weston-super-Mare **148** C 4
Westover (SD.) **118** H 7
West Palm Beach (FL.) **131** OP 8
West Panama City Beach (FL.) **131** HJ 4
West Pensacola (FL.) **130** G 4
West Plains (MO.) **121** O 6
West Point (GA.) **131** J 2
West Point (KY.) **128** F 4
West Point (MS.) **121** R 9
West Point (NE.) **119** M 9
West Point (VA.) **129** P 4
Westport **185** Q 9
Westport **186** C 5
Westport (CA.) **112** B 3
Westport (IN.) **128** F 2
Westport (OR.) **110** B 4
Westport (WA.) **110** A 4
Westray **148** C 3
Westree **105** L 6
West Richland (WA.) **110** F 4
West Salem (WI.) **124** C 6
West Siberian Plain **159** OP 3
West Spanish Peak **115** N 6
West Thumb (WY.) **111** P 6
West Turkistan **162** EF 2
West Union (IA.) **119** R 8
West Union (OH.) **128** H 3
West Union (W.V.) **129** L 2
West Unity (OH.) **125** K 8
Westvaco (WY.) **111** Q 9
Westville (IL.) **124** G 9
Westville (OK.) **121** K 6–7
West Virginia **129**
West Warwick (R.I.) **126** H 7
Westwater (UT.) **114** H 4
Westwego (LA.) **123** N 6
Westwood (CA.) **112** DE 2
Westwood Lakes (FL.) **131** O 9
West Wyalong **183** H 5
West Yellowstone (MT.) **111** OP 6
Wetar, Pulau **177** G 5
Wetar, Selat **177** G 5
Wetaskiwin **103** P 5
Wete **199** F 6
Wetmore (CO.) **115** M 5
Wet Mountains **115** M 5–6
Wetonka (S.D.) **119** K 5
Wetumka (OK.) **120** J 7
Wetumpka (AL.) **131** H 2
Wetzlar **149** E 4
Wetzstein **149** F 4
Wewahitchka (FL.) **131** J 4
Wewak **184** D 2
Wewak **186** A 3
Wewela (SD.) **118** J 8
Wewoka (OK.) **120** J 7
Wexford **148** B 4
Weyburn **103** R 6
Weyland, Pegunungan **177** J 4
Weymouth **148** C 4
Weymouth (MA.) **126** J 6
Whakataki **185** R 9
Whakatane **185** R 8
Whale Cove **103** T 3
Whalsay **148** C 2
Whangarei **185** Q 8
Whangarei **186** C 5
Wharton (TX.) **122** G 6
Wharton Basin **208** C 4
Wharton Lake **103** R 3
Whatcom, Lake **110** C 2
Whatley (AL.) **130** G 3
Wheatland (CA.) **112** D 3
Wheatland (N.M.) **117** N 3
Wheatland (WY.) **118** D 8
Wheatland Reservoir No 2 **118** C 9
Wheaton (MD.) **129** OP 2
Wheaton (MN.) **119** M 5
Wheat Ridge (CO.) **115** M 4
Wheelbarrow Peak **112** J 5
Wheeler (KS.) **120** D 3
Wheeler (MS.) **121** R 8
Wheeler (OR.) **110** A 5
Wheeler (Quebec, Can.) **105** O 4
Wheeler (TX.) **117** Q 2
Wheeler (WA.) **110** F 3
Wheeler Lake **128** D 7
Wheeler Peak (CA.) **112** F 4
Wheeler Peak (N.M.) **117** L 1
Wheeler Peak (NV.) **112** L 4
Wheeler Ridge (CA.) **113** G 7—8
Wheeler Springs (CA.) **113** F 8
Wheeless (OK.) **120** C 6
Wheeling (W.V.) **129** L 1
Whidbey Island **110** C 2
Whiskeytown Lake **112** C 2
Whiskeytown–Shasta–Trinity National Recreation Area **112** C 2
Whitakers (N.C.) **129** O 5
Whitby **148** C 4
White, Lake **182** D 3
White Bay **105** Q 5
Whitebead (OK.) **120** H 8
White Bear Lake (MN.) **119** PQ 5
White Bird (ID.) **110** J 5
White Butte (N.D.) **118** E 4
White Butte (SD.) **118** F 5
White Canyon (UT.) **114** G 6
White City (KS.) **120** J 4
White City (OR.) **110** C 8
Whiteclay (NE.) **118** F 8
White Cliffs **183** G 5
Whitecourt **103** O 5
White Deer (TX.) **117** P 2
White Earth (ND.) **118** F 2
White Earth Indian Reservation **119** N 3
White Escarpment **200** B 4–5
Whiteface (TX.) **117** O 4
Whiteface Reservoir **119** Q 3
Whitefall (MT.) **118** BC 2
Whitefield (N.H.) **126** H 4
Whitefish Bay (MI.) **125** K 3
Whitefish Bay (WI.) **124** G 6
Whitefish Lake (AK.) **108** G 3
Whitefish Lake (MT.) **111** L 2
Whitefish Point **125** K 3
Whitefish Range **111** L 2
White Hall (AL.) **130** H 2
White Hall (IL.) **121** P 3
Whitehall (MI.) **124** H 6
Whitehall (MT.) **111** NO 5
Whitehall (N.Y.) **126** F 5
Whitehall (OH.) **128** J 2
Whitehall (WI.) **124** C 5
Whitehaven **148** C 4
White Heath (IL.) **124** F 9
Whitehorse **102** L 3
White Island **103** UV 2
White Lake (LA.) **123** L 6
White Lake (WI.) **124** F 4
Whiteman Range **185** F 3
Whitemark **184** L 9
White Mountain (AK.) **102** E 3
White Mountain Peak **112** G 5
White Mountains (AK.) **102** H 2
White Mountains (CA.) **112** G 5
White Mountains (N.H.) **126** HJ 4
White Nile **194** E 6
White Nile Dam → Khazzān Jabal al Awliyā' **194** E 5–6
White Oak Late **121** M 9
White Owl (SD.) **118** F 6
White Pass (AK.) **102** L 4
White Pass (WA.) **110** D 4
White Pigeon (MI.) **124** J 8
White Pine (MI.) **124** E 3
White Pine (TN.) **128** H 5
White Pines (CA.) **112** E 4
White Plains (N.Y.) **127** F 7
White River (AR.) **121** O 8
White River (IN.) **128** D 3
White River (NV.) **112** K 5
White River (N.W.T., Can.) **102** J 3
White River (Ontario, Can.) **104** L 6
White River (S.D.) **118** H 7
White River (SD.) **118** H 7
White River Reservoir **117** P 4
White Russia **151** J 5
White Salmon (WA.) **110** D 5
White Sands (N.M.) **117** K 5
White Sands National Monument **117** K 5
Whitesboro (TX.) **122** G 2
Whitesburg (KY.) **128** HJ 4
Whites City (N.M.) **117** M 5
White Sea **158** G 2
White Settlement (TX.) **122** F 3
White Stone (VA.) **129** P 4
White Sulphur Springs (MT.) **111** OP 4
Whitesville (KY.) **128** E 4
White Swan (WA.) **110** E 4
Whitethorn (CA.) **112** B 2
Whiteville (N.C.) **129** N 7
Whiteville (TN.) **128** B 6
White Volta **196** D 3–4
Whitewater (CO.) **115** J 4
Whitewater (KS.) **120** HJ 5
Whitewater (MT.) **111** S 2
Whitewater (N.M.) **116** H 5
Whitewater (WI.) **124** F 7
Whitewater Bay **131** NO 9
Whitewood **183** G 3
Whitharral (TX.) **117** O 4
Whithorn **148** C 4
Whiting (WI.) **124** E 5
Whitlash (MT.) **111** O 2
Whitley City (KY.) **128** G 5
Whitman (NE.) **118** G 8
Whitmire (S.C.) **129** K 7
Whitmore Mountains **203**
Whitney (NE.) **118** E 8
Whitney (Ontario, Can.) **105** M 6
Whitney, Lake **122** F 3–4
Whitney, Mount **112** G 6
Whitney Point (N.Y.) **126** C 6
Whitsett (TX.) **122** E 7
Whitsunday Island **183** H 3
Whittemore (IA.) **119** O 7
Whittemore (MI.) **125** L 5
Whittier **102** H 3
Whittlesea **183** GH 6
Whitwell (TN.) **128** F 6
Wholdaia Lake **103** QR 3
Whiterocks (UT.) **114** H 3
Whyalla **183** F 5
Wiawso **196** D 4
Wibaux (MT.) **118** D 3
Wichita (KS.) **120** H 5
Wichita, Lake **122** E 2
Wichita Falls **122** E 2
Wichita Mountains **120** G 8
Wick **148** C 3
Wickenburg (AZ.) **116** D 3–4
Wickepin **182** B 5
Wickersham (WA.) **110** C 2
Wickham **182** B 3
Wickham, Cape **184** K 8
Wickiup Reservoir **110** D 7
Wickliffe (KY.) **128** C 5
Wicklow **148** B 4
Wicklow Mountains **148** B 4
Widgiemooltha **182** C 5
Wielkopolska **149** G H 4
Wien **153** G 2
Wiener Becken **153** G 2
Wiener Neustadt **153** G 2
Wienerwald **153** G 2
Wieprz **149** H 4
Wiesbaden **149** E 4
Wiezyca **149** G 4
Wiggins (CO.) **115** NO 3
Wiggins (MS.) **130** E 4
Wight, Isle of **148** C D 4
Wigwam (CO.) **115** N 5
Wil **153** E 2
Wilber (NE.) **120** H 2
Wilbur (OR.) **110** B 7
Wilbur (WA.) **110** G 3
Wilburn Dam **128** D 8
Wilburton (OK.) **121** K 8
Wilcannia **183** G 5
Wilcox (PA.) **125** Q 8
Wilcox (WY.) **118** C 9
Wildcat (WY.) **118** C 6
Wilder (ID.) **110** J 7
Wildersville (TN.) **128** C 6
Wild Horse (CO.) **115** P 5
Wild Horse (TX.) **117** M 6
Wild Horse Lake **111** P 2
Wild Horse Reservoir **112** K 1
Wildrose (ND.) **118** E 2
Wild Rose (WI.) **124** E 5
Wildwood (N.J.) **127** E 10
Wiley City (WA.) **110** E 4
Wilhelm, Mount **184** D 3
Wilhelmina Gebergte **139** G 3
Wilhelm-pieck-Stadt Guben **149** FG 4
Wilhelmshaven **149** E 4
Wilkerson Pass **115** M 4
Wilkes-Barre (PA.) **127** D 7
Wilkesboro (N.C.) **129** K 5
Wilkes Land **203**
Wilkins (NV.) **112** L 1
Wilkinsburg (PA.) **125** P 9
Will, Mount **109** N 4
Willaha (AZ.) **116** D 2
Willamette River **110** B 6
Willamina (OR.) **110** B 5
Willapa Bay **110** A 4
Willapa Hills **110** B 4
Willara (UT.) **114** E 2
Willard (MT.) **118** D 4
Willard (N.M.) **117** K 3
Willcox (AZ.) **116** G 5
Willcox Playa **116** G 5
Willemstad **138** E 1
Willeroo **182** E 2
William "Bill" Dannelly Reservoir **130** G 2
Williambury **182** B 3
William Lake (Man., Can.) **103** R 5
Williams (AZ.) **116** D 2
Williams (CA.) **112** C 3
Williams (MN.) **119** NO 2
Williams Bay (WI.) **124** F 7
Williamsburg (IA.) **119** Q 9
Williamsburg (KY.) **128** G 5
Williamsburg (VA.) **129** P 4
Williams Fork Reservoir **115** L 3–4
Williams Lake **103** N 5
Williamson (W.V.) **129** J 4
Williamsport (IN.) **124** G 9
Williamsport (PA.) **127** B 7
Williamston (N.C.) **129** O 6
Williamstown (KS.) **121** K 3
Williamstown (KY.) **128** G 3
Williamstown (W.V.) **129** K 2
Williamsville (IL.) **121** Q 3
Williamsville (MO.) **121** P 6
Willimantic (CT.) **126** G 7
Willis Group **183** J 2
Williston (FL.) **131** M 5
Williston (N.D.) **118** E 2
Williston (South Africa) **200** C 6
Williston Basin **118** D–F 3
Williston Lake **103** N 4
Willits (CA.) **112** B 3
Willmar (MN.) **119** NO 5
Willoughby (OH.) **125** N 8
Willow (AK.) **102** G 3
Willow (OK.) **120** F 7
Willow Bunch **103** Q 6
Willow City (ND.) **118** H 2
Willow Creek (CA.) **112** B 2
Willow Creek (MT.) **111** O 5
Willow Creek Reservoir **112** J 1
Willowdale (OR.) **110** E 6
Willowick (OH.) **125** N 8
Willow Lake (N.W.T., Can.) **103** O 3
Willow Lake (S.D.) **119** L 6
Willow Lake (WY.) **111** Q 7
Willow Ranch (CA.) **112** E 1
Willows (CA.) **112** C 3
Willow Springs (MO.) **121** O 6
Wills, Lake **182** D 3
Wills Creek **183** F 3
Wills Point (TX.) **122** GH 3
Wilma (FL.) **131** K 4
Wilmington (DE.) **127** D 9
Wilmington (IL.) **124** F 8
Wilmington (N.C.) **129** NO 7
Wilmington (OH.) **128** H 2
Wilmore (KS.) **120** F 5
Wilmot (AR.) **121** O 9
Wilmot (S.D.) **119** LM 5
Wilowmore **200** C 6
Wilsall (MT.) **111** P 5
Wilson (AR.) **121** P 7
Wilson (KS.) **120** G 4
Wilson (N.C.) **129** O 6
Wilson (N.Y.) **125** Q 6
Wilson (OK.) **120** H 8
Wilson (TX.) **117** P 4
Wilson, Cape **103** V 2
Wilson, Mount (AZ.) **116** B 2
Wilson, Mount (CO.) **115** JK 6
Wilson, Mount (NV.) **112** L 4
Wilson Bluff **182** D 5
Wilsonia (CA.) **112** G 6
Wilson Lake (AL.) **128** D 7
Wilson Lake (KS.) **120** G 4
Wilson Lake Reservoir **111** L 8
Wilson River **183** G 4
Wilsons Promontory **183** H 6
Wilson's Promontory National Park **183** H 6
Wilsonville (NE.) **120** E 2
Wilton (ME.) **126** J 4
Wilton (ND.) **118** H 3
Wilton (WI.) **124** D 6
Wilton River **182** E 1
Wiltz **148** E 5
Wiluna **182** C 4
Wimbledon (N.D.) **119** K 3
Winamac (IN.) **124** H 8
Winam Gulf **198** E 5
Winbin **183** GH 4
Winburg **200** D 5
Winchell (TX.) **122** D 4
Winchendon (MA.) **126** H 6
Winchester (ID.) **110** J 4
Winchester (IL.) **121** P 3
Winchester (IN.) **125** K 9

Winchester (KY.) **128** G 4
Winchester (NV.) **112** K 6
Winchester (TN.) **128** E 6
Winchester (U.K.) **148** C 4
Winchester (VA.) **129** N 2
Winchester (WY.) **111** R 7
Winchester Bay (OR.) **110** A 7
Wind Cave National Park **118** E 7
Winder (GA.) **128** H 7–8
Windermere, Lake **148** C 4
Windham (ME.) **126** J 5
Windham (MT.) **111** P 3
Windhoek **200** B 4
Windischgarsten **153** F 2
Wind Mountain **117** L 5–6
Windom (MN.) **119** N 7
Windom Mountain **115** K 6
Windorah **183** G 4
Wind River (WY.) **111** Q 7
Wind River(Yukon, Can.) **109** L 2
Wind River Indian Reservation
   111 QR 7
Wind River Peak **111** Q 8
Wind River Range **111** Q 7–R 8
Windsor (CT.) **126** G 7
Windsor (IL.) **121** R 3
Windsor (MO.) **121** M 4
Windsor (N.C.) **129** P 6
Windsor (Nova Scotia, Can.)
   105 P 7
Windsor (Ontario, Can.) **104** L 7
Windsor (U.K.) **148** C 4
Windsor Forest (GA.) **131** N 2–3
Windsor Locks (CT.) **126** G 7
Windthorst (TX.) **122** E 2
Windward Islands (French
   Polynesia) **187** F 4
Windward Islands (Lesser Antilles)
   133 L 4–5
Windy Peak **110** F 2
Winfield (AL.) **128** D 8
Winfield (KS.) **120** J 5
Winfield (W.V.) **129** K 3
Wing (ND.) **118** H 3
Wingen **183** J 5
Winifred (MT.) **111** Q 3
Winisk **104** K 4
Winisk Lake **104** K 5
Winisk River **104** K 5
Wink (TX.) **117** N 6
Winkelman (AZ.) **116** F 4–5
Winlock (WA.) **110** C 4
Winneba **196** D 4
Winnebago (MN.) **119** O 7
Winnebago (NE.) **119** M 8
Winnebago, Lake **124** F 5–6
Winnebago Indian Reservation
   119 M 8
Winnemucca (NV.) **112** H 2
Winnemucca Lake **112** F 2
Winner (SD.) **118** J 7
Winnett (MT.) **111** R 3
Winnfield (LA.) **123** L 4
Winnibigoshish, Lake **119** OP 3
Winnie (TX.) **123** J 6
Winning **182** A 3
Winnipeg **103** S 6
Winnipeg, Lake **103** S 5
Winnipegosis **103** R 5
Winnipegosis, Lake **103** RS 5
Winnipeg River **104** J 5
Winnipesaukee, Lake **126** H 5
Winnsboro (LA.) **123** M 3
Winnsboro (S.C.) **129** K 7
Winnsboro (TX.) **123** H 3
Winona (AZ.) **116** E 2
Winona (KS.) **120** D 3
Winona (MI.) **124** F 3
Winona (MN.) **119** R 6
Winona (MO.) **121** O 5
Winona (MS.) **121** Q 9
Winona (TX.) **123** H 3
Winona (WA.) **110** H 4
Winooski (VT.) **126** F 4
Winooski River **126** FG 4
Winside (NE.) **119** L 8
Winslow (AZ.) **116** F 2
Winslow (Kiribati) **186** D 3
Winsted (CT.) **126** F 7
Winsted (MN.) **119** O 6
Winston (MT.) **111** O 4
Winston (N.M.) **116** J 4
Winston-Salem (N.C.) **129** L 5
Winter (WI.) **124** D 4
Winter Beach (FL.) **131** O 7
Winter Garden (FL.) **131** N 6
Winter Haven (FL.) **131** N 6
Winter Park (CO.) **115** M 4
Winter Park (FL.) **131** N 6
Winters (CA.) **112** C 4
Winters (TX.) **122** CD 4
Wintersburg (AZ.) **116** D 4
Winterset (IA.) **119** O 9
Winterthur **153** E 2
Winthrop (AR.) **121** L 9
Winthrop (ME.) **126** J 4
Winthrop (MN.) **119** O 6
Wintinna **182** E 4
Winton (N.C.) **129** P 5
Winton (New Zealand) **184** P 10

Winton (Queensland, Austr.)
   183 G 3
Winton (WA.) **110** E 3
Winton (WY.) **111** Q 9
Wiscassel (ME.) **126** K 4
Wisconsin **124** G 8
Wisconsin Dells (WI.) **124** E 6
Wisconsin Rapids (WI.) **124** E 5
Wisconsin River **124** DE 6
Wisdom (MT.) **111** M 5
Wise (VA.) **128** J 5
Wise River (MT.) **111** N 5
Wishek (ND.) **118** J 4
Wishram (WA.) **110** D 5
Wisła **149** G 4
Wismar **149** F 4
Wisner (NE.) **119** LM 9
Wissembourg **153** F 2
Wissota, Lake **124** C 5
Wister (OK.) **121** L 8
Witbank **200** D 5
Witchcliff **182** A 5
Withernsea **148** D 4
Withington, Mount **117** J 4
Withrow (WA.) **110** F 3
Witpütz **200** B 5
Witten (SD.) **118** HJ 7
Wittenberg **149** F 4
Wittenberg (WI.) **124** E 5
Wittenberge **149** F 4
Wittenoom **182** B 3
Witti Range **176** E 3
Wittmann (AZ.) **116** D 4
Witu **199** G 5
Witu Islands **184** E 2
Witvlei **200** B 4
Witwatersrand **200** D 5
Wkra **149** H 4
Władys Lawowo **149** G 4
Włocławek **149** G 4
Wodonga **183** J 6
Wogr Sheikh **199** H 3
Wokam, Pulau **177** H 5
Woking **148** C 4
Wolbach (NE.) **120** G 1
Wolcott (CO.) **115** L 4
Wolcott (IN.) **124** G 9
Wolcott (N.Y.) **126** C 5
Wolcottville (IN.) **124** J 8
Woleai **186** A 2
Wolf (KS.) **120** DE 4
Wolf, Isla **138** B 6
Wolf, Volcán **138** B 6
Wolf Creek (MT.) **111** N 3
Wolf Creek (OR.) **110** B 8
Wolf Creek Pass **115** L 6
Wolfeboro (N.H.) **126** H 5
Wolfe City (TX.) **122** GH 2
Wolfforth (TX.) **117** OP 4
Wolf Island **131** N 3
Wolf Lake (MI.) **124** H 6
Wolf Lake(Yukon, Can.) **109** M 3
Wolf Mountain **109** H 2
Wolford (ND.) **118** J 2
Wolf Point (MT.) **118** BC 2
Wolfratshausen **149** F 5
Wolf River **130** E 4
Wolfsberg **153** F 2
Wolfsburg **149** F 4
Wolgast **149** F 4
Wolin **149** F 4
Wollaston, Islas **143** C 10
Wollaston Lake **103** R 4
Wollaston Peninsula **103** OP 2
Wollongong **183** J 5
Wolmaransstad **200** D 5
Wołomin **149** H 4
Wołow **149** G 4
Wolseley **103** R 5
Wolsey (SD.) **119** K 6
Wolstenholme, Cap **105** M 3
Wolverhampton **148** C 4
Wolverine (MI.) **125** K 4
Wolverine Mountain **109** H 2
Wolverine Peak **111** Q 8
Wonarah **183** F 2
Wondo **199** F 3
Wondoola **183** G 2
Wonga Wongué, Parc National de
   197 F 6
Wonju **173** J 3
Wonotobo Falls **139** G 3
Wŏnsan **173** J 3
Wonthaggi **183** H 6
Woocalla **183** F 5
Wood (SD.) **118** H 7
Wood, Mount **111** Q 4
Woodall Mountain **121** R 8
Woodbine (GA.) **131** N 4
Woodbridge (VA.) **129** O 3
Wood Buffalo National Park
   103 OP 4
Woodburn **183** J 4
Woodburn (OR.) **110** C 5
Woodbury (GA.) **131** K 2
Woodbury (MI.) **124** J 7
Woodbury (N.J.) **127** D 9
Woodbury (TN.) **128** E 6

Woodchopper **109** K 2
Woodfords (CA.) **112** F 4
Woodlake (CA.) **112** F 6
Wood Lake (NE.) **118** H 8
Woodland (CA.) **112** D 4
Woodland (WA.) **110** C 5
Woodland Park (CO.) **115** N 5
Woodland Park (MI.) **124** HJ 6
Woodlark **185** F 3
Woodlark **186** B 3
Wood Mountain **116** G 5
Wood River (AK.) **108** G 4
Wood River (NE.) **120** G 2
Wood River Lakes **102** F 4
Wood River Mountains **108** G 4
Woodroffe, Mount **182** E 4
Woodrow (CO.) **115** O 4
Woodruff (S.C.) **129** JK 7
Woodruff (UT.) **114** F 2
Woodruff (WI.) **124** E 4
Woodruff Norrows Reservoir
   111 P 9
Woods, Lake of the **104** H 6
Woodsboro (TX.) **122** F 7
Woodsfield (OH.) **129** KL 2
Woods Hole (MA.) **126** J 7
Woodside (UT.) **114** G 4
Woods Landing (WY.) **118** C 9
Woodson (TX.) **122** DE 2
Woods Reservoir **128** EF 6
Woodstock (AL.) **128** D 8
Woodstock (IL.) **124** F 7
Woodstock (New Brunsw., Can.)
   105 O 6
Woodstock (Queensland, Austr.)
   183 G 2
Woodstock (VA.) **129** N 3
Woodstock (VT.) **126** G 5
Woodsville (N.H.) **126** G 4
Woodville (MS.) **130** C 3
Woodville (OH.) **125** L 8
Woodville (TX.) **123** J 5
Woodward (OK.) **120** F 6
Woody Creek (CO.) **115** KL 4
Woöi **177** J 4
Wooler **148** C 3
Woolgar **183** G 2
Woolsey (NV.) **112** G 2
Woolsey Peak **116** F 3
Woomera **183** F 5
Woonsocket (R.I.) **126** H 7
Woonsocket (S.D.) **119** K 6
Wooramel **182** A 4
Wooramel River **182** A 4
Wooster (OH.) **125** N 9
Worcester (MA.) **126** H 6
Worcester (South Africa) **200** BC 6
Worcester (U.K.) **148** C 4
Worden (MT.) **111** R 4
Worden (OR.) **110** CD 8
Workworth **185** Q 8
Worland (WY.) **111** S 6
World's View → Rhodes Grave
   200 D 4
Worms **149** E 5
Wörther See **153** F 2
Worthing **148** C 4
Worthington (IN.) **128** D 2
Worthington (MN.) **119** N 7
Worthington (OH.) **125** L 9
Worthington Peak **112** K 5
Wosi **177** G 4
Wotho **186** C 2
Wotje **186** C 2
Wour **197** H 1
Wowenda **177** H 5
Wowoni, Pulau **177** F 4
Wrangel Island **202**
Wrangell **102** L 4
Wrangell Mountains **102** J 3
Wrangell Saint Elias National Park
   and Preserve **102** J 3
Wray (CO.) **115** P 3
Wreck Reef **183** K 3
Wrexham **148** C 4
Wright (KS.) **120** F 5
Wright City (OK.) **121** L 8
Wright Peak **112** C 4
Wrightson, Mount **116** F 6
Wrightsville (GA.) **131** M 2
Wrightsville Beach (N.C.) **129** O 7
Wrightwood (CA.) **113** H 8
Wrigley (N.W.T., Can.) **103** N 3
Wrigley (TN.) **128** D 6
Wrocław **149** G 4
Wrottesley, Cape **103** N 1
Września **149** G 4
Wuchale **199** F 2
Wuchang **172** F 4
Wuchang **173** J 2
Wuchuan (GZ.) **172** E 5
Wuchuan **172** E 5
Wuchuan **172** F 6
Wuda **172** E 3
Wudang Shan **172** F 4
Wudaoliang **172** B 3
Wudi **173** G 3
Wuding **172** D 5
Wudu **172** D 4

Wufeng **172** F 4
Wugang **172** F 5
Wugong **172** E 4
Wuhai **172** E 3
Wuhan **172** F 4
Wuhe **173** G 4
Wuhu **173** G 4
Wu Jiang **172** E 5
Wujiang **174** D 1
Wuji **173** G 3
Wukari **197** F 4
Wuliang Shan **172** D 6
Wuling Shan **172** EF 5
Wulong **172** E 5
Wum **197** F 4
Wumeng Shan **172** D 5
Wunnummin Lake **104** K 5
Wun Rog **198** D 3
Wun Shwai **198** D 3
Wuntho **175** G 3
Wupatki National Monument
   116 E 2
Wuppertal **149** E 4
Wuqi **172** E 3
Wuqia **169** K 3
Wuqiang **173** G 3
Wuqing **173** G 3
Wurno **197** F 3
Würzburg **149** F 5
Wurzen **149** F 4
Wushan **172** D 4
Wu Shan **172** F 4
Wusheng **172** E 4
Wushi **169** K 2
Wusuli Jiang **173** K 1
Wutai Shan **172** F 3
Wutunghliao **172** D 5
Wuvulu **184** D 2
Wuvulu **186** A 3
Wuwei **172** D 3
Wuwei **173** G 4
Wuxi **172** E 4
Wuxi **173** H 4
Wu Xian **173** H 4
Wuxing **173** H 4
Wuxuan **172** E 6
Wuyang **172** F 3
Wuyiling **171** N 6
Wuyi Shan **172–173** G 5
Wuyuan **172** E 2
Wuzhai **172** F 3
Wuzhi Shan **172** E 7
Wuzhong **172** E 3
Wuzhou **172** F 6
Wyalusing (PA.) **126** C 7
Wyandotte (MI.) **125** L 7
Wyarno (WY.) **118** B 6
Wyatt (MO.) **121** Q 6
Wye **148** C 4
Wyeville (WI.) **124** D 6
Wylie (TX.) **122** G 2
Wylie, Lake **129** K 6
Wylliesburg (VA.) **129** N 5
Wymer (WA.) **110** E 4
Wymore (NE.) **120** J 2
Wynbring **182** E 5
Wyndham **182** D 2
Wyndmere (N.D.) **119** LM 4
Wynnburg (TN.) **128** B 5
Wynne (AR.) **121** P 7
Wynniatt Bay **103** P 1
Wynona (OK.) **120** J 6
Wynot (NE.) **119** L 8
Wynyard **103** R 5
Wyocena (WI.) **124** E 6
Wyola (MT.) **111** S 5
Wyoming (East) **118**
Wyoming (IA.) **119** RS 8
Wyoming (MI.) **124** J 7
Wyoming (West) **111** P 8
Wyoming (WY.) **118** C 9
Wyoming Peak **111** P 8
Wyoming Range **111** P 7–8
Wyoming Ranges **111** P 9
Wyperfeld National Park **183** G 6
Wysoczyzna Ciechanowska
   149 GH 4
Wyszków **149** H 4
Wytheville (VA.) **129** KL 5
Wyzyna Lubelska **149** H 4

X

Xabyaisamba **172** C 4
Xailongmoin **174** E 2
Xainza **174** E 1
Xai-Xai **201** C 4
Xalapa → Jalapa Enríquez **132** C 4
Xambioá **139** J 5
Xá-Muteba **200** B 1
Xangongo **200** AB 3
Xánthi **154** C 2
Xanthos **154** C 3

Xanxeré **142** F 4
Xapecó **142** F 4
Xapuri **140** C 3
Xarag **172** C 3
Xarba La **174** D 2
Xar Moron **172** F 2
Xar Moron He **173** G 2
Xaundo **200** B 1
Xavantes, Reprêsa de **141** FG 5
Xavantes, Serra dos **141** G 3
Xavantina **141** F 5
Xayar **169** L 2
Xenia (OH.) **128** H 2
Xiachuan Dao **172** F 6
Xiaguan **172** D 5
Xiahe **172** D 3
Xiajin **172** G 3
Xiamen **173** G 6
Xi'an **172** E 4
Xianfeng **172** E 5
Xiangcheng **172** C 5
Xiangfan **172** F 4
Xianghua Ling **172** F 5
Xianghuang **172** F 2
Xiang Jiang **172** F 5
Xiangride **172** C 3
Xiangshan **173** H 5
Xiangtan **172** F 5
Xiangyin **172** F 5
Xianju **173** H 5
Xianning **172** F 5
Xianyang **172** E 4
Xiao'ergou **171** M 6
Xiaogan **172** F 4
Xiao Hinggan Ling **171** N 5–6
Xiaojin **172** D 4
Xiaowutai Shan **172** G 3
Xiaoyi **172** F 3
Xiapu **173** H 5
Xichang **172** D 5
Xichou **172** D 6
Xicoténcatl **132** C 3
Xieng Khouang **175** H 4
Xifeng **173** H 2
Xifengzhen **172** E 3
Xigazê **174** E 2
Xi He **172** D 2
Xiji **172** E 3
Xi Jiang **172** F 6
Xijir Ulan Hu **172** B 3
Xikouzi **170** M 5
Xiliao He **173** H 2
Xilin **172** E 6
Xilókastron **154** B 3
Ximeng **172** C 6
Ximiao **172** D 2
Xin'anjiang Shuiku **173** G 5
Xin Barag Youqi **170** L 6
Xin Barag Zuoqi **170** L 6
Xincai **172** F 4
Xincheng **172** D 3
Xincheng **172** G 3
Xincheng **172** E 6
Xindu **172** D 4
Xinfeng **172** F 6
Xinfengjiang Shuiku **172** F 6
Xing'an **172** F 5
Xingcheng **173** GH 2
Xingdi **172** A 2
Xingguo **172** G 5
Xinghai **172** C 3
Xinghe **172** F 2
Xinglong **173** G 2
Xingning **172** G 6
Xingren **172** E 5
Xingshan **172** F 4
Xingtai **172** F 3
Xingu **139** H 4
Xingu **141** F 3
Xingu **141** F 3
Xing Xian **172** F 3
Xingxingxia **172** C 2
Xingyi **172** D 5
Xinhe **169** L 2
Xinhe **172** G 3
Xining **172** D 3
Xinjiang Uygur Zizhiqu **169** L 2
Xinjin **172** D 4
Xinjin **173** H 3
Xinle **172** F 3
Xinlitun **171** N 5
Xinlong **172** D 4
Xinping **172** D 6
Xinqing **171** N 6
Xintai **173** G 3
Xintian **172** F 5
Xinwen **173** G 3
Xin Xian **172** F 3
Xinxiang **172** F 3
Xinxing **172** F 6
Xinyang **172** F 4
Xinyi **172** F 3
Xinyi **173** G 4
Xinyuan **169** L 2
Xinzheng **172** F 4
Xiong Xian **173** G 3
Xiqing Shan **172** D 4
Xique-Xique **141** H 3

Xishui 172 G 4
Xi Taijnar Hu 172 B 3
Xi Ujimqin Qi 173 G 2
Xiushui 172 F 5
Xiuwu 172 F 3
Xíuyan 173 H 2
Xiwu 172 C 4
Xixabangma Feng 174 E 2
Xi Xian 172 F 3
Xixiang 172 E 4
Xiyang 172 F 3
Xizanq Zizhigu 174 DE 1
XL Ranch Indian Reservation
112 E 1
Xorkol 172 B 3
Xpuhil 132 E 4
Xuan'en 172 E 4
Xuanhan 172 E 4
Xuanhua 172 F 2
Xuanwei 172 D 5
Xuchang 172 F 4
Xue Shan 172 CD 5
Xuguit Qi 170 M 6
Xümatang 172 C 4
Xundian 172 D 5
Xungru 174 D 2
Xun He 171 N 6
Xunke 171 N 6
Xunwu 172 G 6
Xupu 172 F 5
Xur 172 C 3
Xuwen 172 F 6
Xuyi 173 G 4
Xuyong 172 DE 5
Xuzhou 173 G 4

Y

Yaak (MT.) 111 K 2
Ya'an 172 D 4
Yabassi 197 G 5
Yabelo 199 F 4
Yablochnyy 171 Q 6
Yablon 171 V 2
Yablonitse, Pereval 154 B 1
Yablonovo 170 K 5
Yablonovyy Khrebet 170 JL 5
Yablonovyy Range 170 L 4–5
Yabrai Yanchang 172 D 3
Yabrei Shan 172 D 3
Yabrīn 195 H 4
Yabrūd (Syria) 156 B 2
Yabucoa (P.R.) 130 D 8
Yabuli 173 J 2
Yachats (OR.) 110 A 6
Yacuiba 140 D 5
Yacurai 138 E 3
Yadé, Massif du 198 B 3
Yadgir 174 C 4
Yadkin River 129 K 5
Yadkinville (N.C.) 129 L 5
Yadong 174 E 2
Yaeyama-rettō 173 H 6
Yagodnaya Polyana 158 J 5
Yagodnoye 171 R 3
Yagoua 197 GH 3
Yagradagze Shan 172 C 3
Yagtali, Plato 170 G 2
Yahila 198 C 4
Yahisuli 198 C 5
Yahuma 198 C 4
Yahyalı 155 E 3
Yainax Butte 110 D 8
Yajiang 172 D 4
Yakacık 155 E 3
Yakima (WA.) 110 E 4
Yakima Indian Reservation
110 DE 4
Yakima River 110 E 4
Yakmach 169 G 5
Yako 196 D 3
Yakoma 198 C 4
Yakovlevka 170 D 1
Yakrik 169 L 2
Yakt (MT.) 111 K 2
Yakumo 173 LM 2
Yaku-shima 173 K 4
Yakutat 102 K 4
Yakutat Bay 102 J 4
Yakutsk 171 N 3
Yakuttork 171 U 2
Yakuty 159 R 2
Yala (Sri Lanka) 174 D 6
Yala (Thailand) 175 H 6
Yalakköy 155 E 3
Yale Lake 110 C 4–5
Yale Point 116 G 1
Yalgoo 182 B 4
Yali 198 C 5
Yalleroi 183 H 3
Yallourn 183 H 6
Yalnızçam Dağları 155 F 2
Yaloké 198 B 3
Yalong Jiang 172 D 5
Yalova 154 C 2

Yalpukh, Ozero 154 C 1
Yalta 155 E 1
Yalta 155 D 2
Yalu Jiang 173 HJ 2
Yalutorovsk 159 N 4
Yalvaç 154 D 3
Yalym 159 N 5
Yamagata 173 LM 3
Yamaguchi 173 K 4
Yamal, Poluostrov 159 NO 1
Yam-Alin', Khrebet 171 OP 5
Yamal Peninsula 159 NO 1
Yamantau, Gora 159 L 5
Yamarovka 170 K 5
Yamba 198 F 3
Yambering 196 B 3
Yambio 198 D 4
Yambol 154 C 2
Yamburg 159 P 2
Yambuto, Ozero 159 PQ 1
Yambuya 198 CD 4
Yamdena, Pulau 177 H 5
Yamethin 175 G 3
Yamia 197 G 3
Yaminbot 184 D 2
Yam Kinneret (Israel) 156 B 2
Yamm 151 J 4
Yamma Yamma, Lake 183 G 4
Yamoussoukro 196 CD 4
Yampa (CO.) 115 L 3
Yampa River 115 K 3
Yampol' (Ukraine, U.S.S.R.)
154 C 1
Yamsay Mountain 110 D 8
Yamsk 171 S 4
Yamuna 174 D 2
Yamunanagar 174 C 1
Yamzho Yumco 175 F 2
Yana 171 P 1
Yanam 174 D 4
Yan'an 172 E 3
Yanaoca 140 B 3
Yanartaş Dağları 154 D 3
Yanbian 172 D 5
Yanbu' (Saudi Arabia) 156 BC 4
Yancey (TX.) 122 D 6
Yanceyville (N.C.) 129 M 5
Yanchang 172 EF 3
Yancheng 173 H 4
Yanchi 172 E 3
Yan Dağ 154 CD 3
Yandang Shan 173 H 5
Yandja 198 B 5
Yandrakinot 102 C 3
Yanfolia 196 C 3
Yangalia 198 C 3
Yangambi 198 CD 4
Yangarey 159 M 2
Yangbajain 175 F 1
Yangbi 172 C 5
Yangchun 172 F 6
Yanggao 172 F 2
Yanggu 172 G 3
Yangi Emäm (Iran) 157 F 2
Yangiyul' 169 H 2
Yangikishlak 169 H 2
Yangjiang 172 F 6
Yangquan 172 F 3
Yangshan 172 F 6
Yangshuo 172 F 6
Yangtze Kiang 172 F 4
Yang Xian 172 E 4
Yangxiu 172 G 4
Yangzhou 173 G 4
Yanhe 172 E 5
Yanhuqu 174 D 1
Yanis'yarvi, Ozero 150 K 3
Yanji 173 J 2
Yanjin 172 D 5
Yankan, Khrebet 170 L 4
Yanking 173 G 2
Yankton (S.D.) 119 L 8
Yankton Indian Reservation
119 K 7
Yano-Indigirskaya Nizmennost
171 PR 1
Yanov Stan 159 Q 2
Yanqi Huizu Zizhixian 169 LM 2
Yanshan 172 D 6
Yan Shan 173 G 2
Yanshan 173 G 3
Yanshi 172 F 4
Yanshiping 172 B 4
Yanshou 173 J 1
Yanskiy 171 O 2
Yanskiy Zaliv 171 OP 1
Yantai 173 H 3
Yanting 173 H 4
Yanwa 172 C 5
Yany-Kurgan 169 H 2
Yanyuan 172 D 5
Yanzhou 173 G 3
Yao 197 H 3
Yaoundé 197 G 5
Yapei 196 D 4
Yapen, Pulau 177 J 4
Yapen, Selat 177 J 4
Yaptiksale 159 O 2
Yapura 138 D 4
Yaqui, Rio 106 D 6

Yaquina Bay 110 A 6
Yaquina Head 110 A 6
Yaraka 183 G 3
Yaraligöz 155 D 2
Yaransk 158 J 4
Yarda 197 H 2
Yaremcha 154 B 1
Yarensk 158 J 3
Yari 138 D 3
Yarīm 195 G 6
Yarishev 154 C 1
Yaritagua 138 E 1
Yarkant 169 K 3
Yarkant He 169 K 3
Yarkant → Shache 169 K 3
Yarkino 170 G 4
Yarlung Zangbo Jiang 172 B 5
Yarmouth (ME.) 126 J 5
Yarmouth (Nova Scotia, Can.)
105 O 7
Yarnell (AZ.) 116 D 3
Yarongo 159 N 2
Yaroslavl' 158 G 4
Yarraloola 182 B 3
Yarra Yarra Lakes 182 B 4
Yarrie 182 C 3
Yarroto 159 O 2
Yar Sale 159 O 2
Yartsevo 158 F 4
Yartsevo 159 S 3
Yarumal 138 C 2
Yarwa 172 C 4
Yasawa Group 186 C 4
Yasel'da 151 J 5
Yashalta 155 F 1
Yashi 197 F 3
Yashkino 171 P 5
Yashkul' 155 G 1
Yasin 169 J 3
Yasinovataya 155 E 1
Yasinya 154 B 1
Yasnyy 171 N 5
Yass 183 H 5
Yassachnaya 171 S 3
Yasun Burnu 155 E 2
Yata 140 C 3
Yata 140 C 3
Yatağan 154 C 3
Yatakala 196 DE 3
Yates (N.M.) 117 N 1
Yates Center (KS.) 121 K 5
Yates City (IL.) 124 E 9
Yaté-Village 185 J 6
Yatina 140 CD 5
Yatolema 198 C 4
Yatsushiro 173 JK 4
Yatta Plateau 199 F 5
Yatton 183 H 3
Yauca 140 B 4
Yauco (P.R.) 130 C 2
Yauna Moloca 138 D 4
Yauyos 140 A 3
Yavarí 138 D 4
Yavatmal 174 C 3
Yavi, Cerro 138 E 2
Yavita 138 E 3
Yawatahama 173 K 4
Yawng-hwe 175 G 3
Yaxchilán 132 D 4
Ya Xian 172 E 7
Yaya 159 R 4
Yay Gölü 155 E 3
Yayladağı 155 E 3
Yayva 158 L 4
Yazd (Iran) 157 G 3
Yazdān 169 G 4
Yaz-ed Khväst (Iran) 157 F 3
Yazılıkaya 154 D 3
Yazılıkaya 155 D 2
Yazoo City (MS.) 130 D 2
Yazoo River 130 D 2
Ybbs an der Donau 153 G 2
Yding Skovhöj 151 E 4
Ydre 151 G 4
Ydzhid Parma 159 L 3
Ye 175 G 4
Yebawmi 175 G 2
Yebbi Bou 197 H 1
Yecheng 169 K 3
Yecla 152 C 4
Yedarma 170 H 4
Yedashe 175 G 4
Yedinka 171 P 6
Yedintsy 154 C 1
Yedoma 158 H 3
Yedseram 197 G 3
Yeeda River 182 C 2
Yefira 154 B 2
Yeggueba 197 G 2
Yegorlyk 155 F 1
Yegorlykskaya 155 F 1
Yegor'yevsk 158 GH 4
Yegros 142 E 4
Yeha 199 F 2

Yei 198 E 4
Yeji 196 D 4
Yekepa 196 C 4
Yekhegnadzor 155 G 3
Yékiasahal 197 H 2
Yelabuga 158 K 4
Yelan' 158 H 5
Yelanets 154 D 1
Yelantsy 170 J 5
Yele 196 B 4
Yelets 158 G 5
Yelgu 198 E 3
Yelia 184 E 3
Yelimané 196 B 2
Yelizarovo 159 N 3
Yelizavetinka 159 L 5
Yelizovo 171 T 5
Yell 148 C 2
Yellandu 174 D 4
Yellow Dam 111 S 5
Yellowhead Pass 103 O 5
Yellowknife 103 P 3
Yellow Pine (ID.) 111 K 6
Yellow River (FL.) 130 H 4
Yellow River → Huang He 173 G 3
Yellow Sea 173 H 4
Yellowstone Lake 111 P 6
Yellowstone National Park 111 P 6
Yellowstone River 118 D 3
Yellowtail Reservoir 111 R 5–6
Yellville (AR.) 121 N 6
Yel'nya 158 F 4
Yeloguy 159 R 3
Yelovka 171 U 4
Yelua 192 B 4
Yelvertoft 183 F 3
Yelwa 197 EF 3
Yemanzhelinsk 159 M 5
Yemassee (S.C.) 129 L 9
Yematan 172 C 3
Yematan 172 C 3
Yemen 195 G 5
Yemet 171 V 3
Yen 197 G 5
Yenagoa 197 F 5
Yena 150 K 2
Yenakiyevo 155 E 1
Yenanma 175 F 4
Yenashimski Pol'kan, Gora
170 F 3–4
Yen Bai 175 H 3
Yendi 196 DE 4
Yendondin 170 K 5
Yengisar 169 K 3
Yengo 197 H 5
Yengue 197 F 5
Yenice 155 D 2
Yenice 155 D 3
Yenice (Turkey) 155 E 3
Yenice (Turkey) 155 E 3
Yenişehir 154 C 2
Yenisey 159 R 2
Yenisey 170 F 4
Yenisey, Bol'shoy 170 G 5
Yenisey, Malyy 170 FG 5
Yenisey Kryazh 170 F 3–4
Yeniseysk 170 F 4
Yeniseyskiy Zaliv 170 D 1
Yenotayevka 155 G 1
Yentna River 109 H 3
Yeo, Lake 182 C 4
Yeovil 148 C 4
Yepoko 159 OP 2
Yeppoon 183 J 3
Yeraliyevo 168 E 2
Yerbogachen 170 J 3
Yercha 171 R 2
Yerema 170 J 3
Yerema, Bol'shaya 170 J 3
Yerementau, Gory 159 O 5
Yerevan 155 FG 2
Yergeni 155 F 1
Yerington (NV.) 112 F 4
Yerington Indian Reservation
112 F 3
Yerka Inadeyur 159 P 3
Yerköy 155 D 3
Yermak 159 P 5
Yermakovo 159 R 2
Yermakovo 159 O 3
Yermakovskoye 170 F 5
Yermentau 159 O 5
Yermitsa 158 K 2
Yermo (CA.) 113 J 8
Yermo 132 B 2
Yerofey-Pavlovich 171 M 5
Yeroham (Israel) 156 B 3
Yeropol 171 V 2
Yershov 158 J 5
Yertom 158 J 3
Yertsevo 158 H 3
Yerupajá, Nevado 140 A 3
Yerushalayim 156 B 3
Yesa, Embalse de 152 C 3
Yeşil 159 N 5
Yeşilhisar 155 D 3
Yeşilköy 154 C 2

Yeso (N.M.) 117 M 3
Yessentuki 155 F 2
Yessey 159 H 2
Yessey, Ozero 170 H 2
Yöt-Kyuyel' 170 M 3
Yetman 183 J 4
Yetti 192 D 3
Yeu 175 G 2
Yeu, Ile d' 152 C 2
Yeu 196 B 4
Yevlakh 168 D 2
Yevpatoriya 155 D 1
Yevsyavan' 159 M 2
Yeya 155 E 1
Yeysk 155 E 1
Yeyskoye Ukrepleniye 155 E 1
Yezd (Iran) 157 G 3
Yezhikha 158 J 4
Ygyatta 170 L 3
Yialousa 155 D 3
Yialousa (Cyprus) 156 AB 2
Yi'an 171 N 6
Yiannitsá 154 B 2
Yibin 172 D 5
Yibug Caka 174 E 1
Yichang 172 F 4
Yichuan 172 F 3
Yichuan 172 F 4
Yichun 171 N 6
Yichun 172 F 5
Yidu 172 F 4
Yidu 173 G 3
Yidun 172 C 4
Yifeng 172 F 5
Yi He 173 G 3
Yilan 173 J 1
Yıldız Dağı 155 E 2
Yıldızeli 155 E 3
Yilehuli Shan 171 M 5
Yiliang 172 D 6
Yinchuan 172 E 3
Yingde 172 F 6
Yingjiang 172 C 6
Yingkou 173 H 2
Yingshan 172 G 4
Yingtan 173 G 5
Yining 169 L 2
Yin Shan 172 E 2
Yi'ong Zangbo 172 B 4
Yirga Alem 199 F 3
Yirol 198 E 3
Yirshi 170 L 6
Yishui 173 G 3
Yithion 154 B 3
Yitong 173 HJ 2
Yitulihe 171 M 5
Yiwu 172 B 2
Yi Xian 173 H 2
Yiyang 172 F 5
Yiyang 173 G 5
Yizhang 172 F 5
Ylas-Yuryakh 170 J 2
Ylikitka 150 J 2
Yli-li 150 J 2
Ylitornio 150 H 2
Ylivieska 150 H 3
Ylöjärvi 150 H 3
Yngaren 151 G 4
Ynykchanskiy 171 P 3
Yoakum (TX.) 122 F 6
Yoboki 199 G 2
Yoder (WY.) 118 D 9
Yogo Peak 111 P 4
Yogoum 197 H 2
Yogyakarta 176 CD 5
Yojoa, Lago de 132 E 5
Yokadouma 197 G 5
Yoko 197 G 4
Yokoate-jima 173 J 5
Yokohama 173 LM 3
Yokosuka 173 LM 3–4
Yokote 173 M 3
Yola 197 G 4a
Yolombo 198 C 5
Yomba Indian Reservation 112 H 3
Yome 197 H 3
Yonago 173 K 3
Yonaguni-jima 173 H 6
Yoncalla (OR.) 110 B 7
Yonezawa 173 M 3
Yöngan 173 J 2
Yong'an 173 G 5
Yongchang 172 D 3
Yongchuan 172 E 5
Yongchun 173 G 5
Yongde 172 C 6
Yong deng 172 D 3
Yongding 172 G 6
Yonghung 173 J 3
Yongji 173 J 2
Yongjing 172 D 3
Yŏngju 173 J 3
Yongkang 173 H 5
Yongning 172 E 3
Yongping 172 C 5
Yongren 172 D 5
Yongshan 172 D 5
Yongshou 172 E 4
Yongshun 172 E 5
Yongxin 172 F 5

Yongxiu 172 G 5
Yonibana 196 B 4
Yoniveem 108 D 2
Yonkers 127 F 8
Yonne 152 D 2
Yopal 138 D 2
Yopurga 169 K 3
York (AL.) 130 F 2
York (ND.) 118 J 2
York (NE.) 120 H 2
York (PA.) 127 C 9
York (S.C.) 129 K 6–7
York (U.K.) 148 C 4
York (Western Australia) 182 B 5
York, Cape 183 G 1
Yorke Peninsula 183 F 5
York Factory 104 J 4
York River 129 P 4
Yorkshire Moors 148 C 4
Yorkshire Wolds 148 C 4
York Sound 182 D 1
Yorkton 103 R 5
Yorktown (TX.) 122 F 6–7
Yorkville (IL.) 124 F 8
Yoro 132 E 4
Yoron-jima 173 J 5
Yorosso 196 CD 3
Yorubaland Plateau 196 E 4
Yosemite National Park 112 F 5
Yosemite Village (CA.) 112 F 5
Yoshkar Ola 158 J 4
Yost (UT.) 114 D 2
Yŏsu 173 J 4
Yotala 140 C 4
Yotau 140 D 4
Yotvata (Israel) 156 B 3
Youanmi 182 B 4
Youdunzi 172 B 3
Youghal 148 B 4
Youghiogheny River Lake 129 M 2
You Jiang 172 E 6
Youllemmedene 196 E 2
Young 183 H 5
Youngstown (FL.) 131 J 4
Youngstown (N.Y.) 125 Q 6
Youngstown (OH.) 125 O 8
Youngsville (LA.) 123 LM 5
Youngsville (N.M.) 117 K 1
Youngsville (PA.) 125 P 8
Yountville (CA.) 112 C 4
Youshashan 172 B 3
Youssoufia 192 D 2
Youyang 172 E 5
Yozgat 155 D 3
Ypaceraí 142 E 4
Ypeihu 140 E 5
Ypsilanti (MI.) 125 L 7
Yreka (CA.) 112 C 1
Ysabel Channel 185 EF 2
Ystad 151 F 4
Ytterhogdal 150 F 3
Ytyk-Kel' 171 O 3
Yu 'Alliq, Jabal (Egypt) 156 A 3
Yuan Jiang 172 F 5
Yuanjiang 172 D 6
Yuan Jiang 172 D 6
Yuanling 172 F 5
Yuanmou 172 D 5
Yuanping 172 F 3
Yuanqu 172 F 3
Yuanshanzi 172 CD 3
Yuanshi 172 F 3
Yuanyang 172 D 6
Yuba City (CA.) 112 D 3
Yūbari 173 M 2
Yuben' 169 J 3
Yucatán Peninsula 132 E 3–4
Yucca (AZ.) 116 B 3
Yucca House National Monument 114 J 6
Yucca Lake 112 J 6
Yucca Valley (CA.) 113 J 8
Yucheng 173 G 3
Yuci 172 F 3
Yudoma 171 P 4
Yudoma-Krestovskaya 171 P 3
Yudomo Mayskoye Nagor'ye 171 PQ 3–4
Yudomskiy Khrebet 171 Q 3
Yudu 172 G 5
Yueqing 173 H 5
Yuexi 172 D 5
Yueyang 172 F 5
Yug 158 J 3
Yugan, Bol'shoy 159 O 4
Yugorskiy Poluostrov 159 M 2
Yugorskiy Shar 159 M 2
Yugorskiy Shar, Proliv 159 M 2
Yugoslavia 153 G 3
Yugo-Tala 171 S 2
Yuhang 173 H 4
Yu Jiang 172 EF 6
Yukagirskoye Ploskogor'ye 171 ST 2
Yukhnov 158 G 5
Yukhta 170 J 4
Yuki 198 B 5
Yukon (AK.) 102 E 3
Yukon (MO.) 121 O 5

Yukon, Fort 102 H 2
Yukon-Charley Rivers National Preserve 102 J 2–3
Yukon Flats 102 H 2
Yukon Flats National Monument 102 HJ 2
Yukon Plateau 102 K 3
Yukon Territory 102 KL 3
Yüksekova 155 F 3
Yulee (FL.) 131 N 4
Yuli (China) 169 M 2
Yuli (Nigeria) 197 G 4
Yulin 172 E 3
Yulin 172 F 6
Yulong Kueshan 172 D 5
Yulu Rapids 198 C 4
Yuma (AZ.) 116 B 5
Yuma (CO.) 115 P 3
Yuma (U.S.S.R.) 150 K 2
Yuma Desert 116 B 5
Yumari, Cerro 138 E 3
Yumbe 198 E 4
Yumbi (Zaire) 198 B 5
Yumbi (Zaire) 198 D 5
Yumbo 138 C 3
Yumen 172 C 3
Yumenzhen 172 C 2
Yumin 169 L 1
Yumurchen 170 K 5
Yumurtalık 155 E 3
Yunaska 102 C 5
Yuncheng 172 F 3
Yunekit 170 M 3
Yunhe 173 G 5
Yunkai Dashan 172 F 6
Yunling Shan 172 C 5
Yunlong 172 C 5
Yunnan 172 D 6
Yuntra 154 C 2
Yun Xian 172 F 4
Yun Xian 172 D 6
Yunxiao 173 G 6
Yunyang 172 E 4
Yuqing 172 E 5
Yur 171 P 4
Yurga 159 Q 4
Yuribey 159 O 2
Yuriby 159 P 1
Yurimaguas 138 C 5
Yuroma 158 J 2
Yurty 171 U 4
Yurungkax He 169 L 3
Yur'yevka 155 E 1
Yu Shan 172 G 5
Yushan (China) 173 G 5
Yushan (Taiwan) 173 H 6
Yushe 172 F 3
Yushkozero 150 K 3
Yushno Muyskiy Khrebet 170 KL 4
Yushnoye 171 Q 6
Yushu 172 C 4
Yushu 173 J 2
Yusta 155 G 1
Yusufeli 155 F 2
Yuti 140 D 4
Yutian 169 L 3
Yutian 173 G 3
Yuxi 172 D 6
Yu Xian 172 F 3
Yuyao 173 H 4
Yuzhno Chuyskiy, Khrebet 159 R 6
Yuzhno-Kamyshovyy Khrebet 171 Q 6
Yuzhno-Sakhalinsk 171 Q 6
Yuzhno-Yeniseyskiy 170 F 4
Yuzhnyy 155 F 1
Yuzhnyy, Mys 171 T 4
Yuzhnyy Anyuyskiy Khrebet 171 UV 2
Yuzhnyy Bug 154 D 1
Yuznoural'sk 159 M 5
Yverdon 153 E 2
Yvetot 152 D 2
Ywamun 175 G 3

Z

Zabarjad (Egypt) 156 B 5
Zabaykal'sk 170 L 6
Zāb-e Kuchek (Iran) 157 D 1
Zabéré 196 D 3
Zabid 195 G 6
Zabok 153 G 2
Zabol 169 G 4
Zāboli 169 G 5
Zabolotov 154 C 1
Zabřeh 149 G 5
Zabrze 149 G 4
Zaburun'ye 168 E 1
Zabzugu 196 E 4
Zacapa 132 E 5
Zacapu 132 B 4

Zacatecas 132 B 3
Zacatepec 132 C 4
Zadar 153 G 3
Zadetkale Kyun 175 G 5
Zadetkyi Kyun 175 G 6
Zadi 175 G 5
Zadoi 172 C 4
Zadran 169 H 4
Za'faranah (Egypt) 156 A 3
Zafir 195 J 4
Zafra 152 B 4
Zag 192 D 3
Żagań 149 G 4
Zaggūt 193 J 3
Zaghāwa 194 C 6
Zaghdeh (Iran) 157 G 2
Zāgheh (Iran) 157 E 2
Zāgheh (Iran) 157 F 2
Zāgheh-ye Bālā (Iran) 157 E 2
Zāgh Marz (Iran) 157 F 1
Zaghwän 193 H 1
Zagora 192 D 2
Zagorsk 158 G 4
Zagreb 153 G 2
Zagros, Kūhha ye (Iran) 157 EF 2
Zagros Mountains (Iran) 157 F 3
Za'gya Zangbo 174 E 1
Zagyva 154 A 1
Zāhedān 169 G 5
Zahirah (Oman) 157 G 5
Zahl (ND.) 118 E 2
Zahlah (Lebanon) 156 B 2
Zahrān 195 G 5
Zahrez Rharbi 193 F 2
Zair (United Arab Emirates) 157 F 5
Zaire 197 G 7
Zaire 198 C 5
Zaire (Angola) 200 A 1
Zaječar 154 B 2
Zakak 197 E 2
Zakamensk 170 H J 5
Zakataly 168 D 2
Zakharo 154 B 3
Zakharov 171 O 3
Zakharovka 159 O 6
Zakhmet 169 G 3
Zākhū (Iraq) 156 D 1
Zákinthos 154 B 3
Zákinthos 154 B 3
Zakopane 149 G 5
Zakouma 197 H 3
Zakouma, Parc National de 197 H 3
Zakur'ya 170 J 4
Zalābiyah (Syria) 156 C 2
Zalaegerszeg 154 A 1
Zalāf (Syria) 156 B 2
Zalari 170 H 5
Zaleshchiki 154 C 1
Zalesskiy 158 G 4
Zalew Szczecinski 149 F 4
Zalew Wislany 149 G 4
Zalim 195 G 4
Zalingei 194 C 6
Zaliv Akademii 171 P 5
Zaliv Aniva 171 Q 6
Zaliv Chayvo 171 Q 5
Zaliv Kara-Bogaz Gol 168 E 2
Zaliv Korfa 171 V 3–4
Zaliv Kresta 102 B 2
Zaliv Ozernoy 171 U 4
Zaliv Petra Velikogo 173 K 2
Zaliv Pil'tun 171 Q 5
Zaliv Sakhalinskiy 171 Q 5
Zaliv Shelikhova 171 T 3–4
Zaliv Terpeniya 171 Q 6
Zaliv Ushki 171 R 4
Zallah 193 J 3
Zalţan 193 J 3
Zama (MS.) 130 E 2
Zamakh 195 H 5
Zambeze 201 E 3
Zambezi 200 C 2
Zambia 200 D 2
Zamboanga 177 F 2
Zamboanga Peninsula 177 F 2
Zambrów 149 H 4
Zambuè 201 E 3
Zamfara 197 F 3
Zamkowa, Góra 149 H 4
Zamora (Ecuador) 138 C 4
Zamora (Spain) 152 B 3
Zamora de Hidalgo 132 B 4
Zamość 149 H 4
Zamtang 172 D 4
Zanaga 197 G 6
Záncara 152 C 4
Zanda 174 C 1
Zane Hills 108 G 2
Zanesville (OH.) 129 K 2
Zangla 169 K 4
Zanjān (Iran) 157 E 1
Zannah, Jabal az (United Arab Emirates) 157 F 4
Zannone 153 F 3
Zanthus 182 C 5

Zanul'e 158 K 3
Zanzibar 199 F 6
Zanzibar Island 199 F 6
Zaouatallaz 193 G 4
Zaoyang 172 F 4
Zaozernyy 170 F 4
Zaozhuang 173 G 4
Zap 155 F 3
Zap (ND.) 118 G 3
Zapadna Morava 154 B 2
Zapadnaya Dvina 151 J 4
Zapadnaya Dvina 158 F 4
Zapadno 159 OP 3
Zapadno-Sakhalinskiy Khrebet 171 Q 5–6
Zapadno-Sibirskaya Nizmennost' 159 NQ 3
Zapadnyy Sayan 170 F 5
Zapala 143 B 6
Zapata (TX.) 122 D 9
Zapolyarnyy 150 K 2
Zaporosh'ye 155 E 1
Zapug 174 D 1
Za Qu 172 C 4
Zara 155 E 3
Zarafshan 169 G 2
Zaragoza (Colombia) 138 CD 2
Zaragoza (Mexico) 132 B 2
Zaragoza (Spain) 152 C 3
Zaraj 138 E 2
Zaranj 169 G 4
Zaranou 196 D 4
Zarasai 151 J 4
Zárate 142 E 5
Zarauz 152 C 3
Zaraza 138 E 2
Zard Kūh (Iran) 157 F 2
Zarechensk 150 K 2
Zarghat (Saudi Arabia) 156 C 4
Zarghun 169 H 4
Zarghun Shahr 169 H 4
Zaria 197 F 3
Zarma 196 D 1
Zarqān (Iran) 157 F 3
Zarrīneh (Iran) 157 E 1
Zarrīnshahr (Iran) 157 F 2
Zaruma 138 C 4
Zarumilla 138 B 4
Żary 149 FG H 4
Zarya Oktyabrya 168 F 1
Zarzaitine 193 G 3
Zarzal 138 C 3
Zasheyek 150 K 2
Zaskar 169 K 4
Zaskar Mountains 169 K 4
Zaslavl 151 J 5
Zastron 200 D 6
Zaterechnyy 155 G 2
Zatishye 154 CD 1
Zatish'ye 171 T 2
Zatoka Gdańska 149 G 4
Zatoka Pomorska 149 F 4
Zaunguzskiye Karakumy 168 FG 2
Zavala (TX.) 123 J 4
Zavetnoye 155 F 1
Zavitinsk 171 N 5
Zavodoukovsk 159 N 4
Zav'yalova, Ostrov 171 RS 4
Zawiercie 149 G 4
Zāwiyat Masūs 193 K 2
Zawiyat Shammās 194 D 2
Zawr, Ra's az (Saudi Arabia) 157 E 4
Zāyandeh (Iran) 157 F 2
Zayarsk 170 H 4
Zaysan 159 Q 6
Zaysan, Ozero 159 Q 6
Zayü 155 F 4
Zayü Qu 172 C 5
Zduńska Wola 149 G 4
Zdvinsk 159 P 5
Zebak 169 J 3
Zeballos, Monte 143 B 8
Zébar (Iraq) 156 D 1
Zebediela 200 D 4
Zebulon (GA.) 128 8
Zebulon (N.C.) 129 N 6
Zedness, Mont 192 C 4
Zeehan 184 L 9
Zeehan 186 A 5
Zeeland (MI.) 124 J 7
Zeeland (SD.) 118 HJ 5
Zeerust 200 D 5
Zefat (Israel) 156 B 2
Zegdou 192 E 3
Zeila ' 199 G 2
Zêkog 172 D 3
Zelenoborskiy 150 K 2
Zelenodol'sk 158 JK 4
Zelenogorsk 151 J 3
Zelenogradsk 151 H 5
Zelenokumsk 155 F 2
Zeleznodorožny 151 H 5
Zelfana 193 F 2
Zeline 197 F 2
Zell am See 153 F 2

Žemaičiu Aukštuma 151 H 4
Žemaitija 151 H 4
Zemgale 151 HJ 4
Zemio 198 D 3
Zémongo 198 C 3
Zenia (CA.) 112 B 2
Zenica 153 G 3
Zenza do Itombe 200 A 1
Zeona (SD.) 118 F 5
Žepče 153 G 3
Zephyr (TX.) 122 E 4
Zephyrhills (FL.) 131 M 6
Zepu 169 K 3
Zeravshan 169 H 3
Zerav'shanskiy Khrebet 169 H 3
Zerhamra 192 E 3
Zerind 154 B 1
Zermatt 153 E 2
Zernograd 155 F 1
Zestafoni 155 F 2
Zeya 171 O 4
Zeya 171 N 5
Zeya Vodokhranilishche 171 N 5
Zeydābād (Iran) 157 G 3
Zeydār (Iran) 157 G 1
Zeysko-Bureinskaya Ravnina 171 NO 5
Zêzere 152 B 4
Zgierz 149 G 4
Zgorzelec 149 G H 4
Zhag'yab 172 C 4
Zhailma 159 M 5
Zhaksylyk 159 O 6
Zhamanakkal', Ozero 169 G 1
Zhamansor 168 E 1
Zhamshi 159 O 6
Zhanabas 169 H 1
Zhanabek 159 P 6
Zhanang 175 F 2
Zhana-Semey 159 Q 5
Zhanatas 169 HJ 2
Zhangbei 172 FG 2
Zhangguangcai Ling 173 J 1–2
Zhangiz-Tobe 159 Q 6
Zhangjiakou 172 FG 2
Zhangling 171 M 5
Zhangping 173 G 5
Zhangpu 173 G 6
Zhangwu 173 H 2
Zhangye 172 CD 3
Zhangzhou 173 G 6
Zhangzi 172 F 3
Zhanhua 173 G 3
Zhanjiang 172 F 6
Zhantekets 159 Q 6
Zhao'an 172 G 6
Zhaodong 173 J 1
Zhaojue 172 D 5
Zhaoping 172 F 6
Zhaoqing 172 F 6
Zhaosu 169 L 2
Zhaotong 172 D 5
Zhaoyuan 173 J 1
Zhaozhou 173 HJ 1
Zhari Namco 174 E 1
Zharkamys 168 F 1
Zharkova 159 R 4
Zharlykamys 159 P 6
Zharma 159 Q 6
Zhashkov 158 EF 6
Zhatay 171 N 3
Zhaxi Co 174 E 1
Zhaxize 172 C 4
Zhayma 170 F 5
Zhdanov 155 E 1
Zhecheng 172 G 4
Zhejiang 173 GH 5
Zhelaniya, Cape 202
Zhel'dyadyr 169 H 1
Zhelezinka 159 P 5
Zheleznodorozhnyy 158 K 3
Zheleznodorozhnyy 159 M 2
Zheleznodorozhnyy 170 H 4
Zheleznogorsk 158 F 5
Zheleznogorsk 170 HJ 4
Zhen'an 172 E 5
Zheng'an 172 E 5
Zhengding 172 FG 3
Zhenghe 173 G 5
Zhenglan 173 G 2
Zhengning 172 E 3
Zhengxiangbai 172 FG 2
Zhengyang 172 F 4
Zhengzhou 172 F 4
Zhenjiang 173 GH 4
Zhenkang 172 C 6
Zhenlai 173 H 1
Zhenning 172 E 5
Zhenxiong 172 D 5
Zhenyuan 172 E 3
Zhenyuan 172 D 6
Zherdevka 158 H 5
Zheshart 158 JK 3
Zhetybay 168 E 2
Zhicheng 172 F 4
Zhidan 172 E 3
Zhidoi 172 C 4
Zhigalovo 170 J 5

Zhigansk 171 M 2
Zhigulevsk 158 J 5
Zhijiang 172 E 5
Zhitkovichi 151 J 5
Zhitomir 151 J 5
Zhlatyr 159 P 5
Zhmerinka 158 E 6
Zhob 169 H 4
Zhob 169 H 4
Zhodino 151 J 5
Zholymbet 159 O 5
Zhongba 174 D 2
Zhongdian 172 C 5
Zhongning 172 E 3
Zhongshan 172 F 6
Zhongwei 172 DE 3
Zhong Xian 172 E 4
Zhongxiang 172 F 4
Zhongye Islands 176 D 1
Zhongye Qundao 176 D 1
Zhosaly 159 P 5
Zhoukouzhen 172 FG 4
Zhou Shan Qundao 173 H 4
Zhovnino 158 F 6
Zhovten 154 D 1
Zhovtnevoye 154 D 1
Zhuanghe 173 H 3
Zhuanglang 172 E 3
Zhuantobe 169 H 2
Zhubgyügoin 172 C 4
Zhucheng 173 G 3
Zhugqu 172 D 4
Zhujiang Kou 172 F 6
Zhukovka 158 F 5
Zhumadian 172 F 4
Zhuolu 172 G 2
Zhuo Xian 172 G 3
Zhuozi 172 F 2
Zhupanovo 171 U 5

Zhupanovskiy 171 T 5
Zhuralevka 159 N 5
Zhurban 171 N 5
Zhushan 172 EF 4
Zhuya 170 L 4
Zhuzagashskiy 159 P 6
Zhuzhou 172 F 5
Zia Indian Reservation 117 K 2
Ziama Mansuria 153 E 4
Ziārān (Iran) 157 F 1
Ziarat 169 H 4
Zibā (Saudi Arabia) 156 B 4
Zibo 173 G 3
Zicavo 153 E 3
Zichang 172 E 3
Zielona Góra 149 G 4
Zigaing 175 F 3
Zighan, Wāhāt 193 K 3
Zighout Youssef 153 E 4
Zigong 172 DE 5
Zigos Métsevon 154 B 3
Ziguey 197 H 3
Zigui 172 F 4
Ziguinchor 196 A 3
Zihuatanejo 132 B 4
Zilair 159 L 5
Zile 155 E 2
Žilina 149 G 5
Zillah (WA.) 110 E 4
Zima 170 H 5
Zimatlán de Alvarez 132 C 4
Zimba 200 D 3
Zimbabwe 200–201 DE 3
Zimbabwe 201 E 4
Zimi 196 B 4
Zimla 192 E 4
Zimnicea 154 C 2
Zimovniki 155 F 1
Zina 197 G 3

Zinave National Park 201 E 4
Zincirli 155 E 3
Zinder 197 F 3
Zinga (Centr. Afr. Rep.) 198 B 4
Zinga (Tanzania) 199 F 6
Zion (IL.) 124 G 7
Zion National Park 114 DE 6
Zion Reservoir 116 G 3
Zionsville (IN.) 128 E 2
Zipaquirá 138 D 2
Ziqudukou 172 C 4
Ziri 192 C 4
Žirje 153 G 3
Zirkel, Mount 115 L 3
Ziro 175 F 2
Zistonis, Limni 154 C 2
Zitacuaro 132 BC 4
Zittau 149 F 4
Zitundo 201 E 5
Ziwa Magharibi 198 E 5
Ziyanchurino 158 L 5
Ziyang 172 D 4
Ziyang 172 E 4
Ziz 192 E 2
Zizhong 172 E 5
Zlatarsko Jezero 154 B 2
Zlatibor 154 A 2
Zlatiyata 154 B 2
Zlatni Pyaschatsi 154 C 2
Zlatoust 159 L 4
Zlatoustovsk 171 O 5
Zlītan 193 H 2
Złotów 149 G 4
Zmeinogorsk 159 Q 5
Znamenka 155 D 1
Znamenka 158 F 5
Znamenka 159 P 5
Znamenka 159 P 5
Znamenka 170 H 5

Znamenskoye 159 O 4
Znin 149 G 4
Znojmo 149 G 5
Zobeyri (Iran) 157 E 2
Zobia 198 D 4
Zóbuè 201 E 3
Zoekmekaar 200 D 4
Zoetélé 197 G 5
Zogang 172 C 5
Zogqên 172 C 4
Zohreh (Iran) 157 F 3
Zoigê 172 D 4
Zolfo Springs (FL.) 131 N 7
Zolotaya Gora 171 N 5
Zolotinka 171 M 4
Zolotogorskaya 171 TU 3
Zolotogorskiy 159 R 5
Zomba 201 F 3
Zonga 198 B 4
Zonguldak 155 D 2
Zoo Baba 197 G 2
Zorritos 138 B 4
Zorzor 196 C 4
Zouar 197 H 1
Zoulabot 197 G 5
Zouping 173 G 3
Zourate 192 C 4
Zrenjanin 154 B 1
Zruč 149 G 5
Zuara 193 H 2
Zubova-Polyana 158 H 5
Zudanez 140 D 4
Zuénoula 196 C 4
Zuera 152 C 3
Zug 192 C 4
Zug (Switzerland) 153 E 2
Zugdidi 155 F 2
Zugspitze 153 F 2
Zújar 152 B 4

Zuluf (Saudi Arabia) 157 E 3
Zumba 138 C 4
Zumbo 201 E 3
Zumbrota (MN.) 119 Q 6
Zungeru 197 F 4
Zuni (N.M.) 116 H 2
Zuni Indian Reservation 116 H 2
Zuni Mountains 116 H 2
Zunyi 172 E 5
Zuo Jiang 172 E 6
Zuoquan 172 F 3
Zuoyun 172 F 2
Zupanja 153 G 2
Zurbāṭīyah (Iraq) 157 D 2
Zürich 153 E 2
Zurich (MT.) 111 QR 2
Zürich-See 153 E 2
Zurmat 169 H 4
Zurmi 197 F 3
Zuru 197 F 3
Zuwārah 193 H 2
Zuwaylah 193 J 3
Zuwe 200 C 4
Zvishavane 200 D 4
Zvolen 149 G 5
Zwettl 153 G 2
Zwickau 149 F 4
Zwolle 148 E 4
Zwolle (LA.) 123 K 4
Zyranka 170 D 1
Żyrardów 149 H 4
Zyryanka 171 S 2
Zyryanovo 159 R 3
Zyryanovsk 159 Q 6
Zyryanskoye 159 R 4
Żywiec 149 G 5

Symbols

Scale 1:5 000 000, 1 : 6 000 000 , 1:10 000 000

Bombay	More than 5,000,000 inhabitants
Milano	1,000,000 – 5,000,000 inhabitants
Zürich	250,000 – 1,000,000 inhabitants
Dijon	100,000 – 250,000 inhabitants
Dover	25,000 – 100,000 inhabitants
Torquay	Less than 25,000 inhabitants
Tachiumet	Small cities
WIEN	National capital
Atlanta	State capital
————	Major road
————	Other road
– – – –	Road under construction
————	Railway
– – – –	Railway under construction
- - - - - -	Train ferry
	National boundary
	Disputed national boundary
	State boundary
- - - - - - -	Disputed state boundary
	Undefined boundary in the sea
• 7999 ft / 2438 m	Height above sea-level in feet and meters
• 8159ft / 2487m	Depth in feet and meters
	National park
∴ Nineveh	Ruin
≍	Pass
KAINJI DAM	Dam
– – – –	Wadi
┴┴┴┴┴	Canal
—+—	Waterfalls
∩∩∩∩∩	Reef

Symbols

Scale 1:15 000 000, 1:25 000 000, 1:27 000 000, 1:30 000 000

Shanghai	More than 5,000,000 inhabitants
Barcelona	1,000,000 – 5,000,000 inhabitants
Venice	250,000 – 1,000,000 inhabitants
Aberdeen	50,000 – 250,000 inhabitants
○ Beida	Less than 50,000 inhabitants
◻ Mawson	Scientific station
CAIRO	National capital
————	Major road
————	Railway
– – – –	Railway under construction
	National boundary
	Disputed national boundary
————	State boundary
- - - - - - -	Disputed state boundary
	Undefined boundary in the sea
• 11827 ft / 3605 m	Height above sea-level in feet and meters
• 49ft / 15m	Depth in feet and meters
2645	Thickness of ice cap in meters
	Dam
∴ Thebes	Ruin
– – – –	Wadi
┴┴┴┴┴	Canal
—+—	Waterfalls
∩∩∩∩∩	Reef